Creative Living

GLENCOE

TEACHER'S WRAPAROUND EDITION

CREATIVE

CREATIVE *Living*

The Program

Totally rewritten, strengthened, and reorganized, this Sixth Edition of *Creative Living* provides a complete and comprehensive family and consumer sciences program. Students become actively involved in discussions and activities that develop critical thinking skills and encourage responsible and thoughtful decision making in their daily lives.

A strong and extensive ancillary program supports the student text with depth and diversity.

Student Workbook Study guides and activities offer immediate review and reinforcement. Teacher's Edition provides answers.

TEACHER'S WRAPAROUND EDITION
CREATIVE Living

CREATIV Livi

Creative Living
Personal Development Activities

Creative Living
Reteaching Activities

Creative Living
Clothing Lab Activities

Creative
Perform Assess

Creative Living
Foods Lab Activities

Creative Living
Extension Handouts

FAMILY AND CONSUMER SCIENCES
PROFESSIONAL DEVELOPMENT SERIES
Meeting the Special Needs of Students

Creative Livi
Cooperative Le Activitie

Creative Living
Life Skills Activities

School-to-Work

Creative Living
Student Workbook

Creative Livi
Decision-Mak Activities

FAMILY AND CONSUMER SCIENCES
PROFESSIONAL DEVELOPMENT SERIES
Dealing with Sensitive Issues

Creative Living
Student Workbook
Teacher's Annotated Edition

Student Text
Each of 75 chapters focuses on one concept or theme which gives you flexibility in directing your teaching program.

Teacher's Wraparound Edition
Lesson plans, teaching suggestions, discussion activities, research ideas, background information, outreach activities, and multicultural and cross-curricular links are printed around reduced versions of the student pages. This practical format eliminates the need to flip between pages and consult other components.

Teacher's Classroom Resources
This complete package contains new and revised booklets of supplementary materials, a total assessment program, full-color transparencies, and much more. All conveniently organized in this durable canvas tote bag. See back cover for full list.

GLENCOE

CREATIVE *Living*
Teacher's Classroom Resources

Creative Living
Testing Program

Creative Living
Color Transparency Teaching Suggestions

Creative Living
ABC NEWS INTERACTIVE
Bar Code Correlation Activities

Creative Living
Lesson Plans

Creative Living
Color Transparency Package

Creative Living
Testmaker

Testmaker
Macintosh

3M

Testmaker Software
Computer software test bank provides a base of questions (plus you can add your own) that enables teachers to tailor their assessment to the needs of each class.

Student Text

Completely revised and updated with *all* new photos and illustrations, this sixth edition of *Creative Living* reflects today's concerns, issues, and information throughout *all* units. Text revision includes an emphasis on personal development, relationship skills, and consumer skills. Character, skills for career success, making a difference in your community, and meeting the challenges in your life are new topics. A strong focus on family exists, including information on coping with such serious problems as divorce, abuse, and alcoholism. The social impact of clothing and housing has been added. The idea of responsibility is woven throughout the text.

NEW real-life chapter opening examples help make chapters relevant to today's teen.

***NEW* Infographics** — over 50 graphic illustrations combine with text material to explain concepts visually.

STRATEGIES *That Work*

Attitudes for Success

Many people search their whole lives for the secret to success. It's not something you buy or that is given to you. Rather, it's an attitude—a way of approaching life that helps you become a winner. You can't help but have successes when you:

- **Count your blessings, not your misfortunes.** A young high school teacher who fell while hang gliding was paralyzed from the waist down. She sought the positives and formed a company to make wheelchairs that enabled injured people to participate in sports.
- **Work with what you have.** Life isn't fair. Although some people have fewer problems than others, even those who are born into difficult circumstances can succeed. They simply need to show the will, the determination, and the effort.
- **Find the right opportunity.** If you keep looking, you'll find someone who will give you a chance. Don't give up before that happens.
- **Plan to be one in a million.** People may say that you can't succeed where others have failed.

Whatever you attempt, however, remember that it only has to work once—for you.

- **Welcome change.** Don't be afraid to try something new or take a chance. Following the same old routine will not help you achieve goals.
- **Don't be afraid of failure.** Failure is a part of success. It helps you to learn and to become a winner.

Making the Strategy Work

Think . . .

1. Name some people you believe are successful. What traits do they share in common?
2. What successes have you had? What personal qualities led to that success?
3. How might a negative attitude affect a person's achievement?

Try . . .

Choose a goal for yourself. Plan how you will use the guidelines above to achieve your goal. Post your plan where you'll see it regularly. Evaluate your effort and the results.

- Willingness to take reasonable risks to achieve goals. Everyone who attempts something is taking a risk. Confident people know not to take risks that don't make sense. A rollerblader who wants to improve skills may try new twists and turns—these are reasonable risks. The same teen knows better than to rollerblade in car traffic, however. That is not a reasonable risk.
- Healthy self-concept and high self-esteem. Confident people know they aren't perfect, however, they refuse to dwell on their weaknesses. Instead, they feel good about what they have learned and achieved.

Developing Confidence

Confidence grows stronger each time you succeed. This increased confidence makes you more willing to work toward building and strengthening your competencies. In other words, competence builds confidence, and vice versa.

You see this principle in action all the time. A winning team is inspired to practice harder to win again. Making a good grade in class makes a person want to work toward an even better one. Earning extra money from selling garden produce makes a person think about how to raise more vegetables next year. You can put this cycle to work in your life and

CHAPTER 6   Making Changes and Meeting Challenges   71

Figure 25.1

A DAY AT HOME WITH A BABY

6:00 A.M. Time to get up. Baby is awake, crying, and needing a new diaper and clean clothes.

6:30 A.M. Baby cries to be fed. Parent feeds baby and fixes own breakfast.

7:30 A.M. Wide awake, baby wants attention. Baby and parent take time to play.

8:30 A.M. Baby plays while parent cleans kitchen.

9:15 A.M. In need of more attention, baby fusses. Parent talks to baby while sorting laundry, then picks baby up. Time for another diaper change.

10:30 A.M. Baby begins to fidget. Parent rocks baby to sleep. Parent hurries to get some things done and squeezes in a short break.

12:30 P.M. Baby wakes, ready to be changed and fed.

1:30 P.M. Teething pain causes baby to cry. Parent needs a half hour to give comfort.

2:00 P.M. Parent changes baby for a trip to the supermarket.

3:00 P.M. Baby enjoys a teething biscuit while parent puts away food. Time for a diaper change.

4:00 P.M. Must be naptime. Baby is fussy and needs to be rocked and cuddled before sleeping. Parent begins to prepare dinner.

6:30 P.M. Baby is up and ready for a bottle. Baby eats. Then parents have dinner.

7:30 P.M. Playtime.

8:30 P.M. Bathtime.

9:30 P.M. After crying for a while, baby falls asleep.

10:30 P.M. Bedtime for tired parents.

6:00 A.M. Baby wakes, and the day begins again.

254   UNIT 4   Child Care and Development

Strategies That Work takes a tips approach to situations, encouraging students to try out new techniques in their own lives.

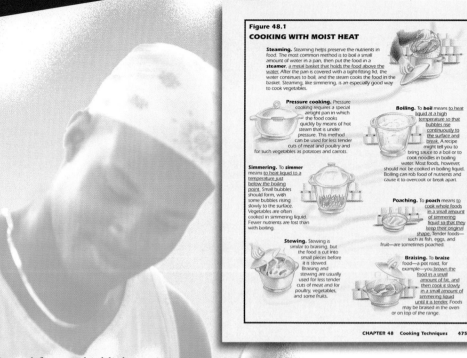

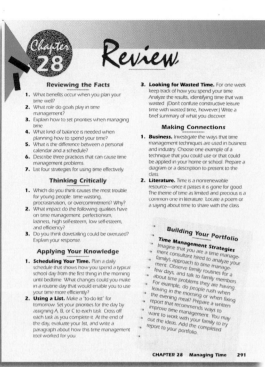

Special features highlight topics teens
want and need to know about.
Topics include:

- *Balancing Work and Family*
- *From School to Work*
- *In Touch with Technology*
- *Strategies That Work*
- *Acting Responsibly*
- *Making Decisions*
- *Managing Your Life*

NEW *Making Connections*
cross-curricular activities link such
subjects as science, math, and social
studies on the chapter review pages.
NEW *Building Your Portfolio*
activities are useful as an alternative
form of assessment.

*Balancing Work and
Family* helps prepare
students to cope with
the demands of school,
work, and family
responsibilities.

Teacher's Wraparound Edition

Valuable teaching aids are placed where you need them . . . right on your teacher's text page. This time-saving Teacher's Edition is packed full of complete *Lesson Plans* and activity ideas to motivate, teach, and assess student learning.

Special Theme Boxes provide information or suggest discussion and activity ideas. Interest-building topics are featured in the teacher's "wraparound" area on each page. Included are:

- Journal Writing
- Cooperative Learning
- Chapter Resources
- Cross-Curricular Activity
- Family and Community Outreach
- Multicultural Perspectives

- Special Needs Strategies
- Using Visuals
- Feature Article Links
- Cross Reference
- Real-Life Application
- Did You Know?
- More About
- Focus On

Feature Boxes

These correlate and supplement text features such as *From School-To-Work*, *In Touch With Technology*, etc. They all work together to spark interest, promote discussion, and expand emphasis on critical life skills!

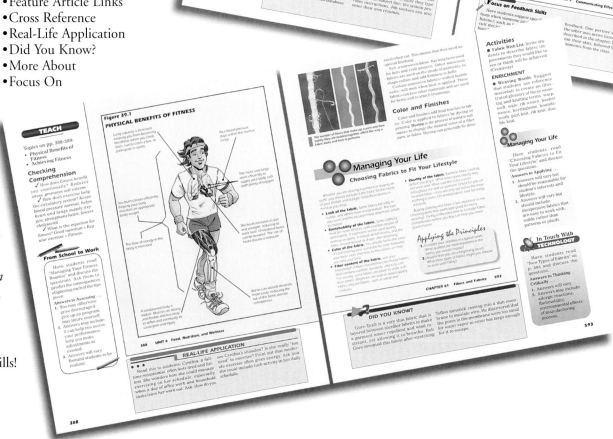

From School to Work identifies skills and shows how they transfer to the work world.

Acting Responsibly encourages students to analyze another teen's actions in a challenging situation and to consider how they might respond themselves.

In Touch with Technology explores advances that relate to chapter topics, such as new fibers developed for exercise clothing.

Managing Your Life offers students guidance in managing their lives effectively, such as organizing time for school-work and leisure.

Making Decisions enables students to practice making difficult decisions in situations they may encounter.

Teacher's Classroom Resources

Now at your fingertips, the updated and expanded *Teacher' Classroom Resources* provides a wealth of information. Conveniently organized in a durable canvas totebag, the 17 booklets offer hundreds of teaching supplements that save you hours of preparation time.

Booklets include:
- Lesson Plans
- Life Skills Activities
- Decision Making Activities
- Cooperative Learning Activities
- Personal Development Activities
- Foods Lab Activities
- Clothing Lab Activities
- Reteaching Activities
- Extension Handouts
- Color Transparency Pkg. — 60 full-color transparencies plus Teaching Suggestion booklet.
- Performance Assessment — includes rubrics
- Testing Program
- Teacher's Annotated Edition of the Student Workbook (answer key)

- School to Work — guides through career planning process and SCANS skills and competencies.
- Meeting the Special Needs of Students — *professional development booklet*
- Dealing with Sensitive Issues — *professional development booklet*
- ABCNews InterActive™ Bar Code Correlation correlates *Creative Living* to the videodisc series *Understanding Ourselves.* This multimedia program combines videodisc, text, and software for each of 7 programs: Alcohol, Drugs and Substance Abuse, Food and Nutrition, Health: AIDS, Teenage Sexuality, Tobacco, and Violence Prevention.

ORDERING INFORMATION FOR CREATIVE LIVING

TEXTBOOK
Student Edition 0-02-642749-4
Teacher's Wraparound Edition 0-02-642751-6
WORKBOOK
Student Edition 0-02-642753-2
Teacher's Annotated Edition* 0-02-642757-5
TEACHER'S CLASSROOM RESOURCES BOX 0-02-642752-4
Lesson Plans* 0-02-642758-3
Life Skills Activities* 0-02-642761-3
Decision Making Activities* 0-02-642762-1
Cooperative Learning* 0-02-642764-8
Personal Development Activities* 0-02-642759-1
Foods Lab Activities* 0-02-642765-6
Clothing Lab Activities* 0-02-642766-4
Reteaching Activities* 0-02-642767-2
Extension Handouts* 0-02-642763-X
Color Transparency Package* 0-02-642771-0
Performance Assessment* 0-02-642768-0
Testing Program* 0-02-642769-9
School to Work* 0-02643043-6
Meeting the Special Needs of Students* 0-02-675461-4
Dealing with Sensitive Issues* 0-02-642798-2
ABCNews InterActive™ Videodisc Correlation* 0-02-642777-X
TESTMAKERS
Macintosh Software 0-02-642754-0
IBM Software 0-02-642756-7
Apple Software 0-02-642755-9
*These components are included in the Teacher's Classroom Resources Box

For more information, contact your nearest regional office or call 1-800-334-7344.

Northeast Region
Glencoe/McGraw-Hill
15 Trafalgar Square #201
Nashua, NH 03063-1968
603-880-4701 • 800-424-3451
Fax: 603-595-0204
(CT, MA, ME, NH, NY,RI, VT)

Mid-Atlantic Region
Glencoe/McGraw-Hill
P.O. Box 458
Hightstown, NJ 08520-0458
609-426-5560 • 800-553-7515
Fax: 609-426-7063
(DC, DE, MD, NJ, PA)

Atlantic-Southeast Region
Glencoe/McGraw-Hill
Brookside Park
One Harbison Way, Suite 101
Columbia, SC 29212
803-732-2365 • 800-731-2365
Fax: 803-732-4582
(KY, NC, SC, VA, WV)

Southeast Region
Glencoe/McGraw-Hill
6510 Jimmy Carter Blvd.
Norcross, GA 30071
770-446-7493 • 800-982-3992
Fax: 770-446-2356
(AL, FL, GA, TN)

Mid-America Region
Glencoe/McGraw-Hill
936 Eastwind Drive
Westerville, OH 43081
614-890-1111 • 800-848-1567
Fax: 614-899-4905
(IN, MI, OH)

Great Lakes Region
Glencoe/McGraw-Hill
846 East Algonquin Road
Schaumburg, IL 60173
847-397-8448 • 800-762-4876
Fax: 847-397-9472
(IL, MN, WI)

Mid-Continent Region
Glencoe/McGraw-Hill
846 East Algonquin Rd.
Schaumburg, IL 60173
847-397-8448 • 800-762-4876
Fax: 847-397-9472
(IA, KS, MO, ND, NE, SD)

Southwest Region
Glencoe/McGraw-Hill
320 Westway Place, Suite 550
Arlington, TX 76018
817-784-2113 • 800-828-5096
Fax: 817-784-2116
(AR, LA, MS, NM, OK)

Texas Region
Glencoe/McGraw-Hill
320 Westway Place, Suite 550
Arlington, TX 76018
817-784-2100 • 800-828-5096
Fax: 817-784-2116
(TX)

Western Region
Glencoe/McGraw-Hill
709 E. Riverpark Lane
Suite 150 • Boise, ID 83706
208-368-0300 • 800-452-6126
Fax: 208-368-0303
(AK, AZ, CO, ID, MT, NV, OR, UT, WA, WY)

California Region
Glencoe/McGraw-Hill
15319 Chatsworth Street
P.O. Box 9609
Mission Hills, CA 91346
818-898-1391 • 800-423-9534
Fax: 818-365-5489
(CA, HI)

Glencoe Catholic School Region
Glencoe/McGraw-Hill
25 Crescent St., 1st Floor
Stamford, CT 06906
203-964-9109 • 800-551-8766
Fax: 203-967-3108

Canada
McGraw-Hill Ryerson Ltd.
300 Water Street
Whitby, Ontario
Canada L1N 9B6
905-430-5000 • 800-565-5758
Fax: 905-430-5020

International
McGraw-Hill, Inc.
International Group
1221 Avenue of the Americas
28th Floor
New York, NY 10020
212-512-3641
Fax: 212-512-2186

DoDDS and Pacific Territories
McGraw-Hill School
Publishing Company
1221 Avenue of the Americas
13th Floor
New York, NY 10020
212-512-6128
Fax: 212-512-6050

Teacher's Manual

Creative Living

Sixth Edition

Consulting Authors

Linda R.Glosson, Ph.D.
Home Economics Teacher
Wylie High School
Wylie, Texas

Janis P. Meek, CFCS
Family and Consumer Sciences Teacher
Warren County High School
Warrenton, North Carolina

Linda G. Smock, CFCS
Supervisor
Family and Consumer Sciences
Pinellas County Schools, Florida

GLENCOE

McGraw-Hill

New York, New York   Columbus, Ohio   Mission Hills, California   Peoria, Illinois

Editorial Development

Co-developed by
Glencoe/McGraw-Hill and
Visual Education Corporation, Princeton, New Jersey

Glencoe/McGraw-Hill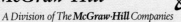

A Division of The McGraw·Hill Companies

Send all inquiries to:
Glencoe/McGraw-Hill
3008 W. Willow Knolls Drive
Peoria, IL 61614-1083

ISBN 0-02-642751-6 (Teacher's Manual)

Printed in the United States of America.

1 2 3 4 5 6 7 8 9   RRDW   03 02 01 00 99 98 97 96

CONTENTS

Creative Living Program Overview

The Sixth Edition of *Creative Living* builds on the outstanding features that have made this program so popular with teachers over the years. From the fundamentals of relationship skills to careers in clothing and textiles, *Creative Living* provides a complete and comprehensive family and consumer sciences program.

This program does much more than present information. Throughout the text, students become actively involved in discussing relevant issues. They strengthen their critical thinking skills through discussions and activities that encourage responsible and thoughtful decision making in their daily lives.

The following have been incorporated in this revised and updated program:

- The content of each chapter guides students to develop their skills in making decisions, setting priorities, and managing their lives.
- Special feature articles within each chapter help students recognize ways to apply the course content and skills. The features are practical, current, and relevant.
- Chapter learning objectives are linked with resources for mastering them and for measuring student performance.
- A strong and extensive ancillary program supports the student text, with several new booklets of activities developed to serve a wide range of skill levels and needs.
- Colorful illustrations and photographs and a bold page design help capture and maintain student interest.

The five program components for the Sixth Edition are completely integrated and include the following:

- **Student Text.** The 768-page fully revised and updated text focuses on the theme of responsible decision making.

- **Teacher's Wraparound Edition.** Lesson plans, teaching suggestions, discussion activities, research ideas, background information, outreach activities, and multicultural and cross-curricular links are printed around reduced versions of the student pages. This practical format eliminates the need to flip between pages and consult other components.
- **Teacher's Classroom Resources.** This complete package contains new and revised booklets of supplementary materials, a total assessment program, full-color transparencies, and much more.
- **Student Workbook.** Study guides and activities offer immediate review and reinforcement.
- **Testmaker Software.** A computer software test bank provides a base of questions and enables teachers to tailor their assessment to the needs of each class.

The Student Text

Written in an engaging, positive voice, the student text has been rewritten, strengthened, and reorganized throughout. The text is supported by special feature articles, all new photographs, and colorful illustrations.

Unit Content

Each of the eight units concentrates on a major area of the family and consumer sciences curriculum.

- **Unit 1: Personal Development.** This unit explores issues that concern teens, including self-esteem, character, and wellness. It also leads students toward responsible decision making and provides tools for setting and reaching goals. New content in the unit focuses on developing positive values, making changes and meeting challenges in life, and career exploration.

- **Unit 2: Relationship Skills.** This new unit helps students improve their relationships with others. Strengthening communication skills is promoted here and throughout the text. Four chapters center on dealing with peer pressure, resolving conflicts peacefully, making a positive difference in the community, and gaining workplace skills.
- **Unit 3: Families and Friendships.** Guidance in strengthening families, adjusting to family changes, developing positive peer relationships, and maintaining responsible dating relationships is offered in this unit. One chapter explores serious problems in family and peer relationships and describes sources of potential help.
- **Unit 4: Child Care and Development.** Unit 4 outlines the physical, intellectual, emotional, moral, and social aspects of child development to help students understand the responsibilities of providing safe and appropriate care for children of different ages. One chapter stresses the realities of parenthood, including the challenges that are especially difficult for teen parents.
- **Unit 5: Management and Consumer Decisions.** This unit helps students learn to manage their resources, especially time and money, so they can reach their goals and also become wise consumers. A new chapter emphasizes the need to keep current with advancing technology.
- **Unit 6: Food, Nutrition, and Wellness.** This unit offers guidelines for nutrition and health in addition to effective techniques for food preparation and meal management. Topics range from making healthful food choices from the Food Guide Pyramid, to kitchen safety, to preparation of foods, to careers in food and nutrition.
- **Unit 7: Clothing and Textiles.** Clothing design, fibers and fabrics, and wardrobe planning, along with step-by-step garment construction are covered in this unit. Chapters explain the use and advantages of both conventional sewing machines and sergers. A new chapter covers the social impact of clothing.
- **Unit 8: Housing and Living Space.** This unit explains ways to organize and care for living space, avoid home accidents, and reduce energy costs. A new chapter helps students understand the impact that housing has on people's lives.

Chapter Components

Each of the 75 chapters in the Sixth Edition deals with one concept or theme and includes these components:

- **Objectives.** To help you define goals for the course, clear behavioral objectives begin each chapter. All chapter content supports these student objectives.
- **Terms to Learn.** New and significant terms in the chapter are listed in alphabetical order. In the student text, each term appears in dark type and is defined with text in italic type. The terms are also defined in the Glossary.
- **Text.** Students will enjoy the anecdotal, interactive, upbeat writing style. The frequent use of headings, lists, and graphics helps maintain interest and readability.
- **Chapter Review.** This full-page, comprehensive review includes these sections:
  Reviewing the Facts. Objective questions check recall of major chapter concepts.
  Thinking Critically. These questions are designed to spark lively discussions related to chapter concepts.
  Applying Your Knowledge. Individual and team activities and projects encourage students to apply what they have learned.
  Making Connections. Chapter-related activities reinforce skills and knowledge in language arts, history, geography, civics, government, social studies, economics, math, science, music, and other areas.
  Building Your Portfolio. These chapter-related projects can strengthen students' grasp of chapter concepts while adding to their portfolios.

Photos and Illustrations

The Sixth Edition of *Creative Living* has an all-new look, created with these components:

- **Infographics.** These full-color illustrations with integrated text give students a visual grasp of concepts and procedures.
- **Photos.** Photos throughout are large, full-color complements to the text. Chosen for visual as well as teaching purposes, these all new photos help draw readers into the text.
- **Illustrations.** Drawings support the text, making content easier to grasp.
- **Charts.** Clear, interesting charts introduce new information and reinforce text concepts.

Feature Articles

Chapters include special feature articles that help students apply concepts to their daily lives. They follow these seven themes:

Balancing Work and Family helps prepare  students to cope with the demands of work and family, exploring such issues as finding good quality child care.

From School to Work identifies skills and shows how they transfer to the work world.

 *In Touch with Technology* explores advances that relate to chapter topics, such as new fibers developed for exercise clothing.

Strategies That Work takes a tips approach to situations, encouraging students to try out new techniques in their own lives.

 *Acting Responsibly* encourages students to analyze another teen's actions in a challenging situation and to consider how they might respond themselves.

Making Decisions enables students to practice making difficult decisions in situations they may encounter.

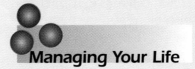 *Managing Your Life* offers students guidance in managing their lives effectively, such as organizing time for schoolwork and leisure.

The Teacher's Wraparound Edition

In the Teacher's Wraparound Edition, each page of the student text has been reduced to allow space for teacher support in the page margins. The outer side columns and space at the bottom provide material for use in classroom management. A lesson-plan format is followed.

Lesson Plans

The lesson plans help you guide students through the chapters and reinforce and enrich their learning. Each chapter's lesson plan has four sections: Focus, Teach, Assess, and Close.

Focus

Chapter Overview. A brief description of the chapter explains its contents.

Motivators. One or two activities stimulate student interest in the chapter.

Objectives. Students are encouraged to comment on the objectives.

Vocabulary. This section explains at least one unfamiliar term from the chapter.

Teach

The components below appear on the main pages of every chapter:

Topics. These summarize the topics on each page spread.

Checking Comprehension. Questions here help you assess students' understanding of the content.

Activities. These activities help foster students' skills, including: critical thinking, decision making, problem solving, maintaining relationships, communicating, observation, and becoming good citizens. Reteaching activities provide an opportunity to review concepts in the text. Enrichment activities can be used to enhance students' learning.

Special Theme Boxes. Each of these has a unique theme and identifying design. Content may provide information or suggest discussion and activity ideas. All are located in side columns unless specified otherwise.

- *Journal Writing*—provides ideas that you might suggest as topics for student writing related to the unit. This theme box is located at the bottom of the unit opener pages.

- *Cooperative Learning*—gives a suggestion for a group activity to use with the unit. This theme box is located at the bottom of the unit opener pages.

- *Chapter Resources*—helps you locate specific items that correlate to the chapter and are found in such components as the Life Skills Activities and Extension Handouts booklets. Assessment materials are also listed. This theme box is located on the bottom of every chapter opening page.

- *Cross-Curricular Activity*—helps students strengthen their academic skills as they explore chapter concepts. An academic skill, such as math, science, or language arts, is identified at the top of each of these.

- *Family and Community Outreach*—encourages students to apply chapter concepts and gather related information outside the classroom.

- *Multicultural Perspectives*— describes how chapter concepts relate to other cultures and encourages students to find out more.

- *Special Needs Strategies*—suggests content-related ideas for working with students who have special needs.

- *Using Visuals*—references text photos and infographics with ideas for discussion.

- *Feature Article Links* —provide answers to questions in the feature articles and may also include ideas for discussion. There are seven of these, each with a title and design corresponding to that of the feature article.

- *Cross-Reference*—directs teachers and students to related information in other chapters.

- *Real-Life Application*—describes a typical situation or decision that teens face and encourages students to make the decision, offer guidance, comment on a teen's actions, or explore the issues involved. This theme box is located at page bottoms.

- *Did You Know?*—offers interesting information and statistics related to chapter content and is located at page bottoms.

- *More About*—includes information to support chapter topics and add interest to chapter discussions. This theme box is located at page bottoms.

- *Focus On*—gives opportunities for students to practice and strengthen such skills as communication and problem solving in relation to chapter content. This theme box is located at page bottoms.

Assess

Review. This section includes a reference to review materials and the Study Guide, plus a chapter review activity.

Evaluation. Suggestions here are for a chapter test and an alternative assessment activity.

Close

Closing Activity. A final activity helps students reflect on the chapter content.

Answers to Reviewing the Facts. Answers are included here to the first part of the Chapter Review.

Answers to Thinking Critically. These are answers to the second part of the Chapter Review. They appear at the bottom of the page.

Teacher's Classroom Resources

The third component of *Creative Living* is the Teacher's Classroom Resources, which contains the booklets listed below. Most of these materials can be reproduced for classroom use. The booklets marked with asterisks were developed especially for the Sixth Edition, while the other booklets have been extensively revised and updated.

- **Lesson Plans.*** This booklet offers a one-page overview of each chapter in the student text to facilitate teacher preparation. The page begins with student objectives, links the chapter to available resources within the program, directs the teacher to applicable reteaching activities, and describes assessment materials. It also provides space to jot down homework assignments.
- **Life Skills Activities.** Designed to provide critical thinking opportunities and encourage students to apply new skills in realistic situations, a life skills activity has

been developed for each chapter, along with possible answers. The activities include group work and cover these nine categories:

Developing Independence
Developing Leadership Skills
Making Decisions
Solving Problems
Thinking Critically
Using Communication Skills
Using Fact Finding Skills
Using Management Skills
Using Relationship Skills

- **Decision-Making Activities.*** This booklet contains 24 handouts, designed to be used with three specific chapters in each unit, such as Chapters 2, 6, and 7 in Unit One. Students may be asked to make decisions related to chapter issues, write endings to stories, complete skits, or answer questions. Students' answers will vary, but possible answers are provided with the activity.
- **Cooperative Learning Activities.** This booklet consists of 36 two-page activities designed for specific chapters in each unit. Students work in pairs or small groups to apply chapter concepts and acquire and practice interpersonal skills. Each activity includes a page of guidelines for the teacher and a reproducible worksheet for students.
- **Personal Development** Activities.* Included here are 22 two-page handouts that coordinate with selected chapters in Units 1-5. Working individually and in groups, students develop personally as they apply chapter concepts beyond the text to their lives, their families, and their communities. Activities engage students in creating handbooks, analyzing literature, conducting interviews, evaluating advertisements, and other challenging chapter-related tasks.
- **Foods Lab Activities.** This is a supplement to the chapters in Unit 6 with hands-on activities that focus on food preparation and meal management. Students practice spe-

cific cooking skills and then learn how to combine foods into nutritious, inviting meals.

- **Clothing Lab Activities.** This booklet extends chapters in Unit 7 with projects that involve sewing by hand and using a conventional sewing machine and a serger. The step-by-step directions and illustrations in each activity allow students to create a useful product as they practice specific skills, such as stitching darts, putting in a zipper, and serging seams.

- **Reteaching Activities.** * One activity for each chapter, plus the answers are included in this booklet. It also includes tables to be completed, concept maps, matching tasks, sentence completions, and other types of activities designed for students who can benefit from this kind of reinforcement of chapter concepts.

- **Extension Handouts.** This booklet consists of 106 handouts with facts, guidelines, tips, and resources correlated to each chapter in *Creative Living.* Many activities include questions requiring critical thinking that encourage students to analyze chapter concepts, examine them in greater detail, and apply knowledge and skills beyond the classroom.

- **Performance Assessment.** * One activity for each chapter enables students to demonstrate what they can do with what they have learned. Students are involved in making decisions and gathering more information, if needed, as they complete a variety of products designed for specific audiences. These products—and the processes students use to create the products—indicate students' mastery of the chapter content.

- **Testing Program.** A two-page test for each chapter and a four-page test for each unit are offered here. Each test is reproducible and consists of objective questions (20 to 25 for chapter tests and 33 for unit tests) and two or three essay questions. Answers are included in the booklet.

- **Teacher's Annotated Edition of the Student Workbook.** This is the answer key to the Student Workbook.

- **School to Work.** This booklet uses activities to guide students through the career planning process and reinforce essential SCANS skills and competencies.

- **Meeting the Special Needs of Students.** Suggestions and strategies for integrating and teaching students with disabilities and learning problems are provided in this booklet. Working with gifted students is also covered. This booklet is part of the Glencoe Professional Development Series, a set of booklets designed to provide special teaching information for educators. This particular booklet has been selected for inclusion with the *Creative Living* supplements.

- **Dealing with Sensitive Issues.** Another booklet from the Professional Development Series, this one prepares the educator for classroom discussions on issues that are generally considered sensitive. Background information and teaching strategies are provided.

- **ABCNews InterActive™ Bar Code Correlation.** This booklet correlates *Creative Living* to the ABCNews InterActive ™ videodisc series *Understanding Ourselves.* Bar codes provide quick access to relevant material on the laser videodisc. *Understanding Ourselves* is a multimedia program combining videodisc, text, and software for each of the seven programs in the series: *Alcohol, Drugs and Substance Abuse, Food and Nutrition, Health: AIDS, Teenage Sexuality, Tobacco,* and *Violence Prevention.*

Color Transparency Package

This package includes 60 full-color transparencies that accompany many of the chapters in *Creative Living.* Graphics vary from computer art, to cartoons, to photography, to illustrations. An accompanying booklet provides an introduction to each transparency plus objectives, teaching suggestions, and an activity that centers on the concept shown in the transparency. This package is included in the Teacher's Classroom Resources or can be purchased separately.

The Student Workbook

To enable students to work individually, a separate Student Workbook contains a study guide and an activity worksheet for each chapter. The study guides consist of fill-in and short-answer questions to help students review the chapter. The worksheets offer activities to reinforce chapter concepts, such as practice in identifying pattern markings.

Printed on perforated paper, the worksheets can be used in class or as homework assignments. Answers for the study guides and worksheets appear in the Teacher's Annotated Edition of the Student Workbook.

The Testmaker

The *Creative Living* Testmaker software package is available in three versions: Macintosh, Apple, and IBM. Its bank contains hundreds of objective questions, and the software allows you to add your own questions. You can construct tests, quizzes, and review sheets and create multiple versions of the same test. The easy-to-use Testmaker will also print an answer key.

Effective Teaching

A comprehensive course in family and consumer sciences is exciting and dynamic to teach because it has so many built-in application opportunities. The subject matter touches the lives of everyone: students, teachers, friends, family members, consumers, workers, and citizens.

Whether you are an experienced teacher or just starting out, you probably already have ideas for teaching with *Creative Living*. Along with the suggestions in the Teacher's Wraparound Edition and the Teacher's Classroom Resources, the guidelines below will help you develop content strategies that will be motivating and effective in your classroom.

The *Creative Living* program can be used for both one-semester and full-year courses. The self-contained chapters provide flexibility in selecting the content that must be covered in the course. In addition, the wealth of support materials enables you to develop lessons that will meet the individual needs of your students.

Emphasis on Basic Skills

A good foundation in basic academic and communication skills is essential for students' success during and after their school careers. The Sixth Edition of *Creative Living* focuses on integrating family and consumer sciences concepts with these basic skills.

Specific cross-curricular activities in each chapter, in combination with the Applying Your Knowledge, Making Connections, and Building Your Portfolio sections in the Chapter Reviews, foster skills in language arts, math, social studies, geography, science, health, art, economics, and other areas.

Here are additional strategies for incorporating basic skill instruction into your family and consumer sciences classroom.

Language Arts

Students get more out of a reading assignment when they have access to background information on topics that especially interest them. A key to promoting students' independent reading is to make books and other resources easily available. The Resource List in this Teacher's Manual includes current books related to each unit of *Creative Living*.

Many of the language arts cross-curricular activities in the chapters of *Creative Living* emphasize writing, as do the Applying Your Knowledge and Building Your Portfolio activities that end each chapter in the Sixth Edition. In addition, the newly developed Personal Development Activities booklet suggests many projects that involve writing and relate to the chapter content.

By encouraging whole-class and small-group discussion, the activities in *Creative Living* help students reinforce and practice their oral communication skills. In addition, after many projects, students are asked to present their findings or conclusions to their classmates orally.

Social Studies and Multicultural Issues

In an increasingly interconnected world, it's vital that students develop knowledge of, and an appreciation for, other viewpoints and other cultures. The social studies cross-curricular activities in the Teacher's Wraparound Edition and Making Connections activities in the Chapter Reviews guide students to study how specific events, inventions, and eras affected people in the United States and other nations.

Multicultural Perspectives in the Teacher's Wraparound Edition encourage students to investigate how something they experience is experienced in other cultures. For example, in various chapters students are asked to research dating customs, gender roles, and communication styles in other cultures. Becoming more aware of other approaches can help prepare students to live in today's world.

Mathematics

Students grasp mathematical concepts more effectively when they are meaningful.

Some of the cross-curricular and Making Connections activities in *Creative Living* encourage students to figure out costs and percentages, appling their math skills to real life situations.

Science

Students learn science best when they are able to conduct experiments and thus witness science in action. Many of the science cross-curricular and Making Connections activities suggest that students devise experiments to examine a certain principle. Encourage students to apply the scientific method by predicting results. Then have them check the validity of their hypotheses by carrying out their experiments. If necessary, help them understand why a hypothesis was incorrect.

Emphasis on Critical Thinking

Teaching has always depended on questioning techniques, but questions take different forms and place different demands on students. Some questions require factual recall and help determine whether students have acquired basic information. Factual questions promote student participation in discussions and can give students a high success rate in answering questions correctly.

Other types of questions build on students' basic understanding by provoking critical thinking. The difference between factual and critical-thinking questions is shown here:

- "What type of nutrient is found in starch?"
- "Why is it important for you to know about the nutrients in food?"

The second question provokes thought by encouraging students to analyze how information affects them. Students tend to learn more when they are asked not only to recall information but to analyze, apply, synthesize, and evaluate it.

Critical-thinking questions are included in the Chapter Review, in the Life Skills Activities booklet in the Teacher's Classroom Resources and in many other ways throughout the program.

Emphasis on Study Skills

Students' study skills strongly influence how much they learn. Low-ability students may need to be taught how and when to use study skills. Encourage students to use the Study Guides in their workbooks to identify and review important points in each chapter. The Special Needs Strategies in the Teacher's Wraparound Edition also offer ideas for helping students grasp concepts.

Emphasis on Career Exploration

Each unit of the Sixth Edition of *Creative Living* concludes with a chapter focusing on career exploration. The progression begins with an overview of career self-assessment and essential interpersonal skills in the workplace and then explores careers in fields related to chapter topics. Careers are discussed in three categories: entry-level jobs, jobs requiring some training, and jobs requiring higher education.

Integrating FHA/HERO Activities

FHA/HERO is an important component of many family and consumer sciences programs. Suggestions for these activities are listed on the opening pages of each unit in the Teacher's Wraparound Edition. The activities can be carried out either during or outside school hours. Many enable students to share what they are learning in the *Creative Living* program with others at school, at home, and in the community.

The FHA adviser training manual offers suggestions for developing additional co-curricular activities. Other resources are available from Future Homemakers of America, Inc.

Scope and Sequence Chart

The chart on the pages that follow show how major themes are woven throughout *Creative Living*. You will find it useful for planning your course, sequencing courses, emphasizing particular course themes, and correlating *Creative Living* to your curriculum.

Scope and Sequence—Unit 1: Personal Development

Topic	Chapter
Career Exploration	7 Thinking About Careers
Citizenship/ Leadership	3 Developing Character 5 Making Responsible Decisions
Communication/ Relationships	1 You and Your World 5 Making Responsible Decisions 6 Making Changes and Meeting Challenges 7 Thinking About Careers
Decision Making/ Life Management	3 Developing Character 5 Making Responsible Decisions 6 Making Changes and Meeting Challenges 7 Thinking About Careers
Health and Safety	2 Health and Wellness 5 Making Responsible Decisions
Managing Resources/ Consumer Skills	2 Health and Wellness 4 Goals and Resources 5 Making Responsible Decisions 6 Making Changes and Meeting Challenges
Personal Development	1 You and Your World 5 Making Responsible Decisions 2 Health and Wellness 6 Making Changes and Meeting Challenges 3 Developing Character 4 Goals and Resources 7 Thinking About Careers
Technology	1 You and Your World 7 Thinking About Careers

Scope and Sequence—Unit 2: Relationship Skills

Topic	Chapter
Career Exploration	13 Skills for Career Success
Citizenship/ Leadership	12 Making a Difference in Your Community
Communication/ Relationships	8 Getting Along with Others 9 Communicating Effectively 10 Peer Pressure and Refusal Skills 11 Conflict Resolution 12 Making a Difference in Your Community 13 Skills for Career Success
Decision Making/ Life Management	10 Peer Pressure and Refusal Skills 11 Conflict Resolution 12 Making a Difference in Your Community 13 Skills for Career Success
Health and Safety	8 Getting Along with Others 10 Peer Pressure and Refusal Skills 11 Conflict Resolution
Managing Resources/ Consumer Skills	8 Getting Along with Others 12 Making a Difference in Your Community 13 Skills for Career Success
Personal Development	8 Getting Along with Others 11 Conflict Resolution 9 Communicating Effectively 12 Making a Difference in Your 10 Peer Pressure and Refusal Community Skills 13 Skills for Career Success
Technology	9 Communicating Effectively 13 Skills for Career Success

Scope and Sequence—Unit 3: Families and Friendships

Topic	Chapter
Career Exploration	20 Careers in the Helping Professions
Citizenship/ Leadership	15 Strengthening Families
Communication/ Relationships	14 The Role of Families 15 Strengthening Families 18 Friendships 19 Responsible Relationships
Decision Making/ Life Management	17 Coping with Problems 19 Responsible Relationships
Health and Safety	17 Coping with Problems 19 Responsible Relationships
Managing Resources/ Consumer Skills	15 Strengthening Families 16 Adjusting to Family Changes 18 Friendships
Personal Development	14 The Role of Families 17 Coping with Problems 15 Strengthening Families 18 Friendships 16 Adjusting to Family Changes 19 Responsible Relationships
Technology	18 Friendships

Scope and Sequence—Unit 4: Child Care and Development

Topic	Chapter
Career Exploration	26 Careers Working with Children
Citizenship/ Leadership	21 Caregiving Skills 23 Care and Safety of Children 25 The Realities of Parenthood
Communication/ Relationships	21 Caregiving Skills 22 Ages and Stages 23 Care and Safety of Children 24 The Importance of Play
Decision Making/ Life Management	21 Caregiving Skills 23 Care and Safety of Children 25 The Realities of Parenthood
Health and Safety	21 Caregiving Skills 23 Care and Safety of Children 25 The Realities of Parenthood
Managing Resources/ Consumer Skills	21 Caregiving Skills 25 The Realities of Parenthood
Personal Development	21 Caregiving Skills 25 The Realities of Parenthood
Technology	24 The Importance of Play

Scope and Sequence—Unit 5: Management and Consumer Decisions

Topic	Chapter
Career Exploration	35 Management and Consumer Careers
Citizenship/ Leadership	34 Consumer Rights and Responsibilities 35 Management and Consumer Careers
Communication/ Relationships	34 Consumer Rights and Responsibilities
Decision Making/ Life Management	27 Managing Resources 31 Using Credit Wisely 28 Managing Time 33 Consumer Skills 29 Managing Technology 34 Consumer Rights and 30 Managing Money Responsibilities
Health and Safety	27 Managing Resources 28 Managing Time 32 Advertising 34 Consumer Rights and Responsibilities
Managing Resources/ Consumer Skills	27 Managing Resources 33 Consumer Skills 28 Managing Time 34 Consumer Rights and 29 Managing Technology Responsibilities 30 Managing Money 35 Management and Consumer 31 Using Credit Wisely Careers 32 Advertising
Personal Development	28 Managing Time 33 Consumer Skills
Technology	29 Managing Technology 30 Managing Money 35 Management and Consumer Careers

Scope and Sequence—Unit 6: Food, Nutrition, and Wellness

Topic	Chapter	
Career Exploration	55 Careers in Food and Nutrition	
Citizenship/ Leadership	55 Careers in Food and Nutrition	
Communication/ Relationships	54 Enjoying Mealtime	
Decision Making/ Life Management	36 Food in Your Life 38 Guidelines for Good Nutrition 40 Healthful Food Choices 41 Planning Meals at Home 45 Getting Ready to Cook	
Health and Safety	36 Food in Your Life 37 Nutrients 38 Guidelines for Good Nutrition 39 Fitness and Weight Management 40 Healthful Food Choices 41 Planning Meals at Home 44 Safety and Sanitation 47 Preparation Skills	49 Microwave Cooking 50 Breads, Cereals, Rice, and Pasta 51 Fruits and Vegetables 52 Milk, Yogurt, and Cheese 53 Meats, Poultry, Fish, Dry Beans, Eggs, and Nuts 54 Enjoying Mealtime
Managing Resources/ Consumer Skills	38 Guidelines for Good Nutrition 39 Fitness and Weight Management 40 Healthful Food Choices 41 Planning Meals at Home 42 Food and the Consumer 45 Getting Ready to Cook 46 Measuring Basics	47 Preparation Skills 50 Breads, Cereals, Rice, and Pasta 51 Fruits and Vegetables 52 Milk, Yogurt, and Cheese 53 Meats, Poultry, Fish, Dry Beans, Eggs,and Nuts
Personal Development	36 Food in Your Life 39 Fitness and Weight Management	40 Healthful Food Choices 54 Enjoying Mealtime
Technology	41 Planning Meals at Home 42 Food and the Consumer 43 Kitchen Principles	49 Microwave Cooking 51 Fruits and Vegetables

Scope and Sequence—Unit 7: Clothing and Textiles

Topic	Chapter
Career Exploration	68 Careers in Clothing and Textiles
Citizenship/ Leadership	67 Redesigning and Recycling
Communication/ Relationships	56 The Impact of Clothing 68 Careers in Clothing and Textiles
Decision Making/ Life Management	58 Wardrobe Planning 59 Clothing and the Consumer 60 Taking Care of Clothing 61 Fibers and Fabrics 62 Selecting Patterns, Fabrics, and Notions 67 Redesigning and Recycling
Health and Safety	56 The Impact of Clothing
Managing Resources/ Consumer Skills	57 Design Basics 59 Clothing and the Consumer 60 Taking Care of Clothing 67 Redesigning and Recycling
Personal Development	56 The Impact of Clothing 57 Design Basics 59 Clothing and the Consumer 60 Taking Care of Clothing
Technology	59 Clothing and the Consumer 60 Taking Care of Clothing 63 Sewing Equipment 61 Fibers and Fabrics

Scope and Sequence—Unit 8: Housing and Living Space

Topic	Chapter
Career Exploration	75 Careers in the Housing Field
Citizenship/ Leadership	69 The Impact of Housing 74 Protecting the Environment
Communication/ Relationships	69 The Impact of Housing 75 Careers in the Housing Field
Decision Making/ Life Management	69 The Impact of Housing 70 Housing and the Consumer 71 Designing and Organizing Space 72 Managing Care and Upkeep 74 Protecting the Environment
Health and Safety	73 Safety in the Home
Managing Resources/ Consumer Skills	70 Housing and the Consumer 71 Designing and Organizing Space 72 Managing Care and Upkeep 74 Protecting the Environment
Personal Development	69 The Impact of Housing
Technology	71 Designing and Organizing Space 74 Protecting the Environment

Correlation to SCANS

The citations in each category below are only representative. The 75 chapters of *Creative Living* and its wealth of supplementary material contain many more links to the SCANS competencies and skills than could be listed here.

Scans Competencies

	RESOURCES: allocating time, money, materials, and staff	

Text Chapter	Page(s)	Topic
1	40	Maintaining balance in your life
4	53-54	Setting priorities and goals
7	75-77	Assessing personal resources
13	138	Managing your life at work
14	146	Running a home office
15	155	Balancing work/family/personal life
16	168	Living in two households
25	246	A day with a baby
26	257	Running a day care center
27	265-272	Chapter on managing resources
28	275-280	Chapter on managing time
30	291-298	Chapter on managing money
31	301-306	Chapter on using credit wisely
33	317-324	Chapter on consumer skills
35	342	Organizing your life
41	397-404	Chapter on planning meals
49	472	Time management in the kitchen
51	488	Conserving food
58	543-548	Chapter on wardrobe planning
59	551-558	Chapter on buying clothing
70	655-660	Chapter on buying housing
72	674-677	Organizing cleaning tasks

Cooperative Learning Activities Booklet

	33-35	Planning an expedition
	51-52	Finding the best buys

Decision-Making Activities Booklet

	17	Time management
	23	Wardrobe decisions

Life Skills Activities Booklet

	59-60	Hunting for good buys
	70-71	Budget cooking for company

Personal Development Activities Booklet

	39-40	Managing study time
	43-44	Sorting out savings and credit

INTERPERSONAL SKILLS: working on teams, teaching others, serving customers, leading, negotiating, and working well with people from diverse backgrounds

Text Chapter	Page(s)	Topic
4	52	Achieving goals through teamwork
6	72	Giving support to others
8	87-94	Chapter on working with others
9	99	Helping disabled people communicate
11	118	Feature on negotiating at work
12	123-128	Chapter on leadership skills
13	138	Getting along with people at work
14	148	Respecting older people
15	151-158	Chapter on family relationships
18	183	Friends of other ages
19	187-196	Chapter on building relationships
21	209-214	Chapter on caregiving skills
22	222	Feature on teaching
22	223	Children who have special needs
23	227-234	Chapter on caring for children
24	238-240	Promoting children's play
25	252	Being a role model
26	255	Working with children
36	352	Respecting other cultures
45	433	Cooperating in the foods lab
47	454	Kitchen ideas for disabled cooks
54	510	Respecting others' mealtime customs
55	520	Handling customer complaints
56	532	Respecting other cultures' clothing
66	624	Adapting clothing for disabilities
67	632	Showing compassion
69	649	Adapting housing for disabilities
69	652	Being a good neighbor
71	670	Sharing a room
75	699	Providing customer service

Cooperative Learning Activities Booklet
All 36 projects in this booklet involve working on teams.

Decision-Making Activities Booklet
8	Getting along with others
26	Being a good neighbor

Life Skills Activities Booklet
23-24	What makes a leader?
33-34	Be a better friend

Personal Development Activities Booklet

27-28	Teach and learn
31-32	The Babysitters' Handbook

INFORMATION: acquiring and using information

Students are encouraged to acquire and apply new information as part of these activities:

- *Teacher's Wraparound Edition:* Cross-Curricular Activities, Multicultural Perspectives, Family and Community Outreach, Enrichment, Critical-Thinking activities, and Real-Life Application.
- *Text:* Thinking Critically, Applying Your Knowledge, Making Connections, and Building Your Portfolio sections of each Chapter Review.
- *Teacher's Classroom Resources Booklets:* Extension Handouts, Clothing Lab Activities, and Foods Lab Activities.

Text Chapter	Page(s)	Topic
7	77-78	Career exploration
17	175	Sources of help
20	199-200	Taking an inventory of skills
26	259	Finding out more about careers
40	394	Interpreting food labels
53	499	Interpreting a meat label
70	660	Deciphering real estate ads

Cooperative Learning Activities Booklet

45-46	The United Nations food court
65-66	Publishing a fashion newsletter

Life Skills Activities Booklet

45	Finding the costs of having a baby
94	Comparison shopping

Personal Development Activities Booklet

25-26	If You Need Help
35-36	Exploring career options

SYSTEMS: understanding complex interrelationships

Text Chapter	Page(s)	Topic
1	23-24	Changes of adolescence
3	44	Influences on values
4	53-54	Identifying goals
7	75-77	Career self-assessment
8	87-89	Influences on relationships
10	105-107	Influences on decisions
11	113-114	Why conflicts occur
14	146-147	Trends affecting families

TECHNOLOGY: selecting equipment and tools, applying technology to specific tasks, and maintaining and troubleshooting equipment

Cooperative Learning Activities Booklet

Life Skills Activities Booklet

SCANS Foundation Skills

BASIC SKILLS: reading, writing, mathematics, listening, speaking

These elements of *Creative Living* directly reinforce basic skills:

- *Text:* Terms to Learn at the beginning of each chapter and in dark type within the chapters; Making Connections and Building Your Portfolio sections in each Chapter Review.
- *Teacher's Wraparound Edition:* Cross-Curricular Activities, Reteaching, and Enrichment.
- *Student Workbook:* Study Guides and worksheets.

In addition, the following pages in the student text and supplementary booklets emphasize basic skills:

Text Chapter	Page(s)	Topic
7	77-78	Reading, interviewing
9	97-102	Chapter on communication skills
10	108-109	Responding to peer pressure
13	134	Basic skills needed at work
15	152-154	Communicating within the family
20	204	Writing a résumé
30	297	Balancing a checkbook
31	304	Comparing finance charges
34	330	Writing letters
41	401	Reading a recipe
42	409-411	Reading food labels
46	438-444	Chapter on kitchen measuring
59	557	Estimating clothing costs
62	579-581	Taking measurements
64	599	Understanding pattern terms

Cooperative Learning Activities Booklet

| 17-18 | Listening clinic |
| 61-62 | Creating a clothing ad |

Life Skills Activities Booklet

| 117-118 | Understanding an electric bill |
| 119-120 | Writing a job description |

Personal Development Activities Booklet

THINKING SKILLS: creative thinking, making decisions, solving problems, imagining, knowing how to learn, reasoning

Cooperative Learning Activities Booklet

Decision-Making Activities Booklet

All 24 projects in this booklet involve decision making.

Life Skills Activities Booklet

Personal Development Activities Booklet

Personal Qualities: being responsible, having self-esteem, being social, managing oneself, having integrity

Resource List

Unit 1: Personal Development

Books

Career Skills by Dr. Joan Kelly and Dr. Ruth Volz-Patton. Columbus, OH: Glencoe, 1991.

Glencoe Health: A Guide to Wellness by Dr. Mary Bronson Merki and Dr. Don Merki. Columbus, OH: Glencoe, 1994.

Growing Up Caring. Columbus, OH: Glencoe and the Kennedy Foundation, 1990.

The Self-Esteem Library, including books entitled *Discovering Self-Confidence, Discovering How to Make Good Choices*, and *Discovering Personal Goals*. Various authors. New York: Rosen, 1991.

Setting Goals by Sandra Lee Smith. New York: Rosen, 1992.

Teen Health: Course 1 and 2 by Dr. Mary Merki. Columbus, OH: Glencoe, 1996.

The Values Library, including books entitled *Citizenship, Compassion, Courage, Honesty, Patriotism, Responsibility, Sportsmanship, and Tolerance*. Various authors. New York: Rosen, 1990.

Videos (unless otherwise noted)

Building Self-Confidence. Sunburst.

Career Values: What Really Matters to You? (filmstrip on video) Guidance Associates.

CHILL: Straight Talk About Stress. Glencoe.

Coming Down: The Aftermath of Doing Drugs. Glencoe.

Gender and Careers. Learning Seed.

Handling Stress—Today and Tomorrow. Cambridge.

Know Yourself: The Secret of Self-Esteem. Sunburst.

Knowing Who You Are—and Liking It. Guidance Associates.

The Leadership Assignment. Glencoe.

Make Up Your Mind: Skillful Decisions. Learning Seed.

Managing Stress. Glencoe.

Mental Wellness: Making It Happen. HRM Video.

Not for Sale: Ethics in the American Workplace. Sunburst.

Nutrition and Exercise for the '90s. Sunburst.

Setting Goals: The Road to Achievement. Sunburst.

Succeeding in the World of Work: Career Awareness, Self-Awareness, Apprenticeship, Freedom to Choose (series of 19 videos) Glencoe.

Teen Health VHS Videos Course 1 (includes *You Can Refuse, Don't Pop Your Cork Mondays* on stress, and *Teenage Suicide*). Glencoe.

Teenagers, Stress, and How to Cope. Sunburst.

What's School Got to Do with It? HRM Video.

Unit 2: Relationship Skills

Books

Advancing in the World of Work by Grady Kimbrell, Dr. Ben Vineyard, and Valerie Putnam. Columbus, OH: Glencoe, 1992.

Everything You Need to Know About Peer Pressure by Robyn Feller. New York: Rosen, 1993.

It's Our World, Too!: Stories of Young People Who Are Making a Difference by Phillip Hoose. Boston: Joy Street Books, 1993.

Surviving on the Job by Jay Como. Columbus, OH: Glencoe, 1991.

Videos (unless otherwise noted)

The Art of Listening. Learning Seed.

Be Your Best Self: Assertiveness Training. Sunburst.

Communication: The Person-to-Person Skill. Sunburst.

Constructive Communication: Talking Your Way to Success. Cambridge Educational.

Coping with Peer Pressure: Getting Along Without Going Along. Guidance Associates.

Don't Put Me Down. Guidance Associates.

Facing Pressure: From Parents to Peers. Learning Seed.

Getting Along on the Job: Interpersonal Work Skills. HRM Video.

Glencoe Health Media Kit, 1993 (includes videos on self-esteem, friendship and dating, decisions, and refusal skills). Glencoe.

Handling Criticism. Learning Seed.

How to Say No Without Losing Your Friends. Guidance Associates.

Just Chill!: Dealing with Anger. Sunburst.

Learning for Earning. Glencoe.

Level with Me: Honest Communication. Guidance Associates/Learning Seed.

Managing Conflicts (filmstrip set). Glencoe.

Peer Pressure, Drugs, and You. Sunburst.

The Problem with People Pleasing. Learning Seed.

Ready for Work: Qualities That Count with Employers. HRM Video.

Refusal Skills: Yes, You Can Say No. Learning Seed.

School-to-Work Transition. Glencoe.

Strength (interracial conflicts). HRM Video.

Team Skills for the New Workplace. Learning Seed.

Teen Health VHS Videos Course 1 (includes *You Can Refuse, Don't Pop Your Cork Mondays* on stress, and *Teenage Suicide*). Glencoe.

Truce: Conflict Resolution. Glencoe.

Valuing Diversity: Multi-Cultural Communication. Learning Seed.

Unit 3: Families and Friendships

Books

Coping in a Single-Parent Home by Bill Wagonseller, Lynne Ruegamer, and Marie Harrington. New York: Rosen, 1992.

Coping with Cliques by Lee Peck. New York: Rosen, 1992.

Developing Responsible Relationships by Dr. Mary Merki. Columbus, OH: Glencoe, 1993.

Drugs and Your Parents by Rhoda McFarland. New York: Rosen, 1991.

Everything You Need to Know About Moving in with Your Grandparents or Other Relatives by Carolyn Simpson. New York: Rosen, 1995.

Families Today by Connie Sasse. Columbus, OH: Glencoe, 1997.

How to Survive Your Parents' Divorce by Nancy O'Keefe Bolick. New York: F. Watts, 1994.

Married and Single Life by Dr. Audrey Palm Riker and Holly Brisbane. Columbus, OH: Glencoe, 1997.

Parental Divorce by Debra Goldentyer. Austin, TX: Raintree Steck-Vaughn, 1995.

Relationships by Elizabeth Tener. Austin, TX: Raintree Steck-Vaughn, 1995.

Your Circle of Friends by Claudine Wirths and Mary Bowman-Kruhm. New York: Twenty-First Century Books, 1993.

Videos (unless otherwise noted)

Are You Ready for Parenthood? Glencoe.

Breaking the Cycle: Child Abuse. Sunburst.

Cool, Smart and Safe: Choosing to Wait. HRM Video.

Coping with Family Crisis: Guidance Associates.

Dangerous Relationships. HRM Video.

Dating in the 90's: Feeling Good About You. Cambridge Educational.

Divorce and the Family. Learning Seed.

Families in Trouble: Learning to Cope. Sunburst.

Getting Help in the Community. Glencoe.

Glencoe Health Media Kit, 1993 (includes videos on self-esteem, friendship and dating, decisions, and refusal skills). Glencoe.

Hotline: Coping with Family Abuse. Glencoe.

Living with Parents: Conflicts, Comforts and Insights. HRM Video.

Real People: Teens Who Choose Abstinence. Sunburst.

Sexual Abstinence: Making the Right Choice. HRM Video.

Sexual Responsibility: A Two-Way Street. HRM Video.

Teen-Parent Conflict: Making Things Better. Sunburst.

Today's Family: Adjusting to Change. Guidance Associates.

Top Secret: A Friend's Cry for Help. HRM Video.

Values and the Traditional Family. Learning Seed.

When Dating Turns Dangerous. Sunburst.

Working Marriage Partners. Glencoe.

Working Parents: Balancing Kids and Careers. Learning Seed.

"You Would If You Loved Me": Making Decisions About Sex. Guidance Associates.

Unit 4: Child Care and Development

Books

Approaches to Preschool Curriculum by Anziano, Soundy, Kostelnik, and Billman. Columbus, OH: Glencoe, 1995.

Careers in Child Care by Marjorie Eberts. Lincolnwood, IL: VGM Career Horizons, 1994.

Careers Inside the World of Homemaking and Parenting by Maryann Miller. New York: Rosen, 1994.

The Child Care Professional by Karen Stephens. Columbus, OH: Glencoe, 1996.

Child Development. Columbus, OH: Glencoe, 1995.

The Developing Child: Understanding Children and Parenting by Holly Brisbane. Columbus, OH: Glencoe, 1997.

Nutrition, Health, and Safety for Preschool Children by Dlugosz, Zuzich, Frank, Giarratano, and Duyff. Columbus, OH: Glencoe, 1995.

Parenting: Rewards and Responsibilities by Verna Hildebrand. Columbus, OH: Glencoe, 1997.

Planning Activities for Child Care by Caroline Spang Rosser. Nasco.

Videos (unless otherwise noted)

Are You Ready for Parenthood? Glencoe.

Child Care Filmstrip Programs: On the Job, Careers Helping Children. Glencoe.

Child Development: Glencoe.

The Child Grows: The First Year. Learning Seed.

Childproof: Home Safety Checklist. Glencoe.

Common Childhood Injuries. Cambridge Educational.

Communicating with Pre-School Children. Glencoe.

Disciplining Children. Glencoe.

Emerging Communication Skills. Glencoe.

Establishing a Child Care Enterprise. Glencoe.

First Aid: Newest Techniques. Sunburst.

The First Aid Video Series. HRM Video.

"I Never Thought It Would Be Like This": Teenagers Speak Out About Being Pregnant/Being Parents. Guidance Associates.

Importance of Play. Glencoe.

The Job of Your Life: The Reality of Teen Parenthood. HLRM Video

Negative Behavior: Positive Discipline. Cambridge Educational.

Observing Children. Glencoe.

Parenting Challenges. Glencoe.

Planning Activities for Children. Glencoe.

Play It Safe: Making Playtime Safe for Your Child. Cambridge Educational.

Preschoolers: How Three and Four Year Olds Develop. Learning Seed.

Promoting Wholesome Sibling Relationships. Glencoe.

Recognizing Children with Special Needs. Glencoe.

Shaking, Hitting, Spanking: What to Do Instead. Learning Seed.

Space for Growth and Development. Glencoe.

Teenage Father. Sunburst.

Tip-Top Tots: The Nutrition Pyramid for Preschoolers. Glencoe.

Toddlers: The Second Year of Life. Learning Seed.

Unit 5: Management and Consumer Decisions

Books

Buyer Beware: Safeguarding Consumer Rights by Binah Brett Taylor. Vero Beach, FL: Rourke, 1992.

Hearing the Pitch: Evaluating All Kinds of Advertising by Carlienne Frisch. New York: Rosen, 1994.

The Information Revolution: Business and Industry by Walter Oleksy. New York: Facts on File, 1996.

The Law and Economics: Your Rights as a Consumer by Michael Walz. Minneapolis: Lerner, 1990.

Marketing Essentials by Lois Farese, Grady Kimbrell, and Carl Wolosyzk. Columbus, OH: Glencoe, 1991.

Money Smarts by Peggy Santamaria. New York: Rosen, 1992.

Videos (unless otherwise noted)

Buyer Be Aware: Avoiding Rip-Offs. Learning Seed.

Checking Accounts: A Guide to Selection and Use. Learning Seed.

Credit Cards: Living with Plastic. Learning Seed.

Invisible Persuaders. Learning Seed.

Making It on Your Own: Managing Your Money. Guidance Associates.

Managing Your Money (filmstrip set). Glencoe.

Money Management Video Series: Stashing Your Cash—Financial Services; Building Your Money Pyramid—Financial Planning; Budgets Aren't for Pushovers—Budgeting, Goal-Setting, and Record Keeping; Don't Shop 'Til You Drop—Credit and Consumerism. Glencoe.

The Paycheck Puzzle. Guidance Associates.

Perils of Plastic: Handling Credit. Cambridge Educational.

Psycho-Sell: Advertising and Persuasion. Learning Seed.

The Road to Wise Money Management. Cambridge Educational.

Understanding Salaries and Benefits: How People Are Paid. Guidance Associates.

Why You Buy: How Ads Persuade. Learning Seed.

Your Credit Record: Keeping It Clean. Cambridge Educational.

Your Rights as a Consumer. Learning Seed.

Unit 6: Food, Nutrition, and Wellness

Books

Discovering Food and Nutrition by Helen Kowtaluk. Columbus, OH: Glencoe, 1997.

Eat Well by Miriam Moss. New York: Crestwood House, 1993.

Exploring Professional Cooking by Ray and Lewis. Columbus, OH: Glencoe, 1996.

Food for Today by Helen Kowtaluk and Alice Kopan. Columbus, OH: Glencoe, 1997.

Food Science and You by Kay Mehas and Sharon Rodgers. Columbus, OH: Glencoe, 1997.

Food Service Skill Series by Michael Pepper, Gilbert Pratt, and Alice Winnick. Columbus, OH: Glencoe, 1993.

Nutrition by Ann Galperin. New York: Chelsea House, 1991.

Videos (unless otherwise noted)

Banquet Preparation and Service. Guidance Associates.

Best Breakfast. Learning Seed.

Buying Nutritious Food. Glencoe.

Careers in Foods and Nutrition (filmstrip set; transfer video). Glencoe.

Controlling Weight Sensibly. Glencoe.

Eating for Life: The Nutrition Pyramid. Learning Seed.

Eating Healthy: What's a Serving? Glencoe.

Ecology in the Kitchen. Glencoe.

The Fast Food Caper: What's in It for You? (nutrition) Cambridge Educational.

The Food Guide Pyramid: Contemporary Nutrition. Cambridge Educational.

Foods from Other Lands. Glencoe.

Handling Food Safely: Basic Rules of Personal Hygiene. Guidance Associates.

An Introduction to Food Science. Glencoe.

Kitchen Safety: Working with Utensils and Equipment. Guidance Associates.

Low Fat Cooking. Glencoe.

Meal Planning: The Food Pyramid in Action. Learning Seed.

Measuring Ingredients and Following Recipes. Guidance Associates.

Nutrients and You. Glencoe.

Read Before You Eat! A Food Package Quiz. Learning Seed.

Read the Food Label. Glencoe.

Supermarket Persuasion: How Food Is Merchandised. Learning Seed.

Timing and Organization in Food Preparation. Glencoe.

Value Shopping: Stretch Your Food Dollar. Learning Seed.

Vegetarianism. Glencoe.

Video Series for Food Service Programs (Employee Skills, Career Opportunities, Management Skills, Food Preparation, Safety and Sanitation). Glencoe.

Unit 7: Clothing and Textiles

Books

Clothing: Fashion, Fabrics, and Construction by Jeanette Weber. Columbus, OH: Glencoe, 1997.

Drawing Fashion by Bill Thames. Columbus, OH: Glencoe, first edition.

Fabric Lab (workbook and swatch kit). Learning Seed.

Fashion: Contemporary Visual Merchandising by Jay Diamond and Ellen Diamond. Columbus, OH: Glencoe, 1990.

Fashion Merchandising by Elaine Stone and Joan Samples. Columbus, OH: Glencoe, 1990.

Know Your Merchandise: For Retailer and Consumers by Wingate, Gillespie, and Barry. Columbus, OH: Glencoe, fifth edition.

Sewing with Nancy: Design and You by Revelli. Atkinson, WI: Nasco, 1994.

Videos (unless otherwise noted)

American Fashion History (transfer video set). Glencoe.

Clothing: An Intelligent Buyer's Guide. Learning Seed.

Clothing Dollars and Sense. Cambridge Educational.

Discovering Fibers and Fabrics: From Fibers to Fabrics and *Fibers, Fabrics, and the Consumer.* Glencoe.

An Introduction to Fashion Merchandising (four related videos also available). Cambridge Educational.

Sewing Today: The Secrets of Sewing (13 videos by Butterick). Glencoe.

Understanding Hang Tags and Labels. Glencoe.

Wardrobe Planning: The Power of Color, The Elements and Principles of Design, and *A Clothing Plan for You* (filmstrip set; transfer video set). Glencoe.

Unit 8: Housing and Living Space

Books

Decor-Aide Space Planner (room-planning kit with hundreds of templates and tips for furniture arrangement) Source: Decor-Aide, P.O. Box 2873, Alameda, CA 94501.

Home Maintenance by Weiss. Columbus, OH: Glencoe, second edition.

Homes: Today and Tomorrow by Ruth F. Sherwood. Columbus, OH: Glencoe, 1997.

How to Clean Practically Anything by Florman. Bridgeport, CT: Consumer Reports Books, 1993.

Room Planning Guide (free kit) Source: Furniture Information Council, P.O. Box HP7, High Point, NC 27261.

Videos (unless otherwise noted)

The American House: A Guide to Architectural Styles. Learning Seed.

Careers in Interior Design. Learning Seed.

Choosing Furnishings and Accessories. Glencoe.

Eye for Design. Learning Seed.

Furnishing and Decorating Your First Home. Learning Seed.

Furniture: A Buyer's Guide. Learning Seed.

Home Safety Series (4 videos). Glencoe.

Paul Ehrlich's Energy Watch. HRM Video.

Styles of American Furniture (slides). Learning Seed.

General Books

Succeeding in the World of Work by Grady Kimbrell and Dr. Ben Vineyard. Columbus, OH: Glencoe, 1992.

Today's Teen by Dr. Joan Kelly and Dr. Eddye Eubanks. Columbus, OH: Glencoe, 1997.

Young Living Nanalee Clayton. Columbus, OH: Glencoe, 1997.

Software

ABCNews InterActive Videodiscs: Understanding Ourselves: Health (DOS and Macintosh programs on AIDS, Drugs and Substance, Teenage Sexuality, Tobacco, Alcohol, Food and Nutrition, Violence Prevention). Glencoe.

Body Awareness Resource Network, interactive programs (IBM, Apple, Macintosh). Glencoe.

Fabric Identification Kit (Apple, IBM). Learning Seed.

Fast Food Microguide (Apple, Macintosh, IBM). Learning Seed.

The Human Sexuality Videodisc (laser disc). HRM Video.

Kaman's Fashions for Less; Merchandising with Microcomputers (IBM). Glencoe.

Making It on Your First Job (video and laser disc). Cambridge Educational.

Mayo Clinic: Sports Health and Fitness. (Windows/MPC). Glencoe.

Multimedia Personal Development: Goals, Self-Esteem, and Decisions (CD-ROM for Windows and Macintosh). Cambridge Educational.

What Did You Eat Yesterday?—The Pyramid Revision (IBM only). Learning Seed.

Audiovisual and Software Companies

These video and software companies will send a current catalog of products at your request. The catalogs contain detailed information about video and software offerings. Several of the companies also offer free previews of videos.

Cambridge Educational
P.O. Box 2153
Charleston, WV 25328
1-800-468-4227

Glencoe/McGraw-Hill Order Department
P.O. Box 508
Columbus, OH 43216
1-800-334-7344

Guidance Associates
P.O. Box 1000
Mount Kisco, NY 10549-0010
1-800-431-1242

HRM Video
175 Tompkins Avenue
Pleasantville, NY 10570-9973
1-800-431-2050

The Learning Seed
330 Telser Road
Lake Zurich, IL 60047
1-800-634-4941

Sunburst Communications
39 Washington Avenue
P.O. Box 40
Pleasantville, NY 10570-0040
1-800-431-1934

Sixth Edition

Creative Living

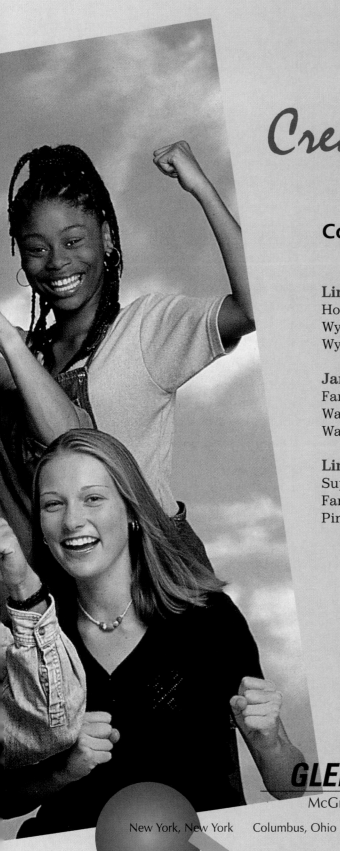

Sixth Edition

Creative Living

Consulting Authors

Linda R. Glosson, Ph.D.
Home Economics Teacher
Wylie High School
Wylie, Texas

Janis P. Meek, CFCS
Family and Consumer Sciences Teacher
Warren County High School
Warrenton, North Carolina

Linda G. Smock, CFCS
Supervisor
Family and Consumer Sciences
Pinellas County Schools, Florida

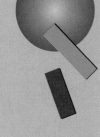

GLENCOE
McGraw-Hill

New York, New York   Columbus, Ohio   Mission Hills, California   Peoria, Illinois

Editorial Development

Co-developed by
Glencoe/McGraw-Hill and Visual Education Corporation,
Princeton, New Jersey

Reviewers

Betty Lou Blackburn
Family and Consumer Sciences Instructor
Broken Arrow Senior High School
Broken Arrow, Oklahoma

Ruth Donna Lewis, CFCS
Vocational Family and Consumer Sciences
  Teacher
Daniel Webster High School
Tulsa, Oklahoma

JoAnna O. Lochen
Home Economics Teacher
South-Doyle High School
Knoxville, Tennessee

Marcia Jean Northrup, M.S., CFCS
Family and Consumer Sciences Educator
Pleasant Lea Junior High School
Lee's Summit, Missouri

Rebecca W. Pierce
Family and Consumer Sciences Teacher
Chilton County High School
Clanton, Alabama

Laura Sarno Porcaro, M.A.
Family Living Teacher
Pascack Hills High School
Montvale, New Jersey

Julie Rosin, M.S., CFCS
Supervisor of Family and Consumer Sciences
Des Moines Public Schools
Des Moines, Iowa

RosaLee Saikley, M.A.
Family Life Instructor
Mira Costa High School
Manhattan Beach, California

Linda Young, M.S.
Consumer Home Economics Teacher
Sullivan South High School
Kingsport, Tennessee

Glencoe/McGraw-Hill

A Division of The **McGraw·Hill** *Companies*

Send all inquiries to:
Glencoe/McGraw-Hill
3008 W. Willow Knolls Drive
Peoria, IL 61614-1083

ISBN 0-02-642749-4 (Student Edition)

Printed in the United States of America.

1 2 3 4 5 6 7 8 9 RRDW/LP 03 02 01 00 99 98 97 96

Table of Contents

Special Text Features

Managing Your Life

Strategies That Work

Charts and Highlighted Topics

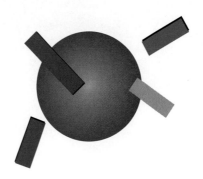

Unit Preview

Unit 1 helps students understand themselves better and prepares them for the future. It explores how personality develops, what behaviors can help teens stay healthy physically, and how values underlie character and guide lives. The unit also helps students learn to set realistic goals, make wise decisions, and develop the competence and confidence they need to meet challenges. Unit 1 ends by encouraging students to begin the self-assessment and exploration that will help them choose meaningful careers.

Content Development

Use these chapters to reinforce the following themes:

Content Strands	Chapters
Career Exploration	7
Citizenship/	
Leadership	3, 5
Communication	1, 5–7
Decision Making	3, 5–7
Health and Safety	2, 5
Managing	
Resources	2, 4–6
Personal	
Development	1–7
Technology	1, 7

Unit Motivator

■ **Skills for Life.** Ask students this question: "What skills do you need for life?" As ideas begin to flow, have students turn to the table of contents in the text and scan the chapter titles. They are likely to see the same ideas and more reflected in these titles.

22

JOURNAL WRITING

Possible topics for student journals:

- What changes do you welcome at this time in your life? Which ones are confusing?
- What, if anything, would you like to change about your physical self?
- What values do you share with your friends? Which values seem more important to you than to other teens?
- Some teens have trouble setting goals. Why do you think that is?
- Are you pleased with the outcome of most of your decisions? If not, what do you think is the problem?
- What kinds of help would you like in choosing a career?

Personal Development

Chapters

1. You and Your World
2. Health and Wellness
3. Developing Character
4. Goals and Resources
5. Making Responsible Decisions
6. Making Changes and Meeting Challenges
7. Thinking About Careers

23

FHA Activities

The following activities can be used with FHA groups or as public relations strategies:

■ **You, Too?** To begin the unit, write each of the sentence starters below at the top of a large sheet of paper. Post the sheets around the classroom. Give students 15 minutes to move around the room and complete as many sentences as possible. When time is up, read and discuss students' responses to each sentence, keeping students' names confidential.

I really like . . . .

I'm confused about . . . .

I'll know I'm successful when I . . . .

When I need to make a decision, I think about . . . .

I wish someone would help me decide . . . .

■ **You Are Special!** After students complete the unit, have groups develop skits to help elementary school children become aware of their uniqueness and gain confidence in themselves and their own positive values. If possible, arrange for several groups to present their skits to elementary classes.

Unit Closure

REVIEW

■ **Keys to Success.** Arrange students into seven groups. Assign each group a chapter and ask groups to summarize the key points in their chapters and write them on a large cardboard key of their own design. They might add small pictures to illustrate points. Display the keys.

EVALUATION

■ **Unit Test.** Have students complete the unit test in the Teacher's Classroom Resources.

■ **Testmaker Software.** You may wish to design a unit test using the *Testmaker Software.*

COOPERATIVE LEARNING

Group Bio. Have groups put together group biographies that include information about every member. Each student should gather information from other group members in order to complete one section of the biography. Ideas for sections are: "Our Early Days," "Ways We Stay Healthy," "Doing Our Part," "Our Best Decisions," and "A Glimpse into the Future." Students may use written reports with photographs or drawings or a documentary (perhaps videotaped), complete with interviews.

FOCUS

Chapter Overview

Chapter 1 discusses the many changes teens experience. It explains factors that affect personality, self-concept, and self-esteem and encourages students to work toward their potential.

Motivators

■ **TV Teens.** Ask the class to think of fictional teens in television shows. Compare these teens' lives to those of the class. Do TV teens share the class' concerns? Discuss.

■ **Word Pictures.** Have students choose and describe one teen pictured in the chapter, suggesting personality as well as physical traits. Explain that in this chapter they will learn more about the components that make each teen unique.

Objectives

Discuss the chapter objectives on this page. Remind students that the objectives focus on important chapter concepts.

Vocabulary

Explain the difference between *self-concept* and *self-esteem*. Tell students they will discuss this difference further as they explore the chapter.

Chapter 1 You and Your World

Terms to Learn

- adolescence
- attitude
- environment
- heredity
- hormones
- peer
- personal development
- personality
- potential
- self-concept
- self-esteem

Objectives

This chapter will help you to:

- **Describe** the changes that take place during adolescence.
- **Explain** how personality is expressed.
- **Analyze** the factors that influence personality.
- **Compare and contrast** self-concept and self-esteem.
- **Explain** how to build self-esteem.
- **Define** potential and explain how to develop yours.

CHAPTER RESOURCES

Student Workbook

Study Guide, pp. 7-8

Activity, *Getting to Know Yourself,* pp. 9-10

Teacher's Classroom Resources

Lesson Plan, p. 5

Cooperative Learning, *What Makes You Proud?* pp. 9-10

Extension #1, *A Realistic Self-Concept,* p. 7

Extension #2, *Coping with Change,* p. 8

Life Skills, *Actions Speak Louder Than Words,* p. 7

Personal Development, *Your Expectations,* pp. 5-6

Transparency 1, *Living in a Changing World*

Chapter 1 Test, pp. 7-8

Performance Assessment, *Growth and Change,* p. 17

Reteaching, *Growing and Changing,* p. 7

See Also:

ABCNews InterActive™ Videodiscs

The journey had been long, but Christy was about to reach her destination. She couldn't wait to see her older sister. It would be a good summer—and it would give her an opportunity to think, to explore, and perhaps to grow.

As the train sped on, Christy thought about the past year. It had been a difficult one. She had concerns about changes that had occurred and about what she had said and done. Spending the summer with her sister would be good. She knew that they would talk for hours and hours.

As the train station in her sister's town loomed into view, Christy felt excited. This journey was about to end, but for some reason she felt that it would be a new beginning for her. Christy had hopes and dreams for her life, and she knew that she was capable of success in the greater journey still ahead.

Teens grow out of childhood and begin to look like adults.

The Journey Ahead

As a teen, you have your whole adult life to look forward to. What will that life be like? It all depends on you and on how you handle your teen years. Few people go through their teens without hitting a few bumps along the way. Some hit more than others. Those bumps can either get you down or get you going. People like Christy develop attitudes, qualities, and skills that help them stay on course and heading for a good future. Your journey can be satisfying—if you make it so.

What attitudes, qualities, and skills do you need for life? That's what much of this text is about. By the time you complete this course, you will have many tools to use. The place to start, however, is with you personally. Take a look at yourself to see who you are and what you are capable of becoming.

Working with Change

Adolescence is a time of exciting changes. This is *the period of life when you prepare to be an adult*. You develop physically, emotionally, intellectually, morally, and socially. Responding to changes in positive ways can make the road to adulthood easier to travel and help you arrive in good condition.

Physical Changes

One look in the mirror tells many teens that adulthood is on the way. Although teens develop physically at different rates, sooner or later they all see changes taking place. Most teens eagerly look forward to becoming an adult. The physical signs show that greater independence is around the corner.

Hormones are the catalysts of physical change. As these *chemicals are released in the body,* males and females begin to take on the forms typical of adults of each gender. Some changes, such as acne and the squeakiness of a developing male voice, are usually only temporary. A sense of humor helps if physical changes make you feel awkward or different. These feelings, too, will pass in time.

CHAPTER 1   You and Your World   25

TEACH

Topic on p. 25:
- **Physical and Emotional Changes**

Checking Comprehension

✓ Why is adolescence both the beginning and the end of a journey? *It ends childhood and begins adulthood.*

✓ What begins the maturing process? *The release of hormones.*

Activities

■ **Too Soon, Too Late.** Ask students why teens may be embarrassed by the changes of adolescence. Guide class to focus on varying growth rates that cause differences among teens. *(Observation)*

RETEACHING

■ **Focus on Changes.** Have students discuss this question in groups, then with class: Which changes of adolescence seem to cause teens more concern: physical or emotional? Guide students to see that each teen's experiences may be different.

ENRICHMENT

■ **It Adds Up.** Have students bring to class print media advertisements that might appeal to teens as they face change. On what kinds of changes do the ads focus? How does this focus help sell products?

DID YOU KNOW?

The average teen grows about 11.5 in. (30 cm) from the beginning of his or her growth spurt until age 18. However, growth rates are different for everyone.

Many societies have formal rites of passage that mark a teen's transition into adulthood. Examples include confirmation and bar mitzvah.

Checking Comprehension

✓ How does teens' thinking change during adolescence? *Becomes more abstract; teens can imagine consequences, options; make better decisions; learn from mistakes; plan better.*

✓ What challenge do parents face as teens undergo these changes? *Provide guidance and support yet give teens more freedom and responsibility.*

SPECIAL NEEDS *Strategies*

Learning in Pairs. Pair students with significant differences, such as cultural backgrounds or talents, to complete the practice activities in "From School to Work." Explain that both partners must be familiar with the pair's ideas because you will choose one partner to share them with the class.

MULTICULTURAL *Perspectives*

Point out that teens from strong ethnic backgrounds must often try to establish their identity in two cultures. The standards and behavior expected of them at school may be very different from those experienced at home. If possible, ask volunteers to share their experiences as teens in this situation.

Emotional Changes

The same hormones that spur physical growth affect emotions. Chad wondered why he felt on top of the world one minute and down in the dumps the next. Learning that hormones can have this effect on teens eased his mind. He could then focus on managing his reactions to the feelings.

Teens learn to adapt to occasional mood swings. For example, most of the time Heather feels very social. She likes to be with friends and family and participate in activities with others. Sometimes, however, a strong desire to be alone builds inside her. Instead of worrying about the feeling, she works with it. Those are the times when she takes a bubble bath, reads a book, or writes in her diary. Later, she is ready to be social again.

Emotional ups and downs tend to diminish as adulthood is reached. That's because the level of hormones becomes more balanced in the adult body. Teens who feel particularly troubled by their changing emotions find help in talking to friends and family members or even to a professional counselor, if necessary.

Many teens find that they need time to be alone with their thoughts.

Intellectual Changes

New intellectual skills allow teens to develop realistic plans. They are able to imagine the consequences of actions and to think about alternatives. Equally important, they develop the ability to reflect on the results of decisions and to learn from mistakes.

Emerging intellect can be very stimulating. As a teen, you are better able to reason and to think in abstract terms. You may begin to ask such questions as "Why is that true?" or "Why not do it this way?" You are ready to test new ideas and to think things through for yourself. You begin to form your own **attitudes**, *thoughts and judgments about the world around you.*

The wise teen realizes that knowing more doesn't necessarily mean knowing it all. To get along well with others, teens respect other people's thoughts and opinions, especially for family members, teachers, and friends.

Moral Changes

In general, teens know the difference between right and wrong. Acting accordingly, however, is sometimes difficult. Because they want to fit in and please others, teens often feel pressured to go along—even when the action is not in their best interest. As teens grow toward adulthood, it becomes easier for them to live by the principles they believe in, regardless of what others think.

In all areas of right and wrong, smart teens are cautious. They learn about the pressures that can surface (as you will learn in Chapter 10). They practice skills that steer them past the challenges without serious mistakes.

Social Changes

Teens typically find themselves drawn more to **peers**—*people their own age.* Time spent with friends increases, often at the expense of time spent with family. Romantic feelings emerge as teens begin to socialize more with friends of the opposite gender.

REAL-LIFE APPLICATION

Ask students to listen to this description of a teen and identify each trait as physical, emotional, intellectual, moral, or social: *Chris is good at math (I), has blue eyes (P), can be moody (E), gets teary in sad movies (E), likes to talk to friends (S), is honest (M), has red hair (P), is a good writer (I), is having trouble getting along with his mother right now (S), and won't go to parties where there are drugs (M).* Summarize by leading students to see that each of them is a unique collection of characteristics from all five groups.

From School to Work

Creative Thinking

What You Learn Today . . .

What does creativity mean to you? You might first think of artistic and musical abilities, but creative thinking can be used in other ways as well. You can find solutions for everyday problems and a wider range of possibilities with creative thinking. Here's how some people think creatively:

- **Brainstorming.** To brainstorm, write down every possible option for solving a problem. Let the ideas flow without evaluating whether they are good or bad. You can brainstorm with others to generate more ideas.
- **Imagining.** Use your imagination to change your perspective. For instance, if you're having problems getting along with someone, imagine yourself as that person and explore the other point of view.
- **Enacting.** With a partner, you can try acting out a situation in order to reach a solution. This allows you to explore options without actually experiencing the consequences.

. . . You Can Use Tomorrow

Businesses encourage employees to use creative thinking in order to generate new ideas. Workers may be charged with solving a job-related problem. They might be asked to develop a new product. Whatever the purpose, creative thinking works. Employees solve problems, save money, and increase sales when they think creatively.

Practicing Your Skills

The more you practice creative thinking, the better you become at it. For a creative workout, try one of these ideas: Think of an unusual use for a familiar object. Prepare a dinner menu that has a color scheme. Make up a nonsense word and then define it. Write a commercial to "sell" a letter of the alphabet. Are you starting to think creatively?

Assessing Your Skills

1. If possible, describe a situation in which you used creative thinking. Why was a creative approach helpful?
2. Now think of a situation in which you could have used creative thinking. How might the outcome have changed?
3. How can creative thinking contribute to your future success?

Reduced reliance on family prepares a teen for eventual independence. This process occurs gradually, with teen and family working together to strike a balance between freedom and responsibility. Teens who realize that this transition time can be confusing for everyone try to understand all points of view. They keep family ties strong while they build new relationships outside the family.

Emerging as an Adult

Development during adolescence is complex. The person who emerges from this stage of life is very different from the one who entered it. You are well on your way through the process. All areas of your development are working together to produce the adult version of you. Everything you do now to promote your development will help you become the capable adult that you need to be.

Personality Development

People come in all shapes and sizes. They also come with distinctive personalities. *The combination of characteristics that makes you different from every other person* is your **personality**.

Often personalities are summed up in a word. People might say that Harry is shy, Tasha is aggressive, and Shannon is outgoing.

ENRICHMENT

■ **Identifying Examples.** Have students write the five areas of change as headings on a sheet of paper. Under each heading, they should list two specific changes in that category. Ask students to describe a benefit and challenge that might result from each change.

From School to Work

Have students read "Creative Thinking." Tell them that the "From School to Work" features in this text focus on how the skills and knowledge they learn today have relevance in their lives later on, especially in the work world. Remind them that making an effort to build their skills and knowledge now has a payoff tomorrow by making them better job candidates and more well-rounded individuals.

Answers to Assessing . . .
1. Possible answers: solving time conflict, finding way to earn money; creativity helps you identify more possible, effective solutions.
2. Answers should explain how a more creative approach would have solved the problem.
3. Answers will vary.

Focus on Creative Thinking Skills

Explain that after creating a list of possible solutions, the next step in problem solving is to examine the ideas and eliminate any unworkable ones, then to weigh the advantages and disadvantages of each remaining solution to identify the best one. The longer the list, the better the chance of finding the best solution. Solutions may be found by combining all or part of two or more ideas.

Checking Comprehension

✓ How do heredity and environment help shape personality? *Inherited traits give you potential to develop in certain ways; environment encourages or discourages traits.*

✓ Why is adolescence a good time to make personality adjustments? *Easier to shape personality now than when you're more set in your ways.*

SPECIAL NEEDS *Strategies*

Impulse Control. Remind students that they express their personalities through their behavior, yet they cannot always act just as they like. Learning to control negative impulses is essential to maturity. Have students list situations where it's difficult to control impulses and offer tips for doing so.

CROSS-CURRICULAR ACTIVITY
Art

Ask each student to create a collage that illustrates his or her personality. Ask them to find pictures or draw their own to show all components of personality.

What are the emotional, social, and intellectual traits of your personality?

Actually, personalities are more complex than this. A closer look will show you in what ways. You will also discover that your personality can be shaped if you make the effort.

Personality Components

Many characteristics are part of personality. In general, they fall into three categories—emotional, social, and intellectual.

Every person feels the same basic emotions, such as fear, happiness, and pain, yet each responds to them individually. When Kara's grandmother died, for example, her sorrow was expressed through tears. Another person might show sorrow in a quiet, reflective way. As you observe how people handle their emotions, you start to form a picture of this part of their personality.

People are also different in how they relate to others. This reveals the social side of their personality, and there is plenty of variation. Some people prefer the company of others rather than being alone. Others are just the opposite. Most people want some combination of the two.

Intellectual traits are the third part of personality. These qualities are influenced by the mind and how it works. One person spends

28   UNIT 1   Personal Development

DID YOU KNOW?

Teen magazines often print personality tests. These tests, however, are designed to sell magazines, not to accurately test personality. Personality testing is best left to professionals in the fields of guidance and mental health. Asking several supportive friends and family members to describe them might provide teens with a better idea of the personality they present than the results of a magazine test.

time in deep thought. Another is creative. Jake, for example, often had people in his class laughing. He saw humor in almost everything and was able to express it in entertaining ways.

The emotional, social, and intellectual traits of personality become apparent to others through behavior. Usually it takes getting to know a person well to see the full depth of that person's personality. For example, a person who is quiet and businesslike in class might be outgoing in a social setting.

The Origins of Personality

When you start thinking about what you are like, you may start wondering why you are that way. Explaining why personalities develop as they do isn't easy. That's because two influences are at work, and no one really knows which one has the greater effect. In fact, the combination of these influences may not be the same for every person.

Heredity is one influence on personality. **Heredity** is *the set of characteristics that you inherit from your parents and ancestors.* "He's just like his father," Mrs. Miller always said about her son Todd, now 17. Since Todd's father had died when the boy was only a year old, heredity explained the resemblances. For Todd, there had been no opportunity to learn these traits from his father.

Other aspects of personality are shaped by what goes on around a person. **Environment**—*the circumstances, objects, and conditions that surround people*—also has an impact on personality. This influence is very strong and very complicated. Home life, for example, affects children's personalities as they grow. People who feel loved and secure are likely to develop more positive personality traits than those who are troubled as they grow up.

Personality Adjustments

Personalities make people interesting. How boring it would be if everyone had the same personality. On the other hand, some personalities are more pleasing than others.

What about you? Are you satisfied with your personality, or is there something—even a small quality—that you would like to change? Most people have at least some personality adjustments they would like to make.

Adolescence is a time for development, and personality is developing right along with everything else. Shaping your personality as you want it to be may be easier

Your self-concept develops as you judge your own strengths and weaknesses and evaluate feedback from others.

CHAPTER 1   You and Your World   29

Activities

■ **Causes of Change.** Ask students what might cause a person's personality to change. *(Critical Thinking)*

RETEACHING

■ **The Effects of Environment.** Have students gather stories about people who came from environments that presented serious obstacles but who managed to succeed in some way. As students share their stories in class, ask them what inherited traits might have helped that person succeed.

ENRICHMENT

■ **Getting to Know Me.** Ask groups to think of ways teens can get to know themselves better. Then have groups share ideas. (Examples include keeping a daily journal, trying out for a play or team, assuming the leadership of a group, and spending some time alone each day.)

FAMILY AND COMMUNITY OUTREACH

Have students ask several people to whom they feel close to write a sentence about the student's positive characteristics, while the student writes a similar sentence about himself or herself. Have students compare their sentences with those that others wrote. Ask them to write a paragraph comparing and contrasting these images of themselves. What does this tell them about their self-concept?

Focus on Relationship Skills

Point out that during adolescence many teens begin to evaluate their parents' attitudes for the first time. Although this is a normal part of maturing, it can be hard on family relationships.

Help students realize that during these kinds of discussions, being fair and reasonable and listening calmly can help everyone express opinions without becoming involved in an argument.

Topics on pp. 30-32:

- Developing Self-Concept
- Building Self-Esteem
- Potential for Personal Development

Checking Comprehension

✓ What is the difference between self-concept and self-esteem? *Self-concept: image of yourself; self-esteem: value you place on yourself.*

✓ Are those with low self-esteem doomed to go through life that way? *No. They can build self-esteem through the approaches in Figure 1.1.*

✓ How is working toward your potential like rolling a snowball through the snow? *You start with small ball of snow. As ball gets bigger, more snow sticks to it, and ball gets bigger yet. Likewise, as you gain skills and knowledge, you can do more in life.*

SPECIAL NEEDS *Strategies*

Inefficient Readers. Ask students to find sentences in this chapter that help them know how a person with high self-esteem and one with low self-esteem might react to: receiving a compliment on a haircut; getting a poor grade on a test; receiving a difficult school assignment; being told they are not tall enough to play basketball.

---

now than later, while change is already in the works. Think about the personality traits that you admire. Just as an athlete builds skills, you can build the personality you want to have, but only if you are determined to do so.

Developing Self-Concept

Suppose that you had to complete this sentence: "I am. . . ." What would you say? You might use many, or just a few, words to describe yourself. *How you define what you are* is your **self-concept**. Sometimes people call this self-image or identity.

When you know who and what you are, then you know how to act. Without a clear idea of who and what you are, then a basis for your actions is missing. You may find yourself confused about what to do in many situations. An example explains the connection between self-concept and actions.

Antonio saw himself as a good student. His family and friends helped him develop this image of himself, which is a typical way for a self-concept to form. Because Antonio saw himself as a good student, he read and he studied. The temptation to watch television when he needed to study was relatively easy to resist. He knew what he had to do to live up to his self-image.

One of the objectives of adolescence is to develop a positive self-concept. Focusing on strengths rather than weaknesses helps you develop the proper perspective. When positive messages come your way, you are more likely to develop the kind of self-concept you need. Danger comes with hearing—and believing—negative messages. All her life, April heard that she was "no good." Hearing those messages, she started to act that way. Then her foster mother helped her realize that she *was* a good person. When her self-concept changed, so did her behavior, and that changed her life.

Figure 1.1

WAYS TO BOOST YOUR SELF-ESTEEM ★★★★★★★★★★★★★★★★★★★★★★★

Here are six things you can do to develop a more positive view of yourself.

Learn to accept praise. When someone compliments you, don't put yourself or your accomplishment down. People praise you because they feel that you really deserve it.

Focus on your strengths. Everyone has talents. One person might play the saxophone or paint well. Another might be a good leader or a good listener. To remind yourself of the things you do well, write down your strengths and talents.

Accept yourself as you are. Accept the fact that you are not perfect and that you have some faults. After all, you accept your friends as they are. Why should you be any harder on yourself?

30   UNIT 1   *Personal Development*

REAL-LIFE APPLICATION

Read this to students: *Charles' father wants him to play football. Charles, however, would rather log on to the Internet than practice a forward pass. Every time his father "catches" him at the computer, Charles feels uncomfortable and has a sense of failure.* Ask: What could Charles do to raise his self-esteem? Refer to Figure 1.1. Ask: Who is more responsible for Charles' feelings? How could communicating help?

Building Self-Esteem

Your self-concept is the picture you have of yourself. Your **self-esteem** is how you feel about that image. It is *the value, or importance, you place on yourself.*

Self-esteem can be high, low, or anywhere in between. Many things affect your level of self-esteem, including your successes, your thoughts about strengths and weaknesses, and the way people react to you. Self-esteem can be higher at some times than others.

Self-esteem matters because it has a strong influence on your behavior and your well-being. When you feel good about yourself, you have more confidence. You believe that you can be successful, and you are willing to try new things. High self-esteem enables you to make the best of your life without becoming arrogant and without harming others.

When self-esteem is lower than it should be, remedies are possible. Give your self-esteem a boost by trying the ideas in **Figure 1.1.**

Realizing Your Potential

The deepest personal defeat suffered by human beings is constituted by the difference between what one was capable of becoming and what one has in fact become.

These words of anthropologist Ashley Montagu have special significance for young people. Today you are looking ahead at life, but what if you could look *back* on your life right now? Would you see mistakes? Regrets? Read what Rita has to say.

"My father begged me not to quit piano lessons, but I just didn't want to practice. I don't even remember how I spent my time. Maybe I talked on the phone or watched television. I could have been a good pianist. My father still talks about how he loved to listen to me play. How could I have been so foolish? Sometimes I envy the people who can play piano at parties or in performances. People say I could start taking lessons again, but it's harder now. I've got so many things I *have* to do at this point in my life."

Activities

■ **Affecting Others.** Have students suggest ways that they affect others' self-concepts, both positively and negatively. *(Relationship)*

■ **Analyzing Efforts.** Have students list at least five things each is doing now toward reaching her or his potential in any area of development. Then have them list five more things each might do to work harder toward that potential. *(Problem Solving)*

ENRICHMENT

■ **Wise Words.** Have groups write a letter from a teen to an advice column. The letter should describe a relationship or self-esteem problem typical to teens. Review the letters for appropriateness. Then give each one to a different group. Have the group write a reply, using knowledge gained from this chapter.

USING VISUALS

Use these questions to help students think about the ideas in Figure 1.1:
1. What should you do when someone compliments you? *Say "thank you" and smile. Don't belittle yourself or your achievements.*
2. How can accepting yourself as you are help you to improve your faults? *You will have more time to work on reducing your faults.*
3. How can helping others build your own self-esteem? *You realize that you are important to others.*

Learn from what you do. Try to see your mistakes as learning experiences, and don't label yourself a failure. Instead, see mistakes as opportunities to figure out how you can do things differently in the future.

Use your strengths to help others. Being a part of activities that help others lets you know that you can accomplish something really important. It also helps you feel good about yourself.

Take responsibility for your own life. Learn how to deal with the different demands that are made of you. Managing your own life successfully will make you feel good about yourself.

CHAPTER 1   You and Your World   31

DID YOU KNOW?

Explain that many communities offer school-based human services centers. (Mention if your school has one.) These centers provide many services for students and parents in a single, convenient location.

MORE ABOUT Community Services

Help students become familiar with the services available to them, which may include teen hot lines, counseling agencies with sliding payment scales, and health clinics.

Review

- **Chapter Review.** Use the contents of the Chapter Review page to help students review concepts, think critically, and apply their knowledge.
- **Study Guide.** Have students complete the Study Guide for Chapter 1 on p. 7 of the Student Workbook.
- **Novel Approach.** Tell students to imagine they are creating two characters with very different personalities for a story. Have students write a description of each character's emotional, social, and intellectual traits, including self-concept and self-esteem. (Application)

Evaluation

- **Chapter Test.** Use the reproducible chapter test provided in the Teacher's Classroom Resources or create your own test using the Testmaker Software.
- **Alternative Assessment.** Have students write a psychological self-portrait by applying the concepts discussed in this chapter to themselves. For example, what is their self-concept? What are they doing to reach their potential? Explain that only you will read these profiles.

CLOSE

- **Then and Now.** Have groups compare and contrast the changes of adolescence today with those their parents faced. Discuss, leading the class to see that physical and intellectual changes are basically the same, but some social factors and problems are different.

Managing Your Life

Adapting to Change

Developmental changes can make any teen feel uneasy. One teen struggles to fit in at school. Another is uncomfortable with a changing body. Still another feels especially sensitive about what people say. If any of this sounds familiar to you, don't worry. You can take steps to make things easier. Here are some ideas:

- **Look ahead.** People sometimes fall into the trap of looking longingly at the past, wishing that changes had not happened. Turning back the clock, however, is simply impossible. Those who look ahead realize that developmental change is moving them in an exciting direction.
- **Think positive.** Changes present opportunity. Try to look at the positive side. Difficult emotions are a sign of deepening emotions that will eventually help you form strong relationships.
- **Take advantage of new abilities.** Use changes to your benefit. Teens' growing moral sense can be used as the basis for making contributions to family, school, and community.

- **Direct change.** Point change toward what you want. Keep in mind your basic desires for your life, and work toward these goals.
- **Get help when you need it.** Almost everyone needs help at one time or another. Adults, who lived through adolescence themselves, can often suggest ways of handling the challenges of this period.

Applying the Principles

1. Why are people sometimes afraid of change?
2. What is wrong with longing for the way things used to be?
3. How have you used—or could you use—one of these ideas to make adapting to developmental change easier?

Like every other person, you have **potential**. This means that you have *the capability of becoming something more than you are right now*. You were born with potential. You have strengths that can be developed. Every person's challenge is to identify those strengths and make use of them.

Like every other person, you can also be sidetracked from reaching your potential. This happens when certain attitudes and circumstances block progress. What problems can you identify in these phrases: "I'll start later." "I've got plenty of time for that." "This will be more fun."

How close you come to reaching your potential is up to you. Things don't have to get in the way if you don't let them. Realizing your potential is a lifelong journey, one that many people fail to take. The time for you to embark is now.

Personal Development

If Cassidy has the potential to be a veterinarian, does that mean she will become one? The answer is no. Potential is simply the capacity you have. What matters is how that capacity is used. *When you work toward your potential*, you aim for **personal development**.

Through personal development, you learn skills and practice them. Growth has a mushrooming effect. The more you learn, the more you are able to learn, and the closer you move toward your potential.

You have an important asset—yourself. By developing the qualities, skills, and attitudes you need, you can build a good life for yourself and your family. You can have a positive effect on the world. Moreover, you will always be able to look back knowing that you made the best of the life you were given.

Managing Your Life

After students read "Adapting to Change," have groups write two scenes in which characters respond first positively, then negatively, to change in their life, based on the guidelines given. Have groups share these and discuss the questions in "Applying the Principles."

Answers to Applying . . .

1. It often requires new, unfamiliar ways of thinking or acting.
2. It makes it harder to adapt; may mean lost opportunities.
3. Answers will vary.

Chapter 1 Review

Reviewing the Facts

1. In what five areas do teens experience changes? Give an example of each kind of change.
2. What three categories can be used to classify personality traits?
3. What factors influence the development of personality?
4. What is the difference between self-concept and self-esteem?
5. List six ways to boost self-esteem.
6. What is a person's potential?

Thinking Critically

1. Can the confidence of someone with high self-esteem be misused? Explain your answer.
2. How can people overcome problems caused by environment?

Applying Your Knowledge

1. **Making Changes.** Identify an area in which you would like to make a personality adjustment. Write down what steps you could follow to achieve the change you want.
2. **Identifying Skills.** List four or five skills that you possess. Write down at least one way that you could improve each skill to help fulfill your potential.
3. **Sending Positive Messages.** Make a list of several statements you made to friends or family members recently when you were commenting on their actions. Evaluate each message. Which ones promoted self-esteem? Which ones did not? Rewrite each negative message to make it more positive without making it untrue.

Making Connections

1. **Science.** In a life science, health, or biology textbook, find a passage that describes one way in which hormones affect a person during adolescence. Summarize what happens for your class. Include ideas for managing and coping with these changes if possible.
2. **Biology.** Investigate how characteristics are passed from one generation to the next. Draw a diagram showing how children inherit a trait, such as eye color, from parents.
3. **Language Arts.** Write a few paragraphs about two people you know, one who has high self-esteem and the other who has low self-esteem. Change the names so that the people will not be recognized. Explore how their level of self-esteem affects their actions.

Building Your Portfolio

Creating a Picture of You
Create a portfolio entry that portrays your personality. Depict your skills, interests, emotions, and attitudes. Include what and how you think and how you get along with others. You may use any media you wish—photographs, drawings, audiotape, videotape, computer software, text, or a combination of more than one of these media. Share your project with the class, and then add it to your portfolio.

ANSWERS TO REVIEWING THE FACTS

1. Physical, emotional, intellectual, moral, social. Students' examples should describe types of changes that teens undergo in each category.
2. Emotional, social, intellectual.
3. Heredity and environment.
4. Self-concept is the picture that each person has of himself or herself. Self-esteem is how much each person values himself or herself.
5. Learn to accept praise; focus on strengths; accept yourself as you are; learn from what you do; use your strengths to help others; take responsibility for your own life.
6. Potential is the capacity to do something; potential may or may not be fulfilled.

ANSWERS TO THINKING CRITICALLY

1. Some people who feel very confident may act inappropriately toward others. They may be arrogant toward those with less ability. They may even use their confidence to influence others into improper behavior. Help students realize that high self-esteem *can* be misused
2. They might overcome their environment by using personal strengths and help from others to work toward their potential.

Chapter 2

Chapter Overview

Chapter 2 introduces wellness and explains how to maintain physical, mental, and social health. The chapter also stresses physical safety and encourages students to actively work toward wellness and safety.

Motivators

■ **Defining Health.** Write on the board: *A healthy person is someone who. . . .* Invite students to finish the sentence. Have them write down their responses and save for future reference.

■ **Well, Well!** Have students study the photo on this page. Ask: In what way is this teen caring for his health? What might motivate him to stay healthy? Lead students to see there are many aspects to health and many ways—and reasons—to stay healthy.

Objectives

Discuss the chapter objectives on this page. Remind students that the objectives focus on important chapter concepts.

Vocabulary

Ask if students have heard the term *wellness*. Discuss how being *well* might be different from being *healthy*.

Chapter 2 — Health and Wellness

Terms to Learn

- addiction
- defensive driving
- hygiene
- stress
- wellness

Objectives

This chapter will help you to:

- Explain **the concept of wellness.**
- Describe **how physical, mental, and health relate to wellness.**
- Combine **the elements of wellness into a personal program.**
- Develop **a plan for incorporating safety precautions into your personal wellness program.**
- Identify **ways to minimize stress.**

CHAPTER RESOURCES

Student Workbook
Study Guide, pp. 11-12
Activity, *Health and Wellness Quiz,*
    p. 13

Teacher's Classroom Resources
Lesson Plan, p. 6

Cooperative Learning, *Corporate Wellness,* pp. 11-12
Decision Making, *Making Healthful Decisions,* p. 5
Extension #3, #4, #5, pp. 9-11
Life Skills, *What Is Wellness?* p. 8
Personal Development, *What Is Your Level of Wellness?* pp. 7-8

Transparency 2, *Hazards Along the Road of Life*
Chapter 2 Test, pp. 9-10
Performance Assessment, *Wellness and Safety,* p. 18
Reteaching, Total Health, p. 8

See Also:
ABCNews InterActive™ Videodiscs

"I've never been what you'd call a fitness freak," Camilla said. "I used to think exercise was only for jocks." Last summer, though, Camilla began meeting with a group of her friends to go in-line skating on weekends. It started out just as something to do, but after a few months, Camilla noticed how much she looked forward to her weekend workouts for other reasons. She discovered that she slept better and felt less stress once the school year started. "I'm *still* no fitness freak," Camilla said, "but I have to admit, I feel better about myself when I'm more active."

Wellness and Health

In the past, people defined *health* as not being sick. Some people still believe that they are healthy if they are free from illness or in good physical condition. However, today good health means more than that. A more accurate way to think of health is in terms of **wellness**—that is, *an overall state of well-being, or total health.*

Wellness involves three main components of health: physical health, including safety; mental health; and social health. These parts are interrelated and affect each other in various ways. By improving her fitness, Camilla found that she was better able to handle stress at school. To work toward wellness, you need to pay attention to all of these aspects.

Each person's ideal level of health is different. Camilla was able to improve her physical health through in-line skating. Her friend on the track team needs to work out even harder—and more often—in order to stay in competitive shape.

The same is true of the mental and social aspects of health. One person may be very private and want more time alone to collect his or her thoughts than someone who is more social. That person may like meeting social needs by joining such organized groups as the 4-H Club. Camilla was happy just to meet informally with her friends.

You need to find the combination of activities that suits you. Whatever this combination is, by making good health decisions, you can achieve the best state of wellness for you.

Physical Health

As you mature, you take more responsibility for your own physical health. For example, you no longer expect your family to ask, "Have you got a sore throat?" or "Is your stomach upset?" You are responsible for paying attention to how you feel and then taking action by getting advice from an adult. In the same way, you make your own decisions about what you eat and about the rest and exercise you need. The more you know about what your body and mind require, the more healthful your decisions will be.

The health decisions you make each day influence your wellness.

CHAPTER 2   **Health and Wellness**   35

MORE ABOUT Healthy People 2000

The Public Health Service finds that among Americans, blood cholesterol levels are down and fewer smoke, but one in three is overweight and one in four never exercises. White Americans' life expectancy is 76.5 years, compared to 69.6 years for African Americans, who have higher rates of teen pregnancy, AIDS, and homicide. Teen pregnancy rates are down for Hispanics, but they have higher rates of AIDS, homicide, and tuberculosis than Caucasians.

Checking Comprehension.

✓ Why is cleanliness especially important for teens? *Combats oily skin and hair, acne, and increased perspiration that physical changes of adolescence can cause.*

✓ Which diseases have been directly linked to smoking or chewing tobacco? *Cancer, stroke, emphysema, heart disease.*

✓ How does alcohol affect the body? *Slows nervous system, interferes with coordination, judgment, decision making. Can cause unconsciousness and death.*

CROSS-CURRICULAR ACTIVITY
Science

Have each student research one aerobic exercise. Have them describe the specific wellness benefits it provides, and if practical, lead the class in the exercise.

SPECIAL NEEDS
Strategies

Inefficient Organizers. Ask students to combine the ideas on these two pages into a list of health tips for teens. Students' tips should include guidance in the areas of nutrition, exercise, sleep, hygiene, and substance abuse.

Nutrition

A balanced diet helps you maintain a state of wellness. When you eat a variety of foods, you have a better chance of resisting infection and disease. You also have more physical and mental energy. By eating right, you can help prevent weight problems, heart disease, diabetes, and some forms of cancer.

A balanced diet takes planning and determination. Every day, at every meal and snack, you have the opportunity to make wise choices. Eating varied, nutritious foods—such as whole-grain breads and cereals, fruits, vegetables, dairy products, beans, poultry, and fish—is essential to achieving wellness.

Exercise

Because the human body is designed for movement, it needs regular exercise. Here are some of the benefits you can expect when you make daily exercise a part of your wellness program:

- More strength and endurance
- Greater agility
- More alertness
- Release of built-up tension
- Easier to maintain an appropriate weight
- Feel and look better

Build your exercise routine around activities you enjoy. Some people like the motivation that comes with group exercise, such as playing team sports or taking aerobics classes. Other people like exercising alone, so they jog, swim, skate, cycle, or lift weights.

No matter what activities you prefer, the key is to exercise regularly. You should exercise 20 to 30 minutes a day, 3 to 5 times a week. You can work exercise into your day-to-day routine in several ways. Omar, for example, enjoys cycling, but he manages to ride only a couple of times a week. He stays fit by being active in other ways. When he rides the bus, he often gets off a couple of stops early and walks the rest of the way. He also tries to take the stairs instead of an elevator whenever he can. When he watches television, he does a few sets of push-ups and sit-ups. Even doing something as simple as vacuuming makes Omar feel more active.

Sleep

Along with regular exercise, your body needs to rest. A good night's sleep allows your body's systems to repair and revitalize themselves. Getting enough rest makes you look and feel better and gives you the energy you need during the day.

Going to bed late now and then will probably not hurt you. Keep in mind, though, that most people require about eight hours of sleep a night to maintain wellness and to feel fit. Research on sleep shows that when people are deprived of sleep, their ability to concentrate declines and their physical coordination suffers.

Many types of exercise from Asia combine physical coordination with mental concentration, making them excellent ways to get into shape and to relieve stress at the same time.

DID YOU KNOW?

A study of 3,000 teens found that males often try to gain weight in order to look older. Two of three females in the study, however, were trying to lose weight to look more like models and actresses. They considered weight gain a sign of failure.

Another study of eighth and ninth graders found that girls who worried about their weight also had lower self-esteem, were less happy, and spent more time alone. None of this was true for boys in the study.

Hygiene

Hygiene means *your level of cleanliness.* Good hygiene helps teens cope with temporary physical conditions, such as acne, oily skin and hair, and increased perspiration. Keeping clean results in better health and a more attractive appearance. A wellness program should include the following habits to promote good hygiene:

- Regular showers or baths
- Use of a deodorant or antiperspirant
- Daily brushing and flossing of the teeth
- Clean hair, hands, and nails

Substance Abuse

Wellness includes choosing not to use harmful substances, such as tobacco, alcohol, and other drugs. All of these substances are bad for your health. They can also lead to **addiction**—*a physical and mental dependence on continued doses of a substance.* Once a person starts using them, it's difficult to stop.

The use of tobacco is directly linked to cancer, stroke, emphysema, and heart disease. Cigarette smoking is the most common preventable cause of death in the United States. Other forms of tobacco use are equally dangerous. Using smokeless tobacco, in the form of chewing tobacco and snuff, damages teeth and gums and causes cancer of the mouth and throat. The use of cigarettes and smokeless tobacco stains teeth and fingers, dulls the senses of smell and taste, and causes bad breath.

Alcohol affects the body by interfering with muscle coordination and mental judgment. Alcohol poisoning causes vomiting, unconsciousness, and even death. Drinkers also cause tragedy to others. Alcohol is involved in one-fourth of all fatal automobile accidents.

The word *drugs* refers to many different kinds of substances, from medicines to illegal marijuana, crack, and heroin. (Alcohol is a drug, too.) People who misuse drugs are abusing themselves physically, mentally, emotionally, and socially. They can develop severe

In many communities, teens are working together to educate others about substance abuse and the advantages of choosing to stay drug free.

health problems, behave in bizarre and dangerous ways, and die from their habits.

As you develop your wellness program, these guidelines will be very helpful to you:

- Take prescription drugs only with a doctor's supervision, and follow the directions for use.
- Choose friends who have also decided to remain drug free.
- Avoid people who want to sell or give you drugs. They threaten your health. Besides, buying or possessing drugs is illegal.
- Prepare yourself for situations in which you may encounter drugs or feel pressured to try them. Knowing in advance how you will react—by leaving the situation or by saying no—will help you make the right decisions.

CHAPTER 2 Health and Wellness 37

Topics on pp. 38-39:

- Accidents, Crime, and Violence
- Staying Safe

Checking Comprehension

✔ Name ways to protect yourself from accidents. *Follow traffic rules; wear safety belt; wear protective gear; follow safety regulations for sports.*

✔ Suggest appropriate ways to express angry feelings. *Talk about or write down feelings; exercise.*

MULTICULTURAL *Perspectives*

According to the Children's Defense Fund, most violence is *not* racially motivated. In cases of homicide, 83 percent of white victims and 94 percent of African American victims are killed by others of their own race. The group's experts believe that violence is more closely related to poverty, discrimination, hopelessness, and lack of education than to race. However, Klanwatch reports the number of school hate crimes in the first five months of 1992 was four times higher than for the same period of 1991. Most racially or ethnically motivated hate crimes are committed by people under age 25.

School programs, support groups, and counselors help many people break the cycle of substance abuse. However, the best way to avoid problems with tobacco, alcohol, and other drugs is never to start using them.

Safety

You can lower risks by avoiding dangerous situations. **Figure 2.1** shows the percentage of teens who engage in certain high-risk behaviors. You can avoid these dangers by:

- **Being prepared.** You are much less likely to get hurt if you know the potential risks in different situations.
- **Resisting pressures.** Don't be afraid to make your own decisions, especially when it comes to your safety.
- **Staying alert.** Accidents are more likely to occur when you aren't paying attention to what is happening around you.
- **Staying within your limits.** Be realistic about your physical condition. For example, if you are new to mountain biking, start by riding a trail for beginners.

Accidents

Accidents are the leading cause of death among teens. Near the top of the killer list are fatal automobile accidents. Sports injuries, though seldom fatal, are also common among young people. Most accidents can be prevented by taking such steps as these:

- Fasten your car safety belt.
- Follow traffic laws.
- Practice **defensive driving** when you become a driver. That means *paying attention at all times to pedestrians, cyclists, and other drivers.* You will be able to avoid surprises and react safely to others' mistakes.
- Wear such gear as helmets, pads, and goggles to prevent sports injuries.
- Never swim alone, and dive only when you've made sure the water is deep enough.

Remember to speak up when someone else is acting in a way that can affect *your* safety. For example, turn down a ride with any driver who has had alcohol to drink.

Crime and Violence

Violence is a serious problem in the United States. According to the National Center for Health Statistics, almost 9,000 young people are killed each year as a result of violent crimes. Many of them were not even directly involved in violent situations. They were simply in the wrong place at the wrong time.

Police forces suggest steps that people can take to protect themselves from random violence. No matter how large or small your

Figure 2.1

Teen Risk Taking

According to a recent report, a substantial number of young people between the ages of 12 and 21 have engaged in behaviors that can endanger their health and longevity.

- About 98 percent of teens did not consistently wear helmets when bike riding.
- About 66 percent did not wear seat belts as passengers in cars.
- About 17 percent had stayed out overnight without permission in the past year.
- About 14 percent had stayed overnight in an at-risk location, such as a bus station, car, or stranger's home.

(Source: National Center for Health Statistics, Centers for Disease Control and Prevention)

DID YOU KNOW?

Drugs often lead to violence and injury. A 1991 national study showed that 70 percent of violence on college campuses is drinking-related. About half of all young males who drown had been drinking. In 1993, hospital emergency room admissions included 4,293 teens who had been using marijuana, 1,583 teens who had been using cocaine, and 282 young users of heroin.

STRATEGIES That Work

Ten Ways to Let Off Steam

Everyone feels angry at times. You can't prevent it—but you can learn to deal with it effectively. Doing so can help prevent arguments from becoming violent.

Taking time to think before you react is a good idea. Take time to calm down and make a good decision about what approach to take. Think about how to communicate your feelings in acceptable ways.

Here are 10 ideas to help you calm down:

- Count to 10. Better yet, count to 20. You could even say the alphabet out loud.
- Breathe deeply, concentrating on your breathing until you feel calmer.
- Call a time-out. Go into another room or outside until you cool off.
- Get a pencil and paper, and write down what caused the anger and why.
- Listen to music.

- Phone a friend. If you can't reach a friend, phone for the weather.
- Be physically active. Do some sit-ups, go for a run, or ride a bike.
- Splash some cold water on your face, or take a warm bath.
- Hug a pillow.
- Lie down on the floor, and concentrate on a spot on the ceiling.

Making the Strategy Work

Think . . .

1. When people routinely blow up in anger, what effect does this have on those around them?
2. How does the saying "Think before you speak" apply to what you just read about anger?
3. On a scale of 1 to 10 (where 1 is poor and 10 is excellent), rate your own ability to manage anger. Explain your reasoning.

Try...

Which technique would be most effective for you when you are angry? Make a pledge to yourself to try using that technique when the need arises. Write your pledge, and place it where it can serve as a reminder to you.

community is, the following precautions can help protect you:

In Public

- If you're walking at night, walk with a companion or a group of friends.
- Choose a route that's well traveled and well lighted. Walk near the sidewalk curb, and avoid dark doorways or alleys.
- Know where you're going. If you get lost, ask directions from a police officer, or go into a store and ask for directions.
- Walk with a confident attitude.
- Keep your valuables, such as your wallet or purse, out of sight. If someone threatens you and asks for your money or jew-

elry, throw your wallet, purse, or jewelry away from you and run in the opposite direction.
- Never hitchhike or pick up hitchhikers when you are driving.

At Home

- Lock the doors and windows.
- Do not open the door for strangers.
- Never give personal information to strangers over the telephone.

Always be aware of what is going on around you. If you spot a situation that looks suspicious, walk away from it. In some instances, you may want to report a dangerous situation to a law enforcement official or to your family.

CHAPTER 2   Health and Wellness   39

Activities

■ **Say No to Injury.** Have students demonstrate assertive behavior that can protect their physical health. Have the rest of the class evaluate the effectiveness of the tactic. (*Relationship*)

■ **Using Strategies.** Ask groups to write a scene in which a teen grows angry. Have groups exchange scenes and list techniques for handling the angry feelings in the situation they received. (If you wish, review the scenes for appropriateness before distributing them for analysis.) (*Problem Solving*)

RETEACHING

■ **Just Looking.** Ask students if they have ever heard someone described as "an accident waiting to happen." Discuss the kinds of actions and behaviors that predictably result in accidents.

STRATEGIES THAT WORK

Have students read "Ten Ways to Let Off Steam." Review the tips provided. Ask students why each helps control anger. Based on their answers, have them suggest other strategies.

Answers to Think . . .

1. They may respond with anger, start to avoid them.
2. Lets you choose words, find solution, respond constructively.
3. Answers will vary but should be supported.

◄ CROSS-REFERENCE ►

For more on expressing feelings in positive ways, refer students to Chapter 9.

Topics on pp. 40-42:
- **Mental and Social Health**
- **Stress**
- **Benefits of Wellness**

Checking Comprehension

✓ How do self-concept and self-esteem relate to mental health? *Self-concept affects self-esteem, and self-esteem affects mental health.*

✓ Is stress negative? *Not necessarily; it can result from positive situations.*

✓ How can contact with others contribute to your wellness? *Supportive relationships contribute to mental and social health.*

✓ How can you contribute to the overall health and wellness of your community? *Volunteer, learn first aid, recycle, help environment.*

The example of Chinese intellectuals (researchers, authors, and scientists) shows how too much stress can be physically harmful. Intellectuals receive bigger apartments and a higher salary than other Chinese and feel great pressure to improve the economy. A study found that a Beijing intellectual typically lives 53 years, 16 less than the national average. At the Chinese Academy of Science's Computer Institute, seven of every ten scientists suffer from a serious long-term illness. At Beijing's Automation Institute, 88 percent of the staff is chronically ill.

Mental and Social Health

Wellness involves not only physical health and safety, but also mental and social health. These components are just as important as physical health and require the same kinds of attention and commitment. What's more, good mental and social health are vital to staying physically healthy and to balancing your total wellness.

Mental Health

Just as there are different levels of physical fitness, there are different levels of mental health. In general, people who are mentally healthy feel good about themselves, are comfortable with other people, and are able to cope with the demands of life. They are conscious of their emotions and can express them in positive, constructive ways.

You can work to improve your overall mental health in the following ways:

- Maintain a positive outlook.
- Focus on your strengths and abilities, not your setbacks and disappointments.
- Treat mistakes as learning experiences.
- Accept the qualities about yourself that you cannot change.
- Make efforts to improve the qualities you can change.
- Develop positive ways to handle your emotions, such as talking about your feelings with a friend or exercising regularly.
- Accept others as they are, and focus on their strengths, not their weaknesses.

Figure 2.2

DEALING WITH STRESS

Get some exercise. When you are starting to feel overwhelmed, go out and run, shoot some baskets, or do some other physical activity that will help you unwind.

Try to relax. Sometimes just getting away from everything and spending time by yourself can help you relax. Take a little time out each week to read a book, listen to music, or just daydream

Plan ahead. If you're nervous about an upcoming event, such as a speech, take time to prepare yourself and rehearse so that you feel more confident.

REAL-LIFE APPLICATION

Read this to students: *Jessie loves music and is intent on a career in that field. She is lonely sometimes but doesn't want relationships to interfere with her goal. Besides, friends have let her down; music never has.* Ask students: How would you evaluate Jessie's mental health? How do her views on friendship affect her social and mental health? How might she increase social contact? *(Make friends with other musicians; do volunteer work that involves music.)*

- Be considerate of other people's feelings and emotions.

Stress

Stress is *your body's response to demands being put on you.* You feel physical and emotional tension. Stress can result from something positive. Giving a speech or going on a date with someone for the first time can produce stress. It can also arise from something negative, such as a death, a divorce, or an argument in the family.

The way you manage stress can affect every aspect of your wellness. For example, Karen was involved in many activities: schoolwork, her job in a video store, band practice, and the school yearbook. She began to feel overwhelmed by all she had to do. Karen became nervous, emotionally drained, and withdrawn.

She even lost sleep and argued with her mother. Karen needed some tools for managing stress. **Figure 2.2** suggests ideas that Karen used and that you can use, too, when stress is a problem.

Social Health

It has been said that "no man is an island." What do you think this means? One view is that people need each other.

Your social health is made up of two main parts, both involving other people. The first includes the people with whom you have direct contact—your family, friends, and neighbors. Studies show that people who have good, supportive relationships with their families and friends are physically healthier than people who live isolated lives.

Think realistically. Your imagination can make situations seem worse than they really are. Ask yourself, "What's the worst thing that could happen? How can I prevent that from happening?"

Learn from the experience. If you're miserable because something didn't go right, think about what you can do better the next time.

CHAPTER 2   Health and Wellness   41

Activities

■ **Ready for Anything.** Explain that planning can help reduce stress. Assign groups a common source of stress (a special date, a driving test) and have them generate a list of ways they could plan and prepare for the situation. Have groups share their three best ideas. (*Creativity*)

■ **Friend in Need.** Have students write a dialogue presenting a realistic scenario in which a teen helps another person cope with a stressful situation. Ask volunteers to read their dialogues aloud. You might combine several dialogues into a "manual" to help other students deal with stress. (*Relationship*)

ENRICHMENT

■ **Acting Out.** Ask students to provide specific responses that demonstrate mental and social wellness in these situations: losing a school election; a good friend moving away; facing serious illness in the family.

USING VISUALS

Have students look at Figure 2.2. Ask them what is happening to the teen in the illustration. What can they do in their own lives to "unwind"?

CROSS-REFERENCE

Chapter 8 will help students develop skills for building and maintaining good relationships.

Review

■ **Chapter Review.** Use the contents of the Chapter Review page to help students review concepts, think critically, and apply their knowledge.

■ **Study Guide.** Have students complete the Study Guide for Chapter 2 on p. 11 of the Student Workbook.

■ **New View.** Have students review the definitions of health they wrote at the beginning of the chapter. Encourage them to change or add to their definitions, based on what they have learned. Explain that the following chapters in this book will help them define the concept of health even further.

Evaluation

■ **Chapter Test.** Use the reproducible chapter test provided in the Teacher's Classroom Resources or create your own test using the *Testmaker Software.*

■ **Alternative Assessment.** Ask students to find an advertisement for a product that promises wellness. Have them explain how that product can and cannot meet wellness needs.

■ **Wellness Checklists.** Form students into three groups. Assign each group physical, mental, or social wellness. Have them create a five-to-seven-item checklist to help teens assess their level of wellness in that area.

Managing Your Life

Maintaining a Balance in Your Life

Finding time for yourself, even a few minutes each day, is good for your mental health. Remember to:

- **Make yourself a priority.** Busy teens and adults often find that life is demanding. A little juggling may be needed to squeeze in some personal time.
- **Choose your time wisely.** When do you feel pressured the most, at the beginning or end of the day? That may be when you most need time for yourself.
- **Use "downtime" to refresh yourself.** Find little bits of time when you can change your focus. Travel and waiting times are perfect for personal thoughts.
- **Enjoy yourself when you do take time.** Put aside your other cares and focus on what you're doing. The good feeling you get will last longer that way.
- **Learn to say no.** Know your limits and simply tell people when you can't do something. Otherwise you may let yourself and others down.

Applying the Principles

1. Take stock of all the demands placed on you from school and other activities. Using a calendar, block out the time periods that are not available. Identify at least 15 minutes every day that you can call your own.
2. Every day Jorge has to walk the family dogs. How can he use that time for himself?
3. Practice saying no. In a notebook, write down ten ways you can politely but firmly tell people that you just don't have the time to do something they want.

The second part of social health concerns your role within society as a whole. When you get involved in your community and help make it a better place, you improve your own wellness while benefiting society.

The Benefits of Wellness

Who is responsible for your wellness? You are. Only you can make the decisions that promote good health. You have much to gain.

People who make smart health decisions tend to have a positive outlook on life. They feel good and have energy for work as well as play. They look better, too. Good health habits bring glow to the skin, shine to the hair, and brightness to the eyes. Healthy people enjoy others, but they don't mind spending time alone. Healthy people handle emotions well and get along with others.

Is this the picture you want for yourself? It can be if you take good health habits seriously.

Managing Your Life

Have students read "Maintaining a Balance in Your Life." Explain that taking time for yourself may be difficult at first, especially if others are used to making demands. Ask: Do you think society supports the need to spend time on oneself?

Responses to Applying . . .
1. Answers will vary.
2. Answers may include: enjoy scenery; reflect; think about something he likes.
3. Answers will vary.

Chapter 2

Review

Reviewing the Facts

1. What is wellness?
2. Describe three behaviors or activities you'd like to fit into your own wellness program.
3. What are two safety precautions that you can follow when you're in public?
4. What are three ways to improve mental health?
5. List three ways to manage stress.
6. Name two ways people benefit from a wellness program.

Thinking Critically

1. What could your school or community do to help promote wellness?
2. What is the danger in thinking that no harm will ever come to you?

Applying Your Knowledge

1. **Identifying Wellness Behavior.** Study newspapers, magazines, and television reports to find at least two examples of people who work to improve their own wellness or the wellness of others. Write a summary of these efforts. Conclude with a statement about how these efforts might apply to you and your community.
2. **Comparing and Contrasting Wellness Attitudes.** In writing, explain what wellness means to you. Exchange papers with a partner. Note the responses that are most interesting to you. Share thoughts with your partner. Then discuss how the responses fit or don't fit what you have learned about wellness.

Making Connections

1. **Science.** Visit a health food store to see what kinds of health-benefit claims are made by the manufacturers of various products. After taking notes, check library resources, such as books or periodicals about nutrition. Based on your research, which products do you think might have exaggerated claims, and why?
2. **Language Arts.** Pick two characters from a short story you read in literature class. Identify ways these characters did or did not assert control over their own physical, mental, or social health. Talk about your conclusions with a group of classmates. What major choices did the characters make that affected their well-being? Why did they make these choices? What were the results of the choices?

Building Your Portfolio

Creating a Personal Wellness Log

On a sheet of paper, list the days of the week across the top. Write 5 to 10 wellness goals in a column on the left. Examples might include: "Eat 5 servings of vegetables," "Exercise at least 30 minutes," or "Spend time with family." Draw lines between the rows and columns to make a grid. Each day, check off the wellness goals you met successfully. At the end of the week, analyze the results in a few paragraphs. Include ideas for how you can continue meeting your goals. Add the log and analysis to your portfolio activity file.

CHAPTER 2   **Health and Wellness**   43

Chapter 3

Chapter 3

Developing Character

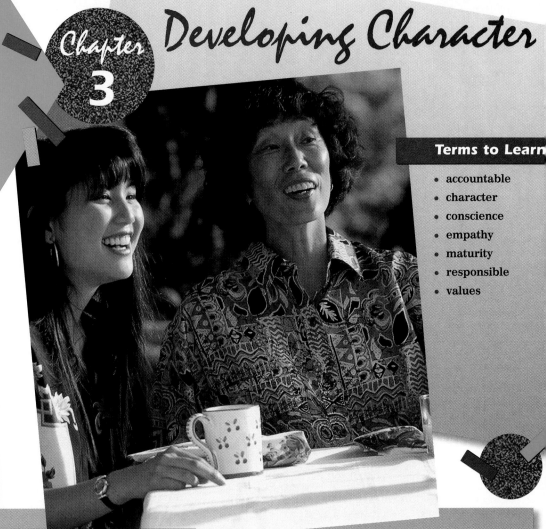

Chapter Overview

Chapter 3 introduces the concept of character and its underlying values. Students learn how values develop, are influenced, and guide their decisions. Chapter 3 also explores responsibilities and the benefits of being responsible.

Motivator

■ **A Teaching Table.** Refer students to the photograph on this page. Ask what the teen might be learning from her parent as they spend time together during a meal. Encourage students to go beyond "the daily news" and "table manners."

Objectives

Discuss the chapter objectives on this page. Remind students that the objectives focus on important chapter concepts.

Vocabulary

Help students distinguish between *conscience* and *conscious*. Explain that *conscience* means "a sense of right and wrong, sensitivity to fairness and justice", while *conscious* means "aware" or "physically awake." Ask volunteers to use the words in a sentence. Prompt them with a sample sentence if needed.

Terms to Learn

- accountable
- character
- conscience
- empathy
- maturity
- responsible
- values

Objectives

This chapter will help you to:

- Define **character.**
- Explain **what values are** .
- Describe **the influences on values and how to choose them.**
- Analyze **your own values.**
- Describe **personal responsibility and give examples of responsible behavior in four areas.**

44   UNIT 1   Personal Development

CHAPTER RESOURCES

Student Workbook
Study Guide, pp. 14-15
Activity, *Positive and Negative Values,* pp. 16-17
Teacher's Classroom Resources
Lesson Plan, p. 7

Extension #6, *Values and the Bill of Rights,* p. 12
Life Skills, *It's Your Choice,* pp. 9-10
Personal Development, *Finding the Hidden Message,* pp. 9-10
Transparency 3, *Examining Values*
Chapter 3 Test, pp. 11-12

Performance Assessment, *What We Value,* pp. 19-20
Reteaching, *Focus on Character,* p. 9
See Also:
ABCNews InterActive™ Videodiscs

Mia listened quietly as her friend Ashley talked. Ashley's mother had been laid off from work, and Ashley was very worried. Mia thought for a long moment. "Did you know that Mr. Dobson is looking for a part-time babysitter after school and on weekends?" Mia asked.

Ashley's eyes brightened. "He is? Why, that would be perfect for me. I'll give him a call tonight. Thanks, Mia. See you tomorrow."

Mia smiled as she walked down the hall. I'll find something else later, she thought to herself as she tossed the piece of scrap paper with Mr. Dobson's phone number on it into the wastebasket.

A Look at Character

What is it about Mia that shows character? The word may not be easy to explain, but most people know it when they see it.

People who have **character** possess *moral strength and integrity*. They show these qualities through their:

- Ability to understand the difference between right and wrong.
- Commitment to doing what is right.
- Acceptance of a set of universal values.
- Demonstration of responsible behavior.

These are the main components of character. As you continue to read, you will see their impact—on you, on others, and on society.

Values As a Guide

Values are the foundation upon which character is built. **Values** are *beliefs, feelings, and ideas about what is important*. Your actions, the decisions you make, and the kind of person you are all reflect your values.

A teen who always remembers the birthdays of family members values thoughtfulness and family relationships. A coach who encourages team

members to work together fosters cooperation. A family that sets aside time to spend together shows respect and caring. As people live each day, they turn to their values to guide them.

Kinds of Values

Some values are mostly a matter of personal preference. For example, Todd and Nikki both wanted to join a school activity. Because Todd enjoys government, he chose to enter the student council. Nikki, on the other hand, likes the outdoors, so she joined the environmental club. Values helped Todd and

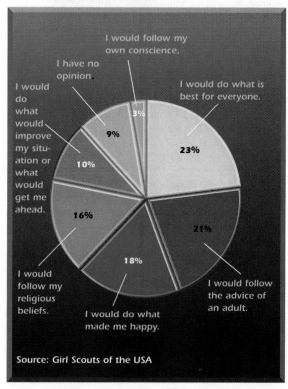

In a recent survey on values, 5,000 young people were asked the following question: "If you were unsure of what to do in a situation, how would you decide what to do?" The pie chart below shows their answers.

I would follow my own conscience.

I have no opinion.

I would do what would improve my situation or what would get me ahead.

I would follow my religious beliefs.

I would do what made me happy.

I would follow the advice of an adult.

I would do what is best for everyone.

3%
9%
10%
16%
18%
21%
23%

Source: Girl Scouts of the USA

CHAPTER 3   Developing Character   45

Topics on pp. 45:
- What Is Character?
- How Values Guide Decisions
- Kinds of Values

Checking Comprehension

✓ Are all values either right or wrong? *No, some are simply matters of personal preference.*

✓ How do the responses of teens to the survey question in the illustration show their values? *Survey asked how teens would make a decision. Values guide decision making.*

Activities

■ **Moral Circle.** Form the class into teams to debate the question: What comes first, values or character? (*Critical Thinking*)

■ **Pop the Question.** Have students repeat the survey in the illustration among schoolmates. Help them determine a representative sample of students (a proportional number of males and females, and of students from each grade). Make one student responsible for surveying one segment of the student body. Have students report their findings to the class and compare them to the survey. (*Communication*)

RETEACHING

■ **Personal Values.** Have the class list values that are matters of personal preference.

ENRICHMENT

■ **Acting Out.** Have pairs of students select two values and create situations that demonstrate them. See if their classmates can determine what values motivated the actions. Remind students that the same value might be described in several ways.

Checking Comprehension

✓ What are some universal values? *Respect, tolerance, compassion, fairness, trust, honesty, responsibility.*

✓ Why might a teen's values change? *Teens begin to explore and clarify them.*

MULTICULTURAL *Perspectives*

Report this clash of values in Australia: The native Aborigines value their land as the living source of all things. To them, veins of metal are Earth's circulation system. When they need ocher or iron, they approach the site with heads bowed in respect and leave by walking backward in their footprints to disturb as little land as possible. Australia is rich in minerals, however. Mining companies have caused great destruction to the land, including many sacred Aborigine sites.

CROSS-CURRICULAR ACTIVITY
Language Arts

Have students pretend they are visitors from another planet. All they know of teens they have learned from television and magazine ads. Have them write about what they might expect teens to value, based on these ads.

Values are shaped in many ways. As this young Jewish woman accepts religious duty and responsibility at her Bat Mitzvah ceremony, she demonstrates the value that religious principles have in her life.

Nikki make their choices. Were they right or wrong? With values like these, there is no right and wrong. Thus personal preference is an acceptable way to choose them.

Many values *are* viewed as either right or wrong. You might look at them as positive or negative. Love and patience are examples of positive values because they are not harmful. In fact, they are helpful to people and bring good feelings. Envy and dishonesty are examples of negative values. These and others like them cause problems in life.

Some positive values are universal to all societies. In other words, they are accepted by nearly all people as right for everyone. Universal values include respect, tolerance, compassion, fairness, trust, honesty, and responsibility. Fundamental values like these guide people and help them live in society.

The interesting, and perhaps most frustrating, thing about values is that they aren't always clearly negative or positive. Even values as strong as those against killing and

stealing are subject to argument. Should you kill in self-defense? Can you steal food to feed your starving family? Issues like these will always be debated. They make the formation of your own value system difficult at times.

Learning Values

You began learning values as soon as you were born. All your life you will be examining your values, living by them, and modifying them when necessary.

Values are learned both directly and indirectly. For example, when a father tells his children not to hit people, but to solve arguments in reasoned, peaceful ways, this is direct teaching. Values can also be learned indirectly, by observing the behavior of others. When Cal was in the eighth grade, for example, his mother went back to school at night, eventually earning a college degree. He and his sisters were proud of her. Her graduation was a very special event in their lives. Through his mother's example, Cal saw the value of his own education.

Influences on Values

People first learn values as children. The family is a fundamental source of values that people use effectively throughout their lives.

Values are also demonstrated by other people you know. What values have you noticed in the behavior of a coach, Scout leader, or neighbor? What values are shown by friends and classmates?

For many people religious beliefs and teachings provide values. These principles offer a base for forming guidelines to live by.

Some values come from cultural backgrounds. For example, many Asian cultures emphasize that young people should respect

DID YOU KNOW?

In a recent study of 8- to 12-year-olds by one life insurance company, 37 percent of the children said they learned their values from their mothers; 21 percent named their fathers. Also, 20 percent of the children reported that they learned their behavior from Mom, 13 percent from Dad. Ask: What influences such results as these? Do you think this changes as children grow older? If so, how?

their grandparents and other elders. Children learn to value the experience and knowledge of older people. Can you identify any values that come from other cultures?

Society teaches values in many ways as well. Laws, for example, very clearly set forth what is important and what isn't. You learn that safety is a value because of laws limiting speed on roads and requiring people to wear safety belts.

The arts and media also send messages that are laden with values. Think about all the attempts by advertisers to have you form specific values. Sometimes these ads give negative values a positive twist. For example, the cigarettes that will eventually give smokers wrinkles, a cough, and perhaps cancer are shown in the hands of vibrant, good-looking people. Can you identify any media messages that operate this way?

As you can see, opportunities to form values are all around you. Sometimes you are aware of choosing values, and sometimes you aren't. With so much information to absorb, you may feel overwhelmed at times. You may even feel pulled in different directions by conflicting values. How can you decide which values to accept as your own?

Developing Values

Think about this situation. Garrett has been hunting with his family and friends for years. As hunting season approaches again, Garrett senses a growing unease about killing animals, and he's wondering what to do.

The teen years are a time for increasing self-awareness. Exploring values is part of that process. Like Garrett, you may be thinking more about your own opinions and ideas about what is right and wrong. How can you make the right decisions?

Comfort comes in knowing that many values tend to become clearer in time. There is danger along the way, however. You will al-

Acting Responsibly

Do You Show Integrity?

Integrity means acting according to a code of values, including honesty. People want integrity in their friends. How would you feel if a friend lied to you? Would you still be trusting? Employers look for integrity in their employees. They want to hire workers they can count on. Voters want integrity in elected officials, who handle taxpayers' money and make decisions affecting whole communities.

Integrity in Action

Sumi sent away for a shirt from a mail-order catalog. When the shirt arrived, it didn't fit properly. Sumi decided to return it for a refund, but the refund didn't come.

After calling the company, Sumi finally got a check in the mail. Then, the next week, she got another refund check. "Their computers are really mixed up," Sumi told her friend Marta. "I bet they don't even know that they paid me twice."

"You're probably right," Marta said. "Why not just cash the check? The company can afford it."

It was tempting to do so, but Sumi wanted to be honest. Instead, she took the time to write a letter explaining the situation. She mailed it to the company with the second check. A few weeks later, she received a thank-you letter from the company and a discount coupon for her next purchase.

Your Analysis

1. Do you think that most people would do what Sumi did? Why or why not?
2. What positive results other than the thank-you letter and coupon might result from Sumi's actions?

Topics on pp. 48-50:

- **A Value System**
- **Growing in Personal Responsibility**
- **Showing Responsibility and Character**

Checking Comprehension

✓ How does empathy influence values? *Allows you to consider others.*

✓ What are the signs of maturity? *Being reliable, accountable; and making wise decisions.*

✓ In what ways can teens show they are responsible? *Care for selves; contribute to family and community.*

✓ In what ways can teens show they are responsible at school? *Follow rules, help others, complete assignments.*

ways face negative influences and pressures to change your values. Here are some ways of choosing values:

- **Aiming for positive values.** Ask yourself: "Will the values I have chosen result in harm to me or to anyone else? Will they cause me to do anything illegal? Will they lead me to regrets? A yes to any of these questions means that the values may not be positive ones.
- **Listening to your conscience.** Your **conscience** is *the inner voice that tells you what is morally right.* Often that nagging feeling that you have when you are about to do something wrong is your conscience trying to steer you in the right direction.
- **Turning to family.** Family is often the first source of guidance on values. Many people think about what they have been taught and then live by those principles.
- **Gaining knowledge.** When faced with a decision involving values, become knowledgeable about the situation. Get the facts before you act.

- **Evaluating the source.** Before accepting someone else's values, look at the source. Is it reliable? For example, would the values suggested in a tabloid newspaper, in an advertisement for beauty products, or by a gang leader be acceptable? Use reason and logic to reach your decision.
- **Talking to others.** When you have doubts or concerns, talk to adults you trust and respect. Reliable people can help you sort things out.

Your Value System

Once you have a strong value system in place, it can work for you. Values continually back up your actions and decisions. Knowing what's important to you gives you confidence to behave accordingly. You can make choices because you know what you believe in.

Why not begin now to explore your values? Try answering these questions:

- What are your best inner qualities?
- What do you like best about your closest friends? Why?
- How do you want other people to treat you?
- If you could do anything in the world, what would you choose?
- What people do you admire most? Why?
- How do you spend your free time?
- What principles would you stand up for?
- What values have been important to your family as you have grown?

Your value system begins with you, but it doesn't end there. Your values affect others—your family, friends, and everyone you meet every day. Your value system has to operate smoothly beside the systems of others. You can accomplish this in two ways. First, use the ideas already suggested for choosing strong, positive values. Second, use empathy.

Empathy is *understanding someone else's feelings and point of view.* In a sense, you place yourself in the other person's shoes.

Many teens, based on their values, act to promote a healthier environment.

48 **UNIT 1 Personal Development**

Sharing Home Responsibilities

When her mother went into the hospital for surgery, Trina had to take over for several weeks. That was when Trina gained a real appreciation for what it means to be a single parent who combines a full day of work with all the responsibilities at home.

Try computing the hours that it takes to manage a household. How many hours a week does it take to do the laundry? What about the cooking? As you think about every task needed to keep a household running, you will soon see that the list is long and time-consuming. You may not even be aware of certain jobs if they haven't been your responsibility. Some tasks are easily taken for granted when someone else does them.

As Trina learned, sharing the workload has benefits. Here are some of them:

- Teens learn skills that they can use in the future. Knowing how to make a casserole, check the oil in the car, and do the laundry without turning everything pink are just a few of the many skills people need to know. Mistakes and frustration are lessened if a teen has learned life skills at home—before becoming independent.

- More shared leisure time may be possible. A tired, overburdened adult may not have the energy to plan or participate in family activities.
- Just as teens feel good when someone works with them to get a job done, so do adults. Family members are likely to have a more positive attitude toward a teen who handles responsibilities well.
- A sense of satisfaction comes with giving support to others.

Suppose That . . .

You are a teen whose parents are divorced and remarried. You live with your mother during the school year and your father during the summer. From September to May, you have a list of agreed responsibilities. During the summer, no tasks are assigned, so you assume that nothing is expected. Your father's wife gets grouchy around late July. What might the problem be? What would you do?

This kind of understanding allows you to recognize that other people can have legitimate values that differ from yours. Out of empathy comes the practice of such universal values as tolerance, compassion, and respect. Without these characteristics, living with others in harmony is difficult.

Personal Responsibility

People who have character live by a positive value system. They also show personal responsibility. When you are **responsible**, you are *reliable and accountable*. People can count on someone who is reliable. They know that such a person will keep his or her word.

People trust someone who is **accountable.** Such a person is *willing to accept the consequences of his or her actions and words.* If you are accountable, you don't blame others when something goes wrong. You simply acknowledge your mistakes and take steps to correct them and learn from them.

Part of Maturity

Alicia has been babysitting for four years. Last summer, the Badillos asked her to care for their children on weekdays while they were working. When they hired Alicia, the Badillos said that she'd been recommended by several friends, who said that she was a

---

Focus on Responsibility Skills

Have groups plan an after-school or Saturday morning project that demonstrates responsibility to the community. They might help older people do their grocery shopping; put on a play or talent show at a child care center; or clean up graffiti and trash in a park. Ask groups to submit their plans to you before they carry them out so you can help them identify and deal with any potential problems.

Review

■ **Chapter Review.** Use the contents of the Chapter Review page to help students review concepts, think critically, and apply their knowledge.
■ **Study Guide.** Have students complete the Study Guide for Chapter 3 on p. 14 of the Student Workbook.
■ **Real Value.** Have students write a letter to a person whom they admire—a world leader, a historical figure, or someone in their daily lives. They should describe the values and qualities of character that the students find admirable. (*Communication*)

Evaluation

■ **Chapter Test.** Use the reproducible chapter test provided in the Teacher's Classroom Resources or create your own test using the *Testmaker Software.*
■ **Alternative Assessment.** Write this poem on the board and have students write a paragraph explaining how it relates to values, responsibility, and character: "Sow a thought, and you reap an act./ Sow an act, and you reap a habit./ Sow a habit, and you reap a character./ Sow a character, and you reap a destiny." (Samuel Smiles, 1887)

■ **Spelling It Out.** Have pairs of students make an acrostic (using the word *character, values,* or *responsibility*) that summarizes what they have learned from this chapter. Make sure at least one pair chooses each word. Have pairs share their work with the class.

Strong leadership creates strong neighborhoods and communities. Why would you want people of good character in leadership roles? How do such people acquire these positions?

mature person. Knowing that they had the confidence in her to do the job well made Alicia feel good.

Alicia's maturity helped her get the job. **Maturity** is reflected in *responsible, adultlike behavior and attitudes.* Making an effort to become more responsible can move you closer to maturity. As this happens, people place more and more trust in you. This results in good feelings, such as those that Alicia had.

Showing Responsibility

Responsibility can be shown in many ways. You show responsibility for yourself by making healthful decisions. Responsibility to family means pitching in with your support. Meeting your responsibilities to others by sticking to your commitments lets them know they can count on you. You can even show responsibility to society as a whole by taking action in your community to make life better for all. How else could you show that you are a responsible person in all of these areas?

50   UNIT 1   Personal Development

Recognizing Character

When values and responsibility come together, they produce a person with character. Character earns people respect and admiration. Not everyone who is respected and admired, however, has character. Some unprincipled people find ways to make others believe in them, sometimes by intimidation and manipulation. At first these people may seem to have character, but a close look shows what they really are.

Genuine character is rooted in positive values. It withstands the tests of time and scrutiny, and it's always there—even when no one else is looking.

DID YOU KNOW?

How can potential employers determine your level of integrity? Some publishers have created tests designed to do just that. Such tests ask questions that aim to evaluate how honest you are. Unfortunately, not all results have been accurate. Many honest employees have been unfairly identified as likely to be dishonest via these tests. Although the tests are frowned upon in some arenas, they are used in others. Improvements and increasing value as an evaluation tool may mean that you will encounter such questions in future job pursuits.

Chapter 3 Review

Reviewing the Facts

1. Define character.
2. Identify three influences on values.
3. What three questions can you ask in order to decide if a value is positive or negative?
4. What are three ways to help you choose among values?
5. Name the four areas in which you can show responsibility, and give an example of each.

Thinking Critically

1. If someone else's values are different from yours, who is right? Explain your answer.
2. What do you think is the most important value for teens in the United States today? Why do you think so? Are there any factors in society that encourage or discourage the value? Explain.

Applying Your Knowledge

1. **Seeing Through Negative Values.**
   Think of an ad or commercial you have seen or heard for a product that is not healthful. Make two columns on your paper labeled "Fiction" and "Fact." In the first, or "Fiction," column, explain how the words and images try to make something negative into something positive. In the second, "Fact," column, write the truth about the product.
2. **Practicing Empathy.** Form a team with another classmate. Take turns describing a situation in which you argued or disagreed with another person. Once you both understand the circumstances of the two situations, act out the scenes. Play the other person, not yourself, in the situation you described. When you're done, write about what it was like to see the other person's perspective from the inside.

Making Connections

1. **History.** Read a biography of someone in history who brought about social change. For example, you might choose a suffragist, a civil rights leader, a politician, or an educator. Write a paragraph or two about this person's achievements. Did the person's values and character affect his or her life? Did he or she experience any conflicts among different values?
2. **Language Arts.** Many fables and folktales from different cultures were told to teach specific values. Aesop's fables from ancient Greece, the African tales of Spider, and countless others use animals, magic, and humor to illustrate moral truths. Choose a short fable from a book at the library. Retell it to your class and explain the values taught.

Building Your Portfolio

Communicating Values
Write a short story that illustrates one or more positive values. You may wish to illustrate it with drawings or cartoons. Add the story to your portfolio.

ANSWERS TO REVIEWING THE FACTS

1. Moral strength and integrity.
2. Any three of these or others that are appropriate: family, other adults, friends, religious teachings, cultural background, society in general, the arts, media.
3. Would this value cause harm to me or anyone else? Is it illegal? Will it cause me to regret my actions later?
4. Any three: aim for positive values; listen to your conscience; turn to family; gain knowledge; evaluate the source; talk to others.
5. Responsibility to self, family, friends, and society; examples should be appropriate.

ANSWERS TO THINKING CRITICALLY

1. Answers will vary; possible responses: neither is right so long as the values are positive or simply a matter of preference; if the other person's values are harmful to that person or to others, however, they are negative values.
2. Answers will vary; student responses should include support of their opinions.

Chapter 4

FOCUS

Chapter Overview

Chapter 4 discusses the need for setting goals. Students learn to distinguish between types of goals, to use values to set priorities, and to identify resources for meeting goals. They are reminded that achieving goals takes ample determination.

Motivator

■ **Goal Point.** Have students describe the goal in soccer (to get the ball into the net). Ask them to imagine playing soccer without a net. Ask: Without a net, what would be the point of the game? If the net were moved to a different location, how would that change the game? Help students see that goals define life's movement and purpose.

Objectives

Discuss the chapter objectives on this page. Remind students that the objectives focus on important chapter concepts.

Vocabulary

Point out that the word *goal* is part of several vocabulary terms for this chapter. Invite students to give examples of goals in sports and in life. Ask: What is the goal of this chapter? (To help students learn about goals.)

Chapter 4 Goals and Resources

Terms to Learn

- fixed goal
- flexible goal
- long-term goal
- prioritize
- resource
- short-term goal

Objectives

This chapter will help you to:

- Explain **why goals are valuable.**
- Distinguish **between long-term and short-term goals and between fixed and flexible goals.**
- Describe **how to use values to set priorities.**
- Explain **how to set effective goals.**
- Identify **the resources you have to achieve goals.**

52   UNIT 1   Personal Development

CHAPTER RESOURCES

Student Workbook
Study Guide, p. 18
Activity, *Goals and Teamwork*, p. 19
Teacher's Classroom Resources
Lesson Plan, p. 8
Extension #7, *Reaching Goals*, p. 13

Extension #8, *Using Resources to Meet Goals*, p. 14
Life Skills, *Getting to Your Goal*, p. 11
Chapter 4 Test, pp. 13-14
Performance Assessment, *Working Toward Our Goals*, pp. 21-22

Reteaching, *Reaching Goals*, p. 10
See Also:
ABCNews InterActive™ Videodiscs

When Nick's grandparents prepared to celebrate their 50th wedding anniversary, the event captured the attention of the whole family. A celebration was planned, and Nick's family really wanted to attend.

Nick had not seen his grandparents in nine years. The anniversary party would be a joyous reunion if they could all be together. The only problem was that the party was in Greece, where Nick's grandparents lived.

For Nick's family, a goal developed. They began to plan for the trip. It would be very costly, but it might be a last chance for them to be together with his grandparents. The family had to make sacrifices to find the money, and each family member had to work toward the goal. They were committed, however, because it meant so much to all of them.

The Need for Goals

A goal is a conscious aim that requires planning and effort to achieve. Goals can be set by individuals, families, businesses, and other groups. The goals that Nick's family chooses are not necessarily the same ones that other families pick. The same is true of individuals. Even though people have different goals, they set them for the same reason.

Goals give direction. Goals provide a focus as people answer such questions as "Where am I headed? What do I want to accomplish?" Without goals, people cannot make progress.

For you personally, goals can keep you from drifting. Think what it would feel like to be much older than you are now and to realize that you haven't done what you wanted in life. That happens to many people. Will it happen to you? It won't if you set goals for yourself and work toward them.

Kinds of Goals

Before you can work with goals, you need to know what kinds there are. A better understanding of what goals are will help you as you practice setting them.

Short- and Long-Term Goals

A **short-term goal** is *something you want to accomplish soon*. Examples of short-term goals are reading a book, fixing a bicycle, and taking a gardening class. A **long-term goal** is *something you plan to accomplish sometime farther in the future, perhaps in six months, a year, or after you finish high school*. Long-term goals might be learning how to sew, rebuilding a classic car, graduating from high school, and becoming a computer technician.

A long-term goal can seem overwhelming if it is viewed as a single task. Amie's junior class, for example, needed to raise several thousand dollars for a class trip. When the class officers first met with the fund-raising committee, they all felt dismayed at the amount of money needed. Not until they started to break their goal down into man-

Todd's short-term goal of practicing the piano for 30 minutes every day can lead him toward long-term goals. What might they be?

CHAPTER 4   **Goals and Resources**   **53**

TEACH

Topics on p. 53:
- **The Need for Goals**
- **Short-Term and Long-Term Goals**

Checking Comprehension

✓ How could a short-term goal be part of a long-term goal? *Short-term goal might be a step in reaching long-term goal.*

✓ Why might you want to divide a long-term goal into several short-term goals? *Makes long-term goal more attainable.*

Activities

■ **Chart a Course.** Ask pairs of students to set a series of short-term goals that would help someone reach each of these long-term goals: raising a grade in one subject area; helping someone learn to speak English; getting along better with someone at school or at home.

CROSS-CURRICULAR ACTIVITY
Language Arts

Remind students of Martin Luther King, Jr.'s pivotal "I have a dream" speech. (Read parts, if possible.) Have students research other people whose goals helped them or others achieve great things. If you wish, allow students to report on people in their own families or community.

DID YOU KNOW?

Benjamin Franklin set a goal of acquiring thirteen virtues, including industry, tranquility, and humility. He decided to master one virtue each week and carried a small book to record his progress. Finding himself "so much fuller of faults than I had imagined," however, he reset his goal to acquiring each virtue in one thirteen-week "course." Mention that, as students will learn, Franklin's method for achieving goals is an effective one.

Checking Comprehension

✔ How might a flexible goal become a fixed goal and a fixed goal, flexible? *Goal becomes fixed when a deadline is set for it, flexible when its deadline is canceled.*

✔ How is learning to prioritize goals a way to take responsibility for your life? *You choose which goals are important and which you can postpone or give up.*

From School to Work

Have students read "Achieving Goals Through Teamwork." Discuss the saying, "Two heads are better than one."

Answers to Assessing . . .
1. Help people work together, share ideas, coordinate tasks.
2. Answers should reflect the principles outlined in the feature.

SPECIAL NEEDS *Strategies*

Inefficient Organizers. Ask students to name one goal they might like to accomplish on the weekend. Have them list everything they need to do to accomplish the goal, arrange their ideas into sequential steps, and put the plan into action.

54

From *School to Work*

Achieving Goals Through Teamwork

What You Learn Today . . .

If you've ever played on a sports team, you know about working toward a common goal—to win—through teamwork. While seemingly easy to understand, teamwork is a skill that needs to be learned and practiced, on and off the field.

Teamwork can be learned in school—and not just through sports. Do you work in small groups in some of your classes? These groups are teams when all members contribute and work toward a common goal. Teams of students can achieve results that they might not achieve alone. Learning how to help a team reach goals is a skill that will always be useful to you.

. . . You Can Use Tomorrow

Businesses recognize the value of teamwork. Business teams accomplish goals that individual workers cannot. At one company, a team figured out how to get a new product to market in half the normal time. In the past, teams were used for special projects. Today many companies are organizing their employees into permanent teams and training them for this style of operation.

Practicing Your Skills

Follow these guidelines the next time you are working with a group toward a common goal:

- Make sure that everyone understands the group's goal.
- Establish rules of behavior that promote cooperation, not individualism.
- Allow every team member to have some say in how the project is organized.
- Identify the particular skills that team members can contribute, and assign tasks accordingly.
- Make sure that everyone has a task and sees how it is part of the overall objective.
- Provide positive feedback to fellow team members. Encourage them to do the same.

Assessing Your Skills

1. How do good interpersonal and communication skills help in teamwork?
2. Think about an occasion when you worked as part of a team. Write a description of what the team did and how it worked. Then analyze whether the team followed the guidelines just described. If not, how well did the team perform? Would following the guidelines have made the team function better?

---

ageable parts did they feel more comfortable. They began to see that bake sales, car washes, and the selling of popcorn at school events were short-term goals that would help them achieve their long-term goal.

What Amie's class found is true for everyone. Whatever the long-term goal, it can probably be divided into some specific short-term goals. Doing so helps make the larger goal easier to attain.

Fixed and Flexible Goals

A **fixed goal** is *one that can be met only at a certain time*. Someone who wants to make

the basketball team needs to be ready to compete when tryouts take place. Fixed goals are often tied to specific dates over which a person has no control.

A **flexible goal,** on the other hand, is *one that has no definite time limit*. Building a savings account, for example, is a flexible goal. It is ongoing, and the amount saved can vary from time to time. If you are saving to buy a birthday gift for a parent, however, the goal becomes fixed.

Fixed and flexible goals can be either short- or long-term goals. Preparing for a piano recital is a fixed, long-term goal. Passing a

54 UNIT 1 Personal Development

MORE ABOUT Needs

Explain that psychologist Abraham Maslow classified needs into five categories, which he arranged into a pyramid. The base of the pyramid is *physical needs* (food, clothing, shelter). Above that is *safety* (protection and security), topped by *love* (both being loved and loving others), then *esteem* (respecting oneself and oth-

ers). At the pyramid's peak is *self-actualization* (developing one's potential).

Maslow believed that people must satisfy lower, more basic needs before they can meet higher-level needs: they must feel physically safe before they can risk loving others, which gives the esteem needed for self-actualization.

math exam scheduled for next week is a fixed, short-term goal. Knowing whether your goals are fixed or flexible helps you manage your time in order to meet them.

Identifying Goals

What dreams and plans do you have for the years ahead? By turning these dreams into goals, you can begin to work toward them.

Goals can shape what you are as well as what you do. In other words, if you can improve yourself, go for it. Kathy Jo had a fear of speaking during class discussions. She made overcoming this fear her goal. She worked at it every day in little ways. Improvement came slowly, but with a clear purpose in mind, she succeeded.

As you think about goals, take a close look at your needs and wants. Needs are those things you must have. Wants are things that you desire. They include your desire for a new sweater and your dreams for your future. People easily fall into the trap of thinking that certain wants are needs. Listen to people as they talk around you. You are likely to hear others say, "I need a . . ." many times in the

As you set goals, can you dream but be realistic too?

course of a day. You may even start to notice how often you say this yourself.

How will you decide which needs and wants to turn into goals? Several principles can help you make these decisions.

Use Your Values

As you know, values are your personal guidelines for living with yourself and others. Your values show what you believe to be important and unimportant. Goals need to be chosen with values in mind.

Set Priorities

You may want to set many goals. Accomplishing all of them, however, may not be possible or even reasonable. You need to prioritize. When you **prioritize,** you *decide which needs and wants are more important than others.* Examine all the possibilities closely. Try to eliminate the imposters—those that you do not really have to have or those that are less important than others. Values will tell you what is important to you. Priorities will tell you what is *most* important.

Be Realistic

Goals should be challenging. They can spur you to learn, grow, and seek new experiences. Goals that are too easy to achieve are likely to be less satisfying than challenging ones. If your goals are too hard to reach or if you set too many, however, you might give up on them in frustration. Disappointment and failure can interfere with future goal setting. That is why a realistic approach is best. Goals should be reachable with a reasonable amount of effort.

Does being realistic mean that you cannot dream? You certainly can. Great achievements can be linked to great dreams. Some people do become award-winning scientists, famous athletes, and world leaders. They are an inspiration to everyone. You can have

CHAPTER 4 Goals and Resources 55

Activities

■ **Meeting Goals.** Have each student list ten personal goals, both short- and long-term. Have them trade papers with a partner and write ideas for prioritizing the goals in order to meet as many as possible. Students may include specific suggestions, such as meeting parts of goals at certain times or meeting several goals at once. *(Creativity)*

■ **What's in a Goal?** Ask students to suggest values that might motivate each of these goals: saving money for karate lessons; collecting items for a family that lost its home in a fire; helping a sibling complete a science project. *(Critical Thinking)*

RETEACHING

■ **Sorting It Out.** Have students name ten items they have seen advertised and categorize each item as satisfying a need or a want. Help students recognize when a single item satisfies both.

MULTICULTURAL *Perspectives*

Point out that cultural background often influences priorities. In some cultures, such as Native American, family holds top priority. Children may be expected to leave school to help support the family. In contrast, education often has a high priority in Asian American homes. School performance is viewed as a reflection on the whole family; children support the family by doing well academically.

DID YOU KNOW?

The word *prioritize* comes from a Latin word meaning both "former" and "superior." This reflects two ways of prioritizing—ranking in terms of both time and importance.

MORE ABOUT Dreams

Writer William Faulker said: "The end of wisdom is to dream high enough to lose the dream in the seeking of it."

Checking Comprehension

✓ How can you aim for great achievements yet be realistic? *Work toward smaller achievements even if major one is out of reach.*

✓ What kinds of resources are available if you don't have much money? *Your own and others' time and skills; some community resources.*

✓ How is determination linked to resourcefulness? *Determined people are resourceful, find alternative ways to reach goals.*

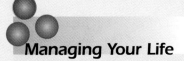

Managing Your Life

Have students read "Handling Disappointment." Ask students to name disappointments teens often face. As a class, have them suggest a positive message that a teen could give himself or herself about each situation.

Answers to Applying . . .

1. Answers will vary.
2. Answers may include: work on interview skills; look in want ads for other job.
3. Answers will vary. Point out that "nothing ventured is nothing gained." Ask what might be gained or learned in defeat.

Managing Your Life

Handling Disappointment

The championship game on television is over. One team is jubilant at victory, but the other experiences defeat. Some players hang their heads, some turn away, and some even react angrily. These players are facing one of the most difficult challenges in life—handling disappointment.

Disappointment can be painful. You can't prevent disappointment, but you can deal with it. Try these suggestions the next time something doesn't work out the way you wish it had:

- **Give yourself a chance to feel the pain—but don't dwell on it.** Allow yourself to accept the loss and move on.
- **Skip the blame.** Groping for something or someone to blame only makes you look bad and may hurt others.
- **Give credit when appropriate.** If someone else wins, recognize their preparation, effort, and skills. That's only fair.
- **Analyze what happened to see if there was something you could have done differently.** Everyone makes mistakes, but some people forget to learn from them. Accept

responsiblity for your mistakes but forgive yourself. Then seek ways to improve your performance.

- **Try again.** You may have to work harder—or smarter—but you can prepare yourself to be more successful the next time.
- **Consider a new goal.** Maybe something else will work out better. Channel your energy in the best directions for you.

Applying the Principles

1. When have you been disappointed in not reaching a goal? Review what happened—how you prepared for it and how you performed. What could you have done differently?
2. Suppose that you were turned down for a part-time job. Identify one way that you could rebound.
3. According to a well-known quotation, "It is better to have tried and failed than never to have tried at all." Do you agree? Explain your answer.

dreams that give you hope and accomplishments to aim for. Often those who pursue dreams accomplish a great deal along the way, even when they do not fulfill their ultimate dream.

To keep yourself in touch with reality as you pursue a dream, you may need to keep an alternative plan in mind. Doug's dream was to become a successful singer. He had been singing in the choir at church and was often asked to sing at special events in his town. He planned to work toward an opportunity to record a song for a nationally recognized music label. At the same time, he also planned to go to college and earn a degree

that would enable him to teach voice. In this way Doug could hold on to his dream without letting go of the realities of life.

Setting Goals

Some people never get beyond the dreaming stage when it comes to goals. You can follow some useful guidelines to prevent that from happening to you.

- **Analyze the goal.** Using what you know about values, priorities, and being realistic, ask yourself whether the goal you want to set is worthwhile. Look at whether it is a short- or long-term, fixed

56   UNIT 1   Personal Development

REAL-LIFE APPLICATION

Read this to students: *Georgia is trying to set a career goal. She loves animals and has thought of becoming a veterinarian. Her aunt's work as a physical therapist, however, also seems very rewarding. Regardless, she knows that finding money for* college *will be a challenge.* Ask students what advice they would give Georgia. Help them see that when goals conflict, learning more about each one can help people make wise choices.

or flexible goal. Do you need to break it down into smaller, short-term goals? Should you save the goal for later or tackle it immediately?

- **Put goals in writing.** Once you identify a goal, write it down. Some goals you might want to put in a visible place. This can be a reminder that will help you stay on track. You could print a banner on a computer and place it on a bulletin board, if you have one, or put a sign on a mirror, where you will see it every day. Some people keep goals and their plans for reaching them in one certain place. A notebook or diary could serve this purpose. By using a designated place to record your goals and your progress, you are more likely to have positive results.

- **Be specific.** To be able to measure your progress in meeting your goals, state them in specific terms. For example, which goal is worded more effectively: "My goal is to help more at home" or "My goal is to fix dinner for my family every Wednesday evening"? The second goal is better because you know exactly what action to take and you can easily determine your progress and level of success.

- **Make a commitment.** It's all too easy to set goals and then abandon them for one reason or another. When you set a reasonable, well-thought-out goal, believe in yourself. Know that you can accomplish it, and then set out to do so.

- **Consider your resources.** A **resource** is *something that you need in order to accomplish a goal.* You need to look for whatever will help you.

Examining Resources

You can identify goals, but if you do not have the necessary resources, you will not achieve them. Resources come in three forms:

- **Human resources.** These come from you as well as others. Your own skills and time are resources. Other people—including family, friends, and teachers—are resources, too.

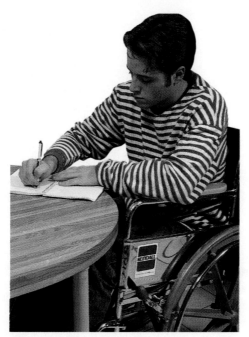

Why is it helpful to write down goals?

- **Material resources.** Tangible items—such as money, tools, and equipment—are another type of resource.

- **Community resources.** These resources are many and varied. You can use community facilities, such as the YMCA, YWCA, and library. Learning opportunities, such as courses offered by schools and colleges, can be useful. Such services as public transportation and government programs are also resources.

Showing Determination

Often the difference between success and failure in reaching goals hinges on a person's determination. Determination shows when people aggressively identify and seek resources that will help them meet their goals. For example, Carlita could have given up on getting a college education because she didn't have the money. Drew could have aban-

CHAPTER 4   Goals and Resources   57

Activities

■ **Financial Fix.** Assign pairs of students one of the following problems. Have them write down their solutions to share with the class: How would you reach your goal if you didn't have the money to . . . buy a shirt that you really liked? . . . take your family out for a special dinner? . . . pay for music lessons? . . . have your car's muffler replaced?*(Problem Solving)*

■ **Bulletin Board.** Have students create a bulletin board on the theme of goal setting or resources. *(Creativity)*

RETEACHING

■ **Natural Resource.** Have students entitle a sheet of paper "My Most Valuable Resource—Me." Have them list what they have that could help them reach goals, including skills, knowledge, possessions, and access to other resources. Ask students to share their lists. As a class, reflect on the many resources within each person that go unrecognized.

ENRICHMENT

■ **Comparing Goals.** Have students ask parents or other adults to identify goals they are currently working toward. Discuss their findings in class. Ask: How do the goals of adulthood compare to those of adolescence? Evaluate one or two adult goals in terms of concepts discussed in this chapter, such as the influence of values and being realistic.

CROSS-REFERENCE

For more help in setting and reaching goals, refer students to material in Chapter 6.

DID YOU KNOW?

School guidance counselors have aptitude tests to help students identify their abilities and interests. This information can guide students in setting goals and exploring careers while still in high school.

MORE ABOUT Specific Goals

The word "measurable" can help with setting goals. You can plan to lose weight or to lose 5 pounds, to be nicer or to do one favor every day, to read more or to read for 30 minutes daily. In each pair, only one can be measured.

Review

■ **Chapter Review.** Use the contents of the Chapter Review page to help students review concepts, think critically, and apply their knowledge.

■ **Study Guide.** Have students complete the Study Guide for Chapter 4 on p. 18 of the Student Workbook.

■ **Noted Goals.** Tell the class: *Jonah wants to play a musical instrument but isn't sure which one, can't afford to buy one, and can't read music.* Have students identify Jonah's long-term goal (to play an instrument), then set up a series of short-term goals to help him reach it. The plan must be realistic and make use of Jonah's resources, which are typical of students in the class. *(Problem Solving)*

Evaluation

■ **Chapter Test.** Use the reproducible chapter test provided in the Teacher's Classroom Resources or create your own test using the *Testmaker Software*.

■ **Alternative Assessment.** Have students write or tape record five guidelines for setting goals that they would give a younger person, including a brief explanation of each one.

■ **Wise Words.** On the board write: "The world stands aside to let anyone pass who knows where he is going." (David Starr Jordan) Have students find other quotations that express what they have learned about goals in this chapter. Encourage them to share and interpret their quotations with the class.

People can use their many resources to accomplish more than one goal at the same time. What kinds of resources are being used here? What goals may be involved?

doned his plan to set up a lawn-mowing service over the summer because he didn't have the equipment. Neither of these teens gave up, however.

Carlita was determined to reach her goal. She found an organization that gave small scholarships to students who agreed that after graduation they would practice nursing in a certain community for three years. That was fine with her, so she applied for and received the help. She financed the rest of her schooling through part-time jobs and a government loan program.

Drew found a lawn mower in good condition at a garage sale. He borrowed the money from his grandfather to buy it. They agreed on

a repayment plan, with interest, that would begin when Drew started to earn money. Drew got permission from the computer teacher at school to use a computer to create an advertising flyer. He even paid his younger brother to help him distribute copies of the flyer throughout the neighborhood.

By wisely seeking and using resources, these two teens accomplished what they wanted to do. So can you. By taking "can't" out of your vocabulary, you may be surprised at what you can do.

58   UNIT 1   Personal Development

MORE ABOUT Resources

Money is a typical resource that people often feel is in short supply. Some people seem to have more to spend because they take care of possessions to keep from having to replace them, they buy quality secondhand items rather than new, and they spend cautiously. Habits like these can make money go further and give a person better control over a valuable resource.

Chapter 4 Review

Reviewing the Facts

1. What purpose do goals serve?
2. Identify the following as short-term or long-term goals: going to a dance this week, getting into college, learning to keyboard, improving grades this marking period.
3. Define and give an example of a fixed goal; define and give an example of a flexible goal.
4. How do you use values to set priorities among goals?
5. List four guidelines for setting goals.
6. List the three main types of resources you might use to accomplish a goal, and give an example of each.

Thinking Critically

1. Identify a goal and then determine what you think is the most important resource for accomplishing that goal. Explain your answer.
2. How might the following affect goal achievement: income level, degree of self-esteem, disabilities, personality?

Applying Your Knowledge

1. **Making Long-Term Goals Manageable.** Choose a long-term goal that requires at least six months of effort to achieve. Identify at least six short-term goals that contribute to that long-term goal.
2. **Weighing Your Priorities.** What is most important to you? List five long-term goals, and state how important each is to you by assigning it a number from 1 to 5 (1 = relatively unimportant, 5 = extremely important). Next think of the resources that you could use to achieve the two most important goals. Then write a brief explanation of your findings.

Making Connections

1. **Business.** Read an article in a business magazine about how teams were used to achieve a goal. Prepare a presentation for your class explaining how the teamwork was structured and whether the effort succeeded.
2. **Health.** Many people set wellness goals for themselves. These may include goals to improve their nutrition, fitness, sleep patterns, or self-esteem. Think of a personal wellness goal, such as eating five servings of fruits and vegetables every day, increasing your upper-body strength, or making a new friend. Write down your goal, the amount of time you think you will need to achieve it, and the specific steps you will take. Keep a daily record of your progress.

Building Your Portfolio

Interpreting a Goal

Choose someone you know who has recently achieved a long-term goal. Examples are a sister who graduated from college and an adult who has a new job. Plan questions for an interview to determine how the person achieved the goal. What short-term goals did he or she set? What resources did he or she use? Interview the person, and ask for permission to make an audio recording of the interview. Place the recording in your portfolio.

Chapter Overview

Chapter 5 addresses the area of decision making. It stresses that most decisions affect both the decision maker and others. It describes a six-step process for making wise decisions and gives ways to avoid interference when making decisions.

Motivator

■ **Hindsight Is.** Ask students to think about a decision they made and later regretted. You may invite volunteers to share their experiences. Ask: What do you think led to your poor decision? Explain that reading this chapter can help them avoid such problems in the future.

Objectives

Discuss the chapter objectives on this page. Remind students that the objectives focus on important chapter concepts.

Vocabulary

Explain that the word *decision* comes from Latin roots that mean "to cut off." Ask students why this might be appropriate for the word *decision*.

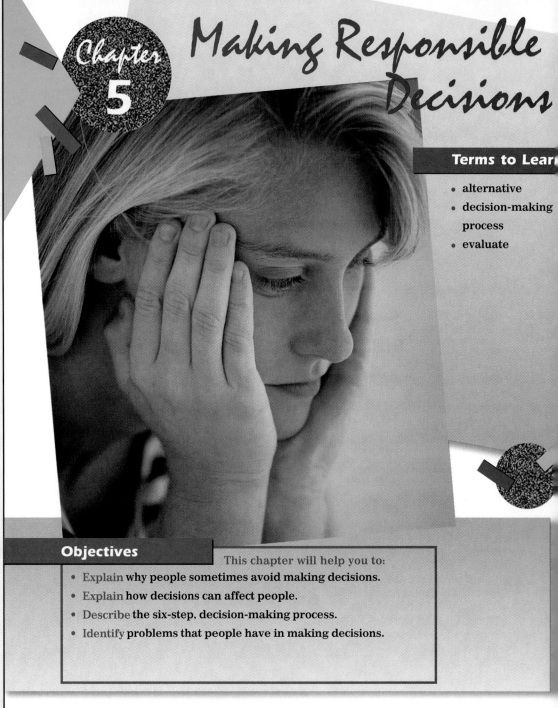

Chapter 5
Making Responsible Decisions

Terms to Learn

- alternative
- decision-making process
- evaluate

Objectives

This chapter will help you to:

- Explain **why people sometimes avoid making decisions.**
- Explain **how decisions can affect people.**
- Describe **the six-step, decision-making process.**
- Identify **problems that people have in making decisions.**

CHAPTER RESOURCES

Student Workbook
Study Guide, p. 20
Activity, *Decision-Making Facts*, p. 21
Teacher's Classroom Resources
Lesson Plan, p. 9
Cooperative Learning, *Making Decisions*, pp. 13-14

Extension #9, *Decision-Making Checklist*, p. 15
Life Skills, *The Pros and the Cons*, pp. 12-13
Transparency 4, *Decision Making*
Chapter 5 Test, pp. 15-16

Performance Assessment, *The Day of Decision*, p. 23
Reteaching, *The Decision-Making Process*, p. 11
See Also:
ABCNews InterActive™ Videodiscs

Decisions can be a real problem. Sometimes they just aren't easy to make—even simple ones. Can you identify with either of these situations?

Melanie stood staring at the menu in the restaurant. As usual, she couldn't make up her mind about what to order.

Clint and his friend Jim were making plans one night. "What do you want to do?" Jim asked.

"I don't know. What do you want to do?" Clint replied.

"I don't care, whatever."

"I don't care either. You decide." The exchange continued without resolution.

Facing Challenge

Some people avoid decision making. One reason is that decision making involves risk. You might not like the food you choose at the restaurant, or you might like what your friend chooses more. You might be afraid of offending someone when you make a decision. What if you pick the movie to go to, and it turns out to be bad? Will you be blamed for choosing it? Sometimes it just seems easier to let someone else decide than to risk the consequences of making a bad decision.

On the other hand, think about people who make decisions with confidence. Most people admire them. It feels good to be with people who can make decisions. You can have that same feeling about yourself.

If you already have decision-making skills, you can work to improve them. If you are weak in this area, now is the time to begin developing those skills. Making good decisions freely and skillfully isn't always easy, but it becomes easier by working at it.

Kinds of Decisions

Imagine the scene in a movie or television show in which the staff in an emergency room makes immediate life-or-death decisions about patients. In a matter of seconds, the medical team decides to administer CPR to someone. The team decides that another pa-

Each day people make many different decisions, such as what to wear. A choice that is easy for one person may be difficult for another.

tient needs surgery immediately. Whatever is needed, these workers always seem to know what to do.

You make decisions all day long, but few are as critical as those just described Everything from clothing, to money, to free time, to schoolwork, to relationships requires that you make decisions. Some decisions are so routine that you are not even aware of making them. Others, however, are bigger decisions that require effort to make.

You can make many decisions on your own. For some decisions, you work with others to make a choice. These decisions can be difficult because different points of view need to be taken into account before agreement can be reached. On the other hand, such decisions are often more effectively made because several people pool their ideas and resources.

CHAPTER 5 **Making Responsible Decisions** **61**

TEACH

Topics on p. 61:
- Facing the Challenge of Decisions
- Kinds of Decisions

Checking Comprehension

✓ Why is decision making hard for some people? *It involves risks; may offend others; some lack experience.*

✓ Identify some areas of life in which you must make decisions. *Family matters, relationships, use of time and money, food and clothing.*

Activities

■ **Decision, Decisions.** Ask pairs to list common teen decisions under these headings: Major Decisions, Minor Decisions, Decisions Made Alone, Decisions Made with Others. (The same decision might be listed more than once.) As classmates share their lists, ask four students to each create a master list of one type of decision.

RETEACHING

■ **Collage Collection.** Have each student create a collage of magazine pictures that represent the types of decisions teens must make.

ENRICHMENT

■ **Degrees of Decision.** Have groups make a time line showing how they have assumed more responsibility for making decisions as they have matured. Have them mark Infancy, Preschool, School Age, and Present on their time line, listing decisions they made or are making at each stage. Have groups compare time lines and discuss the progression of decision making in life.

REAL-LIFE APPLICATION

After reading the following scenario to the class, ask how Eric made his decision and whether the method was sound. After discussing problems with the method, tell students that there is a better way to make decisions. *Eric couldn't decide whether to go to a two-year college and get a certifi-* *cate in air conditioning repair or learn the trade from his uncle. When he finally looked at the college forms, he saw that the application deadline had passed. He decided to work with his uncle and apply at the college next semester.*

Topics on pp. 62-63:
- **The Impact of Decisions**
- **Help with Decisions**
- **The Decision-Making Process**

Checking Comprehension

✓ How can seemingly minor decisions have lasting effects? *Their effects can add up over time.*

✓ In what ways can your decisions affect others? *Decisions about relationships and sexuality involve others; decisions about drug use affect person, friends, and family.*

✓ What kinds of decisions might require input from others? *Those about career, personal relationships, jobs.*

CROSS-CURRICULAR ACTIVITY
Math

Have students write down all the decisions they make in a typical day. Ask them to try to recall unconscious decisions as well as conscious ones. Have students place a check beside those they thought out carefully, then figure these as a percentage of all decisions made that day. Ask: Do you give your daily decisions the attention they deserve?

The Impact of Decisions

How you handle decisions depends on their impact. Decisions can have immediate and long-range effects. They can affect you as well as others. The stronger the impact, the more thought needs to go into the decision.

Effects on You

If you're smart, you won't overlook the significance of some decisions. Jamal, for example, has several ways to get exercise. He can walk to work instead of taking the bus, go to the YMCA to swim, and play tennis in the park. On any given day, the decision to skip the exercise may not matter. If he repeatedly eliminates any of these activities from his routine, however, Jamal threatens his health. If Jamal thinks about the broader picture, he can make better immediate decisions.

The broader picture is relevant when it comes to your career plans too. What you envision for yourself will happen only if you start making the right decisions now. Taking classes in high school that are easy or fun doesn't prepare teens for education and training later on. Planning and preparation for your future career can begin right now.

Some decisions can change your life on the spot. Often decisions that have the greatest impact on a person's life are made with the least thought. Choices about sex, marriage, and substance abuse are among these. What happens to a teen who gets pregnant, gets hooked on drugs, or contracts a sexually transmitted disease that has no cure? That teen's life will never be the same again.

Effects on Others

Your decisions have impact on other people too. Losing sight of this can cause you to hurt others, even if it is unintentional. Nathan, for example, told his younger sister that he would read her a story, but when his friend called and asked him to go out, Nathan left the house. His sister was very disappointed.

Thinking about the impact of your decisions on others will help you make better ones. It may cause you to stop and reconsider before you act. When you care about other people and want them to have a high opinion of you, you will make decisions carefully.

Seeking Help

For difficult decisions, especially, you may need to use the same resources that help you set goals. You might want to ask the opinion of someone you trust. For another decision, you might need to do extensive research. It depends on the decision. Neglecting this effort can mean making an important decision without all the information you need. That's not a good idea.

Other people can often suggest alternatives you might not have considered. Remember, though, that you are responsible for making your own decisions.

62   UNIT 1   Personal Development

MORE ABOUT Decisions

Point out to students that sometimes they will face problems that are complicated. They won't be able to make only one decision in order to reach a solution. By breaking a problem down into several decisions, however, it can be solved more easily. For example, being overweight is a problem that may need to be approached from several angles. Multiple decisions could be made about diet, exercise, attitudes, and lifestyle in order to solve the problem.

Figure 5.1

THE DECISION-MAKING PROCESS

For major decisions, it helps to follow the six-step, decision-making process and to ask yourself a series of questions.

Step 1

State the situation. Ask yourself: "Why do I need to make a decision? Who else is involved?"

Step 2

List the options. Ask yourself: "How many alternatives do I have? What are my resources?"

Step 3

Weigh the possible outcomes. Ask yourself: "How might each alternative affect the final outcome? What would be the positive and negative results based on each alternative?"

Step 4

Consider your values. Ask yourself: "What is most important to me?"

Step 5

Make a decision and act. Ask yourself: "What do I need to do to put my decision into action?"

Step 6

Evaluate the decision. Ask yourself: "Did I make the right decision? How did my decision affect others? Did things turn out the way I wanted? If not, what would I do differently the next time?"

The Process

Even though you won't use it for every decision you make, there is *a procedure you can follow when you have to choose among different options.* This is called the **decision-making process.** The six steps used in this process are shown in **Figure 5.1.**

Sometimes you may use the decision-making process without even realizing it. If you have an important decision to make, however, you need to make a conscious effort to use the technique.

The decision-making process is useful because it helps you focus on the core issue to be decided. You make an effort to identify different possible courses of action and analyze them. Moreover, reviewing the decision can show what worked and what didn't. When you **evaluate** decisions, or *analyze the conse-* *quences* of them, you learn how to make better ones in the future.

How the Process Works

In order to see how the decision-making process works, read how it helped Zachary. Then you can apply the process to your own decisions.

Zachary was working as a server in a restaurant when he learned about a course that he wanted to take. The course, on bookkeeping, was scheduled for eight weeks in the summer and would meet three nights a week. Since Zachary was thinking of becoming an accountant, the course appealed to him. It would be an ideal way to gain skills and learn more about the career. He might also be able to meet some people who could help in his job search later on.

CHAPTER 5 Making Responsible Decisions 63

Activities

■ **Take My Advice.** Many people are eager to help others make decisions; fewer are qualified. Have groups list these people or sources they would turn to for advice in these situations: learning to eat more healthfully; choosing clothes for a formal event; deciding whether to accept a job; deciding what classes to take at school. *(Problem Solving)*

■ **Overdoing It.** Have groups list ten decisions for which they would use the six-step process and ten for which they would not. As a class, reach a consensus about when the process is most helpful. *(Decision Making)*

USING VISUALS

Help students understand the steps in Figure 5.1 by discussing these questions:

1. Why is thinking of options important in decision making? *Having more options increases chance that you will make best decision.*

2. How do you weigh possible outcomes? *Consider possible consequences of each alternative and see which match your goals.*

3. How do your values affect your decisions? *Help you choose options that are important to you.*

4. Why should you evaluate your decision after some time has passed? *To see whether it had expected consequences; to apply this knowledge to future decisions.*

Checking Comprehension

✓ How did Zachary's values and goals help him make a decision? *He decided to take the bookkeeping course to learn more about a potential career, which was his priority.*

✓ Why is it tempting to let others make your decisions? *Lets you blame them for negative consequences.*

STRATEGIES THAT WORK

Have students read "Decision-Making Tips." Encourage volunteers to give examples—from experience, if they like—of how they have used any of the tips to their advantage. Also have students describe any consequences that may result or have resulted from not following the tips.

Answers to Think ...

1. No. Combined, they encourage thoughtful but not excessive deliberation of options.
2. It's the only way to accomplish anything; to evaluate and learn from decisions.

◄ **CROSS-REFERENCE** ►

For more information on peer refusal skills, refer to Chapter 10.

STRATEGIES That Work

Decision-Making Tips

The six-step, decision-making process can help you make good decisions. Here are some other tips that will help you make decisions:

- **Gather information.** To be able to make a good decision, you often need to get some information. If you are thinking about painting your room, for instance, you need to learn about different types of paint and their characteristics before choosing one.
- **Write it down.** Write down every possible option you can think of. Keep a pad of paper handy in case you think of a new option when you are in the middle of something else.
- **Make a table.** Evaluate your options by using a system for ranking them. Suppose that you are planning to buy a new telephone, and you are comparing three different models. List the features you are interested in down the side of a piece of paper. Then list the three models across the top. Use a plus or minus to indicate whether the model has the feature or not. You could also rank each model on a scale of 1 (low) to 10 (high), depending on the quality of each feature for each model.
- **Take a break.** Some decisions can be put off, at least for a while. If you have such a decision to make, list your options but postpone making the

actual decision. Sleep on it. Put it in the background. Sometimes new options can occur to you while you are not concentrating on the decision itself.

- **Set a deadline.** Don't put your decision off indefinitely, however. Before you begin, set a deadline for yourself—for example, "I will make this decision by next Friday." Then do it.
- **Stick to your decision.** Once you've made the decision, stay with it. Unless someone gives you new information—or you start to implement the decision, and it clearly isn't working—give yourself a chance to see what happens before you change your mind.
- **Allow yourself to be wrong.** Don't worry if your decision turns out not to work. If you made it on the basis of the best information available to you at the time, you did your job. Everyone makes mistakes. Just make sure that you learn from those mistakes.

Making the Strategy Work

Think . . .

1. Are the two tips "Take a break" and "Set a deadline" contradictory? Explain your answer.
2. Why is it important to stick to your decision?

Try...

Think of one decision you made, and evaluate whether you followed any of these tips. If you did not, could following one of them have helped you?

Since he worked evenings, Zachary had a problem, however. He liked his job and needed the money, but he wanted to take the class. Zachary was faced with a dilemma that called for the decision-making process. Here's how he used it.

State the Situation

Zachary began by focusing on the problem and putting it into words. Doing this forced him to confront the situation rather than just

let an opportunity pass him by. "Why do I need to make a decision?" he asked himself. The answer was that he really wanted—and felt that he needed—to take the course, but the hours conflicted with his job.

List the Options

At first Zachary thought he had only two **alternatives,** or *options*. He could quit his job in order to take the course or forget about taking the course. By focusing on alternatives,

---

DID YOU KNOW?

Having high self-esteem gives teens the confidence to make their own decisions, stick to them, and allow themselves to be wrong. At the same time, the more skillful and experienced students become at making decisions, the more confidence they gain, which in turn boosts self-esteem.

MORE ABOUT Gathering Information

Discussing alternatives with other people is often helpful as others think of additional options. However, this can become a way of postponing decisions. Teens must know when to stop gathering information and make a decision. If they spend too much time gathering information, they are actually avoiding the decision.

however, Zachary began to realize other possibilities. He could ask the manager about working different hours. He could leave this job and find one with more suitable hours. He could wait another year to take the course.

Exploring the options showed Zachary that he had more than he had originally thought. When he talked about the situation with his aunt, she added another possibility. He could take the course and temporarily accept fewer hours at work.

Weigh the Possible Outcomes

At this point Zachary made a list of all the options. Along with these he noted what would happen if he chose each one. He tried to list both positive and negative effects.

Quitting his job would enable him to take the course, but he couldn't afford to do that. He couldn't afford to cut his hours either. Leaving the job to find another might work, but he liked his job, felt secure, and might not be able to get another one very easily. Waiting to take the course might mean facing the same situation, only a year later. Besides, he was eager to take the course now. Changing his hours would help, if he could find the right times, but he didn't know if his manager would approve.

Consider Your Values

"What is important to me?" Zachary asked himself as he moved toward making a decision. He was examining his values in order to make a sound decision. All his thinking convinced him that he really wanted to take the course. His career goal was a priority. He wanted a solution that allowed him to fit the course into his life now.

Make a Decision and Act

Zachary decided to talk to his manager. He could suggest working longer hours on the nights he didn't have class. He also thought he could volunteer to work every Saturday. That would help the restaurant because many servers didn't like to work Saturdays, but Saturdays were busy nights. Zachary was pleased that his manager agreed to his proposal. She

Making Decisions

Considering Outcomes

Frank had a summer job driving an ice-cream truck. One afternoon, he was about halfway through his route, and the next stop was the community pool. Frank always liked this stop because it was where he usually sold the most ice cream. He got an hourly wage, but he also got a bonus for selling more than his quota. It was especially hot that afternoon, and Frank was sure that the people at the pool would push him well over his quota.

A few streets from the pool, Frank began to hear a grinding noise coming from the back of the truck. "That's funny," he thought, "I've never heard that noise before." He pulled the truck over to the curb so that he could check where the noise was coming from.

With the truck engine turned off, he could still hear the noise. As he walked back toward the freezer, the noise got louder. When he lifted the freezer lid, it didn't feel as cold as it should. Frank felt the ice cream and found that some of the bars were starting to feel soft. Sure that the problem was in the freezer, he knew that he had trouble. The ice cream probably would not stay cold much longer. It might last one more stop, but not for the rest of the route.

The company had a mechanic who could look at the equipment, but if he went back now, he wouldn't meet his quota for the day. That would cost the company extra sales—and lose him his bonus. On the other hand, if he went to the pool and sold what he could, there would still be ice cream left. By the time he got back to the shop, that ice cream would be ruined. "I hate to disappoint the people at the pool," he thought. "I hate to lose my bonus too. If I don't get back soon, though, we may lose even more of the ice cream. If that happens, I could get in trouble. Frank had a decision to make—and little time to make it.

1. What options does Frank have?
2. What serious outcomes may Frank face if he decides to finish the route?
3. What do you think that Frank should do? Why?

■ **Following Others.** Have students work in pairs. Have one student list times when imitating others or following old habits would be helpful for making good decisions, while the other student lists times when these methods would be harmful. Have partners compare lists and discuss points of agreement or disagreement, then share their results with the class.(*Decision Making*)

ENRICHMENT

■ **Decisions Denied.** Form students into teams to debate the following question: It is unfair for society to deny teens certain actions, such as driving a car and voting.

Making Decisions

Have students read "Considering Outcomes." Point out that sometimes a decision doesn't have an answer that is absolutely the right one. In such cases, weighing the possible outcomes helps you choose the best alternative even though it may still have some negative aspects. Ask students how this relates to Frank's situation.

Answers to Questions

1. Sell at the pool; return to the shop; finish route; might phone shop for guidance (perhaps they could send another truck).
2. Pay for ice cream; unhappy boss; possibly loss of job.
3. Encourage students to see that Frank must protect his employer's interests before his own. Going back or calling, if possible, may be best choice.

Focus on Responsibility Skills

Imagine that Zachary's friend Tim also works at the restaurant. Tim wants Zachary to keep working instead of taking a bookkeeping course. Zachary takes the course anyway; then Tim acts hurt. Ask: Should Zachary have passed up the course to please Tim? Suggest that Zachary might come to resent Tim if he passed up an opportunity because of Tim's pressure. Ask: Which teen would then be responsible for Zachary's unhappiness?

Review

■ **Chapter Review.** Use the contents of the Chapter Review page to help students review concepts, think critically, and apply their knowledge.

■ **Study Guide.** Have students complete the Study Guide for Chapter 5 on p. 20 of the Student Workbook.

■ **Step Out.** Ask students which of the steps in the decision-making process could be omitted. After some discussion, have a volunteer try to make a decision without using the step or steps the class has decided to omit. Repeat with other suggested omissions. Help the class conclude that using all six steps is a better approach. *(Problem Solving)*

Evaluation

■ **Chapter Test.** Use the reproducible chapter test provided in the Teacher's Classroom Resources or create your own test using the *Testmaker Software*.

■ **Alternative Assessment.** Have groups perform a skit in which a decision is made using the six-step process. Skits should also show how a troublemaker is overcome.

■ **Decision Do's and Don'ts.** Have groups list five "do's" and five "don'ts" of decision making, based on information in the chapter. As groups share items on their lists, ask several students to create two master lists.

was impressed by Zachary's goal, as well as his effort to be accommodating.

Evaluate the Decision

After taking the course, Zachary felt that he had made the right decision. The course had been worthwhile. His schedule has been heavy, though, and if he had it to do again, he might have asked to cut his hours down a little. Making a small financial sacrifice would have made his life less hectic. He would remember that for future use.

Avoiding Troublemakers

Making decisions would be a whole lot easier if certain things didn't get in the way. Have you ever been hindered by any of these troublemakers?

- **Procrastination.** Some people think too long before deciding and thus lose opportunities. Mariel saw a notice on the bulletin board about a concert. She thought about going but wasn't sure she wanted to. When she finally decided to go, all the tickets were gone.
- **Impulsiveness.** Making a decision too quickly can be as troublesome as putting it off. While in the mall, Lon's friend picked up a small item from a counter and put it in his pocket. Without thought, Lon did too. Later, he regretted his actions. He knew it was wrong and getting caught could have caused him serious trouble.
- **Avoidance.** Fear of consequences or of making the wrong decision may lead people to make no decision at all. The result is that a person lets whatever happens happen. Julie's situation was very serious. A victim of sexual abuse, she knew she should tell someone, but she didn't. As a result, the problem continued.

- **Deferring.** Letting other people make decisions for you can be dangerous. Spence had a close friend who always decided how they would spend their time. When the friend started involving them with people who were constantly in trouble, Spence simply went along. By not thinking for himself, Spence eventually wound up in trouble too.
- **Blaming.** When decisions have negative results, people may feel like blaming others. It's uncomfortable to admit you made a mistake, but it's the right thing to do. After coming home late one night, Luisa told her father that her friends had persuaded her to stay out longer. Luisa's father was disappointed in her because she hadn't simply admitted her mistake and taken responsibility for her own actions.

Your Approach to Decisions

The way you handle decision making is up to you. You have the tools and knowledge to make effective decisions. A responsible approach to decision making will enable you to avoid the troublemakers and choose options and actions that work well for you.

Taking credit for a decision that works is easy. Why can it be difficult to take responsibility for a decision that doesn't work?

REAL-LIFE APPLICATION

In one city (as in many), a teen was ordered by gang members to kill another teen, which he did. Help students see how the decision-making process breaks down in situations like these. The teen did not consider all the consequences, for the victim, himself, and society. He allowed others to control him—to override his compassion for another person and the person's family and friends. After his arrest for murder, he began to see the long-term consequences brought about because he didn't think and act for himself.

Chapter 5

Review

Reviewing the Facts

1. Why do people sometimes avoid making decisions?
2. Give an example of how a decision someone makes can affect others.
3. List the six steps in the decision-making process.
4. Why should you think through all your options when making a decision?
5. Why should you evaluate the effects of your decisions?
6. Identify three problems that people sometimes have in making decisions.

Thinking Critically

1. What effect does self-esteem have on a person's ability to make decisions?
2. How should a person react after making a wrong decision?

Applying Your Knowledge

1. **Applying the Process.** Think about a decision that you are actually going to be making in the future. In writing, apply the six-step, decision-making process to that decision. (Acting on the decision and evaluating it may have to wait.)
2. **Identifying Major Decisions.** Make a list of five decisions that you think are major ones for a teen. For each one, indicate why you see the decision as important. Consolidate your list with classmates, and try to reach agreement on five. Discuss what guidelines can be used to classify decisions as major.

Making Connections

1. **Business.** Businesspeople often conduct market research before introducing a new product or service. They may survey consumers to see if they are interested in the product. Sometimes they produce a small quantity of the product and try to sell it in a limited area to test its acceptance. Make up a new product—a food, a new magazine, or anything else you can think of. Then describe how you might test consumers' acceptance of it.
2. **History.** Choose a significant event in American history, such as the Boston Tea Party, the Louisiana Purchase, or the Civil Rights Act of 1964. Write two or three paragraphs showing how history would have been altered if that person or group had made a different decision.

Building Your Portfolio

Avoiding the Troublemakers
Choose one of the troublemakers described in the chapter—procrastination, impulsiveness, deferring, avoidance, or blame. Write a scenario about a teen who falls into one of these traps when making a decision. Describe the consequences. Then explain how using the six-step, decision-making process would have helped the teen. Share your scenario with your classmates, and discuss why people sometimes fail to make good decisions. Add your scenario to your portfolio.

ANSWERS TO REVIEWING THE FACTS

1. Because decisions involve risk.
2. Possible response: A decision about how to spend money affects family resources.
3. State the decision, list the options, weigh the possible outcomes, consider values, make a decision and act, evaluate the decision.
4. You may find that you have more possible alternatives than you first thought.
5. Evaluation helps you understand the consequences of your decision, decide whether you need to change your decision, and make better decisions in the future.
6. Any three: procrastination, impulsiveness, avoidance, deferring, blaming.

ANSWERS TO THINKING CRITICALLY

1. People with high self-esteem have confidence in their ability to choose a course of action and are more willing to risk being wrong.
2. Take responsibility for the decision and its consequences; take corrective action if needed; try to learn from it.

Chapter Overview

Chapter 6 helps students distinguish between confidence and competence. It explains how both are useful for meeting goals and outlines a practical action plan for making positive changes in life.

Motivator

■ **Changing Times.** To introduce students to the kinds of change that are possible, ask volunteers to describe changes they have made in life, such as learning a new skill. Help students differentiate between changes that happen to them and those they bring about.

Objectives

Discuss the chapter objectives on this page. Remind students that the objectives focus on important chapter concepts.

Vocabulary

Tell students that the term *positive reinforcement* may bring to mind experiments in which mice learn to run a maze to find food. Explain that people also receive positive reinforcement, rewards that motivate them to repeat or improve on some behavior— getting good grades for studying hard, for example. Ask for other examples.

Chapter 6
Making Changes and Meeting Challenges

- action plan
- competence
- confidence
- contracting
- modeling
- positive reinforcement
- rehearsing
- visualizing

Objectives

This chapter will help you to:

- Explain what it means to have confidence in yourself.
- Describe ways to develop a sense of competence.
- List the steps in developing and following through with an action plan to make changes in your life.
- Explain why it is important to overcome barriers by seeing them as challenges rather than obstacles.

CHAPTER RESOURCES

Student Workbook

Study Guide, pp. 22-23

Activity, *Building Self-Confidence,* pp. 24-25

Teacher's Classroom Resources

Lesson Plan, p. 10

Decision Making, *Facing a Challenge* p. 6

Extension #10, *Stories of Courage,* p. 16

Life Skills, *Meeting Challenges,* p. 14

Personal Development, *Facing a Challenge,* pp. 11-12

Transparency 5, *Get Help, Give Help*

Chapter 6 Test, pp. 17-18

Performance Assessment, *Changes and Challenges,* pp. 24-25

Reteaching, *Challenging Changes,* p. 12

See Also:

ABCNews InterActive™ Videodiscs

"Hey, Damon! How's it going?" said Marcus as he slid behind the desk next to Damon. Damon grinned. He liked having Marcus as a friend. They had so much in common.

Damon thought back to how his friendship with Marcus had developed. Damon had never had many friends, especially close ones. He just hadn't been able to make that connection. He realized that he wanted things to be different. The question was how.

He tried a few things. First he just said "hi" to people. He greeted them without waiting for them to speak. The big breakthrough came when he joined the agriculture club. He knew a little about livestock and wanted to learn more. That's how he met Marcus. Over time their friendship grew, and Damon even made several other friends in the club.

Life changed for Damon, and he liked that. Damon knew that he had accomplished something—and *he* had made it happen.

What kinds of changes do you want to make in your life? For some people, it may be something a basic as making new friends.

Taking Action

Some people never get beyond the status quo. They never do anything to make things different than they are right now. If everything is going well, that's OK. If it isn't, however, something needs to be done.

Damon was dissatisfied with his social life. He could have just accepted that, but he didn't. Instead he took action to bring about change. It wasn't easy, but he did it.

Nearly all people can think of ways they would like to make changes in their lives. Wanda, for example, wants to stop biting her nails. Jim wants to get out of the gang that controls him. As you can see, change can involve simple things, but it can also be critical to a person's well-being.

Barriers to Change

Confronting change isn't necessarily easy. Things can get in the way. Sometimes people fear change. "What will happen if I try to end my friendship with Andrea and Carlene?" That's what Kim wondered when she thought about separating from two of her friends who had started to get involved in shoplifting. Kim was afraid of how her friends would react. They might cause trouble for her. On the other hand, she risked much bigger trouble if she joined with them in shoplifting. She didn't want trouble with the law and her family. She had better plans for her life.

Some people feel helpless when they think of making changes. That's how Terrence felt about his father's alcoholism. He saw no way to make his father's behavior change. Terrence and his family needed to see that help existed for them if they would seek it—help that would set them on a path toward making necessary changes in their lives.

Tools for Change

When Abby thinks about her future, she is scared. She doesn't want to live the way her older sister does. Miranda had her first baby at age fourteen. She had two more within a few years. Abby sees how hard it is for Miranda to support herself and the children. Abby wants to do something different with her life, but she worries about making the same mistakes that Miranda and many others around her have made.

Focus on Assertiveness

Help students understand that self-confident people don't need to bully or control others. Their self-image does not depend on feeling superior through intimidation. Self-confident people also do not let others control them; they stand up for what they believe.

MORE ABOUT Change

Many people want to make changes in their lives, but they don't want to experience the difficult part of the change. A shy person might avoid discomfort by not making changes. If results are worth achieving, then discomfort may be worthwhile.

Topics on p. 69
• **Deciding to Change**
• **Barriers to Change**

Checking Comprehension

✓ Was Damon happy with the "status quo"? *No, he wanted more friends.*

✓ Besides those mentioned, what are some other changes young people might want to make? *Possible answers are changes in appearance; improvement in skills, financial situation, grades.*

Activities

■ **Turning Points.** Have pairs create a list of things that motivate people to make changes in their lives. Compare lists in class. Ask: Are there any factors or situations that seem to motivate most people? *(Observation)*

ENRICHMENT

■ **Tokens of Change.** Have students bring in objects that in some way represent a positive change they or others have made in their lives. It could be a personal item or a magazine article recounting the rise of a successful person. Changes may be in external circumstances or in attitude and philosophy. Have students share these items and the stories behind them.

USING VISUALS
Ask students what they think might be going on in the photo on this page. What courses of action might be taken with each of the scenarios they present?

Checking Comprehension

✓ What are some signs of competence? *Showing skill or knowledge in one or more areas.*

✓ What are some signs of confidence? *Willingness to try new things; optimism; assertiveness.*

✓ If you do not feel confident, what can you do? *Gain skills and knowledge that help you succeed. Success builds confidence.*

FAMILY AND COMMUNITY OUTREACH

Have students interview an adult whom they consider to be self-confident. Their goal is to identify factors that encouraged this person's confidence, such as a supportive family or early successes. Give guidelines for asking helpful, appropriate questions. Have students share what they learn with classmates.

What Abby needs—as do all people who want to change their lives—are the tools to do so. Two of these are competence and confidence, and they work hand in hand.

Competence

Have you ever prepared a meal that turned out terrible? Have you ever done poorly on a test in school? In both situations competence may have been lacking. **Competence** means *having the qualities and skills needed to perform a task or participate fully in an activity.*

Developing Competence

People develop competence through learning. In school, you gain skills and knowledge that will remain with you for life. Knowing how to read and write well, for example, will help you in your working life. These skills can help you use your money wisely as well.

A few paragraphs can't describe all the areas of competence a person can have. For example, Bill understands how cars work and can handle many repair and maintenance jobs on his family's car. Katy has built storage cabinets for her family. Heather is a fine volleyball player. Carlos is good with numbers and is preparing himself to learn about investments. The list could go on and on.

Who and what can help you become more competent? School, of course, is an obvious resource. Books, magazines, and newspapers are information resources. People are another good resource. Family, friends, teachers, coaches, counselors, and community members offer many opportunities for you to learn—if you recognize them as resources and let them teach you.

If you already have competence in some areas, that's great. Can you improve those skills or create new ones? Doing so makes you an even more competent person.

Confidence

Another tool that people use to bring about change in their lives is confidence. **Confidence** means *believing in yourself and your abilities.* Actions display this positive

attitude. For example, Ellen's father always said she had a flair for the dramatic. Ellen wondered if she could use that skill in the drama club. Though she worried about stage fright, the thought of performing was exciting. Her confidence won out, and she tried out for a play. When she got a part, she was thrilled.

Qualities of Confidence

Think about the confident people you know. What qualities do they have that make you see them as confident? You can identify certain common characteristics in confident people:

- **Self-assurance.** Because they believe in themselves, confident people stand up for themselves and for what they believe.
- **Self-control.** Since they realize that their actions affect their own lives and the world around them, people with confidence consider carefully what they will do. They use reason, rather than their emotions, to tell them what to do and when to act.

How does practice help you develop your competencies and prepare you for the challenges you must face?

70   UNIT 1   Personal Development

DID YOU KNOW?

Singer Barbra Streisand did not perform on stage from 1967 to 1994—27 years—because she lacked confidence. The reason? She forgot the words of a song during a concert in New York's Central Park. Through determination and years of therapy, she regained the confidence to return to the stage—and to great success. Ask: How does delay affect a shaky confidence? Ask students to recount times that they put off new or frightening experiences.

STRATEGIES *That Work*

Attitudes for Success

Many people search their whole lives for the secret to success. It's not something you buy or that is given to you. Rather, it's an attitude—a way of approaching life that helps you become a winner. You can't help but have successes when you:

- **Count your blessings, not your misfortunes.** A young high school teacher who fell while hang gliding was paralyzed from the waist down. She sought the positives and formed a company to make wheelchairs that enabled injured people to participate in sports.
- **Work with what you have.** Life isn't fair. Although some people have fewer problems than others, even those who are born into difficult circumstances can succeed. They simply need to show the will, the determination, and the effort.
- **Find the right opportunity.** If you keep looking, you'll find someone who will give you a chance. Don't give up before that happens.
- **Plan to be one in a million.** People may say that you can't succeed where others have failed.

Whatever you attempt, however, remember that it only has to work once—for you.

- **Welcome change.** Don't be afraid to try something new or take a chance. Following the same old routine will not help you achieve new goals.
- **Don't be afraid of failure.** Failure is a natural part of success. It helps you to learn and grow, to become a winner.

Making the Strategy Work

Think . . .

1. Name some people you believe are successful. What traits do they share in common?
2. What successes have you had? What personal qualities led to that success?
3. How might a negative attitude affect a person's achievement?

Try...

Choose a goal for yourself. Plan how you will use the guidelines above to achieve your goal. Post your plan where you'll see it regularly. Evaluate your effort and the results.

- **Willingness to take reasonable risks to achieve goals.** Everyone who attempts something is taking a risk. Confident people know not to take risks that don't make sense. A rollerblader who wants to improve skills may try new twists and turns—these are reasonable risks. The same teen knows better than to rollerblade in car traffic, however. That is not a reasonable risk.
- **Healthy self-concept and high self-esteem.** Confident people know they aren't perfect; however, they refuse to dwell on their weaknesses. Instead, they feel good about what they have learned and achieved.

Developing Confidence

Confidence grows stronger each time you succeed. This increased confidence makes you more willing to work toward building and strengthening your competencies. In other words, competence builds confidence, and vice versa.

You see this principle in action all the time. A winning team is inspired to practice harder to win again. Making a good grade in class makes a person want to work toward an even better one. Earning extra money from selling garden produce makes a person think about how to raise more vegetables next year. You can put this cycle to work in your life and

Activities

■ **Chicken or Egg?** Ask students: Which do you think comes first, confidence or competence? Have them write a short paragraph stating and explaining their opinion. (*Critical Thinking*)

RETEACHING

■ **In a Word.** Ask groups to think of four adjectives that describe a competent person and four that describe a confident person. Ask several students to create a master list as groups take turns sharing words from each category.

STRATEGIES THAT WORK

Have students read "Attitudes for Success." Encourage volunteers to share their responses to the activity under "Try." You may begin by telling about a personal goal and your plan for achieving it.

Answers to Think . . .

1. Answers may include: perseverance; taking chances; learning from mistakes.
2. Answers will vary.
3. Could make a person unwilling to recognize or tackle change.

CROSS-REFERENCE

For more about types of resources, refer students to page 57 in Chapter 4.

MORE ABOUT Building Confidence

Confidence can be contagious, infecting an entire community. In 1984, Chanyanya, Zambia, was a poor, deforested fishing village of mud huts and hopelessness. Since then, Habitat for Humanity has helped villagers build 250 houses for low monthly payments. Now confident in the future, the people have built a medical clinic and a school and have begun to reforest the area. Ask: Which inspired more confidence in the villagers—the new homes or the faith that others showed in them?

Topics on pp. 72-74
• A Plan for Action
• Meeting Obstacles and Challenges

Checking Comprehension

✓ What should you do if you are making less progress toward a goal than expected? *Modify your goal or strategies.*

✓ What is the problem with visualizing life as a celebrity? *Such goals are usually unrealistic, waste time, can lead to discouragement.*

✓ What are some possible pitfalls of modeling the behavior of another person? *Person, even if famous, may not be good role model.*

FAMILY AND COMMUNITY OUTREACH

If possible, have the class interview students at a nearby elementary school about their role models: whom do the children admire and why? This can be an informal poll, or you can help students determine a representative sample of children and assign a group to interview each segment of the student body. Have students compare their findings. Ask: Do these results show a positive trend among children? If not, what might teens and adults do to change it?

CROSS-REFERENCE

For a review of types of goals, refer students to pages 53-54 in Chapter 4.

make the changes in your life that you want to make.

Making Changes

Feeling confident and competent provides a sense of power and purpose. You begin to realize that you can take action to become the person you want to be and have the kind of life you want for yourself. Taking action that will lead you in these directions begins with setting goals and continues with making those goals a reality.

Setting Goals

Setting goals is habit forming. Attaining goals is confidence boosting. To give yourself a chance, make sure that your goals can be attained. Follow the suggestions in Chapter 4 for setting reasonable goals for yourself.

Making an Action Plan

To achieve your goals, you need an **action plan**—*a program of behavior for achieving a particular goal.* It should include specific strategies for making change as well as ways to judge whether they are working. Some useful strategies for achieving goals are explained in **Figure 6.1**.

Putting the Plan to Work

Even clear goals and strategies can go wrong if an action plan isn't monitored. Keep these three elements in mind while you are implementing your plan of action:

• **Monitor your progress.** Establish a way to examine how things are going. You might make a chart or record information in a notebook.

• **Provide positive reinforcement.** Successful action plans involve some form of **positive reinforcement**, or *a reward for achievement.* Some people give themselves a treat each time they reach a short-term goal. This technique helps people feel a sense of accomplishment and pride and keeps them motivated.

Figure 6.1
STRATEGIES FOR ACHIEVING GOALS

Modeling involves shaping your behavior after that of another person. A teen who wants to be more outgoing might imitate the behavior of a friend or relative whose social abilities he or she admires.

Contracting involves making an agreement with another person about how you will achieve a goal. For example, a teen whose goal is to gain greater independence by acting more responsibly might agree with her parents to take on additional chores in exchange for a later curfew on weekends. Contracts don't have to be with someone else, however. At times you may make a contract with yourself.

MORE ABOUT Positive Reinforcement

Explain that reinforcement can be extrinsic (given by others) or intrinsic (originating within oneself). Extrinsic reinforcement includes money, grades, and trophies. Intrinsic reinforcement is satisfaction in having done your best or met your goal. Ask: How might a person react if she or he were working for some type of extrinsic reinforcement and it was not given?

- **Evaluate results and decide how to revise the action plan to make it better in the future.** Experience is a good teacher. Only by looking at what worked and what didn't can you decide on a better approach to use the next time.

When you follow an action plan and experience success with it, what will happen? If you said that your confidence will build, you have learned the lesson well. You are likely to discover that you can make things happen in your life when you are willing to try.

The Right Perspective

Some things in life can be changed and some cannot. By accepting that principle, you reduce the frustration that comes with wishful thinking.

Scott, for example, spent many hours daydreaming about what he would do if he were tall. These were wasted hours. Scott had reached his full height, and nothing could change that. Then a friend told him: "Scott, you don't need to be tall. You have a lot going for you. Just pay attention to that instead."

Once Scott learned to accept what he could not change, he found new satisfaction in developing his strengths.

Do you see the difference between what you can change and what you cannot in your own life? This insight is very useful. You can accept some things with peace of mind yet tackle necessary changes with determination.

Overcoming Obstacles

Obstacles are a part of life. Everyone faces them at times. In a perfect world, all obstacles would be easy to overcome, but in the real world overcoming them takes planning and hard work. Sometimes the challenges presented by physical disabilities, discrimination, and socioeconomic conditions seem impossible to overcome, yet there are so many examples of people who conquer them.

A person's attitude toward barriers can mean the difference between giving up and achieving success. People who view their difficulties as challenges rather than roadblocks are in a better position to accomplish the goals they seek.

Visualizing involves imagining yourself doing the task or activity you want to learn. If a person's goal is to master a new dive, for example, she or he might picture herself or himself performing the dive flawlessly.

Visualizing is related to **rehearsing**, which refers to practicing, or learning by doing an activity over and over. A teen might practice a trumpet solo alone at home in preparation for an upcoming concert.

CHAPTER 6   Making Changes and Meeting Challenges   73

Focus on Determination

Queenie Archer is a model for overcoming obstacles. Born with cerebral palsy, she was institutionalized from age 11 to 28. Left alone, Archer often went hungry because she couldn't feed herself, yet her will remained strong. Unable to use her hands, she learned to paint by attaching a brush to a headband. She may spend months on a painting, which can sell for up to $1,000. Now 46, her current goal is to compete in the Ms. Wheelchair contest. A win, she believes, would encourage others with severe disabilities.

Activities

- **Trouble in Sight.** Ask students to identify the built-in problem with these goals:
  - I'm going to win the state spelling championship next spring.
  - Next time I run the 400-meter relay, I won't trip and let everybody down like I did last time.
  - To be as popular as Julie, I'm going to go to the same places she does.
- **Round Robin Goals.** Divide the class into three groups. Have each group make up a character with a clearly defined goal. Have groups pass descriptions to the next group and write an action plan for the character. After another pass, groups should write about how the character monitors progress toward the goal. Read the resulting scenarios aloud.

SPECIAL NEEDS
Strategies

Outlining. Have students rephrase chapter headings into questions and then write answers. For example, "Taking Action" becomes "Why Should I Take Action?"

USING VISUALS

Ask students which of the strategies in Figure 6.1 they have used. Tell them to watch a trained high jumper at a track meet before he or she takes off on an approach. They are likely to see visualization in action.

Review

■ **Chapter Review.** Use the contents of the Chapter Review page to help students review concepts, think critically, and apply their knowledge.

■ **Study Guide.** Have students complete the Study Guide for Chapter 6 on p. 22 of the Student Workbook.

■ **Picture This.** Divide students into six groups. Have each group make a poster illustrating one of the points for giving support featured on page 74. Encourage groups to be creative in choosing a medium and method to deliver their message.

Evaluation

■ **Chapter Test.** Use the reproducible chapter test provided in the Teacher's Classroom Resources or create your own test using the *Testmaker Software.*

■ **Alternative Assessment.** Have pairs prepare and present skits in which characters make, then correct, common errors in setting and working toward goals. Have pairs submit skit ideas for approval to avoid duplication.

■ **Words to Live By.** Have groups share what they have learned about change and challenges by writing short statements of advice that might be read during morning announcements or printed in the school newspaper. Tell groups to focus on advice that other teens might find meaningful. You may assign topics, such as barriers to change, developing competence, and setting goals.

The weight of a challenge is much lighter when shared. Reach out to others, and they will do the same for you.

Mutual Support

No one needs to be alone. As you look toward the future, realize that others are willing to help you reach your goals. Family, friends, school counselors, and teachers are all possible sources of support.

Remember, too, that others need your help. Be ready to listen and encourage friends and members of your family. Giving to others benefits you, making you feel more confident and competent as you see what you can contribute to another person's life.

The Challenges Ahead

Now it's time to get started. You can take charge of your life and make necessary change happen. Large or small, challenges await you. Are you ready to accept them?

Managing Your Life

Giving Support to Others

Just as you need support from others, they also need it from you. You can listen, but you can also advise. Here's how:

■ **Give positive input.** Advice works best if it also recognizes what the person is doing right. He or she will then be more receptive to suggestions on how to do things differently.

■ **Acknowledge past accomplishments.** Point to things that were done well in the past to remind the person of how obstacles were overcome.

■ **Be specific.** Messages need to be understood. Saying "You're cooking the chicken wrong" doesn't help. Saying "Cook the chicken until the juices run clear" is easy to act on.

■ **Recognize the person's style.** Strategies that work for you may not be useful for others. Try to suggest a number of options if you can.

■ **Ask questions.** Even if you don't have a solution, you can help find one. Simply ask some leading questions. Ask questions like: Have you faced a problem like this in the past? How did you solve it? Do you need more information? Where could you get it?

■ **Suggest a break.** Frustration hinders solutions. Tell the person to try again later with a fresh approach when the frustration has passed.

Applying the Principles

1. Imagine that you are teaching a young child how to ride a bike, and she is almost in tears. What advice might you give?
2. Suppose a friend is having a hard time thinking of a topic for an essay assignment. What suggestions can you give?

74   UNIT 1   Personal Development

Managing Your Life

Have students read "Giving Support to Others." Elicit discussion by asking a question such as, "What kind of support do you most appreciate when you have a problem?" or "Can you—or should you—offer help to someone who doesn't seem to want it?"

Answers to Applying . . .

1. Answers will vary but should reflect ideas discussed in the feature.
2. Answers will vary but should reflect ideas discussed in the feature.

Chapter 6 Review

Reviewing the Facts

1. Identify two common barriers to making changes.
2. Describe what it means to have confidence.
3. Identify four strategies for making changes in your life and describe one.
4. What does it mean to monitor your progress when you follow an action plan? Why is it helpful?
5. List three specific conditions that an individual could see either as a challenge to overcome or an obstacle blocking the way.

Thinking Critically

1. What do people who frequently say "I can't" need to know?
2. Explain how high self-esteem could lead to a great sense of competence.

Applying Your Knowledge

1. **Writing a Want Ad.** Write a want ad that begins "Wanted: Confident Person." Describe what kind of person would be able to fill this job, using both traits described in the text and others you think of on your own.
2. **Reading a Biography.** Read a biography or autobiography of someone who faced a lifelong challenge, such as a physical disability or racial discrimination. Helen Keller and George Washington Carver are good examples. After reading the book, summarize the most important ways the person met the challenge he or she faced.

3. **Design a Poster.** Design a poster that raises public awareness of a social problem, such as racial discrimination or age discrimination, that could present a challenge to people trying to reach goals. Display your poster in the classroom or somewhere in the school.

Making Connections

1. **Mathematics.** Choose a good habit that you would like to develop or a bad habit that you would like to break. Keep a record of your successes in increasing or decreasing the frequency of this behavior over three weeks. Display your results in graph form.
2. **Physical Education.** Think of a physical activity or skill you would like to improve in yourself. Use the visualization technique, and report on the results.

Building Your Portfolio

Creating an Action Plan and Predicting Results

Choose a television or movie character who needs to make a change in his or her life. Create an action plan that this individual might follow. Involve one or more of the strategies discussed in this chapter. Place the plan in your portfolio.

Chapter 7

FOCUS

Chapter Overview

Chapter 7 explores career preparation. Students learn to assess their interests and skills in light of job opportunities and required training. They also learn about setting career goals.

Motivators

■ **Big Deal.** Ask students to rate the importance of a person's career choice from 1 (not very important) to 10 (extremely important). Discuss reasons for their ratings.

■ **Why Work?** "We work to become, not to acquire." Ask students to interpret this quotation by Elbert Hubbard. Do they agree?

Objectives

Discuss the chapter objectives on this page. Remind students that the objectives focus on important chapter concepts.

Vocabulary

Entrepreneur is based on an Old French term meaning "to undertake." An entrepreneur undertakes—organizes, manages, and assumes the risks of—running a business. The term is related to both *enterprise* and *enterprising*. Ask: How do those two words relate to running a business?

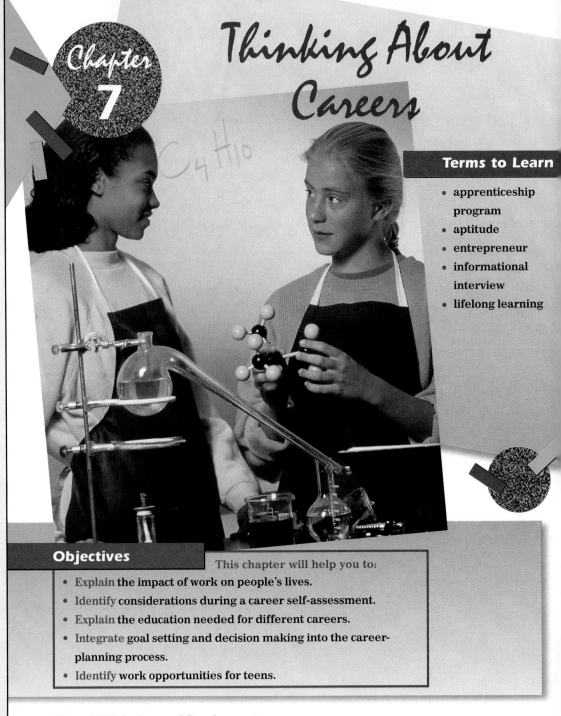

Chapter 7

Thinking About Careers

Terms to Learn

- apprenticeship program
- aptitude
- entrepreneur
- informational interview
- lifelong learning

Objectives

This chapter will help you to:

- Explain the impact of work on people's lives.
- Identify considerations during a career self-assessment.
- Explain the education needed for different careers.
- Integrate goal setting and decision making into the career-planning process.
- Identify work opportunities for teens.

CHAPTER RESOURCES

Student Workbook
Study Guide, p. 26
Activity, *Exploring Career Options*, pp. 27-28

Teacher's Classroom Resources
Lesson Plan, p. 11

Decision Making, *Career Decisions*, p. 7
Extension #11, *Skills, Talents, and Careers*, p. 17
Life Skills, *A Personal Career Profile*, p. 15
Transparency 6, *The Value of Work*

Chapter 7 Test, pp. 19-20
Performance Assessment, *The Steps I'll Take*, p. 26
Reteaching, *Choosing a Career*, p. 13

See Also:
ABCNews InterActive™ Videodiscs

A hundred years ago choosing a career was fairly easy. There were a limited number of well-defined jobs. Everyone knew what a farmer, a shopkeeper, and a railroad engineer did. Many young men followed their fathers into these and other jobs. Young women were usually expected to become homemakers.

Deciding on a career is much more complicated today. In the United States, you can choose from more than 20,000 jobs. What's more, new jobs emerge every day. Robotics engineers, telecommunications specialists, and systems analysts were unheard of only a few decades ago. Many jobs are so technical that they are hard to explain to someone outside the occupation.

In the midst of all this complexity, how can you possibly know which career to choose? Relax! You don't need to choose a career today. However, you do need to start thinking about one. If you begin now to study career options, you will be better prepared to make decisions in the future.

More Than a Paycheck

If you asked classmates why they want a job, most would probably answer, "To make money." Teens often see a job as a way to earn cash for new clothes or for movie tickets or to pay for gas and car insurance. Later, with independence, comes a need to pay for food, housing, health insurance, utility bills, and much more. Someday you may need income to support a family.

Earning a living is an important reason for working. Work satisfies more than physical needs, however. These emotional, intellectual, and social needs are also met:

- **The approval of others.** Performing a job well and receiving praise from coworkers boosts a person's self-esteem.

The jobs of today are different from those of yesterday. What proof of that is shown here?

- **Personal achievement.** Being self-supporting makes a person feel proud and competent.
- **Personal growth.** Jobs provide opportunities to learn new skills and gain knowledge.
- **Social relationships.** Many people form close friendships with coworkers and find a sense of belonging at work.
- **Fulfillment.** Most people want to feel that the work they do is important and that they are making a contribution to society.

Work does more than generate income. It also contributes to a person's overall well-being. Jobs vary in the degree to which they meet physical, intellectual, emotional, and social needs, and no job can satisfy all the needs a person has. Nevertheless, most people want to work not only for the money but also for the opportunity to experience other benefits.

CHAPTER 7   Thinking About Careers   77

DID YOU KNOW?

The types of jobs available vary considerably worldwide. In some developing nations such as Malawi, East Africa, 90 of every 100 workers is involved in growing food to feed the population. In the United States, only 3 of every 100 employees work in farming occupations. The others work at a wide variety of jobs. Ask: What might be some consequences of having a large segment of workers involved in a single area?

Topics on pp. 78-79:

- **Factors Influencing Career Choice**
- **Learning About Careers**

Checking Comprehension

✓ How can your hobbies help you choose a career? *They show your interests.*

✓ How can other people help you choose a career? *They can help you identify your skills and aptitudes.*

How does an informational interview differ from a job interview? *Involves gathering data and impressions, not applying for a job.*

FAMILY AND COMMUNITY OUTREACH

Tell students that, in a 5-year study of 1,200 children in Boston, New Orleans, Virginia, and Washington, DC, about half wanted to go into the same field as one of their parents. More children were interested in their mothers' field than their fathers' because they knew more about the work their mothers did. Ask volunteers to describe how relatives, neighbors, or family friends have influenced their current career goals.

What skills, interests, and aptitudes might these people need for the work they do? What may happen if they don't have them?

Career Self-Assessment

The average person in your generation can expect to work until age 65—and probably longer. That's a big chunk of time! With all those years of working ahead of you, you probably want to find a career that is challenging and enjoyable. How can you know what kind of work is best for you? You can start by looking closely at your interests, skills and aptitudes, personality traits, and values.

Your Interests

Hobbies and what you do with free time reveal your interests. Interests can lead to satisfying careers. For example, Leo enjoys photography, shooting baskets, collecting baseball cards, and watching sports on television. Do you see a way to link these to a career? One possibility for Leo is a career as a sports photographer.

Getting involved in after-school activities can help you develop current interests and discover new ones. Your school and community offer many opportunities in such areas as sports, music, drama, science, and debate. If

you enjoy these activities and develop skills, they may lead you to a fulfilling career.

Your Skills and Aptitudes

Nearly all people have something they do well naturally. *Natural talents and abilities* are called **aptitudes.** A skill, on the other hand, is an ability that results from training and practice. Skills and aptitudes often seem like opposite sides of the same coin. You may learn a skill more easily if you have an aptitude for it. To sharpen your skills to their utmost, however, you need training, hard work, and practice—even if you have an aptitude for that skill. For example, Rachel's natural athletic ability gave her an edge on the soccer field. To become a better player, however, she needed to practice to improve her dribbling and passing.

What are your skills and aptitudes? To find out, ask yourself these questions:

- What school subjects are easiest for me?
- What do I do well?
- Which of my skills were easiest to learn?
- What could I probably learn to do well?
- What skills and aptitudes do my teachers, family, and friends think I have?

Choosing a career that matches your skills and aptitudes is a good idea. Because you're more likely to be good at what you do, you'll be more likely to succeed.

Your Personality Traits

Imagine what might happen if a person who doesn't enjoy talking to people took a job as a salesperson. He or she would probably be happier as a bookkeeper or a truck driver. You need to consider what kind of a person you are when choosing a career. Otherwise, you may wind up in a job that isn't right for

78 UNIT 1 Personal Development

MORE ABOUT Personality Traits

Identifying oneself as more introverted or extroverted can help in choosing a career. Introverts tend to prefer working by themselves, with things or with data. They might be comfortable as machine opera- tors, mathematicians, researchers, or writers. Extroverts tend to be happier in people-oriented positions, such as teacher, medical professional, personnel director, or salesperson.

you. Think about whether you like working alone or with people. Ask yourself whether you prefer working with words, numbers, pictures, objects, or people. Consider whether you would prefer working indoors or outdoors. You can find a career with the right mix of traits for you—but you need to know what traits you're looking for.

Your Values

Values show what is important to you. Some values reflect your personal likes and dislikes. Aim to choose a career that reflects those likes and dislikes. For example:

- If you love the outdoors, you might choose to become a park ranger or a landscaper.
- If you thrive on excitement, you might decide to be a news reporter or a firefighter.
- If you value helping, you might become a member of the clergy or a counselor.
- If you prefer working alone, you might try laboratory work or developing a business you can operate at home.

Other values reflect what you believe is right and wrong and what you believe should have priority in life. Pete became a teacher because he likes children and enjoys helping people learn.

Assessment Tools

Identifying your interests, skills, aptitudes, personality traits, and values isn't always easy. Fortunately, some special assessment tools are available to help you learn more about yourself. See your guidance counselor to find out about these tools.

Career Exploration

When searching for your career, understanding yourself is not enough. You also need to find a career that is a good fit for you. To know how careers match your characteristics, investigate the duties and responsibilities connected to the job. Look at the training or education required, working conditions, salary, and outlook for future employment. You can find this information in several ways.

Reading

Public libraries contain books, pamphlets, and other materials on occupations. Your school library probably has a career section as well. Two resources commonly found in libraries are the *Occupational Outlook Handbook* and the *Dictionary of Occupational Titles.* Both are published by the U.S. Department of Labor. These books give specific information about thousands of jobs.

You can also get information about careers by reading the help-wanted ads in the newspaper. Ads indicate which jobs and skills are most in demand in your area. The biographies and autobiographies of famous people pro-

To learn about a career that interests you, find someone who works in the field. You can ask questions and maybe even get an on-site tour of the facility.

Activities

■ **Piece It Together.** Have students create a puzzle for bulletin board display to show how different factors fit together in finding the right career. After a discussion, have the class select those factors that they believe are most important. These will be the pieces of the puzzle. Have them agree on the dimensions of the puzzle and shape of the pieces. Assign or let groups choose a piece to label and illustrate to reflect the given factor. Assemble and display the puzzle. *(Decision Making)*

■ **Job Search.** Have groups of students choose a skill or an aptitude, such as math ability. Challenge them to see how many occupations they can identify in which that skill would be useful. *(Creativity)*

►CROSS-REFERENCE◄

Note that a career-related chapter appears at the end of every unit in this text. The final chapters in Units 1 and 2 present general information about work and the skills needed to be successful. The career chapters in the remaining units describe specific careers related to each unit's content.

DID YOU KNOW?

About 6 in 10 new jobs result from personal contacts; some are created just for a certain person. Companies with fewer than 100 employees were responsible for 70 percent of all new jobs between 1988 and 1992.

Focus on Career Exploration Skills

Along with general directories, job opportunities are often listed in trade journals. These are as varied as *Automotive News, Logging and Sawmill Journal,* and *Software Canada.* Libraries often carry publications like these.

In Touch with TECHNOLOGY
Technology and Career Planning

New technologies make career planning easier and quicker than ever. Now you can do research on a career just by touching a few buttons.

Are you interested in being a veterinarian? Visit a public library, and check out a videotape about working in an animal hospital. Many libraries stock videotapes and audiotapes about careers. If the library nearest your home doesn't have videos, you may be able to get them through an interlibrary loan.

Many libraries also have computer-based career research centers. If you have access to an on-line service, you can do a computer search for career information. Some services even post want ads and offer help preparing résumés.

Many career-planning centers use computers to score career assessment tests. Some computer programs can automatically print out a list of local companies that hire workers in the areas in which you scored well.

Technology is useful even after a career is chosen. Many people now use computer databases to help them find jobs. Often, people seeking work can enter their own names and qualifications into a database. Then businesses that are looking for workers will learn about them.

No matter what your interest, technology can make your career search swifter and more productive. That's great for you—it leaves you more time to explore your options.

Thinking Critically About Technology

1. What advantages and disadvantages can you see in using technology to research careers?
2. When technological resources are limited, how might an individual increase them?

---

vide another source of career information. You can learn about the work of broadcasters, athletes, government leaders, and scientists as you read these books.

Interviewing

What better picture can you get of a career than a firsthand description? Try talking with someone who does work that interests you. You might talk informally with a relative or family friend who does such work. You also could arrange an **informational interview.**

This is *a meeting in which you can ask people questions and receive advice about careers.* Your guidance counselor may be able to suggest people in your area who are willing to talk to students.

For an informational interview, prepare a short list of questions. You might ask what kind of work the person does, what trends are occurring in the industry, and how to prepare for a career in the field. The person is being gracious in interrupting the workday, so keep your interview brief.

80   UNIT 1   Personal Development

Focus on Computer Skills

One service on Internet offers job listings with hourly updates. More than 3,000 employers post their openings on Internet's On-Line Career Center database. Students can access this database by logging onto Internet and typing in this address: occ@msen.com. After they type "info" on the subject line, the system provides instructions. Job seekers can also enter their own résumés.

Observing

Every day you see people who are at work. Observing them is another good way to learn about jobs. The next time you get your hair cut, for example, watch what the stylist does—cut hair, answer the phone, make appointments, make change. You could even conduct an informational interview on the spot. Why did he or she choose to be a hairstylist? What does the person like and dislike about this job? People generally enjoy talking about their work.

You might be able to arrange a job-visiting day. Spending time with a parent, relative, or neighbor in the workplace gives you a chance to see the worker in action. You may even get to try out a work-related task.

Additional Resources

You can take advantage of still other ways to learn about careers. Look for these:

- Attend a job fair or career day.
- Listen to guest speakers in school talk about different types of jobs.
- Tour factories and other businesses, and talk to employees about their jobs.

Career Preparation

In planning a career, step one is to analyze yourself. Step two is to identify a career. Then it's time for step three: figuring out what education and training you need to enter the career you prefer. Nearly all jobs today require at least a high school diploma. Those that offer the best long-term opportunities and income usually require additional training or education.

A High School Education

You can prepare yourself for a satisfying career by taking vocational courses. You can build the foundation of a satisfying career by taking a college-preparatory program. You can even keep yourself ready for a variety of satisfying careers by pursuing a general course of study.

It is very difficult, however, to have a satisfying career if you drop out of school. Society and the economy are becoming increasingly complex. The few unskilled jobs left, typically have low pay. To survive on these wages, people often need to work at more than one job, taking daytime work with one employer and night work with another. Do yourself a big favor—stay in school.

More Education and Training

Once you have your high school diploma, you have many options for career preparation. Here are some possibilities:

- **Technical institutes.** These train people for hotel management and computer repair, among other fields. Most programs last two years.
- **Trade schools.** These specialize in one field, such as auto mechanics or radio broadcasting.
- **Apprenticeship programs.** In an **apprenticeship program**, *beginning workers learn skilled trades from experienced workers, such as carpenters, electricians, and plumbers.* Many labor unions offer these programs..
- **The U.S. armed services.** The army, navy, air force, marines, and coast guard have training for nearly 2,000 occupations.
- **Community colleges.** These offer two-year degrees, called associate's degrees, in such fields as allied health, travel and tourism, and public service. Many community college graduates move to four-year colleges.
- **Four-year colleges and universities.** These offer bachelor's degrees in academic and professional fields. Teachers, accountants, and engineers need a four-year degree.
- **Graduate schools.** People pursuing some careers—such as lawyers, doctors, and psychologists—need advanced education beyond a four-year degree.

While you're in high school, become familiar with the schools and programs that offer training for careers that interest you. Your counselor has catalogs and brochures from colleges and other schools. If possible, visit the campuses of four-year colleges, commu-

- **Facing Facts.** Give students several minutes to list jobs that pay well and are available for people with no high school education and no training or experience. Discuss the results. *(Observation)*

ENRICHMENT

- **Learn by Mail.** Have students investigate correspondence schools: what courses they offer and how effectively they train people for jobs. Students might analyze ads, talk to people who have enrolled in these courses, and call companies that have hired workers trained in correspondence schools. Provide students time to share what they learn.

SPECIAL NEEDS *Strategies*

Inefficient Organizers. Discuss how to make the most of opportunities to observe people at work. For example, students might take notes or dictate their impressions into a tape recorder while or immediately after observing.

CROSS-CURRICULAR ACTIVITY
Language Arts

Ask students what some of the difficulties connected with writing thank-you notes are. Have students practice writing a sample thank-you note after an interview.

MORE ABOUT Ongoing Education

Many companies offer tuition reimbursement to encourage employees to learn new skills through continued education. Also, some professionals must take courses to maintain their certification. Ask students how paying for employees' education might help ensure the future of both a company and its workers. Explain any continuing education requirements that you must meet as a teacher.

Topics on pp. 82-84:
- Career-Related Goals and Decisions
- Getting Started

Checking Comprehension

✓ Why would you set short-term goals as you are planning your career? *They help you begin career path, work your way into career.*

✓ Identify some advantages and disadvantages of learning about a field through part-time work. *Advantages: Get firsthand experience, make contacts. Disadvantages: May affect grades; job may not represent whole field.*

SPECIAL NEEDS *Strategies*

Learning in Pairs. Have students help each other study chapter concepts by working in pairs to make up 10- to 15-question quizzes—true/false, multiple choice, or short answer—with an answer key on a separate sheet of paper. Have pairs exchange and complete each other's quizzes.

USING VISUALS

Refer students to the bottom photo on page 82. Ask them to imagine themselves as employers. Why would they value a worker who is cooperative and can communicate well with others?

Whether through degree programs or occasional seminars, many adults continue their career training so that they can stay competitive.

Cooperation and communication skills are becoming more and more important in today's workplace.

82   UNIT 1 **Personal Development**

REAL-LIFE APPLICATION

Read to students: *Willis, 16, often helps his uncle in his construction business. He feels competent at the work and knows that it can pay very well. He has decided to work there full-time as soon as he graduates, so he can start earning some money. He isn't considering college or training.* Ask: Is this a wise career move? Suggest that changing technology may affect the field and that Willis may develop different interests.

What kinds of skills can you learn from taking a job or doing volunteer work while you are in high school?

nity colleges, technical institutes, and trade schools. Talk to graduates about the training they received. You might also talk to recruiters at U.S. armed services offices.

Ongoing Education

Many workers—whatever their level of training or education—find that they need to keep their skills and knowledge up-to-date. Their solution is **lifelong learning**, or *education and training that continue throughout life*. This is especially important in today's increasingly complex economy.

Career Planning

After you have considered your interests and explored different careers, you are ready to make a plan. With career planning you actively pursue the career of your choice.

Setting Goals

To begin planning your career, decide what you want to accomplish (your long-term goal) and list the steps to achieve it (your short-term goals). Start by envisioning the type of job you want to have in the future. How will you prepare for it? For example, Mandy's long-term goal is to be a women's fashion buyer for a major department store. Her short-term goals are to:

- Take family and consumer sciences courses in high school.
- Get on the teen fashion board at a department store.
- Earn a four-year degree in clothing and textiles.
- Work part-time and summers in a fabric store while going to college.

Making Decisions

You will make many decisions about careers during your working life. Throughout life, people face decisions about choosing a job, changing jobs, and going back to school. When you make such decisions, use your decision-making skills.

No matter how well thought out a career plan is, obstacles can get in the way. Decision-making skills are extremely important in today's work world, where workers must deal with a job market that is continually changing. Changes include a decline in manufacturing jobs, a rise in service industry jobs, and the growth of technology. More than in the

CHAPTER 7 Thinking About Careers 83

MORE ABOUT Career Changes

Dwight Baldwin was an aspiring minister. When poor health forced him to leave college, he sold organs from a rented wagon. He began to build his own organs, which are now known worldwide. Mary Kay Ash, a retired sales director, opened a tiny store with one shelf of skin creams. She found that women were more likely to buy the creams after she gave them a facial. On this strategy she built Mary Kay Cosmetics into a $54-million-a-year corporation within 15 years.

Review

■ **Chapter Review.** Use the contents of the Chapter Review page to help students review concepts, think critically, and apply their knowledge.

■ **Study Guide.** Have students complete the Study Guide for Chapter 7 on p. 26 of the Student Workbook.

■ **At the Fair.** Discuss with students the purpose of a job fair. Have them write questions they might ask when attending a job fair or a career day program.

Evaluation

■ **Chapter Test.** Use the reproducible chapter test provided in the Teacher's Classroom Resources or create your own test using the *Testmaker Software.*

■ **Alternative Assessment.** Have students select a job that interests them and (1) describe the skills, aptitudes, and experience they could bring to the job; (2) list three specific ways they can find out more about the job; (3) explain the preparation necessary for the job; and (4) set three short-term goals to begin a path toward the job.

■ **Do's and Don'ts.** Have groups list three "do's" and three "don'ts" for career planning. As groups share their suggestions, create a master list. Have students work together using the master list to make a poster entitled "Career Planning Do's and Don'ts."

past, workers can find that their skills have become outdated or that their jobs have been eliminated. In general, fewer opportunities for advancement exist than in the past, as companies operate with fewer employees, merge with other companies, or go out of business.

People's interests and needs also change. They may tire of one career and want a new challenge. Whether by choice or necessity, people today change jobs more frequently than in the past. If these trends continue, you will probably make many career decisions during your life.

Getting Started

Work experiences can help you choose a career. When you work during high school, you learn about different jobs and work environments. You can also discover new interests and aptitudes.

When you are still in school, summer is the ideal time to have a job. Working during the school year can be manageable for some teens. For others, however, it is risky. Lance learned this lesson the hard way. His grades went down when he took a part-time job during the school year. He was forced to quit his after-school activities, too.

Every teen has to look carefully at how to balance work, family, personal, and school life. If work is a reasonable option, here are some ideas:

- **Part-time jobs.** Older teens have opportunities for regular part-time work in a variety of places.
- **Volunteer work.** Many opportunities exist for teens to do volunteer work at school and in the community. They can help

build houses for low-income families, for example, or visit the elderly in nursing homes.

- **Entrepreneurship.** Some teens become entrepreneurs, or *people who start and manage their own businesses.* One teen, for example, started a house-painting service during the summer. Another ran errands for busy people.
- **Cooperative programs.** Schools and businesses may work together to provide on-the-job training for teens. Students may spend part of their day in school and part at work. To qualify, students must maintain a certain grade point average.
- **Youth employment programs.** Many communities create work opportunities for teens, especially in the summer. For example, teens might get paid to build a nature trail.
- **Internships.** Business owners may invite teens to work in their offices. One teen who was interested in a law career, for example, found a summer internship in a law office.

A Clear Focus

Too many people look back on their lives and wonder what happened. Some see years wasted in jobs that weren't satisfying or gave them no chance to advance. Some see struggles with low incomes that didn't provide a comfortable living. Where will you be in 10 or 20 years? Will you be among those with regrets, or will you be one of those who planned well, made strong decisions, and found careers that became a positive part of their lives? It's your choice.

84   UNIT 1   Personal Development

MORE ABOUT Income

According to the Census Bureau, the more you learn, the more you earn. Figures for 1992 showed that people with advanced degrees had average earnings of $48,653. Those with bachelor's degrees av-eraged $32,629. High school graduates managed just $18, 737. Such dramatic differences present a strong case for the pursuit of education.

Reviewing the Facts

1. What needs does work fulfill?
2. What are four factors to consider in career self-assessment?
3. How can you learn more about an occupation that interests you?
4. Name five places where you can get education and training after high school.
5. What are five sources of work experience for teens in high school?

Thinking Critically

1. Should homemaking be considered a career? Why or why not?
2. How might choosing a career be different for you than it was for your parents or grandparents?

Applying Your Knowledge

1. **Evaluating the Media's Portrayal.** As a class, agree to watch a television program that features people in a certain occupation, such as lawyers, nurses, or police officers. The next day, discuss how accurately you think the program portrayed the occupation. If possible, interview a person who works in that field to gain his or her opinion of the program.
2. **Generalizing Job Trends.** Do research in the library to find the 20 fastest-growing occupations in the United States. Good sources for this information include two government publications: Statistical Abstracts of the United States and The American Work Force: 1992–2005. Using this information, write two generalizations about the job trends in the United States.

Making Connections

1. **Geography.** Research how young people in France, Germany, or Japan prepare for a career. Discuss what you like and dislike about the systems with your classmates.
2. **Language Arts.** Using Bartlett's Familiar Quotations or a similar source, find proverbs and sayings about work. For example: "There is no substitute for hard work" (Thomas Alva Edison). Share the proverbs and sayings that you find with the class, and discuss the feelings about work that they convey.

Building Your Portfolio

Making a Career Plan

As you think about your interests, skills, and aptitudes, choose a career idea that seems to mesh with them. Begin to make a career plan by setting a long-term goal related to this occupation. Then make a list of short-term goals that would help you achieve your long-term goal. Include possible work experience and education or training requirements as goals. Place the list in your portfolio.

Unit Preview

In Unit 2, students learn how to strengthen their relationships by analyzing the kinds of relationships they have, building on their communication skills, recognizing and resisting negative peer pressure, and finding ways to resolve conflicts peacefully. The unit also describes how students can make a difference in their community and gain skills that will help them get ahead in the workplace.

Content Development

Use these chapters to reinforce the following themes:

Content Strands	Chapters
Career Exploration	13
Citizenship/ Leadership	12
Communication	8-13
Decision Making	10-13
Health and Safety	8, 10, 11
Managing Resources	8, 12, 13
Personal Development	8-13
Technology	9, 13

Unit Motivator

■ **A Rough Road.** Ask students to suggest some things that can make it difficult for teens to get along with others. After writing their suggestions on the board, ask the class to choose the three most difficult challenges to relationships that teens face. The point is not to reach an agreement but to encourage discussion.

Explain that this unit will help students learn to resolve conflicts more easily. The unit will also give them skills in handling difficult situations that can occur in anyone's relationships—at school, at home, and on the job.

JOURNAL WRITING

Possible topics for student journals:
- Think about a relationship in your life that troubles you. In what ways is this a problem with roles and expectations?
- What is your greatest strength in communicating with others? How does this skill help you?

- What are some ways that peer pressure, positive or negative, affects your life?
- Are you more likely to confront a conflict head-on or to avoid it? What problems has this approach resolved or caused?

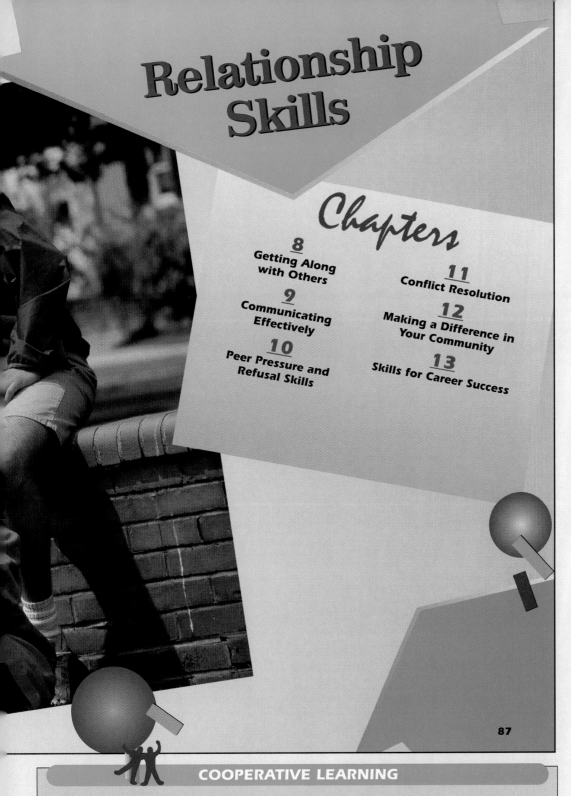

Relationship Skills

Chapters

8
Getting Along with Others

9
Communicating Effectively

10
Peer Pressure and Refusal Skills

11
Conflict Resolution

12
Making a Difference in Your Community

13
Skills for Career Success

87

COOPERATIVE LEARNING

Community Project. Have students plan and carry out a class project that will benefit the community. Students should submit ideas, select one of general interest, and then identify such responsibilities as publicity and cleanup. Set up a system in which groups have assigned tasks. Each group should have one representative who meets regularly with other representatives to monitor progress and resolve any problems. Emphasize the use of strong communication and conflict-resolutions skills as students work together.

FHA Activities

The following activities can be used with your FHA group or as public relations strategies:

■ **Skills How-To.** Have groups create series of panels, like comic strips, that depict relationship problems teens often face and show how teens can deal with them effectively, using skills from this unit. The strip might be published in the school newspaper or posted on a school bulletin board.

■ **Dear FHA.** Set up a school-wide advice column about relationships. Inform students that their letters will remain anonymous. Assign the letters to groups within the class who respond in the school newspaper or on a bulletin board. Have groups remove any identifying details from the letters, and retype them in a standard format.

■ **Peer Mediators.** Arrange for some or all students to receive training in conflict resolution mediation. Then have the trained students serve as peer mediators, helping other students settle their disputes.

Unit Closure

REVIEW

■ **Ready? Action!** Ask groups to act out a segment from a book, a short story, or a movie that demonstrates one or more of the skills described in this unit. One group member tells the class what has happened in the story so far. After the skit, the class should identify each relationship skill that was shown in the skit.

EVALUATION

■ **Unit Test.** Have students complete the unit test in the Teacher's Classroom Resources.

■ **Testmaker Software.** You may wish to design a unit test using the *Testmaker Software*.

Chapter Overview

Chapter 8 stresses that good relationships require caring management. It explores roles and expectations and offers ideas for strengthening relationships. Students are urged to respect differences, reject stereotypes and prejudices, and avoid negative relationships.

Motivator

■ **Adjective Alert.** Ask students for adjectives that describe relationships. Encourage both positive and negative words. Explain that the chapter will help students understand why relationships can be described in so many different ways.

Objectives

Discuss the chapter objectives on this page. Remind students that the objectives focus on important chapter concepts.

Vocabulary

Explain that *relationship* is a form of the root *relate*, meaning to have some connection to. Another "related" word is *relative*, a person connected by blood. Many people think of family when they think of relationships, but the word includes other connections as well.

Chapter 8 Getting Along with Others

Terms to Learn

- compromise
- cooperation
- discrimination
- expectations
- prejudice
- relationships
- roles
- stereotype
- teamwork
- tolerance

Objectives

This chapter will help you to:

- Distinguish **among different kinds of relationships.**
- List **the rewards of good relationships.**
- Describe **how roles and expectations affect relationships.**
- Explain **how to build strong relationships.**
- Determine **when it is best to avoid certain relationships.**
- Analyze **teen relationships with people in authority.**

CHAPTER RESOURCES

Student Workbook
Study Guide, pp. 29-30
Activity, *Relationship Builders*, p. 31

Teacher's Classroom Resources
Lesson Plan, p. 12
Cooperative Learning, *Give-and Take*, pp. 15-16

Decision Making, *Getting Along with Others*, p. 8
Extension #12, *Building Positive Relationships*, p. 18
Life Skills, *From Generation to Generation*, pp. 16-17
Transparency 7, *Wiping Out Stereotypes and Prejudice*

Chapter 8 Test, pp. 21-22
Performance Assessment, *Getting Along with Others*, p. 27
Reteaching, *Recipe for a Good Relationship*, p. 14

See Also:
ABCNews InterActive™ Videodiscs

By the time this day is over, how many people do you think will make contact with you? Probably quite a few. How well those encounters go is largely up to you.

For Dylan, every day brings him frustration with the people around him. He argues with his stepfather. He avoids certain people in school because they annoy him. "The teachers are always on my case," he tells his friends. Even the manager at the bowling alley where he works is hard to get along with in Dylan's eyes. What is going on here? Dylan obviously has problems with his relationships.

Getting along with others isn't always easy. Anyone will tell you that. There are things you can do, however, to make most relationships work well. The better at those skills you become, the stronger and more satisfying your relationships will be.

Kinds of Relationships

Throughout your life you will have many different kinds of relationships. **Relationships** are *the connections you have with other people.* Relationships vary in three basic ways—in their degree of closeness, their purpose, and their form.

Some relationships are casual and some are close, with many variations in between. People tend to need both types in their lives. Strong, close relationships are fulfilling. Most people need at least a few relationships of this type. Whether the relationship is with a sibling or a parent, a friend or a colleague, an advisor or a member of the clergy, people need someone they are close to and can confide in.

Relationships often exist for a specific purpose. Those with teachers, for example, are based on a need to learn. Relationships with classmates might develop during group work. You can probably think of many other reasons why you forge links with other people.

Relationships come in many forms. They may include those you have with children, other teens, adults, and older people. You may have relationships with people of all backgrounds as well. Including a variety of people in your life brings richness and many different rewards.

Rewards of Relationships

What do you gain from the relationships in your life? There is much:

- **Love, affection, and a sense of belonging.** Family, friends, teachers, and counselors can give acceptance and approval.
- **Companionship.** One reason that relationships are so important is that they allow you to share your experiences, ideas, and feelings with others.

Relationships come in different forms. How does the relationship you have with a supervisor on the job differ from other relationships?

Topics on pp. 90-91:
- **Influences on Relationships**
- **Roles and Expectations**
- **Stereotypes**

Checking Comprehension

✓ What are some roles that you have? *Answers will vary but may include son, daughter, sibling, student, and friend.*

✓ Explain the relationship between roles and expectations. *Expectations are based on role and change as role does.*

✓ What should you do if your expectations for a relationship differ from those of others involved? *Talk about differences; try to understand other viewpoints.*

FAMILY AND COMMUNITY
OUTREACH

Have students list five expectations that 8- to 10-year-olds typically have for parents, and five that parents have for the children. Next have students make similar lists of expectations between parents and teens. As students share their lists, ask: How do expectations change on both sides? How do these reflect changes in the relationship itself? Stress that communication about expectations is especially important during the rapid changes of the teen years.

- **Formation of self-concept.** When other people treat you with respect and show appreciation for your efforts, you see yourself in a positive light. Your self-concept, in turn, affects your relationships with others. When you feel good about yourself, you are more likely to be outgoing and friendly—to be the kind of person others like to be around.
- **Broadened horizons.** People can introduce you to new foods, music, celebrations, games, and other activities.
- **Support.** When you have a problem or you simply need to unwind, family and friends can help. The reassurance that someone will be there for you gives a valuable sense of security. It also provides a strong argument for making sure that you keep your relationships strong.

What Are the Influences?

Think of the different ways that you address the people in your life. You may call a close friend by a nickname. You refer to a teacher as "Mr." or "Ms." You might address a police officer as "sir" or "ma'am." This difference illustrates the fact that relationships are not all of the same kind. Certain factors that influence all relationships help determine how you respond in each one.

Roles and Expectations

Your role in a relationship is one factor that influences your behavior. **Roles** are *the parts you play when you interact with others*. Everyone has many different roles. For example, your roles probably include son or daughter, friend, student, and neighbor. You may also have such roles as team member, lab partner, and babysitter. In time, you will probably have the roles of employee and coworker and possibly parent, aunt, or uncle.

Each role carries with it certain **expectations**. These are *the wants and needs that each person believes the relationship will fulfill*. Expectations also affect how a person acts in a given role. For example, members of a sports team are expected to practice, follow

A clear understanding of roles and expectations helps teens and adults get along.

the coach's directions, and work together. Team players, in turn, expect the coach to provide leadership and treat players fairly.

Conflicting Forces

Sixteen-year-old Elaine was confused. As she explained it, "My grandmother has raised me since I was five years old. Now that I have a part-time job, I feel like I can help with expenses, but my grandmother was upset when I suggested it. I thought she would appreciate my offer."

Elaine's grandmother was upset for reasons that were not clear to Elaine. She believed that it was *her* responsibility to provide the basics for Elaine, not Elaine's. What she did want was the same help around the apartment that Elaine used to provide.

MORE ABOUT Diversity and Friendship

Help students see that diversity is already part of their lives. Have them think of a good friend and list three ways they differ physically, intellectually, emotionally, and culturally. Then have each student think of a specific teen he or she doesn't know well and list three qualities they share. Afterward discuss any insights students gained from making these lists.

As with Elaine and her grandmother, problems can arise when roles and expectations conflict. With her new job, Elaine wanted to take on an adult role in the family. This new role, however, caused her to let go of responsibilities at home. Elaine's grandmother wasn't prepared for a change in Elaine's role. She expected Elaine to remain in the child role a little longer and to continue to help at home.

Not until Elaine and her grandmother began to talk about their differing points of view were they able to understand each other and work toward a solution.

Stereotypes

Have you ever lost the opportunity to do something you wanted to do only because someone else felt you were "too young" or "just not right for the job"? If so, you know part of the pain caused by stereotypes.

From School to Work

Working with Diversity

What You Learn Today . . .

Students who attend schools with a diverse student body benefit by getting to know people who are different from themselves. These relationships can expose teens to new points of view.

Whether it's from working together in class, on a team, or in a school club, teens from different backgrounds often form friendships. Learning about the customs of another culture is a fringe benefit of such friendships. Whatever form these relationships take, getting to know people who are different has another, very important, benefit. It prepares teens for participating in the diverse work force.

. . . You Can Use Tomorrow

More and more, the workplace reflects the diversity of society. Where white males once held most jobs, now over half of all women work. More workers are now African Americans, Hispanics, Asian Americans, and Native Americans as well. More disabled people, too, are working now than ever before.

Businesses find that a diverse workforce can generate more innovative solutions to problems. Also, customers are more willing to support companies that employ workers who share their background. Finally, a diverse work force can help a business gain insight into ways to compete in the global economy, and international competition is of increasing importance for businesses. Asian American workers, for instance, may be able to help their employer sell in Asia.

Practicing Your Skills

Try these ideas to become more comfortable with diversity:

- Start a conversation with someone who has a different background from you or who has a disability. Try to find an interest you share to talk about.
- Join or visit a group where you would be in the minority.
- Become active with a group that works with people who have disabilities. Friendship can help you focus on their strengths.
- Learn about another culture by attending a cultural festival.
- Join the group that sponsors your school's foreign exchange student or students.

Assessing Your Skills

1. Some businesses offer employees workshops and seminars in which they receive training on how to get along with coworkers of diverse backgrounds. How might such training be useful?
2. Joining a group in which you are in the minority can help you understand others in two ways. What are they?

Activities

■ **On the Other Hand.** Discuss the possible effects of holding positive stereotypes. During the discussion, make a point of being unduly complimentary toward only one or two students. As students become aware of your tactics (prompt them if needed), ask: How do you feel when you or others receive praise without earning it? How is a positive stereotype simply the "flip side" of a negative one? (*Relationship*)

ENRICHMENT

■ **Play a Part.** Invite pairs to act out a conversation between Elaine and her grandmother. Dialogues should indicate how the misunderstanding developed, identify their conflicting expectations, and suggest a resolution. Ask class members to comment on the pairs' treatment of the situation.

From School to Work

Have students read "Working with Diversity." Ask them to identify specific opportunities to try these ideas in their community.

Answers to Assessing . . .

1. Answers will vary. Generally, they aid understanding and cooperation and provide for personal and professional success.
2. Answers may include: exposes you to other points of view; helps you know how it feels to be in minority.

Topics on pp. 92-93:
- **How Stereotypes Affect Relationships**
- **Building Strong Relationships**
- **Giving and Receiving**
- **Being a Team Player**

Checking Comprehension

✓ What can result from acting on stereotypes? *You might overestimate or underestimate someone, miss out on valuable relationship.*

✓ Why are both giving and receiving important in relationships? *People who feel they are being used by a friend will find others.*

✓ Why is honesty important in relationships? *It allows people to trust each other.*

✓ What are some advantages of being a team player? *You can work easily with others, reach common goals, benefit from their skills and knowledge.*

CROSS-CURRICULAR ACTIVITY
Science

Have students, alone or in groups, report on examples of giving and receiving in the natural world. This might range from the give and take of geologic forces that prevent earthquakes, to photosynthesis, in which plants take in carbon dioxide and give off oxygen. Students might present their findings orally, in writing, or with models.

A **stereotype** is *a set of traits that every person in a particular group is assumed to have.* Stereotypes may be based on gender, age, race, religion, or national origin. They usually result from a lack of contact with, or understanding of, the group of people being stereotyped. Saying that old people are forgetful or that teens are irresponsible is using stereotypes.

Stereotypes have harmful effects on relationships. They can hurt the person who is the object of the stereotype because he or she is not accepted as an individual. That person may also suffer by being denied opportunities.

Stereotypes also hurt the people who accept them. They lose the chance to develop relationships with an entire group of people. Since personal contact is the best way of overcoming stereotypical thinking, these people literally never know what they are missing.

Avoiding stereotypical thinking can, on the other hand, expand your horizons. It allows you to get to know a variety of interesting people and develop rich and rewarding relationships. People who are different can teach you new things, new points of view, and new ways of looking at situations.

Figure 8.1
QUALITIES OF STRONG RELATIONSHIPS
Good relationships are built on a variety of interlinked qualities.

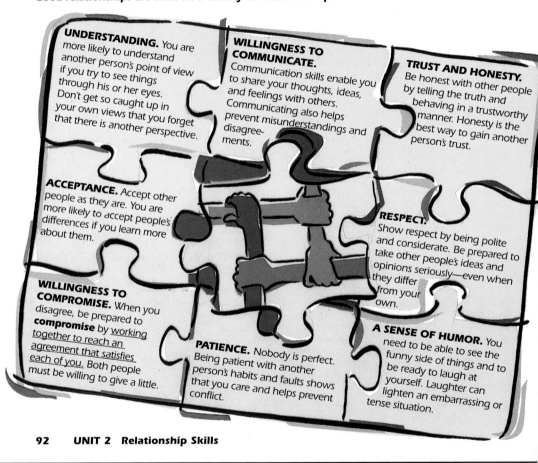

UNDERSTANDING. You are more likely to understand another person's point of view if you try to see things through his or her eyes. Don't get so caught up in your own views that you forget that there is another perspective.

WILLINGNESS TO COMMUNICATE. Communication skills enable you to share your thoughts, ideas, and feelings with others. Communicating also helps prevent misunderstandings and disagreements.

TRUST AND HONESTY. Be honest with other people by telling the truth and behaving in a trustworthy manner. Honesty is the best way to gain another person's trust.

ACCEPTANCE. Accept other people as they are. You are more likely to accept people's differences if you learn more about them.

RESPECT. Show respect by being polite and considerate. Be prepared to take other people's ideas and opinions seriously—even when they differ from your own.

WILLINGNESS TO COMPROMISE. When you disagree, be prepared to **compromise** by working together to reach an agreement that satisfies each of you. Both people must be willing to give a little.

PATIENCE. Nobody is perfect. Being patient with another person's habits and faults shows that you care and helps prevent conflict.

A SENSE OF HUMOR. You need to be able to see the funny side of things and to be ready to laugh at yourself. Laughter can lighten an embarrassing or tense situation.

MORE ABOUT Honesty in Relationships

The discomfort many people feel when they lie causes physical changes in their bodies—increases in blood pressure, heart and breathing rates, and electrochemical impulses to the skin. The lie detector, invented by William Moulton Marston, measures these changes in an attempt to indicate when a person is lying. Other changes may include an unsteady voice and an unwillingness to make eye contact.

What do you think is the most important guideline for working effectively in teams?

Isaac showed that he understood a basic principle of strong relationships: both sides give as well as receive. When one person does all the giving and the other all the taking, the relationship is unlikely to last. This principle applies to more than just friendships. For example, by asking a busy parent how work went and listening to the response, a teen gives support in return for those times that the parent helped the teen.

In strong relationships, giving and getting are united. Giving boosts self-esteem. You feel worthy as a person when you have something to offer. When you receive, you give thanks and show appreciation. The cycle of giving and receiving is ongoing.

One way to help keep relationships strong is to remember to give a word of thanks from time to time to someone who helps you. People can feel hurt or feel that their help is being taken for granted if it isn't acknowledged. For example, Amrit was growing frustrated because his friend Curtis kept calling for help with his homework. When Curtis called one night, Amrit even thought about telling his brother to say that he wasn't home. He was glad he didn't. Curtis had called to say how well he had done on his test and to thank Amrit for his help. Saying those two simple words—"Thank you"—can carry a relationship over rough times.

Becoming a Team Player

Good team players are in demand. Any group is a team, whether it is playing soccer

Building Relationships

Figure 8.1 presents the many qualities of strong relationships. Just as the puzzle needs all of the pieces to make it whole, you need to show all these qualities in order to build a strong and lasting relationship. You can demonstrate those qualities in various ways.

Giving and Receiving

Ben liked to tell this story about his good friend Isaac: "It was Saturday morning after a big storm. Tree branches were all over the yard, which meant I had a full morning of work ahead of me. Then Isaac showed up. He said that since I had offered to drive us to the football game that afternoon, he wanted to save me the trouble of picking him up. He was three hours early, however, and he 'just happened' to have a rake and heavy work gloves with him."

Focus on Teamwork Skills

Explain that in many businesses employees work in teams, sometimes called quality circles. Instead of having a supervisor closely oversee them, team members work together to plan their work, assign responsibilities, solve problems, and make sure their product meets high standards. Perhaps teachers at your school work in teams. Invite students who have worked on teams at their jobs or team teachers to describe their experiences.

Activities

■ **As in a Mirror.** Ask students to write a paragraph describing a time when an interaction with someone else taught them something about themselves. *(Relationship)*

■ **Giving and Getting.** Divide the class into three groups for panel discussions. Assign each group one of the following topics: 1. It truly is better to give than to receive; 2. It is not emotionally healthy to always give and expect nothing in return; 3. Even people who always seem to give gain something in return. Give students several minutes to write questions or points that will generate discussion within their group. *(Critical Thinking)*

CROSS-CURRICULAR ACTIVITY
Social Studies

Ask students to write reports or draw diagrams that explain how various institutions— family, school, business, or government, for example—are like teams. Students should identify team "players," their roles, and responsibilities; describe their goals; and tell how they combine efforts to achieve goals.

USING VISUALS

Ask: Why is the illustration on page 92 presented as a puzzle? How are the qualities related to and part of each other? Have students suggest other pieces they would add to illustrate other qualities they want in their relationships.

Topics on pp. 94-96:

- **Tolerance versus Prejudice**
- **Walking Away from Relationships**
- **Understanding and Relating to Authority**

Checking Comprehension

✓ How can society be hurt by prejudice? *Society loses contributions of those whose opportunities are unfairly limited.*

✓ What are some conditions that favor the development of prejudice? *Being with prejudiced people; having no direct contact with the targets of prejudice; not questioning others' opinions.*

✓ Under what conditions should you walk away from a relationship? *If relationship is harmful to you or others; if person is negative influence.*

MULTICULTURAL *Perspectives*

Northern Ireland is an example of extreme societal intolerance and prejudice. Catholics were the overwhelming majority in Northern Ireland until the early 1600s, when Protestants settling there from England became predominant. Many Catholics still see the Protestants as invaders, and both groups have waged a bloody guerrilla war ever since. They recently have begun to move toward peace, but much hostility remains.

Ask students to research cases of social intolerance. Remind them to be fair and respectful in their investigation.

---

or planning a school celebration. For any team to succeed, each member has to show **teamwork**—*working together to reach a common goal.* Teamwork is valued in the world of work. Employers look for those who understand the need to work well with others and can do so.

Being part of the team requires **cooperation**—*the willingness and ability to work with others.* That cooperation can be shown in many different ways:

- Stick to the group's goals, and put your energy into achieving them. Don't try to outshine others.
- Listen to others in the group; they may have valuable ideas to contribute.
- Give everyone a role so that each is part of the team effort.
- Do your fair share. If you don't, someone else has to make up the difference. That leads to negative feelings toward you.
- Complete your job on time. Otherwise, the group's goal may not be reached.

Showing Tolerance

One key to getting along with others is tolerance. *Tolerance* means **accepting and respecting other people's customs and beliefs.** It helps you recognize that other people have the right to hold beliefs and values that are different from your own. It helps you see that your beliefs and values are not better than theirs, just different.

Tolerance is basic to getting along with all other people—family, friends, acquaintances, and strangers. It helps you listen to other points of view, see things through other people's eyes, and enjoy many different kinds of relationships.

As societies grow more diverse, tolerance becomes more important. It is needed to meet the challenge of coexisting peacefully and productively with many different kinds of people. People who lack tolerance may develop **prejudice**, *bias against an individual or group.* Feelings of prejudice, in turn, can lead to acts of **discrimination**, or *differences in treatment*

Whether cultural celebrations or simple conversations with those from other cultures, people build understanding through knowledge. It is this understanding that leads to tolerance.

REAL-LIFE APPLICATION

Read the following to students: *Chandra, 17, is upset with her father. Most of her friends are allowed to drive, but he won't even let her take the test for her learning permit.* Ask students why Chandra's father might be so protective. What might she do to convince him to let her learn to drive? What things might she do that will probably cause more problems between herself and her father?

Acting Responsibly

Do You Have a Sense of Humor?

Have you ever heard the saying, "Laughter is the best medicine"? Very often, that's true. The ability to find humor in a situation is a valuable quality. When people are tired or discouraged, laughter can restore their spirits. In a tense situation, a light-hearted attitude can be the best way to avoid an unnecessary confrontation.

Sometimes, though, humor is misplaced. Here are some tips for using humor wisely:

- Avoid making jokes on solemn occasions. When someone is seriously ill, for instance, telling a funny story may be inappropriate.
- Be careful not to make fun of someone's problems or weaknesses. Even if the person laughs, it may be quite hurtful.
- Avoid jokes that ridicule certain groups of people. You may unknowingly offend someone.
- Don't become known for making jokes on every occasion. Even at times during a joyful event, such as a wedding or other formal occasion, a respectful mood is advisable.
- Avoid persisting with humor if people are not enjoying it. Watch people's reactions.

A Sense of Humor in Action

As Shawn left school, his thoughts were on the hockey game that afternoon. When Jerome called out to him, he turned abruptly and slid on a patch of ice. The next thing he knew, he was on the ground.

"You're really something," Jerome laughed as he helped Shawn to his feet. "The best hockey player in school, and you can't walk on ice."

Shawn grinned. Then a look of concern crossed his face as he tried to walk. "My ankle hurts."

"Are you okay, Shawn?" asked Cicely, as she hurried over to check.

"I don't know—," Shawn began.

"He's fine," Jerome assured her. "Most people learn to walk and then take skating lessons. With Shawn, it's the other way around."

"Give it a rest, Jerome," Shawn muttered.

Jerome laughed again. "Maybe I should tell the editor of the school paper about your little 'trip'!"

"We get the idea," Cicely said, her voice rising.

Jerome was so absorbed in talking that he didn't see the evergreen branch, heavy with snow, hanging over the sidewalk. As he turned around, it struck him in the face and showered him with snow.

Jerome looked at his friends' smiling faces. "You know what they say," he said. "Eat green, leafy vegetables every day."

Your Analysis

1. Was Jerome's humor always appropriate? Explain.
2. How did Jerome's humor rescue the situation?
3. How do you determine when to use humor?

---

that are based on prejudice rather than on individual merit. Examples of discrimination include refusing to rent housing to someone because of skin color, or refusing to hire someone because of age. Discrimination on the basis of age, gender, ethnic background, and other factors is destructive to individuals and to society. It divides people rather than promoting positive relationships.

Like stereotypes, prejudice and discrimination grow out of ignorance. People who

have little exposure to other ways of life are more likely to see differences in a negative light. You can help combat prejudice by making an effort to increase your knowledge and understanding of all people.

Walking Away

Showing tolerance does not mean that you must—or should—associate with everyone. From time to time, you may decide that you

---

■ **Maybe Not.** Tell students of humorist Will Rogers' remark, "I never met a man I didn't like." Ask: Is it possible to find something likable in every person? Can you like someone without sharing values? If you hold directly opposing views? (*Relationship*)

■ **Powers That Be.** Have students list ideas they associate with *authority*. Write their responses on the board. Evaluate them as positive or negative images. Discuss problems teens commonly have with various types of authority. Ask students to suggest solutions to these problems. You might also explore the dilemma of what to do when an authority figure expects actions that go against positive values. (*Problem Solving*)

RETEACHING

■ **Elements of Inequity.** Have students give examples of teamwork, tolerance, prejudice, discrimination, and stereotypes. Ask them to explain how stereotypes lead to prejudice and then to discrimination.

Acting Responsibly

Have students read "Do You Have a Sense of Humor?" Invite them to share their experiences, successful or otherwise, of using humor to remedy a difficult situation.

Answers to Your Analysis

1. No; Shawn may have been injured.
2. He used it to poke fun at himself.
3. Answers may include: the seriousness of the situation; whether you are with friends; the mood of others involved.

MORE ABOUT Relationships

Ask students to research successful professional relationships, ranging from composers Rodgers and Hammerstein, to investigative reporters Woodward and Bernstein, to local leaders who have

united for community improvement. Have students report on what the partners accomplished. Ask them to try to learn what qualities made the partnership successful and, if it broke up, the reasons it ended.

Review

■ **Chapter Review.** Use the contents of the Chapter Review page to help students review concepts, think critically, and apply their knowledge.

■ **Study Guide.** Have students complete the Study Guide for Chapter 8 on p. 29 of the Student Workbook.

■ **On Second Thought.** Have students review the paragraphs they wrote before studying the chapter, then write a second paragraph describing whether—and how—their ideas about relationship skills have changed.

Evaluation

■ **Chapter Test.** Use the reproducible chapter test provided in the Teacher's Classroom Resources or create your own test using the *Testmaker Software.*

■ **Alternative Assessment.** Have students write or tape record an essay or poem about a teen who gets along with others. The work should describe ways the teen shows respect, demonstrates giving and receiving, and avoids stereotyped thinking.

■ **Ignorance and Prejudice.** On the board write: "Ignorance is the root of all prejudice." Ask students whether they think the information in this chapter supports or contradicts this statement. What is the relationship between ignorance and prejudice?

are better off without certain relationships. People who cause harm to you or others or who perform actions that are illegal should be avoided. Use your values as your guide in deciding what to do.

Even though it may be difficult to break away, that is the best approach. If possible, leave the lines of communication open. You can let other people know that, while you do not agree with their actions or ideas, you still value them as people.

Understanding Authority

As a teen, you are close to becoming an adult. You probably spend more time with adults than in the past. That interaction can be useful. Because of experience alone, adults have much to offer. They can give advice on everything from avoiding mistakes they have made to career success. In turn, teens give adults a youthful view of life. They keep adults in touch with their own past and the way the world is changing.

Sometimes, however, the adult-teen relationship is strained. Adults—whether parents, relatives, teachers, or public officials such as police officers—are in positions of authority. As teens move toward adulthood themselves, they want to increase their own control of their lives. They want to make decisions and act on their own beliefs. Striking a balance between asserting new skills and getting along with those in authority is necessary for teens in order to keep the peace. Staying out of trouble may be an issue as well.

If you have ever done babysitting for young children, you know that you became the authority figure. You enforced rules to keep the children safe and healthy. Your actions, regardless of how the children viewed them, were aimed at living up to the responsibilities of your role. That's the way it is with anyone in authority. Teens who realize this are better

able to get along with adults, who have a job to do. Like you, these people sometimes make mistakes in how they handle situations. Being in charge can be very difficult at times. Looking at the situation from both sides builds understanding as well as the ability to get along.

Aiming High

Troubled relationships provide the theme for many television programs and movies. This theme also runs through the lives of many real people. That doesn't have to be the case for you. The chapters in this unit will point you in the direction of stronger relationships. The rest is up to you. By observing, learning, and practicing, you can have many relationships that enrich your life.

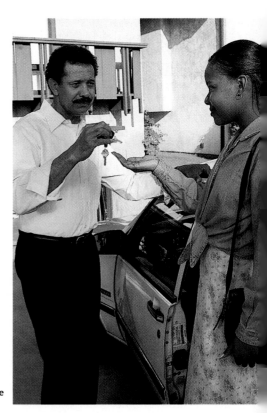

▌ Why are teens' relationships with adults sometimes difficult? What can both teens and adults do to make them easier?

▰▰▰▰ MORE ABOUT Authority

Respect for authority figures is necessary, but are there exceptions? Occasionally people in authority make inappropriate demands. That's when values and good judgment are needed. Think about the soldier ordered by an officer to kill everyone, including women, children, and the elderly, in an enemy village. Think about the gang leader who promotes robbery and fighting. Respect for authority should lead a person to morally acceptable actions. Sometimes the right path is not clearly evident, but it should be carefully sought.

Review

Reviewing the Facts

1. Explain the three ways that relationships differ.
2. What are three rewards of strong relationships?
3. Why is an understanding of roles and expectations important to a relationship?
4. Give at least four examples of the qualities of good relationships.
5. How does being a good team player today help you in the future?
6. When is it best to walk away from a relationship?

Thinking Critically

1. What kinds of actions and attitudes cause problems when people work in groups? Why?
2. How many close relationships do you think that a person needs? Why?

Applying Your Knowledge

1. **Writing a Scenario.** Write a scenario in which two friends demonstrate the necessity of mutual give and take in a relationship.
2. **Planning a Team Project.** Suppose you've been asked to organize either a bake sale or a car wash to raise money for a class gift to the school. What could you do to ensure that all team members participate in the project?
3. **Identifying Stereotypes.** Find examples of stereotyping in advertisements in magazines and on television. In each case, point out in writing what the stereotype is and describe how the message could be changed to eliminate it.

Making Connections

1. **History.** The roles of men and women have changed significantly in the last fifty years. In the past, men generally earned a living outside the home, and women usually stayed at home to raise children and tend the home. Now women and men share the workplace. What effects do you think these changes might have had on marriages? Summarize your ideas in writing.
2. **Language Arts.** Find a short story you have recently read in literature class and study the relationship between the main character and another character in the story. Identify the nature of the relationship and the needs and wants it satisfies for both characters. Do you think it is a balanced relationship? Explain your answer.

Building Your Portfolio

Preparing a Public-Service Announcement

Prepare a public-service announcement urging people to reject stereotyping, prejudice, and discrimination. Choose a particular group that is discriminated against. Then decide how you will raise people's awareness of the injustice against that group. For example, will your message be emotional or informative? Place copies of the completed assignment in your portfolio.

ANSWERS TO REVIEWING THE FACTS

1. In the degree of closeness, in purpose, and in form.
2. Any three: meeting basic needs, providing companionship, broadening horizons, developing self-concept, getting support.
3. A relationship is stronger when people agree on the roles that they are expected to play.
4. Any four of these or others that make sense: patience, respect, willingness to communicate, understanding, trust and honesty, willingness to compromise, acceptance, sense of humor.
5. Team players are welcomed at sports and social events and are more likely to succeed at work.
6. It's best to walk away when the other person does not share important values or wants you to do something that is dangerous to you or others.

ANSWERS TO THINKING CRITICALLY

1. Answers will vary. Possible responses: not doing one's fair share, trying to outperform others, not listening to other group members.
2. Answers will vary. Possible response: One relationship may be enough if it provides someone with whom you can share your deepest feelings.

Chapter 9

FOCUS

Chapter Overview

Chapter 9 focuses on communication, a vital skill in developing relationships. The chapter helps students become more aware of how messages can be sent nonverbally as well as verbally. Students are encouraged to express themselves more effectively through "I" messages and to strengthen their listening skills.

Motivator

■ **More than Words.** Refer students to the photograph on this page. Ask: What means are these teens using to communicate? Guide students to notice facial expressions and gestures.

Objectives

Discuss the chapter objectives on this page. Remind students that the objectives focus on important chapter concepts.

Vocabulary

Explain that the word *communication* is based on a Latin word that means to impart or to participate. Point out that communication not only imparts a message but also requires participation by both the sender and receiver.

Chapter 9

Communicating Effectively

Terms to Learn

- active listening
- body language
- communication
- eye contact
- feedback
- "I" messages
- nonverbal
- verbal

Objectives

This chapter will help you to:

- Define **verbal and nonverbal communication.**
- Distinguish **between "I" messages and "you" messages.**
- Explain **how tone, body language, and image send messages to others.**
- Use **active listening techniques.**
- Describe **how to give feedback.**

CHAPTER RESOURCES

Student Workbook

Study Guide, p. 32

Activity, *Communication Skills,*
  pp. 33-34

Teacher's Classroom Resources

Lesson Plan, p. 13

Cooperative Learning, *Listening Clinic,* pp. 17-18

Extension #13, *Body Language,* p. 19

Extension #14, *Confident Interactions* p. 20

Life Skills, *Diary of a Communicator,* p. 18

Personal Development, *Positive and Negative,* pp. 13-14

Transparency 8, *The Communication*

Equation

Chapter 9 Test, pp. 23-24

Performance Assessment, *Exhibiting Communication Skills,* p. 28

Reteaching, *Communication Terms,* p. 15

See Also:

ABCNews InterActive™ Videodiscs

Sara gripped the weights and prepared to lift. Watching from across the school weight room, her friend Natalie called, "Sara, you can't do that."

Sara's face reddened as she hoisted the weights with determination. She didn't like being told "you can't," especially when she knew she could. Suddenly she felt a sharp pain in the small of her back. Sara dropped the weights and grimaced.

Natalie came to her friend's side. "See. I told you you couldn't do that. You're bound to hurt yourself when you lift weights that way."

Poor communication causes much confusion for people. Do you see what happened with Sara and Natalie? Sara misinterpreted what Natalie was saying. Natalie wasn't trying to tell Sara that she wasn't capable. She only wanted to say that her technique wasn't correct. Unfortunately, the words she chose were inadequate, and Sara took them the wrong way.

The Process

Communication is *the sending and receiving of messages between people.* Often communication is **verbal.** That's when *words are used.* If you've ever seen a mime artist, however, you know that messages can also be conveyed in other ways. **Nonverbal** communication sends messages *without words.* People put together verbal and nonverbal messages in order to understand what is going on around them.

Communication is a two-way street—one person sends messages and another receives them. When all goes well, messages are sent and received correctly. All too often, however, messages aren't transmitted or interpreted as intended, and the kind of confusion Sara and Natalie experienced is the result. Making a serious effort to polish your communication skills can help you avoid such situations—as well as more troublesome ones.

The Messages You Send

Sending clear messages is a skill that can be learned and improved. Here are some ideas that will help you communicate more effectively.

Sending "I" Messages

Steven wanted to play a video game, but his older brother A.J. was using it. "You can have it when I'm finished," he said.

Steven was annoyed. It seemed to him that A.J. always had the first chance at everything. "You always have things your way," he accused. "That's all you care about!"

"That's not true," A.J. shot back. "You're just being selfish!"

Steven and A.J.'s disagreement could have been resolved. Instead, it only produced hurt feelings because they both sent the wrong kind of messages. Steven accused his brother of treating him unfairly; A.J. felt he had to de-

Why are "I" messages better than "you" messages in a disagreement?

CHAPTER 9 **Communicating Effectively** 99

Checking Comprehension

✓ What can result when communication becomes a one-way process? *Confusion and misunderstanding.*

✓ What are the three parts of an "I" message? *I feel. . . when you. . .because. . .*

Activities

■ **Try That Again.** Ask two pairs of volunteers to act out a new dialogue between Sara and Natalie in which both communicate better. One pair can wait outside the classroom while the other performs. Discuss strong points of both presentations.

RETEACHING

■ **It's How You Say It.** Have pairs write an angry message, then translate it into an "I" message. Ask partners to act out for the class how a listener might react in each case. Discuss and ask for reasons for the difference in reactions.

ENRICHMENT

■ **Look and Touch.** Divide the class into two groups. Encourage one group to research the Braille system, while the other learns more about sign language and finger spelling. For their presentations, have each group provide a brief history of the communication method and demonstrate its use for the class.

MORE ABOUT Messages

Mention three habits that discourage communication. Interrupting with trivial questions or remarks; giving unasked-for advice; and topping someone else's story—all discourage a speaker from telling more. Invite students to offer examples of these (and other) barriers to communication and to explain why they tend to inhibit conversation.

Topics on pp. 100-101:
* **Communicating through Tone of Voice**
* **Body Language**

Checking Comprehension

✓ How can the tone of your voice affect what you are communicating? *Can reveal whether you really mean what you say.*

✓ Are people aware of their own tone of voice and body language? *Not always. Can become more aware by concentrating on them and asking others.*

✓ How can nonverbal communication be misleading? *Can be misinterpreted.*

MULTICULTURAL *Perspectives*

Different cultures have different interpretations of body language. For example, most western societies regard eye contact as a signal of attentiveness and honesty. In Arab nations eye contact is so important that people avoid talking to someone who is wearing sunglasses. Yet in many nations, including Puerto Rico, Japan, and Korea, avoiding eye contact is a sign of respect. Ask: Even within a single culture, does eye contact always signal the same thing? Discuss the different messages that may be given by looking someone in the eye.

fend himself. The dispute turned personal and destructive.

Both would have been better off using "I" messages. With **"I" messages,** *you say how you feel and what you think, rather than criticizing someone else.* "I" messages have three parts:

* "I feel . . ." (here you name an emotion—anger, fear, disappointment)
* "when you . . ." (here you say what behavior bothers you)
* "because . . ." (here you explain why it bothers you)

"I" messages work because they avoid raising negative feelings, which interfere with communication. By avoiding attacks, "I" messages help keep a conversation reasonable. That way, both people stay focused on the underlying problem and together they solve it. Using "you" messages dooms a disagreement to attacks and accusations.

The way you carry your body, your facial expressions, and your gestures all send messages, just as your words do.

Using the Right Tone

People send messages with their tone of voice. For instance, Rashone's little brother excitedly says, "Look at the picture I drew!" Rashone answers, "That's terrific." His words contain a positive message, but *how* he says those words is the key to his message.

If Rashone's voice shows enthusiasm, his brother knows Rashone likes the drawing. If his tone of voice is insincere or sarcastic, however, his brother will know that Rashone doesn't really care. He will probably feel hurt.

Be aware of how your words sound. If you are unsure about the impression your tone of voice makes, ask your family and friends. Does your voice sound harsh or friendly? Impatient or polite? Knowing how you sound helps you ensure that you send the messages you intend to send.

Using Body Language

Has someone ever asked you "What's wrong?" before you even said a word? How did the person know that something was wrong? He or she probably sensed that something was different about you. You may have been walking more slowly than usual or looking at the ground. Maybe it was just that you didn't say hello. Somehow you had sent a message that you weren't even aware of.

100   UNIT 2   Relationship Skills

● ● ●   REAL-LIFE APPLICATION

Read this to students: *Ty decides to use an "I" message to tell Milos how he feels. He says, "I feel you were late on purpose, Milos. I think you owe me a big apology for making me wait so long." Ty is surprised* *when Milos glares at him instead of apologizing.* Ask: Does Ty actually use an "I" message? What is the difference between Ty's message to Milos and an authentic "I" message?

In Touch with TECHNOLOGY
Communication for Special Needs

The ability to communicate is easily taken for granted. Fortunately, technology has made great strides in helping people with disabilities communicate. Certain innovations give them greater personal, social, and financial independence. Here are just some of the devices available:

- **Telecommunications Device for the Deaf (TDD).** Hearing-impaired individuals are able to communicate by telephone with the TDD. Users type their messages on a keyboard and read the responses on a screen, both connected to a telephone. A blinking light signals an incoming call. To communicate with someone who does not have a TDD, a service is available that uses telephone operators to type in the other person's message and relay the responses.
- **Talking Glove.** The Talking Glove enhances communication for people who cannot speak. The person wears the glove while making letters and words in sign language. Sensors in the glove detect movement and translate the gestures into speech. From a small microphone worn around the neck, a computerized voice relays the message to the listener.
- **Mechanical "Hand."** This device enables people who cannot see or hear to communicate. The disabled person attaches the hand to his or her own hand while the other person types a message on a computer keyboard. As the words

appear on a screen, the hand translates them into sign language. The user "reads" the message by feeling the movements of the mechanical hand as it shapes words and letters.
- **Voice Synthesizer.** Used with special software, a voice synthesizer can convert written words on a computer screen into spoken words for visually impaired people. They can type their responses using a Braille keyboard.

Thinking Critically About Technology

1. How might these technologies affect other people's attitudes toward those with disabilities?
2. Some people believe computers are making society more impersonal. Do you think learning about these communication devices might change their minds?
3. The Americans with Disabilities Act (ADA) requires all public facilities to be accessible to those with disabilities. Should communication devices such as the ones described here be mandatory in public buildings? Gives reasons for your answer.

Body language refers to *a person's posture, facial expressions, gestures, and way of moving*. Body language affects not only how others see you, but also how they react to your verbal message.

Imagine two students giving a speech. Earl seems relaxed but energetic. He stands up straight with shoulders back. He smiles as he speaks. His gestures are natural yet forceful. Mary Ann stands with her shoulders slumped and her hands behind her back. She shuffles her feet and looks at the floor. What message

about themselves do Earl and Mary Ann send their audience? Whose verbal message receives more attention and respect?

An important element of body language is **eye contact**—*direct visual contact with another person's eyes*. Sandra, for example, looks directly at a new acquaintance. The message she sends is that she is interested, confident, and friendly. Be aware, though, that different cultures have different beliefs about eye contact. In some cultures, it is considered rude to look someone directly in the eye.

DID YOU KNOW?

People in different cultures differ in how much they rely on nonverbal communication. In high-context cultures, including Arabic, Chinese, and Latin American cultures, people gain much information from context—the nonverbal cues that clarify the speaker's words. In low-context cultures, such as the United States, Canada, Germany, and Scandinavia, people rely more on words—verbal communication—to share information. Ask students how this knowledge might be useful in relationships.

Activities

■ **Crystal Clear.** Ask groups to imagine a foolproof system of sending messages verbally and nonverbally. Have them write 6 to 8 characteristics of their system, such as "A (certain gesture) will always mean a (certain message)." If you like, have groups demonstrate part of their systems for the class. (*Creativity*)

■ **Sending Messages.** Have groups present pairs of skits to the class. Each group's skits will use the same words but different nonverbal communication to change the message conveyed. Encourage subtle differences, such as a speaker avoiding eye contact with listeners. Discuss how changes in nonverbal communication affected the verbal message. (*Communication*)

In Touch With TECHNOLOGY

Have students read "Communication for Special Needs." Ask them if they know of anyone who uses the devices described. Can they imagine being isolated in a dark, quiet world? What do devices like these mean to people in these circumstances?

Answers to Thinking ...

1. May become more comfortable with, accepting of, those with disabilities as they increase their ability to communicate.
2. Generally, these devices show how technology can increase human contact.
3. Answers will vary but should be supported.

Topics on pp. 102-104:
- **The Impact of Image**
- **Time and Place**
- **Active Listening**
- **Giving Feedback**

Checking Comprehension

✓ Why is choosing the right time and place important to communication? *Helps ensure message is received as intended.*

✓ Why should you listen with a purpose? *Helps you concentrate on what speaker is saying.*

✓ How can you offer feedback without interrupting the speaker? *Wait until speaker pauses.*

FAMILY AND COMMUNITY OUTREACH

Have students find out which of the services described in "In Touch with Technolgy" on page 101 are available in your community. Does your phone system offer TDDs? Do the police, courts, and hospital emergency rooms have interpreters for the deaf? Do television stations provide closed captioning? What materials are available in Braille or on audiotape? Provide students time to share their findings.

CROSS-REFERENCE

For more information on ways to deal with strong emotions, refer students to Chapter 2, especially "Strategies That Work" on page 39.

Managing Your Image

Controlling body language is one way to manage the image that you project to others. Attending to your appearance is another. How people act and what they say is more important than how they look, but clothes do send a message. When Keesha dresses for her job as a sales clerk in the department store, for example, she wears dress slacks and a matching blouse. When she is with her friends, she dresses more casually. She presents an image appropriate for each situation.

Good grooming plays an important role in image. Washing your face, brushing your hair, and wearing clean clothes contribute to a neat, healthy image. These actions communicate to others that you respect and care about yourself.

Choosing Time and Place

Knowing when and where to communicate can make communication positive as well. Cindy wanted to apologize to Aileen for having to miss her party at the last minute. She decided to call Aileen later that night. She didn't want to wait too long, in case her friend was upset.

Paul, on the other hand, made a poor choice. He wanted to talk to Javier about a problem he had with their coach. Instead of waiting until they were alone, he started talking in the locker room. Another player overheard and told the coach that Paul was criticizing him. Paul got reprimanded—all because he didn't wait for an appropriate time and place.

In choosing when and where to talk to someone, keep these tips in mind:

- Be sure that the person you're talking to is willing and able to listen. Asking your mother something serious when she just arrives home from work isn't a good idea.

102   UNIT 2   Relationship Skills

- Avoid times when emotions will conflict with the message. When you're angry, calm down before talking.
- Make sure the other person isn't distracted. Choose a time and place when the receiver can concentrate on the message.

The Messages Received

Equally important to sending clear messages is accurately interpreting the ones you receive. Other people want you to pay attention to and understand what they have to say. In that way, they are no different from you.

Active Listening

"I heard you; I heard you," Angelo grumbled to his friend, Tanya.

"Yes, I know you heard me talking, but did you really *listen* to me?" Tanya asked in exasperation.

Hearing is just a physical action—receiving sound waves. **Active listening,** on the other

Make an effort to be a good listener. Active listening can strengthen relationships and help you learn more about others.

Cultural differences in interpreting silence have proven fatal. During a time of military turmoil, Egyptian planes requested permission to land at a Greek airport. The Greek traffic controllers responded with silence, which they meant to indicate refusal. To the Egyptian pilots, however, silence meant consent. They landed and were fired on by the Greeks.

hand, is *concentrating on what is said so that you understand and remember the message.* When you listen actively, you give your attention to the person speaking—not thinking about how you are going to respond.

Why is it important to become an active listener? Obviously, the skill helps when you're getting directions at school or work, or working out your schedule with family members. Being an active listener can also enrich your life:

- Active listening helps relationships grow. It promotes real understanding and shows caring when people listen closely to others.
- Active listening helps you grow as a person. People who make an effort to listen to others are less absorbed with themselves. They gain maturity as they learn to appreciate differences in other people.
- Active listening helps you know more about the world. You can learn about people, current events, sports, and many other topics when you pay attention to what other people have to share.
- Active listening boosts self-esteem in others. When you show interest in the speaker's message, you show interest in the speaker. People feel they have something worthwhile to offer.

Now that you know *why* you should become an active listener, you need to know *how.* **Figure 9.1** describes some techniques for active listening.

Feedback

Part of any two-way communication is giving **feedback.** Feedback occurs when *a listener lets a speaker know that he or she is trying to understand the message being delivered.* You can give feedback in many different ways:

- Interject a comment when the speaker pauses.

Figure 9.1
HOW TO LISTEN BETTER

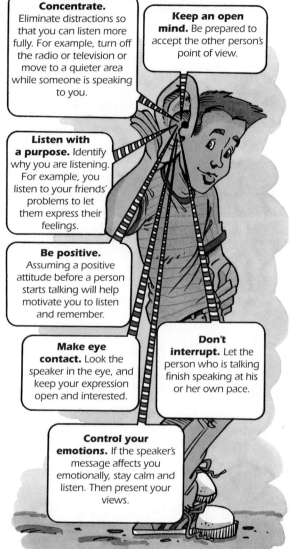

Concentrate. Eliminate distractions so that you can listen more fully. For example, turn off the radio or television or move to a quieter area while someone is speaking to you.

Keep an open mind. Be prepared to accept the other person's point of view.

Listen with a purpose. Identify why you are listening. For example, you listen to your friends' problems to let them express their feelings.

Be positive. Assuming a positive attitude before a person starts talking will help motivate you to listen and remember.

Make eye contact. Look the speaker in the eye, and keep your expression open and interested.

Don't interrupt. Let the person who is talking finish speaking at his or her own pace.

Control your emotions. If the speaker's message affects you emotionally, stay calm and listen. Then present your views.

- Summarize what the other person is saying so it's clear that you got the message. Ask if you interpreted the words right.

CHAPTER 9   Communicating Effectively   103

■ **Chapter Review.** Use the contents of the Chapter Review page to help students review concepts, think critically, and apply their knowledge.

■ **Study Guide.** Have students complete the Study Guide for Chapter 9 on p. 32 of the Student Workbook.

■ **Spread the Word.** Ask students to write a letter to a friend or family member or a journal entry to themselves explaining in a personal way why effective communication is important.

Evaluation

■ **Chapter Test.** Use the reproducible chapter test provided in the Teacher's Classroom Resources or create your own test using the *Testmaker Software.*

■ **Alternative Assessment.** Ask pairs to present or videotape demonstrations that incorporate most of what they have learned in this chapter, including "I" messages, positive nonverbal communication, and active listening.

■ **Personal Disabilities.** Suggest that while limited sight and hearing can make communication a challenge, anyone may be "communication disabled" if they handicap their communication with poor habits such as interrupting or giving unwanted advice. Explore ways that teens can become more aware of, and overcome, these self-imposed limitations.

Acting Responsibly

Do You Show Respect?

Respect is critical to any relationship. Respect is the key to keeping friendships, to political alliances, and to international cooperation. Through respect you show that someone matters to you. Your treatment of others reflects your level of respect for them.

Have you ever been treated with a lack of respect by someone? If so, you know that it's hard to believe the person really cares about you. Someone who shows respect for you, on the other hand, is someone you feel you can count on.

There are many ways to show respect. You can remember details that the person tells you. You can also take the person at his or her word. Listening when someone speaks is another way.

Respect in Action

Five drama club members were meeting to discuss the poster to advertise the school musical. While Mark was explaining his idea, Fran whispered to Bill, "Here we go again. Mark's got one of his so-called brainstorms." As soon as he finished, the two of them started to find fault with his plan.

"That will never work. Nobody will notice it," said Fran.

"It isn't clear and direct enough—too busy." Bill added.

Mark started to protest, but Fran cut him off. "We need something catchier, Mark, something more creative." Then she and Bill began discussing a poster they had seen that they really liked. Mark sank down in his chair.

Allison, who was chairing the committee, called the meeting back to order. "Wait a minute," she said. "Mark's idea may work. You're right, Bill, that there may be too much going on. What can we do to make it more focused?" She looked over at Barry, who was busily sketching. "What have you got, Barry?"

"Well, I had the same thought. If we simplify it and use brighter colors, it could be really effective." He showed his sketch.

Fran and Bill agreed that Barry's version would probably grab people's attention. Allison thought it was great, and said so. She looked inquiringly at Mark, who smiled and said, "Barry, you're a genius."

Your Analysis

1. How did Fran and Bill show a lack of respect for Mark?
2. How did Allison show respect for Mark?
3. What are some examples of respect that you have observed among people you know?
4. What can you do to improve the way you show respect?

• Express your interest by asking questions that lead to more communication.
• When the other person is upset and needs to unload negative feelings, show empathy. Use such phrases as "That's so unfair" or "You must have been hurt." Don't feel you need to solve the problem. Having someone listen may be all that the speaker needs.

Giving summaries and asking questions are particularly effective kinds of feedback. If you're being given directions, for example, wait until the person has finished and then restate them in your own words. By using these techniques, both you and the other person can confirm that you understand the message as it was intended.

The Impact

Relationships seldom thrive without good communication. This is true on a personal level and in society in general. In fact, diplomats from different countries must have excellent communication skills to improve world relations.

When communication produces understanding, people get along better—at home, with friends, and in the community. Understanding fosters good feelings, promoting even better communication.

Acting Responsibly

Have students read "Do You Show Respect?" Ask them whether most disrespectful behavior is accidental or intentional. Give reasons.

Answers to Your Analysis

1. They didn't fully listen to him or consider his idea.

2. She diplomatically cut off Bill and Fran's criticism and tried to work with Mark's idea.

3. Answers will vary.

4. Answers will vary.

Chapter 9

Reviewing the Facts

1. What is nonverbal communication? Give an example.
2. Give two examples of body language and the message each sends.
3. Give three suggestions for sending effective messages.
4. Explain the difference between hearing and listening.
5. Name three benefits of becoming a good listener.
6. Describe two ways to improve your listening skills.

Thinking Critically

1. Why is written communication sometimes less effective than talking to the person?
2. Without interrupting, how can you let a friend know that you are listening when she or he is telling you about a problem over the phone?

Applying Your Knowledge

1. **Creating "I" Messages.** Turn the following "you" messages into "I" messages: (a) "You never pick up your things"; (b) "You're always late"; (c) "You don't give me a chance to talk"; (d) "You won't let me decide for myself."
2. **Creating a Skit on Manners.** Judith Martin writes the popular newspaper column "Miss Manners." Over the years, she has discussed the need for good manners when dealing not only with family and friends but also with coworkers and even political adversaries. In a small group, write a skit in which good manners help people communicate in an adversarial situation. If you like, check some of her columns for ideas.

Making Connections

1. **Civics.** Read a famous, short speech, such as Martin Luther King, Jr.'s "I Have a Dream" or Abraham Lincoln's "Gettysburg Address." In small groups, discuss the purpose of the speech and how specific words and phrases helped get the message across. Each group should then report its findings to the class.
2. **Music.** As a class, discuss how music communicates. What elements make up the language of music? How does the body language of dance enrich the message?
3. **Business.** Experts in business writing advise workers to keep their written communications short. Letters and memos, they say, should be no longer than one page. Write a brief essay explaining why shorter communications may be preferable to longer ones.

Building Your Portfolio

Constructing a Scene
Working with a group, write a scene in which two teens have trouble communicating when: choosing a place to go; talking about a school problem; complaining about a sibling; etc. The problem may involve a faulty message or weak listening skills. Rewrite the scene to show positive communication. Add the scenes and a discussion summary to your portfolio.

Chapter 10

FOCUS

Chapter Overview

Chapter 10 explores internal and external influences on decisions. It describes positive and negative peer pressure, then encourages students to deal with negative pressure by focusing on their values. It gives advice on being assertive and strengthening refusal skills.

Motivator

■ **What Does It Take?** Refer students to the photo on this page. Ask them what might be going on in the photo. Explore the qualities the young man on the left needs to say no to pressure.

Objectives

Discuss the chapter objectives on this page. Remind students that the objectives focus on important chapter concepts.

Vocabulary

Remind students that not only teens have peers. A peer is someone of equal standing, regardless of age. Grandparents have peers, as do preschoolers. People on trial are judged by a jury of their peers—ideally, people of the same status. Peer pressure is positive or negative influence from peers.

Chapter 10 Peer Pressure and Refusal Skills

Terms to Learn

- aggressive
- assertive
- passive
- peer pressure
- refusal skills

Objectives

This chapter will help you to:

- Describe the pressures that influence the decisions you make.
- Explain why peer pressure is such a powerful influence.
- Evaluate a situation involving negative peer pressure.
- Differentiate between passive, assertive, and aggressive.
- Combine assertiveness and refusal skills to resist negative peer pressure.

106   UNIT 2   Relationship Skills

CHAPTER RESOURCES

Student Workbook
Study Guide, pp. 35-36
Activity, *Developing Refusal Skills,* pp. 37-38

Teacher's Classroom Resources
Lesson Plan, p. 14
Decision Making, *Negative Peer Pressure,* p. 9

Extension #15, *Alcohol and Other Drugs,* p. 21
Extension #16, *Assertive Behavior,* p. 22
Life Skills, *Assert Yourself!* pp. 19-20
Personal Development, *Standing Up to Peer Pressure,* pp. 15-16
Transparency 9, *Refusal Skills*

Chapter 10 Test, pp. 25-26
Performance Assessment, *Saying No,* p. 29
Reteaching, *Pressure Profile,* p. 16

See Also:
ABCNews InterActive™ Videodiscs

Rick was getting his lunch out of his locker when his friends Charlie and Tomás came by. Charlie said, "We're skipping classes this afternoon and going to the lake. Come with us."

Rick enjoyed spending time with his friends, and he liked going to the lake. He felt uncomfortable about cutting classes, however. He knew that his parents would be disappointed in him. They trusted him to go to class. Besides, Rick really liked his art class, and he'd miss it if he skipped that day.

Rick made his decision. When he told his friends that he wasn't going with them, Tomás said, "You're a fool. Cutting class isn't a big deal." Tomás and Charlie walked off, leaving Rick to eat lunch alone.

Rick didn't have much of an appetite after that. He kept thinking about his decision. On the one hand, he was glad that he hadn't left with his friends. Then again, maybe cutting a few classes wasn't such a big deal. Rick felt that he had done the right thing—so what was still troubling him?

Both internal and external pressures influence your decisions.

Difficult Decisions

Like Rick, you may have experienced doubts and confusion at times. Rick wanted to keep his friendship with Charlie and Tomás because he liked being with them. They had many good times together. On the other hand, was Rick obligated to do what they wanted him to? Was the friendship worth doing something that he knew was wrong? Rick weighed his decision carefully. He looked at the possible negative consequences in order to reach a good decision, but it wasn't easy.

Teens commonly experience this kind of conflict when facing decisions. So many influences exist that make it difficult to decide.

Influences on Decisions

Decisions are strongly influenced by a number of pressures. How you decide what to do depends on both internal and external pressures. Understanding these pressures and their effect on you can help you evaluate and manage them.

Internal Pressures

Internal pressures are those that come from within you. What you need, what you value, and what you want guide your decisions. Some decisions force you to choose between these different urges.

Ron, for example, always enjoyed playing chess. His older sister taught him the game when he was younger, and he played throughout elementary and junior high school. He thought about joining the chess team in high school because he wanted to try competitive chess.

CHAPTER 10   Peer Pressure and Refusal Skills   **107**

Topics on p. 107:

Topics on p. 107:
- **Conflict in Decision Making**
- **Influences and Pressures on Decisions**

Checking Comprehension

✓ What internal pressures did Rick feel? *Desire to be with friends, go to art class, please parents.*

✓ What are the sources of internal pressure? *Needs, values, wants.*

✓ What are some sources of external pressure? *Media, family, peers.*

Activities

■ **A Delicate Balance.** Have students draw a balance scale with a plate on each side. Above one plate, have them write the pressures Rick felt to go with his friends; above the other, the pressures he felt to stay. Have students share and compare their perceptions of the situation and discuss which side they think should weigh more heavily.

ENRICHMENT

■ **Carefree?** Emphasize the impact of external pressures. Have students describe their daily routine. As they mention actions, tell them to assume they face no external pressure in each situation. No alarm clock wakes them up; no one tells them whether to eat breakfast or go to school. Ask them what would happen without such pressures. What would or wouldn't get done? Would they have more or less stress?

REAL-LIFE APPLICATION

Read this to students: *Many of Angela's friends have part-time jobs and buy new CDs and clothing whenever they like. Angela envies them, yet she knows if she had a job, her grades would probably drop. Her college plans would be threatened.* Ask: What internal pressures does Angela face? What would they do in her situation? Help students see that long-term goals should take priority in decisions.

Topics on pp. 108-109:

- Peer Pressure
- Positive and Negative Pressure

Checking Comprehension

✓ What pressures influenced Ira's decision to give up football? Were these internal or external? *New interests, desire to help children; internal.*

✓ What questions can help you distinguish positive peer pressure from negative? *What are possible outcomes? What are physical and emotional consequences?*

✓ Why should you pay attention to gut feelings? *May tell you suggested activity conflicts with your values.*

FAMILY AND COMMUNITY OUTREACH

Have students interview at least one adult, ideally a family member, about the peer pressure he or she felt as a teen. Students might ask: How did you decide whether the pressure was positive or negative? How did you resist negative peer pressure? Do you think teens face more negative peer pressure today than they did when you were a teen? Have students share their findings in small groups. Ask each group to summarize its findings for the class.

CROSS-REFERENCE

For more information on making responsible decisions, refer students to Chapter 5.

108

Ron also valued doing well in school. He wanted to go to college, and he knew that chess would take away from his study time. On top of that, Ron wanted to have free time to spend with his friends. He also thought about trying out for the school baseball team. He was torn by various internal pressures and had to spend a great deal of time weighing the importance of each.

External Pressures

Everyone feels pressures from external sources. Most of the external pressures that you feel come from the media, your family, and your peers.

- **Media.** As you know, the messages contained in advertisements, television shows, movies, music, and other media influence decisions. If you think back, you may realize that you bought a certain brand of shoes or snack because of an appealing television commercial. Most people don't

even realize how strong the media's influence is on decisions.

- **Family.** Before making a decision, you probably ask yourself what your family will think about your choice. Luisa felt strong pressure from her father when she started dating Brad, a high school dropout. Luisa's father felt that Brad was a bad influence on her. He explained this to Luisa. Luisa valued education and wanted a good future for herself. She also wanted to have a good relationship with her father. His opinion was a large factor in her decision to break up with Brad.

- **Peers.** One of the strongest external pressures on a person is exerted by peers. **Peer pressure** is *influence from friends and people your age to act in a certain way.* Members of a peer group share common interests and form close bonds. Most people want to be liked by others. They want to have friends and thus strive to please them.

Peer pressure can be open and direct, like the pressure Rick felt to go to the lake. It can also be indirect, like the pressure you might feel to look for a summer job when you know that many other teens are already out looking for jobs.

Examining Peer Pressure

Why is pressure from your peers so strong? Why does it play such a major role in the decisions you make? Peer pressure is strong because most teens are sensitive to the opinions of peers—usually, more sensitive than adults. This is because they are still working on their own personal identity. They don't yet have a good sense of who they are, and they are still developing their values.

Many of the consumer decisions you make are strongly influenced by your peers and images of teens in the media. By combining knowledge with good judgment, your buying decisions will be more effective.

108   UNIT 2   Relationship Skills

DID YOU KNOW?

The Search Institute in Minneapolis recently studied 112 communities to see what made some healthier than others. Findings included: in the healthiest communities, 73 percent of teens attended school daily and avoided drugs, alcohol, and people who used those substances. In the least healthy communities, this was true of only 59 percent of teens. Ask students how communities might guide teens to choose positive behaviors.

Ira was a top player on the junior varsity football team in his first year of high school. When he became a sophomore, his attitude changed. He just wasn't enjoying the game anymore. Besides, he wanted to spend some time tutoring young children. He'd had a tutor when he was in fourth grade, which had made a big difference in his schoolwork. For Ira to be a tutor, however, he knew he would have to give up football.

When Ira told his teammates what he was thinking, they were upset. Gilbert refused to talk to him. Leroy threatened to end their friendship. Judd and Ken bargained and pleaded with him to stay on the team. All of this pressure made it very hard for Ira to decide as he did. Leaving the team wasn't easy, but he knew that it was right for him.

Positive or Negative?

Some peer pressure is positive. Jane heard about a cleanup project at a public park. She talked her friends Celeste and Linda into volunteering with her. The word spread to other students in their class. They wanted to be part of the group, so they volunteered too. In the end, 12 students worked in the park. With so many hands, they were able to finish raking leaves and picking up litter in just 2 hours. This is an example of positive peer pressure.

Negative peer pressure comes in conflict with your own wants, needs, or values. Some teens drink alcohol, smoke cigarettes, take illegal drugs, and become involved in sexual relationships because of negative peer pressure. They know that these activities are dangerous and can interfere with their own wants and needs. They know that giving in to this pressure may affect their health, their school performance, and their future. People who haven't learned how to resist negative peer pressure, however, often make the wrong decision and regret it later.

How can you tell if the peer pressure you feel is positive or negative? One way is to determine whether the activity is destructive. Ask yourself the following questions:

Making Decisions

Standing Up to Pressure

Leann and Cassie were walking home through the park. Leann suggested that they go past the softball diamonds, where their friends sometimes played ball on Saturday afternoons. Leann hoped Luke would be there. Luke was new in school. Leann liked him and wanted to get to know him better.

Leann and Cassie slowed as they neared the field where a game was just breaking up. Leann smiled when she saw that Luke was there.

Luke and Ray strolled toward them. "Hey, what do you say?" Ray asked casually as he looked at Cassie. Cassie smiled broadly, and Ray went on. "There's a party tonight—at Ben's place. Should be a good time. Luke and I are going."

Leann glanced at Luke and he smiled back. "Luke will be at the party," she thought to herself, "but I'm not supposed to go to Ben's." Leann remembered the trouble a party there last year had caused. She had not gone, but some classmates had been arrested for drinking alcohol.

"Will you two be there?" Ray asked.

Leann swallowed hard as Cassie elbowed her lightly in the ribs. "What do you think, Lee? It sounds like fun."

What Would You Do?

1. What options does Leann have?
2. What serious outcomes might Leann face if she goes to the party?
3. How can values help Leann make this decision?
4. What pressures might she face in making her decision?
5. What do you think Leann will do? What would you do?

DID YOU KNOW?

A study of 170,000 public school students by the Search Institute found that three-quarters of all parents of sixth-graders ask about homework; slightly less than half the parents of twelfth graders ask. Also, just over half the parents of sixth-graders help with school work; only 10 percent of twelfth graders' parents do. Discuss with students how these changes parallel the increasing importance of peers during this time.

Activity

■ **Peers Through the Years.** Divide the class into three groups (subdivide a larger class into clusters within groups). Assign one group each to list examples of ways that peer pressure might affect a person at age 8, at age 16, and at age 32. Write the ages on the board. As groups share their ideas with the class, add their suggestions under the appropriate age. Review the lists as a class. Ask students to see if they can find a pattern in the influence of peers as a person grows older. (*Relationships*)

Making Decisions

Have students read "Standing Up to Pressure." Ask them if they have ever been in a situation similar to Leann's.

Answers to What . . .

1. Answers may include: go to party; go elsewhere with other friends.
2. Could get in trouble with parents or law, lose self-respect.
3. They offer guidelines for deciding.
4. Answers may include: desire to see Luke, feel independent; concerns about alcohol, parents.
5. Encourage students to realize that choosing safe options that have more positive long-range effects shows a more mature approach than opting for the pleasure of the moment.

- **Using Self-Knowledge**
- **Assertiveness and Refusal Skills**
- **Sticking to Decisions**

Checking Comprehension

✓ How can knowing your own values help you resist negative peer pressure? *Lets you identify and avoid activities that conflict with values.*

✓ How can low self-esteem make people more vulnerable to negative peer pressure? *They may not respect own values; may accept others'.*

✓ Whom do assertive people respect? How do they show this respect? *Respect selves and others; shown by stating opinions confidently and not attacking others.*

STRATEGIES THAT WORK

Have students read "Responding to Come-Ons." Ask them if they have ever thought of the right thing to say when it was too late. Point out that practicing what to say helps you make the right response on the spot. Ask students to suggest responses to the come-ons listed under "Try." *Possible responses are: (a) "You don't know what can and can't hurt me." (b) "But I'll be really sick later."*

Answers to Think . . .

1. Friend can support your efforts to resist or try to wear them down.
2. Answers may include: in dangerous or illegal situation; when it involves someone you don't know well.

- **What are the possible outcomes of the activity?** Some activities have serious consequences. You can be arrested, for example, if you shoplift items or deface property.
- **What are the physical consequences?** Smoking cigarettes and using illegal drugs, such as marijuana and crack cocaine, can be very dangerous. The nicotine in cigarettes is a highly addictive drug, making smoking a difficult habit to give up. Many people have died from using crack.
- **What are the emotional consequences?** Most people feel guilty when they do something that they don't feel good about. Many also worry about being punished for their actions. Usually, these emotional consequences remain strong long after the action.

Another way to figure out whether you are feeling negative peer pressure is to compare your own values with what you are being asked to do. If you have to go against your values to participate in an activity, then the pressure is negative. In the end, it's often just a gut feeling: what you are being pressured to do

It pays to gain the knowledge and self-awareness you need to withstand negative pressures. Some people can resist peer pressure because they have a firm sense of who they are.

110   UNIT 2   Relationship Skills

feels wrong, and you really don't want to do it. The challenge is to be strong enough to trust that feeling.

Peer Pressure and Friendship

Negative peer pressure often disguises itself as friendship. Someone who calls herself your "friend" may demand that you help her cheat on a test or shoplift. She may require it as a test of your friendship, saying, "I can't do this without you. If you were my friend, you'd help me out." This is a difficult form of negative peer pressure. However, *real friends* never expect you to do anything that makes you feel uncomfortable.

Resisting Pressure

Refusing to do something that a peer—especially a friend—wants you to do is not easy. It is hard to say no to someone whose opinion and acceptance you value. In the end, however, you'll feel better about yourself and your friendship if you do what you know is right.

Some people are able to resist pressure. They have a strong sense of themselves and of their values. They know how—and when—to say no. They know how to be assertive. If you do not have these strengths now, you can develop them.

Self-Knowledge

The best way to deal with negative peer pressure is to have a firm sense of who you are. What matters to you? What do you want from life? When you know yourself, you'll find it easier to make decisions and stick to them, no matter how much pressure you feel. People who know themselves will generally have these qualities:

MORE ABOUT Assertiveness

Many people who have made a difference in the world first had to overcome external and internal pressures and follow their own values. Their stories are chronicled in such works as:

American Heroes: In and Out of School, Nat Hentoff (Delacorte Press, 1987); *Great*

Lives series, various authors (Scribners, various dates); and *The New York Times Great Lives of the Twentieth Century,* Gelb, Rosenthal, and Siegel, ed. (Times Books, 1988).

Responding to Come-Ons

When peers pressure you, they play on your emotions and weak spots. They may beg, bribe, threaten, tease, or flatter to get you to do something you're uncomfortable with. Trying to convince you that you'll be "cool" if you do it—and "uncool" if you don't—is another approach.

One way to resist negative peer pressure is to recognize the phrases that peers may use to try to influence you. Each one listed here is followed by a possible response:

- **Come-on:** "What's the matter, afraid?"
  Response: "Not afraid, just smart enough to know that this is dangerous."
- **Come-on:** "Everyone's doing it."
  Response: "No, because I'm not."
- **Come-on:** "How old are you anyway?"
  Response: "I'm mature enough to make up my own mind."
- **Come-on:** "You won't get caught."
  Response: "That's right, I won't—because I'm not doing it."
- **Come-on:** "Aren't you my friend?"

Try...

Suppose that someone wants you to try using drugs. What responses could you give to the following come-ons? (a) "It can't hurt to try it once." (b) "It will make you feel really good."

Response: "Show that you're my friend. Stop trying to force me to do something I don't want to do."

It's important, too, to recognize when to stop responding. Don't be afraid to say that you're tired of the conversation. Real friends know how to take no for an answer. If all else fails, there's nothing wrong with simply walking away.

When you're being pressured, ask yourself, "Who's in control here, anyway?" Remember that it's your life, and you—not your friends—are responsible for making choices that determine where it will lead.

Making the Strategy Work

Think . . .

1. How can being with a friend help you in resisting peer pressure? How can it make it more difficult?
2. Describe two situations in which the best response to negative peer pressure is to say no and walk away.

- **A strong sense of values.** Having a strong sense of values makes it easier for you to know when you're in a situation that makes you feel uncomfortable. It helps you set priorities when someone suggests that you do something questionable. Identifying your values can be challenging, but it's essential to your understanding of yourself.
- **Faith in your judgment.** When you have faith in your own judgment, you know that you are qualified to determine what activities are right for you. You don't

allow yourself to be swayed by negative peer pressure, and you reject alternatives that have destructive consequences.

- **High self-esteem.** When you feel good about yourself, you respect yourself and are not willing to sacrifice that respect to gain the approval of others.

Assertiveness

Self-knowledge helps you to be assertive about your decisions. **Assertiveness** is *the ability to make your own decisions and carry*

Focus on Refusal Skills

Tell students that come-ons are usually emotional appeals. Ask them what emotions come-ons typically appeal to. (You may prompt students by suggesting the fear of not belonging and the de-

sire for independence.) What messages can teens give themselves to strengthen their refusal skills in the face of each type of appeal?

Activities

■ **Making a Statement.** Point out that some teens claim they dress to express their individuality. Have volunteer students come forward to compare the type of shoes—or another item that shows voluntary conformity—worn that day. Discuss how this demonstrates the sometimes subtle power of external pressures. *(Observation)*

RETEACHING

■ **Offer You Can't Refuse.** Have pairs write a come-on that they find difficult to refuse on a piece of paper. Have pairs trade papers and write effective verbal and nonverbal refusals to the come-on they received.

USING VISUALS

Refer students to Figure 10.1 on page 112 for discussion. Then have pairs demonstrate contrasting methods for saying no. They should demonstrate two examples for each of the following: making a refusal with an "I" message and making the same refusal without one; saying "no" with body language that reinforces the message and using body language that weakens the same message; refusing a request firmly and refusing with an apology. Compare the the effectiveness of the messages.

CROSS-REFERENCE

For practice in using "I" messages, refer students to Chapter 9.

Review

■ **Chapter Review.** Use the contents of the Chapter Review page to help students review concepts, think critically, and apply their knowledge.

■ **Study Guide.** Have students complete the Study Guide for Chapter 10 on p. 35 of the Student Workbook.

■ **Under Pressure.** Have students write a paragraph about a time when they pressured a peer. Have them explain whether, after reading the chapter, they would act the same way today.

Evaluation

■ **Chapter Test.** Use the reproducible chapter test provided in the Teacher's Classroom Resources or create your own test using the *Testmaker Software*.

■ **Alternative Assessment.** Have students imagine that a younger relative who lives some distance away is being pressured by friends to take part in a harmful activity. Have them write or tape a letter with advice on recognizing and resisting negative peer pressure.

■ **Mixed Message.** Have students bring in examples of how the media exerts pressure. They might bring a newspaper article about teens doing volunteer work or a written description of a television ad that uses sexual images to sell a product to teens. Ask: Is the media's pressure mostly positive or negative? How is resisting negative media pressure different or more difficult than resisting peer pressure?

112

Figure 10.1
REFUSAL SKILLS

Plan Ahead
Decide in advance what you will do in case certain situations arise.

Take Your Time

Stall if you have to in order to collect your thoughts.

Be Direct
Firmly state how you feel, and keep your statements short.

Make Eye Contact

Look straight at the other person as you talk to show that you mean what you say.

Don't Apologize
You don't need to explain or justify your decision to others. Just stick to your values.

Suggest an Alternative

Reverse the pressure you feel by suggesting another activity, one that is safe and fun.

112   UNIT 2   Relationship Skills

---

them out with confidence. Assertive people state their positions firmly but respectfully.

The opposite of assertiveness is passivity. **Passive** means *keeping your own opinions to yourself and giving in to the influence of others.* Passive people follow the crowd without asking themselves whether they really want to go along with what the crowd is doing.

Have you noticed that once a few students decide certain jeans or running shoes are the best, others start wearing them too? What if you don't like the style? Would you still wear them if everyone else does? Although it's natural to want to fit in with your peers, acting in a certain way just to feel accepted can lead you to make unwise choices.

Assertiveness is not the same as aggressiveness. **Aggressive** people also have strong positions. However, instead of simply stating their positions and standing firm, they *use threats and intimidation to get their point across and achieve what they want.* Aggressive people seldom have strong relationships because they do not respect the feelings and opinions of others.

Refusal Skills

An assertive person has good **refusal skills**, *techniques to resist negative pressure effectively.* When peers try to talk you into doing something you don't really want to do, you need to be prepared. You need the ability to refuse, and you must make sure that people understand and accept your refusal. To improve your refusal skills, try the six strategies shown in **Figure 10.1**.

Sticking to Decisions

Peer pressure is one of the strongest influences on you. Peer pressure can force you to do things you don't really want to do. It's up to you to understand the effects of this pressure and to determine whether it's positive or negative pressure. Learning how to stand up to negative pressures is a skill you need in order to get where you want to go in life.

■■■■

MORE ABOUT Aggressiveness

Aggressiveness is not always viewed the same way in males and females. Often it is tolerated, and even considered acceptable, in males. A female with the same level of aggressiveness, on the other hand, may be criticized for it. Even her assertiveness may be viewed as aggression.

For males and females, a strongly aggressive personality is usually unappreciated. Those individuals who form close relationships with highly aggressive people sometimes take passive roles that welcome control.

 Review

Reviewing the Facts

1. Define peer pressure, and explain why it has such a strong influence on teens.
2. What three ways can you use to tell the difference between positive and negative peer pressure?
3. Give three examples of things teens do because of negative peer pressure.
4. What is the difference between assertiveness and aggressiveness?
5. List the six steps to take when refusing to do something.

Thinking Critically

1. Why is it important to make eye contact when saying no?
2. A friend is pressuring you to try a cigarette. Give an example of an assertive, an aggressive, and a passive response to the pressure.

Applying Your Knowledge

1. **Analyzing Media Pressure.** Look through two magazines geared toward teens. Study the ads, and determine what techniques they use to put pressure on you to buy their products.
2. **Discovering Cause-and-Effect Relationships.** Think of a time when you did something that you did not want to do. Describe the situation. How did it arise? What pressures made you do it? How did you feel? What was the outcome?
3. **Suggesting Assertive Approaches.** Work with a group to list negative pressures you all have felt. Then describe assertive approaches to handling each one.

Making Connections

1. **Social Studies.** Think of a project that you and your peers could do to help your community. Make a list of ways in which you could use positive peer pressure to get others in your school to help you with the project. If possible, implement the project.
2. **Government.** Find out about an issue that your student government recently faced. Interview student leaders to learn about the pressures that played a role in how they voted.
3. **Language Arts.** Many references to peer pressure appear in literature. Find an example, and explain what part peer pressure played in the story and how it affected the characters.

Building Your Portfolio

Portraying Peer Pressure
Imagine that you are a television writer. Write two scenes for a television show that deals with peer pressure. In the first scene, a teen faces negative peer pressure and responds in an aggressive style. In the second scene, a different teen faces negative peer pressure and uses the six-step refusal skill process to resist peer pressure. Include in each scene how the teen is pressured, what each teen says, and what happens as a result. Place the completed scripts in your portfolio.

ANSWERS TO REVIEWING THE FACTS

1. Peer pressure is influence from friends and people your age to act in a certain way. Teens are especially sensitive to their peers' opinions because they are still working on their own identities.
2. Any three: Determine whether the activity you're being asked to participate in is destructive; consider the possible outcomes of the activity, including whether it's legal or healthy; think about its physical and emotional consequences; consider whether the activity conflicts with your values.
3. Any three of these or other negative activities: smoke, drink, cut classes, engage in sexual activity, use drugs, steal, break rules.
4. Both assertive and aggressive people have strong positions. Assertive people simply state their positions and stand firm. Aggressive people may threaten, yell, or get into fights to get their points across.
5. Plan ahead, take your time, be direct, make eye contact, don't apologize, suggest an alternative.

ANSWERS TO THINKING CRITICALLY

1. Looking at the other person shows that you mean what you say, are committed to your decision, and will stand by it.
2. Possible responses: Assertive— Response should be a simple, straightforward statement, such as "No, I don't want to smoke." Aggressive—Response might focus on ridicule or a physical reaction, such as grabbing the cigarette and smashing it. Passive— Response should demonstrate weakness by saying something like, "Well I'm not sure, but if you are, I guess I will too."

Chapter 11

FOCUS

Chapter Overview

Chapter 11 explores the causes and costs of conflict. Students study a six-step process for resolving conflicts satisfactorily. They learn the concepts and practices of negotiation and mediation. The chapter ends by discussing gangs and conflict.

Motivator

■ **Think Back.** Ask students to recall a recent conflict they had with someone. Ask: Was this conflict settled? If not, why not? If so, are you satisfied with the outcome? Explain that this chapter will give them ways to avoid some conflicts and to find satisfying resolutions to the ones that do occur.

Objectives

Discuss the chapter objectives on this page. Remind students that the objectives focus on important chapter concepts.

Vocabulary

Tell students the word *conflict* comes from the Latin *conflictus,* meaning the act of striking together. Conflict is the striking together, or clashing, of different ideas, personalities, or actions. It need not involve physical striking.

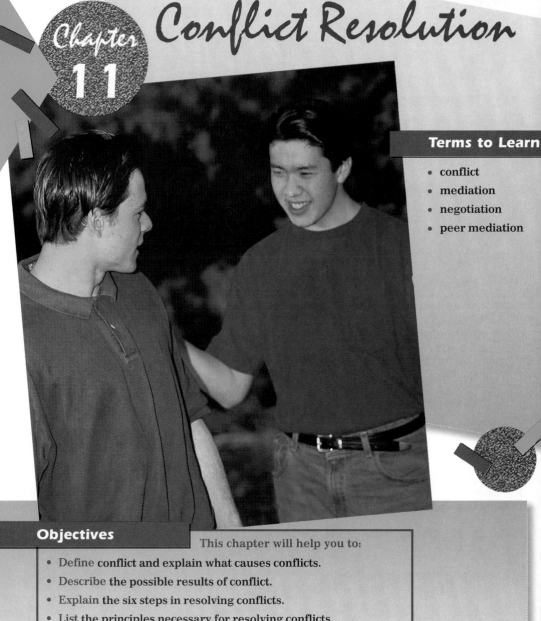

Chapter 11 Conflict Resolution

Terms to Learn

- conflict
- mediation
- negotiation
- peer mediation

Objectives

This chapter will help you to:

- Define **conflict** and explain what causes conflicts.
- Describe the possible results of conflict.
- Explain the six steps in resolving conflicts.
- List the principles necessary for resolving conflicts.
- Use **peer mediation**, when necessary, to resolve a conflict.
- Identify the dangers of gangs.

114   **UNIT 2   Relationship Skills**

CHAPTER RESOURCES

Student Workbook

Study Guide, pp. 39-40

Activity, *Communication "Cooldown,"* pp. 41-42

Teacher's Classroom Resources

Lesson Plan, p. 15

Decision Making, *Resolving Conflicts,* p. 10

Extension #17, *Peer-Mediation Guidelines,* p. 23

Extension #18, *Communicating Feelings,* p. 24

Life Skills, *Dramatic Conflicts,* pp. 21-22

Personal Development, *How to Handle a Conflict,* pp. 17-18

Transparency 10, *Preventing and Resolving Conflict*

Chapter 11 Test, pp. 27-28

Performance Assessment, *Peer Mediation,* pp. 30-31

Reteaching, *Resolving Conflicts,* p. 17

See Also:

ABCNews InterActive™ Videodiscs

As Karlina walked into the youth center, she noticed some of her friends dancing at one end of the room. What she saw made her heart skip a beat. Her close friend Rhonda was dancing to slow music with Marco. Karlina had gone out with Marco for three weekends in a row. She had high hopes that they would continue to see each other—and Rhonda knew that.

Karlina stood inside the doorway watching. She felt hurt and angry—with both of them. How could her friend do this to her? How could Marco? As the feelings grew inside Karlina, many thoughts went through her mind. Part of her wanted to confront them both. Another part wanted to run back outside. Instead, she waited until the music stopped. As soon as Rhonda was alone, Karlina went over to her. "We need to talk," she said.

What Is Conflict?

Karlina's situation had the makings of a conflict. A **conflict** is *a struggle between people who disagree*. That struggle may be verbal, physical, or both. Conflicts range from little disagreements between friends to violent battles between gangs or armies.

Conflicts are not unusual. Everybody argues with someone from time to time. In principle, conflicts are not bad. Through them, people settle disagreements and move toward constructive action. In this way, they are a positive force in people's lives. When conflicts arise for the wrong reasons and when they are not handled well, however, they are an unwelcome part of life.

Disagreements can escalate into conflicts when emotions overcome reason. By talking it over, people move toward solutions.

Why Conflicts Occur

Some conflicts are so trivial that people don't even know how they began. Others have very apparent causes. What creates conflict for one person might not be the same for someone else. In general, conflicts arise from certain basic circumstances. These are situational factors, personality differences, and power struggles.

Situational Causes

Any situation that dissatisfies people can stir conflict. Such situations occur commonly during daily life. Logan always ate lunch with his girlfriend Sonia in the school cafeteria. When she didn't show up for the third time in one week, he was upset. When he saw her in the hall with Rick right after lunch, he was even more upset. A situation was developing that could result in conflict between Logan and Sonia—or between Logan and Rick.

Personality Differences

Personality differences are often at the root of conflict. Values can clash when people express them. If tolerance for differences is low, conflict is even more likely.

CHAPTER 11   Conflict Resolution   **115**

TEACH

Topics on p. 115:
- What Is Conflict?
- Why Conflict Occurs

Checking Comprehension

✓ What causes underlie the conflict that is brewing between Karlina, Marco, and Rhonda? *Misunderstandings, jealousy, hurt feelings, desire for revenge.*

✓ How can conflict be positive? *Can resolve differences, begin constructive action.*

✓ From what three basic circumstances do conflicts often arise? *Situational factors, personality differences, power struggles.*

Activities

■ **No Big Deal.** Ask students for examples of situations in which they personally would give in to another's wishes to avoid conflict. As a class, try to develop guidelines for deciding when an issue is worth a conflict. *(Problem Solving)*

ENRICHMENT

■ **Building on Skills.** Organize the class into three groups. Assign each group Chapter 8, 9, or 10. Have each review its chapter for skills that could help avoid or resolve conflict. As groups share their findings, encourage the class to take notes for reference as they read and discuss Chapter 11.

MORE ABOUT Group Conflict

Group conflict varies with a group's four basic phases. *Orientation,* when members decide how to relate to each other, is often the most harmonious stage. Conflicts arise during *formation,* as members must work together to develop goals. More conflict may occur during *coordination,* as the group does its work, if problems arise and new solutions are needed. In *formalization,* the group finishes its work. Earlier conflict is often forgotten.

Topics on pp. 116-117:

- **Negative Results of Conflict**
- **Violence in Society**

Checking Comprehension

✓ What are some effects of negative conflict? *Illness, negative emotions, regretted messages, damaged relationships, violence.*

✓ What are some social costs of violence? *Financial expense of damages, loss of human potential, fear.*

✓ Why is it important to stay open to other points of view during negotiation? *Increases chance of finding resolution, compromise.*

FAMILY AND COMMUNITY OUTREACH

Ask students to contribute newspaper articles for a bulletin board display. Reserve half of the board for articles about violence in your area, and the other half for articles on regional efforts to help people get along. After students have added to the display for several days, have them compare the number of articles on each side of the display. Have groups choose one article about violence and try to identify the cause of the conflict that led to the violence. After groups have shared their conclusions with the class, discuss the causes that seemed most common.

Becky Lynn was sensitive to the feelings of others. She always tried to speak and act in ways that didn't hurt people. Almost every time that she was around Tina, Becky Lynn could feel anger rising inside. Tina liked to put people down, sometimes even in their presence. Becky Lynn felt that someday Tina was going to go too far, and Becky Lynn would decide to confront her.

Power Struggles

When people feel a need to be in control, a power struggle may result. This, too, can spur conflict.

Every Saturday Steve worked part-time at a drug store. Kelsey was another part-timer, who had worked there a little longer than Steve. On Saturdays Kelsey always had instructions for Steve. She routinely told him to do the jobs that she didn't want to do. This was starting to bother Steve, and he felt that he wanted to do something about it.

The Real Issue

In each of the situations above—and in many others—preventing the conflict is not the issue. Such conflicts are a fact of life. What *is* the issue then? It is the response to the conflict. Conflicts have to be handled appropriately, because when they aren't, individuals and society pay a heavy price.

Negative Results

As Ahmed thought about an argument he recently had with a friend, some of the feelings returned. His muscles tightened, and his stomach felt upset. The disagreement was never settled, and he didn't know if it ever would be.

Like Ahmed, most people are familiar with the negative effects of conflict. What can happen when conflicts occur? Here are some of the results:

- **Negative emotions arise.** Think about the feelings you have experienced during a disagreement with someone. Have you felt anger, frustration, fear, pain, humilia-

tion, sorrow, or bitterness? All of these are unpleasant emotions typically associated with conflicts. You may be able to name others.

- **People can become ill.** Those who are often angry and combative can suffer illness. Sleep and eating patterns may be affected. Conflict causes stress, which is linked to ulcers and heart disease.
- **People say things they don't mean.** In the heat of anger, it is easy to say the wrong thing and hurt another person's feelings. Once the words are said, the damage done is difficult to remove.
- **Relationships suffer.** Conflicts can break up friendships and families. Sometimes feuds last a lifetime when people never find ways to resolve their differences. Damaged work relationships can cause the loss of a job.
- **Violence may occur.** If tempers flare, an argument can escalate to produce physical aggression. Injury, and even death, may be the result. While all the other outcomes of conflict are serious, this one is the most frightening of all.

Violence in Society

"I couldn't believe what I was seeing," Haley said. "I looked out the window and saw a boy being beaten by a teenager. A crowd had gathered and they were actually cheering. No one tried to stop the fight. Wouldn't you think they would care? What if that boy were their brother? It was like a scene in a movie—except this was real life."

The number of people like Haley is growing smaller. The number of people who accept violence and participate in it is growing larger. All over the country, people are expressing their outrage and looking for ways to turn this situation around.

The Cost of Violence

The social cost of violence is too great to measure. As members of society, you and your family help pay the costs—to treat victims in hospital emergency rooms and to put

DID YOU KNOW?

Every year more than 2 million Americans are injured by violence; 500,000 require treatment in hospital emergency rooms. Almost twice as much money is spent caring for victims of violence as for treating people with AIDS. More American teens die from gunshot wounds than from all diseases combined. Alcohol contributes to 55 percent of domestic violence. It is a more likely trigger of violence than are mental disorders.

From School to Work

Negotiating

What You Learn Today . . .

Have you ever persuaded someone to change his or her mind? If so, you may have already used negotiation. **Negotiation** is <u>the use of compromise to reach an agreement.</u> Negotiation is commonly used at all levels of society. Labor unions negotiate with companies. Countries negotiate for peace.

Successful negotiation depends on the willingness of both parties to participate in earnest. They need to be open to opposing points of view and ready to say, "Okay, I'll do this if you'll do that." As with any skill, negotiation improves with practice. Recognizing the benefit of improving these skills, some schools now offer courses in negotiation.

. . . You Can Use Tomorrow

Even before starting a job, negotiation skills can be helpful when salary is discussed. On the job, coworkers may negotiate with each other about getting a project done or managing priorities. A salesperson may negotiate a settlement with a customer who has a complaint.

In the past, each side in a negotiation tried to take whatever it could from the other side. The view was that for one side to win, the other side had to lose. Business experts are now abandoning this "win-lose" attitude in favor of two strategies that benefit both parties. One is called "win-win." With this strategy,

both sides work to satisfy the other. In a conflict, a "win-win" solution is not always possible—differences may be too far apart. With another strategy, called "fair-fair," both sides get some of what they want and give up other things.

Practicing Your Skills

You can learn to recognize "fair-fair" solutions by looking for these features:

- Does the solution specify what each party will do?
- Does the solution specify what must take place to solve the problem?
- Does the solution really solve the problem, and for how long?
- Will the parties be able to do what they pledge to do?
- Are the parties sharing the burden of making the solution work?

Assessing Your Skills

1. What is the benefit of requiring both parties to share responsibility for making a solution work?
2. Think of a negotiation you recently had with your family or a friend that did not result in a "win-win" solution. Would the result have been more lasting had it been achieved with "win-win" negotiation?

---

criminals through the criminal justice system. The loss of human potential is also serious. Fear of violence causes about 160,000 students *each day* to skip classes in school. This lost education causes students to be less prepared for further education and careers. As the number of innocent victims grows, people are afraid to walk in their neighborhoods and let children play outdoors.

Violence among teens, unfortunately, is on the rise. In a recent four-year period, the number of teens arrested for violent crimes

rose from almost 317 out of every 100,000 arrests to over 430. That's an alarming increase of almost 36 percent. In one survey, 40 percent of all teens who responded said they knew someone who had been shot within the last five years.

Violent behavior often comes from people who have no regard for their victims. They are out of touch with the effects of their actions. By not acknowledging the pain and anguish they cause, they enable themselves to continue the behavior.

DID YOU KNOW?

Students who are worried about violence might be interested in an organization called RespecTeen, which encourages teens to write their United States government representatives as part of a *Speak for Yourself* program. These letters (13,000 were counted in 1995) show that violence rose among teens' concerns from seventh in 1993 to first in 1994, where it remained in 1995.

Activities

■ **Voices Against Violence.** Have students collect quotations about violence and conflict from people of a wide variety of cultures and eras. Have them write these on note cards and post the cards in a special area of the classroom over the course of a week. Encourage students to check for new cards every few days. At the end of the week, ask students to identify quotations they find especially meaningful and explain why. Discuss similarities in the attitudes toward violence expressed by people from diverse societies and eras. *(Communication)*

■ **Happily Ever After.** Invite students to suggest possible "win-win" or "fair-fair" solutions to these disputes: 1. You feel you deserve a raise, but your supervisor says the business can't afford it; 2. Both you and another group member want to be project leader; 3. You want to go to a sports event but are expected visit relatives. *(Problem Solving)*

From School to Work

Have students read "Negotiating." Ask students what personal traits and skills would help a person be a good negotiator.

Answers to Assessing . . .

1. Both have interest in successful resolution.
2. Answers will vary, but should show understanding of the advantages of "win-win" solution.

- **Violent Behavior Learned**
- **Six Steps to Conflict Resolution**
- **Ideas for Resolving Conflict**

Checking Comprehension

✓ In what ways can violent behavior be learned? *Through the media, examples of others, song lyrics, games, and sports.*

✓ What are the six steps to resolving conflicts? *See Figure 11.1.*

✓ Why is renegotiation an important part of resolving conflicts? *If need for alternative solution is ignored, conflict may occur again.*

✓ Why should people in a conflict talk to each other away from others? *Others may interfere with those who are trying to resolve a conflict.*

MULTICULTURAL *Perspectives*

Different cultural perspectives can complicate the conflict-resolution process. Ask students to review what they have learned about cultural differences, especially nonverbal communication, and to suggest guidelines for resolving a conflict with a person from another culture. Stress the added importance of making sure people understand each other's actions. Is avoiding eye contact, for example, a sign of embarrassment, deceit, or respect?

Learned Behavior

Violent behavior is learned. Children and teens learn it from adults and see it on television and in movies. Messages in sports, in the lyrics to music, and even in some games reinforce violence. The more violence people see, the more willing they are to act violently.

Fortunately, violent behavior can also be unlearned. Every day many teens are learning and practicing skills in conflict resolution through families, schools, and community programs.

Resolving Conflicts

"In my school we sign a contract not to fight. We take classes on conflict resolution. There used to be a lot of fights in our school, but things are changing."

Avery's comments are shared by many teens today, who are learning better ways to resolve conflicts. They begin with the six-step strategy shown in **Figure 11.1**. This is the basic procedure for settling differences. Much more, however, is involved.

Skillful Resolution

Keep these thoughts in mind as you practice resolving conflicts:

- Use words, not fists. Take pride in your ability to use your mind instead of physical force to settle a disagreement.
- Take charge of the situation. You can make the decision to resolve the conflict peacefully. Don't satisfy the other person's wish to fight if that's what he or she seems to want. Do what you want to do, not what others want you to do.

Figure 11.1

THE CONFLICT-RESOLUTION PROCESS

1 Identify the problem. Make sure that everyone agrees on exactly what the problem is. At times, this step alone can lead quickly to a resolution.

2 Identify possible solutions. Come up with as many possible solutions as you can think of. Accept all suggestions—even those that sound unrealistic. People should feel free to speak without being criticized, judged, or censored.

3 Evaluate each suggested solution. For each proposed solution, ask: Does it solve the problem? Is it practical? Does everyone agree to it? If the answer to any question is no, that solution must be modified or discarded.

REAL-LIFE APPLICATION

Read this to students: *Marlena, who has been dating Leon for two months, tells him that she feels he spends too much time with his other friends and not enough with her. Leon suggests he spend Friday nights with his friends and Saturdays with her.* *She says, "No way. Think of something else."* Ask: Does this approach sound promising? Help students see how it breaks down at Step 2. Have them suggest a more helpful response

- Try to talk in a location where others won't distract you or interfere with your efforts.
- When you talk, take turns. Give the other person a chance to speak, and then use active listening and keep an open mind.
- Show respect in order to get respect back. If the other person doesn't show you respect, set an example anyway.
- Control your voice. Yelling provokes the other person to yell. Staying calm shows strength and character.
- Speak the truth. That's what you want to hear, so that's what you need to deliver.
- Control your tongue. Name-calling and cursing promote conflict rather than helping to settle it. Use "I" messages instead to express your point of view.

- Use body language effectively. Stand firm, showing that you want to work peacefully and can handle the situation. Avoid standing too close, which can be threatening. Make firm but friendly eye contact.
- Value your own safety. Although conflict-resolution strategies work in most situations, occasionally another person is uncooperative and out of control. He or she may not have the skills that you have or may not care. Some of these situations can be dangerous, especially when weapons are involved. That's when you have to say to yourself, "My life and well-being are worth more to me than winning this disagreement." It takes a strong person to walk away from situations like these, but doing so makes you the smarter one.

4 **Pick the best solution.** Make sure that everybody agrees to the solution chosen; otherwise, the conflict has not been resolved.

5 **See if the solution is working.** If any party is not satisfied with the arrangement, you need to renegotiate. Go through the steps again.

6 **If necessary, agree to disagree.** Some conflicts cannot be resolved, but all parties should work to prevent the unresolved issues from escalating the conflict. The best solution here may simply be acceptance.

CHAPTER 11   Conflict Resolution   119

Focus on Negotiating Skills

As a class, list some conflicts that could successfully be resolved through negotiation. Ask groups of two or three students to perform impromptu skits demonstrating one of these situations. Remind students of the guidelines for negotiating. Encourage them to be reasonable and to strive for "win-win" resolutions. After each skit, ask other students to comment on the actors' negotiating skills.

Activities
■ **Simple Solution?** Divide students into teams to debate the following statement: The best way to end violence is to punish the people who cause it. *(Critical Thinking)*

RETEACHING
■ **See for Yourself.** Have pairs write and perform skits showing how a common conflict is resolved through the six-step process. Encourage other students to offer constructive remarks on how well each pair utilized the process.

CROSS-CURRICULAR ACTIVITY
Language Arts

Ask students to write short reports analyzing the conflict in a story they have read recently. What caused the conflict? You might consult the literature teacher for ideas. Why did it escalate? How was it resolved? If the resolution had negative consequences, how might the conflict-resolution process have helped the people involved find a more beneficial and peaceful resolution?

USING VISUALS

Refer students to Figure 11.1. Have them explain how each illustration depicts a step in the conflict-resolution process.

Checking Comprehension

✔ When should you ignore a conflict? *When it's trivial or may lead to a fight.*

✔ How can low self-esteem lead to a bad attitude? *People with low self-esteem are often defensive about how others treat them.*

Making Decisions

Have students read "Keeping Cool." Ask them if the incident is worth fighting about. Why does conflict often stem from insignificant events?

Answers to What ...

1. Confrontation; concerns about reputation.
2. Fight Lawrence or avoid him. Answers will vary. Could have walked away when Lawrence didn't accept the apology. Might have tried to talk to Lawrence before end of day; ask adult for help.
3. Positive values may include safety, peace, academic standing. Negative values may include opinion of peers (in this case), revenge.
4. Answers will vary and may include: physical injury; trouble with school and families; further conflict.
5. Point out that further discussion could help prevent physical violence.

Making Decisions

Keeping Cool

"I'll see you after school behind the stadium," Lawrence growled, as he turned and walked down the hall to his next class.

"Yeah—I'll be waiting," Jerome retorted. Jerome tried to appear confident as he strode along the hall, but his stomach was in knots. How had things gotten so out of hand? Just five minutes earlier, he and Lawrence had been at their lockers. Jerome had accidentally opened his locker door against Lawrence's hand. Even though Jerome had apologized for the accident—and Lawrence wasn't really hurt—Lawrence still got angry. Two of Lawrence's friends, standing by, urged him to not let Jerome *"get away with it."*

That's when Jerome grew annoyed. It had been an accident, after all. He had apologized—what more did Lawrence expect him to do? The two exchanged angry words, their voices rising with each remark. A teacher ordered Jerome and Lawrence—and a crowd of onlookers—to break it up and go to class.

After he cooled down, Jerome wasn't sure that meeting Lawrence after school was a good idea. They could get in trouble and even get hurt.

On the other hand, Jerome thought, avoiding Lawrence might make him look like a coward. What would his friends think? What would Lawrence do? As the afternoon wore on, Jerome felt more and more troubled.

What Would You Do?

1. What role did peer pressure play here?
2. What options did Jerome consider? Can you think of any other possible options?
3. What values are involved in each of Jerome's options? How could Jerome use his own values to make a decision?
4. What serious outcomes might the two teens face if they meet after school?
5. What do you think Jerome should do?

Avoiding Conflict

Many of the disagreements that arise out of everyday life are just small ones. They can escalate into a problem, however, unless you develop an attitude and techniques for keeping them in control.

Minor or temporary conflicts may not be worth the time and effort needed to resolve them. Riley, for example, was annoyed that his friend Tim was always late. Tim said he tried to be on time, but something always came up. Instead of confronting Tim, Riley simply decided to plan on Tim being late. If Tim was supposed to pick him up at a certain time, Riley asked him to come a little earlier, so he could count on leaving on time.

Riley adapted—changing his behavior to suit the needs of the situation—instead of confronting Tim. This approach works best when the situation bothers you more than it does the other person.

Sometimes you can prevent a conflict entirely by avoiding the circumstances that cause it. If you know that a certain person usually tries to provoke you into a fight, you can choose to stay away from that person.

To avoid conflict, you may need to make a pledge to yourself. You can join with your friends and family to take a personal stand against serious conflict. To stand by that pledge, use these tips:

- **See the positive side in situations.** This will decrease the chances of focusing on negative things that cause conflict.
- **Change the subject.** When times get tense, make a deliberate attempt to switch the conversation to another topic.
- **Defuse the situation with confidence.** You can say, "Let's give ourselves some time to settle down and think," or "This isn't important enough to fight about."
- **Don't be easily irritated.** Small things don't really matter. Sometimes a person may simply be trying to antagonize you. If they are successful, they win.

MORE ABOUT Handling Conflict

There are three main ways of handling conflict:

1. *Avoidance* is useful if the dispute cannot be peacefully resolved. However, habitual avoidance can increase anger, risking greater conflict later.

2. *Confrontation* is an aggressive approach. Confronters make sure they are the winner and everyone else the loser.

3. In *problem solving*, outlined in the chapter, people work together for a mutually satisfying solution.

Examining Your Attitudes

According to Seth, "People are always saying things that get under my skin, and I can't take it. I don't want them stepping on me. Sometimes I think they just want to get me angry. Travis says I need an attitude adjustment. Maybe he's right."

People like Seth have a defensive nature that is often rooted in low self-esteem. They pay attention to every remark that comes their way, taking everything personally and often misinterpreting or overvaluing what was said. The result can be frequent conflict and unhappiness.

Seth, however, can make changes. He can follow the suggestions already provided in this chapter. He can also work at building his own self-esteem. If the problem is very serious, he can look to others for help. If he can't handle the problem on his own or with the help of a friend or relative, a counselor can offer professional guidance.

Anyone who is experiencing too much conflict needs to take a closer look at himself or herself. An attitude may be present that invites conflict. If conflict is a problem for you, explore these questions: Do I expect too much from others? Am I too blunt in what I say? Have I alienated people because of conflict? Has conflict become a way of life for me? The answers to questions like these can lead to self-awareness, which can lead, in turn, to solutions.

Mediation

Some attempts to settle conflict aren't successful. That's when mediation helps. Through **mediation**, *an unbiased third party helps settle differences.* You may be able to find a mediator on your own. Friends and family members are often willing to help you think of satisfying solutions to a disagreement.

Peer Mediation

Many schools across the country have programs that use peer mediators to settle differences. **Peer mediation** is *a process in which*

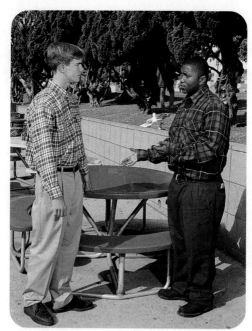

Conflicts can be avoided when you share points of view and listen carefully to each other.

specially trained students help other students resolve conflicts peacefully.

Peer mediators remain neutral. They often see solutions that those in conflict are too upset to see. Keeping everyone calm and productive is one of their goals. Peer mediators are trained to see things through other peoples' eyes. They learn how to ask questions that help people clarify their thoughts and feelings.

Peer mediation sessions are confidential. People feel more free to speak up when they know that others won't hear about what has gone on.

Peer Mediation in Action

Peer mediation helped Sui Lin and John resolve a situation. The two had worked together on an economics fair project. Sui Lin had been responsible for the research, but it had taken longer than expected. John had

■ **In the Huddle.** Discuss: What are some possible advantages and disadvantages of discussing a conflict with several people outside the dispute, but not with the person involved? *(Relationship)*

■ **Amateur Hour.** Have a group of students perform an impromptu skit in which one teen tries to mediate a conflict between two others, both of whom are the first teen's friends. Privately encourage the students portraying the disputing sides to use this relationship to gain favor with the mediator. Afterward ask: What problems arose, for the mediator as well as the two sides, when an untrained individual tried to settle the dispute? *(Critical Thinking)*

FAMILY AND COMMUNITY OUTREACH

Tell students about any in-school mediation services that are available. Invite a representative from a community mediation agency to talk with the class about its services. Alternately, ask interested students to research local mediation services available to teens and their families.

CROSS-REFERENCE

For a review of empathy and active listening, useful skills in conflict resolution, refer students to Chapter 9.

MORE ABOUT Peer Mediation

Peer mediation usually follows a certain process. First each person is asked to calmly give his or her version of the conflict with no interruptions from the other person. Each then states what he or she wants the other to do. The mediator asks if each party is willing to do what is asked. If not, what is the person willing to do? The parties eventually agree on a solution; otherwise, the mediator may suggest adult intervention.

Review

■ **Chapter Review.** Use the contents of the Chapter Review page to help students review concepts, think critically, and apply their knowledge.

■ **Study Guide.** Have students complete the Study Guide for Chapter 11 on p. 39 of the Student Workbook.

■ **A Better Way.** Ask students to cite a conflict they have witnessed or learned of from the news. Have them describe ways the conflict might have been averted using one or more of the strategies they studied in this chapter.

Evaluation

■ **Chapter Test.** Use the reproducible chapter test provided in the Teacher's Classroom Resources or create your own test using the *Testmaker Software.*

■ **Alternative Assessment.** Ask groups to devise a means of teaching children that conflict can be handled in ways that solve the problem instead of making it worse. Groups might create a picture book, videotape, or puppet show. Remind groups to tailor their message to suit a child's intellectual and social skills.

■ **Conflict Guidelines.** Divide the class into four groups. Have two groups each create five guidelines for avoiding conflict, focusing on its causes. Ask each of the other groups to develop five guidelines for living with conflicts that can't be resolved. As each pair of groups shares its guidelines, have volunteers create two master lists and copy them onto poster board for classroom display.

Because mediators are not emotionally involved in a dispute, they are better able to see both sides. What qualities do you think an effective mediator should have?

waited for the research, which he had needed for a display that he was putting together. Their project was late, costing each of them 20 points off the project grade. Disappointed, they began to argue. Resentment grew and threatened their friendship.

Casey, a peer mediator, listened to both. John blamed Sui Lin for the grade because her research was late. Sui Lin claimed that John could have started on the display without waiting. Guiding the discussion, Casey suggested that both could have helped the situation by doing some things differently. She also encouraged them to give up their anger and focus instead on what they needed to do to salvage their friendship.

As they talked, Sui Lin and John discovered that they had more in common in the dispute than they had differences. Both were more upset by the feeling that they had let each other down than they were by the grade. Casey asked them to think of what they could do to set this part of their relationship right. In the end, they decided to talk to their teacher about doing extra credit work to make up for the lost points. With Casey's help, John and Sui Lin were able to deepen their relationship rather than to destroy it.

Avoiding Gangs

Perhaps the most serious link that many young people have with conflict today is through gangs. Gangs thrive on conflict. They promote hatred of outsiders, and that routinely translates into violent acts. Gangs lure teens and even young children into their circle and may not let them leave.

Not allowing yourself to fall under a gang's influence is your best protection. If you live where gang influence is strong, how can you avoid it? First, realize that you can choose to be part of the world outside of gangs. In it, you can stay drug-free, make your own decisions, and be safer. You can build a good future for yourself.

Gangs prey upon people who have a need to belong and who want someone to care about them. People who feel this kind of strong need can fulfill it elsewhere. They can stay away from gang members and the places where they go. They can find other friends who share their desire for a better life and will given them support.

Once you are in a gang, it's very hard to get out. Gangs demand loyalty and use fear for life and safety to keep members. If you are already in a gang, try to move out slowly. Gradually, adopt new activities and friends. It isn't easy, but it can be done over time.

So Much to Gain

Conflicts are not avoidable in life, but the negative consequences are. You know that, but not everyone else does.

Share what you have learned about conflict resolution with others. As you do, your conflicts with the people around you will become easier to settle, and you'll all be healthier and happier for it.

Focus on Mediation Skills

Point out to students that the United States and the United Nations are often involved in mediating conflicts between nations and between groups within nations. With students, identify current or recent examples of such situations in the news. You might locate articles from current newspapers to share with the class or place on the bulletin board. Discuss qualities and skills such governmental mediators must have.

Chapter 11 Review

Reviewing the Facts

1. What are conflicts, and what causes them?
2. What are three possible results of conflict?
3. List the six steps in the conflict-resolution process.
4. Name five principles that underlie resolving conflicts.
5. Name two situations in which it is advisable to avoid conflict.
6. How can mediation help resolve conflicts?
7. Why are gangs dangerous?

Thinking Critically

1. Compromise is necessary to settle conflicts. Are there any situations when you should not compromise?
2. What special skills do you think that a peer mediator needs to have?

Applying Your Knowledge

1. **Taking Another Point of View.** Think of a conflict you had recently with a friend, classmate, or member of your family. Write about the conflict from the point of view of the other person.
2. **Setting up Peer Mediation.** If your school does not already have a peer mediation program, work with three or four classmates and your teacher to see what it would take to set one up. Find out from other schools what training is involved, and develop a training schedule for your program. If your school does have peer mediation, find out how the program works and compare it with programs in nearby schools. How are they similar? How do they differ?

3. **Promoting Nonviolence.** Create a promotional campaign, using posters, public service announcements, videos, handouts, or any other approach, that supports the idea of settling conflicts in nonviolent ways.

Making Connections

1. **Social Studies.** Think about how cultural differences affect conflict by completing this sentence: "When conflict is a problem between people of different cultures, they need to. . . ."
2. **Language Arts.** Write the dialogue for a short radio sketch in which characters come close to fighting but find a way to avoid it.

Building Your Portfolio

Creating a Constructive Debate

With a small group, choose a political or social issue that you feel strongly about. Prepare to debate opposite sides of the issue. Videotape or audio-tape your debate for 20 minutes. Then critique the debate. Did your discussion remain constructive? Did all participants stick with the issue? Did anyone become emotional, stop communicating, or break any other rules of negotiation? Write up your critique, and point out areas where you could do better. Place the tape and your critiques in your portfolio.

CHAPTER 11 Conflict Resolution 123

Chapter Overview

Chapter 12 describes the skills needed for good leadership, along with those of an effective follower. The chapter gives ways teens can make a difference as citizens, students, and volunteers. It reminds students that they can make a positive difference in the lives of family and friends.

Motivator

■ **Making a Difference.** Ask students if they think one teen's actions can make a difference in your school or community. If so, how? If not, why? Encourage students to offer real-life examples. Explain that this chapter will give them ways to show leadership and improve their own and others' lives.

Objectives

Discuss the chapter objectives on this page. Remind students that the objectives focus on important chapter concepts.

Vocabulary

Ask students to define the term *role model*. Confirm that a role model is someone you admire, whose behavior sets an example. Add that positive role models can help teens set goals and make wise decisions.

Chapter
12
Making a Difference in Your Community

Terms to Learn

- citizen
- parliamentary procedure
- role model
- volunteer

Objectives

This chapter will help you to:

- Identify **the skills needed for good leadership.**
- Explain **what it takes to be a good follower.**
- Describe **ways of being a responsible citizen and student.**
- Identify **what you can volunteer to do in your community.**
- Describe **ways to make a difference with family and friends.**

CHAPTER RESOURCES

Student Workbook
Study Guide, p. 43
Activity, *Make a Difference*, p. 44

Teacher's Classroom Resources
Lesson Plan, p. 16
Cooperative Learning, *Making a Difference*, pp. 19-20

Extension #19, *Show Your Interest: Volunteer!* p. 25
Extension #20, *What Makes a Role Model?* p. 26
Life Skills, *What Makes a Leader?* pp. 23-24
Personal Development, *One Small Step*, pp. 19-20

Transparency 11, *A Good Role Model*
Chapter 12 Test, pp. 29-30
Performance Assessment, *Make a Difference*, pp. 32-33
Reteaching, *What Makes a Good Citizen?* p. 18

See Also:
ABCNews InterActive™ Videodiscs

People can make a difference in their community. Those who care about something strongly enough find a way to take action. For example, when Ryan heard that a fire had destroyed the home of a fellow student, he felt concern for the teen and his family. Ryan also felt something else—a sense of helplessness. He wanted to do something for them, but their needs seemed far beyond his capacity to give. He couldn't provide a new home. He couldn't feed them or buy them new clothes. He wanted to take action, but what could he do?

Many people have feelings like Ryan's. Then they move on with their lives and forget those urges. Many others, fortunately, take action. Although he had never done anything like this before, Ryan decided to do something to help the family. He began by talking with other concerned people. In the end, they organized a benefit dance and chili supper to raise money for the family. For Ryan, this successful effort gave him more satisfaction than anything he had ever done before.

The Tools You Need

When Ryan took action, he used skills that he didn't even know that he had. He became a leader.

Leadership skills enable people like Ryan to make things happen. It takes a leader to rouse others to action. It takes followers to get things done. With the skills necessary for leading and following, people can find many opportunities to make a difference in the world.

Leadership Skills

A good leader uses the best talents of a group to achieve the group's goals. The goals might range from organizing a fundraiser to collecting winter coats for disadvantaged children. Whatever the project, an effective leader takes responsibility for getting the job done and enables group members to work together efficiently.

Listed below are some of the main skills that an effective leader needs. As you read through the list, ask yourself, "Which skills have I already developed? How can I improve the ones that I need to work on?"

- **Management.** Good leaders plan, organize, implement, and evaluate a project. They make sure that they have the resources to get the job done. They don't try to do all the work themselves; instead, they use the skills and talents of everyone in the group.
- **Motivation.** A leader is sensitive to the ways that each person can best be motivated. Some people prefer to work independently, for example, while others work best with a partner or group. A good leader also offers guidance, praise, and encouragement to motivate people to do their best.
- **Communication.** Effective speaking and listening are part of leadership. A leader might explain what needs to be done and what role each member will play. A leader is ready to respond to suggestions, problems, and complaints.

How can you begin to acquire leadership skills?

CHAPTER 12 **Making a Difference in Your Community** 125

Topic on p. 125:
- Leadership Skills

Checking Comprehension

✓ How can you tell if a leader is effective? *He or she helps group use talents and work well together.*

✓ What skills help a leader solve problems? *Decision making; conflict resolution.*

✓ Why should a leader know group members personally? *To know each person's talents and motivations.*

Activities

■ **Taking Stock.** Ask students to imagine they faced a situation like Ryan's. What could they offer to a family in such a case? *(Problem Solving)*

■ **Tapping Resources.** Have students suggest resources that group members might have and that leaders might use. Encourage students to name specific talents and contributions. *(Management)*

ENRICHMENT

■ **A Born Leader?** Divide students into teams to debate this statement: Good leaders are born, not made.

CROSS-CURRICULAR ACTIVITY
Social Studies

Challenge the class to find trends in the traits of leaders who have guided nations over the centuries. What qualities were important in ancient leaders? How have requirements for leadership changed? Have they changed at all in some nations? Students might create a time line to show the changes they note.

Topics on pp. 126-127:

- Good Followers
- Making Difference as a Citizen

Checking Comprehension

✓ Why are followers as important as leaders? *Followers carry out the project and get the work done.*

✓ How did Carla fail as a good follower? *Did not complete task, wasn't cooperative, didn't communicate well.*

From School to Work

Have students read "Leadership in the Future Homemakers of America." Can they think of other organizations that offer teens opportunities to practice leadership skills?

Answers to Assessing . . .

1. Encourage each student to identify some leadership experience. Help them see that leadership can be demonstrated in small ways as well as large.

2. The leader needs to take some kind of action. Talking privately with the person to get at the problem might help to begin with. An impersonal request for good attendance during a meeting, with reference to rules on attendance might too. If all else fails, steps may need to be taken to fill the position with someone who is a more willing participant.

- **Problem solving.** Good leaders find solutions to the problems that naturally arise when people work together. They use their decision-making and conflict-resolution skills, and they are willing to look for new ways to achieve goals.

- **Conducting meetings.** A good leader manages a meeting by following a set of rules first developed by the English Parliament. Called **parliamentary procedure**, these rules are *a democratic method for allowing people to voice their opinions in order to reach a majority decision.* Parliamentary procedure has been called "the *right* of the minority, the *rule* of the majority, and the *partiality* to none." Can you put this into other words?

You can practice all of these leadership skills in your everyday activities. For example, you can lead friends in deciding where to go or what to do. You can take part in class discussions and influence others by what you say. You can guide younger and less experienced people in learning new skills.

A leader is a **role model**, *a person who sets an example for others.* Positive role models exhibit such behaviors as fairness, coopera-

---

From School to Work

Leadership in the Future Homemakers of America

What You Learn Today . . .

Participation in organizations is an ideal way for people to test their leadership skills. For more than 50 years, the Future Homemakers of America/Home Economics Related Occupations (FHA/HERO) has allowed students to do just that. FHA/HERO helps students who are interested in careers in family and consumer sciences. Participating in the group allows teens to build job skills by taking leadership roles.

In FHA/HERO, opportunities for leadership are limited only by your abilities and energy. You might be a committee chairperson or a chapter officer, running projects and managing people. If selected by the nominating committee, you can run for office at the district, regional, state, or national level. If elected, you'll speak in front of groups and join in planning and work groups.

. . . You Can Use Tomorrow

Becoming a leader in such organizations as FHA/HERO provides invaluable experience. Interviewing with the nominating committee is good preparation for a college or job interview. Speaking in front of large audiences, managing projects, and dealing with people are skills you can use in your future career. Meeting new people enables you to make connections with others in your field to exchange ideas and grow as a professional.

Many students don't get this experience until they enter the work world. Organizations like FHA/HERO give their members a head start.

Practicing Your Skills

Become a leader the next time you are part of a group. Try the following tips:

- Get everyone's input and identify the group's consensus, or generally agreed-upon decisions.
- Provide each group member with a task that must be completed to reach the goal.
- Set a deadline for completion.
- Follow up to check each person's progress. Offer help to those who need it.
- Motivate members to work toward the goal. Use encouragement, persuasion, and problem solving to get group members over logjams.
- After the project is completed, lead a meeting to assess the outcome. Discuss whether anything could have been done differently.

Assessing Your Skills

1. Describe a situation in which you demonstrated leadership skills. Was it successful? Explain.
2. Suppose that you were leading a group and one officer frequently forgot to attend the meetings. What would you do?

---

126   UNIT 2   Relationship Skills

Focus on Leadership Skills

Have students select one of these quotations and write a brief explanation relating it to leadership skills:

"Leadership is the ability to convince people that they want to do what you want them to do as if they had thought of it themselves."—Eileen Ford, Ford Model Agency; "I suppose leadership at one time meant muscles, but today it means getting along with people."—Indira Gandhi; "A leader is a dealer in hope."—Napoleon Bonaparte; "If you command wisely, you'll be obeyed cheerfully."—Thomas Fuller, M.D.

tion, dedication, and responsibility. As others imitate their example, role models discover that their ability to make a difference extends beyond their own actions.

The Skills of Following

Have you ever heard the expression, "Too many chefs spoil the broth"? This saying illustrates an important point: every successful group project needs followers as well as leaders. Even if you develop strong leadership skills and take a leadership role in your community, you will need to follow the lead of others from time to time.

Good followers are responsible. They complete assigned tasks on time and as directed. A cooperative spirit helps them coordinate efforts and help each other when they can. They use good communication skills.

Carla's experience taught her how important good followers are. She agreed to take photos for a promotional brochure that her hiking club was creating. The committee asked her to reshoot her first photos because the images were too small. In shooting new photos, however, Carla stuck to her own ideas, and the new images were not much better. With no time left, the printer had to use the photos that Carla had submitted. The brochure was costly and ineffective, disappointing the club members—and Carla.

Making a Difference

With leadership skills and the ability to follow effectively, just think what you can do. These skills can be combined with others that you have already learned, such as decision making and problem solving. Putting all your skills together gives you the tools you need to take positive action as a citizen, a student, and a volunteer.

As a Citizen

A society becomes stronger because of good citizens. Sadly, it is weakened by those who are not good citizens.

A **citizen** is a *member of a community, such as a school, city, or nation*. As a citizen, you have certain rights, including the right to receive an education and to be protected by the police. You also have certain responsibilities:

- **Staying informed.** By reading newspapers and listening to news on radio and television, you become aware of what is going on around you. You can then make informed decisions and take responsible actions.

- **Participating in government.** Those who attend public meetings and voice their opinions can change government policies. What the public says influences people who hold office. When you are older, your vote will also count. If you feel that a person in office is not doing the job, complaining does little good. Voting for someone else does. You might even run for office yourself one day.

The police help ensure the safety of people in a community. Cooperating with the police is a responsibility of citizens.

MORE ABOUT Leadership

Leadership can start early, in any number of opportunities. Witness the case of Cynthia Tanguilig, as recounted in *Girls and Young Women Leading the Way: 20 True Stories About Leadership*, by Frances Karnes and Suzanne Bean (Free Spirit, 1993). The teen from Charleston, West Virginia, assumed most of the start-up work of organizing a recycling club at her high school. The project really took off when Cynthia painted the recycling bins to look like giant soda cans. By year's end, under her leadership, the club was the largest and best organized at her school.

Topics on pp. 128-130:

- Making a Difference as a Student and a Volunteer
- Helping Family and Friends
- The Importance of Making an Effort

Checking Comprehension

✔ How do students make schools stronger? *Support school events, be good sports, protect school property, help set policies, start service programs, help others in need.*

✔ Why do helping agencies often need volunteers? *They often have low budgets, cannot afford large staff.*

✔ How can you learn about volunteer opportunities? *Talk to friends, family members, school counselor; read newspaper; call coordinating agency.*

✔ What are some ways you can "volunteer" at home? *Listen to family members' problems; help someone who feels overwhelmed.*

SPECIAL NEEDS
Strategies

Students with Disabilities. Ask students to suggest skills and talents that would be helpful for each of the volunteer activities listed on page 128. Point out that a high level of academic skills is not required for many of the activities. Ask: What volunteer opportunities might exist for students with physical limitations? Remind students that volunteering is a good way for anyone to develop new skills and strengthen old ones.

- **Respecting the rights of others.** Good citizens respect other people—their individuality, needs, and property. You can show respect by helping to keep property that is shared—such as sidewalks and public parks—clean and safe.
- **Obeying the laws.** Good citizens obey the laws, following traffic signs, paying taxes, and refraining from committing crimes. When people obey laws, society functions more smoothly.
- **Fighting crime.** Fighting crime is more than avoiding criminal activity. It begins with prevention, by securing property or joining a neighborhood watch program. It includes reporting crimes when you see them committed and cooperating with police investigations. In these ways, you help prevent further crimes, protecting yourself and others.

As a Student

A school is only as strong as the students and staff make it. All of the responsibilities of citizenship apply at school, just as they do in the larger community. When students work to make their school a better place, it becomes one.

Students who support school events through participation and attendance make school a better place.

How can you make a contribution? You might explore these ideas, or add others to the list:

- Help make school events a success by your support and attendance.
- Be a good sport at school events. Remember that your school's reputation rides on your behavior.
- Protect school property. Money that must be used for repairs is money lost for other programs, such as athletics and music.
- Help set school policies. By participating in school government, you can work toward goals that benefit the entire student body.
- Start a community-service program if one doesn't exist. When a school reaches out to the community, both sides benefit.
- Help students who need assistance with a particular subject.

As a Volunteer

People probably make the greatest difference through volunteer efforts. A **volunteer** is *someone who puts caring into action by offering services free of charge.*

Every community has many needs. Community programs meant to meet those needs often have low operating budgets and must rely on the work of volunteers to survive. How much they can do is directly linked to how many willing hands are extended. A program that supplies meals for the elderly at home, for example, needs people to prepare the meals and people to deliver them.

Although you receive no money for volunteer work, it brings many rewards. You meet new people who share your interests. You can also learn job skills and gain valuable work experience. Also, by keeping a service going now,

---

REAL-LIFE APPLICATION

Read this to students: *Gabriel enjoys woodworking and is considering volunteering to help refurbish houses for Habitat for Humanity. His girlfriend Hope answers calls at a teen hotline and wants Gabriel to join her. Gabriel is a little shy,* but Hope is sure he'll do a good job at the hotline after training. Ask students what they think Gabriel should do. Help them see that he is more likely to feel competent and stay with an activity he enjoys.

Acting Responsibly

Are You Dedicated?

Many people find it easy to act responsibly when it's obviously in their best interest. Driving safely, for example, has its own immediate reward. It takes dedication, however, to invest time and effort when it requires sacrifice. Dedicated people are more likely to follow through with commitments and see a project through difficulties to the end.

Dedication springs from two qualities. One is a belief in what you are doing, the feeling that the job warrants the effort. The other is the personal pride that you take in accomplishing what you set out to do.

Dedication in Action

"Are you entering the competition this year, Julia?"

Julia barely heard her mother's question. She stared at the entry form that had arrived in the mail. For the past two years she had played the piano in a citywide music competition. Julia loved the piano and practiced daily. She had won the contest last year, and she felt she was good enough to win again.

Six months ago, Julia would have felt only excitement about the event. Last spring, however, she and some friends had started volunteering at a food bank that supplied food and nutrition information for lower-income families. At first, Julia had been only mildly interested in the work; she did it mostly to be with her friends. As she met the people who benefited from the program, however, she began to see how important it was. Most of those they served were families with young children. One toddler could have been a twin to her brother Jesse. With every can

of corn and nutrition leaflet, Julia felt that she was helping these families stay strong.

Now came one of the food bank's biggest projects—putting together fifty food baskets for Thanksgiving. All of the volunteers had been asked to help fill baskets on the Saturday before Thanksgiving—the same day as the competition.

"I've worked there every Saturday for the last three months," Julia thought. "I've stacked cans and organized leaflets. I helped collect food. They can do without me this one time."

Then she thought of the parents, working hard to give their children what they needed, and of the child who could have been Jesse's twin.

Julia folded the entry form and tossed it aside. She finally answered her mother. "No, this year I'll give someone else a chance to win."

Your Analysis

1. How had the focus of Julia's dedication changed? Do you think this change showed more maturity? Explain your answer.
2. Can people be too dedicated to a cause? Explain.
3. Describe ways that people show dedication to their families.
4. How might people show dedication to their jobs?

---

you help ensure that it will be available if you should need it later. Finally, helping others brings feelings of self-worth and fulfillment.

Ideas for Teens

Teens are very involved in volunteer efforts these days. Many who want to put their free time to good use are finding ways to make a contribution.

When you choose a volunteer activity, pick something that you believe is worthwhile and

that you think you will enjoy. That way you are more likely to stick with it. For example, do you prefer working inside or outside? Do you enjoy talking with elderly people or playing with young children? Think about the skills you would like to share or learn and the amount of time you have to give.

You can find ideas for volunteering by talking to a school counselor or reading the newspaper. Some communities have an agency that keeps track of volunteering opportuni-

---

Focus on Listening Skills

Ask a pair of volunteers to act out a scene in which Dina helps Franceen make a wise decision. (Dina might first review the steps in decision making in Chapter 5 and good listening skills in Chapter 9.) Then have that or another

pair perform a scene in which Dina's comments drive a wedge between the friends. Ask students to distinguish between giving others caring advice and dictating to them "for their own good."

Activities

■ **Walls Talk.** Have pairs or small groups answer this question: If you were making your first visit to a high school, how could you tell whether the students there cared about their school? Have them list signs of pride or neglect and share their ideas with the class. *(Observation)*

■ **Looking Ahead.** Have students identify volunteer activities that are available to teens and the skills students could learn from them. List these on the board. Then ask how specific skills listed could be helpful in specific careers. *(Critical Thinking)*

RETEACHING

■ **As the Twig Is Bent.** Ask students how the saying "Charity begins at home" relates to this chapter.

Acting Responsibly

Have students read and discuss "Are You Dedicated?"

Answers to Your Analysis

1. Changed from own ambition to good of others; shows maturity in placing others' needs before own wants.
2. Answers will vary. Remind students of need for balance. Suggest that dedication that negatively affects others is type of selfishness.
3. Answers may include: give moral guidance, help with tasks.
4. Answers may include: help other workers, stay late to finish project.

Review

■ **Chapter Review.** Use the contents of the Chapter Review page to help students review concepts, think critically, and apply their knowledge.

■ **Study Guide.** Have students complete the Study Guide for Chapter 12 on p. 43 of the Student Workbook.

■ **Volunteer Profile.** Have students develop and write a profile of a teen volunteer, including the type of activities the teen is involved in and the leadership—and other—skills he or she uses.

Evaluation

■ **Chapter Test.** Use the reproducible chapter test provided in the Teacher's Classroom Resources or create your own test using the *Testmaker Software.*

■ **Alternative Assessment.** Have pairs create acrostics using the words *citizen, student,* or *volunteer.* (Make sure at least one pair chooses each word.) Have the pair use each letter in its word to begin a sentence explaining how someone can make a difference as a citizen, student, or volunteer. Display acrostics in the classroom.

■ **Practicing Leadership.** Ask students how they can use leadership skills without being formally appointed to a leadership position. (Examples include serving as role models for younger people and guiding friends into positive activities.) Discuss ways students can act as "unofficial" volunteers (help a new student learn about the school or spend time with an older neighbor).

130

---

ties in the area. Here are just a few of the many ways you can help.

- Join a recycling program.
- Help at a local food bank, senior citizens' center, or animal shelter.
- Participate in a charity walkathon or race.
- Join Habitat for Humanity, which helps build or renovate houses for lower-income families.
- Form a group to beautify your community by planting flowers or removing *graffiti* (drawings on walls or public places).
- Counsel others on a teen hot line.
- Help with a campaign to combat violence, drunk driving, or drug abuse.

As Family Member or Friend

Making a difference is sometimes easiest and most effective at home. When families and friends help people meet needs, there is less demand on community services.

Making a difference to family members and friends can be as simple as listening to a problem or assuming an extra household chore. You may have discovered that these little things are sometimes the most appreciated.

At times, however, making a difference requires something more. Caring about someone can mean taking risks. For example, Dina listened as her friend Francine talked about "borrowing" her mother's car while her mother was away. Francene thought it would be exciting to take some of her friends out for a ride. Dina grew concerned. Francine did not have much experience driving, much less a driver's license. Although she knew her message would not be welcomed, Dina trusted

in the strength of their friendship. She decided to say something.

"What if you have an accident?" she asked "What if somebody gets hurt?" As they talked, Dina brought up other possible consequences. At first, Francine was irritated. Eventually, however, she realized that Dina was right, and she abandoned her plan.

Every Effort Counts

As you think about making a difference in the world, remember one important point: every effort counts. As a family member, friend, citizen, and volunteer, whatever constructive steps you take are significant.

Starting small is even a good idea. If you set small, attainable goals at first, you are more likely to succeed. As you gain confidence in your abilities, you can set your sights higher.

Whatever you do, don't just sit back and do nothing because you think that the actions of one individual don't matter. They do—to yourself as well as to others. When you develop the habit of helping, you cultivate the attitude of caring. Then you discover that you really can make a difference.

▌ A teen who voluntarily helps at home earns respect, gratitude—and even cooperation—from other family members.

DID YOU KNOW?

In 1992 teens volunteered 1.6 billion hours of service, the equivalent of 966,800 full-time employees with an estimated value of $7 billion.

Over 140,000 people have served in the Peace Corps since it was begun in 1961. It now has 6,500 volunteers (about 10 percent age 50 or older) in 93 nations. Projects range from teaching English to showing people how and why to slow the destruction of the rain forest.

Review

Reviewing the Facts

1. List the main skills that a good leader needs.
2. Describe the qualities of a good follower.
3. Give three examples of ways that you can make a difference as a citizen.
4. List three ways that you can make a difference as a student.
5. What is a reward of volunteering?
6. How can you make a difference to your family and friends?

Thinking Critically

1. What are two excuses people might use for not volunteering? For each one, think of a response that counters it.
2. Some people believe that they are justified in breaking a law that they consider unfair. What are some problems with this attitude?
3. Discuss the adage, "Bloom where you are planted." How might it be applied to the idea of making a difference?

Applying Your Knowledge

1. **Developing a Work Plan.** Suppose that you are working in a group with three other teens to create posters on the rules for conduct at a community center. List the tasks that you need to reach your goal. For each task, identify possible responsibilities of the leader and the followers.
2. **Practicing Parliamentary Procedure.** Obtain a copy of Robert's Rules of Order to learn the rules of parliamentary procedure. With a group of classmates, demonstrate their use.
3. **Helping a Friend.** Suppose that you have a friend who wants to quit her job because she argued with her boss. You believe that this is a minor matter that will blow over. Write an explanation of whether you would or would not tell your friend what you think.

Making Connections

1. **History.** Read about a well-known national or world leader from history. In a brief report, identify the person's leadership skills, illustrating each one with examples of his or her decisions and actions.
2. **Civics.** Use an almanac and other sources to obtain information about voter turnout in the last five presidential elections. Prepare a short report summarizing your findings. Identify any trends and suggest reasons for them.
3. **Language Arts.** Write a public-service announcement aimed at persuading citizens to exercise their right to vote. Think about what appeals or arguments would be most effective. Use persuasive language to put across your message.

Building Your Portfolio

Assessing Your Leadership Skills

Think about an elected office that you believe you are qualified to hold in your school or in an organization to which you belong. Possibilities might include class treasurer, student council representative, 4-H club president, or FHA or FFA officer. Write and tape-record a speech in which you identify your leadership skills, explain why you would be a good choice for the position, and urge others to vote for you. Place the recording in your portfolio.

FOCUS

Chapter Overview

Chapter 13 identifies skills and personal qualities needed for job success and explains why they are valuable. The chapter also describes how personal contacts can help students find a job and do it well.

Motivator

■ **Inventory Skills.** Tell students they may already have some of the skills needed when they begin work such as time management. Explain that this chapter will describe skills and qualities that will help them succeed in their careers.

Objectives

Discuss the chapter objectives on this page. Remind students that the objectives focus on important chapter concepts.

Vocabulary

The term network entered the English language in 1560 and first meant a system of cords or wires. Its meaning broadened to include interconnected communication systems. Only since 1966 has networking been used to mean the exchange of information or services among groups or individuals.

Chapter 13 Skills for Career Success

Terms to Learn

- mentor
- networking
- retrain
- sociability

Objectives

This chapter will help you to:

- Explain **what factors are making changes in the workplace.**
- Describe **what expectations employers have for their workers.**
- Identify **skills needed for career success.**
- List **personal qualities that are valuable at work.**
- Explain **how interpersonal skills can help you work with others.**
- Define **networking and mentor and explain their usefulness.**

132   UNIT 2 Relationship Skills

CHAPTER RESOURCES

Student Workbook
Study Guide, pp. 45-46
Activity, *Help Wanted*, pp. 47-48

Teacher's Classroom Resources
Lesson Plan, p. 17
Extension #21, *Skills for the Workforce*, p. 27

Extension #22, *Authority Figures*, p. 28
Life Skills, *Get Ready for the Working World*, p. 25
Transparency 12, *Put Your Skills to Work!*
Chapter 13 Test, pp. 31-32
Performance Assessment, *Skills for Career Success*, p. 34

Reteaching, *Career Skills You'll Need*, p. 19

See Also:
ABCNews InterActive™ Videodiscs

Discouraged was the best word to describe how Martin felt. Martin had been out of high school for nearly a year, and he was still looking for a job. It wasn't that he hadn't tried. Despite many interviews, though, he never seemed to land anything. He didn't really understand that he lacked the skills employers were looking for.

In the past, a high school diploma and the willingness to work often guaranteed a person a solid job for life. Today, however, employers demand higher-skilled, better-educated workers who are able to keep pace with the rapidly changing work environment. Just as important, they expect workers in all fields to be flexible, adaptable, and able to make smart decisions. Like Martin, a person who lacks these skills will have trouble finding a job.

The Changing Workplace

Imagine what a miner's job is like. Is a laptop computer part of that picture? The fact is, some miners today do use laptops—and cellular phones—to track equipment breakdowns and to monitor water quality. Mining, like many other industries, is changing. Workers in all kinds of jobs are affected by the latest technology.

In many significant ways, the workplace that you need to prepare for is vastly different from the one workers entered a generation ago. Two key reasons are the increasing role of technology and the growth of a global economy.

Technology in the Workplace

You may be familiar with some of the numerous technological changes that have impacted workers in recent years.

Computer literacy is a necessary skill in many jobs.

Offices, for instance, now depend on computers, copiers, and facsimile machines. More and more workers—from managers in offices to salesclerks in department stores—rely on these machines to record, sort, and transmit information. More importantly, more and more decisions are being made by workers at remote locations rather than in a company's main office. As a result, businesses demand workers who have sound decision-making and problem-solving skills.

Technology and Workers' Roles

As technology has allowed workers to do new tasks, their roles and responsibilities have changed. When Lila first began working in an appliance factory, her job consisted of

CHAPTER 13 Skills for Career Success 133

MORE ABOUT Technology

A computer program uses a caller ID phone service to allow a business to route calls from certain customers to certain operators. Caller ID can also limit access to company computers to select callers. In some small towns, caller ID functions as a less expensive 911 system.

TEACH

Topics on p. 133:
- **The Changing Workplace**
- **Technology in the Workplace**
- **Technology and Workers' Roles**

Checking Comprehension

✓ Why is the workplace changing? *Technology is increasing; trade is becoming more global.*

✓ As more companies form teams of employees, will the employees need more or fewer skills? *More, for wider range of roles and responsibilities.*

Activity

■ **Changing Times.** Discuss how workers who did not grow up with high technology can learn to use it on the job. How might the workplace might change in the next generation?

CROSS-CURRICULAR ACTIVITY
Social Studies

Describe philosopher Alvin Toffler's three waves of historical development: The First Wave began with the first permanent human settlements. The Second Wave is represented by the Industrial Revolution, when the techniques of modern production emerged. The Third Wave is the great technological change seen now. Have groups research Toffler's "waves," summarizing the economic and social impact of events that occurred.

Checking Comprehension

✓ For what reasons might workers need to retrain? *New technology has eliminated or changed their job.*

✓ Why is being bilingual an advantage today? *Prepares worker for global economy.*

✓ How might the availability of products and parts from overseas affect United States companies? *Gives them more products and parts to choose from, but increases competition for own products.*

In Touch With TECHNOLOGY

Have students read "Technology on the Job." Ask students to identify possible disadvantages to the advances described in each career area. Ask how these might be countered.

Answers to Thinking...

1. Answers will vary. Students should see that jobs will be limited. Suggest, however, that workers can be trained in new technology.
2. Allows quicker, more efficient production, communication; more business transactions. Examples will vary.

In Touch with **TECHNOLOGY**

Technology on the Job

Chances are, you'll be able to accomplish more at your job than your parents and grandparents did—and you will owe it to technology. No matter what field you choose, new technology will enable you to do more and do it faster. Here are a few examples:

- **Retail.** Not long ago, stores closed down for a day or two every year to take inventory of their stock. Employees had to count and record each piece of merchandise. Today, most stores control their inventory with computers. Each item has a code that is scanned into the computer when it arrives at the store and when it is sold. A computerized inventory makes it easier and faster to identify stock on hand, to track sales, and to determine the need for reorders.
- **Health care.** Today, doctors use many sophisticated scans to diagnose diseases. Another innovation, laser surgery, reduces the need for lengthy hospital stays. With the use of computers, surgeons can improve their skills by practicing laser or traditional surgery on simulated patients. Nurses now take temperatures very quickly with thermometers that are inserted in the patient's ear.
- **Manufacturing.** Factories rely on technology. Automakers use robotics, a system of automatic

machines, to produce vehicles. Those cars, like many products, may also have been designed on computers. Programs are used to design and test new features. Once the design is approved, engineers can print out lists of specifications and materials automatically. Computers and other technology allow products to be customized. For example, a newspaper can print more than 20 different versions of its daily edition, tailoring the news and advertising to each area or suburb.

Thinking Critically About Technology

1. What jobs do you think workers without technological skills will be able to find in the 21st century?
2. How does advanced technology save money for companies that use it? Give examples.

repeatedly performing the same task on an assembly line. Managers made all the decisions about how many appliances were made and how to judge quality.

In recent years, however, the company restructured. Workers formed small, independent teams to oversee each phase of the production of one appliance. Now Lila's team is entirely responsible for the production of one refrigerator model. Team members work together to make decisions about production, manufacture the refrigerator, oversee quality control, and solve problems. They often make suggestions to management about the product's design as well.

134   UNIT 2   Relationship Skills

Technology and Workers' Future

As her role changed, Lila learned new tasks. Suppose, however, that she had been unable to learn them. What if the company began to use machines to make appliances less expensively? What options would Lila have then?

New technology can have negative effects as well. As machines do more work that people once did, jobs are eliminated. Many companies are downsizing, or reducing the number of people they employ in order to save money. If workers are able to **retrain,** or to *learn new skills,* they are more likely to hold their jobs—or to find new ones.

DID YOU KNOW?

Texas Instruments has developed a computerized chip that is attached to a cargo shipment to monitor its progress. It uses satellite transmissions and a two-way radio. If a shipment is delayed, the chip can choose alternative transportation to keep it on schedule. It might, for example, alert a truck driver to take the shipment to a certain airline at a nearby airport. It then arranges for the cargo to be picked up at the destination airport. The system was first developed for the Pentagon, where it was called Total Asset Visibility.

Some workers who leave manufacturing take jobs in service industries. These industries do not provide products but offer services to people. For instance, when Glen lost his job in an auto parts plant, he took a job servicing cars in a garage.

The evolving workplace compels people to adapt quickly to changes. Workers continually have to upgrade their skills. Responsible employers help workers sharpen skills and learn new ones, but preparing for the job market is primarily the worker's responsibility.

Global Connections

Technology has helped spur another trend in the workplace. Telecommunications, computer links, and air travel have allowed businesses to branch out worldwide, altering how business is done.

If you examine the labels on your clothes, you can see the effects of international trade. The fabrics may be produced in one country, then sewn into garments in another country to be sold in countless others. Thanks to telecommunications and overnight shipping, businesses can now look all over the world for the least costly suppliers or materials. A computer manufacturer in England may find that orders for electronic components can be placed and filled as quickly in Asia as in the United States. The price and quality of the components are determining factors in the manufacturer's choice. Clearly, businesses must become more efficient to compete worldwide.

Many businesses have offices and factories in foreign cities as well. Positions in these global enterprises often pay well. However, these workers usually need expertise in their field, fluency in a foreign language, and the ability to work well with people from other cultures.

Skills for Getting Ahead

With all these changes in the workplace, employees have to change, too. Today, simply being available for hire is not enough to make you employable. A U.S. Department of Labor commission determined that tomorrow's workers need to develop a foundation of basic skills, thinking skills, and personal qualities.

Furthermore, the commission established five core areas of ability that workers need. Employees should understand and know how to use resources, information, systems, and technology, plus they have to possess solid interpersonal skills. These five areas are explained in **Figure 13.1.**

By developing a wide variety of skills and abilities, you will be better qualified to per-

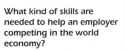
What kind of skills are needed to help an employer competing in the world economy?

CHAPTER 13   *Skills for Career Success*   **135**

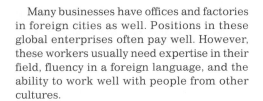

DID YOU KNOW?

How important is international commerce to the United States? The American company Otis Elevator sells 80 percent of its elevators to other nations. Several Japanese car manufacturers have plants in the United States: Honda produces Accords in Ohio; Toyota makes Camrys in Kentucky. Like other American car manufacturers, Ford makes international cars, with parts from Ohio, Mexico, Germany, France, and Belgium.

Figure 13.1

Topics on pp. 136-137:
- Basic Work Skills
- Useful Skills for the Future
- Thinking Skills

Checking Comprehension

✓ Why are reading, writing, math, and communication considered basic skills?" *It's difficult to gain other skills without them.*

✓ What percent of the workday is not spent communicating? *About 25 percent.*

✓ What skills are needed for solving problems? *Ability to find information, get needed help, make observations, weigh evidence, draw conclusions.*

SPECIAL NEEDS *Strategies*

Inefficient Readers. Arrange the class into five groups. Assign each group one of the five "useful abilities" in Figure 13.1. Ask groups to decide which of the basic and thinking skills described on these pages are needed for their assigned ability. Have each group report to the class. Note the overlap of needed skills.

▶▶▶ Useful Abilities in Tomorrow's Workplace

Skill	How It Is Used
• **Managing Resources** Allocating time, money, materials, space, and staff.	Creating schedules and budgets; storing and distributing supplies; evaluating the skills and performance of coworkers.
• **Using Information** Acquiring, organizing, and evaluating data.	Finding data and information; keeping files and records; understanding information presented in spoken, written, graphic, and multimedia forms; using computers to process information.
• **Understanding Systems** Understanding social, organizational, and technological systems; monitoring and correcting performance; designing or improving systems.	Organizing information and resources; working with others toward a common goal; working with various kinds of technological systems.
• **Using Technology** Selecting equipment and tools; applying technology to specific tasks; maintaining equipment; troubleshooting problems.	Using and repairing equipment; using computers as tools; continuing to learn about technology as it changes.
• **Developing Interpersonal Skills** Working in a team; teaching, leading, and negotiating; serving clients and customers; working well with people from culturally diverse backgrounds.	Completing a project with a group; helping others learn their jobs; guiding employees' work; satisfying the needs of clients and customers; appreciating cultural differences as assets.

form in whatever career you choose. What's more, these skills will also be useful to you in other areas of your life.

Basic Skills

Basic skills are just what you might expect—the fundamentals that rank first in importance. People who do not acquire basic skills lessen their chances of finding a job and getting promoted. Fortunately, you have the opportunity to improve these skills every day—right in school. The basic skills that employers want include:

- **Reading.** Reading is as critical at work as it is in daily life. You will need to understand letters, manuals, reports, schedules, and information to do your job correctly. For example, Mariko reads medical journals and product literature in order to keep up in her job with a health care company.
- **Writing.** Despite a greater reliance on electronic communication, people still communicate through the written word. Whether filling out applications and forms, drafting letters and memos, or writing reports, you will express your ideas through writing. In fact, an employer's first impression of you may come from a letter of application and a résumé—two forms of written communication.

136   UNIT 2   Relationship Skills

Read this to the class: *Joel plans to be a truck driver. He was surprised when his counselor recommended he continue taking math and writing classes his last two years in high school.* Ask: Why might the counselor make this suggestion? Lead students to see Joel will need both skills for this job—to figure mileage, estimate cargo weight, write reports to supervisiors—and if he wants to advance or change careers.

- **Mathematics.** While calculators and computer software make performing computations easier, you need basic math skills to use these tools properly. Many jobs require math skills every day—counting change, tallying sales figures, creating budgets, and understanding charts and graphs. Math is needed in any job that uses technology. When Jaime started his own interior design business, he soon found that math skills were essential. He needed to estimate the cost of jobs, pay bills, calculate paychecks, write contracts, balance his books, and prepare his income taxes.
- **Communication.** No matter what the job, you need to be able to communicate to do it well. About 75 percent of an average working day is spent communicating: expressing ideas, dealing with people over the telephone, giving presentations, and exchanging information.

Thinking Skills

If you're a sports fan, you know that a successful athlete has more than just good physical skills. An athlete must be able to concentrate, take initiative, and make lightning-fast decisions.

Likewise, success on the job takes more than basic technical skills. Strong intellectual abilities are at least as valuable. These thinking skills and strategies, which you are developing right now, can help you succeed in the job market:

- **Learning ability.** Training is usually part of any new job; absorbing information and following instructions are skills that help you learn the ropes. Moreover, you are likely to keep learning as long as you are on the job.
- **Problem solving.** Creative problem solving is a valuable asset, no matter what your career. Knowing how to

Upgrading your skills is an ongoing process throughout your career.

figure out solutions—and knowing where to find help when you can't—will help you in many work situations.

- **Reasoning.** To solve problems, you need the ability to make observations, weigh evidence, and draw conclusions. Employers value workers who are skilled at inferring, deducting, and applying what they have learned.
- **Decision making.** The six-step, decision-making process you learned in Chapter 5 is useful in many job situations, such as planning tasks, managing time, and deciding what resources are required to get a job done.

Character

As you learned in Chapter 3, a strong character is founded on positive values. The qualities of character apply as much in the

■ **No More Writing?** Ask students if they think advances in communication technology, such as E-mail, have reduced the need for writing skills. *(Communication)*

■ **Do We Need This?** Point out that teens often think they don't need to know what they are learning in school. Invite students to identify a course they consider irrelevant to their lives. Challenge them to name basic skills and thinking skills they might strengthen by taking this course. *(Critical Thinking)*

RETEACHING

■ **No Skills Required?** Challenge small groups to list jobs that do not require the basic skills discussed here. As they share their ideas with the class, have them consider: What is the outlook for these jobs? What are the chances for advancement for workers who possess no other skills?

FAMILY AND COMMUNITY OUTREACH

Point out that a growing number of people are working out of their homes. Ask students to help you identify people in the community who own a home-based business and use computers extensively, or who "telecommute," using equipment such as a modem or fax machine. Invite these people to speak to the class, perhaps in a panel, about technological and other skills needed for home-based employment.

MORE ABOUT *Skills and Knowledge*

Only about half of the public school graduates in the United States take more than the minimum high school requirements in math and science, yet the need for advanced skills is growing. According to the United States Department of Labor, in 1984, only 6 percent of workers needed to be familiar with advanced calculus, algebra, and statistics. In 2000, 13 percent of workers will need this knowledge.

Topics on pp. 138-140:
- **Character**
- **Interpersonal Skills**
- **Networking and Mentors**
- **Balance**

Checking Comprehension

✓ What aspects of character help employees at work? *Accountability, taking work seriously, high self-esteem, positive attitude, cooperation, initiative, discipline.*

✓ Why are good manners important in the workplace? *Needed for employees to get along with each other and get work done.*

FAMILY AND COMMUNITY OUTREACH

Encourage students to develop or strengthen a network for the future. Have each student identify and contact at least two people they know who work for companies that interest her or him. Have students talk with each contact about potential jobs in that field. They might set up informational interviews. (See chapter 7.)

SPECIAL NEEDS *Strategies*

Attention Deficit. Ask students to name things that could interfere with job performance, such as distractions from coworkers or trouble organizing tasks. Invite students to share strategies they use to cope successfully with such challenges.

No matter where you work, being able to understand and cooperate with a variety of people is an asset.

workplace as they do in other aspects of your life. For instance, employers look for workers who are responsible and honest. Arriving at work on time, taking your job seriously, and being accountable for your work prove to employers that you can be trusted.

People with high self-esteem and a positive attitude are more likely to work well with others. These workers are more likely than those with low self-esteem to ask for help when they need it. Employers also want workers who take initiative without being told what to do. These employers are better problem solvers and decision makers. Finally, employers also want workers who have the self-discipline to complete their tasks.

Using Interpersonal Skills

Once you graduate from high school, you are likely to spend about one-third of your time at work. Will you choose the people you work with during those hours? Probably not. This means that you need to be able to get along with all sorts of people, including those who are very different from you. The inability to get along with others on the job is a common reason why people are fired.

Working relationships can be an asset. They can also be destructive. How you use interpersonal skills to manage relationships on the job makes the difference. Think about how the following interpersonal skills can be put to work for you:

- **Tact.** Working with others may require instructing and correcting them. A tactful person finds ways to say things, even criticism, without hurting others' feelings or attacking them personally.
- **Courtesy.** Courtesy smooths interactions. Employees who show courtesy to customers and clients build repeat business for employers.
- **Respect.** Recognizing the skills and ideas of coworkers builds positive feelings. People are more creative and productive when they feel that they and their contributions are valued.
- **Patience.** Showing patience encourages others to develop valued skills. Be patient with yourself, too, as you try new tasks.
- **Fairness.** Give credit to others for their effort. Accept no more credit or responsibility for something than you are due.
- **Sociability.** *The quality of being friendly and enjoying other people's company,* or **sociability,** is also important at work. Of course, social skills must be applied to getting the job done, not just to finding ways of having a good time at work.

Ted needed these skills to deal with a problem at work. He was part of a team of five coworkers. One team member, Cherie, was able to do excellent work, but she rarely participated in planning meetings. She was re-

Focus on Interpersonal Skills

Arrange the class into four or six groups. Ask half the groups to review Chapter 8, "Getting Along with Others," and half to review Chapter 9, "Communicating Effectively." Have each group write four to six guidelines for the workplace, based on the skills described in its chapter. As groups share their guidelines with the class, create a master list on the board. Encourage students to compare the master list with the skills listed on page 138.

served and preferred to work independently. Parts of her work often had to be redone by other team members to make it useful for their projects. This slowed the entire effort. Others on the team resented the extra work and were troubled by the added stress that resulted for them.

As team leader, Ted had to do something. He arranged a time to talk to Cherie when others were not present. "I was looking at the research that you submitted yesterday, Cherie. It's very impressive and must have taken hours to prepare." After saying this, Ted listened with interest as Cherie described her difficulty in organizing the information. Ted went on, "I hope we can use all your research. It looks as though we'll only need about half of it. I hope you didn't do all that work for nothing." As they talked further, Ted skillfully guided Cherie toward seeing how she could increase her effectiveness as a team player.

Finding Assistance

Just as you make an effort to support others, they can give support in return. Finding a job and building job skills are easier when you develop certain relationships.

Managing Your Life

Developing Effective Work Habits

Good work habits are vital to any successful career. A résumé and interview may secure you a job, but day-to-day performance determines how you fare in the long run. Here are a few basic habits that apply to employees everywhere:

- **Arrive on time.** Employers and coworkers count on your prompt arrival. Determine how much time it takes to get ready for work and to get there. Allow a few minutes for the unexpected.
- **Follow work schedules.** Take only the amount of time established for breaks and meals. If for some reason you need more than the allotted time, arrange to make it up.
- **Earn trust.** Employees earn trust by working as scheduled, completing tasks on time, and using equipment responsibly.
- **Follow directions carefully.** People work more efficiently when tasks are done in established ways. If you have ideas for improvement, clear them with your supervisor first.
- **Be honest with your employer.** Everyone makes mistakes at times. Whatever happens, take responsibility for your own mistakes, and give credit to others for their successes.
- **Respond well to criticism.** Use criticism, even if not tactfully delivered, as an opportunity to correct mistakes and improve performance.

- **Have a positive attitude.** Your ability to see obstacles as challenges and to expect good things from others can set the tone for your coworkers. Employers value this can-do spirit.
- **Be pleasant and cooperative.** People care more about their jobs when they care about their coworkers. Avoid gossip and demonstrate that you are a team player.
- **Present an acceptable appearance.** Dressing appropriately and practicing good hygiene habits shows consideration for others.

Applying the Principles

1. What might be some obstacles to maintaining good work habits? How could an employee work around them?
2. Give three examples of how a habit that helps you succeed in school can be applied to the workplace.
3. How might practicing good work habits lead you to improve habits in other areas of your life?

CHAPTER 13 **Skills for Career Success** 139

139

Review

■ **Chapter Review.** Use the contents of the Chapter Review page to help students review concepts, think critically, and apply their knowledge.

■ **Study Guide.** Have students complete the Study Guide for Chapter 13 on p. 45 of the Student Workbook.

■ **Entering the Workplace.** Ask students to imagine they are starting a job they hope to someday have. Have them write a paragraph describing the technology they anticipate using and the skills and qualities they will need.

Evaluation

■ **Chapter Test.** Use the reproducible chapter test provided in the Teacher's Classroom Resources or create your own test using the *Testmaker Software.*

■ **Alternative Assessment.** Explain to groups that each is in charge of hiring personnel for a large company. They must find ways to determine whether applicants have the basic skills, thinking skills, character, and interpersonal skills to be effective, valued employees. Give groups time to develop a means of assessing these qualities. Then have them share their ideas with the class.

■ **A Slice of Life.** Have each student draw a circle graph (pie chart) with sections showing the skills and knowledge employees need in today's workplace, as indicated in the chapter, plus any others they wish to include. Each section should be assigned a percentage of the whole circle.

Networking

People often call on others they know to help them find jobs and to improve their job performance. **Networking** means *making contacts with others to exchange job information.* Many leads for jobs come through such contacts as relatives, friends, neighbors, teachers, counselors, and people with whom you have worked.

Once on the job, people can use networking to do their jobs well. For instance, Jill, a first-year preschool teacher, was having a discipline problem with one of her students. None of her approaches led the child to better behavior. She called one of her former instructors, a child psychologist, for advice.

Mentors

A **mentor** is *someone who acts as a teacher and a guide.* Often a mentor takes a personal interest in someone and gives support and advice based on experience. Many people who have succeeded in their jobs have had mentors who counseled them along the way. Most mentors work in the same field as the person they are advising. Others can be teachers, counselors, family members, or friends.

Some schools and communities provide mentoring programs. Teens with specific career interests meet professionals in those fields. These people answer questions and explain aspects of their jobs. Sometimes these mentoring programs last a year or more. Such programs help teens make career decisions. They can also introduce teens to people who might help when teens enter the work force.

Finding Balance in Life

Through experience, people have learned that life needs balance. Good health and happiness depend on a successful blend of work, family, and personal life. People need time for each of these. They also need management techniques that prevent one aspect of life from infringing on another.

You might think that balance in life is an adult issue. Often it is. Busy couples struggle to find time for jobs as well as children and leisure activities. People carry work stress home. Personal problems sometimes cause ineffectiveness on the job. These are typical adult problems, but teens can have them too.

In what ways can balance be an issue for teens? Too many hours on a job can interfere with schoolwork and social activities. Too much fun can also mean that schoolwork doesn't get done. Spending too much time with friends can reduce the support of family and cause lack of attention to responsibilities. Even an overemphasis on study and work can get in the way of finding time to relax and enjoy activities that allow you to refresh yourself so that work can be tackled again.

When you recognize the need for balance, you are more likely to take steps to achieve it. You will be better prepared for managing as an adult if you work toward balancing your life right now. You need time for work, family, and yourself. During the course of a week, try to include time for each in a reasonable proportion. If you tend to be more focused on work than play, or vice versa, strive for a better balance. Throughout this text, you will find ideas for managing this need and for helping others you are close to manage as well.

Preparing for Tomorrow

Your future success in a career will be affected by the preparations you make before you ever enter the work world. Many of the skills that you will eventually use on the job are the same ones you use at home and in school. Now is the time to polish them. Practice improving them in your everyday life, and they will be in good condition for use when you make the transition from school to work.

MORE ABOUT Preparing for Work

These nonfiction books are related to this chapter: *Work Ethic,* by Jay Schleifer (Rosen, 1991) and *The Pursuit of Wow!: Every Person's Guide to Topsy-Turvy Times,* by Tom Peters (Vintage, 1994). Students might choose one to read and share what they learn with the class.

Chapter 13 Review

Reviewing the Facts

1. Describe the two main reasons the workplace has changed in recent years.
2. What five abilities will employers look for now and in the future?
3. List four basic skills needed for the workplace.
4. What four thinking skills do employers find valuable in workers?
5. Identify three interpersonal skills that employers seek in workers.
6. What is a mentor?

Thinking Critically

1. What are some ways you could use your interactions with others today to help you when you enter the workforce?
2. Suppose that you are an experienced salesperson. How could you use networking to help you get a new job?

Applying Your Knowledge

1. **Creating Ads.** Scan the help-wanted section of a newspaper, noting the different kinds of skills and qualities employers are seeking in various fields. Write a "seeking employment" ad that highlights your own skills and abilities.
2. **Practicing an Interview.** With a partner, act out a situation in which you are interviewing a job candidate. What kinds of questions will you ask? What abilities will you look for? Would you hire him or her for the position? Why or why not? After you finish the interview, switch positions and have the other person interview you for the same job.

Making Connections

1. **Mathematics.** Government figures show that in 1990, the service industry provided 84.4 million jobs. Manufacturing, construction, and other types of goods production accounted for 25 million jobs. Projected figures for the year 2005 are 107.4 million for service jobs and 25.2 million for production. Show the increase in each of these industries as percentages. If increases occur at the same rate, how many jobs will each industry provide in the year 2020?
2. **Economy.** A growing percentage of the population is over age 65. With a classmate, develop a list of jobs that might be in greater demand due to this increasing older population.

Building Your Portfolio

Developing a Résumé

Jot down a personal profile of all the skills, strengths, and experience that you have. Be sure to include your education, your extracurricular activities, your hobbies, and any jobs you have held. Using a guide from a textbook, encyclopedia, or a book on résumé writing, create your own résumé in a standard format. You may want to include a section describing what sort of career or specific job you would like. Type your completed résumé, and add it to your portfolio activity file.

ANSWERS TO REVIEWING THE FACTS

1. The increasing use of technology and the shift to a global economy.
2. The ability to manage resources, information, systems, and technology and the demonstration of strong interpersonal skills.
3. Reading, writing, math, and communication skills.
4. Learning ability, problem solving, reasoning, decision making.
5. Any three of these or other appropriate responses: tact, courtesy, respect, patience, fairness, sociability.
6. Someone who acts as a teacher and a guide.

ANSWERS TO THINKING CRITICALLY

1. Possible response: By practicing interpersonal skills with family members, you learn to accept responsibility, to solve problems, and to get along with others.
2. Contact former coworkers who are now employed elsewhere to see if they know of any openings.

Unit Preview

Unit 3 focuses on ways that families meet their members' needs and ways that teens can help strengthen their own families. The unit helps students understand better the changes that often occur in families, such as moving and divorce, along with problems that affect both families and individuals, such as divorce and substance abuse. Chapters in this unit guide students in establishing new friendships and in being responsible in their dating relationships. The unit ends by exploring career possibilities for students who enjoy working with people.

Content Development

Use these chapters to reinforce the following themes:

Content Strands	Chapters
Career Exploration	20
Citizenship/	
Leadership	15
Communication	14, 15, 18, 19
Decision Making	17, 19
Health and Safety	17, 19
Managing	
Resources	15, 16, 18
Personal	
Development	14-19
Technology	18

Unit Motivator

■ **Change and Consistency.** Encourage groups to create two lists under these headings: Ways Families Are Changing and Ways Families Have Not Changed. As groups share their ideas with the rest of the class, make two master lists on the board. Ask students what conclusions they might draw as they compare the lists.

142

JOURNAL WRITING

Possible topics for student journals:

- What helpful skill or attitude have you learned from a family member?
- How might you get your family involved in an activity that you all could enjoy?
- Who or what has helped your family cope with a new situation?

- What sources of help are available if you needed guidance in dealing with a serious problem?
- What would convince teens to be more responsible in their dating relationships?
- Would a career that involves helping people suit you?

Families and Friendships

Chapters

143

FHA Activities

The following activities can be used with your FHA group or as public relations strategies:

■ **Family Fun.** Plan a family night, such as playing miniature golf, skating, picnicking at a park, sorting donations at a food pantry, or sprucing up the school flower beds. If an admission charge is involved, the chapter could pay for students who bring at least one family member.

■ **Help!** Have students create a directory of agencies that can help families facing changes or problems. Include the kinds of services offered, phone numbers and addresses, any costs or limitations for services, and a map with the agency locations marked. Distribute the directory schoolwide and leave copies at community libraries.

■ **The Buddy System.** Assign chapter members to each new student at the school. The members' main goals will be to help the student meet new friends, find classes, and learn school procedures.

Unit Closure

REVIEW

Future Families. Have students imagine that they have established their own families and have at least one child. Ask them how they will help prepare that child to deal with the challenges of life. What specific family activities and discussions do they think would help the child handle future relationships successfully?

EVALUATION

■ **Unit Test.** Have students complete the unit test in the Teacher's Classroom Resources.

■ **Testmaker Software.** You may wish to design a unit test using the *Testmaker Software*.

COOPERATIVE LEARNING

Family Versus Friends. Often both family and friends vie for a teen's time. Choosing can produce pressures. Arrange the class into partnerships in which they think of one specific example of such a situation. Have pairs combine into groups of four to discuss the examples and agree on appropriate actions for each example. After a spokesperson for each group reports to the class, have the class agree on four or five guidelines that could help teens manage when activities with family and friends conflict.

Chapter 14

FOCUS

Chapter Overview

Chapter 14 describes different family structures and styles. It explains how all families, regardless of form, meet the developmental needs of their members, and builds appreciation of families.

Motivators

■ **Defining Family.** Write "To me, a family is. . ." on the board and ask several volunteers to complete the sentence. Add their responses to the board. Point out the variety in their definitions.

■ **Growing Up.** Ask students to think of their earliest memories. (They may share these if they like.) Ask how many included family members. Tell students this is so because families have great impact on individuals.

Objectives

Discuss the chapter objectives on this page. Remind students that the objectives focus on important chapter concepts.

Vocabulary

Tell students that one meaning of *nurture* is "nourish." Ask them to name some ways in which the term *nourish* might relate to a family. What kinds of nourishment can a family provide?

Chapter 14

The Role of Families

Terms to Learn

- adoptive families
- blended family
- extended family
- foster families
- nuclear family
- nurture
- sibling

Objectives

This chapter will help you to:

- Recognize **different family forms.**
- Assess **the impact of current social trends on family life.**
- Identify **the functions that families fill for individuals.**
- Explain **the importance of strong families to society.**

CHAPTER RESOURCES

Student Workbook

Study Guide, pp. 49-50

Activity, *Family Plans*, p. 51

Teacher's Classroom Resources

Lesson Plan, p. 18

Decision Making, *Meeting Family Expectations*, p. 11

Extension #23, *Television and the Family*, p. 29

Extension #24, *Sharing Household Responsibilities*, p. 30

Life Skills, *Appreciating Family Differences*, p. 26

Personal Development, *Birth Order*, pp. 21-22

Transparency 13, *What Is a Family?*

Chapter 14 Test, pp. 33-34

Performance Assessment, *Life in My Family*, p. 35

Reteaching, *Types and Functions of Families*, p. 20

See Also:

ABCNews InterActive™ Videodiscs

Nine-year-old Lauren tugged excitedly at her older brother's sleeve. "Look, Beau! I want to show you something."

Beau let his sister lead him through clusters of relatives at the grade school's family night. On one wall hung a row of large posterboard rectangles, each one entitled "My Family Tree." Beau recognized the project that he had helped Lauren complete the week before.

Thinking back, Beau decided that he may have appreciated the assignment more than Lauren did. He had learned so much about his family, including the names of his great-grandparents and the location of the village where they were born. The project had sparked memories, too. Older relatives recalled stories from younger days as they helped Lauren fill in names and dates.

Beau was impressed at how families had changed. He couldn't imagine being one of eight children and marrying at age 19, as his great-uncle had. Beau understood now when older people viewed younger ones with wonder and even concern—their lifestyles were so different. Still, he felt, they were mostly alike. When his grandmother chuckled over her parents' dismay at the "shocking" dress she had ordered from a catalog, Beau recalled his stepmother's reaction to his latest hairstyle.

Lauren held up one corner of her project. "See? Mrs. Abel gave me two gold stars. I think one ought to be yours."

Beau grinned with pride. "Thanks, Lori." He hoped that he remembered this when someone asked *him* for stories for a family tree.

Why Study Families?

Who makes up your family? For Melanie, it includes herself and her parents. Brent would name his mother, stepfather, stepsister, and baby half-brother as his family.

Regardless of size or structure, all families share certain characteristics. By learning about families—what they do, how they are structured, how members interact—you can understand the influence that families have and how you can contribute to family strength.

Types of Families

If you compare a current television show about families to a program from the 1950s or 1960s, you may be surprised at the differences. Due to recent trends and changing attitudes, a wider variety of family forms has become common in society.

Families are too important to be taken for granted. Understanding them and making them strong brings many rewards to individuals and society. Why is this true?

CHAPTER 14   The Role of Families   145

TEACH

Topic on p. 145:
• **Studying Families**

Checking Comprehension

✓ Why should you study families? *Learn about their influence and how to make them stronger.*

Activities

■ **Families on Television.** With the class, survey the situation comedies on television. List programs that involve families and identify the different family forms portrayed. Which ones reflect real life? *(Observation)*

ENRICHMENT

■ **In the Eyes.** Have students ask several young children, teens, and adults for their definition of family. Have students record the definitions, then write a short report comparing views of family from different age groups. Have them note the main qualities or focal points of each group's definition.

CROSS-CURRICULAR ACTIVITY
Language Arts

Have students look through books of quotations for those relating to families. Ask them to find one quotation they agree with and one that they don't. Have students meet in small groups to exchange and discuss quotations as well as their interpretations.

MORE ABOUT Studying Families

Because the "family" is not a subject in the same sense as English, math, and history, students may wonder why they are studying it. The condition of families in this country, however, has weakened. Families are the backbone of society, yet many face destructive problems today. Students may not be aware that concern for families has spurred interest by government, the media, and educators. Hope is high that by studying the family, young people can learn how to make families—and society—stronger.

Checking Comprehension

✓ Why are there so many definitions for the word *family*? *Definitions vary according to personal experience.*

✓ Are single adults part of a family? *Yes, the one they grew up in.*

✓ What is a foster child? *Child who lives with another family for short time.*

✓ What is the "sandwich" generation? *Middle-aged adults who care for aging parents and own children.*

SPECIAL NEEDS *Strategies*

Inefficient Organizers. Ask pairs of students to draw family trees that show how a blended family might be created. Have them begin by drawing family trees for two nuclear families, giving each family member a name. Then have them draw a family tree that includes one parent and some of the children from each family. Ask students to write a description of the various relationships, using correct terms.

Family Forms

For many years—and for many people today—the term *family* meant a **nuclear family,** *a husband and wife and their children.* Other people expand the definition to include the **extended family**—*a family group consisting of parents, children, and other close relatives.* This includes aunts, uncles, cousins, and grandparents. People are increasingly likely to encounter—and become part of—other types of families as well. For example:

- **Blended family.** A **blended family** consists of *a husband and a wife, at least one of whom has at least one child from a previous relationship.* Children become stepchildren to the new spouse, who becomes their stepparent. Any children born to the husband and wife are half-brothers or half-sisters to the others.
- **Single-parent families.** A growing number of families are headed by one parent. Some single parents were never married. Others have lost a spouse through death.

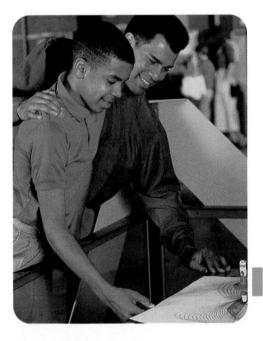

Most single-parent families, however, are created by separation and divorce. The parent who does not live with the children, of course, is still a part of their family, even if some of his or her rights have been legally terminated.

- **Adoptive families.** In **adoptive families,** *one or more children not born into a family are made permanent members of that family by law.* Families may adopt children because they can have none of their own or because they want to give a loving home to a child without one. Occasionally, a child is adopted by relatives.
- **Foster families.** **Foster families** are formed when *a family assumes temporary, legal responsibility for one or more children.* Some foster children have been removed from their homes by state welfare agencies due to abuse, neglect, or other family problems. They return when agency officials are convinced that the situation is safe and healthful for them. Sometimes foster children are available for adoption and may be adopted by their foster families.
- **Couples.** Some married couples choose not to have children.

Trends Affecting Families

Family form is just one aspect of family life that is affected by social trends. As you read about some of the other changes occurring in society, ask yourself what impact each one might have on family relationships and resources of time, energy, and money.

- **Birth rate.** In 1800, the average family included seven children. By the early 1990s, that number had dropped to two. To limit expenses or establish careers, many married couples remain childless or postpone having children for several years.

Just like people, families come in different shapes and sizes. The form of the family doesn't really matter. Just like people, it's what's inside that counts.

DID YOU KNOW?

In a study of 715 adoptive families, the Search Institute in Minneapolis found that most teens who were adopted as infants suffered no ill effects on their mental health. Eighty-six percent were glad they were born; 79 percent had a good sense of self; 72 percent felt a sense of direction. Only 11 percent were confused as to their identity. The teens did best in families that treated adoption as a fact of life. Teens' attachment to their parents was similar whether or not they and their parents were of the same race.

Managing Your Life

Building Relationships with Older People

When large extended families lived under the same roof, teens had regular contact with older relatives. Today's smaller homes and greater family mobility have made this less likely (although the trend is changing). Limited contact can make both age groups feel they have little in common with each other. This mistaken belief prevents teens and older adults from enjoying a most important family resource—each other. Here are some ideas for including older relatives in your life:

- **Listen to them.** Older people have lived lives that some teens can barely imagine. Memories of even ordinary, daily existence 30 or 40 years ago can make fascinating stories. Their years of experience often give them a reasoned, balanced outlook on life's problems, which can help teens see situations in a different light.
- **Learn from their skills.** Older people can pass on valuable skills. A grandmother who sews by hand can show a teen how to alter and personalize purchased clothing. A grandfather accustomed to dealing with others in person instead of by telephone or E-mail can demonstrate good communication skills.
- **Offer to help, but don't insist.** Older people don't like being treated as helpless any more than you would. If you see that an older person is having trouble with a task, ask if you can help.

- **Respect their tastes and wishes.** Older people grew up when some ideas of what is enjoyable and appropriate were quite different from your own.

Remember that older adults also benefit from meaningful exchanges with teens. By listening to older adults, by learning from them, and by treating them with respect, teens remind older people that they still have something to contribute. These actions let older people know that they are valued. That's a feeling that crosses all generational lines.

Applying the Principles

1. Why do you think teens and older relatives sometimes have mistaken beliefs about each other? How can these be corrected?
2. Why do you think older people, especially those who can't get out very often, enjoy the company of teens so much?
3. What could you gain from contact with older people?
4. A friend complains that her grandfather always argues about the music she listens to. What advice might you give her?

- **Women in the workplace.** Most women now work for wages, outside the home and in home offices. This has increased the number of dual-career families.
- **Increasing lifespan.** People are living longer, but not always independently. More and more middle-aged adults are now the primary caregivers for both their aging parents and their own children. Others help support their parents financially. The people who take care of generations on each side of them are often referred to as the "sandwich generation."

- **Mobility.** People are more likely now than ever to change their residence. Some families move several times. They may leave an area where the economy is faltering for one where it is thriving. The trend toward an international economy increases job opportunities in other countries. Improving transportation technology allows people to travel more easily.
- **Divorce.** Once a rarity, divorce is now almost as common as marriage. If divorce rates hold steady, one-half of all current marriages will be legally dissolved.

CHAPTER 14   The Role of Families   147

MORE ABOUT Cultural Differences

Often the role of caretaker for those in the "sandwich generation" falls upon a woman's shoulders. For whatever reasons, women seem to be the first ones to take on the duties of caring for others. People in this position can become heavily burdened with the needs of others. They may be pressured to let many of their own needs go. Sharing the load with people in this position helps. Teens who take on responsibility at home and who participate in the lives of older family members help make things easier for everyone.

Topics on pp. 148-150:

- **How Families Meet Individuals' Needs**
- **Passing On Cultural Heritage**
- **Teens' Contribution to Family Strength**

Checking Comprehension

✓ Do children help meet parents' emotional needs? *Yes, by returning the love and affection they receive.*

✓ How does a family guide moral growth? *By teaching children values and responsibility.*

✓ Why is it important that teens show other family members they care? *It's a form of emotional support.*

BALANCING
WORK AND FAMILY

Have students read "Homework and Working at Home." As students share their responses to Suppose That, encourage them to think of ways to compensate for the disadvantages of each arrangement.

MULTICULTURAL *Perspectives*

Invite foreign exchange students to speak to the class about family forms in their own cultures. Draw comparisons to families in the United States. What can students learn from this information?

BALANCING Work AND Family

Homework and Working at Home

More and more people today are working from their homes. A home office may be either an extension of a separate workplace or business headquarters in its own right.

For students, this is nothing new. School-age children and teens have long been bringing their work home with them. Many have set up study areas—home "offices"—in their rooms or in other parts of the home.

Home workers, both professionals and students, face special challenges. Interruptions—from telephones, neighbors, and other family members—tend to be frequent. Distractions may be more numerous in the home than in a school or business setting. Conflicts over space and privacy can also arise.

Families can help a home worker manage more effectively by adopting a few rules of simple courtesy. For example:

- **Keep the work space as the worker wants it.** People work more efficiently when supplies and equipment can be located where expected.
- **Respect the worker's schedule.** Adhering to a schedule is part of good time management. Many people are more productive when they can work or study at those hours that they have set aside for accomplishing tasks. Staying on schedule is especially important if coworkers or fellow students are relying on them or if their project has a deadline.
- **Be considerate about telephone use.** Some home workers use the family phone as a

business phone. Students also may need to contact other students, libraries, or other sources of information. Family members can help by keeping calls short. They can also learn to take accurate messages when the student or worker is unavailable.

- **Follow rules for using equipment.** In some families, work- and school-related technology—computers, faxes, and copiers—is reserved strictly for that purpose. In others, family members have access to these machines when not in use.
- **Provide a quiet atmosphere.** Avoid creating loud, unnecessary noise during business or study hours. Keep the volume down on music and the television. Limit distractions.
- **Help out when possible.** Mailing a package for a home worker or bringing a student a needed reference book not only helps them complete their work but also shows emotional support.

Suppose That . . .

You want to set up a study area in your home. You decide that the most likely locations are your bedroom, which you share with a sibling; a corner of the living room, which your family uses for entertainment; and a separate room in an unheated, unfinished basement. Identify possible advantages and disadvantages of each arrangement. Select one as the best choice and give reasons for your selection.

Functions of Families

Whatever their form, families have existed throughout history and in every society because they serve a most important purpose. As you know, people develop in five areas: physically, emotionally, intellectually, socially, and morally. The function of families is to **nur-**ture each member, or *to promote development in all areas*, by meeting needs throughout a lifetime.

Meeting Physical Needs

Families supply members with physical necessities like food, clothing, and shelter. Families also provide health care to sick or

MORE ABOUT Family and Work

Some families work together to run a business. Discuss ways that working in a family business might strengthen—and strain—family relationships.

DID YOU KNOW?

In patriarchal societies, the male head of a family makes the major decisions; in a matriarchal society, the female. In societies where neither is predominant, the individuals' personality and cultural background influence their roles.

injured members. They must tend to the ill at home and also seek professional care when necessary.

Families protect members from accidents and other dangers also. In the Bashir family, for example, the adults set rules for the children to keep them safe and to teach them responsible behavior. Fourteen-year-old Armik allows only people he knows into the home. Three-year-old Anwar picks up his toys from the floor when he is finished playing. In these ways, all family members help ensure the physical well-being of others.

Promoting Emotional Growth

Families nurture emotional growth as well. By showing love and acceptance, they help members feel emotionally secure. This is the basis for a positive self-image and high self-esteem.

Families can also be an emotional refuge when people are tired, hurt, or disappointed. In families where acceptance is unconditional, members know they can find a sympathetic, nonjudgmental ear when they need to talk about something troubling them.

Families also teach members how to express emotions. After describing a frustrating day at work, for instance, Mrs. Santo told her family, "I just can't seem to get over it. I'm going to take a long walk." What might her example teach her family about dealing with emotions?

As with meeting physical needs, all family members help determine how a family fulfills emotional needs. When parents show love for their children, for example, their own need for affection is met by the children's show of love in return. A sister feels satisfaction in teaching a younger brother a new skill, and the brother gains self-esteem in learning it. A teen notices when a parent is under pressure and offers an idea that might help.

Shaping Social Development

Families also guide members on how to behave toward others. Basic social skills, such as sharing and communicating, are first learned in the family, then carried over into outside relationships. Sometimes this is done directly, as when a parent instructs a child who is going to a birthday party to say thank you. More often, learning social skills occurs indirectly, through example. A child might overhear an older sibling talk on the telephone or accompany a parent to exchange a purchase at a store. Everything the child hears and observes in the process—words, tone of voice, attitude, and actions—helps form his or her idea of appropriate behavior toward other people.

Preserving Cultural Heritage

Part of helping children grow socially is passing on the family's cultural heritage. Families who value their history encourage younger members to carry on traditions, rituals, and beliefs. For example, William learned about his Cherokee

Many families have a rich cultural heritage that they want to preserve. They do so by passing the cultural history on to young family members.

CHAPTER 14   The Role of Families   149

Activities

■ **Falling Short.** Assign groups to discuss possible reasons why some families have trouble meeting their members' physical, emotional, or intellectual needs. Also ask them to suggest solutions. Have them take notes on their ideas for class discussion. (*Problem Solving*)

RETEACHING

■ **Runs Both Ways.** Have groups list all the ways they can think of that family members meet each others' physical, emotional, and intellectual needs. Have them mark items as the responsibility of parents, of children, or of both. Discuss their lists in class, reminding students that meeting needs is a mutual effort. (*Relationship*)

FAMILY AND COMMUNITY OUTREACH

To demonstrate how unique families are and how much they have to offer, ask several parents to come to class and teach a skill to students. This might range from origami paper folding, to speaking Russian, to filling out an income tax form.

MULTICULTURAL *Perspectives*

Students can help share and preserve their heritage in a class book. Each student might contribute stories, recipes, and copies of family photos that reflect cultural background.

REAL-LIFE APPLICATION

Read this to students: *Over the last four generations, members of Dustin's family have married people from a number of different cultures. Dustin doesn't think he has a clear cultural heritage.* Ask: What would you say to Dustin about this? Lead students to see that Dustin's heritage includes the traditions and customs the family has developed over the years, regardless of origin.

Review

■ **Chapter Review.** Use the contents of the Chapter Review page to help students review concepts, think critically, and apply their knowledge.

■ **Study Guide.** Have students complete the Study Guide for Chapter 14 on p. 49 of the Student Workbook.

■ **Valuable Actions.** Have students list five things they think all families value. Have them select one value and ask: If this were most important for a family, how might it affect the way it fulfilled its functions? Ask for specific examples. Discuss in class.

Evaluation

■ **Chapter Test.** Use the reproducible chapter test provided in the Teacher's Classroom Resources or create your own test using the *Testmaker Software*.

■ **Alternative Assessment.** Have groups write and perform a scene illustrating how a family fosters physical, emotional, intellectual, social, and moral growth. Each group might portray a different family structure. After each group has presented its scene, have other students try to identify how its family promoted growth in each area.

CLOSE

■ **Family Focus.** Ask students why they think four chapters of this textbook focus on families. Why is it valuable to study families? Help students recognize the family's pivotal role in shaping development.

heritage from his grandfather, who related the folklore of the people and the meaning of their customs. Sharing a cultural past in this way gives family members a feeling of stability and unity.

Many families also teach their members to respect and appreciate other cultures besides their own. The Chous and the Rosettis celebrate two new years together—the Chinese New Year in the Chous' home and the western New Year at the Rosettis'.

Aiding Intellectual Growth

The family is a child's first teacher, imparting knowledge, stimulating thinking skills, and encouraging creativity. Parents, other adults, and **siblings**—*brothers and sisters*—can all help young children learn. When formal schooling begins, family members can remain active in the children's education. A parent might take a child to a zoo or a museum; a teen may read with a younger sibling.

All family members can benefit from the intellectual growth of one, at any time in life. Shelly's foster father shared his knowledge of auto maintenance with all his children. Shelly used her computer skills to teach her family how to use a budgeting program.

Guiding Moral Growth

Another important function of families is promoting moral development. Providing children with a code of conduct and a set of values gives them a basis for acting and making decisions as they grow older. Both individuals and society benefit when people have a healthy sense of right and wrong.

As with social skills, families teach morals both directly and indirectly. At first, this teaching focuses on behavior. As children mature, they are given reasons for behavior. They can apply the reasons to other situations. A two-year-old might be told, "In this family, we say please and thank you when we want something." At age 12, the child might learn that this behavior shows respect and consideration for others, which the family values. He or she can then choose to act in other ways that reflect this value.

The Total Picture

No family meets all the needs of its members. Some families are better equipped to meet needs in some areas than in others. A low-income family that has trouble affording health care, for instance, may instill a strong sense of values. Sadly, as you will learn in later chapters, some families provide little or no support in one or more areas. It would be wrong, however, to say that certain family forms are always better than others at meeting members' needs. Caring individuals can build rewarding relationships in a family of any form.

Your Role in the Family

When you think of everything a family provides for its members and of its enormous impact on individuals, you can see why strong, nurturing families are important to society. Throughout life, what a person does or becomes is strongly influenced by the family experience. What happens when children are well cared for physically, supported emotionally, and taught positive social skills and values? These children are not simply better able to adapt to society; they also make society better.

Teens play a part in this experience. While there are some things that they cannot provide for family members, there are needs that, perhaps, only they can meet. A teen with younger siblings can be a valuable, positive example of caring, responsible behavior. Teens whose families are facing tough times can show faith in family members and keep an optimistic attitude. You, too, can make important contributions to your family's life. In the chapters to come, you will learn how.

MORE ABOUT Intellectual Growth

A University of Illinois study shows that babies who are abused or ignored may experience development and behavior problems. The brain produces millions of new neural connections during the first year of life, creating pathways that can increase a child's manual dexterity, visual acuity, and music, math, and language skills. However, unused connections do not survive; they wither over the next 12 years. Those that remain must serve the person for the rest of his or her life.

Review

Reviewing the Facts

1. List four different ways siblings can be related.
2. Name three ways families have changed in recent years.
3. Name three functions that families perform.
4. How do families transmit cultural heritage?
5. What are two ways that families guide social and moral development?

Thinking Critically

1. Why do you think that preserving cultural heritage is considered part of socializing children?
2. Review the discussion of trends that affect families on pages 146-147 of this chapter. Suggest some positive and negative consequences of these social changes.

Applying Your Knowledge

1. **Debating the Need for Families.** Debate this statement, "As people mature and become independent, the family and its functions become less important to them."
2. **Identifying Functions.** Identify some of the ways in which a family might fulfill its functions when family members share a meal. Record your ideas in a chart with columns for each type of function.

Making Connections

1. **Social Studies.** Research a holiday or celebration observed in a different culture, or learn how a holiday in your own culture is celebrated in another. (Your school librarian can suggest resources for this investigation.)

Prepare a short presentation of your findings for the class, describing the holiday and explaining its origins and meaning. Describe the particular role of families in this event. If possible, enhance your presentation with visual or audio aids.

2. **Mathematics.** Using library resources, chart the changes in the national birth rate or in the number of single-parent families every five years over the last fifteen years. (Begin with the most recent year for which this data is available.) Express your findings in a line graph or a series of bar graphs. If you research the number of single-parent families, you may express these numbers as a percentage of all families, using a series of pie charts.

Building Your Portfolio

Recording Family Celebrations
Think about the events you celebrate with your family, and select one that means the most to you. Write a description of how your family commemorates the event. Include drawings or photographs, if possible, illustrating such things as how the home is decorated or the sequence of events in the celebration. Explain what role, if any, your family's cultural background plays in the celebration. Add the completed description to your portfolio.

Chapter 15

FOCUS

Chapter Overview

Chapter 15 describes ways that families show and develop strength. The chapter offers ways to settle family conflicts and to balance family life with work. Students learn how a support system can help a family meet its members' needs.

Motivator

■ **Feeling Strong.** Ask: What does "Strengthening Families" mean to you? How can you tell whether a family needs strengthening? How might you go about doing this? Tell students that this chapter will help them answer questions like these.

Objectives

Discuss the chapter objectives on this page. Remind students that the objectives focus on important chapter concepts.

Vocabulary

Discuss the idea of physical support—of providing a foundation so something can stand on its own. Ask students how people can figuratively support each other.

Chapter 15

Strengthening Families

Terms to Learn

- emotional support
- support system

Objectives

This chapter will help you to:

- Describe **ways to build a strong family.**
- Identify **ways of giving emotional support to family members.**
- Formulate **strategies for balancing family life with other responsibilities.**
- Define and develop **a family support system.**

CHAPTER RESOURCES

The word hung in the air, heavy as a storm cloud. Dying, Erik repeated to himself. Grandma Irwin was dying. Although her health had been poor for a long time, the blow still stung.

"I'll be spending a lot of time at the hospital," Mrs. Cassidy was saying now. "I'll need some extra help from you two at home."

Erik and his sister nodded quick agreement. "Sure, we can do more." Lisa pointed out that she already did some of the laundry, and she and Erik could figure out how to divide other household tasks. "We'll be all right," she assured her mother.

Mrs. Cassidy felt relieved. She knew that the death of a loved one had a strong effect on some people. It could be frightening. Sometimes people acted in ways they later wished they hadn't. Since her mother had entered the hospital, however, Erik and Lisa had seemed to grow stronger and closer. "You two have really come through for me," she told them. "That means a lot."

"Mom?" Erik sounded hesitant. "Could I . . . could I visit Grandma? Do you think she could use the company? Maybe I could read to her or something. You know how she likes stories. It might cheer her up. Even if I can't do that, I'd just like to be with her."

Mrs. Cassidy smiled. She swallowed and nodded. "Yes, I think she'd like that."

What Is Family Strength?

Imagine walking through a park on a summer day and coming across an ancient oak tree. Its trunk is so massive that you cannot circle your arms around it.

What gives a giant oak tree its strength? What about a family?

It reaches up impressively toward the sky and spreads its limbs even wider. Yet even the farthest branches are green with supple, healthy leaves. It must be a hundred years old, you marvel, and could last a hundred years more.

A strong family is similar to this oak tree. Both are deeply rooted in a nourishing environment. Both have a solid base from which spring individual branches, each going off in its own direction. No matter how far from the foundation, however, each shoot draws vitality from that same source. Also like the tree, a strong family can span the generations.

What Creates Strength?

You know what a tree needs to thrive—soil, water, sunshine, and air. Similarly, certain elements are needed for families to grow strong. Remember that each of these qualities is a two-way street. All family members give and receive them, although they may demonstrate them differently.

Respect

People in strong families respect each other's behaviors, abilities, needs, and opinions, even when they do not share them. They

CHAPTER 15   **Strengthening Families**   **153**

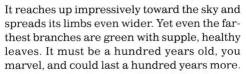
Topics on p. 153:
- **What Makes Families Strong?**
- **Showing Respect**

Checking Comprehension

✓ What is the family equivalent of a tree's roots? Of the branches? *Family history, traditions, values; children.*

✓ What are some ways family members show each other respect? *They appreciate, don't belittle differences; ask to borrow possessions; knock on closed doors.*

Activities

■ **Reaching Out.** Ask students to describe ways that Eric was providing emotional support and to whom he was providing it. *(Relationship)*

■ **Animal Families.** Point out that some animals form families and others do not. Ask each student to describe the "home life" of a species that mates for life or lives in family groups with a species that does not form such bonds. Ask students to compare the survival abilities of young animals born into families with the abilities of those that are not.

CROSS-CURRICULAR ACTIVITY
Language Arts

Ask students if they know what an "analogy" is *(a comparison made of two different things to examine their similarities).* What analogy is made in the text? Why is it effective?

⌕ocus on Relationship Skills

Discuss with students the link between Unit 2 and strengthening families. The same skills they studied and practiced in that unit can be used within the family to build strong relationships and, thus, strong families. Remind students that family relationships are often the ones that are kept for a lifetime. They are worth handling with care and preserving for the future.

Checking Comprehension

✓ In what way is trust mutual? *Family members earn as well as extend trust.*

✓ How can families help build a member's self-esteem? *By showing unconditional love and support.*

CROSS-CURRICULAR ACTIVITY
Language Arts

Ask students to read books or articles about getting along with others, especially family members. (A librarian can help them locate these.) Have students choose three or four tips they consider especially valuable to share with the class.

CROSS-CURRICULAR ACTIVITY
Language Arts

Ask students if they see a link between the words "confidence" and "confide." Point out that one meaning of "confide" is "to have confidence." Ask them if they think it takes confidence to confide in others.

Respect for family members shows through acts of consideration. If you borrow something from a sibling, what actions would show respect? What actions would not?

know that differences don't make any member more or less worthy than another. In fact, they appreciate and value differences. Dana, for example, has an excellent memory. Her mother often relies on Dana to remind her of names and appointments. In turn, Dana admires her mother's gentle, patient way of dealing with people. She is trying to develop this trait in herself.

Members of strong families show respect in other ways also. They ask permission before borrowing possessions. They knock on closed doors before entering a room.

Trust

Family closeness is also built on trust. Family members know they can count on each other for help and support. They can confide in each other—their secrets, ambitions, and weaknesses. They believe in each other's abilities and judgment.

Trust in families grows by degrees. When Manuel was a preschooler, his parents entrusted him with putting out napkins for a family meal and choosing appropriate cloth-

ing from limited options. As a teen, he is trusted with greater responsibility, such as supervising younger siblings and eating healthfully while away from home. When he becomes a young adult, his parents will trust him to make wise decisions about friends and a career.

Manuel, too, has grown in trust. As a child, he believed that his parents would meet his basic needs. Now a teen, he knows that he can turn to them with his problems and fears. He trusts that the rules they set are in his and the family's best interests.

Emotional Support

Kayla recalls her first piano recital: "I was so nervous performing in front of all those people. Then I saw my brother Mike in the front row. I know he's not very fond of music. He came just to make me feel better. It worked, too. I'm sure that I played better just knowing that he cared enough to be there."

Kayla's words capture the essence of one of the most important qualities of strong families: emotional support. **Emotional support** includes *words and actions that reassure others and share positive feelings.* Giving emotional support is like being a personal cheering section for another family member. When people face challenges, when they need confidence, knowing that someone else believes in them can make a big difference.

You can show emotional support in little ways every day. Telling a family member, "You did a great job on that," giving a hug for no special reason, doing a task for someone without being asked (or mentioning it afterward)— you have countless opportunities to show people that they are cared for and valued simply because they are family.

154 UNIT 3 Families and Friendships

REAL-LIFE APPLICATION

Read this to students: *When Garrett didn't make the baseball team, he thought his parents would be terribly disappointed. He told them he didn't have enough time for the team, so he didn't even try out.* Ask: Was Garrett right to "protect" his parents from the truth? How might they react if they found out later? Help students see that trusting others means letting them see your weakness and failings, knowing they will love you anyway.

Showing emotional support even aids emotional growth. People of all ages need to feel unconditional acceptance. Demonstrating emotional support does just that. It provides security and nurtures self-confidence. Self-esteem flourishes when people feel that they are loved just because they exist.

Communication

As you have learned, communicating is basic to any relationship. The more time you spend with people and the closer you are, the more important clear, frequent communication becomes. Communication among family members, then, is essential because sched-

Acting Responsibly

Do You Confide in Your Family?

Confiding in someone can be difficult, especially when you need it the most. Admitting that you have a problem can be the first step to finding a solution. Telling someone of your hopes and dreams can bring the emotional support and practical advice needed to make them come true. Fears seem less threatening when you share them with someone else.

Confiding in others benefits them as well. When other people know about your problems, goals, and insecurities, they understand your actions better. They feel good that you trusted them.

Confiding in Action

Aaron watched his younger brother toy with his dinner, then elbowed him good naturedly. "Better eat up, Dan. The big game is tomorrow."

Daniel only glared in response. He pushed away his half-eaten meal and tossed his napkin on top. "Excuse me," he muttered to his family. He stalked down the hallway and slammed the bedroom door behind him.

Immediately Daniel was sorry: he was still hungry. Still, it was worth it to get away from Aaron. Mr. Perfect, Daniel thought snidely, with his great grades and crowds of friends and scholarship offers from half a dozen colleges. Daniel wished Aaron wouldn't even go to the game tomorrow. It was his game, the regional basketball championship. He was proud of helping his team come this far—and he was scared. What if I can't score a single point, he worried, or let everyone down in the last second, or just look stupid? It was his big moment, and he couldn't even enjoy it.

Daniel heard a rap on the door. He heard the knob turn. "Dan?" Aaron spoke softly. "Are you OK? We're all kind of worried about you."

"It's nothing you would understand," Daniel replied curtly, but he was too full of emotion to keep it in. He began to tell Aaron about his concerns. As he talked—Daniel couldn't believe what he saw—Aaron started to grin.

"I know the feeling," Aaron said. "I used to get queasy before every debate in high school. Before my college interview, I was up half the night thinking of ways to look sick so I wouldn't have to go."

"You?" Daniel said. "What were you afraid of?"

Aaron shrugged. "Failing. Being rejected. I know it sounds silly." He sighed deeply. "I never told anyone that before. Thanks for listening, Dan."

Daniel was still surprised. "No problem." Then he grinned. "But if you get sick the day you leave for college, I'm not buying it."

Your Analysis

1. In this situation, who was confiding in whom?
2. What did Daniel learn about Aaron that surprised him? How do you think this will affect Daniel's experience in the game the next day? How might it affect their relationship?
3. What might have happened to Daniel and Aaron's relationship if they had not confided? To Daniel's relationship with his family?
4. How do you think Aaron felt when he heard of his brother's fears?
5. Is it ever desirable for one person to confide in another without that being reciprocated? Explain.

155

Topics on pp. 156-157:

- **Communication**
- **Sharing Goals and Traditions**

Checking Comprehension

✓ Why might regular family meetings help a family's communication? *Designates a time for a busy family to talk so that communication isn't overlooked.*

✓ How can working on a community project help strengthen a family? *Gives them shared goal, time together, good feelings, bond with community.*

CROSS-CURRICULAR ACTIVITY
Language Arts

Have students explain what the word "assumptions" means. Ask them how assumptions can interfere with good communication. What role did assumptions play in the situation with Ellie and her mother? Discuss how people can guard against problems caused by assumptions.

MULTICULTURAL *Perspectives*

Have groups find out more about traditions and celebrations in other cultures, especially in those of group members. Groups may make class presentations, which might include inviting a knowledgeable person (perhaps a family member) to speak to the class.

ules and feelings are closely affected by other members.

To illustrate this point, note what happened in Ellie's family. Ellie didn't tell her family that she wouldn't be home after school one evening because she needed to work on a research report at the library. When Ellie's mother stopped at home for lunch the same day, she left Ellie a note, saying she had to meet a client at 4:30 P.M. and asking Ellie to pick up her little brother at the babysitter's. That night Ellie's mother came home to an empty house. How do you think she felt? How would you have felt?

Fortunately, family members' closeness also brings many opportunities for communicating. Good communication can be simple and informal. Leaving a note for others where they will see it or writing a schedule on a family calendar kept just for that purpose might have prevented the confusion that Ellie and her mother experienced.

Family meetings work best for some families, especially for topics that need more thorough treatment and for problems and decisions that affect the whole family. Some families hold regular meetings; others meet when any one person feels it's necessary. When Joseph Monti grew concerned about a rise in vandalism at the high school his two sons attended, he called a family meeting to talk about the situation. They discussed why vandalism was wrong. Then Mr. Monti gave the teens some strategies for responding if anyone asked them to join in such acts. He answered their questions and encouraged them to come to him with any concerns—about vandalism or anything else. Communicating not only passed on needed information but also strengthened the family. Mr. Monti expressed his values and helped shape the teens' moral growth. The young men felt the security of having a parent who knew what was happening in their lives and who cared about them.

Sharing

Sharing is one of the first lessons that a child learns when beginning to form relationships. Sharing remains an important tool for building the deepening, more complex bonds of a strong family.

Sharing Goals

Working toward a common goal helps bind family members together. It encourages communication, unites individual efforts, and reaffirms shared values.

Some busy families today make use of ideas that work in business. A regularly scheduled family meeting, for example, gives members a time they can count on for discussing problems and working together on solutions.

156   UNIT 3   Families and Friendships

MORE ABOUT Family Strength

According to research, strong families share four C's. They foster *communication* by talking and listening to one another, especially during meals and family meetings. They show *commitment* by working together toward common goals, dividing up household tasks, and supporting each other's interests. They resolve disputes through *compromise*, meeting each other halfway. Their *celebrations* include traditions, such as favorite meals and bedtime rituals.

The Paulsen's experience illustrates this. Maria Paulsen suggested one spring that the family grow a vegetable garden. The others agreed that this was a goal worth working toward. Each member chose a vegetable to plant. Together they helped prepare the soil, plant the seeds, and dig weeds. Frequently while tending their garden, they commented on how good it felt to be outside, enjoying nature and producing their own fresh, nutritious foods. Those were things the entire family thought were important. As their crops began to ripen, the family harvested more than peppers and tomatoes—they reaped the satisfaction of stronger family ties.

A goal that involves helping others in the community especially increases family closeness. It allows a family to show a united effort before the public. The good feeling that comes from making a positive difference in the world is magnified by each member of the family. The Minehans, for example, often volunteer together serving meals at a homeless shelter. The parents feel good about helping others and about seeing their children do the same. The community recognizes them as a group of caring people, which contributes to their family identity.

Sharing Traditions

Tradition and family seem to go hand in hand. Many traditional cultural and national observances have family togetherness at their core. On Thanksgiving Day, it is traditional for families to gather in celebration. The African-American feast of Kwanzaa emphasizes various qualities that apply to one's family relationships as well as to oneself.

Families also create their own traditions. The Kellys have a family night once a week. Taking turns, one family member selects an activity—playing a game, watching a movie,

Working toward a shared goal is one way to build family strength.

or reading stories—that the whole family can enjoy together.

All traditions, whether recognized by millions or only a few, serve the same purpose for families: to help them build a sense of identity and connection with their past. Sharing special events over time adds to family members' image of themselves, as individuals and as a group. It helps them say, "This is who I am. This is who we are." This strong sense of self is the foundation for making choices that lead to a fulfilling life.

Spending Time Together

To become truly close, family members shouldn't wait for a special occasion or reason for being together. You can form strong bonds in the simple, everyday events in life, if they are shared with a feeling of warmth and caring. As Jesse explains, "I spend weekends with my dad. We used to always try to find something special we could do together, but we realized that the best times are when we're just making dinner or cleaning up

CHAPTER 15   **Strengthening Families**   157

Activities

■ **Blind Spot.** Discuss why it is sometimes difficult to identify the problem that underlies a family conflict. Help students see that anger, lack of reflection, and guilt about one's feelings can blind people to the real source of a disagreement and interfere with good communication. *(Critical Thinking)*

■ **Talk It Over.** Have groups list other situations in which a family meeting like the one Mr. Monti held would be helpful. Have them choose one as the basis of an impromptu skit that demonstrates good communication and resolution skills. *(Communication)*

RETEACHING

■ **What I Meant Was.** Remind students that "I" messages are valuable in communication. (Review Chapter 9's discussion of "I" messages, if necessary.) Have them demonstrate their understanding of this technique by translating these statements into "I" messages:
"You never let me tell my side!"
"Everybody blames me!"
"Do you actually like that music?"
"Can't you see the mess you've made?"
"Why can't you take better messages when someone calls?"

MORE ABOUT Traditions

Family traditions need not be rooted in culture. Families can start their own traditions even when they are not already in place. Here are some ideas that will get students thinking about traditions (simple ones work too) they might like to implement in their own families: an annual holiday picnic (Fourth of July?); breakfast in bed for the birthday person; "family night" once a month; a breakfast supper once a week; a pizza or ice cream outing connected to some event; a joke exchange once a month; a time for sharing during Sunday supper.

Topics on pp. 158-160:
- **Time for Family**
- **Developing a Support System**

Checking Comprehension

✓ Name some free or low-cost family activities. *Reading stories, watching TV or videos, walks or bike rides, visits, doing household tasks, teaching each other skills.*

✓ Give an example of how a person's job can negatively affect family life. *Working long hours could lead to ignoring family.*

✓ Who or what might be part of a family's support system? *Relatives, friends, neighbors, school staff, coworkers, and community agencies.*

CROSS-CURRICULAR ACTIVITY
Social Studies

The term "quality time" has become popular recently among family experts. Ask students to explain the meaning of this term, provide examples, and research current thinking on its importance to families.

USING VISUALS

Refer students to the photo on this page. Ask them to identify roles the man might have. What indications are there that he values his role as a father? How can any person show regard for the roles that he or she has?

158

---

afterward. When we're not trying to have a good time, that's when we relax and just enjoy being together."

As Jesse and his father learned—and as you have probably discovered—family relationships are built on a day-to-day basis. They become strong and rewarding when you take advantage of each day and each opportunity to make them so.

Finding Time for Families

Tanisha was writing the times and places of her debate club meetings on the kitchen calendar when she noticed how full it seemed. Monday afternoons her brother had skating lessons and on Saturday mornings, basketball practice. Thursday evenings her mother volunteered at the hospital. Tuesday was her father's bowling night. There were monthly PTA meetings and twice-monthly meetings of their neighborhood homeowners' association. That didn't even count things like shopping or seeing a movie with friends, Tanisha thought. She asked herself: Is that what life is all about? More and more time spent on other things and less time for family?

Multiple Roles

Like Tanisha, you may have wondered how people can give time and energy to strengthening family relationships when they have so many other obligations. Adults work; younger children go to school; teens often do both. Everyone needs time to enjoy personal hobbies or activities with friends. You need to learn to manage these roles—as brother or sister, parent or child, student, worker, or friend—for two important reasons.

First, each of these roles is necessary. You cannot and probably would not want to give up any of them. You cannot stop being someone's child. You need education to succeed personally and professionally. You need to work to earn an independent living. You enjoy leisure pursuits and time with friends.

People have multiple roles. What roles do both of these family members have?

Second, each role has an effect on the others. A father who feels rewarded by his work and secure in his job is likely to be more relaxed and confident in his role as a parent. On the other hand, you probably have known someone in your family who had a difficult day at work and needed some time away from family and friends.

Strategies for Managing

Balancing roles can be a challenge. Some people feel overwhelmed by trying to identify and respond to the demands of each one. These basic management strategies can help:

158   UNIT 3 Families and Friendships

DID YOU KNOW?

A study of 428 United States families found that about half the mothers of preschoolers work outside the home, many part-time. Yet American mothers spend about 10.7 hours each weekday caring for preschoolers. Fathers totaled less than an hour a day at child care, but thought it was much more. The same study found that fathers in Spain spend two hours a day with their preschoolers, while Belgian and Thai fathers give three hours daily to their youngsters.

- **Set priorities.** Each role has certain "musts." Decide what these are for you and attend to them. You feel less stressed when you meet basic obligations.
- **Allow for variations.** At some times you will need to spend more time and energy on one role than on another. During a family crisis, for instance, you need to place family responsibilities before work or school.
- **Be realistic about what can be done.** Many people want to do it all: do well at work or school; spend quality time with family; entertain friends; and find time for themselves. Set realistic expectations for yourself and others.
- **Seek and give cooperation with other family members.** Few—if any—people cope with all their duties without help. Remember that sharing strengthens family relationships, and friendships also.
- **Plan together how time will be spent.** The family that plans together has more time together. Make an effort to coordinate schedules.
- **Learn to manage stress.** Since the pressures of one role can interfere with your effectiveness in another, it is especially important to keep stress under control.

Support Systems

Just as even strong individuals need families, so do strong families often need outside help to meet family needs and accomplish family goals. A **support system** is *a network of groups and individuals that a family can turn to for help*. This includes family and friends as well as providers of professional and community services.

For many families, a support system begins with their extended family. Grandparents, aunts and uncles, and older cousins may help with child care and transportation. These arrangements are often more convenient and less expensive than other options, although thoughtful families find ways to repay the favor. They also give family members the chance to spend time with, and grow close to, one another.

In today's mobile society, of course, many people don't live near their relatives. Instead, they join with friends and neighbors—other families who are in the same situation—in

Family members support each other in many ways. When you work to keep ties strong, family members are there when you need them.

CHAPTER 15   Strengthening Families   159

159

Seeking outside help is not a sign of family or individual weakness; it is the first step in resolving problems to strengthen the family. Ask students to name problems that might require outside professional help, such as depression and eating disorders, and where they might go for help. Explain that they will learn more about sources of outside help in Chapter 17.

Activities

- **TV or Not TV.** Discuss whether watching television is a good way for a family to spend time together. What are some possible benefits and pitfalls? *(Relationship)*
- **Doing It All.** Discuss advertisements, television shows, and other media in which society seems to imply that working parents, especially mothers, can—and should—do everything, and do it well. How is this message sent in each case? *(Observation)*

ENRICHMENT

- **Time Enough.** Have each student keep a private diary recording how much time his or her family spends together and the activities they share. After one week, ask students to review their logs. (No information needs to be shared.) Ask: Are you surprised at the amount of time your family spends together? They might share their findings with their families and see if they want to find ways to spend more time together.

BALANCING
WORK AND FAMILY

Have students read "Building a Support System" on p. 160. After students respond to Suppose That, ask them to answer similar questions about needs and support in the following situations:

You are new to the community and are looking for ways to get involved.

You notice that several people in your school and neighborhood hold prejudiced views of other cultural groups. You want to increase their appreciation and acceptance of differences in people.

Review

■ **Chapter Review.** Use the contents of the Chapter Review page to help students review concepts, think critically, and apply their knowledge.

■ **Study Guide.** Have students complete the Study Guide for Chapter 15 on p. 52 of the Student Workbook.

■ **Home and Country.** Ask students to suggest ways that ideas for strengthening families could be applied to the community. For example, what civic traditions might they share with others in the community? How could this make the community a better place to live? *(Citizenship)*

Evaluation

■ **Chapter Test.** Use the reproducible chapter test provided in the Teacher's Classroom Resources or create your own test using the *Testmaker Software.*

■ **Alternative Assessment.** Have students set five goals for the family they may someday have. Urge them to be specific—writing, for example, "We will have dinner together and talk about our day at least twice a week," rather than "We will communicate often." Students can share their goals in groups.

CLOSE

■ **Quality Times.** Ask pairs to select five qualities of strong families and then think of three activities that would promote any or all of those qualities. Have pairs share and explain their ideas.

Building a Support System

For families, a support system can keep a challenging situation from becoming a crisis. Unfortunately, too many people wait until they face such a situation before realizing that they have no one to turn to. These suggestions can help you and your family build a support system:

- Get to know your neighbors, classmates, and coworkers. Invite them to your home for a meal or to join you in an activity. Even a few minutes of friendly conversation can suggest ways of helping each other.
- Talk to people about community resources. Remember that a reliable babysitter who lives down the street is as much a "community resource" as the library.
- Help organize a block party or a potluck picnic for neighbors, coworkers, or classmates and their families. You might be surprised at how little people who see each other every day actually know about each other.

- Join a church or a community group that has a worthwhile cause. Families that share common values and goals are more likely to support each other practically and emotionally.

Suppose That . . .

You have an eight-year-old sister who was recently injured in an automobile accident. She will need several months of physical therapy to recover. In the meantime, her doctor recommends that she avoid all unnecessary activity, including going to school. Her doctor also suggests some psychological counseling to deal with any emotional consequences of the accident. Identify the new needs and demands that your family must meet. What members of a support system would be most helpful in meeting these needs? How would they do this?

mutual support and assistance. Parents from the same neighborhood car pool to work or take turns waiting with young children at a bus stop.

Community resources also help families meet needs. Park districts offer recreational activities. Some churches and schools offer after-school programs for young children, as well as family activities that encourage all family members to draw closer.

Professional services may also be part of a support system. Health care providers help family members care for their physical and emotional well-being. Financial institutions help them save for their future and afford the things they need now.

Branching Out

Recall the image of the oak tree at the beginning of the chapter. Now imagine a forest of such trees, part of a healthful environment where other living things thrive. Birds nest in the branches. Wildflowers blossom in the shade. Similarly, a community of strong families can create a positive environment where good things flourish—responsibility, fairness, understanding, and caring. When you work to make your family strong, then, you are actually sharing its benefits with people beyond the family itself. Your simple gestures of kindness and respect to a family member really can make your community a better place.

Focus on Entrepreneurial Skills

Challenge students to think of businesses they could start to help busy families that are trying to manage work, family, and personal responsibilities. For example, they might watch children after school, run errands, or shop for groceries.

Chapter 15 Review

Reviewing the Facts

1. How do respect, trust, and communication contribute to strong families?
2. Give an example of a way to show emotional support for someone in a family.
3. Name two ways that family traditions get started.
4. Identify three strategies to use in balancing family life and other roles.
5. What is a support system?
6. How do strong families help society?

Thinking Critically

1. Debate this statement: "Strong families must begin with parents who model positive traits."
2. How might the qualities described in this chapter be interrelated? For example, how might respect affect communication? How is trust related to emotional support? Suggest and explain other connections.
3. A friend complains that he is outgrowing a certain family tradition: "That was OK when I was younger, but now I think it's boring. My parents don't see that, though." What suggestions might you give him for resolving this problem?

Applying Your Knowledge

1. **Creating Family Traditions.** With a partner, list ten simple activities that could be the basis of a family tradition. Include those your family enjoys and think of new possibilities. Choose one or two of these original ideas and explain how you would transform them into traditions—for example, by choosing a certain night of the week or assigning a specific role to each family member.
2. **Working Toward Family Goals.** Choose a goal that a family might set for itself. Identify one way in which a younger child, a teen, and an adult could help to achieve the goal.

Making Connections

1. **Language Arts.** With one or two partners, write a humorous script depicting one family member's attempt to build good relations with another by demonstrating a quality described in this chapter. (Remember that a happy ending is a traditional element of comedy.) If possible, perform your skit for the class.
2. **Business.** Investigate practices or policies that businesses have developed to help support employees' family or personal lives—for example, on-site child care, alternative work schedules, personal and family benefits, and leaves of absence (family leave). Present your findings to the class, explaining how each policy supports family or personal life.

Building Your Portfolio

Building Trust
Family counselors sometimes uses trust-building exercises to help family members grow closer. Some members of the family might close their eyes, for example, while others lead them over and around obstacles. Develop a trust-building technique of your own. Do research, if necessary. It may be simple or elaborate, using whatever items or locations you choose. It must be safe, however. Write an explanation of your technique. If possible, videotape a demonstration or record it in writing. Add the completed project to your portfolio.

ANSWERS TO REVIEWING THE FACTS

1. Respect means accepting differences without letting them lead to conflict; trust is the basis for reliability; and communication helps people work through problems.
2. An example would be being there to talk through a problem.
3. Any two: cultural traditions, long-standing family practices, enjoying an activity once and then repeating it, learning family history.
4. Any three: Set priorities; allow for variations; be realistic about what can be done; seek and give cooperation with other family members; plan time together; manage stress.
5. People and organizations that help families in need.
6. Strong families help by building a community with a positive environment.

ANSWERS TO THINKING CRITICALLY

1. Ideas may include: a comparison of what happens when parents provide positive role models and when they don't; ideas about other people who serve as role models; thoughts about what makes a strong family.
2. Answers will vary to show what happens as such qualities as respect, trust, and communication work together.
3. Possible answers: share feelings with parents to find compromise in tradition's activities; go along to show maturity and adaptability.

Chapter Overview

Chapter 16 focuses on changes that happen in families, including gaining and losing family members, moving, job loss, divorce and remarriage, illness, and death. It offers students strategies for coping with these events.

Motivators

■ **First-Day Feelings.** Ask the class to think about their first day in high school. How did they feel as the day approached? What did they look forward to? What were their concerns? Point out that changes often cause conflicting feelings.

■ **The Only Constant.** Ask students which they think is greater cause for concern in a family: regular change or no change at all. Help them see that some change is inevitable.

Objectives

Discuss the chapter objectives on this page. Remind students that the objectives focus on important chapter concepts.

Vocabulary

The word *custody* comes from a Latin term for guarding. Ask students how guarding applies to the word as it is used today with regard to children.

Chapter 16
Adjusting to Family Changes

Terms to Learn

- child support
- custody
- joint custody
- launching stage
- traumatic

Objectives

This chapter will help you to:

- Identify **the basic family life cycle and the exceptions to the basic pattern.**
- Describe **the changes that occur in families.**
- Evaluate **ways to adjust to and cope with changes in family life.**

CHAPTER RESOURCES

Student Workbook
Study Guide, p. 54
Activity, *Adding Up the Change,* pp. 55-56

Teacher's Classroom Resources
Lesson Plan, p. 20
Cooperative Learning, *Adjusting to Change,* pp. 23-24

Extension #27, *Solving Family Problems,* p. 33
Extension #28, *Job Loss,* p. 34
Life Skills, *Change and Challenge,* pp. 29-30
Personal Development, *Moving Away,* pp. 23-24
Transparency 15, *Stress in the Family*

Chapter 16 Test, pp. 37-38
Performance Assessment, *Changes Affecting Families,* p. 38
Reteaching, *Dealing with Changes,* p. 22

See Also:
ABCNews InterActive™ Videodiscs

For Cheri, it seemed as though nothing ever stayed the same. When her older brother moved out of the house, it was a sad day. She had always liked having him around, even if he did tease her a lot. The death of her grandfather not long ago had been another difficult time for Cheri. She was very close to her grandfather and looked forward to the regular family gatherings at Grandpa Kimball's. Those times had come to an end.

On the brighter side, some things were better than ever. As of last month, Cheri could drive a car. That was something she had looked forward to for a long time. Now Cheri could be more independent. She liked to pick up her cousin and head for the mall to browse. They always had good times together. That too would end soon, though, because her cousin was starting a full-time job and wouldn't have as much time to spend with her.

The Family Life Cycle

Change is a fact of life. Families experience changes all the time. Some changes have more impact on families than others. Change can be quite routine. It's simply part of the growth that occurs in families.

Social scientists have identified a general pattern to describe how families grow and change over the years. Called the family life cycle, it gives you a basic idea of what happens in families:

1. **Beginning stage.** As a couple establish a home in this stage, they learn about each other. They devise systems for living happily together. These systems may include organizing finances and setting up a schedule for doing household tasks.
2. **Parental stage.** As the couple become parents and raise their children, many changes occur within the family. Parents teach and train their young children and often have less time for activities as a couple. As the children grow up, they start to share in household responsibilities. They also become more independent and begin to prepare for their own adult lives.

3. **Launching stage.** In the **launching stage**, *children leave home to support themselves and develop their own lifestyles.* The family cycle begins for a new generation.
4. **Middle age stage.** After the children have left home, parents have time to focus on being a couple again. During this time, couples may also reassess their careers, take up hobbies, and become more active in their communities.
5. **Retirement stage.** Retirement may mean freedom for travel and leisure activities. Some people find new work to supplement income. Adjusting to the aging process is necessary, often including the death of friends and spouse and moving to a smaller home or retirement facility.

Families often gather to share the major life events of family members. This young woman's coming-of-age ceremony signifies change in her life as well as her family's.

CHAPTER 16   Adjusting to Family Changes   163

Topic on p. 163:
• **The Family Life Cycle**

Checking Comprehension

✓ What does the family life cycle explain? *The basic pattern of stages that families go through in life.*

✓ What happens in the launching stage of the family life cycle? *Grown children leave home to start their own lives.*

Activity

■ **Onstage.** Discuss with students the events that Cheri's extended family is experiencing. What family life cycle stages are they linked to? What impact are these events likely to have on Cheri's family? *(Critical Thinking)*

FAMILY AND COMMUNITY OUTREACH

Have students identify challenges that families face at each stage of the family life cycle. Ask them what they might do to help their own families and the families of people in their community cope with challenges.

CROSS-REFERENCE

Remind students that Chapter 2 has suggestions for ways to deal with stress, including the stress of family changes.

Topics on pp. 164-165:
- **Variations in the Family Life Cycle**
- **Family Changes: New Family Members, Moving, and Job Changes**

Checking Comprehension

✓ What are some variations in the family life cycle? *No children, having children late, divorce, remarriage.*

✓ How can people adjust to moving? *Learn about new community; find others dealing with similar challenge; join school and community groups; keep positive attitude.*

✓ How can a change in a parent's job affect the family? *Might mean moving; give parent less time at home; more responsibilities for other family members; change in income.*

SPECIAL NEEDS
Strategies

Inefficient Organizers. Ask partners to list changes in an average teen's life, categorize them as either minor, moderate, or major. Tell them that having a new teacher is an example of a minor change. A moderate change might be a new family moving in next door. Major changes include those listed in this chapter. As pairs share items from their lists, write them on the board. Encourage students to explain whether they would place an item in a different category. Discuss reasons for their differing perceptions.

How the Cycle Has Changed

Because it is very general, there are many variations in the family life cycle. One family's experiences may be quite different from those of another. For example, some families don't have children. Others are headed by older parents who started having children in their late thirties or early forties. Divorce and remarriage cause families to restructure. Grandparents may raise their grandchildren. Variations such as these are much more common today than in the past. What used to be a basic pattern of family development is now much more complicated.

Families often struggle today because of the changing framework of the family. Events may not be as predictable as they once were. Sometimes families have to look for different methods of operating than earlier generations used. They often have to work out new solutions to fit new situations.

Changes Families Face

Managing change can be a challenge. When changes occur, they affect all members of the family. Young children and teens have their own concerns, just as adults do. Whether the change involves a move, an addition to the family, or a tragedy, effort needs to be made to help everyone make adjustments or repairs and move on.

New Family Members

One of the most common changes that occur in families is the addition of a new member. Whether the new arrival in the home is a baby or an aging grandparent, everyone in the family must make adjustments. All family members have to set different priorities and schedules and take on new responsibilities.

The arrival of a baby is usually a happy event. A new baby can be fun to play with, hug, and hold. Nevertheless, everyone in a family is affected by the 24-hour-a-day job of taking care of a baby. For example, Rodrigo begins preparing dinner while his mother

picks up his infant sister at child care on her way home from work.

Sometimes families adopt an older child or care for a foster child. These children require a period of adjustment, especially if they have lived in several previous homes. They need time to grow accustomed to a different environment and reassurance that they are welcome in the home.

When Carl was adopted by Jessica's family, Jessica helped him feel at home. She showed him where things were kept, introduced him to neighbors and their pets, and gave him some of the toys that had been her favorites when she was Carl's age. In time, Carl felt that he was a real part of the family.

Sometimes relatives come to live with other family members. This move may be made for financial or health reasons. An older person who moves in is sometimes reluctant to give up a home, friends, and independence. Love and support help these individuals get used to having less space and less freedom. When

All families go through a period of adjustment when new members arrive. What changes in a family's routine are needed for a new baby?

Focus on Decision Making Skills

Ask students to imagine they are the main wage earner in a family and have been offered a new job. It includes a pay raise and the opportunity for advancement. However, taking the job means moving to another state and working longer hours. Have groups discuss this situation and develop a family scenario in which they accept the new job and another in which they do not. Have groups explain their scenarios and the values that underlie their decisions.

Moving

Becoming familiar with new surroundings helps people feel more comfortable when they move to a different town or neighborhood.

Moving is a significant change for families, particularly if it involves relocating to another community or state. Moving usually requires adjusting not only to a new home but also to a whole new set of people and places. For example, Amber was concerned when her family planned to return to her father's hometown in South Carolina, where they would be closer to his aging mother. Amber didn't want to leave her school and friends and worried about making new ones. She felt anxious about going to a new school. She hoped it had a science club like her current one. Amber was curious about her future neighbors and what she would do for entertainment.

For people in Amber's situation, adjusting to a move can be made easier. Here are some ideas that help:

- Learn as much as possible about the new community and school. Find out what courses are available and what clubs and sports are offered. If possible, visit the new community before the move is made.
- Talk with staff and students at school to find other new people who are dealing with similar experiences and feelings.
- Join the school newspaper staff, a chorus, a computer club, or another group to meet students with similar interests.
- Join a church or community youth group, or volunteer your time where you'll meet new people.
- Approach the move with a positive attitude; give the new community and people a chance.

Job Change

In the past, people often stayed at one job their entire working lives. Now people may change jobs several times during their careers. Such work-related changes can affect a family in a number of ways.

A job change often requires a family to alter its routines. Family members may have to take on more responsibilities in order to keep

in ill health, older adults may also require assistance and care from family members. In adjusting to the new arrangements, families should be patient and work together.

Older relatives may make positive contributions to families. They offer a source of support and advice. They often share in household tasks, such as child care, and help with household expenses.

When Charlie's grandfather first came to live with the family, Charlie doubted whether the arrangement would work. Their apartment seemed even smaller with one more person living there. One evening, Charlie was struggling to come up with a topic for a U.S. history report. His grandfather started to relate his own experiences as a young man during the Great Depression. Before Charlie knew it, his report—an interview with an eyewitness to the era—had practically written itself. Charlie began to appreciate the other ways that his grandfather had become an asset to the family.

Activity

■ **Welcome Home.** Ask groups to list five questions or concerns they think a foster child or an older adult would have when first coming to live with a family. After each item, have them list two things a teen could do to help that person adjust to the new home. Discuss their ideas in class. *(Problem Solving)*

RETEACHING

■ **Silver Lining.** Have students identify positive aspects of gaining a family member, of relocating, and of having a parent change jobs. Ask: How can a realistic attitude toward a life change help people cope with it?

CROSS-CURRICULAR ACTIVITY
Social Studies

For some families, moving is a routine part of life. Migrant farm workers and their families travel from region to region in the United States, picking crops as they ripen. Have students learn more about the challenges of this life. How does moving often affect children's education? How does it affect parents' ability to obtain credit? What about friendships and other relationships?

Focus on Relationship Skills

Dealing effectively with situations requires tact and respect. Have students demonstrate how they would handle these family changes: a. Your grandfather, who has moved in with you, has a hearing loss and always listens to the television at a very high volume; b. A foster teen living with you is not doing her share of the household tasks; c. Since your family moved to a new city, your 10-year-old brother insists on following you everywhere.

Checking Comprehension

✓ What are some positive ways teens can deal with their parents' divorce? *Stay involved with activities and friends, don't blame selves for divorce, join support groups.*

✓ Why is a positive attitude valuable for members of a blended family? *Expecting good things leads people to act in ways that brings good things about.*

MULTICULTURAL *Perspectives*

Divorce is not the same the world over. Ireland, for instance, only recently legalized the dissolution of marriage. Have students research if and how marriages are ended in other countries.

CROSS-CURRICULAR ACTIVITY
Economics

Workers who involuntarily lose their jobs are often eligible for unemployment insurance benefits, provided by a federal-state program. The amount and duration of payments vary from state to state. Have students learn about benefits for workers in your state. How are these benefits funded?

the household running smoothly. They may have to set up new schedules for having meals and spending leisure time together.

More and more people are working from their homes. If one family member sets up a home office, the others must adjust to less living space and learn to be more quiet during work hours.

A change of job can have deeper impact as well. It can mean a change in income that requires adjustments and decisions about spending.

Job Loss

Loss of a job is especially difficult. People who have lost a job often experience feelings of rejection and depression. They may feel that they have let the family down. If the unemployment lasts a long time, family members may have trouble keeping a positive outlook about finding a new job. The family not only shares this emotional pain, but may face financial problems as well.

Family members need to encourage the unemployed person with understanding and support. Their words and actions should show their confidence in the job seeker and in the family's ability to survive. They can also take positive actions to help.

Job loss, which is usually only temporary, may mean making sacrifices. Family members may have to do without some extras so that the family can afford food, health care, and other necessities. When his mother's company went on strike, Peter volunteered the money he had been saving for a new camera lens.

In many families, people pull together to get past the rough times. Teens may be able to help a little by finding a part-time job or increasing hours on a current job.

Divorce

One of the most painful changes a family can experience is divorce. This is especially true when children are involved and parents disagree over **custody,** or *the legal responsibility for housing and caring for children.*

During separation and divorce, families go through many changes. How well teens and younger children adjust often depends on whether they are able to maintain good relationships with both parents.

The confusion and stress of divorce may be complicated by the custody arrangement. In some cases, a custody decision means the children must move with one parent to a new, unfamiliar home. In other cases, the court divides custody. One child may live with the mother, while the other child lives with the father. The children are then separated not only from one parent, but also from brothers or sisters.

Even when the parents have **joint custody,** or *shared responsibility,* children's routines can be upset. With a joint-custody arrangement, children often move back and forth between homes. If the parents do not work together to make these transitions easy, children can feel that neither place is really home.

166   UNIT 3   Families and Friendships

DID YOU KNOW?

Both the marriage and the divorce rates dropped in 1993. About 2,334,000 marriages—9 per 1,000 people—took place that year, the lowest rate since 1964. About 1,187,000 divorces—4.6 per 1,000 people—were granted, the lowest rate since 1974. Ask: What factors might be responsible for this occurrence? Encourage students to consider social, economic, and personal factors. Ask: Do you think this is the start of a trend? Why or why not?

Conflict over child-support payments also presents problems. **Child support** is *an amount of money that the court orders a parent to pay to help support his or her children.* The monthly payment often goes to the parent with whom the children live. Children often feel anger and disappointment if a parent fails to pay child support. They may also experience serious financial hardship if the parent they live with doesn't earn enough money to support the family.

Reactions to Divorce

When parents tell the family that they are getting a divorce, the news is commonly met with shock and surprise, even if family life has been troubled for some time. Both young children and older ones often experience a wide range of other emotions as well. Some feel angry or resentful toward one or both parents. Many fear that they will no longer be loved or protected. Others also worry about who will care for them.

Young children and teens whose parents are divorcing may lose interest in schoolwork, withdraw from friends, or pick fights with classmates. Young children especially tend to feel guilty and blame themselves for the divorce. They may think that their misbehavior caused the breakup. Young children who feel this way need help in understanding that the parents' own problems are the cause of the divorce. They should be reassured that they are in no way responsible.

In some cases, young children and teens feel relief when their parents separate or divorce. This is especially true when arguments, fighting, or physical abuse have been part of family life.

Coping with Divorce

No matter how family members feel about a divorce, they need time to adjust. Parents can ease this adjustment by not forcing young children or teens to choose loyalty to one parent. By communicating that the divorce is the best way to a better life, parents help everyone to recover. Parents should also be accepting of teens' and younger children's feelings and encourage them to express these feelings in constructive ways. Children should not feel that they must hide negative emotions from parents.

Counseling can also help. School counselors and support groups for children of divorced parents can provide an outlet for sharing feelings and finding ways to cope. By staying active and involved in their own lives, younger children and teens can keep from focusing too much on their parents' divorce.

Remarriage and Blending

The remarriage of a parent requires further adjustments. For one thing, any hope that the children may have had that their divorced parents would get back together must be abandoned.

When families merge and start to share a home and resources, conflicts can occur. Rivalries over territory and possessions may develop. Young children and teens may feel resentful or jealous of a new stepparent.

Blended families can build strength by spending time together. Getting to know new family members may take time, but patience and understanding can lead to positive family relationships.

Activity

■ **Dear Diary.** Ask pairs to assume the identity of an adult who is getting divorced or a young child or teen of divorcing parents. Have them write a diary entry in which this person gives his or her view of the situation and expresses feelings about it. *(Creativity)*

ENRICHMENT

■ **Skills for Coping with Divorce.** Assign groups one or two of the chapters in this textbook that the class has already studied. Ask groups to review their chapters for skills that would help teens experiencing their parents' divorce. Provide time for groups to explain how the skills they have selected would be useful. List these "divorce skills" on the board.

FAMILY AND COMMUNITY OUTREACH

Invite a divorce attorney, family counselor, or custody caseworker to explain the effects of divorce on the family. Ask the speaker to share techniques, approaches, and attitudes that have proven effective—and damaging—in the coping and healing process.

CROSS-REFERENCE

Tell students that Chapter 17 will describe sources of outside help for problems.

REAL-LIFE APPLICATION

Read this to students: *Mae's parents are divorced. Mae spends every other weekend with her father. He always plans a special outing for them, but Mae wishes they could just relax around the house as they used to.* Ask: Why do you think Mae's father makes special plans for their weekends? How should Mae handle the situation? Suggest that Mae's father may feel guilty; he may be trying to make their time "special." He may also be competing with her mother to be a "good" parent.

Topic on pp. 168-170:

- **How Illness, Accidents, and Death Affect Families**
- **Coping Strategies**

Checking Comprehension

✔ How can illness and accidents affect a family? *Members may feel helpless and frustrated. Medical bills may strain finances.*

✔ What does it mean to say a death is traumatic? *Causes severe emotional shock.*

✔ How should you respond to unavoidable change? *Accept and, if possible, prepare for it.*

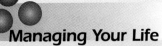

Managing Your Life

Have students read "Living in Two Households." Invite students to offer personal tips on living in two homes.

Answers to Applying . . .

1. Answers may include: try to arrange different work hours or visits; look for other job.
2. Answers may include: talk to parents about situation; find space for belongings out of Amy's reach.

FAMILY AND COMMUNITY OUTREACH

Some hospitals have facilities for families who travel long distances to be with sick or injured loved ones. Ask students to contact local hospitals and see what arrangements are available.

Good communication is essential during this period of adjustment. If members talk to each other and share their feelings in a positive way, the blended family can gradually become united. Here are some additional tips:

- Accept the new arrangement and find ways to make it work. For instance, 14-year-old Dwayne knew his 13-year-old stepsister Angel was sensitive about no longer being the oldest child in the family. He made a point of asking Angel for help and advice with household tasks. He was careful not to use his age against her when they had a conflict.
- Remember that relationships in a blended family will differ. Some will always be closer than others. Respect these differences.
- Work out new ways of managing space and time.

- Get to know new family members by arranging to spend time alone with them. Discover their likes and dislikes, and look for common interests. Don't decide in advance what the relationship should be. Just let it grow into something positive.
- Remember that there will be some difficult moments. No family, whatever its form, is happy all the time.

Illnesses and Accidents

A serious illness or accident can greatly disrupt family life. Family members are naturally worried and upset to see someone they love suffer. They feel helpless and frustrated when they cannot ease that person's pain.

Besides causing emotional distress, a long-term illness or disabling accident can also strain family finances. Huge medical bills increase costs while the family's income may drop while the ill or injured person is unable to work.

Managing Your Life

Living in Two Households

Families today are often split among households. For whatever reason, a teen may have to divide time between two homes. Some live with family members they don't know very well. Adjusting to different sets of rules, routines, and values can be a challenge.

If you find yourself in a situation like this, try to be accepting of others, especially when their habits are different from yours. Learn, respect, and abide by house rules. Offers of help with household tasks will probably be welcomed, and it may increase your sense of belonging.

As new relationships develop in blended families, people often feel the strain. Families need to plan visits carefully to reserve some time for members who do not see each other often. They might share a favorite activity or event.

Friendships can also be challenged when one person is away for long stretches of time. Teens are sometimes torn between spending time with friends or family and may even feel some guilt. One solution is to invite friends for a visit at the "other" home.

People who truly want satisfying resolutions can be creative in solving problems. With the help of good management skills, teens can adapt to living in two households and build relationships with family members in both.

Applying the Principles

1. Suppose that you've been offered a part-time job that requires you to work occasionally on weekends. You want the job, but you spend every other weekend with your father and stepmother who live far from the job. What are your options?
2. Sarah's five-year-old stepsister, Amy, frequently plays with Sarah's belongings and sometimes breaks them. How do you think Sarah should handle the situation?

• • • REAL-LIFE APPLICATION

Read this to students: *Greg hasn't talked to anyone at school about his parents' impending divorce. Talking about it only makes him sad and angry.* Ask: Should Greg wait until he is over his pain to talk about the divorce? Help students see that Greg may not "get over" his pain *unless* he talks about it. It won't "go away" by itself. Suggest that simply acknowledging sorrow and being available may be the best response to a friend in this situation.

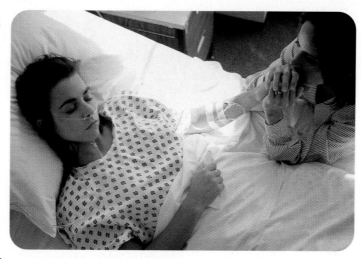

Although it is stressful to have a family member in the hospital, it is important to show love and support. In what ways can family members help a patient recover?

To deal with such a crisis, family members often find strength in one another or in their religious faith. People may discover qualities in themselves and others that they never knew existed. As with other challenges a family may face, sharing feelings and responsibilities helps make difficult times easier.

When Gary's father was seriously injured in a car accident, Gary had trouble coping. At first, he didn't want to go to the hospital. He didn't want to see what his father was going through. When he realized that his mother needed him, however, he went with her. He became determined to be there for his parents, just as they were always there for him. Gary's support proved critical to his father's recovery and his mother's ability to manage through the crisis.

Death

Salim's Uncle Jerry had lived with the family since Salim was a child, and the two were very close. When his uncle died, Salim was unprepared for the rush of conflicting emotions that he felt.

At first, Salim tried to deal with his grief by not thinking about his uncle at all. Later, he felt guilty about the times when he and Uncle Jerry had argued. He wished those moments had not occurred. Sometimes Salim felt angry at his uncle for leaving him; at other times, he felt lonely and sad. All these emotions confused and frightened Salim. Does everyone feel this way? he wondered.

Salim's feelings of denial, guilt, anger, loneliness, and sadness are all natural. A death is

traumatic. It *causes severe emotional shock.* Recovery from trauma is slow.

People who are grieving should accept their feelings and realize that these feelings may last a long time. They should allow themselves to cry, to talk, and to express and share sad feelings. Ignoring these feelings or keeping them inside can result in serious problems later. Even when people do grieve at the time of a death, they should be aware that grief may resurface months or years later.

Members of Salim's family comforted him. He, in turn, reached out to his brother, who also had been close to their uncle. Salim found that sharing memories with his brother made them both feel better.

Some additional suggestions for coping with death are:

- Take responsibility for things you can do. Preparing meals or watching children relieves others of everyday tasks while they attend to more difficult matters.
- Participate in events, such as a funeral or memorial service, that can help you accept the reality of the situation.
- Spend time with young members of the family. Explain what has happened in terms that they can understand. Reassure them that the family will heal in time.

■ **The Unexpected.** Ask students to compare the effects of an expected death, such as after a long illness, with the effects of an unexpected one. What difficulties and challenges does each present? In what ways might each situation be preferable? What emotional reactions occur? (*Critical Thinking*)

ENRICHMENT

■ **Throwing a Curve.** Have each student write a brief description of an imagined family at a certain life cycle stage, then exchange papers with a partner. On the paper each receives, have students designate an event that the family is about to experience and return the papers to their owners. Students should then explain in writing how this change affects the family and how the family copes with it.

STRATEGIES THAT WORK

Have students read "Coping with Loneliness" on p. 170. Invite willing students to share their own experiences in coping with loneliness.

Answers to Think . . .

1. No; loneliness is related to quality, not quantity, of contacts. Might help person avoid dealing with underlying cause of loneliness or lead to harmful relationships.
2. Makes it is easier to reach out to others; makes pitying or blaming oneself for loneliness less likely.

MORE ABOUT Grieving

The grief process generally follows three stages: (1) shock and denial, (2) anger and depression, and (3) reconciliation or acceptance. Ask the class to assume they have a teen friend whose parent has just died. *Discuss: How might the friend express each stage of grief? How might others help this teen cope with grief?*

ASSESS

Review

■ **Chapter Review.** Use the contents of the Chapter Review page to help students review concepts, think critically, and apply their knowledge.

■ **Study Guide.** Have students complete the Study Guide for Chapter 16 on p. 54 of the Student Workbook.

■ **Well-Adjusted.** Divide the class into eight groups and assign each a family change from this chapter. Have groups develop a scenario in which a family experiences the change and successfully adjusts to it.

Evaluation

■ **Chapter Test.** Use the reproducible chapter test provided in the Teacher's Classroom Resources or create your own test using the *Testmaker Software.*

■ **Alternative Assessment.** Arrange the class into eight groups and assign each a family change from this chapter. Have groups list five guidelines for helping a teen deal with this change. As groups present their guidelines, have the class identify the three or four most frequently mentioned as being the most useful for any family change.

CLOSE

■ **Challenging Changes.** Ask students to assume that a family has never experienced any of the situations described in this chapter. Ask: What might be some advantages and disadvantages of such a relatively untroubled life? Help students see that coping with some change as a teen can help them develop the resources and resiliency they may need later.

STRATEGIES *That Work*

Coping with Loneliness

Change is sometimes followed by loneliness. Saying goodbye to old friends when you move, missing a family member after divorce, coping with the loss of someone special after a death—all of these can bring feelings of loneliness.

Most loneliness passes in time. If it turns into depression, low self-esteem, and alienation from others, however, loneliness should not be ignored. Taking steps like these will help:

- Talk to someone about your feelings. A parent, sibling, friend, or trusted teacher or religious leader can help.
- Maintain a relationship with your parents. Share your joys and sorrows. Make an effort to share activities.
- Speak to someone you would like to get to know better. Make the first friendly gesture.
- Find ways to help others. Even small acts of kindness build relationships.

- Get involved in school activities. Volunteer—don't wait to be asked.
- Avoid comparing yourself with others. Focusing on differences tends to isolate people and deepen loneliness.
- Allow for mistakes in forming relationships. The people you are reaching out to make them too.
- Be patient. Relationships take time to grow.

Making the Strategy Work

Think . . .

1. Is surrounding yourself with other people always the best cure for loneliness? What dangers might there be in relying heavily on this approach?
2. How can high self-esteem help people deal with loneliness?

Try...

Think of someone in school you've wanted to get to know but have been afraid to approach. How might you go about meeting this person?

- When a death is due to illness, learn about the disease. Knowledge can bring understanding and reduce fear.

Accepting Change

In all families, change is inevitable. Whether the changes are welcome and exciting or painful and confusing, you will need techniques for dealing with them. General strategies for coping with change include:

- **Cooperate.** Work together with other members of the family to heighten the enjoyment of positive changes and endure the sadness of traumatic ones.
- **Communicate.** Share your feelings with other members of your family. You may be surprised to find that they feel the same

way you do. You may also come to realize that they are willing to work with you to solve family problems once they know how you feel.

- **Follow routines as much as possible.** Try to maintain some stability in the face of change. If possible, continue to do some of the things you like to do.
- **Don't be afraid to ask for help in dealing with difficult times.** Many counseling and support groups are available to help people cope with major changes in life.

Above all, be adaptable. If you resist change, you will face problems at every turn in your life, even positive ones. If you are flexible, you will find that even difficult changes are easier to adjust to.

Review

Reviewing the Facts

1. Name and describe the five stages of the traditional family life cycle.
2. How can you make the adjustment easier when moving to a new community?
3. How can teens help if a parent becomes unemployed?
4. List three common feelings or reactions teens may feel when parents get a divorce.
5. Name five methods families might use for adjusting to change.

Thinking Critically

1. Some people seem to handle change better than others. Do you think adaptability is a natural quality? If not, how might it be acquired?
2. Do you think it is easier or more difficult for young children and teens to adjust to change than for adults and older people? Explain your answer.

Applying Your Knowledge

1. **Interpreting a Statement.** Explain the meaning of this statement in your own words: "Nothing is certain but change." Tell whether you agree or disagree with the statement, and explain why.
2. **Analyzing Family Life Cycle Stages.** Review the five stages of the family life cycle. Identify one positive point and one potential difficulty for families at each stage.
3. **Making a "Welcome" Booklet.** Think of ideas for making a new student feel welcome in your school. Use your ideas to create a booklet that could be distributed to the student body to make others more sensitive to the feelings of a new student.

Making Connections

1. **Social Studies.** Look up the stages of grief and dying identified by Elisabeth Kübler-Ross. Discuss with classmates how these stages apply to other life changes as well.
2. **Economics.** Use library resources to find out what programs are available in your area to help custodial parents get child support payments when the noncustodial parent refuses to pay. Prepare a chart explaining the features of the programs. If possible, include in the chart how effective the programs are.
3. **Social Studies.** Research the rituals and ceremonies performed in another culture when a person dies. Describe these rites in a brief report to the class. Suggest ways that the rituals help people cope with and accept death.

Building Your Portfolio

Writing Creatively
Write a poem that describes the feelings of a teen who is going through one of the changes discussed in this chapter. If you wish, write from your own experiences. Place the completed poem in your portfolio.

CHAPTER 16   Adjusting to Family Changes   171

ANSWERS TO REVIEWING THE FACTS

1. The five stages are beginning, parental, launching, middle age, retirement. See descriptions on p. 163.
2. Learn about the new community, find others in similar situations, join clubs and community groups, be positive.
3. Teens can postpone buying clothes or other items, show support, and/or get a part-time job.
4. They may feel shock, anger, guilt, fear, resentment, withdrawal, or aggression.
5. Five methods could be to cooperate, communicate, maintain as much stability as possible, be adaptable, and seek help if needed.

ANSWERS TO THINKING CRITICALLY

1. Adaptability might be a combination of natural disposition and upbringing. Most people, regardless of natural temperament, can learn adaptability.
2. Younger people tend to be less set in their ways and more accepting. Usually they have less control over changes and less experience with changes, however, and so may be more anxious.

Chapter Overview

Chapter 17 explores serious problems that families and individuals face: abuse, rape, depression, suicide, and substance abuse. It also tells students where families that face these problems can find help.

Motivator

■ **Dominoes.** Discuss: How might a teen's problems affect other family members? How can family problems affect a teen? Help students see that one family member's problem affects all members, directly or indirectly.

Objectives

Discuss the chapter objectives on this page. Remind students that the objectives focus on important chapter concepts.

Vocabulary

The prefix "co" in codependency means with or together. Codependent people become involved with a substance abuser's dependency by assuming the abuser's responsibilities, making it easier for him or her to continue using drugs. They try to fix the problems caused by the abuser's addiction.

Chapter 17
Coping with Problems

Terms to Learn

- abuse
- alcoholism
- codependency
- confidentiality
- date rape
- depression
- neglect
- rape
- substance abuse

Objectives

This chapter will help you to:

- Give reasons why family problems need to be addressed.
- Describe these serious problems that families face and demonstrate appropriate responses to them: abuse, rape, depression, suicide, substance abuse, and alcoholism.
- Identify sources of help for family problems.

CHAPTER RESOURCES

Student Workbook
Study Guide, pp. 57-58
Activity, *Teen Hot Line,* pp. 59-60

Teacher's Classroom Resources
Lesson Plan, p. 21
Decision Making, *When Should You Intervene?* p. 13

Extension #29, *Help or Hindrance?* p. 35
Life Skills, *What Would You Do?* p. 31
Personal Development, *If You Need Help,* pp. 25-26
Transparency 16, *Warning Signs of Suicide*

Chapter 17 Test, pp. 39-40
Performance Assessment, *Seeking Help,* pp. 39-40
Reteaching, Learning to Cope, p. 23

See Also:
ABCNews InterActive™ Videodiscs

Setting the dinner plate on the table, Therese stopped and frowned. She wondered if she should even bother setting a place for Marina.

It wouldn't be the first night that week her younger sister had missed dinner. Since entering the ninth grade a few months before, Marina's manner had gradually changed from cheerful and cooperative to secretive and defensive. She often slipped away without telling anyone. When she returned, she refused to say where she had been or with whom and grew angry if pressed. Several times Therese had seen Marina with a group of older teens whom she suspected were involved with drugs. When she tried to warn her sister, Marina exclaimed, "Mind your own business!"

This frightening change was taking a toll on the whole family. Their youngest brother Paul was afraid of

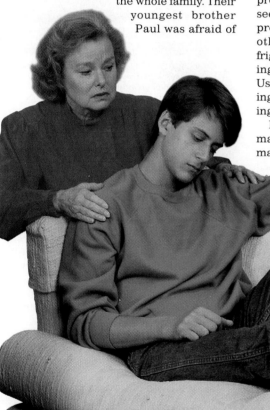

Marina and avoided her. Their father never mentioned Marina's behavior but acted irritable and short-tempered toward the rest of the family. Their mother seemed to take it hardest of all. She always looked drawn and worried.

Her mother entered, glancing at Marina's place and nodding. "Go ahead," she said. "She's a part of our family. I want her to see that there's always a place for her here."

Facing Family Problems

Families are tightly knit groups; the problems of one member touch them all. Despite this fact, people don't always address family problems.

Sometimes people don't recognize that a problem exists. They feel the effects but don't see the cause. Other times people try to hide problems—from themselves as well as from others, Facing problems, after all, can be frightening. It can cause anger and hurt feelings. It may involve making hard decisions. Usually, however, the consequences of ignoring a problem are worse than those of meeting it head-on.

Even after identifying a problem, families may still delay or avoid taking action. They may not know where to go for help. They may be unwilling to burden others with their difficulties.

These obstacles to solving problems interfere with healthy family life; however, they can be overcome. By learning to recognize and deal with family problems, people can work to keep their families strong.

> Facing family problems isn't easy. That's why some problems are never solved. Even if one person in a family is willing to confront the situation by saying something, the chances are better that the family will find happier times ahead.

CHAPTER 17   Coping with Problems   173

Topics on pp. 174-175:

- Abuse
- Rape and Date Rape
- Depression

Checking Comprehension

✔ Name four forms of abuse. *Emotional, physical, sexual, and neglect.*

✔ Why do most homes for battered women keep their addresses secret? *To protect them from batterers.*

✔ Why do some people commit rape? *To show control or power over another.*

✔ Is sadness the same thing as depression? *No, true depression is a long-lasting feeling of hopelessness and weariness.*

CROSS-CURRICULAR ACTIVITY
Language Arts

Have students research and write an article on date rape for the community or school newspaper. Have them include the reasons it occurs, common reactions, steps to take after an attack, and strategies to avoid date rape.

Abuse

Sometimes families become dangerous places. *When one family member threatens the physical or mental health of another,* **abuse** occurs. This abuse can be directed against a child, a spouse, or an older family member.

Abuse takes may forms. Beatings are a kind of physical abuse. Constant threats and criticism constitute emotional abuse. When an older family member forces sexual relations on a child or teen, that is sexual abuse. Another form of abuse is **neglect,** which occurs *when a parent fails to meet a child's basic needs.*

Signs of abuse can be emotional or physical. Abused children often suffer from low self-esteem. They may have been told that they deserve this "punishment," when in fact they have done nothing to warrant such treatment. Some children are afraid to go home. Others have difficulty trusting people. A physically abused child or spouse may have unexplained wounds, such as cuts and bruises in places that are not normally injured.

Abuse is never justified; abusers, however, were often victims of abuse themselves as children. They grow up learning, then repeating, these behaviors with their own children. Unless these people learn positive ways of handling stress and conflict, their abusive behavior is passed on in a terrible cycle.

Fortunately, abuse can be ended, as Victor's family discovered. Victor's father was physically abusive to his wife. When Victor tried to stop him, his father struck him also. Victor's mother finally confided in a caring neighbor, who took Victor and his mother to a shelter for abused women and children. There they were safe until Victor's father agreed to receive counseling to learn positive ways of

Coping with a family problem isn't easy. Finding people who will provide the right support is the key to getting through most tough situations.

dealing with frustration and anger. Victor and his mother also received counseling to help them deal with the emotional scars of abuse. It took courage for the family to admit they had a problem and to accept help in solving it, but they cared enough about one another to take that risk.

Some cases of abuse require more serious intervention. Law enforcement officials are responding more actively to reports of abuse. In some instances, they prosecute a suspected abuser even if the victim does not file charges. Offenders are usually required to seek treatment and sometimes sent to prison.

Rape

Many misconceptions exist about **rape,** which is *sexual activity forced on someone.* One is that rape victims provoke or are re-

DID YOU KNOW?

The National Coalition Against Domestic Violence paints this portrait of an abusive male partner: He has a personal and family history of violence; often uses force to settle arguments; has low self-esteem; "knows" how men and women should behave; is jealous of his wife's family and friends; displays weapons and threatens to use them; expects immediate obedience from his partner; and is sometimes kind and sometimes cruel.

sponsible for the attack. As with abuse, this is not true. Another myth is that rape results from sexual feelings. Rather, it stems from the rapist's desire to control, overpower, and humiliate another person. Also contrary to common belief, the rapist is not always a stranger to the victim; some rapes are committed by neighbors, acquaintances, and even family members.

You can reduce the risk of rape. When going out, stay with a group. Whenever possible, walk only in well-lit places at night, avoiding deserted areas. At home, keep doors and windows locked; avoid letting in strangers. It is also important never to get into a car with a stranger.

If rape does occur, it should be reported to the police immediately. Keeping the attack a secret merely protects the rapist and allows that person to prey on others. The police help rape victims receive medical care, as well as contact crisis centers and other community agencies for counseling. To protect victims' privacy, the media does not include their names in news stories.

Date Rape

One form of rape does not involve strangers, but people who know each other. **Date rape**, also called *acquaintance rape*, occurs when *sexual activity is forced on an individual during a date*. Date rape, like all rape, is an act of violence and a crime.

One way to prevent date rape is to go out in groups. Group dates provide safety in numbers. On a couple date, know the person you go out with and try to stay only in public places. Avoid sexually compromising situations. If you sense a sexual situation is getting out of control, stop it loudly and firmly. Leave the other person if the situation persists.

Depression

Maybe he was imagining it, but Carmine was sure that something was bothering his mother. Recently she had become quiet and withdrawn. She always seemed physically and mentally tired. Sometimes she was still in bed when Carmine left for school, and twice that month she had called in sick to work. Even her favorite hobbies—house plants and ethnic cooking—no longer appealed to her. It seemed that his mother was withering away.

These symptoms could have indicated physical illness, but in this case they were signs of **depression**—*long periods of sadness, hopelessness, and lack of energy*. Depression is more serious than occasional disappointment or "the blues." People with depression have trouble carrying out daily

Feeling low and depression are two different things. Anyone's spirits can be down at times. With depression, however, the feelings are lasting and they affect a person's ongoing ability to carry out daily routines.

CHAPTER 17 Coping with Problems 175

Activities
■ **All in the Family.** Experts believe most abuse is not reported. Also, many people who are abused stay in those relationships. Have students suggest reasons for these behaviors. Then challenge them to find arguments that undermine each one. *(Critical Thinking)*
■ **Help Wanted.** Have groups think of ways to encourage people who are being abused to seek help. Give them time to develop a means of conveying their message, such as a poster or public service ad. Have groups share their ideas. Encourage them to follow through on their projects. *(Communication)*
■ **Rape Prevention.** Group students by gender. Have groups list at least five guidelines, applicable to their gender, that would help them avoid becoming involved in date rape, either as the aggressor or as the victim. After each group has shared its list, discuss the practicality and effectiveness of the guidelines as a class.

CROSS-REFERENCE
Refer students to Chapter 2, pp. 40-41 for a review of stress and how to manage it.

DID YOU KNOW?

In 1994, about 818,000 cases of elder abuse—physical, emotional, sexual, and financial abuse or neglect of older Americans—were reported, up from 1991's estimated 735,000. (Many, no doubt, go unreported.) Like child abuse, elder abuse is an effect of broken families, decreasing respect for others, and economic pressures. Older people hesitate to report abuse for fear of getting younger family members in trouble. Mental confusion and physical dependence may also keep them from asking for help.

Topics on pp. 176-177:
- Helping Others
- Suicide
- Huffing

Checking Comprehension

✓ Why is it sometimes difficult for troubled people to see solutions? *They are too oppressed by the situation to think clearly.*

✓ What is huffing? *Inhaling fumes from household chemicals.*

✓ What kind of reassurance do family members need when someone commits suicide? *That they are not to blame.*

STRATEGIES THAT WORK

Have students read "Lending a Helping Hand." Ask them what benefits they might get from helping someone else solve a problem.

Answer to Think . . .

1. Answers may include: empathy, creativity, communication skills, resourcefulness.
2. No; prevents others from gaining self-confidence, resourcefulness needed to solve problems; can cause unhealthy stress in own life.
3. People may feel less anxious, more confident to solve problems when others show concern and faith in them.

---

tasks. Going to work, maintaining their appearance, and performing household jobs may become difficult for people to do. They may eat or sleep much more or much less than is normal. They may turn to alcohol and other drugs as a way of coping or escaping, although this just compounds the problem. Some entertain thoughts of suicide.

Wisely, Carmine told his mother of his concern. She agreed that something was not right in her life. She first made an appointment with her physician. Finding nothing wrong physically, the doctor referred Carmine's mother to a reputable psychiatrist. After several sessions, the psychiatrist recommended a treatment that proves effective for many people with depression: continued counseling and an antidepressant medication. For Carmine's mother, just identifying the problem—and knowing that she was doing something about it—was the first step in rediscovering her enthusiasm for life.

STRATEGIES That Work

Lending a Helping Hand

Although professional help is usually needed to deal with serious problems, it would be a mistake to assume that <u>only</u> a trained professional can help a person through difficulties. With no specialized training, you can show support for a family member or friend in the following ways:

- Let the person express negative emotions. Bottling up negative feelings can be physically and mentally harmful. Expressing these emotions, on the other hand, can help the person identify their cause. This can make a problem less frightening.
- Encourage the person to focus on the present. Dwelling on past mistakes is defeating. More useful is identifying positive ways of dealing with the problem now and in the future.
- Remind the person of past successes. Recalling challenges that were overcome can provide the encouragement needed to face a new one—and perhaps offer a model for solving it.
- Help the person generate possible solutions. You may be able to offer a fresh, creative approach. Try brainstorming to inspire new ideas. Be willing to help carry out the solution if you can.

- Help divert the person's attention from the problem if it seems to defy solution. Getting involved in some activity—especially one that helps others—can bring needed emotional relief. Physical activity can help work off frustrations and anxiety that interfere with problem solving.

No matter how deeply you care for others and try to help, you may discover that the only "solution" to their problem is learning to live with it. Either way, your support can help others succeed in coping with their problems.

Making the Strategy Work

Think...

1. What personal qualities might be useful in helping people deal with problems?
2. Should you try to solve other people's problems for them? Explain your answer.
3. How might emotional support, even without practical advice, help someone with a problem?

 Try...

With a partner, act out a situation in which two people deal with a problem. One person should assume the role of someone with a problem. The other person should use one or more of the above strategies to help cope with or solve the problem.

Read this to students: *Richard was disappointed with his counseling sessions for depression. At their first meeting, the counselor asked him to describe his feelings; at the next, they discussed his outlook on life. Richard had hoped she would simply tell* *him why he felt depressed and how to cure it.* Ask: Why can't the counselor do what Richard wants? Help students see that the problems in this chapter are complex and deeply rooted. With work and commitment, however, they can be managed.

Figure 17.1

Huffing: It Can Be Lethal

A recent trend in substance abuse is turning common household items into dangerous drugs. Huffing involves inhaling fumes from household chemicals, including gasoline, hair spray, paint thinner, nail polish remover, and lighter fluid. Like other forms of substance abuse, huffing is an attempt to escape from problems that the abuser finds too overwhelming to face. Also like other types of abuse, huffing can have serious consequences. Under the influence of these chemicals, some people become violent. Their physical coordination and mental judgment become impaired. High doses can cause unconsciousness. Short-term aftereffects range from bad breath and fatigue to chronic cough, nosebleeds, and difficulty concentrating. Prolonged abuse can lead to permanent damage to the blood and marrow, the liver and kidneys, and the nervous system.

Huffing has added dangers. The substances used in huffing are poisons; the brain has no tolerance for them at all. Also, these fumes are combustible—they readily catch fire. Huffers have been burned when a buildup of fumes ignited.

For huffers and all substance abusers, the solution lies in identifying the problem that led to the abuse and learning positive ways of coping.

Suicide

Depression is often linked to suicide. In fact, more than 80 percent of suicide victims are thought to have been experiencing major depression at the time they took their lives. Suicide rates are higher than the average among teens, young adults, and the elderly. Suicide is never a solution; it is an act of despair. A person who commits suicide will never discover how their problems could have been resolved.

Signs that someone may be considering suicide include depression, as well as extreme mood swings, giving away favorite possessions, and talk of death or killing oneself. Someone who shows any of these signs needs help. If you suspect someone is thinking of suicide, tell an adult. The person needs direct input from others about the situation.

Help is available in many forms. Counselors, workers at community hot lines, and health care professionals can all provide the needed help or supply the name of someone who can.

When a person does commit suicide, the devastated family members and friends must learn to cope. As with any death, those left behind need to handle feelings of grief, guilt, anger, and loss. They need reassurance that they are not to blame for what happened. Many families help manage their grief by rallying around each other. Many also need counseling to work through their feelings.

Substance Abuse

Substance abuse is *the use of illegal drugs or the misuse of legal drugs.* Illegal drugs include marijuana, cocaine, LSD, PCP, and—for people under 21—alcohol. Legally prescribed medicines, such as tranquilizers, are abused when they are taken in dosages larger than prescribed or by someone other than the per-

MORE ABOUT Suicide

Other warning signs of suicide are: radical personality changes; withdrawal from people and activities; noticeable changes in eating or sleeping habits; neglect of appearance; falling grades; difficulty concentrating; violent or rebellious behavior; drug abuse; physical symptoms, such as stomachache, headache, or fatigue; thoughts of despair, death, or suicide; suicide attempts; verbal hints; putting affairs in order; sudden cheerfulness after long depression.

Activity

■ **Stepping Forward.** Ask students to assume they have a friend who seems to be contemplating suicide. Have each student write what his or her response would be. If verbal, write the exact words. Share responses in class and discuss their potential effectiveness. (Note that authorities say you *should:* take threats seriously, listen, show you care, be direct, remove means of suicide if present, get help, and give reassurance that you will help. Authorities also say that you should *not:* show shock, ask why, debate the morality of suicide, give "empty assurances, or leave the person alone if there is immediate danger.)

RETEACHING

■ **Chain Reaction.** Ask students to explain how rape, depression, and suicide might be linked. Have them suggest ways the progression can be halted.

CROSS-CURRICULAR ACTIVITY
Language Arts

Ask students if they know what the word "invulnerable" means (incapable of being wounded, injured, or harmed). Ask them if they think young people tend to think of themselves this way. Why? Does this affect a teen's willingness to experiment with such potentially harmful activities as huffing? What may result?

Topics on pp. 178-180:

- **Substance Abuse, Including Alcohol**
- **Codependency**
- **Help for Problems**

Checking Comprehension

✓ Can legal drugs be abused? *Yes, if taken in larger doses than prescribed or by person for whom they were not prescribed.*

✓ Why is alcoholism a type of substance abuse? *Alcohol is a drug that changes the way the body works.*

✓ Why might families try to "cover up" for a substance abuser? *They think they are helping, don't want to admit person has problems, don't want others to know of abuse.*

✓ Why is confidentiality important in counseling? *People must know the problems they share won't be revealed.*

Making Decisions

Have students read "Facing a Problem?" Ask: How does the expression "out of the frying pan and into the fire" apply to Chad's plans?

Answers to What ...

1. Interfering with his ability to think rationally.
2. Things will get worse for him and family.
3. His own future; family's welfare.
4. Uses "we" in last question.
5. Answers will vary and may include: relatives, friends, clergy, teacher, school counselor.

178

Making Decisions

Facing a Problem?

His head down, Chad didn't see Darcy walking toward him until he charged into her.

"Hey, Chad! What's the hurry?" Darcy exclaimed.

Chad scowled, too full of emotion to speak. He brushed past her. "I can't talk now. I've got to go."

Darcy recovered herself and raced to catch up. "What's wrong? What's happened?"

Chad stopped, out of breath. "I'm leaving home. I can't take this anymore—and I shouldn't have to."

Darcy winced. She knew what her friend was talking about. "Your mom again?"

Chad nodded and swallowed. "I can't make her stop drinking, and I just can't cover for her anymore. Today she got mad at Jeremy because she found the invitation to parents' night that he was hiding from her. She started yelling that he was ashamed of his mother, and how nobody appreciated her. I tried to make Jeremy feel better, but I couldn't. All I ever do is make excuses for the way she acts, or pretend that it's not so bad. I told Jeremy that I'm getting out."

"You can't just run away," Darcy pleaded.

"Why not?" Chad demanded. "It's got to be better than this."

"Really?" Darcy raised her brow. "Where are you going to stay? How are you going to support yourself? What kind of job do you think you can get?"

Chad squeezed his eyes shut. "I'll figure that out when I get someplace."

"What about Jeremy and your mom?" Darcy persisted. "What's going to happen to them?"

Chad looked wounded. Darcy knew how much he cared about his family. "That's not fair..."

"No," agreed Darcy. "None of this is fair. But it's here. It won't go away by itself. The question is, what are we going to do about it?"

What Would You Do?

1. How are emotions affecting Chad?
2. What outcomes may Chad face?
3. What values is Darcy helping Chad consider?
4. How does Darcy reduce Chad's pressure?
5. What resources can Chad turn to?

178   UNIT 3   Families and Friendships

son for whom they were intended. Many abused substances are addictive, causing a mental or physical dependence that leads the user to crave regular doses. (See **Figure 17.1** for another form of substance abuse.)

Substance abuse is linked to many other problems, including family violence and suicide. Some substance abusers commit crimes to support their habits; others lose their jobs because they are no longer able to work effectively. All these problems harm the substance abuser's family.

People who wish to end substance abuse may enter treatment programs that help them recover from addiction and teach ways of coping with life's difficulties. Sometimes these programs require the person to enter a special facility for intense treatment.

Alcoholism

Alcohol is the most commonly abused substance. **Alcoholism,** *the physical and mental dependence on alcohol,* was once considered a character weakness. Now it is recognized as a disease. Evidence shows that people with a history of alcoholism in their families have an increased risk for developing alcohol problems. Many teens begin to drink because of peer pressure and then find it difficult to stop.

Like other substance abusers, alcoholics must decide to stop drinking for themselves. Sadly, many alcoholics must lose their job, families, and possessions before they seek help. With the support of recovery groups such as Alcoholics Anonymous (AA), alcoholism can be controlled; it is never "cured." Many recovering alcoholics attend AA meetings for the rest of their lives.

Codependency

Alcoholism—and other problems that affect family life—often encourage behavior known as codependency. **Codependency** is *a tendency to allow someone else's problem to control your behavior.* For people who are codependent, how their actions affect the person with the problem is their first concern.

This was the situation in the Breck household. Most people admired and even envied

---

Focus on Coping Skills

For teens who are living with a parent's addiction, here are suggestions: don't deny your parent's alcoholism; realize that you are not alone; understand that you didn't cause the illness nor can you cure or control it; learn more about alcoholism and its effects; become involved in clubs and activities that interest you; talk to a trusted adult; attend an Alateen meeting; be optimistic about your parent's recovery, especially through a treatment program.

Support groups form when people with the same problem unite. Knowing that someone else has had the same experience helps eliminate feelings of isolation. Learning what can be done from people who have been there helps eliminate feelings of helplessness.

■ **Setting It Straight.** Have students counter these misconceptions about family problems:
"People with depression just need something to cheer them up."
"People who talk about killing themselves never do."
"The pills the doctor prescribed for my brother's depression should help me when I feel sad."
"When women say no to sex, they are just playing hard to get." (*Critical Thinking*)
■ **The Doctor Is In.** Ask: How is seeking outside help for a family problem like going to a doctor for a physical problem? Ask students to suggest other comparisons. (*Critical Thinking*)

ENRICHMENT
■ **What Might Have Been.** Challenge students to research and list as many artists, writers, sports figures, and others who have contributed to society whose deaths were related to substance abuse or family violence. As students compare lists, ask them to reflect on the gifts and potential these people left unfulfilled. Stress that this is true of all people, well-known or not.

the family. Their home was clean and quiet. Mrs. Breck always appeared well-groomed and cheerful. Her neighbors and coworkers knew they could count on her, especially in an emergency. Michael and his younger sister Claudia had a reputation for being polite, respectful, and responsible.

Few people knew that the family had adopted this behavior to deal with Mr. Breck's drinking. Mr. Breck was easily angered, especially when he drank; then he could be abusive. His wife and children tried to avoid displeasing him by being the "ideal" family. When problems arose, they relied on themselves and each other. When Michael had a minor accident with the car, for example, he and his mother handled the ticket and the repairs without mentioning it to Mr. Breck.

When his employer finally insisted that Mr. Breck enter a treatment program, his family began to attend a family program. There they learned how much their living habits revolved around Mr. Breck's drinking habit. They had been acting as though they had somehow "caused" Mr. Breck's alcoholism and were responsible for it continuing. In reality, neither was the case.

Support Groups

Many families find their own strength reinforced by joining support groups of others who share their situation. Members of support groups provide each other with encouragement and information in dealing with a particular problem.

Mrs. Breck, for instance, began attending Al-Anon meetings, and Michael and Claudia tried Alateen—two groups for friends and families of alcoholics. They met many members who continued to attend for years after the alcoholic person in their lives had stopped drinking. Other support groups include CODA, specifically for codependents, and Families Anonymous, which helps families of those who abuse other drugs.

Asking for Help

Some people think it is a sign of weakness to ask for outside help. Actually, it takes courage and maturity to admit when you cannot handle a problem alone. Most counselors offer their clients partial or complete **confidentiality,** or *privacy.* Knowing that their iden-

CHAPTER 17   Coping with Problems   179

REAL-LIFE APPLICATION

Read this to students: *Chandra is worried about her older brother Anthony. Several times she has caught him drinking at home while their mother was at work. Some mornings he can't even get out of bed. He tells their mother he has the flu, and she seems to believe him.* Ask: Is this Chandra's problem? Do you think their mother believes Anthony has the flu? What could Chandra do to deal constructively with this problem? What should she avoid doing?

■ **Chapter Review.** Use the contents of the Chapter Review page to help students review concepts, think critically, and apply their knowledge.

■ **Study Guide.** Have students complete the Study Guide for Chapter 17 on p. 57 of the Student Workbook.

■ **Take My Advice.** Have pairs write letters to an advice columnist, writing as someone asking for help with a problem discussed in this chapter. (Letter writers' situations should be realistic.) Have pairs exchange letters, answering the one they receive with advice based on the chapter content.

Evaluation

■ **Chapter Test.** Use the reproducible chapter test provided in the Teacher's Classroom Resources or create your own test using the *Testmaker Software.*

■ **Alternative Assessment.** Divide the class into six groups. Assign each group one of these topics: family violence and abuse, rape, depression, suicide, substance abuse, and outside help. Have them review the chapter and summarize the topic's main points in a three-minute class presentation with an interesting format, such as a debate or call-in talk show.

■ **Equal Opportunity Problems.** Have students recall the causes of family problems and explain why these can occur in any home, regardless of income or ethnicity. Have them identify coping strategies.

WHERE TO GO FOR HELP

Family When faced with a problem or a difficult situation, the best place to start is with a family member. Even grandparents, aunts, or uncles may be able to help you with a problem. When a problem involves the family, it may be better to seek outside help.

Friends Sometimes just talking out a problem with a trusted friend can help your outlook and make you feel better.

Support Groups These groups provide people with a forum to discuss specific problems and feelings. They usually include other people going through a similar crisis. The principle behind these groups is to give and receive support.

Other Adults You Trust If you feel that you need to seek outside help, speak to a teacher, counselor, religious leader, or some other adult you trust. Explain the situation. He or she can put you in touch with social agencies or professionals who can help.

Community Organizations Groups such as the YMCA, YWCA, and the Red Cross often have youth workers experienced in helping teens. Other community resources include clinics and hot lines.

Professional Help Psychologists, social workers, and other professionals in mental health can help with the conflicts teens face.

Figure 17.2

tity and problem will be kept in confidence allows people to be completely open and honest. This is essential to getting at the root of a problem and solving it.

When to ask for outside help depends on how serious the problem is. If the situation is life-threatening—if you fear that someone may attempt suicide, for instance—immediate help is critical. Telephone hot lines can help in these emergencies. Trained staffers offer counseling and suggest immediate actions to take. Many hot lines focus on specific problems, such as family violence, rape, substance abuse, and suicide. The local emergency number (911 if available in your area) or hospital can often give the appropriate hot line number to call. **Figure 17.2** gives additional sources of help.

Family problems sometimes require family counseling, which includes all members in regular discussions. The professional helps family members recognize each other's feelings and identify solutions to the underlying problem.

Pulling Together

Families with problems have a valuable resource—each other. Family members can draw on their mutual love, and responding to a crisis can bring out the best in people. Seeing that the family is threatened, members often put aside smaller differences to focus on what is important—preserving the family and supporting those they love. By pulling together, families can survive—and thrive.

MORE ABOUT Help

Teens can find local assistance for family problems in the yellow pages of the telephone directory. Possible listings to look under are "alcoholism," "drug abuse," "substance abuse," "suicide," "mental health services," "family counselors,"
"abused women and children services," and "rape victim counseling." You may wish to demonstrate to students how such numbers can be located and show them how listings are cross-referenced.

Chapter 17

Reviewing the Facts

1. What is the danger in letting problems in relationships go unaddressed?
2. List four kinds of family violence and give examples of each type.
3. What are warning signs of suicide?
4. How can substance abuse by one person in the family affect the whole family?
5. List three sources of professional help for problems with relationships.

Thinking Critically

1. For several months, Danielle's family has known that her grandmother is having trouble moving about her large home and caring for herself. They have discussed this among themselves but have done nothing about it. What might be preventing the family from taking action?
2. How might a family's codependent behavior contribute to one member's problem?

Applying Your Knowledge

1. **Making Deductions.** Jean looks after her five-year-old cousin in the afternoon while his parents work. Recently she has noticed a change in his behavior. He is reluctant to play with other children and unwilling to try new activities. He tries to hide when his parents come to take him home. Several times he has asked Jean if he can live with her family. What do you think might be happening? What evidence supports your conclusion?
2. **Raising Awareness of Warning Signs.** Create a poster that highlights the warning signs of suicide and how teens can respond when they notice these signs in others.

Making Connections

1. **Government.** Find out how cases of rape are handled by law enforcement agencies in your community. Write a brief report on your findings.
2. **Health.** Alateen has helped many teens in families with alcoholics. Call Alateen to request some material describing the programs they offer and their philosophy about living with an alcoholic. Present your findings to the class.
3. **Language Arts.** Write a short poem describing how one family pulled together to help each other cope with one of the problems discussed in the chapter.

Building Your Portfolio

Creating a Help Referral Database

A database is a collection of information organized for rapid search and retrieval, often by a computer. Create a database of local resources that can help people suffering from any of the following problems: abuse, rape, depression, suicide, substance abuse, and alcoholism. Your database should include: the name, address, and phone number of the help provider; the name of a contact person; a list of services supplied; and any other special information. Add the database to your portfolio.

CHAPTER 17   Coping with Problems   181

Chapter 18

FOCUS

Chapter Overview

Chapter 18 describes some essential qualities of friendship. It explains skills for making and keeping friends, and for responding to challenges in friendship. The chapter stresses the value of diversity and reciprocity in friendships.

Motivator

■ **True or False?** Ask students to respond to this quotation by Samuel Johnson: "If a man does not make new acquaintances as he advances through life, he will soon find himself left alone; one should keep his friendships in constant repair."

Objectives

Discuss the chapter objectives on this page. Remind students that the objectives focus on important chapter concepts.

Vocabulary

Refer students to the term *reciprocity*. Remind students of reciprocals in math: two numbers that, when multiplied by each other, equal one. Ask how this idea might apply to good friends. Suggest that two friends fill in what the other lacks to create wholeness in the relationship.

Chapter 18 — Friendships

Terms to Learn

- clique
- loyalty
- reciprocity

Objectives

This chapter will help you to:

- Define the qualities of strong friendships.
- Suggest ways to meet people and make friends.
- Compare and contrast peer group friendships with cliques.
- Explain the value in having friends of different ages.
- Describe a positive approach to dealing with rejection and changes in friendships.

CHAPTER RESOURCES

Student Workbook
Study Guide, pp. 61-62
Activity, *Friendship Dialogues,* pp. 63-64

Teacher's Classroom Resources
Lesson Plan, p. 22
Cooperative Learning, *Help for New Students,* pp. 25-26

Extension #30, *Qualities of Friendship,* p. 36
Extension #31, *Friendships with Older People,* p. 37
Life Skills, *Be a Better Friend,* pp. 32-33
Personal Development, *Teach and Learn,* pp. 27-28

Transparency 17, *The Value of Friendships*
Chapter 18 Test, pp. 41-42
Performance Assessment, *Keeping Friends,* p. 41
Reteaching, Strong Friendships, p. 24

See Also:
ABCNews InterActive™ Videodiscs

Holly hopped off the school bus and hurried into the school building, shivering and burrowing her hands into her coat pockets. Since moving from Florida to Ohio last month, she had adjusted to a new home, a new school, and even new foods. She wondered if she would ever get used to Midwestern winters, however. To make matters worse, she had lost her new fleece-lined gloves.

Holly scanned the hall hopefully for Mei Lin. Mei, a volleyball teammate, had shown her around school, sat with her at lunch, and introduced her to other students. Holly thought she and Mei could become good friends—which made losing the gloves even harder. They had been a welcoming gift from Mei. She had noticed Holly needed some when Holly drove her home from volleyball practice one night. What kind of friend must she think I am, Holly thought, losing the first gift she gave me, and so soon?

She opened her locker to get her books. Inside was a soft package wrapped in white tissue. Curious, she undid the wrap to reveal a pair of children's mittens, with big clips to attach to the sleeves so they wouldn't be lost. She read the note: "Holly—Hang on to these! Friends with frostbite are terrible at volleyball! Mei."

Holly laughed and began to plot a payback. She knew the name of Mei's favorite music group. Now, she thought, how will I be able to sneak a CD into her book bag?

Qualities of Friendship

Ask ten different people what they like most in their closest friend and you may get ten different answers, such as "She makes me laugh" and "He's always there to help." Look at the responses more carefully, however, and you will discover certain core qualities that are basic to every strong friendship. These qualities include:

- **Common interests.** Friendships form among people with similar interests and outlooks on life. Whether it's a favorite sports team, an interest in astronomy, or a set of values, friends meet on common ground. Sharing interests encourages communication and gives them a focus for spending time together.
- **Loyalty.** Suppose a friend begins experiencing personal problems that make him or her difficult to get along with. Responding with patience and understanding shows **loyalty**, or *faithfulness* to others.
- **Empathy.** Empathy, the ability to experience what someone else is feeling, allows friends to ease each other's pain in hard times and to share the joy of good ones.

Friends share many of the same qualities and interests. Sometimes the quality, not the quantity, of time spent with friends is most important.

CHAPTER 18 Friendships **183**

TEACH

Topic on p. 183:
- **Qualities of Friendship**

Checking Comprehension

✓ What is the difference between reliability and loyalty? *Reliability means people can count on you; loyalty is faithfulness to others.*

✓ Which of the qualities of friendship is most important to you and why? *Answers will vary. Explore reasoning as you discuss the terms.*

Activities

■ **It Shows.** Ask students to leaf through previous chapters of the text and point out those photos that show friendship. Have them explain why friendship is indicated in each. *(Observation)*

■ **What Are Friends For?** On the board, write: "A friend in need is a friend indeed." Discuss with students how this saying relates to any of the six qualities of friendship on pages 183-184. *(Relationship)*

RETEACHING

■ **Between Friends.** Have pairs perform scenes that demonstrate qualities of friendship as the class tries to identify the quality (or qualities) being acted out. Help students see that one interaction can demonstrate several qualities.

ENRICHMENT

■ **Quality Time.** Ask students to record their behavior toward their family members for one week. Have them review their observations, asking which of the qualities of friendship they demonstrated toward their family.

REAL-LIFE APPLICATION

Read each of the following and ask students which quality of friendship seems to be missing:

- Brett considers his lab partner Jeremy as a friend, but he's never sure that Jeremy will do his share of the work.

- Janetta tells Kari all about her day. Kari thinks she has nothing herself worth talking about.
- Kent knows Josh is sensitive about being overweight, yet when a classmate makes a cruel joke about it, Kent says nothing.

Topics on pp. 184-185:

- **Making Friends**
- **Meeting People**
- **Starting a Conversation**

Checking Comprehension

✓ Why might you look for friends among fellow group members? *You share at least one interest that can be a basis for friendship.*

✓ Do you need to be witty to begin a conversation with a stranger? *No. Simple comments and questions typically begin such conversations.*

In Touch With
TECHNOLOGY

Have students read "Friendship On-Line."

Answers to Thinking . . .

1. Diversity of friends; access for those with disabilities.

2. Other relationships may suffer; expensive; limits human contact. Families may set time limits, reserve chatting as privilege.

3. Focus students on specifics: what is "correct" age; how would access be restricted; would restrictions be universal or at parents' request.

4. Answers will vary. May help person overcome shyness, give self-confidence. However, may also help person avoid more personal interaction. Shyness, low self-esteem may make person target for unscrupulous subscribers.

184

- **Dependability.** Friends can count on each other for everything from a ride to school to comfort in a crisis. Friends are not only available for favors, they welcome them.
- **Reciprocity.** Obviously, these and other qualities of friendship must be shown by both people involved. **Reciprocity** is *giving and getting in return*. Good friends are loyal to *each other*. They feel empathy for *one another*.
- **Forgiveness.** True friends understand that each is not perfect. They are willing to accept mistakes and say "I'm sorry" for their own.

- **Caring.** Underlying all these qualities is caring, concern for another person's well-being. It is caring that inspires friends to be loyal, empathetic, and dependable.

Making Friends

Life would be simpler if making friends were like making a cake: combine loyalty and empathy; stir in dependability; season generously with caring. While relationships are more complicated than recipes, you can take certain steps to begin and nurture budding friendships.

In Touch with TECHNOLOGY

Friendship On-Line

Traditionally people had to go out to make friends. Now they can make friends without leaving home by using a computer. Many families who have computers with a modem join on-line services that allow subscribers to talk to each other.

On-line companies have special areas called forums or "chat rooms" where people from across the country can "meet" and talk by typing conversation on their computer keyboard. These areas are organized by specific interests—gardening enthusiasts, for example, or fans of a certain television show. Frequent "chatters" often form friendships with one another.

Friendships formed on-line can offer similar benefits to those made through traditional means, plus the advantage of convenience. They have one major drawback, however. All you know about an on-line friend is what he or she chooses to tell you, which may not be entirely truthful. On-line correspondents must trust in someone's honesty without knowing if that person is trustworthy.

Many parents recognize this concern. On-line communication allows people to enter a home before a parent can decide if they are welcome there. For this reason, many parents monitor on-line relationships. They caution children and teens against revealing personal information, such as

address and telephone number. They want to protect "chatters" from deceptive people and undesirable influences.

On-line services give people another option in forming relationships. Meeting people may now be easier than ever, but true friendships can develop only as individuals learn about and come to appreciate one another fully. Technology can speed up that process, but it cannot replace it.

Thinking Critically About Technology

1. Besides convenience, what other advantages might making friends on-line offer?
2. What might be some drawbacks of spending most of your leisure time chatting on-line? How can teens and parents decide how much time is appropriate?
3. Do you think access to on-line services should be restricted to people over a certain age? Why or why not?
4. Would you recommend on-line friendships for someone who is shy? Why or why not?

184   UNIT 3   Families and Friendships

Focus on Relationship Skills

Have students pretend they have been invited to a party but they know only the person giving the party. Ask them to suggest questions or topics that would help them start conversations and, perhaps, friendships.

DID YOU KNOW?

Teens tend to be especially worried about the impression they make when they first meet others. Suggest that other people often have the same worries. No one really has the time or energy to be critical of others.

Strong friendships tend to develop slowly from the day–to-day encounters people have. Moving from casual to close usually takes time as people learn more about each other and find common interests and traits.

Meeting People

Friendships generally begin when people have something in common. Use this fact to your advantage as you aim to make new friends. Look closely at yourself. What do you like to do? What is important to you? Try to identify ways of meeting people who share those interests.

Many communities have many established groups and clubs. Between school, church, and civic organizations, you should be able to find something that involves one of your interests, whether it is biking, computers, music, or a social cause.

You could also meet people by joining in an effort that seems worthwhile. Is a neighbor collecting canned goods for a food bank? Does a classmate need a study partner? Any of these strategies can help you meet potential friends. Also, getting involved and taking on projects help make you a more interesting, well-rounded person—another quality that people look for in friends.

Starting a Conversation

People can reveal a lot about themselves through conversation, even on such everyday topics as the weather or clothing. Talking to others is a good way to identify people with whom you might begin a friendship.

Many people, however, feel uncomfortable about starting a conversation with someone they don't know. The key to good conversation, especially among acquaintances, is showing interest in the other person without prying. Most people enjoy talking about themselves; after all, it is one subject they are experts on. You must be careful, however, to avoid personal or sensitive subjects.

Don't worry about using a conversation opener that doesn't seem very original. Most people are pleased that you want to speak to them, even if it's just about a class assignment or a television show you watched last night. Other tips for making conversation include:

- Ask open-ended questions, which require more than a yes or no answer. They encourage the other person to keep the conversation going and can lead to other topics.
- Pay attention to what the other person says and respond to it. This shows that you are interested and can also lead to new avenues of discussion.
- Speak with enthusiasm. If you don't, the other person may take what seems like a lack of interest as a sign that you want to end the conversation.
- Avoid controversial topics. When you're just getting to know someone, keep the conversation light. Save serious discussions for people you know better.

CHAPTER 18   Friendships   185

185

Topics on pp. 186-187:
- **Nurturing a New Friendship**
- **Empathy**
- **Rejection**

Checking Comprehension

✓ Is rejection a sign of failure? *No. Not every friendship is meant to be. If it occurs often, a self-examination can lead to positive improvements in the future.*

✓ How should you handle rejection by a potential friend? *Realize you don't share common ground; look for others.*

Acting Responsibly

Have students read "Are You Empathetic?"

Answers to Your Analysis

1. Awkward, uncomfortable. She lacked experience with situation. Empathy allowed her to put self in Vanessa's place and so understand it better.
2. She allowed herself to think about Vanessa's situation and feel as Vanessa might.
3. Vanessa found acceptance and practical help. Anna gained understanding, may have increased self-esteem. Both may have begun friendship.
4. No. Sympathy is pity, feeling sorry for someone. Empathy is deeper, imagining and reacting to a problem as if it were your own.

Acting Responsibly

Are You Empathetic?

Of the people you know, are some sensitive to the feelings of others? Do some try to put themselves in another person's place instead of criticizing or judging? These people are empathetic. Empathy is more than intellectually understanding how another person feels. It is identifying with that person's situation as if it were your own. Combined with caring, empathy can be a great motivator. When you are able to experience what someone else is feeling, you may be moved to action.

Empathy in Action

Anna glanced at the lunchroom clock. She had a little time left. If she could finish these last few algebra problems, she wouldn't have to take the assignment home tonight.

Suddenly the table shuddered. Anna's pencil zigzagged across three lines. She heard, "Sorry," and looked up to see Vanessa trying to work her wheelchair up to the table so she could set her lunch tray on it. As she jostled the table again, Vanessa made a face. "I'm supposed to fit this tray across my lap," she explained, "but that doesn't work real well. I'd rather eat at the table—like everyone else."

Anna hastily gathered her books. "That's okay. I'm done here anyway." She hurried out of the cafeteria. This was the first time she had met Vanessa, who began attending the school three weeks earlier. Anna had seen her several times, however—struggling through doorways, straining to reach her locker, and wheeling herself through the cafeteria line while some students behind her waited impatiently. The school was only gradually becoming wheelchair accessible, as money for needed changes became available.

The encounter left Anna with a tightness in her stomach. I was so rude, she thought. Vanessa was trying to make friendly conversation, and I walked away. I'll bet she gets a lot of that.

All that afternoon, the feeling lingered. Finding a seat for her next class, Anna wondered: What must it be like to always sit at the end of the row because your wheelchair blocks the aisle? She began to think of other things she enjoyed or took for granted—watching a basketball game from the bleachers with friends, riding the school bus, even using the restroom. It's not fair, she thought. She began to feel it personally.

At the end of the day, Anna found Vanessa at her locker. She introduced herself and said, "I'm sorry about the way I acted at lunch. I've never known anyone who used a wheelchair before, and I guess I don't know how to act."

Vanessa smiled. "Act like you would around anyone else."

"I know that now," Anna replied. "I've been thinking about something all afternoon. Tell me what you think. My church has tables in the basement that are higher than the ones in the lunchroom. I think your chair would fit under them, and I'm sure the church wouldn't miss one table. Or maybe a trade would work."

"That would be great. Do you think they'll let us do that?"

"I'm on my way to see the vice-principal now," Anna said. "I wanted to ask you first. That way," she added with a grin, "if he says no, he'll have to explain to both of us why it can't be done."

Vanessa laughed. "Good thinking!"

Anna smiled with satisfaction as the two headed toward the vice-principal's office. It's a small step, she thought, but it's a start.

Your Analysis

1. How do you think Anna felt toward Vanessa before they met? Why did she feel this way? How did empathy change her feelings?
2. How was feeling empathy a choice for Anna?
3. How did both Vanessa and Anna benefit from Anna's ability to empathize?
4. Is empathy the same as sympathy? Explain.

Focus on Communication Skills

Empathy that is felt but not revealed is of little use to others. Ask students how they might reveal feelings of empathy for another.

Figure 18.1

Lessons in Friendship

People learn by the experiences of others. Read what these teens have to say. Are there any lessons to learn?

- **Sheena.** "Delia is this girl in FHA. I thought she was very pretty—but stuck-up. She never spoke to me or even smiled. Then we ended up on a committee together, and I found out what a great person she is. She's kind of shy, but lots of fun when you get to know her."
- **Quinn.** "People used to say to me, 'Why do you even speak to that guy?' Buddy isn't very smart and his clothes are awful, but I've always been nice to him. One cold night I was on the road when my truck broke down. Several cars drove past until one quickly pulled over a few yards ahead of me. It was Buddy."
- **Lynette.** "Taylor and I are good friends now. One time a few months ago I said hello to her, and she just brushed right past me. Later someone told me that she had said something pretty nasty about me. After Taylor and I became locker partners, I learned that both incidents were not what they seemed to be. You just never know for sure."

Taking the Next Step

Meeting people and engaging them in conversation can be the beginning of friendships, but they are only beginnings. Someone has to make the next move.

If you have a promising start with an acquaintance, take the initiative to further the relationship. You may have to make a phone call. Keep the tone casual and low-key.

Remember too that friendship is a slow-growing plant. Any uncomfortable feelings at first eventually give way as familiarity creates a sense of security. Friendships that are allowed to develop at their own rate, in an environment that welcomes other friendships, take deepest root. (See **Figure 18.1** for more about friendship.)

Handling Rejection

Whenever you reach out to another in friendship, you risk being rejected. Not every friendship is meant to be. That's just reality. Accepting that rejection happens to everyone helps give you the strength to keep trying.

Rejection can be painful, shaking your self-esteem and self-concept. An initial response to rejection is often "What's wrong with me?" or "Why don't they like me?" In truth, the problem may be with the other person rather than you.

Some people try to change in order to "get" others to like them. This decision should be made carefully, however. First, changing yourself can be difficult enough when it's done to please yourself. Changing to please someone else is usually even harder. Also, think closely about what you're changing and why. Were you really unhappy with yourself before? Are you making a change for the better?

On the other hand, rejection can be positive, alerting a person to traits that present obstacles to forming relationships. Dominic, for instance, was strong-willed and opinionated. He was constantly telling his new friend Jake which movies they should see, how they should study for a test, and the best way to do things. Jake began to avoid him. When Dominic pressed him for a reason, Jake explained, which forced Dominic to see himself

■ **Down the Drain.** Tell students that many budding friendships don't continue to grow because neither party makes an effort to move beyond the initial introduction. Ask them to list ways other than a phone call to keep a brand new friendship going. Compile a list on the chalkboard.

RETEACHING

■ **Say It Again.** Have students restate the ideas under "Handling Rejection" by completing this sentence in writing: "If someone rejects my attempt at friendship, I will understand that . . ."

USING VISUALS

Refer students to Figure 18.1. Ask them to explain what lesson can be learned from each teen. *Sheena:* You can't judge people by what you see; you need to get to know them. *Quinn:* Reaching out to others has rewards; sometimes the most loyal friendships come with those who seem least likely candidates for friendship. *Lynette:* Make your own judgments rather than relying on others; sometimes things are not as they seem.

REAL-LIFE APPLICATION

Read the following to students: *Amelia had given up on making friends. Every time she tried, something seemed to go wrong. Now she was too afraid to try again. Spending all her free time reading novels seemed to be a safe way to escape the pain of constant rejection.* What advice can students offer to Amelia?

Checking Comprehension

✔ How does a teen friendship change from childhood? *Teens can begin to appreciate differences.*

✔ In what way can cliques be harmful? *Can cause pressures to conform, limit relationships, hurt people's feelings.*

✔ Why do friendships change? *Changing interests, attitudes, experiences.*

CROSS-CURRICULAR ACTIVITY
Art

Invite students to express their feelings about friendship or changes in friendship in any medium they choose. You might suggest a collage of pictures, a clay sculpture, or an arrangement of small items symbolizing friendship. Provide time for students to share their work and explain any symbolism.

► CROSS-REFERENCE ◄

Refer students to Chapter 10 for a review of peer pressure and refusal skills.

---

through his friend's eyes. When he began to consider how his attitudes and behaviors affected others, he became a better friend.

Keeping Friendships Strong

Suppose that in order to feel and look better, you start to eat more healthfully and exercise every day. Your efforts pay off, and you're pleased. As you get used to these improvements, however, you begin to act as though you can maintain your improved look without working at it. What do you think will happen to your health and appearance?

The same is true of friendship. Once established, it needs a maintenance plan to stay healthy. Good friends continue to show the qualities that helped them become friends in the first place: caring, dependability, empathy, and others. They make time for each other, confide in each other, and communicate honestly.

Teen Friendships

Teen friendships evolve, just as teens do. Whereas young children tend to form friendships with others who are much like themselves, teens can begin to appreciate

Accepting yourself for who you are is just as important to friendship as accepting the differences of others. The ability to be yourself helps build trust and honesty in relationships.

differences. Their added maturity and understanding of people allow for deeper, more committed relationships. The process is a gradual one, however.

Friendship Groups

As their twenty-fifth high school reunion approached, Ted's parents talked excitedly about meeting the old gang again. Ted was curious. His parents saw their old classmates only once every five years at reunions; yet after all this time, they still looked forward to seeing each other. What was it about their friendship in those years, Ted asked himself,

---

MORE ABOUT Changes and Friendship

Help students better understand the reasons friendships change. Ask them to think of a person to whom they were once close. Have them write a letter to that person, explaining why the friendship ended and how they feel about it. Remind students to try to be objective and not judgmental. Suggest they review the letter to clarify the reasons to themselves.

that they still care about each other today? He wondered if he would someday feel that way about his current friends.

Chances are, whether or not he stays in touch with them, Ted's friendship group will have a long-lasting effect on him. Teens spend more time with peers than with any other group. Among peers, they continue to form their identity at a time in life when questions about identity are especially important. Teens who make friends with a diverse group of peers not only enjoy interesting relationships, but they also have more chances to learn about themselves and others and to forge their identities.

Cliques

People tend to feel secure with others like themselves. This sometimes results in the formation of a **clique**, *a small exclusive group.* Cliques may come about almost by accident, as when teammates begin to sit at the same table at lunch or when friends from grade school strengthen their ties in high school. They begin to form a group identity that does not easily include others.

You can see how this might damage social growth. Clique members risk developing an "us versus them" attitude that interferes with other relationships. They often feel intense peer pressure from other clique members, which can lead people to negative or unwanted behavior. The teen years are a time to prepare for adult roles and responsibilities. How do you think cliquish attitudes might affect teens' personally and professionally as adults?

Those outside a clique may be harmed also. Rejection of any sort can hurt. When a clique sets itself up as desirable or superior, those it snubs can feel undesirable or inferior.

You can take an active stand against cliques by including a wide variety of people in your friendship group. Show tolerance by treating others with respect and kindness, regardless of ethnic background, disability, or other differences. Remind others—and yourself—that a clique is only as influential as they imagine it to be.

Strong friendships are not limited to those with people your own age. What are the benefits of forming friendships with people of all ages?

Friends of Different Ages

Diversity in friendship can extend to include people of different ages. This, too, helps teens broaden their understanding of themselves and the world. Cass describes one of her closest friendships this way: "Mrs. Jacovic, who lives in our apartment building, tells fascinating stories about growing up in Eastern Europe after World War II. She's taught me how to fix some authentic Russian dishes and now she's teaching me how to crochet. These are things that people my age don't know about."

Of other friends, Cass says: "Liz and Jenna live next door. Since I'm older, I guess they look up to me. I'm showing them how to use the computers at the library and how to swim

CHAPTER 18 Friendships 189

Activities

■ **Work or Play?** Ask students why a friendship might be described as a working relationship. (*Relationship*)

ENRICHMENT

■ **Progress Report.** Have groups trace the progress of a fictional friendship from childhood to adulthood. Encourage students to flesh out their characters as much as possible. Progressions should include demonstrations of the qualities and challenges of friendship, focusing on how these change over the years.

MULTICULTURAL *Perspectives*

Finding friends only among those with whom you share interests may mean that all your friends are duplicates of you and of each other. Invite students to describe friendships they have enjoyed or observed that involved very different individuals, especially people of different cultures and ages. Ask them to suggest factors that helped these people become friends despite their differences. Point out that people who are quite different in some ways are often similar in others. Gaining new interests and skills from others is also an inviting possibility.

REAL-LIFE APPLICATION

Read each situation below to students, having them explain whether the peer pressure is negative or positive:

• Megan welcomes a new student after she sees him talking to her friend Sonya.

• Antonio buys a certain brand of jeans after he notices several friends wearing them.

• Stacy cuts her hair after her friend Elysha comes to school with a short haircut.

• Beatrice starts walking in the morning to be with her friends.

Review

■ **Chapter Review.** Use the contents of the Chapter Review page to help students review concepts, think critically, and apply their knowledge.

■ **Study Guide.** Have students complete the Study Guide for Chapter 18 on p. 61 of the Student Workbook.

■ **New View.** Have students write a short essay on how this chapter has helped them take a fresh look at one of their friendships or form a new one. Ask them to include details to show specifically how the skills and ideas in the chapter guided them.

Evaluation

■ **Chapter Test.** Use the reproducible chapter test provided in the Teacher's Classroom Resources or create your own test using the *Testmaker Software.*

■ **Alternative Assessment.** Have groups create a questionnaire that would help teens evaluate their ability to make friends, keep friends, and handle changes that occur in friendships.

■ **The Company You Keep.** People are often judged by the friends they choose. Ask: Based on what you know about how friendships work, is this fair? Form the class into teams to debate this point.

at the park pool. Sometimes we just talk. I feel good knowing that I have something to offer, and I think Liz and Jenna appreciate the attention I give them."

Growing Apart

The teen years are times of intense emotions and dramatic change, and friendships don't always survive this. As their world opens up, teens naturally acquire new interests, experiences, and outlooks on life—which may not be shared by their friends.

Such was Lee and Brock's situation. The two had been good friends since grade school, sharing a love of sports and a goal of becoming professional athletes. When Lee began covering sports for the high school newspaper, he found he had a talent for writing. His interest grew as he took more literature classes and participated in newspaper workshops with other students.

Brock, still dedicated to sports, could see his friend was changing. They were still close. They still talked often and laughed at the same jokes, but each was accepting the idea that they would eventually go their separate ways. When Lee announced that he wasn't going to try out for basketball so he could spend more time with the newspaper, Brock said, "I guess people will be watching me in the game and reading about it in your column." Both teens felt a twinge of sadness, but each was happy to see his friend move toward his goal.

Friends for Life

Some artists say that "the process is more important than the product." This means that the work that goes into creating a piece of art—the decision mak-

ing and the creativity—is more important than what the artist produces. True art need not be technically well done but has something of the artist invested in it. Creating it has changed the artist or improved the artist's skills.

The same may be said of friendships. In the end, having a lot of friends or having the "right" friends is not what matters. More important is how becoming a friend changes you. When friendship opens you up to others; when it strengthens those qualities that improve character; when it teaches the joy of sharing and giving to others—that friendship is a true masterpiece.

■ What does it take to make a true friendship?

◉ Focus on Communication Skills

Tact is a useful skill in maintaining friendships. Ask students to restate the following more tactfully: "If you weren't so clumsy, you wouldn't keep bumping my desk." *("Is there any way we can keep from bumping each other all the time?")* "Does you sister have to go too? She's a real pain." *("Let's plan something we can do together—just the two of us.")* "That's not the right way to do it." *("Would you like me to help you with that?")* "You made it yourself? It look like it." *("I like the colors you used.")*

Review

Reviewing the Facts

1. What are seven qualities needed for a friendship to last?
2. Explain what empathy is.
3. What needs to happen if a new friendship is to continue?
4. What is a clique?
5. Why is it quite common for teens to change friends?
6. In what ways can a teen benefit from having friends of other ages?

Thinking Critically

1. From your own experience, how do you think friendships change from childhood to the teen years? How might they change from the teen years to adulthood?
2. Some people think that the best way to defeat a clique is to form one of your own. Do you agree? Why or why not?
3. Is friendship by definition a good thing? Are bad "friendships" truly friendships? If not, what would you call these relationships?

Applying Your Knowledge

1. **Icebreakers.** Imagine that there is a new student in your math class whom you want to know better. Suggest three conversation starters that would be appropriate for this situation.
2. **Evaluating Qualities.** Review the qualities of friendship described in this chapter and rank them in your own order of importance. Be prepared to discuss your choice for the most important quality and give reasons for your ranking of the others.

Making Connections

1. **Language Arts.** Writers often try to capture the essence of a concept in a single statement. For example, Kahlil Gibran said, "Friendship is always a sweet responsibility, never an opportunity." Try creating your own one-sentence description of friendship. Begin with "Friendship is . . ." or another opener of your choice.
2. **Technology.** Investigate the effects of technology on friendship. Prepare a chart showing different products of communication technology, such as answering machines, caller ID, E-mail, and TDDs (Telecommunication Device for the Deaf), and telling how such devices have made it easier or harder to form and maintain friendships.

Building Your Portfolio

Defining Friendship

What qualities do you possess that make you a good friend? Write a letter to an imaginary, potential new friend explaining your philosophy about friendship and telling why you believe you would be a good friend. When finished, place the letter in your portfolio.

CHAPTER 18   Friendships   191

Chapter Overview

Chapter 19 explores romantic relationships, from infatuation to marriage. It explains changes that can take place in relationships and suggests ways to deal with them. The chapter also discusses sexual feelings during romantic relationships, urging students to make responsible decisions about sexual activity and to act in ways that show respect for others, for themselves, and for their values.

Motivator

■ **A Little Romance.** Ask students to describe images they associate with the words *romance* and *romantic*. List these on the board. Ask how these images compare with real-life love relationships. What problems might this difference cause?

Objectives

Discuss the chapter objectives on this page. Remind students that the objectives focus on important chapter concepts.

Vocabulary

The word *infatuation* is related to the word *fatuous,* which means both "unconsciously foolish" and "unreal."

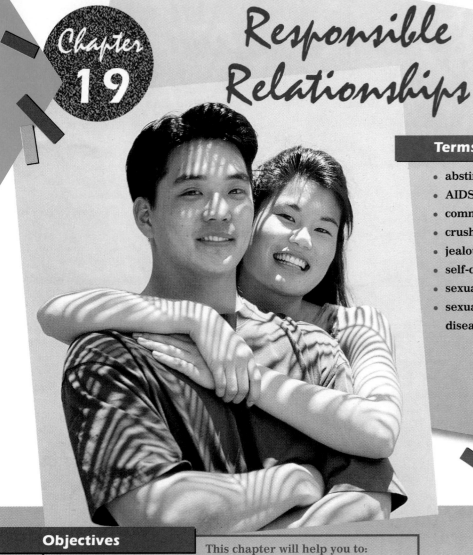

Chapter 19

Responsible Relationships

Terms to Learn

- abstinence
- AIDS
- commitment
- crushes
- jealousy
- self-control
- sexual harassment
- sexually transmitted disease

Objectives

This chapter will help you to:

- Describe **how relationships evolve beyond just friendship.**
- Explain **what to consider before a marriage commitment.**
- Analyze **how certain specific emotions affect a relationship.**
- Demonstrate **positive techniques for ending a relationship.**
- Describe **responsible attitudes and approaches to sexual situations and feelings.**

CHAPTER RESOURCES

Student Workbook

Study Guide, pp. 65-66

Activity, *Righting Relationship Wrongs*, pp. 67-68

Teacher's Classroom Resources

Lesson Plan, p. 23

Extension #32, *Safe and Mature Relationships,* p. 38

Extension #33, *Sexually Transmitted Diseases,* p. 39

Life Skills, *Dear Dateline,* pp. 34-35

Transparency 18, *When Couples Break Up*

Chapter 19 Test, pp. 43-44

Performance Assessment, *A Guide for Relationships,* p. 42

Reteaching, *Responsible Relationships,* p. 25

See Also:

ABCNews InterActive™ Videodiscs

"I think I'm the only girl in school who doesn't have a boyfriend," Jackie sighed.

Her older sister Carole responded. "When I was your age, I didn't have a boyfriend either. Then Devon came along. Do you remember him? We went out for a few months before we broke up. That was really tough at the time. Later on, I realized that I really didn't even like him all that much. It was just sort of—secure. What about Marlie and Tessa? They don't have anyone special, do they?"

"Not Tessa. She's friends with lots of guys, but she doesn't go out with any of them. Marlie had a couple boyfriends, but the relationships didn't last long. She'll find someone new, though. She's not afraid to talk to somebody she likes. Not like me. I'm scared to death."

Carole stifled a smile. "You know, Jackie, you're not as alone as you think. If you really want to change things, though, I'll help. Here, pretend this is the phone." Carole handed Jackie a magazine rolled into a cylinder. "Now, pretend I'm Lance, that guy in your biology class. Start talking."

Jackie smiled weakly. Maybe a little practice wouldn't hurt.

Friendships

On their way to adulthood, teens' social relationships typically start to change. At some point in time, males and females begin to look to people of the opposite gender for closer bonds. Their first link is through friendship.

Jackie's friend Tessa values friendship with the males she knows. Many teens have male-female friendships that don't include romantic feelings. This kind of friendship can be very rewarding.

When people become friends first, they often discover that a romantic relationship later on has more to sustain it.

When two people enter a romantic relationship, they meet a whole set of challenges. They start to examine the extent of caring on both sides. They wonder what each expects of the other. Sexual pressures are likely to appear. With simple friendship, the demands on both parties are usually less. Females and males can learn about each other without the strains of a more serious bond. Tessa and her male friends enjoy talking together about their interests and opinions. These conversations help them understand both males and females better. What they learn will be useful when they eventually move on to romantic relationships.

Friendship is often the first step to a more serious relationship. Two people who don't make good friends probably won't be able to build a successful romantic involvement.

CHAPTER 19   Responsible Relationships   **193**

Topic on p. 193:
- **Different Levels of Relationships**

Checking Comprehension

✓ Do all teens become involved in romantic relationships? *No, some have not found person they want to date; aren't ready or don't have time to date; are happy being friends with opposite gender.*

Activities

■ **Define Typical.** Have students write a few sentences describing what they believe a *typical* relationship between teens of opposite genders is. As they share their responses, stress that many variations exist; however, try to identify at least some qualities that most students agree characterize a typical relationship. *(Relationship)*

■ **Apply Yourself.** Ask students to recall friendship skills in Chapter 18 that they think would be useful in to romantic relationships as well. *(Relationship)*

■ **Shopping Lists.** Ask students to list qualities they would like in a person they go out with. Next ask them to list qualities they would look for in a marriage partner. (See "More About" on p. 197.) Are there any discrepancies between these lists? *(Critical Thinking)*

Focus on Relationship Skills

Have students suggest places and activities where teens could meet or work together without pressure to become romantically involved. Ask volunteers to demonstrate ways to start a conversation with someone of the opposite gender in one of these settings. Remind students that feelings of awkwardness and lack of confidence tend to subside as teens mature and learn more about relating to those of the opposite gender.

TEACH

Topics on pp. 194-195:
- Going Out
- Parental Rules
- Dating: Groups and Couples
- Commitment and Marriage

Checking Comprehension

✓ What purpose does going out serve? *Allows teens to practice relationship, communication skills; to learn which qualities they want in a partner.*

✓ What are some advantages of dating in a group? *Helps you feel less self-conscious; easier to keep conversation going.*

✓ Are there different levels of commitment? *Yes. You can simply commit not to see others or can make a life-time commitment of marriage.*

✓ What makes a successful marriage? *Choosing right partner; good communication, conflict-resolution skills; and making commitment.*

FAMILY AND COMMUNITY OUTREACH

Have students ask older relatives or friends about restrictions their parents imposed when they began dating. After students share their findings, ask if they think today's parents are more or less strict about dating than parents in previous generations. Discuss dating rules they might set for their children.

Going Out

When the time is right, many people want more than just friendship. They are ready for a male-female relationship that involves going out together. The age of readiness for this isn't the same for everyone. Some are interested in their teens, yet some are not ready until much later.

For males and females, going out with each other serves a practical purpose. Before choosing a partner for life, it's a good idea to know what you want. Spending time in several different relationships is one way to find out. You can make observations and practice relationship skills. You can learn what qualities you like in a partner. You can also try out communication skills to see what works and what doesn't. All of this is preparation for a possible long-term relationship in the future.

Establishing Rules

Families often set rules about when a teen is allowed to go out alone with someone. Some teens are eager to begin seeing others at an early age, but they might not realize all the potential for problems. Going out with someone is accompanied by many new and challenging responsibilities.

What if you were the parent of a teen? What concerns would you have? Caring families put safety issues high on the list. Love for a teen and having responsibility for him or her makes many adults in families think carefully about where they will let the teen go, with whom, and for how long. They don't want teens to be in situations that are beyond their ability to control. Responding inappropriately to sexual pressures, for example, could have life-changing consequences for a teen.

What advantages are there to going out with others in a group?

Families don't want teens to get involved in close relationships so soon that important goals lose significance. Aiming for education or training and a positive future needs to be a high priority. Nothing should be allowed to get in the way.

Spending Time with a Group

Going out with others often begins in group settings. Many teens like to associate in groups that include a variety of people. Doing so is usually safer and often less expensive than other situations. They meet for bowling, skating, parties, and movies. In a group, people can relax and have a good time together. Self-conscious feelings are not as likely, and each person has less responsibility for keeping the conversation and the entertainment going. Less nervous, they can enjoy themselves more. Going out in groups is a good option for teens.

194   UNIT 3   Families and Friendships

194

When two people are ready, they often begin to go out as a couple. What are the advantages and disadvantages in this?

derstood date for the weekend and for special events feels comfortable. So does getting to know someone well. There is a downside, however. Such relationships can be limiting. April spent two years in a relationship. When the relationship finally ended, she felt that she had lost a large chunk of time. She wondered how many opportunities to know others she had lost because of her reliance on a single relationship.

Going Out as a Couple

Associating in groups helps people feel comfortable as they begin to explore male-female relationships. Eventually, they may switch to, or include, going out as a couple.

When Mindy and Judd became a couple, they continued to spend time with their group of friends. Maintaining these friendships was important to them even though they started to go places apart from the group at times. After a few months, their relationship ended. Fortunately, they still had friends to be with, since they had never abandoned them. Judd decided that he wasn't really ready for another close relationship. If he started going out again, he decided, he wanted to see different people rather than only one.

Going out with different people gives more opportunities to learn about others. The more a person knows about different people and personalities, the more knowledge is available to use in choosing a long-term partner.

Going out with only one person all the time can bring a sense of security. Having an un-

Commitment

As people go out with others, many find someone special they would like to stay with. Commitment frequently follows.

When two people decide that they no longer want to see others and are ready to stay true to each other, they make a **commitment.** They accept *a state of obligation to each other and a dedication to making the relationship work.* At first they may simply decide not to go out with others. In time, the commitment may be a greater one, becoming a plan for marriage.

Marriage

The success of a marriage is often determined before the marriage ever takes place. How can that be? If you're thinking that choosing the right person to marry is critical, you're right. So many mistakes are made regarding this choice.

When choosing a marriage partner, some people don't spend enough time learning about the person. It often takes a year or more to discover what you will really be like together. You don't see the full dimensions of someone's personality right away. It may take a while to determine how you feel about certain habits and traits. A person can rely on hope and luck, but that's a risk that no one has to take.

CHAPTER 19   **Responsible Relationships**   195

Activities

■ **Is It or Isn't It?** Have students explore the meaning of the word "commitment" in a male-female relationship. Can you have commitments that last a few weeks at a time? Do you have to discuss and agree on a commitment before you are actually committed? Can you end a commitment without telling the other person?

■ **Fill In the Blank.** Ask students to write a response for the blank in this sentence: "If I decide to marry someone, I intend to spend _____ weeks/months/years getting to know my future mate before we actually marry." Poll the class for results.

ENRICHMENT

■ **Fools Rush In.** Ask groups to discuss these questions: Does society pressure teens to begin romantic relationships too early? If so, in what ways? What are some consequences for teens and society when teens date before they are ready? Have a spokesperson from each group summarize the group's conclusions for the class.

FAMILY AND COMMUNITY OUTREACH

Have students interview married relatives or friends about the difficulties, amusing or otherwise, that they have encountered during their first year of marriage. As students share their stories (sources need not be named), look for patterns of problems.

MORE ABOUT Commitment

Teen relationships aren't the only ones challenged by changing interests. Married couples continue to face changes. If these changes take them in different directions, even deeply committed marriages of 20 or 30 years may break up. Ask students to describe some adjustments that couples might have to make after 10, 20, and 30 years of marriage. What specific challenges might a relationship face at each point?

Topics on pp. 196-197:
- Teen Marriage
- Love and Infatuation
- Crushes

Checking Comprehension

✓ What kinds of relationships might teens develop with those of the opposite gender? *Friendship, romance, infatuation, crush.*

✓ What challenges do teens who marry face? *Financial problems; less chance for them to develop socially; limited career choices; pressures of parenthood.*

✓ Are crushes typical? *Yes. Most everyone experiences them.*

CROSS-CURRICULAR ACTIVITY

Language Arts

Ask students to describe in writing a married teen couple they know, without naming them. What signs of caring and commitment does the couple show? How do they treat each other? What adjectives describe the couple? What pressures do they have?

CROSS-CURRICULAR ACTIVITY

Social Studies

Have students create a United States map showing the different state's marriage laws regarding minimum age and parental consent. Have each student research the laws for several states.

A wedding is a happy occasion for two people who have dedicated themselves to building a life together. How can a couple prepare to make the commitment that comes with marriage?

Even choosing the right partner is not insurance for success. Skills and effort make marriages work. Changes in people and circumstances continually test a relationship throughout life. People who learn how communication and conflict resolution work within a marriage have a better chance at success. Watching over the marriage right from the start and not getting sidetracked from this responsibility is essential.

Of course, not everyone chooses to marry. Some people prefer to remain single. They may focus on other fulfilling aspects of life, such as career, travel, or community service. Realizing that marriage is a choice, not an obligation, enables people to look more closely at what they really want out of life rather than what others expect of them.

Teen Marriage

Marriage partners face many challenges. Some people don't take commitment seriously. Many people fail to choose a partner

carefully. All of these situations are especially significant when teens are involved.

Denzel explained his feelings this way: "When I was 17, I didn't think about how many years I had ahead of me to be an adult. I just got in a hurry. Nita and I got married too young. We split for a lot of reasons that I should have seen before we got married. We fought about money, mostly because we didn't have much. We just didn't get along because we were so different, and we changed even more as we got older. Now I'm starting over, but I lost something—time and experiences that I'll never get back. I guess you learn lessons from life, but it's a shame that sometimes you have to lose so much to learn them."

The pressures on teen marriages are so strong that many end in divorce. In one study, almost 40 percent of females who married in their teens ended up in a divorce, a higher rate than among females who married when older. To allow themselves a chance to pursue their education and career goals, many teens feel that it's much better to wait until they are older to marry. Taking the time to learn more about themselves helps them make smarter decisions about what they want in a marriage.

Handling Emotions

At any age the feelings people have in male-female relationships are complex. A high level of attachment to a person can stir intense feelings. When one person cares more than the other, the impact on emotions can be very strong. Understanding emotions and learning how to handle them well strengthens relationships.

Love and Infatuation

"How will I know when I'm in love?" People have long struggled with this question. Love is a special state that people need to be in before they make a commitment to each other.

■■■□□

MORE ABOUT Love

Partners who come from different cultural backgrounds may face added pressures in a relationship. Ask groups to write 5 to 10 question that partners in a multicultural relationship might ask each other—about expectations or religious beliefs, for example—before deciding whether or not to pursue the relationship further.

Is it love or infatuation? Only time will tell.

They may have "loved" everything from hamburgers to spring rain to the color blue, but love in the relationship sense is something different. Love is needed by two people to make a relationship last. Unfortunately, some people don't even try to figure out what it really means to love someone.

Love is based on caring and a desire to work toward common goals together. People build a lasting love when they have mutual interests. Love requires give and take. It takes trust and communication. People associate words like devotion, admiration, and affection with love.

The ability to recognize love is difficult because of an imposter called infatuation. Infatuation can fool people into thinking "this is love" when it really isn't. Although infatuation can turn into love, often it doesn't. Making a commitment based on infatuation rather than love can lead to regrets.

So, how do you tell the difference? Here are some questions to use as a guide:

- Is the relationship based on more than physical attraction? Love needs something more to survive.
- Is the feeling based on the total person? Infatuation is unrealistic, looking only at certain qualities and even ignoring negative qualities and problems.
- Is concern for the other person's well-being and happiness important? With infatuation, self-centered concerns for happiness and fulfillment may take priority over what is good for the other person.

- Has enough time been allowed to tell? Love lasts, but infatuation doesn't.

Crushes

Most people, at some time in their lives, experience *intense, usually short-term feelings of fascination for someone who does not return the feelings*. These **crushes** may be directed toward a person with whom a romantic relationship isn't possible. It may be a friend's older sibling, a teacher, or a celebrity. Very often, the other person isn't even aware of the feelings.

Every week when 16-year-old Kyle went to the doctor's office for his allergy shot, he checked in with the receptionist. He thought she was wonderful. Wednesdays became special to Kyle as he looked forward to seeing Deann. His thoughts often turned to her at other times. Although Deann was friendly to Kyle, she had no idea how he felt about her.

Kyle's crush lasted a few months. For a while, it was even difficult for him. He thought about sending Deann letters and flowers, but he used good judgment and decided against it. Kyle knew that crushes are usually temporary, so he simply let it run its course, and eventually the feelings subsided.

CHAPTER 19   Responsible Relationships   197

Activities

■ **In a Word.** Ask partners to list the different ways people use the word *love*. As partners share their lists with the class, ask: How might this indiscriminate use of the word be confusing for people in romantic relationships? Does it make the word less meaningful? *(Communication)*

■ **Rehearsal.** Discuss: How might infatuation be good "practice" for a romantic relationship? How might it hinder a romantic relationship from developing? *(Relationship)*

■ **Teen Dream.** Bring to class copies of teen fan magazines. Discuss how the articles and ads exploit teens' natural feelings of infatuation.

CROSS-CURRICULAR ACTIVITY
Psychology

According to some researchers, one person in every relationship cares more than the other. Ask students if they think this is true. In a relationship that they have, would they want to be the person who cares more or less? How is the level of caring likely to affect each person's behavior in the relationship?

MORE ABOUT Love

Not all people agree on the most important qualities in a marriage partner. Students can explore their own thinking by ranking these qualities in order of importance: emotionally stable and mature, dependable, similar political background, similar religious background, similar education, sociable, pleasing appearance, pleasing personality, intelligent, ambitious, desire for home and children, healthy, financially stable, good money manager, neat and clean, strong work ethic, moral, good household skills.

Checking Comprehension

✓ Does stalking have to be tolerated? *No. You can contact the police for protection.*

✓ Should you feel jealous when your partner spends time with others? *No; he or she may have interests you don't share; people need time apart.*

✓ Why is lashing out verbally a poor way of dealing with anger? *It can leave lasting emotional scars; doesn't solve problem.*

✓ What might occur when people hold anger inside? *It may fester and erupt later.*

STRATEGIES THAT WORK

Have students read "Ending a Relationship." Have volunteers share the breakup dialogues they wrote for "Try."

Answers to Think . . .

1. Answers may include: lets you identify and avoid behavior that caused it; teaches you about self, expectations.
2. Depends on individuals and nature of relationship, whether partners were good friends before. Is possible, but can lead to jealousy or false hopes of reconciliation.
3. Answers may include: pursue activity you enjoy; learn new skill; volunteer to help others.

Some people have trouble dealing with a crush. The feelings may be extremely strong. Talking with someone can help.

Stalking

Once in a while, the emotions of a crush or an ended relationship cause ongoing problems. A situation known as stalking can result. This occurs when a person is subjected to continued, unwelcomed pursuit by another. A stalker won't acknowledge that a relationship has ended or doesn't even exist. The stalker's behavior may include repeated phone calls and letters, following the person, and loitering around the person's home. Stalking is against the law in many states. If you are bothered or threatened by such a situation, you have the right to protect yourself by contacting the police.

STRATEGIES That Work

Ending a Relationship

Ending a romantic relationship is difficult. Telling someone that you want to end a relationship—or hearing it from another person—can be painful. There are ways of minimizing the pain and leaving both people more comfortable with the decision, however.

If you are the one ending the relationship, make a clean end of it. It isn't fair to the other person to simply stop calling. You can discuss it in person or over the phone, but be sure to make clear where you stand.

When you talk, be straight with the other person. Express your reasons for wanting to end the relationship, using "I" statements to avoid blaming or insulting the other person. Bear in mind the positive feelings you had in the past and be sensitive to the other person's feelings.

At the same time, be firm. If you definitely plan on breaking up, don't say something that suggests the relationship may continue. Doing so leads to false hope and just delays the inevitable pain.

If the other person is the one ending the relationship, avoid using pressure or threats to stop the breakup. Don't cling to the relationship just to keep it going. Someone who wants to end a relationship becomes an unwilling partner. If you continue dating, he or she will probably begin to feel resentful and the relationship will sour.

No matter which partner initiates the breakup, speak fairly about the other person to mutual friends. When they feel rejected, some people say hurtful things about someone they used to go out with. This type of talk reflects badly on the person who does it. Other people may not trust anyone who talks of a former partner that way.

After a breakup, give yourself time to recover from the hurt and disappointment you might feel. Stay busy and spend time with family and friends who will be supportive. Some people move immediately into a new relationship, but relationships that begin on the rebound often do not last. After a while, reflect on the relationship that ended. Consider what you think a successful relationship should be like. In future relationships you can use what you learned from the one that ended.

Making the Strategy Work

Think . . .

1. How can a breakup be a learning experience?
2. Sometimes people try to remain friends after a breakup. Do you think that's possible? Is it a good idea? Why or why not?
3. List several things you could do to improve your self-esteem after the end of a relationship.

Try...

With a partner, practice what you would say when breaking up with someone. Take turns being the one who initiates the breakup. Experiment with ways to respond when someone resists the breakup.

• • • REAL-LIFE APPLICATION

Read this to students: *Derek and April, juniors in high school, have been going together for about a year. Recently April met someone who interests her very much. She sometimes wishes she were not so involved with Derek. She wonders if the feeling will pass.* Ask: How would you advise April? Discuss the difficulties of ending a long-term relationship. Why is it difficult? What may happen if the relationship continues?

other person, especially if nothing out of the ordinary is going on.

Pete felt jealous because his girlfriend Celia spent so much time riding and training her horse while preparing for competition. Celia cared for Pete but had a goal that was important to her. Pete could either get upset with Celia or be supportive. His reaction depended on his own sense of security plus the condition of the relationship.

The best way to handle jealousy is to talk honestly about it. Hearing that the other person really cares is reassuring. Recognizing that the other person has some needs and interests that must be met outside the relationship can help prevent jealousy.

Frequent attacks of jealousy call for self-examination. The jealous person may be expecting too much. In Pete's case, Celia could not fulfill all his needs, nor should anyone be expected to do this. By developing outside interests of his own, Pete was able to put less pressure on Celia and on the relationship.

Anger

Anger is another common emotion that can threaten a couple's relationship. Eliminating all anger is not possible. On the other hand, it is possible to manage anger well.

One rule comes first regarding anger: When anger is felt, physical reactions directed at people are not allowed. You can hit a pillow. You can take a brisk walk. However, you can't injure another person.

Some people feel the pressure to lash out physically or verbally during a conflict. Both of these are destructive. The pain of a physical injury goes far beyond the time it takes to heal. You can't take away the emotional scars that are left. The same is true of verbal attacks. They do nothing to solve the problem, and they live on in people's minds.

People in a close relationship need to balance the time they spend together and apart. Having other friends and separate activities helps each person grow individually and provides a break that can give the relationship a sense of freshness from time to time.

Jealousy

Jealousy is a typical problem in romantic relationships. **Jealousy** is *the feeling that the person you care about is more interested in someone or something else than in you.*

A little bit of jealousy usually won't hurt a relationship. When out of hand, however, it is destructive. Extremely jealous people are usually insecure. They may resent any situation that seems threatening and make their feelings known. This is very wearing on the

Activities

■ **Words of Wisdom.** Have students explain the meaning of this quotation: "In jealousy there is more of self-love than of love to another." (Francois De La Rochefoucauld)

RETEACHING

■ **Couples in Conflict.** Have the class name conflicts that dating teens commonly face and list these on the board. Organize the class into mixed-gender groups. Have each group choose one of the conflicts—avoiding duplication, if possible—and create a scenario that shows how a couple resolves their problem through good communication and conflict-resolution skills. (You may want to refer students to Chapter 2's discussion on handling anger or Chapter 11 for resolving conflict.) After each scenario is presented, discuss the techniques the couple used.

◄ CROSS-REFERENCE ►

Refer students to Chapter 9 for a review of communication skills that would be useful when dealing with jealousy and anger in a relationship.

Focus on Communication Skills

Conflict alone does not end relationships; problems in communicating about conflict do. Ask students to name the most threatening conflicts a marriage could face. List these on the board.

Have students identify specific points for each one that partners need to communicate about to save the relationship. Stress that many serious conflicts can be managed if a couple can focus on the issues.

Topics on pp. 200-202:

- Sexuality and Responsibility
- Sexual Harassment
- Dealing with Sexual Feelings

Checking Comprehension

✓ What physical reason causes strong sexual feelings during the teen years? *Rising levels of hormones.*

✓ Name two forms of "emotional touching." *Being there when someone needs you; being a good listener.*

✓ Why is self-control important? *Lets you overrule emotions and sexual feelings when they threaten to get out of control.*

✓ What actions might be considered sexual harassment? *Making sexual comments, gestures, or looks; touching, pinching, grabbing.*

CROSS-CURRICULAR ACTIVITY
Science/Health

Have students locate current statistics on the sexual transmission of HIV or other sexually transmitted diseases. Ask them to include facts especially pertinent to teens, such as the growth rate of the disease among teens and the percentage of teens who have multiple sexual partners. They may also include a diagram showing how the disease passes from one person to many others through sexual activity.

Physical and verbal responses to anger often occur because people lack the communication and conflict-resolution skills that were described earlier in the text. When these tools have been practiced and are readily available, inappropriate responses to anger are less likely.

For some couples, angry outbursts are not the problem. Instead, holding the anger in causes difficulties. If one person pulls away and refuses to deal with anger, no solution is found. Anger and resentment may simply be stowed away where they will slowly build and later erupt, sometimes over something that is really insignificant. In this situation, too, using communication and conflict-resolution skills prevents problems.

When Relationships End

Do relationships have to end? Yes, they do. It would be unreasonable to expect people to find the relationship they want for life after only one try. That means that endings are inevitable, as is the pain that sometimes accompanies them.

Ending a relationship on a friendly note is ideal, but that doesn't always happen. Breaking up can be very difficult. The information on page 199 suggests ways of handling the end of a relationship.

Sexuality and Responsibility

The subject of sexuality is not an easy one to discuss these days. Opinions and values differ. Nevertheless, information exists that can lead you to certain conclusions. Turning your back on reality isn't smart. It can result in disappointment and often serious consequences.

For people like Tamara, lessons come too late. In her words: "I thought we were in love and that made it OK to have sex. What a joke. The relationship only lasted a few months. The light just seemed to go out after I said yes. Sometimes I don't think he ever really cared about me. Now I feel used. He says he wants

to help raise the baby. I just wish he wanted me too."

Risky Business

Tamara has discovered that sex and risk go hand in hand. Each year about one million female teens in the United States become pregnant. Many had the same thought, "It won't happen to me," but it did.

Pregnancy changes a teen's life dramatically. Tamara and others in her situation face difficult decisions. Finishing school is complicated by the pregnancy and later by the care of a child. Many teens become exhausted as they try to combine parenting with being a student. Some teens drop out of school, only to find themselves lonely and missing their friends and former activities. Worse, they have little money and poor prospects for getting a job because of limited education. Even if they can get a job, they must juggle the demands of working and parenting. Problems with parents, who may feel that their trust has been betrayed, can also occur.

Male teens who father children have similar problems. The law requires them to support their child financially. Consequently, they face the same situation as a working mother: too many demands and too little time.

Sexual activity comes with risks other than pregnancy. **Sexually transmitted diseases (STDs)** are *diseases transmitted from one person to another as a result of sexual contact.* Each year about three million teens are infected with an STD. While some STDs are treatable, they have varied effects on people. Some can even cause blindness, deafness, heart disease, brain damage, sterility, and death.

Because of its impact, the most talked-about STD is AIDS. **AIDS,** or autoimmune deficiency syndrome, is *a disease that attacks the immune system.* This system helps the body ward off infection from other diseases, such as pneumonia and cancer. A person with AIDS is infected with a virus (HIV) that is able to destroy the cells of the immune system. Eventually, the immune system fails to pro-

---

DID YOU KNOW?

Each year about 1 of every 10 teen females becomes pregnant. About 500,000 of them give birth. About 1 in 5 of these teens has another child before the age of 20. In addition, 21 percent of teen females and 8 percent of males who drop out of school do so because they have become parents.

Figure 19.1

Sexual Harassment

When someone imposes *unwanted or unwelcome sexual advances* on another person, this is called **sexual harassment.** Concerns about sexual harassment typically come from the workplace, but the problem can occur anywhere. Sexual harassment can include these behaviors:

- Making sexual comments, gestures, or facial expressions.
- Touching, pinching, or grabbing.
- Leaning over a person or cornering him or her.
- Sending obscene letters, notes, or pictures.
- Pressuring someone to do something sexual.
- Pestering someone for dates after being told no.

When do advances toward someone become harassment? The nature of the behavior, the reaction to it, and how much the behavior persists all determine the answer to that question. Another factor is the relationship between the two people. When the person making the advance is in a more powerful position than the other and uses that power to threaten, harassment has occurred.

Sexual harassment is against the law. People need to be aware of how their own behavior might be interpreted. If you have experienced this kind of treatment from someone else, report it. At school, talk to school officials, who can investigate the matter. At work, you can contact someone in management or personnel. In taking this action regarding genuine concerns, you protect others who might also be harassed.

tect the body, and the person becomes more and more likely to contract a disease that causes death.

HIV is a delicate virus that is transmitted through blood, semen, vaginal secretions, and breast milk. No evidence exists that it is transmitted through any other body fluids. HIV is acquired when infected body fluid enters directly into the body and reaches the blood of an uninfected person. Sexual activity is the most common method of transmission. During intercourse, the virus can enter the blood stream of a person through very small breaks in the skin.

So far, there is no cure for AIDS.

Even if pregnancy and disease are avoided, sexual activity can be emotionally harmful to a teen. Regrets can cause guilt. New rela-

tionships may be harder to form. Reputations can suffer when people don't take sexual responsibility seriously.

Real Pressures

Despite knowing the consequences, many teens become sexually active. Why do they take such risks?

Physical pressures are part of the problem. Adolescence causes many changes in a teen's body. Among them are increased levels of hormones, chemicals that drive many body processes. Some hormones produce strong sexual feelings.

Other pressures add to the problem. Television shows and movies portray sexual activity as casual. Images are explicit and often unconnected to love. Peers put pressure on

■ **Let's Not.** Ask students to give arguments or "lines" people use to pressure partners into greater sexual intimacy. List these on the board. Then ask students to suggest several comebacks to counter each one. *(Communication)*

■ **Reusing Refusal Skills.** Have students review the refusal skills in Chapter 10, page 112. Which of them would be helpful in refusing sexual activity? Which, if any, are not applicable? *(Decision Making)*

CROSS-CURRICULAR ACTIVITY
Social Studies

Divide United States history into 50-year periods and have groups research attitudes toward sex during each one. Have them summarize other important events of that time, such as the Industrial Revolution and the Vietnam War. Ask each group, in chronological order, to share its findings with the class. Help the class relate changes in sexual attitudes to broader changes in society.

MORE ABOUT *Sexual Harassment*

Review the procedures for reporting sexual harassment at your school. Remind students that they do not have to tolerate sexual harassment from anyone of any age.

Review

■ **Chapter Review.** Use the contents of the Chapter Review page to help students review concepts, think critically, and apply their knowledge.

■ **Study Guide.** Have students complete the Study Guide for Chapter 19 on p. 65 of the Student Workbook.

■ **Be Responsible.** Ask groups to list 5 actions and 5 attitudes that characterize a responsible relationship. As groups share their ideas, write a master list on the board. Help students see that a responsible person respects the other person's values, opinions, and feelings.

Evaluation

■ **Chapter Test.** Use the reproducible chapter test provided in the Teacher's Classroom Resources or create your own test using the *Testmaker Software.*

■ **Alternative Assessment.** Divide the class into three groups. Have each one write and perform a skit that demonstrates three guidelines for beginning, enjoying, or ending a romantic relationship. Guidelines should be based on information found in the chapter.

■ **I Didn't Know That.** Ask students to write a few sentences explaining the most important new piece of information they learned from this chapter. Have students share their discoveries as a chapter review.

teens when they act as though "everyone is doing it." Even though this isn't true, teens may feel that there is something wrong with them if they don't have sexual experiences.

As a result of these influences, teens often feel pulled in opposite directions. What can they do when this happens?

Strategies for Handling Sexual Feelings

Because sexual feelings are powerful and confusing, think ahead. Making a decision before the situation demands one is helpful.

Many teens write a pledge to themselves to practice **abstinence,** or *the decision not to engage in sexual activity.* Others have joined campaigns to sign papers making that commitment. Over 200,000 teens have signed such contracts, and thousands more sign each month. These teens recognize that the question is not "What is everybody else doing?" but "What's right for me?"

Other techniques can help a teen handle sexual pressures. Practicing refusal skills is one. This is a way to be ready in advance for troublesome times. Going out in groups and in public rather than being alone with a partner is also helpful. So is spending time at home only when other family members are there too.

You have a right to make your own choices about sexual activity and to communicate them. Talking to your partner makes your wishes clear. The decision will be easier for both of you if you say what you want clearly and honestly. Many teens are relieved to learn that their partner agrees. Having discussed the matter together, couples find it easier to exercise **self-control,** *a person's ability to use sense to overrule emotions.* Teens who are too em-

barrassed to discuss their feelings and wishes honestly are not emotionally ready for sex.

Following these guidelines doesn't mean that teens cannot show affection. Because love is much more than sexual activity, however, there are other ways to express it. Holding hands and hugging are physical ways. Listening to another person's feelings and dreams are emotional ways. In fact, touching someone emotionally, just by doing something nice or by being there when needed, can be very rewarding—for both people. Moments of emotional sharing are the happiest parts of many relationships.

Pride in Yourself

Good feelings come to those who live by their convictions. Many teens who have given in to sexual pressures experience remorse afterward. Going against personal values can lead to harm as well as disappointment in yourself. You are smart enough to make a wise decision on your own, one that is in your best interest. When you act according to positive values, you can feel proud that you are in control of your life.

■ Some commitments can be made just to yourself. A contract for abstinence is one such commitment. Why do you think it could be helpful to a teen?

202   UNIT 3   Families and Friendships

🔍 Focus on Analytical Skills

Have students bring in current musical recordings (with a copy of the lyrics, if possible) that deal with romantic relationships, sexual relationships, or changes in relationships (or locate selected recordings yourself). Ask students to analyze the lyrics and describe the attitudes toward sexual relationships that the songs seem to project. Ask: What effect do you think such lyrics have on teens? Is society the promoter of such messages or a victim of them?

Chapter 19 Review

Reviewing the Facts

1. What are the benefits of opposite-gender friendships?
2. How do infatuation and love differ?
3. What skills are common to handling jealousy and anger in relationships? Why?
4. Name three possible problems faced by teens who marry.
5. Why is it important to decide how you feel about sexual activity before going out with someone?
6. What is sexual harassment?

Thinking Critically

1. Why do you think that it often takes many months to get to know another person well?
2. One couple married two weeks after meeting and had a long, successful marriage. Does this contradict the text? Explain your answer.

Applying Your Knowledge

1. **Identifying Activities for a Group.** Make a list of ten things teens can do with a group. Make columns showing what the activity is, and why you think the activity would be good for a group.
2. **Writing an Advice Column.** Pretend that you write a magazine personal advice column for teens. Write a letter to the column, asking how to handle a relationship problem, such as jealousy or breaking up. Then write your advice.

3. **Analyzing Marriage.** Write your thoughts on the following topic: "Building a successful marriage requires each spouse to make sacrifices." Use specific examples to support your points.

Making Connections

1. **Language Arts.** Write a poem or song lyric in which you describe what love really means.
2. **Art.** Make a poster that offers teens ideas for ways to refuse sexual activity.
3. **Health.** Look up information on a sexually transmitted disease. Report your findings to the class.

Building Your Portfolio

Organizing for Abstinence
Some teens have signed a pledge to abstain from sexual activity. Get a copy of that contract (call 1-800-458-2772) and begin a sign-up campaign in your school. Put a copy of the contract in your portfolio.

ANSWERS TO REVIEWING THE FACTS

1. Two people can enjoy each other's company; each can learn more about relating to the other gender.
2. Infatuation is a one-sided relationship; love involves caring and commitment by both people.
3. Self-analysis and good communication are necessary so that both people can understand their own feelings and needs and are able to express them.
4. Any three: financial troubles, the challenge of raising babies, regret over lost opportunities in life, loneliness, loss of parental trust, loss of opportunity to pursue life goals.
5. The decision will then be clearly thought out and not impulsive; you can also discuss the decision with the other person.
6. Sexual harassment occurs when someone makes unwanted or unwelcome sexual advances toward another person.

ANSWERS TO THINKING CRITICALLY

1. Answers may include: The other person may hide aspects of his or her personality; he or she may be on good behavior; you may not notice some things at first; you might react differently after the relationship becomes more established.

2. These people were lucky that they were compatible. Divorce rates and the prevalence of troubled marriages show that it's wise to be cautious.

Chapter 20

FOCUS

Chapter Overview

Chapter 20 explores careers in the helping professions. It allows students to compare their skills and interests to those needed in the helping field. They are introduced to jobs requiring various levels of training.

Motivators

■ **Filling a Need.** Invite volunteers to share their experiences in helping people—anything from helping friends settle a dispute to grocery shopping for an elderly neighbor. Point out that some people make a career of helping others.

■ **Quality Time.** Ask students to make a list of several qualities they think are necessary for someone in the helping professions.

Objectives

Discuss the chapter objectives on this page. Remind students that the objectives focus on important chapter concepts.

Vocabulary

One of the vocabulary terms for this chapter is *paraprofessional*. Explain that the prefix para- means beside or closely related. Ask: What do you think a *paralegal* is? What is *parapsychology*?

Chapter 20

Careers in the Helping Professions

Terms to Learn

- clients
- entry-level job
- objective
- paraprofessional
- personal inventory
- résumé

Objectives

This chapter will help you to:

- List your personal goals and achievements.
- Identify the interests and skills required for a career in the helping professions.
- Give examples of jobs that involve helping people.
- Create your own résumé.

CHAPTER RESOURCES

Student Workbook
Study Guide, p. 69
Activity, *People Helping People*, p. 70

Teacher's Classroom Resources
Lesson Plan, p. 24
Extension #34, *Careers Helping People*, p. 40

Life Skills, *Try a Career On for Size* p. 36
Transparency 19, *Working to Help People*
Chapter 20 Test, pp. 45-46
Performance Assessment, *Best Foot Forward*, p. 43

Reteaching, *Job Preparation*, p. 26
See Also:
ABCNews InterActive™ Videodiscs

"Bye, Mrs. Canterbury. Enjoy your dinner," Gabrielle said as she turned from the front door of Mrs. Canterbury's house. Of all the stops on her meal-delivery route, her visit to Hazel Canterbury was always the most rewarding. Hazel was an older woman severely afflicted by arthritis, yet she maintained her home, her independence, and her kind-hearted personality. Gabrielle was always inspired by Hazel's positive, informed view of the world.

Actually, Gabrielle enjoyed all the visits on her route. People seemed to open up and respond to her. "And all I do," she thought as she headed for her next stop, "is listen to what they have to say and let them know that I care." Often now, Gabrielle found herself wondering how much more help she could give if she had special training—perhaps as a counselor. The idea excited her. "Maybe I'll talk to the guidance counselor at school," she thought. To help someone else and feel good about herself and earn an income as well—that was a possibility worth investigating.

An Aptitude for Caring

Like Gabrielle, you may feel excited and inspired by the prospect of building a career around helping others. It's a valuable and honorable goal. People in these professions help families solve their problems, see people through personal crises, and assist those who need special help with daily living. All these pursuits can be rewarding to the giver as well as the receiver.

Like other careers, however, the helping professions are not for everyone. The degree of commitment needed to be effective can be physically and emotionally draining. Much of the working day may be spent listening to the problems of patients and **clients**, *people who*

A caring heart is high on the list of qualities needed by those in the helping professions.

use the services of a helping professional. When you involve yourself in someone's life, it isn't easy to put that person's problems out of your mind after business hours. Also, the pay for some jobs has traditionally been lower than many jobs in business that demand similar training and levels of commitment. Those who consider a career in the helping field must weigh both positives and negatives to make the right decision for themselves.

A Personal Inventory

One way to determine whether you would enjoy a career in the helping professions is to take a **personal inventory,** or *a review of your skills and interests.* Organizing your interests, aptitudes, and goals for the future can help you identify a field of work that is rewarding for you. **Figure 20.1** presents one approach.

Topics on pp. 206-207:
- A Personal Inventory
- Résumé Writing

Checking Comprehension

✓ Why is it helpful to do a personal inventory before writing a résumé? *Collected information can be used as the basis for a résumé.*

✓ Would you use the same résumé to apply for a job at a summer camp that you use to apply as an emergency medical technician? *Unlikely. It is best to tailor a résumé to the job you are seeking. Minor changes in employment objective, special skills, and interests and activities are usually needed. While accurate and honest, these should reflect your qualifications for the specific job sought.*

CROSS-CURRICULAR ACTIVITY
Language Arts

Ask students to interview people in the helping professions for a class book of career profiles. Have students clear their choices with you first to avoid multiple interviews in one field. Students might ask: How did you become interested in this job? What qualities help you do your job well? What do you like most and least about the job? After the interviews are written, have groups read and offer feedback on classmates' interviews. Ask students to make any necessary changes before compiling the final version of the book.

206

Figure 20.1

Your Personal Inventory: Finding Out About Yourself

Ask yourself the following questions. Your answers may help give you a sense of what kind of career would be right for you.

What do I like to do?	Do I prefer working with information, things, or people?
What am I good at?	
What skills do I possess?	Do I prefer working indoors or outdoors?
What classes do I enjoy?	
What activities do I enjoy?	Do I prefer working alone or with others?
What hobbies do I like?	
What work have I done?	What jobs do I think that I would enjoy?
What are my goals for the future?	

The ability to listen and empathize is essential in any helping profession. Showing that you care helps build confidence in others as well as yourself.

REAL-LIFE APPLICATION

Read this to students: *Alicia's friends seek her out when they have problems. She always seems to understand how they feel and offers good advice. Recently a good friend confided in Alicia about a very serious family problem. After finding a hotline number for her friend, Alicia sought help and information from the school counselor. She made a special point to listen to her friend and invite her to do things that would get her mind off her troubles for a while. Ask: Would a career in a helping profession seem appropriate for Alicia? Why?*

Managing Your Life

Résumé-Writing Tips

When you apply for most jobs, you may need a résumé, that is, a written summary of your work experience, education, and interests. A résumé allows employers to see your skills at a glance.

A good résumé is usually one page long and is neatly typed and well organized. Most résumés contain the following information, organized into sections:

- **Your name, address, and telephone number.**
- **A brief description of the kind of job you are seeking.** For example, someone applying for a medical-assistant position might write, "Job objective: To work as a full-time medical assistant at a hospital."
- **Current and previous work experience.** Beginning with the most recent experience, list the names and addresses of your employers, the dates of employment, and a short description of your job or duties.
- **Educational background.** List the names and addresses of the schools and training programs you have attended. Include the dates and major subjects or course of study. Résumés prepared prior to high school graduation should include the expected date of graduation.
- **Skills.** Be sure to note any helpful abilities, such as computer skills or the ability to speak and write a second language.

- **Honors and activities.** List any awards, honors, or scholarships you have received. Include volunteer work you have done with civic or charity groups. You may also wish to name extracurricular activities.
- **Personal references.** Many employers ask for the names and addresses of people they can contact to learn more about you and your abilities. It is typical to write "References available on request" on your résumé. Be prepared with a list of people who can speak well of you. Previous employers, teachers, and coaches are all considered reliable references. Ask permission to use their names.

Applying the Principles

1. Using the personal inventory you created earlier and the hints above, create and type your own résumé. Are you able to fill in each of the sections?
2. Are any of the sections in your résumé lacking? What are some ways you could gain work experience and skills?
3. Based on your finished résumé, what sorts of jobs do you think you would be qualified for?

A personal inventory can also form the basis of your **résumé**, *a written summary of your work experience, education, and interests,* which you give to prospective employers. (See the sample in **Figure 20.2.**) Having this organized list of skills and experiences can also be helpful for filling out job or college applications and preparing for interviews.

Qualities and Skills

Another exercise that is valuable for predicting your success in a people-oriented ca-

reer is asking yourself whether you have the specific qualities and skills needed. Those described below offer a good start:

- **Are you interested in people?** Work in the helping professions takes a lot of energy. You must genuinely like people in general and have a strong desire to help them.
- **Do you understand people?** You need considerable knowledge of what "makes people tick." How do they learn? What do they fear and hope for? Why do they be-

---

Focus on Library Skills

Students can find descriptions of jobs that suit their interests in library references. Many books describe educational and training requirements, working conditions, pay rates, and the employ-

ment outlook for the field. Encourage students to locate these books—with a librarian's help, if needed—and bring examples to class.

- **Taking Stock.** Have students take the personal inventory shown in Figure 20.1. When completed, ask them to write a short summary of what the inventories say about them. Ask: What are some other benefits of identifying your skills and interests? Help students see that this information can also be useful in making friends and choosing volunteer work. *(Critical Thinking)*
- **Résumé "Righting."** Prepare as a student handout a résumé with numerous problems: typos, illogical sequences, weak style, etc. (Creating this could be an extra-credit project for advanced students.) Give these to students for correction. Follow up by discussing the value of proofreading, especially by a second party.

Managing Your Life

Have students read "Résumé-Writing Tips." Explain that job seeking is often very competitive today. To stand out amongst candidates, every detail counts. For example, a résumé with typos or smudges could make the difference in not getting a job when candidates are essentially equal. Explain that most libraries have detailed guides on preparing résumés. Many formats are possible. The best choice is one that is clear, concise, and pleasing to the eye.

- **Exploring qualities and skills**
- **Job Categories**
- **Entry-Level Jobs**

Checking Comprehension

✓ Why do people in the helping professions need to be good listeners? *They spend many hours listening and talking to other people with problems.*

✓ How can you have empathy yet remain objective? *You can understand how someone feels without becoming emotionally involved.*

✓ Name the three categories of jobs in the helping professions. *Entry level, paraprofessional, professional.*

✓ Why is the number of entry-level jobs in the helping professions falling? *More and more jobs require some kind of formal training.*

✓ Do workers in most entry-level jobs have any prior training? *No. Most complete on-the-job training.*

SPECIAL NEEDS *Strategies*

Inefficient Readers. Have students create a chart with three columns. At the top of each have them write Entry-Level, Training, Higher Education. As they finish the chapter, have them enter a list of jobs that fall into each category.

Figure 20.2

Sample Résumé

Kara Lynne Faulkner
523 E. Walnut Street
Springdale, MN 12345
(123) 555-1234

EMPLOYMENT OBJECTIVE

To obtain a teacher's aide position in a preschool program.

SPECIAL SKILLS

- Have proven ability to teach young children new skills and lead them in games.
- Organized Little Brother/Little Sister Day at Carmine High School in 1995 and 1996.
- Can speak and write some Spanish.
- Can sign for the hearing impaired.

EDUCATIONAL BACKGROUND

Carmine High School, graduated May, 1996.
CPR training, Springdale YWCA, July, 1995.

WORK EXPERIENCE

Teacher's Aide. Carmine High Lab School, August 1994—May, 1996. Have worked with the children of students and faculty in this preschool program for an average of 8 hours per week.

Child Care Assistant. Valley Methodist Church Child Care Center. Worked as an aide from June through August, 1993 and 1994.

Babysitter. Have been a neighborhood babysitter for five years. Clients have included many families with infants and young children to age eight.

ACTIVITIES AND INTERESTS

Have had roles in class plays at Carmine High School; member of the School Spirit Club for three years; enjoy camping and singing.

have as they do? Some of this knowledge can be gained from studying, but much is also learned through experience.

- **Are you a good listener?** Helping begins with active listening. Clients sense that you care when you make the effort to learn about them. They place confidence in you—and build confidence in themselves—when you accept what they say without judging them.

- **Do you have empathy?** You must be able to truly understand what people are feeling, to see a situation from their point of view. If you can focus only on how a prob-

208   **UNIT 3** *Families and Friendships*

MORE ABOUT Objectivity

"Burn out" is a typical problem among people who work in certain helping professions. Working every day with people who have problems is demanding. The more serious the situations, the greater the strain on professionals. For example, social workers who monitor children in troubled families have a high turnover rate of employment. This type of work is needed in society, but the person who seeks it needs to learn techniques for managing a balance between work and personal life.

lem affects you and how you would react, you cannot help *them*.

- **Are you trustworthy?** Clients must feel that you will respect their privacy by keeping what they tell you confidential.
- **Are you assertive?** When you believe in your own abilities, others are more likely to trust you to help them deal with their problems.
- **Can you be objective?** Although you want to empathize with others, you must also be **objective.** You must be *able to see the facts of a situation without emotional involvement.* People experiencing problems often benefit from talking to someone who sees the situation in a different light. You may point out facts and identify options that they had not recognized.
- **Can you allow people to make independent decisions?** You must respect others and trust them to make the choices that they feel are right. Clients also need to feel supported in their decisions, even if the outcome turns out poorly.
- **Can you handle conflict?** If a problem involves more than one person, disagreements and anger are likely. You must be able to teach people how to use conflict constructively.
- **Are you a skilled negotiator?** You may need to act as a go-between for disputing parties. Being a mediator involves presenting each side's concerns and desires in a reasonable, nonthreatening way. The ability to empathize and understand what is important to each person is essential.

Active Investigation

Sometimes a person doesn't know whether he or she possesses the skills needed in helping professions. Jerome, for example, had always enjoyed entertaining his nieces and nephews when they visited. After taking a comprehensive course in family and consumer sciences, he decided to consider a career in child care. Jerome began to investigate whether he had the personal qualities for such work. He asked his sister what the

everyday care of her young children involved. From his former elementary school teachers, he learned of the rewards and challenges of being an early-childhood educator. His teachers also told Jerome about the training they had needed and the experiences they found helpful. Finally, he volunteered to work at a child-care center run by a social service organization. By reflecting on this information and experience, Jerome was better able to decide on what type of career he wanted.

Opportunities Abound

The future looks bright for those who want to work in the helping professions. The field is expanding rapidly, due partly to the increasing population of senior citizens, who often need services. Jobs in the helping professions fall into three general categories, depending on the training and experience required.

Entry-level jobs are *jobs for which little or no experience is required.* These are often relatively plentiful, but they usually offer the lowest salaries and fewest benefits. Some people begin their careers at this level to learn skills that help them get more specialized jobs later.

Jobs at the next level require some specialized training or experience. This category includes a growing number of **paraprofessionals,** *workers who are trained to assist professionals.* Examples include paralegals, child-care workers, and dental assistants. Training might come from a community college, a vocational-technical school, or a training academy.

The third category includes professional jobs that require at least a degree from a four-year college. Some jobs call for higher degrees as well, such as master's, doctorate, or medical degrees. This category includes some of the highest-paying jobs in the field.

Entry-Level Jobs

Although opportunities in the helping professions are growing, the number of entry-level jobs is going down. This is because more

■ **Getting to Know Me.** Have students list the bulleted questions on page 207-209 on a piece of paper and rate themselves from 1 (weak) to 5 (strong) on each question. Then have partners rate each other using a separate paper. If possible, pair students who know each other fairly well. Follow up by asking students to compare the self-evaluation to the one done by a partner. Are there any surprises?

■ **Born, Not Made?** Discuss: If a person lacks a quality essential to the helping field, can he or she acquire it through practice? If so, how? Will that person ever possess the quality as fully as someone who seems born with it? *(Critical Thinking)*

RETEACHING

■ **Seeing Connections.** Refer students to the qualities listed on pages 207-209. Ask: If a person could have all but one of these qualities, which could most easily be left out? As you discuss their answers, help students see that many qualities are interrelated. Having empathy, for example, is part of understanding people. Stress that a person who is weak in any quality can always work to improve in that area.

MORE ABOUT Jobs

Many high schoolers are familiar with a core list of career ideas but are unfamiliar with others. Here are some job titles in the helping professions that may help trigger thoughts and exploration for students: cardiac rehabilitation specialist, family support police officer, home-care hospice nurse, homeless shelter director, day care provider, obstetric nurse, personal fitness trainer, preschool teacher, refugee resettlement director, retirement complex administrator, retirement park manager, and weight management program coordinator.

Topics on pp. 210-212:
- Jobs That Require Training
- Jobs That Require Education
- Incorporating Values

Checking Comprehension

✓ Identify some positions that require formal training but not a college degree. *Police officer, physical and occupational therapy assistants.*

✓ What makes a career in the helping professions worthwhile? *The satisfaction of helping others achieve happiness, higher self-esteem, and stronger relationships.*

BALANCING
WORK AND FAMILY

Have students read "Family-Friendly Policies of Employers." Point out that, traditionally, family and personal life was the worker's concern alone. Ask students why workers need employers who are concerned about the personal lives of workers? *(The homefront seldom has a stay-at-home parent anymore; work impacts personal life and vice versa; many families face problems today.)* How do both workers and employers benefit? *(Happier, healthier workers and families and better attitudes and productivity on the job.)*

and more entry-level jobs are becoming para-professional positions. However, there are still opportunities for people with no experience to be hired and trained on the job.

Human-services workers help clients obtain social services. This broad category includes social work assistants, mental health technicians, child-abuse workers, and community-outreach workers. Most human services workers are employed by government or private social service agencies.

Duties vary, depending on the job. Agency workers might help clients learn whether they are eligible for government benefits. Residential counselors in a halfway house may supervise adults who are recovering from al-

cohol or drug abuse. Community-outreach workers might organize a youth program or a food bank. While a high school diploma is enough for some of these jobs, an increasing number require more training. Job opportunities in this field are expected to rise sharply over the next several years.

Several health care jobs are growing rapidly. Homemaker-home health aides help people who are elderly, disabled, or ill live independently at home rather than in a hospital or a nursing home. They assist clients with personal care, monitor their health, and help them keep house and prepare meals. Nursing assistants and psychiatric aides perform similar roles in health care or mental health facilities. Medical assistants, who work in physician's offices or in hospitals, handle of-

BALANCING Work AND Family

Family-Friendly Policies of Employers

To help employees with children, many employers have become more flexible about work hours, child care, and family benefits. Some of the more common family-friendly policies that some businesses now offer include:

- **Flexible work hours, or flextime.** Employees can adjust their work schedules to meet family demands. A person may, for example, decide to work from 7 a.m. to 3 p.m., in order to be at work while his or her children are in school.
- **Job sharing.** Two part-time workers can share one full-time job, giving both employees more time for their respective families.
- **Parental leave.** Employees are legally entitled to take time off after the birth or adoption of a child, reducing the strain on the family and allowing parents time to adjust to having a child. Some companies offer paid leave to their employees, while others give workers time off with no salary.
- **Reimbursements for child care.** Workers can afford better child care when they receive financial help.

- **On-site child care.** Employees can stay close to their children while they work, reducing worries about the care their children are getting.
- **Time off with pay to care for sick children.** Employees can stay home to care for sick children without sacrificing their paychecks.

More and more businesses are providing family benefits such as these. Family benefits not only help families, they also help businesses. They lead to higher morale, lower absenteeism, greater productivity, and more successful recruitment of employees.

Suppose That . . .

You are a parent with two young children, and you are thinking about taking a new job. The company recruiting you has invited you to tour its facilities and learn more about the benefits the company has to offer employees. Prepare a list of questions you would ask about the family and child-care policies of this company.

MORE ABOUT Homemaking

Homemaking is a valued helping profession. A homemaker may be an instructor, information source, scheduler, financial and social planner, manager of human resources, social worker, counselor, child-care worker, cook, maintenance worker, nurse, and more. Many families today need or want a second income, leaving them without a full-time homemaker and with the subsequent problems. An interest in homemaking seems to be resurging as people struggle with schedules and child care. For those who have no choice in this matter, solutions come with creative managing.

fice records, record patients' health histories, and prepare patients for medical procedures.

Laws and regulations determine the training and licensing required for these jobs. For example, nursing assistants who work in nursing homes must complete a training course and pass an exam. Most of these workers pursue further education or become certified by a professional organization.

Another entry-level job is that of hot line worker. Many support groups and social service agencies have hot lines, telephone numbers that people can call for emergency help. Hot line workers respond to the callers, helping people who, for example, are thinking about committing suicide or fear that they have HIV. Most hot line programs train their workers, but college courses in counseling improve a person's qualifications.

Jobs That Require Training

You might not think of law enforcement as a helping profession, yet it is. Whether they are responding to a stalled car on the highway or an episode of domestic violence, law enforcement personnel need to react calmly and effectively as they work with people under stress. Women and men who want to work in law enforcement must first pass a number of physical and psychological tests. Then they receive special training at a police academy.

The medical field also includes jobs that require some training beyond high school. Under the supervision of physical therapists, physical therapy assistants use equipment, exercise, and massage to help clients overcome their physical limitations or pain. Similarly, occupational therapy assistants work with occupational therapists to teach skills to people with disabilities. For example, they might teach clients how to feed or dress themselves or help them develop basic job skills. In both of these occupations, individuals may be employed in hospitals, clinics, nursing homes, or schools. Training is offered by community colleges.

Jobs That Require Higher Education

Many jobs in the helping professions require college education—four years or more. Physicians and nurses are among these. Social workers have a bachelor's degree in social work and often a master's degree as well. These professionals help individuals and families deal with a wide range of problems and concerns. As with human services workers, many of these professionals are based in government or private agencies. Some, however,

CHAPTER 20 **Careers in the Helping Professions** 211

Review

■ **Chapter Review.** Use the contents of the Chapter Review page to help students review concepts, think critically, and apply their knowledge.

■ **Study Guide.** Have students complete the Study Guide for Chapter 20 on p. 69 of the Student Workbook.

■ **Seeing Is Believing.** Have students draw caricatures of people in the helping professions, labeled with captions describing the physical qualities shown, such as big ears for listening or a strong spine for assertiveness. Display the caricatures in the classroom.

Evaluation

■ **Chapter Test.** Use the reproducible chapter test provided in the Teacher's Classroom Resources or create your own test using the *Testmaker Software*.

■ **Alternative Assessment.** Ask students to imagine they are adults with several years experience in a helping profession—one mentioned in this chapter or another of their choosing. They have been asked to speak to a high school class about their jobs. Have students write a speech describing their work, their background and training, and the qualities and skills they use on the job.

CLOSE

■ **A Little Respect.** Ask: What signs show that society respects people in the helping professions? What signs point to a lack of respect? How might society demonstrate more appreciation for those who help others?

are employed in schools, hospitals, and other organizations. Many social workers spend much of their time doing field work. They may visit the homes of couples who want to adopt, investigate reports of child neglect, or help families in hospice programs, which serve people who are fatally ill. Others provide counseling or hold classes for their clients.

Counselors assist people with personal, family, educational, and career problems. Depending on the type of counseling they offer, counselors might work in schools, hospitals, clinics, or private practice. Counselors generally need a master's degree in counseling or a related field.

Some counselors provide individual or group therapy for a variety of mental health problems. Others focus on particular specialties. Marriage and family counselors, for instance, help couples and families work through conflicts. Rehabilitation counselors help people overcome alcohol, drug, and gambling addictions. School counselors, also called guidance counselors, help students make decisions about personal, academic, and career issues. Employment and career counselors give advice to those who lose their jobs or change careers.

Many people turn to a religious worker or a member of the clergy—such as a rabbi, minister, priest, or mullah—when they need help. Religious workers can be sources of comfort and advice. Training for the clergy varies from one religion to another, but a college degree and specialized study at a religious school are the usual requirements.

Psychologists and psychiatrists have advanced training in how the mind works and why people behave as they do. Some provide therapy and counseling for clients who have emotional and behavioral problems. These professionals work in hospitals, clinics, private practices, and other settings. Some concentrate on research and teaching. Although they perform many of the same functions, psychologists and psychiatrists differ in the training they receive. Psychologists must earn a doctoral degree in psychology. Psychiatrists are medical doctors who have received additional training in psychiatry. They are the only counselors who may prescribe medication.

Values in Action

When Antonio started to explore opportunities in the helping professions, he was struck by one thing. All the jobs seemed to have a common characteristic. In each one, people were putting their values into action. As one social worker explained, "I do what I believe in. I have the satisfaction of knowing that I can help others achieve happiness, higher self-esteem, and stronger relationships. When you know that your work is truly worthwhile, that's the greatest reward I can think of."

Many people who assume roles in the helping professions work with families to maintain strong family bonds during times of crisis.

MORE ABOUT Psychologists

Psychology includes several fields of specialization. Social psychologists research areas of human behavior and thought. Clinical psychologists counsel people with problems. Industrial psychologists help workers in various areas of business. Educational psychologists study learning patterns.

# Review

Reviewing the Facts

1. What is a personal inventory?
2. List four interests or skills necessary for a career in the helping professions.
3. What kind of preparation might you need for a paraprofessional job?
4. What type of work do human services workers do?
5. Identify three professional careers that involve helping other people.

Thinking Critically

1. Why do you think that such jobs as counselor, psychologist, and psychiatrist require an advanced degree?
2. Which do you think is more important for someone working with people, personal qualities or formal education and training? Why?

Applying Your Knowledge

1. **Simulating a Hot Line.** With a classmate, act out a scene in which one of you is a hot line worker and the other is a caller with a problem. Try to listen to the caller's situation. Ask questions to learn as much as you can about the problem. How would you attempt to solve it? What resources could you suggest that might be helpful? When you have finished, switch roles, using a different problem.
2. **Creating an Informational Chart.** Using the phone book, look up groups that help others under "Social Service Organizations." Identify as many different categories of organizations as you can. Then make an informational chart or poster with a heading for each general category. For example, you may have headings for "Senior Citizens' Groups," "Health and Wellness Groups," and "Religious Groups." Under these headings, list the specific organizations and their phone numbers.

Making Connections

1. **Business.** Write a letter applying for a job that involves helping other people. What personal qualities do you possess that would qualify you for the position? What experience do you have that might help you get the job?
2. **Language Arts.** Write a scene depicting one character helping an individual or a group with a problem. Keep in mind the personal qualities of the characters as you write the scene. How is the problem resolved?

Building Your Portfolio

Comparing Careers

Ask an adult a series of questions about his or her career. What personal qualities, interests, and skills led the person to this work? What duties and responsibilities are there? Write down the responses. Then compare the career to those described in the chapter. How is the work different from, and similar to, a career in the helping professions? Put your comparison in writing, and add it to your portfolio.

ANSWERS TO REVIEWING THE FACTS

1. It is a review of your interests and skills.
2. Any four: an interest in people and the ability to understand them; empathy; a good listener, trustworthy, assertive, and objective; can allow people to make their own decisions; the ability to handle conflict; and negotiation skills.
3. Training might come from a community college, a vocational-technical school, or a training academy. It could also come from work in a skilled-trade apprenticeship program.
4. They help clients obtain social services and provide other types of counseling and assistance. Other duties will vary, depending on the job.
5. Any three: social worker, counselor, religious worker or member of the clergy, psychologist, psychiatrist.

ANSWERS TO THINKING CRITICALLY

1. Helping people with severe problems requires many years of training because the issues are so complex.
2. Education and training give workers a more sophisticated understanding of people's needs and behavior so that they can help people better. On the other hand, workers must relate well to others and possess such personal qualities as maturity, responsibility, and empathy. Students will have their own ideas about whether personal qualities or formal training is more important.

Unit Preview

In Unit 4, students learn about children's needs and developmental milestones when they are infants, toddlers, preschoolers, and school age. The unit prepares students to meet these needs with play activities and guidance appropriate for each stage of development.

Content Development

Use these chapters to reinforce the following themes:

Content Strands	Chapters
Career Exploration	26
Citizenship/ Leadership	21, 23, 25
Communication	21–24
Decision Making	21, 23, 25
Health and Safety	21, 23, 25
Managing Resources	21, 25
Personal Development	21, 25
Technology	24

Unit Motivators

■ **Quick Quiz.** Ask students:

• Should you encourage a two-year-old to play games with friends?

• How would you handle a child's temper tantrum?

• How do you best meet a child's developmental needs?

Discuss responses briefly without providing correct answers. Ask them to review their responses after they complete Unit 4.

■ **Birth of a Parent.** Ask: Do people learn to be good parents or do they naturally have the necessary knowledge and skills? Suggest that people often tend to associate training only with paid employment but that perhaps many problems in families could be lessened if people were better prepared to handle them.

JOURNAL WRITING

Possible topics for student journals:

• What qualities and skills do you have that might help you be a good parent someday?

• Which stage of childhood do you think you will enjoy most if you become a parent? Why?

• Which do you think is the biggest challenge for parents—meeting a child's physical, intellectual, emotional, social, or moral needs?

• Do you think teen parenthood causes more problems for the teens or for their children? Why?

• Would you like to work with children? Why?

Child Care and Development

Chapters

215

COOPERATIVE LEARNING

Class Publication. Ask groups to design and produce age-appropriate concept books for young children. One could teach the alphabet or colors. Another might teach counting or telling time. Each group should identify tasks to be completed and assign them to individuals or teams. The book content might be assigned by types of tasks (writing, illustrating) or by pages. Donate books to an elementary school or child care center.

FHA Activities

The following activities can be used with your FHA group or as public relations strategies:

■ **Saturday Sitting Service.** Encourage students to set up a Saturday morning babysitting service once or twice a month so parents can go shopping, run errands, or attend an older child's soccer game, for example. The service might be free to parents or involve a small fee that would help finance a chapter project. Have students plan a morning of age-appropriate games, songs, and other activities for the children.

■ **Putting Skills to Work.** Arrange for students to volunteer at a community-sponsored child care center. Explain that students will have visits to become familiar with the center. Then they will plan and carry out age-appropriate activities for the children at the center. Work with the center staff to set up a schedule that will not disrupt other center programs.

Unit Closure

REVIEW

In a Perfect World. Discuss with students what the world might be like if everyone in their generation became ideal parents, willing and able to meet all their children's needs. What would these children be like when they grow up? What kinds of problems in society might be reduced or eliminated? Discuss what students might do to increase the number of ideal parents in their generation.

EVALUATION

■ **Unit Test.** Have students complete the unit test in the Teacher's Classroom Resources.

■ **Testmaker Software.** You may wish to design a unit test using the *Testmaker Software*.

Chapter Overview

Chapter 21 examines the role of caregivers and the rewards of helping to shape young lives. The chapter describes personal qualities and skills and identifies resources that can make a caregiver more effective.

Motivator

■ **Define Caregiving.** On the board, write: A child caregiver is someone who ... Have several volunteers complete the sentence with their own ideas on caregiving. If students mention only tasks and duties, ask whether they can name some of its rewards. Point out that caregiving involves responsibilities and rewards, both of which they will explore in this chapter.

Objectives

Discuss the chapter objectives on this page. Remind students that the objectives focus on important chapter concepts.

Vocabulary

Caregiver is a word new to the English language, first used around 1975 to describe someone who gives direct care to others. *Parenting* is a similarly recent addition, formed from the familiar noun *parent*.

Chapter 21

Responsible Caregiving

Terms to Learn

- caregiver
- parenting

Objectives

This chapter will help you to:

- Define **caregiving and explain the roles of parents, guardians, and other caregivers.**
- Identify **the rewards of caregiving.**
- Describe **the personal characteristics of effective caregivers.**
- Explain **the knowledge and skills that caregivers need.**
- Describe **the kinds of resources caregivers use.**

216   UNIT 4   Child Care and Development

CHAPTER RESOURCES

Student Workbook
Study Guide, p. 71
Activity, *What Makes a Good Caregiver?* p. 72

Teacher's Classroom Resources
Lesson Plan, p. 25

Extension #35, *Resources for Parents,* p. 41
Life Skills, *On-the-Scene Caregiving,* pp. 37-38
Transparency 20, *A Caregiving Network*
Chapter 21 Test, pp. 47-48

Performance Assessment, *Caring for Children,* p. 44
Reteaching, *Recipes for Caregiving* p. 27

See Also:
ABCNews InterActive™ Videodiscs

About five minutes after Isabel's nieces went outside to play ball, a softball came crashing through the kitchen window, littering the room with shards of glass. Isabel went outside to see what had happened, but neither Melissa nor Angela would admit to throwing the ball. "I'm sure your mother will be more upset if you don't tell the truth than she will be about the window," said Isabel. "I'm going in now to clean up the glass. Whoever threw the ball should come help me."

Angela slowly followed Isabel into the kitchen, admitting that she had been the one. Melissa came in to help, too. Once Isabel and her nieces had safely cleaned up the glass, Isabel called her sister. "You did exactly the right thing," said Rosa. "Telling the truth is important. Tell the girls that they can't play ball for now. I'll call someone about the window."

Caring for Children

Have you ever done babysitting or cared for young relatives, as Isabel did? If so, you probably realize that children can be a challenge. They can be totally frustrating one minute yet charming the next. Children are full of energy and have a great capacity to learn and to love. Caring for children is easier when you know what to do—and how.

People who take responsibility for raising children on a long-term or short-term basis are called **caregivers**. The job of a caregiver is a critical one because the kind of people children become is largely dependent on the love and guidance received from adults. Capable caregivers tend to raise children who are well adjusted and an asset to society. When caregivers don't handle their responsibilities well, however, children are more likely to grow up with problems.

Caring for children effectively takes a wide range of talents and qualities. Responsible people take child rearing seriously.

Babies begin to learn social skills by interacting with other people.

They prepare themselves for the job. They don't want to learn as they go and discover by trial and error. They realize that the price paid for mistakes can be very high. Because they care, they make a conscious decision to learn about children and gain the skills they need to raise them well.

Kinds of Caregivers

People who have the main responsibility for children are called primary caregivers. These individuals generally make the major decisions about how a child is raised. Usually they are the parents or guardians.

A guardian is someone who has legal responsibility for a child when the parents are unable to provide care. Guardians are often relatives of the child. In this text, references made to parents apply to guardians as well.

For most primary caregivers, raising a child is too much to manage completely alone. They usually need the help of others.

Babysitters offer occasional care for short periods of time. Child-care professionals provide longer-term care

MORE ABOUT Babysitting

Experience in babysitting can help students get other jobs requiring a responsible, caring person. Suggest that students who babysit ask clients to write letters of recommendation. Copies of these letters can be given to potential employers.

DID YOU KNOW?

A guardian is a person who is legally responsible for a child or an adult who cannot handle his or her own affairs. That person is called a ward. Guardians are appointed by the court, which carefully checks their character and background.

Topics on p. 217:
- **Caring for Children**
- **Kinds of Caregivers**

Checking Comprehension

✔ Who serves as a child's primary caregiver? *Parent or guardian.*

✔ How do a babysitter's responsibilities compare with those of a primary caregiver? *Babysitters keep children safe, guide them for short time. Primary caregiver has total responsibility 24 hours a day, even when not with children.*

Activities

■ **One and the Same?** Discuss: Is a child's parent always his or her primary caregiver? Ask for examples of when this would not be so. (*Critical Thinking*)

ENRICHMENT

■ **Better Babysitting.** Have students contact community agencies to learn about any courses for babysitters offered. Students who have completed a course can describe what they learned. The class might make a resource list of classes for those interested in becoming a more responsible babysitter.

CROSS-CURRICULAR ACTIVITY
Math

Have students contact a number of babysitters or parents who hire them regularly to figure the average pay of babysitters in their community. They might also list rates for different circumstances, such as watching different numbers or ages of children.

Checking Comprehension

✓ What are some of the rewards of caregiving? *Playing, learning with children; being part of family; carrying on traditions; watching children reach potential.*

✓ What are some challenges in being a caregiver? *Being patient, consistent, alert, energetic.*

✓ What is the most important quality for a caregiver? *Affection.*

✓ Why is consistency important for children? *Helps them feel comfortable and know how to act.*

BALANCING
WORK AND FAMILY

Finding Quality Child Care. Have students read "Finding Quality Child Care." Have students use the lists developed for the "Suppose That" section to agree as a class on the ten most critical factors.

CROSS-CURRICULAR ACTIVITY
Science

Have students identify the caregiving functions animals perform in raising their young. What behavior do the young learn from their parents?

---

in child-care centers or in family day care homes. Some child-care professionals provide regular care in the child's home while parents are away.

Family members often help with child care as well. Older siblings are a resource. Grandparents offer excellent backup too, as long as parents don't take advantage of them. The fact that many grandparents today are taking on much or all of the responsibility for raising their grandchildren is a mixed blessing. Fortunately, many grandparents fill a critical need. Unfortunately, however, an increasing number of parents are unwilling or unable to care for their children, and this creates a problem in society.

Whether parent, guardian, or another person filling in, the individual in charge of a child fulfills the **parenting** role. In other words, he or she takes on the *responsibility of caring for the child in order to promote development*. Love, guidance, and nurturance are part of the job.

Rewards of Caregiving

Child care has many rewards. Children are creative and enthusiastic and have a distinctive way of seeing the world. Most caregivers enjoy a child's perspective on life. Playing and learning with them can be fun and sometimes surprising.

For many people, children create the kind of family experience they want. Certain emotional needs, such as love, can be fulfilled in part through the parenting experience.

Children also help carry on family traditions and values through succeeding generations. This was especially apparent to Dave after his parents were killed in an automobile

BALANCING Work AND Family
Finding Quality Child Care

Knowing that a child is receiving good care eases the minds of working parents. Finding dependable, quality child care is an important task. If you choose to become a parent someday, you may need to evaluate caregivers and child-care programs.

- **Assess the options.** Talk to people. Recommendations from satisfied parents is an excellent way to locate child-care possibilities. Community resources, such as the agency that licenses child-care facilities, can provide a list of caregivers.
- **Consider values.** Before making a decision, interview the caregivers and center directors to find out if they agree on important aspects of caregiving, such as toys, reading, television viewing, nutrition, and discipline.
- **Observe.** Visit and watch the caregivers at work to judge if they seem to enjoy working with children and understand their needs. Workers

should be nurturing and caring, offering plenty of praise and comfort. Do the children seem to be happy? What is the ratio of adults to children? Also check the physical appearance of the facility—the amount of space, the organization of space, and what toys and equipment are available.

- **Call references.** Contact the parents or guardians of children already at the child-care facility. Listen not only to what is said but how it is said. Sometimes people are reluctant to speak negatively. Long pauses before an answer or cautious-sounding statements may suggest unexpressed dissatisfaction.

Suppose That . . .

You have a three-year-old and are trying to find quality care. Make a list of questions you would ask a prospective child-care provider.

DID YOU KNOW?

Many concerns have been raised recently about the quality of child care. Investigations have revealed mistreatment of children by some caregivers. Some concerned parents have resorted to videotaping in-home caregivers to find out what goes on while they are away. This procedure is not without controversy. Some caregivers welcome videotaping because it offers proof that they are behaving correctly. Others feel that videotaping is an invasion of privacy, especially when done secretly.

accident when he was ten years old. He was raised by his grandparents, making him aware of the family values that both sets of adults instilled in him. When he becomes a father, he hopes to pass along the same values that both generations taught to him.

One of the most rewarding aspects of caregiving is watching a child reach his or her potential. Helping to accomplish this gives caregivers great pride. Few experiences can equal making a contribution to someone else's life and watching children grow into happy, healthy, and responsible adults.

Personal Resources

Chris came home from football practice and was greeted happily by his little sister. When Madison jumped up, though, she knocked over the tower of blocks that she had been building. Their mother calmed her down when she began to cry. No more than a minute later, Madison was whining because the cat wouldn't let her pick him up. Their mother quickly picked Madison up. Watching them, Chris said, "I don't know how you do it, Mom. Here, I'll entertain her for a while. Come here, Squirt. Let's work on that block tower."

As Chris was beginning to notice, taking care of children is not an easy task. Caregivers must have personal qualities that permit them to raise children effectively. They also need knowledge about children and skills to deal with day-to-day challenges.

Personal Characteristics

Not everyone is equipped to care for children. Some people may not be interested in children; others lack the necessary personal qualities. Such individuals need to think twice before taking on parenting.

Effective caregivers, including parents and those who are employed in the child-care field, share many characteristics. Which of these do you have?

- **Affection.** The single most important quality is to care deeply for children.

Caregiving is a tremendous amount of work. Feeling affection for the child makes the work easier. Because Astrid always loved young children's openness and curiosity, she decided to train for a career in child care. Now she finds coming to work every day a joy.

- **Patience.** Next to affection, the most important quality is patience. Caregivers need to understand and accept the limitations that children have. Repeating instructions and reading the same storybook again and again are simply part of child rearing.
- **Self-control.** Caregivers are human, and sometimes they feel impatient. On those occasions they need another quality: self-control. Recognizing that patience is wearing thin, for instance, they can count to ten before speaking or acting.

Taking care of children is a challenge. What kind of knowledge would a caregiver need in this situation?

Activities

■ **Practicing Parenting.** Assign groups to think of ways that teens with younger siblings could help parents with specific caregiving responsibilities, such as feeding or supervising play. Provide groups time to share their ideas with the class. Urge students to carry out one or more ideas. *(Problem Solving)*

RETEACHING

■ **Qualities in Action.** Have groups suggest one behavior that shows each of the necessary personal characteristics for caregivers described in this chapter. Have a volunteer keep a list of the characteristics. Then read the list back as a composite of the ideal caregiver.

FAMILY AND COMMUNITY OUTREACH

Have students ask adults in their family how they learned their parenting skills. For example, did they help care for younger siblings, ask friends for advice, or learn by doing? What are some things they wish they had known when their children were born? What advice would they give new parents today? Have students share their findings with the class.

Focus on Parenting Skills

Caregivers greatly influence a child's developing self-concept. Children who consistently receive attention and praise come to feel good about themselves and believe in their abilities. Children who are continually ignored except to be criticized may resort to misbehavior to get any sort of attention. Such children form a negative self-concept that may stay with them for life. Ask: How might knowing this affect the way a caregiver handles appropriate and inappropriate behavior?

Checking Comprehension

✓ What are some decisions caregivers must make? *When and what to feed the child; how much television child should watch; how to handle sickness and injuries.*

✓ Should parents expect to raise children without consulting others? *No matter how experienced or knowledgeable they are, they can learn from various available resources.*

MULTICULTURAL *Perspectives*

Ask groups to research parenting practices in different cultures, such as the Inuit people and specific African groups. Which values underlie parenting in these cultures? What characteristics does each seek to nurture its children? Model and expect respect for the customs of other cultures.

SPECIAL NEEDS *Strategies*

Attention Deficit. Help students distinguish between the personal characteristics on pages 219-220 and the skills on pages 220-221. Point out that the characteristics are personal traits that caregivers possess. The skills are abilities that caregivers must learn.

Because children are energetic, a caregiver needs energy to keep up with them.

• **Consistency.** Children thrive when they are given routines—the same bedtime, the same rules, the same responses to similar behaviors. Lack of consistency leaves children unsure how to act, which can disturb their sense of well being.
• **Alertness.** Caregivers need to be aware of what children are doing virtually all the time, especially young children. Alertness prevents possible harm. It also allows the caregiver to provide experiences for growth and learning. When Chad showed interest in his father's workbench and tools, Mr. Jacobs used the chance to teach Chad about the use and handling of some of the tools.
• **Energy.** Children require a tremendous amount of attention. Effective caregivers must have the physical and mental stamina to keep up with them.

Knowledge

No one is born with the ability to parent. You must learn and practice how to take good care of children. Effective parenting requires knowing about children. For example, you wouldn't expect a one-year-old to speak in complete sentences. On the other hand, if a three-year old were having difficulty speaking, something could be wrong and help should be sought. Caregivers need to understand the stages of development that children reach at various ages. Then, they have a general idea of what to expect from the child and how to respond.

Skills

Certain skills are needed to care properly for children. Developing the following skills helps parents and other caregivers provide the best care for children:

• **Communication.** Caregivers need to communicate effectively with children. Children cannot learn what behavior is expected of them unless they understand the words. As with people of all ages, making positive statements is far more effective than criticism. For example, making a game of picking up toys is better than saying, "I told you to get this mess picked up!"
• **Conflict resolution.** All children get in occasional disputes with other children. The younger they are, the fewer tools they have to settle their differences. Caregivers need to know how to promote sharing and taking turns.
• **Decision making.** Parents and other caregivers make decisions constantly, from what to feed children to how much television they should watch. At times, such as when a child is sick or injured, a caregiver must make decisions quickly and calmly.
• **Problem solving.** As in other areas of life, problem-solving skills are vital to caregiving. For example, getting Josh to bed was a challenge for his parents. Josh always resisted. When they finally realized that

REAL-LIFE APPLICATION

Read this to students: *Six-month-old Marcus was feverish and crying. His mother Janeen didn't know what medication he should have. She didn't want to ask her mother, who disapproved of Janeen having a baby so young. She couldn't reach her husband at work. She felt foolish calling her pediatrician; she had already done so twice this month.* Ask: What other resources might Janeen use? What personal qualities might help her be a more effective caregiver?

he simply needed more attention, they began taking turns reading a story to him each evening at bedtime. After that change, bedtime became more pleasant.

- **Management.** Time management skills are essential in providing a calm atmosphere for children. No two days are the same, but still Leslie Barnett has a daily routine she follows for her in-home child-care business. Impressed by her skills, a client said, "I don't know how you do it. What do you do if a baby's crying, the phone's ringing, and the other children are hungry." Leslie answered with a laugh, "I pick up the baby, start setting out the sandwiches and fruit prepared earlier in the morning, and let the answering machine get the phone."

Outside Resources

Eve and Paul are new parents. Eve is an only child and had never done babysitting. Unlike his own father, Paul wanted to take an active role in raising little Ben. They are both committed to providing the best environment for Ben, but they lack confidence.

Fortunately for Eve and Paul, caregivers can draw upon many resources to help them in raising children. These resources include the following:

- **Family and friends.** Although caregivers do learn from experience, parenting is easier and can be more rewarding with a support system. Many family members and friends give advice about caregiving. Parents

can weigh the advice and accept what seems most sensible to them.

- **Agencies and organizations.** Several government agencies and programs provide financial, medical, and other support to parents. Other organizations include social services and religious groups, many of which can be found in the yellow pages of the phone book.
- **Support groups.** Talking over caregiving issues with other people can help parents meet challenges. For instance, Parents Without Partners helps single parents cope with many everyday issues of child care.
- **Hot lines.** Telephone hot lines give caregivers immediate answers to questions they have. The hot line for a poison control center, for example, is especially valuable in an emergency.
- **Books and magazines.** Libraries and bookstores have dozens of books and magazines on child care. These resources offer advice and specific information about how to care for children of all ages.
- **Classes and workshops.** Many high schools, community colleges, adult education programs, local health departments,

Classes in child care and parenting skills can be helpful to all caregivers, no matter how experienced they are.

Activities

■ **As the Twig Is Bent.** Ask students to name some factors that influence how parents raise their children. *(Critical Thinking)*

■ **Applying Skills.** Read the following situations aloud. Ask students which of the parenting skills on pages 220-221 would be useful in each situation.

- The three-year-old you are watching says he is hungry. His mother should be home to give him supper in half an hour.
- The two-year-old in your care has been scratched by the family cat. The scratch is not deep, but it is bleeding and the child is crying.
- Your four-year-old niece and her friend, playing in the backyard, are arguing over who will use the swing first. *(Problem Solving)*

CROSS-CURRICULAR ACTIVITY
Language Arts

Ask students to select a current magazine article on parenting and summarize it, orally or in writing. Have them compare the ideas in the article with those in this chapter.

CROSS-REFERENCE

Tell students that they will learn more about the ages and stages of children in Chapter 22, the care and safety of children in Chapter 23, the importance of play in Chapter 24, the realities of parenthood in Chapter 25, and careers involving children in Chapter 26.

Review

■ **Chapter Review.** Use the contents of the Chapter Review page to help students review concepts, think critically, and apply their knowledge.

■ **Study Guide.** Have students complete the Study Guide for Chapter 21 on page 71 of the Student Workbook.

■ **Raising Standards.** Remind students that caregivers have a major impact on children's self-concept and ability to reach their physical and intellectual potential. Then have groups write comparative descriptions of a child who is cared for by a person with the needed caregiving characteristics and skills and a child raised by a person who lacks them.

Evaluation

■ **Chapter Test.** Use the reproducible chapter test provided in the Teacher's Classroom Resources or create your own test using the *Testmaker Software.*

■ **Alternative Assessment.** Ask groups to create ten-item questionnaires to help people determine whether they have the characteristics and skills of responsible caregivers. Each item should be an example of a characteristic or skill, such as "Are you willing to read the same bedtime story every night for two weeks?"

■ **Raising Children.** An African proverb states that it takes a whole village to raise a child. Ask students what they think this means. What view of caregiving does this proverb reflect?

---

hospitals, and such organizations as the Red Cross sponsor courses in parenting skills. These programs provide caregivers with an opportunity to learn from instructors and other students.

A Look at Impact

The overall quality of child care impacts everyone: children, caregivers, families, and even society as a whole. In order to develop properly in all areas, children need to be nurtured by caring adults. When caregivers value children enough to devote time and energy to them, they help ensure that succeeding generations of people will mature into responsible adults. Caring about and for children strengthens society. Indeed, society needs children—healthy and well-adjusted children—to continue to be strong.

You are part of this picture. As a parent, relative, or part of a support system, you are likely to encounter children. Any skills you acquire will be useful. You can begin developing your caregiving skills at any age. Taking care of younger siblings, babysitting for neighbors or friends, and working at a community recreation center—either alone or with your friends—are all good ways to start learning more about children and how to care for them.

Managing Your Life

Baby Basics

Caring for infants calls for some special skills. If you do babysitting or care for an infant in your family, you can use the following hints.

How to Feed Babies

- Set the bottle in warm water for a minute or two. Never warm bottles in a microwave because the milk may become much hotter in some spots than in others.
- Shake the bottle upside down so that a few drops fall on your wrist. It should be warm, not hot.
- Make sure the neck of the bottle is full of liquid so that the baby takes in less air.
- Midway through the feeding, burp the baby to release any air in the stomach. Cover your shoulder with a towel, hold the baby against your shoulder, and pat firmly but gently on the baby's back. You could also place the baby stomach down on your lap and pat gently on the baby's back.

How to Diaper Babies

- Use a clean, flat surface, such as a changing table, a crib, or a towel on the floor. Have all supplies nearby before you begin.
- Never leave the baby or toddler alone on a table or a high surface.
- Remove the diaper. Gently clean the baby with a premoistened wipe or a warm, wet cloth. Be sure to wipe from front to back.
- Apply powder, oil, or ointment—if the parents use it—to prevent diaper rash. Gently shake powder into your hand before applying. Shaking it directly onto the baby can create a dust cloud that could harm the baby's lungs.
- Lift the baby slightly by holding both ankles with one hand and slide the diaper underneath. Fasten a cloth diaper by pinching the material and carefully pinning it, protecting the baby's skin from the point of the pin with one hand.
- Move the baby to a safe location. Discard the used diaper. Wash your hands.

Applying the Principles

1. Why do you think babies shouldn't be put to bed with a bottle?
2. If the baby drops the bottle on the floor, what should you do?
3. How often should a diaper be changed?

Managing Your Life

Have students read "Baby Basics." Invite experienced volunteers to demonstrate feeding and diapering a doll.

Answers to Applying . . .

1. Baby may take in too much air and become uncomfortable; can promote tooth decay; promotes use of food as pacifier.
2. Set baby in safe place before retrieving bottle; continue feeding with clean bottle and nipple.
3. As often as needed.

Reviewing the Facts

1. What is caregiving?
2. List three examples of caregivers.
3. What are two rewards of caregiving?
4. What personal qualities should caregivers possess?
5. Name the skills that caregivers must develop.
6. Identify five outside resources that caregivers might turn to.

Thinking Critically

1. How could observation skills help a person be a more effective caregiver?
2. How could someone's lack of caregiving skills have a negative impact on a child?

Applying Your Knowledge

1. **Defining Caregiving Qualities.** Make a list of questions you would ask if you were interviewing a part-time caregiver for a two-year-old. What qualities would he or she need to have? What would you be concerned about?
2. **Identifying Child-Care Options.** Make a list of five child-care facilities in your area. Include the name and address, the ages of children served, and the approximate number of children and child-care workers.
3. **Finding Resources.** Working in teams, focus on one aspect of child care, such as health issues, reading, ideas for play, or nutrition. Find at least five books or other resources that offer caregivers help and advice in the area you identified.

Making Connections

1. **Government.** Create a chart of child-care support services offered by your local government. For each service, indicate the agency or department responsible, the kind of service supplied, and rules for eligibility.
2. **Literature.** In his poem "My Heart Leaps Up," the English poet William Wordsworth wrote, "The Child is father of the Man." By this, Wordsworth meant that children's experiences, both positive and negative, affect the adults that they become. Write a short poem that deals with the theme of childhood in this regard.

Building Your Portfolio

Performing a Self-Assessment
What skills do you possess that would help you be a responsible caregiver? Make a list of these skills and write at least one example of how you could use each skill to benefit a child in your care. Then, create a list of resources you could use to improve your abilities. You may want to check a phone book, ask people you know, or visit a library to identify some specific resources. How would each of these resources help you become a better caregiver? When you have completed your lists, add them to your portfolio.

ANSWERS TO REVIEWING THE FACTS

1. Taking responsibility for raising children on a long- or short-term basis.
2. Any three: parents, guardians, other relatives, child-care professionals, babysitters.
3. Any two: the pleasure of being with the child; the experience of seeing the world through a child's eyes; the joy of playing and learning with children; the satisfaction of teaching and guiding them; the feeling of accomplishment when children grow into happy, healthy, responsible adults.
4. Affection, patience, self-control, consistency, alertness, and energy.
5. Communication, conflict-resolution, decision-making, problem-solving, and management skills.
6. Any five: family and friends, agencies and organizations, support groups, hot lines, books and magazines, classes and workshops.

ANSWERS TO THINKING CRITICALLY

1. A person could learn caregiving skills from others and better understand children's needs by watching how they behave.

2. Possible response: An ineffective caregiver could raise a child who has problems with self-esteem and poor development.

Chapter 22

FOCUS

Chapter Overview

Chapter 22 outlines the stages of childhood development, describing the physical, intellectual, emotional, social, and moral progress expected at each. The chapter also discusses the special needs some children have and the challenges they face.

Motivator

■ **Children Are.** Ask students to recall familiar expressions relating to children, such as "acting like a child" and "from the mouths of babes." Ask: What does each say about what children are like? Tell students that this chapter will give them an objective understanding of children's abilities and behaviors at different ages.

Objectives

Discuss the chapter objectives on this page. Remind students that the objectives focus on important chapter concepts.

Vocabulary

Large-motor skills and *small-motor skills* are sometimes called gross-motor skills and fine-motor skills respectively. The definitions of these terms are the same, but *large* and *small* are more familiar words than *gross* and *fine*.

Chapter 22

Ages and Stages

Terms to Learn

- cooperative play
- developmental tasks
- eye-hand coordination
- inclusion
- large-motor skills
- morality
- object permanence
- parallel play
- reflexes
- small-motor skills

Objectives

This chapter will help you to:

- List the four main stages of child development.
- Explain the principles that underlie development.
- Describe the physical, intellectual, emotional, social, and moral characteristics of each developmental stage.
- Compare and contrast the needs of children who have special needs with those of other children.

224   UNIT 4   Child Care and Development

Ted hadn't seen his young neighbor's son in a few months, and he was amazed by how he had changed. The last time he saw Tommy, he was always in his mother's or father's arms. He drank from a bottle, and it seemed that his diaper needed to be changed all the time. He could barely sit up and couldn't move around. Now he was a dynamo. Tommy walked across the living room, fed himself, and played patty-cake. Ted couldn't believe what a difference a few months could make.

Areas of Development

As Ted saw with Tommy, the changes that take place in the first few years of life are truly phenomenal. These changes can be grouped into five areas. Physical development includes changes in **large-motor skills,** or *control over the large muscles of the body, such as those in the arms and legs.* Other physical changes involve **small-motor skills**—*control over the small muscles, such as those in the hands and fingers.*

Intellectual development includes the abilities to use language and to understand concepts. With intellectual development, children learn the concentration needed to succeed in school.

Children develop emotionally in tremendous ways. The infant relies on crying to communicate displeasure; the school-age child is able to exercise some control over emotions.

Social development is also noticeable. By the time they are ready for school, young children are able to engage in—and enjoy—a wide variety of different relationships with other people.

Moral development is one of the most remarkable changes in young children. With guidance, they learn to tell right from wrong and to act accordingly.

Stages and Principles

Researchers have identified four main stages that children go through as they develop:

- Infancy (birth to one year)

- Toddlerhood (one to three years)
- Preschool age (three to five years)
- School age (five to ten years)

The first three stages, taken together, are called early childhood.

In each stage, children master *different skills and abilities* that are called **developmental tasks.** For many years, researchers have intensively studied the development of children. As a result, they have identified some principles about how children develop.

- **Development is sequential.** Nearly all children master developmental tasks in the same order. Children build on what they learn, adding layers of ability. Crawling generally comes before walking, and scribbling comes before drawing.
- **Rates of development are individual.** Some children develop more rapidly and some more slowly. Each child has a unique time frame. One child may begin to walk at 15 months while another does so at 10 months. One child may print letters at age four-and-a-half, while another does so at age five-and-a-half.

Children build on previously learned skills as they develop new skills. Crawling helps lead to walking.

CHAPTER 22   Ages and Stages   225

Topic on p. 225:

- **Introducing the Areas of Development**
- **Developmental Stages and Principles**

Checking Comprehension

✓ Which kind of motor skills allow an infant to crawl across the floor? *Large-motor.* To fit one object into another? *Small-motor.*

✓ Can you predict exactly when a child will learn a certain skill? *No; children develop at different rates.*

Activities

■ **Building Skills.** Have students name skills they have acquired over the past several years and explain how they gradually added layers of ability over time. What roles did frustration, repetition, and patience play in acquiring the skills. *(Critical Thinking)*

ENRICHMENT

■ **Switching Sides.** To help students appreciate small-motor skills, ask them to write their names with the hand they don't normally use. Have students name other common tasks and explain whether they require large- or small-motor skills, or both.

CROSS-CURRICULAR ACTIVITY
Social Studies

Have students investigate Jean Piaget's and Maria Montessori's theories of child development. If any students attended a Montessori school, have them describe how learning activities are structured.

Topics on pp. 226-227:
- Infant Development
- Toddler Development

Checking Comprehension

✓ What senses do infants have at birth? *All five—sight, hearing, taste, smell, and touch.*

✓ Why are toddlers' physical skills potentially dangerous to them? *They are unable to recognize when these skills could lead to injuries.*

✓ Can a toddler speak in whole sentences? *Not at first, but by the end of toddlerhood.*

CROSS-CURRICULAR ACTIVITY
Science

Human infants are completely helpless at birth; they take years of development (longer than any other species) to learn survival skills. Have students research what survival skills other species have at birth and write summaries of their findings. Post these throughout the room.

FAMILY AND COMMUNITY OUTREACH

Ask for volunteers to contact local child-care facilities to learn what education or experience they require of their staff. Have students share their data to determine an average level of training for the community.

- **The five areas of development are interrelated.** Many skills require that the child be ready in more than one area. Toileting skills, for instance, include physical control of the bowel and bladder muscles as well as intellectual and emotional readiness.

Infancy

For the first year of a baby's life, growth and development are rapid. The changes that take place during infancy occur more rapidly than at any other stage of life.

Physical Development

When she was only a few days old, An-Lee already was displaying physical characteristics typical of newborns. She had strong **reflexes,** or *automatic, involuntary responses.* If you stroked her cheek, she turned her head toward your hand and sucked. If you placed your finger in her palm, she curled her tiny fingers and grasped it tightly. An-Lee cried to signal discomfort, and she could see, hear, taste, smell, and touch.

Gradually, An-Lee learned about the shapes and textures of her environment by putting objects into her mouth. This activity also helped her develop **eye-hand coordination,** *the ability of the eyes and the hand and arm muscles to work together to make complex movements.* As her large-motor skills developed, she learned to roll over, sit up, and, finally, stand.

Intellectual Development

The intellectual development of an infant can be seen in many ways. At four weeks, An-Lee was awake only for short periods, but she was beginning to notice the world. She would follow a toy with her eyes when it was moved in front of her face. As her vision developed, An-Lee became more aware of the mobile

When you place your finger in a newborn's palm, the newborn's fingers will curl around and grasp your finger. This is an involuntary action called a reflex.

hanging in her crib. Later, she began to imitate the actions of others.

At first, An-Lee's only way of communicating was by crying. Around her third month, she began to use sound to communicate pleasure, gurgling and cooing at familiar people and toys. At the same time, An-Lee was developing important intellectual concepts. For example, when she reached the age of eight months, she learned *that people and things exist even after they are gone from sight.* Most infants learn this concept, called **object permanence,** between 8 and 12 months of age.

Emotional Development

Perhaps the most important emotional task for an infant is to develop trust in the primary caregiver or caregivers. When An-Lee felt warm, dry, fed, and loved, she sensed her caregivers' responsiveness to her needs. This helped her thrive and develop properly.

Social Development

As an infant, An-Lee also developed socially. She smiled for the first time when she was three months old. At seven months, she learned to recognize the difference between familiar and unfamiliar faces. At this time, she also became afraid of new people.

Toddlerhood

Physical growth usually slows a bit as infants become toddlers. During this stage, however, children master an amazing number of physical, intellectual, and social skills. Emotional and moral development also begin to take shape.

MORE ABOUT Language Development

Hearing problems can slow language development. Caregivers can check children's hearing by noting their response to noises. A newborn should be startled by a loud clap; a three-month-old should turn toward a sound.

Toddlers should respond when called, pay attention to sounds around them, and be awakened by loud noises. The child who does not should have a complete hearing test. All infants and children should have their hearing checked during routine physical examinations.

Physical Development

Manuel's first steps were a thrill for him and his family. Once 14-month-old Manuel felt steady, he wanted to walk everywhere. Soon he wanted to run everywhere as fast as he could.

As his small-motor skills developed, Manuel was able to feed and dress himself. Manuel's parents encouraged these efforts. They watched him constantly, because his mobility could get him into dangerous situations. Climbing out of his crib and high chair, for instance, could result in a fall. When Manuel was on the second floor, his parents put up a gate on that floor across the stairs.

Intellectual Development

Improved communication skills mark the intellectual development of toddlers, as young children learn to talk and express their needs, thoughts, and ideas. Manuel went from speaking single words to saying short phrases and, finally, whole sentences. He also began to understand basic intellectual concepts, such as cause and effect. He noticed that if he dropped something, it fell.

As a toddler, Manuel learned about size and space and about how objects relate to one another. When he saw two objects side by side, he learned which was larger, as well as which objects go on top of or inside others. During this stage, children may spend hours putting blocks and toys together and taking them apart, or playing with groups of objects, such as pots and pans.

Emotional Development

Little by little, toddlers acquire the ideas that will form their self-concept: the knowledge that they are unique and have their own feelings and that others have certain feelings about them. Many of Manuel's early attitudes about himself came from people who cared for him. His self-esteem grew as the people around him helped him develop an "I can do it" attitude.

Social Development

Sometimes parents are concerned when they notice that their toddlers seem to play alone instead of with other children. However, this behavior is a natural phase called **parallel play,** *when toddlers play alongside one another instead of together.*

Around age two, children struggle between their dependency on others and their desire for independence. Manuel wanted to do everything for himself even though he couldn't. His favorite word became "no" and sometimes his frustration resulted in temper tantrums.

Moral Development

Toddlers begin to develop a sense of **morality,** that is, *an understanding about what is right and wrong.* They test new behaviors and observe the results of their actions.

Toddlers spend much of their playtime exploring new objects. This toddler is learning about objects that go together.

CHAPTER 22   Ages and Stages   227

Activities

■ **Disturbing Delays?** Ask students why this situation would be of concern: Two-week-old Ruthie does not turn her head and try to suck when her cheek is stroked. *(Problem Solving)*

RETEACHING

■ **Time Line.** Have students bring in pictures of infants and toddlers that illustrate developmental characteristics, such as a toddler's fascination with fitting objects together. Work together to arrange the pictures chronologically as part of a time line of child development. Then write captions that describe the skills depicted. (Students might add to the time line after they study preschoolers and school-age children.)

ENRICHMENT

■ Ask students to observe two or more toddlers playing in the same vicinity. (They might watch at a park or in the mall.) Have them report on what they noticed, including evidence of parallel play.

MORE ABOUT Physical Development

The following heights and weights are typical of toddlers: *age one*—29.8 in. (75.7 cm) and 22.5 lb. (10.2 kg); *age two*—34 in. (86.4 cm) and 27.7 lb. (12.6 kg); *age three*—37.7 in. (95.6 cm) and 32.4 lb. (14.7 kg).

MORE ABOUT Toddlers' Emotions

One typical emotion in toddlers is the fear of being away from parents, familiar caregivers, or even their normal environment. "Separation anxiety" is not unusual and eventually subsides with patient support from caregivers.

- Preschool Development
- Tantrums

Checking Comprehension

✓ Why do two-year-olds often become frustrated? *They are learning new skills but are still mostly dependent on others.*

✓ Why do preschoolers' imaginations sometimes cause them to be fearful? *They are occasionally unable to tell fantasy from reality.*

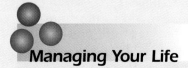

Managing Your Life

Tempering a Tantrum
Have students read "Tempering a Tantrum." Explain that behavior a child cannot control is not "bad." Many adults overreact to tantrums with alarm and anger because they don't understand that these outbursts in a toddler are typical. Children outgrow them when adults use the techniques described.

Answers to Applying...

1. No; she gave in after saying no; this teaches Tim that he can get what he wants by having a tantrum. It reinforces his tendency to have them.
2. Children feel frustrated by limited physical skills; are torn between independence and dependence; may test limits to learn what behavior is acceptable.
3. Child may enjoy attention and feeling of power at provoking strong reaction.

Preschoolers

Preschoolers are more independent than toddlers and have better control over their bodies. Most still lack the intellectual abilities to handle academic subjects, but they are beginning to acquire some understanding that will help them in school.

Physical Development

Preschoolers look different from toddlers because their arms, legs, and trunk lengthen, giving the body different proportions. They also can move with much greater assurance than toddlers do. Preschoolers can hop, pedal a tricycle, and run in even strides. Fine-motor skills are better developed than they were during toddlerhood. In this stage, Katrina was able to use scissors to cut paper and could dress herself fairly well. She could also string beads into necklaces.

Intellectual Development

Preschoolers begin to prepare for their future years in school by learning to count and name colors. Many children also learn to identify the letters of the alphabet. Preschoolers sometimes seem to live in a make-believe world. Katrina loved pretending that she was

Managing Your Life

Tempering a Tantrum

Some people wrongfully assume a young child's temper tantrum means that the child is not being raised properly. These outbursts often occur, however, when children become frustrated because they cannot accomplish something they want to do, such as unbutton a coat. Tantrums also may happen when children are denied something they want, such as a toy or a cookie, or when they are overly tired. They may fall on the floor, cry, and kick for several minutes. Some children also bang their heads against the floor, pull their hair, or hold their breath.

If you take care of a child who has a tantrum, here are some ways to handle it:

- **Ignore the tantrum.** Many child-care professionals believe that the best way to deal with a tantrum is to ignore it. If you walk away, the child has no audience and gets no reward for the tantrum. Usually, the tantrum will not last long.
- **Remain calm.** Remember that occasional temper tantrums are typical of toddlers. Talk soothingly—losing your own temper and yelling at the child will not stop the tantrum—it will only make things worse.
- **Try to distract the child.** If a child wants something that you cannot allow, offer another object. Turn the child's attention to something else.

- **Physically restrain the child.** When children bang their heads or act violently during a tantrum, they may harm themselves physically. These children need to be held or hugged firmly until the tantrum subsides.
- **Remove the child from the situation.** When children throw tantrums in public, the best solution is to pick the child up and leave, or move to a quieter area where others won't be disturbed. If children are taken home, they soon learn that one of the costs of tantrums is losing the pleasure of an outing.

Applying the Principles

1. Ellen is caring for two-year-old Tim. She tells him that he cannot have a cookie before dinner. Tim begins to have a tantrum, and Ellen gives him the cookie after all. Did Ellen do the right thing? Explain your reasoning.
2. Why do you think temper tantrums are most likely to occur between the ages of two and four?
3. How could becoming upset by a child's tantrum encourage future tantrums?

REAL-LIFE APPLICATION

Read this to students: *George wants to give his four-year-old daughter every advantage. He hopes to teach her how to read and write before she finishes kindergarten so she will have a head start when she begins grade school.* Ask: Do you think George will succeed? Help students see that until children are physically and intellectually ready to learn a new task, attempts to teach them will likely lead to frustration.

Between ages three and five, children begin to play together with other children and to form friendships.

different characters—a clown, a fire-breathing dragon, her mother, or a doctor. Her verbal abilities also had advanced tremendously—she spoke in complete sentences and had a much larger vocabulary.

Emotional Development

Katrina's verbal skills helped her control her emotions more than she could as a toddler. Able to express herself better, she no longer had the outbursts of her earlier years. Her love for pretend play also highlighted another emotional development typical of preschoolers: the beginnings of empathy.

Preschoolers experience the full range of emotions, from fear and anxiety to joy and pride. They may display many fears, however, because they are not completely able to distinguish fantasy from reality.

Social Development

During the preschool years, children move from parallel play to **cooperative play,** *seeking out play groups of three or four children.* Around age four or five, a child is likely to single out another child as a best friend. Katrina, for instance, was disappointed when her friend Karen was absent from preschool one day. In day care and preschool, children acquire many social skills. These include how to get along in a group, how to share, and how to solve simple problems together.

Moral Development

The moral development that began in the toddler years continues in the preschool stage. Preschoolers have a rigid sense of right and wrong. They believe that adults—parents, teachers, and other caregivers—set and control rules. Psychologist Lawrence Kohlberg believed that preschoolers behave well to avoid punishment and gain rewards. Other researchers believe that preschoolers can understand basic moral concepts, including fairness, justice, and empathy.

School-Age Children

School-age children—those between five and ten years of age—experience a major change in their world. They spend large periods of time in a very structured setting away from home, interacting with other adults and with many peers.

MORE ABOUT Intellectual Development

Preschoolers have several common intellectual characteristics. They begin to use symbols, learning that objects and words can represent something else. They learn through fantasy as they act out make-believe situations during play. Children at this stage have a self-centered view of the world, which affects the what they say and do. Preschoolers also have trouble focusing on more than one characteristic at a time. Choosing only the red items in a group is easier for them than choosing only the red trucks.

Topics on pp. 230-232:
- School-Age Development
- Children with Special Needs

Checking Comprehension

✓ Does the growth rate increase or decrease for school-age children? *Decreases.*

✓ Why are school-age children less likely than preschoolers to be upset if a rule is broken? *They have begun to realize rules are flexible.*

✓ How can caregivers positively affect the self-concepts of children with physical disabilities? *Treat disability as challenge, encourage children to see selves as capable.*

✓ Why do highly intelligent children need extra help? *So they can reach their potential.*

SPECIAL NEEDS *Strategies*

Visual Learners. Some students benefit by placing key chapter information in a chart form. Have them head four columns on a large piece of paper with each stage of development: infancy, toddlers, preschoolers, and school-age children. They should place the developmental areas (physical, intellectual, social, emotional, and moral) along the left vertical. Then have them enter key words and phrases from the text, class discussion, and other resources that characterize development at each stage. You may supply students with a labeled blank chart.

Physical Development

In the early school years, children continue to grow physically, but at a slightly slower pace than before. Their baby teeth are replaced by permanent teeth. The school-age child's movements are more certain; children at this stage can enjoy games that include more skillful running and jumping. The development of small-motor skills allows children to write and draw more precisely.

Intellectual Development

The exploring and testing that began during infancy continue as a child grows. Young children ask many questions and acquire reasoning skills as they think about why and how things happen.

School-age children build on these skills to master more complex tasks. They learn arithmetic, reading, and the simple principles of science. During the elementary school years, children expand their vocabularies, adding about 5,000 words a year.

Emotional Development

As children develop intellectually during the school-age years and gain a clearer understanding of the world, their preschool fears decrease. Fear, however, often may be replaced by another difficult emotion—stress. Stress can come from academic pressure in school, family problems—such as parents' di-

How does the greater concentration that school-age children possess help them in school?

MORE ABOUT *Intellectual Development*

As part of their intellectual development, school-age children begin to think logically. They use reasoning to think things through. With more advanced thinking skills, they can apply what they know to other objects and situations. Such complex concepts as the passage of time become understandable, and they become curious to learn more. Their thinking skills allow them to become problem solvers and tackle new subjects like biology, geography, and social studies.

From School to Work

Teaching: A Skill for Life

What You Learn Today . . .

Can you show me how you did that?" Can you recall times you have guided someone through a process that was familiar to you? Because you have been a student for so many years, you may never have thought of yourself as a teacher.

Have you ever shown a classmate how to work a math problem or a computer function? Have you demonstrated to a friend how to dive or hold a bat or make a ribbon barrette? As you teach others, you are developing a skill that will always be useful to you.

. . . You Can Use Tomorrow

No matter what career you choose, chances are you will use your teaching skills. In factories and offices, people train new workers. Salespeople often explain the features of products, such as computers and cars, to customers. Child-care professionals and parents impart knowledge to children, as well as skills for independence.

Practicing Your Skills

You can polish your teaching skills using these tips as a guide:

- Think about the age and background of the person you are teaching. For example, use simple words to explain ideas to a small child.

- Find out what the person already knows, and start from there.
- Take your time. Take one step at a time, providing information in a logical sequence.
- Use written explanations, drawings, and demonstrations when they are helpful.
- Preserve self-esteem by not making the person feel inferior.
- Be patient, asking and answering questions.
- Repeat and summarize as necessary. To ensure understanding, ask the person to repeat what you said in his or her own words.

Assessing Your Skills

1. Which of the teaching tips above do you think is most important? Why?
2. Describe a situation in which you tried to teach something to another person. Were you successful? Why or why not?
3. What problem could you encounter if you don't first assess what the person already knows about a subject or process?

---

vorce—and life changes—such as a move to a new city. Children with high self-esteem are more likely to handle stress effectively.

Social Development

School-age children generally have more social opportunities outside the family. They begin to form peer groups and take on more responsibility for their own behavior. During this stage, children work on learning the skills that society values—such as sharing and considering the feelings of others.

Moral Development

During the school years, children begin to understand that many rules are flexible and can be changed. They begin to care about what others think, and most want to be thought of as "good." Children's consciences take on a stronger role.

CHAPTER 22 Ages and Stages 231

DID YOU KNOW?

When school-age children cannot handle their school work, the issue of whether to hold them back a year may arise. Some current research indicates that retention causes social and emotional trauma and increases the odds that a child may eventually wind up in a learning-disability class or drop out of school. The stigma of failure can mark them as well as their own thinking. On the other hand, some believe retention gives children who weren't really ready an extra chance. In either case, examples can be cited to support both sides of this issue.

Review

■ **Chapter Review.** Use the contents of the Chapter Review page to help students review concepts, think critically, and apply their knowledge.

■ **Study Guide.** Have students complete the Study Guide for Chapter 22 on page 73 of the Student Workbook.

■ **Growing Up.** Have students write brief, first-person accounts of a single childhood experience, such as playing with a pet, from the perspective of an infant, a toddler, a preschooler, and a school-age child. Descriptions should reflect the development and abilities found at each stage.

Evaluation

■ **Chapter Test.** Use the reproducible chapter test provided in the Teacher's Classroom Resources or create your own test using the *Testmaker Software.*

■ **Alternative Assessment.** Have pairs prepare a book for parents of newborns. The book should include pages for each developmental stage, with a list of tasks expected at each stage and space for parents to fill in the date they were mastered. Students might also include checklists, fill-in-the-blank sentences, and other features that creatively reflect what they have learned from this chapter.

■ **Two Views.** Ask groups to discuss these two questions and to share their conclusions with the class: Which developmental stage is the most challenging for children? For parents and other caregivers?

Special Needs

For different reasons, some children have special needs. Disabilities, for example, can cause children to be challenged in one or more areas of development. In most ways, children who have special needs are just like all others. With rare exceptions, they have the same need for activity, love, social interaction, stimulation, and guidance that other children have. Supportive caregivers always remember this fact.

Physical Disabilities

Children with physical disabilities usually have strong opinions about how they want to be treated. Although they may need some assistance, they want to be like everyone else. Fitting in to the best of their ability is a high priority.

Parents and other caregivers send subtle messages to children. A physical disability can be viewed as a challenge or as a deterrent in life. The caregiver's attitude often shapes that of the child. The caregiver who takes for granted that a child can do something empowers that child to be successful. André's parents, for example, encouraged him to try things, despite his physical disability. They expected him to live up to his own capabilities, just as they did with their other children. Because they never did anything for André that he could learn to do for himself, he developed confidence.

Mental Disabilities

Children with mental disabilities do not reach normal levels of intellectual development. Mental capabilities develop more slowly, and they often stop at a low level. For example, at age 15, Jolene achieved the mental capabilities of a 6-year-old. She never developed beyond this level, however. The tasks that these children do learn often are accomplished with extra effort, aided by a supportive, caring attitude from caregivers.

Learning Disabilities

Children with learning disabilities have specific problems that interfere with the learning process. For example, Kevin had trouble with reading and math because certain letters and numbers appeared inverted and backward to him. Although he was highly intelligent, he couldn't learn because of interference with the process. Early identification of a learning disability is critical so that the child can get the help needed to prevent falling far behind in school.

Emotional Disabilities

Sometimes a child's behavior—being very withdrawn, afraid, or aggressive—indicates an emotional disturbance. Usually, the behavior pattern is extreme and repeated before signaling a problem. Such children may need professional counseling.

Gifted Children

Children who are highly intelligent also need special attention. Providing extra opportunities and challenges can help keep them stimulated and content. A gifted child may not reach his or her potential without the support of caregivers.

Inclusion

Many schools employ *the practice of placing children who have disabilities and those who do not together in classrooms for all or part of the day.* This is called **inclusion.** Children who have disabilities benefit when they feel accepted instead of set apart. They are challenged and stimulated by contact with other children. Children without disabilities develop greater compassion and understanding for others. They learn that differences do not need to separate people. As long as people work together to overcome any obstacles, inclusion can be successful for the children involved.

MORE ABOUT *Special Needs*

Certain disabilities begin before birth, including cerebral palsy, cleft palate, heart defect, cystic fibrosis, Down syndrome, hemophilia, and sickle cell anemia. Some disabilities are mild or correctable; others result in severe disabilities or death. Some are apparent at birth; others, not until months or years later. For more information, students might contact agencies for specific disabilities or the March of Dimes, 1275 Mamaroneck Avenue, White Plains, NY 10605.

Chapter 22 Review

Reviewing the Facts

1. What are the four stages of child development?
2. Identify the principles of child development.
3. Give one example each of a physical, intellectual, and social characteristic of infants.
4. What kind of play is typical of toddlers, and how would you characterize that play?
5. Name three social skills that preschool-age children learn in preschool or day care.

Thinking Critically

1. Why is it important that caregivers not discourage young children from asking so many questions?
2. Describe one way that caregivers can help young children with special needs develop feelings of independence and positive self-esteem.

Applying Your Knowledge

1. **Identifying Stages.** For each example below, identify the developmental stage of the child who uses language in that way: (a) Combining words to make simple sentences, such as "Me go too." (b) Speaking in complex sentences, such as "I want to come with you." (c) Crying when a caregiver leaves the room.
2. **Comparing Stages.** Suppose that two children both want the same toy. How would the caregiver's responses differ if the children were both infants, both toddlers, or both preschoolers?

Making Connections

1. **History.** Find a book that includes a description of the one-room schoolhouses of early America. Compare the techniques teachers used to foster the intellectual development of children in these early classrooms with what is done today.
2. **Language Arts.** Fear is a common theme in many picture books for preschoolers. Visit the library or the children's section of a bookstore, and find a book that addresses a child's fear of something or someone. Summarize the plot, and describe how the book may help children confront a similar fear.
3. **Art.** Using words and images that you clip from magazines, newspapers, or other sources, create a collage that depicts the development of children from infancy to school age.

Building Your Portfolio

Making a Chart
Create a chart with five columns across the top, one for each area of development. On the left side, write the four stages discussed in the chapter. Fill in the chart with information about which developmental tasks are met in each area at each stage. Add the chart to your portfolio.

Chapter 23

FOCUS

Chapter Overview

In Chapter 23, students learn ways they can aid children's physical, intellectual, emotional, social, and moral growth. The chapter also explores ways to guide children's behavior, to help prevent accidents, and to handle emergencies.

Motivator

■ **Safety Smarts.** Ask students to imagine they are watching a young child. Without knowing what specific actions the parents permit, what rules could they reasonably make for the child's behavior? Explain that common sense, alertness, and knowledge of child development are good guides for keeping children safe.

Objectives

Discuss the chapter objectives on this page. Remind students that the objectives focus on important chapter concepts.

Vocabulary

Write the term *first aid* on the board. Ask students why this kind of treatment is called first aid. Stress that, as the term implies, more extensive treatment ("second aid") may be needed.

Chapter 23
Care and Safety of Children

Terms to Learn

- childproof
- dehydrated
- first aid
- Heimlich maneuver
- immunizations
- time-out

Objectives

This chapter will help you to:

- Suggest ways to meet children's physical, intellectual, emotional, social, and moral needs.
- Explain how caregivers can guide behavior.
- Recommend ways to ensure children's safety.
- Explain how to provide first aid to children and how to handle emergencies.

234   UNIT 4   Child Care and Development

CHAPTER RESOURCES

Student Workbook
Study Guide, p. 52
Activity, *Strong Families*, p. 53

Teacher's Classroom Resources
Lesson Plan, p. 19
Cooperative Learning, *Family Guidelines*, pp. 21-22

Decision Making, *Paul's Decision*, p. 12
Extension #25, *Balancing Work and Family*, p. 31
Extension #26, *Juggling Responsibilities*, p. 32
Life Skills, *Family Help Line*, pp. 27-28

Transparency 14, *Balancing Work and Personal Life*
Chapter 15 Test, pp. 35-36
Performance Assessment, *Family Balancing Act*, pp. 36-37
Reteaching, *Strong Families*, p. 21

See Also:
ABCNews InterActive™ Videodiscs

Six-year-old Tiffany came into the kitchen to ask her mother if she could go outside to play with her friend. Mrs. Cox said, "Of course, but do you remember the rules?"

Tiffany paused and then responded, "Stay in the yard, and don't go close to the street. Come inside if a stranger comes near. That's it, right?" Mrs. Cox nodded and smiled to herself as Tiffany ran out the door.

Caring for children, as Mrs. Cox had found, is no simple task. Caregivers have to provide a loving, stimulating, and safe environment so that children can develop into healthy and secure young people. When caregivers do their job well, children grow, learn, and become confident and self-reliant.

Meeting Needs

Have you ever been a babysitter, a camp counselor, or a mother's helper? Do you think that you will have children of your own or work in the child-care field in the future? If so, you will be helping children develop. Caregiving is like an umbrella that covers the five key areas of children's development: physical, intellectual, emotional, social, and moral.

Physical Needs

Unless a child's physical needs are met, proper development in other areas is threatened. For example, a child who is hungry has difficulty listening to a story and concentrating on the alphabet. When many physical needs are not met, overall development is likely to suffer.

To care for the physical needs of a child, you have to be concerned about sleep, food, comfort, cleanliness, health, and environment. Here are some guidelines caregivers follow:

- **Rest.** Children need more sleep than adults. Most infants and toddlers take naps during the day. Young children may require as much as twelve hours of sleep at night. Getting children to bed can be a challenge when young children fuss and older children look for creative ways to avoid bedtime.
- **Food.** Nutritious foods in reasonable portions promote growth and development. The foods people eat as children greatly determine their likes as adults. If toddlers are given fresh fruits instead of cookies and sweets, for instance, they will probably have healthy eating habits later in life. Foods that could cause choking, such as popcorn, peanuts, and hot dogs, are not appropriate for young children.
- **Clothing.** Since children tend to be messy, a daily change of clothing is necessary. Babies need frequent diaper changes. They generally need one more layer of clothing than older children and adults, except in hot weather.
- **Bath time.** Infants and children should have frequent baths, usually daily. Check the water temperature before placing or allowing children in the water. Never leave young children alone or nearby water, even to quickly answer the phone. Children can drown in just a few inches of water.

Helping children maintain normal routines is part of a caregiver's job.

CHAPTER 23 Care and Safety of Children 235

TEACH

Topic on p. 235:

- **Meeting Physical Development Needs**

Checking Comprehension

✓ What foods can cause choking? *Popcorn, peanuts, and hot dogs.*

✓ What are two important things to remember when bathing a young child or infant? *Never leave child alone in tub; check water temperature first.*

Activities

■ **The Late Show.** Discuss: If children need more sleep than adults, why do they often resist going to bed? *(Critical Thinking)*

■ **Hurrah for Routines.** Have groups list ideas for routines for mealtime, bedtime, bathing, or another activity where it might be useful. *(Creativity)*

ENRICHMENT

■ **Food Fun.** Have groups plan one day's meals and snacks for a toddler, using the Food Guide Pyramid (found in Chapter 40) and any other source they need to determine appropriate serving sizes and caloric intake. Remind students that feeding children is easier when foods are tasty and fun to eat as well as nutritious.

MORE ABOUT Immunizations

All children should be immunized against such diseases as polio, tetanus, and rubella. A vaccine stimulates the body to produce antibodies that fight off a disease. Children need a series of immunizations to fully protect them. Ask why some parents may fail to have their children immunized. Why do schools require up-to-date immunizations?

Topics on pp. 236-237:

- Meeting Intellectual, Emotional, Social, and Moral Development Needs
- Promoting Good Behavior

Checking Comprehension

✓ How can a caregiver help a child learn and develop language skills? *By reading to and talking with the child.*

✓ How can caregivers meet children's moral needs? *Teaching them right from wrong; modeling behaviors they want children to use.*

✓ How can positive statements affect a child's behavior? *They cause the child to feel good and want to repeat the behavior in order to get that good feeling again.*

USING VISUALS

Refer students to the photo on this page. Point out that busy caregivers often want to get household tasks done quickly. They may avoid allowing young children to participate. Ask students how this can affect children. What price may the caregiver pay in the long run? *(Emotional problems of children may cost them more time and energy later.)* Point out that most caregivers want to spend some quality time with children, so incorporating that with routine household tasks can benefit everyone.

Including young children in activities is rewarding. Children learn skills and feel good about themselves. What rewards might the adult experience—now <u>and</u> later?

- **Health care.** Caregivers need to brush young children's teeth for them until they learn how to do a good job on their own. Children start visiting the dentist at about age three. Doctor's exams, of course, begin when they are born. To start school, children must be up-to-date on required **immunizations.** These are *vaccines developed to prevent specific diseases,* such as polio, diphtheria, and measles.
- **Illness.** Sick children need extra rest and sometimes a diet of liquids or soft foods. They must not be allowed to become **dehydrated,** or *too low on fluids.* When children are very sick and require prescribed medicine, follow the doctor's orders exactly.

Intellectual Needs

The mind of a child develops more fully with the help of adults and a rich environment. What happens when a child doesn't get intellectual nurturing from caregivers? The outcomes are serious. Slow intellectual development affects a child's ability to learn in school. Once behind, it's hard for a child to catch up. This can have far-reaching effects on self-esteem and career opportunities.

Effective caregivers read to children. They play games appropriate to a child's age and skill level. They introduce activities that challenge children and stimulate their creativity and problem-solving skills. Simply talking with children helps them develop language skills.

As children grow, caregivers instill the value of good study skills and teach them how to find information. Encouraging children to ask questions helps them learn to think and prepares them for adulthood.

Emotional Needs

A child who grows up feeling loved and successful is likely to become a well-adjusted adult. Failure to nurture a child emotionally sets up the opposite situation—a person who is likely to have low self-esteem or chronic trouble following society's rules. Some techniques caregivers use to promote positive feelings are:

- Listening attentively to what children say.
- Praising children's efforts sincerely.
- Quickly comforting children who are upset.
- Accepting children's fears and concerns as real and deserving of attention.
- Giving a hug or a pat on the head or shoulder to show affection.

236   UNIT 4   Child Care and Development

REAL-LIFE APPLICATION

Read this to students: *Carrie's mother was visiting when Carrie's two-month-old son, sitting in his playpen, began to cry. As Carrie went over to him, her mother cautioned, "If you pick up babies every time they cry, they'll get spoiled."* Ask students if they agree with this approach. Point out that young babies cry from need, and meeting their needs quickly helps them feel secure. Encourage students to consult old and new parenting books for other opinions on the subject.

Social Needs

The ability to relate well to others is useful throughout life. Children who are socially well-adjusted develop strong relationships and get along with people at work and play.

Caregivers address social needs by interacting with children and providing opportunities for them to play with other children. Caregivers talk, play games, and acknowledge the behavior they like. Encouraging children to share toys and take turns teaches cooperation. Children also must learn to communicate and express their thoughts, feelings, and needs in acceptable ways.

Moral Needs

Children need to develop a sense of right and wrong and such basic values as fairness, justice, and empathy. Those who do not learn such values may eventually cause problems for themselves and society.

Parents provide the primary role in fostering their children's moral development. They choose babysitters and child-care workers carefully to ensure that the values they wish to instill are reinforced by others who care for their children.

Moral behavior is better taught by example than by preaching to children. Since children learn through imitation, they are much more likely to follow your actions than your words. If you show respect by considering the child's point of view during a disagreement, the child learns to imitate this behavior with others.

Guiding Behavior

Children learn appropriate behavior by receiving guidance. Because their judgment is undeveloped, children make mistakes that need correction. Guiding children is work, but it's work that pays off. The caregiver who channels behavior appropriately when a child is very young is usually rewarded by having fewer problems with the child as he or she grows older.

Promoting Good Behavior

Modeling appropriate behavior is the best way to promote good behavior in children. Yelling and hitting do not set a good example for children to follow. Children who hear "please" and "excuse me" are more likely to use such expressions themselves.

Acknowledging appropriate behavior is also useful. Notice when a child does something well. Then respond with a positive statement. A parent might say, "Your bed looks so nice, Ryan. I'm proud of the way you made it all by yourself." Simple comments like this encourage a child to repeat the behavior.

Why should caregivers praise children who show desirable behaviors, such as sharing?

■ **Do's and Don'ts.** Have pairs write four sets of instructions for children, each set containing a positive and a negative version of the same rule. (For example, "Don't go in the street," and "Stay on the sidewalk.") Have each pair read aloud one or two sets of instructions. Ask the class to compare the effects of each version on a child. *(Communication)*

CROSS-CURRICULAR ACTIVITY
Language Arts

Write these sentences on the board:
- "Do as I say, not as I do."
- "Actions speak louder than words."
- "Children have never been very good at listening to their elders, but they have never failed to imitate them." (James Baldwin)

Have each student choose one sentence and write a short explanation of how it relates to guiding children.

SPECIAL NEEDS *Strategies*

Inefficient Readers. Divide the class into five groups and assign each group one type of developmental need. Ask each group to present a skit demonstrating how a parent might meet the assigned need. After each presentation, ask students in the audience what other needs the parent might be meeting in the skit. Stress that with one action a caregiver can meet several different needs simultaneously.

MORE ABOUT Moral Training

Often people become upset by the wrong behavior of others, yet the examples they set don't teach the right behavior to their own children. For instance, a parent expressed frustration to his family over a client who left town without paying a bill, but then he snuck his child's friend into the swim club they belonged to so they wouldn't have to pay the visitor's fee. Sadly, children who learn double standards like this apply them later as teens and adults.

Topics on pp. 238-239:
- **Setting Limits**
- **Ways to Handle Misbehavior**
- **Babysitting**
- **Safety**

Checking Comprehension

✓ How should caregivers tell children about limits on their behavior? *Stress what they are expected to do instead of what is forbidden.*

✓ Why should babysitters find out how parents discipline a child? *So they can use the same approach and child's discipline will be consistent.*

✓ What household items can be dangerous for infants and children? *Small objects that can be swallowed, breakable items, unsteady furniture, electric outlets and wires, cleaning products, medicines.*

✓ Why are toddlers likely to find dangerous substances that aren't stored out of reach? *They are curious and like to explore.*

CROSS-CURRICULAR ACTIVITY

Art

Have students create labels that caregivers could put on potentially dangerous products, such as cleaners and medicines, warning children not to touch them. Remind students that the children who most need this warning are not old enough to read. Display students' designs in the classroom.

Setting Limits

Children need to know what they can and cannot do. Although they may complain about limits, children are reassured to know that someone cares. They find security in knowing what is expected of them. For example, if bedtime is always 8:00 P.M., children know what to expect each night.

Some limits protect children's safety. Review the rules frequently with children. Talk about what to do when playing outdoors near water and riding a bicycle. Doing this helps prevent accidents.

Many limits deal with behavior. When children are told to settle disagreements with words rather than with hitting, they learn that words are a tool to use in handling disputes.

Clear and Positive Limits

Limits should be clear. Otherwise, they won't be understood and followed. Limits should also be stated positively. Telling children what they *can* do is more effective than telling them what they *can't* do. For example, saying "You may run all the way to the tree" is more helpful than saying "Don't go too far."

Sometimes you can't enforce a limit with gentle reasoning. If a child is in danger, such as when a toddler chases a ball toward the street, you don't have time to reason.

Handling Misbehavior

Most children do things they shouldn't do on occasion. How should a caregiver respond? Corrective actions should be immediate and fit the misbehavior. In other words, minor punishments fit minor problems with stronger responses saved for bigger ones.

For minor incidents, explaining what was incorrect and reminding the child what behavior is desired is often enough. If the mistake was to leave something undone, the caregiver may ask the child to return to the task. When Vanessa did not pick up the toys in her room, for example, she was sent back to finish.

More serious offenses may require a different approach. Caregivers sometimes take away a privilege as a way of discouraging undesirable behavior. With young children, many caregivers use **time-out.** *The child is required to sit quietly for a period of time, usually about a minute for each year of age.* When used correctly, time-out can help a child learn self-control. Time-out should be presented as an opportunity for gaining composure, not a punishment. In this way, children can feel good about learning a skill that they can use on their own throughout life.

Consistency

Without consistency, attempts to handle misbehavior are likely to fail. Rules and responses need to be carefully thought out so that enforcement can be reasonably managed. When rules and responses continually change, children become confused. They may stop believing the person who enforces a rule one time but not the next. Disregard for rules may occur if children discover they aren't enforced consistently. Multiple caregivers need to agree on rules and responses.

Keeping Children Safe

Safety is a high priority for caregivers. Oversight can cause serious and even fatal accidents.

Childproofing the home ensures a safe environment for children as they explore their world.

MORE ABOUT Setting Limits

Until children learn the needed self-control, rules must be reinforced with careful monitoring. Telling a preschooler, "Play only in the yard," is not enough. The child's play must be supervised.

Focus on Handling Misbehavior

Spanking seldom helps a child learn proper behavior. Too often, adults use spanking to vent their own frustration. Such behavior teaches a child to settle conflicts by force. Most child-care experts recommend that spanking be used sparingly, if at all.

STRATEGIES *That Work*

Providing a Babysitting Service

Babysitting can help you learn how to manage your time, make decisions, and deal with new people and situations, all valuable work experiences. You also gain practice in caring for children and explore the possibility of a child-care career. Of course, you earn money too. For a successful babysitting service, follow these tips:

- **Keep track of jobs carefully.** Record times on a calendar that you keep by the phone. Don't cancel unless it is absolutely necessary. Offer to find a capable replacement.
- **Agree on rates and hours.** Set a rate similar to what others in your area charge. State it clearly when people call. Find out what time to arrive and when the parents expect to return home. Make arrangements for transportation.
- **Get the information that you need.** Before the parents leave, make sure that you know the children's schedules, house rules, and safety procedures. Ask for a list of important phone numbers.

- **Act responsibly on the job.** Don't make or accept personal phone calls while you are babysitting. Don't invite friends over. Stay awake unless the parent suggests otherwise. Leave the house as neat as you found it. Eat only what the parent says you may have.
- **Take a child care or babysitting class.** These are available at hospitals and the Red Cross.

Making the Strategy Work

Think . . .

1. Prepare a list of questions to ask when you are babysitting for a new family.
2. Some babysitters let parents set the rate of pay. Do you think this is a good idea? How might rates vary for different babysitting jobs?
3. What do you think are acceptable and unacceptable reasons for cancelling a babysitting job? Write a short dialogue showing how you would cancel in a businesslike manner.

 Try...

It can be helpful to have a fact sheet about each family that hires you: their name, address, and phone number; names and ages of the children; and special rules of the household. On an index card, create a format for a babysitter fact file.

Childproofing the environment, or *making it safe for children*, reduces chances for accidents. To make an environment safer, explore it on your hands and knees. You may discover dangers not visible at a higher level. Put plastic caps over any unused electrical outlets. Install gates at the top and bottom of stairs until children can climb the stairs safely. Put dangerous objects, such as glass knickknacks, scissors, and matches out of reach. Store any medicines, cleaning products, and dangerous substances in cabinets with safety latches. These are small measures to take in relation to the safety they provide.

Preventing Accidents

Children love to learn and explore, wherever they are, but their curiosity can be dangerous. To prevent possible accidents, follow these guidelines:

- Give infants and toddlers sturdy playthings without small or sharp parts.
- To prevent suffocation, keep plastic bags away from children.
- Restrict crawling children to places that they can explore safely. Prevent them from climbing on tall or unsteady furniture, for example.

CHAPTER 23   Care and Safety of Children   239

DID YOU KNOW?

Most deaths and injuries to infants and toddlers result from traffic accidents. According to National Highway Traffic Safety Administration statistics, more than 600 children under age five died in car crashes in 1993, about 700 in 1994. The proper use of child safety restraints—bucket-type carriers for infants and har-nessed seats for toddlers—could cut the number of deaths and injuries by as much as 71 percent. In some areas, local organizations, such as hospitals or civic groups, provide car seats at reduced cost or no cost to families who cannot afford them.

Activities

- **Stop!** Ask students to describe situations in which a caregiver should forcibly control a child's actions instead of attempting to reason with him or her. *(Management)*
- **Sweets and Strangers.** Discuss with students whether the following practices are wise from a safety perspective: persuading children to take medicine by calling it candy; dressing children in clothing with their name on it; holding a child on your lap while riding in a car; putting children on a "leash" while shopping with them. *(Critical Thinking)*

STRATEGIES THAT WORK

Have students read "Providing a Babysitting Service." Ask them to share the information they included in their fact files. Ask how they might use a similar system to organize and keep track of other important information.

Answers to Think . . .
1. Questions may pertain to household rules, children's preferences and personalities, neighbors' names and phone numbers.
2. Answers will vary. Point out that few professionals allow clients to set rates, and babysitters should think of selves as profe-ssionals.
3. Acceptable reasons would be emergency situations, not social ones. Dialogues should show responsible, respectful attitude.

239

Topics on pp. 240-242:
- Emergencies
- First Aid
- Heimlich Maneuver

Checking Comprehension

✓ In what situations should you call an ambulance? *Child is having trouble breathing; is unconscious, badly burned, or bleeding severely; appears to have broken bone.*

✓ Why must caregivers remain calm in an emergency? *To help keep children calm.*

✓ What should you do if you see or smell a fire while babysitting? *Get children out of the home; call fire department from neighbor's phone.*

Making Decisions

Have students read "Handle with Care." Ask them why adults might not believe a child's claim of abuse. Some adults don't want to believe, or think the child is lying about or misunderstanding the incident.

Answers to What Would You Do?

1. She may have been sexually abused.
2. Situations like these are very sensitive. Gretchen has to decide whether to report the situation.
3. Gretchen should explain her concerns to a trusted adult who will listen and take appropriate action.
4. Gretchen was not actively listening to Jenna, didn't respect her feelings.

Making Decisions

Handle with Care

"Did you have a good time at Aunt Lil's?" Gretchen asked her little sister Jenna. Gretchen was putting away a few dishes in the kitchen. Jenna sat at the table finishing her milk.

"Um-hm." Jenna muttered, her eyes focused on the floor. "Well, not really," she continued. "I don't like that Eddie."

"Oh, sure you do," Gretchen coaxed with a smile. "He's your cousin. You have to like your cousin, don't you?"

Seven-year-old Jenna glanced up at Gretchen. "He's mean," she insisted.

"Well, you know boys," Gretchen laughed. "They're all mean. I never liked boys when I was your age, but you just wait."

"That's not what I mean," Jenna went on. "That's not it." Jenna walked to the window and stood there staring out. She stood silently for a long time, even though there was nothing outside to watch.

"Did Aunt Lil fix her great spaghetti while you were there?" Gretchen asked, hoping to find a subject that would improve Jenna's mood.

"No. She didn't have time. She had to go somewhere. Eddie fixed some soup while she was gone. I didn't even eat it."

"No wonder you and Eddie didn't get along, Jenna. You could have at least eaten the lunch he fixed. He was probably mad."

Jenna said nothing. As she walked slowly through the doorway into the next room, she said very softly, "He touched me." For a long moment, Gretchen didn't move.

What Would You Do?

1. What may have happened to Jenna?
2. If Gretchen decides that Eddie behaved inappropriately with Jenna, what decision does Gretchen face?
3. What should Gretchen do, and why?
4. Why did Gretchen come close to missing the message that Jenna had difficulty conveying?

- Teach the concept of "hot" around the range, fireplace, and heaters. Turn pot handles in when cooking.
- Keep children away from fans.
- Choose playgrounds with well-maintained equipment and soft ground cover. Watch the children, and insist that they follow rules for safe play.
- Secure infants and children in carseats and seatbelts, even when you are traveling only a few blocks. Children who are accustomed to these restraints will learn to feel uncomfortable without them. Set an example by wearing your seatbelt too.

Protecting Children

Unfortunately, children need protection from people who might harm them. Kidnapping and abuse are two frightening situations that require awareness and sometimes action from caregivers. Remember these guidelines:

- Give children clear limits about where they can go alone. Be cautious about what you decide to allow.
- Teach children what a stranger is and to avoid them. Tell them never to get in a car or go anywhere with someone they don't know and to ignore offers of food, drink, or treats. Try not to frighten children as you teach them.
- Make sure you leave children only with people you know well and trust. Pay attention to any uncomfortable feelings you have about anyone.
- Listen to children. Sometimes abusive people threaten children in order to keep their actions a secret. You must respond to any indication from a child that something out of the ordinary is taking place.

When Emergencies Arise

How do you react in an emergency? Remember that children take cues from you. They are more likely to remain calm if you do. Even if you feel upset, try not to show it.

Emergency situations can result from severe weather. Listen to media bulletins for reports.

REAL-LIFE APPLICATION

Read this to students: *Seth was babysitting his two nieces. Four-year-old Candace shrieked and sprinted across the yard, clutching a bleeding finger. Seth tried to ask Candace what happened, but she only sobbed, "It bit me," and began to cry.* Ask: What should Seth do? How can he calm Candace down? What questions might help him learn what happened? What might he do to prevent the situation from occurring again?

Giving First Aid

Minor injuries are common with active children. Caregivers need to know the basics of **first aid**, *emergency care or treatment given right away to an ill or injured person.* See **Figure 23.2** for a list of basic first-aid procedures.

Figure 23.1 illustrates the **Heimlich maneuver,** *the action taken to aid a person who is choking.*

For serious illness or injury, seek help. Call an ambulance immediately if a child has difficulty breathing, is unconscious, is badly burned, appears to have a broken bone, or is

Figure 23.1

HEIMLICH MANEUVER ⸻

This procedure is used to force food or an object that is obstructing a person's breathing from the throat. If the object can be seen, try to remove it, being careful not to push it further back in the airway. If the object cannot be removed easily and the victim is conscious, try the following:

For Infants and Toddlers

Turn the child face down over the length of your arm or on your lap, with his or her head lower than the chest.

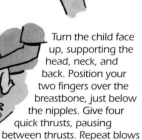

Support the head and neck with one hand. Using the heel of your other hand, give four quick blows between the shoulder blades.

Turn the child face up, supporting the head, neck, and back. Position your two fingers over the breastbone, just below the nipples. Give four quick thrusts, pausing between thrusts. Repeat blows and thrusts if needed. You can also call for help.

For Older Children and Adults

Stand or kneel behind the victim, and place a fist (thumb tucked in) midway between the base of the rib cage and the navel. Have the victim lean forward while you press your fist against the abdomen and give one quick, upward push. This forces the air in the lungs to expel the object. Repeat if necessary. If the object doesn't come out, seek help immediately.

CHAPTER 23   Care and Safety of Children   241

DID YOU KNOW?

Inducing vomiting will add to the injury if a child has swallowed an acid, alkali, or petroleum product, including charcoal lighter, corn and wart removers, dishwasher granules, drain and oven cleaners, floor and furniture polish and wax, gasoline and kerosene, and paint thinner. Suspect these substances if the child has burns around the mouth. Have the child drink milk to dilute the poison. Always try to call a poison control center before administering *any* treatment.

Activities

RETEACHING

■ **Care Quiz.** Have groups write a 10- to 15-item quiz covering the information on one or both of these pages. Have groups trade quizzes and try to complete them.

ENRICHMENT

■ **Picture This.** Have groups prepare picture books teaching young children what to do in a particular emergency, such as a fire or a caregiver suddenly becoming ill. Each page should include a picture and a few short sentences to help readers understand what to do. Display the books in the classroom. They might then be donated to an elementary class.

CROSS-CURRICULAR ACTIVITY
Math

Ask students to research statistics on accidents involving children and to illustrate their findings with graphs. Information might be broken down into type of injuries, age groups, and where accidents occur. Have students extrapolate these statistics to a school of 300 children. For example, how many of these children might suffer burns in the home in a year?

CROSS-CURRICULAR ACTIVITY
Health

Encourage students to assemble a first-aid kit for the home or car, based on the first-aid guidelines on page 242.

Review

■ **Chapter Review.** Use the contents of the Chapter Review page to help students review concepts, think critically, and apply their knowledge.

■ **Study Guide.** Have students complete the Study Guide for Chapter 23 on page 75 of the Student Workbook.

■ **Safety Posters.** Have the class create a series of child safety posters. Students might begin by listing safety tips, then forming teams to illustrate each one. The posters should depict avariety of safety measures and include a slogan to help caregivers remember the safety tip.

Evaluation

■ **Chapter Test.** Use the reproducible chapter test provided in the Teacher's Classroom Resources or create your own test using the *Testmaker Software*.

■ **Alternative Assessment.** Have students plan and describe (orally or in writing) an hour-long outing with a toddler. Activities chosen should be fun and safe and meet developmental needs in at least four of the five categories described in this chapter.

CLOSE

■ **Perfect World.** Assign groups one of these contributing factors to early childhood injuries: unsafe play conditions; children's curiosity and impulsiveness; lack of supervision; and caregivers' lack of safety awareness. Have each group list on the board three suggestions for overcoming its assigned factor. As a class, discuss various ways to combine these ideas in ideal caregiving scenarios.

bleeding severely. Keep emergency numbers by the phone in case you need to call the police, fire department, poison control center, or an ambulance. If 911 is available in your area, use it to seek help.

Fire

In a case of fire, don't take the time to call the fire department or try to put out the blaze yourself. First gather *all* the children in your care and then walk, don't run, to the nearest safe exit. Once you are all safely out, call the fire department from a neighbor's home.

If the residence is filled with smoke, each person should cover his or her face with a damp cloth and stay close to the floor. Feel each closed door that you come to. If the door is hot, don't open it. Find another way out.

Figure 23.2

First Aid

- **Scrapes and bruises.** Clean scrapes with soap and water; apply antiseptic and bandage. For bruises, apply a clean washcloth wrung out in cold water.
- **Nosebleed.** Keep the child seated and leaning forward. (With the head tilted back, the child may choke.) Apply direct pressure on the bleeding nostril. Apply a cold towel to the child's nose and face.
- **Earache.** Cover the ear with a warm towel or a heating pad set on low to relieve pain. Call a doctor.
- **Cuts.** Apply direct pressure to stop bleeding. Wash and apply antiseptic and a bandage. For deep cuts, call a doctor.
- **Bites (insect).** For minor bites, wash the area and apply antiseptic or calamine lotion. For bee, hornet, or wasp stings, scrape against the stinger with a flat object, such as a piece of cardboard, until you pull out the venom sac. Wash the area thoroughly with soap and water. **Caution:** Some people are highly allergic to stings. If a child is short of breath, feels faint, or has stomach pain, seek medical help immediately.
- **Bites (animal or human).** Wash the wound with water. Then clean it with soap and water, and cover it with gauze. Call a doctor.
- **Burns.** For minor burns, immediately run cold water on the burn for about five

minutes. For serious burns, go to the hospital or call an ambulance. Do not try to remove burned clothing.
- **Sprains.** Don't allow the child to walk. Elevate the limb and apply a cold pack. Call a doctor.
- **Broken bone.** If you think that a child has broken a bone, the child needs medical care. Call an ambulance or contact the parents first if you are temporarily in charge.
- **Poisoning.** If a child swallows a poisonous or irritating substance, call the nearest poison control center immediately. Report the name of the substance and the amount swallowed, and follow the instructions you are given. Take the container with you if you go to the doctor or the hospital.
- **Electric shock.** Don't touch the child until his or her contact with electricity is broken, or you will also get a shock. Turn off the electricity if you can, or pull or push the child away from the source of shock with a stick, cloth, or rope, but *never* with anything metal. If the child is not breathing, use cardiopulmonary resuscitation (CPR) if you are trained in the procedure. This is a life-saving technique used when the heart or breathing has stopped.

MORE ABOUT Poison Prevention

Follow these guidelines:
- Store household cleaners out of reach; never below the sink.
- Never store cleaners in containers used for food.
- Keep medicines in cabinets equipped with childproof locks.
- Avoid taking medicine in a child's presence.
- If you must leave the room while using a poisonous product, take the product with you.
- Read labels before using products to learn what to do in case of poisoning.

Review

Reviewing the Facts

1. Name one way in which caregivers might meet each of these needs: physical, intellectual, social, emotional, and moral.
2. Why is it wise to avoid feeding junk foods and sweets to toddlers?
3. What are two reasons that caregivers set limits?
4. Give two examples of limits a parent might set.
5. What are four ways to childproof a home?
6. Describe the basics of accident prevention with infants.
7. What are three emergency situations with children that would necessitate calling the rescue squad?

Thinking Critically

1. Why is careful attention to helping children develop appropriately important to society?
2. Do you think people should be trained for parenting? Explain your reasoning.

Applying Your Knowledge

1. **Making a Poster.** Design a poster that shows how caregivers meet children's needs in the five areas of development.
2. **Ensuring Children's Safety.** Imagine that you are babysitting for a child who wants to go on a bicycle ride with you to the pool for an afternoon swim. What information should you get from the child's parents ahead of time? What precautions do you think that you should take to ensure the child's safety?

3. **Creating a Resource.** Talk to parents of young children you know. Ask them what techniques they have found to be most effective in guiding behavior. Compile a class list of the ten best ideas.

Making Connections

1. **Health.** Find out what immunizations are required for young children, and create a chart that shows when each should be administered.
2. **Language Arts.** Write a brief dialogue that illustrates a caregiver teaching a preschooler not to hit other children.
3. **Geography.** What natural disasters, such as floods, hurricanes, or tornadoes, are possible in your area. For each such emergency, write a three- or four-step plan detailing how to respond.

Building Your Portfolio

Synthesizing Information
Make a "Household Substance Alert" chart. Find out what common household supplies and materials (for example, chlorine bleach, roach spray, paint, or glue) pose danger to children if ingested or inhaled. Determine how to safely store these products and what to do if they are swallowed or inhaled. Make your chart simple and easy to read. Place the chart in your portfolio.

1. Possible responses: *physical*—bathing or feeding children; *intellectual*—playing games or talking with children; *emotional*—providing encouragement and praise; *social*—helping children learn to share; *moral*—setting a good example.
2. Such foods are not nutritious. The children may learn to prefer those foods over healthier choices.
3. To protect children's safety and to control their behavior.
4. Posssible answers are bedtime, outdoor play, behavior. Answers may include specific examples.
5. Place dangerous objects well out of children's reach; place plastic caps over unused electrical outlets; install gates at the top and bottom of stairs; store medicines, cleaning products, and other dangerous substances in locked cabinets or closets.
6. Keep small objects that could accidentally be swallowed away from babies; avoid toys with breakable or sharp parts—choose playthings that are large and soft; when changing diapers, never leave a child alone on a table or bed.
7. Any three of these or other appropriate responses: a child who has difficulty breathing, is unconscious, is badly burned, has a broken bone, or is bleeding severely.

ANSWERS TO THINKING CRITICALLY

1. Guiding children to appropriate behavior helps produce well-adjusted, socially responsible adults.

2. Possible response: Caregivers should be trained because helping children grow and develop is such an important job and learning by mistakes is costly.

FOCUS

Chapter Overview

Chapter 24 explains how play helps infants and young children grow in all developmental areas. Students learn how to plan and guide play that is suitable for a child's developmental level and fosters cooperative behaviors.

Motivator

■ **Early Lessons.** Bring to class some traditional children's toys, such as a squirt gun and doll. Ask: What might children learn from playing with these items? Urge students to go beyond obvious skills and identify attitudes and beliefs. Tell them that this chapter will explain how children learn about the world and themselves through play.

Objectives

Discuss the chapter objectives on this page. Remind students that the objectives focus on important chapter concepts.

Vocabulary

The word *facilitate* is based on a Latin word meaning to do. To facilitate means to make something easier to do. Ask students to name related words and to explain the connection. (For example: *facile*, easy to do; *facility*, a place for doing things.)

Chapter 24

The Importance of Play

Terms to Learn

- active play
- distract
- facilitate
- quiet play
- sensory toys

Objectives

This chapter will help you to:

- **Describe** how playing helps children grow physically, intellectually, emotionally, socially, and morally.
- **Compare** and contrast active and quiet play.
- **Identify** appropriate play for infants and young children.
- **Explain** how caregivers can help children learn from and enjoy their play.

244 UNIT 4 Child Care and Development

CHAPTER RESOURCES

When children play, they are doing much more than simply having fun. Play is as purposeful for children as work is for adults. In fact, some people say that play *is* children's work. Watch a child for a while, and you are likely to see a natural love of play in action. This inborn quality of children helps promote their development.

Play and Development

When children play, they learn about the world, themselves, and others. Different kinds of play also help children act out feelings and needs that they can't yet put into words. As children grow, play spurs progress in all areas of development:

- **Physical development.** Such activities as playing tag and swinging on swing sets help children strengthen their muscles, develop their large-motor skills, burn up energy, and improve coordination.
- **Intellectual development.** Play teaches children about their environment—the shapes, sizes, and number of objects, and how things fit together—as well as such abstract concepts as mathematics and how gravity works. Reading books to children teaches them about letters, words, and ideas. Storytelling, pretend play, and drawing all encourage creativity.
- **Emotional development.** Playing with caregivers helps a child learn to give and receive love, reach out to others, and develop self-esteem. Caregivers can nurture children by initiating a game of patty-cake, making something together, or just cuddling a stuffed animal with them.
- **Social development.** When children play with others, they learn how to make and maintain relationships

and resolve conflicts. Playing board games and group games promotes social skills, such as taking turns, sharing, cooperating, and compromising.

- **Moral development.** Playing with others helps children learn how their actions affect people. Make-believe and other forms of play let children test values and understand the consequences of actions.

Active and Quiet Play

Sometimes children seem like windup toys that never stop. With an abundance of energy, they may keep on going even when they are tired. On the other hand, some children have to be prodded to get moving. For the most part, children need a balance between active and quiet play.

How does quiet play help a child?

CHAPTER 24   The Importance of Play   245

TEACH

Topics on p. 245:
- **Play and Development**
- **Active and Quiet Play**

Checking Comprehension

✓ How does play help children develop physically? *They strengthen muscles, develop large-motor skills, use energy, improve coordination.*

✓ How does play help children develop socially? *Helps them learn to make friends, interact with others.*

✓ What skills does quiet play promote? *Thinking and small-motor skills.*

Activities

■ **The Best Things in Life.** Have groups write the five developmental areas as headings across the top of a piece of paper. Beneath each one, have them list ordinary household items that might safely be used as a toy to promote a child's growth in that area. (*Creativity*)

■ **Three for One.** Have groups think of how one game, toy, or activity could be used to meet at least three developmental needs of children. Have groups share their ideas in class. (*Management*)

MULTICULTURAL *Perspectives*

Invite an exchange student to talk about children's games that are popular in another culture. How do these games meet developmental needs? What beliefs and attitudes do the games promote?

REAL-LIFE APPLICATION

Read this to students: *Melody wants toys that provide stimulating experiences for her four-year-old son Bart. On her tight budget, however, she just manages to feed and clothe them and pay the bills.* Ask: How can Melody acquire toys for Bart without spending a lot of money? How else can she inexpensively provide him with stimulating experiences? Point out that an interested, involved adult can turn everyday activities, such as going to a laundromat, into pleasant learning experiences.

Topics on pp. 246-247:
- Promoting Play with Infants and Toddlers
- Computers and Play

Checking Comprehension

✓ Why is caregivers' attention as important to babies as toys? *Play lead by adults provides entertainment, opportunities to develop, and emotional support.*

✓ Should you be surprised if a toddler takes a toy from another child? *No; toddlers have not yet learned to share and take turns.*

FAMILY AND COMMUNITY OUTREACH

Ask students to bring in older, usable toys for donation. Have students attach a tag to each toy, stating the toy's intended age range, the skills it reinforces, and the knowledge a child might gain from playing with it.

CROSS-CURRICULAR ACTIVITY
Science

Have groups design experiments to determine the sensory appeal of certain toys to infants. Assign each group one sense to test. Have them bring in the toys or pictures of the toys to be tested. Have groups describe their experiments. Discuss the validity of the designs. Will the experiments isolate the sensory reaction that the group is measuring?

Active play is more than just fun for a child. Physical activity also serves other significant purposes. Can you describe what they are?

Active play includes *activities that are primarily physical and employ large-motor skills.* Children might climb on a jungle gym, ride a tricycle, or chase each other around the trees in a park. Although active play is more difficult to manage indoors, it does take place. Anyone who has watched a child use a bed as a trampoline knows that this is true.

Children need active play. Not only does it help them develop their large muscles, but it also allows them to release energy. They are more willing and able to rest at night if they have had opportunities to play hard during the day.

Children also need **quiet play,** which includes *activities that engage the mind and small-motor skills and do not call for much movement.* Quiet play can take various forms. A child may read a book, play with clay, use a bucket and shovel in a sandbox, or play with small figures in an imaginative way. Quiet play helps children develop their small muscles and think in different ways.

Helping children experience both kinds of play is necessary. Good health depends on getting exercise. The ability to concentrate in school depends on learning the self-discipline to sit still and focus on a quiet activity. When both active and quiet play are part of a child's life, the child will be better able to adapt to situations as he or she grows.

Not every child requires exactly the same balance of activities. The age of the child is an influence, and so is the child's personality. Nevertheless, as a caregiver, you need to help children have a variety of experiences for quiet times as well as active ones.

Promoting Children's Play

Play should be tailored to the developmental stage of the particular child. A game that is too advanced for the child's skill level will cause frustration. Play that is more suitable for an earlier developmental stage may make the child bored and cranky. Activities that fit the child's skill and interest level are the most fun. They are also the most stimulating ones.

Infants and Play

Because infants explore the world through their senses, they need sensory-play opportunities. Very young babies like to look at colors, shapes, and patterns. As they reach out

246   UNIT 4   Child Care and Development

DID YOU KNOW?

When children receive new toys, caregivers should put away some of their old ones. A surplus of toys can overwhelm children and confuse them with too many choices. On the other hand, if caregivers put away some of the toys every few weeks, they will seem fresh and fun to the children when retrieved from storage.

for objects, they try to figure out how far away the objects are. **Sensory toys** are *objects that stimulate the senses with different textures, shapes, sounds, and colors.* Mobiles, toys that squeak and rattle, teething rings, and crib "busy-boxes" are examples. Infants explore with their hands, eyes, and mouth, so caregivers must be sure that objects have no sharp edges or parts small enough to swallow.

Playing with an infant also helps the child feel special and loved. Attentive caregivers provide babies with more emotional support than a toy can provide. Infants are particularly interested in seeing faces, hearing voices, and feeling the caring touch of people around them. Cuddling, light bouncing (if the baby seems to like it), talking, singing, playing peekaboo, and making funny faces all make a baby feel valued.

When playing with infants, caregivers should adapt activities to the infants' moods and schedules. Trying to force babies to play when they are hungry, tired, or interested in something else only upsets them. If the baby is busy examining his or her hands or feet, for instance, wait until he or she is finished before introducing a new activity. Caregivers who are sensitive to infants' interests find it easier to engage them in something different.

Toddlers and Play

As you know, toddlerhood is an active time for children. With improved motor skills, they enjoy running, jumping, balancing, climbing,

In Touch with TECHNOLOGY

Computers and Play

Although computers haven't replaced such traditional toys and games as building blocks and tag, they have become part of many children's play. Because many young users cannot yet read, most of the software uses images or sound cues instead of words. Children as young as two can use a computer, since they only need to press a key, touch the screen, or click the mouse.

Playing and Learning

Many software programs stimulate learning and creativity through play. Some programs enable children to solve puzzles, "paint" without a mess, and build a model dinosaur. Other programs help children acquire or improve reading, writing, and math skills. The use of eye-catching graphics, cartoon characters, and lively music helps make learning fun.

While young children usually have a short attention span, they often like to spend time at the computer. Because they need active play, too, parents and caregivers need to monitor the time spent at the computer. Unlike television, computer play can be interactive. The child's touch on the mouse or tap on a key generates a response. The computer then waits for the child's next action. The child directs the play, gaining a sense of power and control.

Computer play can build social skills as well. Adults tend to work at computers alone, but children love to work in pairs or small groups. They can learn to take turns and share ideas for problem solving.

• • • • •

Thinking Critically About Technology

1. Do you think the computer could ever replace traditional toys? Explain your answer.
2. When young students have spent a great deal of time playing computer games, what difficulties might their teachers face?

Focus on Caregiving Skills

Toddlers learn new skills by trial and error, which can be a tedious process. It's easy to become impatient while waiting for a child to put on a shirt or shoes. However, caregivers must resist the temptation to provide help too quickly. Whenever possible, they must allow children to complete tasks at their own speed. Self-esteem can suffer when children think that they cannot accomplish things. Also, they miss out on necessary practice.

Topics on pp. 248-250:
- Preschoolers and Play
- Making the Most of Play
- Providing Play Opportunities

Checking Comprehension

✓ What is meant by distracting children? *Providing safe, interesting activities to keep them from harmful ones and from getting restless.*

✓ Why might a child ask you to read the same story many times? *Familiar stories are comforting to children.*

✓ Why is it a good idea to watch television shows with children? *To monitor child's reactions, explain confusing things, turn off unsuitable shows.*

Preschoolers love pretend play, and it's valuable for them too. Why do you think this is true?

and swinging. Caregivers and toddlers can play catch with a lightweight ball or "dance" to music.

Play can also promote a toddler's intellectual development. Like junior scientists, they explore their physical world, learning such concepts as larger and smaller or full and empty by playing with nesting toys and containers. They learn about shapes by putting together puzzles, and about structures by stacking blocks.

Toddlers love playing with water, sand, modeling clay, dough, and finger paints. Caregivers should encourage these types of activities by giving toddlers a space to work that can be easily cleaned up afterward. This opportunity spurs creativity and helps toddlers develop small-motor skills.

Toddlers like to imitate adults and keep them company while household tasks are performed. Why not give a toddler a cloth to help with the dusting? Letting the child push a toy vacuum or use a broom makes him or her feel grown up.

When playing with toddlers, caregivers should remember that their attention span is short. By changing games or activities when the child seems bored, caregivers keep playtime fun and stimulating. In addition, children at this age have not yet learned to share or take turns, so caregivers should be patient if

a child tries to take toys from another child. By gently correcting self-centered behavior, caregivers help toddlers learn how to get along with others.

Preschoolers and Play

Preschoolers continue many of the interests that began in the toddler years, increasing the variety of play as their skills become more complex and sophisticated. Better small-motor skills make it possible for these children to color in coloring books, draw pictures, and paste colored paper into collages. Blocks that are more elaborate and more complicated puzzles can be enjoyable playthings.

As preschoolers play, their list of accomplishments grows. You will often hear them say, "Watch me!" and "See what I made!" Self-esteem increases when caregivers show sincere appreciation for children's efforts.

At this age, children's creativity expresses itself strongly through pretending. Some preschoolers create imaginary playmates.

248 **UNIT 4 Child Care and Development**

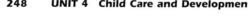

MORE ABOUT Facilitating Play

Caregivers should not become too active in children's play or their choice of activities. Otherwise, children may become dependent on adults for entertainment. They may not learn the social skills provided by playing with others their own age. Also, caregivers may unintentionally "judge" children's play. Children feel inhibited and tailor their behavior to please caregivers, and play loses its expressive, creative value.

You may remember dressing up in old clothing and playing house, school, or any number of themes. This type of play helps preschoolers express their feelings and practice the behaviors they are learning. Often, a new experience is later reenacted through pretend play. For example, after a trip to the circus, preschoolers might pretend to be clowns, acrobats, and circus animals.

Making the Most of Play

A child can play without your help, but think what a difference a caregiver can make. Caregivers can supply play materials, suggest ideas, and join in the fun. Children who spend time with interested, creative caregivers are likely to develop at a faster rate and refine their skills more than children who do not have this input.

Useful Techniques

Children who are busy with safe, interesting play are far less likely to become restless, get into trouble, or test caregivers. You can sometimes **distract** children, or *lead them away from something they shouldn't do*, by creating interest in another activity.

As you plan activities, keep in mind that children need the opportunity to make choices. This helps develop feelings of responsibility and control. For example, you might say: "Would you like to make a puppet out of an old sock or a paper bag?"

Caregivers help children the most when they **facilitate** play. This means that they *help bring about play without controlling what the child does*. Pulling out a box of blocks and saying, "Let's build a house," controls the child's play. Offering the blocks and asking, "What can you make with these?" gives the child the power to choose.

Handling Competition

Most sports and board games have clear winners and losers. Many people feel that competitive play is useful because it motivates children to try their hardest. Others argue that the disappointment of losing can be

Making Decisions

When Playing Becomes Fighting

"Mine!" four-year-old Elena yelled, clutching the toy caterpillar in one hand and reaching out for Carmela with the other.

"No, it isn't!" Carmela, age six, yelled back. "It's just as much mine as yours!" She held the butterfly just out of Elena's reach.

Angelo, who was babysitting for his sisters, looked up from his homework. The object of the dispute was a fuzzy, stuffed caterpillar. Underneath was a zipper, which concealed a colorful butterfly that could be removed. Carmela had grabbed the butterfly and was pretending to make it fly around the room.

"Quiet, both of you," said Angelo. "Can't you play with it together? Uncle Gino sent it for both of you."

"The butterfly is mine," Carmela retorted.

"It has to go together," Elena countered. "I can't play with just one part."

Angelo didn't want to make matters worse, but he sensed that Elena was on the verge of tears. What would their parents do in this situation? He looked at his homework and then out the window. Sighing, he walked toward the girls.

What Would You Do?

1. What options does Angelo have?
2. What do you think would happen if Angelo did nothing?
3. What should Angelo do? Why?

overly painful, spoiling the enjoyment of play. Most agree that too much emphasis on competition is harmful for young children.

Caregivers can help children learn to handle competitive play by emphasizing the pleasure of play—whatever the outcome. Explaining that the outcome of some games is strictly a matter of luck can help ease the

DID YOU KNOW?

Preschoolers respond well to praise and enjoy winning, but they are emotionally unprepared for losing. That's why the preschool years are not a good time to introduce competitive games and sports. Cooperative games that require children to work together toward a goal are more appropriate. For example, having the group see how long they can keep a balloon in the air is one. Libraries have books that explain many possible games of this type.

Activities

■ **Seeing is Believing.** Show a video of an animated series featuring traditional cartoon violence. Ask: What "facts" might a preschooler believe after watching this show? How might such shows affect a child's attitudes toward conflict and relationships? (*Critical Thinking*)

RETEACHING

■ **Timing is Everything.** Read a list of common activities for young children, some energetic, some quiet. Ask whether each would be more appropriate for midmorning or just before bedtime.

ENRICHMENT

■ **Party Time!** In groups have students plan one aspect of a child's birthday party: games, favors, and suggested gifts. Have groups share their plans, explaining why their choices are appropriate. (*Decision Making*)

Making Decisions

Have students read the feature.

Answers to What Would You Do?

1. Answers may include: let girls settle dispute themselves; take toy from both girls; help them compromise.
2. Sisters might continue to fight, without resolution. Not every conflict should be settled by adults; they need to settle their own differences.
3. Answers will vary. Encourage students to see the variety of peaceful outcomes possible.

Review

■ **Chapter Review.** Use the contents of the Chapter Review page to help students review concepts, think critically, and apply their knowledge.

■ **Study Guide.** Have students complete the Study Guide for Chapter 24 on page 79 of the Student Workbook.

■ **A Picture is Worth.** Have each student bring in three or four pictures of infants, toddlers, and preschoolers at play. Ask each student to classify the pictures by age group, then to identify each activity as active or quiet play and explain what skills and knowledge the child might be gaining.

Evaluation

■ **Chapter Test.** Use the reproducible chapter test provided in the Teacher's Classroom Resources or create your own test using the *Testmaker Software.*

■ **Alternative Assessment.** Arrange with a grade school or child care facility to have students inspect its toys and play equipment for safety and suitability. Give groups time to create a checklist of inspection points. Then assign each group one or two items to examine.

■ **Simple Needs.** Tell students that some experts believe the only toys a child needs are a book, a ball, and a doll. Ask students if they think these toys could meet every child's needs. What other toys might they include on an "essential" list?

---

hurt as well. When caregivers set an example by remaining cheerful after, say, losing a simple card game, they help the child learn to accept such results as well.

Reading Books

Reading enhances verbal communication—talking, listening, and vocabulary building—as well as children's imaginations and learning abilities. Reading also fulfills their emotional and social needs. Cuddling in a caregiver's lap, listening to an interesting story, asking questions, and sharing the funny, happy, scary, or sad feelings described in stories, all of these encourage a child's growth and a sense of well-being.

Here are some tips for reading to young children:

• Choose stories that are appropriate for a child's age. If the child doesn't respond well, the book is probably too advanced or too simple.

• Be prepared for a child's request to hear the same story or book over and over. This is a sign that the story is especially important to the child. In time, a new book will seem more interesting.

• Take time to let the child look at the pictures. Ask questions about the pictures, and let the child turn the page when ready.

• Talk about the story, act it out, or refer to it later.

When children are old enough to read simple books themselves, let them read to you. Help them with words they don't know, and praise them for the parts they read well. Don't be too quick to help, though. The child may just need a little extra time to figure out a word.

Using Television Sensibly

Many caregivers use television and videos as babysitters. Letting children watch frees the adult to do things without interruption. Many child-care experts believe, however, that too much television can harm children.

Television demands almost no participation from the child, and little interaction with other people occurs. In addition, many television programs have content that is inappropriate for children.

On the other hand, some children's programming is educational and entertaining for children. To make the most of what television has to offer, you need to manage a child's television watching. Here are some tips:

• Watch television with the child. Ask questions, note the child's emotions, and talk about the programs you watch together.

• Select programs with care. Limit television watching to half an hour or one hour at a time, and limit total time each day.

• If a program seems unsuitable, turn off the set or change the channel.

• When the program ends, or if the child begins to play something else, turn the set off.

• Model good television habits by watching in moderation.

Providing Opportunities

Enriching a child's life doesn't have to be costly, nor does it have to involve exceptional effort. Creative caregivers are continually on the lookout for opportunities to help children develop.

Children need interaction with others their age. Many parents arrange play groups for toddlers and preschoolers who might not otherwise have a chance to be with children.

Routine outings can be turned into positive experiences. For a young child, a ride on the bus or a trip to the grocery store can be an occasion to learn more about the world. Most communities have many free or inexpensive activities that adults and children can enjoy together. Whether it's animals at the county fair or a clown at a restaurant, children are fascinated by new sites. A caregiver who talks about what the child sees in any setting makes the most of such events and gives the child a better start in life.

MORE ABOUT Choosing Books

One-year-olds like short books with big, simple pictures, objects they can name, and textures to feel. Two-year-olds enjoy stories about families and familiar experiences. Three-year-olds enjoy longer, illustrated stories that spark their imagination and help them learn about things. When reading to children, use gestures, facial expressions, and a different voice for each character. A love of reading begun early often lasts a lifetime.

Chapter 24 — Review

Reviewing the Facts

1. Choose one area of development, and explain how play can help children develop in that area.
2. What is the difference between active and quiet play?
3. Define "sensory toys" and give an example of one.
4. How do toddlers benefit from imitating adults?
5. What does facilitating play mean?
6. How can a caregiver turn reading into an active learning experience?

Thinking Critically

1. Do you think that competitive play is useful or harmful to children? Explain your answer.
2. How do you think that a caregiver should react in these situations: (a) a child gets dirty while playing; (b) a toy breaks during play; (c) a child is afraid to join an activity; (d) a child throws a toy; and (e) a child asks for several toys in the store.

Applying Your Knowledge

1. **Everyday Materials.** For each item in the following list, suggest an activity that children might enjoy and learn from: snow, plastic kitchen containers and spoons, cardboard boxes, an empty oatmeal box, old computer printouts, dried beans, paper bags, fruit (apples, bananas), old but clean adult clothing and accessories. Describe the procedure you would use for each activity, and give the age suitable for the activity.
2. **Creating a Play Schedule.** Suppose that you are in charge of a four-year-old for an afternoon. Plan a schedule to cover a four-hour period. Include active and quiet play.

3. **Improvising Play.** Think of a household task that is done with some regularity, such as cooking, doing laundry, food shopping, or cleaning. Describe how a toddler or preschooler could be included in this activity to make it an enjoyable play experience.

Making Connections

1. **Art.** Divide the class into small groups. Each group should bring in a child's drawing. Ask relatives or neighbors for this, if necessary. Discuss the differences among the drawings depending on the age and developmental stage of the child.
2. **Geography.** Find out about a game children play in another culture. Write a brief description of the game, its origins, and the rules for playing it. You may wish to illustrate or demonstrate the game.

Building Your Portfolio

Reading to Preschoolers

Make an audiotape or a videotape of yourself reading a story to a toddler or a preschooler. If possible, choose a story that you enjoyed as a child. (Beforehand, review the hints for reading to children in this chapter.) Afterward, comment on tape about what this experience was like for you. Place a copy of the tape in your portfolio.

ANSWERS TO REVIEWING THE FACTS

1. *Physically*—by giving them the chance to exercise their muscles and improve their large- and small-motor skills; *intellectually*—by teaching them how the world works; *emotionally*—by teaching them how to give and receive caring and to bond with caregivers; *socially*—by teaching them skills for getting along with others, such as sharing and taking turns; *morally*—by encouraging them to learn a sense of right and wrong and understand the consequences of their actions
2. Active play involves using the large muscles; quiet play involves intellectual and small-motor skills.
3. Sensory toys are objects that have different textures, shapes, sounds, and colors, such as mobiles, crib "busy-boxes," rattles, squeak toys, and teething rings.
4. They develop an understanding of how to act in different situations.
5. The caregiver offers a child choices of play but does not control the child's play.
6. By asking questions, encouraging children to share their feelings about stories, asking them to turn the pages, acting out the story after hearing it.

ANSWERS TO THINKING CRITICALLY

1. Can be beneficial as long as children's feelings are safeguarded and they learn to accept losing; more appropriate as children grow older.
2. Possible responses: (a) accept as normal; (b) may comfort child and offer guidance on playing more carefully; consequence may be used for inappropriate behavior; (c) encourage child to join or find another activity; (d) point out the dangers and consequences of throwing; (e) set shopping limits before going to store; say no in a kind, firm way and distract child.

FOCUS

Chapter Overview

Chapter 25 takes a realistic view of day-to-day parenting. It describes the adjustments and responsibilities that come with a baby. It examines the emotional, financial, and personal preparation necessary to be an effective parent, and explains why few teens are ready for this challenge.

Motivator

■ **One to Ten.** Write a scale from one to ten on the chalk board. While students watch, write "very easy" above the number one and "very difficult" above the ten. Then ask students to write down a number that reflects their view about the difficulty level of raising a child. Share these and discuss why they think as they do.

Objectives

Discuss the chapter objectives on this page. Remind students that the objectives focus on important chapter concepts.

Vocabulary

The word *prenatal* combines the prefix *pre-,* meaning before, with *natal,* from a Latin word meaning to be born. Thus, *prenatal* means before birth. Ask students what they think *postnatal* means.

Chapter 25

The Realities of Parenthood

Terms to Learn

- emotional maturity
- fetus
- financial stability
- premature
- prenatal care

Objectives

This chapter will help you to:

- Describe the caregiving and financial responsibilities of parents.
- List and explain some poor reasons for desiring a child.
- Explain what is meant by emotional, financial, and personal readiness for parenthood.
- Describe the special problems teen parents face.

252   UNIT 4   Child Care and Development

CHAPTER RESOURCES

Student Workbook
Study Guide, p. 83
Activity, *Parenting Realities*, p. 84

Teacher's Classroom Resources
Lesson Plan, p. 29
Decision Making, *Deciding to Become Parents*, p. 16

Extension #41, *Teen Pregnancy*, p. 47
Extension #42, *The Development of the Fetus*, p. 48
Life Skills, *The Costs of Having a Baby*, p. 44
Transparency 27, *Parenting Responsibilities*

Chapter 25 Test, pp. 55-56
Performance Assessment, *Parenthood Information*, pp. 48-49
Reteaching, *Responsibilities of Parenthood*, p. 31

See Also:
ABCNews InterActive™ Videodiscs

Mary Lou's day at work had been horrible. After struggling to complete a project, the deadline for delivery had been moved even closer. Because her husband was out of town, Mary Lou had to pick up their son Kerry at the child-care center. She had gotten stuck in traffic on the way to the center and was concerned that Kerry would wonder where she was. Moreover, her late arrival would mean an additional charge for the day.

When she finally arrived, the center's director greeted her saying, "We've been trying to reach you, Mrs. Jolliff. Kerry isn't feeling well. His temperature is 101°." As she hugged Kerry and put him in his snowsuit, Mary Lou knew that the hardest part of her day was ahead. She and Kerry would have to stop for medicine and to pick up some chicken noodle soup for his dinner. The work she'd brought home from the office would have to wait. Making Kerry comfortable was her priority—deadline or no deadline.

Then there was tomorrow to think about. Kerry could not return to the center until his fever had been gone for 24 hours. Driving home, Mary Lou sang to Kerry and considered her options for tomorrow. Her mother-in-law was busy with her own activities, but maybe she'd agree to watch Kerry for the day. Otherwise, Mary Lou would have to stay home from work. She shook her head slowly and gave Kerry a gentle pat.

The Responsibilities of Parenthood

As Mary Lou discovered, parenting is easier on some days than others, yet the responsibility is always there. She and her husband knew from the beginning that being a parent would be a challenge. The realities were no shock to them, but they are to some.

Parents fulfill many roles. Can you name some of them?

Caregiving Responsibilities

The responsibilities of parenthood begin with everyday caregiving. As you have read, children depend on adults for so much. Nurturing a child in all areas of development takes knowledge and skills, combined with the time and energy to do what is needed.

Caring for a child is work, and it's not always fun. Challenges continually arise. Handling behavior, illness, and messiness are all part of the picture. Here's what two parents had to say:

- **Ishmael.** "I couldn't believe how tired we were after a short time into parenting. Our son was up at all times of the night. We kept thinking something was wrong with him, but the doctor said he checked out okay. All I know is that I can't wait to get one whole night of sleep again. Maybe Regina and I could each take a turn at the motel down the street."

- **Cindy.** "My daughter keeps me hopping. I can't take my eyes off her for a second or she's into something. Today it was the big plant in the living room. In less than a minute, she had dirt scattered all over the place. I love her, but I never dreamed how much work parenting would be."

CHAPTER 25   The Realities of Parenthood   253

TEACH

Topics on p. 253:
- **Responsibilities of Parenthood**
- **Caregiving Responsibilities**

Checking Comprehension

✓ Why is it difficult for a parent to work outside the home? *Parent is still responsible for child 24 hours a day; child care is expensive; sick child may cause parent to miss work.*

✓ Why is it important that parents be financially stable? *They must pay own and baby's living expenses, expected and unexpected.*

Activities

■ **Could Be Worse.** Ask students to name some advantages Mary Lou has in her role as a parent, despite the problems she faces. (For example: a two-adult household, a job, transportation.) Have students predict what might happen if she were to lose any one of these. *(Critical Thinking)*

CROSS-CURRICULAR ACTIVITY
Math

Ask groups to calculate the monthly expenses of a young couple and their baby. Have each group research the average cost of one basic living expense, such as housing, food, and insurance. Have groups total their expenses to determine how much a young family can plan to spend in a month. Point out that this figure does not include extras or unexpected expenses.

Topics on pp. 254-255:

- A 24-Hour Job
- Financial Responsibilities

Checking Comprehension

✓ What are some ways that parents handle child-care responsibilities? *One parent is totally responsible; parents share child care; neighbors or families help; parents pay for child care.*

✓ Name some common expenses for parents of a new baby. *Medical bills, formula, clothes, diapers, toys, crib, child care, possibly larger home.*

USING VISUALS

Refer students to Figure 25.1. Ask them if they think the day described is a weekday or one on the weekend. How would the day be different if both parents were employed? What kinds of events are not represented in the timeline?

FAMILY AND COMMUNITY OUTREACH

Have teams determine the options and costs of child care locally. Have them share their findings by filling in a large chart on the board. Ask: Aside from cost, in what cases might each option be the best one for parents?

Figure 25.1

A DAY AT HOME WITH A BABY

6:00 A.M.	Time to get up. Baby is awake, crying, and needing a new diaper and clean clothes.
6:30 A.M.	Baby cries to be fed. Parent feeds baby and fixes own breakfast.
7:30 A.M.	Wide awake, baby wants attention. Baby and parent take time to play.
8:30 A.M.	Baby plays while parent cleans kitchen.
9:15 A.M.	In need of more attention, baby fusses. Parent talks to baby while sorting laundry, then picks baby up. Time for another diaper change.
10:30 A.M.	Baby begins to fidget. Parent rocks baby to sleep. Parent hurries to get some things done and squeezes in a short break.
12:30 P.M.	Baby wakes, ready to be changed and fed.
1:30 P.M.	Teething pain causes baby to cry. Parent needs a half hour to give comfort.
2:00 P.M.	Parent changes baby for a trip to the supermarket.
3:00 P.M.	Baby enjoys a teething biscuit while parent puts away food. Time for a diaper change . . . again.
4:00 P.M.	Must be naptime. Baby is fussy and needs to be rocked and cuddled before sleeping. Parent begins to prepare dinner.
6:30 P.M.	Baby is up and ready for a bottle. Baby eats. Then parents have dinner.
7:30 P.M.	Playtime.
8:30 P.M.	Bathtime.
9:30 P.M.	After crying for a while, baby falls asleep.
10:30 P.M.	Bedtime for tired parents.
6:00 A.M.	Baby wakes, and the day begins again.

254   UNIT 4   Child Care and Development

Focus on Relationship Skills

After the birth of a child, especially the first, the parents' relationship with each other changes. They tend to focus on the child's needs rather than on each other. They have less free time, spend less time together, probably get less sleep, and have more decisions and problems to face. All these demands can strain the relationship. Couples must set aside time to be alone, to talk about things other than the baby, and become reacquainted with each other.

New parents find that their lives change tremendously when a baby is born. Daily routines become focused on the baby's needs. Free time for the parents becomes more limited. **Figure 25.1** shows what it's like to care for a baby full-time.

As children grow older, the demands continue, although the child's specific needs change. Parents often spend a great deal of time helping young children learn to care for themselves, picking up after them, helping with homework, guiding their behavior, driving to after-school activities, and just listening to them.

A 24-Hour Job

Caring for a child is a 24-hour-a-day job. You can't just set the responsibilities aside for a while. Someone has to be responsible for a young child at all times. Many parents today find that mixing parenthood with employment is complicated because of this need. When parents can't be home with children, they have to make alternative arrangements. Here are some options they use:

- Sometimes two parents divide tasks, one caring for the child while the other works at a job that earns a salary. Many families need two incomes, so this arrangement doesn't work well for them unless one parent can work at home.
- Some two-parent families alternate caring for the child. Both might work part-time on alternating days. Another possibility is working different shifts. Child care is covered with this arrangement, but the parents have less time together.
- When relatives are willing and able, some families turn to them for child care. Relatives, of course, are not obligated to take care of a family member's children. Parents who simply expect relatives to babysit can create ill will in a family.
- A growing resource for employed parents is professional child care. Although the services can be costly,

child-care centers and at-home family day care are options. Some employers provide facilities for their employees' children.

Financial Responsibilities

The cost of raising a child is high, and it begins even before a baby is born. As soon as a woman becomes pregnant, she needs to seek **prenatal care**—*care for the mother and the baby before birth.* Prenatal care is necessary to ensure that the child gets the best possible start in life. Pregnant women need frequent medical examinations so that the doctor can make sure that the **fetus**, or *unborn child,* is developing without problems. Doctors also have important advice for the expectant mother on diet and exercise. How well a pregnant woman takes care of herself has a direct impact on her health as well as the baby's. These health needs require expenses that cannot be ignored.

Parents have other expenses as they prepare for a new baby. They need a crib for the

Raising a child is expensive. Who has primary responsibility for raising and caring for a child?

CHAPTER 25   The Realities of Parenthood   255

Activities
■ **Company or a Crowd?** Remind students of the saying "Two's company; three's a crowd." Ask students: Does that apply to having a new baby in the family? Why or why not? *(Relationships)*

RETEACHING
■ **Skills for Parenting.** As a class, name sources of stress and conflict related to the arrival of a baby. List them on the board. Have groups review previous studied chapters for skills that might help parents deal with the conflict and stress identified.

CROSS-CURRICULAR ACTIVITY
Health

Ask students to investigate the possible effects on a fetus when the mother smokes, drinks, uses illegal drugs, takes prescription drugs without her doctor's knowledge, eats a poor diet, does not exercise, or is exposed to x rays. Students might share their findings in oral or written reports or with posters showing the harmful effects of these activities.

SPECIAL NEEDS *Strategies*

Inefficient Readers. Have students create a two-column chart. In the first column, tell them to list the unrealistic reasons for having a child given in the text, plus any others they can think of. In the second column, across from each reason, have them describe the reality.

REAL-LIFE APPLICATION

● ● ●

Read this to students: *Nancy and James, both 20, have been married one year. Nancy feels James is starting to spend more time with his friends than with her. She thinks that if they have a baby, James will pay more attention to her and spend* *more time at home.* Ask: Is Nancy's plan wise? If she becomes pregnant, will James react as she hopes? Suggest that James may spend time with friends to avoid the responsibilities that Nancy is trying to add to their relationship.

Topics on pp. 256-257:
- **Shared Responsibility**
- **Prenatal Care**
- **Wanting a Child**
- **Readiness**

Checking Comprehension

✔ What kind of financial responsibility does a father have for his children? *He is legally required to help support them until they are 18.*

✔ What unrealistic ideas do people sometimes have about having babies? *It will be pleasant all the time because babies are so sweet; gain respect from others; gain purpose in life; feel more grown up; be viewed as adult; will strengthen relationship.*

Avoiding parental responsibilities may be a sign of what? *Lack of readiness.*

STRATEGIES THAT WORK

Have students read "Prenatal Care." Point out that good health before conception is important too.

Answers to Think . . .
1. Encourage mother to get prenatal care, nutritious meals; give emotional support.
2. Added strain may cause pregnancy problems.
3. Call doctor before taking any medications.

CROSS-CURRICULAR ACTIVITY
Science

Find out how paternity tests use blood types and DNA to determine whether a person is the parent of a child.

---

baby to sleep in and a car seat for safe travel. Naturally, the baby needs diapers, clothes, equipment, and furniture. Parents also have to pay for the baby's routine medical examinations and immunizations.

As babies grow, their needs become greater and more costly. They outgrow clothing rapidly. They need food and appropriate toys to stimulate their development. Because parents need a break at times, some arrangements for outside child care are often needed. If help cannot be obtained from other family members or by trading services with other parents, child care must be paid for.

While two people can easily share a small living space, adding a child to that space makes a big difference. Often families want more room after a baby is added to the household, leading to more expense.

A Shared Responsibility

When a child is born, both parents are responsible for financial support. Even a parent who does not live with a child still has financial responsibility. The law requires this parent to contribute to the financial support of the child.

Unfortunately, some parents try to avoid this responsibility. When Miranda had a baby, she and Trent were not married. Although Trent was the father, he was unwilling to support his child. After Miranda hired a lawyer,

STRATEGIES That Work

Prenatal Care

The responsibilities of being a parent begin long before a baby is born. From the moment a child is conceived, the mother must pay special attention to her health. When Ellen became pregnant at age 25, her doctor told her that good care before birth helps prevent low birth weight, premature birth, and other outcomes that would endanger her health and her child's.

Here are some of her doctor's recommendations:

- Get regular prenatal medical care, starting in the early weeks of the pregnancy. Initial visits are monthly. Closer to delivery, visits are scheduled every two weeks and eventually every week.
- Eat a nutritious diet that includes a variety of foods from each of the five food groups.
- Get plenty of rest each night.
- Engage in regular, moderate exercise.
- Take over-the-counter and prescription medication only after consulting with the doctor.

- Don't use alcohol, illegal drugs, and tobacco.
- Avoid secondhand smoke.
- Avoid exposure to X-rays.

Making the Strategy Work

Think . . .

1. How can a father contribute to the health of a child before birth?
2. Many doctors recommend that women exercise only to the extent that they exercised before becoming pregnant. Why do you think they advise against undertaking any new types of exercise?
3. What should a pregnant woman do if she catches a cold?

Try...

Many medicines—even common, over-the-counter drugs—can harm pregnant women or their developing babies. Warnings are printed on their labels. Check five different over-the-counter medicines to see if such warnings are included.

DID YOU KNOW?

In 1993, about 30 percent of all family groups with children were headed by a single parent, up from 12 percent in 1970. Single mothers caring for children outnumber fathers six to one.

MORE ABOUT Child Support

Parents who are awarded child support don't always receive any or all of it. In 1989, for example, only 69 percent of child support due was paid. Judges may authorize automatic deductions of child support from a parent's paycheck.

a judge ordered Trent to contribute a portion of his earnings to Miranda until the child's eighteenth birthday.

The Desire for a Child

Despite all the responsibilities, many people still want to have children. Just the sight of an adorable infant can arouse these desires. Sometimes the reasons behind desires, however, don't make good sense.

The decision to have a child needs to be backed up by sound reasoning. Some people have unrealistic ideas about what having a child can mean to them.

One of Sarina's friends was a mother. Sometimes Sarina thought about what it would be like to have a baby of her own. She could be like Trish, but then—did she really want to be? Sarina had noticed that Trish had much less time to spend with friends after the baby was born. The baby was sweet, but Trish always seemed tired and even worried. Trish was having a difficult time, and Sarina knew that. Having a baby wouldn't be fair to the child—or to me, Sarina concluded.

Although Sarina avoided a mistake, many do not. People often have children for the "wrong" reasons. Some young people have children in hopes that others will treat them more respectfully. They may believe that having a child will make them feel better about themselves and give them a purpose in life. Some want their own parents to view them as grown up. Of course, merely having a baby is not a sign of adulthood.

Babies are not a cure for problems or troublesome situations. Having a child for the "wrong" reasons can lead to regrets when people discover that the child brings a whole new set of concerns to add to the ones they already have.

Some couples think that having a child will strengthen their relationship. The reverse is usually true, however. When two people are having difficulties in their relationship, the added demands of raising a child create more problems.

If these are the "wrong" reasons for having a baby, what are the "right" ones? No reason is "right" unless a person is ready in several ways.

Readiness

One of the problems with parenthood is that some people never really make a careful decision about it. Some simply let it happen—without any forethought. Some people believe they are ready when they really aren't. Giving more thought to the question might change their thinking. Those who do put effort into making a decision about whether and when to have children are more likely to accept the responsibilities of parenthood.

How do you know when you are ready to be a parent? A realistic look at personal qualities and circumstances gives strong clues.

Parenting means giving loving support to children in all situations. Adults must often put aside their own concerns in order to tend to the child. Those who are not emotionally mature may find this difficult to do.

CHAPTER 25   The Realities of Parenthood   257

MORE ABOUT Prenatal Care

Prenatal care is usually provided by an obstetrician or an obstetrician-gynecologist, a doctor who specializes in caring for pregnant women and delivering their babies. One routine prenatal procedure is a painless process that uses ultrasound waves to determine the fetus' size, position, and sometimes gender. The waves bounce off the fetus in the mother's uterus and create an image on a screen. If any problems are apparent, the doctor may recommend drugs, bed rest, or even surgery.

Activities

■ **They Said It.** Write some or all of the quotations below on the board. Have students choose at least one and write a paragraph explaining what it means and whether they agree.

• "A rich child often sits in a poor mother's lap." (Spanish proverb)

• "Your children need your presence more than your presents." (Jesse Jackson)

• "Parenthood remains the greatest single preserve of the amateur." (Alvin Toffler)

• "Insanity is hereditary— you can get it from your children." (Sam Levinson)

ENRICHMENT

■ **Insight from Interviews.** Ask students to interview a parent from their parents' generation. Have them ask: How old were you when your first child was born? Given another chance, would you have had a child or children when you did? Why? As students share the results of the interviews, have them look for clues in the responses that might indicate the age or time in life that people are best prepared to have children.

CROSS-REFERENCE

See Chapter 38 for specific information on guidelines for good nutrition. Point out that the requirements for a pregnant woman are somewhat different than for others, calling for extra nutrients in the diet in order to supply what both mother and child need.

Checking Comprehension

✓ Why is emotional maturity so important for parents? *It helps them make needed emotional adjustments; give baby love without expecting it back; look beyond own needs.*

✓ Why is a teen more likely than an older woman to have a premature baby? *Teen's body is still maturing, may not be able to support developing child; teen is less likely to get prenatal care.*

Acting Responsibly

Have students read the feature. Ask students to describe times they have been role models for young children, intentionally or not.

Answers to Your Analysis
1. Yes; she modeled cooperation, sensitivity, calmness.
2. Answers may include: by cooperating on projects; being open to making new friends; staying calm in unusual situations.

▶ CROSS-REFERENCE ◀
Teens may not realize what it costs to live independently, especially when they have a child. See Chapter 70 for information on costs related to housing.

Acting Responsibly

Are You a Positive Role Model?

Part of readiness for parenting means that a person is willing and able to be a positive role model. This is a critical part of parenting, since children learn by example. Children watch parents for signs of how to act. They notice when parents say one thing and do the opposite.

Even after a tough day at work, a parent must be careful to send the right message. While guiding behavior is primarily a parent's responsibility, the actions of any caregiver are also modeled by children.

A Role Model in Action

Aleta and her two young nephews, Todd and Tyler, were alone at their campsite. Her family and her aunt and uncle's family had driven to the campground in the mountains. After unloading the tent and other equipment, the adults drove to town for supplies. Aleta and the boys were in charge of getting wood for the campfire.

The boys, ages six and eight, had never been camping before. They looked at all the camping gear, then at Aleta.

"All right," she began. "When you go camping, everybody pitches in, because there are lots of things to do. Todd, you look around and collect as many dry twigs and branches as you can find. Tyler, you and I will get things ready to set up the tent."

Todd hesitated, then said, "I'm scared, Aleta."

"OK, I'll go with you," Aleta said. "Tyler, you get the tent poles out of the bag. We won't go far—you'll be able to see us." She and Todd went to the back of the clearing to search for wood. When they returned, each with an armful of wood, there was a sudden scuffling in the leaves. The brothers jumped, but Aleta said, "Oh, how cute!" and pointed to a skunk. "Stay quiet," she told the boys, "don't get close. Just watch him!"

The two boys were quiet as they stared at the skunk. Todd looked sideways at Aleta, but she had a smile on her face, so he exhaled and watched as well. The skunk paid no attention to the campers as it ambled away. When their parents returned, Todd and Tyler bubbled with excitement about their surprise visitor.

Your Analysis

1. Was Aleta a good role model? Explain your answer.
2. How might Todd and Tyler use what they learned at the campground in other situations?

Emotional Readiness

People who are ready for parenthood are emotionally mature. With **emotional maturity** comes *fully developed emotions, or feelings, and the ability to handle them well.* Emotionally mature people possess the inner resources to be able to meet the demands of raising a child. These resources include patience, sympathy, a degree of selflessness, self-control, and self-confidence.

People who lack emotional maturity may not be able to handle a child well because they are still learning to manage their own emotions. Guiding the anger of a child, for example, is difficult when you haven't yet learned to control your own anger. Although some people never reach a high level of emotional maturity, most people do become increasingly mature as they near adulthood.

Financial Readiness

Because raising a child is expensive, financial readiness should come before childbirth. No one should consider having a child until he or she has **financial stability**, *the ability to meet everyday living costs.* Parents must be able to support themselves and their children. They can't expect others to take this responsibility for them.

Focus on Problem Solving Skills

Have pairs list ways that emotionally mature parents might solve the following problems:

- One parent had plans to go out with friends, but the other parent must work late and can't watch the baby.

- One parent, unhappy at work, would like to quit and go to school to learn another trade. The other parent is not working and had planned to stay home with their new baby for at least a year.
- The baby is sick and cannot go to child care. Both parents must go to work.

Personal Readiness

When a baby is born, the child gives the family a new and different focus. Often the parents' needs take a back seat to those of the child. Time that parents could once use for their own activities is less available. People need to be ready to make certain personal sacrifices. If they have had time to become independent and have worked toward their career goals, they are likely to be more content to shift some time and energy to parenting.

Teen Parenthood

Adjusting to parenthood is difficult for anyone, but it can be especially hard for a teen. Teen parents face special problems that parents in their 20s or 30s usually do not face. Teens are not mature enough—emotionally, financially, or physically—to take on the responsibility of caring for another person.

Development in Process

The teen years are personally demanding. Teens have to make the difficult transition from childhood to adulthood. They have a lot on their minds and many decisions to make.

During this time, teens begin to know themselves and understand their values. They start thinking about their goals and what they want from life. Most teens feel strong pressures—from teachers, from parents, from friends, from society, and from within. Because of all these changes, demands, and pressures, most teens are not emotionally prepared to be parents. Most are still learning how to be responsible for themselves.

With all these challenges, having a child can get in the way of a teen's own development. The time and energy that caring for a child requires detracts from the resources available to the teen. Teens have the future before them and can choose from

many paths to pursue. Having a child greatly limits choices.

Michelle has a strong sense of self-awareness. In her heart she still feels young. She doesn't have children, and she plans to keep it that way for a while. She can't really picture herself as a mother. Michelle still wants to enjoy her independence. Although she would like to have children some day, she knows that now is not the time.

Michelle is lucky to have such strong convictions. She realizes that parenthood means making sacrifices that she can't make yet. Having the freedom to go places with friends and work toward a satisfying future is important to her. Michelle wants to be able to take responsibility for herself before she adds to her responsibilities.

Education and Work

Teens are usually not financially prepared to have a child. They tend to have low-paying jobs. Most are still finishing school, so they may work only part-time. A teen who suddenly has the responsibility of raising a child soon finds that a limited income doesn't go very far at all.

Finishing school is extremely important to a teen's future. Generally speaking, the better your education, the better are your career options. Teens who become parents

Being a teen parent usually leaves little time and money to spend with friends. What impact might this have on parent and child?

CHAPTER 25   The Realities of Parenthood   **259**

MORE ABOUT Teen Pregnancy

Some teens are unaware of, ignore, or try to hide their pregnancy. This has strong impact on the baby's health as well as their own when they don't obtain appropriate medical care.

DID YOU KNOW?

Fewer than half of women who have a baby before age 18 ever earn their high school diploma. Teen parents earn half as much money during their lives as people who wait until they are 20 or older before having a child.

Activities

■ **Rough Start.** Discuss: Is having a baby during the teen years fair to the child? (*Critical Thinking*)

ENRICHMENT

■ **Happy(?) Birthday.** Ask students to imagine the situation of a child, born to teen parents, on the child's fifth birthday. In groups have them write a description of that child's life, including family members' relationships, their housing situation, how the child is developing, the child's behavior, and self-esteem. Have groups compare their descriptions.

MULTICULTURAL Perspectives

The percentage of teen births tends to be higher in developing countries than in industrialized nations. For example, in Nigeria 146 teens out of every 1,000 give birth; in Japan, it is only 4 of every 1,000. The teen birth rate in the United States is closer to those in developing nations: 62 per 1,000 teens.

USING VISUALS

Refer students to the photos. Here is what some teen parents said about raising a child:

- "I never realized I would miss out on so much. I'd love to go to a movie, but even if I had the time and money, I'm too exhausted."
- "I don't have much in common with my friends. Jennifer's the only one who still comes around— sometimes."

Review

■ **Chapter Review.** Use the contents of the Chapter Review page to help students review concepts, think critically, and apply their knowledge.
■ **Study Guide.** Have students complete the Study Guide for Chapter 25 on page 83 of the Student Workbook.
■ **Ready or Not?** Ask students to write a description of a couple who is truly ready for parenthood, based on the factors discussed in this chapter and any others they think important. Have a few students share their descriptions with the class. Ask: How closely do the young couples you know fit that description?

Evaluation

■ **Chapter Test.** Use the reproducible chapter test provided in the Teacher's Classroom Resources or create your own test using the *Testmaker Software.*
■ **Alternative Assessment.** Have students use a medium of their choice to illustrate the fantasy versus the reality of parenthood, especially teen parenthood.

■ **Me, a Parent?** Ask students to complete the following sentence in writing: "When I decide to become a parent, it will be because . . ." Ask them to use follow-up sentences as explanation.

Waiting to have children until a couple is ready—emotionally and financially—benefits the entire family.

selves can develop properly. Pregnant teens are more likely than adult women to develop two unhealthy blood conditions, toxemia and anemia. Toxemia is the buildup of poisons in the blood. Anemia is the lack of iron, which leads to fatigue and other problems.

often must change or postpone their career plans because a baby comes along. Finishing high school or going on to technical school or college can be very difficult for a teen parent.

Starting a family before finishing your education can become a lifelong career disability. People who drop out of school and don't find the opportunity to go back later will not have the training and experience they need to get good jobs. Often, they go from one low-paying job to another, with little chance for advancement.

Physical Concerns

Teens who become pregnant run risks, both for the baby and for themselves. Many pregnant teens delay seeking prenatal care from a doctor. Studies show that babies of teen mothers are more likely to be **premature**—*born before they are completely developed*—or have low birth weight. Low birth weight can cause such problems as cerebral palsy and mental retardation.

Very young teens who become pregnant endanger their own bodies. Pregnancy puts a great deal of stress on the body, and teens need food, rest, and energy so that they them-

Planning Ahead

Having a child before you are ready can cause problems. Often, when an unprepared person has a child, both parent and child suffer. The parent may give the baby a poor start in life and be unable to foster the child's growth and development. Even neglect or abuse may result.

Being a parent should be a choice made after much careful thought. Once you choose to become a parent, that decision is permanent. A child's birth changes the lives of the mother and the father—and their families—forever.

Are you ready to be a parent? Think about what it means to be a parent, both the joys and the burdens. Think about your plans for yourself and your future. Where do you want to be in 5 years, 10 years, 15 years? Would having a child fit your plans? If so, when?

Because it takes two people to have a child, be sure to talk it over with your partner when the time comes. Discuss the roles each of you would play in the child's life. Then decide. The happiest and healthiest children are those who are born to parents who honestly want them and who are ready for them.

260   UNIT 4   Child Care and Development

DID YOU KNOW?

A 20-year study of 134,088 pregnant women by the University of Utah found that teens under age 17 were twice as likely as older women to give birth 3 or more weeks prematurely, or to babies with low birth weight (less than 5.5 pounds). Low birth weight is the greatest threat to a newborn. The study ruled out other known causes of prematurity and low birth weight, such as lack of prenatal care.

Chapter 25 Review

Reviewing the Facts

1. Why do people say that parenthood is more demanding than any other job?
2. Give an example of how parenthood can affect a couple's financial resources.
3. What is emotional maturity? Why should parents possess it?
4. Give two poor reasons for having a child.
5. How do unrealistic expectations make parenthood difficult?
6. Describe two problems that teen parents may face.

Thinking Critically

1. Imagine that it's five years from now. Describe what your life would be like if you had a child. Then describe what your life would be like if you did not have a child.
2. What can happen if a parent has no time to meet his or her own needs?

Applying Your Knowledge

1. **Practicing Full-time Child Care.** Babies need to be watched 24 hours a day. To understand how much care they need, get a 10-pound sack of flour and pretend it's your baby for a week. Using the schedule shown in **Figure 25.1**, "feed" the baby, diaper it, and spend time with it as you would a real child. You'll also need to take your baby with you everywhere you go.
2. **Exploring Effects.** Imagine that your long-term goal is to be a journalist. Now imagine that while you are still in college, you are about to become a parent. Write a short essay describing how you think that parenthood will affect your career goal.

Making Connections

1. **Health.** Create a poster that depicts the negative outcomes of teen pregnancy.
2. **Government.** Research laws in your state about fathers who don't take responsibility for their children. What happens in your state to these men? Do you agree with the laws? Explain your conclusions.
3. **Geography.** In some of Israel's kibbutzim, settlements in which much property and labor is shared, children are raised by the entire community, not just their parents alone. What do you think are the advantages and disadvantages of this arrangement?

Building Your Portfolio

Preparing for a Baby

Research what equipment and supplies a parent needs to prepare for a baby's arrival. With your class, agree on a list. Using a catalog, calculate how much it would cost to buy everything on the list. Make two price lists: one for essential items and one for unessential. Total the lists. How might costs be kept down? What must parents consider besides price? In writing, summarize your thoughts about the costs involved. Put your price lists and answers in your portfolio.

ANSWERS TO REVIEWING THE FACTS

1. Possible responses: Parenthood is a 24-hour-a-day job; it takes tremendous amounts of time, energy, and money; you can't quit.
2. Will increase expenses: cost of food, clothing, and more spacious housing; cost of child's medical care.
3. Fully developed emotions, or feelings, and the ability to handle them well; needed in order to meet the demands of raising a child.
3. Possible responses (any two): because friends have babies, to give purpose to life, to strengthen a relationship, to be treated as an adult.
5. Unrealistic expectations create a false image of parenthood, leaving the person unprepared for its real challenges.
6. Any two: lack of emotional readiness for parenthood, neglect of their own development when concentrating on raising a child, financial problems due to incomplete education and low-paying jobs, impaired physical development for females, risks to health of baby.

ANSWERS TO THINKING CRITICALLY

1. Possible response: life with a child—spend a lot of time at home, have less disposable income, settle down; life without a child—start a career, attend college, date different people.
2. Possible response: A parent could be resentful and less able to cope with the demands of parenting.

Chapter Overview

Chapter 26 describes qualities and skills needed for careers working with children. It gives examples of positions requiring various levels of training and education, and suggests ways that students can start preparing for careers in this field.

Motivators

■ **I Could Be.** Point out the title of this chapter. Ask students to name as many jobs as they can that relate to meeting children's needs. List their responses.

■ **Wanted.** Obtain two classified ads for very different child-related jobs, such as nanny and child psychologist. Discuss (and explain, if needed) the training and experience requirements with students. Ask: Does either job sound interesting to you?

Objectives

Discuss the chapter objectives on this page. Remind students that the objectives focus on important chapter concepts.

Vocabulary

The source of the term *pediatrician* is the Greek word *paidos,* meaning child. Help students define *pediatrician*.

Chapter 26

Careers Working with Children

Objectives

This chapter will help you to:

- Identify the interests and skills a person needs to work well with children.
- Describe some jobs that involve working with children.
- Explore the kinds of child-related jobs that might be right for you.

262   UNIT 4   Child Care and Development

CHAPTER RESOURCES

Student Workbook
Study Guide, p. 85
Activity, *Caregiving Careers*, pp. 86-87

Teacher's Classroom Resources
Lesson Plan, p. 30
Extension #43, *Careers Helping Children*, p. 49

Life Skills, *Meet the Caregivers*, pp. 45-46
Personal Development, *Exploring Career Options*, pp. 35-36
Transparency 28, *Working with Children*
Chapter 26 Test, pp. 57-58

Performance Assessment, *Working with Children*, pp. 50-51
Reteaching, *Working with Children*, p. 32

See Also:
ABCNews InterActive™ Videodiscs

Blythe loved her job as a kindergarten teacher, but sometimes it demanded extra imagination. While lining up to play a marching game one day, the children were especially noisy and active. Blythe also noticed some poking and pushing going on.

After a few moments, she said, "All right children, close your eyes and hold your hands out. The 'glue fairy' is going to sprinkle magic glue on your hands." As she walked down the line, she brushed the children's hands lightly with her fingers. "Now, slap your hands down on your thighs. You won't be able to lift them until the fairy comes around again."

With their hands "stuck" to their thighs, the children marched around the room smiling and laughing at the game. Blythe watched with satisfaction.

The Qualities Needed

Children make noise and have abundant energy, and they regularly demand attention. Working with children can be exhausting, but when they accomplish something, the work is worthwhile.

Blythe showed creativity when working with the children in her class. Many other personal qualities have also added to her effectiveness. Anyone who is considering a career that involves work with children needs to take a close look at what interests, qualities, and skills are likely to contribute to success.

- **Do you enjoy children?** A love of children is a common trait of those who decide to work with them. You need to care about children and be interested in how they learn and grow before you

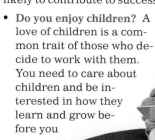

devote yourself to this type of work. Only genuine feelings result in the quality care that children deserve.

- **Do you respect children as people?** You must show children that you value their feelings and that you take their needs seriously. Each child is an individual with unique qualities. Realizing this allows you to respond appropriately to each one.

- **Are you sympathetic?** Can you put yourself in the child's place? Are you able to imagine what your expectations look like to them? If so, you will be able to calm their fears and respond to their needs more effectively.

- **Are you patient, tolerant, and calm?** The repetitive games that children enjoy are much easier to handle when you have these qualities. These qualities are also useful when helping children settle arguments and learn new skills.

- **Are you creative?** Creativity is the ability to use your imagination to do things in new ways. A good imagination can help you think of new and interesting activities for children. Solving problems is also easier when you are creative.

- **Are you enthusiastic and willing to join with children in their play?** Playing with children shows that you think they are important. Children like to act silly and have fun. When adults participate, children's enjoyment increases.

What qualities do child-care workers need to possess?

CHAPTER 26   Careers Working with Children   263

Checking Comprehension

✓ Why should people who work with children respect them? *Children sense respect. It helps them form positive self-concept, and build good self-esteem.*

✓ Why is creativity valuable for people who work with children? *It helps them think of new, interesting activities for children.*

✓ Why must you consider your personal skills and qualities before choosing a career with children? *It helps you select a career that satisfies and suits you.*

Activities

■ **No Go.** Challenge students to name some personal characteristics that might make it difficult for a person to work with children. *(Relationships)*

CROSS-CURRICULAR ACTIVITY
Language Arts

Ask each student to choose two of the qualities on pages 263 and 264, then write a realistic scenario in which a teen working with young children demonstrates both qualities. (Example: A student might describe how a camp counselor shows respect for children and enthusiasm for their activities.)

Focus on Communication Skills

Have students demonstrate the quality indicated in each of these situations:

- A child cries that a big, scary dog is in the yard. You look to see the neighbor's friendly puppy. (Respect)
- A child, watching the rain fall outside, complains of being bored. (Creativity)
- A child begs you to read the same story for the third time in one sitting. (Enthusiasm)
- A child accidentally spills milk, and later a dish of applesauce. (Patience)

Acting Responsibly

Acting Responsibly

Can You Remain Calm?

Have you ever noticed that some people are remarkably calm in an emergency situation? Staying calm can be the key to handling a crisis. It allows people to think clearly and avoid emotional responses. Even if you don't feel calm, you must act calmly when you care for children. They look to the caregiver to set the tone for the situation.

Calmness in Action

Dan was babysitting his swimming coach's young sons. The parents were planning to return about eleven o'clock that night. Although Dan had never taken care of the boys before, he felt comfortable. Their parents had shown him where things were and left a phone number.

At first, everything went fine. The boys had supper, and Dan was playing a board game with them. Halfway through the game, however, lightning and thunder announced that a storm was approaching. Dan turned on the radio for a weather report. Joey, age three, began to fidget and look scared. As the thunder got louder, seven-year-old Jim got edgy—and even Dan felt unsettled. Then the lights went out.

Immediately Joey began to cry, and Jim got rowdy. Dan felt disoriented in the dark house that was unfamiliar to him. He knew that he had to calm the boys, however. As he picked up Joey, he said to Jim, "I

need your help. Do you know where your parents keep a flashlight?"

"No," Jim answered, "but I have one in my room. I think I can find it, even in the dark."

"We'll all go," Dan told the boys. "We'll be explorers looking for treasure. Jim, you be the head explorer and lead the way," he added as he held on to the back of Jim's shirt.

With that, the three "explorers" headed cautiously for the bedroom. "After we find the treasure," Dan said, "we'll use it to help us read a story. Joey, would you like to have a turn holding the treasure when we find it?" Joey was no longer crying, and Jim was happily intent on leading the mission.

Your Analysis

1. How did Dan turn a negative situation into a positive one?
2. What might have happened if Dan had not appeared calm?
3. Suppose that you were caring for a four-year-old who had just fallen off her bike and was crying because of her scraped knee. How would you stay calm and help calm her down?

- **Are you adaptable?** You can always expect the unexpected with children. That calls for adaptability. Children may tire of what they are doing. Behavior may change. Such events call for child-care workers to make adjustments.
- **Do you have a sense of humor?** If you do, you can more easily brighten the mood of a sad or distressed child and help children see the humorous side of situations.
- **Are you willing to learn about children?** To understand a child's behavior and needs, you must know what to expect at each stage of development. Taking classes

and reading books and current articles about children are two ways to learn.

- **Are you interested in a particular career field and how it might apply especially to children?** There are jobs in a variety of fields—for example, medicine, library science, and nutrition—that can involve working with children.

If you have these characteristics, you may be suited for work with children. A sampling of some of the jobs available is given here. Although these describe only a few child-related jobs, you will get a basic idea of the variety of work you can do.

264   UNIT 4 **Child Care and Development**

Topics on pp. 264-265:

- **Career Qualities (Continued)**
- **Entry-Level Jobs**

Checking Comprehension

✓ What jobs could teens hold to find out whether they want to work with children? *Camp counselor, babysitter.*

✓ Describe the job of a nanny. *Lives with and cares for children in their home for room and board, plus salary.*

✓ How might someone prepare to be a child-care worker? *Babysit, take family and consumer sciences courses.*

Acting Responsibly

Have students read "Can You Remain Calm?" Invite students to describe times when they or someone else managed to remain calm in an emergency. What useful tips can they share from the experience?

Answers to Your Analysis

1. He kept calm, showed no fear, encouraged boys to do the same; appealed to sense of imagination and adventure.
2. Boys might have grown frightened, out of control, might have hurt selves in dark.
3. Answers may include: hold child; reassure her she was not seriously injured; have her help in tending to knee.

REAL-LIFE APPLICATION

Read this to students: *To earn extra money during the summer, Hannah accepted a job taking care of five-year-old Troy, her neighbor's child. After a couple of weeks, Hannah noticed that she was starting to "tune Troy out." He asked questions constantly and Hannah got tired of answering them.* Tell students that Hannah has been thinking about becoming a preschool teacher. Ask them to evaluate this idea.

Career Examples

The one job involving children that outranks all others in importance is parenting. Parents have the full-time responsibility for their children's health, safety, learning, and happiness. Parents, however, can't do everything themselves. Teachers, doctors, and child-care workers are among the people who support them. Education and training requirements for these jobs vary.

Entry-Level Jobs

Child-care workers care for children whose parents are employed or who need care for some other reason. Child-care workers generally work in child-care centers and preschools or care for children at home or in the children's home. These workers supervise the children and help them grow in all areas of development. Babysitting experience and family and consumer sciences courses are helpful for child-care jobs.

The type of work done and the training needed depends on the setting. Most child-care centers and preschools are private businesses or are run by nonprofit organizations. Some companies provide child-care facilities for the children of their employees. Child-care and preschool workers need to be skilled with children, but training is not always required. Some employers, however, do require certification and/or a two-year or four-year college degree.

Some people, often stay-at-home parents who are licensed by the state, provide child care in their own homes. The service they provide is called family day care. JoAnne Kemp began by offering family day care to two neighbor children after the birth of her son. Within four years, she was caring for more children, although her son was then in school. She began thinking about renting a separate space and hiring some help.

Private household child-care workers, or nannies, care for the children of a working parent or parents in the family's home. A nanny usually lives with the family, cares for the children in the evenings as well as the day, and receives free room and board as well as a salary. Nannies and family day-care providers need excellent **references**—*written reports about their work from previous employers*—so that parents will trust them with their children.

Camp counselors work with children at summer camps to teach them sports and skills, such as swimming, crafts, and observing nature. Counselors at sleep-away camps are responsible for children's care around the clock. Many children in their care need support, as they experience their first time away from home. Counselors may also work in day camps where the children return home each night. Camp counselors are

Camp counselors must be able to get along with children and make them feel comfortable.

Activities
■ **Who Do You Call?** Discuss the value of references with students. Explain that many potential employers rely on references to help them in making a hiring decision. It pays to develop a good reputation with teachers, coaches, employers, and others who can speak highly of you. Have students try to think of three people they could currently use as references. If they have trouble with this, advise them to think of ways to develop such contacts.

RETEACHING
■ **Spell It Out.** Ask groups to create acrostics from the word *children*, using each letter of the word to begin a sentence or phrase describing a trait or skill needed for people who work with children. Groups might put their acrostics on poster board or a bulletin board for display.

ENRICHMENT
■ **Aptitude Test.** Have students develop a checklist or quiz that would help identify and rate a person's talents and skills for working well with children.

USING VISUALS
Refer students to the photo on this page. Ask them for signs that this young man relates well to children. (*Kneeling down to talk on their level; smiling; using simple, available object in nature to teach.*)

MORE ABOUT Certification

Many states require that certain employees have a Child Development Associate (CDA) credential in order for a child care program to be licensed. This credential is awarded to an applicant after the person demonstrates competency skills in specific areas of child care. You can get information on this credential from the Council for Early Childhood Professional Recognition, 1341 G Street, NW, Suite 400, Washington DC 20005-3105.

Checking Comprehension

✓ What kind of training does a teacher's aide require? *Varies; some earn associate's degrees, others get on-the-job training.*

✓ Name child-related jobs that require college degrees or advanced degrees. *Teacher, children's librarian, pediatrician, dietitian.*

✓ What is the primary difference between a licensed practical nurse and a registered nurse? *LPNs study for 2 years; RNs have college degree and sometimes master's.*

BALANCING
WORK AND FAMILY

Have students read the feature. Refer to the requirements for licensing. Ask students which developmental needs of children are covered by these. Do any of the requirements focus on the intellectual and emotional needs of children.? What responsibilities does a child care provider have in these areas? How can they be addressed?

Answers to Suppose That . . .

Advantages may include: independence; chance to make a difference in children's lives; provide a needed service. Disadvantages: total responsibility for business and children; long hours.

266

BALANCING Work AND Family

Working at Home

Working outside the home isn't always easy to manage for a parent of young children. Some parents have found a solution—they take care of other people's children in their own homes. Many parents believe a homelike setting is an advantage in child care. These caregivers don't have the expense of child care, and they can earn income while being home with their own children.

A family day-care center requires sufficient space. Equipment, such as a changing table and high chairs, is also needed. Toys and creative materials are another investment.

States vary in what they require of providers; it may be necessary to get a license. The standards that must be met to get a license typically include:

- Limiting the number of children.
- Providing adequate space for playing and napping.

- Childproofing the house.
- Installing smoke detectors and planning a fire escape route.
- Keeping the house clean and sanitary.
- Providing nutritious meals and snacks.

An at-home child care operation needs to be run like a business. This means setting regular hours that both the parents and the operator can count on. Following a daily schedule and planning activities for the children is also necessary.

Suppose That . . .

You are exploring the idea of opening a family day-care center after you graduate from school. What disadvantages are there for the operator of such a business? What advantages are there?

---

usually high school and college students. Experience with Boy Scouts or Girl Scouts or babysitting—plus proficiency in a certain sport, craft, or field of interest—is helpful.

As Sonya found, being a camp counselor is a good way to begin exploring an interest in working with children. Working as a counselor for three summers, Sonya found that she enjoyed her job tremendously. She taught the children some simple crafts, led walks in the woods, and, once she got a lifesaving certificate, she helped teach them how to swim. Sonya's experience led her to choose child care as her career.

Cafeteria workers prepare food and serve it to children in school lunchrooms. These workers should enjoy cooking and being with children. Patience and friendliness are a big help too. Many parents with school-age children find this a convenient job, because it allows them to work only during school hours.

Jobs That Require Training

A teacher's aide helps a teacher with preparation and sometimes with actual instruction in the classroom. The training needed for this job varies from one school system to another. Some two-year colleges offer a course of study leading to an associate's degree for teacher's aides. With additional course work, the aide can eventually earn a bachelor's degree and become a teacher. Job openings for teacher's aides are expected to be plentiful in the future.

A team coach works with children who enjoy athletics. Many coaches are hired by school systems, but some work for community parks and recreation departments. Some coaches are volunteers. Coaches instruct children not only in the basic skills of a particular sport but also in the principles of fair play. The training for this job includes experience in

---

DID YOU KNOW?

The Bureau of Labor Statistics in Washington, DC, can provide current information about child-care jobs that will be in demand in the future.

Some vocational programs combine classes on child development with practical experience working with children. Similarly, some child-care agencies offer classes in child-care skills along with on-the-job training.

sports and usually a certain number of college credits. Coaches who are also teachers need college degrees.

Andy Ross works as a coach at a community center. He plans sports activities according to the season, running a T-ball program in the spring, soccer in the fall, and basketball in the winter. The summer is taken up with camps offering more intense instruction and training in the skills each sport demands. Because Andy works with young children ages five to eight, he makes sure that the programs emphasize participation for every child and work in the basic rules and skills of the sport. He doesn't stress winning.

Children's book authors write books for children. They may write picture books for toddlers or novels for teens. There is no single way of becoming a writer, though most writers have college degrees.

Another creative way to work with children is to be a children's performer—a storyteller, a magician, or a clown, for example. These people often have training in acting, singing, or playing instruments. The most important requirements for these jobs are creativity, enthusiasm, and talent.

If you like sports and working with people, a coaching job may be for you.

Jobs That Require Higher Education

Whether they work in a school or a public library, children's librarians help children find books and information and teach them how to use reference materials. Children's librarians also review books and magazines for the libraries to purchase. Many of these jobs require applicants to have a college degree and often a master's degree in library science.

Judy Franks, a librarian at the public library, offers a variety of programs to interest children in books. She loves reading to preschoolers at story time because she enjoys using different voices to make the characters come alive. Judy conducts tours to teach children about the library's many resources. As computer use has increased in the library, Judy has become familiar with the programs so that she can explain them effectively to children.

The *physicians who care for children* are called **pediatricians.** Like all physicians, they have college and medical degrees, as well as extensive additional training in their specialty. Pediatricians may have their own practices, or they may work in a hospital or a clinic.

Pediatric nurses specialize in providing nursing care for children. They may work in a doctor's office, advising parents about how to cope with childhood illnesses or other problems, or they may work in a hospital pediatric ward caring for youngsters. Nurses' responsibilities depend on the level of training they have. Licensed practical nurses usually have two years of study; registered nurses may have a college degree and perhaps a master's degree in their area of expertise.

CHAPTER 26 **Careers Working with Children** **267**

Activities

■ **Best of Both.** On the board list several careers or hobbies not usually associated with children, such as music, law enforcement, or food preparation. Challenge groups to list jobs that combine each interest with meeting the needs of children. Jobs may or may not involve direct contact with children.

ENRICHMENT

■ **Books and More.** Have groups investigate libraries to learn what services each offers to children. Some librarians, for example, teach classes in crafts and computer skills. Libraries may also host special holiday activities. After sharing their findings, have students think of ways to help a library publicize its offerings to children.

FAMILY AND COMMUNITY OUTREACH

Ask students to explore child-related volunteer opportunities in their community. For example, they could help at a hospital or a child-care center. They might also volunteer informally by watching a neighbor's child for free. Encourage students to pursue these opportunities. Later they might discuss the skills they learned, the services they provided, and the satisfaction they received from helping others.

MORE ABOUT Volunteering

Some states require or allow nonprofit agencies to make background checks on volunteers who will spend time alone with children. Applicants are fingerprinted. Then police check their records for past criminal activity, especially child or sexual abuse. An American Bar Association study indicates that only 2.4 percent of volunteers so investigated are rejected, leading some to believe that these checks do little good and only discourage good people from volunteering. Ask students what they think about this practice.

Review

■ **Chapter Review.** Use the contents of the Chapter Review page to help students review concepts, think critically, and apply their knowledge.

■ **Study Guide.** Have students complete the Study Guide for Chapter 26 on page 85 of the Student Workbook.

■ **Say It with Pictures.** Have students use old magazines to collect photos that show the qualities needed by people who work in careers related to children. Have them select the best representative pictures and create a bulletin board display, including labels and captions of explanation.

Evaluation

■ **Chapter Test.** Use the reproducible chapter test provided in the Teacher's Classroom Resources or create your own test using the *Testmaker Software.*

■ **Alternative Assessment.** Have groups create a staff directory for a fictional business in a child-related field, such as a school or a hospital pediatrics wing. Have each student choose one or two staff members about whom to write a brief profile, including job responsibilities, training and education, and experience. Encourage groups to enhance their project with photographs and a cover. Have groups exchange completed directories.

■ **R-E-S-P-E-C-T.** Ask: Does society show respect for people who work with children? What evidence do they see of respect? Of lack of respect? What might attract more people to this field?

Children probably spend more time with their teachers than with any other adults except family members. Teachers are responsible for helping children learn intellectual concepts and skills that they need to succeed in life. Teaching often means spending long hours at home planning lessons and grading papers, yet it can be a very satisfying career. Teachers need a college degree and usually a teacher's certificate. Many also go on to get graduate degrees.

A **dietitian** is *a professional who is educated in food and nutrition and their relationship to health and fitness.* Many dietitians work in hospitals, but some work for school districts.

They plan and direct the purchase and preparation of the food. A school dietitian aims to provide food that appeals to children, satisfies their nutritional needs, and meets the school budgets. Dietitians usually have a college degree in nutrition or food service and must have a master's degree in food service. Management training is also a helpful background for this profession.

Preparing for a Career

If you are interested in a career that involves children, you might like to know that in some of these careers the demand for employees is growing. According to government statistics, the number of jobs for child-care workers is expected to increase by 65 percent by the year 2005. The number of jobs for preschool and kindergarten teachers is projected to increase by 54 percent and for special education teachers by 74 percent.

You can start preparing now for a career that involves children. There are many ways to begin testing your interests and getting experience. You can also explore volunteer opportunities. Any experience you gain will help put you on track for the job you want.

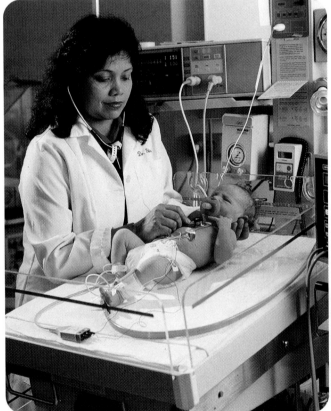

Some people combine a love for children with a medical career. What special qualities might a person need to enter the field of medicine?

MORE ABOUT Careers

For students who might be interested in child-related careers, here are some ideas of places where jobs can be found: battered women's shelters, child-care centers, crisis nurseries, departments of human services, employer-sponsored child-care programs, homeless shelters, hospitals with sick bay child-care services, parks and recreation programs, public and private schools, Salvation Army, United Way, university lab schools, U.S. military bases, Visiting Nurses Association, YWCA, and YMCA.

Chapter 26 Review

Reviewing the Facts

1. Name three personal qualities that are useful in working with children.
2. Name two entry-level jobs that involve working with children.
3. What does a teacher's aide do?
4. What jobs do pediatricians and pediatric nurses do, and where might they work?
5. What experience could you get now to help you know if you would like a career working with children?

Thinking Critically

1. Suppose that you had a seven-year-old sibling. What activities with your sibling would help prepare you for a career in child care?
2. What do you think would be the most difficult part of working with children? Why?

Applying Your Knowledge

1. **Preparing for an Interview.** Experts in job hunting recommend that people prepare for an interview by making a list of their skills and qualities. Then they link each one with an experience that illustrates it. For example, tolerance could be illustrated this way: "As a camp counselor, I helped the ethnically mixed children in my group understand each other better by . . . ." Try making a list of your own skills and qualities. Illustrate three of them with real-life examples.
2. **Identifying Tutoring Opportunities.** Tutoring is a chance to see if you have the ability and patience to teach children. Find out about tutoring programs in your area conducted by schools, churches, or community groups. What are the ages of children who are tutored? In what subjects are they tutored? What abilities are needed in the tutors? Present your findings to the class.

Making Connections

1. **Business.** Some companies have child-care centers on the premises for the children of their employees. Examine this trend by collecting newspaper or magazine articles about such programs, for businesses and for parents. Present your findings to the class.
2. **Language Arts.** Using resources available in the library, read about a children's author or illustrator. Find out how the person works, what training or experience helped the writer or illustrator, and what kind of books the person works on. Describe your findings to the class.

Building Your Portfolio

Investigating a Career

Investigate educational opportunities for a child-care-related field you might like to enter. Check out community colleges and nearby colleges and universities. What courses are required? How many are necessary for a degree or certificate? What is the cost of the program? Summarize your findings in an outline format and place the outline in your portfolio.

Unit Preview

Unit 5 teaches students how to use resources wisely. Students study the four kinds of resources: human, material, community, and natural. Time and money are covered in detail. Students learn the benefits of saving money, establishing credit, using money wisely, how to comparison shop, evaluate advertising, and judge the quality of products and service.

Content Development

Use these chapters to reinforce the following themes:

Content Strands	Chapters
Career Exploration	35
Citizenship/ Leadership	34, 35
Communication	34
Decision Making	27-31, 33, 34
Health and Safety	27, 29, 32, 34
Managing Resources	27-31, 33-35
Personal Development	29, 33
Technology	29, 30, 35

Unit Motivator

■ **Life Management—Part I.** Ask students if they ever forget to do things, run short of money, or have trouble completing assignments on time. What causes these problems? (*Weak management.*) Ask for examples of the trouble students get in when they don't manage resources well. Have them make notes on their own personal management downfalls. Tell students that in this unit, they will be learning some tips for making their lives run more smoothly.

270

JOURNAL WRITING

Ask students to write journal entries at the end of each day on what went well and what didn't. After they have kept the journal for a week, have them look back at their entries and assess their planning and management skills. What ideas for making improvements do they have? During the next week, have students implement their ideas, again keeping journal entries and following up with an analysis of the results.

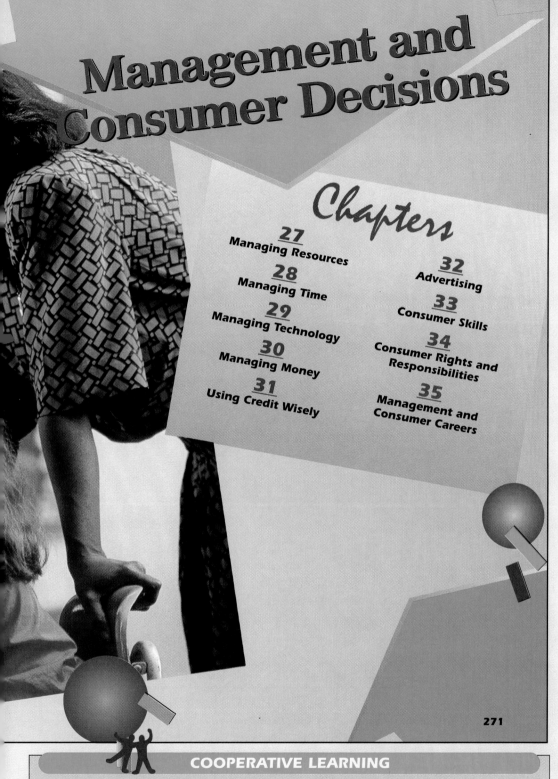

Management and Consumer Decisions

Chapters

271

FHA Activities

The following activities can be used with your FHA group or as public relations strategies:

■ **Better Management Fair.** Sponsor a Live Better Fair at your school. Invite resource people who have information about topics such as time and money management to the school. Have them offer quick lectures on management or set up booths at which they can sit and answer students' questions.

■ **Small Claims Court.** Have students visit a small claims court to find out how cases involving consumer problems are handled.

Unit Closure

■ **Catalog or Store?** Have students look through a mail-order catalog and choose one item they might like to purchase. Have them compare the item's price, quality, and warranty to a similar item in a store. Have them evaluate the advantages and disadvantages of buying through a catalog and through a store.

REVIEW

■ **Life Management—Part II.** Ask students to recall the discussion at the beginning of the unit about management problems they have. What problems did they cite? Did they learn anything in this unit to help them with these problems? Ask students if they have been putting any of this information into practice. If so, what tips can they offer others?

EVALUATION

■ **Unit Test.** Have students complete the unit test in the Teacher's Classroom Resources.

■ **Testmaker Software.** You may wish to design a unit test using the *Testmaker Software*.

COOPERATIVE LEARNING

Advertising Viewpoints. Form groups of three to study points of view in advertising. Each student should assume a role, either advertiser, buyer, or evaluator. Provide copies of the same print advertisement(s), chosen because of their controversial nature. Then have advertisers and buyers join those with the same role to discuss their point of view. Evaluators should make an unbiased analysis of the advertisement's effectiveness. Have students return to their original groups, where advertisers and buyers express their points of view to each other while the evaluator observes and takes notes.

Chapter 27

Chapter Overview

Chapter 27 explores the concepts of locating and using resources. It identifies four kinds of resources—human, material, community, and natural—and explains why and how they are managed. Students learn to use resources wisely by setting goals and making decisions.

Motivator

■ **Using Resources.** Refer students to the photograph on page 272. Ask them what resources the young man is using. The older man? Discuss how one person's resources can become another's.

Objectives

Discuss the chapter objectives on this page. Remind students that the objectives focus on important chapter concepts.

Vocabulary

Explain that the term *resource* comes from the Old French *ressoudre,* to rise again, as a spring of water. Ask: How can a resource be like a spring of water? Suggest that both, well managed, can be kept "flowing" to help meet many needs.

Chapter 27

Managing Resources

Terms to Learn

- backup plan
- barter
- community resources
- conserve
- human resources
- improvise
- material resources
- natural resources
- pollution

Objectives

This chapter will help you to:

- Identify the resources that you have or that are available to you.
- Describe ways to increase your resources and use them effectively.
- Explain how you can exchange resources you have for resources you lack.
- Outline the four steps of the management process.

272   UNIT 5   Management and Consumer Decisions

CHAPTER RESOURCES

Natalie was telling her mother about the sweater she'd seen. "It's a beautiful navy blue cable knit," she said. "It would look great with that navy and red plaid skirt I like so much." The problem was, it cost $70, which Natalie could not afford on her budget.

"You know," her mother said, "Aunt Claire is very good at knitting. If you paid for the yarn, you might ask her to knit something like it for you. Of course, it would take her some time. You should offer to do something in return."

Natalie and her mother talked about various possibilities. They found one that might work. Natalie had painted her own room, and everyone said that she'd done a good job. She might offer to do some painting that her aunt needed done. She could exchange her time for her aunt's.

Natalie called her aunt right away and was delighted when Aunt Claire agreed. Natalie and her aunt arranged to meet at the store the next day to buy the yarn. Natalie could hardly wait.

Your Resources

As Natalie learned, people have many resources. At first, she didn't think that she could have the sweater she wanted because she didn't have the money to buy it. By taking into account other resources she had or could call on—her own time and abilities and those of her aunt—she found that she could achieve her goal.

Resources, as you learned in Chapter 4, are the things you use to achieve your goals. The resources people have can be classified into numerous categories. Everyone has these resources, though in varying amounts. One classmate may not be able to get help from her aunt, as Natalie did. On the other hand, the classmate may be a skillful knitter herself.

Resourceful people find ways to earn money that don't even occur to others. How is this young man earning income?

Human Resources

Human resources include *knowledge, skills, imagination, energy, time, family, and friends*. Your knowledge, skills, and imagination may be the easiest resources to draw on because you have these qualities with you at all times.

- **Knowledge.** Knowledge includes everything you have observed, learned, and remembered. Through learning, your knowledge can grow. Learning takes place all the time—when you are taking classes in school, listening to your friends, talking with your parents, and even being entertained. To learn Spanish, Kim took classes in school, listened to Spanish-language radio, and spent time speaking the language with her neighbors from Puerto Rico.

CHAPTER 27   Managing Resources   273

TEACH

Topics on p. 273:
- **Recognizing Resources**
- **Knowledge**

Checking Comprehension

✓ Name some human resources. *Knowledge, skills, imagination, energy, time, family, friends.*

✓ What does knowledge include? *Everything that you have observed, learned, and remembered.*

Activities

■ **Know-It-Alls?** Have the class list ways they have used knowledge that day. Suggest making breakfast and driving a car to generate ideas, if needed. Begin to write their responses on the board. As the board becomes filled, point out that the list is inexhaustible. What does this say about the value of knowledge? *(Observation)*

ENRICHMENT

■ **Help!** On small pieces of paper, have students write a need or problem people commonly experience. Put the papers in a pile. Have each student draw one and name three resources a person in that situation might call upon.

DID YOU KNOW?

Humans are not alone in using imagination to solve problems. In laboratory situations, chimpanzees can figure out how to use a stick or stand on boxes to get bananas hanging out of reach. Some birds drop shellfish from the air to crack open the shells. Humans, however, have considerable ability to solve problems and make decisions by purely mental means, which gives them a great advantage over other species.

Topics on pp. 274-275:
- **Other Human Resources**
- **Material Resources**
- **Community Resources**
- **Natural Resources**

Checking Comprehension

✓ Why are skills and imagination especially valuable resources? *They are with you at all times.*

✓ What are the two main types of material resources? *Possessions and money.*

✓ Why is caring for community resources especially important? *They are shared with others.*

CROSS-CURRICULAR ACTIVITY
Social Studies

Ask students to research different aspects of welfare: How did it start? Who is served, and by what programs? How often is it used by people in your community? Have students report on their findings.

FAMILY AND COMMUNITY **O**UTREACH

Have students collect flyers, brochures, and other literature describing resources in their community. Ask them to organize the information according to the type of need the resource helps meet and then set up a display of the literature in the school library for other students' use.

- **Skills.** You, like your friends, have a special set of abilities that allow you to perform certain tasks well. Some skills are physical, such as skating. Others are mental, such as playing chess. Skills, like knowledge, can be increased in many ways. Nguyen liked drawing, but he always had trouble drawing human figures. After he watched a three-part television series on drawing the human body—and after he practiced—he improved.
- **Imagination.** Your creativity is a resource too. Did you ever have a conversation with a friend inside your head after a disagreement? If so, you were using your imagination. In fact, using your imagination in this way is frequently helpful. By working through a problem in your imagination, you can think through a situation before you act.
- **Energy.** Energy is the power that helps you get things done. Energy comes from the food you eat and the exercise and rest you get. Energy also depends on your attitude. People with positive attitudes often have a great deal of energy. Those with more negative outlooks often have little energy with which to change something they don't like.
- **Time.** You are reminded of the importance of time every day. First, you think about what you want to do that day. Then you decide how you will go about doing it. Managing time is a vital skill that is described in detail in Chapter 28.
- **Family and friends.** You can supplement your own knowledge, skills, imagination, energy, and time by calling on the resources of others you are close to. That's what Natalie did with her aunt. Family and friends can also offer their time and knowledge to help you solve problems or simply to unwind.

By repairing her own skates, this teen uses personal human resources.

Material Resources

The physical objects you can use to accomplish your goals are your **material resources.** The two main types of material resources are possessions and money.

Possessions are the things you own, which you can use to help you attain some goals. Your clothes, of course, keep you warm in winter. Music, for instance, can either relax or energize you.

Some possessions last a long time. Furniture, cars, homes, and appliances are all examples. Others—for instance, pens, paper, and food—are used up quickly. Caring for both types of possessions will give them a longer useful life, which is especially important with items that are costly to replace. By taking care of them, you save money.

Some possessions enable you to use other resources effectively. A paintbrush and roller can be combined with time, energy, and skill to paint your room. If you become very good at painting, you can use that skill to earn money.

MORE ABOUT Money

Money has taken many different forms throughout the years. Soldiers in the Roman Empire were paid with blocks of salt. On the Pacific Island of Yap, huge stone disks once served as money. In the French Canadian colonies in the late seventeenth century, playing cards signed by the colonial governor were recognized as legal tender.

With money, you can purchase the products created when other people have used their resources. Money makes it easier for everyone in society to trade resources. If you learn to use money well by saving and by spending it wisely, you are taking advantage of the power of money.

Community Resources

Every community has *people, facilities, and organizations that help you enjoy life, improve your skills, and solve your problems.* These **community resources** take numerous forms—schools, libraries, government agencies, houses of worship, and hospitals. Malls, theaters, museums, parks, and mass transit are other community resources.

People in the community provide valuable help. Teachers can expand your knowledge and skills. School counselors and members of the clergy will assist you in handling problems. Doctors, nurses, and dentists help ensure that you stay healthy.

Businesses in your community provide access to many other resources. These include the opportunity to learn skills, earn money, and buy products you need or want.

As with possessions, community resources should be cared for. In fact, caring for community resources may be more important, because these resources are shared with others. This means that you are responsible for keeping them usable. For instance, by disposing of trash after a picnic, you keep the park clean for the next group to use. When people don't take care of community resources, the resources may be eliminated because of the cost of maintaining them.

■ What resources does your community offer?

Natural Resources

Humans have changed their environment tremendously. Where woods and plains used to be, cities now stand. Where rivers once flowed, dams now generate electricity. Despite these changes, **natural resources**—*air, water, soil, plants, animals, minerals, and sources of mechanical energy*—are still an important part of human life.

For that environment to be healthy, though, people need to use resources wisely. Many resources have limits. People need to **conserve**, or *save*, those resources, so that they will last as long as possible. Avoiding waste is one way to conserve. Another way is to prevent **pollution**, *the introduction of dirt and poison into the environment.* Polluted air, water, or soil can destroy other resources, such as plants and animals. They also cause health problems for the people who live near them.

Natural resources provide another important benefit. They create a sense of beauty that enhances the quality of human life. Have you ever marveled at the grace of a flying bird? Have you ever savored the fresh smell of a spring morning? If so, you have sensed the beauty of the natural resources around you.

CHAPTER 27   **Managing Resources**   275

DID YOU KNOW?

More than half the trash collected in the United States is paper. Paper is made from a renewable resource—trees. When you recycle paper, you conserve trees and help keep trash out of landfills.

MORE ABOUT Pollution

The Environmental Protection Agency (EPA) was created by the U.S. government in 1970 to enforce clean-air and -water laws. Pressure from the EPA has led to the banning of aerosol sprays, which damage the Earth's atmosphere.

Activities

■ **Can't Buy Me Love.** Write the following sentence on the board: Money can't buy happiness. Ask for students' comments on the statement. Do they disagree or agree? What evidence do they see that this statement is true or false? Challenge students to make a list of the things that money can't buy. *(Critical Thinking)*

ENRICHMENT

■ **Community Planet.** Have students find out what their community is doing to protect its air, water, and soil. Students might learn about local environmental ordinances, talk to government and business leaders about conservation efforts, and invite representatives from local environmental organizations to explain their respective group's work.

RETEACHING

■ **Routine Resources.** Have students write the different kinds of resources as column headings on a piece of paper. Ask students to describe their daily routine, identifying the resources that they use during various activities and placing these under the correct heading.

MULTICULTURAL *Perspectives*

People in some cultures live simply, in close contact with the natural environment. Have students investigate some of these societies: How do people earn a living, care for their sick, and communicate with other groups? What are some advantages and disadvantages of this way of life?

Checking Comprehension

✓ What is bartering? *Trading resources with someone else.*

✓ What are the benefits of the management process? *Shows you how to best use resources to meet goals; lets you work on several things at a time.*

✓ What are the four steps of the management process? *Planning, organizing, implementing, and evaluating.*

STRATEGIES THAT WORK

Have students read "Managing Your Resources." After discussing the questions, challenge students to apply the concept explored in question 2—using one resource to make the most of others—to other resources.

Answers to Think . . .

1. Answers will vary, but should be realistic and workable.
2. Answers may include: gives you more study time, increasing knowledge; helps you manage part-time job, increasing money; lets you take breaks, increasing energy.
3. Answers may include: ask expert; read book or watch video on subject.

STRATEGIES That Work

Managing Your Resources

You have only so many hours in the day and so much energy to do everything you need—and want—to do. Managing your resources wisely can help. Here are some tips to follow:

- **Knowledge and skills.** Invest some time and energy in gaining useful knowledge. Then practice your skills. Seek solid instruction so that when you practice, you do things correctly.
- **Imagination.** You can increase your imagination and creativity. Think of your imagination as a muscle, one that can gain strength and flexibility through workouts. Build this muscle by brainstorming, either alone or with friends or family.
- **Time.** Curiously, busy people often have the most time. First, they find creative ways to manage their time. Second, they work efficiently. Third, they plan and organize well.
- **Energy.** A high energy level comes with good health habits. You can be at your best by eating a balanced diet, not using harmful substances, and getting plenty of exercise and rest.
- **Family and friends.** You can ask others for help. Of course, you can't pass your own

responsibilities off, but other people can use their resources to help you. You, in turn, should be ready to return the favor.

- **Possessions.** Get the most out of what you own with good care. Possessions last longer and you save money. You can also trade possessions with others.
- **Money.** Careful planning and regular savings helps you use your money well. If a part-time job works for you, you can practice making wise decisions about spending and saving.

Making the Strategy Work

Think . . .

1. Think of a skill you would like to develop or improve. How could you fit several half-hour practice sessions into your weekly schedule?
2. How does using time wisely help you make the most of at least three other resources?
3. Think of a subject or issue you would like to know more about. List specific ways in which you could increase your knowledge on that subject.

Try...

Make a list of your five most valued possessions. Estimate the cost of replacing them. List what you can do to care for each possession so that its life will be extended.

Using Resources

To have resources available to get the job done, you need to handle them properly. First, you need to build a supply of resources. Some resources are more available than others. The potential to expand your knowledge and skills, for example, is always with you.

Some resources, such as time or money, have limits. Using them wisely enables you to make the most of them. The management process described later provides a method for deciding how to use your resources.

People can also exchange one resource for another. That exchange could be the result of **barter,** *trading resources with someone else.* Jeff wanted a ticket to a school football game but couldn't get one. His friend Chad had a ticket he didn't want but wished he had a sweater of Jeff's. Jeff and Chad traded the ticket for the sweater.

People can also exchange their *own* resources. For example, they can use a resource that they have more of rather than one they lack. Carmen enjoys cooking and makes dinner for her family. Preparing a meal every

DID YOU KNOW?

The Industrial Revolution, which swept the developed world during the nineteenth century, was in part a massive attempt to manage and organize manufacturing. It allowed items to be produced more quickly and efficiently. Until then, for example, shoes were made individually, each pair to order. With the set patterns and processes of mass production, one shoe factory worker could cut out dozens of parts that all fit into the finished product.

night cuts into her time for other activities, however. Now she uses Sunday evening to cook four meals—that night's dinner, plus three more she can reheat during the week. By investing more time and energy on Sunday, Carmen frees up more time during the week, when she's busier.

The Management Process

People use resources in everything they do. Whether you use your own energy to walk to a friend's house or mechanical energy to heat your home, you are using resources. The management process is a way to find the best use of your resources in order to achieve your goals. That way, when you finish one task, you will have resources—time or money or energy—left over to tackle another.

The management process has another benefit. By giving you a good grasp of your goals and resources, it enables you to work on more than one thing at a time.

Figure 27.1 illustrates the steps in the management process. They are planning, organizing, implementing, and evaluating.

Figure 27.1

THE MANAGEMENT PROCESS ─────────

Whether you are sorting out scheduling conflicts, planning a party, or preparing a meal, you can use the same four-step management process to make your task easier.

Planning
- Assess the situation.
- Develop a task list.
- Identify your resources.
- Decide on your priorities.

Screen text:
Planning
Organizing
Implementing
Evaluating

Implementing
- Put the plan into action.
- Monitor the plan and your progress.

Organizing
- Develop a schedule.
- Assemble the needed resources.
- Prepare to act.

Evaluating
- Evaluate the plan.
- Evaluate your performance.

Focus on Management Skills

The library is a resource full of other resources, including those needed for managing resources. Ask students to locate library resources that give tips on organizing some aspect of life, from time to kitchen cabinets. Ask them to try some of these ideas. After a few weeks, have them discuss any improvement they have realized in this area.

Checking Comprehension

✓ How do you develop a task list? *List every step needed for achieving goal.*

✓ What are the three steps to organizing? *Develop schedule; assemble needed resources; prepare to act.*

✓ How can improvising help you manage? *Lets you carry out plan if unexpected occurs.*

✓ Why is evaluating important to managing resources? *Helps you devise better plans in future.*

CROSS-CURRICULAR ACTIVITY
Science

Point out to students that the essence of scientific experimentation is having a plan and sticking to it. Ask: What might happen if there were no plan? What would be the value of the results? Ask students to conduct a science experiment or complete a project using the steps outlined on pp. 278-280. Have them write up notes on the work, including an explanation of how the steps were incorporated into various tasks.

Planning

The key to managing your resources successfully is to plan. Danielle often has to rush to finish a homework assignment. That's because she neglects planning. Unfortunately, lack of planning often leads to wasting resources. By planning, you can use your resources more efficiently and effectively.

The principles of planning are:

• **Assess the situation.** Start by writing down what you want to accomplish.

• **Develop a task list.** Expand on each goal by listing every step you need to take in order to achieve it. Don't leave anything out. If you are planning a meal, for instance, you need to include shopping for the ingredients and making whatever preparations are required, as well as cooking.

• **Identify your resources.** Write down all the human and material resources you will need to complete each task. Be sure to think about the other human resources—family and friends—you may be able to use.

• **Decide on your priorities.** Use the advice on setting priorities in Chapter 5 to evaluate different goals and determine those that are most important. When you're done, you can focus your resources on what matters most to you.

Organizing

Once you have planned, you need to organize what you will do. Good organization is essential to make a task go smoothly. This part of the management process has three steps:

1. Develop a schedule. Indicate how much time you will need to perform each item on your task list. Think about which tasks are required to accomplish other tasks. Then you can develop a sequence of events that charts your course of action. If you're working on more than one goal at a time, balance their schedules against each other. This way, you will see how you can juggle tasks and still achieve all your goals.

Planning and organizing are part of good management. Why do leaders need to be skilled in these processes?

REAL-LIFE APPLICATION

Read this to students: *Ann's day seems a constant battle with time. She has trouble waking up in the morning, so she eats little breakfast and is often late for school. As she falls farther behind schedule, she tends to forget commitments. Today she was too busy to fix dinner for her family* and had to buy a prepared meal from the supermarket deli. Ask: What is Ann's poor management costing her? How could Ann better manage her time, beginning when she gets up and throughout the rest of the day?

Acting Responsibly

Are You Resourceful?

Author Mark Twain created a classic example of resourcefulness. Young Tom Sawyer was in charge of whitewashing a fence. He had absolutely no desire to do the work, so he devised a plan. He pretended that painting the fence was great fun. When his friends stopped by and saw how much fun Tom was having as he painted, they were eager to join in. They were so eager, in fact, that they paid Tom for the privilege of doing his work!

Although trickery is not a good idea, the point is that a resourceful person can use creative problem-solving to manage resources in pursuit of a goal. Resourcefulness can be as simple as standing on a stool to reach an object on a high shelf. It can also be complicated. Whatever form the solution takes, the key to being resourceful is to solve the problem creatively.

Resourcefulness in Action

Jordan looked at his calendar and groaned. On Friday he had to turn in his history project. Worse, Sunday was his grandparents' 50th wedding anniversary party, and Jordan had hoped to do something special for them. Time was now running short.

For the history project, Jordan was supposed to describe some aspect of life in the United States in the 1930s. To get it done, Jordan would have to go to the library and do a lot of reading. That would take a long time. This thought made him think of his grandparents. Fifty years seemed like an awfully long time too.

Then Jordan had an idea. His parents had taped his grandparents relating stories about their childhood. Maybe Jordan could turn the stories into a project. He listened to the tapes for about half an hour and decided that he had the answer. By combining stories from different tapes, he could create a family history to give his grandparents. This could also be a story of life in the 1930s for history class. Jordan located some blank tapes and got to work.

Your Analysis

1. How did Jordan show resourcefulness?
2. How could Jordan have managed his time better so as not to find himself with this problem in the first place?
3. Will Jordan be able to use exactly the same tapes for both his grandparents and his project? Explain why or why not.
4. Think of an example of resourcefulness that you have seen or read about. Describe the situation and how creative thinking helped solve the problem.

---

2. **Assemble the needed resources.** Prepare all your resources so that they are ready to use. Check that any equipment you need is in good working order. If you're working with another person, discuss your mutual plans. Be sure to coordinate your efforts.
3. **Prepare to act.** A key to preparing to act is to anticipate possible problems with a plan and develop an *alternative course of action*. This **backup plan** may require the use of resources other than those you originally identified. Having a backup plan helps ensure success, though, be-

cause it prepares you in case something goes wrong.

Implementing

With your planning and organizing done, you are ready to proceed. Now it's time to implement your plan.

- **Put the plan into action.** Using the resources you have assembled, follow the task list according to your schedule.
- **Monitor the plan and your progress.** As you work according to plan, take the time to evaluate how you are progressing. Do

---

Focus on Management Skills

A good manager needs to be well organized. Poor organization can be seen in situations like these: something is always missing or misplaced; appointments and commitments are forgotten; things just don't get done; clutter never goes away; too many situations turn into

crises; plans are so unrealistic that things don't get done. Recognizing the problem is a first step toward solutions. Then, by applying the principles in Unit 5, especially Chapters 27 and 28, better organization can be achieved.

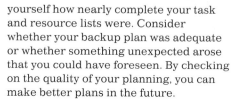

ASSESS

Review

■ **Chapter Review.** Use the contents of the Chapter Review page to help students review concepts, think critically, and apply their knowledge.

■ **Study Guide.** Have students complete the Study Guide for Chapter 27 on p. 88 of the Student Workbook.

■ **Resource Exchange.** Have students identify two of their special abilities and write each one along with their name on a small piece of paper. Place these papers where the entire class can see them. Encourage students to use them to barter or exchange resources (not money) over the course of a week.

Evaluation

■ **Chapter Test.** Use the reproducible chapter test provided in the Teacher's Classroom Resources or create your own test using the *Testmaker Software.*

■ **Alternative Assessment.** Have students research ways that past or current movies or television shows use mismanagement or poor organization as a source of humor. Have students share their findings in groups, then reenact favorite scenes for the class. Ask: How is humor a resource for managing? Suggest that it can be especially valuable for managing relationships.

CLOSE

■ **Management Maven.** Have students make up questions about managing resources for a radio show called "Management Wizard." Have students take turns portraying both callers with questions and the management expert.

---

you need your backup plan for any reason? Has something unexpected come up? If so, you may need to **improvise,** or *come up with a new idea.* For instance, Dustin planned to take his sister to the park one Saturday when he was babysitting. When it rained, he had to devise a new plan. They did jigsaw puzzles together instead.

Evaluating

When you've completed your work, the management process still isn't complete. Just as with the six-step, decision-making method you learned in Chapter 5, you need to take stock of your plan—and how well you performed. Doing so will help you devise better plans in the future.

- **Evaluate the plan.** The first question, of course, is whether you have accomplished your goals. If you haven't, can you do something else to achieve them? If you have, how good was the plan in helping you do so? Ask yourself how nearly complete your task and resource lists were. Consider whether your backup plan was adequate or whether something unexpected arose that you could have foreseen. By checking on the quality of your planning, you can make better plans in the future.

- **Evaluate your performance.** You also need to evaluate how well you followed the plan. Sometimes people have a perfectly good plan, but they miss reaching their goals because of their failure to follow the plan. The answer for them may simply be to keep a copy of the plan handy. That way they'll be sure not to forget what they are supposed to do.

Responsible Management

Over the next few years, you will probably take increasing responsibility for managing your life. As a result, you will be in greater control of your resources. At the same time, greater demands will be placed on those resources. If you go to college or vocational school, you must devote time, energy, and study skills to succeed. You'll need to balance these responsibilities with time for relaxing and being with your friends and family. Once you start working full-time, you will need to use your resources on the job to master the requirements of the job and get ahead.

If you begin learning to manage your resources now, you'll be in a better position to meet these increasing demands. Knowing how to manage your time will help you if you become a spouse and a parent while holding a full-time job. Learning to manage your money will help you handle the increased expenses that come with adulthood and independence.

Practice applying the management process to different tasks now. This practice will help you in the years to come.

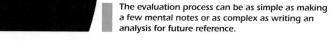
The evaluation process can be as simple as making a few mental notes or as complex as writing an analysis for future reference.

DID YOU KNOW?

In the early twentieth century, Frank and Lillian Gilbreth became famous for their time and motion studies. They began an industrial consulting firm to show companies how to manage industry better. Their work became famous when two of their children, Frank and Ernestine, wrote a book called *Cheaper by the Dozen,* describing their experiences growing up as subjects for their parents' management experiments. The book inspired the movie of the same name.

Reviewing the Facts

1. What are the four main types of resources available to people?
2. What are human resources?
3. How does caring for your possessions help in using your material resources?
4. What is the benefit of exchanging resources? Give your own example of how you could exchange resources.
5. What are the four steps in the management process?
6. What is the benefit of a backup plan?
7. How can practicing the management process now help you in the future?

Thinking Critically

1. How can planning help you increase the time you have available?
2. Which step in the management process do you think is the most important?

Applying Your Knowledge

1. **Promoting Community Resources.** Think of an important resource in your community. It could be a hospital, park, museum, or historic landmark. Write a 30-second radio commercial that makes people in your community aware of this resource and its value to the community.
2. **Caring for Your Resources.** Find the owner's manual for an appliance or electrical device you have at home. Summarize in your own words the proper ways to care for the product.
3. **Persuading Someone to Help.** Suppose that this week it's your turn to clean up after dinner every night, but you have a commitment that conflicts. Write a dialogue in which you persuade a sibling to trade resources so that he or she washes the dishes this week and you do something in return. In your dialogue, assume that your brother or sister isn't interested in the exchange at first. You need to come up with an argument that is very persuasive.

Making Connections

1. **Mathematics.** Many people waste water by taking long showers. Cutting a shower by just 5 minutes can save 20 gallons of water. Assuming that a person showers every day but cuts each shower short by 5 minutes, calculate how many gallons can be saved in (a) a week; (b) a month of 30 days; and (c) a year.
2. **Environmental Science.** Create a poster that urges people to conserve natural resources in order to preserve them for future generations.

Building Your Portfolio

Analyzing a Process

To get used to the idea of including every step on a task list, try this exercise. Choose a simple task—replacing a lightbulb or making a sandwich. Make a list of all resources and steps required. Put the steps in sequence. Then team up with a partner for a class presentation. As you describe each step, your partner will perform the tasks. Ask the class for comments. Did you mention all the necessary resources? Did you include all the needed steps? Did your partner's work produce the desired result? Write a description of your presentation for your portfolio.

ANSWERS TO REVIEWING THE FACTS

1. Human, material, community, and natural.
2. Knowledge, skills, imagination, energy, time, family, and friends.
3. Makes them last longer, thus saving money.
4. Allows you to use a resource you have to obtain one you lack. Examples will vary.
5. Planning, organizing, implementing, and evaluating.
6. Prepares you in case something goes wrong with original plan.
7. Helps you build resource management skills, which become more important in the future, as more demands are placed on your resources.

ANSWERS TO THINKING CRITICALLY

1. Helps you identify and evaluate all options, match tasks to available time, which helps you get more done.

2. Answers will vary.

Chapter Overview

Chapter 28 discusses time management and its benefits. It describes tools and strategies for planning time wisely and helps students and avoid common obstacles to effective time management.

Motivator

■ **Where Does the Time Go?** Ask students to list everything they need or want to accomplish that day and how much time they need or want to spend on each activity. Have them total the time. Can they fit it all into 24 hours? Explain that this chapter gives strategies for getting more—though probably not everything—done in the time available.

Objectives

Discuss the chapter objectives on this page. Remind students that the objectives focus on important chapter concepts.

Vocabulary

Explain that the word *dovetail* derives from the way the tail feathers of a dove fit smoothly together. Ask students to explain how that imagery fits *dovetail* as it is used in this chapter: overlapping tasks to save time.

Chapter 28

Managing Time

Terms to Learn

- deadline
- dovetail
- procrastinating

Objectives

This chapter will help you to:

- Summarize **the benefits of time management.**
- Prioritize **tasks.**
- Prepare and use **calendars, schedules, and lists.**
- Identify **obstacles to good time management.**
- Demonstrate **time management skills.**

282   UNIT 5   Management and Consumer Decisions

CHAPTER RESOURCES

Student Workbook
Study Guide, p. 92
Activity, *A Word to the Wise*, p. 93

Teacher's Classroom Resources
Lesson Plan, p. 32
Decision Making, *Time Management*, p. 17

Extension #46, *Avoiding Time-Wasting Traps*, p. 52
Life Skills, *Scheduling Your Time*, p. 49
Personal Development, *Managing Study Time*, pp. 39-40
Chapter 28 Test, pp. 61-62

Performance Assessment, *Time Management*, pp. 54-55
Reteaching, *Time Management Strategies*, p. 34

See Also:
ABCNews InterActive™ Videodiscs

Just before midnight Denise finally put down her pen. Her chemistry paper was done, but it had been a long night. After working on it frantically for most of the evening, she was exhausted. She knew the paper wasn't as good as she wanted it to be, but at least she had something to hand in the next day.

As she sat at the kitchen table winding down for a few minutes, Denise felt uncomfortable. She had promised Alex that she would call him to make plans for the weekend, but there had been no time. After all, she hadn't even managed to iron her uniform for work or to put away the dinner dishes. "Alex probably won't be very understanding," Denise thought. "This always happens to me. What am I doing wrong?"

Finding Time

For many people time is a problem. There just isn't enough of it—or is there?

Time is a resource, like money and knowledge. Although equipped with the same 24 hours in a day that everyone has, good managers often seem to have more time than other people. They have learned what it takes to make the best use of the time available to them. They have learned about time management.

Experts in time management have developed techniques that work. These can be learned and used by anyone. Like Denise, you may want to learn these techniques. Even if you manage

time well already, you are likely to find ideas for improvement. The benefits will make the effort worthwhile.

The Benefits

What can you gain by improving your time management skills? When people learn ways to manage the time they have, they get more done. Not only do they make time for important tasks, but they also include time for activities that are fun.

People who use time management principles gain respect. These people are often viewed as reliable because they get things done when they are supposed to.

Planning Your Time

It has been said that if there is a job to be done, give it to a busy person. That's probably because people who accomplish much have learned how to manage their time well. What do you think?

Meeting deadlines like those connected with school assignments is easier when you learn and practice time management skills.

CHAPTER 28   Managing Time   283

Checking Comprehension

✓ Why do some people seem to have more time than others? *They've learned how to make the best use of time available.*

✓ What do you gain by planning your time? *Time for important tasks, fun activities; others' respect.*

Activities

■ **Many Roles.** Ask each student to draw a circle and write the word *me* in it, with lines extending from the circle like spokes. Tell students to write at the end of each line a different role they play (student, daughter, friend). Discuss what this diagram tells students about their need to manage time. (*Management*)

RETEACHING

■ **Timely Moments.** Ask students to describe occasions when they felt they used time effectively. How did they feel as a result?

CROSS-CURRICULAR ACTIVITY
Language Arts

Have students write a few paragraphs explaining what they would do if they had three additional hours each day.

REAL-LIFE APPLICATION

Tell students the average workweek has decreased from more than 70 hours in 1900 to about 37 hours today. Ask: How many more hours away from work does that give the average adult each week? (*33 hours*) Add that paid vacations and holidays also give workers more time away from the job.

Ask students to look ahead to when they may be working full-time. Discuss: What job responsibilities, other tasks, and leisure pursuits might they want to spend their time on? How will they manage all these activities?

Topic on pp. 284-285:

• **Setting Goals and Priorities**

Checking Comprehension

✓ How can setting priorities help you manage time? *Helps you identify most important activities and complete them first.*

✓ How do you make a "to-do" list? *Write down what you need and want to accomplish; give each item high, medium, or low priority.*

Acting Responsibly

Have students read "Are You Reliable?" Point out that some people have a higher regard for time and punctuality than others do. Ask students what can happen in a relationship when two people are very different in this way.

Answers to Your Analysis

1. Strong; he is mindful of work commitment even in face of personal concerns.

2. Probably not, due to the seriousness of the situation; can't always count on understanding from others, however.

3. Answers will vary. Employer may see that all situations except last are under worker's control and be unsympathetic; may accept these excuses once.

4. He could be on time; work well; ask for time off well in advance.

5. Answers will vary.

Unfortunately, many people are like Alicia when it comes to time. Alicia takes a casual approach, allowing time to slip by without notice. She does whatever suits her at the moment, without thinking ahead. She doesn't take time to plan.

Setting Goals

Good planning begins with goal setting. Goals become your guide. For example, someone who wants to maintain a strong relationship with a faraway friend finds time to write letters. A person who wants to improve swimming skills schedules time for practice. Someone who wants to have a good job in the

Acting Responsibly

Are You Reliable?

Of the people you know, think about those you would call reliable. What makes them so? Chances are, you know you can count on them. They are there when you need them. When you make plans with them, you know they will follow through.

Reliability means dependability. Reliable people stick to commitments. They manage time well in order to do what is supposed to be done. Not only do they keep appointments, but they also arrive on time.

Of course, the unexpected can interfere with reliability. Reliable people deal with the unexpected in a responsible manner.

Reliability in Action

Andy was on his way to Valleyview Greenhouse. He was excited and a little nervous about his first day on the job. He left the high school at 3:00 P.M. and was headed for work when he heard a news report on the radio.

Part of the roof at the elementary school had caved in after being hit by lightning. According to the report, the children had been loaded onto buses outside the school after the cave-in, but there was no mention of injuries. Andy was worried about his eight-year-old brother.

Knowing that his mother was working away from her office that afternoon, Andy wondered if she had heard the report. He had to know whether his brother Jacob was safe, yet he was expected at work in 15 minutes.

Quickly, Andy decided what to do. He stopped at the nearest phone booth and called the greenhouse. He explained that he had to go to the school to check on Jacob. He also called his mother's office and left her a message.

Within minutes, Andy had parked the car and was walking toward the school. He could see flashing lights and a crowd of people ahead. As he moved closer, Andy saw two figures walking toward him. One was his mother, who was waving with one hand. Her other hand rested securely around Jacob's shoulders.

Andy felt a sense of relief. His brother was safe. Fifteen minutes later, he was on his way to the new job. He was late, but he had already demonstrated reliability—to his employer and his family. In the days ahead, he would demonstrate it even more.

Your Analysis

1. How would you assess Andy's sense of reliability? Why?

2. If Andy had been unable to call, do you think that his new employer would have been upset under the circumstances? Explain your reasoning.

3. Predict what an employer's reaction might be when an employee is late for these reasons: (a) running out of gas; (b) talking with friends; (c) forgetting; (d) running an errand for a parent; (e) an alarm clock not going off; and (f) a doctor's appointment taking extra time.

4. How might Andy continue to demonstrate reliability to his employer in the future?

5. Think of ways that people show reliability in school and at home. Which of these do you practice?

---

284   UNIT 5   Management and Consumer Decisions

DID YOU KNOW?

Ancient peoples used the phases of the moon to measure time, marking periods of about one month. The Babylonians were the first to divide the month into seven-day weeks. The ancient Egyptians are credited with observing a 24-hour day: 12 nighttime hours, 10 daytime hours, and one hour each of dawn and dusk. They varied the number of minutes in an hour according to the season. In winter, when days are shorter, daytime hours were less than 60 minutes long, nighttime hours were more. The trend gradually reversed over spring and summer.

BALANCING Work AND Family

Managing Time in the Morning

In many families, mornings are hectic because everyone must get up, have breakfast, and head for work or school—all within a short time. Making sure that everyone gets prepared for the day and out the door on time takes coordination and effort from the whole family. Here are some tips that some families use to manage "morning madness":

- **Store items in consistent places.** Put keys, backpacks, homework assignments, and schoolbooks, for instance, in the same place every day. This helps eliminate time-consuming searches in the morning.
- **Follow a bathroom schedule.** Each family member could use the bathroom at a specific time. Other rooms can be used for such tasks as drying hair and applying makeup.
- **Plan breakfast in advance.** Breakfast can be quick and easy as well as nutritious when you think ahead. Have cereals, yogurt, fruits, juices,

and breads on hand. In the evening, set the breakfast table, and prepare food that can be warmed up in the morning.

- **Share tasks.** Morning tasks, such as feeding the cat, rinsing the dishes, and turning out the lights, can be rotated among family members. Make a schedule to show who is responsible for each job.

When mornings are hectic, it makes sense to get everyone involved in the solution. Use the time management and organization skills you learn to help make this happen.

Suppose That . . .

You are the oldest child in a household with two adults, three teens, and one bathroom. You are last on the bathroom schedule because your bus for school comes last. The person ahead of you on the schedule, however, takes up to ten extra minutes in the bathroom every morning. What should you do?

---

future includes time to get schoolwork done now. In each situation, a goal is the underlying motivation for the activity.

What do you want to accomplish today? This week? This month? Over the next few years? By setting goals and keeping them in mind, you are more likely to carry out the tasks that will lead to achieving them.

Setting Priorities

Few people have time to do everything they would like to do. That's why they set priorities. They decide which tasks are more important than others. For example, the tasks with immediate **deadlines**—*times or dates by which the tasks must be completed*—usually have higher priority than those with later deadlines or no fixed schedule.

A simple way to prioritize is to make a "to-do list." First write down what you need and

want to accomplish. Then assign one of these categories to each item:

- **A Items**—tasks that must be done.
- **B Items**—tasks that should be done.
- **C Items**—tasks that you hope to do.

To carry out the list of tasks, do the A items first because they have high priority. As time permits, you can also work on B items and then C items. Low-priority items that don't get done may eventually be given a higher priority on future lists. For example, washing a sweater may not be a high-priority item until you want to wear it for a certain occasion.

Balancing Work and Leisure Time

Health experts point out that people need time for leisure activities in order to enjoy life and to control stress. Unfortunately, some people fail to include leisure activities in their schedule. They get so busy with work-related

---

Topics on pp. 286-287:

• **Balancing Work and Leisure**
• **Time Management Tools**

Checking Comprehension

✓ How does leisure fit into time management? *It's needed for good mental health; schedule a reasonable amount.*

✓ Explain how to use a calendar to manage time. *Write down important dates known in advance, all scheduled events and obligations, other activities as they arise.*

✓ What information is recorded on a daily schedule? *Activities, their starting and ending time.*

Different cultures have different priorities regarding time management. For some, tending to immediate needs, especially if they involve others, takes priority over keeping a schedule. Likewise in traditional Asian cultures, where patience is esteemed, waiting for someone is not considered to be as great an imposition as it might be elsewhere. Ask: How would you rate United States society's attitude toward schedules? How did this attitude develop? What contributes to it today? What problems might it present to someone of a different culture?

---

tasks that they forget to have fun too. When planning your schedule, include leisure time. Good mental and emotional health depends on it.

On the other hand, too much time spent on fun at the expense of items on the "to-do list" is equally troublesome. The best answer is to find a suitable balance between responsibilities and relaxation.

Figure 28.1

TIME MANAGEMENT TOOLS

A Calendar

A calendar helps you keep track of appointments and important events on a weekly, monthly, or yearly basis. To use a calendar:

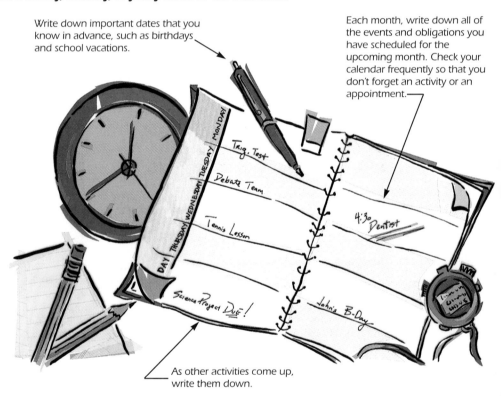

Write down important dates that you know in advance, such as birthdays and school vacations.

Each month, write down all of the events and obligations you have scheduled for the upcoming month. Check your calendar frequently so that you don't forget an activity or an appointment.

As other activities come up, write them down.

Time Management Tools

To help you plan your time, many tools are available. A walk through an office-supply store will show you some.

People use calendars, date books, computer planning programs, and even handheld electronic planners to keep track of their activities and appointments. Some people find that they get more accomplished by following

---

REAL-LIFE APPLICATION

Read this to students: *Jonah is new to time management. He writes down events and commitments on a calendar, so he doesn't see the point of making a schedule* or "to-do list." Ask: What kinds of problems might this cause Jonah? How might it affect his success in accomplishing both long-term projects and daily tasks?

a daily schedule. Others depend on a written list of tasks to be completed. **Figure 28.1** shows how certain time management tools can work for you.

Time Management Troublemakers

Good intentions aren't enough when it comes to managing time. You may have to tackle some troublemakers before you can manage time well.

Wasting Time

Have you ever looked back on a day and realized that you didn't really accomplish anything? Not every day needs to be loaded with accomplishment, but too much wasted time means that goals get lost.

A Schedule

A schedule helps you plan your time on a daily or weekly basis. It shows the starting time and the length of each of your activities. To make a schedule:

Start with a grid that includes a space for every hour in the day.

Block in the starting time and the length of each of your regular activities. Be sure to account for family time.

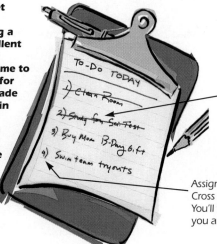

Don't schedule every hour of every day. Make sure that you set aside free time to relax and enjoy yourself.

Odd blocks of time between activities can be used for study time.

A List

When you need to get many things accomplished, writing a "to-do list" is an excellent way to organize your activities. Choose a time to make your list. A list for Wednesday can be made either the first thing in the morning or the night before. Keep in mind that your priorities may change during the day. To create a "to-do list":

Write down the things you plan to do during the day. Include schoolwork, after-school activities, important errands, and tasks to do at home.

Assign each task a priority—A, B, or C. Cross out each item as you complete it. You'll feel good when you see how much you are accomplishing.

TEACH

Topics on pp. 288-290:
- **Trouble Spots**
- **Time Management Strategies**
- **Time Management in Action**

Checking Comprehension

✓ Give some tips for overcoming procrastination. *Do unpleasant tasks first; avoid distractions; set up schedule.*

✓ What's an effective way to tackle a major project? *Break it into smaller parts.*

✓ How do you save time by giving yourself time? *Taking time do to task right is faster than doing it over.*

SPECIAL NEEDS Strategies

Attention Deficit. Dovetailing may not be appropriate for students with attention problems. One activity could distract from the other. Instead, emphasize making a short list of things to do. A student might choose three important things to do today and put them in order in a written list. The list should be placed in a standard location where it will be easily visible all day. As each task is completed, it can be checked off the list. To encourage staying on task, students might reward themselves when all items on the list have been completed. Rewards could be such incentives as watching television, renting a video, going out for pizza, or calling a friend on the phone.

Try to identify what you do that might be considered wasting time. Do you spend too much time talking on the phone or sitting in front of the television? Do you spend more leisure time with friends than you should? All of these can be part of your routine, but when they interfere with the rest of your life, you may need to make some changes.

Procrastination

A common problem when managing time is **procrastinating,** or *putting things off.* People often procrastinate when they are faced with tasks they dislike, even the important ones. You are less likely to procrastinate if you have a clear list of priorities and concentrate on the A items. Here are some additional ways to avoid procrastination:

- **Do unpleasant tasks first.** They seem easier if you do them when you are fresh.
- **Avoid distractions and interruptions.** These can often be hard to resist. Make an effort to stay focused on the task at hand.
- **Set up a schedule.** Establishing a daily routine for such tasks as studying can help you beat the urge to avoid them.

Overcommitment

As a musician, Geoff was always eager to get involved in anything musical that was going on. At the beginning of the school year, he joined the pep band and the youth symphony. He also signed up for keyboard lessons. Later, when some classmates who were auditioning for a school musical asked him to accompany them, he agreed to do so. Combined with other responsibilities, this was just too much. Geoff felt overloaded. Stress began to build.

Taking on too much is a problem for some people. They wind up with so much to do that they can't do anything well, or they spend too much time under pressure. It is better to be realistic with yourself and others than to find yourself overloaded.

If overcommitment is a problem for you, learn how to say no. Practice responses that allow you to decline gracefully. You might say something like, "I'm sorry, but I can't take on another project right now." When people try to make you change your mind, stick to your decision.

You'll be happier if you commit to activities that fit well into your schedule.

288   **UNIT 5   Management and Consumer Decisions**

REAL-LIFE APPLICATION

Read these time conflicts to students and ask them what they would do and why:

- It's Tuesday night. You've planned to study for a Thursday morning math test. Your cousin calls and invites you to tonight's concert by your favorite band.

- A friend asks you to help this evening with a canned food drive. Your schedule shows school until 3:00 P.M., track practice until 5:00 P.M, and finishing a science project that is due tomorrow after dinner.

Strategies To Use

Efficient time managers learn to avoid the troublemakers you have just read about. They also use certain skills that are helpful. To become a skillful manager, try to:

- **Break large tasks into smaller units.** Instead of studying for a big test for two hours the night before the test, plan to study 20 minutes each night for a week.
- **Dovetail activities.** Dovetailing means *overlapping activities in order to save time.* Many possibilities exist for managing time in this way. You can make use of time spent waiting, do something constructive while watching television, or run two errands at once.
- **Allow enough time.** Mistakes are more likely when you rush through tasks. Doing a task right the first time usually takes less time than doing it over again.
- **Be prepared.** Even the best time management plan can fail if you aren't well organized. Before you begin a task, think about what you need to accomplish it. If you're cleaning your room, take the vacuum cleaner and the dusting supplies with you on one trip. Making several trips for supplies slows you down.
- **Evaluate standards.** Is perfection your goal? If so, you may never meet it, no matter how long and hard you try. High standards can be good, but routinely expecting too much can result in frustration and disappointment.
- **Be flexible.** Not everything goes as planned. If you are flexible, you adjust your schedule to include events that occur unexpectedly.

One way to make good use of time is to do two things at once. How is this teen making use of that principle?

Learning from Mistakes

Becoming a good time manager doesn't happen overnight. You need to continually examine your habits and your schedule in order to discover ways to improve. You can also learn by observing others. How would you handle the situations described in **Figure 28.2** on page 290?

A Plan in Action

Putting time management into practice is not as difficult as you might think. Ramon, for example, didn't believe that he could be a good time manager. Then he noticed how his grandmother often made lists to keep track of what she had to do. Ramon decided to try the same technique.

- **Night Owl or Early Bird?** Ask if students have ever heard someone referred to as a "morning person" or a "night owl." Have them write a description of how their energy tends to ebb and flow throughout the day. Ask if this pattern is helpful for accomplishing tasks as scheduled. If not, how can they plan their time and tailor their schedule to take advantage of those times when they feel mentally and physically sharp? Would they be more successful if they tried changing some behaviors to give themselves more energy when their schedule demands it? (*Problem Solving*)
- **Wait a Minute.** Discuss: What is the difference between thoughtful deliberation and procrastination? What is the motive for each one? (*Critical Thinking*)
- **Dovetailing.** Ask students for examples of how Ramon dovetails tasks in his Saturday schedule. *Drops off film on way to doctor; does algebra in doctor's office; reads magazine while waiting for Cindy.* (*Observation*)

ENRICHMENT

- **Expect the Unexpected.** Discuss possible events that might cause Ramon to reassess his schedule. Suppose he does not have time to do his algebra assignment at the doctor's office. What if he discovers a problem with his grandmother's car that needs to be fixed? Ask students how Ramon could rearrange his schedule to deal with these and other problems that may arise. Guide students' responses into including A tasks, at the expense of B and C tasks if necessary; remind them that A tasks still take priority.

Focus on Communication Skills

Remind students that the ability to say no is one very valuable time management skill. Other people can make demands on your time. You must consider your own needs and existing commitments before agreeing to participate in more activities. Have students suggest or act out situations where they face pressure from others to change their schedule, but use good communication skills (explained in Chapter 9) to resist without causing bad feelings.

Review

■ **Chapter Review.** Use the contents of the Chapter Review page to help students review concepts, think critically, and apply their knowledge.

■ **Study Guide.** Have students complete the Study Guide for Chapter 28 on p. 92 of the Student Workbook.

■ **Plan of Action.** Have students choose a long-term activity that they are familiar with, such as putting on a play or doing a crafts project. Ask them to apply the topics discussed in this chapter to that activity. What goals do they set? What time management tools and strategies are helpful?

Evaluation

■ **Chapter Test.** Use the reproducible chapter test provided in the Teacher's Classroom Resources or create your own test using the *Testmaker Software*.

■ **Alternative Assessment.** Ask students to select a personal time management challenge, such as getting ready for school in the morning. Have them write or record a description of how they usually accomplish this task, including any "troublemakers" they face. Ask them to attempt the task applying time management skills, then to describe the skills they used and the result of their efforts.

CLOSE

■ **Get Personal.** Ask students to write a short essay that begins, "Three personal qualities that are helpful for time management are . . ."

290

Figure 28.2

Lessons in Time Management

Read what the following teens have to say. What would you do differently?

- *Angelica.* "I'm so tired of having to do *everything*. It seems like every time there's a project, people expect me to get involved. I just want to have some time to do what *I* want to do for a change. Next Saturday I'm supposed to paint props for the Festival Committee, so I'll miss out on a trip to Chicago with my older sister."
- *Dallas.* "I never get the grade I deserve on research papers. I was up all night finishing one for my literature class. I think I work well under pressure, so I don't know why I just end up with C's."
- *Wendy.* "I've always got a ton of things to do, but I just can't seem to get everything done. Like today. I was supposed to write thank-you notes for the birthday gifts my relatives sent, but by the time I got off the phone with Autumn and watched a little television, it was too late to start."

With another busy Saturday ahead, Ramon made a "to-do list." As you can see here, he assigned an A, B, or C priority to each item:

- Change oil in Grandma Estevan's car. (A)
- Take roll of film to be developed. (C)
- Work on algebra assignment. (A)
- Clean hamster cage. (B)
- Help Roberto with batting. (C)
- Get allergy shot at doctor's office. (A)
- Clean mud off shoes. (B)
- Give Cindy a ride home. (A)

In addition to his "to-do list," Ramon noted two leisure activities that he wanted to include in his day. They were:

- Read new auto magazine.
- Watch NBA game on television.

As Ramon prioritized, he justified categories in his mind. For example, the oil change had high priority because he had promised his grandmother to do it. Developing the film had low priority because he didn't need the pictures right away.

As he looked over the list, Ramon planned his schedule for the day. On his way to the doctor's office in the morning, he would drop off the film. He also decided to take his algebra assignment with him so that he could work on it while waiting in the doctor's office.

During the latter part of the morning, Ramon planned to stop at his grandmother's to work on her car. By not scheduling anything else for the morning, he could stay and talk with her for a while if she had time. After lunch, Ramon planned to clean the hamster cage. This was a low-priority job last week but had higher priority now. If all went well, he would watch the NBA game in the afternoon and suggest that his little brother Roberto join him. If they had time before he had to go pick up his girlfriend Cindy, Ramon would pitch a few balls to Roberto. Otherwise, he would save that for Sunday afternoon. Ramon planned to take the auto magazine with him when picking up Cindy. She was sometimes late getting out, so he could read while waiting for her.

As far as the muddy shoes were concerned, Ramon thought that they could wait. After some second thoughts, however, Ramon decided to clean the shoes first thing, before going to the doctor's office. He just wanted to get that job done.

With planning, Ramon was able to make the most of his Saturday. Without planning, the day probably would have just slipped away. That's the way Ramon's Saturdays used to be, but not anymore.

290   UNIT 5   *Management and Consumer Decisions*

Focus on Critical Thinking Skills

Write one or more of these quotations on the board and ask students what each says about time management:

"The butterfly counts not months but moments and has time enough."—Rabindranath Tagore

"One of these days is none of these days."—English proverb

"It takes time to save time."—Joe Taylor

Chapter 28 Review

Reviewing the Facts

1. What benefits occur when you plan your time well?
2. What role do goals play in time management?
3. Explain how to set priorities when managing time.
4. What kind of balance is needed when planning how to spend your time?
5. What is the difference between a personal calendar and a schedule?
6. Describe three practices that can cause time management problems.
7. List four strategies for using time effectively.

Thinking Critically

1. Which do you think causes the most trouble for young people: time wasting, procrastination, or overcommitment? Why?
2. What impact do the following qualities have on time management: perfectionism, laziness, high self-esteem, low self-esteem, and efficiency?
3. Do you think dovetailing could be overused? Explain your response.

Applying Your Knowledge

1. **Scheduling Your Time.** Plan a daily schedule that shows how you spend a typical school day from the first thing in the morning until bedtime. What changes could you make in a routine day that would enable you to use your time more efficiently?
2. **Using a List.** Make a "to-do list" for tomorrow. Set your priorities for the day by assigning A, B, or C to each task. Cross off each task as you complete it. At the end of the day, evaluate your list, and write a paragraph about how this time management tool worked for you.

3. **Looking for Wasted Time.** For one week keep track of how you spend your time. Analyze the results, identifying time that was wasted. (Don't confuse constructive leisure time with wasted time, however.) Write a brief summary of what you discover.

Making Connections

1. **Business.** Investigate the ways that time management techniques are used in business and industry. Choose one example of a technique that you could use or that could be applied in your home or school. Prepare a diagram or a description to present to the class.
2. **Literature.** Time is a nonrenewable resource—once it passes it is gone for good. The theme of time as limited and precious is a common one in literature. Locate a poem or a saying about time to share with the class.

Building Your Portfolio

Time Management Strategies
Imagine that you are a time management consultant hired to analyze your family's approach to time management. Observe family routines for a few days, and talk to family members about time problems they are having. For example, do people rush when leaving in the morning or when fixing the evening meal? Prepare a written report that recommends ways to improve time management. You may want to work with your family to try out the ideas. Add the completed report to your portfolio.

ANSWERS TO REVIEWING THE FACTS

1. You get more done; have time for duties and leisure; gain respect and reputation for reliability.
2. Help you decide which tasks are most important so you can schedule time for them.
3. List all tasks you want or need to do. Mark them A if they must be done, B if they should be done, and C if you hope to do them. Give A tasks priority over B tasks and B tasks over C when scheduling time.
4. Balance responsibilities with relaxation.
5. Calendar is weekly, monthly, or yearly record of appointments, activities, and events. Schedule is daily or weekly plan showing time and length of each activity.
6. Wasting time—letting leisure interfere with goals; procrastinating—putting off tasks; overcommitment—taking on too many tasks. Also not setting goals or priorities.
7. Any four: break tasks into small units; dovetail activities; allow enough time; be prepared; evaluate standards; be flexible; learn from mistakes.

ANSWERS TO THINKING CRITICALLY

1. Answers will vary.
2. Answers will vary. Generally, perfectionism, laziness, and low self-esteem have negative impact; high self-esteem and efficiency, positive.
3. Possibly; if too many tasks are attempted at once, causing confusion or poor performance response; if you delay tasks until you have others to accomplish at same time—for example, waiting to go to library until you have several things to research may cause you to delay starting a report.

Chapter 29

FOCUS

Chapter Overview

Chapter 29 gives an overview of technology used today for work, home, and consumer needs. It addresses both positive and negative consequences of technology—in terms of time, safety, cost, and utility—and offers ways to manage technology.

Motivator

■ **Modern Life.** Have students list ways they use technology every day. Review their responses. Explain that these are all products of technology; this society has long been a technological one. Add that people often feel overwhelmed by modern technology until they learn to manage it.

Objectives

Discuss the chapter objectives on this page. Remind students that the objectives focus on important chapter concepts.

Vocabulary

Suggest that technological terms, like technology itself, seem designed for efficiency—they are shortened versions of other words. Ask students to identify the "parent" words of *fax* (facsimile) and *Internet* (international and network).

Chapter 29 — Managing Technology

Terms to Learn

- automated teller machine (ATM)
- electronic funds transfer
- fax
- Internet
- point-of-sale terminal
- technology

Objectives

This chapter will help you to:

- Describe some of the technologies that have been developed over the past 30 years.
- Evaluate some of the advantages and disadvantages of new technologies.
- Explain how to manage technology.

CHAPTER RESOURCES

Student Workbook
Study Guide, pp. 94-95
Activity, *The Tools of Technology*, pp. 96-97

Teacher's Classroom Resources
Lesson Plan, p. 33
Cooperative Learning, *Buying a Computer*, pp. 35-36

Extension #47, *Technological Terms*, p. 53
Extension #48, *Security Tips*, p. 54
Life Skills, *Thinking About Technology*, pp. 50-51
Personal Development, *Changing Times*, pp. 41-42
Transparency 30, *Weighing*

Technology's Pros and Cons
Chapter 29 Test, pp. 63-64
Performance Assessment, *Opinions About Technology*, p. 56
Reteaching, *Technology Today*, p. 35

See Also:
ABCNews InterActive™ Videodiscs

When Rick started at his new high school, he became excited about the technology available. Students and teachers used computers in class. In the school's media center, students could watch educational videos and even produce their own video programs. The school library had a computerized catalog and offered an encyclopedia on CD-ROM. Databases that listed grants, loans, and scholarships were available to students who were planning for trade school and college. This was only the beginning.

Rick hadn't had as many opportunities to use computers in his former school, so he was eager to learn more. He bought a book about computers and took a course at the junior college. Gradually, a plan began to form in Rick's mind. He wanted a computer of his own. He could think of all kinds of ways they could make use of one at home, but he knew computers were expensive. Rick began to explore the thought as he examined the resources that might lead him to his goal.

Technological Change

Think of the activities you do each day. How many would you do differently if you did not have the use of technology? **Technology** is *the application of scientific methods to help people meet their needs and wants*. Thanks to technology, people can do many things faster and more easily than they could in the past.

At the Workplace

As you read in Chapter 13, technological changes have revolutionized the way people work. The spread of computers and microchips is probably most responsible for changing all areas of work life. For example, farmers use computers to determine the proper in-gredients for livestock feed and to make planting schedules. Manufacturing companies use computers to design and assemble products and to track shipments. Workers in offices, banks, and stores use computers to serve their customers and stay competitive. Health care professionals rely on computers to conduct sophisticated tests on patients to detect diseases and other conditions.

Computers aren't the only devices that have created major changes in the workplace. Fax machines, voice mail, cellular telephones, pagers, and other communication technologies are also in wide use. A **fax** is *an exact copy, or facsimile, of text or pictures that is sent over phone lines*. Documents can be transmitted by fax machine in a matter of minutes to anywhere in the world.

Computerized robots are usually programmed to perform one or two specialized tasks in a manufacturing process. You can learn basic principles of robotics with models.

CHAPTER 29   Managing Technology   293

Checking Comprehension

✓ How does technology help retail store customers? *Scanners speed checkouts, result in fewer errors.*

✓ Name some ways families use technology. *Answering machines, pagers, cellular phones, computers.*

✓ How does communication technology help keep people safe? *Emergency phone systems (911); car phones quickly summon help when needed.*

FAMILY AND COMMUNITY OUTREACH

Arrange to have a talk by a local police official involved in the 911 emergency communication system. Encourage students to ask the officer to explain how computers and technology are involved in the system's operation. Give students time to prepare questions before the visit.

For Consumers

Technology has radically changed how consumers conduct transactions as well. Today, most bank customers do at least some of their banking at an **automated teller machine**, or **ATM.** This machine is a *computer that allows bank customers to perform banking transactions on their own.* With a magnetically encoded plastic ATM card and a secret personal identification number (PIN), a customer can make deposits and withdrawals, move money from one account to another, and pay bills. ATMs are generally available 24 hours a day, allowing customers to do banking even when the bank is closed.

ATMs use **electronic funds transfers**—*moving money from one bank account to another with the use of computers.* Some customers can make these transfers at home, using their home computers or the telephone.

Another example of electronic funds transfer is the point-of-sale terminal. A **point-of-sale terminal** in a store *is a machine that allows a person to use an ATM card instead of cash to pay for groceries or other merchandise.* When you use your ATM card, the terminal instantly transfers money from your account to the store's account.

Many supermarkets and other retail stores now have electronic checkout scanners. The scanner reads and enters the price of a product into the cash register as the product is passed across the scanner's electronic beam. As a result, checkouts go more quickly, and there are fewer errors than when prices are entered by hand. Stores also use the scanners to keep track of inventory and to tell store personnel when it's time to restock an item.

At Home

Families use high-tech equipment too. Many families have telephone answering machines and other devices to make it easier for family members to keep in touch. Some parents have pagers or cellular phones so that their children can reach them quickly when they are away from home.

Growing numbers of families have computers in their homes. Computers are excellent tools for financial planning because they can calculate figures quickly and accurately. Jackson's mother uses the family computer to keep track of expenses and to figure how much they owe in taxes. Computers can also help with time management. They provide a good way to create, store, and review schedules. Jackson finds the computer handy for writing papers and doing research. With his CD-ROM encyclopedia and other computer-based reference materials, he is able to complete schoolwork at home rather than at the library.

Scanners read data and enter it for use into a computer system. They are used to record purchases and checkouts and to control inventory. If a scanner program is not updated regularly, consumers may be incorrectly charged for purchases.

Focus on Management Skills

Electronic organizers can help students manage time and remember commitments. Features include a scheduler for recording appointments, a memo pad, and a phone book with space for recording additional information.

DID YOU KNOW?

Today 29 percent of all American households have computers. Almost half of all students have access to computers at school, and almost 40 percent of people use computers at work.

Technology has changed other aspects of the modern home as well. Central heating and air-conditioning make some homes comfortable in all weather conditions. Electronic thermostats can be programmed to raise and lower temperature settings automatically.

Electric appliances do everything from kneading dough to disposing of garbage. Microwave ovens defrost and cook food in minutes. Many appliances, such as electronic ovens and coffeemakers, can be set to turn on automatically at a specific time.

For Entertainment

Television, once limited to just a few channels, has become a total entertainment center. With cable television and satellite dishes, households can receive hundreds of stations, with programming choices as varied as cartoons and congressional debates. More widespread are videocassette recorders (VCRs), which people use to tape-record shows when they're not home. They can rent and buy videos too. Many people own videotape recorders, allowing them to tape special family events.

Computers are also a source of entertainment. Many computer games are available for all age groups and ability levels, as are game systems that connect to a television set.

For a Safer World

Technology saves lives and helps people feel safe. Computers are used to regulate airplane traffic and to monitor car traffic in busy intersections. Some cars now have built-in computers that keep the cars functioning properly and warn drivers of problems. The latest car versions can even display maps, give directions, and provide information on driving conditions. Some homes, cars, and

Communication systems, such as the 911 emergency number, allow people to get help quickly when they need it.

businesses have alarms and other sophisticated electronic security systems to alert the police to break-ins.

Safety is also promoted with special communication systems. Thousands of communities across the country have instituted an emergency phone calling system, often triggered by dialing 911, that can quickly summon help when police, fire, or medical personnel are needed. Car phones are another example. When Gene's car broke down late one night on a country road, he called a tow truck from the car phone instead of having to walk a long distance in the dark.

Ideas for Managing

Technology has brought many positive changes, helping to improve the quality of life. That's the positive side of the picture. There is also a negative one, but it is manageable. By examining the negative impacts of technology, you can be prepared for them. You can discover how to make technology work for you rather than against you.

CHAPTER 29   Managing Technology   295

Activities

■ **What's on TV?** Ask students to name some favorite television shows. List these as either network, general access, or other cable station programs. Discuss: How has cable television changed viewing habits for many Americans? What are the advantages and disadvantages of having access to so many choices? (*Critical Thinking*)

RETEACHING

■ **It's Everywhere.** Have groups make a chart with these headings: At Home, At School, As a Consumer. Give them time to fill in the charts with examples of how people use technology in each category. Have groups share their ideas, adding other groups' suggestions to their charts.

ENRICHMENT

■ **Try to Keep Up.** Ask students to research a subject on this page that interests them, such as CD-ROMs or car computers. Have them report to the class on the latest developments in the area and on what to expect next.

CROSS-CURRICULAR ACTIVITY
Consumer Economics

Have students choose one product of technology they think would be a good investment for their family. Have them compare available models on price and features, then select one as the best buy. Have students explain how the product would be useful in their home and why they chose that particular model.

MORE ABOUT the History of Computers

The most important early computing tool was the abacus, which is used to perform mathematical calculations. Invented in China more than 2,000 years ago, the first abacuses were pebbles aligned in grooves in sand; today's model is a wooden frame with beads strung on wires.

The computer debuted in 1945. Called ENIAC, it could do in 20 seconds a computation that would take a human 3 days. Today's fastest computer works with almost unimaginable speed. The Cray Y-MP C90 can complete one billion computations a second.

Topics on pp. 296-298:
- **Managing Technology**
- **Using Technology Ethically**
- **The Internet**

Checking Comprehension

✓ How can a person keep current with technology? *Newspapers and magazines, television programs, classes, talking to others.*

✓ Describe a healthful position for sitting at a computer. *Shoulders straight and back supported.*

✓ How can technology lead to a lack of balance in life? *Allows people to work more; leads them to ignore other aspects of life.*

Making Decisions

Have students read "Using Technology Ethically." Discuss: What other ethical dilemmas do computers and other types of technology present?

Answers to What...

1. Academic suspension or expulsion; parental, possibly legal punishment; loss of self-respect; damaged reputation.
2. Answers may include: study more; extra credit work; summer school.
3. Answers will vary. Students might offer Maria ethical alternative, warn her of consequences.
4. Stress that Maria cannot follow Joe's advice. Such action is wrong and not fair to those who work to earn their grades.

Making Decisions

Using Technology Ethically

As a computer whiz, Maria knew more than most students about computers. A high school junior, she had plans for her future. She wanted to study computer science and become a programmer. She often neglected her homework, however, spending time on the computer instead. As a result, her grades were suffering. She was worried that she might not be accepted at the college she hoped to attend.

Late one night, Maria was connected to the Internet. She was "chatting" with others about computers and careers. Maria mentioned her concern about college and asked advice from anyone on-line who was in a computer career. She read the responses with interest. Then a message that she had not expected was displayed. "Here's a solution for you," it read. "Access the school's computer and change your grades." The message was signed "Hacker Joe." For a long moment, Maria sat in stunned thought.

Then she entered a response. Joe answered right away, explaining that he had done the same thing once and offering to give her some suggestions.

Maria logged off. She needed to think. The idea of changing her grades was tantalizing, but it troubled her at the same time. Of course she wanted to get into a good computer school, but this wouldn't be right. It was just plain dishonest. How would her friends feel if they knew she had done such a thing? If school administrators found out, she would have a serious price to pay. Her reputation and possibly her whole future would be in jeopardy. Maria had to decide.

What Would You Do?

1. What serious outcomes might Maria face by following Joe's suggestion?
2. What other options does Maria have to improve her scholastic record?
3. If you were on the Internet and read the exchange between Maria and Joe, explain what you would do?
4. What do you think Maria should do? Why?

---

296 UNIT 5 Management and Consumer Decisions

Stay Informed

Familiarity can make you more comfortable with the changes going on. Learn about new advances by reading newspapers and magazines, watching informative television programs, and taking classes. Talk to others about technology that is new to you or difficult to understand. This approach can help you prepare for a technological work world. You will also be better equipped to make decisions, such as those concerning health care and buying.

Develop a Positive Attitude

At times technology can be frustrating. Just when you master one thing, something new replaces it. To reach a human voice on the phone, you may have to work your way through a list of messages. After keyboarding for an hour on the computer, you might lose everything because you forgot to save it on the system. Incidents like these can be annoying, but only if you let them.

A positive attitude helps you see that the benefits are real, despite problems. For example, using a computer for word processing is an overall time-saver, even though losses sometimes occur.

Try not to let your expectations get out of hand. The computer user who could once wait several seconds for responses may now find a one-second wait annoying. Ask yourself what difference a few seconds will make. Limits do exist, and you will feel much better if you accept them.

Shop Wisely

The marketplace is full of opportunities to buy products using new technology. Investigating before you buy can save you regrets. Some video recorders, for instance, use tapes that do not fit in regular VCRs. Choosing the right model can save you the frustration of discovering that you need more equipment. Becoming knowledgeable and talking to others before you buy is a good idea.

Remember that not every product of new technology is needed. Having the latest model

---

MORE ABOUT the Internet

Today more than 27,000 computer networks and 20 million users are part of the Internet. One of the easiest ways to access this vast store of information is through an on-line service such as America Online or CompuServe. While these services do not offer access to every part of the Internet, they are user-friendly and relatively inexpensive. Many public libraries also offer free access at library terminals, or through modems that users can access at home.

In Touch with TECHNOLOGY

The Internet

The **Internet** is an <u>international network of computers</u>. Anyone who has a computer, a modem, and the right software can connect to and interact with the Internet.

The Internet was first developed in 1969 during the Cold War. U.S. military scientists in Washington, D.C., were exchanging secret research on nuclear weapons with university researchers in California and Utah. They decided that the most secure way to send such information was directly from one computer to another.

By the early 1980s, the network had grown tremendously, and the military network split off. Now other government agencies, schools, private businesses, and individuals throughout the world have access to the Internet.

Uses of the Internet

The Internet features thousands of electronic bulletin boards called newsgroups. People can post messages for others to read and respond to. Each newsgroup is devoted to a different subject—ranging from the arts, to politics, to travel, to computer technology. Users throughout the world can also engage in political debates and chat about favorite musical groups or television shows.

The Internet also features electronic mail, or e-mail. With e-mail, you can send a message immediately throughout the United States and abroad to people who have an e-mail address.

A vast array of databases and information sources exist on the Internet, including the card catalogs of university and public libraries and the Library of Congress. On-line periodicals and other resources offer up-to-date news, business updates, government documents, and the latest scientific research.

A recent addition to the Internet is the World Wide Web. Businesses, schools, government offices, and individuals can create Web "sites" or "pages" that include words, pictures, sounds, and video images. For example, the Web site set up by the White House offers information about the president and the first family. Some distributors are releasing popular music and movie clips on Internet Web sites. Some people think that, in the future, having a personal Web site will be no more unusual than having a personal phone number.

Cost and Ease of Use

Accessing the Internet may cost money. Colleges and universities and some businesses offer Internet access to students and employees, though only for proper research or business use. Most individuals, though, have to pay for the access software and phone charges for each Internet session.

The Internet has lagged in popularity in the past because access required users to learn a complex set of commands. Now, with ease of use enhanced through the World Wide Web, thousands more people are tapping into the Internet every day.

• • • • •

Thinking Critically About Technology

1. Name three ways you might be able to use the information available on the Internet.
2. Do you think it is necessary to regulate what information people can access on the Internet? Explain your answer.
3. What could a business put on its own Web site?

and keeping up with other people might not be good reasons to buy. Many people have lost interest in items they thought sounded useful before buying them. Examine your needs realistically before investing in new technology.

Examine Costs

Much technology is expensive, especially when it first appears. Health care and cars with high-tech electronic systems are just two examples.

CHAPTER 29   Managing Technology   **297**

---

ocus on Safety Skills

Sadly, ATM robberies are becoming more common. Following safety guidelines can help keep you from becoming a victim. Never keep your PIN, or access number, together with your card. Shield your transaction from the eyes of customers waiting behind you. Be especially careful when using ATMs in secluded locations or at night.

Activity

■ **Caught in the Web.** Have students design their own Web site. Discuss different text or graphics they might include. What would they be comfortable with the rest of the world knowing about them? *(Creativity)*

In Touch With TECHNOLOGY

Have students read "The Internet." Ask: Do lower-income people who can't afford to access the Internet miss out on education and business advantages they need to improve their lives? If so, how can this be remedied?

Answers to Thinking ...

1. Answers may include: for school; entertainment; to learn about careers.
2. Answers will vary. Ask students about specific points: who would regulate information and how; what rights and responsibilities are involved.
3. Answers may include: pictures, promotional material on products; information about ordering.

SPECIAL NEEDS *Strategies*

Gifted Students. Suggest that computer-proficient students give others a tutorial on how to access and navigate the Internet. Alternatively, students could write a user-friendly, step-by-step guide on using the Internet for classmates.

Review

■ **Chapter Review.** Use the contents of the Chapter Review page to help students review concepts, think critically, and apply their knowledge.

■ **Study Guide.** Have students complete the Study Guide for Chapter 29 on p. 94 of the Student Workbook.

■ **Exemplary List.** Help the class identify the main points covered in the chapter. Have students individually list these points along with an example to illustrate each one.

Evaluation

■ **Chapter Test.** Use the reproducible chapter test provided in the Teacher's Classroom Resources or create your own test using the *Testmaker Software.*

■ **Alternative Assessment.** Tell groups to write a "Guide to the Modern World" for a person who has just awakened from a coma after 20 years. The guide should describe technological advances the last 20 years; identify the technology the person is likely to encounter at home, at work, and as a consumer; and briefly explain how the technology works. It should also comment on how technology has affected people's lives and suggest ways to manage technology.

■ **Good Old Days?** Ask students to write an essay describing what a typical day would be like without technology. How would they manage to meet their needs and wants? Could they?

Generally speaking, though, cost goes down as a new technology matures. CD players and VCRs cost much less today than when they were introduced. If you can wait, buying later may be an economical way to go. As newer models are introduced, you can also save by purchasing used equipment.

Technology often comes with costs beyond the initial purchase price. Check carefully to see what additional equipment may be needed or what additional costs might be involved. On-line computer services, for example, can be entertaining, but the time spent on-line can also raise telephone bills.

Protect Yourself

Technology is accompanied by safety concerns. Use caution when managing information about yourself and your finances. Give personal data, such as your address, telephone number, social security number, driver's license number, and bank account numbers, only when you have to. In the wrong hands, the data might be misused.

Report lost ATM cards immediately to the bank. Bank personnel can prevent someone who finds the card from making withdrawals from your account. Then they can issue you a new card and PIN number. Keep careful records of ATM transactions so that you know exactly what occurred. Procedures like these help protect you in a highly technological world.

Consider Your Health

Some technologies have raised health concerns. Extended time in front of a computer can cause eyestrain, back problems, and wrist pain. Sitting with shoulders straight and back supported can help. Taking regular breaks does too.

Whatever the technology, determine any risks to health, then look for reasonable approaches to managing them. A radiology technician in a medical facility, for example, is careful to stand away from the rays. Caution and informed action reduce risks to health.

Getting proper exercise is a health concern that is affected by technology. Because of technology, people are often less active. Televisions, computers, riding lawn mowers, automobiles, and garage door openers contribute to a sedentary lifestyle. As technology reduces physical effort, people need to find ways to get the exercise they need for good health.

The Proper Perspective

With technology, people can accomplish tasks quickly and efficiently. Obviously, this is useful. Some people, however, find that their ability to do more translates into working more. The result can be overwhelming demands on time and energy, with less free time for themselves and for family and friends.

Technology allows people to be reached virtually any time and any place. Conrad's mother works out of her home. Communications technology permits clients to reach her by calling on her cellular phone or by faxing when it's convenient for them—even at night and on weekends.

A fascination with technology is a problem for some people. They are so wrapped up in it that they ignore other aspects of life. The person who spends more time at the computer than doing anything else is a case in point.

When any of these situations occur, life's balance can be lost. People may be pushed into a fast pace that is too much at times. They feel stress. Families suffer when they miss the interaction needed among members.

Recognizing what can happen puts you one step closer to a solution. People need time to relax and get away. They need a change of pace. Simply taking a break or going for a walk may work. Making sure that you include time for family and friends is necessary too. Achieving a balance helps a person maintain relationships and stay emotionally healthy while still making use of what technology has to offer.

Focus on Consumer Skills

Have groups look through ads for technological consumer goods. Ask them to list any specialized or potentially confusing terms or abbreviations, defining those they know. As groups share lists, they can complete their definitions. Challenge students to learn the meaning of any undefined words.

Chapter 29 Review

Reviewing the Facts

1. What is technology, and what is its main purpose?
2. List two uses of computers in business. List two uses of computers in the home.
3. What are some of the communication technologies that have changed the office and home?
4. List three things a bank customer can do with an ATM.
5. Identify one advantage and one disadvantage of new technologies in terms of time.
6. What is the cost disadvantage of adopting a new technology soon after its introduction, and how can this disadvantage be overcome?
7. What are three ways to manage technology?

Thinking Critically

1. One theory about the future is that machines will take over almost all jobs now done by people. Do you think that this outcome is realistic? Explain your answer.
2. What do you think is the greatest advantage of technology? What is the greatest disadvantage? Give reasons for each answer.

Applying Your Knowledge

1. **Analyzing the Media.** Using computers, journalists and photographers can change photographs. They can add and subtract people or objects or blend two or more pictures together. With another student, discuss the danger of this ability to manipulate photos. Also discuss any positive aspects to this technology, and prepare an oral report.
2. **Helping Others Adapt to Technology.** Prepare a list of your own ideas about how someone who feels uncomfortable with technology could learn to adapt to technological changes. Include some reasons why people could benefit from this adaptation.

Making Connections

1. **History.** Technology has made many items obsolete or rare, including the abacus, card catalog, slide rule, typewriter, carbon paper, and horse and buggy. Choose one such item and write about how it worked, why it was replaced, and what replaced it. Can you think of any advantages of the older item over the new technology?
2. **Literature.** Mexican author Octavio Paz said that "alienation . . . is . . . the result of . . . the very nature of technology." In a paragraph, explain what you think the author meant, and state whether you agree or disagree with the statement and why.

Building Your Portfolio

Examining Technology Uses

For one week, make a list of every time you use or encounter technology in some way. Indicate on your list whether the contact was at school, work, or home. As you examine the list, draw conclusions about the impact of technology on your daily life. Write a paragraph describing this impact, and add the list and the paragraph to your portfolio.

ANSWERS TO REVIEWING THE FACTS

1. Application of scientific methods to help people meet their needs and wants. To help people do things more quickly and easily.
2. Business (any two): farmers mix feed, schedule planting; manufacturers design and assemble products, track shipments; banks and stores serve customers, stay competitive; health care workers run tests. Home (any two): keeping financial records; doing schoolwork; managing time; entertainment.
3. Fax machines, voice mail, E-mail, cellular telephones, pagers.
4. Make deposits and withdrawals, move money between accounts, and pay bills.
5. Advantage: enable people to accomplish tasks more efficiently. Disadvantage: can lead to lack of balance between work and relationships.
6. New technology is usually expensive; wait until price comes down.
7. Any three: stay informed; develop positive attitude; shop wisely; protect yourself; consider your health; put technology in perspective.

ANSWERS TO THINKING CRITICALLY

1. Answers will vary. Ask: Might consumers someday have to pay more for personal services where they now pay for technological convenience?
2. Answers will vary. Ask for suggestions for maximizing advantages, minimizing disadvantages.

Chapter 30

FOCUS

Chapter Overview

Chapter 30 discusses the purposes and techniques of money management, including attitudes toward money, setting goals, and living on a budget. Savings and checking accounts are also covered.

Motivator

■ **Where Money Goes.** Bring in a photocopy of a dollar bill. As students suggest common expenses of families and teens, cut pieces out of the dollar. Discuss the results. Did you run out of money before students ran out of ways to spend it?

Vocabulary

The word *budget* derives from the French word *bougette*, a small leather pouch or wallet. Ask: How is the current meaning of *budget* related to the original one? Add that *budget* is also a verb applied to managing other resources—a definition that can help clarify its use in this chapter.

Objectives

Discuss the chapter objectives on this page. Remind students that the objectives focus on important chapter concepts.

Chapter 30

Managing Money

Objectives

This chapter will help you to:

- Describe the benefits of managing and saving money.
- Identify the different attitudes that people have toward money.
- Explain the uses people have for money.
- Create a budget for money management.
- Identify sources of income and categorize expenses.
- Evaluate different types of bank accounts.

CHAPTER RESOURCES

Student Workbook
Study Guide, pp. 98-99
Activity, *Checkbook Basics*, pp. 100-101

Teacher's Classroom Resources
Lesson Plan, p. 34
Decision Making, *Money Management*, p. 18
Extension #49, *Balancing a Checking*

Account, p. 55
Extension #50, *Money Management*, p. 56
LifeSkills, *Balance the Budget*, pp. 52-53
Transparency 31, *Managing Your Money to Reach Your Goals*
Transparency 32, *Writing and*

Recording Checks
Transparency 33, *Understanding a Paycheck*
Chapter 30 Test, pp. 65-66
Performance Assessment, *Money Management*, p. 57
Reteaching, *Money-Management Terms*, p. 36

Thomas left the convenience store soon after his shift ended on Saturday. On his way to meet a friend, he cashed his check at the ATM, stopped at the mall to buy concert tickets, and then walked through a clothing store. There was a sale on jeans, so he decided to buy a new pair. Before he left the mall, he bought a couple of magazines. Then he drove to meet Austin at the coffee shop. Austin greeted him, "So, if it isn't the rich working man." Thomas smiled and ordered a soft drink. It feels great to be earning money, he thought. When he pulled out his wallet to pay, however, he had a sinking feeling. There was only $5 left from his paycheck. Where had all the money gone?

A Case for Management

You don't have to have a great deal of money to practice good management. Money-management skills are as important to the teen with an allowance or a part-time job as to the person with a substantial income.

By becoming good money managers, people like Thomas can avoid that sinking feeling that comes when they realize that the money is gone almost as fast as they earn it. Blowing an allowance or a paycheck is one thing, but just think what it would be like to wake up someday and realize that you have blown everything you earned for many years.

Good habits start early. By becoming a good money manager now, you can make your money work for you. If you put off starting until tomorrow, you may discover that tomorrow never comes.

Learning to Save

"I don't have enough money to save anything." This kind of thinking is faulty. Nearly everyone has the ability to save. The question is not whether to save; it's how much.

Even a very small income has room for savings. Have you ever known anyone who saved pennies in a jar? These add up over time.

The trick to saving is making it a habit. You might save only a dime every week right now, but if you do this regularly, saving a dollar, or even five or ten, later in your life will be more automatic.

The other trick to saving is not spending the money. You need to have money in savings for unplanned expenses. Aim to have more than enough to cover emergencies. By continually building your savings, this aim becomes more realistic. If you save for a special goal, keep that separate from the savings that you want to keep growing.

Using money management skills can help you achieve challenging goals.

Checking Comprehension

✓ How can the need for love affect people's use of money? *They may try to buy love by giving money to others.*

✓ What is a budget? *A plan for spending and saving money.*

✓ What is a flexible expense? *One that doesn't occur regularly, is not always same amount, and can usually be changed.*

SPECIAL NEEDS
Strategies

Inefficient Readers. Explain that numbered items or bulleted lists, such as the budgeting process on these pages, often contain the main points of a text. Paying extra attention to these can help readers glean the most important facts.

FAMILY AND COMMUNITY OUTREACH

Money and budgets can be a source of contention in families. Have groups perform skits showing such a conflict. Ask other students to identify the opposing goals and attitudes toward money that underlie the disagreement.

Attitudes Toward Money

Personalities and attitudes affect the way people manage money. A person who tends to be conservative may be cautious about spending and find that saving is easy. One who takes a more liberal approach may spend more freely and save less. Although some people are clearly one or the other, many fall somewhere in between.

Psychologists could tell you plenty about attitudes and money. Money is often used to fulfill certain emotional needs. This can have positive and negative impact on a person's management skills.

For some people money provides a sense of security. Knowing that money is there to pay bills and cover emergencies is comforting. This is a useful feeling as long as it doesn't become extreme. If money is hoarded while basic needs are let go, that can be a problem.

People who want the feeling of power or status may use money to satisfy their desires. They use money to acquire money and possessions. If this focus becomes an obsession and other dimensions of life are ignored, these people may continually struggle to be happy.

A need for love or respect can also affect the handling of money. Some people believe that they can buy these feelings. Although giving to others is admirable, overemphasis on this may indicate low self-esteem.

This is only a sampling of how attitudes affect the way people manage money. You may be able to think of others. Because people are so different, you will notice many variations.

Sometimes the urge to spend money is very tempting. A budget can help you decide how to best spend and save the money you have.

302 **UNIT 5** **Management and Consumer Decisions**

REAL-LIFE APPLICATION

Read this to students: *Shane wants to buy a car. His current expenses—school supplies, lunches, clothes, entertainment, and a loan from his father for a CD player—take up most of his earnings from a part-time job. Shane has decided to ask for more hours at work.* Ask: Is Shane's decision a wise one? Do you think he will be able to save the extra income? What are his other options? Suggest that cutting expenses may be a wise alternative.

Needs and Wants

Some financial advisors say that a person's ability to handle money well depends mainly on knowing the difference between needs and wants. Only after needs are met should money be spent on wants. Some people make the mistake of spending money on wants first. When they run short of cash, they have to neglect such necessities as healthful meals. They may resort to borrowing money to get by. This can cause serious problems.

Advertisers try hard to convince people that their wants are needs. You have to be smart enough to make that judgment for yourself.

Living on a Budget

Good money managers learn to budget. A **budget** is *a plan for spending and saving your money.* With a budget, you are more likely to spend and save money wisely. Budgeting requires the four basic steps described here.

Step 1: Determine Income

Before you can plan what to do with your money, you need to figure out your income. **Income** is *the money you take in and have available to spend.* Take a realistic look at the sources and the amount of your income. Decide on a period of time—for example, a week or a month—and write down how much money you expect to receive in that time period from each source of income.

Whether it's delivering newspapers or babysitting, many teens depend on part-time jobs as a source of income. For some jobs, the employer takes out money for taxes, social security, and company benefits from the total pay. If you have such a job, use your actual take-home pay, after these deductions are made, as your income figure.

Another source of income for some teens is an allowance. If you receive an allowance, include the full amount of money you receive when you are calculating your income. You will record how you spend it in the next part of your budget.

Finally, list any other regular income you receive. If your income varies, figure out the average weekly amount. For example, if you do errands for people many hours some weeks and not at all other weeks, you will need to estimate average income. Some teens receive gifts of money for birthdays or holidays. If you receive such gifts, you might save this money and not include it in your budget.

Step 2: Record Expenses

The second step in creating a budget is determining your expenses. **Expenses** are *the items that you spend your money on.* Find out what your expenses are by keeping track of each amount you actually spend for a period of time. Using a small notebook or a piece of paper, write down each item you spend money on and how much you spend.

There are two basic types of expenses:

- **Fixed expenses.** These are regular expenses that you have to pay—costs that you are committed to. These might include car payments, car-insurance premiums, music lessons, lunch money, and tuition. They tend to be consistent amounts.

- **Flexible expenses.** These are expenses that do not occur regularly or are not always the same amount. These expenses may be for necessities, such as school supplies and clothes, or they may be for optional items, such as movies and hot fudge sundaes. Flexible expenses can usually be changed. You might want to buy a new sweater, for example, but decide to wait until later.

After you have kept track of your expenses for a week or two, examine them and think about where your money is going. Divide all of your expenses into the fixed and flexible categories. Figure averages if necessary so that you have all expenses calculated for the same period of time—a week or a month, for instance.

You may be surprised at how much money you waste. For instance, Aaron discovered that he spent about $1 a day on snacks. At $30

- **Money Metaphors.** Ask: How does creating and sticking to a budget resemble being on a diet? Challenge students to make other comparisons. (*Creativity*)
- **The Easy Part.** Ask groups to develop a chart, form, or worksheet that could be used to record a monthly budget or spending plan. Have groups compare their forms for completeness and usefulness. (*Management*)

ENRICHMENT

- **The Community Kitty.** Clip and distribute articles about national, state, and local government spending. Have groups or individuals read their article and summarize it for the class. Based on this information, try to answer these and other questions as a class: What expenses does this level of government have? What are the sources of its income? How does a government's budget compare to a family or personal budget?

CROSS-CURRICULAR ACTIVITY
Math

Ask students to find dollar amounts for: a teen who wants to cut back 15 percent on a $40 monthly clothing budget (*$6*); a family that spends 19 percent of its $1600 monthly income on utilities (*$304*); a worker who saves 7 percent of $190 take-home pay (*$13.30*).

Focus on Management Skills

Discuss how insurance policies fit into a budget. Ask: What kind of expense is an insurance premium? (*Fixed*) How can a policy be a source of income? (*You may be able to cash it in or borrow against its value.*) How is a policy a type of savings account? (*It's money set aside for emergencies, for the unexpected.*) How does it differ significantly from a savings account? (*Money isn't there for your use.*)

Topics on pp. 304-305:
- **Creating a Budget**
- **Savings Accounts**

Checking Comprehension

✓ How do good money managers prioritize expenses? *Cover fixed expenses (including savings) first; spend on flexible expenses according to money left and preferences.*

✓ Why do financial institutions pay interest? *As payment for using money to make loans and investments.*

USING VISUALS

Refer students to Figure 30.1. Point out that the amounts under "flexible expenses" are only limits. When creating a budget, you first estimate average expenses. These figures come from the records you keep of what you actually spent for a while. Once a limit is set for a budget, you don't have to spend it all. You may be able to hold down spending and have extra left for savings or some other goal.

FAMILY AND COMMUNITY OUTREACH

Have students discuss with an adult they know well, preferably a family member, how and why the adult saves for different purposes. Stress that students may share this information only if given permission to do so.

Figure 30.1

Weekly Budget

Weekly Income
Allowance	$12.00
Paper route	45.00
Total	**$57.00**

Weekly Expenses

Savings
For emergencies	$ 5.00
For summer class	10.00

Fixed Expenses
Car insurance	15.00
Telephone bill	3.00
Haircut	3.00

Flexible Expenses
Entertainment	8.00
Clothes	9.00
School supplies	4.00
Total	**$57.00**

a month, he was spending $365 in a year. He decided that there were other things he would rather do with $365. Becoming aware of how you spend your money can help you decide which expenses to continue and which ones to change.

Step 3: Create a Plan

The third step is to create a plan for using your money. To do this, you need to know what your short-term and long-term financial goals are. A short-term goal might be buying a picture frame or a birthday gift. A long-term goal might be getting a bicycle or a guitar or having money to pay for technical school.

Fixed expenses have to be covered first. How much of any remaining money you spend on flexible expenses will depend on the amount of money left and on your priorities. Wise savers pay themselves first by considering savings a fixed expense.

Figure 30.1 shows you an example of one person's weekly budget.

As part of the planning step, ask yourself whether you are satisfied with how you have distributed your money. You may decide that you should reduce the amount of one of your flexible expenses so that you can put away money toward reaching a long-term goal.

A realistic budget is one that you can actually follow. When Aaron decided to save more money, he didn't try to cut out all snacks. He simply reduced the amount he allowed himself to spend. He avoided the vending machines by bringing snacks from home. In this way, he saved money without putting unrealistic expectations on himself.

Step 4: Stick to Your Plan

For your budget to be a meaningful money-management tool, you need to keep track of your income and expenses and to check them

Focus on Consumer Skills

Like any business, a bank must sell potential customers on more than its services. Ask students to notice advertisements for banks and other financial institutions. What words or images are used to promote the institution? Ask students to closely observe the lobby the next time they are in a bank. How would they describe the setting? The atmosphere? Help students see that banks want to portray themselves as secure, conservative, and trustworthy.

against your budget regularly. Your budget sets the limits for each category of spending. Check to see that you are staying within those limits and that your actual income matches your budgeted income.

If you aren't able to stay within your budget, you may need to revise it. You should also revise it as you have changes in income or adjustments in expenses.

Remember that you are the person in charge of managing your money. Your budget can be a valuable tool for wise money management if you take responsibility for planning, spending, and saving.

Bank Accounts

After saving money from his part-time job for several months, Jamal realized that he wasn't making good use of the money. He was keeping it in a drawer at home, which was neither safe nor financially smart. He needed a bank account.

Putting money in a savings account can help keep you from spending it and earns money in interest.

Commercial banks, savings and loan associations, and credit unions offer savings and checking accounts that help people manage their money. They offer several advantages: the security of keeping money in a safe, insured place; the convenience of being able to withdraw money when needed; and the advantage of earning extra money.

Savings Accounts

You can protect money you are saving and have it earn money for you by putting it in a savings account. A **savings account** is *an account that holds the money you deposit and pays you interest on it*. **Interest** is *a payment in exchange for the right to use your money*. When you put money in a savings account, the financial institution uses your money to make loans and investments. The institution earns money on these loans and investments, so it pays you for the privilege of using your money.

Generally, there are no limitations on the amount or frequency of deposits or withdrawals with a regular savings account. Some institutions give you a passbook to record your savings account transactions. Others offer statement savings accounts. With a statement account, you use deposit and withdrawal slips and receive a monthly or quarterly statement of your transactions to check against your records. In addition, many financial institutions allow you to use automatic teller machines (ATMs) for savings account transactions.

Activities

■ **Held Accountable.** Bring to class some pamphlets and brochures explaining the various services offered by financial institutions. Have groups read through this literature to learn what types of accounts are available, the terms of each one, and the fees or penalties for violating these terms. Groups might record this information in chart form, by institution or type of account. (*Observation*)

ENRICHMENT

■ **Bank on It.** Have students research one aspect of banking that interests them, such as its history, laws governing bank operations, how and where banks invest money, and famous banks of the world. Ask students to comment on how their topic affects the typical bank customer.

FAMILY AND COMMUNITY OUTREACH

Invite a bank employee, such as a cashier or loan officer, to speak to the class about his or her job duties, the skills or education needed for the job, and career opportunities in the banking field. Have students prepare questions for the speaker in advance.

MORE ABOUT Banking

Automatic transactions have become more common in banking. For example, many employers offer workers direct deposit, automatically depositing their paycheck into their account. Similarly, customers can have regular expenses, from loan payments to charitable contributions, deducted from their accounts every month. Such transactions are convenient for bank and customer alike. However, customers must still make sure that deposits and deductions are made as agreed.

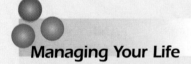
Checking Comprehension

✓ What factors determine the interest money in a savings account earns? *Principal, interest rate, how long money is in account, how often interest is paid.*

✓ Explain whether simple or compound interest earns savers more money. *Compound does; it is interest on both principle and previously earned interest.*

✓ Can you lose money in a savings account? Explain. *Yes; service charges can possibly offset interest.*

Managing Your Life

Have students read "Making Money Grow" and discuss the questions. Ask: Should teens be concerned about investments? If not, when should people begin to invest money? Are investments only for those who are already financially secure?

Answers to Applying . . .

1. Answers may include: own and family's financial stability; possible gain compared to risk.
2. Bonds—guaranteed by government to produce return. Stocks—not guaranteed, greater potential for gain and loss.
3. Answers will vary.

306

How much interest your money earns in a savings account depends on four factors:

- The **principal**, or the amount of money you have in the account.
- The interest rate, or the percentage of the principal, that the institution is paying as interest.
- How long the money is in the account.
- How often the interest is paid.

Suppose that you have $200 in your savings account at an interest rate of 3 percent per year. At the end of a year, your $200 will have earned 3 percent of that $200, or $6. The institution adds that to your account, giving you a total of $206. *Interest that is paid only on the principal* is called **simple interest**.

Managing Your Life

Making Money Grow

People invest their money in the hope that it will increase in value. Many types of investments are available, and each has the potential to earn a profit. Usually, the higher the potential for profit, the higher the risk. Some investments are very safe and guarantee a profit. With others, the investor risks losing the entire investment.

As the conditions of your life change, your investment needs will change. Identify what type of investment is right for you at any given time. To avoid heavy risk, learn in advance the risk factors associated with investments. Never invest more than you can afford to lose.

The following is a list of some of the most popular types of investments, along with their potential risks and returns:

- **Savings bonds.** Because they are issued and guaranteed by the government, savings bonds are a very safe investment. When purchasing a savings bond, you pay half of the face value, or the amount printed on the bond. If you keep the bond for a set number of years, you can then redeem it for its face value. Savings bonds can be cashed in after six months but will not earn as much interest as bonds held longer. Savings bonds can be replaced if they are lost, stolen, or destroyed.
- **Stocks.** When you buy a share of stock, you become a part owner of a corporation. Shares of stock are traded daily, and the value of any stock may go up or down with each day's trading. Investing in stocks can be risky. Investors who sell when the value drops below what they have paid lose part of their investment. Stockholders may

earn a profit in the form of dividends, but that is not guaranteed.

- **Mutual funds.** A mutual fund is a type of investment company. When you purchase shares in a mutual fund, you allow financial professionals to invest your money. The risk of a mutual fund depends on what type of investment the group is making, but most funds diversify, or spread the investments among different types, to reduce the risk of loss. A drop in one investment may be offset by an increase in another. Mutual funds will buy back an investor's shares whenever the investor wishes to sell, but the price of the shares may be lower than when the investor purchased them.
- **Certificates of deposit.** Certificates of deposit (CDs) are a form of deposit that is issued by financial institutions. Depositors must agree to leave a certain amount of money in the bank for a fixed amount of time. CDs are very low-risk investments, but investors must pay a penalty if they remove their deposit before the specified date.

Applying the Principles

1. What is the most important factor to consider when you are planning to invest money?
2. What are the significant differences between savings bonds and stocks as investments?
3. Of the types of investments discussed above, which do you think would be most appropriate for you? Why?

306   UNIT 5   Management and Consumer Decisions

● ● ●   REAL-LIFE APPLICATION

Read this to students: *Alana earns about $30 a week babysitting and doing extra chores around the home. She thinks she could save about $5 a week, but that's too little to open a savings account.* Ask: Is Alana correct? What problems might she encounter in opening an account? How can these be overcome? Suggest that she save enough money to meet a minimum balance requirement, then make regular deposits. Having an account may spur her to save more.

Whenever you use an automatic teller machine for deposits or withdrawals from your savings or checking account, you must record the transaction in your checking or savings register to keep accurate records.

While savings accounts offer many advantages, institutions have varying rules and requirements. Some may have minimum balance requirements and charge service fees if your account falls below the minimum balance. Suppose that they pay 5 percent interest over a year but charge $3 per month for accounts with balances of less than $100. If you have $90 in the account for a year, you will earn $4.50 in interest but pay $36 in service charges. An account with no further deposits could disappear at this rate.

Other institutions calculate the interest based on the lowest amount that was in your account during a certain period of time, no matter what average amount you had in the account during that time. When choosing a financial institution, compare all the accounts that are available.

Traditional savings accounts generally pay relatively low interest rates. Investors can earn higher interest rates by putting their savings into other types of accounts. Many of these require more money to open the account and tie up the money for some period of time. Some are riskier than others. Certificates of deposit (CDs) and government savings bonds are examples of investments that earn higher interest and enjoy no risk.

Once the interest is added on, it becomes part of your principal. For the next year, if you make no additional deposits, your principal is $206, and you will earn 3 percent of that amount, or $6.18. **Compound interest** is *money you earn on your deposit plus previous interest*. The more frequently interest is compounded, the more money your account earns. If the interest is paid quarterly (every three months), your savings will increase faster.

MORE ABOUT Account Insurance

Bank accounts are insured by the Federal Deposit Insurance Corporation (FDIC), an agency created in 1933 in the wake of the Great Depression and its numerous bank failures. The federal government insures customers' deposits in member banks up to $100,000. This includes all accounts (savings, checking, and CDs) under a single name. Ask: How might you protect your funds over $100,000? *Keep joint account; keep accounts in several banks.*

Checking Comprehension

✓ What are some costs of using checks? *Cost of checks; fees and service charges; penalties for bad checks.*

✓ What factors should you consider before opening a checking account? *How often you need checks; costs and convenience of using checks.*

✓ Why should everyone have some knowledge of finances? *In case of death, divorce, separation, illness, or deceit.*

USING VISUALS

Refer students to Figure 30.2. Ask: Why should you write numerals beginning near the dollar sign? *In order to prevent amount from being altered.*

How can the "Memo" blank help you manage expenses? *Shows you what you spend your money on.*

What should you write in your check register besides information about the checks? *Any deposits you make.*

Checking Accounts

A **checking account** is *an account that holds your money and allows you to pay for things by writing a check rather than using cash.* As with savings accounts, checking accounts offer a secure place to keep your money. You don't have to carry cash. Checking accounts also help you keep track of your expenses and income.

To open a checking account, you first deposit money in a bank, savings and loan, or credit union. Then you purchase checks and a booklet, called a check register, for recording each check you write and each deposit you make. Checks can be ordered through the financial institution. A lower cost can often be found through other sources, such as mail-order catalogs.

Shop carefully for a checking account, just as you would for savings. Some accounts require a minimum balance. Many charge a monthly service fee, and others charge a fee for each check written. Almost all charge for printing the checks. Some offer checking accounts that pay interest, but these accounts usually require a higher minimum balance or limit the number of checks a person can write each month.

A checking account can be established so that only one person or more than one can sign checks. Accounts held by more than one person are called joint accounts. Some institutions will not let people open a checking account until they are 18 and have a driver's license, so many young people open joint accounts with a parent or another adult.

If you are thinking about opening a checking account, consider these questions:

- **How often do you need to write checks?** If you write only one or two checks a month, you might pay more in fees than you would benefit from writing checks. Instead of checks, you could make your payments in cash or use a money order. A **money order** is *a piece of paper that can*

be used just like a check. Money orders are sold for a small fee at post offices, banks, and stores. Different fees are charged for money orders, so investigate prices before you purchase one.

- **What will it cost?** Consider the fees and service charges.
- **Will writing checks prove less convenient than paying cash for purchases?** Most businesses accept personal checks only with proper identification, and some do not accept checks at all.

To manage a checking account, you need to know how to make deposits, write checks, keep a record of your transactions, and compare your records regularly with the institution's statements. To make a deposit, list and total the checks and cash you are depositing on a deposit slip, sign the backs of any checks you are depositing, and take these items to the teller or the ATM. Signing the back of a check written to you is called *endorsing* the check. Anyone who receives a paycheck must endorse it before being able to deposit or cash it. **Figure 30.2** shows you how to write a check and how to record the transaction in a check register.

Keep your check register up-to-date. If you forget, your balance may show a figure higher than the amount of money that is actually in your account. If that happens, you could write a check for more money than is in the account, known as an overdraft or a "bounced" check. Some checkbooks come with duplicate checks or with stubs for each check, which help with record keeping.

Writing checks for money you do not have in your account can be costly. You will have to pay not only the amount of the check you wrote, but also a fee to the financial institution. You may also have to pay a substantial "bad check" charge to the business that received the check. Writing a bad check intentionally is illegal. Keeping good records and writing checks responsibly is essential.

MORE ABOUT Checks

Banks that do not return customers' cancelled checks with each statement offer the option of duplicate checks instead. Each check includes a carbon copy, which customers keep as a record of the transaction.

MORE ABOUT Endorsing Checks

Once endorsed, a check can be used like cash—by anyone. A restrictive endorsement helps limit the risk of misuse. For example, writing *for deposit only* along with the endorsement provides some protection if the check is lost or stolen.

Figure 30.2

WRITING CHECKS

You write a check to withdraw money from your account. Always write checks carefully and with nonerasable ink: checks written in pencil can be altered. A correctly written check is shown below.

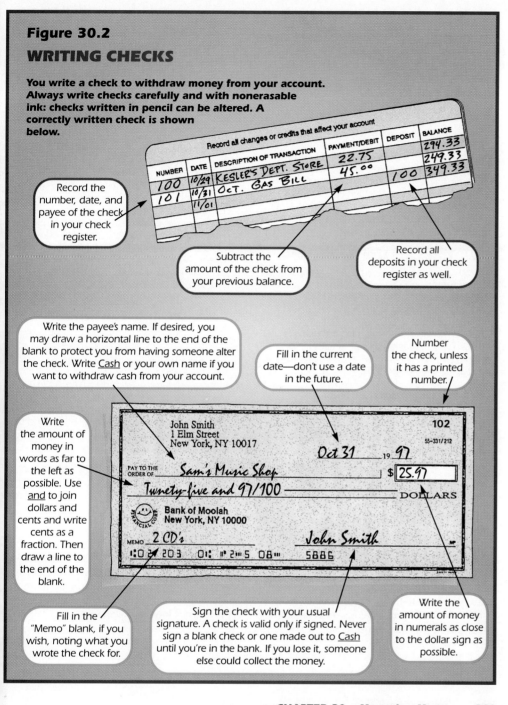

Record the number, date, and payee of the check in your check register.

Subtract the amount of the check from your previous balance.

Record all deposits in your check register as well.

Write the payee's name. If desired, you may draw a horizontal line to the end of the blank to protect you from having someone alter the check. Write <u>Cash</u> or your own name if you want to withdraw cash from your account.

Fill in the current date—don't use a date in the future.

Number the check, unless it has a printed number.

Write the amount of money in words as far to the left as possible. Use <u>and</u> to join dollars and cents and write cents as a fraction. Then draw a line to the end of the blank.

Fill in the "Memo" blank, if you wish, noting what you wrote the check for.

Sign the check with your usual signature. A check is valid only if signed. Never sign a blank check or one made out to <u>Cash</u> until you're in the bank. If you lose it, someone else could collect the money.

Write the amount of money in numerals as close to the dollar sign as possible.

CHAPTER 30   Managing Money   **309**

REAL-LIFE APPLICATION

Ask students to imagine they are parents of young children. What could they do to help teach their children money management skills? What different lessons and experiences would they provide as the children grow older? How would they avoid overemphasizing money or raising fears in children's minds about the family's financial status?

Activity

■ **Checks and Balances.** Give students practice in using checks. Make copies of sample checks and a few pages of a check register for each student. Tell students to begin their accounts with $500 and to write 10 checks for whatever they choose, entering the needed information in the check register. When students are finished, have them trade checks and registers to review for accuracy and correct usage. *(Management)*

From School to Work

Have students read "Balancing Your Checkbook" on page 310 and answer the questions. Ask: Why should you reconcile your account with every statement? What might happen if errors go undetected? Ask volunteers to learn different banks' policies regarding handling of checking account errors.

Answers to Assessing . . .

1. You may have written checks and made deposits since end of statement period. You must update balance on statement with this information and make sure no errors were made.
2. Bank statement would be $10 lower than your register balance.

Review

■ **Chapter Review.** Use the contents of the Chapter Review page to help students review concepts, think critically, and apply their knowledge.

■ **Study Guide.** Have students complete the Study Guide for Chapter 30 on p. 98 of the Student Workbook.

■ **Twenty Questions.** Have groups make up 20 questions using information from the chapter, writing each question on a separate note card and the answer on the back. Have groups try to answer each other's questions.

Evaluation

■ **Chapter Test.** Use the reproducible chapter test provided in the Teacher's Classroom Resources or create your own test using the *Testmaker Software.*

■ **Alternative Assessment.** Have groups create board games in which players advance by correctly answering questions about money management. Games should include a board with a marked path; question cards; chance cards that advance or move players back due to good or poor management; playing pieces; and a rule book. Encourage creativity, especially in board design and game pieces.

■ **Money and Me.** Have students write an assessment of their current financial situation, including their attitude toward money; some of their money management techniques, including use of bank accounts; and whether their current practices will help them in the future.

310

From School to Work

Balancing Your Checkbook

What You Learn Today . . .

Most math classes you take involve practice with basic math skills, even the advanced classes. Taking a careful approach to these skills pays off as you become a money manager. With a checking account, for example, a basic math calculation can trip you up. A simple subtraction error can cause a discrepancy that results in writing a bad check. You will be better prepared to manage money if you learn the basics well.

. . . You Can Use Tomorrow

Money management will be part of your life—at home and possibly on the job. Many people have to prepare budgets and analyze expenses in their work. Accountants, business managers, and business owners are typically responsible for money-management routines—including balancing checkbooks. Your ability to apply math skills to money-management procedures will be useful—perhaps in more ways than one.

Practicing Your Skills

Follow the steps below to learn how to balance a checkbook. If you don't yet have a checking account, ask to balance a family member's. Use the most recent bank statement.

1. Find the ending balance on the statement, and add to it any deposits made to the account since the end of the statement period. You should be able to find the deposits recorded in the checkbook register.
2. Add the amounts, also from the checkbook register, of all the checks written on the account that are not listed on the statement. These are checks that are still outstanding.
3. Subtract the total amount of the outstanding checks in number 2 from the total balance in number 1. The result should be the same as the current balance in the checkbook register. If it isn't, check all the figures in the register and on the bank statement to find the error.

Assessing Your Skills

1. When you get a statement from the bank, why can't you just compare the ending balance on the statement with the current balance in your checkbook register?
2. Suppose you forgot to record a $10 check in your checkbook register. If that was the only error you made, how would your checkbook register balance compare with the balance on your next bank statement?

Taking Financial Responsibility

Managing money is a skill you can and should develop. Learning to rely on someone else to make these decisions for you is a mistake. You have to look out for your own interests. Males and females alike, even when they form partnerships, need to be aware of finances. Death, divorce, separation, illness, deceit—all of these and more can result in a person's need to know. Those who have neglected this need have often had later regrets. This doesn't have to happen to you.

REAL-LIFE APPLICATION

Read this to students: *Emily has been married for six years. Her husband always pays the bills and balances the checkbook each month. Emily doesn't know the amounts of their bills. She has never learned how to balance a checkbook. Emily's husband says they have a savings account, but Emily has never seen any of the bank statements.* Ask students what they think about this situation. Help them see that Emily would have trouble taking over if she had to. Also, she is not making sure their income is being well handled.

Chapter 30 Review

Reviewing the Facts

1. What is a budget and what is its main purpose?
2. List the four steps in creating and living on a budget.
3. What are the advantages of keeping money in a savings account? In a checking account?
4. What are the consequences of "bouncing" a check?
5. What are the main reasons for learning sound money management?

Thinking Critically

1. Do you think that people need money to be happy? Explain why or why not.
2. Why do advertisers attempt to turn wants into needs?

Applying Your Knowledge

1. **Maintaining a Check Register.** Jean had a balance in her checking account of $150. On June 15 she wrote a check to All-Star Records for $41.45 for some compact discs. On June 17 she wrote a check to Outdoors Outfitters for $33.95 for a sweater. On June 20 she deposited $100. On June 21 she wrote a check for $57.19 to the phone company. Calculate the new balance in Jean's account.
2. **Distinguishing Needs and Wants.** Make a list of 15 items that cost money. Include both necessities and luxuries. On a separate piece of paper, identify each of your items as a need or a want and tell why. Exchange lists with another student. Identify the items on the other student's list as needs and wants. Compare your decisions on both lists with those of the other student. Examine how you each categorized items on the two lists, and draw conclusions about how different people view needs and wants.

Making Connections

1. **Literature.** Benjamin Franklin once wrote, "A penny saved is a penny earned." In a brief essay, explain what Franklin meant about the value of savings.
2. **Mathematics.** Assume that you have a savings account that pays 5 percent interest per year and that you have $500 in the account. Calculate how much you will have in your account after one year, two years, and five years, if you make no additional deposits, assuming that the bank adds the interest to your account at the end of each year.

Building Your Portfolio

Create a Personal Budget
Make a weekly budget for yourself. Follow the steps you have learned for creating a budget. Try living on your budget for two weeks or more. Keep track of your actual income and expenses, and compare them to your budget. Write a short report describing any difficulties you had in preparing or living on your budget. Describe any problems you anticipate in staying within your budget. Discuss how you expect to handle these difficulties, and describe any revisions you propose in your budget. Add your budget and your report to your portfolio.

ANSWERS TO REVIEWING THE FACTS

1. Plan for spending and saving money. Help you manage your money to meet present needs and wants and save for future.
2. Determine income, record expenses, create plan, and stick to plan.
3. Savings account: keeps money safe, readily available, and earning interest. Checking account: keeps money safe; gives flexibility of check writing; helps you keep track of income and expenses.
4. You pay amount of check, fee to bank, and possibly fee to business check was given to.
5. Meet current and future financial goals; for self-reliance and self-protection.

ANSWERS TO THINKING CRITICALLY

1. Answers will vary. Ask: Does happiness come from money or things money can buy? Does having money or these things guarantee happiness?
2. To increase sales by convincing people they need what they may only want.

Chapter 31

Chapter Overview

Chapter 31 describes some of the different types of credit available to consumers. Students learn about choosing, obtaining, and using credit, and the consequences of misusing it.

Motivator

■ **Charge!** Have students discuss ads they have seen that involve credit, such as credit card ads or ads for sales or products that stress credit terms. What advantages to using credit are emphasized? Point out that these ads ignore the responsibilities and negative aspects of credit.

Objectives

Discuss the chapter objectives on this page. Remind students that the objectives focus on important chapter concepts.

Vocabulary

The word *credit* comes from the Latin verb *credere,* to trust. When people use credit, they are being trusted to pay what they owe to whomever gave them the credit. Ask students to identify and define related words, such as credible, credulous, and credence.

Chapter 31

Using Credit Wisely

INFINITI C

Terms to Learn

- annual percentage rate (APR)
- co-signing
- credit
- credit application
- credit limit
- creditor
- finance charge
- grace period
- lease

Objectives

This chapter will help you to:

- Explain what credit is.
- Describe different types of credit.
- Compare different credit plans to find the best terms for you.
- Describe steps you can take to build a good credit record.
- Identify ways to use credit wisely.

CHAPTER RESOURCES

Tony signed the papers where the first "X" appeared, then handed them to his father. Mr. Cannova signed his name, smiled at his son, and passed the loan agreement back to the loan officer. "I'll be right back with your copies and a check," she said.

While she was gone, Tony thought about how hard he had worked during the summer to save for the down payment on a car. He had been so relieved when his father agreed to co-sign the loan. In just a little while, he would be driving home in his own car. It might be ten years old, but it was going to be *his*.

Gasoline companies offer credit cards that their customers can use to pay for gas, oil, and other services.

What Is Credit?

Credit is *an arrangement in which some-one receives money or merchandise now and promises to pay for it later.* Tony's situation illustrates how credit works. He couldn't afford to pay cash for a car. A **creditor**—*a bank, fi-nance company, credit union, business, or in-dividual to whom money is owed*—agreed to advance Tony the money he needed. In turn, Tony agreed to repay the bank in affordable installments over a period of time. When credit is extended by a store, it works in the same way. The consumer receives the prod-uct and makes regular payments.

Buying with credit is serious business be-cause the buyer is committing future re-sources. Tony, for instance, is guaranteeing that he will use part of his future income to repay the loan. He is re-sponsible for making sure that in-come is available.

By buying on credit, Tony is also agreeing to pay more than he would if he had paid cash for the car. When they issue credit, cred-itors add a **finance charge.** This is *an addition to the purchase price that is the cost of using the credi-tor's money.* Tony's car cost $2,500. He paid $500 as a down payment to the car dealer and borrowed the rest from the bank. He has to repay the bank more than $2,000, though. The total amount he will pay is $2,327.52. The additional $327.52 is the finance charge.

TEACH

Topic on p. 313:
• Using Credit

Checking Comprehension

✓ How does credit work? *Someone receives money or merchandise and promises to pay for it later.*

✓ Why is the finance charge of concern to credit users? *It must be paid along with amount borrowed.*

Activity

■ **Buy Now.** Discuss whether it would be appropriate to take out a loan to: buy a car; pay for a vacation; finance a college education; pay off an-other debt. *(Decision Making)*

FAMILY AND COMMUNITY OUTREACH

Ask students to dis-cuss with the adults in their family their philos-ophy about credit. Do they use it? If so, for what reasons? How do they de-cide what type of credit to use, and how much credit debt is acceptable? Tell students they may share what they learn only with permission from the adults

Focus on Critical Thinking Skills

Write this statement from p. 313 on the board: "Buying with credit is serious business because the buyer is commit-ting future resources." Ask students to read and think about that assertion.

Ask: Do you think most teens are able to "commit future resources"? Are they in a position to anticipate what resources they will have? What credit situations might teens be able or unable to handle?

Checking Comprehension

✓ What is deferred billing? *Store sells item with no payments due for several months, at which time payments with finance charges begin.*

✓ What is a disadvantage of leasing compared to using credit? *You don't own item at end of lease.*

✓ In what two ways must creditors express finance charges? Why? *As actual amount and annual percentage rate (APR), for easier comparison of credit costs.*

SPECIAL NEEDS
Strategies

Learning in Pairs. Have each student of a pair outline the information on types of credit on pp. 314-315. Have partners trade and critique each other's work, then together make one outline that incorporates the better parts of their individual efforts.

Types of Credit

Consumers can choose from among many types of credit. The most common are credit cards, loans, deferred payments, layaway plans, and leasing agreements. Each type has advantages and disadvantages. Each type is used for particular kinds of transactions.

Credit Cards

Credit cards are issued by banks and stores. Those issued by banks can be used for many different purchases—meals in restaurants, clothes from department stores, and equipment from electronics stores. Store charge cards can usually be used only in different branches of the chain of stores that issues them. Whether a store or a bank, the company issuing the card gives the cardholder a **credit limit**, *a maximum total that can be charged.*

Credit cards have several advantages. They enable people to buy products and services without having to carry large sums of cash. They help people take advantage of sale prices even if they don't have the cash required at the time. They allow people to buy goods by telephone and can be helpful in an emergency.

Credit cards have disadvantages too. Finance charges can be high. Also, because credit cards are so easy to use, people sometimes charge more than they can afford to repay.

Loans

For large purchases, such as cars and homes, consumers take out loans. Loans are available from banks, credit unions, and consumer-finance companies. Some consumers are able to borrow money against their life insurance.

While credit cards can be used to purchase a variety of goods and services, loans are generally made to finance one purchase in particular. The borrower usually has to apply separately for each new loan. Lenders occasionally charge a fee to process the loan application.

Loans tend to be for larger sums of money than most purchases made by credit cards. They usually have lower interest rates than credit cards do.

Many stores offer an installment plan, which works like a loan. Consumers can buy furniture, computers, and appliances this way. Sometimes the store offers deferred billing to stimulate sales, often at the end of the year. They may sell a consumer a television, with the promise that no payments are due for several months. When payments do begin, they include a finance charge.

Layaway

Denise wanted to buy a new winter coat, but she didn't have all the cash that she needed. Instead, she bought the coat using a layaway agreement with the department store. Denise gave the store a portion of the coat's cost at the time of purchase. The store then reserved the coat for her so that no one else could buy it. For each of the next three months, Denise gave the store another payment. After that time, the coat was completely paid for, and she could take it home.

Leasing

People do not always use credit to purchase goods. Sometimes they **lease,** or *rent,* a product. Leasing cars, for instance, has become increasingly popular. Many businesses lease equipment, such as copying machines and computers.

With a lease, the consumer often puts some money down when the product is received. The remainder of the cost of the lease is paid in regular monthly payments. Those payments include funds to cover the use of the product plus a finance charge. Many leases include a buyout option at the end of the lease. By paying off the product's value at the end of the lease term, the consumer owns the product.

Monthly payments for leased cars may be lower than car payments made to a bank. One drawback, however, is that when the leasing period is up, the car is not yours without ad-

MORE ABOUT Credit Cards

Credit card issuers try a number of promotions to interest consumers in their product. One is the sports card, a bank's card that features the logo of a local team. Some issuers arrange with airlines to give customers frequent-flyer miles for purchases made with their card. Nonprofit organizations have begun to issue cards that return a small portion of amounts charged on them to the group. These cards may carry higher interest charges than some bank-issued cards.

By using a layaway plan, consumers can spread payments out over a period of time.

Activities

■ **The Meaning of It All.** Write the words *credit, creditor, finance charge, credit card,* and *credit limit* on the board. Challenge students to write a single sentence that uses all of these terms correctly. Ask students to read their sentences to the class.

RETEACHING

■ **Credit Chart.** Have groups make a chart with these headings: Credit Cards, Loans, Layaway, and Leasing. Under each heading, have students write the characteristics of that type of lending and when it is most likely to be used. Have students use their answers to complete a large chart on the board.

ENRICHMENT

■ **Take It to the Limit.** Assign students to contact banks that issue credit cards to learn how credit limits are determined for individual customers. Have these students explain the process to the class.

ditional cost. As a result, you have no vehicle to trade in to buy another car.

Sellers are required to inform consumers of all the costs associated with a lease. Still, comparing the cost of a lease to the cost of buying the same product outright—even if the purchase is financed—is difficult. Wise consumers read lease agreements carefully and ask questions to ensure that they fully understand their terms and conditions of the lease.

Shopping for Credit

Shopping for credit is just like shopping for a product. You need to comparison shop to find the credit terms that offer you the best combination of cost and services.

Comparing Finance Charges

Not every creditor handles finance charges the same way. Some charge more than others. If you don't watch carefully, you may pay more than you want to.

Comparing finance charges has not always been easy. When two creditors expressed the charges in different terms, consumers were confused. The Fair Credit and Charge Card Disclosure Act of 1988 greatly simplified comparison shopping for finance charges.

Creditors are required to specify the amount borrowed, the amount of each monthly payment, the number of payments that must be made, the date that payments are due, and what, if any, extra charges are incurred for late payments. To allow consumers to compare finance charges, the law requires creditors to specify the actual amount of the finance charge and state the finance charge as a percentage called the annual percentage rate.

The **annual percentage rate** (or **APR**) *shows how much the finance charge is in relation to the amount borrowed.* A finance charge of

CHAPTER 31   Using Credit Wisely   315

● ● ●   REAL-LIFE APPLICATION

Read this to students: *Claire and Trevor are furniture shopping. They saw a newspaper ad for one store that offers six months of interest-free financing on any amount they charge. It sounds like a great deal.* Ask: Should the couple take advantage of this deal? What else do they need to know about it? What other factors should influence their decision? Point out that such deals often have inflated finance charges after the initial grace period.

Checking Comprehension

✓ Why might using a credit card with a high APR be acceptable? *When you pay off charges each month and card has no annual fee.*

✓ What problems may arise from using credit unwisely? *Lose of purchase; difficulty getting credit in future; bankruptcy.*

✓ For what types of expenses is credit use wisest? *Needs rather than wants, especially emergencies and large, long-lasting purchases.*

FAMILY AND COMMUNITY OUTREACH

Ask students to learn whether their community has nonprofit groups or businesses that help people who are overwhelmed by debt. If so, what services are offered? Suggest they begin their search in the yellow pages under the heading Credit.

SPECIAL NEEDS Strategies

English as a Second Language. Pair a native speaker with an ESL student to list the important words discussed on these pages. Have the ESL student work on definitions for these words to be reviewed by the partner.

Shopping for the best APR helps consumers save money when buying merchandise on credit.

see, borrowers save money by shopping for the lowest APR possible.

Analyzing Added Charges

It may seem that a credit plan with a lower APR is better than one with a higher APR. That's not the only thing to look at when shopping for credit, however.

Some credit cards charge annual membership fees. These may range from $20 to $25 or even more. A credit card with no annual fee may be more attractive, but not if the APR is much higher than that for the card with a fee. Of course, if the balance due is always paid off on time, the finance charges are not incurred. In that case, the no-fee card would be a better choice.

Another consideration with credit cards is the **grace period.** This is *the period of time in which the money can be repaid without incurring the finance charge*. Most credit cards allow consumers a month to repay charges before the finance charge is added. Some, however, begin adding the finance charge on the day of the purchase. These cards are more expensive to use.

Many bank credit cards allow cardholders to use the account to obtain cash. This feature can benefit consumers who have an emergency need for money. Often cash withdrawals are treated differently from purchases, however. Cash loans may incur finance charges from the date that the cash is received, with no grace period, for instance. The APR for borrowing cash is often higher than that for making purchases.

Some credit arrangements also include

late fees. As much as $20 may be added to the monthly payment when that payment has not been received by the bill's due date.

Getting and Using Credit

To get credit, a person has to fill out a **credit application.** This is *a form asking for details about an applicant's job, bank accounts, and credit history*. The creditor examines that information and performs a credit check. The credit check is often carried out by contacting a business called a credit bureau. This agency keeps records on how people pay

MORE ABOUT Credit Ratings

Consumers Union reports that the following factors improve a credit rating: owning a home; owning a car; living in one place for many years; having the same job for several years; and earning a high income. Consumers can receive a copy of their credit report, which influences their credit rating, by writing to: TRW IS&S-NAC, P.O. Box 2106, Allen, Texas 75013.

Making Decisions

Are Rebates Good Deals?

Another credit card offer in the Marshall's mail, Laura noticed. The flyer said that the company paid a rebate on any purchases made with the card. It pointed out that the more times you used the card, the more money you got back.

When her mother got home from work, Laura showed her the offer. "Look at this, Mom," Laura said. Then she explained what it said about a rebate.

"That does sound good," said Mrs. Marshall. "Let's read more about it."

Laura and her mother sat down to read the brochure. It explained that at the end of the year, the company would pay each cardholder 1 percent of all amounts charged to the account for purchases. The APR for the card was 19.8 percent. The card that the Marshalls currently had charged only 15.9 percent. "That means that if we don't pay the full amount at the end of the month, we'll be paying more in interest," Laura pointed out. Her mother added, "Right, and that 1 percent rebate doesn't really erase the difference."

Laura then pointed to another feature of the card—there was no annual membership fee. Their current card charged $25 a year to keep the account open. "So we'll save money there."

"You know, we usually pay our credit card balances in full each month," Mrs. Marshall said. "If we do that using this card, the higher interest rate won't matter. We really will be getting some money back on what we buy."

"What do you think we should do?" Laura asked.

"I think we should have dinner," her mother answered. "This decision can wait for a while."

What Would You Do?

1. What might happen if the Marshalls take the card with the rebate and then cannot pay for purchases in the grace period?
2. Why is it necessary to read all information about an offer such as this one?
3. What do you think the Marshalls should do?

---

their bills. The creditor may also contact employers to verify the job information on the application. These checks help businesses extend credit only to those people who are likely to pay them back.

Any consumer who is turned down for credit has the right, by law, to be told why. Sometimes a credit-bureau report needs updating or correction. By contacting the credit bureau, the consumer can see about having a problem corrected.

Getting Credit

You can begin to build a good credit record today. A first step is to open a savings account—and regularly deposit money into it. This shows that you know how to manage money.

When you get a job and open a checking account, this will help to establish that you are worthy of receiving credit. Some stores allow young people to obtain a store credit card. By using that account wisely—especially when you are careful to make payments on time—you can show that you are responsible enough to meet your commitments.

Rebates are offered on credit card purchases as well as on products you buy in stores.

Activities

■ **Credit Counselor.** Have groups write scenarios in which people are considering taking on debt. Scenarios should include details about the characters' financial situation, credit history, and other relevant or complicating factors. Have groups exchange scenarios and suggest possible ways to handle the situation that they received. *(Problem-Solving)*

■ **Predictions.** Have students complete the following statement: "When I am on my own, I will use credit for . . ." Ask them to add additional statements as necessary to explain their position.

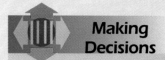

Making Decisions

Have students read "Are Rebates Good Deals?" and discuss the questions. Ask: Would it be advisable to use both cards? In what situations would they use each one? What might be some advantages and disadvantages of this option?

Answers to What ...

1. They will pay more in interest.
2. You need to understand all terms to get the best deal, make an informed choice, avoid unexpected charges.
3. Answers will vary.

Focus on Critical Thinking Skills

Many credit card companies send applications to recent high school and college graduates, even before they have full-time jobs, just when they are least likely to be able to afford credit. Ask: Is it ethical for credit card companies to target this audience, or do students benefit from the chance to establish credit with limited credit history?

Review

■ **Chapter Review.** Use the contents of the Chapter Review page to help students review concepts, think critically, and apply their knowledge.

■ **Study Guide.** Have students complete the Study Guide for Chapter 31 on p. 102 of the Student Workbook.

■ **Credit Primer.** Ask groups to prepare a five-minute consumer report for radio that explains the various types of credit, how and when to use credit, and the pitfalls of using credit unwisely.

Evaluation

■ **Chapter Test.** Use the reproducible chapter test provided in the Teacher's Classroom Resources or create your own test using the *Testmaker Software.*

■ **Alternative Assessment.** Have groups write two profiles of people seeking credit—one good candidate and one poor one—based on information given in this chapter. Encourage students to be subtle but not deceptive. Collect and randomly distribute profiles. Have groups identify the profiles they receive as either good candidates or poor ones and cite details from the profiles to support their decision.

■ **Give Credit.** Ask students to identify in writing the three most practical points about using credit that they learned from this chapter and explain how they can apply them in their lives now and in the future.

Some young people need a large loan to buy a car or fund education after high school. These teens may be able to get the needed money from a bank, but the lender often requires that a parent or guardian co-sign the loan. **Co-signing** means that a person is *agreeing to be responsible for loan payments if the other party fails to make them.*

Credit Problems

Credit is a valuable tool if used wisely. People who charge too many purchases on their credit cards or borrow too much can suffer. If they cannot make the required payments, serious consequences may occur. Someone who fails to meet car payments, for instance, may lose his or her car, which goes to the creditor. A poor credit history may make it impossible later to obtain a car or home loan.

Credit problems may mushroom, as consumers continue borrowing money to pay off earlier debts. When people no longer have the ability to repay debt, they may have to declare bankruptcy. A judge may say that they don't have to repay their former debts, but it is extremely difficult for these consumers to receive credit again for years.

Tips for Using Credit

Credit problems can be avoided with wise habits. Use these tips:

- Try to reserve credit for meeting emergencies when money in savings is not available. The ideal approach is to have money saved in case something goes wrong, but that is not always possible. When sudden expenses come up, credit can help.
- Avoid using credit for goods and services that you simply want rather than need. Racking up large credit card bills on concert tickets, CDs, and entertainment

equipment is a poor use of credit.
- Use credit for expensive purchases that have a long lifetime, such as a refrigerator or car. Because these products give many years of use, it is more reasonable to pay the extra cost of finance charges for them than for products that will not last so long.
- Pay credit card charges within the grace period to avoid unnecessary finance charges.
- Make payments on time to avoid costly late fees.
- Remember to shop wisely for credit, looking for the best overall terms. By holding finance charges down, you can save yourself money.

Safeguard Your Rating

Your credit rating is a valuable asset that you control. As you earn and spend money in the coming years, your borrowing decisions will affect whether your credit is good or bad. Some credit card companies now target teens as new customers. If you choose to accept or apply for a credit card at some time, keep in mind that it is a serious responsibility. The way you repay your debts will follow you for a long time.

Focus on Decision-Making Skills

Have groups list five purchases, large and small, that are often made with credit. Have groups trade lists. For each item, have them write an explanation of which type of credit they would use to purchase it.

Chapter 31 Review

Reviewing the Facts

1. Why do creditors charge finance charges for credit?
2. Name two kinds of businesses that issue credit cards.
3. Explain how buying on layaway works.
4. How does using the APR help consumers shop for credit?
5. What are three steps that a teen can take to begin establishing a good credit history?
6. List two ways of using credit wisely.

Thinking Critically

1. How does getting a loan differ from using credit cards?
2. Stacy, a high school senior, wanted her boyfriend's birthday gift to be really special. A chain store had special one-day discounts on stereos, with no payments for six months. With income from her part-time job, Stacy felt that the purchase was within her budget. Her mother and sister tried to discourage the idea. With whom would you side, and why?

Applying Your Knowledge

1. **Comparing Credit Terms.** Suppose that you are buying a new guitar, which costs $450. If you buy the guitar using the store's layaway plan, you will have to pay $60 up front plus $65 a month for six months. Then you can have the guitar. If you buy the guitar using a credit card and pay it off over the same seven months, it will cost $70 a month. Which plan would you choose? How much more would charging the guitar cost?
2. **Judging Credit Histories.** Tom attends community college while living at home and working 20 hours a week. He opened a savings account when he became a newspaper carrier at age 12. Jennifer earns more than Tom, working at the full-time mall job she's had for three months. She and a friend split their apartment rent. Jennifer pays toward her credit card bill each month, but not always on time. Both young adults are applying for a car loan. Whose loan application do you think the bank would approve. Why?

Making Connections

1. **Mathematics.** The Hoffmeyers took out a bank loan of $5,000 to renovate their house. They have to repay the loan in 36 monthly payments of $168.47. How much are the Hoffmeyers paying in finance charges?
2. **Government.** The government has passed a law called the Equal Credit Opportunity Act. Research this law, and write a few paragraphs explaining how it protects consumers.

Building Your Portfolio

Determining Credit Needs
Suppose that you are moving into your own apartment. Make a list of some of the items you will need—furniture, cooking equipment, and so on. Choosing three items from your list, indicate whether you think you would buy each with cash or credit. For the credit purchases, indicate what kind of credit—credit card, loan, layaway, or lease—you would use. Give reasons for each of your choices.

CHAPTER 31   Using Credit Wisely   319

ANSWERS TO REVIEWING THE FACTS

1. As fee for using creditor's money.
2. Any two: banks, stores, gasoline companies.
3. Buyer pays part of item's price to store, which holds item. Buyer makes regular payments, taking item home when completely paid for.
4. Helps them compare finance charges of different credit plans to find most economical one.
5. Any three: open savings account, make regular deposits; get a job; open a checking account; and get a store credit card and use wisely.
6. Any two: use credit for emergencies; for needed goods and services; for expensive purchases that have a long lifetime; pay charges within the grace period; shop wisely for credit.

ANSWERS TO THINKING CRITICALLY

1. Loan is money borrowed for one specific use; must be applied for individually. Credit card is open account that can be used for many purchases made at any time.
2. Answers will vary. Help students see that buying a substantial gift on credit doesn't fall in the category of "need." Cash for a smaller gift is probably more appropriate, especially if relationship could possibly end.

Chapter 32

FOCUS

Chapter Overview

Chapter 32 looks at advertising and its effect on consumers' tastes, habits, and attitudes. It describes the most common advertising media and methods, tells how this industry is regulated, and offers strategies for evaluating advertisements.

Motivator

■ **No Ads.** Ask students to imagine there were no advertisements—not even pictures on product packages. How would they learn what an item was for or whether they might want to buy it? Point out that for wise consumers, advertising is a valuable tool for making informed choices. This chapter will help them learn how to use—and not feel used by—advertising.

Objectives

Discuss the chapter objectives on this page. Remind students that the objectives focus on important chapter concepts.

Vocabulary

Write the term *bait and switch* on the board. Ask students to define each word and then to use the words together to try to define the term. Compare their definition to the actual one.

Advertising

Terms to Learn

- bait and switch
- consumer
- direct mail ad
- image ad
- "infomercial"
- information ad
- media

Objectives

This chapter will help you to:

- Explain the purposes and benefits of advertising.
- Describe the kinds of advertising media.
- Contrast the basic types of advertisements.
- Explain different advertising techniques
- Identify the agencies and groups that regulate advertising.
- Evaluate advertisements using consumer strategies.

320   UNIT 5   Management and Consumer Decisions

CHAPTER RESOURCES

Tamara furrowed her brow as she looked at the small, rectangular box in her hand. Tamara had been using the same brand of toothpaste since she had had teeth to brush and was generally satisfied with it. The ads for a new toothpaste, Dazzle, intrigued her, however. They claimed that its formula was "most effective" for preventing cavities as well as promising a "whiter, brighter smile." The model that appeared in the ads certainly had a beautiful smile. Even the jingle was memorable. What's more, the store where Tamara shopped advertised the toothpaste as being on sale, which made the price match her regular brand.

Tamara sighed. Even simple decisions, she thought, weren't always easy to make.

The Purposes

All advertising is designed for one main purpose: to make people want to buy what the advertiser is trying to sell. Businesses spend tens of billions of dollars each year to promote their products and services. In addition, large amounts of money are spent by individuals and groups to influence behavior and public opinion. Included in these groups are candidates for political office and special interest groups promoting various political, social, and charitable causes.

Some advertising is directed from one business to another. Most, however, is meant to appeal directly to the consumer. **Consumers** are *people who buy and use products and services.* Their ability to make decisions about where and when to spend their money gives consumers great power in the marketplace. If too few consumers buy a product, for example, it will be taken off the market. The manufacturer loses money and may even go out of business. With so much at stake, stores and manufacturers compete for the public's dollars by advertising.

Consumers can use advertising to compare prices, features, availability, and location of products and services.

Advertising can be helpful to shoppers because it provides a wealth of information about products and services. Some advertisements inform people of new products or businesses. Some announce improvements in existing products and services. Others give information about sales and special promotions. Often shoppers can use advertisements to compare one product with another.

Advertising Media

Advertisements are communicated through numerous **media,** or *means by which ads are broadcast or displayed.* These media fit into three main types: print, electronic, and direct mail. In addition, advertisers use many other formats that help them capture consumers' attention.

Print Advertising

Advertisers using print media buy space in newspapers and magazines for their ads. Newspapers are especially useful to local advertisers—such as supermarkets and department stores—that want to reach nearby residents.

CHAPTER 32 Advertising   321

Topics on p. 321:
- **Advertising and Its Purpose**
- **Print Advertising**

Checking Comprehension

✓ Why do businesses advertise? *To compete for consumers' dollars and survive financially.*

✓ Define media and name the three main types. *Means by which ads are broadcast or displayed. Print, electronic, and direct mail.*

Activities

■ **Ad Appeal.** Have students write a paragraph describing their favorite ad and explaining its appeal. Ask students to read their paragraph to the class. Discuss what techniques seem most effective, noting any trends among students of the same gender or those having similar interests. *(Critical Thinking)*

■ **The Right Place.** Ask students to suggest the most effective place for print ads for: a sale at an appliance store; a new menu item at a restaurant; the release of a postage stamp honoring American quilting; a discount on student holiday travel; a state senator's political campaign; a new soap.

MORE ABOUT Impact of Advertising

Those who doubt the power of advertising might consider how easily it becomes part of popular culture. Political candidates paraphrase advertising slogans to challenge opponents; comedians make jokes that refer to ad campaigns; preschoolers recite jingles as readily as nursery rhymes. Certain advertisements become a kind of shared experience that brings people together, much like popular music or other forms of entertainment.

Checking Comprehension

✓ Why might sellers place ads in general interest magazines? *For broad exposure to national audience; allows for colorful, glossy ad.*

✓ How is advertising sold in electronic media? *By time.*

✓ Give three examples of direct mail advertising. *Catalogs, circulars, and coupon booklets.*

In Touch With TECHNOLOGY

Have students read "Advertising Goes On-line" and discuss the questions. Ask: What items or businesses might be best suited for advertising on the Internet? Would a pet store do well? A computer support service?

Answers to Thinking ...

1. Advantages may include: can reach millions of people; can directly reach target audience. Disadvantages: few buyers; poor visuals; lack of consumer access; possibly cost, especially for small businesses.
2. Answers will vary. Suggest that local advertising of either form will likely be less affected than national. Direct marketing may be particularly hard hit.

322

Unlike most newspapers, magazines can reach a wide national audience. Some, such as weekly news magazines, reach a general audience. These are ideal for advertising a product of interest to many people, such as life insurance. Other magazines that reach a smaller, specific group of readers—such as teens or retired people, cooks or stamp collectors—appeal to advertisers selling a product of interest to that magazine's readers. In general, magazine ads are more colorful and glossier than ads in newspapers.

In Touch with TECHNOLOGY — Advertising Goes On-Line

With more and more people buying home computers, advertisers have discovered a new medium for reaching customers. Many companies, from computer-software producers to clothing retailers to automobile manufacturers, are advertising on-line.

Computer users can access these ads through commercial on-line services and through direct connections to the Internet, the largest international network of computers.

In electronic malls, shoppers can read advertisements describing food, clothing, and other consumer products. In some cases, full-color images of the products are available. Ordering instructions are also provided.

Companies that advertise their products directly on the Internet may do so through a site, or page, on the World Wide Web. Some sites are "superstores." In these superstores, one product category, such as compact discs or cars and trucks, is advertised. For example, one site presents a catalog offering the largest selection of music albums in the world. It gives the song titles in each album, track lengths, information about the artists, and images of the album covers.

In addition, some companies that have sites on the Web sell advertising space to other businesses on their Web pages. A site that provides information to college students might sell advertising space to companies whose products appeal to young adults.

Thus far, many people are browsing—but not buying—through these on-line ads. Some worry that if they give their credit card number over the computer, it may be misused. Another drawback is that the visual presentation of the product is not as clear and detailed as it would be in a glossy catalog or print ad. Finally, many computer users do not have the high-capacity connections needed to access the visuals in the ads. Nevertheless, companies expect this form of advertising to grow as they work to improve credit card security and the quality of visual transmissions.

Thinking Critically About Technology

1. What are the advantages and disadvantages to advertisers of presenting products on-line?
2. How might on-line advertising affect print and direct mail advertising?

Electronic Advertising

The electronic media consist primarily of radio and television. Advertisers buy airtime instead of space—usually 30 to 60 seconds during or between programs. Some commercials are 30 minutes in length. Called **"infomercials,"** these *programs are usually devoted to selling one product and include product demonstrations and ordering information.* Some cable TV channels feature nothing but "infomercials."

322   **UNIT 5   Management and Consumer Decisions**

MORE ABOUT Electronic Advertising

The television sweeps periods, which happen three times a year, help set advertising rates. "Network premieres" of recent movies and other special programming are aired to draw more viewers, which allows networks to charge more for advertising time.

DID YOU KNOW?

In early 1996, several on-line services created new technology that protects personal information, including credit card numbers, sent through modems by shoppers on the Internet. This came to allay consumer fears about the security of on-line buying.

If there is a place to put an advertisement where it will catch the public eye, advertisers will find it. Have you seen ads on bus stop benches and on barn roofs? Where else have you seen them?

In recent years new technology has brought advertising to another electronic medium—the computer. Thousands of companies advertise their products and services in this way.

Direct Mail Advertising

The third major type of advertising is **direct mail ads**, or *ads delivered directly to consumers' homes*. Some types of ads are catalogs from mail order companies, circulars for local businesses, and coupon booklets.

Other Advertising Formats

Do you see students wearing clothing with the designer's name or symbol on it? Do you drive past giant billboards or a business's neon sign? These are also advertising formats. To promote their message, advertisers may use the phone book yellow pages; store window and point-of-sale displays; signs on buses and taxis and in subways; and even blimps and race cars.

Making Decisions

Mail-Order Clubs

Phil was browsing through Luis's CD collection after the two teens returned from ball practice one Saturday morning. "Put on anything you want," Luis called.

"You've got a lot more than the last time I was here," Phil noted. "Some really good ones, too. When did you get independently wealthy?"

Luis laughed. "I meant to tell you. I joined one of those mail-order music clubs a few months ago. I got ten CDs for a dollar, just for joining. Now all I have to do is order five CDs at regular price every year, plus shipping and handling. Let's see if there are any you want on the latest order form."

Luis found the new order form, and the two teens began scanning the selections. "I don't know," Phil said. "There's not much here that I'm interested in."

Luis nodded, looking disappointed. "They had a better selection in that big ad that I used to join. But this one might be good." He pointed to one title. "And what about these? I might get them."

"I thought you only had to buy five more all year," Phil pointed out. "Maybe you should spend your money on something you really want."

Luis shrugged. "I'm making enough money, and if I really need to, I can put in some more hours at work." He laughed and added, "Or borrow from Mom."

Phil shook his head. "It sounds good," he admitted, "but I have trouble just scraping together my car-insurance payments every three months."

"You should join, Phil," Luis urged his friend. "It doesn't really cost that much, and it's easy."

Phil was thoughtful. Oh, it's easy, he said to himself—maybe too easy. On the other hand, the idea of ten new CDs was extremely tempting.

What Would You Do?

1. Why can clubs like the one Luis joined offer so many CDs at such a low price?
2. What potential problems can occur?
3. Would buying CDs on sale be better?
4. Would you join a similar club? Explain.

CHAPTER 32   Advertising   **323**

Topics on pp. 324-326:
- Advertising Types and Techniques
- Advertising Laws
- Evaluating Ads

Checking Comprehension

✓ Why are testimonials not always reliable? *Sometimes made by paid celebrity, actor portrayed as authority.*

✓ What groups help ensure ads are truthful? *Federal government, advertising associations, consumers.*

✓ When can a sale price be misleading? *When it is discount on inflated original price.*

✓ How does bait-and-switch work? *Advertised item is out of stock or of poor quality; buyer is steered to more expensive model.*

CROSS-CURRICULAR ACTIVITY
Health

Ads for nutritional supplements, such as vitamins and diet aids, are often good examples of misleading advertisements. Have students choose one such ad and research the claims with books, articles, and interviews with health professionals. Have them report their findings to the class.

Types of Advertisements

The first step toward making wise choices among advertisements is to understand the types of advertising and how they work. Advertisements—whether on television, in a magazine, or in other media—are of two general types:

- **Information ads.** An **information ad** is *one that highlights specific information about a product, such as its size, color, price, and special features.* An information ad for a service—a health club, for instance—might mention the classes offered, schedules, and fees. Because information ads supply facts, they are helpful in learning about and comparing products or services.

- **Image ads.** **Image ads** are *ads that attempt to associate a product with a popular image or positive emotion.* These ads might feature glamorous people driving luxurious cars or sports figures sipping soft drinks.

Advertising Techniques

Advertisers use many techniques to grab your attention and influence your purchasing habits. Understanding these techniques can help you separate facts from advertiser's claims. Frequently used techniques include:

- **Attention-getting headlines.** "Best Deal in Town!" "Tremendous Savings!" "Lose 10 Pounds in One Week!"—these kinds of headlines lure you into reading the rest of the ad. They often do this by promising some remarkable benefit.

- **Demonstrations.** Demonstrations might be used in information ads. They aim to show one or more advantages of a product or service, such as the strength of paper towels.

- **Testimonials.** Celebrities and famous athletes are paid to endorse a product, seemingly based on their own experiences. Testimonials are also made by customers who have used and liked a product. In some commercials, a testimonial is made by an expert or an actor who is portrayed as an authority—a doctor, a scientist, or a technical expert.

- **Animation.** This technique encourages consumers to identify a product with a cartoon character. The character may be a figure that children and adults recognize, or it may be one created specifically for a particular ad campaign.

- **Presenters.** Presenters give facts about a product. They may be professional announcers, officials with the company selling the product, or a personality created by advertisers. An example of a created personality is an actor portraying the chef who tells a customer how a certain spice makes all his dishes mouth-watering.

- **Emotional appeals.** An emotional appeal is a technique used in image ads. In an emotional appeal the advertiser promises that you will be happier, smarter, more popular or attractive, or a better athlete if you buy a specific product or service.

- **Slogans and jingles.** Catchy slogans and jingles—slogans set to music—are used to reinforce the image of a product in the listener's memory.

Regulating Advertising

You may have seen movies or read stories about fast-talking salesmen who used to peddle amazing cure-alls from the back of a covered wagon. These concoctions, they promised, could cure ailments, improve health, and renew people's energy. A hundred years ago, advertisers could make such outrageous claims for their products. Buyers had no assurance that the claims were true. Today, advertisers can be challenged legally for making false or misleading representations about their products. They are regulated by the federal government, advertising associations, and consumer action.

Advertising is regulated by several federal government agencies, most notably the Federal Trade Commission (FTC). These agencies can force advertisers to prove their claims or to remove or modify a false or misleading ad.

DID YOU KNOW?

Traveling salesmen once sold "patent medicines," said to cure all kinds of ailments. Some were merely flavored syrups, others primarily alcohol. A few contained poisons. Now a *patent medicine* is a drug that can be sold without prescription.

The United States' advertising industry is the world's biggest, with a yearly outlay of more than $131 billion. Madison Avenue, the New York City address of many ad agencies' main offices, has become a synonym for the industry.

Commercials airing on nationwide television have the potential of reaching 40 or 50 million viewers at one time.

claims it "can make your hair fuller, thicker, and shinier" is not necessarily guaranteed to do so. "A $59 value" may mean only that the advertiser values the item at that price, not that it is worth that amount.

- **Misleading sale pricing.** Some businesses may advertise a sale price that is not the bargain it seems to be simply because they state a higher-than-normal retail price in comparison. When advertisers compare a sale price with a retail price, the retail price should be the prevailing price in the area.
- **Bait and switch.** Beware of a fraudulent sales practice called **bait and switch,** *advertising that is used to draw the buyer into a store under false pretenses.* The buyer soon learns that the low-priced product shown in the ad is out of stock or of poor quality. The salesperson then steers the buyer to a more expensive model.

The advertiser may be required to run a new ad to correct false claims made in earlier ads. Individual states have similar regulations.

The advertising industry also regulates itself. Advertising associations establish ethical codes of standards and guidelines for their members to follow. The National Advertising Review Council asks advertisers to volunteer in preventing deceptive advertising.

In addition, consumers may complain when they believe that an ad is deceptive. They may go to a local consumer assistance agency, to the advertiser, or to the place where the ad appeared.

Making Evaluations

As you read or listen to an ad, try to separate the facts from the fiction designed to influence you. Be skeptical of promises that seem too good to be true. **Figure 32.1** describes some tips for evaluating advertising. Here are some additional warning signals:

- **Unclear wording.** Words such as *can, often, many,* and *value* sometimes point to misleading information. A shampoo that

If you suspect that an ad has given an inflated retail price, compare the price to that of a similar item in other stores.

Activities

■ **It Says Here.** Have pairs choose two ads and analyze them to separate fact from opinion. Have them identify those statements that are factual, those that express an opinion, and those that blur the line between the two (for example, the phrase, "two out of three doctors recommend"). *(Critical Thinking)*

RETEACHING

■ **Analyzing Ads.** Ask students to list 10 ads they see in the next day. Have them analyze each ad. What is the medium? Is it an image ad or an information ad? What advertising techniques are used? Have students compare findings in class.

FAMILY AND COMMUNITY OUTREACH

Invite someone in the advertising field to talk to the class about the process of turning a client's needs into an ad. Consider a person who works for an ad agency or in the advertising department of a newspaper; freelance artists and photographers are other possibilities. Have students prepare questions for the guest in advance.

DID YOU KNOW?

Like advertising, the purpose of public relations is to present clients in a favorable light. Public relations (or PR) experts place ads and encourage news outlets to feature clients in positive stories in their publications or programs. They advise clients on how to deal with the media and with consumers. Increasingly, ad agencies are including public relations among their services. Ask students how advertising techniques might be used to "sell" a person or a company.

Review

- **Chapter Review.** Use the contents of the Chapter Review page to help students review concepts, think critically, and apply their knowledge.
- **Study Guide.** Have students complete the Study Guide for Chapter 32 on p. 105 of the Student Workbook.
- **Junior Ad Execs.** Ask groups to create both an image and an information ad for any product they choose, using the most effective techniques and media. Have groups perform, display, or describe their ads for the class, explaining their choice of media and techniques.

Evaluation

- **Chapter Test.** Use the reproducible chapter test provided in the Teacher's Classroom Resources or create your own test using the *Testmaker Software.*
- **Alternative Assessment.** Have groups develop advertising campaigns for their school, imagining that they are trying to attract new students and teachers. Tell each group to identify the school's best qualities and promote them. Campaigns should use at least three different media. Have groups present their campaigns to the class as an ad agency pitching its ideas to a client.

CLOSE

- **Ad Diary.** Ask students to keep a diary for a few days in which they assess the ads they encounter for technique and informative value. Do they think, overall, that advertising educates or manipulates consumers?

Figure 32.1

SOME STRATEGIES FOR EVALUATING ADVERTISEMENTS

Remember that the main purpose of advertising is to entice you to buy.

"WIN BIG WITH ALL-PRO GRANOLA BARS!" says Manitoba's star quarterback, Chip Tucker.

Put Testimonials in Perspective. Remember that the famous athletes, actors, and musicians who endorse products are well paid for telling you how wonderful the products are. They may sincerely like the products they are advertising, but they may not know about the nutritional content or effectiveness of one product versus another.

Recognize Emotional Appeals. Read and listen carefully. Then ask yourself which parts of the message are facts and which are opinions and emotional appeals. In which category would you place the granola bar's ingredients and nutrients? Where would you put the advertiser's statement that the granola bar makes the athlete play his best? What about the idea that eating a certain brand of granola bar will enable you to become a spectacular athlete?

Look for the Facts. Remember that advertisers talk only about the best features of a product. If a great-tasting granola bar is high in fat and calories, the advertiser isn't going to tell you that.

Focus on Communication Skills

Ask students to think of an ad that they find misleading, unfair, or offensive. Have them write a letter to the product manufacturer or service provider expressing this opinion. Remind students that they must be clear in describing the ad and explaining how or why they find it inappropriate—in effect, "selling" their argument—but respectful and businesslike. Ask students to read their letters in class. Do they make a successful pitch for their position?

Reviewing the Facts

1. What are two main purposes of advertising?
2. In what ways do advertisements help consumers?
3. Compare ads in newspapers with those in magazines.
4. Explain the difference between an image ad and an information ad. Present an example of each.
5. Name five common advertising techniques.
6. Explain the steps an advertiser may have to take if the Federal Trade Commission questions the truthfulness of an ad.

Thinking Critically

1. What techniques might some television advertisers use to encourage children to ask their parents to buy products advertised during children's programming? Give examples.
2. Why do you think that you see more information ads in newspapers than on billboards?
3. Why might advertisers use cartoon characters to promote a product?

Applying Your Knowledge

1. **Distinguishing Fact from Opinion.** List four statements you recall from advertisements. Categorize each statement as either fact or fiction. Give reasons for categorizing each statement as you did.
2. **Evaluating Product Endorsements.** Consider the advertisements you have seen on television in which celebrities endorse products. Consider why each celebrity was chosen for the particular product. Choose one product and explain in writing why you think that the advertiser did or did not make a wise choice.

Making Connections

1. **Government.** Presidential and congressional elections have grown increasingly costly during the last 10 years. Much of the increase has been attributed to television and radio campaign commercials. In addition, several recent election campaigns have been criticized for the personal attacks used in their advertising. If you were given the responsibility for setting rules for election campaign advertising, what rules would you choose?
2. **Civics.** Advertisements or announcements that promote ideas for the common good are called public service announcements (PSA). Write a PSA flyer to promote a school fund-raiser or a community function. How will you create interest in the event?

Building Your Portfolio

Writing Persuasive Advertising
Pick a product that you think would make a good subject for a television commercial. Write the script of the commercial, basing it on others you find persuasive. Explain what advertising techniques were used to capture the attention of consumers and sell your product. Be sure to include descriptions of the person you might choose to star in your commercial. What types of music would you use? What would be the location? List any special effects you would want. Add the script to your portfolio.

CHAPTER 32   Advertising   327

Chapter 33

Chapter Overview

Chapter 33 explains how planning purchases helps consumers get the most value for their money. The chapter compares several ways of shopping and different kinds of stores. Students learn strategies for comparison shopping for quality.

Motivator

■ **They Want You.** Explain that sellers often target teens because they tend to have more disposable income than any other age group. Ask: What are some advantages and disadvantages of so many businesses vying for your dollar? Stress that to withstand such pressure to buy, students need consumer skills.

Objectives

Discuss the chapter objectives on this page. Remind students that the objectives focus on important chapter concepts.

Vocabulary

Note that the term *seconds* has several meanings in different contexts. Ask students for some of these. Then tell them the definition in this chapter: slightly flawed or out-of-production items.

Chapter 33

Consumer Skills

Terms to Learn

- hidden costs
- impulse buying
- seconds
- Underwriter's Laboratory (UL)
- warranty

Objectives

This chapter will help you to:

- Identify **the resources you can use to help plan your purchases.**
- Explain **ways to avoid impulse buying.**
- Evaluate **store sales.**
- Summarize **the different types of stores and other places to shop.**
- Develop **comparison-shopping strategies.**

CHAPTER RESOURCES

Student Workbook

Study Guide, pp. 109-110

Activity, *Purchasing Power*, pp. 111-112

Teacher's Classroom Resources

Lesson Plan, p. 37

Cooperative Learning, *Starting a Student Store*, pp. 37-38

Extension #54, *What Is a Warranty?* p. 60

Extension #55, *Comparison Shopping*, p. 61

Life Skills, *The Most for Your Money*, pp. 57-58

Transparency 35, *Comparison Shopping*

Chapter 33 Test, pp. 71-72

Performance Assessment, *A Word About Math Skills*, pp. 60-61

Reteaching, *Improving Shopping Skills*, p. 39

See Also

ABCNews InterActive™ Videodisc

Warren looked at all the sleeping bags, but he wasn't sure what to buy. He was about to go on his first camping trip with a group of friends. Warren had decided that he needed a sleeping bag. There were so many, however, he didn't know what to do. "What are the differences?" he asked the salesclerk.

"We have nylon and cotton, heavy-duty and lightweight, waterproofed and insulated," the clerk replied.

This response only raised more questions. Was there any advantage to nylon bags over cotton? Did Warren need waterproofing and insulation? He described his situation. "I only need it for a few nights—at least for now. Actually, these seem kind of expensive. I'm not sure I want to spend that much on something I probably won't use very often."

When the clerk stepped away for a minute, a man looking at camping gear nearby said, "I couldn't help hearing that you need a sleeping bag. Have you tried looking through the want ads? If you don't mind buying a used one, you can find one for much less."

"Thanks," Warren said. "I might try that."

Planning Purchases

Like Warren, consumers are bombarded daily with an almost unlimited number of goods and services. Consumers who plan their purchases usually get good value for their money. They are also likely to be satisfied with their purchases.

You need not plan every purchase you make. For instance, if you need a pen, you can pick one up at the store the next time you go. However, for major purchases that are expensive and that you expect to keep for a long time, it's wise to plan ahead.

By planning your purchases, you will be happier with the choices you make.

Using Consumer Resources

Wise consumers use their resources to learn about a product before buying. What resources do you have?

One way to gather information is to talk to friends and family members who have used any of the products and services that interest you. For such services as tailoring, you might ask to see a sample of the work.

You can also do some research in consumer magazines, such as *Consumer Reports* and *Consumer Research*. These periodicals test, evaluate, and rate a wide range of products and services. They offer detailed, objective reviews. The *Consumer Index,* available in most libraries, lists which products and services have been reviewed in consumer magazines. In addition, special interest magazines, such as photography and computer publications, evaluate products for their readers.

No matter how much research you do, the final decision is usually up to you. To make the best decision, use your own skills in talking to store clerks, examining merchandise, and

Topics on p. 329:
- **The Importance of Planning**
- **Resources for Planning**

Checking Comprehension

✓ When should you make a plan for a purchase? *Especially for expensive item you expect to keep a long time.*

✓ How can consumer magazines help you plan purchases? *Test, rate, and review wide range of products and services.*

Activities

■ **Testing, Testing.** Have pairs choose one article from a consumer magazine that describes a test or comparison of products. Have them summarize the article for the class, explaining the testing methods or points of comparison. Have pairs note how—or if—the assessment is fair and objective. Ask the class what else they would like to know about the product. *(Critical Thinking)*

ENRICHMENT

■ **What Should Warren Do?** Have students discuss Warren's situation. What would they do and why?

Focus on Consumer Skills

The telephone is a most accessible consumer resource, saving other resources of time, energy, and gasoline. By comparison shopping over the phone, you can learn not only which store has the best price on the product you want to buy, but you may also connect with a helpful sales associate. By getting the associate's name and asking for that person when visiting the store, you can often get personal attention—another benefit of planning purchases.

Checking Comprehension

✓ How do stores tempt shoppers to buy on impulse? *Place items in noticeable locations, at eye level; make special offers; give product samples and demonstrations.*

✓ Give four tips for shopping sales wisely. *Be sure you really need item; compare sale price to other stores' regular price; check return policy; ask about replacement parts.*

✓ How does a specialty store differ from a department store? *Specialty store sells only a certain kind of merchandise, usually at higher price. Department store offers wide selection of many types of goods.*

FAMILY AND COMMUNITY OUTREACH

Have groups prepare a shopper's guide for consumers in their community. Have each group research one type of store, recording the names, locations, and any special information about the types of products offered. Students might include additional information, such as business hours and whether the store is accessible to those with disabilities. Have groups edit and compile their findings into a booklet.

330

reading labels. This way, you can find out as much as possible about a product. Don't be afraid to ask questions. Keep in mind that, since money is a limited resource, you'll want to get the best value for your dollar.

Avoiding Impulse Buying

Stores intentionally display goods to tempt you toward **impulse buying**—*purchasing something that you did not intend to buy*. They place items in noticeable locations, such as checkout lanes and center aisles—and at eye level. They make enticing offers, such as "Buy one, get one free." Stores may even offer samples and feature demonstrations to attract your interest.

How can you defend against impulse buying? A shopping trip Leo took offers some clues. He decided to get some things he needed at the mall during his lunch hour. Before leaving, Leo took some practical steps. First, he made a list of exactly what he needed. He estimated how much money the items would cost and took only a little more than that with him. He even ate lunch before going, in order to avoid the temptation of the mall's eateries.

As he shopped, Leo noticed a tie that looked good but was more expensive than the one he planned to purchase. Leo knew that sometimes he was tempted to buy something to reward himself for some reason or to make himself feel good on a "down" day. That kind of purchase would have been easy to justify. Yet Leo passed it by. He was determined not to let that happen this time.

Before leaving the mall, Leo noticed a jacket he liked. He hadn't planned to buy one, but it did look like a good buy. Instead of buying it, however, Leo asked the sales associate to hold the item for a day so that he could think about it.

Leo's efforts helped him get through the shopping trip without regrets. The defenses he used can be followed by anyone to avoid the trap of impulse buying.

Getting Value at Sales

Stores have sales to attract customers and clear out merchandise to make room for new inventory. The managers hope that while you're in the store, you will buy regular-priced items as well. Sales often occur at specific times, or they are timed to coincide with certain events throughout the year. These sales include end-of-season sales, back-to-school sales, and special promotions, such as grand openings.

Just because an item is on sale doesn't mean that it's a bargain. Consider the following ideas before buying at a sale:

- Be sure that you really need and can use the item. For instance, you may want to buy a jacket that fits poorly because it costs only $20. Chances are, you won't wear it once you get it home. You could have put the $20 toward a jacket you would wear often.
- Compare sale prices. One store's "sale" price may be higher than another store's regular price. The same holds true for coupons, rebates, and other special offers.
- Find out whether you can return the item you want to buy. Some items are sold "as is," or they are part of a final sale, with no returns allowed.
- If the model has been discontinued, ask if replacement parts are still available.

Where to Buy

As a senior citizen, Edith Anderson tells her 14-year-old granddaughter Lisanne, "In the town where I grew up, we didn't even have a department store." For Lisanne, this idea is startling. Like other people today, Lisanne can choose from many ways to shop—at department stores and factory-outlet malls and even through mail-order catalogs and the television set.

MORE ABOUT Outlet Shopping

The growing popularity of factory outlets has an unfortunate side effect: stores with no connection to a manufacturer lease space in outlet malls. Shoppers must check—not assume—that a store truly offers merchandise from factories at discounted prices.

DID YOU KNOW?

Sometimes an item sold as irregular or "as is" has only cosmetic defects. The product's appearance may suffer, but not its performance. It may carry the same warranty as a regularly priced item.

Making Decisions

Risky Business

"This year," Rolanda told her younger sister Kim, *"Mom's birthday should be special. How about a television set for her room?"*

"Perfect!" Kim agreed. Excited, the two decided on the features they wanted and how much they could spend. After checking the ads, however, they realized how expensive the televisions were.

A few days later, Rolanda noticed a *"Going Out of Business Sale"* sign in the window of an appliance store. She had never been in the store before, and her family had never purchased anything there.

Later, as they entered the store, the sisters saw signs proclaiming *"Everything Must Go"* and *"50-75% Off All Merchandise."* They squeezed through cluttered aisles to the television display. There they found an affordable but unfamiliar model. The set was marked 50 percent off.

A salesclerk told Kim and Rolanda that the set was a floor model—the last the store had in stock. The teens examined the set carefully. They turned it on, testing the picture, sound, and controls.

"This is fine," Rolanda said. *"Just that little nick on the side that we can stain over."*

Kim was less convinced. *"What if it doesn't work as well later? Will Mom think we spent too much?"*

"But we're not spending that much," Rolanda pointed out. *"If she doesn't like it, maybe we can bring it back."*

Kim shook her head. *"Rolanda, the store is going out of business. Will this place even be here if we bring it back?"*

What Would You Do?

1. What options do Kim and Rolanda have?
2. What might happen if they purchase the set at the store that is closing?
3. What do you think the sisters should do?

Stores and Outlets

For many people, shopping means going to a store. This option offers several advantages. You can see and examine numerous brands of the product you're interested in before buying. You can even get advice from knowledgeable salespeople. Some stores provide such additional services as gift wrapping and home delivery. Choosing the right type of store can help you make the purchase that best suits your needs:

- **Specialty stores.** A specialty store sells only a certain kind of merchandise, such as craft supplies, shoes, or clothing and accessories. It carries a wide selection of those products, but it often charges higher prices than other kinds of stores.
- **Department stores.** A department store offers shoppers a wide selection of goods, often in different price ranges, under one roof. Some department stores issue their own credit cards and provide additional customer services.
- **Discount stores.** A discount store carries nationally advertised brands at reduced prices. This kind of store also sells lines of clothing and shoes at a lower price— though often of lesser quality—than are found in department stores.
- **Factory outlets.** At factory outlets, manufacturers sell their products directly to shoppers usually at prices lower than those charged by department stores. Some items may be **seconds,** which are *items that are slightly imperfect or out of production.*
- **Warehouse clubs.** Warehouse clubs charge lower prices than do supermarkets or department stores because they buy in bulk and furnish their stores sparsely. Customers pay a membership fee, which also helps offset the store's costs. Club stores may carry a variety of goods, from bulk groceries to clothing to home furnishings.

Activities

■ **What's Going On?** Ask students why stores do the following: periodically change the location of items; place items in aisles for sale; create aisles that lead you in different directions rather than straight through the store.

RETEACHING

■ **Stores at a Glance.** Have groups make charts with the headings: Type of Store; Items Sold; Advantages; and Disadvantages. Have them complete their charts with information from p. 331.

Making Decisions

Have students read "Risky Business" and discuss the questions. Ask: What kinds of items might be good buys at clearance or going-out-of-business sales? What items should shoppers beware of buying?

Answers to What...

1. Answers may include: buy set; buy other gift; buy small gift now, continue saving money for more reputable set.
2. If problem occurs with set, they will have no recourse from store; may be able to use warranty.
3. Answers will vary. Suggest that the television is an expensive item and seems to be a risky purchase; since teens want to please mother, they should consider what she would want them to do; find other birthday treat she would appreciate.

Topics on pp. 332-333:
- Mail-Order Shopping
- Other Shopping Methods

Checking Comprehension

✓ How does mail-order purchasing work? *People order goods from catalog, by either mail or phone; goods are shipped directly to them.*

✓ What is electronic shopping? *Ordering goods shown on home-shopping channels on cable TV or on-line on computer.*

✓ What should you remember when buying at flea markets or auctions? *You probably can't return the merchandise.*

STRATEGIES THAT WORK

Have students read "Smart Mail-Order Shopping." Ask volunteers to share their experiences with buying items through catalogs. Would they recommend shopping by mail to others?

Answers to Think . . .

1. Answers may include: elderly people; those with disabilities; those who can't get to stores during day.
2. Answers may include: talk to others who have used catalog; learn about company from consumer magazine or BBB.
3. Answers may include: they can examine item before buying; knowledgeable sales staff can answer questions.

Mail-Order Companies

Although going to a store remains the most popular way to shop, millions of people now buy from mail-order companies. In addition, some department and specialty stores send customers catalogs. Most mail-order businesses, however, rely solely on catalog sales for their income.

Mail-order catalogs are as varied as stores. Some feature a particular type of item, such as clothing or electronics. Others offer a wider variety of goods. People select the items they want, then either phone or mail in their order. In addition to the cost of the item, customers usually pay shipping and handling fees and sometimes a sales tax. Customers can usually return an item if they are dissatisfied. Generally, though, they must pay to ship the item back.

STRATEGIES That Work

Smart Mail-Order Shopping

Shopping from catalogs offers certain advantages. Catalogs often have a wider variety of goods, and you can find what you want without taking the time to go out and shop. With many catalogs you can order by phone any time of day. Delivery can be made right to your home or workplace.

You have to consider the disadvantages too. For example, items may be out of stock or may become lost during shipment. With some items, such as very large or insured items, you may have to be home to accept delivery.

To get the best value for your money when you shop by mail, follow these tips:

- Buy only from companies with whom you have done business or whose reputation you know.
- See whether the company offers toll-free 800 numbers for phoning in orders and calling customer service. If not, consider the charge for the call when you calculate the price of the item.
- Be sure to include sales tax and shipping and handling fees as you add up the cost. These fees can vary widely from catalog to catalog.
- Find out the company's policy on returning items. Can you return items for refund or exchange? Do you have to pay return-shipment charges? How long do you have to decide whether you want to keep an item?
- If you mail your order, include all requested information. This will help prevent delays. Provide your phone number on the order form.
- Pay by check, money order, or credit card. Never send cash through the mail.
- Ask how packages are shipped. If the item is lost while being shipped, will the company send you a replacement at no extra charge? Will you be able to cancel your order?
- Keep a record of your order—what you ordered, when, the order number, and the amount you paid.

Making the Strategy Work

Think . . .

1. Which people do you think are most likely to shop from catalogs?
2. If you wanted to buy from a catalog you weren't familiar with, what could you do to limit your risk?
3. Why do you think some people prefer to shop at stores rather than from catalogs?

Try. . .

Look through a catalog that you, a friend, or a relative has received. Note the company's pricing, shipping, and return policies. Using the tips given here, list any information not included in the catalog that you feel is important. Decide whether you would order from the company.

332 UNIT 5 *Management and Consumer Decisions*

MORE ABOUT Electronic Shopping

Infomercials, or informercials, are a growing segment of electronic selling. Infomercials often run early in the morning or late at night, when air time is less expensive. These programs, sometimes hosted by celebrities, resemble cooking shows or talk shows until it becomes clear that the topic is a product or service. Infomercials often appeal to the wish for instant or effortless fame, looks, or success. As with any form of selling, consumers must beware of such claims.

What are the advantages and disadvantages of buying used merchandise? What about antiques?

Electronic Shopping

In recent years, cable television has offered a new type of selling: home-shopping channels. These channels broadcast 24 hours a day, with a presenter telling viewers about many types of products—everything from collectible dolls to furniture. Customers order products by calling a toll-free number. They pay by credit card or by check. As with mail-order catalog companies, customers can return items they don't want.

As you read in Chapter 32, companies are presenting their goods on-line to computer users. However, at this time, more people are looking than buying.

Direct Sales

Direct sales, represented by the door-to-door salesperson, bring merchandise to your doorstep. At one time, cosmetics, encyclopedias, magazine subscriptions, vacuum cleaners, and other products were commonly sold this way. In recent years, however, direct sales have decreased. This is due in part to mail-order and electronic shopping options, which allow people to shop at home more quickly and conveniently.

Companies that use direct sales often set up appointments with customers rather than knock on doors randomly. Alternately, individuals who have home-based businesses bring such products as carpet and fabric to the buyer's home and show the samples right where the products will be used.

Other Shopping Alternatives

People can often find bargains at yard and garage sales. There, people sell what they no longer need or want for low prices. Bargaining between buyer and seller may reduce prices further. Some other sources of bargains are flea markets and swap meets—places where people rent tables to sell new or used goods at low prices. Used goods are also sold at auction, where an item goes to the highest bidder. Another good source of previously owned goods—from fine china to old cars—is the classified ad section of newspaper and magazines.

In each of these shopping places, you should purchase carefully. You will probably not be able to return items later.

Comparison Shopping

Suppose that you are shopping for a denim jacket. You find one you really like, but the price is higher than you're willing to pay. Do

Activities

■ **Call Now!** Have students watch a home-shopping show for half an hour and take notes to answer these questions: What kinds of items are advertised? What can you tell about the quality of these items? How do the hosts try to induce viewers to buy? Have students compare and offer conclusions from their notes. *(Observation)*

■ **Sounds Good.** Have students find ads for sales, auctions, and individual items in a newspaper classified section. What details do sellers include to attract customers? Have students write an ad to sell one of their own possessions. Challenge students to condense their ads into a limited number of words or lines, as those in newspapers. *(Communication)*

MULTICULTURAL *Perspectives*

Encourage students to visit an ethnic marketplace, festival, or street fair. Ask them to note the types of items sold, the prices, and whether any bargaining is expected. Students who have experienced such events as part of their own culture might make a presentation to the class with pictures and examples of the items commonly sold. They might invite a person involved in these events to speak to the class.

REAL-LIFE APPLICATION

Read this to students: *Browsing at a flea market, Edgar noticed a framed, autographed baseball card of his favorite player. It was priced at $20; Edgar believed it was worth at least five times that. The seller said the man who sold her the card claimed it was authentic.* Ask: Do you think the card is genuine? (Caution students that many items like these are fakes.) What factors besides monetary value are involved in Edgar's interest in the card? Discuss the role of emotions in buying items, especially when they seem like a "steal."

Topic on pp. 334-336:

- **Comparing for Quality**

Checking Comprehension

✓ How can you check for performance before buying an item? *Ask for demonstration; try on apparel.*

✓ What hidden cost might be in a store's exchange policy? *Repair or replacement costs if you cannot exchange defective item.*

✓ What should a warranty tell you? *Whom to contact about problems; exactly what it covers; its length; how to use it; your responsibilities; length of time manufacturer has to fix problem.*

SPECIAL NEEDS
Strategies

Inefficient Readers. Refer students to Fig. 33.1. Explain that visuals often reinforce the text and provide another way to understand it. Here, the questions in the diagram show one way of using the text information on pp. 334-335. Have students demonstrate their understanding by asking questions about the visual that are answered in the text. For example: How can you learn how well the hair dryer works? *Ask for demonstration.*

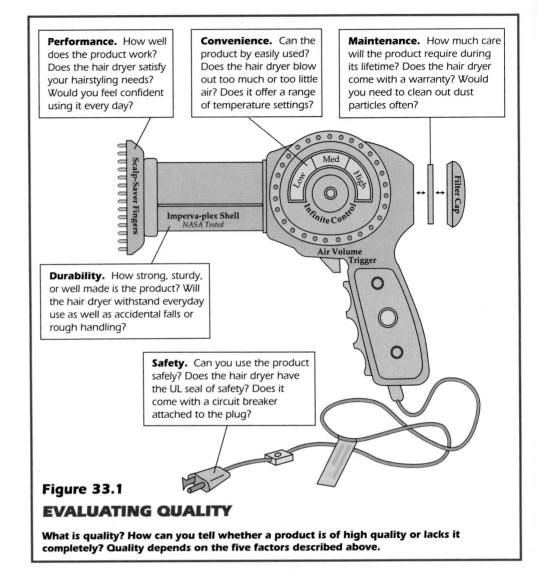

Performance. How well does the product work? Does the hair dryer satisfy your hairstyling needs? Would you feel confident using it every day?

Convenience. Can the product by easily used? Does the hair dryer blow out too much or too little air? Does it offer a range of temperature settings?

Maintenance. How much care will the product require during its lifetime? Does the hair dryer come with a warranty? Would you need to clean out dust particles often?

Durability. How strong, sturdy, or well made is the product? Will the hair dryer withstand everyday use as well as accidental falls or rough handling?

Safety. Can you use the product safely? Does the hair dryer have the UL seal of safety? Does it come with a circuit breaker attached to the plug?

Figure 33.1
EVALUATING QUALITY

What is quality? How can you tell whether a product is of high quality or lacks it completely? Quality depends on the five factors described above.

you buy the jacket anyway? Do you settle for a less expensive, perhaps less attractive jacket? You have another option. You can comparison shop—comparing products for quality, price, and warranties before buying them. Comparison shopping helps you get the best value for your money. You are also likely to be more satisfied with your purchase.

Quality

To check for quality, look at performance, convenience, maintenance, durability, and safety (**Figure 33.1**).

Performance

One way to test performance is to ask for a demonstration in the store. This is appropri-

Focus on Listening Skills

Buying from professional salespeople or private sellers often means paying attention to what claims are *not* made. Have students portray someone trying to sell an item of dubious quality, such as a car that runs poorly or a reputed antique that may not be one. Have them write statements that avoid or gloss over the item's defect without actually lying about it. As students share their statements, ask the class to identify the incomplete facts or ambiguities.

ate for such merchandise as cameras, computers, musical instruments, and stereo equipment. Clothing and shoes can be tested by trying them on and examining the work.

Convenience, Maintenance, and Durability

You can compare the durability and amount of care items require by looking at care labels and service manuals. Labels on clothing sold in the United States tell what fibers the garment contains and how it should be cleaned.

Appliances should come with service manuals. These booklets describe the kind of care the item requires. They also indicate the location of repair centers. In case of a problem, having a repair center nearby may be more convenient and less expensive than shipping the item for service. If you're buying something that needs assembly, be sure that instructions are included. You might ask whether the item can be assembled at the store.

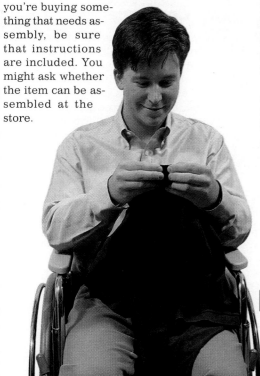

Consider the cost and care needs of purchases before you buy.

Safety

One way to compare products for safety is to see whether they have the Underwriter's Laboratory seal. The **Underwriter's Laboratory (UL)** is an agency that tests electrical products for safety. On clothing and furniture, for example, check the labels to see whether they are made of flame-retardant or flame-resistant fabrics. You can also check for fibers you may be allergic to.

Price

How do you decide what you're willing to spend on a product? It's helpful to remember that the lowest-priced item is not necessarily the best buy. On the other hand, a higher price doesn't automatically translate as better quality.

To help determine how much a particular product is worth to you, think about which features you must have and which are less important. If you know that you need only two temperature settings on a hair dryer, you may not need to look at models offering three or four settings.

Besides the actual price of the item, consider **hidden costs**—*expenses of time, energy, and money not included in the purchase price.* Hidden costs include:

- **Travel.** Consider the time and cost of traveling to make a purchase. Paying a low price at a discount store may not be worthwhile if you have to travel far to get there. On the other hand, you may have to pay more for a product or service if the store is within walking distance of your home.

Activities

■ **Warranty Watch.** Have students bring in a warranty from an item at home and locate each of the sections described in the text on p. 336. *(Observation)*

ENRICHMENT

■ **Rave Reviews?** Ask students to think of a major purchase they or their family would like to make. Have them use the *Consumer Index* to try to locate issues of consumer magazines that rate models of that item. (Consumers Union, publisher of *Consumer Reports,* also publishes a yearly compilation of its recommendations.) After reading the reviews, have students tell which model they would buy and why.

FAMILY AND COMMUNITY OUTREACH

Have students help their families develop a filing system for warranties, owner's manuals, and receipts from major purchases. If families use such a system already, ask students to try to think of improvements.

DID YOU KNOW?

If merchandise being returned is lost en route, the consumer must either pay for the lost item or provide proof that it was mailed, such as a post office, Federal Express, or UPS receipt.

MORE ABOUT Product Testing

The Good Housekeeping Seal of Approval is another sign of product quality. *Good Housekeeping* magazine has a laboratory that checks the claims of various products; those that pass the test can show the label.

Review

■ **Chapter Review.** Use the contents of the Chapter Review page to help students review concepts, think critically, and apply their knowledge.

■ **Study Guide.** Have students complete the Study Guide for Chapter 33 on p. 109 of the Student Workbook.

■ **Don't Leave Home.** Have students make a list of the most important questions to ask themselves as they make purchases, based on the information in this chapter. Suggest they copy their lists onto small pieces of poster board for their wallets—next to their money and credit cards.

Evaluation

■ **Chapter Test.** Use the reproducible chapter test provided in the Teacher's Classroom Resources or create your own test using the *Testmaker Software*.

■ **Alternative Assessment.** Have groups choose an item to buy and use chapter information to make a wise, imaginary purchase. Have them give a written or oral report explaining how they used consumer resources; whether they took advantage of sales; from what type of store or other source they "bought" the item; and how they determined its quality.

■ **If I Knew Then.** Ask students to recall a significant purchase they made before reading this chapter. Have them assess that purchase in light of what they have learned, explaining whether they would do anything differently in planning or making the purchase.

- **Maintenance.** When you're buying an item that needs periodic maintenance, you should find out the cost of this care beforehand. A reasonably priced wool sweater may seem like a real bargain, for example, until you figure in dry cleaning costs. Likewise, after saving up for the car you've always wanted, you may discover that you can't afford replacement parts.
- **Extras.** Consider the price of such items as batteries and accessories when figuring costs.
- **Exchanges.** Find out before you buy whether you can exchange a defective item. If you don't, you may end up having to repair or replace the item at your own expense.

Warranties

Many products, especially appliances and electronic equipment, come with a written statement of guarantee called a **warranty.** This is *the manufacturer's or retailer's promise to repair or replace a defective product, or to refund the customer's money.* To protect yourself, check that the warranty includes:

- The name and address of the company and the person to contact with questions or for repairs.
- A precise account of what is covered. For example, will the manufacturer pay for all parts and labor? Are certain types of repairs excluded?
- The length of the warranty.
- Specific procedures to follow, such as how to wrap and ship the product and who will pay the return-freight charges.

- Any requirements the purchaser must meet.
- The length of time the manufacturer has in which to remedy the problem.

A limited warranty promises replacement or repair of certain parts within a specified time. Usually, labor costs are not covered. Under a full warranty, the product is replaced or repaired within a reasonable time, normally set by federal guidelines. A consumer may also choose to purchase an extended warranty, which provides protection after the manufacturer's warranty expires. Extended warranties are usually offered by sellers of large appliances. Whatever options are available, it is the consumer's responsibility to determine whether the warranty meets his or her particular needs.

The Careful Consumer

A marketplace that offers so many types of so many items presents consumers with great advantages—and great challenges. If you plan and compare before you buy, you have a very good chance of purchasing a quality product or service that meets your needs and fits your budget.

Carefully review the warranties of products you purchase. Keep them in a safe place along with sales receipts.

Focus on Critical Thinking Skills

On the board, write the quotations below. Ask students how each relates to the content of this chapter.

"Penny-wise and pound-foolish."

"Bargain: something you can't use at a price you can't resist." (Franklin P. Jones)

"A fool knows the cost of everything and the value of nothing."

"When reason rules, money is a blessing." (Publilius Syrus)

Review

Reviewing the Facts

1. What are the main resources consumers use to make wise choices?
2. How can you avoid buying on impulse?
3. Name two reasons why stores have sales.
4. At which types of stores would you be most likely to find low prices?
5. What are the five factors you should check when determining the quality of a product?
6. What are three ways you can gather information when you are comparison shopping?

Thinking Critically

1. Discuss the meaning of the expression "You get what you pay for." Do you agree with the statement? Give reasons for your answer.
2. When may it not be appropriate or desirable to comparison shop?

Applying Your Knowledge

1. **Comparing Shopping Methods.** Create a chart showing the advantages and disadvantages of shopping in stores and shopping from home through catalogs and television.
2. **Negotiating.** At swap meets and yard sales, buyers often bargain for a lower price with sellers. Create a script in which you negotiate with a seller to get a guitar at a price lower than is listed on the tag.
3. **Developing a Questionnaire.** Devise a ten-item questionnaire you could use to get information from a salesperson about an appliance you might buy.

Making Connections

1. **Language Arts.** Choose an article of clothing or an appliance that you own. Write a consumer magazine article in which you evaluate the appliance's features and rate it. Be sure to keep your article unbiased and offer solid facts to back up your rating.
2. **Math.** Compare the savings on these two items: a VCR that regularly costs $189.95 and is being sold at a 25 percent discount and one that has a regular price of $250.00 and is now 35 percent less.

Building Your Portfolio

Selecting a Product
Choose a product you would like to buy. Prepare a checklist of the features you'd like the product to have. Then select three or four brands of the product, and check off on your list which features each product has. Include in your checklist a column for price. Explain in writing which brand you would buy. Add your checklist and explanation to your portfolio.

CHAPTER 33   Consumer Skills   337

Chapter Overview

Chapter 34 discusses consumer rights and responsibilities. Students learn what they may expect from sellers and manufacturers, what recourse they have if they feel they've been treated unfairly, and what they are obliged to do—and avoid doing—as conscientious consumers.

Motivator

■ **Page-Turner.** Tell students you are researching a book to be called *Consumer Nightmare*. Ask them to contribute stories of their worst shopping experience. After several stories, tell the class this chapter can help them avoid—or handle effectively—such problems in the future.

Objectives

Discuss the chapter objectives on this page. Remind students that the objectives focus on important chapter concepts.

Vocabulary

The word *vandalism* comes from the Vandals, a Germanic tribe that looted Rome in A.D. 455. A modern vandal willfully destroys property.

Chapter 34
Consumer Rights and Responsibilities

- Better Business Bureau (BBB)
- boycott
- chamber of commerce
- consumer action panels (CAPs)
- recall
- redress
- return policy
- shoplifting
- small-claims court
- vandalism

Objectives

This chapter will help you to:

- Describe **the six rights of consumers.**
- Explain **three ways to make a complaint.**
- Describe **sources of help for consumers with complaints.**
- Analyze **consumer actions to determine whether they are considerate and honest.**
- Explain **consumers' responsibility to use products safely.**

CHAPTER RESOURCES

Student Workbook
Study Guide, pp. 113-114
Activity, *Caveat Emptor*, pp. 115-116

Teacher's Classroom Resources
Lesson Plan, p. 38
Cooperative Learning, *Consumer Responsibilities*, pp. 39-40

Extension #56, *Writing a Letter of Complaint*, p. 62
Life Skills, *Consumer Hot Line*, pp. 59-60
Personal Development, *Writing a Letter of Complaint*, pp. 47-48
Transparency 36, *Shoplifting Hurts Everyone!*

Chapter 34 Test, pp. 73-74
Performance Assessment, *Resolving Consumer Problems*, pp. 62-63
Reteaching, *Rights and Responsibilities*, p. 40

See Also:
ABCNews InterActive™Videodiscs

Gabriel hung up the telephone in disgust and frowned at the figures he'd written down. He knocked on the door of his mother's home office.

"I was talking to Millie Bryce at the insurance company," he said. "She told me that my car insurance premium would be $50 higher if I took out my own policy than if we kept my car on yours—just because I'm 18. Does that sound right?"

His mother turned from her computer with a slight smile. "Don't take it personally. Insurance companies can set different rates for different groups. Statistically, teens have more automobile accidents than people my age. The company has a right to protect itself."

"Yes, but *I* haven't had any accidents. It doesn't seem fair."

"What you can do," his mother suggested, "is call another company and compare rates. There's no law that says you have to use my insurance agent."

Consumer Rights

Gabriel's mother is right. In fact, there *are* laws that protect Gabriel's right to choose another agent. There are also laws requiring those agents—like all businesses—to act responsibly and honestly toward their customers.

Spurred by public-interest groups, consumer advocates, and businesses, federal and state governments have enacted laws to protect consumers. These wide-ranging laws regulate the sale of many goods and services, from food and cars to health insurance and home mortgages.

The various laws that protect consumers are based on six basic consumer rights. They are:

- **The right to safety.** Consumers should not face undue risk of being harmed by a product. For instance, the Con-

sumer Product Safety Act allows the government to ban the sale of products considered unsafe.

- **The right to be informed.** Businesses must give consumers the facts about goods and services. The Truth-in-Lending Act, for example, requires that lenders state clearly how much they charge for credit. Consumers are also protected from false and misleading advertising.

- **The right to choose.** Federal and state laws forbid businesses from taking actions that limit competition. These laws help give Gabriel the chance to find lower auto insurance rates.

- **The right to redress.** Redress is the *right to have a wrong corrected*. For example, consumers can receive refunds or replacements for products that don't work properly. They can take legal action against a business that has treated them unfairly.

Have you ever opened a product package only to find certain parts missing? As a consumer, you have the right to have the problem corrected.

CHAPTER 34   Consumer Rights and Responsibilities   339

MORE ABOUT the Right to Be Heard

Before voting on a consumer-oriented bill, legislators offer a period of public comment. During this time, consumers may present their positions and urge lawmakers on how to vote.

TEACH

Topic on p. 339:
- **Consumer Rights**

Checking Comprehension

✓ What is the right to be informed? *Businesses must give consumers facts about goods and services.*

✓ How can consumers use the right to redress? *Receive refund or replacement for defective product; take legal action against unfair business.*

Activity

■ **Use 'Em Or.** For each consumer right, have students write or describe a brief scenario showing what happens to a character who should have exercised that right but did not. (*Creativity*)

FAMILY AND COMMUNITY OUTREACH

Invite a representative from the district office of the Federal Trade Commission or the state attorney general's office to speak about what the agency does to protect consumers. Have students prepare questions for the guest.

Topic on pp. 340-341:

• Making a Complaint

Checking Comprehension

✓ Whom should you first contact when making a complaint? *Salesperson, manager, someone in customer service.*

✓ Why should you act promptly when making a complaint? *Lends credibility to claim; avoids chance that item will be unavailable.*

✓ Why is it better to leave a store than accept an unsatisfactory solution to a problem? *You have other options for getting satisfaction.*

CROSS-CURRICULAR ACTIVITY
Social Studies

Have students research and write a short report about one aspect of the consumer movement in the United States, such as: the Food and Drug Administration; Ralph Nader; Sinclair Lewis' *The Jungle;* the Consumer Product Safety Commission; and the Consumer Federation of America.

• **The right to consumer education.** Consumers have a right to learn about consumer issues. Many states have laws requiring that schools teach basic consumer skills.

• **The right to be heard.** Consumers can speak out when they aren't satisfied. They can campaign or lobby to help shape consumer laws and regulations.

The key to protecting consumer rights is exercising them responsibly. As you continue reading, you will learn ways to use your power as a consumer wisely.

Handling Problems

"It was not one of my better shopping trips," Robbie recalled. "The salespeople were rude. They didn't give me the sale price, and the toaster I bought didn't even work. I was tempted to bring two pieces of burned toast when I returned it."

Robbie's experience illustrates some of the mishaps that can occur in the marketplace. Fortunately, Robbie's problems, like most, can be resolved. Businesses want satisfied customers. A businessperson who fears losing you as a future customer will work to settle a complaint to your satisfaction.

Figure 34.1

THE PROCESS OF MAKING A COMPLAINT

1. See if the problem is covered in the warranty. If it tells you to return the item to the manufacturer, follow the directions for doing so. If you must return the item to the store, or if you are unsure whether the problem is covered, follow the next four steps.

2. Write down exactly what is wrong with the product. Use these notes to guide you as you describe the problem in person.

Focus on Critical Thinking Skills

Tell students that until this century, few laws protected consumers from irresponsible and greedy sellers. The last 30 years, however, have seen a proliferation of laws and government and private agencies that protect consumer rights. Ask: What do you think caused this change? Do you think, as many do, that society has gone to the other extreme? What guidelines might be used to distinguish consumers' responsibilities from seller's?

Making Complaints

When you have a consumer complaint, your first step is deciding whom to contact. You might begin by approaching the original salesperson. If the complaint is about that person, or if you can't get any results that way, you may need to talk to the manager. You might see someone in a customer service department. This department is staffed by employees trained to handle consumer complaints.

How you go about making a complaint can affect the results. Regardless of whether you complain in person, by phone, or by letter, you are likely to be more satisfied if you follow the four rules listed here.

- Act as soon as you recognize a problem. Quick action lends credibility to your claim. Also, by waiting, you risk that the model you bought will be sold out, back ordered, or discontinued.
- Have a specific goal in mind; know in advance what will satisfy you. Do you want to have the item replaced or repaired? Do you want a refund, or do you want a credit toward another purchase?
- When you buy a product, always keep your sales receipt and warranty. You may need them if a problem arises.
- Keep the product's original packaging at least as long as the warranty period. You might need it for shipping the product back.

3. Return the product to the store where you bought it, along with the receipt, warranty, and original packaging. Ask to speak to the person who handles complaints or returns.

4. Explain your problem briefly and clearly. Be polite but firm. Remember that you have bargaining power. Stores usually try to settle consumer complaints to keep shoppers' business.

5. Propose the solution you want, knowing in advance what will satisfy you.

CHAPTER 34 **Consumer Rights and Responsibilities** **341**

Topics on pp. 342-343:

- **Complaining in Person, by Phone, and by Mail**
- **Further Actions**

Checking Comprehension

✓ To what groups can consumers turn for help when they have problems? *See p. 343*

✓ What are two ways consumers can band together for redress? *Letter-writing campaigns and boycotts.*

From School to Work

Have students read "Handling Consumer Complaints." Ask: Has new technology, which speeds communication, made writing skills less important or more so? Suggest that although— and because—messages can be quickly sent, they must be carefully considered and expressed. Many adults who placed little value on writing skills as teens have later found themselves in jobs where their lack of writing skills caused them embarrassment.

Answers to Assessing . . .

1. Lists will vary but should be extensive, indicating the importance of writing skills.
2. Letters should include all facts, take conciliatory tone, and persuasively offer alternative solution.

In Person

Figure 34.1 outlines the procedure to follow when making a complaint in person.

You may have to explain your problem more than once before it's resolved. Adrienne had bought a sweater at a small clothing store. When she opened the box at home, she noticed that the color was not uniform on one sleeve. She returned to the store with the sweater and talked to a salesperson. That worker, however, had no authority to accept a return. Adrienne had to explain the problem again to the store manager.

If you must explain the problem more than once, try to be calm and patient each time. Treat the store personnel as *you* would like to be treated. That way, you're more likely to gain satisfaction.

No matter how many times you explain your problem, remember that you have a specific goal in mind. If you're not satisfied, be prepared to leave the store. Leaving is better than accepting an unsatisfactory solution, especially when other options are available.

By Phone

Sometimes taking your problem to a store isn't possible. Karin's clock radio needed a replacement part that was covered by the warranty. At the store where she bought the item, however, a salesperson explained that the store no longer carried that manufacturer's products. Karin would have to go to a store that did. Ken subscribed to a magazine. After three months, though, he still hadn't received

From School to Work

Handling Consumer Complaints

What You Learn Today . . .

Good writing skills are vital to success in school. Most school assignments and exams, for example, require that you express yourself in writing. Putting words on paper encourages organization of ideas, as well as expressing them clearly and concisely.

. . . You Can Use Tomorrow

Good writing is also a valued skill at work. Much communication on the job is done in writing: memos, letters, evaluations, and reports. In each case, clear and thorough communication gets better results than confused or unimportant information.

Practicing Your Skills

If you worked in customer relations for a company, good letter-writing skills would be essential. Writing a letter in response to a complaint is a good way to practice your writing skills. An effective response:

- Uses calm, reasonable language.
- Is businesslike but polite in style and tone.

- Clearly conveys the decision about how the complaint is being handled.
- Carefully describes any steps that the customer should take to help resolve the complaint.
- Convinces the customer that the solution is fair.
- Offers reassurance that the customer's business is valued.

Assessing Your Skills

1. With your classmates, make a list of jobs that use writing skills in some way. What does the list tell you about the need for writing skills?
2. Assume that you work in customer service for a watchmaker. A customer's watch has stopped working, but the warranty has expired. Since the watch is beyond warranty, the company declines to replace it. As a gesture of goodwill, your manager says that you can offer a $20 discount toward the purchase of a new model. Write a letter that declines the customer's request for a replacement but includes the company's offer.

Focus on Relationship Skills

Have pairs perform impromptu skits in which a consumer makes a complaint to a store employee. Have students trade roles and repeat the performance. Afterward, ask students what they learned about each character's point of view.

MORE ABOUT Complaining by Phone

Many major companies have a toll-free number specifically for consumer questions. To find if a company has such a number, call directory assistance (toll-free) at 1-800-555-1212.

an issue. He had no store to take his complaint to. In such cases as these, it's more effective to make a phone call to the manufacturer or supplier of an item or service.

Making a complaint over the phone is similar to doing it in person. Have all the necessary information available: when, where, and how you purchased the item; what the problem is; and what solution you want. Describe the problem clearly and calmly. Politely but firmly ask for a satisfactory solution.

If your complaint concerns a product, look for the manufacturer's phone number in the printed material that came with it. If that doesn't work, you can consult reference books in the public library. *Standard and Poor's Register of Corporations, Directors, and Executives* is one source you can check. For a local company, look in the phone book.

By Letter

If making your complaint in person or by phone hasn't worked, you can write a letter. Find the company's address either in the printed material that came with the product or at the library.

An effective complaint letter includes your name and address plus the name and job title of the person you're writing to. It contains the

same information you would give in a phone call. Include copies of the sales receipt and warranty; keep the originals for yourself. You should also keep a copy of the letter.

Remember that the tone and appearance of a complaint letter are particularly important. A polite, reasonable tone and correct grammar and spelling are more likely to produce successful results.

Taking Further Action

Sometimes consumers are unable to settle their problems in person, by phone, or by letter. Fortunately, there are other sources of help.

Local Business Groups

The **Better Business Bureau (BBB)** is *an organization of businesses that promise to follow fair business practices.* One function of the BBB is to help resolve consumer complaints against its members and other businesses in the community. The BBB has more than 170 branch offices.

People can also get help from the local **chamber of commerce.** This is *a member organization that represents and serves businesses in a town or city.* You might call the chamber to locate a certain type of business in your area.

National Business Groups

If you have a complaint about a professional, such as an accountant, lawyer, or contractor, you can contact the professional association that person belongs to. **Consumer action panels (CAPs)** are another source of help. These are *groups formed by industries to handle consumer complaints.* If a consumer is not satisfied after talking directly with the manufacturer, the CAP will try to help. You can find the names and addresses of CAPs in the library.

When well prepared, a letter of complaint can bring you the results you want.

Checking Comprehension

✓ What is small-claims court? *Court where consumers present own claims and judge decides outcome.*

✓ How does vandalism affect consumers? *Results in higher prices.*

✓ How can shoplifting be punished? *Arrest, conviction, fine, and prison.*

✓ How can consumers learn if an item has been recalled? *Fill out registration cards; stay informed through the news.*

CROSS-CURRICULAR ACTIVITY
Language Arts

Suggest to students that while consumers are more likely to write a letter of complaint than one of praise, both are effective in shaping store policy. Have students write and mail a letter praising a business for something they appreciate.

Government Agencies

Federal, state, and local governments all have agencies that help protect consumers. At the national level, for instance, the Consumer Product Safety Commission handles complaints about product safety. Call or write the nearest Federal Information Center to learn which federal agency can best help with your particular problem.

Agencies of municipal, county, and state governments also protect consumers. Some inspect restaurants and other food-service establishments to ensure that they are sanitary. Others make rules governing the operations of banking, credit, and insurance companies. These state and local agencies are listed in the phone book.

Joining with Other Consumers

Another way to seek redress is to band together with other consumers. Businesses recognize the power of word of mouth. They

know that unhappy customers are likely to tell friends and family, costing the business sales.

Letter-writing campaigns can influence businesses to change their practices. In recent years, for instance, fast-food restaurants have begun to package their foods in more environmentally responsible ways. They are doing this in response to consumer campaigns. Another method is the **boycott**, *a technique in which consumers organize to refuse to buy a company's products.* These actions should be taken, however, only when you have a justifiable complaint and only after other avenues for redress have been exhausted.

Legal Action

If a serious complaint is not settled, you can seek legal help. Hiring a lawyer can be expensive, but local legal aid agencies can sometimes be used. These groups provide free legal help to consumers who cannot pay attorneys' fees.

Consumers with minor complaints can take the case to **small-claims court.** These are *proceedings in which consumers present their own claims and a judge decides the outcome.* The claim must be under a certain dollar amount, which varies from state to state. Because you must serve as your own lawyer, there are no legal fees. You do pay the court a fee of between $5 and $50, which may be paid back if you win the case.

Consumer Responsibilities

Teen buying power is very impressive. In the United States, young people ages 12 to 19 have an estimated $60 billion to spend annually. Busy parents give their children another $28 billion for family grocery shopping. Teens also influence their parents' purchasing decisions. Naturally, with this purchasing power comes responsibility.

What responsibilities accompany the power that teens command in the marketplace?

MORE ABOUT Consideration

Showing consideration for store owners is possible in many ways. You can: refrain from opening packaged items to examine the contents (ask a clerk for help instead); look at breakable items without handling them; shop with clean hands; try on clothing carefully to keep garments free of makeup and to prevent tearing; and put items back on appropriate shelves. Consideration extended to customers is more likely when shoppers follow such practices as these.

Showing Consideration

One of a consumer's first and easiest responsibilities is showing consideration. Considerate consumers realize that a store and its merchandise are meant to be used and enjoyed by many other people. For example, have you ever brought a product home, only to find that a piece was missing? It may have been lost when a thoughtless shopper opened the package in the store. Considerate consumers ask to see a floor model instead. They try on clothes carefully to avoid soiling or damaging the articles.

Consideration extends to store owners as well. Responsible consumers recognize that the store and everything in it belong to someone else. They refrain from acts of **vandalism**, which is *deliberately destroying or damaging the property of others.* Such acts as smashing windows and ruining merchandise force owners to raise prices in order to cover losses.

Acting Honestly

Marisa was listening to her friend recount her experience at a music shop. "The cashier thought the CD was on sale. It wasn't, but she gave me 30 percent off. I wish I'd bought two!"

"That's dishonest. You should have said something," Marisa said firmly.

"Why?" her friend demanded. "It was only a few dollars. They can afford it."

"When they lose money like that," Marisa countered, "they have to charge more to make up for it."

Acting Responsibly

Are You Ethical?

When you act ethically, you examine principles of right and wrong as you decide what to do. Personal and family values guide these decisions. You can also be guided by the values that are generally held by people in every society. Honesty, responsibility, and respect for others, for example, are qualities that people have long valued and admired.

Another test of ethical behavior is how a decision affects others. No one lives in a vacuum. Everything you do has an impact on others, positive or negative, insignificant or long-lasting. An ethical person considers those consequences, as well as personal beliefs, when choosing how to act.

Ethics in Action

Jessica had been looking forward to the prom all year. She already had her dress but wanted a special pair of earrings to wear with it. While browsing in a store with her friend Shelby, Jessica found some earrings that she thought were perfect.

"Those earrings are gorgeous," Shelby said. "I think you should get them."

"But look at the price," Jessica replied. "I can't spend that kind of money on a pair of earrings."

"There's a way," Shelby responded, her voice softening to a near whisper. "Just buy them and return them after the prom."

Jessica looked silently at Shelby, then down at the earrings. They would look nice with her dress. What harm would there be if she took good care of them? Jessica thought for a long moment.

"I can't," she said as she placed the earrings back in the display case. "It's not right. I just wouldn't feel comfortable wearing them. Besides, they wouldn't be new anymore. I might even scratch one or lose it. No, I can't do that."

As they turned from the counter, Shelby shrugged her shoulders. "Come on," Jessica said smiling. "Let's look some more—for a pair I can afford."

Your Analysis

1. What negative outcomes could have come from Shelby's suggestion?
2. What actions show that Jessica is an ethical person?
3. What positive outcomes are connected to Jessica's ethical behavior?

Focus on Reading Skills

Consumers are responsible for understanding warranties and for using products as directed, both of which require good reading skills. Have students bring in warranties and directions from product packages. Read several in class.

Discuss whether the packager made the directions clear. How is the warranty written to cover most possibilities without being cumbersome? Can students find any potential sources of misunderstanding in either?

Activity

■ **Reasonable Response?** Discuss: How far may merchants go to prevent theft? Should they be allowed to inspect shopping bags? Purses? Set up security cameras outside changing rooms? (*Critical Thinking*)

FAMILY AND COMMUNITY OUTREACH

Ask students to interview merchants about what consumer behavior they most dislike and most appreciate. Have students compile a chart or master list of merchants' responses.

Acting Responsibly

Have students read "Are You Ethical?" Ask students why so many people disregard how their actions affect others. Lead them to see that when people care about what happens to others and act accordingly, good things result.

Answers to Your Analysis

1. Answers may include: store would have used, possibly damaged, merchandise; might raise prices to offset losses; Jessica might lose self-respect, respect of others.
2. She refused dishonest option, based on own values and effect on others.
3. She maintains self-respect; store does not suffer loss; Shelby may learn from her example.

■ **Chapter Review.** Use the contents of the Chapter Review page to help students review concepts, think critically, and apply their knowledge.

■ **Study Guide.** Have students complete the Study Guide for Chapter 34 on p. 113 of the Student Workbook.

■ **Give Yourself Away.** Have groups develop a list called "Consumer's Dozen: You Know You're a Good Consumer If..." that gives twelve examples of good consumers in action: one for each right and responsibility, and three related to making a complaint. Encourage students to be creative and to use humor if they like.

Evaluation

■ **Chapter Test.** Use the reproducible chapter test provided in the Teacher's Classroom Resources or create your own test using the *Testmaker Software.*

■ **Alternative Assessment.** Have groups develop rubrics for consumers (similar to those in the *Performance Assessment* booklet in the Teacher's Classroom Resources). Have students use the chapter to identify traits of good consumers and write brief descriptions of how these are shown by excellent, good, fair, and poor consumers.

■ **Know Your Responsibilities.** Ask students to write a paragraph that begins: "What I want most to remember about consumer rights and responsibilities is . . ."

■ How is using products safely a consumer responsibility?

Marisa was right—and right to be angry. Like vandalism, such cheating is not only wrong but costly—to everyone. Stores make up for the money lost to dishonest consumers by charging more.

Marisa's friend took advantage of an innocent mistake. Some consumers are more deliberately dishonest. They abuse a store's **return policy,** its *rules for returning or exchanging merchandise.* They may buy a product "as is," then demand a refund when they discover that it is damaged or defective. Some consumers switch price tags on items to pay a lower price. This is illegal and dishonest.

An even more extreme type of dishonesty is **shoplifting,** or *stealing items that are displayed for sale in a store.* Shoplifters cost stores over $30 billion a year. To combat shoplifting, stores install security cameras to monitor customers. Some attach a small plastic tab to clothing articles, which sets off an alarm unless it is removed by sales staff when the item is purchased. Many stores have customers check their bags at the service counter when they enter. All these measures cost consumers not only in money but in added inconvenience and loss of privacy.

More and more merchants are prosecuting shoplifters, even young offenders. Once arrested, shoplifters are taken into police custody. At the police station, they are searched, questioned, fingerprinted, and photographed.

If convicted, they can be fined and imprisoned. Because convictions become part of a permanent criminal record, their effect can last a lifetime.

Using Products Safely

Consumer responsibility continues after you leave the store. It includes how you use the products you buy. Responsible consumers follow manufacturers' instructions. Many products, such as tools and electronic equipment, can be dangerous if used improperly. Using them correctly protects not just you but others.

Consumers also need to stay informed about safety issues. News reports tell about products that have been found to be unsafe. Sometimes these products are **recalled,** or *returned to the maker to be fixed or destroyed.*

To make recalls easier, many manufacturers include registration cards in the product packaging. By filling out and sending in these cards, you register yourself with the company as the owner of that product. This allows the company to contact you should there be a recall. If this happens, you should follow the instructions given. Continuing to use a recalled product could be dangerous.

If you discover a faulty product or service, report it to the manufacturer. If the manufacturer shows no interest in your concern, contact a government agency. By taking action, you may be saving others from injury.

A Two-Way Street

Thoughtful consumers pay as much attention to their responsibilities as they do to their rights. They realize that fair treatment is a two-way street. Businesses need the cooperation and consideration of their customers in order to offer reasonable prices and good service. Responsible consumers recognize this. They realize that their actions have a strong impact on what businesses provide.

When a serious problem arises, however, a consumer has the responsibility for taking action. Doing so protects more than just that person's rights. It can protect all consumers.

Focus on Problem-Solving Skills

Have groups perform skits depicting a consumer experience—including a shopping trip and purchase, some type of consumer problem, and its resolution—that incorporates the points raised in this chapter. Roles might include a consumer, store personnel, and a customer service representative (reading aloud a complaint letter). Have the class take notes on how various consumer responsibilities and rights are demonstrated in the skit for later discussion.

Reviewing the Facts

1. Name the six consumer rights.
2. List the steps in making a complaint in person.
3. What basic information do you need when making a complaint, regardless of whether it is in person, by phone, or by letter?
4. Identify three actions that can be taken if a business does not act on a complaint.
5. How does shoplifting harm consumers?

Thinking Critically

1. Why should consumers bother to be considerate to store owners, employees, and other consumers?
2. Marco bought his brother, Drew, a remote control car for his birthday. Drew had played with the car only a few minutes when it hit a bump in the street and lost a wheel. Would it be fair for Marco to return or exchange the car? Why or why not?

Applying Your Knowledge

1. **Handling a Consumer Problem.** Suppose that you bought a new camera by mail. At a friend's wedding, you find that the built-in flash does not work. Make a list of the procedure you would follow to solve the problem.
2. **Writing a Complaint Letter.** Suppose you bought a new radio from a retailer that claimed to match the advertised price of any store, even two weeks after purchase. You paid $79 and one week later saw the same model advertised at the same store for $59. You asked for a $20 credit, but the customer-service worker refused it. The service representative said that the offer doesn't apply to changes in price at this store, only to competitors' prices. Write an effective letter to the store's manager requesting the $20 credit.

3. **Making a Poster.** Make a poster that highlights the benefits of consumers acting responsibly.

Making Connections

1. **Business.** Find the address and phone number of the Better Business Bureau office nearest you. Visit the office if you can, and obtain a brochure outlining the group's services. Report your findings to the class.
2. **Language Arts.** Write an article or opinion piece for the school newspaper that warns teens about the possible consequences of vandalism and shoplifting.
3. **Government.** Research a consumer-protection law, such as the Truth-in-Lending Act, and prepare a brief report on its provisions.

Building Your Portfolio

Organizing Consumer Action

Suppose that you subscribed to cable television and your local cable carrier decided to eliminate from its service a network you very much enjoyed. You could write a letter to the company, but hearing from one consumer may not carry any weight with the company. What other steps could you take? Plan a strategy in which you try to convince the company to reverse its decision. Write out the steps you would follow. Add these steps to your portfolio.

ANSWERS TO REVIEWING THE FACTS

1. The right to safety, to be informed, to choose, to redress, to consumer education, to be heard.
2. Check if problem is covered by warranty; write down what's wrong; ask for help at store; explain problem; propose solution.
3. When and where you bought item; whom to contact; problem with purchase; how you want problem solved.
4. Any three: contact the BBB or possibly chamber of commerce; contact professional association or CAP; contact government agency; band together with other consumers; take legal action.
5. Forces businesses to raise prices; adds inconvenience.

ANSWERS TO THINKING CRITICALLY

1. Answers may include: from simple decency; from self-interest, since it helps transactions go more smoothly and saves money.
2. Could argue both ways. Was the car poorly constructed for the cost and unable to withstand reasonable play? Was Drew playing inappropriately with the car? Did any instructions dictate appropriate use?

Chapter Overview

Chapter 35 examines careers in management and consumer-related fields. It outlines the characteristics, interests, and abilities helpful for pursuing these careers. It describes specific jobs available at various levels of education and training.

Motivators

■ **Job Experience.** Stage an opportunity for students to manage or work with you. Then give their service a job title. For example, ask them to suggest a CD that you might buy for a younger relative. Then tell them they have acted as consumer consultants for leisure activities. Tell them they may have a future in consumer relations.

■ **In Training.** Write on the chalkboard "I manage people when . . ." and "I work with people when . . ." Ask students to finish these statements with examples from their daily lives. Explain that these experiences will help them if they decide to pursue a career like the ones described in this chapter.

Objectives

Discuss the chapter objectives on this page. Remind students that the objectives focus on important chapter concepts.

Vocabulary

The term *administration* may be unfamiliar to some students. Point out that its root is *minister*, to attend to others' needs or to perform the functions of an office. People in administration have both of these responsibilities.

Chapter 35

Management and Consumer Careers

Terms to Learn

- administration
- capital

Objectives

This chapter will help you to:

- Discuss **the interests and skills suitable for management and consumer-related careers.**
- Name **several examples of management careers.**
- Identify **several consumer-related careers.**

CHAPTER RESOURCES

Student Workbook
Study Guide, p. 117
Activity, *Consumer Careers*, pp. 118-119

Teacher's Classroom Resources
Lesson Plan, p. 39
Extension #57, *Career Choices*, p. 63

Life Skills, *Entrepreneur Profile*, pp. 61-62
Chapter 35 Test, pp. 75-76
Performance Assessment, *Management and Consumer Careers*, p. 64
Reteaching, *Thinking About Careers*, p. 41

See Also:
ABCNews InterActive™ Videodiscs

Annalise carefully laid down the necklace she had just finished making. Stopping by her work area, her father smiled with pride. "Beautiful," he said as he looked over the necklaces on the table. "They're all different too."

Annalise nodded. "This one is for Aunt Helen. She said she wanted something to wear with her blue sweater. That one is for Mary Ellen. She likes the outdoors. So I thought shells would be just right."

"Have you ever thought of selling these?" her father asked.

Annalise smiled. "Do you think I could?"

"I don't see why not," her father said. "You do great work. You take the time and effort to make what people like. Judging from the way your friends are always asking you to make them something, there's definitely a market for it. You might design and sell your own line of jewelry."

Annalise laughed, but the idea was exciting. Being her own boss was almost as appealing as being paid for doing something she enjoyed.

The Qualities Needed

Who knows? Annalise's skills and interests may guide her to pursue a management or consumer-related career. These careers share several features. Both types involve working with other people and explaining information to others. Managers organize the way work is performed. They explain projects and tasks to

Some customer service representatives talk to consumers on the telephone all day. Although they have no direct contact with the public, these employees must enjoy speaking with and helping people.

their subordinates and evaluate how workers do their jobs. People who work in consumer-related careers provide products and services to other people, or they advise people how to use those products and services.

Both types of careers involve resources other than human resources. Managers make decisions about how best to use time, money, energy, and equipment. Many workers in consumer careers help consumers use their time and energy effectively. Many are also concerned with helping consumers get the most for their money.

As you read this section, think about whether you have any of the skills or interests described here. If so, a management or consumer-related career may be right for you.

Interests

If you enjoy organizing tasks and managing your time, you may be suited for one of these careers. Most important, though, someone who enters a management or consumer-related career should enjoy working with people.

TEACH

Topic on p. 349:
• Qualities Needed

Checking Comprehension

✓ How are management and consumer careers similar? *Both involve working with, explaining things to, others; using resources other than human.*

✓ What are a manager's job duties? *Organizing and explaining tasks, evaluating workers' performance.*

✓ What help do those in consumer careers offer consumers? *Using time and energy effectively, getting most for their money.*

Activity

■ **Using Qualities.** Have pairs list five people in consumer or management jobs whom they have encountered. For each position, have each student name one of the qualities discussed on p. 349, while the partner suggests a job situation where that quality would prove helpful.

FAMILY AND COMMUNITY OUTREACH

The qualities needed for consumer relations are also those that help family members relate to each other. Ask students to try, for one day, to treat their family as clients whose needs they want to meet. Have them reflect on and write about this exercise. Did they notice a difference in family members' behavior or attitudes? What did they learn about relationship skills?

MORE ABOUT Service Jobs

Service jobs will continue to be the fastest-growing sector of the job market. Most employment growth will come from retail sales, including restaurants; business services, which include temporary help services and computer services; building systems maintenance; and home health care. While these jobs require little or no additional training or education, they also offer the lowest wages.

Topics on pp. 350-351:

- **Personal Interests and Skills**
- **Entry-Level Management Jobs**
- **Management Jobs That Require Training**

Checking Comprehension

✓ What does leading people involve? *Guiding, directing others toward achieving goal.*

✓ Why do people in consumer-oriented jobs need good time management skills? *To plan use of own time, supervise how others use theirs.*

✓ What do administrative assistants do? *Prepare reports; schedule meetings and travel; communicate with other workers.*

- **Do you like leading others?** Have you ever led a group in a project and felt rewarded by the experience? If so, you were learning techniques all managers must know: how to guide and direct other people toward accomplishing a goal.

- **Do you like working with other people?** People in management and consumer careers work closely with coworkers and often with the public. For example, a sales manager of a large company might supervise 100 salespeople. A manicurist might interact with 20 or more customers every day. Anyone in these careers must genuinely like people and know how to treat them with courtesy and respect.

Skills

Four kinds of abilities are central to management and consumer careers. They are:

- **Communication skills.** If you have ever successfully explained to a friend how to change the oil in a car or send E-mail on the computer, you know how to give clear directions and be a good listener. Managers must have these skills. Sales workers need them, too, when they listen to a customer's needs or explain how a product works. Good communication includes good writing skills, since much business communication is in written form.

- **Math skills.** While management and consumer workers don't always need to be math whizzes, they do need good basic math skills. Bank tellers and store clerks count out money all day as part of their jobs. Most managers are responsible for budgets. Math skills are essential in all these jobs.

- **Goal-setting and planning skills.** Planning and organizing are vital to people in management and consumer careers. Managers must organize the activities of teams of people. Salespeople need to keep merchandise neatly organized so that shoppers can see it easily. Teens can begin to develop these skills. For example, when Julio joined a walkathon, he had to plan how to contact donors, organize their pledges, and contact them again after the walkathon took place. Then he had to collect the money and turn it over to the sponsoring organization. Through planning, he reached his goal.

- **Time management skills.** People in management and consumer jobs need to make the best use of their time. People who sell insurance, for instance, need to balance seeing clients with getting paperwork done. Sometimes workers must supervise how others use *their* time. For example, a restaurant manager must plan the schedule of all the servers, making sure that enough are available to serve the customers expected.

Good communication and time management are two skills that effective managers must possess.

DID YOU KNOW?

The service industry is becoming more concerned with customer satisfaction. One sign of this is the greater demand for service quality managers, who strive to make every customer a satisfied one. Concern for service is further shown in the number of books on the subject for companies and their employees. Such strategies as training employees to deal with irate customers, rewarding them for good service, and testing customer service with company "spies" are also popular.

Management Careers

Management jobs exist in virtually every field—from high technology and manufacturing to the performing arts and journalism. **Administration** is the term sometimes used to refer to *management in institutions and public agencies.* For an idea of the duties of management, imagine what the technical support department of a computer software company is like. A staff of 20 operators fields calls from customers with questions about using the programs published by the company. The manager has to train these operators so that they know how to answer customers' questions. The manager must also run weekly meetings where staff members can discuss problems as well as manage the department budget for salaries and office equipment.

Entry-Level Jobs

Many retail stores and fast-food restaurants hire management trainees who work with the store manager. Trainees learn to create schedules, track inventory, organize daily receipts, and develop in-store promotions and special events. When their training is complete, they become full-fledged managers.

In many offices, administrative assistants help managers by preparing reports, scheduling meetings and travel, and communicating with other workers. Administrative assistants must be well organized. They have to be good at managing their time since they often switch between tasks.

Jobs That Require Training

Employment agents help people find jobs. They also help employers find qualified job candidates. Many work for private employment agencies or "temp" agencies, which provide companies with temporary personnel.

Entrepreneurs start their businesses based on their interests and skills. What advantages and disadvantages do you think there are in owning your own business?

Employment agents maintain computerized files of job openings, conduct interviews with applicants, and arrange interviews for qualified people with prospective employers. While some employment agencies require a college degree for positions as agents, many hire high school graduates.

Entrepreneurs

Most management jobs are found in companies that already exist. Suppose, however, that you don't want to work for someone else. People who want to be their own bosses become entrepreneurs. They are people who own their business, providing a product or

Activities

■ **Just Practicing.** Have students make lists or charts with examples of how they use the following skills, needed in management and consumer careers, in their everyday lives: communication skills; math skills; goal-setting and planning skills; and time management skills. *(Observation)*

ENRICHMENT

■ **Handle with Care.** Ask groups to discuss how they would respond in the following management and consumer-related situations. Have them share their ideas with the class.

- A job applicant whom you are interviewing is very nervous and knocks over a glass of water on your desk.
- A once-reliable employee has begun missing work, making mistakes, and acting irritable. You need to learn why.
- A parent brings a child to the health clinic where you are the receptionist. The parent's language skills are poor, however, and you cannot understand what the child needs.
- You are the senior sales associate at a small clothing store. The manager asks for ideas on promoting a line of sweaters that isn't selling well.

MORE ABOUT Personnel Managers

Personnel managers at some companies perform exit interviews with employees who leave the company. At these interviews, they discuss the employee's experiences with the company, especially those related to the worker's leaving. Managers use this information to gain insight into how to choose employees more wisely and serve them better in the future.

Checking Comprehension

✔ What do controllers do? *Manage company's financial operations; make financial reports; direct investments.*

✔ How can the law be a consumer-oriented career? *Lawyers may represent consumers in product safety and consumer rights cases.*

✔ How can teens begin preparing for a management or consumer-related career? *Get part-time job; stay in school.*

STRATEGIES THAT WORK

Have students read "Becoming an Entrepreneur." Ask them whether they think intelligence or industriousness is more important to becoming a successful entrepreneur.

Answers to Think . . .

1. Answers may include: savings; loans; part-time job; selling possessions.
2. Answers should include places parents (potential customers) frequent, such as supermarkets and play parks.
3. Lead students to see that honoring work commitment is ethical and wise business decision.

---

service they think people will want or need. Entrepreneurs work for themselves rather than other people. As a result, they set their own goals. The money they make depends on how profitable their business becomes.

Being an entrepreneur involves numerous risks, pressures, and responsibilities. Usually, entrepreneurs use their own savings or a loan from a bank as **capital**, or *money to start and run a business*. If the new business fails to do well, the entrepreneur loses the money that was invested.

STRATEGIES That Work

Becoming an Entrepreneur

People who run their own businesses need to be businesslike. Even teens can become entrepreneurs. If you start your own business, get off on the right foot with the following techniques:

- **Identify expenses.** List everything you will need to start your business, from equipment and materials to advertising and transportation. Determine how much you expect to spend on each area.
- **Find sources of money.** You might use your savings or the income from a current job. Maybe a family member can offer a loan.
- **Make your business known.** Let people know that you are ready to work. Hand out advertising flyers or cards. Post them on a community bulletin board too.
- **Keep a calendar.** Writing down appointments helps you be prompt and prepared. Schedule your social events on the same calendar. That way, you'll make sure that your professional and personal commitments do not conflict.
- **Keep your commitments.** Show up on time, finish on time, and do the job right. That's the best way to build repeat business.
- **Be polite and cooperative.** You are working for the people who hire you. Show them that pleasing them is what matters to you.
- **Make a customer file.** Use a separate card for each customer to record all important

information, including name, address, and phone number. Also, note things you want to remember about that customer's personal preferences. If your business is walking dogs, for example, you might note that a neighbor's dog is afraid of trucks.

- **Keep accounts carefully.** Even if you don't give bills and receipts, keep track of hours worked, services performed, and fees owed or paid. This helps your business run smoothly and avoids questions about payment. If you do present customers with a bill, be sure to keep a copy and note when it is paid.
- **Ask for referrals.** Ask satisfied customers to refer you to their friends. This can build your business.

Making the Strategy Work

Think...

1. What are some ways you could get start-up money for a business?
2. If you were starting a babysitting business, where would you post notices about your services? Why?
3. Suppose that you were scheduled to mow a neighbor's lawn on Saturday afternoon for the first time, but a friend invited you to a party that same afternoon. What would you do?

Try...

Imagine that you are the operator of Odds 'n' Ends, a business that specializes in running errands for customers. Create file cards for two imaginary customers. Include two notes on the personal preferences of each customer.

REAL-LIFE APPLICATION

Read this to students: *Carmi is a talented singer and wants to make that her career. Professional singing is a very demanding, competitive field, however, so Carmi is also thinking about becoming a voice or music teacher.* Ask: What factors besides singing ability should Carmi consider before making her decision? Lead students to see that she must also be good with people and able to help them learn if she decides to teach. A career as a service provider should not be chosen by default.

Many people start a business based on a personal interest, as Annalise may do with her jewelry making. To give themselves the best chance to succeed, many take courses in business management and financial planning. Community colleges offer courses in these areas, plus marketing, business law, and many other subjects. Some government agencies and business groups provide training and advice to entrepreneurs.

Jobs That Require Higher Education

Most companies have a personnel manager to handle the company's employee needs. These managers set performance standards for hiring and firing and for employee behavior on the job. They oversee the company's health insurance plan along with any other benefits the company gives its employees. Personnel managers usually have a college degree in business or a related area. Many have a graduate degree.

Controllers hold the highest financial position in a company. Sometimes they are called "treasurer" or "chief financial officer." Controllers manage all the financial operations of the company, which may include supervising the people who work in accounting and bookkeeping. They are responsible for financial reporting, such as annual reports to stockholders, and for directing the company's investments. The typical controller has a college degree in accounting or finance. Most hold an advanced degree in accounting.

Brand managers handle the advertising and marketing for a specific brand of a product, such as pasta, soap, or athletic shoes. They develop budgets to account for all expenses related to advertising and marketing the product. These managers decide what advertising media should be used and review all ads. They may devise coupon programs through magazines or direct mail, that is, promotional pieces sent directly to consumers' homes. Brand managers typically have a business degree.

Consumer Careers

Many people work with and for consumers. They may provide goods and services to consumers or help consumers get the most for their money. Some give help to consumers in specialized fields, such as interior design, buying a home, cooking, or vacation travel. Whether these people work for a company or for themselves, they must be able to get along well with customers.

Entry-Level Jobs

Darren, who is interested in working in a bank, has started out as a bank teller. He is training on the job, handling deposits and withdrawals for bank customers. Darren must be extremely careful in his work, or he might make mistakes. He hopes that his job will lead to a management position, such as a branch manager, where he would be in charge of all the operations at a particular branch of a bank. Another possible future career is that of a loan officer. This worker oversees customers' applications for personal loans and mortgages.

Victoria is a market researcher. She conducts surveys at public places, such as shopping malls, to see how people might respond to a new advertising campaign or a new product. Market researchers should be friendly and willing to work with the public. They also have to be careful to record consumers' responses accurately.

Jobs That Require Training

Many magazines and newspapers print articles evaluating new products or describing how to manage resources. The reporters write articles based on the research done. Sometimes they interview experts. For example, a reporter writing an article about inexpensive decorating ideas may interview an interior designer or upholstery expert. Reporters sometimes attend trade shows, where different companies set up booths to show their products and services. Sometimes they

Activities

■ **That's Genius!** Have groups list entrepreneurial ideas for teens. Tell students to accept any idea that fills a need and could be managed by one or two teens; encourage them to have fun with the activity. Have each group select one idea and create a start-up plan, identifying immediate needs and possible sources of financing, information, and other kinds of support. Have groups share their ideas with the class. *(Creativity)*

RETEACHING

■ **Charting a Career.** On the board make a chart with the following headings: Entry-Level, Requires Training, and Requires Higher Education. Read a list of jobs described in this chapter and have students place each one in the proper category.

MULTICULTURAL *Perspectives*

Experience in a minority culture can bring success in management and consumer-related careers. It can be a bonus when working among the general public, as in police work, or as the basis of a business venture, such as an ethnic food shop. Ask students to suggest other ways that an ethnic identity could be an advantage in a consumer-oriented or management job.

MORE ABOUT Consumer Advocates

People may become consumer advocates after studying law, political science, family and consumer sciences, or government administration. Some have training in public information, research, or community education. All levels of government hire consumer advocates. In the private sector, they work for citizens' groups or lobbying organizations. For further information about careers in consumer advocacy, write: Consumer Federation of America, 1314 14th Street NW, Washington, DC 20005.

Review

■ **Chapter Review.** Use the contents of the Chapter Review page to help students review concepts, think critically, and apply their knowledge.

■ **Study Guide.** Have students complete the Study Guide for Chapter 35 on p. 117 of the Student Workbook.

■ **On the Job.** Ask students to imagine they are writing an article on someone who works at a specific management or consumer-related job. Have them make up a character and use information from the chapter to write the story.

Evaluation

■ **Chapter Test.** Use the reproducible chapter test provided in the Teacher's Classroom Resources or create your own test using the *Testmaker Software.*

■ **Alternative Assessment.** Have pairs write a dialogue between a personnel manager interviewing a candidate for a specific consumer-related position. The personnel manager's manner and questions and the candidate's responses should all reflect what students have learned from this chapter about the qualities, education, and duties these jobs require.

■ **Make Arrangements.** Have groups bring in classified ads for consumer-oriented or management jobs. Have them arrange the ads on a sheet of paper in some logical but creative way, such as from entry- to higher-level jobs or by qualities needed. Have groups explain their arrangement to the class.

354

test the products. At other times, they compile the results produced by a separate testing group. Consumer reporters must be able to write clearly and engage the attention of their readers. Generally, they have at least a high school diploma. Most have a degree in journalism or communications from a community college or a four-year school.

Credit managers for department stores, gas companies, or credit card companies review applications for credit. They decide whether people should receive the credit they desire. Some credit managers have attended college, but most of their experience comes with on-the-job training.

Jobs That Require Higher Education

Many lawyers work on behalf of consumers. They study laws and court decisions about product safety and consumer rights. They may practice alone or as part of a group. To become lawyers, they must earn a college degree, then attend law school for three years.

Consumer specialists, formerly called "home economists," have numerous job options. Some teach in public and private schools. Nearly every county in the United States employs a consumer specialist through the Cooperative Extension Service. These specialists answer consumer questions and develop family living programs. Many businesses hire these workers as well. They advise families on managing their resources, as well as writing pamphlets on the use and care of appliances or how to cook with various foods. Stores and manufacturers also hire them to work with the public, explaining new products or new uses for existing products. Consumer specialists have college degrees.

Preparing for a Career

If you think that you might pursue a management or consumer-related career, you can start preparing for it now. Some teens begin their career preparations by getting part-time

Many consumer specialists are employed by food, cookware, or appliance companies to educate the public about their products.

jobs. The single most important step, though, is education.

Most of the jobs described in this chapter require at least a high school diploma. So, by staying in school, you're already on your way to becoming qualified. For those who need additional education, programs in many fields are provided by technical schools, community colleges, and universities. You can write away for brochures and catalogs containing detailed descriptions of what each school offers. By preparing yourself today, you can help make sure that you have a rewarding work life tomorrow.

354   UNIT 5 *Management and Consumer Decisions*

REAL-LIFE APPLICATION

Ask students to explain what skill or interest needed for management and consumer-related jobs is demonstrated or lacking in each of these situations:

• Brendan stops by the library on his way to work to pick up a book he reserved last week. (*Time management*)

• When working in the science lab, Alexis prefers experiments that she can run alone, without a partner. (*Lacks desire to work with others*)

• Luisa scans her supermarket receipt to make sure she has not been overcharged. (*Math skills*)

Chapter 35

Reviewing the Facts

1. What two people-related skills are essential for those in management and consumer careers?
2. Give an example of an entry-level job in the management field. Briefly describe the job's responsibilities.
3. Name two activities of personnel managers. What level and type of education do they need?
4. How do consumer reporters get the information they need for the articles they write?
5. Name four job options open to people who have a college degree in family and consumer sciences.

Thinking Critically

1. The ability to work as part of a team is important in management and consumer-related positions. Why do you think that this is so?
2. Suppose that you are interested in becoming a clothing buyer for a department store. What two things might you do to prepare yourself for this career?

Applying Your Knowledge

1. **Practicing Communication Skills.** The ability to explain things clearly and simply is a part of virtually every management and consumer job. Choose a simple task—such as operating a washing machine or repairing a puncture in a bicycle tire—and describe the steps needed to get the job done.
2. **Relating to Others.** Suppose that you are a customer-service worker for a mail-order company. A customer calls to complain that she received only four of five articles of clothing she'd ordered, and one came in the wrong color. Describe how you would handle the situation.

Making Connections

1. **Language Arts.** Choose a career described in this chapter, and write a "help-wanted" ad for it. Include the interests, skills, training, and education required.
2. **Science.** Choose a career described in this chapter. What type of technology is used by someone in that position? How might the person have done his or her job 100 years ago, without that technology?
3. **Government.** For many jobs in the federal government, applicants must take a civil service exam. This exam evaluates basic skills, including reading, writing, and problem solving. Find out how to go about taking the civil service exam and what types of jobs are available to people who pass. Present your findings to the class.

Building Your Portfolio

Constructing a Business Plan

Entrepreneurs generally have to write a business plan that describes the product or service they will provide and how they will reach and build a client or customer base. Entrepreneurs show these plans to banks or investment firms in order to raise the capital needed to start their businesses. Imagine that you are an entrepreneur. Write a one-page business plan describing a management or consumer-related business you might start. What product or service will you provide? Who might your target client or customer be? Place your business plan in your portfolio.

ANSWERS TO REVIEWING THE FACTS

1. Leading people; working with them.
2. Answers may include (any one): trainee—make schedules, track inventory, organize receipts, develop special events; administrative assistant—prepare reports, schedule meetings and travel, communicate with other workers.
3. Any two: set standards for hiring, firing, and employee conduct; oversee company's benefits program. Usually have college degree, may have graduate degree, in business or related area.
4. Use own or existing research; interview experts; attend trade shows; test products; compile others' test results.
5. Could teach; work for the Cooperative Extension Service; write and advise on resource management and cooking for business; promote products for store or manufacturer.

ANSWERS TO THINKING CRITICALLY

1. People in these fields must work with others to accomplish tasks and meet goals. Teamwork skills, such as cooperation and communication, are needed for this.
2. Answers may include: get job as salesperson; finish high school; take courses in business, fashion, or family and consumer sciences.

Unit Preview

Unit 6 introduces students to the relationship of diet, exercise, and rest to health and wellness. Students explore the factors that influence food choices and learn about the Food Guide Pyramid.

Content Development

Use these chapters to reinforce the following themes:

Unit Motivator

■ **Eat Your Spinach.** Have students ever been told by a parent or another adult to eat something because it's good for them? Ask students what kinds of foods tend to be urged on them. Do they know why? Tell students that people who urge them to eat things like green vegetables have a reason. Tell students they will learn more about the role of these foods in keeping them healthy.

356

JOURNAL WRITING

Possible topics for student journals:
• Have students keep track of what they eat for one week and why. Then have them analyze their habits. Could they eat better? How? • Have students record their reactions to different kinds of foods. Does a meat-heavy meal give them energy or make them sluggish? Does a candy bar perk them up or just make them sleepier? What foods make them happy? What foods do they associate with negative experiences? What did they learn from their records?

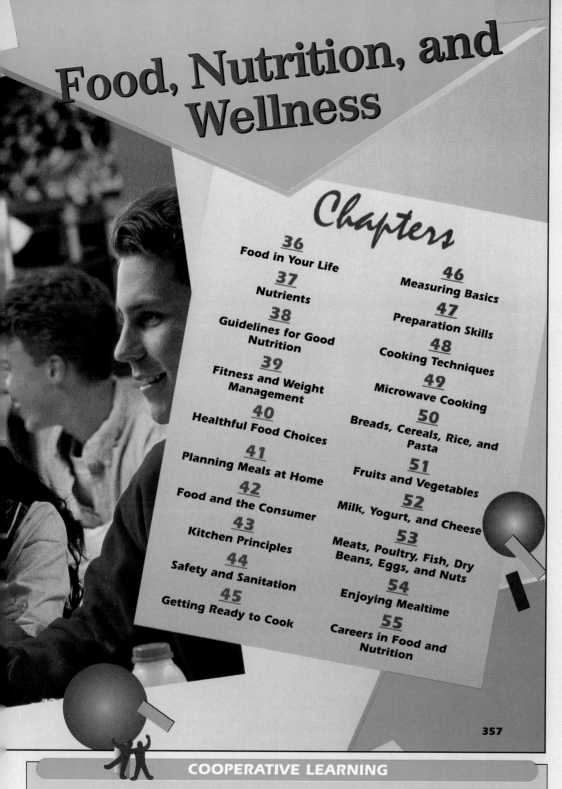

Food, Nutrition, and Wellness

Chapters

357

FHA Activity

The following activity can be used with your FHA group or as a public relations strategy:

■ **Low-Cost Meals.** People with limited incomes often have trouble coming up with inexpensive meals that are healthful and appealing. Have students plan meals that are appealing, nutritious, low cost, and easy to fix. Then have them compile these into a booklet that could be offered to a community center for use by people who want to stretch their food dollars and still cook healthful yet pleasing meals.

Unit Closure

■ **What You Need to Know.** Have students condense the most important information in this unit into a brochure called "Food: The Facts." In this brochure, students should offer, probably in list style, the most important pointers from this chapter about selecting, storing, and cooking various foods.

REVIEW

■ **More Food Choices.** Remind students of their introduction to unusual foods at the beginning of the unit. Ask them to list foods that are now familiar to them but weren't before. Also ask students to list facts about food that they learned from this chapter. You might want to make a list on the board as students talk.

EVALUATION

■ **Unit Test.** Have students complete the unit test in the Teacher's Classroom Resources.

■ **Testmaker Software.** You may wish to design a unit test using the *Testmaker Software*.

COOPERATIVE LEARNING

Potluck Lunch. Divide students into small groups to carry out a potluck lunch. Give these assignments to groups—salad, vegetable, main dish, dessert, and organization. All but the organization group should choose a dish to prepare and learn its nutritional value. The organization group should obtain drinks, cups, plates, utensils, napkins, and trash bags. They should plan the room arrangement and make a cleanup assignment chart that designates cleanup duties for all students in the class. Follow up with an analysis of the event's success.

Chapter Overview

Chapter 36 examines various needs that are satisfied by food and some influences on food choices. It encourages students to analyze their eating habits and to consider how those habits contribute to their overall health.

Motivators

■ **Fond Memories.** Ask students to describe some memorable experiences involving food, both positive and negative. You might share some of your own. Ask: Does that experience affect the way you feel about the food now? How? Point out that food can be more to people than a way to satisfy hunger or a source of nutrition.

■ **On the Menu.** Ask students to name foods they regularly eat. List these on the board. Discuss: Why do we eat some plants and animals and not others? Tell students that this chapter will explain why people eat as they do to help students be more aware of their own food choices.

Objectives

Discuss the chapter objectives on this page. Remind students that the objectives focus on important chapter concepts.

Vocabulary

People often speak of "going on a diet" to lose weight. Stress that the word *diet* refers not only to a weight-loss program, but to everything a person eats. There are many sorts of diets, such as low sodium, low cholesterol, or vegetarian.

358

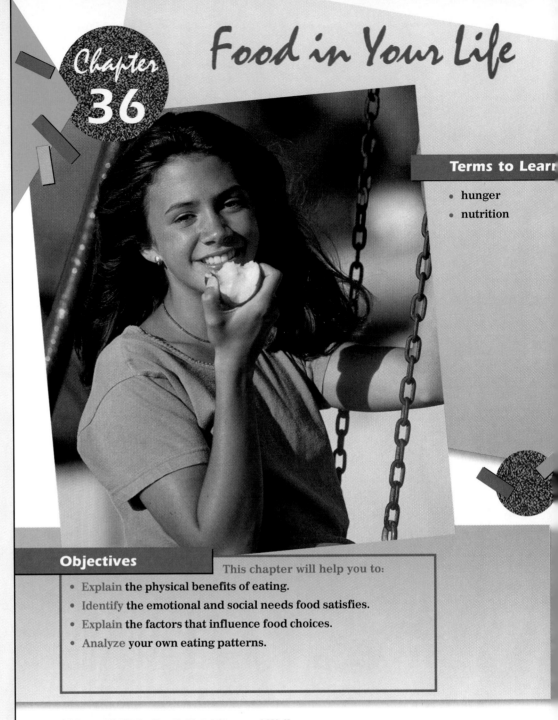

Chapter 36 — Food in Your Life

Terms to Learn

- hunger
- nutrition

Objectives

This chapter will help you to:

- Explain the physical benefits of eating.
- Identify the emotional and social needs food satisfies.
- Explain the factors that influence food choices.
- Analyze your own eating patterns.

CHAPTER RESOURCES

Student Workbook
Study Guide, pp. 120-121
Activity, *The Food in Your Life*, pp. 122-123

Teacher's Classroom Resources
Lesson Plan, p. 40
Extension #58, *Why Do People Overeat?* p. 64

Life Skills, *Do You Eat on the Run?* p. 63
Chapter 36 Test, pp. 77-78
Performance Assessment, *Many Foods, Many Choices*, p. 65
Reteaching, *Needs and Influences*, p. 42

See Also:
ABCNews InterActive™ Videodiscs

Food is so much a part of daily life that people often take eating for granted. They do not think about their own attitudes toward food, their food choices, and the ways these factors influence them now and in the future.

Now is a good time for you to think carefully about the foods you put into your body. What kinds of needs does food fulfill? What influences the choices you make about food? What kinds of eating habits are you forming? How will they affect you now and, just as important, in the future?

Food Fills Many Needs

Nutrition refers to *the way the body uses food.* When people talk about getting good nutrition, they mean eating the foods that keep them healthy and help their bodies perform most efficiently.

Food has many purposes. Besides meeting basic physical needs, nutritious food helps you stay healthy. Eating helps fulfill emotional and social needs as well.

Physical Needs

Like other living things, people need nourishment to live. Food supplies the energy needed for day-to-day activities, from automatic actions such as breathing and sleeping to more demanding activities such as sports. Eating the right foods each day helps your body perform vital functions. What you eat and drink helps your heart to beat, your temperature to remain within the normal range, and your cuts and bruises to heal.

If you go without eating for too long, you become tired, irritable, and unable to concentrate. You may get a headache or feel pain and an unpleasant rumbling in your stomach. In other words, you feel hungry. **Hunger** is *your body's physical signal that it is short of energy and needs food.*

Food does more than just keep your body functioning from one day to the next. It affects your health over a long period of time. Even before babies are born, they need nourishment to develop normally. Children who do not get adequate amounts of the right foods

Good nutrition allows children to grow to their full height.

may experience growth problems and diseases of the bones and skin. Wise food choices during the teen and adult years help people avoid heart disease and other long-term problems. No matter what your age, a well-nourished body is better equipped to heal properly and combat disease than a poorly nourished one is.

Emotional Needs

Physical needs are not the only ones people satisfy by eating every day. People often feel the urge to eat even when they're not hungry. This happens because food satisfies emotional needs, including the need for comfort, security, happiness, and well-being.

People start to make associations between food and feelings very early in life. Infants quickly learn to associate feeding with physical contact and a sense of security. Such emotional links with food continue throughout life.

CHAPTER 36   Food in Your Life   **359**

Checking Comprehension

✓ Why should you think now about your food choices and habits? *They affect you now and will in future.*

✓ Why is proper nutrition important to young people? *Helps prevent growth problems, bone, skin, and heart disease; aids healing and resistance to disease.*

CROSS-CURRICULAR ACTIVITY
Math

Have students graph their hunger patterns for three days, using either three separate graphs or color-coding all three days on a single graph. Have them write their waking hours across the bottom of the graph, and the numbers 1 through 10 (10 representing their hungriest) up the left side. Have students use a dot to indicate how hungry they feel at each hour and an X to note when they eat. Have them connect the dots to form a line graph. Ask them to write a few sentences summarizing the patterns the graph reveals.

MORE ABOUT Hunger

For much of the world's population, hunger is a prelude to starvation. World hunger is increasing due to many complex situations: a global population growth rate that outpaces food production; changing weather conditions in certain areas; rising costs of importing food and fertilizer; poor farming practices; and inadequate storage and transportation systems. Many private and government agencies are working to alleviate hunger through food-aid programs, agricultural assistance, and nutrition education.

Checking Comprehension

✓ Why might people eat when they're not hungry? *To comfort themselves, to relieve stress or boredom.*

✓ Why are certain dishes associated with certain regions? *The foods were plentiful there.*

✓ How can religious beliefs affect eating habits? *Special foods eaten on religious holidays; forbidden foods, fasting part of some religions .*

Acting Responsibly

Have students read "Are You Respectful of Other Cultures?" and discuss the questions. Ask: How might asking about culture show disrespect? Suggest that displaying a judgmental attitude and asking about inappropriate subjects may be deemed disrespectful.

Answers to What Would You Do?

1. She learned about it, helped others appreciate it also.
2. Answers will vary. She might give information to correct false ideas.
3. Answers may include: support person among friends; avoid ethnic jokes.
4. Answers will vary. Sharing meal creates social atmosphere, encouraging conversation (food choices are convenient topic) and learning.

Just the smell or sight of food can trigger in people a desire to eat certain foods in order to fill an emotional need for comfort or a sense of well-being. What foods do you think of as "comfort" foods?

For example, people who are recovering from an illness may crave a food that a parent or other caregiver made for them when they were younger. They connect the idea of that food with the feeling of being loved and cared for.

Although there is an emotional element to everyone's enjoyment of food, allowing emotions to control eating habits can affect an individual's health. Some people eat to comfort themselves whenever they are tense or upset. Others eat to relieve boredom. People who are sad or grieving may lose their appetites entirely. Allowing emotional ups and downs to control food intake can create health problems over time. You can avoid letting emotions rule your eating habits by being aware of the feelings that stimulate you to eat. You will learn more about how to monitor your eating habits later in the chapter.

Social Needs

Food serves social needs as well as physical and emotional ones. People often combine eating with the company of friends and family because both experiences are pleasurable. Do you ever stop with friends for a snack after school? Do you have a favorite relative or friend you enjoy talking to over a meal? In some families, mealtime is the only time of day that the whole family can be together. For many workers, lunch is an important opportunity to discuss business or just to relax with one another.

Food also plays a significant role in maintaining social traditions. Many special occasions are associated with specific foods—birthday cakes, Thanksgiving turkeys, or Fourth of July cookouts. Wedding receptions and religious holidays may be celebrated with special foods. These traditions provide links between food and social activities.

Influences on Choices

People fulfill their needs for food in many different ways. What they choose to eat is affected by both social and personal influences.

Social Influences

Social influences play an important role in the food choices you make. These outside influences include the region you live in; your cultural, ethnic, and religious background; your family and friends; and the media.

Regional Traditions

People are strongly influenced by the foods available to them. The Inuit, for example—an Arctic people who lack a growing season—are primarily meat eaters. People in the United States probably eat a wider variety of foods than people in any other part of the world. The size of the United States, the variety of its people, and the existence of an excellent transportation network to ship foods account for this fact.

360   UNIT 6   Food, Nutrition, and Wellness

DID YOU KNOW?

Just a few of the foods associated with various countries include: Great Britain—roast beef, fish and chips; France—crepes, bouillabaisse; Germany—sauerbrauten, sauerkraut; Italy—antipasto, spumoni, pasta; Norway and Sweden—herring, lingonberries; Lebanon—kibbe, baklava; India—curry, dal; Mexico—tortillas, tamales; China—stir-fries, hot pot; Japan—sushi, tempura; Jamaica—rice and beans, plantains.

Acting Responsibly

Are You Respectful of Other Cultures?

Showing respect means demonstrating high regard for others. One way of showing respect for another person's culture is to learn about it. Ask people who follow certain traditions to explain them. They will appreciate your interest.

You can help teach others, too. Use what you have learned about a culture to explain the traditions to others and help spread understanding and awareness.

Respect for Cultures in Action

Janice's family had agreed to host an exchange student from India. Janice was excited about having Fala live with them and go to her school, but she knew very little about Indian customs.

To prepare for Fala's arrival, Janice decided to learn as much as possible about Indian culture. She was especially interested in food preferences because she liked to cook and sometimes prepared family meals.

Janice began by learning the dietary laws of Fala's religion, Hinduism. She found a specialty store that sold Indian foods. She also suggested that her family sample different foods at an Indian restaurant. Janice wanted to make meals that both Fala and the rest of the family would enjoy.

Janice wanted Fala to feel comfortable at school too, so she invited a few classmates to a party the family gave when Fala arrived. Janice prepared a buffet of Indian food, encouraging everyone to sample the dishes. Her friends were fascinated by Fala's interesting stories and enjoyed her sense of humor. Janice had helped her friends appreciate Fala's culture. They, in turn, had helped Fala feel more at home in a new land.

Your Analysis

1. How did Janice show respect for Fala's culture?
2. What might Janice say to people who show disrespect for Fala?
3. What might you do to show respect for a classmate who comes from a different culture?
4. Why do you think sharing a meal is a good way to help people get to know each other?

Many food specialties developed because certain foods were plentiful in certain regions. Although most foods can be found all over the United States, certain dishes are still associated with specific regions. Have you ever tried New England clam chowder, Texas barbecue, or Louisiana gumbo?

Cultural and Ethnic Background

Because the United States is a nation of immigrants, foods from many cultural and ethnic groups are available here—in people's homes, in restaurants, even in specialty supermarkets. Can you easily locate Chinese or Italian restaurants where you live? Do you know where to find German sausages or Mexican tortillas? Does your region include In-

dian, Japanese, or Korean restaurants or grocery stores?

Religious Customs

Your religious customs may also influence your choice of foods. Families often eat special foods on their religious holidays—lamb at Passover or egg dishes at Easter, for example. Religious rules may forbid the eating of particular foods or require fasting—going without food—for designated periods of time.

Family

One of the greatest influences on how and what you eat is your family. Besides the ethnic and religious traditions that families follow, some families develop eating habits unique to

- **Just Not the Same.** Have students write a description of a celebration with family or friends in which a big meal or special foods play a prominent part. Ask them to explain how—or if—the event would be less meaningful if these foods were not included. *(Critical Thinking)*

RETEACHING

- **Why We Eat.** On the board, write the headings Regional Traditions, Cultural and Ethnic Background, Religious Customs, and Family. Ask students to recall foods they have eaten recently and explain how one or more of the influences listed played a role in their food choice.

ENRICHMENT

- **Regional Foods.** Ask students to research a food known as a specialty of the region. Have them learn how that food became associated with their part of the country. Students might make the dish at home and share it with the class.

REAL-LIFE APPLICATION

Read this to students: Rajeed is a *Muslim; most of his friends are not. Rajeed observes the month of Ramadan by refraining from eating and drinking from sunrise to sunset, as his religion prescribes. During this time, his friends avoid inviting* him to their homes or to activities that might include eating. Ask: Why might Rajeed's friends act this way? How would you feel if you were Rajeed? How would you respond?

Topics on pp. 362-364:
- Social Influences
- Personal Influences
- Evaluating Eating Habits

Checking Comprehension

✔ How can friends positively influence each other's food habits? *Introduce them to new cooking styles, to foods they wouldn't try; encourage nutritious habits.*

✔ Why might teens be vulnerable to ads for nonnutritious foods? *May be more concerned with immediate wants than future effects.*

✔ What can a food diary reveal? *How often you eat, foods you choose, social setting in which you eat.*

BALANCING
WORK AND FAMILY

Have students read the feature "Sharing Time Together." For each tip in the feature, ask volunteers to suggest ways they could apply it to their own family meals.

Answers to Suppose That...

Answers may include: help sibling find ways to earn money for bike; inject humorous tone into debate; tell sibling he has 30 seconds to argue for bike, then must talk about something else.

Many people enjoy foods that have cultural links even when they come from a different cultural background.

them. For example, some families always eat certain meals on certain days, such as fish on Wednesdays. Other families combine certain foods, such as always serving spinach and mashed potatoes with meat loaf. What people eat is also influenced by the family's food budget and the amount of time the family has to spend preparing and eating meals. Often, the eating habits of families are imitated by the children when they grow up and start their own families.

Friends

Friends have considerable influence on people's food choices. You may have friends whose family backgrounds are different from yours. They can introduce you to new foods and styles of cooking that you may not have known about. Friends can also encourage you to eat something you may not think you like. However, you should be careful not to eat what your friends are eating if you know that a particular food is not healthful. If you know that friends are eating too many unhealthful foods, you may be able to persuade them to try something that is nutritious as well as tasty.

Media

Food is frequently the subject of articles in newspapers and magazines and of programs on television and radio. These articles and programs offer many suggestions about preparing foods and eating for good health.

Food is also sold through advertising in these media. You will be tempted to try certain foods because the ads make them look inviting and appetizing. As you read in Chapter 32, you must evaluate these ads to be sure that the advertisers aren't hiding the poor nutritional value of the food. Teens are especially vulnerable to such pressure if they are more concerned about having what they want right now than about how it will affect them in the future.

Personal Influences

All the social influences combine to help you create an eating style and food preference that is yours alone. Among the personal influences on food choices are lifestyle, personal taste, physical changes, and medical conditions.

Lifestyle

Your way of life affects what you eat. A person who often works late may choose a simple sandwich or take-out dinner rather than prepare a complicated evening meal. Students with part-time jobs may not have time for family meals. They may have to pick up a quick meal at a fast-food restaurant. For some people, their food choices depend on whether they enjoy preparing and eating food or would rather spend their time doing other activities.

Personal Taste

Personal taste also influences the range of your food choices. You may love fish and eat it often, but you may not be able to eat spicy

Focus on Coping Skills

Some parents show love or reward children by giving them sweets or snack foods. As a result, many people turn to these foods when they want to reward or feel good about themselves. Ask:

What problems can this habit lead to? What might be a better way for parents to show love and approval? How else can people reward themselves besides eating favorite foods?

Sharing Time Together

In many families, hectic work and school days leave mealtime as the only time people spend together. Family meals, then, should be a chance to nurture relationships as well as nourish the body. Eating in a relaxed setting aids digestion, and sharing enjoyable family meals helps people form positive associations with both meals and family. Here are some tips for making mealtime moments count:

- **Try to eat at least one meal a day together.** If you can't all be together, arrange your schedules so that as many people can be present as possible.
- **Set aside a place for the meal.** Choose a comfortable place where it's easy to make conversation.
- **Create a pleasant atmosphere.** You might play some quiet background music, but avoid the distractions of television or reading.

- **Tell your family about your school or work day.** Take turns sharing the interesting things that have happened or are planned for that day.
- **Avoid discussing unpleasant or difficult topics.** If you have bad news or a problem that needs to be addressed, find a more suitable time.
- **Take turns choosing an interesting topic of conversation for each meal.** Select something that is appropriate for everyone and, if possible, that everyone can offer an opinion on.

Suppose That . . .

Your younger sibling has been using mealtimes to bring up his desire for a new bike. Your father gets upset because the money isn't available. An argument always starts. What could you do to defuse this situation and make mealtimes happier occasions?

foods because they cause you discomfort. You may prefer the crunchy texture of raw vegetables to the softer texture of cooked ones. Whether you like a particular food may also be affected by past associations. For example, if you were forced to eat brussels sprouts as a young child, you may never want to eat them again. Some people are adventurous eaters who like to try new foods. Others prefer to eat only foods they are familiar with and know they like.

Physical Changes and Medical Conditions

Physical changes you experience as you grow can have an impact on the way you eat.

> Some people enjoy sampling different foods. Are you willing to take a chance and try food you've never had before?

CHAPTER 36   Food in Your Life   363

Activities

- **What's So Funny?** Have groups write parodies of television ads for nonnutritious foods in which they put a positive slant on an unhealthful quality. Encourage students to use satire and other forms of humor. For instance, they might tout a high-sugar cereal as "supplying your quick energy needs for the entire week." *(Communication)*

RETEACHING

- **Food for Thought.** Have students list five foods they regularly eat. For each one, have them explain how one or more of the social and personal influences discussed on pp. 361-363 affect their choice.

ENRICHMENT

- **Filling Foods.** Have students watch food advertisements on television (or find them in newspapers and magazines) and determine which needs the ad appeals to. Some snack foods are often shown in a party setting, for example, appealing to social needs.

CROSS-REFERENCE

Good eating habits are essential for good health. For more information about health and wellness, see Chapter 2.

DID YOU KNOW?

Sugar originally was an item on a druggist's shelf, used to disguise the taste of medicine, and considered a drug itself. Sugar was first sold as candy in about 1200—in sugar-coated almonds, the creation of a French druggist.

The word *diet* comes from the Greek *diata*, which means to lead one's life. Ask: How can food choices reflect a person's approach to life in general?

Review

■ **Chapter Review.** Use the contents of the Chapter Review page to help students review concepts, think critically, and apply their knowledge.

■ **Study Guide.** Have students complete the Study Guide for Chapter 36 on p. 120 of the Student Workbook.

■ **Focus on Foods.** Ask students to keep a food diary for several days. Have them review each entry to identify what needs each meal or snack met and what influences contributed to their choosing that food. Have students write a short report summarizing the affects of these two factors on their eating habits, using examples from their diary.

Evaluation

■ **Chapter Test.** Use the reproducible chapter test provided in the Teacher's Classroom Resources or create your own test using the *Testmaker Software.*

■ **Alternative Assessment.** Have groups use the major points of this chapter to create a survey of eating habits. Groups may focus on a certain population, such as male or female teens, younger children, or student athletes, and tailor their questions to that group.

■ **New Food View.** Ask students to write a paragraph describing the greatest impact this chapter has had on their awareness of food choices, and how they plan to use this new understanding when choosing foods.

During a period of growth, you may notice that you eat more food or more of a particular type of food. Such conditions as food allergies and diseases may limit your food options.

Eating Habits

Do you tend to reach for the same foods whenever you're hungry? Are you a snacker? Do you eat regular, balanced meals? Your everyday patterns of eating are your eating habits. Because, as you just read, some influences can lead to poor food choices, it's important to develop healthful eating habits.

Some eating habits are established when you are very young. Other habits develop from factors in your current lifestyle. Understanding your eating habits is the first step in managing them.

Analyzing Your Own Habits

The best way to become aware of your eating habits is to keep a food diary—a record of everything you eat. For two or three days, write down:

- What you ate, as precisely as you can.
- When you ate each food.
- What else you were doing while eating.

When you review this record, you will see how frequently you eat, what foods you tend to choose, and the social circumstances in which you eat. When you look over your food diary, ask yourself:

- What foods do I choose most often?
- What foods do I eat during family meals?
- What foods do I eat when I'm with my friends?

Try to make healthful snacks a part of your daily routine. What foods do you snack on now that are good for you?

- When do I snack, and what snacks do I choose?
- Do I eat out? What foods do I choose?
- Do I eat more when I'm alone or when I'm eating with others?
- What foods do I eat when I'm in a hurry?
- How many daily activities involve food?
- Are what and when I eat affected by my moods?

By answering these questions, you will begin to get a picture of your eating habits.

Good and Bad Habits

Good eating habits, like any good habits, develop through regular practice. By beginning to choose nutritious foods in a conscious way, you will start the process that allows these choices to become second nature. Bad eating habits result from making poor food choices over a period of time. Developing good habits has real benefits. Proper nutrition can help you look and feel better and have more energy. It may even prevent you from getting diseases later in life.

As you read the rest of this unit, you will learn to make wise food choices. You will learn the importance of exercise and good eating habits. You'll also learn to control your weight and improve your fitness. You will find out how to prepare meals and snacks for yourself, your family, and your friends. You will then be able to take more responsibility for what you eat and get the maximum enjoyment and benefits that food can provide.

Focus on Problem Solving Skills

Ask students to imagine that after keeping a food diary for three days, they decide they are eating too many unhealthful snacks. What information from the diary could they use to change this habit, and how? *Might look at snacks they choose and find similar but more healthful replacements; could look at social settings and avoid, change, or prepare for them.*

Review

Reviewing the Facts

1. How does food fulfill your body's physical needs?
2. Name three emotional needs food helps satisfy.
3. Explain how a food association made early in life may affect food choices later in life.
4. How does food serve social needs?
5. Name three social influences and three personal influences on food choices.
6. Why is it important to start now to develop good eating habits?

Thinking Critically

1. What foods are considered typical of the region in which you live? How do you think they became popular there?
2. Why do you think that some people are unwilling to try new foods? Give some reasons for and against trying something you've never eaten before.

Applying Your Knowledge

1. **Identifying Cultural Influences.** Create a chart that lists and illustrates or describes foods you and your family eat that are related to your cultural and ethnic background. Indicate whether you eat these foods regularly or just on special occasions. Share the chart with the class.
2. **Ranking Social Influences.** Rank in order of importance the social influences on your eating habits. Explain in a paragraph your reasons for ranking them in the order you did.
3. **Recognizing the Importance of Foods.** Native Americans grew foods unknown to the settlers from Europe—for example, corn, peanuts, tomatoes, potatoes, pineapples, and avocados. Prepare a report on how American eating habits would be different today if Native Americans hadn't taught the settlers how to cultivate these foods. Include some dishes you like that use these foods as ingredients.

Making Connections

1. **Social Studies.** Do research on food restrictions or dietary laws of a particular religion or cultural group. Write a short report on your findings.
2. **Economics.** Companies spend billions of dollars annually to advertise their products. Consider several advertisements for food products you have seen, read, or heard recently. Explain how the ads try to convince people to buy the product. State whether you were impressed enough to try the product, and why.

Building Your Portfolio

Celebrating the Harvest

Harvest celebrations such as Thanksgiving, Kwanzaa, and Sukkoth are a part of nearly every culture. Research these three celebrations to discover their basic purposes, as well as the traditional foods that are served.

Use a chart, table, or narrative to explain basic information about each celebration. Then write a paragraph telling what needs you think such celebrations satisfy for the people who share them. Add your comparison and paragraph to your portfolio.

ANSWERS TO REVIEWING THE FACTS

1. Helps the body perform vital functions; promotes normal growth, healing, resistance to disease.
2. Any three: comfort, security, happiness, well-being, love.
3. Child who learns to associate food with positive feelings may turn to that food later to experience same emotions; may avoid foods associated with negative emotions.
4. Meals and snacks give families, friends, and co-workers chance to relax together. Food also is prominent in many social traditions.
5. Social (any three): regional traditions, cultural background, religious customs, family, friends, media. Personal (any three): lifestyle, personal tastes, physical changes, medical conditions.
6. Good eating habits take time to develop and will affect the rest of your life, helping you look and feel better, have more energy, and stay healthy.

ANSWERS TO THINKING CRITICALLY

1. Answers will vary. Point out that certain dish may be associated with area when ethnic group that settled there created it using native foods, such as jambalaya, a spicy, Creole rice-and-seafood dish.
2. Answers may include: For—share customs of friend or host; learn about different culture; enjoy new taste. Against—religious prohibition; personal bias; fear of illness or upset.

Chapter 37

FOCUS

Chapter Overview

Chapter 37 describes the importance of nutrients in food. It presents the six classes of nutrients—carbohydrates, proteins, fats, water, vitamins, and minerals—and explains how each contributes to good health.

Motivator

■ **Nutrition IQ.** Ask students to identify foods they believe are healthful and those they believe are not. List these on the board. Ask students why each food named is good for them. Keep a copy of the list and reasons for reevaluation after studying the chapter.

Objectives

Discuss the chapter objectives on this page. Remind students that the objectives focus on important chapter concepts.

Vocabulary

Many of the words associated with nutrition have Latin origins. *Nutrient* and *nutrition* both come from the Latin verb nutrire, to feed. The word *vitamin* is derived from the Latin *vita*, which is life. Ask: How is each of these modern English words related to its Latin root in meaning?

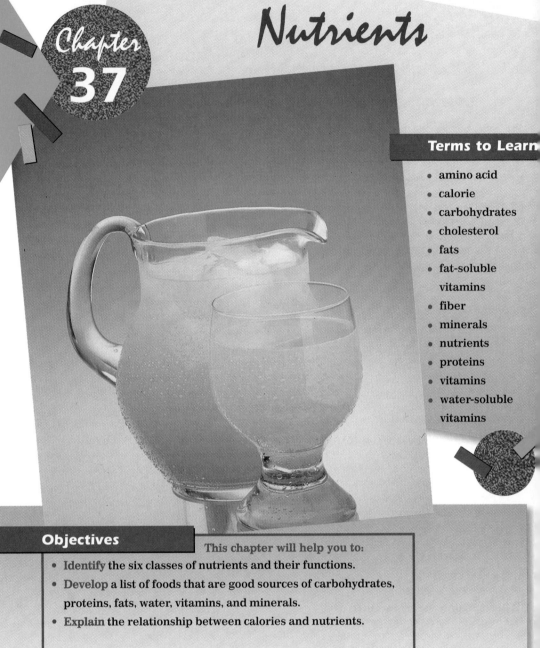

Chapter 37 — Nutrients

Terms to Learn

- amino acid
- calorie
- carbohydrates
- cholesterol
- fats
- fat-soluble vitamins
- fiber
- minerals
- nutrients
- proteins
- vitamins
- water-soluble vitamins

Objectives

This chapter will help you to:
- **Identify** the six classes of nutrients and their functions.
- **Develop** a list of foods that are good sources of carbohydrates, proteins, fats, water, vitamins, and minerals.
- **Explain** the relationship between calories and nutrients.

366 UNIT 6 Food, Nutrition, and Wellness

CHAPTER RESOURCES

Student Workbook
Study Guide, pp. 124-125
Activity, *Nutrition on the Menu*, pp. 126-127

Teacher's Classroom Resources
Lesson Plan, p. 41
Cooperative Learning, *Good Nutrition*, pp. 41-42

Extension #59, *Minerals at a Glance*, p. 65
Extension #60, *Calcium and Phosphorus*, p. 66
Life Skills, *Keeping Your Bones Healthy*, p. 64
Transparency 37, *Vitamins at a Glance*

Transparency 38, *Minerals at a Glance*
Chapter 37 Test, pp. 79-80
Performance Assessment, *Tips for Healthful Eating*, pp. 66-67
Reteaching, *Naming Nutrients*, p. 43

See Also:
ABCNews InterActive™ Videodiscs

Nutritionists, scientists who study food and its effects on the body, have found that food contains a number of nourishing substances called nutrients. **Nutrients** are *chemicals found in food that help the body work properly*. Nutrients are needed to maintain good health and to fight disease.

More than 40 key nutrients have been identified. They can be grouped into six classes: carbohydrates, proteins, fats, water, vitamins, and minerals. Each nutrient has specific jobs, which it carries out as a member of a team to help the body work properly.

Carbohydrates

Carbohydrates are *the nutrients that provide your body with ready energy*. Food containing carbohydrates should be a major part of your food choices. Grains, vegetables, fruits, and dry beans and peas are high in carbohydrates and also provide other nutrients, making them particularly valuable.

Carbohydrates are your body's most efficient fuel. If you don't eat enough carbohydrates, your body has to get energy from other nutrients or from its reserve supplies in body tissues. However, these sources are not able to provide energy as quickly. To keep your body functioning at its peak, you need carbohydrates throughout the day.

There are many ways that you can include carbohydrates in your daily meals and snacks. Sugars and starches are the two main categories of carbohydrates.

Starches

Starches are called complex carbohydrates. Rice, potatoes, bread, and pasta are examples of foods high in starch. Starch is digested to form a simple sugar called glucose, which is a major source of energy for your body.

Sugars

Glucose can also be formed from sugars, or simple carbohydrates. Foods such as fruits, grain products, and milk provide natural sugars as well as other valuable nutrients.

Sugar that has been removed from its natural source and processed, or changed from its raw form, is called refined sugar. Table sugar is an example. Refined sugar is found in cakes, candy, cookies, and many processed foods. Too much refined sugar can lead to weight gain and dental problems. Refined sugar can also cause problems for people with certain health conditions, such as diabetes. For good health, get your energy from starches and natural sugars instead of refined sugars.

These foods contain complex carbohydrates. You should eat a variety of these foods every day to give your body the energy it needs to perform well.

CHAPTER 37 Nutrients 367

TEACH

Topics on p. 367:
• Carbohydrates

Checking Comprehension

✓ What happens if you don't eat carbohydrates often enough? *Body must draw energy from other nutrients or body tissue.*

✓ Name four foods that are high in starches. *Rice, potato, bread, pasta.*

✓ Why is an apple a better source of carbohydrates than a cookie? *Apple has natural sugars, other nutrients; cookie has refined sugar, linked to weight gain, dental problems, problems for people with some health conditions.*

Activity

■ **Carbo Count.** Ask students to record the information on carbohydrate content from the labels of eight foods they find at home. Have them note also whether these are simple or complex carbohydrates. Have students use their findings to complete a large chart on the board. Ask students what conclusions they can draw from the information in the chart. *(Critical Thinking)*

MORE ABOUT Breakfast Cereals

Nutritionists have long been critical of cold breakfast cereals and their high sugar content. While cereal makers are responding by producing varieties that are lower in sugar—and by promoting those that have always been—some cereals contain up to a tablespoon of refined sugar per one-cup serving. Encourage students to note the sugar content of cold cereals they eat. Tell them to read the ingredients list to learn the amount of sugar in relation to other ingredients.

Topics on pp. 368-369:
- Fiber
- Proteins
- Fats

Checking Comprehension

✔ What does fiber do? *Helps move food through digestive system; may help reduce risk of heart disease.*

✔ Why is protein so important to young people? *They're still growing, and protein is needed for building tissue.*

✔ Do people need body fat? *Yes; to insulate body from cold, protect vital organs, provide reserve energy.*

Making Decisions

Have students read "Choices for Good Health" and discuss the questions. Ask volunteers to role-play Cory trying to convince Mike to change his pregame meal. What approach might be successful in changing Mike's mind?

Answers to What You Do?

1. He can do nothing; talk to coach; warn teammates; talk to Mike.
2. Team may not perform as well; members may develop health problems.
3. He may worry about losing friends, offending Mike, seeming unsupportive.
4. He might place nutritional pamphlets in locker room; ask coach to have nutrition expert talk to team.
5. Answers will vary.

368

Making Decisions

Choices for Good Health

Cory and his teammates had just finished practice. "We're going to the top this year," one player commented as they headed for the lockers.

"Listen to me and we just might," Mike responded. Cory said nothing. Since joining the team, Mike had been a strong influence on the rest. His confidence commanded attention. The players listened to Mike, even though his ideas were not sound.

Cory had learned a great deal from his father, who was a nutritionist. Some of Mike's ideas contradicted what Cory's father said, as well as the coach's words.

For one thing, Mike rarely drank water during practices and games, saying that it caused stomach cramps. Cory knew that as hard as the team played, they needed regular drinks of water to avoid dehydration and weakness.

Cory had also heard Mike advising teammates to take very large doses—megadoses—of vitamins. Cory knew that even very active athletes can get all their required nutrition from balanced meals. Megadoses of some vitamins could be harmful.

"We need a real protein boost before regional competition," Mike said. "Let's make steak and eggs our pregame meal." As Cory listened, he remembered his father's suggestion that a meal high in complex carbohydrates digests more quickly and supplies energy for endurance.

I like Mike, Cory thought to himself, and so does everyone else, but his advice is hurting the team, not helping it. Cory pondered what action to take.

What Would You Do?

1. What choices does Cory have in this situation?
2. What might be the consequences of not acting?
3. Why might Cory be reluctant to act?
4. If Cory decides to provide information that contradicts Mike, how can he do so without making an enemy out of him?
5. What do you think Cory should do? Why?

Fiber

One of the benefits of eating certain carbohydrate foods is that they contain *indigestible threadlike cells* called **fiber.** Fiber is not strictly a nutrient, but it performs several important jobs. One type of fiber helps move food through the digestive system. Another type seems to help reduce the risk of heart disease. Whole-grain cereals and breads are excellent sources of fiber because they use almost the entire grain seed, or kernel, and contain almost all of the grain's original nutrients. Other good sources of fiber are fruits and vegetables, especially the peels and seeds.

Proteins

Proteins are *the nutrients necessary for building and repairing body tissues.* Proteins are the basis of all the body's cells and form the major part of hair, nails, and skin. Proteins are especially important for children and teens, because they are growing. Getting enough proteins is crucial, however, for people of all ages.

Complete and Incomplete

Your body needs many different types of protein, but all proteins are made from the same basic chemicals. These *chemicals in proteins* are called **amino acids.** Twenty-two different kinds of amino acids have been identified by scientists.

While your body uses all the amino acids, only 9 of them must be obtained from food. The other 13 can be created by your body from other food substances. The 9 amino acids that you must obtain from food are called the essential amino acids. The foods that contain essential amino acids—such animal proteins as meat, poultry, fish, eggs, and milk—are said to have complete proteins.

Dry beans and peas, nuts, seeds, vegetables, and grains are said to be incomplete proteins. They contain some, but not all, of the essential amino acids. You can get the essential 9, however, by combining certain incom-

---

MORE ABOUT Cholesterol

Scientists have identified two kinds of blood cholesterol: "bad" cholesterol (LDLs, or low-density lipoproteins) and "good" cholesterol (HDLs, or high-density lipoproteins). High amounts of HDLs are associated with lower risk of heart disease. HDL cholesterol levels can be raised by exercising, controlling your weight, avoiding cigarettes, eating plenty of soluble fiber, and limiting intake of animal products and tropical oils.

Most Americans eat more protein foods than they need. Excess protein is stored in the body as fat.

plete proteins. For example, you can combine beans with rice, or you can combine dry beans or peas with grains, nuts, or seeds. This process is called protein complementing. People who do not eat animal products can use protein complementing to get the protein necessary for good health. Incomplete proteins do not have to be combined in the same dish or meal. They should just be eaten during the same day.

You can combine certain incomplete proteins, such as rice and beans, to form a complete protein.

Fats

Fats are *the nutrients that are the most concentrated sources of energy*. They are needed by the body for several reasons. Fats allow your body to transport and store certain other nutrients. They also help regulate body temperature and growth. Without dietary fats, people can develop problems with their skin and hair.

After the body has used the fat it needs for these purposes, it stores the rest as body fat. Some body fat is needed to insulate the body in cold weather, protect vital organs, and serve as a reserve supply of energy.

Although some fat is needed for good health, most Americans eat too much fat. Eating food with too much fat over a period of time, combined with little or no exercise, will make you gain weight. Excess weight can lead to heart disease and other serious health problems.

CHAPTER 37   Nutrients   369

Activities

■ **Eye on Fiber.** Ask students to bring in the nutrition panel from packages of grain products. Make a large chart on the board comparing amounts of fiber, sugar, calories, and fat per serving of the products they have identified. Have students draw conclusions about each food as a source of fiber, especially when balanced against the sugar and calorie content.

RETEACHING

■ **Find the Fats.** Have students look through cookbooks and identify recipes containing fats. Have students tell which ingredient contributes the fat to the dish.

Have students compare the amount and types of fat in traditional diets of other cultures to the typical American diet. What food choices or eating habits account for differences in fat intake? Have students write recommendations based on their findings on how Americans could follow the example of some other cultures to lower the fat in their diets.

REAL-LIFE APPLICATION

Read this to students: *Terri would like to try a vegetarian diet. Her brother claims the family will have to spend a lot of money on hard-to-find foods. Her mother says if Terri wants special vegetarian dishes, she will have to prepare them herself.* Ask: Are the family's concerns well-founded? Help students see that while vegetarians must be careful to meet protein needs, most other nutritional requirements can be met with a balanced diet of readily available foods.

Topics on pp. 370-371:

- **Saturated and Unsaturated Fats**
- **Water**
- **Vitamins**

Checking Comprehension

✓ Why are saturated fats undesirable? *May lead to high levels of blood cholesterol, increasing risk of heart disease, high blood pressure, other problems.*

✓ What single nutrient accounts for most of body weight? Where in the body is it found? *Water; in every cell.*

✓ True or false: vitamins give people extra energy. *False.*

CROSS-CURRICULAR ACTIVITY
Science

Vitamin supplements usually contain synthetic vitamins, those made in a laboratory. Encourage students to investigate this process. Ask them to formulate an opinion as to whether synthetic vitamins are less beneficial than naturally occurring ones.

Figure 37.1

Vitamins at a Glance

Vitamin	Function	Source
Vitamin A	• Builds good vision, healthy teeth and gums, and strong bones • Helps immune system resist infection	• Yellow-orange fruits and vegetables—such as cantaloupes, apricots, carrots, and sweet potatoes—and dark green leafy vegetables—such as broccoli and spinach (these fruits and vegetables contain beta-carotene [BAY-tuh-CARE-uh-teen], which the body uses to make vitamin A) • Eggs, liver, milk products
B Vitamins: Thiamine (B1), Riboflavin (B2), Niacin, Vitamin B6, Vitamin B12, Folate (folic acid), Pantothenic acid, Biotin	• Helps nerve and brain tissue work well • Aids in digestion	• Milk products, meats, breads and cereals, dry beans and peas, dark green leafy vegetables
Vitamin C (Ascorbic Acid)	• Helps body build cells—aids in healing cuts and bruises • Helps form healthy teeth and gums and strong bones	• Citrus fruits (oranges and grapefruits), strawberries, cantaloupe, tomatoes, potatoes, broccoli, raw cabbage
Vitamin D	• Helps body use minerals, such as calcium and phosphorus • Helps form strong bones and teeth	• Your body makes it if skin is exposed to enough sunlight • Added to many milk products
Vitamin E	• Helps keep red blood cells healthy	• Vegetable oils, grains, nuts, dark green leafy vegetables
Vitamin K	• Helps blood to clot	• Broccoli and other dark green leafy vegetables, cauliflower, egg yolks, liver

370   UNIT 6   Food, Nutrition, and Wellness

Focus on Critical Thinking Skills

Claims for vitamins range from plausible to extreme. Certain vitamins are said to heal injuries or prevent disease. Megadoses—large amounts of vitamins, which can be dangerous—are touted as cures for colds or other illness. Have students make a bulletin board display with examples of extravagant claims for vitamins. Discuss the language used: How does the ad try to convince readers that it is true? What promises are actually made?

Fats are present in many foods. Those especially high in fat include butter, margarine, cream, sour cream, fried foods, and salad dressings made with oil. Other high-fat foods include some meats, some poultry, peanut butter, nuts, whole milk, cheese, baked goods, and many processed snack foods. Some fats are easy to spot, such as butter or the layer of fat on the edge of a pork chop. Other fats are hidden in such foods as eggs, french fries, ice cream, and chocolate.

Saturated and Unsaturated

There are two types of fats: saturated and unsaturated. Saturated fats are found in animal foods such as meat, milk, and butter, as well as in coconut and palm oil and other tropical oils. Most saturated fats are solid at room temperature. Unsaturated fats are liquid at room temperature. They are found mainly in oils from vegetables, nuts, and seeds, such as corn, olive, peanut, and sesame oils.

Saturated fats are particularly undesirable in the diet because they may lead to high levels of cholesterol in the blood. **Cholesterol** (kuh-LESS-tuh-rahl) is *a white, waxlike substance that plays a part in transporting and digesting fat.* High cholesterol levels can lead to heart disease, high blood pressure, and other health problems. Whenever possible, unsaturated fats should be substituted for saturated fats.

Water

Nearly 70 percent of your body weight is made up of water. Water is found in every cell and is the basic material of your blood. It transports nutrients throughout the body and carries away waste products. Water also helps to move food through the digestive system and to regulate the temperature of your body.

Your body loses water continually, so it is important that you take in enough. Foods especially high in water include milk, soups, and many fruits and vegetables. In addition, health professionals recommend drinking between six and eight glasses of water daily. You need additional water when it is hot and when you exercise or do physical work.

Unless a health professional advises supplements, it's better to get your daily intake of vitamins and minerals by eating nutritious foods such as these.

Activities

■ **Water, Water Everywhere.** Have students investigate bottled water. They might evaluate nutritional and other claims on the labels; compare prices; and conduct a taste test with tap water and various brands of bottled water. Discuss: What are some advantages and disadvantages of using bottled water? For whom might bottled water be a good option? (*Critical Thinking*)

■ **Meal-in-a-Pill.** Bring in the label from a multivitamin supplement. Have students plan a day's menu that would supply the same vitamins and minerals as does the pill. Discuss the nutritive value of a poor diet and a vitamin pill as compared to a balanced diet without the supplement. (*Management*)

ENRICHMENT

■ Many people in developing nations, and in regions of industrialized nations, suffer from illnesses due to vitamin deficiencies, such as scurvy, pellegra, and rickets. Ask students to explore this situation, focusing on where these problems are most common and what efforts are being made to alleviate them.

DID YOU KNOW?

Human milk is deficient in vitamin D. Scientists speculate this is because humans originated in warmer climates where they could get the vitamin D they needed from the sun. Children who do not get enough sun may develop rickets, a softening of the bones due to vitamin D deficiency. This is one reason the nutrient is added to commercially processed milk.

Topics on pp. 372-374:
- **Vitamins (continued)**
- **Minerals**
- **Calories**

Checking Comprehension

✓ What health concern do water-soluble vitamins present? *You need daily supply since not stored for later.*

✓ If osteoporosis usually appears later in life, why is it a concern for teens? *It can start if you skimp on calcium when you're young.*

✓ What affects a food's calorie count? Give one example. *Nutrients it contains. Food with more fat (steak, butter) has more calories than water- or carbohydrate-based food (potato).*

In Touch With
TECHNOLOGY

Have students read the feature. Ask: Would a simpler version of the software be more useful? What features would consumers want most?

Answers to Thinking Critically
1. Answers may include: organizes complex information for ease of use; lets professionals evaluate patients' habits and needs quickly.
2. Answers may include: need for updating; may be more detailed and expensive than needed.
3. Answers will vary. Average consumer may not need or want such detailed information.

In Touch with TECHNOLOGY
Nutrition Computer Software

Computers help health professionals, educators, and food service professionals determine whether their clients are getting proper levels of essential nutrients. Available now are several software packages containing databases that provide information about the calories and nutrients in many foods.

One program has almost 3,000 items. They include ethnic, vegetarian, and fast-food items, specific brands of convenience foods, and the latest low-fat and nonfat products. Users can add foods to the database also. The program provides information about two dozen individual nutrients.

Users retrieve data in many forms, ranging from a simple nutrient analysis of a single food to personalized recommendations for improving eating habits. They can evaluate nutrient intake based on age, gender, height, weight, and activity level. Users can also get printouts of average nutrient intake for several days.

Programs like these make it easy to create recipes, meals, and menus that meet an individual's special needs, such as a low-sodium diet.

Thinking Critically About Technology

1. What do you think is the greatest benefit of this type of computer software?
2. What might be a drawback to this type of program?
3. Do you think this product would be useful to individual consumers?

Vitamins

Vitamins are *nutrients that help the body stay healthy, function properly, and process other nutrients.* Vitamins do not provide energy or form body tissues, but they are necessary for good health. They are needed in very small amounts. Not getting enough of certain vitamins can lead to a number of problems, including diseases of the eyes, skin, and bones. **Figure 37.1** on page 370 shows common vitamins along with the functions and good food sources of each.

Getting too many vitamins can be just as harmful as not getting enough. The body is able to get rid of some unneeded vitamins, but others can build up to dangerous levels in the body. What makes the difference is whether the vitamins are water soluble or fat soluble.

Water-soluble vitamins *are easily absorbed and can move through the body dissolved in water.* Since water is constantly lost from the body through urine and perspiration, you need fresh supplies of these vitamins every day. Excess amounts are not stored for later use. Vitamin C and the B vitamins, which are a group of eight nutrients, are water-soluble vitamins.

Vitamins A, D, E, and K are **fat-soluble vitamins.** *They travel through the bloodstream in droplets of fat.* They can also be stored in fat cells for long periods of time.

Minerals

Minerals are *simple substances that form part of many tissues and are needed to keep body processes operating smoothly.* **Figure 37.2** on page 373 shows common minerals and the functions and good food sources of each.

Your body contains large amounts of some minerals and tiny quantities of others. For ex-

372   UNIT 6   Food, Nutrition, and Wellness

DID YOU KNOW?

Mineral deficiencies are fairly rare, possibly because minerals are difficult to destroy. Unlike vitamins, they aren't lost by cooking, processing, or exposure to air. Two notable exceptions are iron and calcium. Iron deficiency is the most common mineral-related problem in the United States. It is most often seen among children and especially among poor children. An iron deficiency can cause attention problems in young children, which may lead to poor school performance.

Figure 37.2

Minerals at a Glance

Mineral	Function	Source
Calcium	• Builds and maintains healthy bones, teeth, and muscles • Keeps heartbeat regular • Helps blood clot normally	• Dairy products (including milk, cheese, and yogurt), dark green leafy vegetables, canned fish with soft bones (such as sardines, salmon, and mackerel)
Phosphorus	• Works with calcium to help build and maintain strong bones and teeth • Helps body obtain energy from other nutrients	• Dairy products (including milk, cheese, and yogurt), meats, fish, poultry, dry beans and peas, whole-grain breads and cereals
Potassium	• Regulates muscle contractions and transmission of nerve signals • Helps regulate fluid in cells • Works with sodium to regulate blood pressure	• Oranges, bananas
Sodium	• Helps regulate blood pressure • Helps regulate fluid balance in body	• Table salt, processed foods
Magnesium	• Helps body build strong bones • Regulates nervous system and body temperature	• Whole-grain cereals and breads, dry beans and peas, dark green leafy vegetables
Iron	• Builds red blood cells, which transport oxygen through body	• Liver, spinach, red meat, eggs, raisins, dry beans and peas, nuts, grain products
Zinc	• Is needed for proper growth • Affects senses of taste and smell • Helps wounds heal	• Shellfish, meat, eggs, dairy products, whole-grain breads
Iodine	• Helps thyroid gland, which produces substances that help the body obtain energy from nutrients, to work properly	• Iodized salt, seafood

Activity

■ **Do Meals Measure Up?** Ask students to list all the foods they recall eating in the past two days, grouping them as high in either carbohydrates, protein, or fat. Refer students to the discussion of nutrients and calories on p. 374. Point out the calories contained in each nutrient. Ask: How do your food choices compare with nutritionists' recommendations?

FAMILY AND COMMUNITY OUTREACH

Ask students to interview people from different areas of the health and nutrition field, such as a nutritionist, a trainer at a health club, and the owner of an organic food store, about their views on vitamins and minerals. (Approve students' choices in advance to ensure a variety of respondents.) Students might ask: What benefits do you believe vitamins and minerals provide? From what foods or other products do you recommend people get these nutrients? On what research or experience do you base your beliefs? Have students compare their findings. Do any opinions conflict? How would students decide whose advice to follow?

MORE ABOUT Sodium

Sodium is a mineral—and a villain to some. Sodium is vital to maintaining a balance of fluid in the body; yet in excess it can cause a host of problems, from swelling of the hands and feet to high blood pressure. Sodium-conscious consumers must be vigilant: sodium—in the form of table salt and additives such as sodium phosphate and sodium nitrite—lurks everywhere, especially in processed foods. Some brands of soup have over 800 mg per one-cup serving.

Review

■ **Chapter Review.** Use the contents of the Chapter Review page to help students review concepts, think critically, and apply their knowledge.

■ **Study Guide.** Have students complete the Study Guide for Chapter 37 on p. 124 of the Student Workbook.

■ **In Other Words . . .** Refer students to the chapter objectives listed on p. 366. Have them rewrite each objective as a question and then answer it.

Evaluation

■ **Chapter Test.** Use the reproducible chapter test provided in the Teacher's Classroom Resources or create your own test using the *Testmaker Software.*

■ **Alternative Assessment.** Tell students they are writing the "Today's Specials" insert to a health food restaurant menu. Have them choose six likely items and write appealing descriptions of the nutrients they supply. (Pasta in tomato sauce might be "a zesty combination of carbohydrates and vitamin C.") Use in real menus as examples of descriptive style and tone.

■ **Presenting . . .** Have students create a new food, using the information in this chapter on nutrients and their sources. Students' creations should comprise parts of existing foods to include all the nutrients discussed. For example, a food might be part liver for iron, part spinach for calcium. Encourage students to provide sketches of their new food.

374

---

ample, calcium is the mineral that is present in the body in the largest quantities. Iron is present in only very small, or trace, amounts. Maintaining the proper level of both of these minerals, as well as all other essential minerals, is vital to good health. Calcium and iron are of particular importance during adolescence because of the great increase in growth during this time.

Although calcium is found in many foods, all too often teens take in too little calcium. This is particularly true for females, who need more calcium than males.

A condition known as osteoporosis (AHS-tee-oh-puh-ROH-sus) can develop later in life if you skimp on high-calcium foods when you are young. When osteoporosis occurs, bones lose their density and become brittle. Bones in this condition are much more likely to fracture. Osteoporosis is common in older people, especially women. By taking in enough calcium throughout life and exercising regularly, people can help prevent osteoporosis.

Iron is vital for building red blood cells. It is important that teen girls get enough iron to replace losses during menstruation. Teens, especially boys, need iron to accommodate growing muscle mass. People who do not get enough iron develop iron-deficiency anemia—their blood cannot carry enough oxygen, and they experience a lack of energy and low resistance to infections.

Nutrients and Calories

As you have read, some nutrients provide energy. The energy in food is measured in calories. A **calorie** is *a unit of heat energy*. The number of calories found in a particular food is an indicator of the amount of energy the food provides. This energy may be used by the body or stored as body fat.

The calorie count of a particular food depends on what nutrients the food contains. There are 4 calories in every gram of protein and 4 in every gram of carbohydrate. In every gram of fat, however, there are 9 calories. Water, vitamins, and minerals have no calories at all.

A comparison of calories in equal amounts of steak, baked potato, and butter shows that calorie content is greatly affected by the nutrients that make up a food. A 5-oz. (140 g) baked potato, for example, is mostly water and carbohydrates. It has approximately 130 calories. A 5-oz. sirloin steak, which is 18 percent fat by weight, has close to 400 calories. Finally, 5 oz. of butter, which is more than 80 percent fat by weight, has over 1,000 calories.

Nutritionists recommend that people get 55 percent or more of their calories from carbohydrates. Of that amount, the greater percentage should be from complex carbohydrates. The recommended percentage from protein is 12-15 percent. From fat, 30 percent or less is recommended. Of the percentage from fat, less should be from saturated than from unsaturated fats.

Making Choices for Health

If you start now to eat foods that contain sufficient nutrients, you will help protect yourself from heart disease and other serious illnesses later in life. You will also find that you have more energy now to do the things you want to do.

Focus on Critical Thinking Skills

Divide the class into six groups, one for each nutrient. Give each student a copy of the school's lunch menu for the week. Have groups list those foods identified in the chapter as sources of their assigned nutrient, then look for these foods, or recipes made with them, on the menu. Have each group report to the class whether, after this brief evaluation, they think the school lunches meet students' needs for that nutrient. Have them give reasons for their opinion.

Reviewing the Facts

1. List the six classes of nutrients. What is a major function of each?
2. What are the two major types of carbohydrates? What substance do they form when they are digested by the body?
3. What is the difference between a complete protein and an incomplete protein? Describe protein complementing.
4. Describe the two types of fats.
5. What is the difference between fat-soluble and water-soluble vitamins?
6. What do calcium and phosphorus have in common?

Thinking Critically

1. Why do you think that nutritionists recommend that people get the greatest percentage of their calories from carbohydrates?
2. What factors can you think of that may contribute to the high amount of fat in the American diet? What alternatives are available that might help people lessen their fat intake?

Applying Your Knowledge

1. **Preparing a Chart.** Create a chart that shows the six classes of nutrients and some of the foods that are good sources of nutrients from each category. Identify foods on the list that you enjoy eating. Note which categories of nutrients your favorite foods contain.
2. **Making Predictions.** Suppose that you have a friend who eats no animal products. Predict the health consequences to your friend if he or she does not eat enough complete protein. Identify how your friend can get complete protein from sources other than animal products.
3. **Designing a Poster.** Make a poster that illustrates why it is necessary for everyone, including teens, to get enough calcium in foods.

Making Connections

1. **Language Arts.** With a classmate, write an article for a nutrition magazine on one of the following topics: "The Truth About Saturated Fats" or "Sugar: The Inside Scoop." Be sure to include in the article the dangers of eating too many foods that contain fat or sugar.
2. **Math.** Calculate the approximate number of calories in each of these foods: a chicken dish that contains 30 g of protein, 3 g of carbohydrate, and 3 g of fat; a green bean dish that contains 7 g of protein, 10 g of carbohydrate, and 2 g of fat; a macaroni and cheese dish that contains 15 g of protein, 28 g of carbohydrate, and 11 g of fat.

Building Your Portfolio

Preparing a Pamphlet for Good Nutrition

Health professionals have found that there is a direct connection between what you put into your body and how well your body functions. The foods you choose affect how well you feel now and whether you will stay healthy later in life. Taking the part of a nutritionist, prepare a pamphlet that you could distribute to people to help them choose foods that are high in vital nutrients. Include in the pamphlet the reasons that the nutrients are important to good health. Add the pamphlet to your portfolio.

CHAPTER 37 Nutrients 375

ANSWERS TO REVIEWING THE FACTS

1. *Carbohydrates*—give quick energy; *proteins*—build and repair body tissue; *fats*—transport and store other nutrients, help regulate body temperature and growth; *water*—moves food and nutrients through body, removes waste; *vitamins*—keep body healthy and functioning, process other nutrients; *minerals*—form part of many tissues, keep body processes running smoothly.
2. Starches and sugars; glucose.
3. Complete protein contains all 9 essential amino acids; incomplete contains some but not all. Protein complementing—eating incomplete protein foods which together form complete protein.
4. *Saturated*—solid at room temperature, found in animal foods and tropical oils. *Unsaturated fats*—liquid at room temperature, found in vegetable and nut oils.
5. *Fat-soluble*—travel through the bloodstream in droplets of fat; stored in fat cells for long time; can build up dangerously. *Water-soluble*—move through body dissolved in water; excess amounts excreted; must be replenished daily.
6. Both help build and maintain strong bones and teeth.

ANSWERS TO THINKING CRITICALLY

1. Answers may include: carbohydrates are most efficient fuel; allow body to maintain energy stores from other nutrients; none of the health risks of fats.
2. Answers may include: Americans eat many processed, high-fat foods due to busy lifestyle; include high-fat snacks in many social and leisure activities. Alternatives include: seasoned popcorn without butter; selected salad bar items at fast-food restaurant; low-fat snacks, either homemade or store-bought.

Chapter Overview

Chapter 38 explains the Food Guide Pyramid. Students learn how to use the Pyramid and other strategies to plan nutritious meals and achieve a balanced diet.

Motivator

■ **Foods of a Feather.** Ask students to name ways people group foods, such as health foods, breakfast foods, and desserts. Ask: What quality is each method of grouping based on? How would you group foods if good nutrition were your aim? For this purpose, it helps to group foods by their source and the nutrients they provide—like the Food Guide Pyramid.

Objectives

Discuss the chapter objectives on this page. Remind students that the objectives focus on important chapter concepts.

Vocabulary

Point out that the term *legume* applies only to dry beans and peas. This is because these foods are higher in nutrients when matured, as opposed to eaten fresh, and so "earn" the designation.

Chapter 38
Guidelines for Good Nutrition

Terms to Learn

- Dietary Guidelines for Americans
- enriched
- Food Guide Pyramid
- fortified
- legumes
- moderate
- nutrient density

Objectives

This chapter will help you to:

- Identify **the five major food groups in the Food Guide Pyramid.**
- Recognize **the nutrients that each of the five major food groups supplies.**
- Identify **the Dietary Guidelines for Americans and explain how they contribute to good health.**

CHAPTER RESOURCES

Student Workbook
Study Guide, pp. 128-129
Activity, *Watching What You Eat*, p. 130

Teacher's Classroom Resources
Lesson Plan, p. 42
Cooperative Learning, *Healthful Choices*, pp. 43-44

Extension #61, *Vegetarians and Food Choices*, p. 67
Extension #62, *Improving Nutrient Density*, p. 68
Life Skills, *Personal Nutrition Profile*, p. 65
Transparency 39, *The Food Guide Pyramid*

Transparency 40, *Hidden Ingredients*
Chapter 38 Test, pp. 81-82
Performance Assessment, *Where Are the Nutrients?* p. 68
Reteaching, *Good Food Choices*, p. 44

See Also:
ABCNews InterActive ™ Videodiscs

When Janet was studying foods and nutrition in school, she decided that she wanted to make more of an effort to choose foods that would help her maintain her good health. As she started to read brochures from the library and magazine articles about healthful eating, she was at first somewhat confused by all the advice that was available. She was happy to find out that the government puts out guidelines and diagrams that help consumers choose healthful foods in the right amounts. This chapter introduces these guidelines and diagrams that have been developed to make it easier to eat right for good health.

Food Groups and the Food Guide Pyramid

Eating for good health is a matter of selecting nutrient-rich foods and then knowing how much of each food to eat. Nutritionists have helped make this two-step goal easier to reach by dividing foods into five basic groups, according to the nutrients that different foods contain. The five food groups are:

- Bread, cereal, rice, and pasta.
- Vegetables.
- Fruits.
- Milk, yogurt, and cheese.
- Meat, poultry, fish, dry beans, eggs, and nuts.

Nutritionists have also developed the **Food Guide Pyramid,** which *places the food groups in a pyramid shape according to the amount of food you need each day from each group.* The Food Guide Pyramid is shown in **Figure 38.1** on page 378. The base of the Pyramid represents the largest amount of food needed each day. The top of the Pyramid represents the smallest amount needed.

The Food Guide Pyramid recommends a certain number of daily servings from each of the food groups. How do you measure a serving? **Figure 38.2** on page 379 indicates the serving size of a few sample foods from each food group. Using first the Food Guide Pyramid and then the sample serving sizes chart makes it easy to know what and how much to eat from the five food groups.

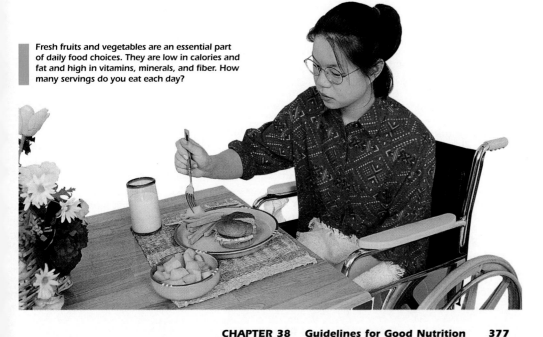

Fresh fruits and vegetables are an essential part of daily food choices. They are low in calories and fat and high in vitamins, minerals, and fiber. How many servings do you eat each day?

CHAPTER 38   Guidelines for Good Nutrition   377

TEACH

Topics on p. 377:
- **The Food Guide Pyramid**

Checking Comprehension

✓ What are the two steps to eating nutritiously? *Select nutrient-rich foods; eat them in proper amounts.*

✓ How are foods in the Food Guide Pyramid arranged? *According to amount of food you need each day from each group.*

Activities

■ **Food Guide Square?** Nutritionists chose the pyramid shape to illustrate the desired ratio of servings from each food group. Challenge students to create another design to convey this same information. *(Creativity)*

ENRICHMENT

■ **In the Beginning . . .** The Food Guide Pyramid went through a lengthy stage of public comment before it was chosen. Have students research the history of the Food Guide Pyramid and write a paragraph on how it came to be adopted.

MULTICULTURAL *Perspectives*

Have students learn what foods are popular in a certain ethnic cuisine and place them in the Food Group Pyramid. Ask: Does this cuisine seem to fit in with the Pyramid? Why or why not?

REAL-LIFE APPLICATION

Read this to students: *Stephen is trying to use the Food Guide Pyramid to make food choices. He was glad to see that his favorite snacks, doughnuts and cookies, are both from the Bread, Cereal, Rice, and Pasta Group.* Ask: Has Stephen correctly categorized these foods? Does he seem to understand the purpose of the Pyramid? Help students to see that not every food in a group is a wise choice. Challenge them to suggest more healthful alternatives.

Checking Comprehension

✓ What factors determine how many daily servings a person needs? *Age, gender, size, activity level.*

✓ Why should a diet be based on bread, cereal, rice, and pasta? *They're rich in carbohydrates.*

✓ What parts of plants may be eaten? *Roots, stems, leaves, flowers, seeds, fruits.*

FAMILY AND COMMUNITY OUTREACH

Suggest that students learn whether the grain products their family buys are whole-grain. If not, they might investigate and recommend whole-grain alternatives.

CROSS-CURRICULAR ACTIVITY
Social Studies

Have students report on the history of one type of grain. Who or what group is credited with first cultivating it and using it as a major food source? In what cultures is it popular today, and why?

Food Pyramid

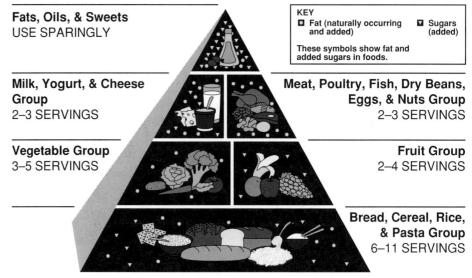

Fats, Oils, & Sweets
USE SPARINGLY

KEY
☐ Fat (naturally occurring and added)   ☑ Sugars (added)
These symbols show fat and added sugars in foods.

Milk, Yogurt, & Cheese Group
2–3 SERVINGS

Meat, Poultry, Fish, Dry Beans, Eggs, & Nuts Group
2–3 SERVINGS

Vegetable Group
3–5 SERVINGS

Fruit Group
2–4 SERVINGS

Bread, Cereal, Rice, & Pasta Group
6–11 SERVINGS

Figure 38.1

The range of daily servings of each food group in the Food Guide Pyramid varies. For example, 6 to 11 servings from the Bread, Cereal, Rice, and Pasta Group are recommended. How do you know how many servings are right for you? It depends on your age, gender, body size, and activity level. For example, many inactive women and some older adults need only 6 servings from the Bread, Cereal, Rice, and Pasta Group. Most children, teen females, active women, and many inactive men need 9 servings. Teen males, many active men, and some very active women need 11 servings from this group.

Bread, Cereal, Rice, and Pasta

The Bread, Cereal, Rice, and Pasta Group makes up the base of the Food Guide Pyramid, because foods from this group are the foundation of a balanced diet. Bread, cereal, rice, and pasta are the richest source of carbohydrates, the energy nutrient. Foods from this group also provide B vitamins, vitamin E, iron, fats, incomplete proteins, and fiber.

Many grain products are processed before being sold. Processing strips away some of the nutrients from grains. For the most nutritional value, select foods with the following labels:

- **Whole-grain,** which means that the natural nutrients were never removed.
- **Enriched,** which means that *many of the lost nutrients have been replaced.*
- **Fortified,** which means that *additional nutrients have been added.*

The recommended number of servings to be eaten daily from the Bread, Cereal, Rice, and Pasta Group is more than from any other food group. You will learn more about these foods in Chapter 50.

DID YOU KNOW?

- While some breakfast cereals are quite good sources of fiber, others have less one gram per serving. Always read the label when choosing a breakfast cereal for its fiber content.

- Vegetables that are popular in other cultures include the calabaza, a West Indian pumpkin; the potato-like malanga, enjoyed in Cuba and Puerto Rico; the boniato, a tropical sweet potato; and the chayote, a tropical summer squash.

Vegetables

Three to five servings of vegetables are recommended daily. Vegetables are valuable sources of carbohydrates and are high in fiber. They provide many important vitamins and minerals, including vitamins A and C, iron, and calcium.

All vegetables are plant products. Different parts of plants are harvested as edible foods.

- **Roots.** Carrots, beets, turnips, and potatoes grow underground.
- **Stems.** Asparagus, broccoli, and celery have edible stalks.
- **Leaves.** Leafy vegetables include lettuce, chicory, romaine, spinach, and cabbage.
- **Flowers.** Broccoli and cauliflower are both flowers of plants.
- **Seeds.** This group includes corn, beans, and peas.
- **Fruits.** Some foods that are eaten as vegetables, such as tomatoes and peppers, are actually the fruits of plants.

Figure 38.2

Food Guide Pyramid Serving Sizes

Use these serving sizes as guidelines when you decide how much food from each food group to eat every day.

Bread, Cereal, Rice, and Pasta Group

1 slice bread
1 oz. (28 g) ready-to-eat cereal
½ cup (125 mL) cooked cereal, rice, or pasta
5-6 small crackers

Vegetable Group

1 cup (250 mL) raw leafy vegetables
½ cup (125 mL) other vegetables, cooked or chopped raw
¾ cup (175 mL) vegetable juice

Fruit Group

1 medium apple, banana, or orange
½ cup (125 mL) chopped, cooked, or canned fruit
¾ cup (175 mL) fruit juice

Milk, Yogurt, and Cheese Group

1 cup (250 mL) milk or yogurt
1½ oz. (42 g) natural cheese, such as cheddar
2 oz. (56 g) process cheese

Meat, Poultry, Fish, Dry Beans, Eggs, and Nuts Group

2-3 oz. (56-85 g) cooked lean meat, poultry, or fish, such as:
- 1 hamburger patty
- 1 chicken leg or one-half medium chicken breast
- piece of halibut

Foods that can substitute for 1 oz. (28 g) of meat, such as:

- ½ cup (125 mL) cooked dry beans or peas
- 1 egg
- 2 Tbsp. (30 mL) peanut butter

CHAPTER 38   Guidelines for Good Nutrition   379

Checking Comprehension

✓ What are the two main minerals provided by milk, yogurt, and cheese? *Calcium and phosphorus.*

✓ What foods in the Meat, Poultry, Fish, Dry Beans, Eggs, and Nuts Group can be combined to form complete protein? *Legumes plus nuts or seeds.*

✓ Why don't fats, oils, and sweets form a basic food group? *They are not needed for good health.*

CROSS-CURRICULAR ACTIVITY
Science

Have students research noncaloric sweeteners. How and of what are they made? How do they provide sweetness? What issues or conflicts are associated with their use? Students could use their research to debate the safety or healthfulness of these products.

Three servings of milk products are recommended for teens each day. Drinking a glass of low-fat milk for a snack or with a meal is a good way to get a serving from the Milk, Yogurt, and Cheese Group.

Fruits

Fruits contain many of the same nutrients as vegetables. They are good sources of fiber and carbohydrates and provide essential vitamins and minerals, especially vitamin A, vitamin C, and potassium. Two to four servings of fruits are recommended every day. You will learn more about cooking fruits and vegetables in Chapter 51.

Milk, Yogurt, and Cheese

Two to three servings from the Milk, Yogurt, and Cheese Group are needed each day. Milk is a source of carbohydrates, fat, and protein. It is rich in riboflavin, one of the B vitamins, as well as vitamin A, and it is often fortified with vitamin D. Drinking milk is an excellent way to get calcium and phosphorus.

Milk is available in a variety of types, including whole milk, low-fat milk, skim milk, and powdered or dry milk. Yogurt and cheese are made from milk and are also available in many varieties. These foods are nutritious, but the amount of nutrients and calories they contain varies, depending on how they were processed. You will learn more about these foods in Chapter 52.

Meat, Poultry, Fish, Dry Beans, Eggs, and Nuts

The foods in this group are all sources of protein and B vitamins. They also provide vitamins A and E, iron, and other minerals. Many foods in this group contain saturated fats, though excess fat can be removed. Two to three servings of food from this group are needed each day.

Here are some facts about the different foods in this group. You will read more about some of them in Chapter 53.

- Meats include beef, lamb, and pork. Meat is a good source of complete protein and B vitamins, especially thiamine and riboflavin. It also provides iron and several other minerals. Liver is especially high in iron and vitamin B12.
- Poultry includes chicken, turkey, and duck. Poultry is a good source of complete protein. It also supplies the B vitamin niacin and the minerals iron and phosphorus.

MORE ABOUT Food Group Systems

Different countries have developed their own food group systems. For instance, a German health newsletter outlines seven food groups. Five of them are similar to the food groups in the Pyramid, except that potatoes are placed in the same group with grain products. There is also a fat group and a "miscellaneous" group.

- Fish is an excellent source of complete protein as well as the minerals iodine, iron, potassium, and phosphorus.
- Eggs provide complete protein and significant amounts of almost every nutrient except vitamin C.
- *Dry beans and peas* are also called **legumes.** Kidney beans, lentils, split peas, and chickpeas are legumes. Green beans, wax beans, and fresh green peas are classified as vegetables, not legumes. Legumes are rich in carbohydrates, B vitamins, and iron, as well as incomplete proteins. Your body can make use of these incomplete proteins as long as you also eat grain products, nuts, seeds, or complete protein foods.
- Nuts are high in incomplete proteins and B vitamins. They are also high in fat and should therefore be used sparingly.

Fats, Oils, and Sweets

The smallest section at the top of the Food Guide Pyramid represents fats, oils, and sweets. Foods in this category include cream, butter, refined sugars, sweet desserts, candy, soft drinks, and salad oils and dressings. These foods do not form a food group because they are not needed for good health. Nutritionists advise people to eat the foods at the top of the Food Guide Pyramid sparingly. The few nutrients they provide can be obtained easily from the five food groups.

The circles on the Food Guide Pyramid represent naturally occurring and added fats. The triangles represent added sugars. These symbols appear mainly in the small section at the top of the Pyramid. They also appear in each of the other sections because fats and sugar are found in some foods in each food group.

These foods are high in sugar, salt, and fats and low in other nutrients. How many servings of these foods do you have each day?

CHAPTER 38 **Guidelines for Good Nutrition** 381

Activities

■ **Makes Sense.** Discuss: Many protein-rich foods also tend to be high in fat. Should this be a problem for people? Stress that low-fat items are a wise choice. Add, however, that many people eat too much protein. Might excess fat and associated health risks be less of a concern if people ate only the recommended amounts of protein? *(Critical Thinking)*

■ **Fat-Finding Tour.** Ask students to read labels of foods in their home to learn whether a food contains fats. If so, have students record the type of fat (corn oil, butter, etc.), whether it is saturated or unsaturated, and the percentage of calories from fat. Have them also list the foods they checked that do not contain fat. Have students share both lists in class. Are they surprised at their findings? *(Observation)*

■ **Sweets in Disguise.** Refer students to the statement on p. 381 that "fats and sugars are found in some foods in each food group." Review the groups of the Pyramid and ask students to name foods from each that support this claim. List these on the board. Add examples of your own if needed to lengthen the list and impress upon students the truth of the text's statement. *(Observation)*

REAL-LIFE APPLICATION

Read this to students: *To limit fat and sugar in her family's diet, Josie replaced their favorite dessert—pound cake, strawberries in sweet syrup, and whipped cream—with angel food cake, fresh strawberries, and strawberry yogurt.* Ask: How did Josie maintain the dessert's appeal while improving its healthfulness? Help students see the new foods are still good-tasting, but lower in sugar (the strawberries) and fat and cholesterol (the cake and yogurt).

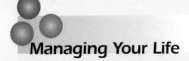

TEACH

Topics on pp. 382-384:
- Nutrient Density
- Dietary Guidelines

Checking Comprehension

✓ What is nutrient density? *Relationship between the number of calories in a food and amount and types of nutrients it provides.*

✓ Why is eating a variety of foods important? *No one food provides all nutrients in amounts needed; keeps meals from becoming boring.*

Managing Your Life

Have students"Getting Enough Fiber" and discuss the questions. Review the suggestions in the feature. Ask how students could apply—or have applied—those and others to their own eating habits.

Answers to Applying . . .
1. Answers will vary but should total more than 11 g.
2. Answers may include: helps reduce fat and cholesterol, add variety to diet.
3. Answers may include: they think it's "rabbit food" bland or limited. People can be educated about variety of flavorful high-fiber foods.

Foods at the tip of the Food Guide Pyramid share one important trait: low nutrient density. **Nutrient density** is *the relationship between the number of calories a food has and the amount and types of nutrients it provides.* Foods in the fats, oils, and sweets category tend to be high in calories, yet they provide few nutrients other than fat and sugar. In contrast, foods such as whole-grain products, fresh fruits and vegetables, lean meats, legumes, and low-fat and skim milk have high nutrient density. They are rich in nutrients such as complex carbohydrates, protein, vitamins, and minerals, so their calories provide more nutritional value.

Dietary Guidelines

The Food Guide Pyramid is an easy and convenient way to keep track of the foods you need. The Pyramid is set up to help you follow the **Dietary Guidelines for Americans** that have been developed by the United States government. These are *guidelines that offer a number of recommendations for improving eating habits.* The guidelines are:

Managing Your Life

Getting Enough Fiber

Dietary fiber promotes healthy digestion and reduces the risk of cancer and heart disease. Experts estimate, however, that the average American adult gets only 11 g of dietary fiber daily—far less than the National Cancer Institute's recommended 20 to 35 g per day.

Why do Americans get so little fiber? One reason is that people in industrialized nations include more foods from animal sources in their diets. People in less industrialized nations base their diets on foods that are high in fiber—whole grains, fruits, vegetables, and legumes.

Foods are considered to be good sources of fiber if they contain at least 2 g of dietary fiber per serving. This table gives some examples:

Food and Serving Size	Dietary Fiber (g)
1½ cup (125 mL) baked beans	10
1 medium pear with skin	4
1 medium orange	3
1 medium sweet potato	3
¾ cup (175 mL) oatmeal	3
½ cup (125 mL) broccoli	2
2 Tbsp. (30 mL) peanut butter	2

Part of managing your life is managing your diet. Why not find ways to add foods that are good sources of fiber to your daily diet? You might try these suggestions:

- Keep a bowl of fruit within easy reach on the kitchen counter or the refrigerator.
- Take fresh fruit, cut-up fresh vegetables, or a package of raisins to school as a snack.
- Choose whole-grain varieties of breads and breakfast cereals.
- Buy brown rice instead of white rice, whole-wheat noodles instead of regular ones.
- Add canned legumes to salads and casseroles.

Applying the Principles

1. From the list of foods above, suggest three combinations that supply more than 11 g of fiber.
2. What are other health benefits of eating more high-fiber foods and fewer high-protein foods?
3. What negative associations or mistaken ideas might some people have about dietary fiber? How do you suggest overcoming these

---

DID YOU KNOW?

Cola drinks typically contain 30 to 46 mg of caffeine per can, compared to 100 mg found in a cup of coffee. Diet sodas frequently have more caffeine than those containing sugar.

MORE ABOUT Sugar

On food labels, sugar goes by many different names: sucrose, glucose, maltose, dextrose, lactose, fructose, or corn syrup. Honey and molasses are also sugars.

The Dietary Guidelines suggest ways to improve your eating habits. How might these foods fit into the recommendations?

1. **Eat a variety of foods.** No single food provides all the nutrients in the amounts you need. Even within a single food group, the nutrients provided by specific foods differ. When choosing foods within a food group, don't limit yourself to only a few foods. Branch out! By eating a wide range of foods within each group, you'll get the nutrients you need—and you won't be bored by good eating.

2. **Balance the food you eat with physical activity—maintain or improve your weight.** Eating the right amount of nutritious foods and exercising regularly can help you achieve and maintain the weight that's right for you. Being overweight or underweight can lead to health problems. You will learn more about managing weight in Chapter 39.

3. **Choose a diet with plenty of grain products, vegetables, and fruits.** Following the Food Guide Pyramid will help you do this.

Starchy foods—such as potatoes, pasta, and breads—provide carbohydrates for energy. Fibrous foods—fruits, vegetables, and whole-grain products—keep your digestive system working well. Eating foods high in fiber can help you lower the risk of colon and rectal cancers, extreme overweight, and heart disease.

4. **Choose a diet low in fat, saturated fat, and cholesterol.** Dietary fats, especially saturated fats and cholesterol, can contribute to high blood pressure and heart disease. Within each food group, look for the low-fat choices. For example, choose lean meats and poultry, and trim off excess fat and skin. Substitute legumes for meats at least a few times a week. Choose low-fat or skim milk instead of whole milk. Choose broiled or baked foods rather than fried foods. In addition, watch out for high-fat toppings, such as butter, sour cream, and oily salad dressings.

Activities

■ **Good for You?** On the board write the headings Best Choices, Good Choices, and Special Treat Only. Name some food items, some healthful, some less so. Have students place each food under the best heading, if the student was to try to follow the Dietary Guidelines. Ask students to continue by offering their favorite foods or other, more challenging items. *(Critical Thinking)*

ENRICHMENT

■ **Snack Smart.** Challenge students to think of foods or food combinations that would make nutritious, nutrient-dense snacks. List their ideas on the board. Encourage the class to copy the list and post it at home for their families.

STRATEGIES THAT WORK

Have students read "Cutting Back on Caffeine" and discuss the questions. Ask: Why do some people prefer caffeinated drinks? How might they get the same effects without the possibly harmful side effects?

Answers to Think . . .
1. Answers will vary.
2. Answers will vary.
3. Answers may include: caffeine has been linked to health problems; more healthful drinks could be substituted for caffeinated ones.

Focus on Critical Thinking Skills

Have students compare nutrition panels, ingredient lists, and prices of a product's regular and low-fat versions. How great is the difference in the amount of fat in each? Point out that while percentage-wise the reduction may sound significant, if the original item has only a small amount of fat, the "savings" may be negligible. See if students can determine how fat was reduced by comparing ingredients. Compare prices. What might be some reasons for price differences?

Review

■ **Chapter Review.** Use the contents of the Chapter Review page to help students review concepts, think critically, and apply their knowledge.

■ **Study Guide.** Have students complete the Study Guide for Chapter 38 on p. 128of the Student Workbook.

■ **School Lunch Spotlight.** Have each of five groups make a chart with the six guidelines as column headings. Distribute copies of that week's school lunch menu. Have each group review one day's lunch, decide which guidelines the items promote, and list foods in the appropriate columns. Repeat the activity using the Food Guide Pyramid.

Evaluation

■ **Chapter Test.** Use the reproducible chapter test provided in the Teacher's Classroom Resources or create your own test using the *Testmaker Software*.

■ **Alternative Assessment.** Have students plan and follow one day's menu that meets both the Food Guide Pyramid and the Dietary Guidelines. Afterward, discuss the experience. What was difficult? Enjoyable? Do they feel better about themselves? Could they continue on this type of diet?

■ **Dietary Double-Team.** Have students write a paragraph explaining how the Pyramid and the Guidelines complement each other. How does adhering to one make it easier to follow the other?

STRATEGIES That Work

Cutting Back on Caffeine

How often have you heard people ask, "Regular or decaf?" or "Is that cola caffeine-free?" Many people today are interested in avoiding caffeine. Just what are the facts about this substance?

Caffeine is a chemical found in coffee, tea, and many carbonated soft drinks. It is also used in some headache, cold, and allergy remedies. Cocoa and chocolate products have smaller amounts.

As a stimulant, caffeine can increase alertness. It can also cause nervousness and trouble sleeping. Researchers are studying possible links between caffeine and other health problems.

If you think caffeine may be causing problems for you, try these suggestions for cutting back:

- Cut back on caffeine consumption gradually. Otherwise you may have headaches or other withdrawal symptoms.
- Switch to decaffeinated coffee or tea, caffeine-free cola, or herbal tea.
- Instead of carbonated drinks, have 100 percent fruit, vegetable juice or skim milk. You'll get less caffeine and more nutrients.
- Boost energy from exercise, not caffeine.

Making the Strategy Work

Think . . .

1. What foods and beverages containing caffeine do you consume on a regular basis?
2. Have you ever experienced side effects from caffeine? If so, what are they?
3. Why should people cut back on caffeine even if they are feeling no negative effects?

 Try...

Choose one day this week to be caffeine-free. Try several of the suggestions listed above. Can you develop habits that help you extend the one-day trial?

5. **Choose a diet moderate in sugars.** No food is "bad" in itself, including sugar. However, eating too much of some foods is a poor choice. **Moderate** use means *avoiding extreme amounts.* Too much sugar can lead to cavities in your teeth as well as to weight gain. If you want to discover more about the amount of sugar you consume, check the ingredients labels of the foods you eat. Sucrose, glucose, maltose, lactose, fructose, and syrups are all forms of sugar. As an alternative to foods high in added sugar, try fresh fruit. It will provide plenty of nutrients along with natural sweetness.

6. **Choose a diet moderate in salt and sodium.** Sodium, found in table salt, plays an important part in controlling the movement of water in your body. Too much of it, however, can disrupt the system and may lead to high blood pressure in some individuals. Check food labels for the amount of sodium, and choose foods lower in salt. Enjoy the natural flavor of foods, or use herbs and spices as seasonings instead of salt.

By following these suggestions, you will be better able to make healthful food choices. In turn, you will increase your chances of leading a long and healthy life.

Focus on Communication Skills

Divide the class into six groups; assign each group one Guideline. Explain that they have been asked by the school board to think of a way to promote that guideline among middle school students. They might consider changes in the school lunch program, a school-wide project, an informational campaign for parents—any effective, appropriate means of teaching children about the guideline and encouraging them to follow it. Have groups plan a detailed strategy and present it to the class.

Reviewing the Facts

1. Name the five major food groups, and identify one or more of the chief nutrients each group supplies.
2. How many daily servings of food from each food group are recommended?
3. What role do variety and moderation play in healthy food choices?
4. Why is it so important to include fiber, which is not a nutrient, in your eating choices?
5. Name four ways you can reduce your intake of fats.

Thinking Critically

1. Why do you think that some people eat more than moderate amounts of foods that are high in fat, sugar, and salt content?
2. Since scientists are continually making new discoveries about nutrition, how do you think that it is possible to know what to eat?

Applying Your Knowledge

1. **Understanding the Dietary Guidelines.** List each of the Dietary Guidelines for Americans. Next to each guideline, name one step you could take to improve your eating habits. For example, next to "Choose a diet with plenty of grain products, vegetables, and fruits," you might say, "Try to eat vegetables two more times each week."
2. **Adopting Nutritious Eating Habits.** Using the Food Guide Pyramid and the Dietary Guidelines, devise an eating plan for one day. Include an explanation of how your plan follows the Food Guide Pyramid and the Dietary Guidelines.

Making Connections

1. **Business.** Many products are labeled as low-fat, cholesterol-free, or enriched in an effort to attract the health-conscious consumer. It is often what is not stated that is more important. Some foods never had cholesterol, for example. Others, such as low-fat yogurt, have had sugar added while the fat content has been reduced. Choose three food labels and report on the hidden messages.
2. **History.** Food choices have changed dramatically over the past century. Using old cookbooks, old advertisements for food products, or encyclopedia articles about foods and eating choices of the last century, compare today's eating habits with the past. Report your findings to the class.

Building Your Portfolio

Writing a Public Service Message

Imagine that you have been hired to write a public service message about reducing the amount of fat in the food people eat. Aim your message at teens by focusing on tips for reducing fat that are most relevant for this age group, such as how to choose low-fat fast foods and low-fat snacks. Put a copy of the public service message in your portfolio.

CHAPTER 38   Guidelines for Good Nutrition   385

Chapter 39

Chapter Overview

Chapter 39 discusses fitness and weight management. Students learn the benefits of fitness and how to determine a healthful body weight. They explore issues in weight management: losing and gaining weight; eating disorders; and changing eating habits for better health.

Motivator

■ **Beauty Is . . .** Show students a picture of a Reubens painting featuring a typically large woman. Compare this to a photo of a present-day actress or model. Explain that Reubens' depiction was once considered the ideal weight. Ask: How does society decide what weight is desirable? Why do these standards change? Was Reubens' ideal a healthful one? Is today's?

Objectives

Discuss the chapter objectives on this page. Remind students that the objectives focus on important chapter concepts.

Vocabulary

The term *bulimia* has Greek origins: *bous*, ox, and *limos*, hunger. Ask: How do you think this words combined came to be applied to bulimics?

Chapter 39

Fitness and Weight Management

Terms to Learn

- aerobic
- anorexia nervosa
- basal metabolism
- bulimia
- eating disorders
- fad diet
- fitness
- obese

Objectives

This chapter will help you to:

- Identify **the benefits of fitness.**
- Describe **three types of exercise that contribute to fitness.**
- Name **the factors that determine an individual's healthy weight.**
- Identify **the factors that affect weight loss and gain.**
- Explain **eating and exercise plans for weight management.**
- Describe **the eating disorders anorexia nervosa and bulimia.**

UNIT 6   Food, Nutrition, and Wellness

CHAPTER RESOURCES

Study Guide, pp. 131-132
Activity, *Information or Misinformation?* p. 133

Teacher's Classroom Resources
Lesson Plan, p. 43

Decision Making, *Food and Good Health,* p. 20
Extension #63, *Eating Disorders: Warning Signs,* p. 69
Extension #64, *Which Body Is Better?* p. 70
Life Skills, *Are You a Couch Potato?* p. 66

Chapter 39 Test, pp. 83-84
Performance Assessment, *Weight and Fitness,* pp. 69-70
Reteaching, *What's So Great About Fitness?* p. 45

See Also:
ABCNews InterActive™ Videodiscs

Sara has a busy life. She has several hours of homework each night, and she is active on the school newspaper as a sportswriter. She also has a part-time job on weekends as a short-order cook. Because Sara's days and evenings are so full, she has trouble finding the time to exercise regularly. She also does not always take time to eat healthful meals. It's not unusual for Sara to feel tired during the day even though she usually gets enough sleep each night. She is wondering what she can do to feel more energetic so that she can handle all of her commitments.

Sara needs to take steps to become fit. **Fitness** is *your ability to meet the demands of day-to-day life*. Healthful eating habits and regular exercise are important components of fitness. In addition, both are key factors in reaching and maintaining a healthy body weight. Sara needs to look more closely at what and when she eats and to make time for regular exercise.

The Benefits of Fitness

Fitness is important for everyone. When you are fit, you are strong and healthy enough to participate in a wide range of physical activities. Your body can work at its best. You look good and feel well. Fitness helps improve your physical health, as described in **Figure 39.1** on page 388.

Fitness has benefits besides physical ones. It improves other aspects of your life too. You also have the strength to handle mental and emotional demands that arise. When you are fit, you are better able to stay calm when things aren't going well and to relax when you need to. In other words, you are able to handle stress.

Exercise that you enjoy is the best kind. That way you will stick with it. What kind of exercise is right for you?

CHAPTER 39   Fitness and Weight Management   387

Topics on pp. 387:
• **Importance of Fitness**

Checking Comprehension

✓ What is fitness? *Ability to meet demands of day-to-day life.*

✓ Identify two main elements of fitness. *Healthful eating habits, regular exercise.*

Activities

■ **Harshest Critic?** Ask students to write a brief evaluation of their own weight and fitness. Explain this critique is for self-awareness only; it will not be shared. Suggest students review this evaluation after reading the chapter. Do they still feel it is accurate? *(Critical Thinking)*

SPECIAL NEEDS *Strategies*

Physically Disabled. Students with physical disabilities can easily feel left out or self-conscious in a discussion of physical fitness and exercise. Stress the importance of achieving one's own optimal fitness. Encourage volunteers with disabilities to demonstrate special or modified exercises they perform, or to discuss obstacles to fitness they find in an able-bodied society.

MORE ABOUT Nutrition and Fitness

The correlation between adequate nutrition and mental alterness and health, as well physical health, has been indicated in studies. Children who are undernourished often have trouble concentrating in school. Chronic malnutrition, particularly protein deficiency, can result in permanent mental retardation. Adults who do not eat properly tend to suffer from depression, irritability, and apathy.

Topics on pp. 388-389:
- **Physical Benefits of Fitness**
- **Achieving Fitness**

Checking Comprehension

✓ How does fitness benefit you emotionally? *Reduces stress, promotes self-esteem.*

✓ How does exercise help the circulatory system? *Keeps blood pressure normal; helps heart and lungs supply oxygen; strengthens heart; lowers cholesterol.*

✓ What is the equation for fitness? *Good nutrition + Regular exercise = Fitness.*

From School to Work

Have students read "Managing Your Fitness Routine" and discuss the questions. Ask them to predict the consequences of ignoring each of the tips given.

Answers to Assessing . . .
1. You may otherwise grow discouraged, give up on program; may injure yourself.
2. Answers may include: it can help you assess your performance; help you make adjustments as needed.
3. Answers will vary. Remind students to be realistic.

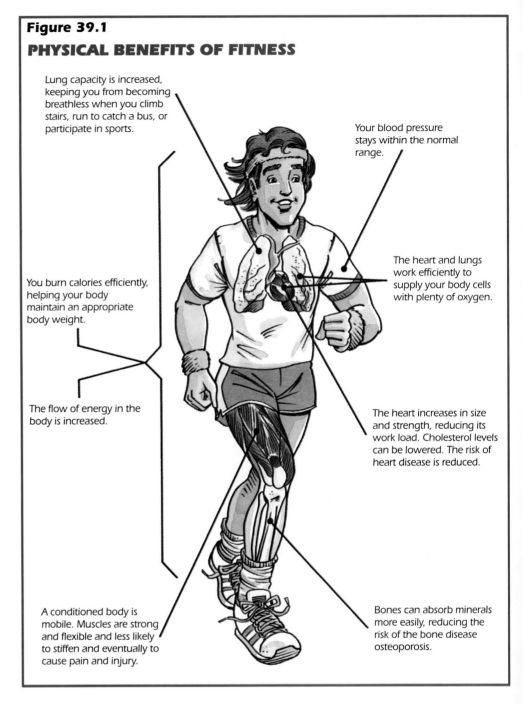

Figure 39.1
PHYSICAL BENEFITS OF FITNESS

Lung capacity is increased, keeping you from becoming breathless when you climb stairs, run to catch a bus, or participate in sports.

Your blood pressure stays within the normal range.

You burn calories efficiently, helping your body maintain an appropriate body weight.

The heart and lungs work efficiently to supply your body cells with plenty of oxygen.

The flow of energy in the body is increased.

The heart increases in size and strength, reducing its work load. Cholesterol levels can be lowered. The risk of heart disease is reduced.

A conditioned body is mobile. Muscles are strong and flexible and less likely to stiffen and eventually to cause pain and injury.

Bones can absorb minerals more easily, reducing the risk of the bone disease osteoporosis.

388   UNIT 6   Food, Nutrition, and Wellness

• • • REAL-LIFE APPLICATION

Read this to students: *Cynthia, a full-time receptionist, often feels tired and listless. She wonders how she could manage exercising on her schedule, especially when a day of office work and household tasks leave her worn out.* Ask: How do you see Cynthia's situation? Is she really "too tired" to exercise? Point out that moderate exercise often gives energy. Ask how she could include such activity in her daily schedule.

Fitness also promotes high self-esteem, which improves overall outlook and attitude. Think about fitness as having physical, mental, and emotional benefits—helping you stay healthy, think clearly, and feel confident and at ease with yourself and with others.

Achieving Fitness

How can you achieve fitness? An easy way to think about becoming fit is this equation:

Good nutrition + Regular exercise = Fitness

As you have learned in earlier chapters, proper nutrition gives your body the fuel it needs to get through the day. Regular exercise keeps your heart, lungs, and muscles healthy and helps you feel more energetic.

Fitness and Exercise

Three types of exercise can help you achieve your fitness goals. A well-rounded exercise program includes all three types.

- **Strengthening exercises.** Exercises of this type help build strong muscles. Muscle strength is measured by the amount of

Managing Your Fitness Routine

What You Learn Today . . .

In physical education and health education classes, you learn how to exercise, how to eat nutritiously, and why both are needed for good health. In addition, you discover ways to assess your level of fitness, to set fitness goals and monitor your progress, and to motivate yourself to follow your program.

. . . You Can Use Tomorrow

Setting personal fitness goals and demonstrating the self-discipline needed to reach them has practical value in the workplace. When you feel fit, you have the energy to be more productive. Attaining good health builds self-esteem, which helps give you confidence to do well at your job. The self-management skills of self-assessment, goal setting, and self-monitoring make you more effective in any work setting.

Practicing Your Skills

Try these tips for setting up a fitness program and sticking to it:

- Evaluate your present status accurately.
- Set up a schedule. Rearrange your day, if necessary, to make time for exercise and proper meals.

- Be realistic in your goals and expectations.
- Start slowly. Gradual improvement generally lasts the longest.
- Don't compare yourself to other people.
- Make your fitness program a permanent part of your daily routine.
  Remember that improving your health is something you do for yourself. If you do it only to please someone else, you're less likely to succeed.

Assessing Your Skills

1. Why do you think it is so important to be realistic about your goals when setting up a fitness program?
2. Explain how self-management can be valuable even in an entry-level job in which tasks and schedule are dictated by a supervisor.
3. What could you do to make fitness a permanent part of your lifestyle?

Activities

- **Step One.** Discuss: Why do people avoid exercising? What strategies might help them overcome these obstacles? *(Problem Solving)*
- **Had Enough?** Have students list all the exercise they get on a daily basis. Ask: Do you think you are getting enough regular exercise? How could you include more physical activity in your daily routine? *(Management)*

RETEACHING

- **Why Exercise?** Have students work in pairs. Tell them to take turns using their partner as a model to explain to the class how exercise benefits different parts of the body.

CROSS-CURRICULAR ACTIVITY
Math

Have students learn their target heart rate—the pulse rate, while exercising, that provides the most benefit—using this formula: subtract your age from 220; multiply this number first by 70 percent and then by 85 percent. Their target rate is between these two figures.

Focus on Management Skills

Many people, students included, claim they have no time for exercise. Point out that physical activity can be included in regularly scheduled events. They can take stairs instead of elevators when shopping; relax by gardening instead of watching TV; choose miniature golf instead of a movie as a leisure activity. Challenge students to think of other ways of fitting physical activity into their schedules. Encourage them to report periodically on their progress.

Topics on pp. 389-391:
- Types of Exercise
- Determining An Appropriate Weight

Checking Comprehension

✓ Why are stretching exercises important? *Promote flexibility; help prevent muscle pulls, other injuries.*

✓ Describe a positive attitude toward body weight and size. *Accept own weight and build; focus on maintaining healthful weight.*

✓ What are some dangers of being underweight? *Reduced strength and resistance to infection, poor general health, malnutrition.*

SPECIAL NEEDS *Strategies*

Outlining Suggestion. These pages offer a good opportunity to practice outlining. Point out the two sizes of headings. "What Affects Your Weight?" is larger than "Basal Metabolism," for example, so basal metabolism is one factor that affects weight. Show students how to organize this information in an outline on the board. Then ask for main points that belong under the heading "Basal Metabolism."

---

work your muscles can do at one time. Strengthening exercises help improve your ability to perform all types of physical activity, from kicking a soccer ball farther to lifting a heavier bag of groceries. They also help prevent muscle injuries during physical activity. Strengthening exercises include weightlifting, push-ups, and sit-ups.

- **Aerobic exercises. Aerobic** (uh-ROE-bik) exercises are *sustained, rhythmic exercises that improve the efficiency of your heart and lungs.* These exercises increase the intake of oxygen into the body. They help improve the circulation of blood and oxygen through the body. This type of exercise also helps control weight by increasing the rate at which the body uses energy, even at rest. It increases the amount of lean tissue in the body and reduces body fat. Exercises that improve heart and lung endurance include walking, running, bicycling, and swimming. Aerobic exercises must be done at least 3 days a week, 20 minutes at a time, to be effective. Over time, aerobic exercises increase endurance, or staying power.

- **Stretching exercises.** Stretching exercises help promote flexibility, which is important in many sports and in dance. Flexibility also helps prevent muscle pulls and other injuries. Examples of stretching exercises include ones targeted at specific muscle groups, such as calf stretches.

Are these kinds of exercises part of your weekly routine? Setting aside time for exercise will help you improve fitness. Before you begin any exercise program, however, check with your doctor to make sure that the routine you have chosen is safe for you.

Each workout should begin with warm-up activities, such as walking followed by gentle stretching. A cool-down period after exercise with slower movements and additional stretching will help prevent muscle cramps and soreness.

People come in all shapes and sizes. The best weight for your friend may not be best for you. Learning what is best for you will help you avoid unrealistic expectations.

MORE ABOUT Basal Metabolism

Basal metabolism is determined by a type of measurement called calorimetry. Calorimetry determines the number of calories burned in the body by measuring the amount of oxygen breathed into the lungs and the carbon dioxide breathed out. This measurement is taken when the individual is lying absolutely still, in a comfortable temperature, 12 hours after eating.

A Healthy Body Weight

By eating well and exercising regularly you can stay fit. You can also reach and maintain the best weight for your body. Determining that weight can be difficult, however. Many components contribute to an individual's weight.

What Is Your Best Weight?

Healthy weights vary from person to person, depending on such factors as:

- **Your height.** The taller a person is, the more he or she can expect to weigh.
- **Your age.** Adults typically weigh more than teens of the same height.
- **Your gender.** Males generally weigh more than females of the same height.
- **Your bone structure.** People with larger body frames usually weigh more than those with smaller body frames. You can judge the size of your frame by looking at your wrist. If it is slimmer than that of most people your age, gender, and height, you have a small frame. If it is sturdier, you have a large frame.
- **Your body build.** People who are muscular tend to weigh more than those who are not. That is because muscle is denser than body fat.

A physician or another health professional is the best person to decide what is a healthy weight for you. Charts that give weight ranges can be misleading.

Try not to compare your weight and appearance with those of models, superathletes, or other famous personalities. Television, movies, and magazines have helped paint an unrealistic picture of the "ideal body." In real life, few people are as slim or as muscular as models and athletes—nor do they need to be. Instead, focus on accepting your own body build and maintaining a weight that is healthy for you.

Overweight and Underweight

People who are overweight weigh 10 to 20 percent more than the healthy weight recommended for them by their physician. **Obese** people *weigh at least 20 percent more than the healthy weight that is recommended by their physician.* People who are obese have too much body fat. This fat puts them at risk of developing serious health problems, including heart disease, high blood pressure, and certain cancers.

People who are underweight weigh at least 15 percent less than the healthy weight recommended by their physician. Underweight people have lowered resistance to infection and reduced strength. Often their general health is poor, and in some cases malnutrition develops.

Although thinness often is associated with glamour and beauty, a thin person is not necessarily a fit person. The body needs a certain amount of body fat and muscle to maintain good health. In trying to remain thin, some individuals—especially teens, who are still growing—may be robbing their bodies of essential nutrients.

What Affects Weight?

How much weight you gain or lose over time is affected by several factors. These include your basal metabolism, the amount you exercise, and the food you eat.

Basal Metabolism

Basal metabolism refers to *the minimum amount of energy required to maintain the automatic functions of your body.* These include breathing, blood circulation, maintenance of body temperature, and cell growth and repair. These automatic functions account for over half of the energy you use each day—that's more than the energy you use for exercise and all other activities combined.

MORE ABOUT Body Shapes

A recent theory about body shape suggests that people are born with body types that predispose them toward leanness or heaviness. Three body types are identified: *endomorphs* tend to be round and soft, and most disposed toward weight gain; *mesomorphs* have heavy bones and muscles; and *ectomorphs* are slight and fine-boned, and least likely to gain weight.

Topics on pp. 392-393:
- **Metabolic Rate**
- **Weight and Calories**
- **Exercise**

Checking Comprehension

✓ Is drastic food restriction effective for long-term weight loss? *No, slows metabolism, making weight loss more difficult.*

✓ Why is exercise effective for losing weight? *Burns calories; raises metabolic rate for up to 12 hours after.*

✓ How can exercise help you gain weight? *Increases muscle, can stimulate appetite.*

FAMILY AND COMMUNITY OUTREACH

Ask students who have family members or friends who are trying to lose or gain weight to interview these people about their diet strategies. (Interviewees' identities should not be revealed.) Have students compare the dieter's techniques to those described in this chapter and to predict whether that person will be successful in losing and keeping off weight.

Basal metabolism, like other characteristics such as hair color or height, differs from individual to individual. Some people have a high metabolic rate, often called a "fast" metabolism. Their automatic body functions naturally burn energy at a high rate. These people may be able to eat large amounts of food yet not gain weight. Other people have a low metabolic rate, or a "slow" metabolism. These individuals do not burn calories as quickly, and so they gain weight more easily.

Whatever a person's natural metabolic rate, exercise can increase it and help burn up energy faster. After vigorous exercise, your body continues to use energy at a faster rate, even when you are resting. In addition, muscles require relatively larger amounts of energy for maintenance than does body fat. So a person who has more developed muscles, that is, one who is more physically fit, will burn calories at a faster rate than one who does not.

Drastically lowering your food intake, on the other hand, which some weight-loss diets promote, can lower your metabolism and make it difficult to lose weight. When a person reduces food intake, the metabolic rate slows to conserve energy. This enables the body to survive on the lower amount of food that the person is eating. As a result, weight loss slows or stops.

Exercise and Food

Exercise and food intake have direct effects on body weight. Exercise uses up energy; food provides it. Weight loss or gain depends on the balance between the two. Therefore:

- If you generally take in fewer calories each day than your body burns, over time you will lose weight.
- If you generally take in more calories each day than your body burns, over time you will gain weight.

Figure 39.2

Calories Burned in Various Activities

Activity	Calories burned per hour (for a 150-lb. [67.5-kg] person)
Housework	180
Bicycling (5½ mph [9 km/h])	210
Walking (2½ mph [4 km/h])	210
Mowing the lawn (power mower)	250
Rowing a boat (2½ mph [4 km/h])	300
Swimming (¼ mph [0.4 km/h])	300
Badminton	350
Ice-skating	400
Tennis	420
Basketball	500
Skiing (10 mph [16 km/h])	600
Squash and handball	600
Running (10 mph [16 km/h])	900

MORE ABOUT Losing Weight

You must burn 3,500 calories more than you consume, or reduce your intake by the same, to lose one pound of weight. This is best done gradually; very low calorie diets are rarely successful. Over 90 percent of those who try to live on an unreasonably restrictive diet experience the "boomerang" effect, regaining the weight within a year.

If you want to lose weight, choosing nutrient-dense foods is especially important. Choose lean, baked poultry or fish rather than fried, a plain baked potato rather than french fries, a piece of whole-grain bread rather than white bread, and fresh fruit rather than fruit pie for dessert.

Activities

■ **Put Down the Donut.** Ask students if they think it is possible to lose weight without reducing calorie intake. Tell them to suppose they normally consumed 3,000 calories a day and wanted to burn an extra 500 calories daily. Referring to Figure 39.2, point out that 4,000 calories is the equivalent of mowing a lawn for 16 hours. Ask students to make similar calculations using other activities to illustrate the need for eating less to lose weight. *(Management)*

CROSS-CURRICULAR ACTIVITY

Social Studies

Encourage students to research the history of dieting to lose weight. What are the earliest known incidents of dieting? What methods were used? What different motives have people had for losing weight? How have science and technology affected weight-loss methods?

- If you generally take in the same amount of calories as are burned, you will maintain your weight.

You can see that a change in the amount of calories you consume (the food you eat) or the calories you burn (the exercise you get) will affect body weight.

Weight Management

Teens who weigh significantly more or less than the healthy weight recommended by their physician will probably want to consider a weight management plan. The healthiest approach is to develop both new exercise habits and new eating habits. Modifying old habits can be difficult, but wise choices can benefit teens for the rest of their lives. Teens who plan to lose or gain more than a few pounds should always consult a physician or another health professional first.

Exercise

If your goal is to lose weight, increasing your activity level will help you achieve your goal. Vigorous activity not only burns calories while you are doing it, but it also increases your metabolic rate for up to 12 hours after you finish exercising. Different types of activities burn calories at different rates. **Figure 39.2** shows how many calories are burned in various common activities.

Even if you are trying to gain weight, exercise should be part of your plan. Moderate exercise can stimulate the appetite. As you build muscle strength, you will be gaining weight in a healthful way.

CHAPTER 39   Fitness and Weight Management   393

⌕ocus on Critical Thinking Skills

Science is answering many questions about some people's difficulty in losing weight and reshaping their bodies. Body shape and basal metabolism, for example, seem more a product of heredity than was once believed. Ask: How can this new information help people who want or need to lose weight? How might it discourage them? Do you think many people use this research as an excuse to not get fit? Do they abuse it, looking for ways to lose more weight than is healthful?

Checking Comprehension

✓ Why are nutrient-dense foods especially important on a weight-loss diet? *You must get all needed nutrients in fewer calories.*

✓ What is a safe rate of weight loss? *1-2 lbs. (0.5-1 kg) weekly.*

✓ What are the two keys to successful, life-long weight management? *Good exercise and eating habits.*

Making Decisions

Have students read "The Price of Success?" and discuss the questions. Ask: Is society biased in favor of thinness? What evidence of this do you see?

Answers to What Would You Do?

1. Answers will vary. Help students see actions are short-sighted and hazardous.
2. Must decide whether to act and, if so, what to do.
3. Christa could become dangerously underweight, develop eating disorder, become addicted to pills. Therese might feel guilt.
4. Answers may include: tell parent or other adult; get Christa information on diet pills and eating disorders.

Exercise alone, however, is not always enough to help you manage your weight. You may also need to change your eating habits.

Losing Weight

To lose weight, you must take in fewer calories than your body uses for energy each day. How can you lose weight safely and still get the proper amount of nutrients?

• Be sure that you get at least the minimum number of daily servings from each food group in the Food Guide Pyramid, as explained in Chapter 38.
• Choose low-fat, low-calorie foods that are nutrient-dense. Nutrient-dense foods are those that provide a large amount as well as a variety of nutrients relative to their

calories. Such foods include whole-grain products; vegetables; fruits; legumes; lean meat, poultry, and fish; and low-fat dairy products.

• Watch out for foods with low nutrient density, such as potato chips, soft drinks, and ice cream. They should be limited in any eating plan, but especially in one that has weight loss as a goal.

Some people try to lose weight by following *diets that promise quick and easy weight loss.* These are often called **fad diets.** Some fad diets limit you to special diet bars or milk shakes. Other fad diets include large amounts of one nutrient, such as protein, but almost no others. Still other fad diets are based on the mistaken idea that certain foods, such as grapefruit, help the body burn fat.

Avoid any diet or weight-loss plan that excludes one or more of the five basic food groups or that calls for eating 800 calories or less per day. Such diets can be very dangerous to your health, and they may encourage you to develop poor eating habits. You should also avoid diet pills. Some contain drugs that can cause serious health problems.

The only way to lose weight safely and effectively is to lose it slowly—just 1 or 2 lbs. (0.5-1 kg) per week. Although it will take longer to reach your weight goal, the weight loss is much more likely to be permanent. Weight that is lost quickly is more likely to return. An effective weight management program involves developing good exercise and eating habits that you can use throughout your life.

An exercise program is often more effective with a friend. You can motivate each other to continue while you have a good time together.

REAL-LIFE APPLICATION

Read this to students: *Bradlee is looking for the quickest, easiest way to lose weight. He's impressed by advertisements for a diet shake that supplies many needed nutrients for under 300 calories. He would drink two shakes a day in place of two regular meals.* Ask: Does this sound like a good idea? What are some drawbacks? Stress that to keep weight off, Bradlee must adopt eating habits he can live with. "Diet" foods or meals do not encourage this.

Gaining Weight

Some of the same cautions that apply to weight loss apply to weight gain as well. Weight should be gained slowly and steadily, and the foods chosen should be low in fat and nutrient-dense.

Here are some additional tips:

- Plan meals around foods you like.
- Try to eat more frequently and to eat larger portions at each meal and snack.
- Snack on hearty, nutritious foods, such as yogurt and fresh or dried fruit and sandwiches on whole-grain bread.
- Make sure that you include foods from all of the major food groups.
- Be sure to take time to relax around mealtimes and to get enough sleep.

As with weight loss, it is important to consult a physician about a weight-gain program. Avoid any solutions, such as steroids, that promise speedy results. They could be very dangerous to your health.

Maintaining Your Weight

Once you have reached your goal weight, your next challenge is to maintain it. It is important that you make healthy eating habits and regular exercise a permanent part of your daily life. If you find your weight changing, reexamine the amount and types of food you are eating and whether you are getting the exercise you need.

Eating Disorders

Weight management is a good goal, but it can become a problem when it gets out of control. Some people develop **eating disorders,** which are *extreme eating behaviors that can lead to serious health problems and even death.* In many cases, people with eating disorders hide them from friends and family members. Although people of either gender can have eating disorders, they are more common among females than males. They generally occur during the teen years and young adulthood.

Making Decisions

The Price of Success?

Christa and April slid into a booth at the restaurant. "You're so lucky to have been away all summer doing something you love," April said. "Acting at drama camp must have been exciting." She opened the menu. "Shall we have the usual?"

Her friend shook her head. "Just a small salad. I realized this summer that I need to lose a lot of weight—the sooner, the better."

April was surprised. "You look like you've already lost weight—not that you needed to. You're practically a stick."

"Not compared to the other girls at drama camp." Christa sounded envious. "They were all so slim. And the thinnest girls got the best parts."

"Christa, you don't have to worry. You always get a good part in the school plays," April reminded her.

"High school plays are no big deal," Christa said impatiently. "If I'm going to be an actress, I have to be a lot thinner. Besides, there's nothing wrong with dieting, and it's not hard. A girl at camp gave me this to help." She pulled a bottle from her purse.

April read the label. "Diet pills?"

Christa smiled. "My secret weapon against fat. They're terrific—I've lost 10 pounds already."

April didn't know what to say. She knew that some diet pills contained amphetamines—"uppers." From health class, she knew the physical and emotional damage these drugs could cause.

"What's in these?" she demanded anxiously.

Christa shrugged. "I don't know—I just know they work." April sat in stunned silence.

What Would You Do?

1. Evaluate the decision Christa is making.
2. What decision does April now face?
3. What might be the consequences if April does nothing?
4. If you were April, what would you do?

Review

■ **Chapter Review.** Use the contents of the Chapter Review page to help students review concepts, think critically, and apply their knowledge.

■ **Study Guide.** Have students complete the Study Guide for Chapter 39 on p. 131 of the Student Workbook.

■ **Fitness Files.** Have groups write clinical profiles of individuals who need to lose or gain weight and improve their fitness. Profiles should include the person's age, height, weight, and details about his or her physical condition. Have groups exchange profiles and write suggestions to help the person become more fit.

Evaluation

■ **Chapter Test.** Use the reproducible chapter test provided in the Teacher's Classroom Resources or create your own test using the *Testmaker Software.*

■ **Alternative Assessment.** Tell groups they have been asked to speak at a meeting of Couch Potatoes Anonymous, a self-help group for people who want to become more fit and active. They must prepare a presentation on the benefits of fitness and exercise and on safe, effective weight management. Encourage groups to include demonstrations and visual aids.

■ **Take It Personally.** Have students write a short essay that begins, "The three most important ideas in this chapter for me are . . ."

Anorexia nervosa is *an eating disorder that involves an extreme urge to lose weight by starving oneself.* People with anorexia nervosa drastically reduce the amount of food they eat. At the same time, some greatly increase the amount of exercise they get. People with this disorder have a distorted self-image. When they look in the mirror, they see themselves as fat even when they are painfully thin. They resist the efforts of parents and friends to get them to eat more.

Bulimia is *an eating disorder that involves bouts of extreme overeating followed by attempts to get rid of the food eaten.* The periods of overeating, called bingeing, are often done in secret. Then, because the people feel guilt and fear of losing control over their weight, they get rid of the food by using laxatives or forcing themselves to vomit. These practices are very damaging to the body.

Eating disorders can be life threatening if left untreated. Teens who think that they themselves or someone they know may have an eating disorder should seek help from a health professional. Once an eating disorder develops, it is not easy to overcome. Medical, nutritional, and psychological counseling and the continued support of family and friends are important in the recovery process.

Changing Your Habits

Teens who work toward fitness and weight management are taking the first important steps toward a lifelong program of regular exercise and healthful eating. Remember that you don't need to be athletic or join a sports team to get the exercise you need. Your fitness activities may include dancing, canoeing, or walking the dog. Just find something you enjoy and do it regularly. (See **Figure 39.3.**)

Think about simple changes you could make to improve your fitness. Could you choose an apple or a banana instead of candy for a snack? Could you walk to your friend's house instead of going in the car? Make fitness an enjoyable, rewarding challenge that will pay off in the years to come.

Figure 39.3

Learning from Others

What can you learn from others about fitness and weight management? Read what these teens have to say:

- Jenna Lynn. "I always hated exercise. P.E. class was not my thing. Sometimes I forced myself to exercise because I knew it was right. I took an aerobics class that left me weak. Every session was a nightmare. Then I discovered hiking. My boyfriend is an avid hiker, so he influenced me. We followed local trails and then found some new ones in our state. I love the outdoors, learning about the plants, and watching the animals. I walk all over now and feel better than I ever have."
- Shawn. "For years my father skipped breakfast and grabbed fast food and candy bars for lunch. He worked hard and never wanted to take time to eat—except at night. Then he ate big meals and snacks. In the last few years he's developed all kinds of problems, with his heart, diabetes, and more. Now that his life is threatened, he's changed his ways. I just hope it isn't too late."
- Kira. "I'm the only one in my family who's overweight, and that has always hurt. Last summer I went to a camp for young people with weight problems, and I learned a lot. For one thing, I learned that the real me—the one that counts—is inside, not outside. Liking myself was sort of a first step to being able to change the habits that were harming me."

396 UNIT 6 **Food, Nutrition, and Wellness**

REAL-LIFE APPLICATION

Read this to students: *Steffi has been on a diet-and-exercise program for six weeks. She feels better than before, but is starting to grow bored with her routine. She is also frustrated because, after she lost 10 pounds in the first month, her weight* *seems to have stabilized.* Ask: How would you encourage Steffi to stay with her program? How could she vary her routine? Should she be discouraged by her inability to lose more weight?

Review

Reviewing the Facts

1. List four benefits of fitness. Include at least one each of physical, emotional, and mental benefits.
2. Name the three types of exercise that should be part of a complete fitness program, and give an example of each type.
3. What five factors help determine what weight is best for each person?
4. What factors affect how much weight you gain or lose over time?
5. Give two tips for how to modify eating habits for safe and effective weight gain and for safe and effective weight loss.
6. Briefly describe anorexia nervosa and bulimia.

Thinking Critically

1. Why do you think that so many people strive to look like famous personalities?
2. If you had a friend who was about to go on a fad diet, what would you do to convince the person that he or she should not take that approach to weight loss?

Applying Your Skills

1. **Providing Incentives for Fitness.** Prepare a list of low-cost or no-cost activities or items that you could treat yourself with to encourage you to stick with your fitness program.
2. **Creating a Public Service Announcement.** Prepare a 60-second announcement that might be given over your school's public address system. The announcement should tell students about the importance of including in their fitness program exercises that improve strength, endurance, and flexibility.
3. **Examining Obstacles to Fitness.** List as many lifestyle factors as you can think of that cause people not to eat properly and not to

get enough exercise. Next to each item on your list, write a suggestion for a way to change that factor for a healthier lifestyle.

Making Connections

1. **Government.** Diet aids, along with other over-the-counter medications, are regulated by the federal government. Find out what kinds of regulations apply to makers of such products. Then write a paragraph explaining why such laws are important and what might happen if there were no such limitations.
2. **Mathematics.** Using the table of food values in the back of this book, plan a menu of approximately 2,000 calories for one day. Be sure that it includes foods from the major food groups as recommended in the Food Guide Pyramid (Chapter 38). The menu may include any number of meals and snacks that you choose.

Building Your Portfolio

Evaluating Weight-Loss Programs
In the library, find books or magazine articles that describe two weight-loss programs. Analyze how safe and healthful each is. Make a list of good points about each program. Then list any unsound features of each program and what changes you would make to improve them. Include copies of your completed analyses in your portfolio.

ANSWERS TO THINKING CRITICALLY

1. Answers may include: famous people are admired for their looks; seem to lead happy, exciting lives.

2. Answers may include: point out dangers and ineffectiveness of fad diets; ask trusted adult to intervene; offer support if sensible weight-loss diet is advisable.

ANSWERS TO REVIEWING THE FACTS

1. Any four: *Physical* (at least one)—increases heart and lung capacity; lowers cholesterol; helps blood pressure; helps with weight control; increases energy; helps prevent injuring; helps bones absorb minerals. *Emotional* (at least one)—helps with stress; improves self-esteem. *Mental*—helps you think clearly.
2. *Strengthening* (any one)—weight lifting, push-ups, sit-ups; *aerobic*—(any one)—walking, running, bicycling, swimming; *stretching*—(any one)—calf stretches, other exercises targeted at specific muscle groups.
3. Height, age, gender, bone structure, body build.
4. Basal metabolism, amount of exercise and of food eaten.
5. *Weight gain* (any two): plan meals around favorite foods; eat more frequently and larger portions; snack on heart, nutritious foods; include foods from all groups; relax at meals and get enough sleep. *Weight loss*: get at least the minimum number of servings from each food group; choose low-fat, low-calorie, nutrient-dense foods; limit foods with low nutrient density.
6. Anorexia nervosa: drastic weight loss by self-starvation and excessive exercise. Bulimia: bingeing, then laxative use or vomiting to rid body of food.

Chapter 40

FOCUS

Chapter Overview

Chapter 40 gives guidelines for establishing healthful eating habits, suggestions for eating well throughout the day and throughout life. Students learn of the special food needs of vegetarians, athletes, and those on medically indicated diets. They also learn how to make healthful choices when eating out.

Motivator

■ **They Say . . .** Have students recall and discuss sayings about food and nutrition, such as "An apple a day keeps the doctor away" and "You are what you eat." Why are there so many food aphorisms? Is there any truth to them?

Objectives

Discuss the chapter objectives on this page. Remind students that the objectives focus on important chapter concepts.

Vocabulary

Point out that *malnourished* does not necessarily mean thin. Ask: How can an overweight person be malnourished? *By consuming too many "empty" calories, not exercising enough.*

Chapter 40

Healthful Food Choices

Terms to Learn

- lactose-intolerant
- malnourished
- meal patterns

Objectives

This chapter will help you to:

- **Explain** how you can follow healthful meal patterns.
- **Distinguish** among healthful eating patterns at different life stages.
- **Give** examples of special lifestyle and medical diets.
- **List** guidelines for eating healthful meals and snacks away from home.

398   UNIT 6   Food, Nutrition, and Wellness

CHAPTER RESOURCES

Student Workbook
Study Guide, pp. 134-135
Activity, *Order Your Health*, pp. 136-137
Teacher's Classroom Resources
Lesson Plan, p. 44
Cooperative Learning, *International Food*, pp. 45-46

Decision Making, *Choosing Food Wisely*, p. 21
Extension #65, *Pregnancy and Diet*, p. 71
Extension #66, *What Does the Menu Say?* p. 72
Life Skills, *Restaurant Review*, p. 67

Chapter 40 Test, pp. 85-86
Performance Assessment, *A Good Day's Eating*, p. 71
Reteaching, *Prescriptions for Good Health*, p. 46

See Also:
ABCNews InterActive™ Videodiscs

The chapters of this unit have helped you understand how what you eat affects your health and fitness. You have learned about the needs that food satisfies, the nutrients that food includes, and guidelines you can follow to stay healthy and fit.

Now it is time for you to look at practical ways to apply this knowledge to your own life. How do you approach making healthful food choices every day? How carefully do you consider what you eat? What types of foods do you think you should be eating at this time in your life, and how might your food choices be similar or different in the future? This chapter will discuss answers to these and other questions about healthful food choices.

Meal Patterns

What you eat affects your health, but when and how often you eat affects it too. Do you often eat on the run, skip breakfast, or snack too often? Your **meal patterns,** or *daily routines for eating,* have an effect on your energy level and overall health and fitness.

Different families follow different meal patterns. Many families have a relatively light breakfast and lunch, with dinner in the evening as their main meal for the day. Other families have their main meal at midday and eat a light supper in the evening.

One meal pattern is not necessarily better than another. Following a regular pattern of meals and snacks, however, allows your body to prepare itself to digest food at specific times. It also allows you to plan how you will obtain your daily servings from the five major food groups. Skipping meals is not healthy and often leads to overeating and poor food choices later in the day.

 What food groups are included in this teen's breakfast?

Breakfast

The day's first meal is particularly important. Your body, which may have gone 10 to 15 hours without food, needs fuel to get started. Nutrients that the body cannot store, including the water-soluble B vitamins and vitamin C, become depleted. In addition, when carbohydrates are not replaced, the body begins to burn protein for fuel. Since protein's more important job is to build and repair tissue, this can cause problems.

A good breakfast restores these nutrients and energizes you for the day ahead. Eating a good breakfast will even help you do better in school. By choosing a variety of foods, you

Topics on p. 399:
- **Mealtime Patterns**
- **Breakfast**

Checking Comprehension

✓ What are meal patterns? *Daily routines for eating.*

✓ Why are eating patterns helpful? *Let body prepare itself to digest foods; let you plan to obtain needed daily servings.*

✓ How can you help stimulate your appetite for breakfast? *Try variety of non-traditional foods.*

Activities

■ **Perfect Patterns.** Have students agree on qualities of a healthful meal pattern; list these on the board. Ask: What obstacles prevent people from following such a pattern? How could they be overcome? *(Problem Solving)*

RETEACHING

■ **Positive Patterns?** Have students describe their own meal pattern, including its strengths and weaknesses. Have them conclude whether their pattern is essentially a healthful one.

DID YOU KNOW?

Eggs are a traditional breakfast food, but they are high in cholesterol, as well as protein and other nutrients. You can reduce cholesterol intake by substituting two whites for every other egg in an omelet. Egg substitutes, which contain no cholesterol, are aslo available.

Focus on Creative Thinking Skills

Have students use cookbooks and other sources to come up with innovative, healthful breakfasts. Have them try some with their family and report the results to the class.

Topics on pp. 400-401:
• Lunch, Dinner, and Snack Patterns
• Eating for a Lifetime

Checking Comprehension

✓ What purpose should dinner serve in meeting nutrition needs? *Should fill gaps in day's nutrient needs.*

✓ Why is lunch an important meal? *Supplies body with nutrients for rest of afternoon.*

✓ How can eating right now help you later in life? *May help you stay healthier and avoid problems such as cancer and heart disease.*

MULTICULTURAL *Perspectives*

Have students research eating patterns in other cultures. Ask them to note in particular how the pattern fits into the people's way of life. How does it complement other aspects of their culture?

CROSS-REFERENCE

Have students review the information about the five basic food groups and the food pyramid in Chapter 38.

will get a good start on meeting your daily nutritional needs.

If you don't have much appetite for traditional breakfast foods, you still can have a nutritious morning meal. Instead of cereal or eggs, try yogurt with fruit, peanut butter on whole-wheat toast, or even an English muffin pizza.

Lunch

By midday your body has used up much of the energy it gained from breakfast. You need a nutritious lunch to help keep you going through the afternoon hours. It is important that you do not skip lunch or just have a candy bar and a soft drink. Traditional foods for lunch include sandwiches, soups, and salads. Along with these items, many people enjoy fresh fruit and low-fat milk.

Whether you eat at home, pack your lunch to take to school or work, eat out at a restaurant, or buy from the school cafeteria, follow the guidelines for food choices that you learned about in Chapter 38. Later in this chapter, you will learn some tips for making healthful food choices when you are eating at school.

Dinner

Many people in the United States eat their largest meal in the evening. This isn't necessarily the best plan, since most of the day's activities are usually over at this point. No matter what its size, the last meal of the day should fill in any gaps in your nutrient needs for the day.

By dinnertime, for example, William still needed three servings of grains, two of vegetables, and one each from the meat and beans group and the milk group. The family meal that evening was spaghetti with meatballs, Italian bread, and a salad. By eating one serving of spaghetti and two slices of bread, William got his three remaining servings of grains. A large bowl of salad provided the two servings of vegetables he needed. The meatballs in the spaghetti provided his remaining serving from the meat and beans group, and a glass of milk gave William his milk group serving.

When packing a lunch, include foods from all five food groups. What are some other food choices you could include for a nutritionally balanced lunch?

DID YOU KNOW?

The potato chip, that champion of snack foods, was invented in Saratoga Springs, New York, in 1853. According to legend, a chef was riled by a customer who kept returning his French fries, complaining they were too thick. The chef decided to make fries so thin the diner couldn't spear them with a fork. The plan had a surprising result: the diner was delighted with the thin, crispy creation.

Low-fat yogurt makes an excellent snack. Experiment by mixing a few spoons of crunchy, whole-grain cereal or some diced fruit into yogurt to get the taste you like best.

- Remember that snacks count as part of your total daily servings of food, along with breakfast, lunch, and dinner.

You can use snacks to include servings from food groups that you may have missed in your meals. Here are a few healthful snack ideas:

- A banana, some melon or pineapple, or any fruit.
- Celery sticks with low-fat cream cheese and raisins.
- Whole-grain bread with peanut butter.
- Raw vegetables with yogurt dip.
- Plain popcorn.
- Dry-roasted, unsalted nuts.
- A handful of granola or sunflower seeds.
- A slice of pizza with vegetable toppings.

Eating for a Lifetime

Good nutrition is essential for health at all times of the day and at every stage of life. If you do not get enough of the nutrients you need over a long period of time, you will become **malnourished,** or *impaired in health, growth, or functioning because of inadequate nutrient intake.* People of all ages need the same basic nutrients. The amount of nutrients and calories individuals need varies from one age to another, however, as growth rates and activity levels change. The way you eat now as a teen should be different from how you ate as a child and how you will eat as an adult.

Eating well throughout life will help you avoid some of the problems that may occur later in life. For example, the fiber, vitamins, and other components of fruits and vegeta-

Snacks

Teens are growing rapidly and may need more nutrients and calories than three meals a day can provide. Snacking is a good way for teens to get what they need. The key is choosing the right snacks—a variety of low-fat, low-sugar, nutrient-dense foods. Foods that are nutrient-dense provide a large amount and variety of nutrients relative to their calories. The following tips will help you snack in healthful ways:

- Snack midway between meals—not right before mealtime—so that you don't spoil your appetite for regular meals.
- Choose snacks from the five major food groups. Avoid foods with low nutrient density, such as candy and potato chips.

■ **How You've Grown!** Ask students to list their typical food choices and meal patterns from about five to seven years ago, then to list those of today. Have students compare the lists and write a few sentences answering these questions: How have your meals and patterns changed? Were they healthful then? Are they more or less so now? What might account for the changes you notice? *(Observation)*

■ **Planning Ahead.** Ask students to identify the benefits and drawbacks of planning meals a week in advance. Consider this in terms of both families and individuals. Do any students plan what they will eat at least a day at a time?

■ **Mind Your Munchies.** Ask students to list five foods they usually eat for snacks, then analyze the foods for healthfulness, using the tips on p. 401. Have students identify any poor choices and suggest more nutritious substitutes, using the list of snack ideas on on page 401. *(Problem Solving)*

■ **Come for Brunch.** Brunch, a combination of breakfast and lunch, is a popular weekend meal. Have students use cookbooks and other sources to plan a healthful brunch menu. *(Management)*

Focus on Problem Solving Skills

Point out that in many European cultures, the largest meal is served at midday—which, as the text suggests, may be a more healthful eating pattern. This is followed by a longer lunch break and later business hours. Ask: Could such a meal pattern work in the United States? How would it affect other aspects of daily life? What might be some advantages and disadvantages?

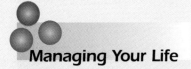
Checking Comprehension

✓ In what order are new foods introduced to infants? *Milk; rice cereal; pureed vegetables; fruit; cooked, pureed meat; finger food.*

✓ Besides nutrition, what is the value of giving preschoolers regular meals? *Teaches good eating habits.*

✓ Why do breast-feeding women need extra nutrients? *For own health; to supply nutrients to baby through milk.*

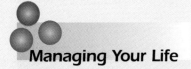

Managing Your Life

Have students read "Interpreting Food Label Claims" and discuss the questions. Ask them to describe other health claims they find confusing or misleading. What definitions do they suggest for these?

Answers to Applying . . .

1. No, food may still contain considerable fat; people may eat more of it.
2. Answers may include: nutrition facts; ingredients; recipe ideas.
3. No, food can be healthful without advertising the fact.

Managing Your Life

Interpreting Food Label Claims

Food labels can be an asset when it comes to managing your diet. They supply the information you need to make wise dietary choices—if you know how to interpret them.

In the past, words such as reduced and lean meant whatever the food manufacturer wanted them to mean. Now guidelines from the federal government have standardized these terms so that each one means the same thing no matter where it appears. Some of the most common food label claims are:

- **Free.** The product contains only a very small amount of fat, saturated fat, cholesterol, sodium, or calories. A product labeled "fat-free" has less than 0.5 g of fat per serving. A food claiming to be "99 percent fat-free" contains 1 g of fat per 100 g of the product.
- **Low.** A person can eat this food frequently without exceeding recommended amounts of the specified nutrient.
- **Lean.** "Lean" and "extra lean" meats, poultry, and seafood must have less than certain specified amounts of total fat, saturated fat, and cholesterol per serving.

- **High.** A food contains 20 percent or more of the recommended amounts of the specified nutrient per serving. "Good source" means a food provides 10 to 19 percent of the recommended amount per serving.
- **Reduced, less, fewer, more.** These comparison words must state what food or group of foods the product is being compared with. For example, the label "reduced-calorie mayonnaise" must also contain a statement such as "half the calories of regular mayonnaise."
- **Light.** The food has been altered to contain one-third fewer calories or half the fat of the original product; or the sodium content of a low-fat, low-calorie food has been reduced by half.

Applying the Principles

1. Does eating only foods labeled "lower in fat" ensure a low-fat diet? Explain.
2. What other helpful information might a label give?
3. Are foods without health claims on the labels necessarily poor choices? Explain.

bles may reduce your risk of some types of cancer. Choosing foods that are low in saturated fats and cholesterol may reduce your risk of heart disease.

Childhood

During childhood, the body is growing rapidly, and activity levels are high. At each stage—infant, toddler, and preschooler—children need an increasing number of calories to build body tissue and provide fuel for physical activity. For example, a six-month-old infant needs about 850 calories per day, a two-year-old about 1,200, and a five-year-old about 1,500. Nutrient needs also change. For

example, toddlers need large amounts of calcium and phosphorus to develop strong bones and teeth. Older preschoolers need more protein, more vitamins A, C, and K, and more magnesium and iodine than toddlers. Inadequate nutrients or calories in childhood can result in poor growth and decreased resistance to infection.

Infants obtain most of the energy and nutrients they need from formula or breast milk. Between four and six months, infants can begin to make the gradual transition to eating solid food. They begin with semisolid food, usually rice cereal specially formulated for infants. Then, one at a time (to check for aller-

MORE ABOUT Feeding Children

Toddlers and preschoolers tend to be picky eaters. Forcing a young child to eat rarely works and often creates an unpleasant scene. Also, evidence indicates that mealtime power struggles can lead to eating problems later on. To minimize mealtime conflict, provide a nutritious array of foods from which the child may choose. A child who insists on having dessert can be offered—with the rest of the family—an appealing choice of fruit.

gic reaction), strained, pureed vegetables are introduced, followed by fruits (which have a sweeter taste), and then cooked and pureed meats. Next come finger foods, such as soft toast, arrowroot biscuits, graham crackers, and tidbits of banana.

During the toddler, preschool, and elementary school years, children develop eating habits they are likely to carry into adulthood. Growth slows, but activity levels usually increase, so nutrient and calorie needs are still relatively high. During this time caregivers can help children develop healthy eating habits by providing a variety of nutrient-dense foods and establishing regular, consistent meal patterns. Allowing children to help in the kitchen or creating simple cooking activities with them (such as making easy snacks) helps make learning about food and nutrition fun.

Children often need frequent small meals instead of a few large ones. These children are learning that healthful snacks can be delicious.

Adolescence

Teens are growing rapidly and need even more vitamins and nutrients than children do. For example, the need for calcium to grow strong bones is greater than at any other time of life. Teens need 1,200 milligrams of calcium daily, while children need 800. Once girls begin to menstruate, their iron needs increase. Teen boys and girls need more iron as the amounts of blood and muscle tissue in their bodies increase.

Adulthood

As people get older, they are no longer growing, and some tend to become less active. While adults of all ages continue to need the same nutrients as children and teens, they need them in smaller amounts. If they continue to eat the same amount of food they did when they were still growing, they are likely to gain weight.

Elderly adults continue to need to make well-balanced food choices. They need nutrient-rich foods for meals and snacks to maintain their health and appropriate weight. Eating right for good health must continue throughout life.

Pregnancy

Good eating habits are especially important when a woman is pregnant. During pregnancy, nutrient needs increase as the fetus grows and develops. In addition to an extra 300 calories per day for the last six months of pregnancy, extra protein, vitamins, and minerals are necessary. Poor nutrition during pregnancy, as well as the use of tobacco or alcohol, can negatively affect the health of both mother and child.

A woman who is breast-feeding needs an extra 500 calories per day. She also needs ad-

Activities

■ **Different Strokes.** Have students make a chart with the column headings Infants; Children; Teens; Adults; and Pregnant and Breast-Feeding Women. Have them complete the chart by naming a health concern for each group and suggesting a to address it. Have students share ideas in class. (*Problem Solving*)

ENRICHMENT

■ **Teach Your Children.** Ask groups to select one good eating habit that children should know. Have them develop a plan for presenting this information in a way that would appeal to six- to eight-year-olds. You might suggest a song with accompanying actions, a puppet show, or an art project. Have groups share their plans with the class.

CROSS-CURRICULAR ACTIVITY
Math

Have students use calorie charts and additional information on children's food needs to write a day's menu for two different children: a two-year-old and a five-year-old. Meals should supply needed nutrients and calories.

MORE ABOUT Care During Pregnancy

What pregnant women avoid is as important as what they consume: alcohol can cause fetal alcohol syndrome; tobacco can contribute to dangerously low birth weight; and drugs, even legal ones, can lead to a host of serious problems.

Focus on Critical Thinking Skills

Ask: How can malnutrition be a problem in wealthy nations? Help students see that some parents don't know how to feed children well; some older adults have physical problems that keep them from shopping or eating right; people may not realize nutrient needs change.

Topics on pp. 404-405:
- **Vegetarian Choices**
- **Nutrition for Athletes**

Checking Comprehension

✓ What nutrients must vegetarians be especially careful to include in their diets? *Protein, vitamin B 12, vitamin D, iron, calcium.*

✓ How can vegetarians get enough calcium? *From legumes, leafy green vegetables, fortified soy milk.*

✓ When and what should athletes eat before a competition? *Three to four hours before; variety of foods high in complex carbohydrates, low in fats.*

FAMILY AND COMMUNITY OUTREACH

Encourage students to plan a nutritious vegetarian meal, with input from their families, and serve it at home. Ask volunteers to discuss their family's reaction with the class.

CROSS-CURRICULAR ACTIVITY
Health

Ask students to learn from coaches at school what they recommend their athletes eat before competition, then to compare these recommendations with the guidelines in the text.

Prenatal health care includes getting extra vitamins and minerals. A female who has taken good care of her health even before pregnancy, of course, is better prepared for this event.

ditional vitamins and protein, as well as calcium. The higher the intake of nutrients, the more nutritious the breast milk will be and the healthier the mother and baby.

Special Food Needs

You have looked at the effects that meal patterns and the stages of life have on your food needs and choices. Other factors are also at work. In Chapter 36 you looked at the way regional and ethnic factors influence eating patterns. Some people follow special food customs for religious reasons. Although such customs may limit food choices, they do not have to compromise good nutrition.

Lifestyle choices also affect what foods people eat. People who are vegetarians, who are training for athletic events, or who have certain medical conditions must make thoughtful food choices.

Vegetarian Food Choices

Vegetarians have special dietary concerns because their food choices include few or no foods from animal sources. People may choose to become vegetarians for religious, ethical, or health-related reasons. Not all vegetarian eating plans are the same, but most fit into one of the following categories:

- Eating foods from plant sources—grain products, legumes, vegetables, fruits, nuts, and seeds.
- Eating foods from plant sources *plus* milk products.
- Eating foods from plant sources *plus* eggs.
- Eating foods from plant sources *plus* both milk products and eggs.
- Eating vegetarian foods most of the time but occasionally eating meat, poultry, or fish.

Vegetarians must make food choices that provide nutritional balance and variety. It is crucial that they get enough of the nutrients that they would otherwise get from meat, poultry, fish, eggs, and milk products. These include protein, vitamin B12, vitamin D, iron, and calcium.

Vegetarians can get complete protein by eating a variety of incomplete protein foods, such as legumes and grain products. The

DID YOU KNOW?

Evidence suggests that prehistoric humans were vegetarians, surviving mainly on fruits, nuts, seeds, tubers, roots, berries, grains, and other foods they gathered. The popular image of early humans as hunters probably arose from archaeological digs that uncovered bones from the meat the cave dwellers infrequently ate, as opposed to vegetable matter, which had long since decomposed.

combination supplies all the essential amino acids, just as complete proteins in animal products do. Nutritious vegetarian dishes with complete proteins include:

- Black-eyed peas and rice.
- Hummus (a spread made of ground chickpeas) and pita bread.
- Succotash, a casserole of lima beans and corn.

Here are some examples of how vegetarians can meet their needs for certain vitamins and minerals:

- **Iron.** Legumes, dried fruits, and grain products provide iron. Foods rich in vitamin C help the body absorb iron.
- **Calcium.** Legumes, green leafy vegetables, and fortified soy milk are sources of calcium.
- **Vitamins B12 and D.** Vegetarians may need supplements if they eat no animal products at all. Physicians can offer advice on this need.

Nutrition for Athletes

Athletes who are actively training need the same nutrients as other people, but they need

By combining hummus and pita bread, you can get complete protein.

extra calories. No one food or nutrient builds muscle or increases speed, but complex carbohydrates—such as breads, pasta, rice, and starchy vegetables—are the best source of the energy an athlete's body needs.

Physical activity also requires extra fluids, especially during hot weather. Drinking plenty of fluids prevents dehydration and heatstroke. Most fluids should be taken in as water, but fruit juices, milk, and foods with high water content, such as lettuce and oranges, are good sources of extra fluid.

Many athletes wonder what they should eat before competition to improve their performance. Eating a meal three or four hours before competition is best because it gives the body time to digest the food. The meal should have a variety of foods from the five major food groups and should be high in complex carbohydrates and low in fats.

There are many misconceptions about the nutritional needs of athletes. A common one is that athletes need to take supplements for extra protein. In fact, normal eating patterns meet their protein needs. Furthermore, if athletes eat a balanced variety of nutritious foods, they do not need vitamin or mineral supplements or salt tablets.

Medical Diets

Many medical conditions, such as diabetes and food allergies, are treated with special diets. Sometimes certain foods must be eliminated from the diet to avoid problems. Other conditions require special foods to be included in the diet.

Diabetes

Diabetes is an incurable disorder that impairs the body's ability to use carbohydrates. It is caused by an inadequate production of the hormone insulin. While some diabetics must take insulin injections, many can control their condition through their diet.

It used to be assumed that people with diabetes could never eat sweets. However, current guidelines have created a meal plan exchange system that offers a variety of foods,

CHAPTER 40   Healthful Food Choices   405

Activities

■ **Living Green.** Ask students to plan a day's menu for a vegetarian teen who eats only foods from plant sources. The meals must meet the teen's daily nutritional needs. *(Problem Solving)*

ENRICHMENT

■ **Athletic Success vs. Safety.** Have students research drugs, vitamin supplements, etc. that are sometimes used by athletes. What are the side effects of these substances? What dangers are associated with their use?

CROSS-CURRICULAR ACTIVITY
Science

Have groups learn more about why athletes need more water than nonathletes. What is dehydration and what are the signs? What are the dangers of dehydration?

REAL-LIFE APPLICATION

Read this to students: *Your neighbor says, "We saw this coming: now that Josh has started preschool, he wants to have a birthday party like all his friends. They'll expect cake, and Josh is allergic to milk and eggs."* Ask: How do you advise your neighbor? What imaginative, festive alternatives can you suggest? Stress that children are often receptive to an adult's creativity and positive approach.

Topics on pp. 405-408:
- **Medically Indicated Diets**
- **Food Choices Away from Home**

Checking Comprehension

✓ Explain the exchange system of controlling diabetes. *Foods are divided into 6 groups, based on calories and nutrients; foods within group are interchangeable.*

✓ What foods might you use for a nutritious sandwich? *Whole-grain bread or roll; tuna; lean meat or poultry; cooked vegetables; lettuce, onion, tomato, bean sprouts.*

✓ Name some healthful choices from vending machines. *Beef stew, vegetable soup, apple, yogurt, raisins.*

FAMILY AND COMMUNITY OUTREACH

Suggest that students to make a survey of the contents of vending machines they notice and report their findings to the class. Students might compile a vending machine guide, similar to a food critic's restaurant guide, indicating the machine's location and contents and awarding stars for nutritious choices. If the class is not satisfied with the number or variety of healthful choices, encourage them to contact the company that stocks the machines and argue their case.

including some sugars. This system divides foods into six major groups, each consisting of foods with similar calorie and nutrient content. A food in any group may be traded for another in the same group.

Like everyone else, people with diabetes should eat a variety of foods, including adequate amounts of complex carbohydrates and high-fiber foods. They should limit foods high in fats, sugars, and sodium.

Although the tendency to develop diabetes may be inherited, overweight is a factor contributing to the development of one type of diabetes. Weight control is thus an important factor in the prevention of diabetes.

Food Allergies

Sometimes the body's immune system reacts to a particular food substance as though it were a foreign invader. When this food is eaten, the body produces substances that irritate the system and may even be life threatening. Common reactions include stomach pain, diarrhea, rashes, itching, swelling, or nasal congestion.

Foods that most often cause allergic reactions include nuts, eggs, milk, wheat, shellfish, and soybeans. Once a food allergy is identified—either through allergy testing or by keeping a food diary—the food can be eliminated from the diet. Nutrients supplied by that food can be made up by substituting other foods.

Lactose Intolerance

When people say they are allergic to milk, they may actually mean that they are **lactose-intolerant,** or *unable to digest lactose, the form of sugar that is found in milk.* Digesting lactose requires the enzyme lactase. People who cannot digest lactose usually have low levels of that enzyme. When lactose-intolerant people drink milk, they may experience gas, bloating, abdominal pain, or diarrhea. To avoid the symptoms, people with lactose intolerance may need to limit the amount of milk in their diets, use special lactose-free milk products, or add a lactase enzyme preparation to regular milk.

Eating Out

When you eat away from home, it can sometimes be difficult to make healthful food choices. Your choices may be limited, and you may not be able to find out the fat, sugar, or sodium content of a particular food. If you select carefully, however, you will be able to enjoy tasty, healthful foods when you eat out.

Restaurant Meals

If you are eating in a restaurant, you can take several steps to get the nutrition you need:

- Look for a restaurant that has a large selection of menu items. The more choices you have, the easier it will be to find healthful foods.

Salad bars can provide healthful alternatives—just watch the dressings and the extras, such as potato or macaroni salad, toppings, and croutons.

406   UNIT 6   Food, Nutrition, and Wellness

MORE ABOUT Dietary Fat

Though much maligned, fat is a nutrient. It provides reserve energy, allows the body to store and use other nutrients, and helps regulate body temperature. Many high-fat foods also provide other essential nutrients. However, for most Americans, one tablespoon of fat meets the daily nutritional requirement. In that tablespoon are essential fatty acids the body cannot produce. Meeting this requirement is a problem only for those on extremely low-fat diets or who have eating disorders.

- To avoid excess fat, choose a main dish that is broiled, grilled, steamed, or baked instead of fried. If possible, ask to have your entrée prepared without added fat.
- Have soup and a dinner salad instead of an entrée. Broth- or tomato-based soups are lower in fat than creamed types.
- If a portion served is much larger than your usual serving, have some wrapped to take home for lunch the next day.
- Order such side dishes as a baked potato and a tossed salad instead of french fries.
- Choose fresh fruit for dessert. If you don't see fruit on the menu, ask if it is available.

Fast Foods

In the past, fast-food restaurants had a limited selection, and the foods were often high in fat, sodium, and sugar. Today, to meet consumer demand, fast-food restaurants have added many low-fat, healthful choices to their menus. They include broiled hamburgers, roasted chicken, fresh salads and salad bars, plain baked potatoes, "light" entrées with reduced fat and calories, low-fat shakes, fruit juice, and skim milk. Many restaurants also make nutrient information about the menu choices available to customers.

STRATEGIES That Work

Fast Food: Cutting the Fat

Eating at a fast-food restaurant doesn't automatically mean splurging on fat and calories. You must choose carefully, however, to avoid nutritional pitfalls. For example:

- A baked potato makes a good substitute for french fries, unless it's loaded with butter, sour cream, grated cheese, or cheese sauce. Try toppers like chives, broccoli, or salsa. A sprinkle of vinegar adds tang.
- Fast-food fish and chicken items are often breaded and deep-fried, adding fat and calories. Order broiled fish with no breading; flavor it with lemon juice, not tartar sauce. Choose grilled chicken dishes.
- When choosing Mexican foods, avoid items dripping with cheese—it's high in saturated fat. A chicken fajita (without cheese) in a flour tortilla is a better choice.
- Pizza can be an acceptable fast-food choice—if it's topped with mushrooms, onion, green pepper, and other vegetables. Pass on the pepperoni, sausage, and extra cheese.

- Watch out for salad bars. Among the lettuce may lurk high-fat items including potato and pasta salads made with mayonnaise or oil; bacon bits and croutons (they look harmless, but can contain more than 50 percent fat); and creamy, high-fat dressings. Smarter choices include salad greens, vegetables, fruit, plain pasta, raisins, and low-fat dressing.
- When you crave a milk shake, ask for low-fat or fat-free frozen yogurt instead.

Making the Strategy Work

Think . . .

1. What are some ways consumers can influence what foods a fast-food restaurant offers?
2. Why do you think so many fast foods are high in fat?
3. Would you be willing to pay more for a more healthful fast-food meal? Why or why not?

Try...

Using nutritional information from a fast-food restaurant menu, sign, or brochure, plan three low-fat meals that you could order there.

■ **Veggies to Go.** Ask groups to design a menu for a fast-food restaurant that serves only healthful foods. Remind students that fast-food restaurant customers want inexpensive food that is available quickly and easy to eat. Have groups present their menus to the class. *(Creativity)*

RETEACHING

■ **Eat and Run.** Ask students to imagine it is a hectic day. They pick up breakfast at a fast-food restaurant, have lunch at school, and get dinner from a vending machine. Have students name the healthful food choices they make.

STRATEGIES THAT WORK

Have students read "Fast Food: Cutting the Fat" and discuss the questions. Ask: Do people really expect—or want—healthful choices at fast-food restaurants? Do you order these items? Have you seen others order them?

Answers to Think . . .
1. Answers may include: talk to manager; write to chain's president or marketing director; order only healthful items.
2. Answers may include: many are fried because it's easy and inexpensive; high-fat foods are popular.
3. Answers will vary. Ask: Why would healthful items cost more? Could consumer pressure lower prices?

MORE ABOUT Healthful Dining

Try these tips for dining out. First, don't fill up on breads and rolls. Try ordering a few nutritious appetizers and have them served when others get their entrées. Ask for salad dressings and sauces on the side. Share large portions with a companion.

DID YOU KNOW?

Vending machines may date from as far back as 200 B.C., when Hero of Alexandria wrote about a machine in an Egyptian temple that gave holy water in exchange for coins. Today, vending machine sales total more than $26 billion annually.

Review

■ **Chapter Review.** Use the contents of the Chapter Review page to help students review concepts, think critically, and apply their knowledge.

■ **Study Guide.** Have students complete the Study Guide for Chapter 40 on page 134 of the Student Workbook.

■ **Pick and Choose.** Have groups create a character who: is either a vegetarian, an athlete, or on a special diet; is a child, a teen, or pregnant; and averages one meal daily from a restaurant, fast-food restaurant, or vending machine. Have groups create a one-day menu that meets this person's nutritional needs.

Evaluation

■ **Chapter Test.** Use the reproducible chapter test provided in the Teacher's Classroom Resources or create your own test using the *Testmaker Software*.

■ **Alternative Assessment.** Have students ask an adult friend to be the subject of a case study that applies topics covered in this chapter. Students should indicate the person's age, gender, and other relevant life conditions, then describe his or her eating habits and food choices. Students should explain whether these are healthful habits and, if not, suggest improvements.

■ **Top Ten.** Have students compile a one-page list of ten tips for healthful eating to cover these topics: meal patterns; changes in eating habits over a lifetime; special food needs; and eating out.

Eating at School

Today nutritionists plan many school lunch programs. They consider nutrition and they follow the Dietary Guidelines for Americans. When you select your lunch from the offerings in the school cafeteria, keep in mind the number of servings you need for the day from each food group.

If you bring food from home instead of eating cafeteria food, here are ideas for packing nutritious lunches:

- Instead of white bread, choose whole-grain breads—whole-wheat, multigrain, rye, pumpernickel, or oatmeal.
- For variety, choose rolls, pita pockets, or tortillas instead of sliced bread.
- Instead of high-fat cheese and luncheon meats, choose sandwich fillings with less fat and sodium—water-packed tuna; lean meat or poultry; chopped or shredded vegetables; mashed, cooked dry beans mixed with chili powder and dry mustard; or low-fat cottage cheese mixed with chopped fruit or vegetables.
- Instead of adding mayonnaise, ketchup, or other high-fat or high-sodium condiments to sandwiches, try lettuce, onion, tomatoes, or bean sprouts.
- Round out your lunch with low-fat milk or fruit juice and additions such as fresh fruit, plain popcorn, fig bars, yogurt, or a bran muffin. Pass up the potato chips, soda, and cookies.

Vending Machines

Making healthful choices at a vending machine may be easy or impossible, depending on what the machine offers. Although some sell only candy and gum or soda, larger vending machines in public areas such as malls, airports, and office parks may have more nutritious choices. If you eat a snack or meal from a vending machine that you think may be high in calories, sodium, or fat, make sure that the rest of the food you eat that day is low in calories, sodium, and fat. Consider these examples of good vending machine choices:

- **Vending machines that offer main dishes.** Beef stew and vegetable soup are high in sodium but are good sources of vitamin A.
- **Vending machines that offer refrigerated foods.** An apple is high in fiber and has no fat. Yogurt is low in fat and sodium and provides calcium and riboflavin.
- **Vending machines that offer snack foods.** Raisins, if available, are a healthful choice, with only 40 calories and a trace of fat and sodium.

No matter where or when you eat, think of food as many parts of a balanced whole. For example, if you haven't had a serving of fruit by afternoon, grab an orange for an after-school snack and include fruit at dinner. If you munched on oil-popped, salted popcorn at a movie, make sure that your next meal is low in fat and sodium. Making healthful food choices requires creativity, thoughtfulness, and a basic knowledge of nutrition.

■ When buying snacks from a vending machine, try to avoid foods that are high in sugar, salt, or fats.

REAL-LIFE APPLICATION

Ask students to imagine that a friend in this class tells them, "Actually, all this stuff about making healthful food choices sounds like a lot of work. It takes the fun out of eating. Am I supposed to go around with the Food Guide Pyramid and a nutrition book and look up everything I eat?" Have students write a paragraph in response that suggests a more positive, less rigid approach to choosing foods, but that still promotes good health.

Review

Reviewing the Facts

1. Why is breakfast such an important meal?
2. What role do snacks play in nutritious food choices?
3. Why do people need different amounts of nutrients at each stage of life?
4. How should teens who are training for athletic events eat?
5. What is a food allergy? What are some of the symptoms of a food allergy?
6. List three ways you can be sure to follow the nutrition guidelines when eating in a restaurant.

Thinking Critically

1. Why might introducing vegetables before fruits help infants develop good eating habits?
2. Many teens skip meals and fill up on nonnutritious snacks. What do you think are the reasons behind these poor eating habits?

Applying Your Knowledge

1. **Taking a Survey.** Take a survey of students in your school to find out what nutritious snacks they would purchase, if available, from the vending machines in your school. Present a summary of your findings to the school staff in charge of the vending machines.
2. **Analyzing Your Meal Patterns.** For a week, keep a diary describing your regular routine for eating meals. At the end of the week, look for meal patterns. Do you think that you have a healthy eating routine based on what you now know? How could you improve it?
3. **Planning Better School Lunches.** Write a list of "Do's and Don'ts" for someone eating in your school cafeteria who wants to make healthful choices. For example, you might write, "Make a salad with diet dressing" or "Ask for the broiled chicken without sauce."

Making Connections

1. **Health.** Imagine that you are a preschool teacher. Plan an activity that would teach four-year-olds about making healthful food choices. How will you involve the children in the activity? What materials will you need? Remember that young children have a short attention span. Your activity should take no longer than 20 minutes.
2. **Language Arts.** Create a menu for a restaurant that would cater to one of the special diets discussed in this chapter. Do additional research as needed to discover what kinds of offerings your restaurant should have. Use descriptive language to make the menu items sound appetizing to customers.

Building Your Portfolio

Creating a Snack Cookbook
Collect recipes for nutritious snacks from friends, cookbooks, or magazines, or develop your own. Assemble enough recipes so that each of the five food groups is included at least twice. The recipes should be easy to prepare and appealing to teens. Try each recipe, and put copies of the three best recipes in your portfolio, along with an analysis of what nutrients they provide.

ANSWERS TO REVIEWING THE FACTS

1. Restores nutrients depleted during long break since last meal; provides energy for the morning's activities.
2. Low-fat, low-sugar, nutrient-dense snacks can help provide needed nutrients and calories.
3. Growth rates and activity levels change.
4. Need same nutrients but extra calories, especially from carbohydrates; extra fluids for physical activity.
5. Immune system responds to certain food as though it were foreign invader. Stomach pain, diarrhea, rashes, itching, swelling, nasal congestion.
6. Any three: eat at restaurant with a varied menu; avoid fatty foods; have soup and a dinner salad rather than an entrée; take part of large portions home; have fresh fruit for dessert.

ANSWERS TO THINKING CRITICALLY

1. Allows child to develop taste for vegetables before becoming accustomed to sweet taste of fruit, encouraging good eating habits.

2. Answers may include: snacks taste good, are readily available, heavily advertised; teens have busy schedules, don't think about how food choices will affect health later.

FOCUS

Chapter Overview

Chapter 41 covers the basics of meal planning. Students learn to combine foods in healthful, appealing ways that make good use of available resources. They learn to locate and choose recipes that will help them plan and prepare successful meals.

Motivator

■ **Good Enough to Eat.** Ask students to describe their favorite meals. Draw out details related to meal appeal, such as appearance, texture, and flavor. Add that an appealing meal can be nutritious. Tell students this chapter explains how to combine elements to create successful meals.

Objectives

Discuss the chapter objectives on this page. Remind students that the objectives focus on important chapter concepts.

Vocabulary

A *recipe* was once the ingredients a pharmacist combined to make a prescribed medicine. In England, a *recipe,* the cooking term, is known as a *receipt.* Ask: How is the American definition of *receipt*—a list and amount of items purchased—related to its English usage?

Chapter 41 Planning Meals at Home

Terms to Learn

- entrée
- ingredient
- menu
- recipe
- yield

Objectives

This chapter will help you to:

- **Describe** the main factors to consider for successful meal planning.
- **Name** five ways to make meals appealing.
- **Explain** strategies for choosing recipes.

410   UNIT 6   Food, Nutrition and Wellness

CHAPTER RESOURCES

Student Workbook
Study Guide, pp. 134-135
Activity, *Order Your Health*, pp. 136-137

Teacher's Classroom Resources
Lesson Plan, p. 44
Cooperative Learning, *International Food*, pp. 45-46

Decision Making, *Choosing Food Wisely*, p. 21
Extension #65, *Pregnancy and Diet*, p. 71
Extension #66, *What Does the Menu Say?* p. 72
Life Skills, *Restaurant Review*, p. 67
Chapter 40 Test, pp. 85-86

Performance Assessment, *A Good Day's Eating*, p. 71
Reteaching, *Prescriptions for Good Health*, p. 46

See Also:
ABCNews InterActive™ Videodiscs

As they get ready for school and work each morning, Elena and her family usually know what they'll be having for dinner that night. Elena's mother does the weekly meal planning and Elena's older brother shops for groceries once a week. When the family is going to have fresh vegetables, Elena's father stops at the farmer's market on his way home. Sometimes Elena's mother buys fish from the fish market near the office where she works.

Elena, her parents, and her brother take turns preparing and cleaning up the evening meal. Because they plan ahead, Elena can count on the kitchen being stocked with the food she needs when it is her turn to prepare a meal.

Meal Planning

Many families, like Elena's, find it useful to plan meals a day or a week ahead. Planning meals well in advance can result in well-balanced, nutritious meals that are appetizing and attractive. Through planning, families can satisfy everyone's needs and schedules while staying within their food budget.

Planning meals involves choosing a **menu,** or *list of foods that will be included in the meal.* A common meal-planning strategy is to first select an **entrée** (AHN-tray), or *main dish.* Then you can select side dishes that work well with the main dish.

When planning meals for your family, it helps to know:

- How many people will be eating at each meal? Do some require larger- or smaller-than-average servings?
- Will everyone be eating at the same time,

The person planning meals should take into account food allergies and other medical reasons that certain foods must be avoided.

or will food have to be kept warm or re-heated later?
- What are family members' food preferences?
- Does anyone have dietary restrictions or the need for special foods?

In addition, several factors are essential for planning any meal. They include the nutrition and appeal of the foods included and the resources you have to prepare the meal.

Nutrition

As you know, good nutrition is vital to good health. If you plan your daily meals and snacks in advance, you can be sure to get the variety of foods you need each day for good nutrition. As recommended in the Food Guide Pyramid, each day everyone should have:

- 6 to 11 servings from the Bread, Cereal, Rice, and Pasta Group.
- 3 to 5 servings of vegetables.
- 2 to 4 servings of fruits.
- 2 to 3 servings from the Milk, Yogurt, and Cheese Group.

CHAPTER 41   Planning Meals at Home   411

TEACH

Topics on pp. 411:
- **Meal Planning**
- **Nutritional Concerns**

Checking Comprehension

✓ What are the benefits of planning meals? *Families can have meals that meet everyone's nutritional needs and schedules and stay within budget.*

✓ Besides family preferences, what should meal planners consider? *Foods' nutrition and appeal, available resources.*

Activities

■ **Family Chef.** Have students make a chart by writing the four meal-planning questions, in abbreviated form, across the top as column headings, then listing their family members in a column on the left. Have students fill in the charts accordingly. *(Management)*

FAMILY AND COMMUNITY OUTREACH

Invite a dietitian who plans menus at an institution, such as a nursing home or school, to speak to the class. What factors does he or she take into consideration? How does this task compare with planning meals for a family?

DID YOU KNOW?

- Taste buds detect only four basic sensations: salty, sweet, bitter, and sour. The distinction of flavors is actually made from smelling the food rather than tasting it. That's why taste is impaired when the nose is congested.

- Preserving food gives cooks options in meal planning. One of the oldest methods is salting. Meat, for example, was soaked in a strong brine solution or covered with large pieces of salt. In England, these salt chunks were called corn—hence the name corned beef.

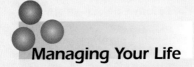
Checking Comprehension

✓ What five qualities contribute to a meal's appeal? *Flavor, color, shape and size, texture, temperature.*

✓ True or false: Textures of foods in a meal should be similar. *False.*

✓ Why is it important that meals have appeal? *People are more likely to eat nutritious foods that look and taste good.*

Managing Your Life

Have students read "Planning Meals for Busy Families" and discuss the questions. Refer them to the meal plan on page 418. Ask how they could apply the tips in the feature to each meal described.

Answers to Applying . . .
1. Answers may include: meal must be planned to be ready when diners are; foods may take different amounts of time to prepare; some foods can be prepared ahead when more time is available.
2. Answers may include: have them suggest meals for weekly plan; let them help prepare meals.
3. Answers may include: serve cold dish if preparation time is limited; combine take-out food with homemade.

Be sure to include nutritious snacks as part of daily meal planning.

- 2 to 3 servings from the Meat, Poultry, Fish, Dry Beans, Eggs, and Nuts Group.

With practice, you'll find that it's easy to plan meals based on the Food Guide Pyramid. To get three servings of fruit in a day, for instance, you could have banana slices on your cereal at breakfast, some melon at lunch, and pineapple juice as an afternoon snack. By planning, you won't let a day go by without

Managing Your Life

Planning Meals for Busy Families

Families today seem busier than ever with work and school activities, leaving little time to prepare meals. Management skills can help families plan healthful meals that are as easy to prepare as they are tasty to eat. Try these timesaving tips:

- When advisable, chop, slice, or otherwise prepare ingredients for a meal ahead of time. Cover and store them until needed.
- Combine convenience foods and fresh foods in recipes. Use canned beans in chili, for instance, instead of cooking dry beans.
- When preparing a recipe, make enough for several meals. Freeze the extra to use when time is short.
- Plan appliance use to manage time. Plan meals that can be made with time- or energy-saving appliances, such as slow cookers.
- Plan entrées that provide leftovers for future, preferably varied, meals. Leftover roast chicken can be cubed for stews, shredded for salads, or sliced for sandwiches.
- Plan one-dish meals often. They usually take less time to prepare than separate entreés and side dishes.

- Create a collection of easy-to-make recipes. Cookbooks and magazines often feature recipes that take 30 minutes or less to prepare.
- Take advantage of other people's schedules as you plan meals. A family member who is home early on a certain day, for example, might be asked to start dinner.

Applying the Principles

1. Why is timing, as well as use of time, important to meal planning?
2. Projects such as meal preparation are most efficiently completed when the skills of everyone are used to their fullest. How could you interest and involve younger family members in meal planning and preparation?
3. Add one more timesaving tip to the list above.

MORE ABOUT Creating Appeal

Herbs and spices add taste and color to foods. Favorite herbs include rosemary, parsley, oregano, chives, and basil. Use three times as much fresh herbs as dried. Spices include cinnamon, pepper, cloves, and paprika. Herbs and spices may be combined in special blends, such as curry or chili powder. Garnishes also add color, increasing visual appeal. Popular, edible garnishes include parsley, lemon wedges, orange slices, radishes, cherry tomatoes, carrot curls, and pickles.

Figure 41.1

MEAL APPEAL

When planning a meal, remember that flavor, color, shape, texture, and temperature are characteristics of food that should be varied. A successful meal looks as good as it tastes.

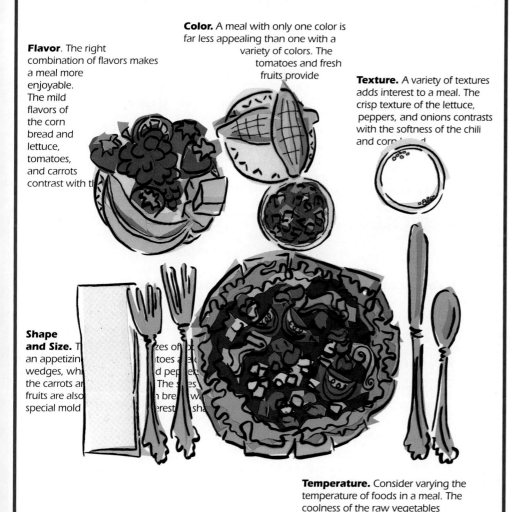

Color. A meal with only one color is far less appealing than one with a variety of colors. The tomatoes and fresh fruits provide

Flavor. The right combination of flavors makes a meal more enjoyable. The mild flavors of the corn bread and lettuce, tomatoes, and carrots contrast with th

Texture. A variety of textures adds interest to a meal. The crisp texture of the lettuce, peppers, and onions contrasts with the softness of the chili and corn

Shape and Size. T___ ___ ___ ___zes of ___ an appetizin___ ___toes a___ ___ wedges, wh___ ___ ___d pepp___ the carrots a___ ___ ___. The s___ fruits are also ___ ___ ___ bre___ w___ special mold ___ ___ ___erest___ sh___

Temperature. Consider varying the temperature of foods in a meal. The coolness of the raw vegetables contrasts with the hot chili and warm bread.

Activities

■ **Food Combos.** Have students make a list of food combinations that would provide an interesting and appealing contrast in each of the following areas: color, flavor, temperature, shape, and texture. *(Creativity)*

RETEACHING

■ **Today's Special.** Ask students to look at a restaurant menu that lists complete meals (as opposed to à la carte) and to rate the meals on their appeal, based on the criteria given on p. 413. Alternately, have students order appealing meals à la carte.

MULTICULTURAL *Perspectives*

Have students create a meal of an ethnic cuisine (other than their own, if applicable) that uses the five elements of meal appeal to advantage. Have students describe their meal to the class, explaining its ethnic origin and how it satisfies the different criteria.

Focus on Planning Skills

Point out that for meal appeal, how students' choice of any one dish affects their options for the others. If they promise one family member mashed potatoes for dinner, they should plan on not serving applesauce as well. Ask students to describe and give examples of foods they would plan to serve with: corn on the cob; creamed corn; iceberg lettuce salad; cottage cheese; onion soup.

Topics on pp. 414-415:
- **Meal-Planning Resources**
- **Preparation Options**

Checking Comprehension

✓ True or false: the most nutritious meals are also the most expensive. *False.*

✓ Why should you limit convenience foods in your menus? *Most cost more than homemade; some are high in fat, sodium, and sugar.*

✓ Name two sources for recipes. *Any two: cookbooks; newspapers and magazines; food packaging; family and friends.*

From School to Work

Have students read "Maintaining Information" and discuss the questions. Ask: What problems arise from failing to maintain information properly? What impression does readily finding and using information create?

Answers to Assessing . . .
1. Answers will vary. Stress that such skills are useful for any task, especially when time is limited.
2. Answers will vary. Challenge students to name jobs where these skills are not needed.
3. Answers will vary.

getting the essential nutrients you need to stay healthy.

Meal Appeal

The way a meal looks and tastes affects what people eat and how much they enjoy their food. When you plan nutritious meals that look attractive and appetizing, you help ensure that people will eat the foods that are good for them. **Figure 41.1** on page 413 shows how the five characteristics of an appealing meal are combined in a meal consisting of a Mexican chili salad with corn bread and salsa, fresh fruit for dessert, and skim milk.

Your Resources

As you plan meals, try to be realistic about your resources. If you are, the result is much more likely to be a meal you can be proud of. Consider these four factors as you make your meal selections:

- **Time.** If you do not have much time, plan simple meals that involve few preparation steps and short cooking times.
- **Preparation skill.** If you're a beginning cook, plan meals that are easy to prepare using basic cooking skills. As you gain experience and confidence, you can begin to expand your skills by preparing more complicated dishes.
- **Money.** Plan your meals within the family food budget. Few people can afford to dine on steak and lobster every day. Fortunately, it's not hard to plan nutritious, tasty meals using less expensive foods. (You'll find tips for smart food shopping in the next chapter.)

Maintaining Information

What You Learn Today . . .

Do you realize how much you rely on your ability to maintain information throughout the day? For school work, you receive information from teachers and research sources. At home, you need to keep track of schedules and tasks to help keep the household running. Your social life includes remembering dates, appointments, and other obligations. In all these areas, your success depends on storing information in an orderly fashion for ready use.

. . . You Can Use Tomorrow

Information-recording skills are an asset in the workplace. People who run businesses and work in them must maintain information in an organized way. They record inventory and maintain computer files on customers and employees, among many other processes. Smooth operation and profitability rely on effective handling of such procedures.

Practicing Your Skills

What techniques do you use to handle information? You might want to try these:

- Don't rely on memory. Use lists, notebooks, calendars, and other record-keeping tools.
- Categorize information using methods such as alphabetizing, color coding, or grouping by type—whatever method you find easiest for retrieving the material.
- Make notes on your records. These serve as reminders about any changes, special details, or unusual circumstances.

Assessing Your Skills

1. Describe a situation in which you would find organizational skills helpful. Explain why.
2. Name several jobs in which you could use your ability to organize and maintain information.
3. What method of organizing information works best for you?

REAL-LIFE APPLICATION

Read this to students: *Matthew is serving turkey patties, steamed broccoli, and biscuits for dinner. His options are using either frozen patties or fresh ground turkey; frozen broccoli pieces or whole fresh broccoli; and refrigerated rolls or homemade biscuits.* Ask: What resources does Matthew need in each case? How can he combine options to use resources most efficiently? What other factors might influence his choice?

Pizza is a handy convenience food. How could you add nutritional value to a frozen pizza?

• **Supplies and equipment.** Before deciding on a menu, be sure you have or can get the foods and equipment you need. Sometimes you can substitute for an item that's missing. For example, if fresh sweet corn is unavailable, you could serve frozen corn instead. If you wanted homemade mashed potatoes but your electric mixer was broken, what alternatives could you use? Some cookbooks may offer ideas for making conversions.

Preparation Options

As you plan your meals, consider not only what foods you want to include in the menu but also what options you have for purchasing and preparing them. For example, if you're planning to have a pizza with vegetable toppings, you could:

• Order pizza from a restaurant.
• Heat up a frozen pizza.
• Use a packaged crust or a mix for the crust and sauce and add your own toppings.
• Make the pizza entirely from scratch.

Each of these options has benefits and drawbacks. Ordering a pizza is the easiest option but also the most expensive. A frozen pizza would be ready in the least amount of time but might not be as tasty or nutritious as one you make yourself.

Today, convenience foods provide more choices than ever before. You can buy everything from mashed potato flakes to frozen mashed potatoes, from muffin mixes to prewashed, premixed salad greens. Convenience foods can save you time and effort, but they are not always the best choice. Using them usually costs more than making a meal from scratch. Some convenience foods are high in fat, sodium, or sugar. For good nutrition, limit your use of convenience foods or choose ones that are more healthful.

Choosing Recipes

When you prepare foods yourself, you will use **recipes** to give you *detailed instructions for preparing particular foods*. Recipes are found in many places:

• **Cookbooks.** General cookbooks may offer suggestions for planning entire meals. They often have instructions on cooking methods and equipment. Some cookbooks are specialized, with recipes only for salads, vegetarian meals, or regional food, for example.

Activities

■ **Do You Have What It Takes?** Have students choose a recipe and give examples of specific resources they would need to prepare it, based on the four resources listed on p. 414. Have them explain whether they think they would be able to make the recipe. *(Critical Thinking)*

ENRICHMENT

■ **File Follows Function.** Challenge students to create a recipe filing system that reflects the way their family lives and eats. Ask them to identify four or five different categories, not necessarily traditional ones, and a few foods their family often serves for each category.

MULTICULTURAL *Perspectives*

Cookbooks featuring foods from another country offer insights into that culture. Using such cookbooks, ask students to analyze the foods and recipes in comparison to American cookbooks. What types of foods predominate in each? What flavors and ingredients are popular? What measurement systems are used (or would be used in that country)? What terms? Provide a dictionary for students to look up any unfamiliar words.

MORE ABOUT More About Cookbooks

Beautiful color photographs in cookbooks help "sell" the recipes—and thus the cookbooks. They can be informative by showing cooks how a recipe should look. Amateurs can grow discouraged, however, comparing their results to the creations of experienced professionals that are made using state-of-the-art equipment and photographed in picture-perfect settings. Show students some examples of this. Ask: Are photos are more a help or a hindrance?

Topics on pp. 416-418:
- Choosing and Evaluating Recipes
- Long-Range Meal Planning

Checking Comprehension

✓ Identify at least five types of information found on recipes. *Any five: ingredients and amounts; appliance settings; equipment; times; directions; yield; nutritional information.*

✓ How can you tell if a recipe is healthful? *Provides many nutrients with relatively few calories; low in fat, sugar, and salt.*

✓ How can you learn what equipment you need to make a recipe? *Look in directions for equipment named, or used but not mentioned.*

CROSS-CURRICULAR ACTIVITY
Language Arts

Have students write an anecdotal essay describing the consequences of using a poorly written recipe, or of not following recipe correctly. The story may be either true or fictional. Encourage students to share their stories with the class.

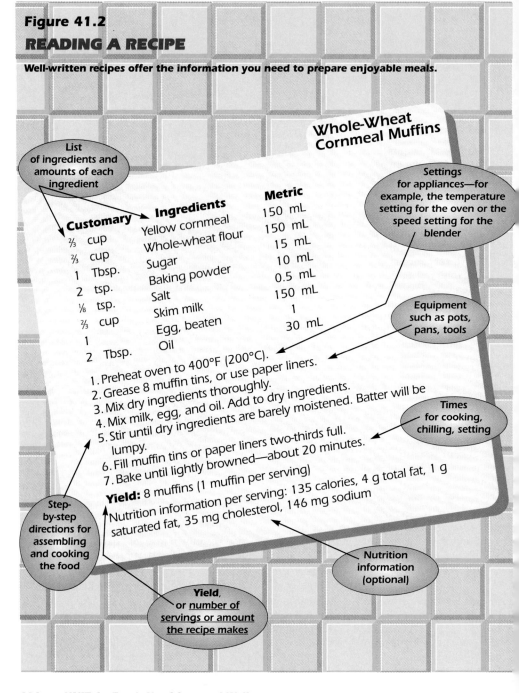

Figure 41.2
READING A RECIPE

Well-written recipes offer the information you need to prepare enjoyable meals.

List of ingredients and amounts of each ingredient

Settings for appliances—for example, the temperature setting for the oven or the speed setting for the blender

Equipment such as pots, pans, tools

Times for cooking, chilling, setting

Step-by-step directions for assembling and cooking the food

Yield, or number of servings or amount the recipe makes

Nutrition information (optional)

Whole-Wheat Cornmeal Muffins

Customary	Ingredients	Metric
⅔ cup	Yellow cornmeal	150 mL
⅔ cup	Whole-wheat flour	150 mL
1 Tbsp.	Sugar	15 mL
2 tsp.	Baking powder	10 mL
⅛ tsp.	Salt	0.5 mL
⅔ cup	Skim milk	150 mL
1	Egg, beaten	1
2 Tbsp.	Oil	30 mL

1. Preheat oven to 400°F (200°C).
2. Grease 8 muffin tins, or use paper liners.
3. Mix dry ingredients thoroughly.
4. Mix milk, egg, and oil. Add to dry ingredients.
5. Stir until dry ingredients are barely moistened. Batter will be lumpy.
6. Fill muffin tins or paper liners two-thirds full.
7. Bake until lightly browned—about 20 minutes.

Yield: 8 muffins (1 muffin per serving)
Nutrition information per serving: 135 calories, 4 g total fat, 1 g saturated fat, 35 mg cholesterol, 146 mg sodium

---

Focus on Problem Solving Skills

Ask students to imagine they are reading a recipe in a magazine that sounds very good. Unfortunately, the page on which the recipe is continued is missing. They have only the recipe title and list of ingredients. What would they do? Help students see that, depending on their cooking skills, they might improvise the directions; use the title as a clue and look for similar recipes; or locate another copy of the magazine. They have options other than giving up.

- **Newspapers and magazines.** You can clip recipes featured in newspapers and magazines and keep them in a loose-leaf binder or copy them onto file cards.
- **Food packaging.** Boxes of macaroni, soup cans, bags of rice, and other packages may provide recipes.
- **Family and friends.** Some of the meals your family likes best have probably been made from recipes passed on from relatives or friends.

With many recipes to choose from, how can you decide which ones to clip and save or which to use on a particular day? As when planning a menu, consider your resources—the time available, the skills you have or want to develop, your food budget, and the supplies and equipment you have or can obtain. You'll also want to ask yourself:

- Does the recipe sound good?
- Is the recipe healthful?
- Is the recipe complete?

Does the Recipe Sound Good?

Sometimes just reading a recipe makes your mouth water. You know it will taste good. If you are preparing a meal for other people, what you know about their tastes—rather than your own—helps you choose one recipe over another. Searching for recipes to prepare during her grandfather's visit, Andrea found one for a spicy meat loaf that sounded delicious. She kept looking, though, remembering that he wasn't fond of garlic and was watching his cholesterol carefully.

Is the Recipe Healthful?

Try to choose recipes for foods that provide many nutrients without too many calories. Look for recipes that are low in fat, sugar, and salt. Some recipes provide nutrition information that tells you the amount of calories and nutrients per serving. Sometimes you can modify a recipe to make it more healthful. For example, you could substitute fat-free sour cream for regular sour cream in a recipe for beef stroganoff.

Is the Recipe Complete?

Check to see that a recipe contains all the information you need to make the dish. The information may be arranged in several ways. In the most commonly used format, the **ingredients,** which are *the individual food items needed to make a recipe,* are listed first. The assembly directions follow the list of ingredients. Other, less common formats combine the ingredients and directions.

No matter how a recipe is written, it should include certain basic information. **Figure 41.2** on page 416 indicates the main parts of a recipe. Note that measurements are often abbreviated in recipes. You will learn about the measurements in Chapter 46.

Using Management Skills

Long-range meal planning is a useful management technique. It helps you use your resources, especially time, energy, knowledge, and money, wisely. Through planning, you can achieve the goal of eating healthful, enjoyable meals.

Set aside a regular time and place to plan meals each week. Be sure your meal plan takes into account all the activities that you and others have scheduled during the week. See **Figure 41.3** on pages 418 for a sample

MORE ABOUT Meal Planning

Until the last 100 years, meal planning was was limited by local availability. People mainly ate foods that could be raised in their area, supplemented by native game and plants. Time of year was also a factor. Fruits and vegetables were eaten in season, unless, like squash and potatoes, they kept well for winter. Ask students to learn what foods they might serve for dinner if they were living in this area on this date 200 years ago.

Review

■ **Chapter Review.** Use the contents of the Chapter Review page to help students review concepts, think critically, and apply their knowledge.

■ **Study Guide.** Have students complete the Study Guide for Chapter 41 on p. 138 of the Student Workbook.

■ **Analysis A la Carte.** Have groups make charts with the column headings Servings from Food Guide Pyramid, Meal Appeal Rating, and Resources Needed. Give each group a cookbook. Have each member choose a recipe from a different category. Have groups complete the charts, based on the information in the recipes. Challenge the class to combine their meals into a weekly meal plan.

Evaluation

■ **Chapter Test.** Use the reproducible chapter test provided in the Teacher's Classroom Resources or create your own test using the *Testmaker Software.*

■ **Alternative Assessment.** Have students create informational ads, either print or electronic, that promote a recipe based on topics discussed in this chapter. Ads might show how the recipe can be adapted to different schedules; how it uses available resources; and ways it can fit in a weekly meal plan.

■ **Family Plans.** Have students write a short essay assessing their family's skill in planning single and weekly meals, based on the topics discussed in this chapter, and suggesting at least one improvement.

418

Figure 41.3

A Sample Weekly Meal Plan

	Breakfast	Lunch	Dinner	Snacks
Monday	Bagel with nonfat cream cheese, orange juice, skim milk	Chicken salad sandwich on whole-wheat bread, green pepper strips, apple, skim milk	Spaghetti and white clam sauce, tossed salad with low-fat dressing, garlic bread, skim milk	Popcorn, pretzels
Tuesday	Bran cereal, banana, whole-wheat toast, skim milk	Tuna salad sandwich with tomato on multigrain bread, carrot sticks, pear, skim milk	Turkey cutlet, mashed potatoes, broccoli, tossed salad, rye roll	Graham crackers
Wednesday	Oatmeal, grapefruit juice, blueberry muffin, skim milk	White bean salad with spinach and red sweet peppers, oat bran biscuit, orange, skim milk	Lentil soup, grilled salmon steaks, brown rice, green beans	Frozen yogurt, rice cakes
Thursday	Cold cereal and milk, eggs, pineapple juice, rye toast	Grilled cheese sandwich with low-fat cheese, apple, vegetable juice	Beef and vegetable stir-fry, rice, skim milk	Oatmeal raisin cookies
Friday	Grapefruit, corn muffin, skim milk	Vegetable salad in pita pocket, banana, skim milk	Lamb with chickpea salsa, baked potato, zucchini	Grapes, cheese, mixed nuts
Saturday	Melon, western omelet, rye toast, skim milk	Burger on roll, potato salad, tomato juice	Split-pea soup, sesame bread sticks, tossed salad, skim milk	Angel food cake, mango slices
Sunday	Pancakes with applesauce, orange slices, skim milk	Pizza topped with mushrooms and green peppers, tossed salad	Roasted chicken, noodles, three-bean salad, rolls, skim milk	Banana

Note that schedules may not allow all family members to follow a meal plan like this one for every meal. Adjustments need to be made for packing certain meals and eating some meals away from home.

Focus on Teamwork Skills

Many nonprofit organizations put out cookbooks featuring members' favorite recipes as a money-making project. Ask students to develop a plan to organize such a project among themselves. Have them first identify tasks—such as soliciting and editing recipes, determining nutritional values, and writing suggested weekly meal plans—and then assign them to groups or individuals. Supply other similar cookbooks as models. Students could follow through on their plan and "publish" a class cookbook.

Chapter 41

Reviewing the Facts

1. What are three considerations to be taken into account when planning meals for families?
2. How can advance meal planning help you get proper nutrition?
3. Name five qualities of food that you can vary to make an appealing meal.
4. What are four important personal resources you should evaluate as you are planning meals?
5. What are two advantages and two disadvantages of using convenience foods in your meal plans?
6. Name four factors you should consider as you determine whether you will choose to prepare a recipe.

Thinking Critically

1. Which of the five qualities that affect meal appeal do you think is most important to vary for a successful meal? Which is the least important to vary? Explain your choices.
2. Why do you think that most recipes present the ingredients and the assembly directions separately?

Applying Your Knowledge

1. **Cookbook Review.** Choose a cookbook and write a review that answers these questions: What types of recipes and other information does the cookbook include? How complete is each recipe? How clear are the directions? What types of illustrations, if any, are included? Overall, how would you rate this cookbook? What type of user is it most appropriate for? Why?
2. **Creating Appealing Meals.** Plan a simple meal that incorporates the five factors of meal appeal. Describe how you are using

each of the elements in your meal. If you wish, draw a picture that illustrates your meal.

Making Connections

1. **Language Arts.** Suppose that you are the foods editor of a daily newspaper. Write a column advising readers about how meal planning can save them time and money.
3. **Math.** Find a recipe for a main dish that is also available in convenience form. Estimate the recipe's cost per serving, based on the prices of the main ingredients. (You do not have to calculate the cost of ingredients used in very small amounts, such as spices.) Also calculate the cost per serving of a convenience form of the same main dish. Then estimate how much time each will take to prepare. Present your results in the form of a table.

Building Your Portfolio

Creating a Meal-Planning System

Make a weekly meal plan. Explain how you considered nutrition, food preferences, variety, schedules, meal plan. Add your meal plan to your portfolio.

1. Any three: how many people are eating meal; when they are eating; family food preferences; dietary restrictions.
2. Lets you plan how to get variety of foods and essential nutrients.
3. Five qualities you can vary are flavor, color, texture, temperature, and shape and size.
4. Time, skill, money, and supplies and equipment.
5. *Advantages:* Provide more options; save time. *Disadvantages:* usually expensive; may be high in fat, sodium, or sugar.
6. Your resources; whether recipe sounds good; is healthful; is complete.

ANSWERS TO THINKING CRITICALLY

1. Answers may vary.
2. Answers may include: makes it easier to identify ingredients for planning; to determine whether it sounds good and is healthful; to refer to ingredients or directions during preparation.

Chapter 42

FOCUS

Chapter Overview

Chapter 42 discusses the decisions people face when buying food. It offers suggestions for choosing where to shop; judging food quality; interpreting package labels; and getting the most value for your food budget.

Motivator

■ **Food Drill.** Bring in a common food item (one that students can share as a snack, if you like). Ask: Where do you think this food was bought? How much did it cost? How do you know if it's any good? What is it made with? Accept all responses. Explain that reading this chapter will help students answer those questions more confidently.

Objectives

Discuss the chapter objectives on this page. Remind students that the objectives focus on important chapter concepts.

Vocabulary

Stress the difference between the terms *additives* and *preservatives*. *Additives* are substances added to food as it is being processed. *Preservatives* are a kind of additive. They are designed to keep foods from spoiling.

Chapter 42

Food and the Consumer

Terms to Learn

- additives
- daily value
- expiration date
- generic product
- national brands
- organically grown
- preservatives
- pull date
- staples
- store brands
- unit price

Objectives

This chapter will help you to:

- Explain **how a shopping list promotes efficient shopping.**
- Evaluate **the different stores available for food shopping.**
- Judge **the quality and freshness of foods.**
- Interpret **product labeling to get the most nutritious foods.**
- Differentiate **among the three types of products available.**

CHAPTER RESOURCES

Student Workbook
Study Guide, pp. 140-141
Activity, *Read the Label!* pp. 142-143

Teacher's Classroom Resources
Lesson Plan, p. 46
Cooperative Learning, *Making a Shopping List*, pp. 49-50

Extension #68, *Buying the Right Amount*, p. 74
Extension #69, *What Are Additives?* p. 75
Life Skills, *Is Bigger Better?* p. 70
Transparency 42, *Unit Pricing*
Transparency 43, *Nutrition Facts Labels*

Chapter 42 Test, pp. 89-90
Performance Assessment, *Shop with the Experts*, pp. 74-75
Reteaching, *Be a Smart Food Shopper*, p. 48

See Also:
ABCNews InterActive™ Videodiscs

You've probably gone food shopping dozens of times, either alone or with someone in your household. Whether you are buying a week's worth of groceries or picking up a last-minute item, food shopping requires decision making at every step.

You have to do some planning ahead of time, by deciding what items you need and where you'll go to get them. Other decisions are made in the store: Does the lettuce look fresh? Should I buy canned or frozen peas, single-serving or family size? How do prices compare? Efficient food shopping helps you make these decisions by selecting the highest quality foods and saving time and money.

Making a Shopping List

Before shopping, it is wise to prepare a shopping list. Having a list helps ensure that you get the food and other products you need. It also helps you avoid impulse buying, which can add unnecessarily to your shopping bill.

Begin your list by reviewing the ingredients you need for the menus you've planned. If you don't have all the ingredients on hand, make a shopping list. Include the specific amounts of each item you need. Then look over your supplies of staple foods. **Staples** are *basic food items you use regularly,* such as flour, sugar, rice, and pasta. These items do not spoil easily. Most people keep them on hand at all times. Add to the list items you keep on hand for emergencies, such as frozen meals, and such nonfood items as paper products and cleaning supplies.

Remember to organize your list logically. One way is to group similar types of food together: fresh vegetables and fruits, pasta and grains, meats, and so on. If you shop often at the same store, try listing foods in the order that they are arranged in the store. This technique helps save time when you are shopping.

Where to Shop

Once you've decided what food to buy, you need to determine the best place to shop. Different kinds of food stores fill different consumer needs. Prices, quality, and service can vary widely.

When you want a special food item, where might you find it in your area?

CHAPTER 42   Food and the Consumer   421

TEACH

Topics on p. 421:
• Making a List

Checking Comprehension

✓ Describe an efficient way of making a list. *Review ingredients needed for planned meals; add staples, emergency foods, nonfood items.*

✓ Describe two ways of organizing a shopping list. *List like foods together; list foods as arranged in store.*

Activities

■ **Make a List.** Give students a long shopping list and ask them to organize it in a logical manner. Ask them to explain the reasoning behind their choice of organization. *(Management)*

RETEACHING

■ **Shopping for Dinner.** Tell students to imagine they are preparing dinner for four people. Give them a menu of four or five dishes to be served along with any relevant recipes. Have students draw up a shopping list that includes all the ingredients needed to make the foods you named, and the approximate amount to be purchased.

Focus on Communication Skills

To avoid confusion and wasted time and money, shopping lists need to be precise, especially when several different people contribute to them. Ask students to rewrite these items to be more clear: peas; crackers; cereal; cold cuts; pasta.

DID YOU KNOW?

Surveys have shown that a person who goes into a supermarket without a list and plans to buy three items usually walk out with eight to ten. Making a list *can* save time and money.

Topics on pp. 422-423:
- Places to Shop
- Judging Quality

Checking Comprehension

✓ How are warehouse stores and discount supermarkets similar? *Both have lower prices but usually have a smaller selection than do supermarkets.*

✓ What do specialty stores offer? *Large selection and high-quality of one type of product.*

✓ Is it safe to buy a product on its pull date? Explain. *Yes, date gives consumer reasonable amount of time to use product.*

FAMILY AND COMMUNITY OUTREACH

Ask students to comparison shop for five items their families regularly use, checking prices at three different stores if possible. Have students record the prices in a chart and then total their list for each store to reveal which is most cost-effective. What other factors should be considered in choosing where to shop?

Supermarkets

Supermarkets are large stores that sell many types of food and household products. In fact, supermarkets can serve as "one-stop shopping" for all food needs. Aisles are stocked with a range of items from fresh produce to paper products. Refrigerated areas sell meat and fish, dairy items, and beverages. Huge freezers store frozen vegetables and prepared meals. Many supermarkets even have such special areas as bakeries, delis, salad bars, and coffee bars. Some include florist shops, pharmacies, and video departments. Because of their size, supermarkets can offer a wider selection and lower prices than most other food stores.

Very large supermarkets are also known as superstores. Some sell small appliances, automotive supplies, and many other goods in addition to groceries.

Warehouse stores also sell many food products. They often sell their goods for less than supermarkets do, but they do not have as wide a variety of food products as supermarkets do. Some of these stores are clubs that require consumers to pay an annual membership fee before they can shop at the store.

Some communities have discount—or "no frills"—supermarkets. These stores usually have discount prices, but they may stock

Managing Your Life

Finding the Best Buys

Faced with the tremendous variety of foods and appetizing choices, some consumers spend more money than they had intended when they go shopping. These guidelines can help you manage your food budget:

- Take advantage of sales. Stores often have weekly specials or "buy one, get one free" sales on selected items. They also reduce the price of items as they near their pull dates.
- Make a list before you shop, but be flexible. Consider revising your original menu if you find comparable, less expensive foods.
- Resist the impulse to buy items you don't need. Avoid tempting store displays designed to lure you into making unplanned purchases.
- Use coupons for items that you buy regularly. You can find coupons in newspapers, advertising flyers, and on some product packages. Some stores have small dispensers that offer instant coupons. Look for stores that double or triple a coupon's value.
- Check unit prices to determine whether or not an item is truly a good buy.
- Buy a store brand or generic item when you have no real preference. They are generally less expensive than national-brand items and may be equal in quality.

- Plan meals around low-cost main dishes, such as those made with beans and rice.
- Compare prices of different available forms of food, such as fresh, frozen, and canned.
- Buy fresh fruit and vegetables in season, when quality is usually higher and prices lower.
- Consider joining a preferred-shopper club or a warehouse club, which offer savings by selling products in bulk. This can be very economical, especially for items that don't spoil.

Applying the Principles

1. When might an item marked "buy one, get one free" not be a good buy?
2. Why do you think that certain items, such as meats and milk, are often placed in the back of a supermarket?
3. Do you think that it is best to shop at one store regularly or to shop at different stores? List the pros and cons of each method.

MORE ABOUT Convenience Stores and Supermarkets

The popularity of convenience stores has cut into supermarket profits. In response, many supermarkets have extended their hours—up to 24 hours a day in some cases—and offer express lanes for customers buying only a few items.

Focus on Consumer Skills

For high-quality, nutritious food, try to shop the "edges" of the supermarket. That's where the fresh produce, meat, poultry, seafood, and dairy products are located. These are often the least processed and most nutritious choices.

fewer brands of basic items and offer fewer services than regular supermarkets. At many discount supermarkets, customers select some items from cardboard boxes or barrels. Customers may also have to bag their own groceries or bring their own shopping bags in which to take their purchases home.

Convenience Stores

A convenience store is a small store with a limited selection of basic items. Some serve customers 24 hours a day and are open on holidays when other food stores are closed. Convenience stores are handy if you need to pick up a few last-minute items, but prices are usually much higher than in other stores and the selection is limited.

Specialty Stores

Stores that sell only one type of product are called specialty stores. Although their prices may be higher than at a supermarket, these stores offer an excellent selection of high-quality goods in their specialty.

- Fish stores and butcher shops specialize in fish and meat. Some allow customers to special order particular types of fish or cuts of meat in advance.
- Natural food stores sell a variety of whole-grain products, fresh produce, and other items popular with some consumers. Many of these products are carried with minimal packaging and can be bought in bulk.
- Some towns and cities have farmers' markets, where shoppers can buy fruits and vegetables from local growers. The produce is very fresh and prices may be low because the consumer is buying directly from the people who grow the products. This avoids the shipping costs that supermarkets have to pay.
- Fresh fruits and vegetables are also sold from roadside stands next to farms. In some places customers may purchase produce that they pick themselves from fields or orchards.

- Some people belong to food co-ops. A co-op (or cooperative) is a group of shoppers who join together to purchase basic food items in large quantities, allowing members to pay discount prices.

Judging Quality

Wherever you decide to shop, wise shopping requires good decision-making skills. Your first task as you select food items is to judge their quality. Fruits and vegetables, for example, begin to lose nutrients as soon as they are picked, and they continue to lose their freshness while being shipped to the stores. Look for firmness, proper color, and lack of bruises and breaks in the skin. Tips on buying fresh foods from all five major food groups are included in Chapters 50 through 53.

Watch for signs that packaged foods may be spoiled. Eating such foods could make you sick. **Figure 42.1** describes telltale signs to look for.

Product Dating

Dates stamped or printed on food packages can also help you to judge freshness. Two different types of dates may appear on food products:

- A **pull date,** or "sell by" date, is *the last day a product may be sold.* Pull dates are usually found on products that spoil quickly, such as dairy products and meats. The product will still be good for some time after this date, since the date allows a reasonable amount of time for the consumer to store the product at home before using it.
- An **expiration date,** or "use by" date, is *the last day a product is considered fresh.* These labels often say "Best if used by [date]." A food may still be safe to eat after this date, but its taste and nutritional quality may have suffered. Check all foods stored at home from time to time to make sure that no foods have passed their expiration dates.

MORE ABOUT Product Dating

Pull dates are found on breads, most dairy products, and delicatessen meats. Expiration dates are more common on eggs, some snack foods, and packages of yeast.

MORE ABOUT Expiration Dates

Occasionally products that are marked down as the near their expiration date. These may be good buys if they will be used within a few days or if the store will take back products that prove spoiled or otherwise inedible.

- Evaluating Food
- Reading Food Labels
- Brand Names and Generics

Checking Comprehension

✓ How can a consumer calculate the unit price of an item? *Divide total cost of package by number of units.*

✓ In what order are ingredients listed on food labels? *By weight, with predominant ingredients listed first.*

✓ Why might a food contain additives? *To help keep it fresh; make it look or taste better.*

✓ What are some examples of natrional and store brands? How can generic brands be identified? *Answers will vary; by their plain packaging.*

SPECIAL NEEDS
Strategies

Inefficient Readers. Examine a nutrition label with students. Point out that some facts, such as calories, calories from fat, and sodium content, may be more useful than others. Ask students to find this information on the label.

Figure 42.1

Warning Signs

You should not buy products that show any of the characteristics listed here:

- Bulging or dented cans may contain dangerous bacteria.
- Rusty cans may be old. They may have rust on the inside as well.
- Soft or soggy frozen food packages may be thawing.
- Frozen food packages that are stained, covered with ice, or irregularly shaped may have been thawed and refrozen. The safety and quality of the food may have suffered.
- Packages of any kind that have been opened in any way may have been tampered with.

Judging Value

Most stores help you judge the value of an item by providing **unit prices.** A unit price is *the price per ounce, pound, or other accepted unit of measure.* This information makes it easy to compare the cost of products in different-sized packages.

Unit prices are usually displayed on labels attached to the front of the shelf where the item is found. By comparing the unit prices on two items you can discover which is a better bargain.

You can calculate unit prices yourself by dividing the total cost of a package by the number of units. A 42-fl. oz. bottle of dishwashing liquid, for example, that costs $1.29 has a unit price of 3 cents per oz. ($1.29 ÷ 42 = 0.031). A 22-oz. bottle that costs $0.99 is not as good a value, because its cost per oz. is almost 5 cents ($0.99 ÷ 22 = 0.045).

Reading Labels

Nutritional value is just as important as the quality and the price of the foods you buy. Food labels give information about the contents and the nutritional value of a product. This enables an informed shopper to make good food choices.

Basic Information

Almost every food label contains certain basic information:

- The name of the product.
- The amount of the food, by weight or by volume.
- The name and address of the manufacturer, packer, or distributor.
- A list of ingredients.

Ingredients are listed in order by weight—the ingredient that weighs the most proportionately is listed first. The federal government now requires full ingredient labeling on all processed, packaged foods.

You may also see other numbers or letters on packages of food, especially cans. These codes indicate where and when the product was made. If there is a problem with a product, its origin can be traced, and other foods made at the same time can be located and taken off the shelves.

Nutrition Labels

By law, about 90 percent of processed food and many raw foods must contain nutrition information in a label titled "Nutrition Facts." You can use these labels to see how the product fits into your daily plan for nutritious eat-

MORE ABOUT Labeling Laws

The FDA exempts more than 300 food items from ingredient listing because manufacturers have agreed to use a standard recipe. Tomato products, margarine, jellies, and cheese are among these items.

MORE ABOUT Additives

Food colorings are among the most controversial additives because their use is purely cosmetic. In improving a food's appearance, they may mask poor quality. Some synthetic dyes (derived from coal tars) are even suspected of causing cancer.

Figure 42.2
UNDERSTANDING NUTRITION LABELS

Serving Information. The serving size is given in both customary and metric measurements. The nutrient amounts given here are for one serving. The package may contain more than one serving, as shown.

Nutrition Facts

Serving Size 1 cup (228g)
Servings Per Container 2

Amount Per Serving

Calories 260	Calories from Fat 120

	% Daily Value *
Total Fat 13g	20%
Saturated Fat 5g	25%
Cholesterol 30mg	10%
Sodium 660mg	28%
Total Carbohydrate 31g	10%
Dietary Fiber 0g	0%
Sugars 5g	
Protein 5g	

Vitamin A 4%	•	Vitamin C 2%
Calcium 15%	•	Iron 4%

*Percent Daily Values are based on a 2,000 calorie diet. Your daily values may be higher or lower depending on your calorie needs:

	Calories:	2,000	2,500
Total Fat	Less than	65g	80g
Sat Fat	Less than	20g	25g
Cholesterol	Less than	300mg	300mg
Sodium	Less than	2,400mg	2,400mg
Total Carbohydrate		300g	375g
Dietary Fiber		25g	30g

Calories Per gram:
Fat 9 • Carbohydrate 4 • Protein 4

Calorie Information. The label shows both the total number of calories in one serving and the calories that come from fat.

Nutrient Information. The amount of each nutrient is given in grams or milligrams (metric units of weight).

Percent Daily Value. Nutrient amounts are also listed as a percentage of the daily value. The **daily value** is a <u>reference amount for a particular nutrient based on recommendations of health experts.</u> The "percent daily value" number lets you see how the amount of a certain nutrient in the food compares with the daily minimum or maximum recommended for the "average" person. In this example, the 13 g of fat in one serving of the food represent 20 percent of the amount of fat recommended for a whole day.

Daily Values. The daily values, or reference values, for each nutrient are shown in the columns in the lower portion of the label. The numbers in the column under "2,000" represent minimum or maximum amounts of nutrients for a person who needs 2,000 calories a day. These numbers are used to calculate the percent daily values above. Larger labels, like this one, also show daily values for a person who needs 2,500 calories a day. This information helps the consumer make adjustments based on his or her calorie needs.

Conversion Guide. This information at the bottom of the label helps consumers learn the caloric value of the energy-producing nutrients—fats, carbohydrates, and proteins.

CHAPTER 42   Food and the Consumer   425

Activities

■ **Ingredients: Water . . .** Collect packages from a variety of foods, including soup, spaghetti sauce, pancake syrup, chocolate cake mix, and canned stews or casseroles. Ask students to list ingredients for each product as they would expect to read them on the label. Then read the actual package label. How accurate were students' lists? Were they surprised at what they learned? *(Critical Thinking)*

■ **Don't Touch.** Food-tampering scares have impelled manufacturers to seal food packages to prevent people from contaminating the products. Ask students to describe some tamper-proof packages they have seen. Are there any disadvantages to tamper-proof packages? *Additional materials and cost; may be difficult or impossible for some people to open. (Observation)*

CROSS-CURRICULAR ACTIVITY
Science

Encourage students to research the additives listed on a food label. What is the chemical composition of each? What is its function in that food?

MORE ABOUT Packaging

"Reduce, reuse, and recycle" means a cleaner environment—and profits for wise manufacturers. Polls show that consumers are more inclined to buy products that claim to protect the environment, whether or not the claim is true.

DID YOU KNOW?

The numbered arrows-chasing-arrows recycling emblem on the bottom of plastic containers is part of the resin-coding system of the Society of Plastics Industry. The number allows the various resins to be separated for recycling. Ask which plastics can be recycled in your community.

Review

■ **Chapter Review.** Use the contents of the Chapter Review page to help students review concepts, think critically, and apply their knowledge.

■ **Study Guide.** Have students complete the Study Guide for Chapter 42 on page 142 of the Student Workbook.

■ **My Hero!** Have groups perform skits in they act as "grocery superheroes," patrolling the aisles of a supermarket, "rescuing" consumers from poor shopping habits by explaining more helpful techniques. Situations portrayed should deal with the topics of where to shop; getting quality and value; and reading labels.

Evaluation

■ **Chapter Test.** Use the reproducible chapter test provided in the Teacher's Classroom Resources or create your own test using the *Testmaker Software.*

■ **Alternative Assessment.** Have students create a parody of a contemporary television talk show in which guests admit to past poor shopping habits and describe an enlightening experience that inspired them to mend their ways.

■ **Food Q & A.** Ask students to enact a radio call-in show called "Shop Smart." Have them make up questions about the topics in this chapter and then take turns playing the shopping expert and the callers.

ing. They can also help you compare the nutrition of different versions of the same food. **Figure 42.2** shows how to interpret the information on a typical nutrition facts label.

Food Additives

Among the ingredients may be food **additives.** These are *substances that are added to the food before it is sold.* Additives serve many different purposes. Food colors, sweeteners, and flavorings make foods look or taste better. Some additives are **preservatives,** which *keep foods fresh longer.*

In the United States, all additives must be approved by the Food and Drug Administration (FDA), a federal agency. Because additives appear in the ingredients list, consumers may avoid particular additives.

It is possible to choose foods that have been **organically grown,** or *produced without the use of manufactured chemicals.* These foods generally cost more than foods grown using chemical fertilizers or pesticides.

Brand Names and Generic Products

When shopping for food, you often have a choice between three types of products:

- **National brands** are *products sold across the country.* They are advertised in national media, which adds to their price.
- **Store brands** are *products produced especially for the store or chain that sells them.* These usually cost less than national brands.
- **Generic products** are *goods that have a plain package and are less expensive than national or store brands.*

You may find differences in quality among these three types of products. Such differences may be important to you in some cases but not in others. For example, some people prefer a national brand of peanut butter but use generic canned tomatoes for a stew. The choice is up to you.

■ When you look for a product to buy, you often have many brands to choose from. How will you decide?

Focus on Management Skills

Have groups design shopping organizers, similar to school or office organizers, to help consumers food shop efficiently. Have students use information from this chapter to decide what features the organizer should have, such as sheets of paper for shopping lists and a reference guide to community stores. Organizers may be as simple or elaborate as students wish.

Chapter 42 Review

Reviewing the Facts

1. What are two advantages of making a list before shopping?
2. Name three kinds of food stores. What is one advantage of each?
3. What warning signs should you look for to avoid buying spoiled canned and frozen foods?
4. What is the difference between a pull date and an expiration date on a food package?
5. How are consumers helped by having information about serving size and number of servings per container on a nutrition label?
6. How can the percent daily value information on a nutrition label be used by consumers to help manage the amount of fat they eat?
7. What is the difference between a national brand, a store brand, and a generic product?

Thinking Critically

1. Rising food prices have a major effect on an average family's budget. What can people do to keep costs down while ensuring that their families eat a nutritious diet?
2. What would you do if the frozen food packages in the supermarket where your family shops were often coated with ice?

Applying Your Knowledge

1. **Comparing Prices.** Choosing three common food items—chicken soup or spaghetti, for instance—compare the prices of national and store brands and generic versions of the same product. How large is the price difference between the three versions?
2. **Using Nutrition Labels.** Compare the nutrition labels for two ready-to-eat cereals. Explain which product you would choose on the basis of nutrition and why.

Making Connections

1. **Mathematics.** Search newspapers and magazines for coupons that would save your family money on products it normally buys. How many coupons did you find, and how much money would be saved if you used them? What would be the savings if you received double the face value of the coupons? If you saved a similar amount of money every week, what would the savings be after a whole year?
2. **Economics.** Compare the prices found in circulars from at least two local food stores for six different products, such as paper towels, chicken, or carrots. Create a chart that shows the product and the price. Indicate whether the prices advertised are for different brands. Write a summary of your findings, and compare it to those of classmates. Are one store's prices generally higher or lower than another's?

Building Your Portfolio

Explaining Nutrition Labeling
Write an easy-to-read brochure that would help other teens understand food labels. Use words, pictures, sample labels, or any other resources to create the brochure. Add the completed brochure to your portfolio.

Chapter 43

FOCUS

Chapter Overview

Chapter 43 explains some basic principles of setting up and using a kitchen. It describes refrigerators, ranges, and the efficient planning of work centers and storage space that are organized around them.

Motivator

■ **In the Bag.** Bring in a variety of food items—a few boxes, cans, and some delicate items, such as bread. Ask a volunteer to place them in a grocery sack. Afterward, ask how the student decided how to arrange the items. Explain that this chapter shows how in kitchens also, a wise arrangement can lead to success.

Objectives

Discuss the chapter objectives on this page. Remind students that the objectives focus on important chapter concepts.

Vocabulary

Stress to students the difference between *appliances and utensils.* Appliances are pieces of kitchen equipment run by electricity or gas. Utensils are tools, cookware and containers. Ask students for examples of each.

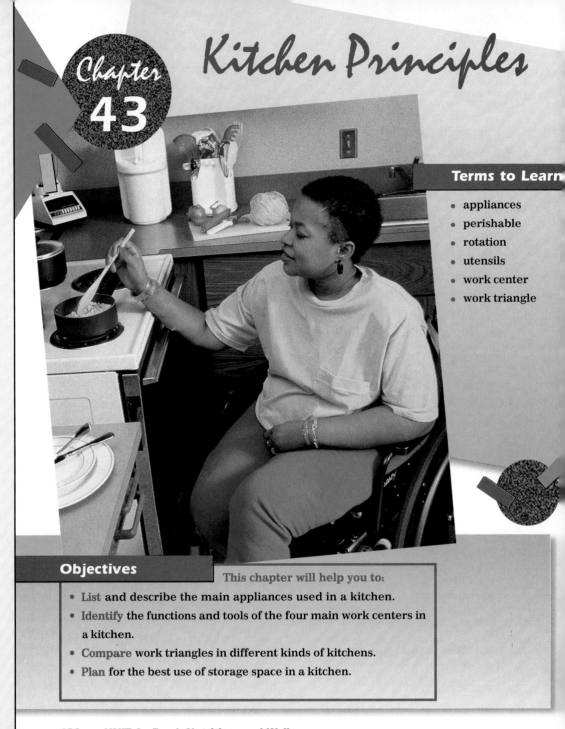

Chapter 43 Kitchen Principles

Terms to Learn

- appliances
- perishable
- rotation
- utensils
- work center
- work triangle

Objectives

This chapter will help you to:

- **List** and describe the main appliances used in a kitchen.
- **Identify** the functions and tools of the four main work centers in a kitchen.
- **Compare** work triangles in different kinds of kitchens.
- **Plan** for the best use of storage space in a kitchen.

428   UNIT 6   Food, Nutrition, and Wellness

CHAPTER RESOURCES

Student Workbook

Study Guide, pp. 144-145

Activity, *Energy Wise,* pp. 146-147

Teacher's Classroom Resources

Lesson Plan, p. 47

Cooperative Learning, *Finding the Best Buys,* pp. 51-52

Extension #70, *Choosing Small Appliances,* p. 76

Life Skills, *Appliance Shopping Spree,* p. 71

Transparency 44, *Planning Kitchen Space*

Chapter 43 Test, pp. 91-92

Performance Assessment, *An Ideal Kitchen,* p. 76

Reteaching, *What's in the Kitchen?* p. 49

A kitchen is a workshop in which you complete the tasks associated with preparing and serving food. A well-planned kitchen is both convenient and pleasant to work in. It contains a number of **appliances**—*kitchen equipment run by electricity or gas* and has a ready supply of **utensils**—*tools and containers such as knives, measuring cups, pots, and pans.*

Efficiency in the kitchen involves carefully planned work areas, easy access to the appliances and utensils you use most frequently, and safe and convenient food storage. In this chapter you will see how a well-planned kitchen can make food preparation easier and more enjoyable.

Kitchen Appliances

Kitchens are organized around major appliances. Almost all kitchens contain the two basic major appliances—a refrigerator for storing food and a range (or cooktop and oven) for cooking it. Most kitchens also have other appliances.

Refrigerators and Freezers

In most kitchens, the largest appliance is the refrigerator-freezer. The freezer section might be at the top, at the bottom, or on one side. Some kitchens also have a separate freezer for storing large quantities of frozen foods. Some freezers are self-defrosting; others need to be emptied and thawed regularly.

Many refrigerators have humidity-controlled compartments for storing fruits, vegetables, meats, and dairy products. Separate sections for storing bottles and other tall containers may also be included. Some also have automatic ice makers, which dispense ice either in the inside compartment or through the door.

Refrigerators and freezers are easy to use and maintain. You need to keep them clean and defrosted. You also need to know how long you can store different kinds of foods and how to prepare and pack foods for storage. Storage is discussed later in this chapter.

Ranges, Cooktops, and Ovens

For basic cooking, most kitchens have either a range or a separate cooktop and an oven built into a wall or cabinet. These appliances can be gas or electric.

- **Ranges and cooktops.** A range usually consists of a cooktop with three or four burners, an oven, and a broiler. Separate dials control the heat of the different burners. For the oven, you can set the exact temperature you need. The cooktop should be cleaned after each use. Some modern cooktops have smooth surfaces that are easier to clean than the traditional cooktops with electric coils or gas jets.
- **Ovens.** Ovens are used for baking and roasting foods, reheating cooked foods, and keeping foods warm. Three main kinds of ovens are used in kitchens today: conventional, convection, and microwave. The conventional oven works by heating the air that surrounds the food. A convection oven works like a conventional oven, except that it has a fan that circulates the heated air and speeds up cooking. A microwave oven turns electricity into microwaves that cause food molecules to vibrate and heat the food. Microwave ovens work faster than other ovens.

Other Appliances

Other common kitchen appliances are dishwashers, garbage disposals, and trash compactors. Many small appliances are also available to make food preparation easier or more efficient. These include toasters, toaster ovens, blenders, food processors, electric skillets, and mixers. Many of these appliances have multiple uses. Toaster ovens, for example, can both toast and bake. Food processors do several preparation tasks.

The appliances you choose to have in your kitchen will depend on the kinds of foods you prepare, what you can afford, and the space

TEACH

Topics on pp. 429:
- Kitchen Appliances

Checking Comprehension

✓ What maintenance do refrigerator-freezers need? Cooktops? *Cleaning and defrosting; cleaning after each use.*

✓ What is the difference between an oven and a range? *An oven may be part of a range, or separate. It is used to bake and roast.*

✓ How can you reduce the amount of energy your appliances consume? *Care for and use them properly.*

Activities

■ **Scouting Report.** Have students look through appliance and department store catalogs and fliers to learn more about the features available in refrigerators and ranges. Have them explain which features would be most useful for their families. Also have them compare the price of each model. *(Decision Making)*

MORE ABOUT the Range

The first gas range was invented in 1802 in Germany by Frederick Albert Winson. His early models had a serious drawback: they leaked gas fumes and regularly exploded. As a result, Europeans would not exchange coal fires for gas for nearly 30 years. In the United States, the gas stove did not became common until the 1860s. More recent range innovations include quartz halogen burners, a range-top hibachi, and various other grills.

Checking Comprehension

✓ Describe an efficient work triangle. *Refrigerator, sink, and range form the corners; sides as equal as possible, with total length of 12-22 ft. (4-7 m).*

✓ What are the goals of proper storage? *Safe food storage, effective use of storage space and aids.*

In Touch With TECHNOLOGY

Have students read "Cooling Trends" and discuss the questions. Discuss social changes that have affected—and may continue to affect—the manufacture of refrigerators and other appliances.

Answers to Thinking Critically

1. Answers may include: safety to consumers and environment; cost-effectiveness.
2. Replacing pump with sound waves leaves fewer parts to malfunction; no liquid circulation may mean less danger of leaks.
3. Answers may include: more individual temperature control for different sections; easier access to all areas; small, modular units for in different work centers.

In Touch with TECHNOLOGY

Cooling Trends

Traditional refrigerators work by relatively old technology. Substances called coolants are compressed into a liquid, then released into tubes that circulate through the refrigerator. There the coolant expands, absorbing large amounts of heat energy (called latent heat) and lowering the temperature inside the refrigerator. The coolant is then drawn from the tubes by an exterior pump and compressed back into a liquid, giving off heat to the air outside. It circulates back to the tubes and the process begins anew.

Refrigerator technology has been slow to evolve. Consumers' main demand was for durability, rather than convenience or efficiency. New concerns however, are changing that. Traditional coolants—called chlorofluorocarbons (CFCs)—have been found to damage the earth's protective ozone layer. Refrigerator pumps use a great deal of energy—almost 10 percent of the electric power used in the United States, according to some calculations. The noise from the pumps is now considered a source of noise pollution in the home.

Newer technologies are being introduced in response to these problems. Great advances already have been made in finding new coolants to replace CFCs and developing quieter, energy-saving pumps. In some refrigerators, the coolant is compressed by silenced sound waves instead of electric pumps. Totally new cooling processes are also being implemented. In thermoacoustic cooling, for example, the coolant does not circulate. Instead, it is compressed and expands very quickly. Heat is pulled away by a heat exchanger at each compression.

Thinking Critically About Technology

1. What might a manufacturer want to know about a new technology before using it in a refrigerator?
2. What additional benefits might the new cooling technologies described above offer?
3. What other improvements to traditional refrigerators can you suggest?

available for storing the appliances. You also need to weigh the pros and cons of using a particular appliance. For example, it is generally more energy-efficient to heat a small amount of food in a toaster oven than in a conventional oven. However, a toaster oven takes up counter space. It is quicker to use an electric mixer than to mix foods by hand, but an electric mixer uses energy and requires storage space.

All appliances use energy in some form. Caring for your appliances and using them properly, however, can reduce the amount of energy they consume. Chapter 74 provides more information on using appliances without wasting energy.

Planning Work Areas

You perform many tasks in the kitchen. If you organize your tools and equipment around the major groups of tasks you do, your job will be easier. Most kitchens are divided into work centers.

Work Centers

A **work center** is *an organized area where specific kitchen tasks are performed.* Ideally, everything needed to perform those tasks—major equipment, counter space, and storage for related utensils and supplies—is provided within the center. The work centers in a typical kitchen are:

Focus on Consumer Skills

Many single-use appliances, such as hot-dog cookers, ice-cream makers, and bread bakers, are now available. Ask students what they think of these items. Which, if any, might be useful for their family? Help students see that families should decide how often they will use a piece of equipment and whether it will be worth the cost and kitchen space before buying it. Point out that some small appliances duplicate jobs done by equipment already owned.

In which work center would you expect to find a trash compactor?

- The food storage center, organized around the refrigerator.
- The mixing center, organized around counter space.
- The cleanup center, organized around the sink.
- The cooking center, organized around the range.

Figure 43.1 on page 432 provides more information about each of these work centers.

Some kitchens include additional work centers. For example, there might be a baking center with a special work surface for rolling out pastry. A planning center might include a desk, cookbooks, and recipe files. Some kitchens include space and equipment for tasks other than food preparation, such as a laundry area.

The Work Triangle

When you are preparing a meal, you make many trips back and forth between the refrigerator, the sink, and the range. *The paths connecting the refrigerator, sink, and range* form the **work triangle.** Expert kitchen planners have studied how the work triangle relates to kitchen efficiency. They suggest that the three sides of the work triangle should be as equal as possible, and that their total length should be between 12 and 22 ft. (4 and 7 m). If the work triangle is too large, you will waste time and energy going from one work center to another. If the work triangle is too small, some work centers may not have enough storage and counter space. **Figure 43.2** on page 433 illustrates the concept of work triangles.

Planning Storage Space

Efficiency in the kitchen also involves the proper storage of food and equipment. The main goals of proper storage are:

- Safe storage of food.
- Efficient use of storage space.
- Effective use of simple storage aids.

Storing Food Safely

A large portion of most kitchens—the refrigerator, the freezer, and considerable shelf space—is devoted to storing food. Storing food properly can save you money and time.

CHAPTER 43   Kitchen Principles   431

DID YOU KNOW?

Kitchens have always evolved to meet people's needs. The first "kitchen" was simply an open fire. In the Middle Ages, when people often lived together in large, extended families, home life centered around its warm kitchen hearth. In the 1800s, large, well-equipped kitchens were essential to wealthy English landowners who invited many guests for country-house weekends. In the 1900s, kitchens began to shrink as designers learned how to do more with less space. What are today's trends in kitchens?

Topics on pp. 432-434:
- Work Centers
- The Work Triangle

Checking Comprehension

✓ How is counter space used in the cleanup center? How is it used in the cooking center? *Cleanup—washing dishes; cooking—set down ingredients, hot pots and pans.*

✓ What is the main disadvantage of corridor kitchens? *Difficult for two people to work at same time.*

✓ What is the basic rule for storing equipment? *Keep it near work center where it is used most often.*

SPECIAL NEEDS *Strategies*

Physically Disabled. Students with physical disabilities may have had frustrating experiences with conventional kitchen design. If they are comfortable discussing it, ask these students to point out problems that typical kitchens create for people with their disability. Ask them to describe design adaptions that would make a kitchen more efficient for them.

Figure 43.1
KITCHEN WORK CENTERS

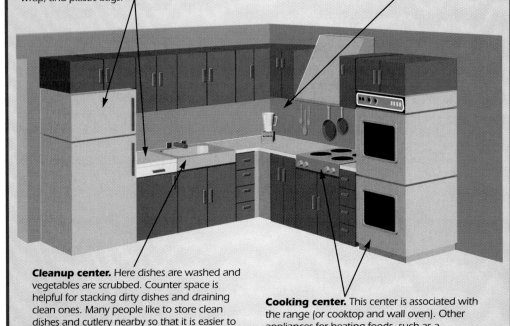

Food storage center. Counter space is needed for taking foods in and out of the refrigerator, putting down grocery bags, and wrapping foods. Shelves for canned and packaged foods should also be in this center or nearby. Supplies stored in this center might include storage containers, plastic wrap, and plastic bags.

Mixing center. This center is used for such tasks as chopping, measuring, and mixing ingredients. There should be enough counter space to work comfortably. Utensils stored in this center include bowls, knives, and measuring cups and spoons. Small appliances such as a blender, mixer, or food processor would also be used here.

Cleanup center. Here dishes are washed and vegetables are scrubbed. Counter space is helpful for stacking dirty dishes and draining clean ones. Many people like to store clean dishes and cutlery nearby so that it is easier to put them away.

Cooking center. This center is associated with the range (or cooktop and wall oven). Other appliances for heating foods, such as a microwave oven or slow cooker, also may be found here. Storage space for pots and pans, cooking tools, and hot pads should be provided. Counter space is needed for setting down hot pots and pans safely.

MORE ABOUT Kitchen Planning

Kitchen planners are in growing demand. These designers plan for safety and efficiency, using knowledge of space planning and some structural engineering. Certification requires seven years of experience and education, including at least two years of designing and supervising kitchen installation. Designers must provide work samples and references from clients and pass a day-long exam. Interested students can call the National Kitchen and Bath Association at 800-FOR-NKBA.

Figure 43.2
WORK TRIANGLES

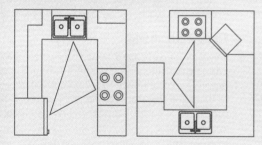

U-shaped kitchen. The U-shaped kitchen has work centers arranged on three adjoining walls. It has an uninterrupted work triangle with sides of similar lengths and provides room for two people to work at the same time. Some U-shaped kitchens also have an island, which is a freestanding unit, or a peninsula, which is an extension of a counter. The layout on the near left shows a peninsula.

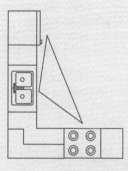

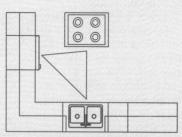

L-shaped kitchen. The L-shaped kitchen has work centers arranged along two adjoining walls. The work triangle is uninterrupted, and more than one person could work in this space at the same time. Some L-shaped kitchens have an island, which changes the shape of the work triangle.

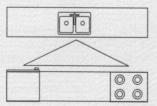

Corridor kitchen. The work triangle in a corridor kitchen generally has one side that is much longer than the other two. This layout does not lend itself to having two people working in the kitchen at the same time.

CHAPTER 43   Kitchen Principles   **433**

■ **A Place for Everything.** Present pairs or small groups with a typical kitchen storage problem, such as too many dishes for the cabinet space available. Have them suggest solutions, using diagrams, if needed. Refer students to the tips on p. 434 for ideas. You might have groups make up problems for others to solve. *(Problem Solving)*

Activities

RETEACHING

■ **Start From Scratch.** Ask students to imagine that some friends are remodeling their kitchen. They ask the student for suggestions for making the kitchen safe and efficient. What principles about kitchen design would students share with their friends? What design features would they recommend, and why?

ENRICHMENT

■ **New Stuff.** Suggest that students visit a local kitchen design center to take notes and collect information on the latest trends in kitchen design. Have students report on their trip to the class.

Focus on Management Skills

Some kitchen designs promote resource management with features for storing recyclable and compost materials. Special drawers that tilt out hold different kinds of recyclables. Some counter tops have a small chute for compost leading to a removable bin underneath that can be taken outside daily to a compost bin or heap. Ask: Where in a kitchen would you locate each of these features? *Recyclables might be kept near a back door or garage; a compost bin, near the sink.*

Review

■ **Chapter Review.** Use the contents of the Chapter Review page to help students review concepts, think critically, and apply their knowledge.

■ **Study Guide.** Have students complete the Study Guide for Chapter 43 on p. 144 of the Student Workbook.

■ **You'll Be Sorry.** Ask students to write a short, possibly humorous scene depicting at least five consequences of poor kitchen design or inefficient storage techniques. Students might exchange scenes, identify the problems, and suggest solutions.

Evaluation

■ **Chapter Test.** Use the reproducible chapter test provided in the Teacher's Classroom Resources or create your own test using the *Testmaker Software.*

■ **Alternative Assessment.** Have groups perform skits in which sellers show buyers the kitchen of a new house. Sellers should point out design features, while buyers ask questions to assess the kitchen's efficiency and comment on how they might equip it with appliances.

■ **Start to Finish.** Have students outline the preparation of a meal, highlighting the necessary tasks; the work center where each is done; and the large and small appliances used to complete the meal.

A general principle to follow with all food storage is "first in, first out." Set up a system of **rotation** so that *older supplies are used before newer ones.* For example, when you purchase a new carton of milk, place it behind the carton that is already in the refrigerator so that you will be sure to use the older milk first. Look for "sell by" and "use by" dates on all food containers. Be sure to use up food before the "use by" date has passed or within a reasonable time after the "sell by" date.

Many fresh foods are **perishable,** meaning that they *tend to spoil easily.* Perishable foods are usually stored in the refrigerator or freezer. They should be stored in tightly covered containers to prevent them from drying out. Freezer burn, in which food dries out and loses its flavor, can result from improper packaging of foods stored in the freezer. Leftover cooked foods should be wrapped in airtight packages of aluminum foil, plastic wrap, sealed plastic bags, or covered bowls.

Not all foods should be kept in the refrigerator. Some perishables, such as potatoes and onions, do better in a cool, dry place. Packaged and canned goods can be stored at room temperature on shelves. Cabinets under the sink or above the range generally are not recommended for food storage.

Using Space Efficiently

Kitchen space is needed not only for storing food but also for storing all the equipment used in preparing the food. The basic rule for storing equipment is to keep items near the work center where they will be used most often. For example, storage bags and containers will be kept near the food storage center, while mixers and mixing utensils will be kept near the mixing center.

Other general principles for efficient use of storage space include the following:

• Items that you use most often should be the easiest to reach.

• Heavy items should be kept on low shelves so that you don't have to move them down from high shelves.

• If counter space is limited, keep out only the appliances that you use frequently. Store less frequently used appliances in cabinets.

Storage Aids

Many people find that they don't have enough storage space in the kitchen. Fortunately, you don't have to spend a lot of money to increase the storage space available. Simple ideas for adding or improving storage space include:

• Open shelving, which costs much less than cabinets. Items stored on open shelves are visible and accessible. However, they will get dusty.

• Wall storage, in the form of gridded racks or boards with hooks.

• Cabinet aids, such as roll-out shelves or turntables, to make better use of inaccessible space.

• Baskets placed on shelves or counters or hung from the ceiling to provide additional inexpensive storage.

■ There are many creative ways to handle storage space in a kitchen.

REAL-LIFE APPLICATION

Have groups plan and equip an efficient kitchen for a specific family, such as: a single mother with little space, a limited budget, and two teenage sons; an urban couple with a large income who cook and entertain often; or a large family in the country who grow much of their own food.

Chapter 43 Review

Reviewing the Facts

1. Name and explain the features of the main appliances you are likely to find in any kitchen. What determines the number and variety of appliances in a kitchen?
2. List the four main kitchen work centers, and tell what each one is organized around.
3. What is the relationship between the work triangle and kitchen efficiency?
4. What is the function of a rotation system in food storage?
5. Give three examples of inexpensive ideas that can increase or improve kitchen storage.

Thinking Critically

1. Think about how your family stores food, dishes, and utensils in your kitchen. How could you rearrange these items to create work centers that would save time and energy when working in the kitchen?
2. Imagine that you have a very large kitchen. What centers, other than the basic four work centers, would you include? Explain your choices.

Applying Your Knowledge

1. **Collecting Data.** Select a type of small kitchen appliance that your family is thinking of buying or would like to buy someday. Find a recent report about it in a consumer magazine, and compare the different brands for quality, features, cost, care, and warranty information. Report to the class which one you would recommend to your family and why.
2. **Sharing Storage Ideas.** The last section of this chapter discussed simple storage aids. Describe to your classmates three simple storage techniques you or someone you know uses at home.

Making Connections

1. **History.** In colonial America, kitchens were sometimes separate from the main house. Why might this have been done? What advantages and disadvantages might a separate kitchen have had? Write down your ideas, and be prepared to discuss them in class.
2. **Social Studies.** Consider how economics, climate, culture, and religion might affect the setup and arrangement of a kitchen. For example, what special food storage techniques might be needed in a very hot climate, or how might dietary restrictions affect how a kitchen is set up? Choose a cultural group from another part of the world, and find out how a typical food preparation area in that culture is organized. Share your findings with your classmates.

Building Your Portfolio

Designing Kitchens for the Twenty-First Century

Imagine that you have been asked to design a kitchen that is appropriate for the 21st century. You have no budget limit. Design your visionary kitchen, and list the design principles and social developments you have taken into consideration. You might want to think about wheelchair access, recycling, and automation. Draw your kitchen layout, or use pictures from magazines. Place your completed design in your portfolio.

ANSWERS TO REVIEWING THE FACTS

1. *Refrigerator-freezer:* humidity-controlled compartments for storing produce, meats, dairy products; section for tall containers; ice maker; self-defrosting freezer. *Range* (or cooktop and oven): three to four burners with separate heat-control dials; broiler; oven with temperature setting. The type of foods prepared; expense; available storage space.
2. *Food storage*—refrigerator; *mixing*—counter space; *cleanup*—sink; *cooking*—range.
3. Too large a triangle wastes energy and space, too small lacks space; both detract from efficiency. Most efficient triangle has equal sides and total length of 12-22 ft (4-7 m).
4. Ensures that older supplies are used before newer ones.
5. Any three: open shelving, wall storage, cabinet aids, baskets.

ANSWERS TO THINKING CRITICALLY

1. Answers will vary but should reflect principles described in the chapter.
2. Answers will vary. Ask how students might incorporate a serving or eating area, a laundry center, or a play center for children.

Chapter 44

FOCUS

Chapter Overview

Chapter 44 teaches students safety and sanitation principles that help prevent kitchen accidents and illness. Students learn how to prevent cuts, burns, fires, and electric shocks, and how to control the spread of food-borne illness.

Motivator

■ **Safe at Home?** Tell students that studies repeatedly show the kitchen to be one of the most dangerous rooms in the home. Ask why this might be. *Working in the kitchen often involves electricity, water, sharp objects, and people hurrying at tasks.* Tell students this chapter will help them recognize hazards and develop good safety practices.

Objectives

Discuss the chapter objectives on this page. Remind students that the objectives focus on important chapter concepts.

Vocabulary

The word "borne", as in *food-borne illness,* is not often used. Tell students it is the past participle of "to bear." Ask what "to bear" means. *(To carry.)* Ask how a food-borne illness is transmitted.

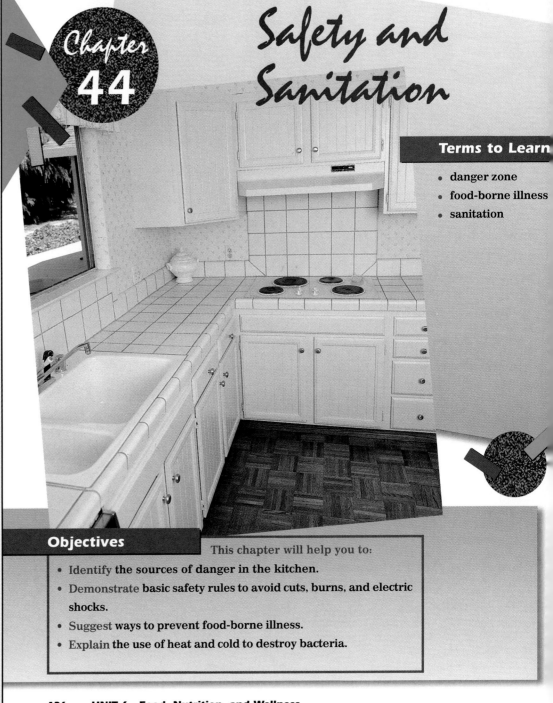

Chapter 44

Safety and Sanitation

Terms to Learn

- danger zone
- food-borne illness
- sanitation

Objectives

This chapter will help you to:

- Identify **the sources of danger in the kitchen.**
- Demonstrate **basic safety rules to avoid cuts, burns, and electric shocks.**
- Suggest **ways to prevent food-borne illness.**
- Explain **the use of heat and cold to destroy bacteria.**

CHAPTER RESOURCES

Student Workbook
Study Guide, pp. 148-149
Activity, *Food Safety—Cold and Hot,* p. 150

Teacher's Classroom Resources
Lesson Plan, p. 48

Extension #71, *Getting Rid of Kitchen Pests,* p. 77
Life Skills, *A Safety Checkup,* p. 72
Transparency 45, *Kitchen Dangers and Precautions*
Chapter 44 Test, pp. 93-94

Performance Assessment, *Kitchen Safety,* p. 77
Reteaching, *An Ounce of Prevention,* p. 50

See Also:
ABCNews InterActive™ Videodiscs

Safety and sanitation are vitally important whenever you work in the kitchen. Safe work habits can help you avoid accidents such as burns, cuts, electric shocks, and falls. **Sanitation** means *keeping harmful bacteria from growing in food* by keeping the kitchen, appliances, tools, and yourself clean, as well as washing, cooking, and storing food properly.

Safety and sanitation rules are especially important when you are preparing food with a group, such as in the food preparation lab. By following rules, you can prevent injuries and the transmission of illness to yourself or your classmates. Proper safety and sanitation practices are equally important when you are preparing food at home.

Kitchen Safety

Knowledge is one of the most useful resources for working in a kitchen. Knowing what dangers might occur will help you avoid them. If you pay close attention to your work, develop careful work habits, and follow safety rules consistently, your kitchen will be a safe and pleasant place.

Sources of Danger

Some kitchen dangers are obvious. Knives and open cans are sharp, and an oven or range gets hot rapidly when it is turned on. However, there are also other, less obvious dangers. Grease on the floor can cause you to slip and fall. Metal pots, pans, and tools can get very hot very quickly. Even food can be so hot that it can burn.

Many electric appliances can cause shock if they have frayed cords, are used without following instructions, or are used near water. In addition, leaks from gas appliances, such as ranges, are very dangerous because they can cause explosions and fires.

Finally, cleaning products stored in the kitchen can cause serious injuries. Many common cleaning agents are poisonous if they are swallowed. They can cause irritation or injury if they splash into a person's eyes. These products can be very dangerous, especially to young children.

Simple safety devices can be purchased and installed to prevent children from opening drawers with dangerous contents.

CHAPTER 44   Safety and Sanitation   437

TEACH

Topics on p. 437:
- **Importance of Kitchen Safety**
- **Sources of Danger**

Checking Comprehension

✓ How do you practice kitchen sanitation? *Keep kitchen, appliances, tools, and self clean; wash, cook, and store food properly.*

✓ How can you promote kitchen safety? *Pay attention to work; work carefully; follow safety rules.*

Activity

■ **Think Safety.** Have students list possible hazards in making a meal of fried chicken, mashed potatoes, and steamed carrots. Ask students to share their lists and to save them to review after reading the chapter, when they may be able to add ideas. (*Critical Thinking*)

SPECIAL NEEDS *Strategies*

Visual Learners. Discussions on procedures and techniques offer advantages to students who learn best by seeing or doing. Look for ways to include teacher and student demonstrations in these lessons.

MORE ABOUT Kitchen Safety

In the kitchen, dressing for success means dressing for safety. Rubber-soled shoes help prevent slipping; closed toes and heels help protect against cuts and burns. Keep shoes tied and clothes a reasonable length to avoid tripping. Avoid wearing dangling hair jewelry, which can become caught.

Topics on pp. 438-439:
- **Safety Precautions**
- **Food-Borne Illnesses**

Checking Comprehension

✓ How can you prevent cuts when using knives? *Hold knife by handle; cut away from fingers; use cutting board.*

✓ How should pots on a cooktop be arranged? *With handles over center of range or counter.*

✓ Describe two ways of safely putting out a grease fire. *Turn off heat and cover pan; use fire extinguisher.*

✓ How is salmonella often spread? *Through improperly cleaned cooking utensils and cutting boards.*

FAMILY AND COMMUNITY OUTREACH

Suggest students contact the health department to learn how it investigates suspected cases of food poisoning. How does it identify the bacteria responsible and track down its source?

Safety Precautions

The following safety rules will help prevent cuts, burns, electric shock, and other serious injuries that can occur in the kitchen. The list is long, but learning and following these rules can help you, your family, and your friends and classmates prevent kitchen accidents.

To prevent cuts:
- Always hold a knife by its handle and cut by moving the knife blade away from your fingers. Use a cutting board.
- Wash knives separately from other dishes or utensils.
- Insert beaters into a mixer and cutting blades into a food processor before plugging in the appliances.
- Watch out for sharp edges on the lids and rims of opened cans.

To prevent burns and scalding:
- Use a plastic-handled spoon to stir hot foods—metal handles can get too hot.
- Use pot holders to handle hot pots, pans, utensils, and oven racks.
- Keep pan handles turned in over the center of the range or over a counter so that the pans won't get knocked off the range.
- Lift the far side of a pan's cover first so that the steam won't burn you.

To prevent fires:
- Keep paper, dish towels, cleaning cloths, and all other flammable materials away from the range.
- Keep your sleeves and other parts of your clothing away from flames and hot burners. Tie back long hair. Don't wear loose, flowing garments while working in the kitchen.
- Clean all grease from the surfaces of the oven and the range top. Check and clean the vent above the burners, where grease collects.
- Smother a grease fire by turning off the heat source and covering the pan. Never use water.
- Keep a fire extinguisher handy.

To prevent electric shocks:
- Plug only one electric appliance into an outlet at a time.
- Unplug appliances when they are not in use. Unplug them by pulling on the plug, not on the cord.
- Don't use appliances with frayed cords, and don't drape cords over the edge of a countertop.
- Keep electric appliances away from water, and don't touch them with wet hands.

Keep the handles of cooking pots turned so that you do not jar them and so that children cannot pull the contents over on themselves.

438   **UNIT 6   Food, Nutrition, and Wellness**

MORE ABOUT Food Borne Illness

Other bacteria of concern to cooks include staphylococcus and E. coli. Staphylococcus live on human skin and in the mouth and throat. Spread by coughing, sneezing, and touching with unclean hands, they can cause nausea, vomiting and diarrhea. E. coli may contaminate water, raw ground beef, and unpasteurized milk. They produce a toxin that can cause cramps, bloody diarrhea, and vomiting. Basic sanitation can prevent the spread of both of these bacteria.

- Don't stick metal objects such as knives or forks inside a toaster or other electric appliance.

To prevent other kinds of injuries:
- Wipe up spills immediately.
- Never leave anything on the floor where someone might trip over it.
- Stand on a ladder or stool, not on a chair or box, to reach a high shelf.
- Turn all range or appliance controls to "Off" when you have finished cooking.
- Never turn on a gas range if you smell gas. Leave the building, report a gas leak to your gas company immediately, and follow the company's instructions precisely.
- Store dangerous chemicals well out of the reach of children. Keep cabinet doors closed and, if necessary, secure them with childproof locks.

Kitchen Sanitation

Most of the dangers you have read about so far are visible. Microscopic bacteria, however, can grow unseen in foods and cause serious, even fatal, illnesses. Fortunately, you can prevent the growth of harmful bacteria.

What Is Food-Borne Illness?

Harmful bacteria can grow in food until the food becomes unsafe to eat. These bacteria are tiny living things that multiply rapidly and can be seen only with a microscope. A **food-borne illness** is *an illness caused by eating food that is contaminated with harmful bacteria.* Examples of food-borne illnesses include salmonella poisoning and botulism.

Salmonella is a bacterium that grows in such foods as poultry and eggs. It is often spread from one food to another by improper cleaning of cooking utensils and cutting boards. Symptoms of salmonella poisoning include nausea, diarrhea, mild to severe cramps, and fever.

Botulism is a more serious, often fatal type of food-borne illness. It affects the nervous system. Improperly canned (often home-

Making Decisions

Reporting Sanitation Problems

As Julio entered the restaurant, he recalled his interview with Jed, the kitchen manager. "Show me that you can do the job," Jed had told him, "and you'll move up in this business fast." Julio had plans for himself. He was very interested in learning the restaurant business.

As Julio settled into his work at the salad station, he noticed something that startled him. One of the cooks tasted the soup with the stirring spoon, then put it back in the pot. Later in the day he noticed another worker use one knife to cut both meat and vegetables without washing in between.

Julio was hesitant about saying anything, but later he talked to Jed. "Don't worry about it, OK?" said his boss. "You do your work and let the others do theirs. We don't want any problems here."

Julio said nothing, but it wasn't easy when he began to notice other basic sanitation rules broken repeatedly. Julio's mind was swirling. Everyone at his last job had been so careful. Were they the exception? Was what he was seeing here more realistic? Maybe it wasn't such a big deal. On the other hand, what if someone got food poisoning? Should I call the health department, Julio wondered, but what about my job?

What Would You Do?

1. What options does Julio have?
2. Suggest some possible short- and long-term consequences of each option you identified.
3. Should risks to others carry more weight than those to yourself when you decide how to act? Explain.
4. What would you do if you were Julio? Why?

canned) foods are usually the source of botulism. Symptoms include difficulty breathing, trouble swallowing, and double vision. Never taste or eat food from leaking or bulging cans or cracked jars.

CHAPTER 44   Safety and Sanitation   439

Activity

■ **Picture of Health.** Have students draw kitchen scenes depicting health and safety problems. Have them trade pictures and identify the problems. *(Observation)*

Making Decisions

Have students read "Reporting Sanitation Problems" and discuss the questions. Discuss incidents of unsafe practices at restaurants that students know of. As consumers, how do they respond to such news?

Answers to What Would You Do?
1. Answers may include: say nothing; talk to restaurant owner; talk to coworkers; inform health department; quit.
2. Answers may include: saying nothing, he may keep job and advance in career, but many others may become ill; kitchen's poor standards may be found out anyway. Speaking up may cost his job but save others from illness or death.
3. Answers will vary. Ask: Would number of others affect your decision? Likelihood of risk or the severity of consequences?
4. Answers will vary. Ask: Might speaking up help Julio's reputation and career? How might he feel in long run if he keeps quiet?

DID YOU KNOW?

The Food and Drug Administration (FDA) sets sanitation standards for the food industry. The agency employs professionals to develop tests for food contamination and methods to prevent pest infestation during food processing.

Contaminated food may not look, smell, or taste bad. However, if you suspect food to be spoiled, follow the adage: "When in doubt, throw it out." The cost of wasted food is much less than the cost of illness.

Topics on pp. 440-442:

• Basic Sanitation

Checking Comprehension

✓ When should you wash your hands while handling food? *Before working with food; after coughing, sneezing, or using rest room.*

✓ Give two tips for handling cooked food. *Keep hot until eaten; cover and refrigerate leftovers within two hours.*

✓ Does refrigeration stop bacteria growth? *No, only slows it down.*

CROSS-CURRICULAR ACTIVITY
Social Studies

Have students research and report on methods people use to keep food safe without refrigeration. Students might coordinate reports to show the progression from traditional methods such as curing and drying, to more recent developments such as aseptic packaging and irradiation. Encourage students to use visual aids and demonstrations where feasible.

STRATEGIES That Work

Safe Packed Lunches

Without refrigeration, a packed lunch can be a source of food-borne illness, especially if kept in a warm place, where bacteria thrive. You can take precautions, however, to pack lunches safely.

Using an insulated lunch container extends the time that your lunch is safe by helping keep foods either hot or cold. It also enhances their flavor.

Some foods and drinks—such as yogurt, milk, and juice—can be kept cold in a vacuum bottle. If you chill the bottle in the refrigerator before filling it, the contents will stay cold longer.

Another way to keep foods cold is to pack them frozen or pack them next to frozen food. You can make and freeze a sandwich the night before, for instance, as well as portions of juice or fruit. These will thaw by lunchtime and keep other foods cool. An ice pack or gel freezer pack in your lunch container also helps keep the contents cold.

If your lunch must be kept at room temperature longer than four hours, avoid sandwiches made with eggs or meat. Peanut butter and aged cheeses are safe alternatives. You can also pack portion-sized cans of tuna or meat along with bread and make your sandwich just before eating it.

Such hot foods as spaghetti and stew—fresh or leftover—also make nutritious packed lunches. You can freeze portion-sized containers of leftovers several months before, then microwave as needed. To keep foods hot, use a widemouthed vacuum bottle. Prepare the bottle by filling it with clean hot water and letting it stand for two minutes. Heat the food to steaming hot. Pour the water from the bottle and add the food. Be sure the food still feels hot to the touch at lunchtime.

Making the Strategy Work

Think . . .

1. What would be a safe way to pack a garden salad or fresh fruit salad for lunch?
2. What containers would you need if you wanted hot leftovers for your packed lunch?
3. The beef stew in your vacuum bottle is only lukewarm at lunchtime. A friend says that it is still safe to eat because it was thoroughly cooked before. Do you accept this reasoning? Why?

Try...

Make a list of foods you like that would be good leftovers for a packed lunch. How could you store and transport them safely?

Sanitation Practices

Careless sanitation practices not only spread food-borne illness but also can pass on other types of illness in raw or undercooked food. To prevent the spread of any illness when preparing food, use these basic rules:

• Use hot, soapy water to wash tools, utensils, cutting boards, and other surfaces every time you prepare food. Be especially careful to clean items that come in contact with raw poultry or eggs.

• Wash fresh fruits and vegetables thoroughly under cold, running water to remove dirt and insecticides. Wash the tops of cans before opening them.

• Use a clean plate for cooked food. Never use the same plate that held the raw food.

• Keep pets out of the kitchen, especially off counters and tabletops where you prepare food.

• Wash your hands well before working with food and after using the rest room.

MORE ABOUT Bacteria Growth

Bacteria grow by splitting in two, a rapid means of reproduction. They grow best in foods containing fats and proteins—such as eggs, milk, meats, and fish—and less well or not at all in dried, highly sugared, or highly salted foods. (Thus salting as a method of food preservation.) Also, food that is frozen, thawed, and then refrozen will have a higher level of bacteria contamination than it had when first frozen.

- Use separate towels for wiping dishes and drying your hands.
- Use a tissue when you must sneeze or cough, and turn away from the food. Then wash your hands.
- Keep your hair out of the food. If your hair is long, tie it back.
- Use a separate spoon, not your fingers, for tasting food. If the spoon has been used for tasting once, wash it thoroughly before using it again.
- Avoid touching the eating surfaces of plates, flatware, and glassware when you set the table.

Dealing with Pests

Pests, another kitchen concern, are insects or small animals that carry dirt and bacteria. Ants, cockroaches, mice, and rats contaminate foods and surfaces with their eggs or with diseases they carry.

Methods for combating pests vary. Always choose a method that is both effective and safe. Insecticides are available in both sprays and traps. If you use a spray, don't spray it in places that come in contact with food. In fact, don't allow insecticides in *any* form to come in contact with food. If the pest problem persists, call a professional exterminator to deal with it.

Proper Temperatures

Bacteria grow to dangerous levels most rapidly within a particular range of temperatures. The **danger zone** is *a range of temperatures between 60°F and 125°F (16°C and 52°C)*. Do not keep perishable and cooked foods within this temperature range for more than two hours. Heating and storing foods properly can avoid potential problems. **Figure 44.1** shows you safe and unsafe temperatures for handling food.

Heating Foods

High temperatures, such as those reached when boiling food, can kill most harmful bacteria. Length of cooking time and degree of temperature will vary, de-

Figure 44.1
GERM WARFARE

°F	°C	
250	121	Canning temperatures in pressure canner.
240	116	
212	100	Canning temperatures for fruits, tomatoes, and pickles in water bath canner.
165	74	Cooking temperatures destroy most bacteria. Time required to kill bacteria decreases as temperature is increased.
140	60	Warming temperatures prevent growth but allow survival of some bacteria.
125	52	Some bacterial growth. Many bacteria survive.
		DANGER ZONE Temperatures in this zone allow rapid growth of bacteria and production of toxins by some bacteria.
60	16	
40	4	Some growth of food-poisoning bacteria may occur.
32	0	Slow growth of some bacteria that cause spoilage.
		Freezing temperatures stop bacteria growth but allow survival. Don't store food above 10°F (-12°C) more
0	-18°	than a few weeks.

CHAPTER 44 Safety and Sanitation 441

RETEACHING

■ **Safety Quiz.** Have students write a 10- to 15-item quiz on sanitation practices. Have students exchange and complete the quizzes. Discuss in class to clarify any points of confusion.

ENRICHMENT

■ **Pros Know Safety.** Have students arrange to observe sanitation techniques practiced at a local restaurant or the school kitchen. Have students report their findings to the class.

STRATEGIES THAT WORK

Safe Packed Lunches. Have students read "Safe Packed Lunches" and discuss the questions. Suggest they observe other students at lunch who have brought meals from home. Do others use techniques described here?

Answers to Think . . .
1. In widemouthed thermos; insulated lunch container; in carrier containing ice or gel freezer pack.
2. Portion-sized container for refrigerating or freezing and microwaving; widemouthed thermos for packing in lunch container.
3. No; bacteria can grow on cooked foods in warm conditions.

REAL-LIFE APPLICATION

Read this to students: *You and a friend are dining at a cafeteria. Tasting your potato salad, you discover it is warm and tangier than you had expected. You suspect it has gone bad, but your friend is doubtful: a restaurant wouldn't serve un-* *safe food.* Ask: What do you do? Is your friend right? Suggest that while the salad may simply be an unfamiliar recipe, restaurants do on occasion serve tainted food. Urge students to take their concerns to management in such a situation.

Review

■ **Chapter Review.** Use the contents of the Chapter Review page to help students review concepts, think critically, and apply their knowledge.

■ **Study Guide.** Have students complete the Study Guide for Chapter 44 on page 148 of the Student Workbook.

■ **On T.V.** Have groups perform humorous skits showing a cooking show chef who pays the consequences of following poor safety and sanitation practices. Afterward, ask the class to identify the health-related errors dramatized and describe the correct procedure for each one.

Evaluation

■ **Chapter Test.** Use the reproducible chapter test provided in the Teacher's Classroom Resources or create your own test using the *Testmaker Software*.

■ **Alternative Assessment.** Ask pairs to imagine they are health department officials inspecting a restaurant kitchen. Have them create a checklist that would help them determine the level of safety and sanitation in the establishment. The checklist should include items on both the state of the facilities and workers' habits.

■ **Safety Courses.** Have groups write a four-course dinner menu. Have them outline the preparation of each course, highlighting the safety and sanitation concerns that apply at each step.

pending on the type of food. For example, pork must be cooked until its internal temperature is 170°F (77°C). If it is not cooked until this temperature is reached, tiny worms that may be in the pork may survive, causing a serious disease called trichinosis. All tools used to cut or grind raw pork should be washed with hot water and soap.

Once food is cooked, keep it hot until it is eaten. Then cover and refrigerate leftovers in two hours or less. Be especially careful with poultry stuffing. Recent research shows that stuffing should be cooked separately from chicken and other poultry to avoid possible salmonella contamination.

Cooling Foods

Low temperatures slow down, but do not stop, the growth of bacteria. For this reason, food stays fresh in the refrigerator, but only for a limited time. **Figure 44.2** lists the refrigerator storage times for some common foods.

Take extra care with foods that spoil quickly, such as milk and meat. Egg-rich foods, such as custards, provide bacteria with a rich environment in which to grow. Always refrigerate these foods promptly, especially in hot weather.

Freezing food does not kill bacteria but keeps it from growing. During and after thawing frozen foods, take care to avoid the danger zone. The bacteria may still be alive and could grow to harmful levels if not handled properly. Chapters 50 to 53 provide additional information on how to properly handle many foods.

Figure 44.2

Refrigeration Storage

One to two days	Two to three days	Three to five days	Up to one week
poultry	berries	broccoli	tomatoes
fish	cherries	lima beans	cauliflower
ground meat	asparagus	spinach	celery
variety meats (liver, kidneys, etc.)	raw egg yolks or whites	green onions	lettuce
sausage		green peas	bacon
leftover cooked poultry	**Three to four days**	grapes	whole ham
gravy and meat broth	leftover cooked meats and meat dishes	peaches	hard cooked eggs
store-cooked convenience meals	ham slices (fully cooked)	apricots	hot dogs (opened package)
sweet corn		fresh meats	cottage cheese
		cold cuts	
		milk and cream	**Up to two weeks**
		store-prepared salads	butter
			dried beef, sliced
			lemons
			carrots (tops removed)
			cabbage
			hot dogs (unopened package)

Focus on Observation Skills

Plant safety and sanitation errors in the foods lab, such as too many appliances plugged into an outlet and plastic pests in cabinets. Challenge students to find them.

REAL-LIFE APPLICATION

Encourage students to survey their kitchen at home for safety and sanitation practices and to alert their families to any problems. Volunteers may also wish to share their findings with the class.

 Review

Reviewing the Facts

1. What are four types of accidents that can occur in the kitchen?
2. List three ways to prevent burns.
3. Name two types of food-borne illness, and briefly describe the symptoms of each.
4. List at least three sanitation practices you should follow when handling food.
5. What is the purpose of washing fresh foods before cooking them?
6. What is the danger zone for food, and why is it called that?

Thinking Critically

1. Injuries from cuts and burns can happen in the food preparation lab. How would you respond to each type of injury?
2. Incidents of some types of food-borne illnesses, which were not common in the past, are increasing. Why might this be occurring?

Applying Your Knowledge

1. **Creating a Safety Advertisement.** Write a one-minute TV commercial to promote safety. Feature one aspect of kitchen safety in your commercial. Suggest what visuals should be shown on camera, and create a brief script. If a video recorder is available, tape your commercial.
2. **Writing Sanitation Captions.** Cut out three pictures of foods from a magazine. Write a caption for each, explaining some sanitation practices to follow when preparing the food shown.
3. **Promoting Public Safety.** Food safety is especially important on picnics, when food may be left outside for some time. Make a list of safety recommendations for people having a picnic.

Making Connections

1. **Health.** At the library, research a food-borne illness not mentioned in this chapter. Find out the most frequent causes and the common symptoms. Look for information about how to prevent the illness. Present an oral report to your class.
2. **Language Arts.** Choose a kitchen appliance, and prepare a safety brochure about it. The brochure should include a description of the appliance, its uses, and safety precautions.

Building Your Portfolio

Creating a Safety Checklist
Prepare a safety and sanitation checklist that could be posted in your kitchen at home. The checklist should address the appliances and tools that you have and areas of potential danger in your kitchen. Suggest solutions for problems whenever possible. Add the finished checklist to your portfolio.

ANSWERS TO REVIEWING THE FACTS

1. Cuts, burns, fire, and electric shock; also slips and falls and poisoning.
2. Any three: use plastic-handled spoons; use pot holders; turn pan handles toward the center of range or counter; lift lids away from you.
3. *Salmonella*—nausea, diarrhea, stomach cramps, fever. *Botulism*—difficulty breathing and swallowing, double vision.
4. Any three: wash tools and surfaces in hot, soapy water; use a plastic cutting board for cutting raw poultry; wash fresh fruits, vegetables and tops of cans thoroughly; use clean plate for cooked food; keep pets out of kitchen; wash hands before working with food, after using rest room; use separate towels to wipe dishes and hands; sneeze or cough into tissue, away from food, wash hands afterward; keep hair out of the food; use clean spoon for tasting food each time; and avoid touching eating surfaces of tableware.
5. To wash off dirt and insecticides.
6. Temperatures between 60°F and 125°F (16°C and 52°C), where bacteria can grow to dangerous levels and cause illness.

ANSWERS TO THINKING CRITICALLY

1. Cuts: apply direct pressure to stop bleeding, wash cut, apply antiseptic and bandage. Minor burns: run cold water on the burned area for about five minutes. Remind students these and other first-aid practices are found in Chapter 23.
2. Answers may include: more accurate reporting and diagnosing of illnesses; insufficient health department staff to inspect increased number of restaurants; more people eating out.

Chapter Overview

Chapter 45 explains the value of planning when working in the kitchen. Students learn how to prepare meals efficiently by using a work plan and a schedule to identify, sequence and coordinate food preparation tasks.

Motivator

■ **Ready, Set . . .** Ask students to recall a task they perform, such as writing a report or doing laundry. Ask volunteers to describe how they prepare to undertake it this task. Point out that tasks are simpler and often more successful when people make some sort of preparation.

Objectives

Discuss the chapter objectives on this page. Remind students that the objectives focus on important chapter concepts.

Vocabulary

The word *sequence* derives from the Latin *sequi*, meaning to follow. This can help students understand its definition. A helpful, related word is sequel. Students might remember that steps follow one another in sequence as a movie sequel follows the original.

Chapter 45

Getting Ready to Cook

Terms to Learn

- sequence
- work plan

Objectives

This chapter will help you to:

- **Describe and create** a work plan for meal preparation.
- **Create** a schedule for preparing a meal and explain why it is useful.
- **Explain** efficient kitchen work techniques.

CHAPTER RESOURCES

Student Workbook

Study Guide, p. 151

Activity, *Cooking and Baking Success*, p. 152

Teacher's Classroom Resources

Lesson Plan, p. 49

Cooperative Learning, *Planning a Meal*, pp. 53-54

Extension #72, *Kitchen Time Management*, p. 78

Life Skills, *Planning a Special Meal*, p. 73

Chapter 45 Test, pp. 95-96

Performance Assessment, *Planning and Preparing a Meal*, p. 78

Reteaching, *The Cook's Ladder*, p. 51

Fifteen minutes before Karen expected her friends to arrive, she started preparing lunch. The kitchen was such a mess, however, that she first had to spend precious minutes cleaning it up.

While she was preparing the soup, the tuna melt sandwiches began to burn. As she started to make more sandwiches, the soup boiled over and spilled on the range. When she went to the refrigerator for salad ingredients, she discovered that she was out of lettuce.

"What a disaster!" Karen thought. "What am I going to do?" As she stood pondering what to do next, Karen's guests arrived.

Karen's meal didn't turn out well because she didn't have a plan of action. She neglected to think ahead about what she needed to do and when. In other words, she was not ready to cook. As you will learn in this chapter, organization and timing are as vital for meal preparation as cooking skills.

Making a Work Plan

You learned in Chapter 41 about how useful advance daily or weekly meal planning is to ensure that you have nutritious, attractive meals for yourself and your family. Equally important is the short-term planning you do to be sure that each meal is completed according to directions and on time. Management of time and equipment in the kitchen is vital to putting together a meal that everyone, including the cook, can enjoy.

To be sure that you accomplish this objective, a wise first step is to have a **work plan**, or action plan. This plan is *a list of all the tasks you will have to do to prepare each dish in the meal and how long each task will take.* To learn what the tasks are, read the package directions or the recipe for each food dish. Then estimate how much time each task will take. As you gain experience, you will in-

Figure 45.1

Vegetable Lasagna

Customary		Ingredients	Metric	
½	lb.	Lasagna noodles	480	g
1	lb.	Zucchini	960	g
2	cups	Low-fat cottage cheese	500	mL
1		Egg	1	
1	Tbsp.	Parsley	15	mL
1	tsp.	Basil	5	mL
2	cups	Tomato sauce	500	mL
½	cup	Parmesan cheese	125	mL

1. Cook lasagna noodles according to package directions and drain.
2. Spray bottom and sides of 2-qt. (2 -L) casserole dish with vegetable oil cooking spray.
3. Slice zucchini into thin pieces, about 1/4 in. (6 mm) thick.
4. In bowl mix together cottage cheese, egg, parsley, and basil.
5. Layer in casserole dish: noodles, cottage cheese mixture, zucchini, tomato sauce, and Parmesan cheese. Use one-quarter of each ingredient for each layer. Top last layer with noodles, sauce, and Parmesan cheese.
6. Bake uncovered at 400°F (200°C) for 30 minutes, or until top is brown and sauce bubbles.

Topics on p. 445:
• Making a Work Plan

Checking Comprehension

✓ What are the two steps to making a work plan? *Learn tasks from package directions or recipe; estimate time needed for each one.*

✓ How does a cook's experience affect the amount of detail in a work plan? *Less experienced cook should include more detail.*

Activities

■ **"Work" Plans?** Have students list the steps of a work plan they might use to prepare a favorite breakfast food, sandwich, or snack.

CROSS-CURRICULAR ACTIVITY
Language Arts

Ask students to read Chapter 11 of *Little Women*, "Experiments," describing Jo's attempt to make a fancy dinner. Talk about how, with planning, she could have turned the meal from a disaster into a triumph.

MORE ABOUT Work Plans

A work plan is valuable for revealing the "hidden" time needed to prepare a recipe most successfully. Banana bread, for example, tastes better with very ripe bananas, which cooks might plan to buy ahead of time. Also, more than one cook has been dismayed to learn that the lovely dessert just prepared for this evening's meal needs to chill overnight. The moral: a work plan is best put together not an hour before the meal, but a day.

Checking Comprehension

✓ Why does Binh include in his work plan details not mentioned in the recipe? *These steps also take time, must be figured into preparation time.*

✓ Name the two main steps in making a schedule for preparing a meal. *Decide best way to organize tasks; determine starting and ending time for each task.*

✓ Why is deciding the sequence important in preparing a meal? *You can arrange steps in a time- and energy-efficient way.*

FAMILY AND COMMUNITY OUTREACH

Short-order cooks are masters at planning tasks. Help small groups of students arrange to observe a short-order cook in a diner or restaurant . Ask students to make notes about how the cook saves time and motion while working. Have students report what they learn to the class.

---

crease the accuracy of your time estimates. Allow just a little more time than you think you will actually need. Then you will be able to handle any unexpected events that come up.

The level of detail of your plan will be determined by how experienced a cook you are and how often you have made the dishes before. If you are inexperienced, you may want to include in your work plan turning on the oven and washing your hands before you start working with the food, as well as each step of the directions on the package or in the recipe.

A Sample Work Plan

Binh is planning to invite three friends over for lunch. He is going to serve vegetable lasagna along with a tossed salad, apples and pears for dessert, and milk as a beverage. The recipe for the vegetable lasagna is given in **Figure 45.1** on page 445. The salad is a simple one of lettuce, shredded carrots, and sliced cucumbers, with bottled low-fat Italian dressing. Notice that the work plan Binh creates for this meal, shown in **Figure 45.2**, includes not just the directions mentioned in the lasagna recipe, but many other details as well, such as the time needed to boil the water for the lasagna noodles and the tasks involved in preparing the salad.

Making a Schedule

A schedule helps you manage the meal preparation so that all the tasks listed in the work plan can be coordinated and all the

Figure 45-2

▶▶▶ Work Plan for Vegetable Lasagna Meal

Task	Time Needed (approximate)
Wash hands.	1 minute
Gather ingredients and equipment.	8 minutes
Boil water for lasagna noodles.	10 minutes
Cook and drain lasagna noodles.	15 minutes
Preheat oven.	10 minutes
Spray lasagna casserole dish.	1 minute
Wash and slice zucchini for lasagna.	5 minutes
Measure and mix other lasagna ingredients (cottage cheese, egg, parsley, basil).	3 minutes
Layer lasagna ingredients in dish.	8 minutes
Bake lasagna.	30 minutes
Wash salad greens and pat dry with paper towels. Break leaves into pieces.	8 minutes
Wash and cut cucumbers for salad.	5 minutes
Wash and shred carrots for salad.	6 minutes
Assemble salad and add dressing.	4 minutes
Wash apples and pears and pat dry. Put in bowl.	4 minutes
Pour milk into glasses.	2 minutes
Set table.	8 minutes
Bring food to table.	2 minutes

🔍 Focus on Management Skills

Making a schedule is an excellent exercise in assessing and managing resources. For instance, if you lack a certain utensil (a material resource), how could you use your creativity (a human resource) to find a substitute? How would this affect your available time (another human resource)? Ask students to give other examples demonstrating this interplay of resources in work plans and schedules.

From School to Work

Cooperation in the Foods Lab

What You Learn Today . . .

When you cook a meal with others in a foods laboratory, you learn more than how to work in the kitchen: you also learn how to work as a team. Sharing tools, ingredients, appliances, and—most importantly—responsibilities with classmates is good practice in cooperation.

. . . You Can Use Tomorrow

Cooperation is important not only in the foods lab, but also in the workplace. Increasingly, employers want people who can work as members of a team. For example, workers from a manufacturer's marketing, engineering, and testing departments may combine their knowledge to develop a new appliance.

Practicing Your Skills

Whenever you work as part of a foods lab team, follow these guidelines to help things go smoothly:

- **Plan ahead.** Prepare a work plan and a schedule to list what tasks must be done, when, and by whom. Consider work space, equipment, and individual skills. ·
- **Carry out your assignment.** Show that you take your responsibility seriously by doing your tasks efficiently, safely, and well.
- **Follow the rules.** Following the rules lessens the chance for mistakes. You work more safely as well as more effectively.
- **Communicate.** Communication is also important to both safety and teamwork. You need to inform others about potential hazards, such as a slippery floor. You may need information or help with a problem. Remember, exchanging help and ideas is one of the purposes of teams.
- **Be courteous.** Working with others means establishing good relationships. Showing respect—by being patient, helpful, and tactful—builds positive feelings and loyalty among team members.

Assessing Your Skills

1. Give an example of how good communication can prevent a potentially dangerous situation in the foods lab.
2. What would you do if you saw a student leave a work center without cleaning it up?

foods will be ready to eat at the same time. Making a schedule is a two-step process. First, decide on the best way to organize the tasks in your work plan. Then determine what time you will need to start preparation and complete each task.

Organizing the Tasks

Before you make the schedule, look over your work plan to see how you can make it simpler and more efficient. Part of this process includes deciding the **sequence**, or *order in which you will perform the tasks you*

CHAPTER 45   Getting Ready to Cook   447

Activities

RETEACHING

■ **Package Deal.** Provide small groups with an empty food package with cooking directions. Have them make a work plan based on the instructions given.

From School to Work

Have students read "Cooperation in the Foods Lab" and discuss the questions. Ask: How is working together on a project different from studying together? Stress that sharing tasks means accommodating not only others' physical presence, but their way of doing things.

Answers to Assessing . . .
1. Answers may include: warn others when you have hot dish; remind them of safety rules.
2. Answers will vary. Help students see that tactfully reminding student to clean up and offering to help would be most cooperative course of action.

DID YOU KNOW?

Large professional kitchens provide work stations for various tasks: a bake station for making breads and desserts; a hot-food station for hot items and final cooking; a cold-food station for cold dishes and appetizers; and more. Professional chefs often start their careers in huge kitchens where they specialize in one kind of food preparation. In a well-known restaurant, an apprentice chef may spend a year simply tearing up salad ingredients or making stock for sauces and soups.

Topics on pp. 448-450:

- **Making a Schedule**
- **Efficient Kitchen Habits**

Checking Comprehension

✓ How does dovetailing same time? *Lets you complete more than one task at the same time.*

✓ How do you determine a starting time for each step in a schedule? *Figure time needed for task; work backward from time you want meal to be ready.*

✓ Give two tips for working efficiently with a partner in the kitchen. *Have separate work area for each person; alternate tasks at work center.*

Managing Your Life

Have students read "Preparing a Meal for Guests" and discuss the questions. Ask: May you ask guests to help with food? What might be some of the advantages and disadvantages of doing so?

1. Answers may include: helps you remember additional, unusual tasks; helps you feel confident, relaxed.

2. Answers will vary. Ask students how freezing, chilling, or reheating might affect dishes or ingredients.

3. Answers may include: use humor; don't dwell on problem.

listed on the work plan. When you are determining the sequence, think about ways you can save time and effort. Notice how Binh can take quite a few minutes off his preparation time by following these tips:

- **Dovetailing tasks.** You may recall that when you dovetail tasks, you combine them in such a way that one task overlaps another. Doing this saves you time and makes it possible for you to have all the foods in the meal ready at the same time. Binh, for example, decides that he can prepare the cottage cheese mixture, spray the baking dish, and set the table while the noodles are cooking.

- **Grouping similar tasks.** It is a good idea to group tasks together that are similar or that use the same tools or equipment. Binh decides that it will be more efficient to measure out all the ingredients for the lasagna at one time. He also decides to group the tasks of cutting the cucumbers for the salad and the zucchini for the lasagna.

- **Preparing some items ahead of time.** Sometimes food can be prepared earlier in the day or even the day before it is served. If Binh's time was limited on the day of the lunch, he could assemble the lasagna the day before, leaving only the baking for the day of the meal.

Managing Your Life
Preparing a Meal for Guests

Making a work plan and schedule is always a good idea when working in the kitchen, especially when preparing a special meal for guests. In fact, you may want to plan and schedule such tasks as inviting the guests, making extra ice, and finding a centerpiece.

When you entertain, your goal is to provide a relaxed, enjoyable time for everyone—yourself included. This is easier when everything is done on time and recipes turn out right. The following tips can help you achieve those goals:

- Choose recipes that you know and trust. When you are familiar with preparing a recipe and know that it tastes good, you feel more confident. You avoid unpleasant surprises.
- Choose dishes that can be prepared ahead of time. Some salads and desserts may be prepared a day in advance and refrigerated. Some casseroles can be assembled ahead of time, refrigerated, and then baked for the meal. Do other tasks, such as preparing ingredients and setting the table, ahead of time also.
- If you have one complicated or time-consuming recipe, make the rest of the menu simple. That way you spend less time in the kitchen and more time with your guests.

- A day or so in advance, try to free up refrigerator space for the foods you have prepared ahead.
- If you're planning a large party, check ahead to see that you have enough tableware for everyone. If not, consider borrowing what you need from family or friends. (Return borrowed items promptly and in good condition.) Also be sure that you can provide enough seating.

Above all, stay relaxed and flexible. Remember that a cheerful attitude and good company are the most important ingredients for a special meal.

Applying the Principles

1. Why are a work plan and a schedule especially valuable when preparing a meal for guests?
2. Select two or three of your favorite recipes and tell how they can be entirely or partially made ahead.
3. If something should go wrong during a party, what might you do to put your guests at ease?

MORE ABOUT Pre-Preparation

When appearance of foods is especially important, remember to toss cut fruits, such as apples and pears, with a little lemon juice and refrigerate to help prevent darkening. Peeled potatoes retain their cream color when kept in water. Rinse just before using them. Mix soft sandwich fillings in advance and assemble the sandwiches nearer serving time. Spread condiments between slices of a meat or cheese filling to keep the bread from getting soggy.

Figure 45-3

Schedule for Vegetable Lasagna Meal

10:40	Wash hands.
	Gather ingredients and equipment.
10:50	Put water on to boil.
	Wash and slice zucchini for lasagna and cucumber for salad.
	Refrigerate cucumber slices in plastic container.
11:00	Place noodles in boiling water.
	Measure and mix cottage cheese, egg, parsley, and basil.
	Spray lasagna casserole dish.
	Set table.
11:15	Preheat oven.
	Drain noodles.
	Layer lasagna ingredients in casserole.
11:25	Put lasagna in oven.
	Wash salad greens and pat dry with paper towels. Break leaves into pieces. Refrigerate in plastic container.
11:35	Wash and shred carrots for salad. Refrigerate in plastic container.
11:45	Wash apples and pears and pat dry. Put in bowl.
11:50	Assemble salad and add dressing.
11:55	Pour milk.
	Remove casserole from oven.
	Bring lasagna and salad to table.
NOON	Enjoy the meal.

Scheduling the Tasks

As you decide on an efficient sequence of preparation tasks, make a new list of tasks in the order you plan to do them. This list will become your schedule. The next step is to write down a starting time for each task or group of tasks on the schedule. To do this, work backward from the time you want the meal to be ready. For example, Binh wants to serve his lunch at noon. One of the last items on his list is taking the lasagna out of the oven, so he schedules that for 11:55. Since the lasagna needs to bake for 30 minutes, he will have to put it in the oven at 11:25. He uses the same strategy to schedule the rest of the tasks on his list.

A Sample Schedule

Binh's schedule for the lasagna meal is shown in **Figure 45.3.** By using scheduling shortcuts, such as dovetailing, Binh is able to cut almost by half the total preparation time listed in the work plan. Done separately, the tasks in the lasagna meal would take 130 minutes. As the schedule shows, Binh needs only 80 minutes.

Activities

■ **Sequence of Events.** Ask groups to plan a three-course meal and then to write a schedule for cooking and serving it. Have them write their menu on an index card, and each step on separate cards. Have groups exchange cards and try to order the steps correctly based on the menu. *(Critical Thinking)*

RETEACHING

■ **Dinner Plans.** Write the following menu on the board: spaghetti with meat sauce, salad, garlic bread, and chocolate pudding. Provide package directions for the pasta and the pudding. Tell students the meat sauce is a prepared, store-bought variety. Have them then write a schedule for preparing this meal.

ENRICHMENT

■ **Dinner Committee.** Have the class agree on a dinner menu and a serving time. Assign groups the task of writing a work plan and schedule for one of the courses. Afterward, have the class share their plans to identify how tasks could be dovetailed and space and equipment shared. Have them write a revised schedule incorporating all the steps needed to prepare every course.

Focus on Consumer Skills

Using convenience foods can save a cook time in the kitchen. Some foods such as pudding mixes or chopped nuts may be similar or superior in quality to the homemade versions; however, other prepackaged foods lack more in quality than they offer in convenience. A bag of peeled carrots or cut broccoli, for instance, has lost vitamins from being cut and exposed to light. Consumers should fully realize what they give up when they opt for convenience.

Review

■ **Chapter Review.** Use the contents of the Chapter Review page to help students review concepts, think critically, and apply their knowledge.

■ **Study Guide.** Have students complete the Study Guide for Chapter 45 on p. 151 of the Student Workbook.

■ **Home Cooking.** Have students write a plan for a meal they could make in 45 minutes or less. Have them write a sequence for the meal, underlining the ways in which they save time by using tips in this chapter.

Evaluation

■ **Chapter Test.** Use the reproducible chapter test provided in the Teacher's Classroom Resources or create your own test using the *Testmaker Software.*

■ **Alternative Assessment.** Have groups perform a skit showing students in a foods lab, some of whom follow a meal preparation schedule and work smoothly in the kitchen; and others who have no plan and suffer the consequences. Encourage students to use humor. Remind them to be obvious enough that classmates can identify examples of using a plan or working without one.

■ **Lunch Crowd.** Have students think of a nutritious school lunch that could be partly or completely made ahead of time. Have them write the steps for making this lunch.

Working Efficiently

Once you have your work plan and schedule, you are ready to prepare the meal. You will be better able to ensure that meal preparation goes smoothly if you develop these efficient kitchen work techniques:

- If you are working with another person, have a work area for each person or alternate tasks at the sink or range so that you don't get in each other's way.
- Clear the kitchen counters to give yourself room to work. For good sanitation, wipe off the counters and range.
- Reread the recipe or package directions for each dish. Make sure you have all the ingredients you will need and that they are close at hand.
- Locate the right utensils or appliances for each task. Be sure you know how to use them correctly. The chapters that follow will describe food preparation tasks and the equipment to use for each.
- Check off each task in your schedule as you complete it so that you don't leave out any steps.
- Clean up as you work, so that there won't be so much to do afterward. Rinse bowls, utensils, and pans immediately after using them. Then place them in hot, soapy water to soak until you can wash them. Do not, however, place knives in the water. You may cut yourself as you reach into the water.
- Leave the kitchen clean and uncluttered, ready to be used to prepare the next meal.

Reviewing Your Efforts

By preparing a work plan and a schedule and working efficiently, you help ensure that your meal will be a success. Be sure to keep your plan and schedule to use again. If there are any improvements or changes you want to make, note them on your schedule. As you gain experience, you may need to make schedules only for meals you have not prepared before or meals you are serving to guests.

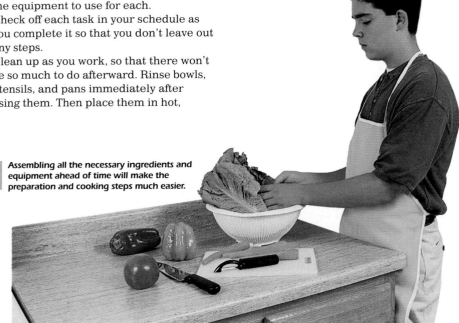

Assembling all the necessary ingredients and equipment ahead of time will make the preparation and cooking steps much easier.

REAL-LIFE APPLICATION

Tell students that the best plans have back-up plans to deal with unexpected events. Ask how they might "plan for the unplanned" and avoid potential mealtime disaster, if. . . the dessert they plan to serve doesn't turn out right. *(Keep cookies, ice cream, or fruit on hand.)* . . . the oven quits working an hour before you plan on baking the entrée. *(Plan main dish that can be prepared on cooktop.)* . . . as you begin to serve the main-dish quiche, a guest announces she is allergic to eggs. *(Plan variety of dishes.)*

Reviewing the Facts

1. What is a work plan?
2. From where do you get the information you need to make a work plan for a meal?
3. What two factors should you consider when you are deciding how detailed your work plan should be?
4. What is the purpose of making a schedule for preparing a meal?
5. What are three ways to simplify the steps in a work plan as you use the plan to make your schedule?
6. List two work techniques that will help meal preparation go smoothly.

Thinking Critically

1. Karen's lunch for her friends, described at the start of this chapter, was a disaster. If you were having the same meal for your friends, what would you do differently? Be specific in your response.
2. For what other tasks would the principles of kitchen efficiency be useful?

Applying Your Skills

1. **Making a Work Plan.** Choose one of your favorite main dishes. Make a work plan for preparing the dish, including all tasks and the estimated time needed to complete each task.
2. **Making a Schedule.** Change the schedule shown in Figure 45.3 on page 449 to show how you would prepare the meal with the help of a second person. Indicate how much time, if any, is saved.
3. **Designing Forms.** Design one form for a work plan and one for a schedule that could be used in a foods lab class.

Making Connections

1. **Science.** Find out why some steps for making such foods as yeast breads and cakes are altered if they are made at higher altitudes. Write a summary paragraph that explains your findings.
2. **Math.** Take the work plan you made for your favorite main dish in item #1 of "Applying Your Skills." Make a schedule that will allow you to serve the dish on time, assuming that the meal will be served at noon.

Building Your Portfolio

Planning a Meal
Decide on a meal that you would like to cook for three of your friends. Consult cookbooks for recipes for the meal. Then create a work plan and a schedule for it. If possible, prepare the meal. Write a paragraph explaining why you selected the foods you chose. If you do prepare the meal, add a paragraph to your report telling whether you think that the meal was a success and why. Include your recipes, work plan, schedule, and written report in your portfolio.

ANSWERS TO REVIEWING THE FACTS

1. List of all tasks you must do to prepare each dish in meal and how long each task will take.
2. Recipes and package directions.
3. Amount of cooking experience you have; how often you have made dish before.
4. To coordinate all tasks listed in work plan and have all foods ready to eat at same time.
5. Dovetail tasks; group similar tasks; prepare some foods ahead of time.
6. Any two: have separate space or alternate tasks for each preparer; clear and clean space on counter; double check directions and ingredients; locate needed equipment; check off tasks as completed; clean up as you work; leave kitchen clean.

ANSWERS TO THINKING CRITICALLY

1. Answers may include: list and make sure all ingredients are on hand; make work plan and schedule; clean kitchen early in day; assemble equipment ahead of time.
2. Answers will vary. In general, principles are useful in any task that involves multiple steps, allows for dovetailing, or involves items that can be assembled in advance.

Chapter Overview

Chapter 46 explains how to measure ingredients for cooking. Students learn what type of equipment is needed for measuring different quantities, and when and how to use each type. The chapter also offers instructions for adjusting recipe measurements.

Motivator

■ **Measure Up.** Ask how many students weigh their breakfast cereal or measure teaspoons of ketchup for sandwiches. Ask: When is measuring foods important? Help students see that recipes need the correct proportion of ingredients to turn out well.

Objectives

Discuss the chapter objectives on this page. Remind students that the objectives focus on important chapter concepts.

Vocabulary

The *metric system* is so named because its basic unit of measurement is the meter, equal to about 39 inches. The word metric comes from the French *mètre*, which in turn derives from the Greek word *metron*, meaning a measure.

Chapter
46

Measuring Basics

Objectives

This chapter will help you to:

- Identify **the two major systems of measurement.**
- Identify **the features and uses of measuring equipment.**
- Explain **how to measure liquid and dry ingredients accurately.**
- Adapt **recipes for smaller or greater amounts.**

CHAPTER RESOURCES

Student Workbook
Study Guide, pp. 153-154
Activity, *Measure for Measure*, p. 155

Teacher's Classroom Resources
Lesson Plan, p. 50

Extension #73, *Common Equivalents*, p. 79
Life Skills, *Measuring Techniques*, p. 74
Chapter 46 Test, pp. 97-98

Performance Assessment, *Measuring Tips*, p. 79
Reteaching, *Measuring Up*, p. 52

When Ernesto was very little, he loved to play with his grandmother's measuring cups and spoons while she prepared the family meals. Wonderful smells surrounded him as he sat on the kitchen floor, pouring make-believe foods into bowls and stirring the air with a spoon.

This year, Ernesto was accepted into a highly respected cooking school. He is on his way to a career as a master chef. His whole family celebrated the news of his acceptance into the chef's program. At a dinner in his honor, his grandmother gave him a special gift: her now worn and battered set of measuring cups and spoons. Ernesto was touched by his grandmother's gift and grateful for her support.

Units of Measure

In order to follow a recipe, whether in a professional or home setting, you must know how to measure ingredients. If you don't measure exactly, the food won't turn out the way that you expect. Before you can make accurate measurements, however, you must understand units of measure.

Two different systems of measurement may be used to give the ingredient amounts in a recipe. The **customary system** is *the standard system of measurement used in the United States*. The **metric system** is *the system of measurement used in most of the world*. The metric system is also used by American scientists, nutritionists, and other health and food professionals.

Remember that the two measurement systems are just different ways of expressing the same amounts. It is helpful to know how to measure using both systems. The recipes and other measurements in this book give the customary measurement first, followed by the metric measurement. Both customary and metric units can be used to measure volume, weight, temperature, and length.

Volume

In recipes for home use, most ingredients are measured by **volume**, or *the amount of*

space taken up by an ingredient. Following are some units of volume and their abbreviations or symbols:

Customary	Metric
teaspoon (tsp.)	milliliter (mL)
tablespoon (Tbsp.)	liter (L)
fluid ounce (fl. oz.)	
cup (c.)	
pint (pt.)	
quart (qt.)	
gallon (gal.)	

Weight

Solid ingredients in recipes are often described in terms of their weight. Units of weight and their abbreviations or symbols include the following:

Customary	Metric
ounce (oz.)	gram (g)
pound (lb.)	kilogram (kg)

Notice that the term *ounce* is used as a measure of weight as well as volume. Remember that these two kinds of ounces are not the same. As a rule of thumb, if an ingredient is a liquid or if the measurement specifies fluid ounces, you can assume that ounces refer to volume. With solid foods, the same term will most often refer to weight.

Temperature and Length

Temperature is used to gauge the heat of appliances (such as ovens and electric skillets) as well as the heat of foods such as candy and meat as they cook. In the customary system, temperature is measured in degrees Fahrenheit (°F). The metric system uses degrees Celsius (°C).

You may also use length measurements as you work with ingredients. For example, you may be asked to cut carrots into strips of a certain size or to use a pan of a particular length and width. Length may be measured in inches (in.) or using metric units such as millimeters (mm) and centimeters (cm).

Equivalent Measurements

In working with recipes, it is important to understand equivalents. An **equivalent** is *the*

Topics on p. 453:
• Units of Measure

Checking Comprehension

✓ When does the term *ounce* in a recipe refer to weight? To volume? *When ingredient is liquid; when ingredient is solid.*

✓ When might a recipe use length measurements? *In describing ingredient preparation and pan size.*

Activities

■ **Fight the System.** Point out to students that most people seem comfortable buying soft drinks in 2-liter bottles. Ask what other items they have seen marked with both customary and metric units. Do students feel they could make the trasition to the metric system? Explain that the United States attempted to convert to the metric system some years ago, with limited success. Ask: Why might people be resistant to change? *(Critical Thinking)*

RETEACHING

■ **Take a Reading.** Have students read three recipes and identify all units of measurement as indicating volume, weight, temperature, or length.

MORE ABOUT the Metric System

The metric system is a decimal system; all units are multiples of ten. The measure's prefix tells its relationship to the base unit. For example, *centi-* means one one-hundreth, *kilo—* is one thousand. Ask: What is a centimeter? A kilogram?

DID YOU KNOW?

The metric system was first proposed by Gabriel Mouton in France, 1670, and put into practice in 1795. The customary system is based on the British Imperial System. Great Britain, incidentally, is gradually converting to metric.

TEACH

Topics on pp. 454-455:
- Equivalent Measurements
- Measuring Equipment

Checking Comprehension

✓ What is the advantage of knowing equivalents? *Lets you measure foods with different units of measurement, convert one form of food to another.*

✓ Are nonstandard utensils useful for measuring? *No, they are inaccurate.*

✓ Should you measure liquids over a bowl of ingredients? *No, any spillage will go into bowl.*

USING VISUALS Have students use the equivalents given in Figure 46.1 to convert a favorite recipe from customary to metric measurements.

Figure 46.1

Measurement Equivalents

Customary Measure	Customary Equivalent	Metric Equivalent (approx.)
¼ tsp.		1 mL
½ tsp.		2 mL
1 tsp.		5 mL
1 Tbsp.	3 tsp.	15 mL
¼ cup	4 Tbsp.	50 mL
⅓ cup	5 ⅓ Tbsp.	75 mL
½ cup	8 Tbsp.	125 mL
¾ cup	12 Tbsp.	175 mL
1 cup	16 Tbsp. or 8 fl. oz.	250 mL
1 pt.	2 cups	500 mL
1 qt.	4 cups or 2 pt.	1000 mL or 1 L
1 gal.	4 qt.	4 L
1 lb.	16 oz.	500 g
2 lb.	32 oz.	1000 g or 1 kg

same amount expressed in a different way, using a different unit of measure. For example, 16 ounces is the same amount as 1 pound or about 500 grams. **Figure 46.1** lists some common equivalents.

Another type of equivalent chart is found in many cookbooks. This type of chart is useful when you want to compare a specific food's weight to its volume or to compare one form of the food to another. For example, suppose a recipe calls for 6 cups (1.5 L) of cored, sliced apples. Using a food equivalent chart, you can calculate that you'll need to buy about 2 lb. (1 kg) of apples.

Measuring Equipment

Many different tools are used for measuring, and each plays a vital part in food preparation. **Figure 46.2** shows common measuring tools and describes their uses. Always use standard equipment when measuring. Serving or eating utensils, such as teacups, will not give accurate results.

Measuring Techniques

Correct measurements depend on using the right equipment in the proper way. Different techniques are used for measuring liquids, dry ingredients, and fats and for measuring by weight.

Liquid Ingredients

To measure liquids, use a clear glass or plastic liquid measuring cup. Place it on a level surface and add the liquid. Check the measurement at eye level by crouching down to look through the side of the cup. Never lift the cup to check the measurement, because you might tilt it and get an inaccurate reading. If necessary, pour some liquid out or add more until the liquid reaches the right mark on the cup.

REAL-LIFE APPLICATION

Ask students to imagine they want to use a recipe that calls for 4 oz. of flour. They don't have a kitchen scale, only measuring cups and spoons. However, the nutrition panel on the sack of flour lists one serving as a quarter of a cup, or 30 grams. How can they find out how much flour they need in an amount they can measure? *Convert grams to ounces to find how many ounces are in a quarter cup, then how many cups equal four ounces. Thirty grams is about one ounce, so they need about one cup of flour.*

Figure 46.2
MEASURING EQUIPMENT

Liquid measuring cups. Used to measure liquids, these are made of glass or clear plastic. Markings on the sides show portions of a cup, fluid ounces (fl. oz.), and milliliters (mL). Extra space at the top and a pouring spout help prevent spills. Common sizes include 1 cup (250 mL) and 2 cups (500 mL).

Dry measuring cups. Used to measure dry ingredients, these are made of plastic or metal and are usually sold in sets. A typical customary set includes ¼ cup, ⅓ cup, ½ cup, and 1 cup sizes. A typical metric set includes 50 mL, 125 mL, and 250 mL sizes.

Measuring spoons. These are used to measure small amounts of liquid and dry ingredients. They usually come in sets. Customary sets include ¼ tsp., ½ tsp., 1 tsp., and 1 Tbsp. sizes. Metric sets include 1 mL, 2 mL, 5 mL, 15 mL, and 25 mL sizes.

Kitchen scale. Used to measure ingredients by weight, these are usually marked in both customary and metric units. Both electronic and traditional scales are available.

Meat thermometer. This measures the internal temperature of meat or poultry to determine when it has finished cooking. Many thermometers show both degrees Fahrenheit (°F) and degrees Celsius (°C). They also indicate the recommended final temperatures for a variety of meats and poultry.

RETEACHING
■ **The Systematic Sort.** Make a chart on the board with the column headings Volume, Weight, Temperature, and Length and rows labeled Customary and Metric. Read the different units of measurement mentioned on pp. 453-454 and have students tell you where in the chart each belongs.

ENRICHMENT
■ **An Eye for Measurement.** Measure different amounts of dry ingredients and place them on a sheet of paper. Have students identify the amount by placing the correct measuring tool beside the ingredient.

CROSS-CURRICULAR ACTIVITY
Language Arts

Ask students to imagine they are writing a letter to a friend about a visit to a European country. Have them mention different instances of using metric measurements in daily life in that country. Observations need not be confined to cooking situations. Ask volunteers to read their letters to the class.

DID YOU KNOW?

Cookbook writer Fannie Farmer revolutionized cooking when, in 1896, her self-published *Boston Cooking School Cook Book* introduced precise measurement to the American kitchen. Known as "the mother of level measurement," she replaced terms such as *handful* and *dash* *with level tablespoon and ¼ teaspoon.* She told cooks to "bake at 400 degrees for 30 minutes" instead of "bake until done." Thanks to Farmer, even inexperienced American cooks could follow a recipe with success.

Topics on pp. 454, 456-458:

- Measuring Techniques
- Adjusting Measurements

Checking Comprehension

✓ How should you measure dry ingredients? *Fill measuring cup or spoon above brim; level off with flat side of knife or spatula.*

✓ Briefly explain measuring fats by water displacement. *Combine enough water and desired amount of fat to equal one cup.*

✓ Give three tips for adjusting recipes. *Write ingredient adjustments first; adjust equipment; adjust cooking time.*

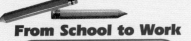

From School to Work

Have students read "Math Applications" and discuss the questions. Ask: What other math skills might you need for baking? Point out that finding the volume of pans can also be useful.

Answers to Assessing . . .

1. Answers may include: measure 7 ½ tsp.; measure ¼ cup and subtract 4 ½ tsp.
2. Answers may include: use 6 Tbsp.; measure ¼ cup and add 2 Tbsp.

Why must you check the measurement of a liquid at eye level while the container is on a level surface?

Small amounts of liquid are measured with measuring spoons. Select the correct size spoon and fill it to the brim. As you do, hold the spoon away from the bowl of other ingredients. If any extra spills over, it won't fall into what you are making. An extra amount of any ingredient could affect the results.

When measuring honey, syrups, and other thick liquids, coat the measuring cup or spoon first with cooking spray or a bit of cooking oil. You'll be able to remove all of the liquid more easily. Use a rubber scraper, if needed.

Dry Ingredients

Dry ingredients—such as flour, sugar, baking powder, and spices—can be measured in dry measuring cups or in measuring spoons. Select the correct size cup or spoon. Hold it over waxed paper or the ingredient's container to catch any spills. Fill it slightly above the brim. Then use a knife or spatula to level it off even with the top of the cup or spoon.

Sometimes recipes call for an amount that is smaller than your smallest measuring spoon. Suppose that your recipe calls for ⅛ tsp., and you have only a ¼ tsp. measure. Fill and level the ¼ tsp. measuring spoon. Then use a knife to divide the ingredient amount in half, and push one half off the spoon.

The following dry ingredients require special measuring techniques:

- **Flour.** Always spoon flour gently into a dry measuring cup. Avoid dipping the cup into the flour or shaking it once you have filled it. This causes the flour to pack down and gives you more than the required amount. If the recipe calls for sifted flour, sift the flour onto waxed paper, and then measure it.
- **Brown sugar.** Spoon the sugar into a dry measuring cup, and press the sugar down firmly. Continue adding and packing down sugar until the cup is slightly more than full. Level off the top.

Solid Fats

Fats, such as butter, margarine, and shortening, can be measured several ways:

- You can spoon the fat into a dry measuring cup, packing it firmly. Level off the top, then scrape it out using a rubber spatula.
- A second technique is the water displacement method. To measure ¼ cup of shortening, for example, fill a liquid measuring cup to the ¾ cup mark with water. Add the fat until the water level reaches the 1 cup

MORE ABOUT Equivalents

With recipes asking for so many different forms and measures of ingredients, knowing these basic equivalents can save time and trouble:

3 medium apples = 1 lb.
1 slice bread = ¼ c. fine dry crumbs

2 sticks butter or margarine = 1 cup
4 oz. semihard cheese = 1 cup shredded
1 square baking chocolate = 1 oz.
3 ½ c. all-purpose flour = 1 lb.
1 c. dry kidney beans = 6 c. cooked
1 c. uncooked noodles = 1 ¾ c. cooked

line (¾ cup water + ¼ cup shortening = 1 cup). Then drain the water and remove the shortening with a rubber scraper.

- The stick method can be used for fat that comes in ¼-lb. (125-g) sticks. The wrappers on these sticks are marked in tablespoons, and you can cut off the amount you need.

Measuring by Weight

If a recipe specifies an amount by weight, such as 1 lb. (0.5 kg) of turkey, you may not need to measure at all. The weights of many packaged foods are given on the label. If you do need to weigh the ingredient, use a kitchen scale. First place an appropriate empty container on the scale. Turn the adjustment knob until the scale reads zero. Then add the ingredient to the container until the scale shows the desired amount.

Adjusting Measurements

Sometimes you need to prepare a recipe for more or fewer people than the recipe serves. In these cases, you might adapt the recipe by adjusting its measurements.

Adjusting measurements works well for mixtures of foods, such as stews, salads, casseroles, and some desserts. Ingredient amounts can be rounded up or down without affecting results. For example, if your con-

From School to Work

Math Applications

What You Learn Today . . .

Throughout your school years, you have been learning math skills. These skills can help you do well in many classes. They also help you to solve practical problems, such as estimating your car's gas mileage and comparing supermarket prices.

. . . You Can Use Tomorrow

Almost every job involves some knowledge of math. A salesclerk needs to make change and may keep track of inventory. A construction contractor has to calculate the amount and cost of building materials. Of course, math is basic to accounting and banking. In any field, using math skills to help solve problems and save money is essential.

Practicing Your Skills

In the class you are now taking, you use and practice math skills when working with recipes. When adjusting a recipe, you may end up with amounts that aren't included in conversion charts. You may also find that you do not have a measuring tool marked with the amount. You can still make the recipe work.

For example, suppose you are dividing recipe ingredients by two. The original recipe asks for ⅓ cup yogurt. Dividing by two gives you ⅙ cup. How would you measure that? You need to convert it to smaller units, such as tablespoons or teaspoons. Knowing there are 16 Tbsp. in 1 cup, and 3 tsp. in 1 Tbsp., you can make the following calculations:

⅙ cup x 16 Tbsp.	=	16/6 Tbsp.
	=	8/3 Tbsp.
	=	2 ⅔ Tbsp.
	=	2 Tbsp. + 2 tsp.

Suppose again that you need to measure ⅝ cup of flour. You could measure part of the amount in a ½ cup measure (½ = 4/8), leaving ⅛ cup to convert into smaller units. You would calculate:

⅛ cup x 16 Tbsp.	=	16/8 Tbsp.
	=	2 Tbsp.

You would add 2 Tbsp. to ½ cup for ⅝ cup.

Assessing Your Skills

1. How would you measure 2 ½ Tbsp. of flour if you did not have a tablespoon available?
2. How would you measure ⅜ cup of water?

Activities

■ **Well Adjusted.** Give students a recipe that is easy to adjust. Have them increase or decrease the recipe by halves, thirds, or quarters. *(Problem Solving)*

Acting Responsibly

Have students read "Are You Careful?" on page 458 and discuss the questions. Ask them to describe situations where ignoring details could cause an entire task to fail.

Answers to Your Analysis

1. Any three: he began preparations early; increased ingredients exactly; included extra serving; followed recipe; checked pans for fit.
2. Shows concern for producing good result; for others' enjoyment, convenience, or safety.
3. Answers may include: patience, good judgment, respect for self and others.

REAL-LIFE APPLICATION

Read this to students: *Moira is preparing a stew recipe that instructs her to cut the meat and vegetables into one-inch (2.5-cm) cubes. Moira wants larger pieces, so she cuts the ingredients to about twice that size. She follows the rest of the recipe as it is written.* Ask: How will this change affect the stew, if at all? Help students see that larger pieces take longer to cook. Unless Moira cooks the stew longer, she risks serving an unsavory—and possibly unsafe—meal.

Review

■ **Chapter Review.** Use the contents of the Chapter Review page to help students review concepts, think critically, and apply their knowledge.

■ **Study Guide.** Have students complete the Study Guide for Chapter 46 on p. 153 of the Student Workbook.

■ **Spoonful of Sugar?** Copy a recipe on the board. For each ingredient, have students identify an appropriate measuring tool and describe the measuring procedure. Ask: How might doubling or halving the recipe affect the tools used for each ingredient? How might it affect pan size? Baking time?

Evaluation

■ **Chapter Test.** Use the reproducible chapter test provided in the Teacher's Classroom Resources or create your own test using the *Testmaker Software.*

■ **Alternative Assessment.** Ask students to create or redesign a measuring tool to make it more useful for the functions discussed in this chapter, including measuring both metric and customary units; measuring by weight; and measuring dry and liquid ingredients. Have students describe these features in writing and with sketches.

■ **Must-Haves.** Ask students to choose five measuring tools as most essential and to write a paragraph defending their choice.

version calls for half an egg, you could use a whole egg without causing a problem. Recipes for certain baked products, however, such as breads and cakes, may be harder to adapt. Good results depend on exact proportions of ingredients.

Use your math skills to find out how much to increase or decrease the ingredients in the recipe that you want to adjust. For example, if your recipe makes 4 servings and you need 8, multiply all ingredient amounts by 2. If the recipe yields 12 servings and you need only 4, divide each figure by 3. Then convert the results to amounts that are easy to measure. For example, you may need to convert 12 Tbsp. of sugar to ¾ cup.

The following pointers will help you achieve good results when you adjust recipes:

• Adjust the recipe before you begin to cook. Write down the adjusted measurements so you won't forget them as you follow the recipe.

• Make any needed adjustments in equipment. If you increase a recipe, you will need either more containers or larger containers for mixing and cooking. For smaller recipes, use smaller containers.

• Adjust the cooking time, if needed. Cooking time depends on the depth of food in the pan. If you double a casserole recipe and use a larger, deeper baking dish, the casserole will need to bake longer (but not twice as long). When doubling a recipe for bread or cake, it's better to use two pans of the original size and bake for the usual time.

Acting Responsibly

Are You Careful?

When you're in a hurry or beginning a large project, you may feel that you haven't the time to be careful, especially with details. Paying attention to all aspects of a job, however, can save you work, worry, and energy in the end.

Carefulness in Action

Gil was returning some notes that he had borrowed from Darnell. He found his friend poring over a cookbook, jotting down figures on a piece of paper.

"Your next chemistry experiment?" Gil joked.

"Not quite," Darnell explained. "My music teacher is retiring next month, so we're all giving him a surprise dinner. His wife told me this is his favorite recipe, but it only serves four. Since there'll be eleven of us, I'm tripling it, just to be sure."

Gil glanced at the recipe. "Hmm—chicken, pineapple, soy sauce. That sounds good. Spicy brown mustard might be better than plain."

"Maybe," Darnell replied, "but I know Mr. Weber likes this recipe, so I think I'll follow it." He took two nine-by-thirteen-inch dishes from the cupboard.

"These should hold six servings apiece." He arranged them in the oven. "Yes, these should work just right."

Gil shook his head. "You don't leave anything to chance."

Darnell shrugged. "I'm kind of new at this, and I just want to get it right."

"In that case," Gil said, "you really should try this recipe first. Now, my dad and I just happen to be free for dinner tomorrow . . ."

Your Analysis

1. Identify three ways in which Darnell showed carefulness.
2. How does carefulness show consideration for others?
3. What personal qualities are related to carefulness?

Focus on Citizenship Skills

Have students contact members of nonprofit groups to obtain their recipes for fund-raising meals. Discuss the recipes in class: the amounts of ingredients used; how are they measured; and how they compare to those used for family recipes. Ask: What other adjustments are necessary to prepare this meal? *(Number of utensils, size of pots and pans.)* Encourage students to volunteer to help prepare such a meal for a cause they support and to report the experience to the class.

Reviewing the Facts

1. Name the two major systems of measurement.
2. Give two examples each of customary and metric measurements for volume and weight.
3. Briefly describe four types of kitchen measuring equipment.
4. Explain the proper technique for measuring liquids.
5. How is measuring flour similar to measuring brown sugar? How is it different?
6. When adjusting recipes for smaller amounts, would you probably have more success with a recipe for chili or for biscuits? Why?

Thinking Critically

1. What might happen if you did not wash and dry a measuring spoon that you had used to measure one ingredient before dipping it into another ingredient?
2. Do you think more people in the United States should use the metric system for recipe measurements? Why or why not? What would be the advantages and disadvantages?

Applying Your Knowledge

1. **Computing Equivalents.** Using the information in Figure 46.1, compute metric equivalents for the following: 2 lb. pears, 8 oz. grated cheese, 1½ cups applesauce, 4 fl. oz. milk. Prepare a two-column chart to record your equivalents.
2. **Practicing Measuring Techniques.** Working with a partner, take turns using standard measuring equipment to measure the following: ⅔ cup water, ⅛ tsp. salt, ½ cup flour, ¼ cup shortening, 12 oz. uncooked macaroni. Be sure to follow the techniques described in the chapter. Have your partner check your work.

3. **Finding Equivalent Information.** Look through cookbooks and other sources to find information about equivalents of foods in different forms. (For example, 4 large eggs equal 1 cup of eggs.) Compile a list of these equivalents that could be posted in your cooking class.

Making Connections

1. **Math.** Read the recipe for vegetable lasagna in Chapter 45. Imagine that you are going to serve the lasagna to 10 people instead of 4. Calculate how much of each ingredient you will need. Make a list of the amounts.
2. **Science.** Identify the units of measure, equipment, and techniques used in your school's science lab for measuring volume, weight, and temperature. How are they similar to those used for food preparation? How are they different and why?

Building Your Portfolio

Preparing a Brochure of Measuring Equipment
Prepare a brochure describing the features and uses of the pieces of measuring equipment that you have learned about in this chapter. Also include in the brochure pieces of equipment that you would like to see produced by a manufacturer, along with explanations of how these pieces would make meal preparation easier. You may include drawings of the pieces. Add the brochure to your portfolio.

ANSWERS TO REVIEWING THE FACTS

1. Customary and metric.
2. *Volume*: customary (any two)—teaspoon, tablespoon, fluid ounce, cup, pint, quart, gallon; metric—milliliter, liter. *Weight*: customary—ounce, pound; metric: gram, kilogram.
3. Any four: liquid measuring cups—glass or clear plastic, portions marked on side, extra space and spout for pouring, 1 and 2 cups (250 mL and 500 mL); dry measuring cups—plastic or metal, sold in sets of ¼, ⅓, ½ and 1 cup (50, 125, and 250 mL); measuring spoons—sets of ¼, ½, and 1 tsp. and 1 Tbsp. (1, 2, 5, 15, and 25 mL); kitchen scale—both customary and metric markings, traditional or electric; meat thermometer—both Fahrenheit and Celsius, final temperatures for meats and poultry.
4. Place cup on level surface, add liquid to desired mark, check measurement at eye level.
5. Both use dry measuring cup. Flour is spooned gently to avoid packing; brown sugar is purposely packed.
6. Chili. Mixtures of food can be varied with less effect on results; baked goods require more precise proportions.

ANSWERS TO THINKING CRITICALLY

1. Measurement of second ingredient would be affected if some of first ingredient stayed on tool. Supply of the second ingredient could be contaminated.
2. Advantages may include: would save time, effort and money associated with conversion in international trade; metric system is more logical, easier to learn. Disadvantages may include: conversion would cause initial confusion for individuals, expense for industry; may result in higher prices for consumers, at least temporarily.

Chapter Overview

Chapter 47 explains how to cut and mix foods for recipe preparation. It gives terms and describes techniques and tools for both skills, highlighting safety. Separating eggs and breading foods are also explained.

Motivator

■ **Recipe Skills Repertoire.** Choose a recipe that calls for some of the skills described in the chapter. Ask: What is the difference between sliced and diced apple? What tools shred cheese? Tell students that this chapter will help them master more preparation skills to make a greater variety of recipes.

Objectives

Discuss the chapter objectives on this page. Remind students that the objectives focus on important chapter concepts.

Vocabulary

Write the Terms to Learn on the board. Explain that all the terms are verbs that have special meanings in food preparation. Encourage students to suggest definitions for each term. Compare these with actual definitions in the chapter.

Chapter 47 — Preparation Skills

Terms to Learn

- beat
- chop
- cream
- cut in
- fold
- grate
- mince
- pare
- puree

Objectives

This chapter will help you to:

- Identify equipment and describe techniques used for cutting.
- List safety precautions to be followed when cutting.
- Identify equipment and describe techniques used for mixing.
- Give tips on mixing foods properly.
- Describe two special techniques used in food preparation.

460   UNIT 6   Food, Nutrition, and Wellness

CHAPTER RESOURCES

Student Workbook
Study Guide, p. 156
Activity, *Which Tools to Use?* p. 157

Teacher's Classroom Resources
Lesson Plan, p. 51

Extension #74, *Gathering Cooking Equipment,* p. 80
Life Skills, *Kitchen on a Shoestring,* p. 75
Chapter 47 Test, pp. 99-100

Performance Assessment, *Equipment for Cutting and Mixing,* p. 80
Reteaching, *Kitchen Terms,* p. 53

See Also:
ABCNews InterActive™ Videodiscs

Have you ever seen a professional chef prepare food? At some Japanese restaurants, you can watch as the food is prepared and cooked at your own table. The skillful way the chef cuts, cooks, and arranges foods is an impressive display of showmanship. A chef who can do this knows a great deal about food preparation—both techniques and equipment.

How does your knowledge compare? Do you know the difference between dicing and mincing? Can you distinguish between blending and folding? Each term names a technique for using certain equipment in specific ways to get the right results. When using a recipe, you will often find terms such as these. To follow the recipe and to get good results, you need to know:

- What the terms mean.
- What equipment to use.
- How to perform the necessary tasks correctly and safely.

Cutting Foods

Many food preparation tasks involve cutting food into smaller pieces. Specialized tools and appliances have been developed for this task. Knowing what each tool or appliance can do will help you choose the right one for each job.

This chapter will also help you understand cutting terminology—the difference between chopping and mincing, for example. Always follow safety rules when performing cutting tasks. The tools you use are sharp and can cause serious injury.

Equipment for Cutting

A well-stocked kitchen has several types of knives, most of which can be used for many tasks. Other tools—such as shears, peelers, and pizza wheels—are used for specific types of cutting jobs. In addition, cutting appliances such as blenders and food processors can be used to perform many tasks. The photographs in **Figure 47.1** on page 462 will help you identify the equipment used for cutting.

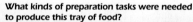
What kinds of preparation tasks were needed to produce this tray of food?

CHAPTER 47   Preparation Skills   461

Topics on p. 461:
- Cutting Foods

Checking Comprehension

✓ What must you know to get good results from a recipe? *Meaning of terms; equipment needed; how to perform tasks.*

✓ Why are there some may different types of cutting tools, such as pizza wheels? *Each has been developed for a specific type of cutting job.*

Activities

■ **Kitchen Cut-Ups.** Have groups list as many different kitchen cutting tools as they can think of. Invite groups to share their lists. If any list includes an unfamiliar tool, ask the student who suggested it to describe it to the class. *(Observation)*

■ **"Fracture Celery"?** Have students list words other than the vocabulary terms that describe ways of severing or breaking things into smaller pieces. Discuss which seem appropriate for recipes. *(Communication)*

MORE ABOUT Sharpening Knives

Sharp knives are essential to safe, efficient cutting. Newer devices for sharpening knives often leave nicks in the blade, so most experts recommend a sharpening steel—a long cylindrical tool with a brushed metal appearance. Many cooks sharpen knives this way before each use. Demonstrate correct use of a sharpening steel.

Topics on pp. 462-463:
- **Cutting Equipment**
- **Cutting Safety**

Checking Comprehension

✓ Give two reasons for using a cutting board. *Protects countertop, keeps food from slipping when cutting.*

✓ What is the best tool to use for cutting dried fruits? *Kitchen shears.*

✓ Explain which are safer—dull knives or sharp. *Sharp; dull knives more apt to slip, cause injury.*

✓ How should you catch a knife that you drop? *You shouldn't; let it fall.*

STRATEGIES THAT WORK

Making Do. Have students read "Making Do" and discuss the questions. Ask: When should you not substitute tools? Help students see that substitutions should not compromise safety.

Answers to Think . . .
1. Answers may include: it usually does job more easily and quickly; may be safer.
2. Answers will vary.
3. Answers may include: grater, chef's knife, paring knife.

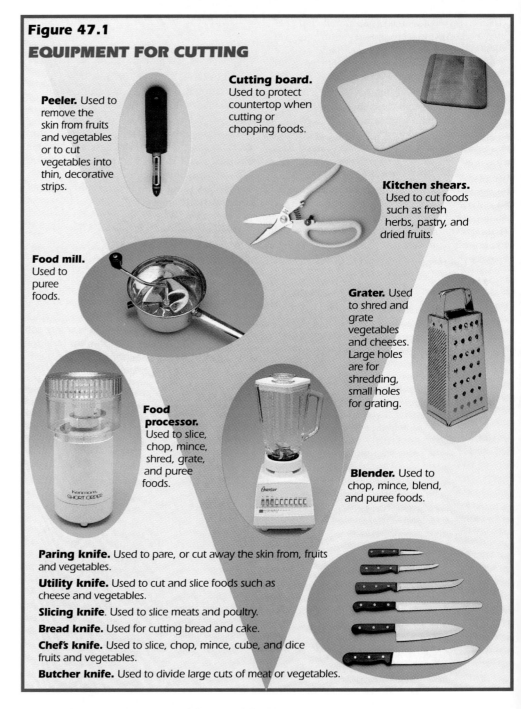

Figure 47.1
EQUIPMENT FOR CUTTING

Peeler. Used to remove the skin from fruits and vegetables or to cut vegetables into thin, decorative strips.

Cutting board. Used to protect countertop when cutting or chopping foods.

Kitchen shears. Used to cut foods such as fresh herbs, pastry, and dried fruits.

Food mill. Used to puree foods.

Grater. Used to shred and grate vegetables and cheeses. Large holes are for shredding, small holes for grating.

Food processor. Used to slice, chop, mince, shred, grate, and puree foods.

Blender. Used to chop, mince, blend, and puree foods.

Paring knife. Used to pare, or cut away the skin from, fruits and vegetables.

Utility knife. Used to cut and slice foods such as cheese and vegetables.

Slicing knife. Used to slice meats and poultry.

Bread knife. Used for cutting bread and cake.

Chef's knife. Used to slice, chop, mince, cube, and dice fruits and vegetables.

Butcher knife. Used to divide large cuts of meat or vegetables.

🔍 Focus on Safety Skills

These safety tips can help prevent injuries when cutting. First, always suit the knife to the task—use a heavy-bladed knife for large, dense foods, a light-bladed knife for smaller foods. When cutting potatoes, first cut them lengthwise, then place them on the cutting board cut-side down. This prevents slippage. Likewise, peel or slice a thin layer down the length of a carrot before cutting to help keep it in place.

Techniques for Cutting

When cutting food you need to know not only which tool to use but also what technique to apply. There are many different techniques for cutting food, ranging from slicing and dicing through peeling and shredding. By learning the terminology and practicing your skills, you can become an expert in cutting. **Figure 47.2** on page 464 shows techniques for cutting.

Safety When Cutting

Cutting requires the use of sharp knives and other hazardous equipment. Always follow these safety precautions in order to avoid accidents:

- Keep knives sharp. Dull knives are more likely to slip and may cause you to cut yourself.
- Always cut with the blade of the knife slanting away from you.
- Always hold foods with your fingertips tucked in.
- Always use a cutting board when you use a knife. Its surface has a rough texture that prevents foods from slipping.
- Never cut foods while holding them in your hand.
- If you drop a knife, step back and let it fall. Never try to catch it on the way down.
- Wash knives one at a time with the blade pointing away from your hand. Never place them in soapy water where they cannot be seen.

Making Do

You may not always have the right tool for a particular job. Even a professional kitchen—let alone a single household—doesn't always have all the tools and equipment needed. Substituting is the answer. Try these ideas if you can't find a:

- **Peeler.** Use a sharp paring knife to remove the skins of firm fruits and vegetables. Work carefully to peel only the skin and to avoid cutting yourself.
- **Wire whisk.** Try a fork or rotary beater for beating eggs. To blend a sauce or beat cake batter, use a long-handled spoon.
- **Sifter.** Use a fine mesh strainer to sift flour or other dry ingredients. Gently tap the strainer, or press the ingredients through with a spoon.
- **Pastry blender.** Try using two small knives to cut shortening into flour. Grasp one knife in each hand. Press your forefinger against the back to

steady it. Cross the knives in an X, then slice through the ingredients repeatedly, pulling the knives past each other as you cut. Occasionally push the mixture together again with the flat sides of the knives.

Making the Strategy Work

Think . . .

1. What are the advantages of using the proper kitchen tool if it is available?
2. If your kitchen could have just three different knives, what types would you choose? Why?
3. Name two hand tools that could be used to do some of the work done by a food processor.

Try...

Demonstrate the substitution principle for your class. Think of other specialized kitchen tools that might not always be available, such as a potato masher, a garlic press, a food mill, or a rolling pin. Show how a substitute tool or technique might work.

- **Try Your Technique.** Have students name and demonstrate one cutting technique. Have them tell what tool they are using and how it is suited to the task, as well as any precautions to take.

ENRICHMENT

- **Cut and Save.** Ask students to look through cooking magazines or catalogs for unusual cutting tools. Have students save and share their pictures or descriptions, possibly in a classroom display.

USING VISUALS

Refer students to the knives illustrated in Figure 47.1 on p. 462. Ask: Why do you think the bread knife blade is serrated? *To saw bread without tearing it.* Why do you think the blade of the butcher knife is shaped as it is? *Lets you make deep initial cut in large piece of meat.*

SPECIAL NEEDS
Strategies

English as a Second Language. Suggest that ESL students keep a notebook for listing terms and tools they are familiar with, in both their native language and English. Students might also draw pictures of tools that have no equivalent in their first language and write the English term beneath.

MORE ABOUT Knife Safety

The best-quality—and safest—knives are those with a blade that runs well into the tang, or handle, and is riveted in place. These blades are less likely to break off under pressure.

DID YOU KNOW?

To remove the skin from foods that resist a peeler, such as tomatoes and almonds, try blanching. Submerge the food in boiling water for 10 to 20 seconds; rinse in cold water. The skins should peel off quickly and easily.

Topics on pp. 464-465:

- Cutting Terms and Techniques
- Mixing Foods

Checking Comprehension

✓ Compare and contrast cubing and dicing. *Both involve slicing, stacking, and cutting foods in different directions; diced pieces are smaller.*

✓ Why do recipes call for different mixing methods? *Different methods produce different results.*

✓ How does the speed of mixing affect a recipe? *The higher the speed, the more air introduced into mixture.*

Figure 47.2

CUTTING TERMS AND TECHNIQUES

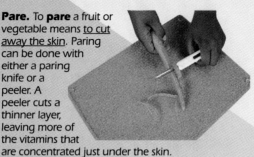

Pare. To **pare** a fruit or vegetable means <u>to cut away the skin</u>. Paring can be done with either a paring knife or a peeler. A peeler cuts a thinner layer, leaving more of the vitamins that are concentrated just under the skin.

Slice. A sharp knife and a cutting board are usually used to slice food. Steady the food with one hand or with a fork, and use the other hand to cut the food into thin, flat pieces. A food processor may be used to slice some foods.

Chop and mince. To **chop** food is <u>to cut it into small, irregular pieces</u>. The recipe may tell you what size pieces you need—coarse, medium, or fine. To **mince** is <u>to chop food until the pieces are as small as you can make them.</u> A food processor may also be used for chopping and mincing.

Cube and dice. To cube or dice foods, cut them in three directions. First, slice the food. Next, stack the slices, and cut them first in one direction and then the other. To cube, make the cuts about ½ in. (13 mm) apart. To dice, make the cuts about ¼ in. (6 mm) apart, or as specified in the recipe.

Puree. To **puree** (pyu-RAY) is <u>to mash food until it is smooth.</u> Vegetables are usually cooked before being pureed. Use a food mill, food processor, or blender to puree foods.

Shred and grate. Foods such as carrots and cheese can be shredded using a grater. When you push the food firmly across the grater's large holes, fine shreds will fall away. Foods such as lettuce and cabbage can be cut into shreds with a knife. A food processor—with the proper blade inserted—is useful for large shredding jobs. To **grate** food is to <u>make very small particles</u> by rubbing the food against the small holes of the grater.

464   UNIT 6   Food, Nutrition, and Wellness

Focus on Management Skills

Ask students how using different cutting tools and techniques in a recipe might affect meal planning. Dicing a food may take more time than chopping, for instance, but the food will cook more quickly. Ask students for other such examples Refer them to Chapter 41 for information on choosing recipes and Chapter 45 for a discussion on scheduling preparation tasks to generate ideas.

Managing Your Life

User-Friendly Kitchen Tools

Many of the tools described in this chapter are difficult for some people to use. Imagine someone with arthritis, for example, trying to use a vegetable peeler. Even a temporary injury can turn a common kitchen task into a challenge.

To overcome such problems, several companies produce lines of kitchen utensils that can help disabled people live independently. Here are a few examples:

- Knives and peelers with large, ribbed, rubber handles are easily gripped by a hand with limited motion. Some handles are angled to suit an inflexible wrist or can even be adjusted to fit a particular hand.
- Cutting boards equipped with suction cups keep them from sliding on the counter. Some have stainless steel spikes or raised edges to help keep food in place.
- Power peelers work with very little pressure.
- Lightweight electric mixers with rechargeable batteries are good for one-handed use; they also save users from having to reach for an electrical outlet.

- Some can and jar openers can be worked with one hand.

Sometimes you can solve the problem by applying ingenuity to equipment you already have. If your hand cannot grip a knife firmly, wrapping the handle with a cloth may give you a more comfortable grasp. Arrange the cloth to keep it clear of your work and tape it securely. A damp cloth or a nonslip rubber mat placed under a cutting board or a mixing bowl helps hold it steady if you cannot.

Applying the Principles

1. An older neighbor who enjoys cooking now has trouble seeing small details, such as the print in cookbooks and the lines on measuring cups. How might this difficulty be overcome?
2. Aside from the practical value, why is it important that people with disabilities be able to work in the kitchen?

- When working with a food processor or blender, don't put your hand or a tool inside while the blades are moving or the motor is turned on.

Mixing Foods

Mixing, or combining ingredients, is a skill frequently used in food preparation. A recipe should clearly explain how and in what order to combine the ingredients. Stirring slowly will produce very different results from beating vigorously. These are just two of the common mixing methods used in food preparation.

Equipment for Mixing

Mixing tools include bowls, spoons, and other stirring tools. Some mixing tasks require specialized equipment, such as an electric mixer. **Figure 47.3** on page 466 highlights the equipment most often used for mixing. Blenders and food processors, shown earlier, also may be used for mixing.

Techniques for Mixing

When mixing foods, you need to know the speed at which the mixing should be done. The speed of mixing affects the amount of air that is introduced into the mixture. High-

CHAPTER 47   Preparation Skills   465

Topics on pp. 466-468:
• **Mixing Equipment**
• **Mixing Terms and Techniques**
• **Special Techniques**

Checking Comprehension

✓ For what is a pastry blender used? *To cut shortening into flour for biscuits and pie crusts.*

✓ Describe two ways of breading foods. *Roll food in coating; add food to breading mixture in plastic bag, close tightly and shake.*

✓ Why do you fold ingredients into a mixture? *To keep the air in air-filled ingredient.*

CROSS-CURRICULAR ACTIVITY
Music

Play students excerpts from Rimsky-Korsakov's "Flight of the Bumblebee." Ask how the music is reminiscent of its title. Encourage students to find selections from musical pieces that likewise describe mixing tasks explained on p. 486 and to share them with the class.

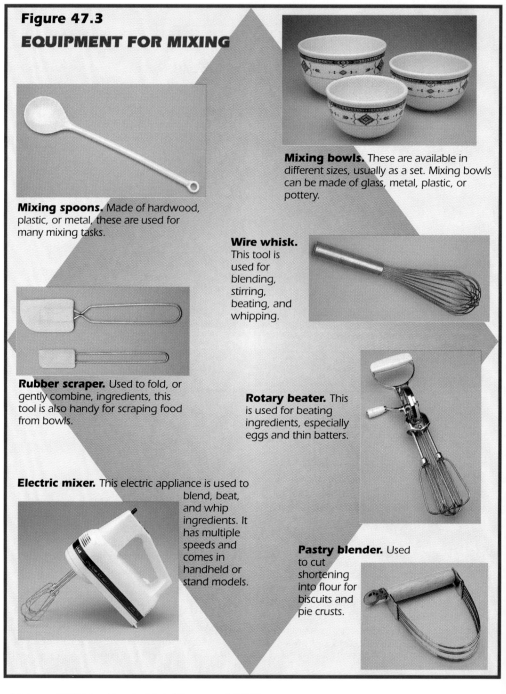

Figure 47.3
EQUIPMENT FOR MIXING

Mixing spoons. Made of hardwood, plastic, or metal, these are used for many mixing tasks.

Mixing bowls. These are available in different sizes, usually as a set. Mixing bowls can be made of glass, metal, plastic, or pottery.

Wire whisk. This tool is used for blending, stirring, beating, and whipping.

Rubber scraper. Used to fold, or gently combine, ingredients, this tool is also handy for scraping food from bowls.

Rotary beater. This is used for beating ingredients, especially eggs and thin batters.

Electric mixer. This electric appliance is used to blend, beat, and whip ingredients. It has multiple speeds and comes in handheld or stand models.

Pastry blender. Used to cut shortening into flour for biscuits and pie crusts.

466   **UNIT 6   Food, Nutrition, and Wellness**

MORE ABOUT Separating Eggs

When separating more than one egg, catch each white in a separate bowl before adding it to the others. That way, you can keep stray bits of yolk from making the rest of the whites unusable.

DID YOU KNOW?

Choose mixing bowls carefully for beating egg whites. Using an aluminum bowl will cause the whites to turn gray. Whites may not beat to full volume in plastic bowls if they still contain any oil from previous foods. Glass and stainless teel are good choices.

speed mixing usually introduces more air than mixing at slow speeds. **Figure 47.4** on page 468 illustrates and describes mixing techniques.

Tips for Mixing

Proper mixing of ingredients contributes to good-tasting results. Here are some mixing tips:

- Choose a bowl that is the right size for the job. Base your decision on both the amount of the ingredients and the method of mixing. Beating or whipping will require a larger bowl than stirring.
- Choose the best tool or appliance for the job. You might use a wire whisk to blend eggs but an electric mixer to make cookie dough.
- Place a wet cloth under your mixing bowl to keep it from sliding.
- When adding dry ingredients to a wet mixture, add a small amount at a time. Mix until the dry ingredients disappear before adding more.
- Use a rubber scraper to remove food from a mixing bowl.

Special Techniques

Two other techniques used in food preparation deserve special mention. Mastering these techniques will be useful for many recipes:

- **Separating eggs.** When you separate an egg you divide the white from the yolk. The most sanitary method is to use a tool called an egg separator. Lay the egg separator across the rim of a small bowl. Then tap the egg lightly on the edge of the bowl—just enough to crack one side of the shell. Hold the egg over the round part of the egg separator and carefully pull apart the halves of the shell. Gently transfer the yolk to the egg separator, allowing the white to drip into the bowl. Place the yolk in a separate dish.
- **Breading.** Foods such as fish and chicken are sometimes breaded, or covered with a light layer of flour, crumbs, or cornmeal before cooking. You can either roll the food in the coating or place the breading mixture in a plastic bag, add the food, close the bag tightly, and shake.

When separating an egg, work gently so that you do not break the yolk.

CHAPTER 47   *Preparation Skills*   **467**

Activities

RETEACHING

■ **Tools of Choice.** Have students read recipes to identify tasks that require mixing tools. Have them tell what tool or tools they might use for each task, and why.

ENRICHMENT

■ **Mixed Results.** Choose a recipe for a baked good that could be mixed with an electric mixer, a spoon, or a whisk. Have small groups each use one of the tools to make the recipe. Have the class compare the results for taste, texture, and appearance. What might account for one method producing better results, in this recipe or in others?

CROSS-CURRICULAR ACTIVITY

Language Arts

A single term may have many different meanings, depending on the field of study it refer to. Challenge students to find examples of this with regards to mixing terms. What is the scientific definition of a mixture? What does beat mean to a musician?

REAL-LIFE APPLICATION

Read this to students:

Looking through her grandmother's recipes, Greta came across a cake recipe that she wanted to try. The ingredients included sugar, shortening, eggs, flour, spices, baking soda, and buttermilk. However, the directions read simply "Mix all together." Ask: How might Greta decide now to procede? What different tools and techniques might Greta use to mix these ingredients? Refer students to p. 466 and p. 468 for guidance.

Review

■ **Chapter Review.** Use the contents of the Chapter Review page to help students review concepts, think critically, and apply their knowledge.

■ **Study Guide.** Have students complete the Study Guide for Chapter 47 on p. 156 of the Student Workbook.

■ **"Dice Until Blended."** Have groups choose a recipe and rewrite it, mixing up all the cutting and mixing terms or techniques. Have groups exchange and correct recipes to make sense.

Evaluation

■ **Chapter Test.** Use the reproducible chapter test provided in the Teacher's Classroom Resources or create your own test using the *Testmaker Software*.

■ **Alternative Assessment.** Have groups perform skits depicting customers and sales staff in a cookware shop. The situations and dialogue created should allow students to show what they have learned from the chapter about cutting and mixing ingredients.

■ **All-Purpose Advice.** Ask students to review the techniques described in this chapter. Have them suggest three general guidelines, applicable to all techniques, for performing these tasks safely and efficiently.

Figure 47.4

MIXING TERMS AND TECHNIQUES

Stir. This is a slow mixing technique done in a circular motion with a spoon or a wire whisk.

Blend. To blend is to thoroughly combine two or more ingredients until the mixture has a uniform appearance. Blending may be done with a spoon, wire whisk, egg beater, electric mixer, or electric blender.

Beat. To **beat** is <u>to mix ingredients vigorously, which introduces air into them.</u> To beat by hand with a spoon or wire whisk, use a quick, circular, over-and-under motion that lifts the mixture on each rotation, adding air. Beating can also be done with a rotary beater or electric mixer.

Whip. Whipping is a very rapid beating that incorporates so much air that it increases the volume of the product. For example, whipped cream is twice the volume of the original heavy cream. To whip, use a wire whisk, rotary beater, or electric mixer.

Cream. To **cream** is <u>to beat shortening or another fat with sugar until the mixture is light and fluffy.</u> Creaming is done with a spoon, a rotary beater, or an electric mixer.

Fold. Use a spoon or rubber scraper to **fold**, or <u>gently add an air-filled ingredient to a mixture.</u> For example, you might fold whipped egg whites into cake batter. Gently cut down through the mixture and across the bottom. Then, without lifting the utensil out, bring some of the mixture up and over. Repeat, keeping the utensil in the mixture, until the ingredients are combined.

Cut in. To **cut in** is <u>to mix a solid fat, such as shortening, with dry ingredients using a cutting motion.</u> You can use a pastry blender or two knives for this task.

Toss. To toss a salad, tumble the ingredients lightly together using a spoon or fork. This delicate handling keeps the lettuce from bruising.

468 **UNIT 6 Food, Nutrition, and Wellness**

Focus on Consumer Skills

Point out that many of the cutting and mixing tools described in this chapter duplicate tasks. Have students identify examples of this and select those tools that would allow them to perform all of the tasks described in the chapter without buying unnecessary equipment.

Review

Reviewing the Facts

1. Name and describe the functions of six types of knives.
2. What are the differences between chopping, mincing, and cubing?
3. List four safety rules for cutting foods.
4. What tools could you use to blend, to beat, and to fold?
5. How do you separate an egg?

Thinking Critically

1. Why do you think that there are so many specific terms for cutting and mixing? What might happen to people who don't understand them?
2. Compare the advantages and disadvantages of using a hand tool instead of an electric appliance for cutting or mixing. Give some examples to back up your reasoning.

Applying Your Knowledge

1. **Identifying Words.** Prepare a 20-term matching exercise or crossword puzzle, using words for food preparation techniques and equipment that you learned in this chapter. Exchange your paper with a classmate to see how well you both know your terms.
2. **Making Comparisons.** Use an electric mixer to prove the connection between the speed of mixing and the amount of air introduced into the food product. Pour a small amount of heavy cream into a mixing bowl, and mix for 1/2 minute on a slow speed. Observe the effect. Now mix for 1/2 minute at a fast speed. Write a brief report of your findings.
3. **Recommending Equipment.** A friend is moving into her own apartment and asks your advice on buying cutting and mixing equipment. The friend has a limited budget and wants to buy only essentials. Based on

what you have learned in this chapter and on your own experiences at home, write your recommendations, giving specific reasons for your selections.

Making Connections

1. **Health.** Working with knives can be dangerous. Follow safety rules, but know what to do in case an accident occurs. Using a book on first aid as your source, find out the recommended emergency procedures for dealing with cuts. Present your findings in class.
2. **Social Studies.** Find a book in the library on the cuisine of a particular country or culture, such as India or Japan. As you look through the book, find descriptions of food preparation tasks that are different from those described in this textbook. Write down two of the tasks, and describe or demonstrate them to the class.

Building Your Portfolio

Designing a "How-to" Booklet for Mixing

Have you ever seen one of the special cookbooks designed just for young children? These colorful cookbooks usually have simple directions, as well as clear pictures that show how to perform certain tasks. Choose two mixing tasks mentioned in this chapter. Design a booklet that would describe simply how to perform these tasks. Use color and simple drawings to make your booklet interesting. When it is finished, add the booklet to your portfolio.

CHAPTER 47   Preparation Skills   469

ANSWERS TO REVIEWING THE FACTS

1. *Paring*—cut skin from fruits and vegetables; *utility knife*—cut and slice; *slicing knife*—slice meats and poultry; *bread*—cut bread and cake; *chef's*—slice, chop, mince, cube, and dice; *butcher*—divide large cuts of meat or vegetables.
2. *Chopping*—cutting food into small, irregular pieces; *mincing*—cutting pieces as small as possible; *cubing*—cutting food into half-inch (13-mm) cubes.
3. Any four: Keep knives sharp; cut with blade slanting away; keep fingertips tucked in; use cutting board; never cut foods in your hand; never try to catch falling knife; wash knives one at a time with blade pointing away; don't put hand or tool inside running food processor or blender.
4. *Blend*—spoon, wire whisk, egg beater, electric mixer, electric blender; *beat*—spoon, wire whisk, rotary beater, electric mixer; *fold*—spoon, rubber scraper.
5. Set egg separator across rim of bowl; tap egg on edge of bowl to crack one side; allow yolk to slip into separator while white drips into bowl below.

ANSWERS TO THINKING CRITICALLY

1. There are many terms because there are many different techniques, some of which produce very different results. People who don't understand terms risk spoiling a recipe.
2. Answers may include: hand tool saves electricity, is easier to clean and learn to use, but takes longer to perform task. Electric appliance is easier to use and performs task more quickly, but costs more to buy, run, and replace. Examples will vary.

Chapter 48

Chapter Overview

Chapter 48 describes various types of cookware and bakeware and their uses. It explains the basic methods of cooking food and provides guidelines for determining doneness.

Motivator

■ **Panoramic Views.** Bring in a few of the cookware and bakeware items described in this chapter. Ask: How is this used? What features do you think make it especially fit for that use? Explain that this chapter will help students learn not only about cooking methods and equipment, but how to match the two for successful results.

Objectives

Discuss the chapter objectives on this page. Remind students that the objectives focus on important chapter concepts.

Vocabulary

Point out that the terms *sauté* and *braise* are of French origin. French cooking has long been considered the height of elegant cuisine—another French word—but the techniques are used in any number of recipes and can be learned by most cooks.

Chapter 48 Cooking Techniques

Terms to Learn

- boil
- braise
- broil
- casserole
- poach
- sauté
- simmer
- steamer
- stir-fry

Objectives

This chapter will help you to:

- Identify **equipment used for cooking and baking.**
- Compare and contrast **different methods of cooking using moist heat, dry heat, and fat.**
- Explain **how to determine when foods are done.**

CHAPTER RESOURCES

Student Workbook

Study Guide, pp. 158-159

Activity, *A Day at the Restaurant,* pp. 160-161

Teacher's Classroom Resources

Lesson Plan, p. 52

Cooperative Learning, *Cooking Techniques,* pp. 55-56

Extension #75, *The Tool for the Task,* p. 81

Life Skills, *What Did I Do Wrong?* p. 76

Chapter 48 Test, pp. 101-102

Performance Assessment, *Cooking Equipment and Methods,* p. 81

Reteaching, *Cookware and Bakeware,* p. 54

Have you ever had a boiled steak or a roasted egg in its shell? What about broiled spaghetti? You can probably tell just by reading this that these foods wouldn't be very appealing. Boiled steak would be watery and grayish. A roasted egg would probably explode. Broiled spaghetti would be crisp and inedible. Why?

There are many different ways to apply heat to foods. Each method has characteristics that make it a good choice for cooking some foods and a poor choice for others. When you know these characteristics, you can choose the best method for a particular food. This chapter describes equipment and techniques used in conventional (nonmicrowave) cooking. Microwave equipment and techniques are discussed in the next chapter. Chapters 50 through 53 explain in more detail how all of these techniques can be used to cook various foods.

Cooking Equipment

Will you heat food in cookware or bakeware? It depends on what you are preparing and the cooking method chosen.

Cookware and Bakeware

Items used for cooking on top of the range, such as pots and pans, are called cookware. Bakeware is used in the oven. Some items can be used as both cookware and bakeware. Cookware items come in many sizes. They have some similarities, however.

- Most have covers to retain steam and nutrients during cooking.
- Most have handles for safe and easy lifting when the pot or pan is hot. A saucepan has a long handle that you can lift with one hand. Larger pots have a small handle on each side. Use these han-

These tools will make cooking easier.

Colander. Used to drain liquid from foods, such as vegetables or cooked pasta.
Strainer. Used to remove solid particles from liquids, such as broth.
Steamer. Used inside a covered saucepan to steam vegetables.

Tongs. Used to lift and turn hot foods without piercing the food.
Cooling rack. Used to cool cakes, cookies, and breads.
Turner. Used to flip foods, such as pancakes and hamburgers.
Ladle. Used to dip out soup or stew.
Long-handled fork. Used to lift or turn hot foods.
Cooking spoon. Used to stir hot foods.
Slotted spoon. Used to lift food out of a liquid.

CHAPTER 48   Cooking Techniques   471

Topics on p. 471:
- **Features of Cookware and Bakeware**
- **Helpful Tools**

Checking Comprehension

✓ Why are different cooking methods used for different foods? *Each method has characteristics that make it better for some foods than for others.*

✓ What is the difference between cookware and bakeware? *Cookware is used on top of range; bakeware in oven.*

✓ Describe two features found on most cookware items. *Covers to retain steam and nutrients; handles for safe and easy handling.*

Activities

■ **Pan Appreciation.** Ask students to list the foods in their favorite meal and then all the cookware and bakeware used to prepare them. How aware are students of the items needed to create the foods they enjoy? *(Observation)*

■ **Just What I Need.** Have students review recipes for tasks that require the tools shown on p. 471. Have them identify the task and the tool needed to complete it. *(Management)*

Checking Comprehension

✓ Why is it good to know what material cookware or bakeware is made of? *Material affects looks, heating properties, durability, care.*

✓ What is the difference between a pot and a saucepan? *Pot has two handles; saucepan has one long handle.*

✓ What might you bake in a loaf pan? *Bread, cake, meat loaf.*

Dutch oven. Large, heavy pot used for slow cooking of meats and poultry.
Griddle. Flat surface used for cooking eggs and pancakes.
Skillet. Low-sided pan; has a handle and usually a cover; comes in several sizes. Used for frying foods.

Double boiler. Two saucepans, the inside one for the food, the outer one for water. Used for heating foods that burn easily.
Saucepan. Comes in several sizes; has one long handle and a cover. Many uses.
Pot. Larger than most saucepans; has two handles and a cover. Used for cooking pasta, soups, and corn on the cob.

 Cookware is used on the range.

dles to lift the pot with both hands. Always use a hot pad or mitt when lifting cookware that has been on the range. Even if the handle is not hot, the metal pot will be.

Like pieces of cookware, bakeware items come in many sizes. Some dishes, called **casseroles,** *can be used for both cooking and serving.* Casseroles usually have covers and small handles. Other pieces of bakeware, such as loaf pans, may have a ridge around the edge to allow you to grip them easily. Hot pads or mitts are essential for removing bakeware from the oven.

Know Your Materials

Cookware and bakeware can be made from many different materials. Each material has its own characteristics. These affect how it looks, how well it conducts heat, how long it will last, and how it should be cleaned. The thickness of some materials also affects cooking quality.

Many cookware and bakeware items are made of aluminum or stainless steel, but enamel, cast iron, glass, and plastic are also used. Each material has advantages and disadvantages.

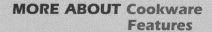

DID YOU KNOW?

The oldest nonstick material is soapstone, or steatite. It has been used for hundreds of years, particularly for griddles. This rock is made up mostly of talc, so it is easily shaped and slightly oily—two excellent qualities in a nonstick surface.

MORE ABOUT Cookware Features

For safety and efficiency, cookware should have heat-resistant, easy-to-grasp handles or knobs and snug-fitting covers to hold in steam. The bottom should be flat to heat evenly and help keep the item from tipping over.

Roasting pan. Large, shallow pan with rack. Used for roasting meat and poultry.
Broiler pan. Shallow pan with slotted grid for fat to drip through when broiling foods.
Casserole. Dish used for baking and serving. Comes in a variety of shapes and sizes.
Loaf pan. Deep, rectangular pan. Used for baking bread, cake, or meat loaf.

Baking sheet. Large, flat metal pan, sometimes with narrow sides. Used for baking cookies.
Muffin pan. Has individual cups for baking muffins or cupcakes.
Pie pan. Round pan with sloping sides. Used for baking pies.
Cake pan. Round, square, or rectangular in shape. Used for baking cakes, brownies, and bar cookies.

 **Bakeware is used in the oven.**

- Aluminum is both lightweight and durable and heats rapidly and evenly. It darkens and stains easily, however.
- Stainless steel is attractive, tough, durable, and easy to clean, but it heats slowly and unevenly.
- Enamel pots and pans are attractive, but they may chip easily, and most cannot be scoured.
- Cast-iron pots and skillets are durable and heat well, but they are heavy and may rust if they are not dried thoroughly.
- Glass and glass-ceramic items are durable and attractive. Many can go from freezer to oven to table and are microwave-safe. If dropped, however, they may chip or break.
- Plastic cookware is durable, stain-resistant, and easy to clean. Some plastic equipment, however, is intended for microwave ovens only and is not suitable for use in conventional ovens.

Many cookware and bakeware items are available with nonstick surfaces. These surfaces make cleanup easy. They also allow you to brown or fry some foods without using fat. Nonstick surfaces scratch easily, however, so always use nylon or plastic utensils with them.

CHAPTER 48   Cooking Techniques   473

Checking Comprehension

✓ When might you cook with moist heat? *When food needs to absorb water; to tenderize; to blend flavors.*

✓ Why is boiling not advised for most foods? *Causes nutrient loss, overcooking.*

✓ Why is poaching a good choice for tender foods? *Uses small amount of simmering liquid so foods keep shape.*

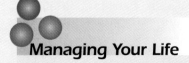

Managing Your Life

Have students read "Stocking Your Kitchen" and discuss the questions. Ask: How do the needs and concerns of established households compare with those of young singles?

Answers to Applying ...

1. Answers will vary but should include small, basic, useful items.
2. Answers may include: friend may know your needs better; is not interested in selling particular product.
3. Answers may include: plan is successful if cookware meets needs; if all items are useful.

Managing Your Life

Stocking Your Kitchen

When you're ready to buy your first items of cookware and bakeware, you may face two obstacles: lack of experience and a limited budget. This need not stop you from stocking your kitchen well, however. All you need is a management plan.

How will you know which items to buy? Start by thinking of what you like to eat and what you can cook. Write down the sizes of pots, pans, and other items that you might use to prepare those foods. Also note any equipment that you already own.

Next, check on the items' availability and cost. Buying a packaged set of cookware usually costs less than buying the same pieces separately. Purchasing individual pieces may be wiser, however, if you need only a few. Browse in stores, asking salespeople for help.

Another good management tool is human resources. Ask friends and relatives which cookware and bakeware items they consider indispensable. While each cook's needs vary, some pieces are essential.

If your list exceeds your resources, you will need to set priorities. Ask yourself:

• Do I expect to cook mainly for myself, or for others too? This affects the size of the cookware that you will need.
• How much can I afford to spend, and what can I get for that amount of money?
• Must these utensils be microwave-safe?
• What items are most versatile and useful?

Most people start with the basics and add to their collection as their skills and interest in cooking increase. Evaluate your equipment from time to time to identify additional items that you need.

Applying the Principles

1. What cookware items might you recommend to a single person who does little entertaining?
2. What are the benefits of asking a friend, instead of a salesperson, about cookware?
3. How can you evaluate the success of your management plan for purchasing cookware?

Different Methods

There are many methods for cooking food, but most fall into one of three basic categories. They are:

• Cooking with moist heat.
• Cooking with dry heat.
• Cooking with fat.

Different techniques are best for different foods, and many foods can be cooked using more than one technique.

Moist-heat cooking methods—such as boiling, simmering, and stewing—involve the use of liquids or steam to cook the food. Such foods as rice and dry beans are cooked in moist heat so that they can absorb water and soften. Moist heat is also a good choice for making meats, vegetables, and other foods tender. Another advantage of moist heat is that it helps flavors to blend, as in a sauce or soup. **Figure 48.1** explains the different moist-heat cooking methods.

Focus on Management Skills

Atmospheric pressure drops as altitude increases. This causes water to boil at a lower temperature at higher elevations. Thus boiled foods take longer to cook. Ask: Which other cooking methods would this condition most affect? How might this affect the planning and timing of a meal served in Charleston, South Carolina (altitude 9 ft.) as compared to Denver, Colorado, the "Mile-High City"?

Figure 48.1

COOKING WITH MOIST HEAT

Steaming. Steaming helps preserve the nutrients in food. The most common method is to boil a small amount of water in a pan, then put the food in a **steamer**, <u>a metal basket that holds the food above the water.</u> After the pan is covered with a tight-fitting lid, the water continues to boil, and the steam cooks the food in the basket. Steaming, like simmering, is an especially good way to cook vegetables.

Pressure cooking. Pressure cooking requires a special airtight pan in which the food cooks quickly by means of hot steam that is under pressure. This method can be used for less tender cuts of meat and poultry and for such vegetables as potatoes and carrots.

Boiling. To **boil** means <u>to heat liquid at a high temperature so that bubbles rise continuously to the surface and break.</u> A recipe might tell you to bring sauce to a boil or to cook noodles in boiling water. Most foods, however, should not be cooked in boiling liquid. Boiling can rob food of nutrients and cause it to overcook or break apart.

Simmering. To **simmer** means <u>to heat liquid to a temperature just below the boiling point.</u> Small bubbles should form, with some bubbles rising slowly to the surface. Vegetables are often cooked in simmering liquid. Fewer nutrients are lost than with boiling.

Poaching. To **poach** means <u>to cook whole foods in a small amount of simmering liquid so that they keep their original shape.</u> Tender foods— such as fish, eggs, and fruit—are sometimes poached.

Stewing. Stewing is similar to braising, but the food is cut into small pieces before it is stewed. Braising and stewing are usually used for less tender cuts of meat and for poultry, vegetables, and some fruits.

Braising. To **braise** food—a pot roast, for example—you <u>brown the food in a small amount of fat, and then cook it slowly in a small amount of simmering liquid until it is tender.</u> Foods may be braised in the oven or on top of the range.

MORE ABOUT Braising

In braising, the liquid should simmer just enough to create steam. If steam escapes around the edge of the pan lid, the liquid is boiling. Reduce the heat and add more liquid if necessary to prevent evaporation and scorching.

DID YOU KNOW?

Special plastic, vapor-proof cooking bags are available for cooking less tender meats in the oven. A small amount of liquid is added to the bag with the food. Follow instructions carefully to prevent bursting or splattering.

Activities

■ **Moist-Heat Menu.** Have groups write a one-day menu that includes as many moist-heat methods as possible. Remind students that the method should suit the food, enhancing its appeal and nutritional value. *(Management)*

■ **Method Match-Up.** On the board, list the moist-heat methods described on p. 475. Quiz students by naming a food and asking if it is suited to a particular method. For example, could pasta be braised? Could potatoes be simmered? Ask students to explain their answers. *(Critical Thinking)*

ENRICHMENT

■ **Moist and Methodical.** Have groups experiment with preparing the same food using different moist-heat methods: simmering and steaming rice, for example, or stewing and braising meat. Have groups prepare enough for others to share and compare on taste, texture, and appearance. Can they draw any general conclusions about matching specific methods to certain kinds of foods?

Topics on pp. 476-478
- Dry-Heat Cooking
- Cooking with Fat
- Judging Doneness

Checking Comprehension

✓ Name two ways to broil food. *In oven broiler unit; on outdoor grill.*

✓ Why is stir-frying a more healthful way to fry foods? *Uses less fat than sautéing or deep-fat frying.*

✓ Describe two signs of doneness in cakes. *Spring back when lightly pressed; toothpick inserted in center comes out clean.*

Figure 48.2
COOKING WITH DRY HEAT

Roasting or baking. Roasting and baking both mean cooking food uncovered in the oven. Many foods can be baked—breads, fruits and vegetables, cakes, cookies, pies, casseroles, and fish, for example. The term roasting is used primarily to refer to large pieces of meat or poultry. Foods that are roasted or baked often have a crisp, brown crust and are tender and flavorful inside.

Broiling. To **broil** means <u>to cook food directly under or over a glowing heat source.</u> For example, the heat source might be the broiler unit of an oven. The food is placed on a broiler pan, which has slots that allow fat to drain away during cooking. Grilling food on an outdoor grill is another method of broiling. Broiling is often used for tender meats, such as steaks and hamburgers, and for poultry and some fruits and vegetables.

With dry-heat cooking methods, such as roasting and broiling, the food is cooked uncovered without adding liquid. Foods cooked with dry heat get brown and crisp on the outside but remain moist and tender on the inside. **Figure 48.2** explains dry-heat cooking methods.

Cooking with fat is a quick method that produces flavorful foods. However, it has the disadvantage of adding fat and calories to the food. When cooking with fat, choose oils that are low in saturated fats. Olive oil and canola oil are healthful cooking oils. Nonstick cooking spray is also a good choice. **Figure 48.3** explains three methods of cooking with fat.

DID YOU KNOW?

Some ovens have hot spots, places that are hotter than the temperature set. Locating these spots allows cooks to adjust cooking times or position food racks and bakeware accordingly.

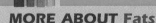

MORE ABOUT Fats

When fats used in frying start to smoke, they have reached their smoking point, at which they begin to break down and taste and smell bad. Butter, olive oil, and margarine have the lowest smoking points, which can be raised by blending in other vegetable oils.

Figure 48.3
COOKING WITH FAT

Sautéing or panfrying. To **sauté** (saw-TAY) means <u>to cook small pieces of food in a small amount of fat over low to medium heat.</u> For example, chopped onions are often sautéed until they become soft and transparent. Panfrying means using a similar method for larger pieces of food, such as tender meats, fish, or eggs.

Deep-fat frying. With this method, food is cooked by immersing it in hot fat. French fries and doughnuts are examples of deep-fat fried foods.

Stir-frying. To **stir-fry** is <u>to stir and cook small pieces of food very quickly at high heat in very little fat.</u> This method is used for vegetables, meat, poultry, and fish. Because it uses less fat, stir-frying is a more healthful way to cook with fat than either of the other two methods.

■ **To a T.** Have students write a few paragraphs explaining how they determine doneness in their favorite foods cooked with dry heat. Have them describe the foods' taste, texture or appearance when it is done just right. They might contrast this with the same foods when they are undercooked or overcooked. *(Observation)*

RETEACHING

■ **Is It Done Yet?** Have students name three foods not mentioned on p. 478 that could be tested for doneness using the methods discussed. For example, pancakes and some cookies can be judged by appearance.

FAMILY AND COMMUNITY OUTREACH

Have students obtain nutritional information from fast-food restaurants to compare menu items that are prepared using dry heat (such as roasted chicken or grilled hamburgers) to those that are fried. Discuss their findings in class. Ask: Do health-conscious consumers have enough options among fast-food outlets in the community?

MORE ABOUT Testing Doneness

Some whole poultry is sold with a built-in thermometer that is designed to pop up when the bird is done. These are not always reliable, however. Another test is to try moving a leg in the socket. When it moves easily, the bird is done.

MORE ABOUT Frying

If frying fat catches fire, turn off the heat immediately and cover the pan with a lid or pour baking soda or salt over the flames. The fire will die from lack of oxygen. Never pour water on a grease fire or try to grab the pan.

Review

■ **Chapter Review.** Use the contents of the Chapter Review page to help students review concepts, think critically, and apply their knowledge.

■ **Study Guide.** Have students complete the Study Guide for Chapter 48 on p. 158 of the Student Workbook.

■ **Chef's Choice.** Have students plan a menu consisting of a main dish; a vegetable; a rice or potato dish; biscuits; and a fruit dessert. Have them list the cookware and bakeware they would need to prepare this meal, and explain which cooking method would be appropriate for each item.

Evaluation

■ **Chapter Test.** Use the reproducible chapter test provided in the Teacher's Classroom Resources or create your own test using the *Testmaker Software*.

■ **Alternative Assessment.** Have groups develop a flow chart showing how to choose cookware or bakeware for a specific need by asking a series of questions about the food and the method used. The first question might be "Are you cooking in the oven or on the range top?" followed by "Are you using moist heat or dry?" Successive questions should be increasingly specific, leading the reader to the most suitable choice.

■ **Recipe Writers.** Give each student the name and ingredients list of a recipe. Have them suggest cookware or bakeware and cooking methods that would help them prepare the recipe successfully.

478

When Food Is Done

How do you judge when food is cooked properly? Your guide, of course, will be the time listed in the recipe, but actual cooking times may vary. Therefore, experienced cooks depend on other doneness checks as well. Here are some suggestions for determining when food is done:

• **Look at the food or touch it.** You can tell when many foods are done by the way they look or feel. Meat and poultry, for example, should not be pink inside. A loaf of yeast bread is done when you hear a hollow sound as you tap it with your knuckles. You can test some cakes for doneness by pressing lightly on the top of the cake with one finger. If the cake springs back, it is done. When touching foods to check doneness, use clean hands and take care not to burn yourself.

• **Pierce the food with a fork.** You might pierce vegetables—such as potatoes, carrots, beans, or asparagus—with a cooking fork. If the vegetables are done, the fork will go in and pull out easily. When you pierce meats and poultry, juices should run clear. Fish should flake easily with a fork.

• **Use a thermometer.** Foods such as meats and poultry must reach a specific internal temperature in order to be safe to eat. Some meat thermometers are designed to be left in the meat or poultry while it cooks. Others are used to check the temperature after cooking. Thermometers are also used when making some other foods, such as candy.

• **Use a wooden or metal tester.** When cakes and some breads are done, a toothpick or skewer inserted into the center will come out clean. Use a knife in the same way to test custards.

• **Taste a sample.** Remove a piece of vegetable or pasta, let it cool slightly, and taste it. Vegetables should be tender-crisp; pasta should be slightly chewy.

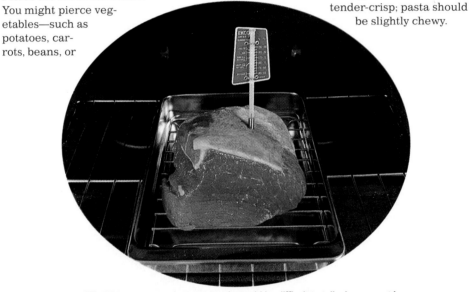

Without a meat thermometer, it would be difficult to tell when a roast is done. As the meat cooks, the thermometer rises. A scale shows how far the thermometer must rise to completely cook various meats. Once the proper temperature is reached on the thermometer, the meat is done and can be removed from the oven.

Focus on Creative Thinking Skills

A particular type of cookware or bakeware may not be available, especially if one's budget is limited. Encourage students to think of items that might substitute for cooking pans; some breads, for example, are baked in coffee cans. Remind students that containers must be safe and sanitary as well as flame-proof or oven-proof.

Review

Reviewing the Facts

1. Give four examples of cookware and four examples of bakeware.
2. Name three materials used for making cookware and bakeware. What is one characteristic of each?
3. Why is simmering often a better cooking method than boiling?
4. What is the difference between braising and baking?
5. What are three ways to tell when a food is cooked?

Thinking Critically

1. Cookware is generally used on top of the range while bakeware is generally used in the oven. What are the main differences between the two types of equipment as a result of this difference in use?
2. Foods such as potatoes, fish, eggs, and chicken can be successfully cooked in several different ways. Assuming that each method results in food that tastes equally good to you, which cooking technique would you favor for each of these foods? Why?

Applying Your Knowledge

1. **Making a Chart.** Make a chart summarizing the cooking methods discussed in the chapter. Include what foods are prepared by each method, how the technique is done, and what equipment is used for each method.
2. **Selecting Equipment.** Based on what you have learned in this chapter about cookware and bakeware, make a list of the items you would need in your starter kitchen in order to be able to cook the meals you most like to prepare.
3. **Analyzing Recipes.** Using a cookbook or magazine, find three recipes that each use a different cooking method. Describe the method used in each recipe, and tell why you think it is appropriate for that type of food.

Making Connections

1. **Science.** Do research into the properties of some of the materials—such as aluminum, steel, enamel, iron, copper, glass, and plastic—that are used for making cookware and bakeware. Find out the advantages and disadvantages of the materials and why they are suitable for cooking equipment. Prepare a report on your findings.
2. **Language Arts.** Choose one of the cooking methods described in this chapter. In your own words, explain what equipment is needed, how the food should be cooked, and how to determine when the food is done.

Building Your Portfolio

Understanding Other Cooking Methods

Use cookbooks, encyclopedias, or other resources to research the cooking methods of other countries or cultures. Find information on at least two cooking methods that are unfamiliar to you. Prepare a short report or a taped speech that describes these cooking methods and their similarities to, or differences from, methods described in this chapter. Add the finished report or tape to your portfolio.

ANSWERS TO REVIEWING THE FACTS

1. *Cookware: any four—* saucepan, pot, Dutch oven, double boiler, skillet, griddle. *Bakeware: any four—*roasting pan, broiler pan, casserole, cake pan, muffin pan, pie pan, loaf pan, baking sheet.
2. Students might list aluminum, which is lightweight but may stain; stainless steel, which is attractive but heats slowly and unevenly; enamel, which is attractive but chips easily; cast iron, which is durable but may rust; glass-ceramic, which is attractive but may break; plastic, which is durable but not always suitable for conventional ovens.
3. When simmering, food retains more nutrients than when boiling and is less likely to overcook or break apart.
4. Braising is a moist-heat method using a small amount of liquid. Baking is a dry-heat method.
5. Any three: looking at or touching the food, piercing it with a fork, using a thermometer, inserting a tester, and tasting a sample.

ANSWERS TO THINKING CRITICALLY

1. Students might suggest that because cookware is exposed directly to heat, it needs to be heavier than bakeware. Also, long handles on some cookware, designed for easier lifting, would not fit in an oven. Bakeware does not have to be so heavy, and therefore lighter, less expensive materials are used.

2. In their answers, students should consider factors such as tenderness, cooking ease, speed of preparation and cooking, energy costs, and nutrition.

Chapter Overview

Chapter 49 gives guidelines for using a microwave oven. It describes suitable cookware and helpful techniques; variables that affect cooking time; and precautions to take.

Motivator

■ **Micro Quiz.** Ask students true/false questions about microwave ovens, such as "Any food can be microwaved" and "Microwave ovens give off radiation." Encourage debate. Tell students this chapter will help them answer questions like these.

Objectives

Discuss the chapter objectives on this page. Remind students that the objectives focus on important chapter concepts.

Vocabulary

A *microwave* is a very short, high-frequency radio wave. Ask: How else is the word *microwave* used? *As a noun, shorthand for a microwave oven; an adjective showing relationship to microwave cooking; a verb meaning to cook using microwaves.*

Chapter 49

Microwave Cooking

Terms to Learn

- arcing
- microwave
- rotate
- shield
- standing time
- variable

Objectives

This chapter will help you to:

- Explain **how microwaves cook food.**
- Describe **the uses of the microwave oven.**
- Describe **various techniques for microwave cooking.**
- Identify **the variables in microwave cooking and explain how they affect the cooking time.**

CHAPTER RESOURCES

Student Workbook
Study Guide, pp. 162-163
Activity, *Facts About Microwave Ovens,* pp. 164-165

Teacher's Classroom Resources
Lesson Plan, p. 53

Cooperative Learning, *Comparing Ovens,* pp. 57-58
Extension #76, *Microwave Cooking Utensils,* p. 82
Life Skills, *Make It in the Microwave,* pp. 77-78
Chapter 49 Test, pp. 103-104

Performance Assessment, *Effective Use of a Microwave Oven,* p. 82
Reteaching, *Using the Microwave Oven,* p. 55

Microwave cooking continues to be very popular in the home kitchen. Because the microwave oven performs many cooking tasks faster and more easily than a conventional oven, people can cook a meal in minutes or prepare a snack in seconds. Microwave ovens are also cleaner and more economical to operate than conventional ovens.

Most microwave ovens are best suited for cooking relatively small amounts of food; large amounts usually call for a conventional oven or range. Microwave ovens are also ideal for reheating cooked foods and defrosting frozen foods. To use a microwave oven to its best advantage, you need to understand how it works and learn the special techniques of microwave cooking.

How a Microwave Works

Microwave ovens vary in size, features, and available power, but all work in a similar way:

- When you turn on a microwave oven, you activate a magnetron tube that converts electrical energy into microwaves. A **microwave** is *a type of energy wave, similar to a radio wave, that operates at a very high frequency.*

In Touch with TECHNOLOGY
A New Wave in Microwave Cooking

Microwave ovens have come a long way since 1945, when Dr. Percy Spencer discovered the melted candy bar. Experimenting with magnetron tubes in his Waltham, Massachusetts, laboratory, he found the candy bar in his pocket had melted, though he had felt no heat. He tried several other foods near the tube, including popcorn. He soon encased the tube in a cabinet, creating the first "radar range."

Microwave ovens have always cooked foods quickly. Early models, though, were heavy, less powerful, and tended to cook unevenly. They were also more expensive. In 1981, prices ran upwards of $400; today they average about one-third of that.

Today's designs are also more sophisticated. These are some of their technological highlights:

- Turntables, now a standard feature, provide automatic rotation for more even cooking.
- Ovens can cook foods at the correct power level for the time needed when you punch in the type of cooking job and the food's weight.
- Moisture sensors can automatically stop the cooking process by sensing when enough moisture has escaped from food to indicate that it is done.

- Instant touch pads allow you to press a single spot for common tasks, such as popping corn or preparing a frozen waffle.
- Multistage cooking features let you program several different cooking times and power levels into one operation—cooking a meal at 100 percent power for two minutes, for example, then at 50 percent for seven more.
- Memory settings let you program power levels and cooking times for foods you prepare often.

Thinking Critically About Technology

1. How do you think the advances in microwave ovens have changed families' food preparation and eating habits? Have these changes been more positive or negative? Explain.
2. How has the food industry adapted to the increased use of microwave ovens?

CHAPTER 49   Microwave Cooking   481

MORE ABOUT Microwaves

Microwaves are less than 5 inches in length. As radio waves, they operate in both positive and negative directions, reversing direction 2.45 billion times a second. Like a magnet, they attract oppositely charged food molecules. This attraction, combined with the microwaves' change in direction, causes heat-producing friction. Heat spreads through the food by conduction, as in a conventional oven, cooking the food.

Checking Comprehension

✓ Name some advantages of microwave cooking. *Faster, easier, cleaner, more economical than conventional cooking; foods retain colors, may be more healthful.*

✓ What features are common on newer microwaves? *Digital control panel; different power settings; convenience settings; temperature probe.*

✓ Can you use metal foils in a microwave oven? *Only when called for in recipe and allowed in owner's manual.*

SPECIAL NEEDS *Strategies*

Physically Disabled. Portable microwave ovens can be positioned for use by students with physical disabilities. If possible, situate microwave ovens in the foods lab for the convenience of all students.

- A stirrer blade, or fan, in the top of the oven distributes the waves throughout the oven. Some waves hit the food directly, and others bounce off the metal walls, floor, and ceiling of the oven and then enter the food. (Microwaves can pass through most materials, but not metal.)
- When microwaves penetrate the food, they cause the molecules in the food to vibrate or rub against each other. This produces heat, which cooks the food.

Microwave ovens cook foods without greatly changing their appearance. Usually this is an advantage—broccoli and carrots, for example, retain their bright colors. Because less fat and water are used in microwave cooking, foods may have fewer calories than those prepared in traditional ways and may retain more of their nutrients. On the other hand, microwave ovens do not brown foods as conventional ovens do. Some microwave ovens do include a special browning element, however.

Settings

Microwave power is measured in watts. The maximum power of most microwave ovens today is 700 to 850 watts, although some large models may offer up to 1050 watts. You can find the wattage rating for a microwave oven on the back of the oven and in the instruction manual.

Microwave ovens usually have a number of power settings. Some models require you to select the power setting and the cooking time. More sophisticated models also have automatic settings for specific tasks.

Some recipes, especially ones written ten or more years ago, may assume lower power settings, 750 watts or less. The rule of thumb is, the lower the wattage, the longer the cooking time. The higher the wattage, the shorter the cooking time. You may need to experiment with some recipes to get the cooking time just right.

The power control on older microwave ovens was a single dial; models sold now use a digital control panel. These newer models generally have a number of different settings; the percentage of power provided by similar settings on various brands may not be the same. Some models also have convenience settings for cooking specific items—such as

---

MORE ABOUT *Successful Microwaving*

In *Mastering Microwave Cookery*, Marcia Cone and Thelma Snyder offer this simple "hot spot" test for microwave ovens: Place a ready-to-bake pie crust on waxed paper; microwave on high power for seven minutes. Check the underside of the crust for brown spots, which indicate where the oven heats more quickly. (This tendency is exaggerated by the fat in the crust.) If your microwave oven has hot spots, be sure to rotate food during cooking.

Special microwave cookware is available, but you can use many dishes and containers that you already have. Check for "microwave-safe" labels. Most foods should be covered to hold in moisture.

popcorn and baked potatoes—and for reheating and defrosting. Some manufacturers include a temperature probe that can be placed directly into a food. It monitors the internal food temperature and automatically adjusts the power level.

Cookware

Not all cookware is suitable for microwave cooking. Ceramic, glass, plastic, and paper containers are usually appropriate, but look for a label indicating that they are microwave-safe.

Microwave-safe ceramic, glass, and plastic are unaffected by microwaves. They are also heat-resistant, so they do not crack or melt when the food becomes hot. Ceramic dishes that are not microwave-safe may shatter in a microwave oven.

Metal pans and bowls should *never* be used in a microwave oven. Because microwaves cannot pass through metal, some parts of the food will not be heated. As a more serious concern, metal containers may cause **arcing** (ARK-ing), *sparks that can damage the oven and start a fire.*

Some dishes have metallic trim or a metallic glaze, and they, too, should not be used. Avoid using recycled paper in a microwave oven, because it may include metal fragments or chemicals that could catch on fire. Use metal foils only when a recipe specifically calls for their use in the microwave oven *and* when the owner's manual for your oven indicates that this will not harm your oven. Then, follow recipe directions carefully. (See the section on "Shielding" in this chapter.)

483

Activities

■ **Countdown.** Have students run the cycle for defrosting meat or poultry on a microwave oven. What do they notice about the power settings? Why do they think settings change as they do? *(Critical Thinking)*

RETEACHING

■ **Name That Feature.** Show students a large picture of a microwave oven from a store ad or catalog. Have them identify various features and briefly explain their function.

MULTICULTURAL Perspectives

Challenge students to learn whether microwave ovens are as popular in other cultures as in their own. Can they find ethnic recipes written for the microwave oven?

CROSS-CURRICULAR ACTIVITY
Science

Have students research other uses for microwaves, including the operation of radios, remote controls, and mobile telephones.

MORE ABOUT Successful Microwaving (continued)

Another test shows students whether cookware is suitable for use in a microwave oven. Set the cookware and a glass bowl containing half a cup of water in the oven. Microwave on high power for one minute. Tell students that if the water is hot and the cookware is not, the cookware may be used for microwaving. Ask why they think this is so. *Warm cookware and cool water indicate that cookware is absorbing energy. It will not transfer heat to food efficiently and may crack.*

Checking Comprehension

✓ Why are foods covered during microwave cooking? *To hold in moisture, prevent splattering.*

✓ Why is standing time important to microwave cooking? *Allows food to finish cooking.*

✓ Why should you be careful when biting into a microwaved jelly doughnut? *Sugary center may be much hotter than surrounding dough.*

FAMILY AND COMMUNITY OUTREACH

Students may have older relatives who are unfamiliar with, and hesitant about, using a microwave oven. Encourage students to give these relatives a short course in how microwave ovens work and tips on using them.

Microwave Techniques

Microwave cooking requires special techniques. Because food heats up so quickly in a microwave oven, moisture also builds up rapidly, which may cause improperly prepared foods to burst. Another concern is the evenness of cooking.

Stirring and Rotating

Microwaves penetrate food to a depth of about 1½ in. (4 cm). The heat generated by the vibrating food molecules is then conducted toward the center of the food. That is why the center of food cooked in a microwave oven takes longer to cook than the outer edges.

Soups, stews, and other foods containing liquids heat evenly if you stir them occasionally. For best results, stir from the outer edge toward the center. When food cannot be stirred, use **rotation,** or *turning the dish a quarter- or a half-turn* partway through the cooking. This maneuver allows the microwaves to penetrate the food on all sides.

In some cases you may need to rearrange food pieces or turn them over. For example, you would rotate a tuna casserole, rearrange baking potatoes, and turn over a ham.

Defrosting

How long it takes a food to defrost depends on the size and density of the food and on the temperature at which it was frozen. Most microwave cookbooks provide a defrosting chart. Some models of microwave ovens have automatic defrost features that set the defrosting time and power level based on the food weight.

Defrosting is a useful function of a microwave oven because it cuts down on meal preparation time. Menus can be more easily created or changed at the last minute. Also, individual servings or whole meals can be prepared ahead of time, frozen, and then thawed and reheated when needed.

Covering

Most foods should be covered in a microwave oven to hold in moisture and prevent spattering. You may cover foods with several different materials:

To keep food from drying out in the microwave oven, cover the dish. Why is the corner of this plastic wrap turned back?

484   UNIT 6   Food, Nutrition, and Wellness

• • • REAL-LIFE APPLICATION

Read this to students: *Vince was preparing his dinner in the microwave oven. He began cooking a piece of chicken. When it was halfway done, he put in a small dish of peas and continued cooking. When the chicken was almost done, he added a cup of custard.* Ask students to give reasons for the order in which Vince cooked the foods. Point them toward the effects of food density and volume, moisture, fat, and sugar content on the cooking time of each course.

- Paper towels or napkins work well for covering bacon, sandwiches, and appetizers. Wrapping breads in paper towels prevents them from becoming soggy. Use towels that are marked "microwavable."
- Waxed paper is often used on casseroles to hold in some moisture while letting steam escape.
- Microwave-safe dishes with covers are ideal for vegetables and casseroles.
- Microwave-safe plastic wrap can be used to cook any food. Because it forms a tight seal, however, pierce the wrap or turn it back at one corner. This will keep it from bursting.

Puncturing

Foods that are encased in a skin or sealed in plastic should be pierced before they are placed in a microwave oven. Otherwise, steam will build up inside the food and cause it to burst. Piercing foods with a fork or making a small knife slit will prevent pressure buildup. Puncture whole potatoes, egg yolks, sausages, hot dogs, tomatoes, and apples, as well as vegetables that are to be cooked in plastic pouches.

Shielding

As you know, metal is not usually used in a microwave oven. You may, however, use small pieces of aluminum foil to **shield,** or *cover parts of food that might overcook.* For example, you might shield the tips of chicken wings and drumsticks or the corners of a rectangular casserole. To prevent arcing, be careful that the foil does not touch the sides of the oven. Always check the instruction manual for any cautions before you shield food.

Standing Time

A mistake that many people make when using a microwave oven to cook foods is to ignore the standing time called for in a recipe. **Standing time** is *the time allowed for the food to continue to cook after the microwave oven is turned off.* As the foods stands, the molecules inside the food continue moving and

cooking it. Standing time is almost as important as cooking time to ensure that the food turns out properly.

Recipe cooking times are usually slightly less than what is needed for doneness. That way, the center of the food can cook some more during standing time and the outer edges won't dry out.

Variables in Cooking

Many factors influence how food cooks in a microwave oven. Understanding these **variables,** or *conditions that determine how long a food needs to be microwaved and at what power level,* will help you use your microwave oven effectively:

- **Food moisture, fat, and sugar content.** Because these elements are heated quickly by microwave ovens, foods high in water, fat, or sugar heat quickly. Areas of foods with high fat or sugar content attract microwave energy and cook faster, creating "hot spots." That is why you may burn your tongue on the filling inside a microwaved breakfast roll even though the surrounding dough may not be warm. Salt also attracts microwaves, so salt food *after* microwaving it, not before.
- **Food density.** The denser the food, the longer it takes to cook. Rolls or cakes cook faster than similarly sized meats or potatoes.
- **Food volume.** The more food you are cooking, the longer it takes to cook because microwaves of the same intensity are cooking more food. For this reason, cooking a large amount of food often takes just as long in a microwave oven as in a conventional oven.
- **Food shape.** Shape also determines how foods cook. Unevenly shaped food will cook unevenly; corners or thinner pieces may overcook before other areas are done. When you are cooking foods that are uneven in thickness, place the thin pieces toward the center of the pan or dish and the thick pieces toward the out-

Activities

■ **Rotate and Wrap.** For each of the following foods, have students suggest techniques that would be helpful for microwave cooking and explain how they would be used: potatoes; drumsticks; sliced carrots; beef stew. *(Problem Solving)*

■ **Variable Verities.** Ask students to bring in recipes written for use in a microwave oven. Have them work in groups to add their own hints for success, based on what they learned about the variables in microwave cooking. *(Critical Thinking)*

RETEACHING

■ **Check It Out.** Have students develop checklists for use with microwave ovens in the foods lab. Checklist items should help students allow for variables in cooking and follow safety rules.

FAMILY AND COMMUNITY OUTREACH

Suggest that students contact the Cooperative Extension Service in their area for more tips on microwave oven use and safety. They might also ask the Service and local cookware shops about microwave cooking classes. Ask students to share their information with the class.

MORE ABOUT Microwave Cooking

For best results when converting conventional recipes, choose moist foods or those cooked in sauces, reducing the liquid by about one-quarter. Avoid food that should be crispy or crusty, such as hash browns, especially if they require frying in fat. Frying should never be attempted in a microwave oven. In fact, fats are generally used only as desired for flavor. Cover foods loosely if you need to keep in moisture. Reduce cooking time by one-quarter to one-third.

Review

■ **Chapter Review.** Use the contents of the Chapter Review page to help students review concepts, think critically, and apply their knowledge.

■ **Study Guide.** Have students complete the Study Guide for Chapter 49 on p. 162 of the Student Workbook.

■ **Micromanagement.** Have students create a dinner menu that includes a main dish; a vegetable; a potato dish, rice dish, or rolls; and dessert. Have students create a work plan or schedule that indicates how they might use a microwave oven in their preparations.

Evaluation

■ **Chapter Test.** Use the reproducible chapter test provided in the Teacher's Classroom Resources or create your own test using the *Testmaker Software.*

■ **Alternative Assessment.** Divide the class into groups to debate the pros and cons of microwave cooking. Ask students to use only facts mentioned in the chapter in their arguments.

■ **Very Advanced Model.** Have students write a letter "from" a microwave oven to its owner. The "oven" should explain how it works; the kinds of foods it "likes" to cook; and microwaving techniques and precautions that will make theirs a rewarding relationship.

side. Placing uneven foods in a spoke arrangement will allow them to cook more evenly.

• **Food starting temperature.** Foods that are at room temperature cook faster than foods that are refrigerated or frozen. Because most recipes are designed for foods at room temperature, you may have to add to cooking time if the food has been refrigerated.

Safety Considerations

Microwave ovens are a great help to today's cooks. There are, however, safety precautions to follow when using them:

• Always remove the cover from microwaved food by lifting the side farthest away from you so that the escaping steam doesn't burn you. The tighter and less porous the cover, the greater the buildup of steam.

• Avoid using dishes that are not microwave-safe because they might shatter.

• Do not use an extension cord with a microwave oven. The oven should be grounded with a three-prong plug and should not be on the same electrical circuit as other appliances.

• Keep your microwave oven clean and in good working order. Spattered food left on the inside walls will increase cooking time because it will absorb waves. Call an authorized repair person if the door does not seal tightly or if the oven makes any unusual sound when it is turned on.

Why do you think the broccoli and chicken legs have been arranged as shown here?

MORE ABOUT *Safe Microwaving*

For successful microwaving:

• Never operate the oven when it is empty.

• Don't attach magnets to the oven. They can interfere with the controls.

• Keep the door seal clean so the door can close securely.

• Loosen tight-fitting caps or covers on food containers to prevent steam build-up.

• Don't reuse the microwavable containers of commercially frozen foods. Discard the food if the package turns brown during cooking.

Chapter 49

Review

Reviewing the Facts

1. How do microwaves cook food?
2. What rule of thumb guides cooking times based on the wattage of the microwave oven?
3. What cookware can be used for microwave cooking? What material should you not use?
4. How does stirring food at intervals during microwave cooking help it to cook more evenly? How should you stir the food? When foods cannot be stirred, what can you do to help them cook faster and more evenly?
5. Why should you puncture certain foods as well as plastic wrap covering before placing them in the microwave oven?
6. Why would you use aluminum foil to shield part of some food? What resource should be checked before using foil for shielding?
7. Name four variables in microwave cooking, and describe how each affects cooking time.
8. What are four safety precautions you should be aware of when using a microwave oven?

Thinking Critically

1. If you had to choose between a microwave oven and a conventional oven, which would you choose and why? Explain your answer.
2. Suppose that you had to warm a frozen casserole that contained both large chunks and small bits of meat. Would it be better to warm it in a microwave oven or a conventional oven?

Applying Your Knowledge

1. **Comparing Results.** Cook broccoli, carrots, and baked apples in a microwave oven and by conventional methods. Compare the appearance and taste of each item. Which method of preparation do you prefer, and why?

2. **Explaining Techniques.** From cookbooks or magazines, find five recipes that use microwave techniques discussed in this chapter. Review the recipes, and be prepared to explain why the particular technique or techniques are important in preparing that dish.

Making Connections

1. **Science.** Find out these facts about microwavesand report to the class: what they are, other ways they are used, and what (if any) dangers they pose.
2. **Social Studies.** What elements of the American lifestyle make microwave ovens especially popular in the United States? Make a list of the social and economic realities of family life that contribute to the widespread use of this appliance.

Building Your Portfolio

Comparison Shopping
Suppose that you are about to buy a new microwave oven for your home. Consider in advance what features are important to you. Then visit an appliance store and take notes on at least three models. Write down the wattage, the number of power settings, and any other features, as well as the price and the terms of the warranty. Prepare a chart comparing these features for all the ovens. Write a paragraph describing which oven you would recommend buying and explaining why. Add the chart and the paragraph to your portfolio.

CHAPTER 49 Microwave Cooking 487

Chapter 50

Chapter Overview

Chapter 50 discusses foods in the Bread, Cereal, Rice, and Pasta Group. Students learn more about the processing and nutritional value of foods in this group, the wide variety available, and how to store and prepare these foods.

Motivators

■ **Grains Galore.** Bring in samples of flours and cereals for students to examine. Ask them to name baked goods or other items made with these products that they enjoy.

■ **Very Al Dente.** Offer students a bowl of raw rice or pasta as a snack. Ask: What must you do to these foods to make them edible?

Objectives

Discuss the chapter objectives on this page. Remind students that the objectives focus on important chapter concepts.

Vocabulary

The many uses of the word *bread* illustrate the importance of bread to life. *Bread* is slang for money; to *break bread* means to make peace. Since the 1820s, the term *breadbasket* has meant the stomach.

Chapter 50
Breads, Cereals, Rice, and Pasta

Chapter 50

Terms to Learn

- gluten
- knead
- quick breads
- yeast breads

Objectives

This chapter will help you to:

- Identify and select foods from the Bread, Cereal, Rice, and Pasta Group.
- Explain how to store breads and other cereal foods properly.
- Describe the best methods for preparing breads and other cereal foods.

CHAPTER RESOURCES

Student Workbook
Study Guide, p. 166
Activity, *Invent a Better Breakfast*, p. 167

Teacher's Classroom Resources
Lesson Plan, p. 54
Extension #77, *Types of Pasta*, p. 83

Foods Lab Activities, pp. 5-8
Life Skills, *Feeding the World*, pp. 79-80
Chapter 50 Test, pp. 105-106
Performance Assessment, *The Breads, Cereals, Rice, and Pasta Group*, p. 83

Reteaching, *Breads Cereals, Rice, and Pasta*, p. 56

See Also:
ABCNews InterActive™ Videodiscs

Among the five major food groups, the Bread, Cereal, Rice, and Pasta Group is significant for many reasons. In addition to providing carbohydrates for energy, this food group supplies protein and important vitamins and minerals. These foods are also a valuable source of fiber. Many food products—breakfast cereals, pasta, pita bread, tortillas, pancakes, and even pizza crusts—come from grains. Grains and grain products should be an important daily food choice because of the nutrients they provide.

Selecting

In most markets, you can choose from a wide variety of breads and cereals. Your decisions may be based on personal taste, convenience, price, or nutritional value. The grains from which bread and cereal products are made are rich in nutrients. During processing, however, nutrients can be lost.

Nutrient Composition

A grain kernel, or seed, has four parts. **Figure 50.1** on page 490 shows a typical kernel of grain. The germ, which is at its core, contains vitamins and minerals, such as vitamins B and E, iron, and zinc. Surrounding the germ is the endosperm. Its nutrients would nourish the seed if it were allowed to sprout. These nutrients include complex carbohydrates and most of the grain's protein. Outside of the endosperm are layers of bran, covered by a protective case called the hull. The germ, bran, and hull contain cellulose, or fiber.

TEACH

Topics on p. 489:
• **Nutrients in Grains**

Checking Comprehension

✓ What nutrients are found in the germ of a grain kernel? *Vitamins B and E, iron, zinc.*

✓ Why is the endosperm high in carbohydrates and protein? *To nourish seed if it were to sprout.*

Managing Your Life

Have students read "Meeting Your Whole-Grain Goal" and discuss the questions. Point out that despite the benefits of whole grains, many people still prefer more processed grain products. Ask why this might be.

Answers to Applying . . .

1. Answers may include: makes it easier to include them in meals; makes meals more enjoyable.
2. Answers may include: price, availability; own and family's preferences and eating habits.
3. Answers will vary.

Managing Your Life

Meeting Your Whole-Grain Goal

Knowing the advantages of eating whole grains should spur you to include more of them in your diet. By reading food labels, you can identify products made from the entire grain. Look for ingredients such as whole-wheat (or graham) flour, whole-oat flour, rolled oats, wheat germ, and various kinds of bran. Rely on food ingredients rather than color. A dark-colored bread labeled "wheat bread" may be made with refined—not whole wheat—flour, and the dark appearance due to added coloring.

Be resourceful and creative in considering all your whole-grain options. Could you try brown rice instead of white, or use whole-wheat flour for part of the white flour in recipes? Explore the wide variety of grains and grain products. Which of these items are available to you?

- **Wheat berries.** Cook and serve these tasty whole-wheat kernels as a hot cereal, or use them as you would rice.
- **Bulgur.** Popular in the Middle East, bulgur is made from whole-wheat kernels that are precooked, dried, and cracked. It is eaten as a side dish or used in main dishes and salads.

- **Barley.** Often added to soups and stews, this grain also makes a flavorful side dish.
- **Kasha.** Coarsely ground buckwheat, or kasha, is common in Eastern European cooking. Eat it as a breakfast cereal or in place of rice.
- **Wheat germ.** Although not a whole grain, wheat germ is a nutrient-rich part of the grain. Sprinkle these crunchy granules on breakfast cereal or yogurt, or use in recipes.

Applying the Principles

1. What are the advantages of including a variety of whole-grain products in your diet?
2. What factors might influence your decision about which whole-grain foods to choose?
3. Plan a one-day menu of meals and snacks that provides at least six servings of whole-grain foods. Include some of those mentioned above.

MORE ABOUT Wheat Germ

Wheat germ is removed from grains because it contains oil that can become rancid and cause spoilage. Wheat germ is available in vacuum-packed containers in grocery stores. When added to foods as a topping or in baking, it increases the food's nutritional value, and fiber content, but also its fat content—an unusual quality for a grain product. Therefore, wheat germ should be used sparingly.

Topics on pp. 490-491:
- Processing Methods
- Breads, Breakfast Cereals, and Rice

Checking Comprehension

✓ Give an advantage and a disadvantage of refining grain products. *Lets them last longer but removes important nutrients.*

✓ What are whole-grain products? *Those made from entire grain, including bran and germ.*

✓ Name two basic types of breakfast cereal. *Cold or ready to eat; cooked or hot.*

✓ What is a nutritional advantage of serving converted rice? *Contains nutrients from the bran.*

Activities

■ **Whole-some Grains.** Ask students to list the grain products they've eaten in the past 24 hours and to circle the whole-grain products. Ask: About what percentage of your daily grain product choices are whole grain? Challenge students to write down whole-grain substitutes for the other items on their list. *(Critical Thinking)*

Figure 50.1

A GRAIN KERNEL

A grain kernel measures no more than ¼ in. (0.5 cm), yet it is packed with nutrients.

- BRAN
- ENDOSPERM
- HULL
- GERM

Many grain products sold in the United States are made of white wheat flour, which is the endosperm of wheat. This type of flour has been refined, meaning that the bran and the germ are removed from the kernels of wheat to give the flour a finer texture and make it last longer.

Together with removing the bran and the germ, refining removes important nutrients, such as iron and B vitamins. Because federal law requires that nutrients lost in processing be replaced, the refined flour is then enriched. Enrichment replaces lost nutrients. Some cereals are fortified, which means that nutrients have been added that were not in the grain originally or were not in the grain in large amounts.

Whole-grain products are made from the entire grain, including the bran and the germ. Whole-grain products often have a nutlike taste and are higher in fiber than refined flour products.

Breads

There are many types of breads—white, whole-wheat, rye, pumpernickel, and oat bran are a few examples. Bread products include rolls, muffins, and biscuits, as well as loaves.

In addition to bread that has been commercially baked, you can buy bread mixes or ingredients to make the bread yourself. For extra convenience, you can also purchase frozen bread products such as waffles or rolls. These merely need thawing or heating to be ready to eat.

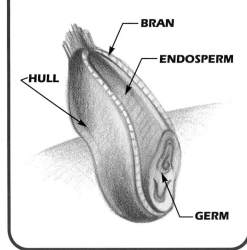

Pasta comes in assorted shapes and is a good source of complex carbohydrates. What types of pasta have you tried?

MORE ABOUT Rice

Rice is the single most widely consumed food in the world, the mainstay of half the planet's population. Nutritious and inexpensive, it grows in wet, marshy areas that cannot support other crops, livestock, or industry. Its popularity also stems from its versatility. It absorbs flavors well, from spicy Indian curries to sweet rice puddings, and so is easily assimilated into the cuisine of many cultures.

Breakfast Cereals

Breakfast cereals are made from grains such as wheat, oats, corn, rice, and barley. Some are ready to eat—wheat flakes or rice puffs, for example—and can be served with milk and fruit. Others are cooked in water or milk and served hot. Some hot cereals are instant—only requiring the addition of boiling water for preparation. Breakfast cereals vary greatly in their nutritional content.

Read the labels carefully for nutrition and ingredient information. Whole-grain cereals are a good choice, but many processed cereals are fortified with added nutrients. Watch out for cereals that contain large amounts of sugar and salt.

Rice

White rice has had its outer coverings, the hull and the bran, removed by polishing. Because most of the vitamin B and fiber are in the bran layer, enriched rice, like enriched bread, has had the vitamins put back in. You can also buy brown rice, which has been hulled but still has the bran. Rich in fiber, brown rice has a nutlike flavor similar to that of whole-wheat products.

Precooked, or instant, rice is made from rice that has been cooked and dehydrated, thus decreasing the cooking time for the consumer. Converted rice is partly cooked before the bran is removed. This allows nutrients from the bran to enter the endosperm. It

STRATEGIES That Work

Winning Ways with Pasta and Rice

When your goal is to eat 6 to 11 servings of grain products each day, you need more to choose from than just bread and breakfast cereal. Pasta and rice are two popular, versatile alternatives that can help you plan nutritious, economical meals. The next time you prepare rice or pasta, cook extra portions, moisten with a little cooking oil or broth, and refrigerate, covered. Try it in some of these recipe ideas:

- Warm spaghetti with cooked, diced ham, chicken, or beef for a hot meal.
- Stuff green peppers with rice and lean ground beef for a main-course dish.
- Combine pasta or rice with beans, lentils, or other legumes for meatless dishes with complete protein.
- Add rice, macaroni, or other types of pasta to soups and stews to make these dishes more nutritious and satisfying.

- For cold salads, mix pasta with seafood and a small amount of mayonnaise, or toss it with chopped fresh vegetables, olives, and low-fat Italian dressing. Mix rice with cooked, diced chicken, pineapple, and chopped green peppers or with canned shrimp, onions, and celery. Season as desired and toss with low-fat dressing. Most pasta and rice salads keep well, making them good choices for packed lunches, picnics, and make-ahead meals.

Making the Strategy Work

Think . . .

1. Why do you think pasta and rice are so versatile?
2. Suggest ways of adding other grains to recipes to create easy, nutritious dishes.
3. Pasta, a nutritious food, is often topped with high-fat, high-calorie sauces. What healthful toppings could you use instead?

Try...

Choose a favorite recipe and think of how you might add rice or pasta to it. Explain which product you would add and why, how you would include it, and any changes you would make in preparation. Try preparing the dish at home.

CHAPTER 50   Breads, Cereals, Rice, and Pasta   491

Topics on pp. 492-494:
- Pasta and Flour
- Storing Grain Products
- Preparing Grain Products

Checking Comprehension

✓ How should dry cereals be stored? *Store them in tightly closed packages or airtight containers.*

✓ Why do rice and cereals retain their nutrients when cooked? *They absorb cooking liquid.*

✓ How are ingredients for quick breads usually mixed? *Liquid and dry ingredients combined separately, stirred together just until dry ingredients are moistened.*

CROSS-CURRICULAR ACTIVITY
Math

Tell students to imagine they are cooking pasta for a family get-together. They plan on a 2-oz. serving for each of 10 people, plus 8 oz. for extra servings and leftovers. If the pasta comes in 1-lb. boxes, how many boxes will they need? *(Two.)* If they need 2 qts. of water for every 8 oz. of dry pasta, how much water will they need? *(7 qts.)*

---

takes longer to cook than regular white rice. Rice also comes packaged with a sauce or seasoning packet. As with cereals, you should check labels carefully, since many seasoning packets contain large amounts of sodium.

Pasta

Macaroni, spaghetti, and noodles are also in the grain products group. These products are called pasta, which comes from the Italian word for dough. Most pasta keeps its shape and stays firm even after it has been cooked because it is made from a special flour called semolina. Semolina is a type of wheat flour that is high in gluten. **Gluten** is *an elastic, protein substance found in wheat flour.*

Pasta comes in all sizes and shapes—from thin strands of spaghetti to little shells and pieces that look like wagon wheels. Some pasta products have spinach or tomatoes added to the dough for color. Most pasta tastes the same, but the difference in texture or appearance may be important in a recipe.

Flour

You can purchase several kinds of flour for making bread products. All-purpose flour is used for general baking and cooking. Self-rising flour is an all-purpose flour with baking powder and salt added.

Other types of flour include buckwheat, rye, oat, and whole-wheat. The germ, endosperm, and bran are all retained in whole-wheat flour, which can be used for bread, crackers, pasta, and other products. Cornmeal is used for baking corn bread, tortillas, and hush puppies (small balls of deep-fried cornmeal dough).

Cook pasta in a large pot so that water circulates around it freely and will not cause the pasta to stick together. Bring the water to a boil, then add the pasta slowly so that the boiling does not stop. Why is it important not to rinse pasta after cooking?

Storing

Products in the Bread, Cereal, Rice, and Pasta Group generally are easy to store. Many items keep well for long periods of time without refrigeration.

Breads

Bread tastes best when it's fresh, but it can also keep for some time if properly stored. Always wrap breads tightly and store them in a cool, dark place (such as a bread box or cabinet). In hot weather, keep bread in the refrigerator to slow down the growth of mold. Since refrigeration causes breads to dry out, avoid storing them this way unless it is necessary. Keep refrigerated rolls in the refrigerator after you bring them home from the store.

Tightly wrapped bread freezes well and can be kept in the freezer for several months. Bread products that come frozen should be kept in the freezer until they are used.

MORE ABOUT Freezing Breads

Homemade breads can be frozen for up to three months without losing their flavor. Cool to room temperature first, then wrap in aluminum foil, plastic wrap, airtight plastic bags, or freezer wrap, with the air pressed out of the package. If using a plastic bag, you can close off all but a narrow opening and suck out the air through a straw.

Cereals, Rice, Pasta, and Flours

Dry cereals keep well in tightly closed packages or airtight containers. Rice, pasta, and flours also stay fresh for a long time if their containers are airtight. Refrigeration is not needed for most cereal products except in hot, humid weather or if insects are a problem. Whole-grain flours, however, should be refrigerated. The fat content of the germ that remains in whole-wheat flours can cause spoilage and limit storage time.

Preparing

Foods in this group may be prepared in several ways. They may be cooked in liquids, baked, or heated in the microwave oven. Learning how to prepare these foods correctly will give the finished foods good taste, texture, and appearance.

Cooking in Liquids

Many cereal products—including rice, pastas, and hot breakfast cereals—are cooked in water or other liquids. The package will tell you how much liquid to use and how long to cook the product.

Rice and breakfast cereals absorb all the liquid used to cook them, so no nutrients are lost during cooking. In contrast, pasta is cooked in a large amount of boiling water that is drained after cooking. Use 2 qt. (2 L) of water for every 8 oz. (224 g) of pasta. Add the pasta slowly to boiling water.

Pasta is done cooking when it has expanded and softened but is still firm to the bite. Overcooking destroys the texture and nutritive value. Drain pasta, using a colander. To avoid loss of nutrients, do not rinse pasta or rice.

Baking

When a loaf of bread, muffins, or biscuits are baked, chemical and physical changes take place. The dough rises or puffs up because ingredients in the dough release gases and steam. There are two basic types of breads: quick breads and yeast breads. Each type uses different ingredients to make the dough rise.

Quick Breads

Quick breads *use baking soda or baking powder to rise.* Because these ingredients work quickly, the bread is ready for baking right away. Examples are muffins, biscuits, pancakes, waffles, and banana bread. Most quick breads are made by combining the dry ingredients in one bowl and the liquid ingredients in another. The liquid is poured all at once into the dry ingredients. The mixture is then stirred only until the dry ingredients are moistened. Overmixing will cause the baked product to be tough.

To make some types of biscuits, cut the shortening into the flour mixture using a pastry blender and a cutting motion. Then add the liquid to this mixture. After all of the ingredients are mixed together, knead the dough on a lightly floured surface. To **knead** the dough, *use the heels of your hands to press the dough down and away from your body.* Rotate the dough one-quarter turn, fold the dough toward you, and then knead again using the above motion. Kneading develops the gluten, which forms the structure of the bread. Finally, use a rolling pin to roll out—or flatten—the dough until it is about ½ in. (1 cm) thick.

Yeast Breads

Yeast breads are *breads that rise through the action of yeast, a tiny fungus.* They take longer to make than quick breads because the dough must be left to rise, often for half an hour or more, before it is put into the oven. Common yeast breads include white bread, whole-grain bread, raisin bread, rolls, and pizza crusts.

To make a yeast bread, combine the ingredients according to the recipe. Mixing the yeast with warm water causes it to become active. Active yeast releases carbon dioxide, which makes the dough rise.

After combining the yeast with the flour and other ingredients, knead the dough for at

Activities

■ **Testing, Testing.** Have students experiment with storing pieces of bread in different ways, such as in a brown paper bag, a plastic container, and aluminum foil. After 24 hours, have them compare the bread and judge which method kept it freshest. Encourage students to continue their observations for several days. (*Observation*)

RETEACHING

■ **Method Match-Up.** Have small groups create quizzes that involve matching steps for preparing quick bread, muffins, rice, or pasta with the appropriate food. Quizzes may be true/false, matching, or fill-in-the-blank. Remind groups to word items carefully so that only one answer is correct, or to accept several responses. Have groups exchange and take the quizzes. Discuss the results to check for accuracy.

ENRICHMENT

■ **Fresh Forever.** Ask students to design an ideal container for storing either bread, cereal, rice, or pasta. Have them specify the size, shape, and material they would choose, and explain their choices.

CROSS-CURRICULAR ACTIVITY
Science

Ask students to investigate the chemical and biological processes by which baking powder, baking soda, and yeast cause baked goods to rise.

Focus on Management Skills

Making yeast breads is good practice in planning and managing time. Ask: What are the advantages and disadvantages of baking yeast breads for time management? Have students find recipes for yeast breads and make schedules for preparing them. Schedules should be based on the kneading, rising, and baking times given, and on students' estimation of the time they need for other preparation tasks.

Review

■ **Chapter Review.** Use the contents of the Chapter Review page to help students review concepts, think critically, and apply their knowledge.

■ **Study Guide.** Have students complete the Study Guide for Chapter 50 on page 166 of the Student Workbook.

■ **Grain Guide.** Have students create a chart showing the different types of grains; how to select and store them; and some common products made with them. Display the chart for reference.

Evaluation

■ **Chapter Test.** Use the reproducible chapter test provided in the Teacher's Classroom Resources or create your own test using the *Testmaker Software.*

■ **Alternative Assessment.** Have groups produce a news program revolving around foods in the Breads, Cereals, Rice, and Pasta Group. Top stories might be cautionary tales about people who have used or stored grain products improperly; a human interest story might feature a blue-ribbon winner in a county fair baking competition.

■ **Bread-Cereal Summary.** Have students write a list entitled "Top 10 Reasons for Including Grain Products in Your Diet." Lists may be straightforward or humorous, but should reflect facts discussed in the chapter.

To knead dough, first fold the dough over toward you. Then press down on the dough with the heel of your hand. Next, give it a quarter turn, fold, and press down again. Repeat these steps throughout the kneading process. What do you think the advantages are of homemade bread over store-bought bread?

least eight to ten minutes. Then allow the dough to rise. After some time, punch down and shape the dough. Allow it to rise a second time. This process may be repeated more times for heavier breads. Finally, put the dough into the oven and bake it.

You can test yeast breads for doneness by tapping the crust with your knuckles. A hollow sound means the bread is done baking.

Microwave Cooking

A microwave oven can be used to defrost or warm prepared rolls, pancakes, waffles, bagels, and other breads. You can add chopped nuts, cinnamon and sugar, low-fat cream cheese, fruit spread, or frosting as a topping. Baking breads is possible in a microwave, but the loaves will be pale in color, not brown.

Microwave ovens are useful for cooking hot breakfast cereals. Always make sure that your dish is microwave-safe and large enough to allow for expansion of the cereal.

Microwave ovens are not usually used for rice and pasta because they take as long to cook in a microwave oven as on the range. These products need time to absorb liquid and soften. Precooked rice and pasta, however, can be quickly reheated in a microwave oven. In addition, some frozen packaged rice and pasta entrées and side dishes can be cooked in a microwave in much less time than is needed in a conventional oven.

Focus on Creative Thinking Skills

Ask students to think of how grain products could be substituted in recipes. Encourage them to consider unusual substitutions, such as raw rice for oats in a quick bread. Ask: How would this affect the finished product? What changes would you make in ingredients or procedures to increases chances of success?

Chapter 50

Reviewing the Facts

1. What are the four parts of a kernel of grain?
2. What is the difference between bread and cereal products that have been enriched and those that have been fortified?
3. List two tips for bread storage.
4. What is the difference between quick breads and yeast breads?
5. How are yeast breads tested for doneness?
6. How is a microwave oven best used for preparing bread and cereal products?

Thinking Critically

1. Bread has often been referred to as the "staff of life." What do you think this means? How do breads fit into the meal plans of most people today? Discuss your answers with the class.
2. What are some ways to incorporate whole grains into daily menus?

Applying Your Knowledge

1. **Summarizing Information.** Draw a large circle on a piece of paper, and divide it into four quarters. Write the labels "Breads," "Cereals," "Rice," and "Pasta"—one for each quarter of the circle. Using information from this chapter, in each section give an example of a food product or dish, list the nutrients it provides, and state one way you might incorporate it into your daily food choices.
2. **Investigating Recipes.** Bulgur, or cracked wheat, is the pasta of the Middle East. Kasha, or ground buckwheat, is used in Eastern European countries. Consult cookbooks specializing in foods of these regions to find two recipes for each grain. What ingredients make these recipes unique? How could you incorporate these recipes into daily meal plans?

Making Connections

1. **Social Studies.** One way to enjoy the cultural diversity of the United States is to try some of the traditional foods of various ethnic groups. Find out about ethnic breads and grain dishes. You might consult recipe books, talk to people from other cultures, or visit ethnic food stores. If possible, join with a partner or group of classmates to prepare a dish or obtain a bread that can be sampled by the class.
2. **Science.** To learn how one common type of yeast—active dry yeast—works, try this experiment. Fill two bowls with ¼ cup (50 mL) water, one at 45° to 55°F (7° to 13°C) and one at 105° to 115°F (40° to 46°C). Sprinkle 1 Tbsp. (15 mL) of active dry yeast on the surface of each bowl, and let it dissolve three to five minutes. Compare the results. Which bowl of water activates the yeast? Why do you think this happened?

Building Your Portfolio

Develop a Press Release
Press releases alert the media to news, events, and items of interest. Imagine that you work for a public relations firm with clients in the food industry. One client, a company that makes whole-grain food products, wants you to write a press release to generate public interest in breads, cereals, rice, and pasta. Use information in this chapter to explain the nutritional value of whole-grain foods. Include tips and ideas for incorporating these foods into meal plans. Add the press release to your portfolio.

ANSWERS TO REVIEWING THE FACTS

1. Germ, endosperm, bran, and hull.
2. *Enriched*—nutrients lost in processing have been replaced; *fortified*—nutrients increased or other nutrients added.
3. Any two: store tightly wrapped in cool, dark place; refrigerate in hot weather; freeze tightly wrapped.
4. Quick breads use baking soda or baking powder to rise. Yeast breads rise through action of yeast.
5. Sounds hollow when tapped on crust.
6. To defrost or warm prepared foods; cook hot cereals; reheat cooked rice and pasta; cook frozen packaged dishes.

ANSWERS TO THINKING CRITICALLY

1. Breads provide many important nutrients and fiber; they are common to most cultures throughout history. They should be significant part of daily food choices.
2. Answers may include: use whole-wheat flour instead of white for baking; brown rice instead of white in recipes; whole-grain products such as barley, bulgur, and whole-wheat kernels in place of white rice or pasta.

Chapter Overview

Chapter 51 looks at fruits and vegetables, both fresh and processed. It gives suggestions for selecting, storing, and preparing fruits and vegetables for maximum nutritional value.

Motivators

■ **Attitude Survey.** Explore students' attitude toward vegetables. Ask: Did you like vegetables as a child? Now? What images or feelings do you associate with the word?

■ **Good Enough to Eat?** Bring in a piece of fresh fruit. Ask: How can you tell if this is ripe? Good to eat? Tell them this chapter will help them choose quality fruits and vegetables and prepare them for full flavor.

Objectives

Discuss the chapter objectives on this page. Remind students that the objectives focus on important chapter concepts.

Vocabulary

Point out that in this chapter *concentrate* and *produce* are used as nouns, not verbs. Call on volunteers to use these in sentences as verbs, then as nouns.

Chapter **Fruits and Vegetables**

Chapter **51**

Terms to Learn

- concentrates
- produce
- seasonal
- spoilage

Objectives

This chapter will help you to:

- Identify **foods in the Fruit Group and the Vegetable Group.**
- Explain **how to store fruits and vegetables.**
- Describe **how to retain nutrients when preparing fruits and vegetables.**

CHAPTER RESOURCES

Student Workbook
Study Guide, pp. 168-169
Activity, *Facts About Fruits*, p. 170

Teacher's Classroom Resources
Lesson Plan, p. 55
Extension #78, *Microwaving Vegetables*, p. 84

Foods Lab Activities, pp. 9-16
Life Skills, *Purchasing Produce at Its Peak*, p. 81
Transparency 46, *Selecting Fresh Fruits and Vegetables*
Chapter 51 Test, pp. 107-108

Performance Assessment, *Varieties of Fruits and Vegetables*, p. 84
Reteaching, *Facts About Produce*, p. 57

See Also:
ABCNews InterActive™ Videodiscs

Plants have provided people with important foods for thousands of years. Early peoples wandered great distances to find roots, stems, leaves, berries, and fruits to eat. Today refrigerated transportation brings a wide array of fruits and vegetables right to neighborhood stores.

Fruits and vegetables are valuable sources of vitamins and minerals. For example, oranges, tomatoes, and green peppers are rich in vitamin C. Carrots, cantaloupes, and apricots contain large amounts of vitamin A. Collard and turnip greens are valuable sources of vitamins A and C, calcium, and iron. Dark yellow and dark green fruits and vegetables are also high in beta-carotene, a nutrient that fights damage to body cells.

In addition, fruits and vegetables are excellent sources of carbohydrates, including starches, sugars, and fiber. Most fruits and vegetables contain small amounts of incomplete protein and little or no fat.

How fruits and vegetables are handled, processed, and cooked can affect the nutrients they contain. Therefore, learning how to select, store, and prepare fruits and vegetables will do more than improve the taste of meals and snacks—it will also add to their nutritional benefits.

Selecting

There is probably more variety in the Fruit Group and the Vegetable Group than in any of the other food groups. Most people who shop at a supermarket can easily name ten fruits and vegetables found in the produce section. **Produce** (PROH-doos) is a term used to describe *fresh fruits and vegetables.*

New transportation techniques are increasing the variety of produce available in supermarkets. Next to the familiar fruits and vegetables, you may also find varieties from around the world. The kiwifruit from New Zealand; the carambola, or star fruit, from South America; winged beans from the Philippines; and the chayote, or vegetable pear, from Latin America are some selections in the produce sections in today's supermarkets.

You can buy fruits and vegetables in several forms: fresh, frozen, canned, and (sometimes) dried. Many fruit and vegetable juices are also available.

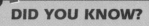

Examine fresh vegetables and fruits for color, ripeness, and texture. Don't buy any that are wilted, bruised, spotted, or damaged—they have lost nutrients and will not keep well.

CHAPTER 51   Fruits and Vegetables   497

TEACH

Topics on p. 497:
- **Value of Fruits and Vegetables**
- **Varieties of Produce**

Checking Comprehension

✓ What nutritional benefits do fruits and vegetables offer? *Good sources of vitamins A and C, calcium, iron, beta-carotene; traces of protein; little or no fat.*

✓ How does the variety of fruits and vegetables compare with that of other foods? *Probably most varied group; selection is increasing.*

Activity

■ **Trade-off.** Very ripe produce is often reduced in price for quick sale. Ask: Is the money saved worth possible nutrient loss? How can you decide whether overripe produce is a good economic and nutritional buy? (*Critical Thinking*)

MULTICULTURAL *Perspectives*

Ask students to learn where their favorite fruits and vegetables originated and to locate these regions on a world map. Encourage those who have lived in or visited another country to tell about popular produce there.

Focus on Consumer Skills

Bags of prewashed and cut produce are increasingly popular with consumers. Have students look for this form of produce and compare the prices to that of loose produce. How much more do consumers pay for convenience? Do they sacrifice anything in nutrition?

DID YOU KNOW?

Water in produce (80 to 95 percent of its content) is an often overlooked but vitally important nutrient. It transports other nutrients in the blood and is needed throughout digestion.

Checking Comprehension

✓ Why is freshness important in choosing produce? *Some vitamins deteriorate after harvest; freshest-looking are most nutritious.*

✓ Why might you choose processed fruits and vegetables? *When fresh are unavailable, in poor condition, expensive; for convenience.*

✓ What should you look for when buying juices? *Products that are 100 percent juice, with no added water and sweeteners.*

In Touch With TECHNOLOGY

Have students read "Bioengineered Foods" and discuss the questions. Ask if they can supply other facts about the subject. Encourage them to do more research and to share it with the class.

Answers to Thinking Critically

1. Answers may include: increase food supply by allowing imports to stay fresh; help economy by creating foods adapted to country's climate.
2. Answers will vary.
3. Answers will vary. Ask: Who should decide limits? How could they be enforced?

What main dishes and desserts could you make with canned, dried, or frozen fruits and vegetables?

Fresh

Fresh fruits and vegetables—crisp, tart apples, steaming baked potatoes—have tastes and textures that many people find irresistible. Fresh fruits and vegetables are usually more nutritious than processed ones, since fruits and vegetables can lose some nutrients during processing. Some of the vitamins in fresh produce deteriorate after harvest, however, so you should select fruits and vegetables that look fresh and crisp.

Fruits and vegetables should also have a healthy color and no bruises, spots, or sticky areas. Fruit that is soft to the touch may be overripe. Choose fruit that is relatively heavy for its size, since this usually indicates that the fruit will be juicy.

Carrots, salad greens, and some other fresh vegetables are available, cut and prewashed, in sealed bags. These are convenient for meal preparation or healthful snacking. They usually cost more, however, than loose produce.

Seasonal produce is *more plentiful at certain times of the year,* during its peak growing season. At other times it may not be available at all, or it may be more expensive

Processed

Sometimes, processed vegetables may be a good choice. Perhaps you want a particular kind of produce, but in its fresh form it is either unavailable, in poor condition, or expensive. Maybe you want to stock up on fruits and vegetables so that you don't have to go to the store so often. You may prefer the convenience of frozen, canned, or dried fruits and vegetables.

- **Frozen.** Frozen fruits and vegetables retain almost as many nutrients as fresh produce. In addition, they keep their flavor and color better than canned products. However, frozen fruits usually have a softer texture than fresh fruits. Frozen vegetables are available whole, cut in pieces, and in special sauces. Be aware, however, that sauces often add fat, sodium, or sugar—and calories—to the fruit or vegetable.
- **Canned.** Fruits and vegetables in cans also come in many forms, such as whole, halved, sliced, or in pieces. The form you choose depends on how you will use the item. Whole fruits and vegetables usually

because it has been shipped a long distance. Fresh corn, for example, is in season during the summer. Buying fruits and vegetables in season can provide you with top-quality produce at a relatively low price.

REAL-LIFE APPLICATION

Explain that many food traditions originated in a time when seasonal produce was the only type available. Pumpkin pie at Thanksgiving is one example; ask students if they can name others. Point out that now a variety of fruits and vegetables are available year-round. Ask: What fruit or vegetable would you associate with different events or holidays? Why would it be appropriate?

cost more than those in pieces. Many canned fruits are sold in a heavy sugar syrup. For less sugar and fewer calories, look for fruits packed in their own juices. Keep in mind that canned fruits and vegetables lose some of their nutritional value during the canning process.

- **Dried.** Many fruits and vegetables—from raisins and apricots to mushrooms, tomatoes, and onions—are available dried. All can be used in cooking, and dried fruits can be eaten as snacks.

- **Juices.** Apples, oranges, tomatoes, and carrots are some of the many fruits and vegetables that are commonly made into juices. Juices may be sold fresh, canned, or as frozen **concentrates**—*juice products from which most of the water has been removed.* Concentrates may be less costly than other forms of juice. Try to select 100 percent juice products. Products with names other than "juice," such as "fruit drinks," may have only a small amount of juice plus added water and sweeteners. Also keep in mind that juices lack the fiber content of fresh produce.

In Touch with TECHNOLOGY

Bioengineered Foods

A ripe, red tomato or a juicy orange at the height of its freshness is a marvel of nature. Increasingly, nature is getting an assist by a relatively new field of science. Genetic engineering, or bioengineering, uses sophisticated technology to develop higher-yield crops and to produce more healthful, less perishable foods.

As in humans, many of a plant's unique characteristics are programmed in their genes. Genetic engineers take the gene for a particular characteristic from one organism and place it into another. This allows them to improve the quality or quantity of food products in a number of ways:

- A gene inserted in a tomato turns off the tomato's natural tendency to rot, keeping it tasty and juicy for ten days instead of the normal three days.
- A gene from a cold-water fish can protect tomatoes from damage in freezing temperatures.
- A silkworm gene inserted into a potato can protect it from the disease soft rot.
- Potatoes can be modified so they absorb less fat when fried.
- Genetic engineering may someday produce feed grains with complete protein, allowing chickens to lay low-cholesterol eggs.

Genetic engineering does raise some questions. For example, people who avoid eating animal products may face a dilemma if animal genes are inserted into a food plant. Some people are concerned about possible negative consequences of genetically altering plants and animals. Some wonder how informed people will be about the genetic makeup of the foods they eat. Other people feel that the benefits outweigh any concerns. For example, making crops more resistant to disease could reduce the need for chemical pesticides.

Thinking Critically About Technology

1. How might genetically engineered foods help people in developing countries?
2. Do you think that most people will accept genetically engineered foods? Why or why not?
3. What, if any, limits do you think should be placed on genetic engineering? Explain your answer.

MORE ABOUT Seasonal Produce

While most produce is more abundant during spring and summer, different fruits and vegetables are more readily available during different months. Look for strawberries and rhubarb from late May to early June. Cherries are ripe and ready later in June. Tomatoes and peaches are juiciest in July and zucchini proliferates in August. Apples and "winter" squashes (including acorn squash and pumpkin) are bountiful in late summer and early autumn.

Checking Comprehension

✓ How should you store leafy greens? *Refrigerate in airtight containers.*

✓ Name two fresh fruits and two vegetables that keep well for a month or longer. *Apples, oranges; potatoes, onions.*

✓ Should you soak produce when washing it? *No; the produce may lose vitamins and minerals.*

✓ Give three tips for simmering produce. *Leave skins on; use little water; use heavy-bottomed pan.*

CROSS-CURRICULAR ACTIVITY
Art

Vegetable dyes are an ancient medium for coloring yarn and cloth. Have students research vegetable dyes and experiment with making their own vegetable-tie-dyed cloth.

Storing

Storing fruits and vegetables properly helps prevent **spoilage,** *damage caused by bacteria, yeasts, or molds that make food look or smell bad.* Some tips on storing fresh and processed fruits and vegetables to prevent spoilage follow.

Fresh

Many fresh fruits and vegetables need refrigeration. Lettuce and other leafy vegetables should be refrigerated in airtight containers to retain their moisture. Some unripe fruits, such as bananas, can be left at room temperature to ripen. Store potatoes and onions in a cool, dry, dark area.

Unless they are very dirty, fresh fruits and vegetables should not be washed until you are ready to use them. If you do wash produce before storing it, dry it thoroughly. Otherwise it may get slimy or moldy.

Use most fresh produce within a few days of buying it. Apples, however, can stay fresh in the refrigerator for three or four weeks, while oranges and other citrus fruits can keep for five weeks in the refrigerator. Stored properly, potatoes and onions can be kept up to two or three months. If you have a question about a specific product, ask the produce manager at your supermarket.

Processed

Frozen produce keeps well for several months if the temperature in the freezer or freezing compartment is no higher than 0°F (-18°C). If the temperature is 10° to 15°F (-12° to -9°C), foods purchased frozen can be stored for several weeks.

Canned fruits and vegetables keep for a year or more if they are stored in a cool, dry place. A temperature no higher than 70°F (21°C) is recommended.

Dried products keep well on the cabinet shelf, tightly wrapped. In humid weather, refrigerate dried fruit.

Juices should be stored according to the package directions. Canned and bottled juices can usually be stored on the shelf until they are opened. After opening, they should be kept in the refrigerator. Frozen juices should be kept frozen until use, but they should not be stored for more than 12 months.

The crisper drawer in your refrigerator is the best place for many vegetables, especially ones that have a high water content.

Preparing

You can prepare and serve fruits and vegetables in many ways. Whether served raw or cooked, with proper preparation these foods will retain their flavor, texture, and nutritional value.

Washing Fresh Produce

All fresh produce should be washed under cool running water just before you use it. Use a vegetable brush to scrub potatoes. Soaking produce in water is not recommended because vitamins and minerals may be lost.

MORE ABOUT *Saving Nutrients*

Preserving nutrients is always a concern when preparing vegetables. Nutrients in and under the skin may have to be sacrificed if the produce is caked with dirt or has been exposed to pesticides or chemical fertilizers. Such fruits and vegetables need to be scrubbed or perhaps peeled. Nutrients lost when vegetables are cooked in water can be recovered by using the water to make gravy, sauce, or soup.

Serving Raw Produce

Many fresh fruits and vegetables may be eaten raw as snacks, in salads, as appetizers, as side dishes, or for dessert. For snacking, produce such as apples and grapes can simply be washed and served. Often, however, produce must be peeled, pared, or cut before being eaten.

Some cut fruits and vegetables darken in color if they are not eaten or cooked immediately. This is especially true of apples, bananas, peaches, and avocados. You can prevent darkening by sprinkling the cut surfaces with lemon juice or wrapping the produce in plastic or another airtight covering.

Salad greens should be washed, drained thoroughly, and torn into bite-size pieces before tossing. To prevent wilting, add dressing to greens just before the salad is served.

Cooking with Moist Heat

Vegetables are often steamed or simmered, and fruits are sometimes poached. Remember that vitamin A, vitamin C, and the B vitamins are easily destroyed or dissolved by water, heat, and air. Follow the cooking suggestions provided in Chapter 48. In addition, take the following steps to preserve nutrients:

- Whenever possible, leave the skins on fruits and vegetables and leave them whole during cooking. If you cut them, make the pieces as large as your recipe will allow.
- Use as little water as possible. Steaming is ideal for most vegetables, because nutrient loss is minimal.
- When simmering fruits and vegetables, use a heavy-bottomed pan so that they can cook at a low, even temperature. Add a minimal amount of water. Cover the pan to prevent steam from taking valuable nutrients with it.
- To cook frozen vegetables, bring a small amount of water and the vegetables to a full boil in a saucepan. Reduce heat and simmer five to seven minutes or until the vegetables are tender. Do not overcook.

Canned vegetables are already cooked and need only to be heated. The liquid from canned vegetables may be used in soups and stews.

Baking

Baking is an excellent way to cook many fruits and vegetables because it preserves the nutrients well. You can bake pears, apples, potatoes, and all forms of squash. Sometimes a very small amount of liquid is added to the

Before using fresh fruits and vegetables, wash them carefully under cold running water to remove dirt, bacteria, and pesticides.

CHAPTER 51   Fruits and Vegetables   501

Activity

RETEACHING

■ **Step by Step.** Ask students to write instructions for cooking one kind of vegetable in its fresh, canned, and frozen forms. Remind students to aim for maximum flavor and minimum loss of nutrients.

Acting Responsibly

Have students read "Do You Conserve?" and discuss the questions. Ask for ways their families have discovered of conserving food.

Answers to Your Analysis

1. Any three: used microwave instead of conventional oven; saved broccoli; made stock; composted. *Benefits:* saved family money; made meals more nutritious; reduced need for chemical fertilizers.
2. Answers may include: when it compromises safety or sanitation; when it seriously diminishes food quality or nutrient value.
3. Answers will vary. Ask students what they can do to promote food conservation in their community.

DID YOU KNOW?

Many fruits ripen more quickly when placed in a paper bag.

You can hasten ripening of avocados by burying them in flour, and of bananas by wrapping them in a wet dish towel.

Place paper towels on the bottom of the crisper in the refrigerator to absorb excess moisture and keep produce fresh longer.

Lemons refrigerated in a tightly sealed jar of water will be juicier.

Review

■ **Chapter Review.** Use the contents of the Chapter Review page to help students review concepts, think critically, and apply their knowledge.

■ **Study Guide.** Have students complete the Study Guide for Chapter 51 on p. 168 of the Student Workbook.

■ **Produce Check.** Have students write the name of a fruit or vegetable on a slip of paper. Collect the papers. Draw them individually and choose one student to supply a fact about that fruit or vegetable, based on or supported by information found in the chapter.

Evaluation

■ **Chapter Test.** Use the reproducible chapter test provided in the Teacher's Classroom Resources or create your own test using the *Testmaker Software.*

■ **Alternative Assessment.** Ask students to create a new kind of produce, combining the qualities they most enjoy in existing fruits and vegetables. Have them give suggestions for choosing, storing, and preparing this food item, using information found in the chapter.

■ **Treat Them Right.** Ask students to imagine they are buying their favorite fruit and vegetable. Have them write a paragraph for each that explains how they choose, store, and prepare it.

---

pan to prevent the skins from becoming too dry. Potatoes, however, are baked entirely dry after their skin has been pierced to release steam.

Stir-Frying

Stir-frying—cooking quickly in very little fat—is another popular method of preparing vegetables. Cut the vegetables into small, even pieces for quick cooking. Stir-fried vegetables should not be overcooked; they should remain slightly crisp when pierced with a knife or fork.

Microwave Cooking

Microwave cooking is well-suited to fruits and vegetables. Because the microwave cooks quickly and requires very little, if any, added water, nutrients are not lost.

Fruits and vegetables will cook more evenly in the microwave if pieces are equal in size. When microwaving whole, unpeeled apples or potatoes, slit or pierce the skins to prevent bursting. For even cooking, foods usually should be stirred or rearranged once or twice. Fruits and vegetables should be taken out of the microwave while they are still slightly underdone and allowed to stand a few minutes to complete cooking.

Acting Responsibly

Do You Conserve?

Just as people conserve energy and other resources, they can also conserve food. Conserving food needn't mean accepting poor quality or skimping on nutrients. It does mean buying only those items that you will use, storing them properly to maintain their quality, and using them creatively.

Conservation in Action

"I need to get some things ready for dinner before we study," Jeanette said as her friend Sylvan set their textbooks on the table.

"Want some help?" Sylvan offered. "What are you fixing?"

"Grilled chicken, steamed broccoli, baked potatoes, and applesauce."

"Sounds good. We should start the potatoes now," Sylvan noted. "What oven temperature do you use?"

"I'll put them in the microwave oven later," Jeanette said, "since I don't need the oven for anything else. You can clean the broccoli while I bone the chicken."

Sylvan rinsed the broccoli and began cutting the flowerets into the steamer basket. "You can put in part of the stalks, too," Jeanette told him. "Just slice them thin."

"OK," Sylvan agreed as Jeanette put the chicken bones in a pot. "What are you doing with the bones?"

"We like soup made with homemade stock," she explained.

Sylvan laughed good naturedly. "You don't waste anything, do you?" He scooped up the tough broccoli stubs that had fallen into the sink. "Now I know you don't eat these—do you?"

"No," Jeanette shook her head and smiled. "We do have our limits." Then she uncovered a large coffee can from under the sink that was half full of coffee grounds and egg shells. "That we compost for the vegetable garden."

Your Analysis

1. Identify three ways in which Jeanette and her family conserved when preparing food. How do you think this benefited the family?
2. When might it be inadvisable to conserve on food or food preparation?
3. How would you describe society's attitude toward conserving food? Does society encourage or discourage it? Explain.

MORE ABOUT Exotic Produce

While many types of produce are making inroads in American markets, others have a way to go. Seaweed is one example. Long a staple of the Japanese diet (as a side dish or in soups and fish dishes), this sea vegetable is high in B vitamins and rich in calcium, iodine, iron, magnesium, potassium, and other minerals. Common varieties include agar-agar, carragheen (both used as thickeners in some commercial products) and kelp. Ask students how they would use seaweed in recipes.

Reviewing the Facts

1. Name five forms in which you can buy fruits and vegetables.
2. Describe three features to look for when you are buying fresh produce.
3. What does the term seasonal mean?
4. Name advantages of buying fresh fruits and vegetables, of buying frozen, and of buying canned.
5. Why should you cook vegetables in a covered pan or pot?
6. Why is microwave cooking a good method of cooking fruits and vegetables?

Thinking Critically

1. What would you say to encourage a person to eat a wider variety of fruits and vegetables?
2. Deep-fat frying is a common way of cooking some vegetables. Why do you think that this might not be the ideal method?

Applying Your Knowledge

1. **Using Reference Materials.** Select a fruit or vegetable, and find four recipes that use your choice in these dishes: an appetizer, a side dish, a main dish, and a dessert or snack. Make a poster showing the versatility of the fruit or vegetable by listing the various recipes.
2. **Explaining Storage Techniques.** Create a quick guide to storage techniques that a supermarket could give away in its produce section. Fold a piece of paper in half. On the left side, write the head "Fruits." On the right side, write the head "Vegetables." Then list several different types of fruits and vegetables, followed by short suggestions of how to store each. Use art, too, if you wish.

Making Connections

1. **Mathematics.** Locate the weekly food advertisements in a newspaper. Compare prices of fresh, frozen, and canned forms of one fruit and one vegetable. Estimate an equivalent amount, remembering that with fresh produce you may discard some of the fruit or vegetable before you use it. Which form is least expensive? Is the fresh form currently in season in your area? Write a brief report on your findings.
2. **Chemistry.** Using library resources, find out what happens to fruits and vegetables as they spoil. Write about the chemical changes that occur, and tell how proper storage techniques guard against spoilage.

Building Your Portfolio

Researching the Uncommon
Find information in cookbooks, encyclopedias, and other reference sources on three of the fruits and three of the vegetables listed at the end of this paragraph. Prepare a report that gives information about the food, including where it is grown or widely used, what it looks and tastes like, and what part of the plant it comes from. Fruits to choose from are cherimoya, guava, kumquat, persimmon, pomegranate, prickly pear, and carambola. Vegetables to choose from are artichoke, bok choy, celeriac, chayote, jicama, and kohlrabi. Add your finished report to your portfolio.

CHAPTER 51   Fruits and Vegetables   503

FOCUS

Chapter Overview

Chapter 52 focuses on milk and cheese: different types; proper storage; and tips for cooking with these products. It also describes other foods from the Milk, Yogurt, and Cheese Group.

Motivators

■ **Never Outgrown.** Point out that milk is the first food of all mammals—including humans. What might that say about the importance of milk products for nutrition?

■ **Milk and More.** Bring in clean, empty containers of dissimilar milk products, such as mint ice cream, cherry yogurt, and blue cheese. Ask: What do all of these items have in common?

Objectives

Discuss the chapter objectives on this page. Remind students that the objectives focus on important chapter concepts.

Vocabulary

Ask if students know the origin of the term *pasteurize*. Explain that Louis Pasteur, a French chemist of the late 1800s, discovered the method of destroying disease-producing microorganisms by partial sterilization.

Chapter 52

Milk, Yogurt, and Cheese

Terms to Learn

- coagulate
- dehydrated
- homogenized
- pasteurized

Objectives

This chapter will help you to:

- Identify and select **foods in the Milk, Yogurt, and Cheese Group.**
- Explain **how to store milk, yogurt, and cheese.**
- Describe **the best methods of preparing milk, yogurt, and cheese.**

504   UNIT 6   Food, Nutrition, and Wellness

CHAPTER RESOURCES

Student Workbook
Study Guide, pp. 171-172
Activity, *Milk Facts*, pp. 173-174

Teacher's Classroom Resources
Lesson Plan, p. 56

Extension #79, *Cheeses from Around the World*, p. 85
Foods Lab Activities, pp. 17-20
Life Skills, *Choosing New Cheeses*, pp. 82-83
Chapter 52 Test, pp. 109-110

Performance Assessment, *Milk and Milk Products*, p. 85
Reteaching, *Varieties of Milk*, p. 58

See Also:
ABCNews InterActive™ Videodiscs

The Milk, Yogurt, and Cheese Group is unique among the food groups in that it includes products made from just one substance: milk. In the United States, milk usually means cow's milk. In some other countries, people drink milk that comes from goats, camels, sheep, and llamas.

Milk is an excellent source of many nutrients. It provides carbohydrates, complete proteins, and water. It also provides fat—the amount varies depending on how the milk is processed. Milk is also an excellent source of calcium and phosphorus. In combination with vitamin D, these two minerals make bones and teeth strong.

Milk is also rich in several essential vitamins. It is a good source of riboflavin, a B vitamin, as well as vitamin A. (Since vitamin A is fat soluble, milk from which the fat has been removed must be fortified with vitamin A.) Most milk is also fortified with vitamin D, a nutrient that must be present for calcium and phosphorus to be used by the body. Because vitamin D occurs naturally in very few foods, adding it to milk makes it possible for people to get enough.

Selecting

Milk products come in many varieties. You can buy whole milk, milk with less fat, or milk with nearly all fat removed. You can choose from yogurt and hundreds of varieties of cheeses. In addition, many delicious flavors of ice cream, frozen yogurt, and low-fat ice cream are available.

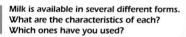
Milk is available in several different forms. What are the characteristics of each? Which ones have you used?

Milk

Milk can be purchased in liquid or **dehydrated** form, meaning that *all of the liquid has been removed*. Milk sold as a liquid is usually **pasteurized** (PASS-chuh-ryzed), or *heated and cooled to kill harmful bacteria*. It is also **homogenized** (hoe-MAH-juh-nyzed), which involves *suspending the fat particles into the liquid*. Here are some of the types of milk available:

- **Whole milk.** Whole milk has all the original nutrients of milk and at least 3.5 percent fat. None of the fat has been removed from whole milk. One cup (250 mL) of whole milk contains 150 calories.
- **Low-fat milk.** Low-fat milk has less fat than whole milk but more than skim milk. Low-fat milk comes in different varieties—2 percent and 1 percent fat content are the most common. One cup (250 mL) of 1 percent low-fat milk contains 100 calories. Although low-fat milk is a little higher in calories than skim milk, many people prefer its flavor and texture.

CHAPTER 52   Milk, Yogurt, and Cheese   505

TEACH

Topics on p. 505:
- **Milk in the Diet**
- **Types of Milk**

Checking Comprehension

✓ Why is milk fortified with vitamin D? *Vitamin D occurs naturally in very few foods and is needed for the body to use calcium and phosphorus.*

✓ What other nutrients does milk contain? *Carbohydrates, complete protein, water, fat, calcium, phosphorus, riboflavin, vitamin A.*

✓ Why is milk pasteurized? *To kill harmful bacteria.*

Activity

■ **Taste Test.** Bring in samples of whole, 2 percent, 1 percent, and skim milk. Conduct a blind taste test with volunteers, asking them to describe and identify each sample. Afterward discuss: were students surprised at the results? Do those who usually drink whole milk feel that drinking lower-fat varieties is a "sacrifice"? Did those who drink other types enjoy whole milk? Do the health advantages of lower-fat milk outweigh anything students feel it lacks in taste or texture? *(Critical Thinking)*

MORE ABOUT Types of Milk

By law, all milk sold in interstate trade must be pasteurized. Unpasteurized—"raw"—milk may be sold within some states if the herds have been "certified"—declared free of brucellosis, an infectious disease that can be transmitted to humans. Many people believe raw milk has a superior, more natural taste. The practice remains controversial, however. Young children, older adults, and pregnant women are cautioned against drinking unpasteurized milk.

Checking Comprehension

✓ Which kind of liquid milk might a person on a diet choose? *Why? Skim; has most of nutrients, little fat, and fewer calories than whole milk.*

✓ What is an advantage of UHT milk? *Needs no refrigeration until opened.*

✓ What is ripening? How does it affect cheese? *Aging; gives cheese special taste, texture, appearance, depending on length of time.*

STRATEGIES THAT WORK

Have students read "Getting Enough Calcium" and discuss the questions. Ask: Do you think teens know that—or how—they can get calcium from sources other than milk products?

Answers to Think . . .

1. Answers may include: aren't aware of dietary sources; think of milk as a "kid's" drink.
2. Answers may include: poor bone and tooth development, osteoporosis, dental problems.
3. Answers may include: the body may absorb calcium in foods better; calcium-rich foods provide other needed nutrients; supplements may be expensive.

- **Skim milk.** Skim milk is whole milk from which almost all the fat has been removed. It has most of the nutrients supplied by whole milk, except for fat, and it is fortified with vitamin A. One cup (250 mL) of skim milk contains only 85 calories, much less than whole milk.

- **Cream.** Cream is a high-fat liquid separated from whole milk. It contains at least 18 percent fat. Heavy cream has more fat than light cream. Just 1 Tbsp. (15 mL) of heavy cream contains 80 calories.
- **Half-and-half.** Half-and-half is a mixture of cream and milk. It offers some of the rich taste and texture of cream with less fat and fewer calories.

STRATEGIES That Work

Getting Enough Calcium

You need more calcium in the teen years than at any other time of life. Yet many teens don't get enough. How can you avoid becoming one of them?

Milk products are undeniably one of the best dietary sources of calcium. One cup (250 mL) of skim milk supplies about 300 mg of calcium—one-fourth of a teen's or young adult's daily calcium needs. Choosing milk in place of a soft drink even once a day significantly boosts your calcium intake. Yogurt and cheese are also calcium-rich.

Some teens, however, must avoid milk products due to allergies, lactose intolerance, or other reasons. Even teens who include milk products in their diets may not be getting enough calcium. Fortunately, many other foods also provide this nutrient. Here is a partial list:

Food and Serving Size	Calcium (mg)
½ cup (125 mL) tofu	258
3 oz. (84 g) canned salmon	181
½ cup (125 mL) cooked collard greens	178
½ cup (125 mL) cooked spinach	149
½ cup (25 mL) baked beans	77
1 cup (250 mL) raw spinach	55
1 bran muffin	54
1 orange	52

Calcium-fortified foods are another option. For example, calcium-fortified orange juice has about as much calcium as milk.

If in doubt, discuss your calcium needs and food choices with your physician. He or she may recommend calcium supplements in addition to calcium-rich foods.

Making the Strategy Work

Think . . .

1. What are some possible reasons why many teens don't get enough calcium?
2. What might be the long-term consequences of not getting enough calcium?
3. What are the advantages of getting calcium from the foods you eat instead of relying only on calcium supplements?

Try...

Identify three specific ways to increase your own calcium intake through your food choices. Try these ideas over a period of several days. Which do you think could become long-term habits?

506   UNIT 6   Food, Nutrition, and Wellness

DID YOU KNOW?

The bacteria *Lactobacillus acidophilus* in yogurt aids in digestion by breaking down milk sugar into lactic acid. The acidic environment promotes mineral absorption and prevents the growth of harmful bacteria. Not all yogurt has live *Lactobacillus acidophilus*. Check the label.

Nonfat dry milk is added to some varieties of low-fat milk to increase their protein content. These are labeled "high protein" or "protein fortified."

- **Evaporated milk.** Canned evaporated milk is whole milk that has been heated to remove 60 percent of the water. By adding the right amount of water, you can create a product similar to fresh whole milk. The calorie content is about the same as that of whole milk.
- **Sweetened condensed milk.** Canned sweetened condensed milk has about half the water removed and added sugar. It is a rich concentrated milk that can be used in baked desserts and candy.
- **Nonfat dry milk.** This is milk from which all the moisture and most of the fat have been removed before packaging. Nonfat dry milk is an inexpensive powder that contains all the nutrients found in skim milk with about half the calories of whole milk. It can be used for cooking and, with water added, for drinking.
- **UHT (ultra-high-temperature) milk.** This milk has been heated to very high temperatures to kill all the bacteria. It comes in cartons but needs no refrigeration until after the carton is opened.

Cheese

Cheese is made from the milk of cows or goats. The type of cheese depends on what milk it is made from and how it is made. There are hundreds of types of cheeses.

Some cheeses, such as cottage or cream cheese, are fresh or unripened and must be used within a short time. These cheeses have soft textures and mild flavors. Other cheeses, such as Swiss, Cheddar, and Parmesan, are aged or ripened for as long as two years. Each type of cheese requires a specific length of time and temperature to develop. This gives the cheese its special flavor, texture, and appearance. The longer the cheese ages, the sharper the flavor becomes. A short ripening time produces a mild-flavored cheese.

Cheese is a milk product and is a good source of complete protein, carbohydrates, and calcium. For example, the calcium content of 1 cup (250 mL) of milk can be provided by about 2 cups (500 mL) of cottage cheese or by 1½ oz. (42 g) of Cheddar cheese. These equivalent amounts of cheese, however, are higher in calories than milk. Although many cheeses have a high fat content, low-fat varieties are becoming increasingly available.

Almost all cheeses can be put into one of these four categories:

- **Soft.** These range in flavor from mild types—such as cottage cheese, cream cheese, and ricotta—to the tangy French Brie (BREE) and Camembert (KA-muhm-behr). Some soft cheeses are flavored with garlic, herbs, or pepper.
- **Semisoft.** Mild cheeses such as Muenster (MUHN-stur), Monterey Jack, and mozzarella (maht-suh-REH-luh) are semisoft. So are many strong-flavored blue cheeses, including Roquefort, Stilton, and Gorgonzola.
- **Hard.** Hard cheeses range from mild to sharp flavors. They include Cheddar, provolone, Swiss, and Parmesan. Their hard, granular texture makes them excellent for grating.
- **Processed.** These are mixtures of different natural cheeses, blended by hot or cold processing methods. Sometimes they are combined with flavorings such as pepper, spices, or olives. Pasteurization stops the aging of the natural cheese, giving processed cheese a consistent flavor and texture and a longer period of freshness.

Other Milk Products

Some milk products are formed by adding new ingredients to milk, while others are developed through a freezing process.

- **Cultured milk products.** The flavor and texture of milk and cream can be changed by the addition of certain harmless bacteria. These bacteria, grown in colonies called cultures, turn milk and cream into products that have a tangy taste and a thick texture. That is why yogurt, sour cream, and buttermilk are called cultured milk products. Sour cream is made from cream, buttermilk is made from skim or low-fat milk, and yogurt can be made from either whole or

Activities

ENRICHMENT

■ **Cheese Challenge.** Encourage students to experiment with making their own cheese. Recipes and ingredients can be found at natural foods stores. Invite volunteers to share the results.

MULTICULTURAL *Perspectives*

Cheeses are a source of great pride, even renown, for the country that produces them. Have students research one well-known cheese and write a brief description on a small piece of paper. Have them post their descriptions on a world map.

MORE ABOUT Cheese

Cheese is made by souring milk through heating, adding lactic acid, or both. Rennet (an enzyme from calves' stomachs) is added, causing the curds (milk solids) to separate from the whey (liquids). The whey is drained and the curds broken up. Cream or milk is added to the curds to make fresh cheeses. Aged cheeses are made by further draining or pressing out the whey to achieve the desired hardness, then allowing the curd to ferment—up to three years for some types.

Topics on pp. 508-510:
- Storing Milk Products
- Cooking with Milk and Cheese

Checking Comprehension

✓ What are the nutritional concerns about frozen milk products? *Have more sugar and calories than other products; some have more fat.*

✓ How do warmth and light affect fresh milk? *Warmth allows harmful bacteria growth; light destroys riboflavin.*

✓ How should soft cheeses be stored? For how long? *Refrigerate tightly covered for a few days.*

✓ How can you prevent cheese from toughening when added to sauces? *Use low heat; chop, grate, or slice; add last; stir constantly until melted.*

FAMILY AND COMMUNITY OUTREACH

Ask students to record the milk products their family usually consumes. Suggest they consult with family members to decide on new products to try and possibly add to their diet.

---

skim milk. Yogurts come in both plain and flavored varieties.

- **Frozen milk products.** Ice cream, ice milk, and frozen yogurt are all popular desserts made from milk. Ice milk and frozen yogurt contain less fat and fewer calories than ice cream. All three, however, are usually sweetened with sugar and contain more calories than liquid milk or regular yogurt.

Storing

Once you get milk products home, keeping them fresh is important. Most dairy products are perishable. Storing them properly helps you use them safely, enjoy their flavor, and avoid wasting money. Most milk products will stay fresh for up to a week if properly stored.

Milk

Fresh milk should be kept in the coldest part of the refrigerator to retain nutrients and freshness for as long as possible. Putting the milk container away as soon as you have used what you need is important, since warmth and light both harm fresh milk. Warmth allows the growth of harmful bacteria, while light destroys the riboflavin, a B vitamin, in milk. To protect milk from light, buy milk in opaque cardboard cartons instead of translucent plastic jugs. Low-fat milk is especially subject to nutrient loss. Cream and half-and-half should also be refrigerated.

Evaporated and sweetened condensed milk as well as UHT milk can be stored for long periods of time on the cabinet shelf. Once you have opened the cans, however, refrigerate any unused portions, and finish them within a day or two. It is best to store the unused portions of canned products in clean glass or plastic containers and to dispose of the used cans.

Nonfat dry milk keeps well on the shelf as long as it is stored away from moisture. After adding water to dry milk to restore it to liquid form, use or refrigerate it right away, just as you would fresh milk.

Cheese and Other Products

Keep all cheese in the refrigerator. Soft cheeses, such as cottage cheese, stay fresh for a few days if tightly covered. Hard cheeses, such as Cheddar and Swiss, remain fresh for weeks or even months if they are tightly wrapped in plastic or foil and stored in the coldest part of the refrigerator. Whole blocks of cheese will keep better than sliced cheeses. Be sure to wrap strong cheeses well, since their odors can be absorbed by delicately flavored foods.

Cultured milk products also need refrigeration. Although they keep longer unopened than fresh milk, once opened they spoil quickly. Use them by the dates stamped on the packages.

Canned milk has a long shelf life. What should you do with leftover milk after the can has been opened?

MORE ABOUT Storing Milk Products

Although fresh cheeses do not freeze well, some hard cheeses such as Cheddar do, as does milk. Milk and cheeses can be frozen successfully for up to three months, while ice cream and ice milk are best used within a month.

DID YOU KNOW?

Heating slightly affects the nutrient value of milk; boiling renders milk an incomplete protein. Pasteurization, which involves a low heating temperature, does not destroy proteins in milk.

Managing Your Life

Safe Handling and Storage of Milk

Using resources wisely is an important part of management. Food lost to spoilage is a resource wasted. Eating spoiled food is even more costly. Fresh milk is an excellent example. It is one of the most nutritious of all foods, but also one of the most perishable. In addition to the guidelines given in the chapter, follow these tips to be sure the milk you buy is safe to drink and cook with:

- Always check the "sell by" date on the milk container when you buy it, and buy no more milk than you can use within about five days after that date. A large container may cost less per ounce, but it's not a better buy if it spoils before you can use it.
- Get the milk home from the store and into the refrigerator quickly. Keep the thermostat of your refrigerator set at 38°F (3°C).
- Always return milk to the refrigerator as soon as you use it. Milk left at room temperature longer than two hours should be discarded. If you pour milk into a pitcher for serving, pour out only as much as you will use. Don't return leftover milk to the original container.
- Never drink directly from the milk container. Bacteria flourish in milk.

- If you must store milk for more than five days beyond the "sell by" date, consider buying evaporated, nonfat dry, or ultra-high-temperature (UHT) milk. Until opened or reconstituted, these forms of milk have a shelf life of six months or more.

Applying the Principles

1. What form of milk would be the best choice for a camping trip? Why?
2. Suppose your younger brother has a habit of drinking milk directly out of the carton. What might you say to convince him that this is not only rude but unsafe for the family's health?
3. If you lived alone and the only milk you used was a few ounces for cereal each morning, what is the largest-size container of milk you should you buy?
4. What are some ways to use up milk when it is nearing five days beyond the "sell by" date?

The freezer, of course, is the place for ice cream, ice milk, and frozen yogurt. If the freezer temperature is above 0°F (-18°C), the product should be used within a few days. Freezing milk products that are not meant for freezing—cheese, sour cream, and fresh yogurt, for example—may damage their flavor and texture.

If ice cream is kept in the freezer too long, it loses flavor and texture. For most people, eating it in time is not much of a problem.

MORE ABOUT Using Cheese

Usually, mild-flavored cheeses combine better with other foods in a recipe. More pungent varieties such as Brie and blue are better in appetizers, salads, and desserts. When substituting cheeses, choose those with similar textures for best results.

DID YOU KNOW?

The home remedy of drinking a glass of warm milk to cure insomnia has some validity. Milk contains tryptophan, an amino acid that helps people fall asleep naturally. Whether the milk is warm or cold doesn't seem to matter.

Review

■ **Chapter Review.** Use the contents of the Chapter Review page to help students review concepts, think critically, and apply their knowledge.

■ **Study Guide.** Have students complete the Study Guide for Chapter 52 on p. 171 of the Student Workbook.

■ **Milk on the Menu.** Have students plan a one-day menu—three meals and a snack—that includes at least one milk product in every meal. Have students note why they chose that particular product; how they would store it before and after use; and, if applicable, the procedure for preparing it.

Evaluation

■ **Chapter Test.** Use the reproducible chapter test provided in the Teacher's Classroom Resources or create your own test using the *Testmaker Software.*

■ **Alternative Assessment.** Have groups create a game show requiring contestants to answer questions about choosing, storing, and using milk products. Encourage groups to be creative in pursuing a "milk" theme throughout their plans. A correct answer, for example, might be indicated by a ringing cow bell, an incorrect one by a mooing cow.

■ **Ode to Cheddar?** Ask students to write a poem about selecting, storing, and using milk products. Encourage them to use humor.

Preparing

Milk products can be served in a variety of ways. They may be eaten fresh or used in cooking. Proteins **coagulate,** or *change from a fluid state to a thickened mass,* when they are heated. In order to prevent milk proteins from becoming tough and stringy at high temperatures, low heat is the rule for cooking milk and milk products.

Cooking with Milk

Because milk can scorch, or burn, easily, cook milk products in heavy pans that allow slow, even heating. In addition to preventing scorching, this also keeps milk from boiling over. A double boiler, a type of pan in which one pan is nested inside another, can also be used to heat milk. The heat from boiling water in the lower pan cooks the food in the upper pan without scorching or coagulating it.

Low temperatures and stirring also prevent a skin from forming over the surface of the milk. If a skin begins to develop, stir it vigorously back into the milk to avoid losing valuable proteins. Covering the pan during cooking also discourages skin formation. Covering the pan also helps retain the milk nutrients, since light quickly destroys riboflavin, a B vitamin.

To cook milk and milk mixtures in a microwave oven, follow the same general rules but watch the mixture very closely. Because milk boils over easily, the glass or bowl used to heat milk should be no more than two-thirds full. Puddings will scorch if they are cooked in the microwave too long.

Puddings and custards are another way to enjoy the benefits of milk.

Many packaged convenience products use milk in their preparation. Milk is often added to rice and noodle dishes and packaged soups. Follow the package directions to ensure the best preparation of these dishes.

Cooking with Cheese

Cheese can be served in dozens of ways. It can be served uncooked, melted in a sandwich, or added to a sauce. It can also be grated and sprinkled on top of casseroles or vegetables near the end of the cooking time. Cheese can also be baked in pasta, beef, chicken, or vegetable casseroles. Baking or boiling quickly melts the cheese. As with milk, the rule to remember when cooking cheese is to cook it slowly over low heat.

Cheese toughens when it is overcooked. To allow it to melt swiftly, chop, grate, or slice the cheese into small pieces before adding it to liquid in a recipe. The cheese should be added last to a mixture and stirred constantly until it melts. Overheating may cause the protein in some cheeses to coagulate and separate from the mixture.

Cheese toppings need to be watched carefully for signs of overcooking or toughening. Top casseroles with cheese during the last five or ten minutes of baking. Bake cheese-topped casseroles no higher than 375°F (190°C). Cheese that is broiled should be placed several inches from the heat source and broiled only until the cheese softens. The same principles apply to cooking cheese in a microwave oven.

Focus on Critical Thinking Skills

Have students read nutritional information from the labels of nondairy substitutes for dairy products, such as margarine, coffee lighteners, and dessert toppings. What are these products made of? What are some advantages and disadvantages, in terms of nutrition and convenience, of using them instead of the dairy products they replace?

Chapter 52

Review

Reviewing the Facts

1. Describe the main characteristics of five types of milk.
2. What are the four basic categories of cheese? Name a type of cheese from each category.
3. How are cultured milk products produced? How does this process affect the flavor of milk?
4. Describe the recommended way to store hard cheese.
5. Explain how to store fresh, canned, and dry milk.
6. How should milk and milk products be cooked? Why?

Thinking Critically

1. What do you think are some of the advantages and disadvantages of adding cheese to vegetables and sauces?
2. What are three suggestions you might make to someone who is interested in trimming his or her fat intake while still enjoying milk and milk products?

Applying Your Knowledge

1. **Making a Chart.** Make a chart that compares the different types of milk in terms of fat content, storage directions, and typical uses in cooking. Use information from your textbook as well as other sources.
2. **Uses for Yogurt.** Plain low-fat or nonfat yogurt is a healthful alternative to sour cream on a baked potato. Using cookbooks and other resources, find at least five other specific ways to use yogurt as a topping or in recipes. Share your findings with your classmates.
3. **Nutrient Comparison.** Compare the nutrition information on packages of three different versions of the same dairy product. For example, you might compare regular, reduced-fat, and fat-free Cheddar cheese.

What is the difference in fat and calories per serving? How do the amounts of other nutrients compare? What items in the ingredients lists might account for the differences in nutrient content? Write a summary of your findings.

Making Connections

1. **Science.** Investigate how the pasteurization process takes place. Create a chart illustrating this process. Write a brief summary of the benefits of pasteurization.
2. **Health.** Research the use of rBGH (recombinant bovine growth hormone) to increase the milk supply. How does rBGH work? What health concerns have been raised about its use? What evidence has been presented by those who oppose the hormone's use and by those who support it? Report your findings to the class.

Building Your Portfolio

Creating a Reference Chart

Create a reference chart identifying at least ten different types of cheese. List the name of each cheese, its country of origin (when applicable), the type of milk it's made from, a description of its flavor and texture, and several ways that it might be used in preparing food. Consult encyclopedias, cookbooks, and other food references found in the classroom for information about these cheeses. If possible, use drawings or photos to illustrate the chart before adding it to your portfolio.

ANSWERS TO REVIEWING THE FACTS

1. Any five: *whole milk*— at least 3.5 percent fat content, 150 calories per serving; *low-fat*—1 or 2 percent fat, 100 calories per serving; *skim milk*— almost no fat, fortified with vitamin A, 85 calories per serving; *cream*—at least 18 percent fat, 80 calories per Tbsp. (15 mL); *half-and-half*—mixture of cream and milk; *evaporated milk*—whole milk with 60 percent of water removed; *sweetened condensed milk*—half of water removed, sugar added; *nonfat dry milk*— powdered, all nutrients of skim, half the calories of whole; *UHT milk*—heated to kill bacteria, no refrigeration until opened.
2. Examples may include (any one): *soft*—cottage or cream cheese, ricotta, Brie, Camembert; *semisoft*—Muenster, Monterey Jack, mozzarella, blue; *hard*— Cheddar, provolone, Swiss, Parmesan; *processed*— blend of naturals with pepper, spices, olives.
3. Harmless bacteria added to milk and cream; gives tangy taste.
4. Wrap tightly in plastic or foil, store in coldest part of refrigerator.
5. *Fresh*—in coldest part of refrigerator; *canned*—on cabinet shelf until opened, then refrigerate in glass or plastic; *dry*—on shelf away from moisture until reconstituted, then refrigerate.
6. With low heat and regular stirring to prevent proteins from coagulating, scorching, becoming tough and stringy.

ANSWERS TO THINKING CRITICALLY

1. Advantages may include: adds nutrition; gives flavor; improves texture. Disadvantages: adds calories and fat; could scorch or toughen.

2. Answers may include: choose low-fat milks and cheeses; use small amounts of strong-flavored cheese; buy ice milk or frozen yogurt instead of ice cream.

Chapter Overview

Chapter 53 discusses the protein-rich foods of the Meat, Poultry, Fish, Dry Beans, Eggs, and Nuts Group. It offers tips for selecting and storing these foods in their various forms and for choosing appropriate cooking methods.

Motivator

■ **Portrait of Protein.** Show students three pictures: a cut of meat, a piece of fish, and a beans-and-rice (or other complementary protein) dish. As you hold up each one, ask: Is this a good source of protein? Explain that each can be a good way to get protein, depending on a person's preferences and circumstances.

Objectives

Discuss the chapter objectives on this page. Remind students that the objectives focus on important chapter concepts.

Vocabulary

Ask students for examples of the different uses of the word *cut*. Tell them they can add another definition—a particular section of an animal carcass that is used for food. Ask them to name some cuts of meat.

Chapter 53 Meat, Poultry, Fish, Dry Beans, Eggs, and Nuts

Terms to Learn

- cut
- marbling
- processed meat
- variety meat

Objectives

This chapter will help you to:

- Identify **foods in the Meat, Poultry, Fish, Dry Beans, Eggs, and Nuts Group.**
- Explain **how to store protein foods.**
- Describe **recommended methods for cooking protein foods.**

CHAPTER RESOURCES

Student Workbook
Study Guide, pp. 175-176
Activity, *Protein Basics*, pp. 177-178

Teacher's Classroom Resources
Lesson Plan, p. 57
Cooperative Learning, *The Five Food Groups*, pp. 59-60

Extension #80, *Useful Cooking Techniques*, p. 86
Foods Lab Activities, pp. 21-24
Life Skills, *Protein Sources*, p. 84
Transparency 47, *Beef on the Hoof*
Chapter 53 Test, pp. 111-112

Performance Assessment, *The Many Sources of Protein*, p. 86
Reteaching, *Protein Foods*, p. 59

See Also:
ABCNews InterActive™ Videodiscs

The Meat, Poultry, Fish, Dry Beans, Eggs, and Nuts Group offers a wide variety of food choices. All of these foods are important sources of proteins. Proteins are the nutrients that maintain healthy muscles and tissues—in fact, they are involved with all the cells in your body. Most foods in this group also provide iron and important vitamins, such as the B vitamins and vitamin A. Legumes (dry beans) are rich in carbohydrates and fiber.

Selecting

Whether you eat meat or are a vegetarian, this food group is full of choices to make delicious dishes for every meal. From roast chicken to a western omelet, you can easily find some foods in this group to enjoy every day.

Meats

Beef, veal, lamb, and pork are the most common types of meats. Beef and veal come from cattle, lamb comes from sheep, and pork comes from hogs.

Each type of meat is sold in many different **cuts,** which are *sections or parts of the meat carcass.* The meat is first divided into large sections, called wholesale cuts, and then into smaller retail cuts for purchase. For example, pork loin is a wholesale cut. It is divided into retail cuts, such as chops, ribs, and roasts. The price label on the meat package lists the type of meat first, then the wholesale cut, and finally the retail cut. **Figure 53.1** shows a typical meat label.

Tenderness is an important consideration when buying meat because it affects cost and cooking method. Cuts that are naturally ten-

Figure 53.1

INTERPRETING A MEAT LABEL

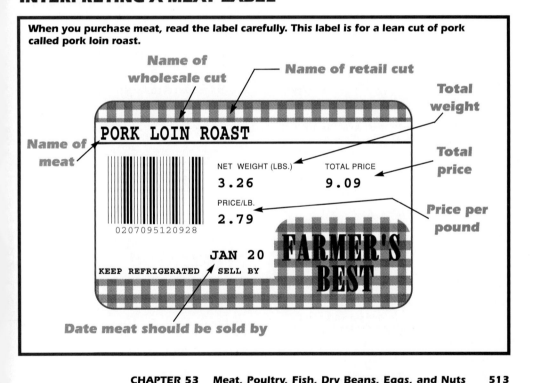

When you purchase meat, read the label carefully. This label is for a lean cut of pork called pork loin roast.

Name of wholesale cut

Name of retail cut

Name of meat

Total weight

Total price

Price per pound

PORK LOIN ROAST

NET WEIGHT (LBS.)
3.26

TOTAL PRICE
9.09

PRICE/LB.
2.79

0207095120928

JAN 20

KEEP REFRIGERATED   SELL BY

FARMER'S BEST

Date meat should be sold by

TEACH

Topics on p. 513:
- **Types of Meat**
- **Meat Cuts**
- **Reading Meat Labels**

Checking Comprehension

✓ What are the most common types of meat? Where do they come from? *Beef and veal—cattle; lamb—sheep; pork—hogs.*

✓ What is the difference between wholesale and retail cuts? *Retail cuts are smaller sections of wholesale cuts; purchased by consumers.*

✓ What information is found on the meat label? *Type of meat and cuts, total weight, total price, price per pound, "sell by" date.*

Activities

■ **Make a Diagram.** Have pairs use drawings from cookbooks or other resources to make diagrams showing where different cuts of meat come from. *(Observation)*

CROSS-REFERENCE

Chapter 37 tells more about the role of proteins in maintaining health. Chapter 38 gives guidelines for including protein foods in your daily diet.

DID YOU KNOW?

Why is cattle called beef when it comes to the table, and pig called pork? The animal names originated in the Saxon language of England, in the ninth century and earlier. When William of Normandy conquered England in 1066, the Norman (French) language became predominant, especially among the ruling classes. The Saxon farmers kept their names for their livestock; Norman chefs and aristocrats used the French, translated into modern English as beef, veal, lamb, mutton, and pork.

Topics on pp. 514-515:
- **Choosing Meats, Poultry, and Fish**

Checking Comprehension

✓ How can you limit fat intake when buying cuts of meat? *Choose lean cuts; choose meat with little marbling; trim fat before cooking; look for statement of fat content on label; choose grades Choice or Select.*

✓ Name some nutritional benefits of eating poultry. *Complete protein, B vitamins, and iron; skinless has less fat than most meats.*

✓ What are the different form of fresh fish? *Drawn, dressed, steaks, fillets.*

MULTICULTURAL *Perspectives*

Have students learn more about meat sources in different cultures, including their own. Ask them to find out why a particular animal became a popular food source and how it is often prepared.

---

der include those from the rib, loin or short loin, sirloin, and leg or round. These cuts usually are more expensive than others. Less tender cuts, such as those from the chuck or flank, are relatively inexpensive. Long, slow cooking in moist heat can make them more tender.

Leanness is another consideration. Although meat is nutritious, it can be high in saturated fat. Often there is a visible layer of fat around the edge of the cut. Some fat is also present as **marbling**, *fine streaks and flecks of fat within the lean area of the meat.* Mar-

bling adds flavor and juiciness. However, meat with less marbling can be just as delicious when properly cooked.

To reduce your fat intake, choose lean cuts. Examples include beef round, loin, sirloin, and chuck arm; pork tenderloin, center loin, and ham; most cuts of veal; and lamb leg, loin, and foreshanks. Look for meat with little visible fat, and trim away as much as you can before cooking. When buying ground meat, look for a statement of fat content on the label.

Another way to judge fat content is by the grade of meat. Beef, lamb, and veal are graded. The top three grades are:

Managing Your Life
Meals with an All-Star Cast

Many people think of meat, poultry, or fish as the "star" of a meal—one reason, perhaps, that they eat more of these foods than is necessary or healthful. Of course, protein foods from animals provide many valuable nutrients—not only protein, but B vitamins, iron, zinc, and more. Still, eating large portions of these foods has two drawbacks.

First, it can make your food choices "top-heavy" when it comes to the Food Guide Pyramid. As you know, most of your servings of food should come from grain products, vegetables, and fruits. These food groups form the base of the Pyramid—and of a healthful diet. Protein foods are equally necessary, but in smaller amounts. If you eat a lot of meat, poultry, and fish, you may get too much protein and fat and not enough of the fiber and nutrients that grains, vegetables, and fruits provide.

Also, a diet based on meat, poultry, and fish is an expensive one. Eating less of these foods can help you manage your food budget.

How can you learn new ways of eating in which meat, poultry, and fish share the stage with other nutritious foods instead of stealing the limelight? Here are some suggestions:

- Become familiar with the recommended serving size: 2 to 3 oz. (56 to 84 g) of cooked lean meat, poultry, or fish. One serving of meat is about the size of a deck of cards.

- Fill at least two-thirds of your plate with grain products, vegetables, and fruits—then take a serving of meat, fish, or poultry.

- If you want seconds, don't automatically have another drumstick or pork chop. Help yourself first to more of the meal's high-carbohydrate foods, such as rolls or fruit salad.

- In dishes such as casseroles, stews, stir-fries, and main dish salads, think of meat, poultry, or fish as a flavorful addition rather than the main ingredient. Use a little less of these foods than you're used to. Make your favorite chili with less ground beef, for example, and more beans and tomatoes.

- Plan meals around plant proteins, such as dry beans, more often. They are lower in fat—and usually in cost—than animal proteins.

Applying the Principles

1. How does the idea of eating less meat, poultry, and fish relate to management skills?
2. What foods could you use to replace some of the meat in a recipe for meat loaf?
3. Give two examples of how you can reduce the amount of poultry or fish in a recipe.

MORE ABOUT Grades of Beef

All beef sold in the United States is inspected by the USDA, but grading is a voluntary program. About half of all beef is graded, with USDA Choice the most widely sold at retail.

MORE ABOUT Fish and Fat

While fish tends to be lower in fat than meat, some have more fat than others. Firmer-fleshed fish, such as mackerel and trout, are highest in fat. Lean varieties include flounder, grouper, halibut, snapper, sole, and turbot.

- **Prime.** This grade has the most marbling and is the most expensive. Most is sold to restaurants.
- **Choice.** This grade has less marbling than prime and is less expensive.
- **Select.** This grade has less marbling and costs less than prime or choice. "Select" is used for beef, "good" for lamb and veal.

Check fresh meat for color. Meat that looks brown and dry is probably not fresh. Read the label to learn the weight of the package, cost per pound, and total price. The weight given includes any bone and fat in the package. Boneless meat usually costs more but gives more servings per pound.

You also can choose from **variety meats,** which are *organ meats such as liver, heart, and kidney,* and **processed meats,** which *have been seasoned, smoked, or prepared in some other way before sale.* These include hot dogs, bacon, sausages, ham, and luncheon meats.

Poultry

Poultry includes chicken, turkey, duck, and other birds. These foods, like meats, are good sources of complete protein, B vitamins, and iron. Chicken and turkey, when eaten without the skin, are lower in fat than most meats.

Stores sell fresh, frozen, and canned poultry products. Poultry can be bought whole, cut up, or in packages of separate pieces (such as legs, breasts, or wings). Ground turkey and chicken are also available. Processed forms of poultry include chicken hot dogs and turkey cold cuts.

The names for chicken are clues to age and tenderness. Broiler-fryers are young and tender, roasters are older, and stewing chickens are the oldest and toughest. The names also suggest the best cooking methods.

Whole poultry generally costs less per pound than cut-up poultry. Boneless pieces usually cost the most per pound but have less waste than whole poultry.

Fish

Fish are divided into saltwater and freshwater fish, depending on where they come from. Tuna, flounder, and other saltwater fish come from the oceans. Freshwater fish, such as trout and catfish, come from lakes, rivers, and streams. This food group also includes shellfish, such as clams, scallops, shrimp, and lobsters. Fish and shellfish are good sources of complete protein, the B vitamins, and important minerals, such as phosphorus.

Fish is available fresh, frozen, or canned. Fresh fish is commonly sold in four forms:

- **Drawn.** This is a whole fish with the scales and insides removed.
- **Dressed.** The head, tail, fins, scales, and insides have been removed.
- **Fillets.** These are lengthwise slices cut from the sides of the fish.
- **Steaks.** These are crosswise slices cut through the middle of the fish.

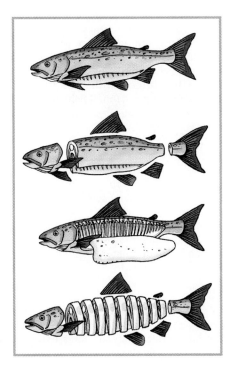

Before you purchase fresh fish, familiarize yourself with these forms: (top to bottom) drawn, dressed, fillets, and steaks.

Activities

■ **The Spice of Life?** Have students find recipes for variety meats. Based on the cooking method used and the other ingredients in the recipe, what can students infer about the meat's tenderness, flavor, and other qualities? *(Critical Thinking)*

Managing Your Life

Have students read "Meals with an All-Star Cast" and discuss the questions. Ask: How do you think meat came to feature so prominently in American diets? Suggest that ample grazing land and affluence play a part.

Answers to Applying...

1. Answers may include: may affect meal planning, food budgeting, storage needs; recipes may have to be adjusted or replaced.
2. Answers may include: oatmeal, bread crumbs, tofu.
3. Answers may include: less chicken, more rice in casserole; stretch tuna salad by adding vegetables.

Checking Comprehension

✓ Compare legumes with nuts as protein sources. *Both are incomplete proteins; legumes are low in fat; nuts are high in fat and calories.*

✓ How should eggs be stored? For how long? *Refrigerated in original covered container; up to three weeks.*

✓ Why are dry beans soaked before cooking? *Improves flavor, texture, appearance, digestibility; reduces cooking time.*

When buying fresh fish, look for flesh that is firm. No strong smell should be present.

Fresh fish should not have a strong smell, and the flesh should be firm when pressed. Frozen fish and shellfish also are available. Some are sold completely cooked, both plain and batter-dipped with breading. Tuna, salmon, and other canned fish come packed in water or oil.

Legumes

There are many varieties of legumes, including soy, navy, pinto, lima, and kidney beans, as well as split peas and lentils. Legumes are excellent sources of B vitamins, iron, and fiber, and they are low in fat. Legumes are also excellent and inexpensive sources of protein, as long as grains or nuts and seeds are also eaten. Legumes are available dry and canned.

Eggs

Eggs are a source of complete protein, vitamin A, B vitamins, and iron. Egg yolks contain fat and cholesterol. Eggs usually are bought fresh by the dozen in cartons. They come in various sizes, but the most common are large and extra large. Both brown and white eggs are available; the two varieties have exactly the same quality and taste. Many stores also sell dried eggs, which keep for a long time, and egg substitutes, which have reduced fat and cholesterol.

Nuts and Seeds

Nuts and seeds provide incomplete protein. They are high in minerals, such as iron and magnesium, but also have high levels of fat and calories. Nuts and seeds are sold in packages or loose from bins. Shelled nuts are convenient but usually more expensive. They may be whole, halved, slivered, or chopped.

Storing

Proper storage is the first step in using protein foods wisely. Fresh meat, poultry, and fish should be left in the original store wrapper and placed in the coldest part of the refrigerator. If you purchase large quantities of meat, you may wish to rewrap smaller portions in plastic wrap.

Most fresh meat should be used within three to four days of purchase. Ground meat, variety meats, poultry, and fish should be used within one to two days. Storage times for processed meats vary, so check the date on the package.

For longer storage, meat, poultry, and fish can be frozen. Wrap the food tightly in freezer paper or heavy-duty foil, and write the date of storage on the package. When you thaw the product, do so in the refrigerator or microwave oven—not at room temperature.

Eggs should be refrigerated in their original covered carton to keep them from absorbing food odors. They will stay fresh in the refrigerator for up to three weeks.

MORE ABOUT Freezing Meat

For best results, meat should be frozen rapidly. Slow freezing allows cells to expand and rupture, robbing the meat of natural juices. Wrap meat for freezing carefully. Improperly wrapped meat is subject to freezer burn, resulting in a dry, discolored product with a decidedly "off" taste.

Dry beans, nuts, and seeds will stay fresh at room temperature if they are kept in a tightly sealed container. Canned meat, poultry, fish, and beans keep well on cool, dry shelves until they are opened. Some canned hams, however, need to be refrigerated. Check the label.

Cooking

The general principles for cooking protein foods are based on how proteins react to heat. Proteins usually are sensitive to heat. Cooking at too high a temperature can make the food tough. The cooking method you choose is also important. Moist heat, dry heat, and fat are all used to cook the foods in this group.

Moist Heat

Protein foods are often cooked with moist-heat methods—those that use liquid or steam to cook the food. Moist-heat methods are a good way to tenderize tougher cuts of meat and poultry. For example, pot roasts are braised in a small amount of liquid. Flavorful soups and stews can be made by simmering

small pieces of meat or poultry in liquid and adding vegetables and seasonings. Browning the meat first adds more flavor. Corned beef and cabbage is another popular combination cooked in moist heat.

Moist-heat methods may also be used to add flavor to tender cuts of meat, poultry, or fish. Examples include poached salmon, sausage simmered with sauerkraut, and chicken cacciatore, an Italian dish of braised chicken and tomatoes.

Legumes must be simmered in a large amount of liquid so that they can absorb water and soften. Dry beans may take one to three hours or longer to cook. Some people prefer to soak dry beans first to improve their flavor, texture, appearance, and digestibility and to reduce the cooking time. Split peas and lentils cook more quickly than dry beans and need not be soaked.

Eggs can be cooked with moist heat in or out of the shell. To make hard-cooked eggs, place eggs in a pan and add cool tap water to an inch above the eggs. Bring water just to a boil and remove pan from heat source. Cover pan and let sit for 15 minutes. Remove eggs from the pan and run cold water over them to stop the cooking. Poached eggs are made by breaking eggs into simmering water and cooking them until firm.

To poach eggs, slip them into a simmering liquid, cook them for several minutes, and then remove them to drain the liquid. Special pans for poaching eggs and other foods can also be purchased.

Activities

■ **The Seedy Side.** Ask students to list as many edible nuts and seeds as they can. Then have them think of healthful ways of adding nuts or seeds to recipes, such as stirring them into yogurt or using them to top vegetables and casseroles. *(Creativity)*

RETEACHING

■ **Protein Providers.** Have students identify protein foods in recipes and tell what other nutrients they add to the dish.

ENRICHMENT

■ **All Created Equal?** Have groups choose one of the protein sources discussed on pp. 513-516 and learn the nutritional value of three foods from that source. Nutritional analyses should include calories, protein, carbohydrates, fiber, fats, cholesterol, and sodium. Remind students to indicate serving size also. Have students compare their findings. What are the pros and cons of getting protein from each source?

Focus on Management Skills

Eggs are sized according to minimum weight per dozen. One dozen medium eggs weigh at least 21 oz.; large eggs, 24 oz.; extra large, 27 oz. Ask: Would a cake recipe be significantly altered by using two large instead of medium eggs? *Possibly; total weight of eggs would change from about 3 ½ oz. to about 4 oz.—a 15 percent increase that could affect a baked good. Increase varies with actual weight of each egg.*

Topics on pp. 518-520:

- **Dry-Heat Cooking of Protein Foods**
- **Cooking Protein Foods with Fat**
- **Microwave Cooking**

Checking Comprehension

✓ How should you check for doneness in hamburgers? In fish? *Hamburger—make sure the juices are clear and the meat is not pink in center. Fish—flakes easily with fork.*

✓ What is the most healthful way to cook proteins using fat? Why? *Stir-frying; uses little fat, often includes vegetables.*

✓ What are some advantages and disadvantages of cooking meats in a microwave oven? *They stay moister, shrink less, but do not brown as well.*

CROSS-CURRICULAR ACTIVITY
Science

Ask students to learn the scientific basis for the guidelines for cooking protein foods given on pp. 517-520. Why does meat toughen? How does moist heat tenderize? Why does fish flake when cooked?

STRATEGIES *That Work*   Roasting a Turkey

Roast turkey, a favorite for special meals, can be enjoyed anytime. It's not difficult to prepare—if you know a few basic facts and plan ahead.

Whole turkeys are sold fresh, frozen, or prestuffed and frozen. When buying a fresh or frozen turkey without stuffing, allow 1 lb. (0.5 kg) per person. For a prestuffed frozen turkey, allow 1¼ lb. (0.6 kg) per person.

<u>Do not</u> thaw prestuffed frozen turkeys before cooking. Follow label directions for preparation.

To prevent bacterial growth, thaw a frozen turkey that is not stuffed by one of these methods:

- Place the turkey in a pan in the refrigerator. Allow about 24 hours for every 5 lb. (2 kg) of turkey.
- To save time, place the wrapped turkey in a sink or large container and cover it with cold water. Allow about 30 minutes per lb. (0.5 kg). Change the water every 30 minutes to keep cold.
- You can thaw a turkey in the microwave oven, if it fits. Check the manufacturer's instructions for the recommended time and power setting. Cook the turkey immediately after microwave thawing.

To prepare the turkey for roasting, remove the plastic bags containing the neck and giblets from the cavity. Check for two bags, one inside the turkey and one in the neck cavity. (You can save these to make gravy.) Rinse the turkey inside and out under cold running water. Remember to wash your hands, utensils, and work surfaces after handling raw poultry.

Season the bird, if you wish. If you plan to serve stuffing, remember that it's safer to cook the stuffing separately, not inside the turkey. Authorities recommend that you not stuff a turkey because of the risk of bacterial growth.

Place the turkey, breast side up, on a rack in a shallow roasting pan. Insert an ovenproof meat thermometer in the thickest part of the thigh muscle, not touching bone. Set the oven temperature no lower than 325°F (160°C). Cooking time varies according to the turkey's weight, whether it is stuffed, and other factors. Consult the package label or a cookbook for estimated cooking times and other preparation tips.

The turkey is done when the meat thermometer registers 180°F (82°C). Note the time you remove the turkey from the oven. Leftovers should be refrigerated or frozen in shallow containers within 2 hours of that time. Let the turkey stand for about 20 minutes, loosely covered with foil, then carve and enjoy the results of your efforts.

Making the Strategy Work

Think . . .

1. What challenges does roasting a turkey present to planning and time management?
2. What might happen if you do not use a meat thermometer when roasting a turkey?
3. What common mistakes can be avoided by learning how to prepare a turkey correctly?

Try...

Make a plan for preparing a turkey (without stuffing) for 12 people. What size turkey should you buy? Consult a cookbook to estimate the cooking time. To serve the turkey at 2:00 P.M. on Sunday, when should you put it in the oven? When should you put it in the refrigerator to thaw?

DID YOU KNOW?

When you roast nuts, set the oven temperature below 300°F (150°C). Low temperatures minimize the loss of the amino acid lysine, which is sensitive to heat.

MORE ABOUT Cooking Eggs

Cooking eggs successfully takes a fine sense of timing. Egg white solidifies at 140°F (60°C), the denser yolk at 150°F (65°C). It takes experience and attention to cook an egg so that both are firmly set and neither is rubbery.

Dry Heat

Tender meats, poultry, and fish can be cooked with dry heat. Dry-heat cooking methods are healthful because they allow fat to drain away.

Whole poultry and large, tender cuts of meat can be roasted on a rack in a shallow, open pan. The rack allows fat to drip down into the pan during cooking. Set the oven temperature to at least 325°F (160°C). Insert a meat thermometer deep into the center of the roast or the thigh of the bird, not touching bone. Cook meat to at least 160°F (71°C) and whole poultry to 180°F (82°C).

Smaller pieces—steaks, chops, hamburgers, poultry pieces, and fish—can be baked in the oven or broiled on a broiler pan. Follow these tips:

- Check steaks, chops, hamburgers, and poultry pieces for doneness by cutting into the center. Juices should run clear, and the meat should not show any pink color.

- Fish cooks quickly. It's done when you can easily separate the flesh with a fork. If overcooked, fish will dry out and toughen.

Eggs also can be cooked in dry heat. Remove them from the shell and bake them in individual dishes. Baked eggs need to be timed according to a recipe. They will toughen if overcooked.

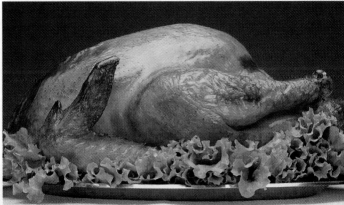

Roast turkey is a traditional meal component for holidays and special occasions in many families.

Chicken pieces can be roasted in the oven. Which cooking method is this?

CHAPTER 53   Meat, Poultry, Fish, Dry Beans, Eggs, and Nuts   519

Review

■ **Chapter Review.** Use the contents of the Chapter Review page to help students review concepts, think critically, and apply their knowledge.

■ **Study Guide.** Have students complete the Study Guide for Chapter 53 on p. 175 of the Student Workbook.

■ **See the Sights.** Have students give an oral or written "tour" of a kitchen, highlighting areas where different protein foods are stored or prepared. At each "stop" on the tour, students should identify the food and explain how it is kept or cooked. Tell students to include as many foods as possible.

Evaluation

■ **Chapter Test.** Use the reproducible chapter test provided in the Teacher's Classroom Resources or create your own test using the *Testmaker Software*.

■ **Alternative Assessment.** Have groups perform skits that take place at the Gone Wrong Diner, where workers store and prepare protein foods in inadvisable ways. Have the rest of the class note the errors to discuss after the performance.

■ **Protein Pointers.** Ask students to think of three favorite recipes that each use a different type of protein food. For each recipe, have them write three guidelines for choosing and storing the food and for preparing the dish.

Cooking with Fat

Meat, poultry, and fish also can be cooked with fat. Common methods include stir-frying, panfrying, and deep-fat frying. Fat should always be very hot so that the foods will cook quickly without absorbing the excess fat. Sometimes chicken and fish are breaded before being fried.

Of the different methods for cooking with fat, stir-frying is the most healthful because it uses only a small amount of oil. Meat, poultry, and fish should be thinly and evenly sliced before stir-frying. Often a variety of sliced vegetables are stir-fried along with the meat, poultry, or fish. Then the mixture is served over rice. The result is a nutritious, low-fat main dish that is almost a complete meal in itself.

Eggs can be fried in a small amount of fat or beaten first to make scrambled eggs. It is important to watch fried eggs and scrambled eggs closely as they cook. If they are undercooked, they will be soft and runny; overcooked eggs are tough and rubbery.

Microwave Cooking

Meats remain more moist and shrink less in a microwave than they do in conventional cooking. However, they do not brown as well. Hamburger patties can be placed on a plate, covered with waxed paper, and microwaved. Moist meat dishes—such as

When you cook pieces of poultry with fat, use no more than 1 tsp. (5 mL) of oil or vegetable oil spray in the pan.

stews, pot roasts, and Salisbury steaks—should be covered with plastic that has been pierced or vented to let the steam escape.

Poultry can be microwaved whole or cut up into pieces. If the poultry is in pieces, place the thicker, meatier parts toward the outer edge of the dish. Cover them with waxed paper or vented plastic wrap. If the microwave does not have a turntable, rotate the dish every few minutes for even cooking.

Fish must be watched carefully because it cooks quickly. Remove fish from the microwave before it is fully cooked. It will continue to cook during standing time.

Never microwave eggs in the shell—they can burst during or after cooking. To make baked eggs in a microwave, break them into a bowl and pierce the yolks to keep them from bursting. Scrambled eggs also can be cooked in a microwave oven.

Legumes may be cooked in a microwave oven. However, they require about the same amount of time as they would to simmer on the range.

Focus on Decision-Making Skills

Ask: If you could use just one cooking method—moist heat, dry heat, frying, or microwaving—which would you choose? Have students discuss factors that help determine which option might be best for them, such as: What types of protein foods does your family enjoy? How willing are you to try new ones? What foods could you conveniently store? What are your health concerns? Your cooking skills?

Review

Reviewing the Facts

1. What is a cut of meat? Why is it important to know the cut when choosing a cooking method?
2. What is the significance for the consumer of the different names given to types of chicken?
3. List four forms in which fresh fish is sold.
4. How should you store fresh meats, poultry, and fish if you plan to use them very soon?
5. When should moist-heat and dry-heat cooking methods be used for protein foods?

Thinking Critically

1. How can being knowledgeable about cuts of meat and cooking methods help you nutritionally and economically?
2. What steps could you take to reduce fat when choosing and preparing protein foods?

Applying Your Knowledge

1. **Your Point of View.** Some people strongly object to eating meat and poultry or even foods that come from animals (such as milk and eggs). Others believe that there is nothing wrong with eating meat. Write a paragraph that expresses your view on this topic. Use examples and details to support your opinion.
2. **Comparing Fat Content.** Prepare hamburger patties of equal weight from different types of ground beef, such as ground round and ground chuck. Broil each patty separately for the same length of time. Compare the weight of each patty after cooking and the amounts of fat in the broiler pan. Write a summary of your findings and conclusions.

Making Connections

1. **Mathematics.** Using supermarket advertisements, note the cost per pound for four different types of meat, poultry, or fish. Use reference materials to find out the number of servings per pound for your choices, and compute the cost per serving for each. Make a bar graph or other type of diagram to illustrate your results.
2. **Technology.** Advances in packaging technology have greatly increased grocery store offerings. Research the technology behind modified-atmosphere packaging. What are its advantages? How is this technology being used with protein foods? How might it be used in the future?

Building Your Portfolio

Writing a Script
Write a script that could be used to teach preschool children about the foods in the Meat, Poultry, Fish, Dry Beans, Eggs, and Nuts Group. Use any method you like (such as having each type of food speak about itself). Remember that children of this age will not understand words such as protein unless you explain them or paraphrase them. When your script is completed, put a copy in your portfolio.

ANSWERS TO REVIEWING THE FACTS

1. Section or part of meat carcass. Cut affects tenderness of meat and thus appropriate cooking method.
2. They are clues to age and tenderness; suggest best cooking method.
3. Drawn, dressed, steaks, fillets.
4. In original store wrapper, in coldest part of refrigerator.
5. Moist heat—to tenderize tougher cuts; add flavor to tender cuts; for legumes. Dry heat—for tender cuts.

ANSWERS TO THINKING CRITICALLY

1. Answers may include: can help you control fat in diet, preserve nutrients, make good-tasting dishes of both expensive and less expensive cuts.
2. Answers may include: choose lean cuts; trim visible fat; read package labels for fat content; choose cooking methods that use least amount of fat; choose legumes more often.

Chapter Overview

Chapter 54 gives information to help students feel more confident and relaxed at mealtime. It familiarizes them with different table settings and serving styles. It outlines table manners and mealtime etiquette, and offers tips for dining in restaurants.

Motivators

■ **Family Table.** Ask students for words or phrases that describe a typical family meal, their own or in general. List these on the board.

■ **P's and Q's.** Ask students what they think of when they hear the word etiquette. Tell them to remember as they read this chapter that etiquette is meant to add to mealtime enjoyment.

Objectives

Discuss the chapter objectives on this page. Remind students that the objectives focus on important chapter concepts.

Vocabulary

Point out that the words *buffet* and *etiquette* are French words. Paris has long been considered a major cultural center. As a result, many French mealtime conventions have been adopted throughout the Western world.

Chapter 54 — Enjoying Mealtime

Terms to Learn

- buffet
- etiquette
- family style
- flatware
- place setting
- table service
- tipping

Objectives

This chapter will help you to:

- Explain **the significance of mealtime customs.**
- Describe **an attractive and well-ordered table.**
- Describe **the ways in which a meal can be served at home.**
- List **important points of table manners and etiquette.**

CHAPTER RESOURCES

Student Workbook
Study Guide, pp. 179-180
Activity, *Enjoying Mealtime,*
   pp. 181-182

Teacher's Classroom Resources
Lesson Plan, p. 58

Extension #81, *Making the Most of Mealtimes,* p. 87
Foods Lab Activities, pp. 25-48
Life Skills, *Adapting Eating Styles,*
   p. 85
Transparency 48, *Making Mealtimes Pleasant*

Chapter 54 Test, pp. 113-114
Performance Assessment, *Mealtime Manners,* p. 87
Reteaching, *At the Table,* p. 60

Pablo was nervous about eating dinner at Peter's house for the first time. Peter, his parents, and his sister had just moved into the neighborhood in September. Pablo and Peter had become friendly almost immediately because both of them were interested in raising tropical fish.

As they sat down at the table, Pablo watched to see what would happen next. Peter's mother asked Pablo for his plate and began serving. Pablo was surprised—in his family, his father was always served first. As the meal progressed, Pablo finished his first helping and wondered if he could have more. He saw that Peter's sister simply asked to have the serving dishes passed to her when she wanted seconds, so he did the same.

Pablo enjoyed his dinner with Peter's family that night. Although he was unfamiliar with their customs, Peter's family made him feel at home.

Mealtime Customs

Lighting candles, sitting in a certain place at the table for every meal, and eating in the kitchen instead of the dining room are examples of mealtime customs. Mealtime customs are as varied as the families that follow them. A family's ethnic background, religious beliefs, or family history may influence mealtime customs. Some customs are simple, while others are more complex. All, however, bring together the families that practice them. These customs are a way for families to share in the mealtime experience.

For many families, mealtime provides a rare opportunity to be together. At mealtime people can relax, talk about the day's events, share ideas, and enjoy each other's company. In today's busy world, dinnertime—when most people in the United States eat the largest meal of the day—may be the only time when a family can be together.

Mealtimes also can have benefits beyond being with your own family. Lessons that you learn from eating with your family can contribute to success in social situations. Family dinners are a good place to learn how to participate in a group conversation, express interest in what others are saying, and show respect for the ideas and feelings of others.

Family mealtimes also provide an opportunity to establish healthful lifetime eating patterns. Studies show that relaxation while eating helps the digestive process. The pleasant atmosphere of a family meal can help you make the association between a balanced, healthful meal and an enjoyable time.

Setting the Table

Most families set the table in similar ways. Traditional rules for setting the table make it easy for people to know what to expect, no matter where they eat. Special touches can provide a pleasant atmosphere for any meal.

Table setting begins with the dishes you have available. How would you create an attractive table setting based on the design of this plate?

CHAPTER 54   Enjoying Mealtime   523

Topics on p. 523:
• **Mealtime Customs**

Checking Comprehension

✓ Why do families follow mealtime customs? *To bring members together and share the mealtime experience.*

✓ How can pleasant family meals promote healthful eating? *Links nutritious meals with enjoyable time; relaxation aids digestion.*

Activity

■ **Food and Family.** Ask students to describe family customs they have heard of and tell how they bring family members closer or strengthen their identity as a family. Why might the linking of family with food be especially significant? *(Relationship)*

Checking Comprehension

✓ How is flatware arranged around a dinner plate? *Forks on left; knife, then spoons on right; first-used utensils outermost.*

✓ What might you add to enhance a table setting? *Tablecloth or place mats; flowers, fruit, green plant; candlelight.*

USING VISUALS

To give students "practice" with using a table setting, refer them to Figure 54.1 on p. 524 and ask: Would you start this meal with the main dish or the salad? How can you tell? *Salad; salad fork is outside dinner fork.* Between what pieces of tableware would you reach to pick up your beverage glass? *Water glass, cup and saucer.* Where would you set a roll? Why? *On dinner plate; no bread plate used.*

Place Setting

Sit-down meals require individual place settings for every person. A **place setting** is *the arrangement of tableware that each person needs for a meal.* Tableware for a simple place setting includes a plate, glass, napkin, and **flatware**—*knife, fork, and teaspoon.* Depending on the foods served, a more formal place setting might include several forks or spoons, a bread plate, a salad plate, two glasses, and a coffee cup and saucer. **Figure 54.1** shows how the tableware is arranged for a place setting.

In addition to the place settings, most tables include salt and pepper shakers. Place them together in front of one of the place settings. When dishes of food are put on the table, the serving spoons and forks should be placed to the right of each dish until they are used during serving.

Figure 54.1

SETTING THE TABLE

Each piece of tableware has a certain place.

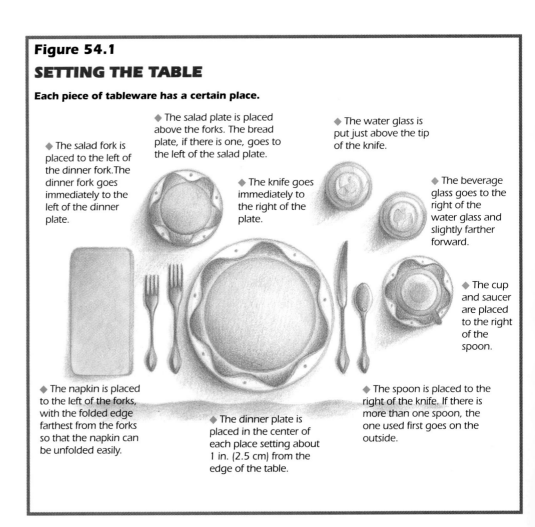

◆ The salad fork is placed to the left of the dinner fork. The dinner fork goes immediately to the left of the dinner plate.

◆ The salad plate is placed above the forks. The bread plate, if there is one, goes to the left of the salad plate.

◆ The water glass is put just above the tip of the knife.

◆ The knife goes immediately to the right of the plate.

◆ The beverage glass goes to the right of the water glass and slightly farther forward.

◆ The cup and saucer are placed to the right of the spoon.

◆ The napkin is placed to the left of the forks, with the folded edge farthest from the forks so that the napkin can be unfolded easily.

◆ The dinner plate is placed in the center of each place setting about 1 in. (2.5 cm) from the edge of the table.

◆ The spoon is placed to the right of the knife. If there is more than one spoon, the one used first goes on the outside.

Focus on Critical Thinking Skills

Point out that buffets, including salad bars, are increasingly popular in restaurants. Ask: Why might this be so? What are some advantages and disadvantages for restaurants and diners? Help students see that a buffet is more economical for restaurants because it requires less wait staff; it offers diners more choices and a more relaxed setting. However, food quality and safety may be compromised as foods sit for long periods and are handled by many customers.

Special Touches

Families can add special touches to their table settings to make daily or holiday meals stand out:

- **Table covering.** A snowy linen tablecloth—clean, pressed, and hanging evenly around the table—adds formal elegance to a meal. You can also choose solid or patterned fabrics for less formal occasions (for example, a red-checked cloth and napkins). Another table-covering option is to use place mats instead of a tablecloth.
- **Table decoration.** A simple floral arrangement adds sparkle to the table and enhances your enjoyment of the meal. Alternatives to a flower arrangement include a bowl of fresh fruit or a simple green plant.
- **Lighting.** Using candlelight is probably the easiest way to create a dramatic effect, whether the occasion is formal or informal. Place several candles in candleholders, or try floating votive candles in a simple glass bowl of water—floating an additional flower or two adds a classic touch.

Serving Styles

Although family mealtime customs differ greatly, most families serve their meals in similar ways. One of the most common styles of meal service is family style. Other styles include plate service and buffet.

- **Family style service.** When serving **family style,** *food is brought to the table in bowls and on serving platters, which are passed from person to person* until everyone is served. To avoid confusion at the table,

In family style service, food is passed around the table in serving dishes. As dishes are passed to you, continue to pass them to the next person until everyone has been served.

serving bowls and platters are passed to each person's right. Each place setting has a plate, flatware, glassware, and a napkin.

- **Plate service.** Plate service is used when table space is limited. The table is set with the appropriate flatware, glassware, and napkin for each diner. Food is put onto each person's plate in the kitchen, and the plate is then brought to the table.
- **Buffet service.** When using **buffet** service, *all the plates, flatware, and food—in serving bowls and on platters—are arranged on a serving table.* Dinner plates are placed at one end of the buffet table, and people serve themselves as they walk along the table. People pick up flatware, napkins, and beverages at the other end of the buffet table or at a separate table. Diners may then find a place to sit down to eat their meal. This style of service is useful when there is not enough seating space for people to sit around one table.

CHAPTER 54   Enjoying Mealtime   525

Activities

- **What's the Point?** Discuss: When family members' schedules prevent them from sharing meals, they often do not use place settings. Is it worthwhile to set a table for one or two people? *(Critical Thinking)*

RETEACHING

- **The Set-Up.** Have students practice setting the table. Begin with simple settings, gradually adding pieces and flatware for more formal service.

ENRICHMENT

- **Special Centerpieces.** Ask students to design centerpieces for different occasions, such as a particular holiday, a birthday, or a wedding. Have students describe their ideas with sketches and written details. Encourage them to create the actual centerpiece if possible.

MORE ABOUT Table Setting

When setting the table, line up flatware so the bottom is even with the dinner plate, about an inch from the edge of the table. Turn the knife blade to face the plate. If you set out a dessert fork or spoon, place it above the plate; it is not recommended to have more than three pieces of flatware on either side of the plate. When placing full dinner plates or serving plates before guests, serve from the right. Remove used plates from the left.

Topics on pp. 526-528:

• Using Good Manners

Checking Comprehension

✓ What is the purpose of good manners? *Add to diners' comfort, enjoyment; show thoughtfulness, respect.*

✓ May you ever begin eating before others do? *Only if urged by parent or host.*

✓ How should you signal that you are finished eating? *Place flatware across center of plate, napkin at left of plate.*

Acting Responsibly

Have students read "Do You Have Good Manners?" and discuss the questions. Ask: How might Miki or the Morrows have responded had the other shown poor manners?

Answers to Your Analysis

1. She was on time; brought gift; washed hands; complimented food; joined in conversation; offered to help clean up; thanked hosts.

2. Mrs. Morrow thanked Miki for flowers, used them on table; Beth described dish; Paul asked Miki about herself; Mr. Morrow helped clean up.

3. Answers may include: write thank-you note; invite Beth to her home.

4. Reflects thoughtfulness a good host shows; respect shown by guests.

Using Good Manners

The food, style of service, and appearance of the table all help make a meal a success, as does the behavior of the people who are eating the meal. Good manners are important at mealtime because they enable people to have a comfortable and enjoyable experience.

Thoughtfulness toward others is the basis for good manners. The way you look, the way you eat, and the way you talk with others all indicate your respect for them and for yourself. The good manners you practice at home will be an asset as you enjoy meals in social settings away from home.

Appearance and Hygiene

Good mealtime hygiene is important both for your own health and for the health of others. Always wash your hands before you eat. When passing food to others, you should do

Acting Responsibly

Do You Have Good Manners?

Manners have been called the oil in the social machine—they help relationships run smoothly. Volumes have been written on etiquette. When you accept an invitation to a meal in someone's home, you accept the responsibility of showing the same respect and consideration that you would like to receive.

Good Manners in Action

Miki checked her watch as she rang the Morrows' doorbell. It was almost 6:00 P.M., the time her friend Beth had asked her to arrive for dinner. Beth's mother answered the door and took the bouquet of tulips that Miki had cut from her yard and now offered. "Thank you, Miki, these are beautiful," Mrs. Morrow said. "I'll put them on the table as a centerpiece. You and Beth can visit until we're ready to eat."

At dinnertime, Miki excused herself to wash her hands, then asked Mrs. Morrow where she should sit. As the food was passed around the table, Miki eyed one dish curiously. "This looks interesting," she commented, placing a spoonful on her plate.

"It's sweet potato casserole," Beth said, "made with apple cider and cinnamon."

Miki took a bite. "I like it. The flavors are really good together."

Beth's younger brother Paul began talking about a movie he had seen. "Have you seen it?" he asked Miki.

"No," she replied. "What was the best part?"

Paul went on at length about why he liked the movie until Mrs. Morrow nudged him gently. "What kind of movies do you like, Miki?" she asked.

At the end of the meal, Beth's stepfather rose and began stacking the dirty dishes. Miki gathered the plates on her side of the table. "I'll help you wash the dishes."

"No, that's okay. Paul and I are just going to let these soak in the sink. They can wait."

"Right," Paul agreed. "Beth told us you've lived in Germany. I want to hear all about that."

The family and their guest spent the rest of the evening in conversation. When Miki glanced at her watch again, it was almost 9:00 P.M. "I've had a really nice time," she said, "but I've got to get up early tomorrow. Thank you all so much for inviting me."

Beth walked Miki to her car. "Your friend is very nice," Mr. Morrow said when Beth returned. "She's welcome here anytime."

Your Analysis

1. What did Miki say or do that showed good manners?

2. Identify at least one way in which each member of the Morrow family showed good manners.

3. What might Miki do to continue to show good manners toward Beth and her family?

4. According to an old saying, "A gracious host makes guests feel as if they are at home. Gracious guests remember that they are not." How does this relate to good manners?

MORE ABOUT Manners

The name Emily Post is synonymous with good manners. *Emily Post's Etiquette* was first published in 1922; new authors have assumed her name for the book's many revisions. "Emily's" classic pointers include:

• A man should never tuck his napkin in his collar, in his belt, or between the buttons of his shirt.

• You may sop bread into gravy by putting a small piece into the gravy and eating it with a fork.

• Don't crook your finger when picking up your cup. It's an affected mannerism.

STRATEGIES That Work

Handling New Situations

Should you use your fingers to eat an artichoke? Are edible garnishes really meant to be eaten? Questions like these can make people hesitant to try new foods or food experiences. The all-purpose guidelines below can help make you more comfortable and open to new food situations:

- Tell your host or hostess in advance if there are foods that you cannot eat due to special dietary needs or food allergies. Those preparing the menu can then plan accordingly.
- Watch your host for guidance if you are unsure about how to eat a food or how to act in a formal situation.
- Unless you have special dietary restrictions or food allergies, accept at least a small portion of every dish being served when eating in another person's home.
- Ask for advice if you need it. A gracious host or hostess will gladly answer a few polite questions.
- Keep a sense of humor if you are having difficulty. Make light of your own inexperience; however, don't make jokes that might offend the people who prepared or served the dish.

- Offer guidance when others are unfamiliar with a situation that you are knowledgeable about. For example, you might tell them how a food is prepared and describe its distinctive flavors.

Making the Strategy Work

Think . . .

1. Some new friends invite you to their house for dinner at the last minute. When you arrive, you discover that the main course is a casserole made with milk and cheese. You are allergic to dairy products. How do you handle the situation?
2. Eating at a friend's house, you are served an artichoke. You are not sure how to eat it or whether you will like it. What do you do?
3. When you are not sure if others are familiar with a situation, how can you offer guidance without insulting them or implying that they are incompetent?

Try...

Using a book on etiquette, learn how to handle a dining situation that you are unsure about. Demonstrate the appropriate response for the class.

---

so with clean hands. If you need to comb your hair or freshen makeup, do it before you come to the table, not after you sit down.

When you need to cough or sneeze, cover your mouth or nose with a napkin and turn away from the table. If a problem continues, excuse yourself from the table.

Etiquette at the Table

Etiquette (EH-tih-ket) refers to *accepted rules of behavior in a culture.* Each rule is designed to make mealtime comfortable and en-

joyable for everyone. The following rules are generally accepted in North America:

- Use the serving forks and spoons, not your own flatware, to serve yourself.
- Ask for serving dishes to be passed to you instead of reaching in front of someone or across the table.
- Start with the outermost fork, spoon, or knife and work toward the plate when the place setting is formal. Flatware for the first course is always farthest from the plate.

CHAPTER 54 Enjoying Mealtime 527

Review

■ **Chapter Review.** Use the contents of the Chapter Review page to help students review concepts, think critically, and apply their knowledge.

■ **Study Guide.** Have students complete the Study Guide for Chapter 54 on p. 179 of the Student Workbook.

■ **Dining Dilemmas.** Have groups write scenarios of difficult dining situations. Have them exchange scenarios and enact a response that shows good manners.

Evaluation

■ **Chapter Test.** Use the reproducible chapter test provided in the Teacher's Classroom Resources or create your own test using the *Testmaker Software*.

■ **Alternative Assessment.** Have students observe and describe their family's behavior during an ordinary family meal. The next time the family shares this meal (breakfast, lunch, or dinner), have students replace their usual tableware with paper plates and plastic utensils, and again record their behavior. Repeat using formal place settings. Ask students to compare their findings for the three meals. Did the table setting seem to affect behavior?

■ **Why Bother?** Ask students to write a paragraph that begins, "Knowledge of table etiquette is valuable because . . ."

- Start eating only after everyone has been served. If, however, a parent or host urges you to start, go ahead and do so.
- Chew and swallow food before talking. Do not speak with your mouth full.
- Sit up straight at the table. Don't rest your elbows on the table while you eat.
- Keep your napkin on your lap, except when you need to use it.
- Cut several pieces of food at a time. Then place your knife on the edge of the plate, and eat the food with your fork.
- Break breads or rolls into pieces with your hands instead of cutting them or biting off pieces.
- Eat finger foods, such as chicken or french fries, with your fingers at home or at informal restaurants. At more formal meals and restaurants, however, only a very few foods are considered finger foods. These include celery and carrot sticks, olives, pickles, crisp bacon, sandwiches, bread and rolls, cookies, and some small appetizers.
- Signal that you have finished by placing your flatware across the center of your plate and your napkin to the left of the plate.

Conversation

Conversation is an important part of dining. Meals are a time for warmth and friendship, not for arguments or disputes. Discuss topics of interest to everyone, and avoid discussing unpleasant experiences.

When you're a guest in someone's home, thank your hosts before you leave. A special word of thanks for the food and hospitality is always appreciated. For some occasions, you might want to bring a simple gift for the hosts.

Etiquette at a Restaurant

Good manners are also important when eating out. When entering a restaurant for the first time, look to see if it is an informal restaurant where guests seat themselves. Often a sign indicates whether someone will lead you to a seat.

In many nice restaurants, the bill comes in a folder or case, which is used to pay the server right at the table. The tip may be placed in the folder along with money for the bill.

When you are seated, review the menu—the list of foods that the restaurant offers. Ask the server any questions that you have about the food (such as how it is prepared or what ingredients are used). Some servers will suggest what to order if they are asked.

To get the attention of a server, speak in an ordinary voice as he or she passes your table. If the server is across the room, raise your hand to catch his or her eye.

After receiving the bill, quickly add it up to be sure that the total is correct. If there has been a mistake, which sometimes happens, politely and quietly bring the error to the server's attention.

Tipping, *giving extra money to servers in appreciation of good service,* is customary in all restaurants that offer **table service,** in which *servers take your order at the table, bring the food, and clean up after the meal.* Usually, 15 percent of the cost of the food (before taxes) is an acceptable tip. Many customers tip 20 percent in more expensive restaurants. Some restaurants automatically add a 15 percent tip to any check when there are six or more people at a table.

Focus on Critical Thinking Skills

Remind students that the purpose of manners is showing consideration and making others comfortable. Ask groups to list five actions that might violate the law of good manners (such as using the wrong fork), but not the spirit. Have groups share and defend their choices.

Chapter 54

Review

Reviewing the Facts

1. Identify two benefits of family mealtimes.
2. Describe a simple place setting.
3. What is the difference between a family style dinner and a buffet?
4. At a formal dinner, how do you decide which pieces of flatware to use first?
5. What are two guidelines for appropriate mealtime conversation?
6. How should you get a restaurant server's attention?
7. Why should you tip restaurant servers? What is the usual amount for tipping?

Thinking Critically

1. Suppose you are dining at someone else's house. You would like to have another piece of chicken, but there is only one piece left. What would you do? Why?
2. When someone else is treating you to a meal in a restaurant, should you order one of the most expensive dishes, one of the least expensive, or one that falls somewhere in between? Explain your answer.

Applying Your Knowledge

1. **Table Manners Skit.** In a group, write a skit in which the Goodmanners family and the Badmanners family are dining together in an elegant restaurant. Have your skit demonstrate as many of the points of etiquette discussed in the chapter as possible. Include a server and other restaurant patrons if your group is large enough. Act out your scene for the class.
2. **Compare and Contrast.** Compare and contrast the serving styles described in this chapter. Which is easiest for the host? For the diners? Write a paragraph that evaluates the advantages and disadvantages of each.

Making Connections

1. **Social Studies.** Mealtime customs differ around the world. Look in a reference source to find at least one mealtime custom that you are not familiar with. Write several sentences describing this custom and naming its culture of origin.
2. **Language Arts.** Create a mealtime etiquette brochure suitable for teens. Include the basics of good table manners in a format that would capture the interest of your peers. Include the benefits of using good manners.
3. **Mathematics.** Using the standard 15 percent rate, calculate the amount of a tip for family meals costing $17.25, $24.50, and $43.95. Round your numbers up to the nearest five cents.

Building Your Portfolio

Entertaining Friends

Assume that you are planning and serving a meal for three friends and yourself. Write the menu for your meal on a sheet of paper. On a separate sheet, draw your table setting. Include the type of table covering, table decorations, and tableware needed for individual place settings. Draw your table setting exactly as you would set the table. On a third sheet of paper, list possible topics of conversation that interest you and your friends. What questions might you ask to stimulate conversation? Assemble your plans, and place them in your portfolio.

CHAPTER 54   Enjoying Mealtime   529

ANSWERS TO REVIEWING THE FACTS

1. Any two: time for family togetherness; teach social skills; teach good eating habits.
2. Plate, glass, napkin, and flatware. Knife and spoon at right of plate; fork and napkin at left; glass above knife.
3. *Family style*—food is brought to table in serving bowls and platters and passed from person to person. *Buffet*—food and tableware arranged on a serving table, people serve selves and sit elsewhere.
4. Start with the outermost pieces.
5. Any two: avoid arguments; discuss topics of general interest; avoid unpleasant topics.
6. If server is close by, speak in ordinary voice as he or she passes; if across room, raise your hand to catch his or her eye.
7. As appreciation of good service; 15 percent of cost of food.

ANSWERS TO THINKING CRITICALLY

1. Answers may include: ask if anyone wants piece; ask if someone wants to split piece with you; wait until it is offered to you.
2. Answers will vary. Suggest that ordering most expensive dish may seem to take advantage of host's generosity, ordering least expensive may seem to insult it.

Chapter Overview

Chapter 55 introduces students to careers in food processing and food service. It identifies the interests and skills required for a career in these fields; it gives examples of a few of the many jobs available and the training required for each. The chapter also suggests ways students can begin preparing for a career in food and nutrition.

Motivators

■ **Just a Job?** Ask students with jobs related to food to explain their tasks and share some experiences.

■ **In a Can of Peas.** Hold up a common food product, such as a can of peas. Ask students to name all the people whose work helped make the item available.

Objectives

Discuss the chapter objectives on this page. Remind students that the objectives focus on important chapter concepts.

Vocabulary

Inventory comes from the Latin word *invenire,* to find. Store employees take inventory to learn how many of each kind of item is on hand. Ask: How is finding related to taking inventory?

Chapter
55

Careers in Food and Nutrition

Term to Learn

• inventory

Objectives

This chapter will help you to:

• Identify **the interests and skills required for careers in food and nutrition.**
• List **examples of jobs in food processing.**
• List **examples of jobs in food service.**
• Describe **how to prepare for a job in the food industry.**

530   UNIT 6   Food, Nutrition, and Wellness

CHAPTER RESOURCES

Student Workbook
Study Guide, p. 183
Activity, *Job Opportunities,* p. 184
Teacher's Classroom Resources
Lesson Plan, p. 59

Extension #82, *Food and Nutrition Careers,* p. 88
Life Skills, *Jobs in Foods and Nutrition,* pp. 86-87
Chapter 55 Test, pp. 115-116

Performance Assessment, *Finding the Facts About Careers,* p. 88
Reteaching, *Careers in Food and Nutrition,* p. 61

"Dolores! I didn't know you worked here!" Gina stared at her classmate in surprise. Dolores was wearing a crisp new uniform and was standing behind the counter of a fast-food restaurant.

"I work one school night and on weekends. I like it a lot! I'm earning money and making new friends too."

"Every time I apply for a job, they want to know if I have experience. Have you worked at a place like this before?"

"No, this is different. There's a training program here. They hired me based on my school activities and an interview."

The Qualities Needed

Do you love to concoct your own recipes or bake for friends? Are you interested in how food is grown and harvested? The career field of food and nutrition includes an enormous variety of jobs. Positions range from farmworkers and school dietitians to supermarket managers and food technologists. Fruit pickers, meat cutters, caterers, and chefs are all part of the food and nutrition industry.

Jocelyn volunteers on weekends for an organization that distributes hot meals to older people who cannot shop or cook for themselves. She likes helping people eat well, and she loves chatting with the older people. Jocelyn's interests and skills might make her a good candidate for a career as a nutritionist for a retirement community or an administrator for a nonprofit agency that helps fight hunger.

This chapter will discuss jobs in the two major divisions of the industry: food processing and food service. Both are related to food, but different interests and skills apply to each field.

Interests and Skills

People who work in the food-processing industry produce and sell food products. By asking yourself these questions, you can begin to identify personal qualities that are suited to a job in the food-processing industry:

- **Do you like working outdoors?** Some people in the field of food processing, such as farm laborers and workers on fishing boats, spend many hours outdoors.
- **Can you pay close attention to details?** Stock clerks must put the right foods in the right places. People who check the quality of food before it leaves the plant must look carefully for problems.
- **Do you like working with machinery?** Many food-processing jobs today use complex machinery. Machine operators have to be both knowledgeable and careful in their work.

What might happen if a stock clerk wasn't attentive to detail?

TEACH

Topics on p. 531:
- **Interests and Skills for Food-Processing Jobs**

Checking Comprehension

✓ What is meant by food processing? *Producing and selling food products.*

✓ Give two examples of when food-processing workers must be being careful and attentive. *Any two: stocking foods; checking food quality; operating machinery.*

Activity

■ **This Could Be You.** Refer students to the qualities listed on p. 531. Ask them to give examples of how these traits might be shown by teens in their schoolwork, their choice of hobbies, and other common activities. *(Creativity)*

Topics on pp. 532-533:

- **Interests and Skills for Food Service Jobs**
- **Entry-Level Food-Processing Jobs**

Checking Comprehension

✓ How might creativity be used in food service? *To devise fresh menus; to write about foods.*

✓ Would food service be a good field for a person who likes to work alone? *No; it requires much contact with coworkers, sometimes public.*

✓ Identify some entry-level food-processing jobs. *Farm laborer; jobs in canning, freezing, packing; stock clerk; cashier; bagger; deli clerk.*

Acting Responsibly

Have students read "Do You Have a Positive Attitude?" and discuss the questions. Ask: Is a positive attitude simply being cheerful? Is it more than that?

1. Answers may include: management (coordinating staff); personal relationships (dealing with customers); humor (joking with waitress).
2. Helped both cope with difficulty and disappointment, evidenced by diner's and cook's later remarks.
3. Answers may include: short-term—angry customers, ill feelings among staff; long-term—loss of business, resulting in possible loss of jobs.

The interests and skills needed for a food service job are very different from those needed for a job in food processing. You are more likely to work closely with other people, both coworkers and customers. Special qualities are needed. Can you answer yes to many of the following questions?

- **Do you have good math skills?** Food servers need to add checks accurately so that the customer's bill is correct.

- **Are you calm under pressure?** Remaining calm when a lot is going on around you isn't easy. A restaurant kitchen can be a very hectic place. The same is true of a restaurant dining room. Remaining calm will help you do your job effectively.

- **Are you creative?** Chefs often must devise fresh menus to attract new customers. Food writers have to describe food in appetizing ways that will make people want to try new dishes or go to a particular restaurant.

Acting Responsibly

Do You Have a Positive Attitude?

When a problem arises, how do you respond? Keeping a positive attitude is often harder than giving in to feelings of anger and frustration, but always more beneficial. Remaining optimistic and upbeat prevents a difficult situation from growing worse. You are more open to possible solutions. You can help reassure others and provide a model for constructive action. You even gain respect.

A Positive Attitude in Action

It was already a busy night in the restaurant where Loni worked as a hostess. Between seating new arrivals, soothing impatient customers, directing the servers, and checking with the kitchen staff, she felt that she could barely catch her breath.

"You must be exhausted," a waitress told her.

Loni mustered a smile. "Let's just say we're all getting our exercise tonight."

Around 7:30 a waiter quietly summoned Loni to the kitchen. The head chef was peering inside one of the ovens. "This oven isn't working," she said impatiently. "I just took out a cake that looked like pudding. What are we supposed to do?"

Loni sighed. This was the last thing she needed. "Get on the phone," she directed. "See if we can get a repair service in here. In the meantime, make do as best you can. Does the range still work? Can you use the grill instead? You're the pros here, so I'll leave that up to you. I'll deal with the customers."

With the help of the staff, Loni went to the patrons who had ordered dishes that couldn't be prepared.

"We do have many other excellent dishes. Our soups and stews are very popular, and we make all kinds of sandwiches—we did get the bread baked this afternoon!"

A few people expressed their disappointment, but others made up for it. "This was kind of an adventure," one man told her. "I probably never would have tried your French onion soup, and it was delicious. My son now thinks spaghetti sauce on Italian bread is better than pizza."

After the long evening, Loni thanked the staff for their extra effort. To the chef she added, "Sorry about your cake."

The chef laughed. "Oh, it wasn't a total loss, just a little moist. We can serve it with a little cream and call it bread pudding!"

Your Analysis

1. By staying positive, what other personal qualities was Loni able to demonstrate? Give examples.
2. What effect do you think Loni's attitude had on her coworkers? On the customers? Cite evidence for your answer.
3. What might have been some short- and long-term consequences if Loni had not stayed positive?

REAL-LIFE APPLICATION

Ask students to imagine that one of their friends is growing discouraged with his job as a supermarket bagger. "It's such a simple job," he explains, "and I'm not learning anything." Ask: Is he correct? What valuable job skills might he be developing? Help students see that bagging groceries takes organization skills; dealing with shoppers takes relationship skills; even double-bagging and offering shoppers help takes initiative.

- **Can you work well and get along with others?** Few people in the field of food service work alone. A restaurant staff is a team made up of waiters and waitresses, hosts and hostesses, food preparers, buspersons, bartenders, and dishwashers. The ability to cooperate is essential.
- **Are you friendly?** Many food servers work with the public. Some are paid directly by their customers—in tips. A pleasant attitude helps ensure that patrons are satisfied and encourages them to return.
- **Are you willing to learn more about food and food preparation?** A short-order cook must know how to grill hamburgers rare, medium, or well-done. The dishwasher must know how to make plates and utensils sanitary. No matter how much you know about food and nutrition now, you need to be willing to learn more.

Jobs in Food Processing

The field of food processing involves producing, canning, freezing, drying, packaging, and selling food products. Some people who work in food processing never see the customers who purchase the food. These workers may spend their time hauling produce or checking the quality of canned goods in the factory; they do not work in the store that actually sells the fruit or the canned goods. Others, such as those who sell food in supermarkets, deal directly with the consumer.

Entry-Level Jobs

The food-processing field includes many jobs for people without prior experience. Farm laborers, for example, learn their skills on the job. Positions in canning and packing also may be entry-level jobs. Food-canning and food-freezing workers prepare foods that are sold in cans, jars, and cartons. Tasks such as washing, peeling, pitting, and cooking the food may be done by hand or machine. Most packing is done by machines, although hand packers are needed for some fruits and vegetables. Some of these jobs are seasonal.

Stock clerks keep supermarket shelves and refrigerated units stocked with food. They also unpack food shipments, label items with prices or codes, and help keep the store clean by wiping up spills and broken glass. Other entry-level positions include cashier, bagger, and deli clerk. Many are part-time positions instead of full-time ones, making these good options for homemakers, retired people, or people who are in school or who are looking for a second job in addition to a full-time one.

Jobs That Require Training

Managers are needed in all aspects of food processing. Food-processing plants use line managers, department managers, and plant managers. Managers are also needed to run supermarkets. These workers oversee staff members and make sure that jobs are done properly and that the business makes a profit.

 Many jobs in a food-processing plant involve operating specialized machinery.

CHAPTER 55   **Careers in Food and Nutrition**   533

 **Activities**

Activities
■ **A Fly in My Soup.** Ask students to write and present skits that illustrate the interests and skills needed by food service workers. For example, they might act out a restaurant scene contrasting a food server who is friendly, accurate, and calm with one who lacks those characteristics. *(Creativity)*

ENRICHMENT
■ **Resident Stock Clerk.** Have students take inventory of the food in their refrigerator or full-size freezer at home. Tell them to record all the items in a detailed, organized list. Ask: What skills did you use to perform this task? How do both families and businesses benefit by knowing exactly what items are in stock? *(Management)*

FAMILY AND COMMUNITY OUTREACH
Encourage students to contact a local community college, trade school, or university to learn what opportunities it offers for further study in the field of food processing. Suggest they ask what high school courses are recommended for students who plan to study food processing at that school.

DID YOU KNOW?

Budding food scientists may find a career with the United States Food and Drug Administration (FDA). Established in 1907, the agency's original purpose was monitoring food purity and sanitation in the food-processing industry. Today FDA scientists test the safety and usefulness of drugs and chemicals, including those used in foods. They also study the effect of pesticides that may enter the food supply.

Topics on pp. 534-536:

- **Food-Processing Jobs That Require Training and Higher Education**
- **Food Service Jobs**
- **Preparing for a Career in Foods**

Checking Comprehension

✓ How might a store manager get training for the position? *Learn through entry-level jobs; take college courses; get special training offered by employer.*

✓ Name some of a head chef's responsibilities. *Order food; accept deliveries; plan menus; hire chefs; direct workers.*

✓ How do dietitians' and nutritionists' jobs differ? *Dietitians plan menus for certain groups; nutritionists teach about nutrition.*

SPECIAL NEEDS
Strategies

Gifted Students. Gifted students with an interest in a food-related career may be able to take college courses now to advance toward their goal. Help these students learn what courses they need and whether they are available at local colleges.

In businesses such as retail food stores, managers are also responsible for keeping track of **inventory**—*the amount of each product that is in stock at any one time.* Some businesses close down for a few days and hire extra staff when they conduct the yearly inventory, which is a careful counting of all items. Computers help managers keep track of inventory throughout the year.

Supermarket managers often have taken college courses. Many are promoted from cashier to department head and then to store manager. In addition to college courses, managers often receive special training through the companies they work for.

Other positions are earned through apprenticeships. An apprentice is an employee who studies a position under the supervision of a senior worker. For example, meat cutters (workers who cut and package meat) learn their jobs this way. Meat cutters must be very careful because they work with dangerous equipment. Training for such jobs may also occur in vocational or trade schools.

Quality control inspectors make sure that the taste, texture, and appearance of products meet plant standards. Other inspectors work for the government to monitor the safety and cleanliness of food-processing plants. These workers are usually trained on the job.

Jobs That Require Higher Education

Many people who work in food and nutrition careers have college degrees. Food scientists study nutrition, biology, and chemistry. They try to improve methods of canning, freezing, packaging, and storing foods so that fewer nutrients are lost. At the same time, they are concerned with preserving a food's flavor, texture, and appearance.

Agronomists are scientists who try to improve the process of growing crops. They often have advanced training beyond a four-year college degree. They study ways to make crops produce higher yields and work to develop disease-resistant plants. These researchers may work for the government, universities, or private companies.

Jobs in Food Service

Food service is the other major branch in the field of food and nutrition. People in these careers work mostly in restaurants and cafeterias, making sure that customers get the foods they want and enjoy their meals. Others work for large institutions. For example, they may work in hospitals, making sure that the special nutritional needs of patients are met each day.

Math skills are important to food service workers, especially servers and cashiers.

534   **UNIT 6   Food, Nutrition, and Wellness**

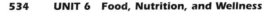

MORE ABOUT Dietitians

Not all dietitians work in institutions; many are in private practice. They may be hired to provide nutritional advice to professional athletes, lecture to clubs and organizations, and consult with food companies in developing new products.

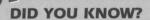

DID YOU KNOW?

Restaurant franchises offer opportunities for entrepreneurship in the food industry. The franchise company provides the site and equipment, operations assistance, advertising, and an established name; franchise owners manage daily operations.

Entry-Level Jobs

Waiters and waitresses, also called servers or wait staff, take customers' orders and bring them their food. The job goes beyond this, however. Many customers ask their servers to recommend selections. How much people enjoy the dining experience often begins with how comfortable the waiter or waitress makes customers feel.

Restaurants also offer other entry-level positions. Dishwashers work in kitchens cleaning plates, glasses, and utensils. They also wash the mixing bowls, pots and pans, and other preparation equipment the cooks have used. Buspersons, also called dining room attendants, clear dirty dishware from tables and bring it to the kitchen for washing.

Hosts and hostesses greet customers and show them to their tables. They also take reservations and, in some places, operate the cash register. Cafeteria attendants—who serve food in school, office, and institutional cafeterias—also may be hired without prior experience.

Restaurant jobs can be full- or part-time positions. Dining room attendants, waiters, and waitresses are normally paid a low hourly rate that is supplemented with tips. Other workers are paid by the hour or given salaries.

Jobs That Require Training

In restaurants, entry-level jobs often open doors to higher positions. Openings for assistant managers, kitchen managers, and floor managers frequently are filled by promoting and training hard workers from within the restaurant.

Some chefs earn their positions by working their way up through the kitchen; they learn from other chefs and through their own experiences. Many chefs, however, attend culinary institutes or take vocational courses. Some restaurants hire chefs with specialties, such as pastry chefs.

The head chef often manages all of the kitchen activities. He or she may order the food, accept deliveries, plan menus, and hire

What skills do you think a person needs to be a chef in a large restaurant?

subordinate chefs. When the restaurant is open, the head chef may direct the team of workers who prepare customers' meals.

Jobs That Require Higher Education

Many food service jobs require college degrees. Dietitians and nutritionists study and apply nutrition principles to food management. Dietitians use their knowledge of food and nutrition to prepare appealing, healthful meals for people on special diets. Hospitals, nursing homes, schools, and other institutions rely on dietitians.

Nutritionists study how the body uses food. They are usually more involved with teaching about nutrition than with planning particular menus. They are employed in schools, hospitals, and public health agencies, as well as in

■ **Food Writer.** Have students write a short article that might appear in a food magazine about the opportunities in food service .

■ **Climbing the Rungs.** Have students sketch a diagram of the career ladder that a person in the food service field might climb. Explain that each successively higher rung of the ladder should represent a more advanced position that can be reached with experience, training, and education.

In Touch With TECHNOLOGY

Discuss with students ways in which they have seen technology at work in regular restaurants and fast-food restaurants. Ask whether any students have had experience with the technology mentioned on page 536 or with other kinds of technology in food-service jobs.

Answers to Thinking Critically

1. Answers may include: operations could be seriously disrupted, depending on restaurant's reliance on computers; staff would revert to previous methods. Train staff in traditional techniques also.
2. Answers may include: restaurants might prefer to offer customers more personal touch; may want to avoid expense, effort of installing computer system and training employees to use it.

MORE ABOUT Restaurant Jobs

Jobs in fast-food restaurants offer real, often unrecognized benefits. Tasks and training are fairly uniform within a franchise, so employees can work in franchise restaurants in any location; they have "portable" jobs. Fast-food restaurants are usually open long hours, offering more flexibility in scheduling. Workers can also learn a variety of food preparation and kitchen management skills, sometimes changing tasks from week to week.

Review

■ **Chapter Review.** Use the contents of the Chapter Review page to help students review concepts, think critically, and apply their knowledge.

■ **Study Guide.** Have students complete the Study Guide for Chapter 55 on p. 183 of the Student Workbook.

■ **Can of Peas Revisited.** Give students copies of the list of workers they made at the start of the chapter. Ask them what other jobs they can add. Stress that there are even more "behind-the-scenes" workers not discussed in the chapter.

Evaluation

■ **Chapter Test.** Use the reproducible chapter test provided in the Teacher's Classroom Resources or create your own test using the *Testmaker Software.*

■ **Alternative Assessment.** Tell groups to imagine they are opening a restaurant. Have them make a chart showing the different jobs they would need to fill and the skills, training, and experience each worker would need.

■ **Thanks, but No Thanks?** Have students write a paragraph explaining whether they think they might enjoy a job in food processing or food service, and if so, which ones.

---

the food industry. Dietitians and nutritionists have college degrees, and many have graduate degrees.

Food writers and editors help the public learn about food and nutrition. They write newspaper and magazine articles explaining new ways of using food or describing the latest discoveries in nutrition. They also write books and prepare reports for food manufacturers. People in these jobs usually have college degrees, often with training in English or journalism.

In the food service industry, many companies rely on the expertise of people from other fields. Restaurant chains may hire licensed real estate experts to study locations for future franchises. Financial experts analyze the special structure of the food service corporation to better manage its earnings.

Preparing for a Career

Have you discovered any food-related careers that seem interesting to you? If so, try one of these ideas. Look for a summer job as a server, counter worker, or stock clerk, or consider volunteering at a hospital or nursing home where you can observe food preparation and service. In these ways, you can learn firsthand what some food-related careers are like.

In Touch with TECHNOLOGY — Better Service Through Science

Increasingly, restaurants are using some impersonal technology to help them give more personal attention. Consider these examples:

- **Pager systems.** Some restaurant personnel wear wrist pagers. With these devices, customers can change an order or request the check, servers can find out whether food is ready, and managers can tell kitchen staff to pick up the pace. Some restaurants use pagers to tell waiting customers that their tables are ready.
- **Reservation software.** One computer program tracks reservations, shows who has arrived, and estimates the wait for walk-in customers. The system can even store a frequent diner's preferred table or favorite dish in memory.
- **Point-of-sale computers.** Introduced during the past decade, these computers have changed food delivery techniques. After taking an order, a server enters the information—table location, number of customers, and the order (including specific requests)—on a computer terminal. The order is printed or displayed in the kitchen. Each station gets its own instructions, with one kitchen worker coordinating the order. The computer

prints the check. National Restaurant Association statistics show that these systems are used by more than half the table-service restaurants with average checks of $25 or more.

Fast-food restaurants have long used computers to take customer orders. Over time, other types of restaurants have seen the benefits in coordination, documentation, and inventory control. With computerization, no diner gets the wrong order due to illegible handwriting, and the check is added correctly.

Thinking Critically About Technology

1. What is the potential effect on restaurants that use computers if the system "goes down," or ceases to function? How could they plan ahead to lessen the difficulties?
2. Why might a restaurant, even a large one, choose not to use this technology?

REAL-LIFE APPLICATION

Help students invite a variety of workers in food processing and food service to speak to the class, for a round table discussion, if possible. Tell students to explain to the guests that they want to learn about the skills, qualities, and training that help them succeed on the job, as well as their job responsibilities.

Chapter 55 Review

Reviewing the Facts

1. List and describe four qualities that are useful for a career in food and nutrition.
2. Describe two jobs in food processing, and tell whether each is an entry-level position or a position that requires some education or experience.
3. Explain the term inventory.
4. Describe two jobs in food service, and tell whether each is an entry-level position or a position that requires some education or experience.
5. Describe two ways you could prepare for a job in food and nutrition.

Thinking Critically

1. Which would you prefer: a career in food processing or one in food service? Give reasons for your choice.
2. When you are a customer in a restaurant, what expectations do you have of a waiter or waitress? What personal traits and knowledge should he or she have? How might these traits and knowledge benefit the server, the customers, and the restaurant?

Applying Your Knowledge

1. **Preparing for a Job Interview.** Even when experience is not a requirement, employers like to hear about things you have done that show you have qualities that would be useful in that job. Make a list of traits, experiences, and interests that might help you get a job in food-processing or food service.
2. **Developing Interview Skills.** With a partner, take turns acting out the roles of interviewer and job candidate. The interviewer should state his or her needs to the applicant, and the candidate should explain how these would be met.

Making Connections

1. **Business.** Pretend you are an efficiency expert brought in to increase business in a supermarket. Make a list of specific suggestions you might offer these workers to help them serve their customers more effectively: cashier, stock clerk, produce manager, meat manager. Have at least two suggestions for each worker.
2. **Government.** The Food and Drug Administration (FDA), as well as food associations, such as the National Fisheries Institute and the International Apple Institute, are responsible for making sure that the food people buy is safe to eat. Imagine that you work for the FDA or a food association. Name two food safety issues that you would be concerned about. Be prepared to discuss these issues with the class, stating how you might address them.

Building Your Portfolio

Writing a Restaurant Review

Food writers often do restaurant reviews. Find two reviews in newspapers or magazines, and read them closely. What aspects of dining do reviewers discuss?

Select an eating facility—such as the school cafeteria, a restaurant, or even your own home. Imagine that you are a food critic. Write a review of at least one page about a meal and the way it was served, supporting your opinions with details. Share your findings with the class. Place a copy of your written review in your portfolio.

Unit Preview

Unit 7 begins by helping students see the impact that clothing has on their lives. They learn how to use the elements of design to highlight their best features and how to plan their wardrobes to make the best use of their resources. The unit also explores a range of fibers, fabrics, and finishes. Five chapters in Unit 7 guide students through garment construction, from selecting a pattern to sewing on the buttons. Another chapter describes ways to recycle fashions, and the unit ends with an overview of careers in clothing and textiles.

Content Development

Use these chapters to reinforce the following themes:

Content Strands	Chapters
Career Exploration	68
Communication	56, 68
Decision Making	57-59, 61, 62, 67
Health and Safety	56
Managing Resources	58-60, 64-67
Personal Development	56, 58-60
Technology	59, 61, 63, 68

Unit Motivator

■ **Sewing Expectations.** Gather garments that are in need of repair to show to the class (button hanging by thread, broken zipper, stained fabric, loose hem, open seam, ripped fabric, etc.). Ask how many students know how to correct the problems. Discuss the value of having these skills.

538

JOURNAL WRITING

Possible topics for student journals:

- How does your clothing express your personality?
- Which elements of design could help you?
- What might you do differently the next time you shop for clothes?
- What do you do to take good care of your clothes?
- Do you prefer natural or manufactured fibers? Why?
- Which part of sewing do you enjoy most? Why?
- Which aspect of sewing presents the biggest challenge to you? How can you master it?

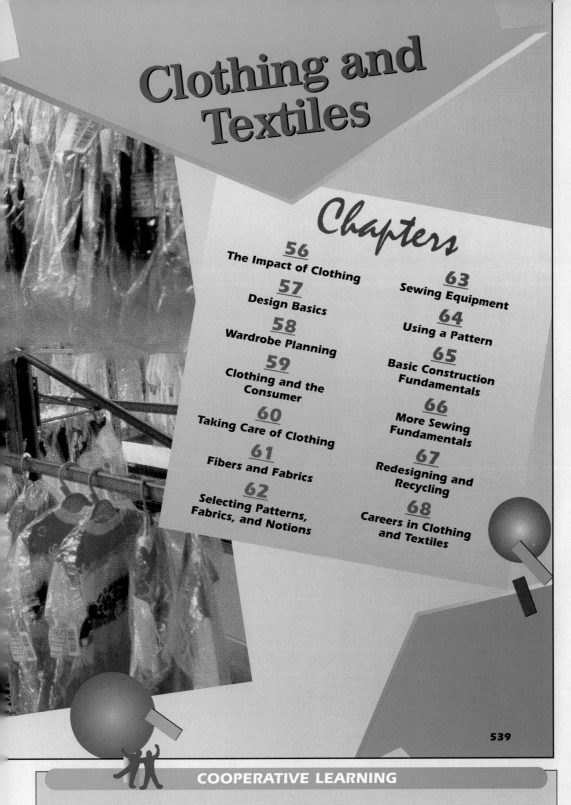

Clothing and Textiles

Chapters

539

FHA Activities

These activities can be used with your FHA group or as public relations strategies:

■ **Clothes Clinic.** Set up a "clinic" at school and invite students and staff to bring in "sick" clothes—clothes that need minor repairs or alterations, such as a button replaced or a hem shortened. Set a small charge for these services and donate the money to a nonprofit clothing recycling center.

■ **Wheelchair Pockets.** As a community project, have students design and sew carryalls for wheelchair-bound residents of nursing homes. Students might produce several styles in a variety of easy-care fabrics, with decorative hand and machine stitches.

■ **Sharing Skills.** Arrange for students to teach children, perhaps fourth graders, how to replace buttons on their clothing. Your class might begin by writing the steps on posterboard and teaching each other for practice.

Unit Closure

REVIEW

Review in the Round. Organize the class into 13 groups and assign each group a chapter from Unit 7. Explain that each group will have four minutes to present the main points or demonstrate the skills explained in its chapter, using visuals. When the groups are ready, have them sit in order in a large circle. Start with Chapter 56 and go quickly around the circle.

EVALUATION

■ **Unit Test.** Have students complete the unit test in the Teacher's Classroom Resources.

■ **Testmaker Software.** You may wish to design a unit test using the *Testmaker Software*.

COOPERATIVE LEARNING

Send a Problem. Have teams write problems pertaining to unit content on index cards (along with a team name and problem number, such as A-1) and send them to other teams. Encourage teams to be creative in developing problems that require application of knowledge to solve. The receiving teams should write responses on separate cards, identifying each problem by name/number. Teams continue to write problems and pass them along as time permits. Follow up by reading problems and discussing responses.

Chapter Overview

Chapter 56 helps students understand the many roles of clothing—its personal, social, and practical functions. The chapter also describes influences on clothing choices and provides clothing guidelines for social situations.

Motivators

■ **Agree or Disagree?** An old Latin proverb states: "Clothes make the man." Have students respond to this saying.

Objectives

Discuss the chapter objectives on this page. Remind students that the objectives focus on important chapter concepts.

Vocabulary

Explain that the word *status* is based on the same Latin word as state. *Status* can refer to someone's position in society, or it can mean the state or current condition of something. For example, if someone asks, "What is the status of that report?" she or he is probably wondering whether the report is finished, not whether it is important.

Chapter
56

The Impact of Clothing

Terms to Learn

- conform
- designer
- dress code
- formal clothing
- garment industry
- individuality
- status

Objectives

This chapter will help you to:

- Interpret **personal statements expressed through clothing.**
- Explain **the social significance of clothing.**
- Establish **guidelines for choosing appropriate clothing.**
- Identify **health and safety issues regarding clothing and describe how to respond to them.**
- Assess **the impact of the fashion industry.**

CHAPTER RESOURCES

Student Workbook
Study Guide, pp. 185-186
Activity, *Fashion Facts*, pp. 187-188

Teacher's Classroom Resources
Lesson Plan, p. 60
Cooperative Learning, *Creating a Clothing Ad*, pp. 61-62

Extension #83, *Dressing Appropriately*, p. 89
Extension #84, *Clothing Purchases*, p. 90
Life Skills, *Analyzing a Clothing Ad*, pp. 88-89
Transparency 49, *Influences on Clothing Choices*

Chapter 56 Test, pp. 117-118
Performance Assessment, *Appropriate Dress*, pp. 89-90
Reteaching, *Influences on Clothing Choices*, p. 62

See Also:
ABCNews InterActive™ Videodiscs

Kendra grimaced as she studied herself in the mirror. "My feet hurt!" she exclaimed.

"With those shoes, it's no wonder," her friend Lana said. "They look too small."

"Yes, but I love this style. I'm not so sure about the dress, though. The label says this is my size, but maybe I should have bought a larger size."

Lana tugged on the hem of Kendra's dress, trying to pull it into place.

"I saw a pink one that I liked better," Kendra went on, "but the salesclerk at Kramer's said they just got this style in. It's the same one that's on page 37 of this magazine. Let me show you. Besides, I know this is Derrick's favorite color."

Kendra leafed through the magazine until she came to page 37. There a tall, thin model wearing the same dress leaned against a tree. Lana looked from the photo to her friend, then back. She barely recognized the dress.

Kendra sighed and frowned. She studied the picture, then turned again to the mirror. "Maybe if I wear my hair the same way as hers. . . ." She looked hopefully at Lana.

Lana didn't reply. She had some things that she wanted to say, but she wasn't sure where to begin—or even if she should.

Exploring the Issues

Kendra and Lana were both responding to the impact of clothing. You have experienced this impact also, to various degrees in different situations. You know, perhaps without realizing it, that clothing serves functions other than keeping you warm in cold weather and dry in a rainstorm. When you explore the issues that surround clothing, you may discover that they are even more complex than you imagined.

What personality characteristics might you perceive about this teen based on clothing choices?

A Personal Statement

Every time you put on an article of clothing, you do more than simply get dressed. You are revealing something about who you are, what groups you are a part of, and even how you feel about yourself.

Clothing choices are often clues to individual personality. For example, people who combine colors and styles in unusual ways may be expressing a creative, independent attitude. Someone wearing a cap and a T-shirt with the name of a sports team is clearly demonstrating a personal interest.

Clothing can reflect personal values. Rebecca feels strongly about protecting the environment. She often buys clothing at secondhand shops and chooses items made

---

Focus on Decision-Making Skills

Remind students that making clothing choices involves evaluating their needs, goals, and values. Chapter 57 will help students choose clothing that looks good on them. Chapter 58 explains how to identify the clothing items they really need, not just what they want. Chapter 59 will help them avoid shopping pitfalls.

TEACH

Topics on p. 541:
- **Exploring the Issues Around Clothing**
- **How Clothing Makes a Personal Statement**

Checking Comprehension

✓ Why does Kendra want to buy the dress she is trying on? *It looks good on a model in a magazine; it's her boyfriend's favorite color.*

✓ What can be reflected by your choice of clothing? *Your personality and self-concept, your values and interests, the groups you belong to.*

Activities

■ **Reflecting Feelings.** Have students suggest a number of clothing choices that might show they feel good about themselves. *(Relationship)*

RETEACHING

■ **Sending Messages.** Ask students to suggest specific clothing teens might wear to show that:
They feel depressed.
They care about animals.
They are proud of their culture.
They don't care how they look.
Music is their passion.
They like to be comfortable.

ENRICHMENT

■ **Snap Judgment.** Ask students if they have ever had a bad first impression of someone based on his or her clothing but changed their opinion when they got to know the person better. What kinds of clothing can lead to a negative first impression? A positive first impression? How can you avoid making snap judgments about people based on their clothing?

Checking Comprehension

✓ What are some examples of a written dress code? *School or military dress codes; signs in restaurants requiring men to wear jackets; dress requirements in offices.*

✓ What are three examples of clothing that would identify you as a member of a group? *Team or band uniforms; skirts (gender group); club jackets or T-shirts; certain brands favored by a group.*

✓ What is the difference between individuality and conformity in clothing? *Individuality means you think for yourself in choosing your clothing and enjoy being original. Conformity means you dress like the people around you; being part of a group makes you feel comfortable.*

CROSS-CURRICULAR ACTIVITY
Language Arts

Discuss how students currently use clothing to express their individuality, to show their interests and values, to indicate group membership, and to reflect their positive or negative moods. Have students write analyses of how particular clothing items or combination of items fulfill one or more of these functions. Or have them write a description with this title: "This Outfit Is the Real Me."

542

---

of natural, durable fibers. She feels that these choices are in keeping with her views on recycling and reducing waste.

Clothing can also be used to show pride in cultural heritage. Some African Americans, for example, accent their wardrobes with garments made of kente, a traditional African fabric. A Native American might favor hand-woven articles with authentic Navajo designs.

Clothing choice sometimes indicates how you feel about yourself and the world. Certain garments may reflect an angry or depressed state or show low self-esteem. On the other hand, some choices give the impression that the wearers are self-assured and comfortable.

They aren't worried about the impression they make on others. Can you think of garments that might reflect such images?

When you look at clothing as an insight to personality, remember that it is a clue at best. Judging someone on the basis of clothing alone, without knowing all the facts, is unfair and often inaccurate. You may think that a friend is wearing old sweatpants and a sweatshirt because she is depressed, when in reality she was only getting ready to clean out her garage.

Social Aspects

In 1851, Amelia Bloomer stunned society by wearing "Turkish pantaloons"—baggy trousers—under her knee-length skirt. In the mid-19th century, it was an outrage for a woman to wear pants. Amelia Bloomer's action had a purpose, however. A women's rights activist, she wanted to demonstrate her belief in the equality of men and women. She chose to wear pants because she recognized the value of clothing as a social symbol.

Reinforcing gender roles (or, in Amelia Bloomer's case, challenging them) is only one function of clothing in society. People also use dress to express membership in other social groups.

Dress Codes

What do the servers in an elegant restaurant and the fans at a country and western music concert have in common? Both are probably following some sort of **dress code,** *a set of rules describing required or appropriate clothing.*

Clothes are a means of self-expression. Adding your own designs to clothing reflects your individuality.

542   UNIT 7   Clothing and Textiles

DID YOU KNOW?

People wear clothing for:
- Protection—clothes provide protection from the weather and injuries.
- Modesty—clothes cover parts of the body, but standards of modesty vary by activity and culture.
- Identification—clothes can identify people as members of a group.

- Status—clothes can show the level of a person's standing in a group or the community.
- Decoration and self-expression—clothes can improve people's appearance and express their uniqueness and their self-concepts.

A dress code may be written (for example, for a military academy). There are also "unwritten rules" of attire that people accept and adhere to. It is understood, for example, that you wouldn't wear the same clothing to a formal dinner that you would to a picnic.

Dress codes are designed not only to show membership in a certain group, but also to promote a desired atmosphere or environment. Schools that require uniforms or that permit only certain types of street clothes are trying to foster an orderly environment for learning. They encourage students to focus on their education, not on what they and other students are wearing. Likewise, restaurants that require men to wear suit jackets are trying to achieve an atmosphere of formality and refinement for the enjoyment of their customers. In many offices, managers expect people to dress professionally but allow a dress-down day once a week when everyone can dress casually.

Some people dislike dress codes. They believe that requiring some garments and forbidding others infringes on their freedom of expression. Some students, for example, feel that dress codes hinder **individuality**—*the unique way of being and expressing yourself.* Unless the clothing is offensive or interrupts the learning atmosphere, they argue, students should be allowed to wear whatever they like. Similarly, others claim that dress codes in restaurants and other public establishments promote exclusiveness and division. People who don't own or can't afford the required garments are made to feel inferior.

The issues surrounding dress codes are not likely to be resolved. You may find yourself in situations where dress codes seem too loose or too restrictive. If adapting to a dress code saves you hassle and trouble, that may be the best approach to take.

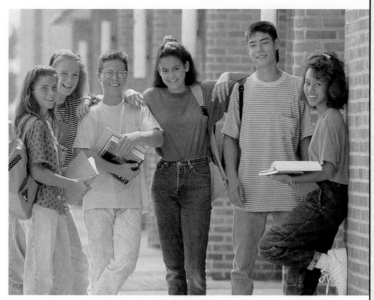

How does peer pressure influence the way many teens dress? What are the pros and cons of following the crowd in terms of dress?

Peer Pressures

The pressures of a peer group can act as an unwritten dress code. Wearing a style that is popular with your peers can help meet a need for belonging. The desire to **conform,** or *go along with current custom,* is natural in all people and often especially strong among teens.

Conformity in clothing choice can be healthy. Wearing a team uniform, for instance, helps unite members in focus and goals; it shows pride in membership. Conformity is also harmlessly expressed by following general clothing habits—when male teens favor pullover sweaters instead of cardigans, for example, or when females wear skirts at a certain length.

Conformity can carry negative consequences, however. Suppose that many of your peers are dressing in ways that make you uncomfortable. What if following the latest trend means buying clothes that you think are over-

■ **Adults Have Peers, Too.** Discuss whether students think peer pressure to dress alike is stronger for teens or for adults. (Also explore why teens tend to be more susceptible to peer pressure than adults.) *(Relationship)*

CROSS-CURRICULAR ACTIVITY
Language Arts

Ask students to collect magazine and newspaper clothing ads that use status as a selling point. Have them analyze the effectiveness of several of the ads and the wants and values to which the ads appeal. Discuss the reasons why students would or would not buy the item in each ad.

FAMILY AND COMMUNITY OUTREACH

Encourage students to classify the clothing they have at home into these two categories:

• Items they chose because their friends were wearing them or because the item looked good on a model in an ad or on television.
• Items they chose because the items fit their clothing needs and looked good on them.

Have students write a brief report explaining what they learned from this activity. How much are their clothing choices influenced by outside pressure?

DID YOU KNOW?

Research shows that people's ideas about appropriate dress for different activities are strongly and subconsciously affected by television advertising. This is true even when the advertising is for products other than clothes.

Ask students if they think television ads affect their clothing choices. If so, in what ways? Also discuss how the wardrobes of popular singers, musicians, movie actors, and characters on television shows might influence teens' clothing choices.

Topics on pp. 544-545:
- **Clothing and Relationships**
- **Dressing for Occasions**

Checking Comprehension

✓ How can your clothing choice show respect for others? *When you choose clothing that is appropriate for the occasion, you show respect for others' values and feelings.*

✓ How can your clothing choices help you get a job or gain admission to a college? *Wearing appropriate clothing can make a good impression on an employer or an admissions director.*

✓ How can you find out what is appropriate to wear to a religious service or a cultural event? *Ask knowledgeable people.*

Acting Responsibly

Have students read "Are You Sensitive?" Have them explain what they might have done if they had been in Vasant's position. What if they had been Lisa?

Answers to Your Analysis

1. They may have been uncomfortable with Vasant's different appearance; they may not have learned to be sensitive to the feelings of others.
2. Helping others can help you feel good, too; you might gain a friend.

Acting Responsibly

Are You Sensitive?

The word sensitive has several meanings. People who are irritated by perfumes and soaps are said to have sensitive skin. If you react strongly to teasing, friends may accuse you of being overly sensitive.

Sensitivity also describes an understanding and appreciation of the feelings and needs of others. A sensitive person is someone who notices when a person feels uncomfortable and tries to help.

Sensitivity can be an issue whenever people interact, whether they are teens or senior citizens. Even close friends may say things—intentionally or accidentally—that are hurtful.

Sensitivity in Action

Vasant has lived in California all her life. She loves being an American citizen, but she has always been proud of the Indian traditions she learned from her parents. Vasant usually dresses in typical American clothing, but at least once a week she enjoys wearing a sari—a traditional Indian garment.

During Vasant's sophomore year, her family moved. She didn't know anyone at the new school, but she began to make new friends right away. When she wore her sari to school one day, the reactions of some of her new classmates surprised Vasant. A few people laughed and made loud comments to each other. One teen asked Vasant whether she was an American or a foreigner.

A new friend from Vasant's homeroom stepped forward. Lisa wasn't familiar with Indian traditions, but she knew she didn't like seeing the way Vasant was being taunted. She could tell that Vasant was confused and upset. Lisa told the others to leave Vasant alone. After all, she pointed out, isn't it the American way for people to be able to express themselves in whatever way they like? Lisa's sensitivity set an example for the others. Some students just walked away, but a few apologized to Vasant. One girl even asked her to show her how to put on a sari sometime.

Your Analysis

1. Why do you think Vasant's classmates made fun of her?
2. Obviously, treating others with sensitivity helps other people. How does it help you?

priced and unattractive? With clothing, as with all choices, you need to establish your own priorities and act on your own values. Some teens become so concerned with getting into the "right" crowd that they lose sight of who they are and what's important to them. When you feel these pressures, ask yourself whether inclusion in a group is worth putting aside your personal beliefs and goals.

Clothing and Relationships

"Unusual" is how Tara described her fashion sense. Her parents had other words for it. A typical outfit for Tara consisted of a red and green plaid vest over a satiny, bright blue blouse, with a flowing black skirt and low-heeled boots. A carved wooden necklace and a feather barrette completed the effect. Tara was considered a trendsetter by her friends, but they would not have recognized her at the party for her great-aunt's 80th birthday. She wore a rose-colored dress with a simple gold pin and pale blue pumps.

Tara explained the change this way: "I knew Aunt Jessie and a lot of other people in my family would be offended if I dressed the way I usually do. To me, it wasn't worth upsetting the people I care about just to wear certain clothes for a few hours. *I* decide how I dress, and I decided to wear something to

REAL-LIFE APPLICATION

Read each situation below and ask students to suggest ways that the person named might retain his or her individuality while showing respect for others:

- Anthony is expected to attend his younger sister's graduation from middle school.

- Janetta will be part of a student panel presentation at the parent-teacher open house.
- Mark will be an usher at his brother's wedding.
- Randolph has volunteered to drive senior citizens to a musical production at a downtown theater.

make Aunt Jessie happy. In the end, it's not so much what you wear as why you wear it."

An attitude like Tara's is helpful when issues concerning choice of clothing arise in a family. Now that you are a teen, you have a greater say in deciding what clothes look good and are appropriate, especially if you pay for the articles yourself.

At the same time, however, you are better able to empathize. Teens can recognize when a situation calls for flexibility. They can be responsible enough to care about others, not just themselves. A simple, temporary adjustment like Tara's can work wonders. When conflicts over clothing occur, both teens and adults can take comfort in remembering that such disagreements are nothing new. Many adults can look back to their teen years and remember wearing styles that their parents didn't like.

Dressing the Part

Imagine that you have volunteered to help a conservation group pull up shrubs and bushes in an area so that native plants may take root and flourish. How do you dress for the job? You need sturdy clothing that you don't mind getting dirty, such as jeans, work boots, and heavy gloves. If the temperature is especially hot or cold, you need clothing that protects you from either extreme. In this situation, your clothes should show that you understand and are prepared for the task. Appropriateness, then, is another important influence on clothing choice.

Meeting the Occasion

What would you think if, at a graduation ceremony, some of the students accepted their diplomas wearing flannel pajamas? This, of course, would look strange. Obviously, clothing may be appropriate in one setting but not in another. Described below are some sit-

uations that you may encounter in which you will want to pay special attention to your choice of clothing:

- **Job and school interviews.** Your clothes can help to create a positive first impression on an employer or an admissions director. Dressing neatly and conservatively tells the interviewer that you are serious and determined to succeed. Sloppy dress indicates a lack of concern and interest.

- **Weddings and proms.** These events vary greatly, according to the personal tastes of the bride and groom or the wishes of the student body. Traditionally, however, they call for **formal clothing**—*clothes worn for dressy occasions. These may include suits and ties, tuxedos, dresses, or gowns.* Guests at weddings are not usually as formally dressed as the members of the wedding party. The time and place of the ceremony are often clues to what type of dress is appropriate.

How does paying careful attention to the way you dress for an interview show your future employer that you are serious about obtaining a job?

CHAPTER 56   The Impact of Clothing   545

Topics on pp. 546-548:

- **Dangerous Dress**
- **How the Fashion Industry Influences Clothing Choices**
- **Raising Clothing Consciousness**

Checking Comprehension

✓ How does the fashion industry help make a certain clothing item a status symbol? *By making it more expensive than a similar item; by placing distinctive emblems or the designer's name on the garment; by getting someone famous to model it.*

✓ What are some types of clothing that are worn for safety reasons? *Helmets, hard hats, goggles, padding, fireproof suits, latex gloves.*

✓ What does the garment industry include? *The many companies involved in designing and manufacturing clothing.*

STRATEGIES THAT WORK

Have students read "When Dress Is Dangerous." Ask them for other examples of situations in which clothing could cause problems.

Answers to Think . . .

1. Answers will vary.
2. Answers will vary. Responses should show an understanding of the complex issues involved.
3. Don't wear expensive items; never walk alone through an unfamiliar area; stay on well-lighted streets; walk confidently.

- **Funerals.** Black is the traditional color for people in mourning. Any simple, neutral-colored clothing is usually considered appropriate, however.
- **Religious services.** Most services that take place inside a house of worship require tasteful, respectful attire. In addition, some religions have strict rules for dress. In the Jewish religion, for example, males must wear a yarmulke (YAH-muh-kuh), or a skullcap, when inside a house of worship. If you plan to attend a religious ceremony, ask about clothing requirements ahead of time.
- **Multicultural events.** Many cultures have specific rules about what may and may not be worn. Some of these contrast dramatically with prevailing American customs. As with religious services, ask beforehand if you are unsure about how to dress. This shows that you respect the culture and traditions of the people hosting the event.

Addressing Health Concerns

Sometimes protecting your physical health is your primary aim in dressing. The climate where you live and the amount of time you spend outdoors help determine which practical garments belong in your wardrobe.

In cold weather, wearing several layers of clothing helps insulate the body so that it retains heat. Covering your head reduces the

STRATEGIES That Work

When Dress is Dangerous

Dressing safely is usually a matter of dressing for the weather or wearing safety gear for a job or sport. In some situations, however, dressing safely is more complicated. Wearing the "wrong" clothes in some settings can provoke violence.

Gangs commonly use clothing to signal membership. In neighborhoods where gang rivalries exist, wearing a combination of colors or turning a cap a certain way can target a person for an attack—even for nonmembers. People have been injured and killed in attempts to steal their jackets and athletic shoes.

It might seem that suggestions for dressing with caution end up blaming the victim instead of the attacker. The thief who grabs the gold chains from around a young woman's neck is clearly the one at fault. Nevertheless, decisions about what to wear need to be based on possible consequences, the same as any other decision. Just as you would not willingly walk alone through a dark, deserted area, you should also think twice about wearing a team jacket or cap that is a known gang symbol.

Growing up safely means balancing the need for personal expression with the challenges of living in a world with people whose actions you cannot control.

Making the Strategy Work

Think . . .

1. Describe incidents you know of that seemed to be prompted by the victim's apparel.
2. What are your own views about the balance a person should take between personal expression and the need for safety? Give an example.
3. What three clothing and behavior guidelines would you offer someone who must travel through a dangerous area?

Try...

Contact the police department or neighborhood watch group for behavior guidelines for living and working safely in areas that are considered dangerous. Ask for a description of clothing that has a gang connotation.

546   UNIT 7   Clothing and Textiles

DID YOU KNOW?

Remind students of the significance of supply and demand in a market economy. Suggest that they contribute to consumer demand possibly without being aware of it. Have students explain how teens have helped to decide which styles and brands are available in stores today. Discuss what would happen to a certain fashion, style, or brand name if few people bought it.

loss of body heat by over one-half. These measures guard against hypothermia, which occurs when body temperature becomes dangerously low. Boots and gloves protect the feet and hands. These areas, along with the ears and nose, are particularly vulnerable to frostbite, or freezing of the skin tissues.

In hot weather, loose-fitting, loosely woven garments allow the body to cool itself through perspiration. Without such cooling, sunstroke and heatstroke, two serious conditions, can occur. Overexposure to the sun, in both warm weather and cold, has been linked to skin cancer. Protect yourself by keeping your arms and legs covered. In addition, shield your face with a wide-brimmed hat or a cap with a bill.

Dressing for Safety

Clothing not only protects against the elements; it also helps prevent injury during high-risk activities. Many workers need protective clothing to guard against on-the-job hazards. Scientists wear goggles and latex gloves when handling dangerous chemicals. Construction workers and carpenters wear masks to avoid inhaling dust and wood particles and bright colors so they can be easily seen.

Some sports also call for protective clothing. Contact sports, such as football and hockey, require helmets and several kinds of padding. Helmets are also advisable for other activities where falls are a threat, from in-line skating to horseback riding.

Fashion in Your Life

Have you ever browsed in a clothing store or paged through a clothing catalog wondering who decides which styles are fashionable? Why are skirt lengths long or short? Why are baggy garments "in" one year and "out" the next? Whether or not you are concerned with wearing the latest style, the fashion industry influences your life.

What Influences Fashions?

Clothing fashions are created by the **garment industry**—*all of the companies involved in the design and manufacture of clothing.* The production of a particular garment begins with the **designer,** *a person who creates clothing styles.* Designers are inspired by many sources: history and current events; books, movies, and television; and the styles of other cultures. They may also be influenced by styles already worn by others. For example, the popularity of Western boots worn with blue jeans and fleece-lined, rawhide vests is a trend based on the everyday attire of farm and ranch workers.

When a designer's work becomes popular, perhaps merely for the way he or she combines colors or uses certain fabrics, companies not connected with that designer often try to capitalize on that success by imitating the style. This is how a style spreads from its premiere at fashion shows to clothing stores around the country.

Some kinds of clothing protect people from danger.

CHAPTER 56   The Impact of Clothing   547

Activities

■ **Promises, Promises.** Discuss ways that the fashion industry takes advantage of some people's low self-esteem and lack of self-confidence. *(Relationship)*

RETEACHING

■ **Industry Influences.** Have students explain at least four ways that the fashion industry affects everyone, even people who avoid buying current fashions.

CROSS-CURRICULAR ACTIVITY
Art

Have pairs of students learn more about the contributions of one of these fashion designers: Cristobal Balenciaga, Bill Blass, Pierre Cardin, Coco Chanel, Liz Claiborne, Oscar de la Renta, Christian Dior, Perry Ellis, Betsy Johnson, Hubert de Givenchy, Halston, Kenzo, Calvin Klein, Ralph Lauren, Issey Miyake, Mary Quant, Yves Saint Laurent, or any other recognized designer. Have pairs create a display of the designer's work and report on his or her influence.

FAMILY AND COMMUNITY OUTREACH

Have students interview adults about the types of clothing that were considered status symbols when they were teens. What was most important: styles, brands, fabrics, or another aspect of clothing?

DID YOU KNOW?

Students probably do not realize that World War II greatly affected clothing fashions. Mobilizing a huge army required the rationing of fabrics, which were needed for soldiers' uniforms and parachutes. In 1942, the United States Congress tried to conserve fabric by passing a law making it illegal to manufacture clothing with patch pockets, cuffs, or wide hems.

Review

■ **Chapter Review.** Use the contents of the Chapter Review page to help students review concepts, think critically, and apply their knowledge.

■ **Study Guide.** Have students complete the Study Guide for Chapter 56 on p. 185 of the Student Workbook.

■ **Assessing the Impact.** Ask groups to discuss this question and summarize their thoughts for the class: In what ways does a person's choice of clothing impact his or her life?

Evaluation

■ **Chapter Test.** Use the reproducible chapter test provided in the Teacher's Classroom Resources or create your own test using the *Testmaker Software.*

■ **Alternative Assessment.** Ask each student to choose four important influences on clothing choices from this chapter. Have students explain by writing a report or by dictating into a tape recorder how these four influences do or do not affect their own clothing decisions.

CLOSE

■ **Defining Yourself.** Ask students to explain this saying: You are what you eat. (Your health depends to a great extent on what you eat.) Ask students if they think this version of the saying is true: "You are what you wear." If it is, what does this tell them about their clothing choices?

Influence of the Industry

Even if your way of dressing is totally independent of the latest fashion trends, the fashion industry affects you. At the very least, you are limited by what manufacturers decide to produce. Older adults, for example, are often frustrated by trying to find clothes that fit. The body changes shape as it ages. For example, the shoulders and back may become rounded. So far, however, few manufacturers have attempted to meet the needs of this growing group of consumers.

The designer system also affects people economically and socially. Some people feel they are forced to pay more for clothing simply because of the designer's name on the label. Others buy clothing by a certain designer as a way of attaining **status,** *position in society.* Manufacturers play on this emotional need by placing logos, or even the designer's name, prominently on articles of clothing.

The fashion trade can exert an additional, more subtle influence. Look, for example, at clothing catalogs and advertisements. Most, if not all, the models you find there are tall, slim, and attractive. This seems to imply two things. First, it suggests that wearing a particular shirt or pair of pants will make you as attractive and happy as the people in the photos appear to be. This, of course, is unrealistic.

Second, by using models with certain physical features, clothing manufacturers make a statement that these features are the most desirable ones. Although the same message is found in other types of advertising, it is especially powerful when promoted by the fashion industry, where appearance is a main reason for buying the product.

What effect might such advertising messages have on a person's self-concept and self-esteem? What do they tell people about the way they and others "should" look? Consider these questions, and let your values be your guide as you make clothing choices.

Wearing It Well

Teens are sometimes accused of being too concerned with wearing the "right" clothing. Clothing consciousness, however, is valuable for personal satisfaction and success in certain situations. Understanding what influences your clothing choices helps you make better ones.

Choose clothing that makes you look and feel good, not necessarily what looks good on models in fashion advertising.

548   UNIT 7   Clothing and Textiles

MORE ABOUT the Garment Industry

The garment industry is very large and complex. Designers and fashion models are only the most visible members of an industry that employs more than two million workers. This industry's three main tasks are making textiles, producing clothing, and selling clothing to stores.

Reviewing the Facts

1. Describe four things clothing can reveal about a person.
2. Summarize the arguments for and against having dress codes.
3. Identify three types of social occasions and the appropriate dress for each.
4. Describe two situations in which health concerns or safety guidelines dictate clothing choice.
5. Explain the effects of the fashion industry on individuals in our society.

Thinking Critically

1. Some teens are concerned about wearing what their peers like but not about what adults like. How would you explain this seeming contradiction?
2. Many female fashion models become celebrities, while the names of male models are lesser known outside the industry. What social attitudes or messages might this situation convey?

Applying Your Knowledge

1. **Predicting Clothing Needs.** Imagine that you are going on a three-day camping trip. You will be hiking, swimming, and canoeing. The days will be warm, but the nights will be chilly. Suggest six articles of clothing that would be appropriate for this trip. Keep in mind possible safety and health needs.
2. **Analyzing Motives.** Sixteen-year-old Jeremy is expected to attend his grandparents' anniversary dinner, which will be held in an expensive restaurant. Jeremy agrees to go but dresses for the occasion in jeans and motorcycle boots. How do you explain his behavior? What are possible outcomes of his actions—for Jeremy and others?

Making Connections

1. **Science.** Investigate one way that scientific research has led to the development or improvement of health- or safety-related clothing (for example, heat-resistant suits worn by firefighters and ironworkers). Prepare a brief report on your findings.
2. **History.** Research the clothing trends of a historical era. (If you choose a recent time period, you might ask older family members to help.) Write a paragraph or a short essay describing one garment worn in that time. Include such facts as who wore it, how it was made, and why it became popular. Include photos or drawings, if possible. Also tell of any social significance (such as Amelia Bloomer's wearing of pants to protest unfair treatment of women) attached to its popularity.

Building Your Portfolio

Analyzing a Garment

Select a favorite garment from your wardrobe to analyze. After reviewing the points discussed in this chapter, what do you think the garment says about you? For what situations is it appropriate? Does it serve any health- or safety-related purpose? How do others react when you wear it? Bring the item to class, and have your classmates evaluate it in the same way. Record your analysis and your classmates' opinions for inclusion in your portfolio.

CHAPTER 56   The Impact of Clothing   549

Chapter Overview

Chapter 57 decribes the effects of design elements and principles on appearance. Students learn how to use these concepts to choose clothing that complements their features and presents the desired image.

Motivators

■ **Looking Good.** Ask: Why did you choose the clothes you are wearing today? When appearance is mentioned, ask volunteers how they feel a certain garment enhances their looks. Tell them these effects demonstrate certain elements and principles of design, which they will study in this chapter.

Objectives

Discuss the chapter objectives on this page. Remind students that the objectives focus on important chapter concepts.

Vocabulary

Alert students that *complementary* is not the same as *complimentary*. Complimentary means showing praise; complementary (like *complete*) means supplying what something else lacks. Complementary combinations often earn compliments.

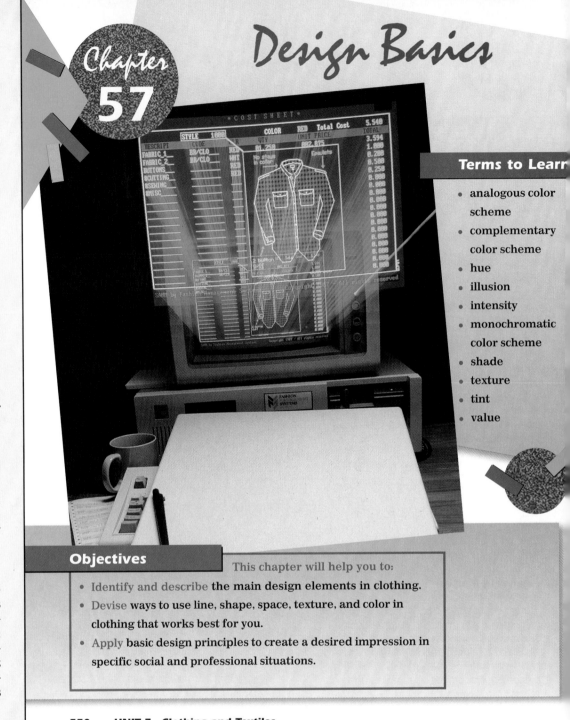

Design Basics

Terms to Learn

- analogous color scheme
- complementary color scheme
- hue
- illusion
- intensity
- monochromatic color scheme
- shade
- texture
- tint
- value

Objectives

This chapter will help you to:

- Identify and describe the main design elements in clothing.
- Devise ways to use line, shape, space, texture, and color in clothing that works best for you.
- Apply basic design principles to create a desired impression in specific social and professional situations.

550   UNIT 7   Clothing and Textiles

CHAPTER RESOURCES

Student Workbook
Study Guide, pp. 189-190
Activity, *Working with Color,* pp. 191-192

Teacher's Classroom Resources
Lesson Plan, p. 61
Extension #85, *Creative Color and Design,* p. 91

Life Skills, *Be a Fashion Consultant,* pp. 90-91
Transparency 50, *The Color Wheel*
Transparency 51, *Analogous Colors*
Transparency 52, *Complementary Colors*
Transparency 53, *Putting Elements of Design to Work for You*

Chapter 57 Test, pp. 119-120
Performance Assessment, *A Fashion Advertisement,* p. 91
Reteaching, *Clothing Counseling,* p. 63

When Maria went shopping for clothes with her Aunt Selena, she watched in awe as her aunt put together outfits that made Maria look and feel terrific. Aunt Selena kept saying, "It's you!" to Maria, and she was right.

Selena knew what looked right on Maria's frame—and what would match her personality. The next time Maria went shopping, she bought a dress that looked like one she had admired in a fashion magazine. When she got home, however, Maria realized that the dress really wasn't "her"—as her aunt would say. Maria returned the dress the next day.

Have you ever wondered why you look better in some clothes than others? Why doesn't everyone look great in the same outfit? You will discover the answers to these questions in this chapter as you study the elements of clothing design.

Elements of Design

Deciding what to buy and which articles of clothing to combine with others are some of the most common clothing decisions that you will make. Good choices are not good luck; informed decisions, made with an understanding of the basic elements of design, will always create pleasing effects in clothing. Maria's aunt applied these guidelines to choose styles that would make Maria look her best.

If you study any garment closely, you can pick out the five elements of design: *line, shape, space, texture,* and *color.* **Figure 57.1** on pages 552-553 shows how these elements affect the way clothing makes you appear to yourself and others.

Line

The stripes on a shirt, the creases in a pleated skirt, and the seams on a pair of jeans are examples of line. Line can be used to create an **illusion**—*an image that fools the eye.* The line of a garment directs the eye of the viewer. Therefore, it is possible to de-emphasize certain features by directing the eye toward others.

Making Decisions

How Do You Choose the Right Style?

"I can't go tonight," Scott said to Will, who had just stopped by to see if Scott wanted to go for a ride. "I'm going to tryouts for 'How to Succeed in Business Without Really Trying'."

Will smiled. "That's the one about the guy trying to climb the corporate ladder, right? The lead role has lots of singing. With your voice, you'd be great."

"Thanks. They might think I'm too young though. I've seen some of their productions. I could be one of the youngest ones trying out."

Will looked thoughtfully at Scott. "You might want to rethink what you're wearing then," he said.

"What's wrong with these clothes?" Scott asked, looking down at his black T-shirt and black jeans. His athletic shoes were half unlaced.

"In that outfit, you might get a job as a stagehand," Will said, only half joking.

Scott looked concerned. "What do you mean? They're just going to listen to me sing. That's what counts."

Will pointed out that Scott needed to look the part, too. "You've got lots of other clothes. Why don't you wear the suit you bought for your sister's wedding?" he suggested. "It would make you look older, taller, and more—well, businesslike."

After Will left, Scott glanced at his image in a mirror. "I do want that part," he thought.

What Would You Do?

1. What are Scott's options?
2. If Scott wears his jeans and T-shirt, what impression will he make at the audition?
3. Do you think Scott's apparel would be as important if he were 30 years old instead of 18?
4. What would you wear?

Topics on p. 551:
- **Why Study Design?**
- **Line**

Checking Comprehension

✓ What is the value of understanding design? *Helps you create pleasing effects with clothing.*

✓ Give some examples of lines in clothing. *Stripes on shirt, skirt pleats, seams on jeans.*

✓ How can lines create illusions? *They direct attention to some features and away from others.*

Making Decisions

Have students read "How Do You Choose the Right Style?" and discuss the questions. Ask: Why is "dressing the part" important in real life?

Answers to What Would You Do?

1. Wear what he has on or take Will's advice.
2. He may seem too small and young, not right for part; may seem unfamiliar with play.
3. Answers will vary. Suggest that while it may not be as important, it would still be helpful to dress the part.
4. Answers will vary.

REAL-LIFE APPLICATION

Read this to students: *Tisha and her friend Amy were shopping for dresses. Tisha tried on one that she thought suited her, but Amy said, "Don't get that one. It makes you look kind of fat."* Ask: Do you find Amy's remark hurtful or helpful? Should Amy have expressed her opinion? If so, in those words? What was Amy implying by discouraging Tisha from buying a dress that made her look "fat"?

Topics on pp. 552-553:

- Space, Shape, Texture, and Color

Checking Comprehension

✓ How is line related to space? *Line breaks up space into different shapes.*

✓ Explain three ways to define a color. *Hue—specific color name; value—its lightness or darkness; intensity—its brightness or dullness.*

✓ How does a shade differ from a tint? *Shade is darker value of hue, created by adding black; tint is lighter value, created by adding white.*

CROSS-CURRICULAR ACTIVITY
Math

Figure drawings used to illustrate clothing designs, called croquis (CRO-kees), are based on standard body proportions. Have students draw a four-inch (10-cm) figure on graph paper using these proportions: the head, from the top to the chin, is one-eighth of the height of the figure; the underarm starts one-quarter of the height from the top; the waist is drawn three-eighths of the height from the top; the widest part of the hips falls exactly in the middle; the knee line is one-quarter of the height from the soles of the feet.

Vertical lines lead the eye up and down. Horizontal lines—waistbands, belts, and wide horizontal stripes—lead the eye from side to side. Diagonal lines can give the illusion of height or width, depending on the length and angle of the lines. Curved lines, as used in the curved front of a vest, create a softer effect than vertical or horizontal lines. They may also suggest movement.

Shape

The outline of a garment is its shape. A dress that is loose and full at the top and narrow at the bottom creates an inverted triangular shape. A dress that is fitted on top and fuller on the bottom creates an A-line shape. A shirt that hangs straight from the shoulders creates a boxy shape, or the T shape found in a T-shirt. The overall shape of a garment can distract from, or draw attention to, whatever features the wearer chooses.

Space

Space is the entire area within a garment. Garment lines break up this total space. Pockets, seams, buttons, and trim divide a garment into different shapes. A dress with a simple neckline and no waistband uses space in a different way from a dress with large pockets or a belt.

Texture

Texture is *the way the surface of a fabric looks and feels.* Satin has a smooth and slippery texture. Denim is rough and rugged. Corduroy is ribbed and bulky.

Some textures—such as bulky wools found in sweaters—are usually associated with casual wear. Fabrics that reflect light and have a shimmery texture—such as velvet, satin, and taffeta—are traditionally more dressy and suitable for formal occasions.

Figure 57.1

ELEMENTS OF DESIGN

Line: Vertical lines can make the wearer look taller and thinner. Horizontal lines make the wearer seem shorter and broader.

Texture: Texture can create illusion. Bulky fabrics add width. Silk, rayon, and other smooth, lightweight fabrics add length.

Shape: The tubular shape of this outfit is created with vertical lines, straight-legged pants, and very little width variation overall.

REAL-LIFE APPLICATION

Ask students to suggest uses of space, line, or texture to create the following impressions: authority; casual and comfortable; unconventional and attention-getting.

Focus on Observation Skills

Design elements can be used in garment features as well as in the garment itself. Have students point out examples on their own clothes that show the use of line, shape, space, texture, and color in collars, neck openings, pockets, sleeves, and other features.

Color

Color, the fifth element of clothing design, has many visual effects. Special terms—such as hue, value, shade, tint, and intensity—are used to describe the effects of color.

Hue is *a specific color name.* Green, red, and blue-violet are examples of hue. A color wheel is an arrangement of basic hues. It shows how the colors are related to each other. Although there are hundreds of hues, they are all blends of three primary colors: red, yellow, and blue, as shown in the color sheel on page 554.

When two primary colors are equally mixed, a secondary color results. The secondary colors are orange, green, and purple. Orange is a mixture of red and yellow and appears on the color wheel halfway between those hues. Green is a mixture of blue and yellow, and purple is a mixture of red and blue.

It is possible to create an infinite number of hues on the color wheel simply by mixing the primary colors in different amounts. For example, by adding more blue to a blue-yellow mixture you will obtain a bluish green commonly known as turquoise. By adding more yellow, you will get a bright yellow-green color often called chartreuse (shahr-TROOS).

White, black, and gray are considered neutrals. They are not included on the color wheel, but they are used to create different values of a hue. **Value** is *the lightness or darkness of a color.* Adding black to a color results in a *darker value,* or **shade,** of that color. Burgundy is a shade of red, for example. Adding white to a color results in a *lighter value,* or **tint,** of that color. Pink is an example of a tint of red.

Intensity is *the brightness or dullness of a color.* Hot pink and lemon yellow are bright. They are high in intensity. Navy blue and rust are examples of subdued colors that are low in intensity.

Color: A solid color outfit generally makes a person appear taller. Complementary colors—such as a yellow shirt and dark purple pants—break up the line of an outfit and make a person look shorter.

Space: The space within a garment can be defined in many ways. A jacket worn with a skirt divides the total space, making the wearer appear shorter than she would in a flowing garment. Pockets, belts, and trims further define space.

CHAPTER 57 Design Basics 553

DID YOU KNOW?

Color blindness, the inability to distinguish between red and green, is due to a lack of substances in the eye that are sensitive to red and green in light rays as they enter the eye. More than 4 of every 100 males and 1 of every 200 females experience some degree of color blindness. It is almost always hereditary and congenital. Color blindness may be treated with colored or filtered lenses that sharpen contrasts. Though incurable, the condition usually does not greatly hamper daily life.

Topics on pp. 554-556:
- Color Schemes
- Emphasis and Proportion
- Using Design

Checking Comprehension

✓ What are the effects of warm and cool colors? *Warm—make things seem larger; cool—make them seem smaller.*

✓ In what two ways is proportion a concern when choosing clothes? *Parts of design should relate well to each other and to whole; clothes should be in proportion to person.*

✓ What should be your aim in using design to choose clothing? *To highlight most positive features.*

From School to Work

Have students read "Conceptualization" and discuss the questions. Point out that not everyone is equally adept at conceptualizing. Ask: How might a person strengthen conceptualization skills?

Answers to Assessing ...

1. Answers may include: planning to run errands; packing for a trip; organizing a report. Save time and money by letting you work through possible solutions before committing resources to them.
2. Answers will vary.

Figure 57.2
COLOR SCHEMES

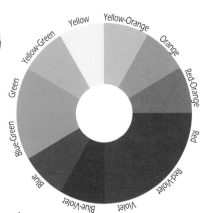

1. A **monochromatic color scheme** uses tints and shades of only one color. If you wore a light blue sweater and dark blue pants, your outfit would be monochromatic.

2. An **analogous** color scheme uses two or more colors that are next to each other on the color wheel. If you topped your blue pants with a blue-green sweater, your color scheme would be analogous.

3. A **complementary color scheme** uses colors that are direct opposites on the color wheel, such as blue and orange. Using different values and intensities can create an interesting effect. With pants that are navy blue (a shade of blue), you may choose a peach (a tint of orange) sweater for a pleasant complementary color combination.

4. A split-complementary color scheme uses one color (such as blue) along with the two colors on each side of its complementary color (in this case, orange). In this color scheme, with blue pants you would use tints or shades of yellow-orange and red-orange.

5. A triadic color scheme uses any three colors that are an equal distance apart on the color wheel. With navy blue pants, you could use a pale yellow sweater and a bright red scarf.

Color Schemes

How do you put colors together to create a pleasing effect? **Figure 57.2** can help you make up combinations, or color schemes. Some of the most common color schemes are shown here.

Visual Effects of Color

Color, like the other elements of design, can be used to create an illusion. Warm colors—such as red, yellow, and orange—give the illusion of increased size. Cool colors—such as blue, green, and purple—give the illusion of decreased size.

To make the best use of your wardrobe, it is a good idea to learn which hues, values, and intensities look best on you. You might experiment with colors you've never worn before. Some people look best in bright, bold

REAL-LIFE APPLICATION

Refer students to Figure 57.2. After discussing and studying the color wheel, challenge them to identify the color schemes of the clothing they and others are wearing. Encourage students to apply this critique to their clothing at home. Does their wardrobe allow for a variety of color schemes? Do these colors complement their best features?

colors, while others find that softer pastels are more attractive. Colors that are right for you will highlight your best features, such as your eyes, hair, or skin tone. If you have trouble deciding about color, ask someone you trust for advice.

Principles of Design

The elements of design can be combined effectively in your own clothing if you use them according to certain guidelines known as the principles of design. These principles focus on proportion, balance, rhythm, and emphasis. Emphasis and proportion are most often associated with clothing. The other principles are closely related to interior housing design and will be covered in Chapter 71.

Here are some ways that the principles of emphasis and proportion are used in clothing design:

- **Emphasis.** Emphasis draws attention to the point of greatest interest. The elements of line, color, and texture might all be used for emphasis. For example, a contrasting collar uses color to draw attention to the wearer's face. A woven belt uses line and texture to emphasize the waistline. Emphasis can help you enhance your best features.

From School to Work

CONCEPTUALIZATION

What You Learn Today . . .

Have you ever done a geometry problem in your head before you worked it out on paper? Do you picture how you want to lay out a project sometimes before you begin working with the materials? If so, you have conceptualized.

Conceptualization allows you to manipulate ideas in your mind before you touch them or move them around with your hands. By working a problem out this way, you can often decide how to proceed and solve it. You use conceptualization skills when you think about how an outfit might look on you or how it will coordinate with other garments you own.

. . . You Can Use Tomorrow

Conceptualization is a skill you are likely to use frequently on the job. Jobs that involve planning for equipment and personnel require people to consider solutions in their minds before committing their plans to paper or trying them out on the job. Clothing designers and interior decorators picture outfits and room arrangements mentally before they draw or create them. Computer specialists work out programming problems in their minds before they sit down to write and run the programs on the computer.

Practicing Your Skills

One way to practice your conceptualization skills is to imagine how different clothing combinations will look. Find a few garments you like in advertisements or catalogs. Think about clothes you already have that might look good with each garment you select. Consider how the elements and principles of design used in the garments will look on you. Then try to conceptualize how each outfit would look.

Assessing Your Skills

1. How do you use conceptualization skills? Can you think of ways they save time and money?
2. Think of a favorite outfit, and conceptualize how it would look in different colors. Which color combinations would look best on you? How might the colors change the way you appear to others?

CHAPTER 57 **Design Basics** 555

Activities

■ **Clothing Critique.** Have students list some questions teens could ask themselves as they evaluate the latest styles, based on the discussion of principles of design on pp. 555-556.

ENRICHMENT

■ **Chameleons.** Have students experiment with swatches to see how colors affect each other. How does a violet swatch, for example, change in appearance when placed on swatches of yellow, red, blue, and various neutral colors? How might this phenomenon affect clothing choices?

FAMILY AND COMMUNITY OUTREACH

Invite someone familiar with color charting, such as a cosmetologist or an art teacher, to help students identify the colors and color schemes that look most attractive on them.

MORE ABOUT Proportion

Based on detailed studies of the human body, Leonardo da Vinci (1452-1519) developed certain standards of proportion. He held that the palm was as wide as four fingers. The distance from the elbow to the tip of the middle finger equaled six palms. From the tip of the thumb of an outstretched hand to the tip of the nose was one yard (about one meter). The arms stretched out to the sides spanned one fathom (two yards or about two meters). Have students measure themselves to find how they compare with da Vinci's standards.

Review

■ **Chapter Review.** Use the contents of the Chapter Review page to help students review concepts, think critically, and apply their knowledge.

■ **Study Guide.** Have students complete the Study Guide for Chapter 57 on p. 189 of the Student Workbook.

■ **Design Studio.** Have groups design an outfit for one of the following people: a slightly-built man of below-average height with fair hair and skin who wants his shoulders to appear broader; a short, rather heavy woman with a dark complexion who wants to appear taller. Have groups explain how they used design elements and principles to suit the features and meet the goals of that person.

Evaluation

■ **Chapter Test.** Use the reproducible chapter test provided in the Teacher's Classroom Resources or create your own test using the *Testmaker Software*.

■ **Alternative Assessment.** Have students compile scrapbooks with examples of design basics. They might include paper folded using different proportions and color swatches showing different color schemes.

■ **For Your Own Good.** Ask students to write a paragraph explaining how knowing the basics of design can save time, money, and frustration when choosing clothes.

Figure 57.3
PRINCIPLES OF DESIGN

Proportion is the way that one part of a design relates in size, shape, or space to another part or the whole design. Uneven proportions are generally more pleasing to the eye.

Emphasis draws attention to the point of greatest interest in a garment. A tie or collar can emphasize the face while an interesting belt can emphasize the waist.

• **Proportion.** The way one part of a design relates in size, shape, or space to another part and to the whole design is called proportion. Proportion in a suit would be the length of the jacket in relation to the length of the pants or skirt. Unequal proportions are generally the most pleasing to the eye. For example, a jacket that divides an outfit exactly in half is usually less appealing to the eye than one that divides an outfit into smaller and larger sections. The elements of line, shape, and space can be used to create effective proportion. Clothing should also be in proportion to a person's size. For example, a wide collar or oversized pockets might seem to overpower a person who has a small frame.

The Impact of Design

The lines, shapes, and spaces in your clothing, combined with texture and color, affect your appearance. When you know how these elements work together, you can choose clothes that are right for you.

How could you use the elements and principles of design to achieve a desired effect for certain situations? Suppose that you are applying for a job working in an office. You might choose a jacket with clean, uncluttered lines in a muted color that says to your prospective employer, "I am organized and calm, and I will get the job done for you." For a social situation, a person who is feeling anxious before a party might stick with a casual, comfortable outfit that gives a calm impression.

You can make almost any impression you want through clothing choices, simply by using the elements and principles of design. Be realistic about your clothing goals. By using the elements and principles of design, you probably will not look like your favorite movie star or media figure. You *will*, however, highlight your most positive features and know that you look your best.

Ask students how to respond when current fashions conflict with your clothing needs, as you have identified using elements and principles of design. What do you do when you have determined that straight lines work best for you, but the trend is for baggy clothing? Must you buy what retailers offer? What are your other options? What resources might be helpful in this situation?

Reviewing the Facts

1. What are the five elements of clothing design?

2. How does line in clothing affect a person's appearance?

3. Define texture. How does texture in clothing affect a person's appearance?

4. Name the primary and secondary colors.

5. Give an example of each of the five common color schemes.

6. How can emphasis affect the way you look?

Thinking Critically

1. Based on your knowledge of the elements and principles of design, how would you describe the look of clothing that is popular right now? Do you feel that this clothing works well for you? Why or why not?

2. Suppose that a friend has asked you to go shopping with him to help him pick out some clothes. He is taller than most people his age. What styles and colors would you suggest that he choose? What should he avoid?

Applying your Knowledge

1. Writing a Description. Assume that you are a fashion journalist who must critique a mail-order clothing catalog or one issue of a fashion magazine. Using the elements and principles of clothing design, write your review. Bring in the catalog or magazine, and share your review with the class.

2. Create a Color Wheel. Using tempera or watercolor paints, create your own color wheel. Begin with the primary colors, then create the secondary colors and tertiary colors until you have completed the wheel. Select and complete two color schemes that you feel enhance your appearance. These graphics will help you as you select clothing colors that work well for you.

Making Connections

1. Language Arts. Make a list of ways in which color is used to describe emotion, such as "seeing red" or "feeling blue." Choose five colors, and describe what effect they would create in clothing choices. Yellow, for example, might give a sunny and upbeat impression.

2. Science. Different types of light affect colors. Examine several colored fabrics under incandescent light, fluorescent light, and natural sunlight. Describe any differences in the value and intensity of each color. What similarities do you observe?

Building Your Portfolio

Applying Your Knowledge of Design Principles to Life Skills
Have you ever heard the expression "Dress for Success"? Choose three different jobs (for example, babysitter, office worker, health club attendant or lifeguard), and imagine that you are going on an interview for each one. How would you dress for each interview? Make your three job choices as varied as possible. Then write a description of what you would wear to each interview. If you prefer, sketch each outfit or clip and mount examples from catalogs. Add the clothing descriptions and sketches to your portfolio.

CHAPTER 57 Design Basics 557

Chapter 58

FOCUS

Chapter Overview

Chapter 58 helps students create a wardrobe that meets their needs. Students learn how to assess the clothing they already own and how to expand their wardrobe creatively and economically.

Motivators

■ **Why Buy?** Ask students how they decide whether to buy a new item of clothing. What needs are they usually trying to meet? How far ahead do they plan? What factors do they consider? Are they usually satisfied with their choices? What kinds of mistakes have they made? Write down students' responses to use for the review activity at the end of the chapter.

Objectives

Discuss the chapter objectives on this page. Remind students that the objectives focus on important chapter concepts.

Vocabulary

Explain that a *wardrobe* originally was a tall cabinet for storing clothes or a small room for one's finery. Eventually the word came to mean both the clothes and the cabinets in which they were kept.

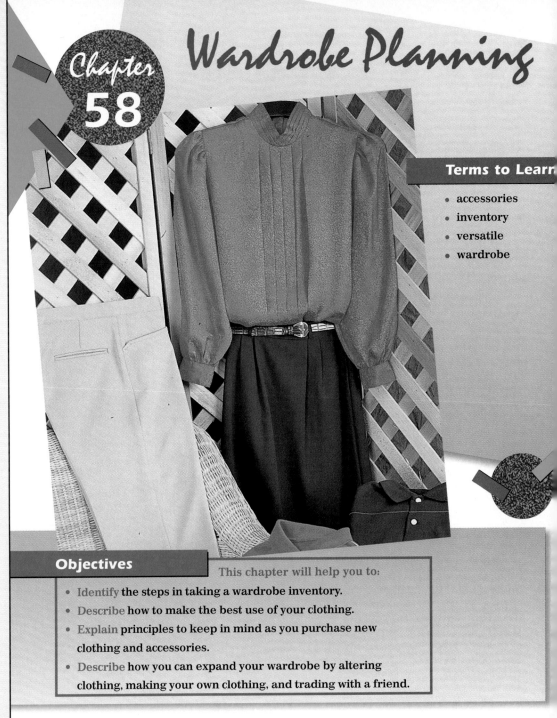

Chapter 58

Wardrobe Planning

Terms to Learn

- accessories
- inventory
- versatile
- wardrobe

Objectives

This chapter will help you to:

- Identify the steps in taking a wardrobe inventory.
- Describe how to make the best use of your clothing.
- Explain principles to keep in mind as you purchase new clothing and accessories.
- Describe how you can expand your wardrobe by altering clothing, making your own clothing, and trading with a friend.

558   UNIT 7   Clothing and Textiles

CHAPTER RESOURCES

Student Workbook
Study Guide, p. 193
Activity, *Wardrobe Inventory*, p. 194

Teacher's Classroom Resources
Lesson Plan, p. 62
Cooperative Learning, *Adaptability*, pp. 63-64

Decision Making, *Wardrobe Decisions*, p. 23
Extension #86, *New Life for Old Clothes*, p. 92
Life Skills, *Buy or Sew?* pp. 92-93
Transparency 54, *Planning Your Wardrobe, Step-by-Step*

Chapter 58 Test, pp. 121-122
Performance Assessment, *Ways to Stretch a Wardrobe*, p. 92
Reteaching, *Wardrobe Planning*, p. 64

Donna was the lucky winner in a drawing at a local clothing store. The prize was a five-minute shopping spree at the store. When the clock started ticking, she began to select items that appealed to her. She didn't have time to think much about colors or items that matched each other or about what she already had. Later, as Donna stood in front of her closet, she asked herself: "How can I possibly not have anything I want to wear?"

Needs and Wants

Donna had plenty of new clothes, but nothing that seemed appealing. Although Donna was under a time pressure to make her clothing decisions, most people are not. You can not only make purchases carefully, but you can also take time to assess the wardrobe you have now.

Planning a **wardrobe**, *the clothes that you own*, requires making many decisions as you think about how you live your life. Do you tend to wear casual clothes, such as jeans and T-shirts, most of the time, or does your lifestyle call for dressy clothes too? What about changing fashions, the changing seasons, and your own changing moods?

Other factors to consider in planning your wardrobe are your resources—both financial and personal. Do you have the money to buy the new items you want? Or are there other ways to add new life to your wardrobe? By looking closely at the clothes you have and carefully determining what you need, you can use your resources wisely.

Taking Inventory

One way to decide what clothes you need is to take an inventory of the clothes you already have. An **inventory** is *a detailed list of everything on hand*. Clothing stores know exactly what they have by taking inventory, and it's a method you can use at home too. Don't forget to include items that are in the wash or at the dry cleaner's. Your inventory can help you analyze your wardrobe and learn which clothes are best suited for you and your lifestyle.

Assessing Clothes You Have

Begin your inventory list by taking stock of what you have. Go through your closet and drawers and divide your clothes into three groups:

- Group A: Clothes in good condition that you like to wear.
- Group B: Clothes that you like, but that need to be repaired.
- Group C: Clothes that you don't wear because you don't like them, they no longer fit, or they are beyond repair.

Make a list of the clothes in each group, noting the type of clothing (sweaters, shirts, pants, for example) as well as the color of

How might your list differ from this one?

GROUP A	GROUP B	GROUP C
Blue sweater	Green plaid shirt—needs buttons	Navy pants—too small
White shirt	Black dress pants—repair seam	Red shirt—worn collar, sleeves too short
Denim shirt		

Focus on Management Skills

Remind students that complex tasks can be broken down into more manageable units. For example, making a clothing inventory can be simplified by beginning with one category of clothing, such as school clothes or summer clothes.

DID YOU KNOW?

An increasing number of public schools are requiring their students to wear uniforms to school. The goal is to avoid clothing as a status symbol and as a way to identify gang membership.

TEACH

Topics on p. 559:
- **Considering Needs and Wants**
- **Taking Inventory**

Checking Comprehension

✓ What factors should you consider when planning your wardrobe? *Lifestyle; changing fashions, seasons, moods; resources.*

✓ Into what three groups should you sort your clothes for an inventory? *Clothes in good shape that you like to wear; clothes you like that need repairs; clothes you don't wear.*

Activities

■ **Defining Terms.** Ask students to explain the difference between wardrobe needs and wardrobe wants. (*Critical Thinking*)

RETEACHING

■ **Closed for Inventory.** Have students begin an inventory of their own wardrobes from memory. After classifying several clothing items into the three categories, they should note why each item was placed in Group B or Group C. Also ask students to record when they usually wear each item.

ENRICHMENT

■ **Common Clothes.** Ask students why it might be difficult to describe a typical teen's wardrobe. Along with gender, what other factors influence which clothes are included in a teen's wardrobe?

Topics on pp. 560-561:
• **Taking Inventory**
• **Buying Clothes**

Checking Comprehension

✓ Why should you have a goal of eliminating Groups B and C in your wardrobe inventory? *Your wardrobe will then contain only clothes you like and can wear.*

✓ What is the advantage of determining characteristics of clothes you like? *You will have a set of standards to apply in making future clothing choices.*

✓ Why would examining the clothes that you don't like in your wardrobe be helpful? *You can avoid making a similar purchase in the future.*

✓ Why is it helpful to categorize your clothing in terms of use? *To identify gaps in your wardrobe.*

FAMILY AND COMMUNITY OUTREACH

Encourage students to identify community groups that accept used clothing. Examples may include charitable organizations, community fund-raisers, recycling centers, consignment shops, and agencies that help people who have lost their belongings in fires or natural disasters. Have students find out specifically how, where, and when these groups collect clothing.

---

each item. Which group has the most items: A, B, or C? Your goal should be to eliminate Groups B and C so that you'll be left with one list—Group A—an active wardrobe that includes clothing that works well for you.

Start by looking at the clothes you listed in Group A—the clothes you like. These are the clothes you reach for all the time. They seem to go with everything. Many of these items are **versatile**—that is, they *can be used in many different ways*. These items may also be more comfortable than other clothing you own. The fabrics in this group may be able to be worn in more than one climate or season. If you think about why you like some clothes, you will have set a standard for judging your entire wardrobe.

Now take a close look at the garments in Group B—the clothes you like but that need to be repaired. Is a favorite shirt at the back of your closet because it needs a button? By removing a stain or mending a tear, you can make these clothes wearable again and move them up to your A list. Simply by stitching a seam on an item you like, you can move it back into your active wardrobe. You will read more about clothing care and repair in Chapter 60.

Finally, look at the list of clothes in Group C—clothes you don't wear. Set aside the clothes that no longer fit and the clothes that are worn out. If you look closely at what remains in Group C—the clothes that you simply don't like—you will learn the most about your purchasing habits. Some of these clothes can probably be described as mistakes. You can't remember why you bought them. Others you may have been talked into buying. Some of these clothes match nothing else you own, and others are fad items that are now out of date.

Eliminating Items

Take a closer look at the items in Group C that you have set aside. Discard the clothing that is completely worn-out. If the fabric is still good, recycle it to make other garments or accessories.

(Attractive fabric can, for example, be made into ponytail holders or fabric book covers.) Offer some clothing to a younger sibling or relative who is the right size. Give other clothing to a shelter or organization that can use them. If there is anything left that you might still want to wear, move these garments into Group A or Group B.

Categorizing by Type

Once you have created an inventory list, you'll want to know if your wardrobe is useful for all your activities. Do you have enough school clothes and dressy clothes for special occasions? What about work clothes for a job or for working around the house and specialty clothes, such as a uniform for an after-school job or a sports activity? If you think about your clothing in terms of use, you'll be able to fill in the gaps in your wardrobe.

How might assessing each article of clothing you own help you determine what you need?

MORE ABOUT Coordinating Clothing

Explain that successfully combining two or more prints, stripes, plaids, or checks requires harmony in color, size, or shape of the pattern. For example, two plaids could be combined if they are the same color and design but differ in pattern size. Without an element of harmony, however, combinations can be too confusing. Encourage students to use catalog pictures, fabric scraps, or hand-drawn patterns to show effective ways to mix and match patterns.

STRATEGIES That Work

Coordinating Your Purchases

Candace's closet has only half the clothes that Melanie's does, yet Candace seems to have more to wear than Melanie. Candace spends less than Melanie, too. Her secret? It's the thought she puts into coordinating her wardrobe. For adding items that will coordinate well with your wardrobe, try these tips:

- Whenever you consider buying something new, think about how it coordinates with what you have. Try not to buy things that can be worn with only one other item in your wardrobe.
- Pay attention to garments that are always in style. A cardigan sweater or a simple vest in a fabric and color that is suited to your personal style can be a smart addition.
- Jackets are good wardrobe additions when they can be worn with several other items. Males can wear one sport jacket with different jeans and slacks. Females can pair a jacket with pants, a skirt, or even a dress.
- Shirts and blouses with a finished bottom edge can be worn out and belted for a more casual look or even worn as lightweight jackets.

- Choose patterned fabrics carefully. Small patterns are easiest to mix. To coordinate prints, plaids, and stripes, use different patterns that contain the same or related colors.
- Cotton T-shirts are versatile since they can be mixed with vests, jeans, pants, and skirts. In colder weather, sweaters can be used in similar ways.

Making the Strategy Work

Think . . .

1. If you could add two pieces of clothing to your wardrobe, what would they be? Explain your choices and describe at least two items you already have that could be worn with each.
2. Describe the last "mistake" you added to your wardrobe. Why did you buy it?
3. Determine which colors and patterns are most common in your wardrobe. What new items might coordinate best with them?

Try...

Write a short list of buying tips that you could use as you expand your wardrobe. It should help you buy coordinated items based on what you already have.

Expanding A Wardrobe

Now that you have looked at your wardrobe to see what you own and have eliminated what you don't want, you can decide what to add. After taking inventory, make a list of the clothing you think you need. How will you obtain these items?

The easiest way to add to your wardrobe is to buy new items. You can buy ready-made clothes from stores and catalogs. Buying ready-made clothes allows you to build your wardrobe with little work.

When you purchase new clothes, however, think about how you can maximize your wardrobe with a minimum of expenditure. Can you purchase items that serve more than one purpose? A football jersey, for example, is a specialty item that can be combined with a pair of jeans for a casual outfit.

CHAPTER 58 Wardrobe Planning 561

MORE ABOUT Making Clothing Decisions

Tell students that complex decisions are sometimes easier to make if they first decide what *not* to do. Have each student develop personal guidelines for how *not* to buy clothing, based on his or her experience, new knowledge, and wardrobe inventory.

Activities

■ **Buying Boo-Boos.** Have students suggest reasons why teens sometimes buy clothing they never wear. Do students think adults make the same mistakes? Why or why not? (*Decision Making*)

RETEACHING

■ **Making Connections.** Have students list as headings on a sheet of paper three items that they wear frequently. Then have them list under each item all the clothes in their wardrobes that they can coordinate with that item. Encourage them to explain why the items coordinate. After students complete their charts, ask them to share any insights they gained about what makes some clothing items more versatile than others.

STRATEGIES THAT WORK

Have students read "Coordinating Your Purchases" and discuss the questions. Ask them to share their own lists of wardrobe buying tips.

Answers to Think . . .

1. Answers will vary. Encourage students to follow the listed tips when making their choices.
2. Answers will vary. Help students analyze why each item was a mistake and how they might avoid similar mistakes in the future.
3. Answers should reflect the strategies given in the text.

Topic on pp. 562-564:
• **Other Ways to Expand a Wardrobe**

Checking Comprehension

✓ What are some ways to add to your wardrobe? *Buy new clothes, combine clothes in different ways, add accessories, alter clothing to update it, make new clothing, trade with friends.*

✓ What should be the main goal in purchasing clothes? *Create a versatile wardrobe.*

✓ How can an accessory change an outfit? *By updating it, making it dressier, brightening neutral colors, focusing attention where you want it.*

✓ Why should you be sure you don't want an item of clothing that you trade with a friend? *Asking for something back can strain a friendship.*

CROSS-CURRICULAR ACTIVITY
Art

Challenge each student to design a male or female paper doll with a wardrobe of clothing. Provide time for students to demonstrate the versatility of their dolls' wardrobes. They might duplicate their dolls and wardrobes on a color copier and donate them to a local day-care center.

How would you combine some of these items to create two different outfits?

Your goal is to have a versatile wardrobe. A shirt that can be worn in three different combinations is more practical than an item that can be worn with only one other item. When you plan purchases, keep this thought in mind. Chapter 59 has more about shopping for clothing.

Combining Clothes

One way to expand your wardrobe without buying new clothes is to combine items to make new outfits. Look again at the clothes in Groups A and B—the clothes you like. Try looking at these clothes with a fresh eye. You may find that you can mix and match your clothes in new ways.

Sometimes different combinations of clothes won't occur to you because you are used to wearing certain pieces together as an outfit. A favorite sweater might go with jeans, a skirt, and a pair of pants. If you have a two-piece outfit, try wearing the

top with different bottoms and the bottom with different tops. You will be surprised at how many different outfits you can create this way.

Think of the variety of ways that clothes can be combined. Combine a dressy item—a suit jacket, for example—with a plain white cotton T-shirt. By creating new combinations, you'll get more use out of your dressy garments and achieve an interesting new look as well.

Using Accessories

Experiment with accessories too. **Accessories** are *scarves, belts, ties, jewelry, hats, and other items that enhance an outfit.* Accessories can completely change the look of an

Accessories expand a wardrobe by giving one outfit varied looks. They also allow you to adapt an outfit for different occasions.

562   UNIT 7   Clothing and Textiles

REAL-LIFE APPLICATION

How could these dilemmas be solved?
• *Emilio's family has moved from a ranch to the city, and Emilio has been chosen for the soccer team at his new school. His wardrobe now has gaps.*
• *Nina has a part-time job in a greenhouse and will also be helping with the fall orientation for new*

students at school. She can't seem to find the clothes she needs in her closet.
• *Jill has a summer job as a camp counselor. Every weekend her family attends religious services and eats out. She has birthday money for clothes, but doesn't know what to buy.*

outfit. Creative use of accessories helps you express your personality. Use accessories to:

- Update a classic or favorite outfit with new fashion colors.
- Make a quick change from a school outfit to a dressier outfit.
- Brighten neutral colors.
- Focus attention wherever you want it.

Check fashion magazines and clothing catalogs for new styles and colors of accessories. Select accessories that are appropriate for a person of your size. If you are short, for example, choose a neck scarf with a delicate pattern rather than a longer scarf with a large print. Also, use accessories to set the tone of your look. A hat or a belt in an unusual or bright color can add an element of fun to your appearance.

Carry your inventory list when you shop for accessories. If you have them, fabric samples from clothing will help you match accessories. In addition, think of new ways to use accessories you already own. Wear a tie or a scarf as a belt, for example, or twist two scarves together for a colorful look.

Altering and Sewing

There are other ways to freshen your wardrobe and use your creativity too—sometimes without purchasing anything. Here are some possibilities:

- **Altering new and old clothing.** By lengthening or shortening clothing you already own, you can make it stylish again. Chapter 67 has more ideas on how to turn old clothing into new. It is also possible to

Managing Your Life

Dressed for Every Occasion

Suppose that you're being picked up after school today to drive to a relative's surprise birthday dinner. Would what you are wearing right now be appropriate at a nice restaurant?

Some days your schedule may require you to dress in different ways. When there's no time to go home to change clothes, thinking ahead can allow you to adapt an outfit quickly and easily. To plan a wardrobe that is adaptable to many different situations, remember several things:

- **Include a few basic styles in solid colors.** These might include a white shirt, black pants, a gray or beige sweater, and a black or brown jacket. Such basics are the building blocks of a flexible wardrobe. A shirt and pants in basic colors can be dressed up with a jacket or dressed down with a casual sweater.
- **Use shoes and accessories to dress up or dress down wardrobe basics.** A sleeveless dress worn to school could be made more suitable for a restaurant meal by adding a jacket, necklace, or dress shoes. The same dress could be worn to a pool party by changing to flat sandals.

- **Select a bag with compartments for carrying accessories with you.** Experiment at home with clothing and accessories to see what simple changes will give the looks you want. A scarf, for instance, can make an outfit look more casual, more tailored, or more dressy, depending on whether it is worn as a belt or around the neck.

Applying the Principles

1. Select three activities you might have during the day (walking to school, playing in a band concert, and working after school, for example). Describe two versatile outfits that could take you through the day. Explain how you would store items not being worn.
2. How could you dress up a plain white shirt or turtleneck for a job interview and then dress it down to meet friends to watch a ball game?

■ **Benefits and Drawbacks.** Discuss the advantages and disadvantages of buying, altering, sewing, and trading clothing. *(Decision Making)*

■ **Last Resort.** Ask students why they should try combining clothes in new ways, using accessories, altering clothes, and trading clothes before making any new purchases. *(Critical Thinking)*

ENRICHMENT

■ **Needs Rating.** Have students list their own clothing needs, considering both their activities and seasonal requirements. Then ask them to mark each need with a plus (+) if their wardrobes meet that need or a minus (-) if clothing additions are required. Have them describe specific clothing items that would meet each minus need. Ask them to star items that would meet more than one need.

Managing Your Life

Have students read "Dressed for Every Occasion" and discuss the questions. What techniques have they used or oberved for adapting an outfit to suit different situations?

Answers to Applying . . .

1. Outfits will vary depending on the activities chosen. Students might suggest placing items in a garment bag or duffel bag and storing them in their school locker.
2. Possible answer: Dress up the shirt by wearing it with dress pants and a blazer. Dress it down by pairing it with jeans and a sweatshirt.

Focus on Creative Thinking Skills

Bring to class an assortment of old hats, belts, vests, and other accessories. (You might acquire these from garage sales and secondhand stores or ask students to bring unwanted items from home.) Also supply materials such as fabric scraps, artifiicial flowers, assorted trims, glue, and fabric paint. Challenge student teams to update the old accessories with their own creative touches. Have each team display their creation and demonstrate how it could be used to enhance an outfit.

Review

■ **Chapter Review.** Use the contents of the Chapter Review page to help students review concepts, think critically, and apply their knowledge.

■ **Study Guide.** Have students complete the Study Guide for Chapter 58 on p. 193 of the Student Workbook.

■ **Making Better Buys.** Review with students their responses to the Motivator activity, Why Buy? (p. 558). What kinds of problems were revealed by their responses? What have they learned about factors to consider in adding to their wardrobes? What kinds of mistakes are they now prepared to avoid?

Evaluation

■ **Chapter Test.** Use the reproducible chapter test provided in the Teacher's Classroom Resources or create your own test using the *Testmaker Software*.

■ **Alternative Assessment.** Have students imagine they have graduated from high school and are starting an entry-level job in the office of an architectural firm. Ask them to plan a wardrobe of eight basic pieces that would enhance their professional image and provide maximum versatility. Students should describe each item, explain their choice, and show how the items can be combined into a variety of outfits.

■ **When Less Is More.** Discuss why one teen with a small wardrobe might seem well dressed, while another with a closet full of clothes.

customize ready-to-wear clothing by making minor changes. Knowing how to alter clothes allows you to make use of hand-me-down clothing from a family member.

- **Sewing new clothing.** You may also choose to make your own clothes. Being able to sew gives you a chance to make a garment that's exactly what you want. Begin by purchasing patterns based on styles that you like. By selecting colors and fabrics that work well for you, you'll be able to customize your wardrobe in an easy way. Chapters 62 through 66 introduce you to basic sewing skills.

Trading with a Friend

Another way to add to your wardrobe is to trade with a friend or family member. You may have something that you don't wear because you don't like the color or it doesn't coordinate with anything else in your wardrobe. Maybe it just isn't comfortable. Someone else may admire something you own that you no longer want. In turn, that person may have something he or she no longer wants but that you like.

When trading clothing, make sure that you no longer want the item you're giving up. Asking for something back is a sure way to strain a relationship.

What Went Wrong—or Right?

Creativity and cooperation can expand a wardrobe—if handled in the right way. What went right and wrong in these situations?

Tara. "Jennie and I started trading clothes a few months ago. Everything was going just fine until she begged me to trade for the dress my grandmother gave me for my birthday. It actually looked better on Jennie than it did on me, so I traded for a jacket she had that I liked. Then last week my grandmother asked me why she hadn't seen me wearing the dress. When I asked Jennie, to trade it back, she didn't want to. You'd think she would have wanted to help me out. She's supposed to be my friend."

Ellis. "I guess I just don't care about clothes the way my mother would like. My friend Judd and I are always wearing each other's clothes. I just leave things at his place sometimes and he wears them. He does the same thing here. My mother's not too happy about it. I left a new shirt at Judd's last week, and now he can't find it. Mom says she's not buying anymore new clothes until I learn to appreciate them."

Dawn. "I always hated my sister's hand-me-down clothes. I just didn't want to wear them. Then I discovered that I had a knack for design. I started giving garments a totally new look. I actually began to hint that I wanted certain clothes that Katrina wasn't quite ready to give up. My family thinks my changed attitude is amazing. They're always telling people what I do. Now I get clothes from my cousin too."

Wynneta. "Since my friend Rachel and I are the same size, it's easy for us to trade clothes. We came up with a system. Every few months, we each make a list of a few clothes that we would like to trade. Then we sit down and bargain for just what's on the list. That way we don't trade away something that we really want to keep just because the other person asks for it."

MORE ABOUT Trading Clothes

Strongly caution students not to trade clothing, in or out of school, without first discussing the transaction with their parents or guardians. They should also check before giving any clothing to community groups. Many parents feel angry when they learn that their teens have traded or given away relatively new pieces of clothing, especially if they had purchased the clothing at the teens' urging.

Chapter 58

Review

Reviewing the Facts

1. What is the benefit of taking a wardrobe inventory?
2. What are the steps in taking a wardrobe inventory?
3. Why should you look carefully at the clothes in your wardrobe that need to be repaired?
4. What is the advantage of mixing and matching different clothing items?
5. How can you make wise choices when purchasing new clothing and choosing accessories?
6. List two advantages of sewing your clothes.

Thinking Critically

1. What do you think is the most versatile item in a typical teen's wardrobe? Why?
2. What accessories could make the clothes you are wearing right now more versatile? What accessories work for both males and females?

Applying Your Knowledge

1. **Deciding What You Need.** Imagine that you have been invited to a family reunion that will take place during the next school vacation. You can take only 10 articles of clothing and two accessories with you. You will need three outfits: one to travel in, a dressy outfit for the reunion itself, and a casual outfit for the day after the reunion. What 12 items will you pack?
2. **Managing Your Budget.** Examine your own wardrobe, and determine which items of clothing you will need to purchase during the next six months. List an appropriate price for each item, using advertisements from the newspaper or mail-order catalogs for reference. What is the total of the estimated costs? Which are the most important items you will need to buy? How could you reduce some of your costs by altering clothing you

already own or trading with a friend? Prepare a report that describes your conclusions.

Making Connections

1. **Language Arts.** Select a novel or a play that you are currently studying in class or reading for fun. Select one character, and describe the character's wardrobe needs throughout the story.
2. **History.** Research the clothing of a period of history that interests you. Find out how people in earlier periods obtained and reused clothing. Are similar methods in use today? Which of the reuse methods might be adapted to expand your own wardrobe? Prepare a short oral report telling what your research revealed.

Building Your Portfolio

Making a Wardrobe Plan
Follow the steps in the chapter for taking a wardrobe inventory. Go through your clothing, placing items in the groups described. For each item, make a brief notation that explains why it is in the category (for example, "never worn because it doesn't fit right") or what you might do with it ("replace all buttons"). At the end of the inventory, write a short paragraph that tells how taking this inventory will help you plan your wardrobe in the next few months. Place a copy of the plan and the summary paragraph in your portfolio.

CHAPTER 58   Wardrobe Planning   565

Chapter Overview

Chapter 59 helps students to make wise decisions about buying clothing. It compares different sources of clothing and recommends times to shop. Students learn how to choose quality clothes that fit them and their budgets.

Motivator

■ **Nothing Up the Sleeve?** Invent a pretext (you want to see if it will fit your teen niece; you're playing "fashion show") for asking a volunteer to try on a jacket. In one sleeve place a dollar bill that the student will find when trying on the garment. Lead a discussion about how buying quality clothing is like finding money—the money you save by making a wise choice.

Objectives

Discuss the chapter objectives on this page. Remind students that the objectives focus on important chapter concepts.

Vocabulary

This chapter begins to introduce students to specific sewing terms: *facing, hem, inseam,* and *seam.* Stress that these terms are relevant for anyone who wears clothes, not only for those who sew them.

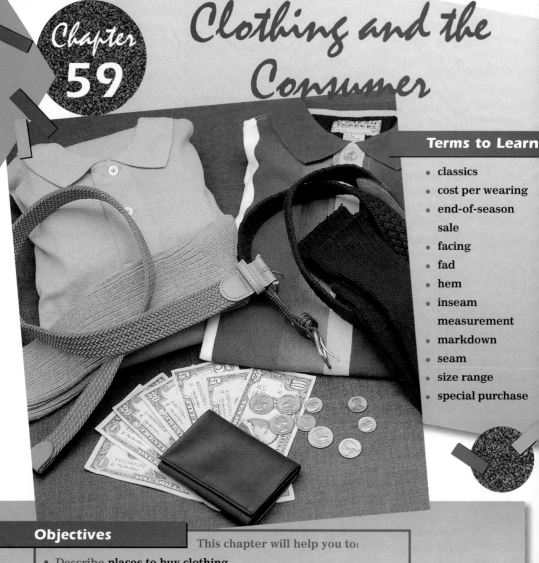

Chapter 59
Clothing and the Consumer

- classics
- cost per wearing
- end-of-season sale
- facing
- fad
- hem
- inseam measurement
- markdown
- seam
- size range
- special purchase

Objectives

This chapter will help you to:

- Describe **places to buy clothing.**
- Describe **sales that are useful for making clothing purchases.**
- Explain **how to determine clothing size.**
- Evaluate **clothes for fit and quality.**
- Evaluate **clothing cost.**

566   UNIT 7   Clothing and Textiles

CHAPTER RESOURCES

Student Workbook
Study Guide, p. 195
Activity, *Garment Checklist,*
  pp. 196-197

Teacher's Classroom Resources
Lesson Plan, p. 63

Cooperative Learning, *A Fashion
  Newsletter,* pp. 65-66
Extension #87, *Shopping for Bargains,*
  p. 93
Life Skills, *Comparison Shopping,*
  p. 94
Transparency 49, *Influences on
  Clothing Choices*

Chapter 59 Test, pp. 123-124
Performance Assessment, *Clothes-
  Shopping Savvy,* pp. 93-94
Reteaching, *Wise Clothing Choices,*
  p. 65

Standing in front of her closet one day, Tanisha sighed in frustration. She wanted some new looks, but all she saw were the same old outfits. She was determined to find a way.

Deep in thought, ideas began to come to her. What if she bought a couple new garments that would go with different clothes? One possibility might be a shirt or turtleneck, or even a skirt, in a neutral color. Tanisha's finances were limited, so she couldn't buy much, but one or two of the right garments could give her new opportunities to mix and match. If she watched the advertisements, she might find a good sale. She could also look at resale shops, where quality clothing sells secondhand for a fraction of its original cost.

Later, before she went shopping, Tanisha put on a sweater that she seldom wore because hardly anything went with it. She also took with her a vest and a skirt belt made of the same fabric as the skirt. These would help her find the matches she wanted. By thinking and planning ahead, Tanisha was confident that she could revive her wardrobe without great expense. What's more, it would be fun.

Where to Shop

Knowing where you might shop for clothes is useful. Like Tanisha, you can look for bargains that still suit your purpose. The store you choose has an effect on the selection, the quality, and the cost. You'll also want to consider convenience and a store's atmosphere when you decide where to shop. Today's shopper has quite a few choices:

- **Department stores.** These stores are divided into sections that offer many clothing styles and sizes for men, women, and children. They also sell accessories. Most offer extra services, such as store credit cards, gift wrapping, and free delivery. Department stores may have slightly higher prices than some other stores, but they almost always have certain items on sale.

- **Factory outlets.** These stores are run by a manufacturer or factory. Prices are generally lower than in department and specialty stores, because fewer customer services (such as individual dressing rooms) are offered. Some factory outlets may not accept credit cards, checks, returns, or exchanges.

When shopping for specific items at factory outlets, it is useful to know the original price of the items you want.

Stores differ in type of merchandise, prices, and services offered. Which stores best meet your needs?

Topic on p. 567:
- **Where to Shop**

Checking Comprehension

✓ Why is your decision where to shop important? *Affects selection, quality, price of clothes; convenience and atmosphere of shopping trip.*

✓ Why do department stores tend to charge higher prices? *Customer pays for large selection and extra services.*

✓ How does a factory outlet differ from a department store? *Run by manufacturer; prices generally lower; fewer services.*

Activities

■ **One Roof.** Ask students to name some advantages and disadvantages offered by shopping malls. *(Critical Thinking)*

RETEACHING

■ **Our Town.** Ask students to categorize local stores according to the descriptions on pp. 567-568. Can they think of stores that combine elements of several types?

Focus on Relationship Skills

Invite students to describe the customer services they most appreciate when shopping for clothes. What help do they want from sales personnel? What are some polite, effective ways to ask for or refuse assistance? How can they make a complaint without offending store staff and still get a problem resolved? Ask students who have worked as sales associates in clothing stores to describe customers' attitudes and actions that help them help customers with their shopping.

Topics on pp. 568–569:
• **More Places to Shop**
• **When to Shop**

Checking Comprehension

✓ Describe the quality of clothing at a factory outlet. *Varies from high to slightly imperfect to noticeably flawed.*

✓ What is meant by selling clothes on consignment? *Owner of the clothing receives part of selling price.*

✓ What is a disadvantage common to resales shops, yard sales, and flea markets? *Items cannot be returned.*

✓ Name an advantage and disadvantage of buying clothes at the start of a season. *Greatest selection but highest prices.*

MULTICULTURAL *Perspectives*

Have students find out where or how United States residents who are of another culture find traditional clothing of their native country. Where might a native of Japan, for instance, buy a kimono? Are there special stores in the United States? Are items imported or homemade? Provide time for students to share what they learn.

Then you'll know if you're getting a bargain. A mix of merchandise is generally found in these stores, from high-quality clothes to clothing labeled "seconds" or "irregulars." These are items with imperfections. If the flaws aren't noticeable, the item may be worth buying. If you have sewing skills, you can repair some imperfections.

• **Specialty stores.** These stores sell only one type of clothing, such as sportswear, shoes, children's apparel, or a particular brand of clothing. A specialty store may carry labels that most department stores do not stock. Prices may be higher than at a department store, but many specialty stores offer extra personal services and handle special orders.

• **Mail-order catalogs.** Many stores and companies send out these magazine-style booklets. You may find it convenient to order items from a catalog, but it may take a few days to several weeks for an order to be delivered. In addition, you must think carefully about what size to order. Catalogs usually explain how to measure for your correct size and give a toll-free number to call if you want the advice of a customer-service representative. Catalog prices vary, and you will usually have to pay shipping charges. It's a good idea to compare catalog prices with those in local stores.

• **Resale shops.** Secondhand shops sell garments that often look new. Some may specialize in antique or designer clothing. A resale shop may be sponsored by a charitable organization, or it may be a consignment shop where the person bringing the clothing to be sold will get a percentage of the selling price. Clothing from resale shops cannot be returned.

• **Garage, yard, and rummage sales.** These are other sources of used clothing. Clothing items at these sales often can be purchased for a few dollars or less. Items cannot be returned, so you must check carefully to make sure they are not stained or worn beyond repair.

• **Flea markets.** Everything from first-quality merchandise to seconds and irregulars can be found at flea markets. Some items labeled "designer" may be poor-quality copies. Prices are usually below retail-store prices, but many flea markets do not allow customers to try on or return items.

• **Art and craft fairs.** If you like original, one-of-a-kind designs, art and craft fairs may be places for you to shop. You may find hand-painted, quilted, patchwork, handwoven, or hand-knitted garments, as well as handcrafted jewelry and accessories. Although you will pay a premium price for these unique designs, a special item may be worth the cost.

You are likely to find a large selection of a particular item in a specialty store.

Focus on Decision-Making Skills

Recognizing options is a necessary step in making decisions. Some people, however, let biases (sometimes unjustified) limit their shopping options. They feel that unless an item is a name brand, bought new from a department store, it is somehow inferior. Ask: Why might people feel this way? What clothes-buying options are they overlooking? How can failing to recognize options make any decision more difficult?

In Touch with TECHNOLOGY

Shopping by Computer

Although some people like to shop, others don't and some have little time. That's when a personal shopper can come in handy.

Finding such a service can be as simple as connecting a computer with an on-line service. Once a user logs on and enters a membership code, a pizza can be ordered or flowers may be sent out of state. For clothes shopping, you can choose from an array of department stores, specialty stores, mail-order catalogs, or even a cable television shopping network.

With more sophisticated shopping software add-ons, you simply enter the type of product you want, your size, and a price limit. The software analyzes the information, recommends a brand, and then lists sources for it.

Shopping with the aid of a computer has a few drawbacks. The first is the cost. Software for conducting a specialized search is expensive. Moreover, the user pays for every minute on-line,

whether or not a purchase is made. Another drawback is that items usually need to be charged to a credit card. Some people are apprehensive about giving credit card information when they use on-line services. Like any catalog shopping, buyers aren't able to first try on the garment.

●●●●●
Thinking Critically About Technology

1. What effects might widespread use of computerized shopping have? Do you think it could eliminate jobs for salespeople?
2. What benefits does shopping in person have over on-line shopping?
3. Would there be times you could save money by using a computer to shop? Give examples.

When to Shop

Just as important as *where* to shop is deciding *when* to shop. Stores generally market clothes for different seasons, so the time of year that you shop affects prices and selection. At the beginning of each season, for example, prices tend to be at their highest, yet a large selection of clothing is available. As the season progresses, selection decreases and prices usually go down.

In addition, many stores hold sales at regular times throughout the year. If you are aware of the sale schedule, you can plan ahead for more expensive purchases, such as a winter coat. These are some sales you can watch for:

- An **end-of-season sale** is *a sale that is held to clear out merchandise to make room for the next season's styles*. Winter coats, sweaters, and ski clothes usually go on sale in February; bathing suits and summer sportswear generally go on sale in July.
- Annual holiday sales, such as those on Labor Day or Washington's Birthday, aim to bring in business on a day when more customers can shop.
- **Markdowns,** or *reduced-price items*, are available year-round. These are clothes that, for some reason, didn't sell as fast as planned. The longer an item remains in the store, the more it is marked down.

CHAPTER 59   Clothing and the Consumer   569

Focus on Consumer Skills

Point out that some stores apply sale prices retroactively: customers can get a partial refund on an item's price if that item goes on sale within a given time period, perhaps 30 days, after they bought it. On the other hand, some stores state that "sale prices do not include previous purchases." Ask students why a store might favor one policy over the other. Which is better for the consumer?

Activities

■ **All Sales Are Final.** Ask students why they think clothing bought at resale shops and yard sales usually cannot be returned. *(Critical Thinking)*

In Touch With TECHNOLOGY

Have students read "Shopping by Computer" and discuss the questions. Ask: How might people react to this shopping option? Do you think they felt similarly about other innovations, such as home shopping networks, when those options first appeared?

Answers to Thinking Critically

1. Answers will vary. Encourage students to consider ripple effects in such fields as building and related industries, career training, and software development. Suggest that people with selling skills will always be needed, though they may not work in stores.
2. Answers may include: attention and advice from sales staff; actually inspecting goods before buying; good buys offered in retail stores but not on-line.
3. Answers may include: could save transportation expenses if stores are distant; buyers could find on-line sales.

Checking Comprehension

✓ What is the difference between junior and misses sizes? *Junior— odd numbered, for trimmer, shorter-waisted figure. Misses—even numbered, for a well-proportioned figure.*

✓ Which size should you choose if you fall between two sizes? Why? *Larger, to allow for growth.*

✓ In what areas should you check a garment for fit? *Neck, waist, legs, hem, hips, sleeves, shoulders, fasteners, chest, back.*

• **Special purchases** are *items that the store has bought for a lower-than-usual price.* The store then passes on the savings to its customers.

Sales are important to anyone buying clothes. However, stores have sales in the hope that customers will also buy regularly priced items during a sale. Whenever you are shopping, remember that no item, no matter how low-priced, is a bargain if you have no use for it.

Sizing Things Up

You've decided where and when to shop, and now you are ready to look at items of clothing. To do this, you need to know your **size range**, or *the category you fit into.* If you shop in the right size range, you'll get a better fit. For teens there are several possible size ranges.

Size Ranges

Clothing stores use many terms to size clothing. Here are some guidelines to help you determine which size range will fit you best:

• **Female sizes.** Most female teens wear either a junior, misses, or petite size. Junior sizes are odd numbered (3, 5, 7, 9, 11, 13, 15) and cut for a trimmer, shorter-waisted figure. Misses sizes are even numbered (4, 6, 8, 10, 12, 14, 16) and designed for a well-proportioned figure. Petites are for women 5 feet 4 inches tall and under. The size range is not just for women with small frames—petite sizes are cut for the person's height, not weight. Teen sections in some department stores carry clothes made for developing teen figures.

• **Male sizes.** Male clothing comes in men's and boys' sizes. Some stores have special teen departments with clothing sized for this age group. Men's and boys' pants are sold by waist and **inseam measurement—** *the length of the pants leg from the bottom to the seam where the two legs meet.*

• **Special sizes.** Some manufacturers make special sizes (such as *women's, slim, husky, tall,* and *short*) to better fit different body shapes.

How to Find the Right Size

Sizes in ready-to-wear clothing are based on the measurements of typical bodies. No one is typical, so finding the right size can be difficult. Some clothing is marked *extra-small, small, medium, large,* or *extra-large.* These categories will fit two or three standard sizes. For example, a *small* usually fits sizes 6 and 8 in women's sizes; a *medium* fits sizes 10 and 12. In men's sizes, which are usually given in waist measurements, an *extra-large* can span a 44- to 46-inch (110- to 115-cm) waist. Because of manufacturers' variations in sizing, it's best to try clothing on before buying.

If you have trouble choosing between two sizes, it's smart to buy the larger size. Because you're probably still growing, you will be able to wear the item longer. Allow for growth by looking for skirts and pants with wide hems. You'll be able to let the hems down later to lengthen the garment if you grow taller.

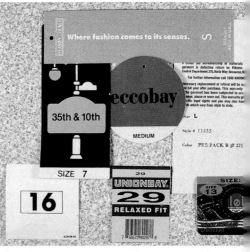

Since sizes are not necessarily the same for all manufacturers, it's always a good idea to try on a garment before buying.

MORE ABOUT Fit

People with physical disabilities have additional concerns about fit. They may need clothing that can accommodate a leg or neck brace. People with multiple sclerosis and other muscular disorders appreciate clothing that is easy to put on and take off, as do those who use wheelchairs. Constant sitting in a wheelchair can broaden the waist; elastic waistbands make garments more comfortable to wear.

Evaluating Your Choice

After finding clothing in your size that you want to buy, how will you know if you're getting good value? Fit, fabric quality, construction details, and cost all determine the value of a garment.

Checking the Fit

To find out if a garment fits properly, you need to try it on. When you are in the dressing room, don't just stand still. Move around, sit down, reach up, bend over. If you cannot do any of these things easily, or if the garment sags, gaps, or pulls anywhere, it doesn't fit properly. **Figure 59.1** illustrates what to keep in mind when checking clothes for fit.

Never compromise on fit. An ill-fitting garment will end up at the back of your closet and never be worn.

Figure 59.1

CHECKING CLOTHES FOR FIT

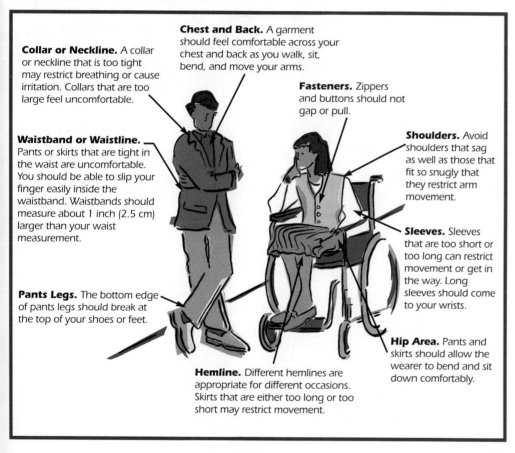

Collar or Neckline. A collar or neckline that is too tight may restrict breathing or cause irritation. Collars that are too large feel uncomfortable.

Waistband or Waistline. Pants or skirts that are tight in the waist are uncomfortable. You should be able to slip your finger easily inside the waistband. Waistbands should measure about 1 inch (2.5 cm) larger than your waist measurement.

Pants Legs. The bottom edge of pants legs should break at the top of your shoes or feet.

Chest and Back. A garment should feel comfortable across your chest and back as you walk, sit, bend, and move your arms.

Fasteners. Zippers and buttons should not gap or pull.

Shoulders. Avoid shoulders that sag as well as those that fit so snugly that they restrict arm movement.

Sleeves. Sleeves that are too short or too long can restrict movement or get in the way. Long sleeves should come to your wrists.

Hip Area. Pants and skirts should allow the wearer to bend and sit down comfortably.

Hemline. Different hemlines are appropriate for different occasions. Skirts that are either too long or too short may restrict movement.

Activities

■ **No Perfect Fit.** Point out that few garments fit perfectly in every way. Refer students to Figure 59.1. Ask: In which of the areas described could you accept a less than exact fit? Which areas could be corrected to fit better? In which areas would you demand an exact fit? *(Decision Making)*

■ **Insider's View.** Have two student volunteers each write a short description of how they think the clothing they are wearing fits. Then have them critique the fit of each other's clothes. How does the wearer's opinion compare to the observer's?

ENRICHMENT

■ **How You've Grown!** Have students research and chart the change in people's average height and weight over the centuries. Discuss the impact of these changes on clothing sizes and fit.

DID YOU KNOW?

A team at Cornell University is developing a new, more detailed sizing system. It uses size clusters based on 15 variables in body proportion, such as a short waist or long legs. Each cluster represents a different combination of these proportions. Nearly everyone fits into one of these clusters.

MORE ABOUT Checking for Fit

As with clothes, shoe and boot sizes vary by manufacturer. Try on both shoes and walk around before making a purchase. You should be able to wiggle your toes, the heel should be snug without rubbing, and the sole should fit the shape of your foot.

- **Clothing Fabric and Construction**
- **Calculating Cost**
- **Avoiding Pitfalls**

Checking Comprehension

✓ What should you look for when checking hem construction? *Smooth edges; stitches invisible from right side; no wrinkles or puckers.*

✓ How do you figure cost per wearing? *Add purchase price to cleaning cost; divide sum by number of wearings.*

✓ What style elements do classic garments often display? *Clean lines, less detail.*

✓ Is there any advantage to buying fad items? *Yes; they can update wardrobe inexpensively.*

CROSS-CURRICULAR ACTIVITY
Art

Ask students to choose an item that typically has a high cost per wearing, such as prom clothes and other formal attire, and design a garment that is suitable for that occasion and others as well. Suggest they look at fabrics, styles, and accessories that would dress up or dress down a garment for different events. Ask students to present their ideas in their choice of media.

Figure 59.2
CHECKING FABRIC AND CONSTRUCTION

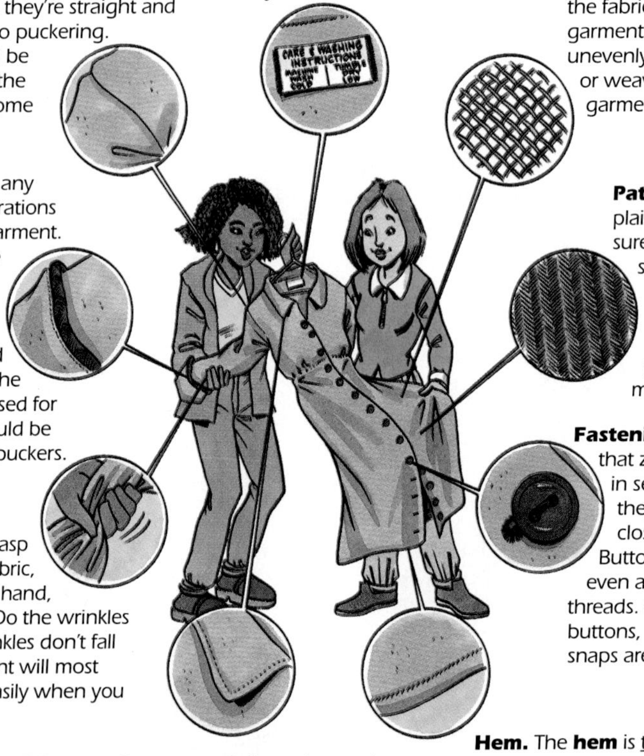

Seams. Check each **seam**, _the line of stitching that joins the pieces of a garment together._ Make sure that they're straight and smooth with no puckering. Stitches should be secure so that the seams won't come apart.

Care information. Look at the garment labels for the fiber content and care information. Clothes that you wear often should be made of easy-to-care-for fabrics.

Wearing qualities. Hold the garment up to the light. If patches of light come through the fabric unevenly, the garment will probably wear unevenly. The tighter the knit or weave, the better the garment will hold its shape.

Trims. Look at any trims, the decorations sewn on the garment. They should be attached with even, secure stitches. Top-stitching thread should match the fabric, unless used for contrast. It should be even, without puckers.

Pattern. If the fabric is a plaid or a print, make sure that the pattern is straight and even all around. The pattern should run in the same direction in all pieces. Plaids should match at the seams.

Fastenings. Make sure that zippers are sewn in securely, and that they slide open and closed smoothly. Buttonholes should be even and without loose threads. Check to see that buttons, hooks, eyes, and snaps are firmly attached.

Wrinkling. Grasp a handful of fabric, crush it in your hand, and release it. Do the wrinkles stay? If the wrinkles don't fall out, the garment will most likely wrinkle easily when you wear it.

Edges and corners. Collar points and lapels should be flat and smooth, without bulk or puckers. Some edges, such as necklines and armholes, have **facings**— _extra pieces of fabric sewn on the outside and turned to the inside to finish an edge._ Facings should lie flat and be anchored to the seams so that they won't show when the garment is worn.

Hem. The **hem** is _the bottom edge of the fabric that is turned up and sewn to the wrong side of the garment._ Hemmed edges should be smooth. Stitches should be invisible from the right side, with no wrinkles or puckers.

REAL-LIFE APPLICATION

Read this to students: *Jana wants a pair of nice jeans for school and work. She found a pair that cost $35; however, she also found a pair of dry-clean-only dress pants for $20.* Ask: Which pair of pants is a better buy? Help students see that Jana should consider other factors, including how much use she would get from each pair; what other items in her wardrobe match each one; how well each pair fits.

Checking the Fabric

The fabric quality of a garment also contributes to its value. Before buying, take a close look at the fabric. As **Figure 59.2** shows, you should look for wrinkling, pattern, wearing qualities, and care information.

Checking the Construction

Next you should consider how the garment is made. **Figure 59.2** reminds you to check the construction in the seams, edges and corners, hems, fastenings, and trimmings.

Calculating the Cost

The value of a garment also depends on the overall cost. When deciding to purchase an item, you should ask:

- Is the price within my budget?
- How long will I wear it?
- How long will it last?
- Can I buy something similar for less?
- Can I buy it for less elsewhere?
- Could I save money by waiting for it to go on sale?
- Could I make the item?

Estimating Cost Per Wearing

The more times you wear a garment, the more value you will get from the money you spend on it. One way of finding that value is to compute the **cost per wearing,** or *the total of the purchase price and the cost of cleaning divided by the number of times you wear a garment.*

Suppose that you bought a sweater and a pair of pants. The sweater had been marked down to $24.99. The pants cost $25.00. In two years, you wear the sweater 15 times, the pants 64 times. Over that same time, you have the sweater dry-cleaned four times, at a total cost of $16.00. The pants are washable, so their cleaning cost is only a small fraction of the cost of doing the family laundry—about a dollar a year.

Making Decisions

To Buy or Not to Buy?

As members of a singing quartet, Toni and Alex needed to make a purchase. The group had decided to wear white shirts with black skirts or pants for their performances. Neither Toni nor Alex owned a white shirt in good condition.

As they walked through the department store, Toni noticed the coats. She had been saving for a new one. "Wait a second, Alex," she said. "The coats are on sale, and this blue coat is just the color I want. I have to try it on."

The fit was perfect, but Toni's heart sank when she calculated that, even with 20 percent off, the coat would take every penny she had saved. The salesperson standing by remarked, "That coat looks perfect on you. Did you know the coat sale ends today?"

Alex frowned as he said, "Toni, what about the shirt? You can't show up without one. The coat might go on sale again later. Maybe you'll even see one you like better."

Toni hesitated, mumbling, "My sister has a white shirt that would work—but she won't let me borrow her clothes."

What Would You Do?

1. What options might Toni have?
2. What are the likely outcomes of each one?
3. What could happen if Toni doesn't find a white shirt?
4. What would you do if you were Toni?

CHAPTER 59   Clothing and the Consumer   573

Review

■ **Chapter Review.** Use the contents of the Chapter Review page to help students review concepts, think critically, and apply their knowledge.

■ **Study Guide.** Have students complete the Study Guide for Chapter 59 on p. 195 of the Student Workbook.

■ **Be Prepared.** Have students make two lists of guidelines, entitled "Before You Shop" and "Before You Buy," that summarize the ideas discussed in this chapter. Ask students to try to list the guidelines in chronological order.

Evaluation

■ **Chapter Test.** Use the reproducible chapter test provided in the Teacher's Classroom Resources or create your own test using the *Testmaker Software.*

■ **Alternative Assessment.** Have student write a humorous poem or monologue in which the speaker reveals poor motives, choices, and practices in buying a garment. Invite students to share their writing and the rest of the class to identify the errors.

■ **In Retrospect.** Have students review their latest clothing purchase in light of what they have learned in this chapter. Did they buy the garment at a type of store and a time that promoted savings? Did they check for fit and quality as described? How might they improve their technique next time?

To figure out the cost per wearing, add the purchase price and the cleaning cost. Then divide by the number of wearings.

Sweater

	$24.99 (purchase price)
+	$16.00 (cleaning cost)
	$40.99
÷	15 (number of wearings)
	$ 2.73 (cost per wearing)

Pants

	$25.00 (purchase price)
+	$ 2.00 (laundering cost)
	$27.00
÷	64 (number of wearings)
	$ 0.42 (cost per wearing)

The cost per wearing of the sweater is $2.73 and of the pants is 42 cents.

| By shopping carefully for clothing, you can choose lasting styles that will be suitable for more than just a few months of wear.

Avoiding Pitfalls

When shopping for clothes, always ask yourself how long each garment will remain in style. Some garment styles are **classics,** or *styles that stay popular for a long time.* Examples of classic styles are blazers, pullover sweaters, pleated skirts, and polo shirts. **Fads** are *styles that are popular for a short time.* Unlaced high-top athletic shoes, oversized sweatshirts, and baseball caps worn backwards are examples of recent fads. Other styles, such as the short skirt, seem to go through fashion cycles, or periods when they are in and out of fashion.

It takes experience to be able to judge which styles will stay popular for a while and which will disappear quickly. You can learn about fashion trends by talking with salespeople and reading fashion magazines. Styles with clean lines that are less detailed usually last longer: a basic skirt, a solid-color blazer, and a classic shirt with a simple collar and cuffs.

Most wardrobes contain both classics and fads. Carefully chosen fad items can add sparkle to a wardrobe; inexpensive belts, scarves, jewelry, hats, and T-shirts allow you to keep up-to-date without spending more than you can afford. While fad items may be appealing at the moment, use the guidelines in this chapter to avoid regrets.

Focus on Critical Thinking Skills

Remind students that chapters in a unit build on one another. Information from previous chapters can be integrated into a current discussion. Ask:

How can knowing basics of clothing design, discussed in Chapter 57, help you be a better consumer of clothing? How can having a wardrobe plan, described in Chapter 58, improve your shopping skills?

Chapter 59 Review

Reviewing the Facts

1. What are two ways to prepare for a shopping trip?
2. List six places to buy clothes. Provide an advantage and a disadvantage for each.
3. Describe how to choose clothing that is the right size.
4. How should you check the fit of a garment?
5. Name five factors to consider when evaluating a garment for quality fabric and construction.
6. How does determining the cost per wearing help you judge the value of a garment?

Thinking Critically

1. How can you benefit from reading advertisements when you're planning wardrobe purchases?
2. When you are shopping for clothes, which two of the following factors are most important to you: price, style, fit, color, fiber content and care, appearance, quality? Explain your answer. Why should you consider all these factors?

Applying Your Knowledge

1. **Analyzing Quality.** Examine a garment that you recently purchased. Check the quality of the fabric and construction. Write an analysis of your purchase that compares it with the garment being examined in Figure 59.2 on page 572. Tell why you did or did not make a good purchase.
2. **Drawing Conclusions.** Where do you buy most of your clothes? Make a list of your five favorite places to shop. List the reasons why you shop in these places. Which factors—convenience, price, quality, service, selection, advertising, or peer pressure—have the greatest influence on you? Why? Compare your list with those of your classmates.

Making Connections

1. **Language Arts.** Have you had any clothing shopping disasters, such as a new shirt that came apart at the seams or a sweater that shrank when washed as directed? Write a letter to the store or manufacturer outlining the problem and stating the action you would like to be taken. You might ask for a full refund, a replacement item, or a store credit. Use your most persuasive writing technique.
2. **Business.** What you've learned in this chapter will help you evaluate accuracy and completeness of information in advertisements. Collect five clothing advertisements from newspapers or catalogs. Compare the information they give. What technique does each one use to persuade customers to buy?

Building Your Portfolio

Preparing to Shop
Decide on three items of clothing that you might buy, such as a washable sweater, a pair of cotton pants, and a leather belt. Look through catalogs and go to several stores, checking prices for each item. Where did you find the items you wanted for the best price? Write an analysis of your findings, and include clippings or sketches of the items you chose. Place the text and pictures in your portfolio.

Chapter Overview

Chapter 60 discusses basic clothing care. It includes tips for preventive maintenance and making minor repairs, and explains different washing and drying techniques. Dry cleaning and caring for borrowed clothing are also covered.

Motivators

■ **A Small Problem.** Borrow or buy cheaply a child's garment. Tell students it's yours. Complain that "it got dirty" the first time you wore it, so you washed it in hot water to make sure it got clean. You don't understand what happened—do they? Begin a discussion about the price of mishandling clothes compared to the time and effort of taking care of them.

■ **I Give Up!** Bring in or recite numerous examples of fabric content descriptions and instructions from clothing care labels. Ask: Does treating clothing right seem confusing? Tell students this chapter gives basic guidelines for clothing care which, with practice, they can master.

Objectives

Discuss the chapter objectives on this page. Remind students that the objectives focus on important chapter concepts.

Vocabulary

The root of the term *detergent* is not *deter* but *deterge,* a seldom used English verb meaning to wash off or cleanse. Adapted from the French, *deterge* is based on a Latin verb with the same meaning.

Chapter 60

Taking Care of Clothing

Terms to Learn

- detergent
- dry-clean
- ironing
- mildew
- pressing
- pretreatment
- snag

Objectives

This chapter will help you to:

- Explain **why you should take care of clothing.**
- Distinguish **between daily, occasional, and seasonal clothing care.**
- Describe **simple clothing repairs.**
- List **points to remember in washing, drying, and pressing clothes.**

CHAPTER RESOURCES

Student Workbook
Study Guide, pp. 198-199
Activity, *Clothesline*, pp. 200-201

Teacher's Classroom Resources
Lesson Plan, p. 64
Decision Making, *Clothing Care*, p. 24

Extension #88, *Money-Saving Cleaning Tips*, p. 94
Life Skills, *Laundry Know-how*, p. 95
Chapter 60 Test, pp. 125-126
Performance Assessment, *Caring for Clothing*, p. 95
Reteaching, *Caring for Clothes*, p. 66

Lynn and her friend Felicia were finding a seat at the movie theater. Soon after they sat down, Felicia gasped. "Lynn, I think there's something sticky on the arm of my seat." Sure enough, there was a wad of gum stuck partly to the seat and partly to the elbow of Felicia's cotton jacket.

"Don't worry," Lynn said. "I think we can save it. Go ask for some ice at the snack bar."

"Ice? Why?" Felicia asked.

"It's something my mother taught me," Lynn said. "Ice will harden the gum. When it gets hard, scrape if off with this." Lynn handed Felicia the nail file she kept in her purse. "When you get home this afternoon, put some prewash spray on it right away and then launder it."

"If I can get the gum off this jacket before it sets," Felicia said, "it will be worth missing the first couple minutes of the movie."

Reasons for Care

As Felicia knows, there are good reasons to act quickly when clothing is stained. It is disappointing and costly to lose a favorite jacket or dress to a stain or a tear.

Just as your clothes reflect who you are, so does the way you care for them. Taking the time to properly repair, clean, and press garments shows that you care about your appearance. Establishing a maintenance routine for your wardrobe has other benefits too:

- **Your clothing will last longer.** Protecting the clothing you wear can extend its life. Putting clothes on and taking them off carefully, for example, can prevent accidental tears. By opening zippers completely, they are less likely to break.

- **Your clothing will look better.** Garments look crisp the first time you wear them. Proper care can keep them looking that way. Regular washings make a sweater look neat; if it is neglected, the elbows and shoulders will stretch and sag.

- **You will save money.** Taking care of your wardrobe saves money. As you get older, you will have many financial goals to meet. Spending less on clothing can help you reach your goals sooner.

- **You'll have a selection of clothes to wear.** Most people have taken a garment out of their closet at some time only to find that it is missing a button or has an obvious rip. Repairing and maintaining your clothes properly ensures that whatever you have will be available to wear.

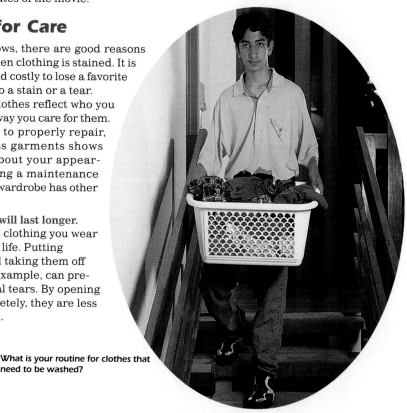

■ What is your routine for clothes that need to be washed?

CHAPTER 60   Taking Care of Clothing   577

TEACH

Topic on p. 577:
- **Why Care for Clothing?**

Checking Comprehension

✓ Why should you take care of your clothing? *It lasts longer, looks better; you save money, have greater selection.*

✓ What does caring for your clothes say about you? *You care about appearance.*

Activities

■ **Clothes Talk.** Ask students if they think others judge them by the condition of their clothing. If so, is that fair? *(Relationship)*

■ **Visible Signs.** Discuss ways that students can tell whether others do or do not take care of their clothing. *(Observation)*

• • •   **REAL-LIFE APPLICATION**

Read this to students: *After hearing her mother again tell her to pick her clothes off the bedroom floor and hang them up, Kelli shot back, "Why should you care? I don't care if my clothes are dirty or wrinkled when I want them. I just find some-thing else to wear."* Ask: What might be some consequences of Kelli's attitude? Why should her mother care? Point out that unless Kelli buys and washes her own clothes, her actions cost others in money and time.

Topics on pp. 578-579:

- **Daily, Occasional, and Seasonal Care**

Checking Comprehension

✔ How does personal hygiene relate to clothing care? *Clothes stay cleaner when you do.*

✔ How should clothes in drawers be stored? *Light on top of heavy; fluffy wools in tissue paper.*

✔ Why should clothes be clean and dry when stored for long periods? *Perspiration, skin oils weaken fabric; food stains attract insects; wet clothes can mildew.*

Managing Your Life

Have students read "Buying Easy-Care Clothes" and discuss the questions. Ask: Besides the care label, where can you find information about caring for fabrics? Suggest salespersons, clothing magazines, family and consumer sciences teachers and texts.

Answers to Applying . . .

1. Twelve times (6 cleanings at $5 each).
2. Answers will vary.

Managing Your Life

Buying Easy-Care Clothes

Comparison shopping is a skill Alana learned from her mother. After buying a silk blouse for half its original price, Alana couldn't wait to show her mother the great bargain. After its markdown, the silk top was the same price as a polyester blouse Alana had also tried on.

Reluctantly, Alana's mother pointed out that the blouse would have to be dry-cleaned, according to the care label. Alana knew how expensive that can be. Realizing that she could launder the polyester blouse at home for pennies, Alana thought about exchanging the silk blouse.

When buying new clothes, consider what they'll cost—in money and in time—to keep them looking nice. If special care is required, you'll probably wear them less often, making them a poor investment. For easy care, look for:

- **Washable fabrics.** Check the care label and choose clothes that can be laundered in the washing machine. Dry cleaning is expensive, and hand washing takes extra time.
- **Smooth, tightly knit fabrics.** Garments made of such fabrics are more durable than those constructed with loose knits that may pull or snag easily and need to be repaired frequently.
- **Permanent-press fabrics.** Unless you truly like to iron, clothes that come out of the dryer too wrinkled to wear may stay that way for weeks. Look for fibers and blends, such as acrylic, polyester, nylon, and cotton/polyester.
- **Hidden costs.** Some garments require special treatment when they're cleaned, adding even more to the cost of their care. Most dry cleaners charge extra to press pleats, for example, and leather is very expensive to have cleaned. Check trims and read content labels carefully.

If you value the coolness of cotton or the look of wool enough, you may not mind the extra care they require. You should be able to find a balance in your wardrobe that's right for you.

Applying the Principles

1. Dry cleaning Alana's new silk blouse costs $5; she estimates she would have it cleaned every other wearing. How many times could she wear the blouse before she's paid the purchase price of $30 in dry-cleaning bills?
2. Consider the time you would spend ironing if you bought a cotton shirt that needed to be ironed instead of a cotton/polyester blend that did not. Would it be worth it?

General Care

If you devote just a few minutes each day to caring for your clothing, your wardrobe will show the difference. There are three basic types of clothing care. Some tasks must be carried out every day, others only occasionally, and still others only seasonally.

Daily Care

The first step in responsible clothing care is the development of daily routines. Bathing daily and using deodorant helps keep garments fresh. Perform the following tasks every day for good clothing care:

- **Air clothing out.** If you will be wearing a garment again before you have to clean it, air it out before putting it away. Spread it out on a bed or drape it over a chair.
- **Inspect clothing.** Brush off lint. Check each garment to see if it needs repairs. A small rip or a loose button takes only a few minutes to fix. If you ignore it, however, the repair may become a major job.
- **Set aside dirty clothes.** Keep a laundry basket or bag for clothing that can be machine washed. Set aside any clothing that has to be dry-cleaned and hand-washed. Always take care of stains immediately.

578   UNIT 7 Clothing and Textiles

MORE ABOUT Daily Care

Clothing can be aired out quickly by using an electric fan, a hair dryer on low heat, or the tumble cycle on a clothes dryer with the heat turned off. Lint removers, brushed or rolled with the fabric's grain or nap, remove lint and hair. Using padded hangers prevents unsightly ridges in the shoulders left by wire hangers. You can make your own by wrapping wire hangers in yarn or fabric.

Buttoning a jacket or blouse on a hanger prevents the front from sagging and wrinkling.

- **Put away aired clothes.** Once clothes have aired, hang or fold them and put them away. Don't crowd the closet so much that clothing becomes wrinkled. In drawers, stack the lighter garments on top of heavy ones to prevent crushing. Wrap fluffy wools in tissue paper so they won't shed on other clothes.

Occasional Care

Set aside some time each week for occasional care. This is the time to make repairs as well as to hand wash garments that can't be machine washed.

It's a good idea to keep all clothes that need mending or ironing in one place, such as a basket or a drawer. Then, when you have some time to spare, you can make repairs or iron these items.

Seasonal Care

When seasons change, people often put some clothes into storage and take others out. Winter coats, for example, are usually worn only for a few months. When clothes are not worn for a long period of time, they can become damaged if they are not stored properly. Insects can damage fabrics; strong light can discolor them. Such hazards can be avoided by taking the following precautions:

- **Clean clothes before storing them.** Clothing to be stored should be clean, dry, and stain free. Perspiration and skin oils can weaken fabric. Food stains may attract insects, such as silverfish, which damage fibers.
- **Prevent moth damage.** Treat woolens and other natural fibers with moth repellents—or store them in a cedar box or closet—to prevent moth larvae from eating holes in them.
- **Prevent mildew. Mildew** is *a fungus that grows on damp fabric, causing stains that appear as small black spots.* To prevent mildew, make sure that clothes are completely dry before putting them away. Always store clothes in a dry place.
- **Use clothing bags or boxes.** These protect your garments from insects, airborne soil, light, and air that is either excessively humid or too dry.

Storing seasonal clothing properly helps keep garments looking new longer. How do you care for seasonal clothes?

Topics on pp. 580-581:
* **Storing Clothes**
* **Stain Removal Tips**

Checking Comprehension

✔ How can you remove wax from items before washing? *Scrape with dull knife; place fabric between paper towels, melt wax with iron.*

✔ What unusual pretreatment helps remove ink stains? *Sponge with rubbing alcohol; spray with hair spray that has alcohol.*

✔ When should you use bleach on clothing? *For blood stains; when stain remains after washing.*

FAMILY AND COMMUNITY OUTREACH

Challenge students to design systems for storing their family's clothing at home. Suggest they begin by identifying garments, their storage requirements, and storage space available. They might then incorporate ideas from "Storing Your Clothes," as well as their own, into a plan for storing clothes in an organized way.

STRATEGIES That Work

Storing Your Clothes

When you take off your clothes, where do they wind up? On the bed or the floor? Stuffed in a dresser drawer that wasn't meant to hold another thing? For some people, even getting clothes onto a hanger doesn't necessarily mean the garment will stay attached.

Such hasty actions may seem acceptable at the time, but there are drawbacks. The next time you want to wear a garment, it may not be in very good shape for wearing, and if you can't find it, that's even worse. Moreover, garments that aren't stored carefully may not hold up as well over time.

You can prevent the frustration that comes with poor storage of clothing. Following these tips can keep your garments always looking good and ready to wear when you want them:

* Take an extra minute to put garments where they belong when you remove them. This prevents the accumulation of a stack that takes a long time to put away.
* As recommended in Chapter 58, free up storage space by eliminating garments you no longer wear from closets and drawers.
* Check to see if you're hanging garments that could be folded and placed in a drawer, trunk, or box. Or are you putting things in drawers when they belong on hangers?
* Hang similar items together in the closet for ease in finding them.
* Remove extra hangers from the closet in order to maximize hanging space.
* Install hooks and over-the-door hangers as extra hanging space if you need it. You can even purchase rods that hang like a hanger from the

permanent rod. Such devices help relieve overcrowding in closets.
* For extra drawer space, consider obtaining an under-the-bed, cardboard storage box for folded items.
* Store collections of small items, such as mittens or socks, in old pillowcases with their contents marked in large letters. Attach a loop and hang on a convenient hook.
* To prevent creases in pants and skirts, hang them from the waistband on special hangers with clamps.
* Use padded or heavy wooden hangers for special clothing items. This helps separate them from other garments in the closet, keeping them from getting crushed. It also helps maintain the shape of the garment's shoulders. Coats, suits, and jackets, in particular, need the support that comes with shaped wooden hangers.
* When storing a garment for a while, help keep the shape of shoulders and sleeves by stuffing with paper.

Making the Strategy Work

Think . . .

1. Maya has to touch up nearly every item in her closet with the iron before wearing. What might be the reason for this?
2. Jerry has numerous cotton T-shirts hanging in his closet. Why might this be a problem?
3. On a scale of one to ten, with ten "excellent," rate your own handling of clothing storage. What improvements, if any, could you make?

 Try...

Visit a department or discount store to get ideas about organizing a closet. Then make a plan for implementing one inexpensive idea in the closet you use. If possible, try out your idea.

MORE ABOUT Removing Stains

Catsup and other tomato-based stains are treated the same as chocolate stains. Coffee or tea stains are soaked in cold water, then in a presoak, and finally in bleach if the fabric allows. Bleach or ammonia will remove mildew. (Do not combine bleach with ammonia. The combination can produce hazardous gases.) Rub rust spots with lemon juice and salt, then place the garment in the sun for a while before washing.

Figure 60.1

 ## Tips for Stain Removal

When pretreating stains, place garments stain side down on paper towels. Sponge the stain from the back side, replacing the paper towels frequently. Take care not to rub too hard, especially on delicate fabrics.

Stain	Cleaning Method
Blood	Soak in cold water and detergent or enzyme presoak. Wash using bleach that is safe for fabric.
Candle wax	Scrape off the wax on the surface with a dull knife. Place fabric between layers of paper towels with the wax side down, and press with an iron to melt the wax into the towels. Replace the towels frequently to absorb additional wax. Apply a prewash stain remover. Blot and let dry. Launder.
Chewing gum	Harden by rubbing with an ice cube. Then scrape off with a dull knife. Apply prewash stain remover, rinse, and launder.
Chocolate	Soak in cold water, or use a prewash stain remover. Rub detergent onto the stain and wash. If the stain remains, wash using bleach that is safe for fabric.
Cosmetics	Pretreat with a prewash stain remover. Rub detergent or bar soap on the stain and wash.
Grease	Sponge with cleaning fluid, or use a prewash stain remover. (Rinse out cleaning fluid before washing.) Rub detergent into the stain and wash. If the stain remains, wash using bleach that is safe for fabric.
Ink	Sponge with rubbing alcohol, or spray with hair spray containing alcohol. Rinse. Rub any remaining stain with detergent and wash.
Nail polish	Never use polish remover on acetate fabrics. Sponge with amyl acetate and wash. If necessary, sponge with alcohol mixed with a few drops of ammonia (or nail polish remover if it is safe). Rinse and launder.

Simple Repairs

No matter how careful you are, you will need to make some clothing repairs. Buttons pop off and sweaters get snags. Here are some examples of simple repairs you can make:

- **Repairing snags.** A **snag** is *a loop of yarn that gets pulled out of a knit.* You should grasp the snag from the back with a crochet hook and pull it through to the underside of the garment.

 ### DID YOU KNOW?

In many regions, conservationists recommend using soap rather than detergent. Soap is natural and biodegradable, while detergents often contain high concentrations of phosphate salts, which can upset the chemical balance in water and soil.

DID YOU KNOW?

The first commercial laundry in the United States was probably Contra Costa Laundry, opened in 1851 to serve prospectors in the California Gold Rush. Entrepreneurs also set up hand laundries on creek banks. Some forty-niners, sent dirty laundry to Hawaii, waiting up to six months for its return.

Activities

■ **Better Late Than Never?** Point out that many people treat stains just before the garments go into the washer. Discuss the consequences of this approach. (*Problem Solving*)

 **CROSS-CURRICULAR ACTIVITY**
SCIENCE

Have groups set up experiments comparing commercial spot removers, trying several brands and forms—spray, liquid, and stick—on the same stains to test their relative effectiveness. Have groups write and test a hypothesis and chart their results.

STRATEGIES THAT WORK

Have students read "Storing Your Clothes" and discuss the questions. Tell them that some people who take good routine care of other possessions, such as jewelry and books, take a "fend-for-themselves" approach to their clothing. Ask why people might have this attitude. How can they be reminded that storage is part of clothing care?

Answers to Think . . .

1. Could be overcrowding, storing in drawer instead of hanging, using wrong type of hangers.
2. Could overcrowd closet; T-shirts may be stored folded.
3. Answers will vary.

581

Topics on pp. 582-583:
- **Making Simple Repairs**
- **Preparing to Wash**

Checking Comprehension

✓ What clothing repairs can most teens learn? *Fixing snags; mending seams; patching holes; replacing fasteners.*

✓ What is the quickest, most accurate way to learn how to wash a garment? *Read care label.*

✓ What is the general rule for sorting clothes? *Wash like items together.*

FAMILY AND COMMUNITY OUTREACH

Encourage students who are proficient in mending to contact a charitable group that collects used clothing, such as the Kidney Foundation, and offer to do simple repairs on collected items so more may be resold. They might also offer their services to elderly neighbors or nursing homes.

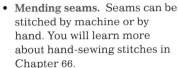

Why should you look at care labels before deciding to buy a garment?

- **Mending seams.** Seams can be stitched by machine or by hand. You will learn more about hand-sewing stitches in Chapter 66.
- **Patching holes.** For jeans and casual clothes, use iron-on patches. For dressier clothes, cut a piece of fabric from a hem or seam allowance and place it behind the hole. Turn torn edges under, and stitch around the opening with tiny, almost invisible, hand-sewing stitches.
- **Replacing fasteners.** Most common fasteners—such as buttons, hooks, and eyes—are available from fabric stores. You may need to repair the fabric under the fastener as well.

For repairs that are beyond your skill level, check with a dry cleaner. Many keep tailors on staff to provide mending and altering services to customers. Ask the price of the repair first. Then determine whether the garment is worth the expense of repair.

Cleaning Clothes

All clothes need to be cleaned, but different garments require different methods. A pair of jeans with an ink stain requires different handling from a shirt that is slightly soiled.

To choose the correct method for washing a piece of clothing, check the care label inside the garment. Laws require clothing manufacturers to provide permanent labels that tell what fibers the clothing is made of and how to care for the fabric.

The care label tells you what procedure to follow, such as "Machine Wash," "Hand Wash," or "Dry-clean Only." It also indicates what water temperature to use and whether the

clothing can be machine dried. The label may even state whether the garment needs ironing. Some labels include cautions. For example, a label may warn "Do not bleach" or "Wash separately with like colors."

Removing Stains

Stains are areas where dirt is concentrated. If they are not treated properly, they can become permanent. **Figure 60.1** on page 581 lists some common stain-removal procedures. Most of these methods require **pretreatment,** *applying stain-removal techniques before laundering a garment.*

Fresh stains can be pretreated by using a commercial prewash stain remover. These come in the form of sprays, liquids, and rubbing sticks. Chemicals in these products surround soil and lift it away from fabric. Regular cleaning methods can then more easily wash the stain away. Before using any pretreatment product, read the label carefully.

The sooner you treat a spot, the more likely you are to remove it. A quick rinse with cold water can help remove stains from washable fabrics. For nonwashables, the garment should be taken for dry cleaning as soon as possible.

MORE ABOUT Sorting Clothes

Sorting by color is important because different fabrics have different levels of wash fastness, the resistance of the dye to bleeding into wash water. Dyes that are chemically bonded to the fiber or that do not dissolve in water have the highest wash fastness.

REAL-LIFE APPLICATION

Declare a mending day. Discuss the kinds of garment repairs students are capable of, then have each student bring in one or two garments to mend, plus any needed materials. Encourage students to exchange advice before repairing their own or classmates' clothes.

Sorting Clothes

Sorting clothes before you wash them helps prevent them from damage in the wash. The basic rule to remember is to wash items that are alike together. Clothing of different colors or combined fabrics may have different washing requirements.

First, separate clothing according to care labels. Put together all clothing that must be washed at the same temperature, for example, or that must be hand washed. Keep in mind the weight of each fabric. Although a delicate shirt and a pair of jeans are both cotton—and perhaps even the same color—they should not be washed together.

Next, sort laundry by size and by the degree to which it is soiled. For example, wash sheets and other large items together, since they may get tangled with other clothes. Group heavily soiled clothes together and lightly soiled clothes with other lightly soiled items. Then separate fabrics that leave lint—such as towels and corduroys—from other garments.

Finally, sort by color. Dyes from bright colors can stain lighter clothes—even after many washings. Just because a red T-shirt has the same care instructions as white slacks does not mean they should be washed together. Can you imagine what would happen if you did?

After sorting laundry into washer loads, the work is easier. You may have quite a few piles: sheets, light colors, dark colors, heavily soiled clothing, and delicate fabrics, such as laces and sheers.

Washing Clothes

Washing cleans clothes by pushing water between yarns and fibers. The water dissolves some soils and lifts others away from the fabric. This is true for both machine and hand washing.

Cleaning Agents

Cleaning agents are usually added to help remove soil. Two products, soap and detergent, perform the same function but are chemically different. Soap is made from fat and alkali, a type of salt that can be dissolved

Read product labels carefully when choosing laundry products.

CHAPTER 60   Taking Care of Clothing   583

Checking Comprehension

✓ Why might you use an enzyme presoak? *To remove protein stains.*

✓ When in doubt, should you wash in hotter or colder water? Why? *Colder; cannot harm clothes, while hotter temperatures might; also saves energy.*

✓ Give tips for caring for borrowed clothing. *Inspect before and after wearing; avoid stains; wash after wearing; mend if needed; return promptly.*

USING VISUALS

Refer students to Figure 60.2 on p. 584 and ask questions such as: What does the load size selector control? *Amount of water machine uses.* Why are two temperatures given for each water temperature setting? *For wash and rinse cycles.* What do the numbers on the cycle selector indicate? *Length in minutes of each cycle.*

in water. **Detergent,** the most common choice of consumers today, is *a chemical cleaner that removes soil and holds it in suspension in water.* Some brands now have special features, such as built-in fabric softener, added bleach, and protection from fading colors.

The following are additional laundry products that can be used for special purposes:

- Enzyme presoak solutions help remove such protein stains as egg, meat juices, and blood. The clothes sit in the presoak solution before the cleaning cycle begins.
- Disinfectants kill bacteria. They are helpful if hot water is unavailable or if there is an illness in the family.
- Water softeners soften hard water, which has mineral deposits that prevent thorough cleaning.
- Bleach removes tough stains and acts as a disinfectant. Chlorine bleach should be used only on sturdy, white, 100 percent cotton fabric; it can take the color out of others. Nonchlorine bleach is available for darker fabrics.

- Fabric softeners decrease static electricity and make fabrics feel softer. Many also add fragrance to clothing. Add liquid softener to the washer; add softener sheets to the dryer.

Always read the directions on any product label before adding it to your laundry. Many carry cautions about when and how they should be used.

Washing Machines

Washing machines are fairly simple to use once you are familiar with the settings. **Figure 60.2** shows the options typically found on machines. Machines in laundromats usually have instructions on the inside of the cover. Whether you are using a machine in your home or in a laundromat, follow these steps:

1. **Select water temperature.** Follow directions on care labels. Using colder settings than suggested cannot harm your wash, but using hotter ones can. Colder settings save energy.

Figure 60.2

WASHING MACHINE CONTROL PANEL

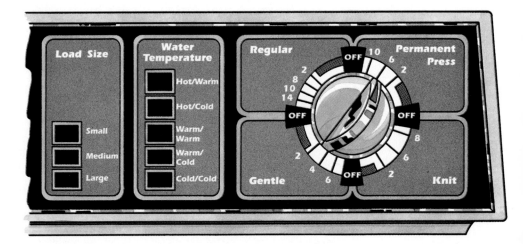

MORE ABOUT Laundry Products

Measure laundry soap and detergent carefully. Using more than is needed is not only wasteful, but may damage the machine. A buildup of soap or detergent in clothes can leave them dingy and harmful to the skin. Too much bleach or cleaning fluid can weaken fibers, discolor items, and damage the eyes and skin of launderer and wearer alike. Laws require manufacturers to print warning labels on product packaging; heed them.

2. **Add clothing and cleaning agents.** Read the directions for loading the machine and for adding cleaning agents. Some machines require adding the detergent or soap first; others suggest adding the clothing first. In top-loading machines, be sure to distribute clothes evenly, or the machine will not wash properly. Never fill a machine more than three-quarters full with clothing. If you do, water will not circulate well enough for cleaning.

3. **Adjust the water level.** Choose small, medium, or large load size. If you are not washing a full load, reduce the setting to save water.

4. **Select cycle.** Long cycles (12 minutes or longer) are for dirtier clothes; short ones (2 to 6 minutes) are for delicate fabrics or less-soiled loads.

5. **Turn on the wash cycle.** Refer to the owner's guide or follow the directions on the machine.

Hand Washing

Some clothes need very delicate care and should be washed by hand. To hand wash a garment, first soak it in a sink or tub of water and detergent. Garments with colors that may bleed should be soaked in cool or cold water. Heavily soiled garments may be soaked for half an hour or longer, as long as the colors do not run.

After soaking, drain the water and add fresh water. Then gently squeeze the sudsy water out of the garment. Be sure to rinse the garment until no soap or detergent remains.

Drying Clothes

Recheck care labels as you take clothing out of the washer, if necessary. Clothes may be machine dried, line dried, or dried flat. For machine drying, first choose the proper fabric and temperature setting for the load you are drying. (Check the instructions for the machine.) Shake out each laundered garment before putting it in the dryer. Remove clothes from the dryer as soon as they are dry. Fold them or hang them up immediately to pre-vent wrinkling. Some clothes, such as jeans, will be less wrinkled if you take them out when they are slightly damp. They can be hung up to air-dry in your laundry area or bathroom or outside on a clothesline.

Line drying can give clothes a fresh smell. Place clothespins so they don't leave marks that can be seen when the garment is worn. For example, shirts and dresses can be hung upside down, with pins placed along the hems. Placed at the shoulders, the clothespins leave an indentation. Some clothes can be hung on hangers.

Sweaters and delicate garments are often dried flat. The best way to do this is with a mesh drying rack. When one is not available, place a thick towel over a waterproof surface, such as a countertop or a kitchen table. Lay the garment down and gently reshape it. Every few hours or so, turn it over and replace the towel with a dry one.

Pressing or Ironing Clothes

Some fabrics require pressing or ironing. Both are done with an iron. **Pressing** is *lifting the iron and setting it back down on the fabric*. Knits and wool are pressed so that they do not stretch. **Ironing** involves *sliding the iron over the fabric to smooth out wrinkles*.

The proper heat setting depends on the garment fabric. If it's a fabric blend, such as polyester and cotton, choose the lowest suggested setting. An iron that is too hot can damage clothes. Iron collars, cuffs, and sleeves before large flat surfaces, such as shirt backs and skirts.

Dry Cleaning

Dry cleaning is done with equipment and materials you do not have at home. Clothing that is **dry-cleaned** is *cleaned with special chemicals rather than soaps or detergents and water*. Clothing is then placed on a form in the shape of a body, and steam is blown through the clothing to remove wrinkles. Special touches, such as trouser creases, are added with steam-pressing machines or handheld steam irons.

Activities

■ **Do You Care?** Remind students of the statement on p. 577 that "the way you care for (clothes)" shows whether "you care about your appearance." Ask: What does the way you care for borrowed clothes say about how you care about the owner? *(Relationship)*

RETEACHING

■ **This Is the Way We Wash the Clothes . . .** Have students give skits demonstrating proper machine-washing, hand-washing, and drying techniques.

ENRICHMENT

■ **Wash Out.** Encourage students to compare the effectiveness of hand washing, machine washing, and (if feasible) coin-operated dry cleaning for different types of fabrics. Have them soil a large piece of each fabric, cut it into thirds, and clean each piece using a different method. What conclusions do students draw from the results?

DID YOU KNOW?

Although dry cleaning is not really dry, it does not use water. Clothes are put into a spin washer that usually contains solvents instead of soap and water. Afterward a special dryer removes most of the solvents, which can be reused.

REAL-LIFE APPLICATION

Have students make sure they know how to use the washers and dryers in their homes or at the laundries their families use. Ask students to develop a personal checklist of precleaning tasks, sorting practices, and washing and drying reminders they can follow to handle or to help with the family laundry.

Review

■ **Chapter Review.** Use the contents of the Chapter Review page to help students review concepts, think critically, and apply their knowledge.

■ **Study Guide.** Have students complete the Study Guide for Chapter 60 on p. 198 of the Student Workbook.

■ **Care in Action.** Have groups create a chart that explains how to prevent and to treat these clothing problems: food spill, body odor, loose button, ripped seam, fallen hem, hair and dandruff, wrinkles, moth holes, and mildew.

Evaluation

■ **Chapter Test.** Use the reproducible chapter test provided in the Teacher's Classroom Resources or create your own test using the *Testmaker Software.*

■ **Alternative Assessment.** Have groups put on a series of interactive skits, each scene depicting either tips for clothing care or correct laundering techniques. Have students stop the action at certain points in the scene so classmates can direct the actors to the proper procedure, depending on the context of the scene.

■ **Clean Up My Act.** Have students explain, by writing or tape recording, the clothing-care techniques from the chapter that they already use. Then have them set specific goals for following any new techniques they have learned. Ask them to include a timetable with their goals.

Point out spots or stains to the dry cleaner when you bring in the clothing. If you know what caused the stain, say so; this may help the dry cleaner to remove it. Certain fabrics should not be dry-cleaned, and this will be stated on the care label.

Some laundromats feature coin-operated dry-cleaning machines. This method costs less than professional dry cleaning and removes most soils quite well. No special treatment, however, is given to spots and stains.

Caring for Borrowed Clothes

At one time or another, you may ask to borrow a piece of clothing from a friend or a family member. Certain occasions—such as weddings—call for clothes you may not wear again. Borrowing can be an economical alternative to purchasing an item. In addition, friends sometimes trade clothing with each other to add variety to their wardrobes.

Borrowing clothes carries a special responsibility. When someone loans you clothing, he or she is trusting you to care for something of value. When you borrow clothing, you can show your appreciation for the loan by following these rules:

- **Inspect it.** Examine the garment before you wear it. Make a note of any problems, such as torn seams or missing buttons.
- **Avoid stains.** When you eat while wearing the garment, put a napkin in your lap to catch spills. Immediately treat any spots that do occur.
- **Launder it.** Clean the garment before returning it, following the directions on the care label. You do not have to dry clean a garment, however, unless you have stained it.

Always return a garment clean and in good repair. It only takes a few minutes to preserve a garment—and a friendship.

- **Inspect it again.** Has your use of the garment caused any new problems?
- **Mend it.** Mending a minor problem that existed when you borrowed the garment is one way to say thanks for a loan. If you have damaged the item and can repair it, you should. If you can't, ask someone for help. If a garment is badly damaged, offer to replace it.
- **Return it promptly.** Always return an item as soon as you can after using it.

Focus on Relationship Skills

Point out that some young people think keeping their clothes clean and in good repair is unimportant because "My real friends don't care how I look." Discuss whether students agree. Should friends care whether their clothes are clean and neat-looking? Why or why not? Should you dress "for" friends? Acquaintances? Adults? If so, in what situations?

Chapter 60

Review

Reviewing the Facts

1. What are four steps you can take every day to care for your clothes?
2. Explain how care labels found inside garments can help you take care of your clothes.
3. Describe how to repair a snag and patch a hole.
4. How should clothes be sorted before you wash them?
5. How can you be sure to dry your clothing properly?
6. What is the correct way to iron clothes?

Thinking Critically

1. What do you think are the most important reasons to take care of your clothing? Why?
2. How much responsibility do you think teens should take in caring for their own clothing? Explain your answer.

Applying Your Skills

1. **Classifying Your Clothing-Care Needs.** Examine the care labels on your own clothes, including jackets and coats. What kinds of care methods does your wardrobe require?
2. **Making a Clothing-Care Timetable.** Consider your daily, occasional, and seasonal clothing-care needs. Do many of your clothes need ironing? Which of your clothes require only seasonal cleaning? Make a chart that shows what you should be doing daily, weekly, and seasonally.
3. **Creating a Clothing-Care System.** What is your method for storing soiled clothes, clothes to be ironed, and clothes to be mended between wash days? How well does it work? Describe what you do now. Suggest how you could improve on this system or describe a new one.

Making Connections

1. **Mathematics.** Collect information on the brand of detergent you use at home or a brand a friend or relative uses. Using information on the package, calculate the price per wash load, and be prepared to compare this brand with others researched by your classmates. Are you using an economical brand? What factors, other than price, would you need to consider in choosing a brand of detergent?
2. **Economics.** Using the yellow pages of the telephone book, classified advertisements, and other advertisements, list the different services you find available. For example, do laundromats offer a wash-and-fold service? Do individuals sell ironing services from their homes? Does the dry cleaner also offer seasonal clothing storage?

Building Your Portfolio

Writing a Résumé

Imagine that you are applying for a job as the clothing-care manager of a busy household. Create a résumé showing your clothing-care skills. You should include what you can do (your abilities), where you have done this work before (your experience), how well you do it (your expertise), and where you have learned to do it (your education). Place your completed résumé in your portfolio.

Chapter Overview

Chapter 61 discusses characteristics of natural and manufactured fibers, and how these qualities make certain fibers suitable for certain types of garments. Students also learn how fabric construction and finish affect fabric use.

Motivator

■ **Selected Use.** Show students a large piece of plastic. Ask: Would you like to wear a shirt made of this material? Suppose it were raining. Would such a garment be more useful then? What qualities make the material suitable for one garment but not the other?

Objectives

Discuss the chapter objectives on this page. Remind students that the objectives focus on important chapter concepts.

Vocabulary

Point out that *blend* and *finish* are two words that "are what they do": they can be used as nouns (as in the chapter) or verbs. A blend is a yarn made by blending different fibers; a finish is a substance that adds final characteristics to fabrics.

Chapter **61** Fibers and Fabrics

Terms to Learn

- blend
- dyeing
- fabric
- fiber
- finish
- manufactured fiber
- natural fiber
- yarn

Objectives

This chapter will help you to:

- Differentiate **between natural and manufactured fibers.**
- Identify **the characteristics of natural and manufactured fibers.**
- Describe **the construction of woven, knit, and nonwoven fabrics.**
- Explain **how added finishes affect fabric appearance and performance.**
- Evaluate **the suitability of particular fabrics for clothing.**

588   UNIT 7   Clothing and Textiles

CHAPTER RESOURCES

Student Workbook

Study Guide, p. 202

Activity, *Fabrics and Fibers*, p. 203

Teacher's Classroom Resources

Lesson Plan, p. 65

Extension #89, *Care for Delicate Fabrics*, p. 95

Life Skills, *Fabrics and Their Uses*, p. 96

Chapter 61 Test, pp. 127-128

Performance Assessment, *Fabric Facts*, p. 96

Reteaching, *Fabric and Fiber Terms*, p. 67

When Jeff bought an acrylic warm-up suit, it looked great in the store and appeared to be just what he wanted. When he got very little wear out of it, however, Jeff had second thoughts. The suit was a problem to clean. It had to be washed in cold water, hung to dry, and then pressed with a warm iron. He rarely wanted to go to that much trouble.

One day Jeff ignored the care instructions, thinking it wouldn't really matter. Taking the suit out of the dryer, Jeff realized he had created a hand-me-down for his younger brother. It was now one size smaller.

Jeff could have avoided his mistake if he had paid more attention to fabric. Knowing about fabrics can help you:

- Be a smarter shopper.
- Look and feel better in your clothing.
- Get more use from the clothing you make.
- Care for garments correctly so that they look better and last longer.

Knowing how the fiber content and the finish of a garment affect its appearance and performance can be helpful knowledge.

Fibers

The basic components of all fabrics are **fibers,** *the tiny strands that, when twisted together, make up yarns.* Fibers are made into yarns, yarns into fabrics, and fabrics into clothing. There are two kinds of fibers: natural and manufactured.

Natural Fibers

Natural fibers are *fibers that come from plants or animals.* Each natural fiber has its own special characteristics. **Figure 61.1** on page 590 describes these characteristics. All natural fibers absorb moisture and allow air to reach your skin. They are comfortable to wear, keeping you warm in winter and cool in summer. Natural fibers usually require more care, however, than manufactured fibers. These are the most common natural fibers:

- Cotton is the most common plant fiber. It comes from the seedpod of the cotton plant.

- Linen is another common plant fiber. It comes from the stalk of the flax plant.
- Wool comes from the fleece of sheep. Camels, alpacas, goats, and rabbits also provide hair that is used for special types of wool.
- Silk is made by an insect called the silkworm. The fibers come from the cocoon that the silkworm spins.
- Ramie comes from the stems of China grass.

Manufactured Fibers

Until the end of the 19th century, all fabrics were made of natural fibers. Today many fabrics are made of manufactured fibers. **Manufactured fibers** are *fibers formed completely or in part by chemicals.*

Many manufactured fibers were created to replace or copy natural fibers. For instance, nylon was made to look like silk, and acrylic is a substitute for wool in sweaters and blankets. One advantage of manufactured fibers is that many of them are easy to care for. **Figure 61.1** on page 591 describes characteristics of common manufactured fibers.

Cotton, a natural fiber, comes from the seedpod of this plant.

CHAPTER 61   Fibers and Fabrics   589

Checking Comprehension

✓ Trace the progression from fibers to clothes. *Fibers twisted into yarns, yarns made into fabrics, fabrics into clothes.*

✓ Name some plants and animals that produce natural fibers. *Cotton plant, flax plant, sheep, camels, alpacas, goats, rabbits, silkworms, China grass.*

✓ Why were some manufactured fibers developed? *To replace or copy natural fibers.*

Activity

■ **Figuring Out Fibers.** Ask students if they think many consumers pay attention to fiber content when buying clothes. Of those who do, do students think they understand the properties, advantages, and disadvantages of each? Why else might people choose one type of fiber over another? *(Critical Thinking)*

DID YOU KNOW?

Recycled plastic bottles now make up 50 to 89 percent of the content of fake fur, fleece, and other fluffy fabrics. A fleece jacket can be made entirely from melted-down bottles—about 25 per jacket. Recycled plastic can also be made to resemble denim, pointelle, broadcloth, jersey blends, and canvas. One company recycles 2.4 billion bottles a year into polyester fiber, saving enough raw petroleum to power the city of Atlanta for a year while producing strong fibers that resist fading, wrinkling, and moths.

- Fiber Characteristics
- Yarns
- Fabric Construction

Checking Comprehension

✓ Name one advantage of blends. *Have best qualities of both fibers.*

✓ What added expense may come with garments made of wool, silk, and acetate fibers? *Dry cleaning.*

✓ What three basic methods are used to make fabrics? *Weaving, knitting, bonding.*

USING VISUALS

Refer students to Figure 61.1 on pp. 590-591. Ask questions such as: Why do you think wool is warm and water-repellent? *To protect sheep from elements.* What qualities of nylon make it good for stockings? *Strong, holds shape.* Would acetate look good in a formal dress? *Yes, it's silklike, drapes well.*

SPECIAL NEEDS
Strategies

Inefficient Organizers. Encourage students to make charts showing the information in Figure 61.1. Have them list the fibers down the left side of the chart and the characteristics across the top, using check marks to show which fibers have which characteristics.

590

Yarns

Yarns are *strands that are formed when fibers are twisted together.* Long, straight fibers usually create smooth, silky yarns. Short, curly fibers tend to make softer, fluffier yarns. The thickness of the yarn also depends on how tightly the fibers are spun together. The qualities of the fiber and yarn affect the wear and care of the fabric.

A **blend** is *a yarn made from two or more different fibers.* The blend can be made of natural fibers (such as cotton and linen), manufactured fibers (such as rayon and acetate), or natural and manufactured fibers (such as cotton and polyester). Blends combine characteristics of both fibers.

The percentage of each fiber in a blend determines which characteristics will dominate. A common blend for shirt fabrics is 60 percent polyester and 40 percent cotton. The result is

Figure 61.1

FIBER CHARACTERISTICS

Characteristics of Natural Fibers

Cotton is soft, comfortable, and absorbent. It is strong even when wet and takes finishes well. It is easily washed but wrinkles and shrinks unless it is treated with wrinkle-resistant or shrink-resistant finishes.

Linen is very durable. It is comfortable and absorbent. It is easily washed but wrinkles and shrinks unless it is treated with wrinkle-resistant or shrink-resistant finishes.

Wool is warm because it retains body heat. It resists wrinkles and is naturally water-repellent. It can shrink with heat and moisture, however, and can be damaged by moths. Wool usually must be dry-cleaned but is sometimes washable.

Silk is lightweight and flexible but strong, with a natural luster. It can be damaged by perspiration. Most silks must be dry-cleaned. Some are washable but are damaged by chlorine bleach.

Ramie is very strong and absorbs moisture. It has a natural luster. Ramie is washable. It is often combined with other fibers.

590 **UNIT 7 Clothing and Textiles**

MORE ABOUT Fabric Quality

For both natural and manufactured fibers, one important test of quality is how it feels to the touch. This is called its hand. High-quality fabrics are made from tightly spun or woven fibers. They tend to feel soft and smooth and hang well, flowing smoothly over the body. A tightly spun cotton can feel like expensive cashmere. Manufactured fibers also can produce quality garments that breathe like cotton, hang like fine wool, and retain color better than silk.

a shirt that has the good looks and comfort of cotton and the easy-care features of polyester. This combination does not require ironing but may not be as comfortable as a shirt that is 100 percent cotton.

Fabric Construction

Yarns are made into **fabric,** which is *material or cloth.* Most fabrics are made by one of three basic methods: weaving, knitting, or

bonding the yarns or fibers together. **Figure 61.2** on page 592 illustrates the basic types of fabric construction.

Woven Fabrics

You may have seen people weaving fabric by hand on a loom. Weaving is the interlacing of yarns to form woven fabric. The yarns are interlaced at right angles. The warp, or lengthwise, yarns are lined up in parallel rows on a loom. Crosswise yarns, called the filling,

Characteristics of Manufactured Fibers

Acetate has an attractive silklike look and is soft and drapes easily. It may wrinkle and fade, however, and it is sensitive to heat. Usually it must be dry-cleaned.

Acrylic is soft and lightweight, yet warm. It resists wrinkles, and it blends well with other fibers for added bulk. Acrylic is nonallergenic. It is sensitive to heat and can be dry cleaned or washed.

Nylon is strong and holds its shape well. It does not absorb moisture. It is washable and dries quickly but is sensitive to heat.

Polyester resists wrinkles but retains pleats. It blends well with other fibers. It is washable and dries quickly but holds oily stains.

Rayon is soft, comfortable, and highly absorbent. It wrinkles easily. Rayon is usually dry-cleaned but may be washable.

Spandex has a high degree of stretch and recovery. It combines well with other fibers. Spandex is washable, but is weakened by chlorine bleach.

CHAPTER 61   Fibers and Fabrics   591

DID YOU KNOW?

Processing and bleaching cotton adds to the pollution in the environment. A few manufacturers are now offering environmentally friendly cotton that is unbleached and undyed. Others are trying to devise ways to dye fabric naturally with berries, nuts, clay, mud, leaves, and insect shells. The most promising approaches are recycling soda bottles (see p. 589) and making clothes from rags and remnants.

(see p. 589)

Activities

■ **Fiber Survey.** Have students check accessible labels on each other's garments for fiber content. How many students are wearing clothing made of natural fibers? Manufactured fibers? Blends of both?

RETEACHING

■ **Fitting Fabrics.** Have students suggest fabrics that would be suitable for: a bathing suit; a winter coat; a knapsack; and pajamas. Ask students to give reasons for their choices.

CROSS-CURRICULAR ACTIVITY
Science

Have students compare natural and manufactured fibers under a microscope. Students should see individual cells in the natural fibers, while the manufactured fibers will look more uniform. Ask students to examine strands of their own hair under the microscope. Which kind of fiber does hair more closely resemble?

CROSS-CURRICULAR ACTIVITY
Social Studies

Point out that the United States exports far more textiles than garments, while importing far more garments than textiles. Ask students to learn why this imbalance exists. How does it affect both consumers and the American garment industry?

Checking Comprehension

✔ What are two advantages of woven garments? *Stronger, hold shape better than knits.*

✔ Why do the edges of nonwoven fabrics need no special finishing? *Edges don't fray or unravel when cut.*

✔ When are dyes added in the fabric-making process? *At any point.*

USING VISUALS

After students study Figure 61.2, challenge them to reproduce one or more of the weaves, using yarn, strips of colored paper, or colored drawings that show how each length of yarn lies under and over other lengths of yarn.

CROSS-CURRICULAR ACTIVITY
Art

Invite students to try their hands at textile printing, using inks or pigments specially developed for fabrics. Their projects could range from tie-dyeing T-shirts, to making potato prints on fabric, to painting designs on silk.

are passed over and under the warp yarns. **Figure 61.2** shows and explains how the three basic types of weaves—plain, twill, and satin—are constructed.

Fabrics are woven on industrial looms that produce many variations of the basic weaves. Each weave produces a different fabric. For example, pile fabrics—such as corduroy and velvet—are made from three sets of yarns. The extra set of yarns forms the pile, or cut surface, on a plain or twill weave base.

The type of weave, along with the type of fiber and yarn, determines whether the fabric is soft or crisp, smooth or textured. Woven fabrics generally hold their shape better and are stronger than knits.

Knit Fabrics

Unlike weaving, knitting can be done with a single strand of yarn, just as people do by hand with knitting needles. Many kinds of clothing, from sport shirts and dresses to T-shirts and underwear, are made of knitted fabrics. **Figure 61.2** shows the construction of knitted fabrics.

Knitted fabrics are comfortable because they can stretch with movement and return to their original shape. They don't wrinkle easily. Although knits do not fray or unravel, some may run if snagged.

Nonwoven Fabrics

The fibers of nonwoven fabrics are matted or bonded (see **Figure 61.2**). They all share one special quality—their edges do not fray or un-

Figure 61.2
FABRIC CONSTRUCTION

Twill weave. Each filling yarn passes over two to four warp yarns, producing a diagonal line in the fabric.

Knit. Loops of yarn are interlocked, one row after another, on special knitting machines.

Plain weave. Each filling yarn passes over and under a warp yarn.

Satin weave. Each filling yarn passes under four or more warp yarns, then usually over one warp yarn.

Nonwoven fabric. Fibers are matted or bonded with heat, moisture, agitation, pressure, chemicals, or adhesives.

DID YOU KNOW?

Tell students that bonded fabrics are simply two fabrics glued together. Laminated fabrics have three layers: the fabric, a sheet of foam, and a backing. During lamination, heat melts the foam, causing the fabric and its backing to stick together.

MORE ABOUT Dyeing

Some dyed yarns and fabrics are colorfast; others bleed so easily the color rubs off on hands or other clothing. Many conditions affect color permanence, including sunlight, acids in perspiration, airborne chemicals, and heat.

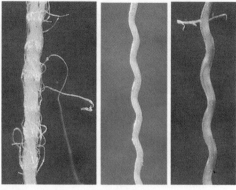
The number of fibers that make up a yarn and how tightly they are twisted together affect the way a fabric looks and how it performs.

ravel when cut. This means that they need no special finishing.

Felt, a nonwoven fabric, has long been used for hats and craft projects. Other nonwoven fabrics are used on the inside of garments, to shape collars and add firmness to belts.

Certain nonwoven fabrics—called fusible webs—will melt when heat is applied. These fabrics can fuse other materials and are used for hems and to attach trimmings.

Color and Finishes

Color and finishes add final touches to fabric. Color is applied to fabrics by dyeing or printing. **Dyeing** is *the process of using a substance to change the natural color of a fiber, yarn, or fabric.* Dyeing can generally be done

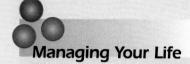

Activities

■ **Fabric Wish List.** Invite students to describe fabric improvements they would like to see or think will be achieved. *(Creativity)*

ENRICHMENT

■ **Weaving Words.** Suggest that students use reference materials to create an illustrated glossary of these weaving and knitting terms: warp, weft, wale, rib weave, basket weave, herringbone, houndstooth, purl knit, rib knit, double knit.

Managing Your Life

Choosing Fabrics to Fit Your Lifestyle

Whether you are sewing a garment or buying an outfit, you should consider if the fabric fits the needs of your lifestyle and budget. Keep these points in mind as you shop:

- **Look of the fabric.** Some fabrics fall softly in curves, and others have a crisp texture. The look you want and the occasion help determine which to choose.
- **Stretchability of the fabric.** Some clothing must be made of fabric with a certain degree of stretchability. If a garment will be used during exercise or sports, it should stretch readily, and the fabric should recover its shape after stretching.
- **Color of the fabric.** You already know the value of coordinating your wardrobe by color. Knowing your best colors and how to mix colors can help you look your best.
- **Fiber content of the fabric.** Use your knowledge of fiber characteristics to choose fabrics that combine comfort, durability, and easy care. For sewing, some fabrics are easier to work with than others. Beginners are wise to avoid slippery fabrics and pile fabrics, such as velvet and corduroy.

- **Quality of the fabric.** Examine fabric carefully before you buy it. What looks good initially may not wear well. Make sure the color is even throughout the bolt or garment. Check for pills on brushed fabric—they will only get worse the more clothing is worn. On knitted fabrics, look for snags and pulls.

Buying clothing and fabric is too expensive to risk choosing items that won't look good for many wearings. Taking a little extra time to consider fabric characteristics before you buy can help you make good choices.

Applying the Principles

1. Consider your activities in a typical week. What qualities are most important in the fabrics you would choose?
2. Assume that you are a beginning sewer. What three types of fabrics might you choose to work with? Why?

CHAPTER 61   Fibers and Fabrics   593

Managing Your Life

Have students read "Choosing Fabrics to Fit Your Lifestyle" and discuss the questions.

Answers to Applying . . .

1. Answers will vary but should be reasonable for student's interests and lifestyle.
2. Answers will vary but should include inexpensive fabrics that are easy to work with, solids rather than patterns or plaids.

In Touch With
TECHNOLOGY

Have students read "New Types of Fabrics" on p. 594 and discuss the questions.

Answers to Thinking Critically . . .

1. Answers will vary.
2. Answers may include: allergic reactions, flammability, environmental effects of manufacturing process.

DID YOU KNOW?

Gore-Tex® is a very thin fabric that is layered between sturdier fabrics to make a garment water repellent and wind resistant, yet allowing it to breathe. Bob Gore invented this fabric after stretching Teflon nonstick coating into a thin membrane to insulate wire. He discovered that the pores in the membrane were too small for water vapor to enter but large enough for it to escape.

Review

■ **Chapter Review.** Use the contents of the Chapter Review page to help students review concepts, think critically, and apply their knowledge.

■ **Study Guide.** Have students complete the Study Guide for Chapter 61 on p. 202 of the Student Workbook.

■ **Made for Each Other?** Have students write an appropriate or inappropriate fiber-garment pairing on a slip of paper. Collect the papers. Have students draw one, read the combination, and explain whether it is a suitable one. Also have the student identify the fiber named as natural or manufactured.

Evaluation

■ **Chapter Test.** Use the reproducible chapter test provided in the Teacher's Classroom Resources or create your own test using the *Testmaker Software.*

■ **Alternative Assessment.** Have groups list five or six questions shoppers should ask themselves about fibers and fabrics before they buy clothing or material. Have groups exchange and answer questions, explaining options, consequences, or issues as appropriate.

■ **Knowledge Is Power?** Ask students how they would respond to a classmate who says, "Why should we learn about fibers and fabrics? As long as the manufacturers know what to use for clothes, what does it matter to us?"

In Touch with TECHNOLOGY

New Types of Fabrics

Before nylon became available in 1939, most fabric was constructed of natural fibers. Textile chemists followed with other manufactured fibers, such as acrylics and polyester. In recent years, more specialty fabrics have been developed.

- **Water-repellent fabrics.** Fabrics and finishes that repel water are not new, but they have been greatly improved. Many advances use microfibers. As the name implies, microfibers are made of threads that are spun very tightly and are therefore extremely fine. Fabric constructed of microfibers is lightweight, durable, and water-repellent. Microfibers can be made into 100 percent manufactured fabrics or woven in blends with cotton, linen, and other natural fibers.
- **Insulating fabrics.** Great strides have been made in insulating fabrics that are lightweight, flexible, and breathable. Fabrics with a high insulation factor protect the wearer against wind, while letting body moisture escape.
- **Sun-protection fabrics.** Did you know the sun's rays can pass right through the holes in many loosely woven fabrics? Typical summer clothing does not provide total protection from

ultraviolet rays—about the equivalent of a sun protection factor (SPF) of 5 to 15. A new process, in which fabrics are bathed in a special chemical solution, produces fabrics with SPFs of 50 or more. The sun protection is supposed to last through numerous washings.

- **Antibacterial fabrics.** Textile manufacturers have developed fabrics that resist bacteria. In sports clothing, these treated fabrics can act as a built-in deodorant, since the chemical treatment destroys the bacteria that cause perspiration odors. An even more significant use is in hospitals, where sheets with built-in resistance to bacteria can reduce the spread of disease.

Thinking Critically About Technology

1. Which new fabric would you most like to try? Why?
2. What kind of safety hazards do textile manufacturers need to consider as they come up with new fabrics and fabric treatments?

at any stage of fabric making. Both natural and manufactured fibers and yarns can be dyed, or an entire finished fabric can be soaked in a dye bath. Designs can also be printed on the surface of fabrics.

A **finish** is *a substance added to a fabric to change the appearance, feel, or performance of the fabric.* Some finishes make the fabric look or feel more appealing. In a napped fabric, such as flannel, the fabric is brushed to raise the fiber ends. The result is a smooth, soft look. Upholstery and drapery fabrics often are finished with chemicals to allow them to resist dirt and look new. Other finishes make a fabric shinier or crisper.

Some finishes affect the performance of a fabric. Wool is often made shrink resistant

through the application of chemicals. Fabrics used for raincoats and all-weather bags usually have water-repellent finishes. Other finishes are applied to provide resistance to wrinkles, stains, and flames.

A finish may be permanent or temporary. Special care might make the finish last longer. Some finishes, such as one that repels water, can be renewed at home or by a professional dry cleaner.

When you purchase fabric, check the care label. Fabric sold by the yard includes a label on the end of the bolt that lists fiber content and any special finishes. The salesperson has a special care label that you can sew into the seam of a garment you construct.

Focus on Creative Thinking Skills

Ask students to imagine they have discovered a way to create a "Superfabric of the Future." It is made by blending any combination of existing fibers, retaining only the best characteristics of each one, into the most versatile clothing material known. Have them select five qualities they find most valuable in a fabric, then suggest possible fiber combinations that will result in such a product.

Chapter 61 Review

Reviewing the Facts

1. How will you benefit from knowing the fabric content of a garment?
2. What is the difference between natural fibers and manufactured fibers? Name four natural fibers and four manufactured fibers.
3. List two advantages of natural fibers and two advantages of manufactured fibers.
4. What is the difference between a woven fabric, a knit fabric, and a nonwoven fabric?
5. Why are finishes used on some fabrics? Give three examples of added finishes that affect the possible uses of a fabric.
6. What information is included on a care label? Give several examples of specific fabric care.

Thinking Critically

1. Think about the clothes you wear most frequently. Do you prefer garments made of natural or manufactured fibers? Why? Consider the pros and cons of each type.
2. What fabric characteristics would you look for in a warm-up suit? Which fiber, or combination of fibers, would you choose? Consider what added finishes might be appropriate. Explain your choice.

Applying Your Knowledge

1. **Examining Characteristics.** Without looking at the labels, can you tell whether the garments you are wearing are made from natural or manufactured fibers? Describe how the garments look and feel, and predict fiber content. Check the care label to see how accurate you are.
2. **Comparing Fabric Performance.** Select a woven and a knitted fabric made of the same fiber—cotton or polyester, for example. (Choose fabric scraps or pieces of clothing that are no longer worn.) Test each fabric for

wrinkle resistance by crushing and releasing a corner of the fabric in your hand. Test stretchability by stretching and releasing the fabric. What conclusions can you draw about the characteristics of weaves and knits?

Making Connections

1. **History.** Investigate the history of silk production—when and where it was first used. Discuss modern silk production and how it differs from the way that silk was produced in the past.
2. **Fabric Technology.** Imagine that you have been asked to develop a new fabric. List five qualities this fabric should have to make it most useful to the average consumer. Explain why you chose these qualities over others.

Building Your Portfolio

Identifying Fabric

Collect at least six fabric swatches, or samples. Include woven, knit, and nonwoven fabrics. Mount the swatches in a notebook, and write a description identifying each according to type of weave or knit, name of fabric, fiber content, and characteristics. Add this collection to your portfolio.

ANSWERS TO REVIEWING THE FACTS

1. You can be better shopper; look and feel better in clothing; get more use from clothing you make; know how to care for garments so they last longer, look better.
2. *Natural fibers*—come from plants or animals; include *(any four)*: cotton, linen, wool, silk, ramie. *Manufactured fibers*—made from chemicals; include *(any four)*: acetate, acrylic, nylon, polyester, rayon, spandex.
3. *Natural* (any two): absorb moisture; let air reach skin; cool in summer, warm in winter. *Manufactured:* easy to care for; mimic qualities of natural.
4. *Woven fabrics*—made of yarns interlaced at right angles. *Knits*—made by interlocking loops of yarn. *Nonwoven*—made by matting or bonding fibers together.
5. To enhance fabric's look, feel, or performance. *Any three:* napped fabric is brushed; upholstery, drapery made dirt resistant; wool made shrink resistant; raincoats made water-repellent; other finishes resist wrinkles, stains, flames.
6. Fiber content and finishes. Examples of fabric care may be extrapolated from information in Chapter 60 and Figure 61.1, including: wash in cold water; dry clean only; do not bleach.

ANSWERS TO THINKING CRITICALLY

1. Answers will vary.
2. Answers may include: warm-up suit should be soft, comfortable, absorb perspiration, somewhat elastic, washable. Cotton knit or cotton blend might be good choice, finished to add softness, resist stains.

Chapter Overview

Chapter 62 begins the garment-sewing process. Students learn how to take body measurements; interpret pattern envelopes; and select suitable patterns, fabrics and notions.

Motivators

■ **Wouldn't It Be Nice.** Show students pictures of beautiful objects—a piece of jewelry, a painting. Ask: Would you like to be able to make something like this? Show a picture of an attractive garment; repeat the question. Suggest that any of them may be able to create something equally appealing.

■ **Just Add Water?** Read students the directions from a box cake mix. Ask: Could you make a cake using these directions and what's inside this package? Repeat with the back of a pattern envelope. Tell students to think of a pattern as a "clothing mix"; this chapter helps them follow the directions.

Objectives

Discuss the chapter objectives on this page. Remind students that the objectives focus on important chapter concepts.

Vocabulary

Tell students that the word *pattern* comes from the Medieval Latin word *patron*, who was someone worthy of imitation. Ask: How does this definition apply to sewing patterns?

Chapter 62 Selecting Patterns, Fabrics, and Notions

Terms to Learn

- figure type
- multisized pattern
- notions
- pattern
- pattern catalog
- view

Objectives

This chapter will help you to:

- Take **accurate body measurements and determine what size pattern to buy.**
- List and explain **considerations when selecting a pattern.**
- Describe **factors that affect the choice of fabric.**
- Explain **how to select notions.**
- Estimate **the cost of a project.**

596   UNIT 7   Clothing and Textiles

CHAPTER RESOURCES

Student Workbook
Study Guide, pp. 204-205
Activity, *I've Got a Notion*, pp. 206-207

Teacher's Classroom Resources
Lesson Plan, p. 66
Cooperative Learning, *A Versatile Pattern*, pp. 67-68

Extension #90, *Tips for Buying Fabric*, p. 96
Life Skills, *Examining a Pattern Envelope*, p. 97
Chapter 62 Test, pp. 129-130
Performance Assessment, *Planning a Sewing Project*, p. 97
Reteaching, *Selecting What You Need*, p. 68

Tim had finally built up enough nerve to ask Jenny to the prom, and she had said yes. Although he had already rented a tuxedo, Tim wanted to add something to make his outfit special. The accessories offered at the formal-wear store weren't really what he had in mind. Also, expenses for the prom had left little money for any extras.

Since Tim also needed a final sewing project for his family and consumer sciences class, he thought that he might be able to make something to add a special touch to his tuxedo as his class project. Tim decided to check out the pattern catalogs at a fabric store. As he turned the pages in the easy-to-sew section of a catalog, a vest caught his eye. The pattern was designed for beginners.

With the pattern envelope in hand, Tim started looking at fabric. He finally chose one that would complement the colors in Jenny's dress. Since his other projects had turned out well, Tim was sure that this one would, too.

Like Tim, you might first think of sewing your own clothes in order to save money; however, saving money is not the only benefit. Creating a garment in the size, style, and color that best suits you and your wardrobe, provides enjoyment and great personal satisfaction. Armed with a little knowledge about taking measurements, selecting patterns, and sewing skills, you can be well on your way to creating garments you'll enjoy wearing.

Body Measurements

An item of clothing may be the first sewing project you decide to tackle. To do this, you must select a pattern. A **pattern** is *a set of written directions and printed paper pieces that shows you how to put a garment together.* The pattern also indicates how much fabric is needed and how to lay out and cut the pieces. To determine pattern size, you must first know your body measurements.

Taking Measurements

Measuring accurately is easy once you know how. Use the tips below for taking accurate measurements every time:

- Ask someone to help you take your measurements and write them down for you.
- Wear smooth-fitting clothes when measuring. Do not measure over a bulky sweater or jacket.
- Wear shoes for all measurements except your height. This will make your posture close to what it will be when you wear the clothing.
- Tie a string or a piece of narrow elastic around your waist. You will use it to locate your waist and for measuring the length of your back, hips, and legs.
- Stand straight and tall.
- Keep the tape measure parallel to the floor when taking measurements around the body.
- For accurate measurements, pull the tape measure snugly, but not too tightly, around your body.
- Double-check any measurement before writing it down.

As a first step, measure your height. In your bare feet, stand tall against the wall. For pants or skirt measurements, wear shoes. Have another person make an erasable mark on the wall that is level with the top of your head.

When measuring around your body, make sure that the tape measure is parallel to the floor and snug but not tight.

MORE ABOUT Accurate Measurements

Cloth tape measures can stretch enough that they no longer measure accurately. Suggest students check old cloth tape measures against a yard stick or plastic tape measure for accuracy.

TEACH

Topics on p. 597:
- **Why Sew?**
- **Body Measurements**

Checking Comprehension

✓ What are some advantages of sewing your own clothing? *Saves money; garment suits own tastes and wardrobe; personal satisfaction.*

✓ What does a pattern include? *Written directions, paper pieces for assembling garment, directions for laying out and cutting; information on amount of fabric needed.*

✓ Should you wear shoes when taking measurements? *Yes, for all but height; for height when measuring for pants or skirt.*

Activities

■ **Measure for Measure.** Ask pairs to put on skits demonstrating the tips for taking measurements listed on p. 597. Skits should include dialogue indicating the proper procedures. Point out that students need not take actual measurements.

Checking Comprehension

✓ How can you learn your figure type? *Look at pattern size chart in back of pattern book.*

✓ Is height or proportion more important for identifying your figure type? Why? *Proportion; lengths can be altered if your height varies.*

USING VISUALS

Refer students to Figure 62.1 to answer these and other questions: Why should you bend your arm while length is being measured? *To make sleeves long enough for movement.* How do females identify the waist? How do males? *Females—the narrowest point; males—where belt or waistband feels most comfortable.* How should the measurement of the inseam compare to that of the outseam? *Should be shorter.* Which measurement will vary depending on whether you are long-waisted or short-waisted? *Back waist length.*

Figure 62.1

TAKING MEASUREMENTS

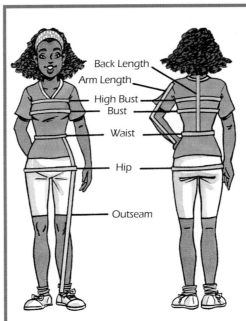

Measuring the Female Body

Back waist length. Measure from the base of the neck (the point at which a collar seam falls on the neck) to the waistline.

High bust. Measure around the body, under the arms.

Bust. Measure at the fullest part of the bustline.

Arm length. Bend the elbow slightly. Measure from the top of the shoulder, over the bent elbow, down to the wrist.

Waist. Tie a string or piece of elastic around the waist to identify the narrowest point. Measure around the waist at this location.

Hip. Measure around the fullest part of the hips, 7-9 in. (18-23 cm) below the waist.

Outseam. Measure along the outside of the leg from the waist, over the hips, to the desired length of the skirt or pants.

Measuring the Male Body

Neck. Measure around the fullest part of the neck, adding ½ in. (1.3 cm) for wearing ease. Compare to neckband measurement.

Back waist length. Measure from the base of the neck to the waistline.

Arm length. Bend the arm up. Measure from the base of the neck at the center back, across the shoulder to the crook of the elbow, and up to the wrist bone. Use this measurement to compare with pattern to see if alterations in sleeve length are needed.

Chest. Measure the fullest part of the chest.

Waist. Measure around the natural waist at the location a belt or waistband feels most comfortable.

Hip. Measure around the fullest part of the hips. This is usually 8 in. (20.5 cm) below the waist.

Inseam. Measure a pair of pants that fits well and is the correct length, measuring from bottom of one leg to the seam at which the two pant legs are sewn together.

Outseam. Measure along the outside of the leg from waist to desired length of pants.

DID YOU KNOW?

While fewer people are sewing their own clothing today, many more are discovering the great savings advantage of sewing their own home decorations. At Simplicity, home-decorating and craft patterns make up 25 percent of all pattern sales. At House of Fabric, a nationwide chain of fabric stores, 30 percent of its sewing classes focus on home decoration. Do-it-yourself decorators can now enjoy Ralph Lauren or Laura Ashley designs at minimal cost.

Measure from this point to the floor. See **Figure 62.1** for guidance in measuring other parts of your body.

Figure Types and Sizes

Compare your measurements with the pattern size charts found in the back of a **pattern catalog**, *a book in a fabric store that shows all the patterns available from one company*. Pattern sizes are divided by **figure types**, *size categories determined by height and body proportions*. The major pattern companies use common figure types based on height and figure development. Which description most closely describes your figure type? (Note tht patterns can be altered for length if you are shorter or taller than the heights mentioned.)

- Misses' patterns are designed for the well-proportioned figure—5'5" to 5'6" in height.
- Girls' patterns are for the petite figure—5'1" or shorter.
- Men's patterns are for the average adult build—about 5'10" tall.
- Teen boys' patterns are for boys who are still growing.

STRATEGIES That Work

Choosing the Right Pattern Size

Taking your measurements and knowing your figure type are essential steps in choosing the right pattern size. Sometimes, it's still not an easy task. Several general guidelines can help:

- **Understand differences between brands.** All pattern brands are based on the same basic measurements, but some brands are likely to fit you better than others. Try different brands to determine which are best for you.
- **Consider the type of garment you're sewing.** One measurement is often more important than the others. For skirts, pants, and shorts, rely on the waist measurement. If, however, your hips measure two sizes larger than your waist, use the hip measurement. Taking a garment in at the waist is easier than letting it out at the hip. For dresses and blouses, use the bust measurement. For males, use the chest or neck size for determining a pattern size for shirts. Coat and jacket patterns assume that the garment will be worn over other clothing. Choose these patterns according to your normal measurements.
- **Consider all the factors.** Many people find that their measurements fall between pattern sizes. They need to consider the project itself and their bone structure. The fabric that has been chosen makes a difference. Personal preference about fit is also a factor.

Making the Strategy Work

Think . . .

1. How could you determine the pattern brand that fits you best without spending much money?
2. How might current fashion trends affect your choice of pattern size?
3. Assume that you want to sew a swimsuit coverup and your measurements put you between pattern sizes. Would you go up or down in size?

Try...

Jayne and her younger sister have similar taste in clothing and weigh the same—120 pounds. Do you think their mother should expect them to be able to share patterns? Explain in a paragraph.

CHAPTER 62 **Selecting Patterns, Fabrics, and Notions** 599

Topics on pp. 600-601:

• **Factors in Selecting a Pattern**

Checking Comprehension

✓ How can you get an idea about a pattern's style? *Study pictures in catalog for line, shape, length, fit; read description.*

✓ What details mark a style as more difficult to sew? *Cuffs, collar, fly-front zipper, extra darts, tucks, topstitching.*

✓ What information does the front of a pattern offer? *Pattern views; figure type and size; pattern number; price.*

CROSS-CURRICULAR ACTIVITY

Art

Challenge students to draw different views of a garment that is in their wardrobe. They might show the article in different colors or fabrics, with various sleeve lengths or necklines.

CROSS-REFERENCE

Chapter 57 described design elements students should consider in choosing a style that will look good on them.

Because each person's body is built differently, you may not always be able to match your measurements exactly to a pattern size. Choose the size within your figure type that comes closest to your measurements. Some patterns are not identified by a single size but by measurements, such as by waist size for pants. Others may be sized small, medium, large, and extra large.

Selecting a Pattern

Pattern catalogs provide a lot of information about patterns. First, look for the type of garment or item you want to sew. Clothes patterns usually are grouped according to the type of garment (such as sportswear or dresses) or by figure type (men or misses). There are also sections devoted exclusively to top fashion designers so that you can duplicate the designs of Paris, Milan, or New York.

Other categories are based on sewing skill, such as easy-to-sew patterns. Catalogs also have sections for gifts, home decorating, toys, accessories, and crafts. Each catalog page has drawings or photographs showing how the project will look when sewn. These illustrations often include a number of views. A **view** is *a variation on the pattern design.* For example, a shirt pattern may include views for long and short sleeves, or a garment may be shown in one color or contrasting colors.

■ *Examine patterns carefully to select a style that is best for you.*

Be sure to look at patterns that may be shown on special display racks in the store. These may be best-selling patterns, seasonal selections, or easy-to-sew patterns.

Choosing for Style

When you buy a shirt or pair of pants in a store, you can see the style, color, and fabric together. You can also try the item on to see how it looks and feels. When selecting a pattern, you must rely on the way the garment looks in the pattern catalog. Study the photographs and illustrations carefully. Check the design lines, as well as the shape, length, and fit. Read the description under the pat-

600   UNIT 7   Clothing and Textiles

MORE ABOUT Patterns

Traditional pattern making is a time-consuming task. The designer's sketches are redrawn into various views using different fabrics. The garment is sewn and modeled to check for appearance and fit. A master pattern is created and converted into various sizes. Sketches or photographs for the pattern catalog are made and fabric layouts developed. Today, manufacturers save time by using computer-aided design (CAD) for many of these steps. Ask: For which steps would computers be most helpful?

tern. This tells how it fits. Is it snug-fitting or loose? Pattern catalogs also feature a drawing of the back of the garment.

You may still wonder if the garment will look good on you. One clue might be whether the item is similar to something you've worn in the past. If it isn't, look for a similar garment in a store and try it on. That way, you can select a pattern that really suits you.

Choosing for Sewing Skills

When picking a pattern, consider your sewing skills. If you're a beginner, look for patterns marked "easy to sew" or "very easy." The number of pattern pieces is a clue to the pattern's difficulty. The fewer the pieces, the easier the pattern. Such details as shirt cuffs, collars, fly-front zippers, extra darts, tucks, and topstitching make a pattern more difficult to complete. If you have some sewing experience and are confident that you could handle some of these details, they will add interest to a garment and challenge to your work.

Using the Pattern Envelope

The pattern department in most stores is self-service. That means you find the pattern you want in large file drawers. The drawers hold the patterns in order by number. When you have found the right number, be sure to select the correct size. Most stores will not allow you to exchange or return a pattern.

Once you've chosen your pattern, take a good look at the pattern envelope. The outside of the envelope contains important information:

- **Front of the envelope.** The front of the envelope shows the same drawings and photographs of the pattern views that were in the catalog. You will also find the figure type and the size the pattern is made for, along with the pattern number and the price.
- **Back of the envelope.** On the back of the envelope, the garment description lists design details that may not be obvious in

Making Decisions

Deciding Whether to Make or Buy

"Guess what?" Amanda said to Heather at the bus stop. "I just found out my dad and I are going to a special reception and dinner after my brother's graduation. It's going to be at a very nice off-campus restaurant. Now the dress I was going to wear just doesn't seem right."

"I'll go shopping with you," Heather suggested.

"I don't know," Amanda hesitated. "I saw this pattern for a dress and I love it. Maybe I could make it."

Heather's eyebrows raised in response. "You've only got two weeks. Is it a simple pattern? Maybe you should just go over to Cher's Boutique. Their dresses are on sale."

"Really?" Amanda asked with renewed interest. "That would be great, but Cher's is kind of expensive and their selection isn't always good."

"Well, you'll need to decide soon. What do you want to do?" Heather asked.

What Would You Do?

1. What are Amanda's options?
2. What are the advantages and disadvantages of each option?
3. Why would Amanda be wise to check the fabric store as well as the dress shop?
4. Can you think of any other options that Amanda hasn't considered?
5. Assuming you had intermediate sewing skills, what would you do?

the illustration. A sketch is given of the back of each pattern view, along with a size chart of the body measurements for each pattern size. The measurements of the finished garment may also be listed.

- **Things Get Tricky.** Provide two patterns of the same brand for the same type of garment, such as a shirt. Choose one pattern labeled "easy" and one labeled "difficult." Have groups compare them to determine what makes one more challenging. *(Critical Thinking)*

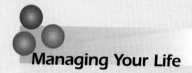

Managing Your Life

Have students read "Deciding Whether to Make or Buy" and discuss the questions. Ask: Is this a good situation in which to try a challenging project? Why or why not?

Answers to What Would You Do?

1. To sew dress or buy one.
2. *Sewing*—advantages: lower cost; choosing style and fabric; personal satisfaction. Disadvantages: limited time and skills. *Buying*—advantages: faster; easier; more certain. Disadvantages: limited selection; higher cost.
3. At fabric store she can see what patterns, fabrics are available; find helpful resources to make informed decision. At shop she can learn styles, prices of dresses.
4. Answers may include: borrow dress; ask experienced sewer to help; try other type of store.
5. Answers will vary.

DID YOU KNOW?

Another advantage of sewing instead of buying clothes is that pattern sizes are standard; ready-to-wear clothing sizes, as students have probably discovered, are not. One clothing manufacturer's size 8 dress might be larger or smaller than another dress maker's. It might also be similar to a pattern size 6 or 10, depending again on the dress manufacturer.

Topics on pp. 602–604:

- **Selecting a Pattern (continued)**
- **Selecting Fabric**
- **Choosing Notions**
- **Estimating Cost**

Checking Comprehension

✓ How are multisized patterns different from others? *They include three or more separate cutting lines for different sizes.*

✓ What fabrics might a novice sewer want to avoid? *Those with one-way design or nap; plaids; those that ravel easily.*

✓ Describe signs of poor quality in a fabric. *Torn threads, snags, holes, stains, wrinkles easily, knit does not hold shape.*

✓ Should notions be the same color as the fabric? *Threads, zippers, and others should be; buttons may contrast.*

What information can you find out about a project just by reading the pattern envelope?

- **Other information.** The back of the pattern envelope provides your shopping list. The yardage chart shows how much fabric you'll need for each pattern size. It will tell you whether you need extra fabric when using napped fabrics, such as corduroy, velvet, and velveteen. Under "Fabrics," you will find listed the types of fabric appropriate for the pattern. In addition, this paragraph states whether a fabric such as a plaid or a diagonal is suitable. Finally, you'll find information on the notions that you'll need to buy. **Notions** are *the smaller supplies needed to complete a project, such as thread and zippers.*

Multisized Patterns

Some patterns are designed especially to make size selection easier or to help you get a better fit. One of these is the **multisized pattern,** which is *a pattern that has three or more separate cutting lines for three or more pattern sizes on each pattern piece.* As an example, a multisized pattern for a girl's shirt might be labeled "Size 8-10-12." A man's pattern might be labeled "Size 34-36-38." You could buy this pattern if you wear any one of these sizes. Some people choose multisized patterns because different parts of their bodies fit different sizes. They can buy only one multisized pattern for a garment that includes separate items, such as a shirt and pants.

Focus on Consumer Skills

Ask students to visit a fabric store to make comparisons of fabric value. Have them identify two of the most and least expensive fabrics available and note the price, care requirements, quality, and suggested uses of each one. (Encourage students to ask sales staff if they need information or help.) Do students think the price difference is justified? For what other reasons might one fabric be priced higher than another?

Selecting a Fabric

The array of different fabrics in a store can seem so overwhelming that you may not know where to start. Perhaps you have some idea based on the illustrations in the pattern catalog. However, there are other factors that will help you choose the right fabric.

What the Pattern Tells You

The back of the pattern envelope suggests the types of fabrics that are most suitable for the shape and style of the garment. A soft fabric, such as challis (SHA-lee), might be suggested for a soft, gathered shape. For casual clothes, the pattern might suggest a more durable, sturdy fabric, such as denim or sailcloth, or a comfortable fabric, such as sweatshirt fleece or a T-shirt knit. Dressier fabrics will be recommended for a special occasion item. You might use taffeta or satin, for example, to make a formal prom dress.

Using Your Knowledge

In trying to determine which fabric is right for your project, remember what you learned in the previous chapter about the characteristics of different fabrics. In addition, you should consider:

- **Personal style.** Your feelings about yourself and the clothes you wear will help you make a decision about fabric. What feels comfortable? What best expresses your personality? An active person who spends a lot of time outdoors might choose durable, plain fabrics. Someone who likes to express his or her individuality might choose a bold print or a bright color.
- **Look and feel.** Find a mirror and drape the fabric over your shoulder to see how it looks on you. Consider not only the color, but also the softness or firmness. Does it drape nicely for a garment with soft gathers? Is it crisp enough for the details in the pattern?

- **Seasonal wear.** The climate in which you live will influence your choice of fabric. You wouldn't want a heavy wool for summer or a lightweight cotton fabric for winter. If you plan to wear the garment often, you'll want a fabric that wears well.
- **Fabric care.** If you don't want to spend time hand washing and ironing, pick an easy-care fabric. If your budget is limited, avoid a fabric that needs dry cleaning. To find out about fabric care, read the label at the end of the bolt of fabric.
- **Sewing difficulty.** Some fabrics are easier to work with than others. Fabrics with a one-way design or a nap are more time-consuming to lay the pattern on. The top edges of the pattern pieces must be placed in the same direction so that, when the pieces are sewn together, the nap or design will retain the same look throughout the garment. Because plaids need to be matched at the seams, they are more difficult to lay out and cut. Fabrics that ravel easily can also be frustrating to work with.

Checking for Quality

When you've found a fabric you like, examine it for flaws, such as torn threads, snags, holes, and grease stains. Crumple the fabric in your hand. Do the wrinkles disappear when you release it? If it's a knit, stretch the fabric across the cut edge, then see if it goes back into shape when you let go. If a fabric does not meet these quality standards, don't buy it.

Buy the best quality fabric you can afford. It is a waste of time and money to work with fabric of poor quality. By choosing a high-quality fabric, you'll enjoy sewing and end up with a garment that is a pleasure to wear.

Deciding How Much Fabric

Check the chart on the back of the pattern envelope. It will tell you the amount of fabric to buy. That amount will depend on the view and the size you'll be using, as well as the fab-

Activities

- **Bits and Pieces.** Tell students that a remnant is a piece of fabric left over after the rest has been sold. Larger remnants are big enough for some projects. Ask: What are the advantages and disadvantages of buying remnants? (*Critical Thinking*)
- **Fashion On the Cheap.** Ask students to describe ways they might use—or have used—notions to inexpensively update their clothing. (*Creativity*)
- **Margin of Safety.** Ask students why, if a pattern view calls for 2 ¾ yards of fabric, they might buy three yards. Remind students that even experienced sewers, and especially beginners, are wise to allow for mistakes. (*Critical Thinking*)

RETEACHING

- **Sewing Run.** Ask students to write a paragraph describing a fictional trip to a clothing store to buy fabric and notions, incorporating the information and suggestions given on pp. 603-604.

MORE ABOUT Thread

Cotton-wrapped polyester thread is best for sheer, lightweight, and medium-weight fabrics made of manufactured fibers and blends. Mercerized cotton is best for such fabrics made from natural fibers. Heavy-weight fabrics of either kind need heavy-duty cotton and cotton-polyester thread.

MORE ABOUT Zippers

In 1893, Whitcomb L. Judson debuted the slide fastener. This was the forerunner of today's zipper, with at least one significant difference: it ran sideways, across the opening. Sales were low because it opened under stress and sometimes tore the garment.

Review

■ **Chapter Review.** Use the contents of the Chapter Review page to help students review concepts, think critically, and apply their knowledge.

■ **Study Guide.** Have students complete the Study Guide for Chapter 62 on p. 204 of the Student Workbook.

■ **What Happened?** Have students write one- or two-statement descriptions of errors that may occur in a finished homemade garment. Have the class suggest how these might have happened. Where in the process of measuring or selecting a pattern or fabric might a mistake have been made?

Evaluation

■ **Chapter Test.** Use the reproducible chapter test provided in the Teacher's Classroom Resources or create your own test using the *Testmaker Software*.

■ **Alternative Assessment.** Ask groups to imagine that, as part of a campaign to promote home sewing, they are to develop a series of posters showing how to take body measurements and choose a pattern and fabrics. Have groups sketch their ideas on sheets of paper, annotated if needed. Remind them that they want to make these tasks seem fun or interesting.

■ **I Know Better.** Ask students to write two paragraphs: one describing how they would have taken measurements and chosen a pattern and fabric before reading this chapter; the other telling how they would do those tasks now.

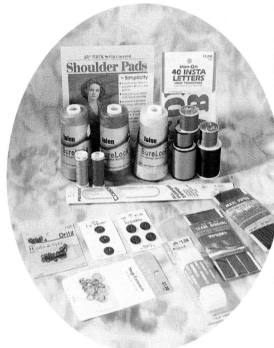

Notions are essential to give your garment the finishing touches.

ric width. To be sure you purchase the right amount, circle the amount you need on the pattern envelope.

Selecting Notions

At the same time you buy the pattern and fabric, you should buy the notions you'll need to complete the project. The pattern envelope provides a list of specific notions: thread, zippers, buttons, elastic, and trimmings.

Choosing Colors

Always coordinate notions with your fabric. When buying thread, zippers, seam binding, or bias tape, pick a color that matches or that is slightly darker than the fabric. Buttons can match the color of the fabric or they can contrast with the fabric for accent. If you're not sure what style or color notions to buy, get some ideas by looking at ready-to-wear clothing.

Choosing Thread

The thread you use depends on your fabric. All-purpose thread, such as cotton-wrapped polyester and 100 percent polyester, can be used for almost all fabrics. These threads are strong, stretch slightly, and don't shrink. They're especially good for knit and stretch fabrics, as well as for fabrics made from manufactured fibers.

If you will be using a serger, or overlock machine, buy special serger thread on cones. Because three or four cones of thread are used at once, serger thread is finer and lighter weight than all-purpose thread.

Specialty threads are available for machine embroidery, quilting, topstitching, and sewing on buttons. In addition, there are cotton, silk, rayon, and nylon threads for other specialty sewing.

Estimating the Cost

Once you've decided on all the elements of your project, you should estimate the total cost. Multiply the cost per yard of the fabric by the number of yards needed. Then add the cost of the pattern and thread, plus buttons, zippers, and any other notions required. If the total cost is more than you planned to spend, look for a less expensive fabric, or shop at another store.

604 **UNIT 7 Clothing and Textiles**

REAL-LIFE APPLICATION

Ask students to think of a garment they would like to own. Challenge them to act on what they have learned in this chapter to prepare to make that article. They can take their measurements, locate a pattern and fabric, pick out notions, and determine the cost of the project. Caution students not to actually purchase anything, but encourage them to save notes on their "research" to use as they gain knowledge and experience.

Chapter 62 Review

Reviewing the Facts

1. How can you be sure that the measurements you've taken are accurate?
2. Why does a page in a pattern catalog often have several different views of a garment?
3. Describe some strategies you would use when choosing a pattern.
4. List three pieces of information you can obtain from the pattern envelope.
5. List three factors you should consider when choosing a fabric for a particular garment.
6. How can you be sure to select the right notions for your sewing project?

Thinking Critically

1. Suppose that you and a friend buy a pattern together. You don't want to dress alike, however. How could each of you use the same pattern but come up with garments that are unique?
2. Why is it a good idea to estimate the cost of a project before making a final decision on the type of fabric you will use?

Applying Your Knowledge

1. **Taking Body Measurements.** Have someone help you take your measurements, following the guidelines in this chapter. Using the pattern size charts found in a pattern catalog, determine the best figure type and pattern size for you to use.
2. **Making a Shopping List.** Study a pattern envelope provided by your teacher. Choose a pattern size and view, then write a list of the fabric and notions you would need to make the item. Describe the color of the fabric and the type of notions you would need. Trade patterns and lists with another student. Check each other's work.

Making Connections

1. **Business.** Your class wants to raise money to help sponsor a local Special Olympics team. You've decided to sell stuffed animals. Draw up a brief plan that describes the pattern you would use, the supplies needed, and how you would market your product. Present your plan to the class.
2. **Math.** Use the back of a pattern envelope to determine how much fabric you will need to make a garment in your size that has at least two variations, such as length of sleeves or skirt. Assume that the fabric you've chosen costs $7.98 a yard. Determine how much the fabric would cost for each garment variation. Determine how much the fabric for the garment would cost if it were on sale for 20 percent off.

Building Your Portfolio

Estimating the Cost of a Project
Take the shopping list you made in "Applying Your Knowledge" #2, or make up a new list following those directions. Then find prices for each item on your list. Estimate the total cost of making the garment you chose. Write a summary of your findings. Include the summary and any lists and worksheets in your portfolio.

Chapter 63

Chapter Overview

Chapter 63 introduces students to the sewing machine and the serger—their parts, operation, accessories, and care. The chapter also describes smaller sewing tools and their uses.

Motivator

■ **Leadfoot?** Ask: Do you think learning to use a sewing machine is any more difficult than learning to drive a car? What advantages are common to acquiring both skills? What added benefits are there in knowing how to use a sewing machine? Encourage students to look at this chapter as a kind of "driver's education."

Objectives

Discuss the chapter objectives on this page. Remind students that the objectives focus on important chapter concepts.

Vocabulary

Point out that some terms in this chapter are picturesque: they help students envision their definition. Ask: What do you think *feed dogs* do? *Feed fabric along machine.* What does a *lockstitch* look like? *Interlocked in the middle.*

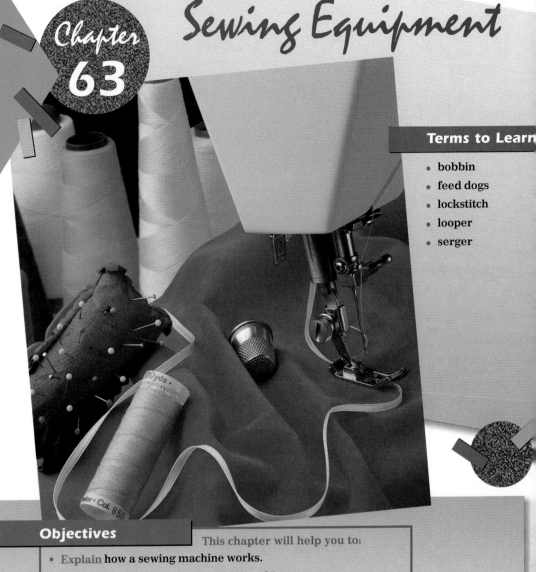

Chapter 63

Sewing Equipment

Terms to Learn

- bobbin
- feed dogs
- lockstitch
- looper
- serger

Objectives

This chapter will help you to:

- Explain **how a sewing machine works.**
- Describe **how to care for a sewing machine.**
- Distinguish **between the way a serger works and the way a conventional sewing machine works.**
- Identify **the correct sewing tools for measuring, marking, cutting, and pressing.**

CHAPTER RESOURCES

Student Workbook
Study Guide, pp. 208-209
Activity, *Machine Parts*, pp. 210-211

Teacher's Classroom Resources
Lesson Plan, p. 67

Clothing Lab, pp. 36-48
Extension #91, *Common Sewing Machine Problems*, p. 97
Life Skills, *Sewing Machine Shopping*, pp. 98-99
Chapter 63 Test, pp. 131-132

Performance Assessment, *Using Sewing Equipment*, pp. 98-99
Reteaching, *Sewing Machine or Serger?* p. 69

Have you ever stopped to think about how people made clothing before there were sewing machines? Early people used stone and bone needles and thread made from animal sinews. The Chinese are credited with first using needles made from steel. By the end of the 17th century, needle making was an important industry in England.

Machines capable of some types of sewing were patented in Europe as early as 1790. Until after 1850, however, most sewing was still done by hand. Elias Howe, with his 1846 patent, is usually credited with inventing the sewing machine. Howe was actually one of several inventors who contributed to the creation of the machine that revolutionized how clothing has been made over the years.

Today, electronic, computerized sewing machines and high-speed overlock machines (usually called sergers) are available for home use, helping individuals create clothing, accessories, and home decorations. In this chapter, you will become familiar with the basic operations of these machines and other basic sewing equipment.

The Sewing Machine

A sewing machine is one of the most important pieces of sewing equipment. Although sewing machines vary in capabilities and accessories, each one has the same basic parts and controls. Refer to **Figure 63.1** on page 608, which shows the parts of a sewing machine, as you read this chapter.

How It Works

Sewing machines join pieces of fabric together with a **lockstitch,** *a stitch that uses a thread above the fabric to join another thread (the bobbin thread) coming from below the fabric.* These two threads are linked, or locked, in the middle of the fabric layers. A tension control device on the sewing machine helps keep the stitches even.

The fabric is moved along by a part of the machine called the **feed dogs,** *two small rows of metal teeth that advance the fabric evenly for each stitch.* The process of stitching and positioning is repeated over and over to create a row of stitching.

Sewing machines are operated by a foot or knee control. A handwheel raises and lowers the needle as you begin and end stitching. More advanced machines allow you to raise and lower the needle by tapping the foot control. **Figure 63.1** identifies additional machine parts and their functions.

Threading the Machine

Every sewing machine model is threaded a bit differently. The basic steps, however, are the same for all machines. Thread goes from the spool, to the upper tension control, to the take-up lever, and then down to the needle. Thread guides keep the thread from tangling along the way. Diagrams in the machine manual will explain exactly how to thread the particular machine.

You must also wind and insert the **bobbin,** *a small spool that holds the bottom thread.* Wind the bobbin and insert it in the bobbin case according to the directions supplied in the manual.

Adjusting the Stitch

As you begin each sewing job, you may need to adjust the type and length of stitches, depending on the fabric and type of job. Every sewing machine has controls to make these adjustments. In recent years, most sewing machine manufacturers have converted the length controls to the metric system. Instead of the number of stitches per inch, manufacturers now list the number of stitches per centimeter. A comparison of stitches per inch (in.) to stitches per centimeter (cm) is included in the list below.

Here are four main types of stitches (shown in **Figure 63.1**) that are commonly used:

- **Regular stitch.** This is a medium-length stitch (10-12 stitches per in. or 3-5 stitches per cm) used for most purposes.
- **Basting stitch.** This is a long stitch (4-6 stitches per in. or 1-2 stitches per cm) used for temporarily holding layers of fabric together and for gathering.

CHAPTER 63   Sewing Equipment   607

TEACH

Topics on p. 607:
- **How a Sewing Machine Works**
- **Threading the Machine**
- **Stitches**

Checking Comprehension

✓ What is the function of the feed dogs? *To move fabric into position for next stitch.*

✓ When would you use a basting stitch? *To temporarily hold fabric layers together; to make gathers.*

Activity

■ **Tense Situation.** Ask students to predict what would happen if the tension between the upper thread and the bobbin thread were uneven. (*Critical Thinking*)

MULTICULTURAL *Perspectives*

Point out that groups of people in some parts of the world still do not have ready access to electricity. Ask the class if and how these people might still use sewing machines. Under what conditions do students think sewing machines would be helpful additions to such cultures? Under what conditions might sewing machines cause harmful disruptions?

MORE ABOUT Bobbins

Some machines have winders built into the bobbin case, but most bobbins must be removed from their cases to be refilled with thread. Show students how to place the bobbin on the winder and wrap it with thread, holding the end of the thread until the bobbin winder spins a few seconds and catches the thread securely. Advise students to make sure the thread winds evenly, perhaps by guiding it between their fingers, until the bobbin is about three-quarters full.

- **Sewing Machine Parts**
- **Stitches (continued)**
- **Needles and Accessories**
- **Sewing Machine Care**
- **Sergers**

Checking Comprehension

✓ What is the main difference between the regular, basting, and reinforcement stitch? *Length.*

✓ How can you tell when the tension of the stitches is even? *Stitches look the same on both sides of fabric.*

✓ Describe the two types of sewing machine needles and their uses. *General purpose (universal)—sharp, used on most fabrics; ballpoint—rounded point, used for knits.*

✓ What are sergers used for? *Making special stitches on garment seams and edges.*

SPECIAL NEEDS *Strategies*

Inefficient Readers. Review Figure 63.1 with students before practicing with an actual machine. Quiz them on the definitions of some parts. Have them trace the path of the upper thread from the spool to the needle.

608

Figure 63.1
PARTS OF THE SEWING MACHINE

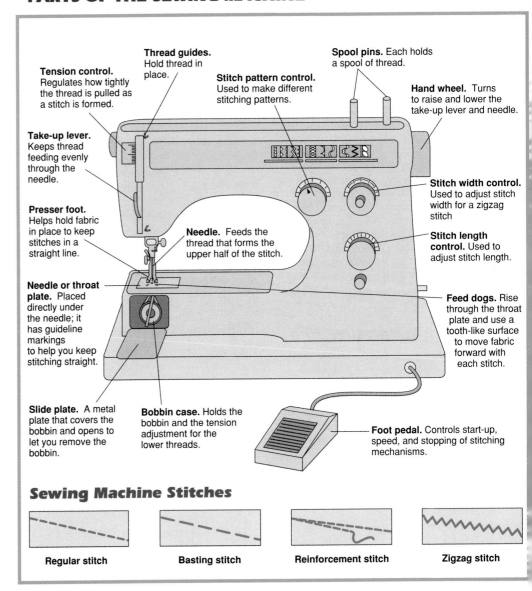

Tension control. Regulates how tightly the thread is pulled as a stitch is formed.

Thread guides. Hold thread in place.

Stitch pattern control. Used to make different stitching patterns.

Spool pins. Each holds a spool of thread.

Hand wheel. Turns to raise and lower the take-up lever and needle.

Take-up lever. Keeps thread feeding evenly through the needle.

Stitch width control. Used to adjust stitch width for a zigzag stitch

Presser foot. Helps hold fabric in place to keep stitches in a straight line.

Needle. Feeds the thread that forms the upper half of the stitch.

Stitch length control. Used to adjust stitch length.

Needle or throat plate. Placed directly under the needle; it has guideline markings to help you keep stitching straight.

Feed dogs. Rise through the throat plate and use a tooth-like surface to move fabric forward with each stitch.

Slide plate. A metal plate that covers the bobbin and opens to let you remove the bobbin.

Bobbin case. Holds the bobbin and the tension adjustment for the lower threads.

Foot pedal. Controls start-up, speed, and stopping of stitching mechanisms.

Sewing Machine Stitches

| Regular stitch | Basting stitch | Reinforcement stitch | Zigzag stitch |

DID YOU KNOW?

Some computerized sewing machines allow sewers to use preprogrammed decorative stitches or to design their own. Manufacturers are now seeking ways to link sewers' machines with their home computers, to store custom stitches in the computer's memory. Other features include a special motor that allows sewers to stitch on thick fabrics; an electronic sensor to signal that the bobbin is nearly empty; and other sensors that adjust thread tension to match the fabric and stitch selection.

- **Reinforcement stitch.** This is a short stitch (18-20 stitches per in. or 7-8 stitches per cm) used to strengthen a corner or a point.
- **Zigzag stitch.** This is a sideways stitch used to finish seam allowances, make buttonholes, and sew special seams. Stitch width and length are adjusted according to the desired result.

Specialty stitches are built into some machines and used for hemming, stitching stretch fabrics, and decorative stitching. Attachments, such as embroidery patterns, can be added to computerized sewing machines for more options. In addition to controls for the stitch length and type, some machines have controls to adjust the width of zigzag and other specialty stitches.

You can adjust the tightness and looseness of the stitches with the tension control on the upper thread. This control affects the location at which the top and bobbin threads interlock. If one thread lies flat against the fabric while the thread on the other side forms loops, the tension needs adjusting. When the stitches look the same on both sides of the fabric, the tension is balanced.

Machine Needles

Machine needles come in two basic types. General purpose, or universal, needles have a sharp point for use with most fabrics, woven or knit. Ballpoint needles have a rounded point and are used for knits.

Needles also come in a range of sizes. You will see both European sizes (ranging from 70 to 110) and American sizes (ranging from 9 to 18) marked on the package. In both systems the lower the number, the finer the needle.

A bent or damaged needle will not stitch properly. If a needle seems dull, replace it right away to prevent damage to the fabric and the machine.

Accessories

Modern machines perform many sewing tasks. You may need separate attachments for some operations. To sew zippers, for example, use a zipper foot that allows you to stitch close to the zipper teeth. Special attachments may also be used for hemming, gathering, and attaching bindings.

Caring for the Machine

A sewing machine is a finely engineered piece of equipment that requires regular maintenance and careful handling. After each use, unplug the machine. Put it away in its cabinet or case, or cover it.

Clean it regularly with a soft sewing machine brush to keep moving parts free of dust and lint. Keep lint away from the area around the feed dogs and the bobbin case. Directions for cleaning the machine are in the owner's manual.

Oil the machine occasionally with sewing machine oil. Refer to the manual to see where and how often to oil the machine. After oiling, carefully wipe away excess oil to avoid spotting your fabric.

The Serger

The **serger,** or overlock sewing machine, is *a machine that trims, sews, and overcasts in one step.* It creates the special stitches used on the seams and edges of ready-to-wear garments. Sergers sew at twice the speed of conventional sewing machines—up to 1,500 stitches per minute—and use from 2 to 5 threads to make a stitch. Refer to **Figure 63.2** on page 610, which shows the parts of a serger, as you read this section.

Sergers use two basic types of stitches: overlock and overedge. An overlock stitch is used for seams. It locks the fabric layers together at the edge of the seam allowance, fin-

---

Focus on Troubleshooting Skills

Alert students to these problems and their remedies:

Skipped stitches: make sure needle size and type are right for fabric; rethread machine; loosen tension.

Bunching of thread: hold thread ends behind presser foot when starting to stitch.

Puckering: loosen tension; replace needle; shorten stitch length.

Thread breaks: check threading and needle; begin stitching more slowly.

Machine jams: check threading, needle position, and bobbin.

Topics on pp. 610-611:
- Parts of the Serger
- Capabilities of the Serger

Checking Comprehension

✔ Name and describe the two basic serger stitches. *Overlock—locks fabric layers together at edge of seam allowance and finishes edges; overedge—finishes edge of single piece of fabric.*

✔ How are sergers used in sewing projects? *In addition to sewing machine; for its particular capabilities.*

USING VISUALS

Refer students to Figures 63.1 and 63.2 to answer these questions: What parts do sergers and sewing machine have in common? *Thread guides, spool pins, hand wheel, needle, feed dogs, tension controls.* What are the major differences? *More threads, knives on serger.*

How many tension controls would a three-thread serger need? *Three.*

How do the serger's knife blades function like scissors? *One blade remains stationary, other moves against it.*

Figure 63.2
PARTS OF THE SERGER

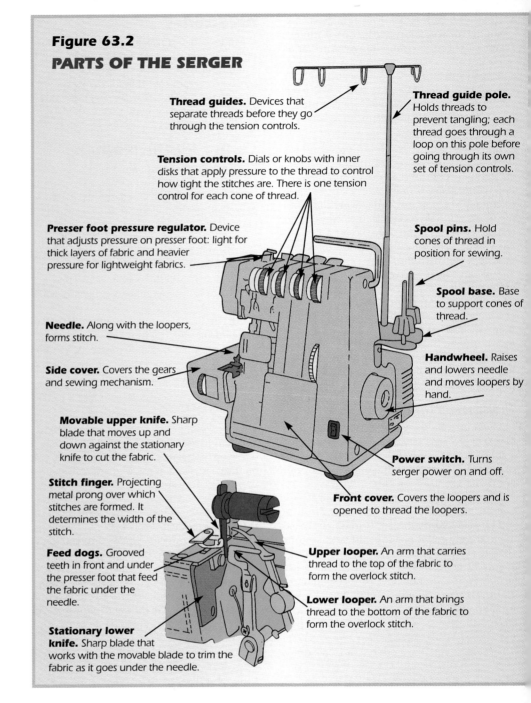

Thread guides. Devices that separate threads before they go through the tension controls.

Tension controls. Dials or knobs with inner disks that apply pressure to the thread to control how tight the stitches are. There is one tension control for each cone of thread.

Presser foot pressure regulator. Device that adjusts pressure on presser foot: light for thick layers of fabric and heavier pressure for lightweight fabrics.

Needle. Along with the loopers, forms stitch.

Side cover. Covers the gears and sewing mechanism.

Movable upper knife. Sharp blade that moves up and down against the stationary knife to cut the fabric.

Stitch finger. Projecting metal prong over which stitches are formed. It determines the width of the stitch.

Feed dogs. Grooved teeth in front and under the presser foot that feed the fabric under the needle.

Stationary lower knife. Sharp blade that works with the movable blade to trim the fabric as it goes under the needle.

Thread guide pole. Holds threads to prevent tangling; each thread goes through a loop on this pole before going through its own set of tension controls.

Spool pins. Hold cones of thread in position for sewing.

Spool base. Base to support cones of thread.

Handwheel. Raises and lowers needle and moves loopers by hand.

Power switch. Turns serger power on and off.

Front cover. Covers the loopers and is opened to thread the loopers.

Upper looper. An arm that carries thread to the top of the fabric to form the overlock stitch.

Lower looper. An arm that brings thread to the bottom of the fabric to form the overlock stitch.

610   **UNIT 7   Clothing and Textiles**

DID YOU KNOW?

Sergers were developed in the early 1900s by manufacturers of military uniforms made of serge, a cloth woven in a twill pattern from woolen fibers. Sergers enabled the clothing manufacturers to provide a great many uniforms quickly and inexpensively.

MORE ABOUT Sergers

The numbers used to identify a serger refer to the number of threads it uses. A 4/2-thread serger uses two or four threads; a 4/3-thread serger, three or four threads. Both types have two needles and two loopers.

ishing the edges as it stitches the seam. Some machines make a chain stitch, or a safety stitch, along with the overlock stitch. This gives added strength to seams. An overedge stitch, the other basic stitch, finishes the edge of a single piece of fabric.

A serger is used along *with* a sewing machine, not as a replacement for conventional sewing. Each serger has special capabilities that determine how the machine will be used in a sewing project. Although a serger can be used for all seams, a conventional sewing machine is used for buttonholes, straight-stitch application of a zipper, and topstitching detail. Whenever you are unsure of a garment's

fit, temporarily stitch the garment with the regular machine, using basting stitches. Once a seam is serged, no seam allowances remain. You won't be able to let out a serged seam to make the garment fit better.

Sergers also differ from conventional sewing machines in other ways. Sergers have several unique features:

- **More threads.** A conventional sewing machine uses two threads. Sergers use two, three, four, or five threads, depending on the type of machine. Each thread goes through a separate tension control. A four-thread serger meets the needs of most sewers.

In Touch with TECHNOLOGY

New Serger Technology

Thanks to computerization, sergers can perform many complicated functions that make it easier to create high-quality, professional-looking garments. Some new developments in serger technology include:

- **Automatic tension adjustment.** The computer automatically adjusts tension settings.
- **Automatic shutoff.** Power is shut off if, for example, the presser foot is up or a looper cover opens.
- **Panel display.** An illuminated digital panel displays such information as the stitch selection and the needle stop position.
- **Easier threading.** Some machines self-thread through tube-shaped loopers. Thread will not slip out of these loopers.
- **Computer-enhanced stitch selection.** Some machines can memorize custom stitches. In others, preprogrammed stitches can be supplemented with a card containing additional stitch techniques, as well as empty spaces for saving your own stitches.
- **Computerized sewing guidance.** After entering information about the stitch you want and the fabric you are using, the machine

provides guidance. It tells which needle to use, how to thread the machine and adjust tension, and what settings to use for the differential feed and stitch length.

Various serger models offer different features. If you're shopping for a serger, compare and test several models. Be sure to ask about local service, lessons, and additional technical support. If you're replacing a serger, see if the dealer accepts trade-ins.

Thinking Critically About Technology

1. Do you think the new features available on sergers makes choosing a machine even more complicated? How would you choose?
2. Why would it be unwise to select a serger based on price alone?

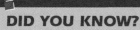
DID YOU KNOW?

A ruffling attachment on a serger can make it easier to sew ruffled pillows or curtains. The serger can gather fabric, attach the ruffle, and finish the seam, all at the same time. The serger's rolled-hem stitch finishes sheer curtains for a delicate, billowy look.

Focus on Consumer Skills

New sewers should buy a less expensive sewing machine and trade up as their skills improve. Many dealers take trade-ins and apply them toward the price of a new machine. As you consider buying a sewing machine or serger, try it out using fabrics you want to work on.

Three-thread overlock stitch

Four-thread overlock stitch

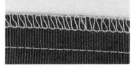
Five-thread overlock stitch

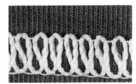
Flatlock stitch

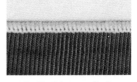
Rolled hem stitch

These examples show what serger stitches look like. All are overlock stitches except for the rolled hem stitch, which is overedge.

TEACH

Topic on pp. 612-614:

- **Serger Features**
- **Measuring, Marking, and Cutting Tools**
- **Equipment for Pressing and Sewing**

Checking Comprehension

✓ What parts on a serger correspond to the bobbin of a sewing machine? *Loopers.*

✓ What is the advantage of retractable knives? *Lets you make decorative stitches without cutting fabric.*

✓ Which is lighter in weight—serger or regular thread? Why? *Serger; up to five may be used in one seam.*

✓ What are three ways to mark fabric? *With tracing paper and wheel; chalk; liquid marking pens.*

✓ What is a tailor's ham used for? *Pressing curved seams and darts.*

CROSS-CURRICULAR ACTIVITY
Science

Suggest that students learn why cutting paper dulls the blades of scissors and shears much faster than cutting fabric. How does this knowledge help them to keep the blades sharp? Have students share their findings with the class.

- **Loopers.** Sergers do not have bobbins. Instead they have **loopers,** which are *parts that perform as bobbins do on conventional sewing machines.* One or two threads in a serger go to the needles. Two or three threads go through loopers. Looper threads loop around each other and are interlocked with the needle thread.

- **Cutting knives.** Sergers also use two sharp knife blades, one movable and the other stationary, to trim and smooth the fabric to the width of the stitch just before it goes under the needle and loopers. These knives assure ravel-free seams and seam finishes. The knife blades can be retracted for some stitches so that you can sew along an edge without cutting the fabric.

- **Special edge finishes and decorative stitching.** Sergers can do narrow rolled hems, like the hems on napkins or silk scarves. Sergers also can produce a blind hem stitch and a flatlock stitch. The flatlock stitch can be used to decorate lingerie, T-shirts, and sweatshirts. Some sergers can stitch a cover stitch, a decorative stitch used on the outside of sportswear. This stitch is common on seams that connect ribbing to flat knit fabric. The decorative stitches are made without engaging the knife blades.

- **Special threads.** Sergers use special threads that are cross wound on cones or tubes for smoother feeding. Because up to five threads may be used in one seam, serger thread is lighter weight than regular thread. The loopers also can handle special threads (such as metallics) and narrow ribbons for decorative stitching and edges.

- **Differential feed.** Some sergers have a differential feed. It provides different speeds for feeding the upper and lower layers of fabric. This makes such fabrics as sheers and silks easier to handle, allowing seams that are smooth and free of puckers.

Other Tools

Every sewing project requires equipment for measuring, cutting, marking, pinning, hand stitching, and pressing. **Figures 63.3 and 63.4** on pages 613-614 display basic tools that will help you complete your sewing projects successfully.

Focus on Decision-Making Skills

Ask students to imagine they want to sew a shirt. They have a tape measure, scissors, and a box of pins; they have access to an older but working sewing machine, an iron, and ironing board. After buying a pattern, fabric, and notions, they have enough money for two or three additional, basic sewing tools or one piece of equipment. Ask: Which item or items would you buy? Why?

Figure 63.3

MEASURING, MARKING, AND CUTTING TOOLS

Measuring Tools

Tape measure. Needed to take body measurements. It should be flexible and 60 in. (1.5 m) long.

Yardstick/meter stick. Used to measure fabric, check grainlines, mark hems, and draw long lines. Yardstick measures 36 in. (91.5 cm); meter stick measures 1 meter (39.5 in.).

Ruler. A 12-in. (30.5-cm) ruler with ⅛-in. (3-mm) markings can be used to measure and mark lines. A see-through plastic ruler is practical to use with a rotary cutter to cut pieces and strips for quilting and patchwork.

Sewing gauge. A 6-in. (15-cm) ruler with an adjustable sliding marker used to measure seams or hems.

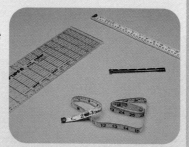

Marking Equipment

Tracing paper. Comes in several colors. Choose a color that will show up on the fabric without being too dark. Double-faced tracing paper allows you to mark two layers of fabric at one time.

Tracing wheel. Used with tracing paper to transfer pattern markings. Wheels with sawtooth edges can be used for most fabrics. Smooth-edged wheels are best for delicate fabrics.

Chalk. Chalk can be used to mark most fabrics. The markings can be brushed off or will disappear when pressed with an iron. Chalk is available as colored squares, pencils, or powder. Chalk wheels that hold powdered chalk are popular because they produce a fine line and keep hands clean.

Liquid marking pens. Used to mark tucks, darts, pleats, and pocket locations. Use the type that washes off with cold water. Heat may set the marks permanently, so remove markings before pressing.

Cutting Tools

Pinking shears. Shears with zigzag-shaped blades used to finish the edge of firmly woven fabrics.

Shears. Used to cut fabric, these have long blades, and the two handles are shaped differently. Bent-handled shears are easiest to use because the fabric can stay flat on a surface as you cut.

Scissors. Used for trimming and clipping, these are smaller than shears. Both handles are the same shape.

Seam ripper. Used for removing stitches, this is a tool with a sharp, pointed end and a small blade on the handle.

Rotary cutter. A fabric cutter that looks like a pizza cutter, with a sharp, round blade for accurately cutting several layers of fabric. It should always be used with a special plastic cutting mat.

Cutting mat. A plastic mat to use with the rotary cutter. It does not dull the rotary blade or mar the cutting table. Some mats are called "self-healing" because the cutting lines from the rotary blade disappear and do not mark the surface.

CHAPTER 63   Sewing Equipment   613

Activities

■ **Bare Essentials.** Ask students which of the tools in Figure 63.3 they think are essential even for beginning sewers. *(Decision Making)*

RETEACHING

■ **Tool Time.** Ask groups to write five- to seven-item quizzes about sewing tools and their uses. Have them write the answers on a separate sheet of paper. Have groups exchange and complete the quizzes. Review the answers in class for accuracy.

ENRICHMENT

■ **Watch Those Fingers.** Ask groups to list five safety guidelines for using the items in Figures 63.3 and 63.4. Have groups share their tips with the class. Explain that they will learn more about using these items safely in Chapter 64.

USING VISUALS

Refer students to figures 63.3 and 63.4 to answer these questions: What tool would you use to double-check the hem of a long skirt? *Yardstick or meter stick.* How and why should you wash garment marked with a liquid marking pen? *In cold water; to remove marks before pressing, which may set them permanently.* What items are especially useful for pressing the shoulders of garments? *Tailor's ham, sleeve board.* What is the difference between pins and needles? *Pins have heads; needles have eyes.*

MORE ABOUT Pins

Brass or stainless steel pins are best for sewing; they won't rust easily. For delicate fabrics, use "silk" pins; they are very fine and don't leave puncture marks. Remind students that loose pins can cause damage if they fall into sewing machine mechanisms; they can break the needle if stitched over. Encourage students to wear small pincushions on their wrists for convenient last-minute removal.

Review

■ **Chapter Review.** Use the contents of the Chapter Review page to help students review concepts, think critically, and apply their knowledge.

■ **Study Guide.** Have students complete the Study Guide for Chapter 63 on p. 208 of the Student Workbook.

■ **What Am I?** Write the name of each machine and tool in this chapter on a separate note card. Duplicate some, if needed, so every student has a card. Have students draw a card and describe the function of the item while the class tries to identify it. If a student has described an item earlier, those with duplicate cards must describe it in another way.

Evaluation

■ **Chapter Test.** Use the reproducible chapter test provided in the Teacher's Classroom Resources or create your own test using the *Testmaker Software*.

■ **Alternative Assessment.** Have groups read the guidelines from a pattern and decide which of the machines, tools, and pieces of equipment discussed in the chapter they would need to sew the garment. Have groups explain their choices in a presentation to the class, using the pattern and other available visual aids.

■ **Qualified Personnel.** Have students describe personal qualities or skills that would be helpful for using the items discussed in this chapter. Have them explain using specific examples.

614

Figure 63.4

EQUIPMENT FOR PRESSING AND SEWING

Pressing Equipment

Steam iron. An iron that steams and sprays at any setting gives the best results.

Ironing board. Your ironing board should have a well-padded, clean cover. It also should be adjustable for your height.

Press cloth. For some fabrics a press cloth is needed to prevent shiny marks caused by the iron's heat. Dampen the cloth to provide additional steam for hard-to-press fabrics.

Tailor's ham. This firm cushion, shaped like a ham, is used for pressing curved seams and darts.

Sleeve board. This small ironing board enables the whole sleeve to be evenly pressed and is convenient for small pieces.

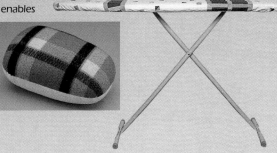

Other Small Sewing Equipment

Pins. Used to hold the pattern on the fabric for cutting and to hold fabric layers together for stitching. Straight pins with colored heads are easy to see and use.

Needles. Needles for hand sewing come in a variety of sizes and lengths. The smaller the number, the larger the needle. Sizes 7 and 8 are good for most purposes.

Pincushion. Traditional pincushions hold pins so that they can't spill. Some have a small emery-packed section to keep needles sharp.

Magnetic pin grabbers are convenient to use and are handy for picking up spilled pins.

Thimble. A thimble made of metal or plastic protects your finger while it pushes the needle through the fabric when hand sewing. Wear it on your middle finger.

614   UNIT 7   Clothing and Textiles

Focus on Consumer Skills

Like sewing machines and sergers, other tools and equipment come in various models and prices. Have pairs select one group of items from Figures 63.3 and 63.4 and one area fabric store or fabric department. (Approve choices in advance to ensure variety in both. You might also contact the stores to ensure they have the items students have chosen.) Have students list the models of items in that group that the store carries and the price of each. Have the class compile their research into a chart to be copied and distributed for students' use.

Review

Reviewing the Facts

1. How does a sewing machine join pieces of fabric?
2. How should a sewing machine be cared for between uses?
3. Compare the ways sewing machines and sergers are used.
4. Why is it often a good idea to baste a garment's seam before serging it?
5. Describe at least one sewing tool that is used for each of the following tasks: measuring, marking, cutting, and pressing.
6. What is the difference between scissors and shears?

Thinking Critically

1. What factors should you consider when purchasing a sewing machine or a serger?
2. Why is it important to learn how to operate and maintain a sewing machine properly?

Applying Your Knowledge

1. **Comparing Features.** Think about the sewing machines you have used or seen advertised. What five features would you consider most valuable? Why?
2. **Comparing Costs.** List any sewing tools and equipment that you already have. What additional tools would you need to begin a sewing project? Estimate the cost of the tools. If the cost is too high, what other options might you have?
3. **Following Instructions.** Depending on the make and model, there is some variation in the way sewing machines are threaded. Demonstrate how to thread several different sewing machines. Use the machine itself or a photocopy of the machine diagram from the owner's manual. Remember to include directions for threading the bobbin.

Making Connections

1. **Economics.** Look through sewing magazines for advertisements that display sewing machines. Make up a chart that compares features and prices of three different models. Recommend a purchase based on your research.
2. **History.** It wasn't until the mid-1860s that a cotton thread strong enough for machine sewing was developed. The new thread was labeled "O.N.T." (for "our new thread") and still retains that label. Why do you think sewing machines require stronger thread than hand sewing?

Building Your Portfolio

Making a Sewing Sample
Today many types of thread are available; choose three different types of thread, and hand sew a line of running stitches with each. How does each one handle? Predict how each one might perform in a sewing machine or serger. Then use the threads to sew a sample of stitches on a sewing machine or serger. What differences do you notice with each thread? Label your sample, and add it to your portfolio.

CHAPTER 63   Sewing Equipment   615

ANSWERS TO REVIEWING THE FACTS

1. With lockstitch: thread above fabric joins one from below, linking between fabric layers.
2. Unplug; cover or put into cabinet or case; clean regularly with soft brush; oil occasionally.
3. Sewing machines can do all types of sewing tasks. Sergers sew special seams and edges quickly; can't be used for some tasks, such as making buttonholes, applying zippers.
4. So you can adjust for fit; serged seam has no allowance, so adjusting is impossible.
5. See pp. 613-614.
6. Scissors are smaller than shears; both handles are same shape. Shears' handles are shaped differently, may be bent.

ANSWERS TO THINKING CRITICALLY

1. Answers may include: price; sewing needs and skills, now and in future; features of different models; dealer's and manufacturer's reputation.
2. Incorrect use could result in poor quality garment, damage to machine, injury.

Chapter 64

FOCUS

Chapter Overview

Chapter 64 helps students prepare to sew. They learn how to check and adjust patterns; prepare fabric; lay out, pin, and cut pattern pieces; and transfer pattern markings to the fabric pieces. Illustrations lead students through the steps.

Motivator

■ **Changing Times.** If possible, gather a number of old patterns. Show these, along with new patterns, to students. What differences do they note as they examine all the patterns? Help students see that there are not only style changes, but differences in the patterns themselves.

Objectives

Discuss the chapter objectives on this page. Remind students that the objectives focus on important chapter concepts.

Vocabulary

Point out that the word *selvage* comes from "self edge," meaning the narrow woven border on the long edges of fabric. This self edge prevents the fabric from raveling. Also help students distinguish between *selvage* and *salvage,* meaning to save or rescue.

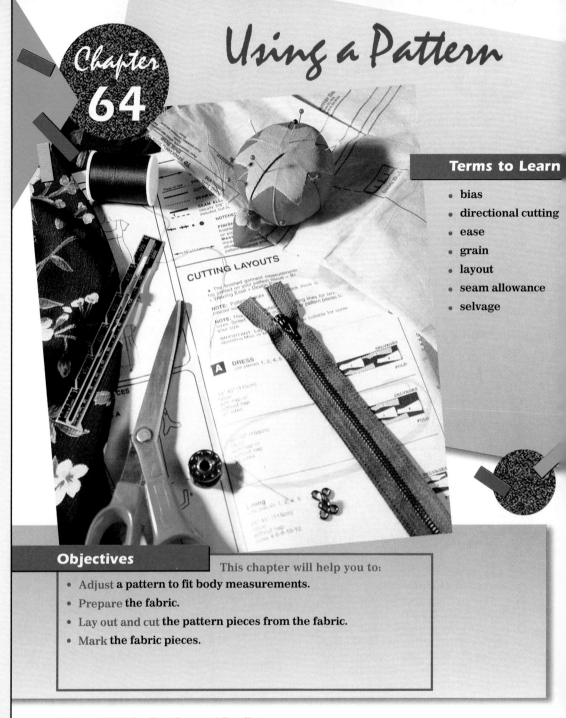

Chapter 64

Using a Pattern

Terms to Learn

- bias
- directional cutting
- ease
- grain
- layout
- seam allowance
- selvage

Objectives

This chapter will help you to:

- **Adjust** a pattern to fit body measurements.
- **Prepare** the fabric.
- **Lay out and cut** the pattern pieces from the fabric.
- **Mark** the fabric pieces.

616   **UNIT 7   Clothing and Textiles**

CHAPTER RESOURCES

Student Workbook
Study Guide, p. 212
Activity, *Identify Pattern Markings,* p. 213

Teacher's Classroom Resources
Lesson Plan, p. 68
Clothing Lab, pp. 5-6

Cooperative Learning, *Getting Ready to Sew,* pp. 69-70
Extension #92, *Making the Most of Patterns,* p. 98
Extension #93, *Sewing Safely,* p. 99
Life Skills, *Stop! Before You Cut . . . ,* pp. 100-101

Transparency 55, *Identifying Pattern Markings*
Chapter 64 Test, pp. 133-134
Performance Assessment, *Using a Pattern,* pp.100-101
Reteaching, *Pattern Markings,* p. 70

You have selected your pattern, fabric, and notions. Your sewing equipment is ready. Before you can actually begin sewing on the machine, however, four steps should be completed. You need to:

1. Prepare the pattern.
2. Prepare the fabric.

3. Lay out the pattern pieces and cut the fabric.
4. Mark the fabric.

By following these steps, you will make sure that your finished project looks good and fits well.

Figure 64.1
PATTERNS AND PATTERN TERMS

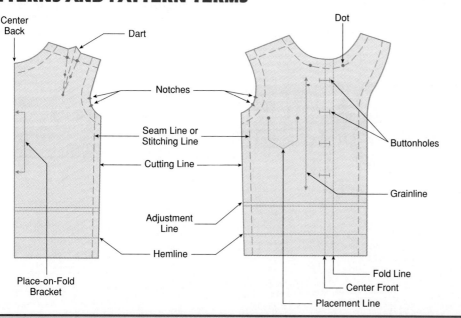

Adjustment line. Double line showing where the pattern may be lengthened or shortened.

Buttonholes. Areas marked by lines that show the exact location and length.

Center front and center back. Solid lines that show the center of the garment.

Cutting line. The heavy outer line along which you cut.

Dart. Two broken lines (stitching lines) and dots (for matching).

Dots. Markings used for matching seams and construction details.

Fold line. Solid line showing where the fabric is to be folded.

Grainline. The heavy solid line with arrows at each end that shows the direction of the grain.

Hemline. Solid line indicating the finished edge of the garment.

Notches. Diamond-shaped symbols along the cutting line that are used for matching fabric pieces to be joined.

Placement line. Line showing the exact location of pocket, fastener, zipper, or trim.

Place-on-fold bracket. Symbol that shows that the pattern piece is to be placed along a fold of fabric.

Seamline or stitching line. Broken line 5/8 in. (1.5 cm) inside the cutting line (unless otherwise noted).

Checking Comprehension

✓ What four steps do you have to complete before you start sewing? *Prepare the pattern; prepare the fabric; lay out the pattern pieces and cut the fabric; mark the fabric.*

Activity

Finding Examples. Have students examine their own pattern pieces for the markings shown in Figure 64.1. Ask them to search their pattern pieces for any other kinds of markings, too, so the class can discuss them and learn what they mean.

USING VISUALS
Patterns and Pattern Terms. Refer students to Figure 64.1. Discuss these questions to check their understanding: Why do some pattern pieces have dots in the seamlines? *For matching the seams of two fabric pieces.* What marking might help if you are long waisted? *Adjustment line.* Should you cut a pattern piece along the hemline? *No, that's the finished edge of the hem. Cut on the marked cutting line.* Should you fold a pattern piece on a fold-line? *No, that's where the fabric will be folded, not the pattern piece.*

DID YOU KNOW?

Early patterns were much simpler—and less helpful—than today's. Before World War II, patterns were mostly blank pieces of tissue. Tiny holes showed dart placement. Other holes indicated pieces that were to be placed on the fabric fold. Instead of step-by-step directions, the instructions were mostly sketches and arrows. Pattern makers used a sort of shorthand to guide sewers. For example, the directions might say, "Use a regulation side-placket closing." Sewers were supposed to know what that meant. Modern sewing techniques are not only less complicated, but also more clearly explained.

Checking Comprehension

✓ Where would you find the meaning of a symbol on a pattern piece? *Front of the pattern guide sheet.*

✓ Why might pattern pieces be larger than the measurements on the pattern envelope? *For ease in wearing the garment.*

✓ How could you lengthen a pattern? *Cut at adjustment line on front and back, move pieces apart, and tape tissue paper between them.*

✓ How can you tell whether to preshrink fabric? *Check label on the fabric bolt; if fabric will shrink more than 1 percent or if label does not mention shrinkage, preshrink.*

✓ What can happen if you don't straighten the grain of fabric? *Finished garment may twist to one side or hang unevenly.*

STRATEGIES THAT WORK

Have students read "Sewing Safely." Ask whether anyone can add safety tips to those listed in the feature

Answers to Think . . .

1. Examples are tripping over an iron cord and getting burned and getting cut by picking up a rotary cutter with an uncovered blade.
2. Teach children about dangers and put away equipment in safe places.

Preparing the Pattern

To begin, take the pattern guide sheet out of the pattern envelope. This sheet gives step-by-step information for laying out, cutting, marking, and sewing the garment or accessory. The front of the guide sheet contains general instructions, information about pattern symbols, and diagrams for laying out the pattern pieces. Circle the layout for your pattern size, view, and width of fabric.

Write your name on the pattern envelope, all the pattern pieces, and the guide sheet. Then select the required pattern pieces and look them over. You will need to become familiar with the terms shown in **Figure 64.1** on page 617. Use a warm—not hot—dry iron to press pattern pieces smooth and flat.

Now, find the measurements that you took before you bought the pattern. Compare them with those listed on the pattern envelope to see if you'll need to adjust the pattern to fit your measurements.

Checking Measurements

If your body measurements do not exactly match those listed on the back of the pattern envelope, you may have to make pattern adjustments. This involves changing the pattern so that the finished garment will fit properly.

Sewing Safely

Sewing tools and equipment require special care and handling. By following the tips below, you can help prevent accidents and injuries:

- Never hold pins by placing them in your mouth or attaching them to your clothing or the arm of a chair. Use a pincushion or a magnetic pin holder. If you drop a pin or needle, pick it up immediately.
- Keep scissors, shears, rotary cutters, and seam rippers closed or covered when not in use.
- Pass cutting tools by clasping the blades and extending the handles to the other person.
- Use rotary cutters only with their special self-healing mat and ruler; always cut away from your body in one smooth motion.
- Use a slow machine speed until you are an experienced sewer.
- Keep your fingers away from machine needles and cutting knives; avoid leaning too close to the machine needle in case it breaks.
- Never machine sew or serge over pins.

- Keep sewing machine, serger, and iron cords where you cannot trip over them. Unplug when they aren't in use.
- Keep your fingers and face away from the steam from an iron. Touch only the handle.
- Rest an iron on its heel when not in use. Let it cool completely before emptying water and storing it.

Making the Strategy Work

Think . . .

1. Give specific examples of how improper handling or storage of sewing tools might cause accidents and injuries.
2. What further safety precautions would have to be taken when children or pets are present in the household?

Try...

Visit the fabric store to look for safety devices for sewing. Do you have any alternative items at home that could be used for sewing safety?

REAL-LIFE APPLICATION

Read the following list to students and have them explain or research appropriate actions to take:

- a cut caused by a seam ripper or the sewing machine needle;

- a burn caused by a hot iron;
- an electrical shock that occurred while plugging in an iron;
- smoking fabric caused by an iron that was left face down.

If there is a difference of 1 in. (2.5 cm) or more between your measurements and the size measurements on the envelope, you will probably have to adjust the pattern. Check with your instructor to be sure, since a loose pattern style may not require adjustment.

You can also compare your measurements to those of the pattern by measuring the pattern pieces. Measure only from seam to seam, without including the **seam allowance**—*the fabric between the line for cutting and the line for stitching.* For clothing, the seam allowance is ⅝ in. (1.5 cm) from the cutting line. If your pattern is multisized and has three or more sizes printed on it, the seam allowance is not marked. You will have to measure it yourself. When you make accessories or crafts, particularly when using a serger, any seam allowance measurements that differ from the usual ⅝ in. (1.5 cm) will be indicated on the guide sheet and pattern pieces.

Remember that clothing patterns include **ease,** *extra room that allows for clothing to fit comfortably.* Because of the ease, pattern pieces measure larger than size measurements. The difference might be 3 to 4 in. (7.5 to 9.5 cm) at the bust or chest, ¾ to 1 in. (2 to 2.5 cm) at the waist, and 2 in. (5 cm) at the hips. Thus, a pattern for 34-in. (86.5-cm) hips would actually measure 36 in. (91.5 cm). Patterns for "activewear"—such as bathing suits, leotards, tights, and biking shorts—will have little or no ease because they fit close to the body.

Simple Adjustments

Shortening or lengthening a pattern is the easiest adjustment to make. An adjustment line is printed on many pattern pieces to show where the piece can be folded or cut.

Shorten a pattern piece by measuring the amount to be shortened up from the adjustment line and drawing a line parallel to the adjustment line. Fold the pattern so the two lines meet, and then tape the fold.

To lengthen a pattern piece, cut it apart at the adjustment line. Then insert and tape a strip of tissue paper to one of the pieces and extend the grainline arrow through the tissue. Attach the remaining piece, matching the grainline, and tape it in place. Don't forget to adjust both the front and the back.

Adjusting for width is a little more complicated. An increase or decrease of an inch (2.5 cm) or less can be done at the side seams. Divide the amount of increase by the number of seamlines. For example, if you want to decrease width by 1 in. (2.5 cm) and have two seams, each seam will be decreased by ½ in. (1.3 cm). Draw new seamlines ¼ in. (6 mm) inside and parallel to the old ones.

You may need to add tissue paper to increase width. If you have to add or subtract more than 1 in. (2.5 cm), get assistance from your instructor. Multisized patterns with three or more separate cutting lines make it easier to adjust the width by gradually blending from one size to the next.

Preparing the Fabric

Determine if the fabric needs to be preshrunk by reading the label on the bolt of the fabric. If the fabric will shrink more than 1 percent or if no information is given, preshrink it before cutting. To preshrink washable fabric, wash and dry it according to the manufacturer's instructions. Fabrics that cannot be washed must be taken to a dry cleaner for preshrinking.

Next, determine if the fabric **grain**—*the direction in which the threads run*—needs to be straightened. Lengthwise and crosswise grains should meet at right angles. If the fabric is not straightened before the pieces are cut, the hemline may hang unevenly or the garment may twist to one side.

To check the grain in a woven fabric, cut crosswise along one thread from one *finished edge of the fabric,* or **selvage,** to the other selvage just below the cut edge. If you cannot see individual threads, clip one selvage and pull out a thread. The missing thread will show as a line; cut along this line. Repeat at the other cut edge. (For knitted fabric, cut along a row of loops at each edge.) Then fold the fabric in half, matching selvage to selvage and cut edge to cut edge. If the fabric isn't smooth and corners don't match, it is off grain.

■ **Wrinkle Remover.** Discuss the benefits of ironing pattern pieces before using them. What might happen if you don't iron them? *(Critical Thinking)*

■ **Emphasis on Fit.** Have students use pattern catalogs to identify several garments that would require precise fitting and several that would forgive small differences between the pattern size and the wearer's measurements. Ask them to locate patterns that are flexible in width and in length, along with patterns that could be worn by both long-waisted and short-waisted people. *(Observation)*

ENRICHMENT

■ **Maladjusted Patterns.** Ask students why they think there are limits to the amount of pattern adjustments they should make. Have them describe how a large adjustment in one area might affect the way other pattern pieces fit together. For example, greatly increasing or reducing the width of a blouse can affect the size of the armholes, making it difficult to fit the sleeves.

CROSS-CURRICULAR ACTIVITY
Math

Have students measure the appropriate areas of pattern pieces and calculate the bust, chest, waist, and hip measurements of their patterns. Remind them not to figure in seam allowances or areas that will be modified by darts and so on. Have students compare these actual measurements with those on the pattern envelope and see how much ease has been allowed. As a class look for trends in the ease allowed.

REAL-LIFE APPLICATION

Read this to students: *Marcella worked carefully because she wanted her dress to fit right. She pinned the pattern pieces together and tried them on before she cut her fabric. The top of the dress seemed way too big, so when Marcella cut the fabric pieces, she took about an inch off each side seam.* Ask students what surprises may await Marcella.

Topics on pp. 620-621:
- **Straightening Grain**
- **Laying Out, Pinning, and Cutting**

Checking Comprehension

✓ What's the difference between the selvage and the bias? *The selvage is the finished edge of the fabric; the bias is a line that is diagonal to the lengthwise and crosswise grain.*

✓ What is a layout? *A diagram that shows how to place pattern pieces on the fabric.*

✓ Why should you lay out all the pattern pieces before you cut any? *To make sure there is room for all of them.*

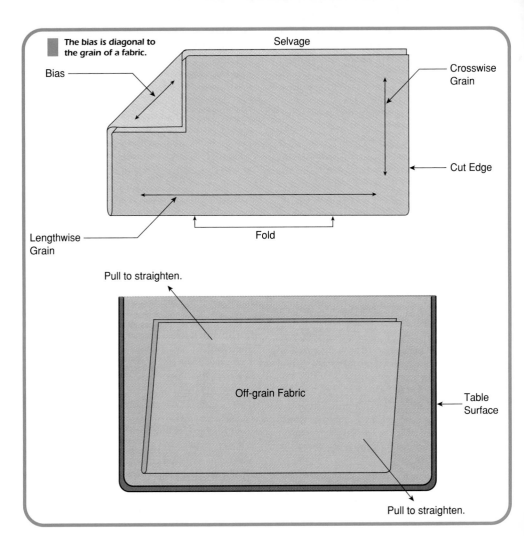

The bias is diagonal to the grain of a fabric.

Bias

Selvage

Crosswise Grain

Cut Edge

Lengthwise Grain

Fold

Pull to straighten.

Off-grain Fabric

Table Surface

Pull to straighten.

Off-grain fabric can be straightened by pulling it on the **bias,** *the diagonal line that intersects the lengthwise and crosswise grains.* You may also be able to straighten the grain by steam pressing. Pin the fabric along the selvages and along both cut ends. Press from the selvage toward the fold, being careful not to iron a center crease in the fabric. Fabrics that have a permanent finish cannot be straightened.

Laying Out, Cutting, and Marking

Lay out the pattern and cut out the fabric in a comfortable place. It is best to work in a well-lighted room on a large, flat surface, such as a table topped with a cutting board.

DID YOU KNOW?

Another term for straightening the grain of fabric by steam ironing is *blocking*.

Laying Out and Pinning the Pattern

The pattern **layout** is *a diagram that shows how to place the pattern pieces on your fabric.* It allows you to use the fabric as economically as possible. Special layouts may be given for fabrics with a nap, such as corduroy, or a directional print.

Fold the fabric with the right sides together, as shown on the layout you circled. Smooth the fabric flat on a surface that is large enough to hold the entire fabric width. Arrange the pattern pieces on the fabric, following the layout. To avoid mistakes, lay out all the pieces before starting to pin and cut. Parts A and B of **Figure 64.2** on page 622 show how to lay out and pin pattern pieces.

Cutting the Fabric

Before cutting the fabric, make sure that all the pieces are properly laid out and are placed on grain. Part C of **Figure 64.2** shows you how to cut fabric properly.

Follow the cutting line exactly. If you are using a multisized pattern, be sure to cut on the line for your size. Mark the proper cutting line with a highlighting marker. If you are between two sizes, draw a new line between two cutting lines. If you want to blend from one size to another, gradually taper from one cutting line to another.

Managing Your Life

Setting Up a Sewing Area

An entire room to devote to sewing is a luxury most people don't have. Sewers often find space wherever they can. Whether it's in the dining room, a corner of the basement, or even in a walk-in closet, a well-organized sewing area helps you work more efficiently. Whatever area is used, it should be comfortable and well-lighted.

The need for a large surface (preferably at least 3 ft. x 6 ft.) for layout and cutting makes it desirable to have a table of some kind nearby. Protect a wooden dining room table with a vinyl tablecloth, table pad, or heavy paper. When storage space is not a problem, a sheet of plywood laid on a smaller table or on sawhorses makes an excellent surface. By padding the board with blankets and covering it tightly with a sheet, it can double as a pressing table. Another option sold at fabric stores is a folding table designed for sewing.

Wherever the sewing area is, the sewing machine and ironing board need to be positioned close to electrical outlets. If there is a window, position the sewing machine nearby to take advantage of natural light. Place a portable sewing machine on a sturdy table. Choose a stool or straight-backed chair without arms when you sew. Keep tools, small equipment and supplies, and a wastebasket within easy reach of the sewing machine.

If your sewing area must be dismantled when not in use, try to store everything in one place, preferably close to the sewing area. A lightweight cart can be helpful. It can be wheeled out for sewing projects.

Fabrics and old patterns can be stored outside the sewing area, if there are space constraints. Plastic bags and shoeboxes are ideal for them. Plastic drawer dividers designed for the kitchen can house spools of thread. For storing other small items, such as scissors, thimbles, and notions, use a sewing box or organizer. Many inexpensive ones are now available.

Applying the Principles

1. How can storing sewing tools and supplies in one place make sewing more enjoyable?
2. If you don't already have a sewing area at home, draw a floor plan for setting one up. If you do have one, list ways you could improve it.

Activities
- **Napped or Not Napped?** Have students study their pattern guidelines and figure out how layouts for napped fabrics are different from other layouts. *(Observation)*
- **Which Is Up?** Show students how to find the right side of a fabric: Fold back one edge and compare the two surfaces. The right side will have a more pronounced weave, more nap, a brighter and clearer print, or more shine. For knitted fabrics, stretch an edge that has been cut crosswise. The edge will usually roll to the right side of the fabric. *(Observation)*
- **Fold Facts.** Discuss why fabric should always be folded with the right sides together before laying out the pattern pieces. *(Critical Thinking)*

ENRICHMENT

Working Without a Net. Ask students to pretend they are going to make a garment without using a pattern. Have them sketch their ideas for the garment and then explain what they would do next. After some discussion, have students list some problems they might encounter if they tried to sew without a pattern. *(Wasted time and fabric, poor fit, frustration.)*

Managing Your Life

Have students read "Setting Up a Sewing Area."

Answers to Applying . . .

1. You would always know where to find them; sewing tasks could be completed more quickly and efficiently.
2. Students' plans and improvements should reflect the guidelines in the text.

● ● ●   REAL-LIFE APPLICATION

Read this to students: *Jill doesn't have room on her fabric to place the sleeve pattern piece so that its grainline is parallel to the selvage. However, she can fit it in at an angle.* Ask students whether this is a good idea. What advice would they give Jill? *(They should advise Jill to check the layout to make sure other pieces are positioned correctly. She should then rearrange the pieces until all grainlines are parallel. Otherwise, the garment may not fit or look right.)*

Checking Comprehension

✓ What is directional cutting? *Cutting with the grain of the fabric.*

✓ What should you do before using any marking system? *Make test marks on a scrap of fabric to see if they show and can be removed.*

USING VISUALS

Have students study Figure 64.2. Discuss these questions to check their understanding:

1. What does a bracket arrow mean? *Place that edge of the pattern piece on the fabric fold.*
2. How can you tell if you have placed a pattern piece on the grain? *If the distances between each point of the grainline arrow and the selvage are equal.*
3. What should you do if you have two layers of fabric to mark? *Use two pieces of tracing paper or fold one in half.*
4. Why would you use contrasting thread to mark placement lines on the right side of the fabric? *Can be easily seen and then removed after using the markings.*

Figure 64.2

LAYING OUT, CUTTING, AND MARKING

When pinning a pattern to the fabric, there are several general rules to remember. Fold the fabric with the right sides together. As you pin, be sure to insert the pins perpendicular (at right angles) to the fold lines and the cutting lines. The exception to this rule is to insert pins diagonally into all corners. In general, place pins every 6 in. (15 cm) along the edges of the pattern pieces. The tips of the pins should not extend into or over the cutting lines. As you begin the layout, cutting, and marking process, follow the directions on your pattern guide sheet.

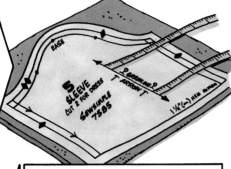

A. First lay out pattern pieces that go along the fold line of the fabric. These pieces have a bracket arrow on a straight edge. Pin the pieces along the fold line. Next, lay out pattern pieces with grainline arrows. To be sure each pattern piece is exactly on grain, measure the distance from each end of the grainline arrow to the selvage. If the distances are not equal, move the pieces and remeasure. Pin grainline arrows to hold pieces in place.

B. Smooth out the pattern pieces pinned to the fold. Then pin any corners. Pin along the remaining edges, smoothing the pattern as you go. Next, smooth out the pattern pieces that are pinned on the grainlines. Pin the corners, then around the edges, smoothing the pattern as you pin.

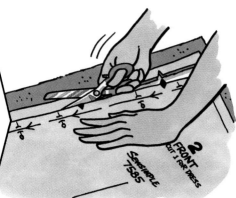

C. Using a sharp shears, cut along the cutting line with long, even strokes. With your free hand, hold the fabric flat on the table. Cut with the grain of the fabric. The direction of the grain may be shown on the pattern by arrows or by illustrations of tiny scissors on the cutting line. Use the points of your shears to cut corners, curves, and notches. Always cut notches <u>outward</u> from the cutting line. Cut double and triple notches together as one long notch.

DID YOU KNOW?

Not every sewer uses pins to hold a pattern in place. Students might like to try other methods, such as weights made for holding a pattern in place. These work best on simple projects. Sprays can be purchased that temporarily attach the pattern to fabric.

D. When marking pattern pieces with tracing paper and wheel, slide the tracing paper under the pattern so the color is against the <u>wrong</u> side of the fabric. If you have two layers of fabric to mark, use two pieces of tracing paper, or fold one in half. Roll the tracing wheel once along the line that you want to mark. Use a ruler to keep the lines straight. Mark dots with an X.

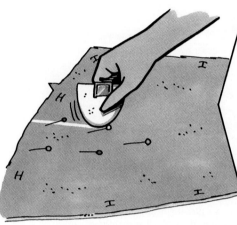

E. When marking with pins and chalk, push a pin through the pattern and fabric at the symbol to be marked. Then, make a mark using a piece of chalk or a chalk wheel on the wrong side of both fabric layers at the pin markings. Fabric pens can also be used instead of chalk to mark fabric. These special liquid marking pens allow temporary markings to be made on fabric. Some markings can be removed with cold water; others fade within a few hours. Always test these markers on a fabric scrap to be sure the markings will all come out.

F. Some pattern markings, particularly placement lines for pockets and fold lines for lapels, need to show on the right side of the fabric. If this is the case, you may use contrasting thread to hand sew long running stitches along the lines you have marked on the wrong side of the fabric.

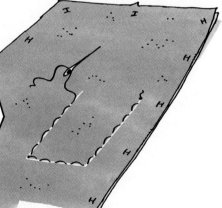

CHAPTER 64   Using a Pattern   623

DID YOU KNOW?

Here's a tip for a time when the marking chalk can't be found. A sliver of bar soap can do the job. Tell students that they can save leftovers from soap to use on their sewing projects.

Activities

■ **No Margins.** Tell the class that some people cut out pattern pieces along the cutting lines before placing the pieces on the fabric. Explore the pros and cons of this practice. *(Decision Making)*

■ **Cut That Out!** Ask students what problems might result from cutting notches inward from the cutting line. *(Critical Thinking)*

RETEACHING

■ **Step by Step.** Organize the class into three groups. One group should demonstrate how to lay out and pin a pattern; one, how to cut the fabric; and one, how to mark the pieces. All three groups might work on the same project, taking responsibility for different tasks. The groups should explain the steps as they carry them out and offer the class special tips to make students' future sewing more accurate and efficient.

CROSS-CURRICULAR ACTIVITY
Language Arts

After students cut their fabric, have them analyze whether their layout directions are clear and complete. Did they have trouble identifying which pattern pieces to lay out? Could they tell how many of each piece to cut? Did they realize that some pattern pieces were to be placed upside down or on only one thickness of fabric? What tips would they add to make the instructions clearer?

Review

■ **Chapter Review.** Use the contents of the Chapter Review page to help students review concepts, think critically, and apply their knowledge.

■ **Study Guide.** Have students complete the Study Guide for Chapter 64 on p. 212 of the Student Workbook.

■ **Paper Patterns.** Distribute an unlabeled diagram of a pattern piece and have partners add the following labels in the appropriate places: seamline, cutting line, seam allowance, adjustment line, grainline, foldline bracket, notch, dot, dart.

Evaluation

■ **Chapter Test.** Use the reproducible chapter test provided in the Teacher's Classroom Resources or create your own test using the *Testmaker Software.*

■ **Alternative Assessment.** Have students follow the steps for preparing a pattern and fabric. Then ask them to lay out the pattern, cut the pieces, and mark them. Remind students to use methods that are appropriate for their fabric. Ask partners to help evaluate each other's work as each completes the steps in the process.

■ **Life Patterns.** Discuss how the use of patterns changes with experience. When the guide says to sew the darts, for example, an experienced sewer will know what to do without studying the illustrations as carefully as a beginner should.

Use **directional cutting,** which is *cutting with the grain of the fabric.* Double-check to be sure that you have cut each pattern piece as many times as necessary. Do not remove the pattern from the fabric pieces after cutting, since the pattern markings must be transferred to the fabric first.

Marking the Fabric

Each pattern piece contains markings that must be transferred to the wrong side of your fabric. You will use these markings as you stitch the pieces together after the pattern has been removed. Several marking methods are available, including:

• Tracing paper and wheel
• Pins and chalk wheel or chalk
• Fabric pens
• Thread

Choose the method most suitable for your fabric. Always test the method first on a fabric scrap. Parts D through F of **Figure 64.2,** pages 622-623, show these methods.

A Careful Approach

When you create a garment or other project, you put time, energy, and expense into the process. No one wants to waste such resources by creating something that doesn't turn out as expected. A careful approach helps—right from the start. This can save disappointment, as you can see from the teens' comments in **Figure 64.3.**

Figure 64.3

What Would You Have Done?

Whether through impatience, eagerness to see results, or lack of knowledge, some people make costly mistakes on sewing projects. Even mistakes made in the early stages of a project can be ruinous. What can you learn from these beginning sewers?

• *Chelsey.* "When my dress was done and I put it on, I couldn't believe how funny it looked. It seemed all out of shape, but I didn't know what went wrong. When my mother asked me if I had followed the grainline on the layout, I realized that I had forgotten to do that. The fabric had kind of a loose weave and it had stretched where it shouldn't have."

• *Lyle.* "I just got in a hurry when I was working on my project. Cutting around notches seemed like a waste of time. When I put my project together, though, I had a hard time matching pieces. I even had to redo some seams because I put some pieces together wrong."

• *Conchita.* "The fabric I chose for my project was so pretty. The color was pale teal. I was so disappointed when I saw the red marks running alongside the darts. I had marked the stitching lines on the right side of the fabric with tracing paper. My teacher says the marks might not wash out. I hope they do, since I put so much work into my project."

• *Brian.* "I guess you could say I don't have a delicate touch. I just grabbed the fabric and lifted it several inches off the table while cutting out my project. I didn't realize that I was changing the size by doing that. Oh, well, that's not the first mistake I've ever made."

MORE ABOUT Patterns

Patterns first came into use about 1850. The garment industry needed patterns in order to mass-produce ready-to-wear clothing. In time, the use of both patterns and sewing machines spread from the garment industry to the general public.

Today's sewers spend roughly $3 billion a year on fabric, patterns, sewing machines, and other equipment and supplies. Catalogs offer patterns not only for clothing, but also for crafts and home decorating.

Review

Reviewing the Facts

1. Before sewing, what four steps should you follow?
2. Why do pattern pieces measure slightly larger than the size measurements?
3. Describe two simple adjustments you can make to a pattern.
4. What two characteristics of the fabric need to be determined before laying out the pattern? How would you deal with each one?
5. What does the pattern layout show you? Where is it found and why is it important?
6. Why should you transfer markings from the pattern to your fabric? Give an example of when markings might appear on the right side of the fabric.

Thinking Critically

1. What do you think would happen if you began to sew without properly adjusting the pattern? Without following the pattern layout? Without marking the fabric pieces?
2. Suppose that you wanted to make the same garment for yourself and two friends. Each of you wears a slightly different size, however. List two ways you might solve this problem.

Applying Your Knowledge

1. **Identifying Details.** Using two or three pieces from any pattern, identify, list, and define all the markings and pattern terms.
2. **Testing Marking Tools.** Not all marking tools may be suited to a particular fabric. Choose a piece of fabric and mark it using different methods. Compare the marks. Are they easy to see? Are they removable? Which would be best to use? Why?
3. **Solving Adjustment Problems.** Joelle is making a skirt. Her measurements are 1 in. (2.5 cm) larger at the waist and hips than shown for the pattern size. She also needs to

make the skirt 1 ½ in. (3.8 cm) longer. The skirt pattern has three pieces—a skirt front, a skirt back, and a waistband. How should she adjust the pattern so the skirt will fit?

Making Connections

1. **Geometry.** The lengthwise and crosswise grains of a fabric form a right, or 90°, angle. The true bias of a fabric is a diagonal line that intersects the two grainlines and should, therefore, create two 45° angles. Straighten an off-grain piece of fabric. Use a protractor to evaluate the result.
2. **Language Arts.** Write a brief instruction leaflet for a sewing tool described in this or an earlier chapter. Be sure to include step-by-step instructions on its proper use. Give several examples. Illustrate the safe versus unsafe use of the tool.

Building Your Portfolio

Adjusting a Pattern

Trace several pattern pieces onto tissue paper. Use these tissue paper pattern pieces to demonstrate how to adjust a pattern in the following ways: shortening, lengthening, increasing width, and decreasing width. Prepare each pattern piece as you would if you were going to make the garment, and write a short paragraph to accompany each piece telling what you did and why. Add the pieces and the written material to your portfolio.

CHAPTER 64   Using a Pattern   625

Chapter Overview

Chapter 65 explains basic garment construction, from staystitching to finishing the seams. After explaining the advantages of unit construction, the chapter describes how to sew darts, tucks, gathers, pleats, and seams and how to add facings and interfacings.

Motivator

■ **Fit to Wear.** Drape a fabric length over you or a student volunteer and ask the class to suggest ways to make that fabric fit the shape of the body. Ask them to suggest how cutting the fabric into different pieces and taking "nips and tucks" would help.

Objectives

Discuss the chapter objectives. Remind students that the objectives focus on important chapter concepts.

Vocabulary

Tell students that the sewing term *dart* has nothing to do with its meaning as a verb (to move suddenly). Instead, the term is taken from the shape of the darts that are thrown at a target as part of a game. The pointed end of these darts is similar to the shape of a sewn dart.

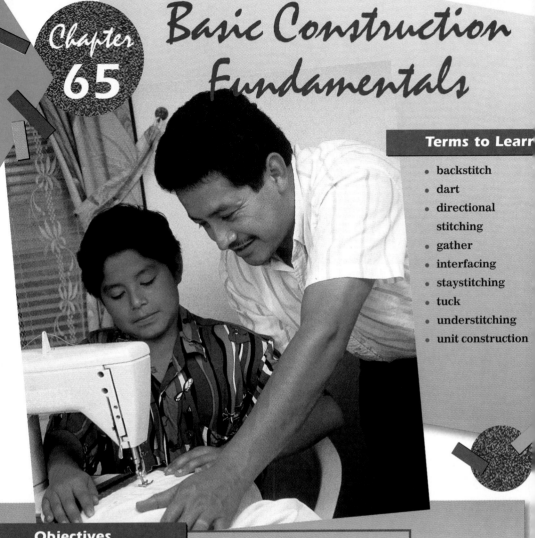

Chapter 65
Basic Construction Fundamentals

Terms to Learn

- backstitch
- dart
- directional stitching
- gather
- interfacing
- staystitching
- tuck
- understitching
- unit construction

Objectives

This chapter will help you to:

- Explain the concept of unit construction.
- Describe the sewing techniques used to fit garment pieces.
- Identify the five basic seam finishes.
- Describe how to apply interfacings.
- Describe how to apply facings.
- Explain how to press garments as you sew them.

CHAPTER RESOURCES

Student Workbook
Study Guide, p. 214
Activity, *Basic Construction Terms*, p. 215

Teacher's Classroom Resources
Lesson Plan, p. 69

Clothing Lab, pp. 7-12
Extension #94, *The Language of Sewing*, p. 100
Life Skills, *Giving Expert Advice*, pp. 102-103
Chapter 65 Test, pp. 135-136

Performance Assessment, *Basic Construction Techniques*, p. 102
Reteaching, *Shaping and Finishing*, p. 71

Now that you have marked your fabric, you are ready to assemble your project using a basic technique called unit construction. In **unit construction,** *you prepare the separate garment pieces first, and then assemble them in a specific order.* For example, a shirt has a back piece, two front pieces, two sleeves, and perhaps a collar. Each piece is a unit, and each unit is constructed separately. To complete the project, you simply put all the units together.

Staystitching

The first step in assembling a project is to prepare the fabric pieces. First look for all edges that are curved or cut on the bias. Curved edges can stretch as you work with them unless you put a row of stitching on these edges to prevent them from losing their shape. This type of stitching is called **staystitching,** *or sewing a row of regular machine stitches through one layer of fabric.* The stitches are placed in the seam allowance ½ in. (1.3 cm) from the edge of the fabric. The pattern guide sheet generally shows which areas to staystitch.

Whenever you staystitch or sew seams, always use **directional stitching,** *or stitching in the same direction as the grain in the fabric.*

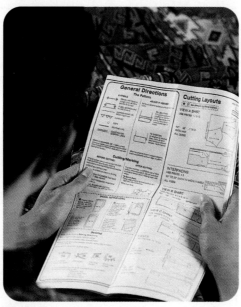

When constructing a sewing project, follow the directions on the guide sheet carefully.

For example, stitch from the shoulder to the center of the neckline. Many patterns include arrows to help you determine directional stitching.

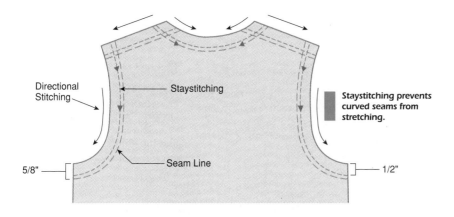

Directional Stitching

Staystitching

Staystitching prevents curved seams from stretching.

Seam Line

5/8"

1/2"

CHAPTER 65   Basic Construction Fundamentals   627

TEACH

Topic on p. 607:
- Staystitching

Checking Comprehension

✓ Regarding unit construction, what are the main units in a shirt or blouse? *Back, front, sleeves, and perhaps collar.*

✓ What is a disadvantage of using bias-cut edges and how can you prevent this disadvantage? *Bias-cut edges can stretch as you work with them. Staystitching prevents stretching.*

✓ In what direction should you staystitch? *In the direction of the grain, usually from the wider to the narrower part of a piece.*

Activities

■ **Why Cut on the Bias?** Discuss why anyone would cut a pattern piece on the bias, since bias-cut edges stretch easily. *(Decision Making)*

■ **Seams Okay.** Ask what might happen if staystitching is done on the seam line. *(Critical Thinking)*

RETEACHING

■ **Seeing Is Believing.** Ask students to measure and then sew together two long, bias-cut edges without staystitching and measure how much they stretch. Then have them staystitch two similar bias-cut edges, sew them together, and measure the length. Discuss.

ENRICHMENT

■ **Looking at Length.** Have students experiment with stitches of different lengths to determine which best prevents the stretching of bias edges of different types of fabric. They might summarize their findings in a chart.

MORE ABOUT Bias

Explain that pattern pieces that are meant to stretch are often cut on the bias. A bias-cut edge allows the fabric to curve and fit the body. It also allows narrow strips of fabric to be tied more easily into knots and bows. However, stretching a bias-cut edge as it is sewn can pull the fabric out of shape. Bias-cut edges are less likely to ravel than edges cut on the lengthwise or crosswise grain.

- **Shaping**
- **Darts**
- **Tucks**

Checking Comprehension

✓ What are some ways to shape a flat piece of fabric to fit the body? *Darts, tucks, pleats, and gathers.*

✓ Where do darts usually appear on a garment? *Waistline, bustline, back of the shoulder, and elbow.*

✓ How are darts and tucks similar and different? *Both are folds in the fabric. A dart tapers to a point; a tuck is the same width its entire length. For a dart, the fold is on the inside of the garment. For a tuck, the fold might be on the inside or outside of the garment.*

MULTICULTURAL *Perspectives*

Ask students to visit museums or find reference books that show clothing from other times and cultures. Ask them to observe how darts, tucks, and gathers were used in these garments.

SPECIAL NEEDS *Strategies*

Gifted Students. Challenge students to use the fabric-shaping techniques on these pages to design clothing that fits a stuffed animal. Have them create their own pattern pieces. Then ask students to use their patterns to construct the clothing.

628

Figure 65.1
SEWING DARTS

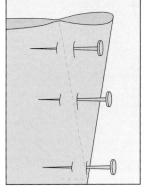

1. Fold the dart in half with the right fabric sides together, and match the markings. Pin in place.

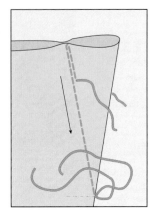

2. Machine stitch from the wide end of the dart to the point, backstitching only at the beginning of the dart. Remove the pins as you sew. Leave thread ends approximately 3 in. (7.5 cm) long at the point of the dart.

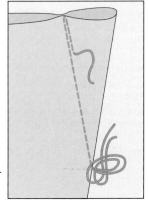

3. Tie a small knot at the point of the dart. Then clip the thread ends ¼ in. (6 mm) from the point. Press.

Shaping to Fit the Body

There are several different methods for shaping flat pieces of fabric to fit the body. The most common methods include darts, tucks, and gathers. Each is used to create a different effect.

Darts

A **dart** is *a triangular fold of fabric stitched to a point.* Darts help shape the fabric to body curves. They are usually located at the waistline, the bustline, the back of the shoulder, and the elbow. Darts can also be used to shape curved areas in such accessories as caps and tote bags.

628   **UNIT 7 Clothing and Textiles**

🔍 **Focus on Sewing Skills**

Show students how to pin a dart by placing the pins with the heads toward them (toward the point of the dart) so they can remove the pins easily as they sew. Explain that some darts, such as those in dresses or jackets without seams at the waistline, taper at both ends. In this case, students should stitch from the center toward each end of the dart. Lines that form a dart can be curved instead of straight in order to shape the fabric to the body. Stress that students should follow these lines exactly so the dart will be shaped correctly. Curved darts often must be clipped so they will lie flat.

Figure 65.2
SEWING TUCKS

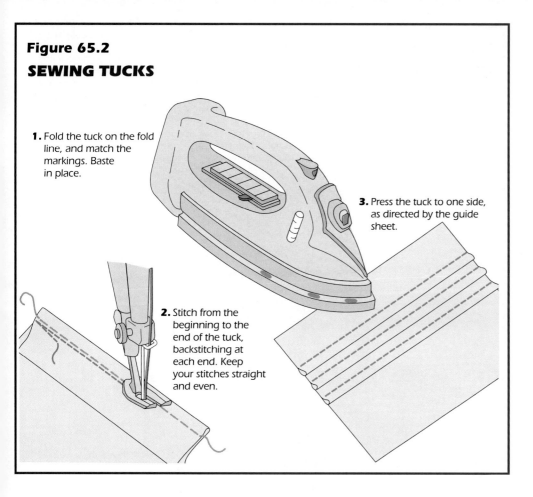

1. Fold the tuck on the fold line, and match the markings. Baste in place.

3. Press the tuck to one side, as directed by the guide sheet.

2. Stitch from the beginning to the end of the tuck, backstitching at each end. Keep your stitches straight and even.

On the outside of the garment, darts should look like short seams. They should not have bubbles or puckers at the points. For this reason, do not use a serger to sew darts.

Darts on the right and left sides of a garment should be the same length, and they should be the same distance from the center of the garment. **Figure 65.1** on page 628 shows the procedure for sewing darts.

Tucks

A **tuck** is *a fold of fabric stitched from top to bottom and used to shape a garment.* It does not taper to a point at the end. Tucks make small, stitched pleats in the fabric. Several tucks are generally used together—down the front of a shirt, for example—to shape a garment.

Activities

■ **Matching Darts.** Ask students why the darts on the right and left side of a garment should be the same length and the same distance from the center. *(Observation)*

■ **A Tuck in Time.** Have students explain how a garment might be affected if the stitching on tucks is not straight. What will result if the stitching is just inside the stitching line? *(Critical Thinking)*

■ **Thinking of Fabrics.** Discuss the kinds of fabric that are appropriate and inappropriate for darts and tucks. For example, what might happen if you put darts in a sheer fabric? How might a heavy wool garment look with a series of tucks? *(Critical Thinking)*

ENRICHMENT

■ **Types of Pleats.** Explain to students that pleats are another type of body shaping method. Have them find out what is meant by box pleats, accordion pleats, knife pleats, and kick pleats. Students could use folded paper to illustrate each variation. They might also research pleats used in draperies, such as pinch pleats, French pleats, and box pleats.

CROSS-CURRICULAR ACTIVITY
Math

Have students solve this problem: The material on one side of a shirt front measures 27 inches wide. The finished side should measure $19\frac{7}{8}$ inches with a $\frac{5}{8}$ inch seam and threetucks with $\frac{1}{4}$ inch between each tuck. How wide will the tucks be? *(About 2 inches each.)*

REAL-LIFE APPLICATION

Read these problems to students and have them suggest solutions:

• Jennie has made a blouse for herself, but it's too full in the front and the back. *(Add darts in the front and back.)*

• Karen has made a skirt with tucks, but the fabric is so soft that the skirt seems to be gathered. *(Make the tucks longer.)*

Topics on pp. 630-631:

- **Gathers**
- **Stitching Seams**
- **Using Good Judgment**

Checking Comprehension

✓ How are gathers used to shape a garment? *To control fullness along a seam line; to fit a larger piece of fabric to a smaller one.*

✓ On what part of a garment might you use gathers? *At waistlines, cuffs, shoulders, and sleeves.*

✓ How are gathers created? *By sliding fabric along a line of basting stitches until it is the same width as a smaller piece of fabric.*

✓ How is a standard or plain seam sewn? *With a regular machine stitch length, using directional stitching.*

✓ Why should you backstitch at the beginning and ending of each seam? *To secure the stitching.*

CROSS-CURRICULAR ACTIVITY
Math

Tell students that for gathering you usually use a length of fabric two to three times the finished length. Then have students solve this problem: You want to make a gathered skirt to fit a 24-inch waistband. How many inches wide should the fabric be for the skirt? *(48 to 72 inches)*

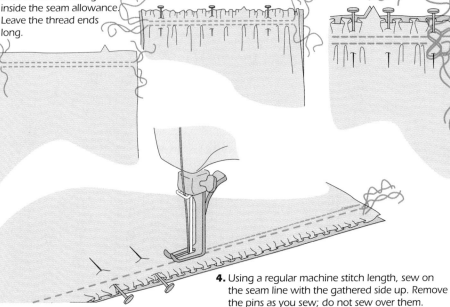

Figure 65.3
SEWING GATHERS

1. Stitch two rows of machine basting. One row should be just next to the seam line and the other ¼ in. (6 mm) away from the first stitching inside the seam allowance. Leave the thread ends long.

2. Pin the piece to be gathered to the straight piece with the right sides together, and match notches, markings, raw edges, and seams.

3. Pull up both bobbin threads at one end of the gathered piece, and gently slide the fabric along the threads. Repeat at the other end until the gathered piece of fabric is the same length as the straight piece. Distribute the gathers evenly. Secure the thread ends by wrapping them around a pin.

4. Using a regular machine stitch length, sew on the seam line with the gathered side up. Remove the pins as you sew; do not sew over them.

Tucks may be stitched with the fold on the inside for shaping or with the fold on the outside for decorative detail. Sergers can be used to make decorative tucks, but the fold of the fabric must be kept clear of the knives. The width of the tuck and the spacing between tucks varies depending on how the garment is to be shaped. **Figure 65.2** on page 629 illustrates how to sew tucks.

Gathers

Gathers are *small, soft folds of fabric created by sliding fabric along two parallel rows of machine basting.* Gathers control fullness along a seam line and are often used at waistlines, cuffs, shoulders, and sleeves. Ruffles on clothing, pillows, and place mats are also gathered.

Gathers are used to fit a larger piece of fabric to a smaller one. **Figure 65.3** illustrates how to sew gathers.

MORE ABOUT Gathering

Explain that another word for gathering is *shirring.* Although many people use the machine's longest stitch for gathering all fabrics, professionals often use a shorter stitch for soft, sheer fabrics, such as chiffon. The shorter stitch makes gathers more even on soft fabric.

Assembling the Pieces

After staystitching the pieces and building in the shape, you can begin assembling the garment. In unit construction, garment assembly begins with the seams.

Stitching Seams

A standard seam is ⅝ in. (1.5 cm) wide and is sometimes called a plain seam. To sew a standard seam, first pin the two layers of fabric together with the right sides facing each other, and match the notches. With a regular machine stitch length, use directional stitching to sew the seam. To secure the stitching at the beginning and end of the seam, **backstitch**, or *sew in reverse by using the reverse lever on your machine.*

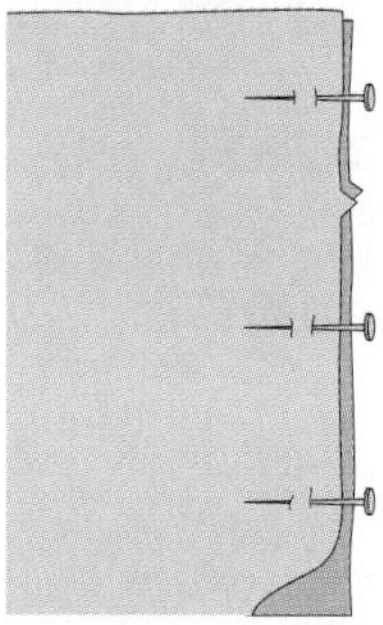

Backstitching about ½ in. (1.3 cm) secures the beginning and the end of the seam.

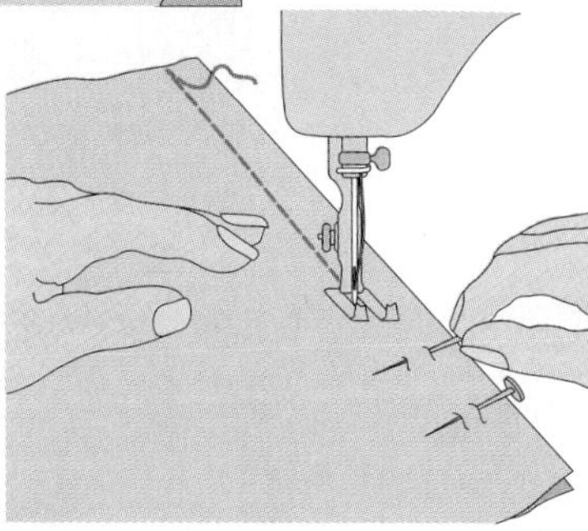

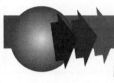

Acting Responsibly

Do You Use Good Judgment?

In the sewing lab, everyone shares the school's equipment. Naturally, students need to act responsibly with the machines to keep them in working order. When students aren't sure what to do in a situation, they must weigh the options and try to use good judgment.

Good Judgment in Action

Caitlin was hurrying to finish sewing a side seam on her shirt project before the bell rang. She was looking forward to watching her sister play in the volleyball championship at her middle school. Leaving straight from class would give her just enough time to get there. Caitlin finished sewing and pulled the fabric out of the machine only to find that she had jammed the upper and lower threads together.

Panicking, her first impulse was to leave everything and go to the game. Caitlin realized, though, that someone would need the machine the next morning.

Caitlin went to her teacher and explained the problem. Ms. Stedman told Caitlin that they could fix the jam together. After explaining about the volleyball game, Caitlin asked if she could come in first thing in the morning during homeroom to fix the machine. Ms. Stedman agreed.

Your Analysis

1. How would you assess Caitlin's judgment?
2. If Caitlin had not told her teacher about the jammed machine, what might have occurred?
3. Have you ever broken something you were using that belonged to someone else? What did you do? What should you do?

Activities

■ **Oops.** Discuss what might happen if students do not secure the thread ends of a gather before sewing or if they try to sew the material with the gathered side down. *(Problem Solving)*

RETEACHING

■ **Sewing Samples.** Have students use fabric scraps to make samples of darts, tucks, and gathers. They might show vertical, horizontal, and diagonal darts; broad and narrow tucks on the inside and the outside of garments; and tight and loose gathers.

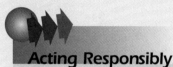

Acting Responsibly

Have students read "Do You Use Good Judgment?" Ask them to name other sewing situations in which good judgment is required. What impact does good judgment have in all areas of a person's life?

Answers to Your Analysis

1. She used good judgment in bringing the problem to the teacher's attention and working out a solution.
2. The next student to use the machine would have been inconvenienced and possibly blamed for the problem; the teacher would have had to take time during class to fix the machine.
3. Answers will vary. Emphasize the need to take responsibility for your own mistakes. Positive long-range effects outweigh the temporary comfort of denying responsibility.

MORE ABOUT Gathers

Students may wonder about the need for sewing two rows of basting stitches when gathering material. Point out that there are several reasons for doing so. Final sewing is easier and neater when the fabric is pulled together with two sets of stitches. The gathers are more even, and the fabric is less likely to slip out of place and get caught under the needle. Gathering creates tension on thread. With two threads, there is less pressure on each and less chance for breakage.

- Seam Techniques
- Finishing Seams

Checking Comprehension

✓ At what point are such sewing techniques as trimming, grading, clipping, and notching used? *After stitching a seam but before pressing and completing other sewing details, such as topstitching.*

✓ What should you do to make inward-curving seams lie flat? *Clip them, making small, evenly spaced cuts through the seam allowance.*

✓ Why do seams need to be finished? *To prevent fabric edges from raveling and to improve the appearance of seams that will show in the finished garment.*

✓ What type of finishing is appropriate for most fabrics? *Zigzag stitch.*

CROSS-CURRICULAR ACTIVITY
Language Arts

Have students pretend they are filming a video (or actually film one) to help people learn basic sewing techniques. Arrange the class into groups and have each group write the script for a different construction technique, such as gathering fabric or using a certain seam finishing method. Have one person from each group demonstrate the technique to the class, following the group's script.

Figure 65.4
SEAM TECHNIQUES

Trimming. Cut the seam allowance (both layers togther) to half its width.

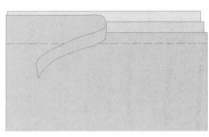

Grading. Cut one layer of seam allowance narrower than the other.

Clipping. Clip seam allowances on inner curves up to staystitching.

Notching. Cut notches on outer curves to allow seam allowances to spread and lie flat.

Press the seam before going on to sew the next one. First press the seam flat, just as it was stitched. Then press the seam allowance open. See page 635 for more information on pressing.

Additional Seam Techniques

Trimming, grading, clipping, and notching help seams to lie flat and smooth by reducing fabric bulk. It is often necessary to use one or more of these techniques when stitching collars, necklines, and waistbands. They are used after stitching a seam, but before pressing and completing other sewing details, such as topstitching. **Figure 65.4** illustrates the following techniques:

- **Trimming.** When trimming, cut the seam allowance to half its width.

- **Grading.** To grade, cut each layer of a seam allowance slightly narrower than the previous layer. Leave at least ⅛ to ¼ in. (3 to 6 mm) on the narrowest layer of the seam allowance to prevent raveling. Grade seam allowances if the fabric is thick or if the seams have three or more layers.

- **Clipping.** After trimming, clip seam allowances that curve inward. This will allow the fabric to lie flat. Clip by making small, evenly spaced cuts up to, but not through, the staystitching line.

- **Notching.** Notch the seams that curve outward. To notch, cut evenly spaced, V-shaped wedges out of the seam allowance no closer than ⅛ in. (3 mm) to the seam line.

REAL-LIFE APPLICATION

Have students suggest effective ways to finish the seams on each of the garments below. Point out that several methods are appropriate for some of the garments. Ask students to explain the reasons for their suggestions.

- Seersucker shorts
- An unlined, lightweight wool skirt
- A heavy corduroy jacket
- A felt puppet
- A chiffon scarf
- A cotton shirt
- An unlined cotton/polyester jacket
- A terrycloth robe

Figure 65.5
WAYS TO FINISH SEAMS

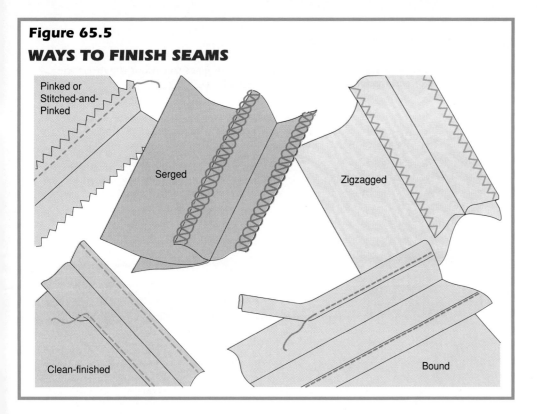

Pinked or Stitched-and-Pinked

Serged

Zigzagged

Clean-finished

Bound

Finishing Seams

Seams need to be finished to prevent fabric edges from fraying or raveling. Finished seams create a neat appearance. **Figure 65.5** illustrates the following techniques:

- **Pinked or stitched-and-pinked.** Trim the edges of the seam allowance with pinking shears. For fabrics that ravel easily, stitch ¼ in. (6 mm) from the edge of the seam allowance before pinking. Use this finish on lightweight, woven fabrics.
- **Zigzagged.** Sew a zigzag machine stitch close to the raw edge of the seam allowance. This finish is appropriate for most fabrics. Use a narrow width zigzag stitch for lightweight, closely woven fabrics; use a wider zigzag stitch for bulky or loosely woven fabrics.

- **Clean-finished.** A narrow hem forms along the raw edge of the seam allowance when it is clean finished. To clean finish, turn the edge of the seam allowance under ⅛ in. (3 mm), and press it flat. Then stitch along the folded edge. Use this finish on lightweight and medium-weight fabrics.
- **Bound.** To make a bound finish, put double-fold bias tape strips over the raw edge of each seam allowance. Place the slightly narrower folded edge of the tape on top, and stitch through all the layers. Use this method for heavyweight fabrics.
- **Serged.** Using a serger, sew along the raw edge of the seam allowance, trimming away ⅛ in. (3 mm) or less. Use this finish for bulky fabric or fabric that ravels easily.

CHAPTER 65   Basic Construction Fundamentals   633

Topics on pp. 634-636:
- Applying Interfacing
- Constructing Facings
- Pressing

Checking Comprehension

✓ What is the purpose of interfacing? *To prevent stretching and give edges extra body and shape.*

✓ What types of interfacing fabrics are commonly used? *Fusible and sew-in.*

✓ *Where in a garment might you use facing?* Neck-lines, armholes, or waistlines, where raw edges need to be finished.

✓ *How do you make a facing lie flat and smooth?* By trimming, grading, clipping, or notching the seam allowance; after the facing is turned inside, you understitch or sew a row of stitches on the facing through the seam allowances.

✓ *What is the difference between ironing and pressing?* Ironing involves moving a hot iron back and forth over the fabric. Pressing means lowering the iron on the garment and then lifting it. Pressing the fabric does not stretch it, but ironing may.

✓ *Why should you remove any pins before pressing?* To avoid scratching the iron or marking the fabric.

► CROSS-REFERENCE ◄
Remind students that interfacing requirements listed on the back of the pattern envelope, as they learned in Chapter 62.

Figure 65.6
APPLYING INTERFACING

For each type of interfacing, use the appropriate pattern piece to cut out the interfacing. Then follow the directions for fusible or sew-in interfacings.

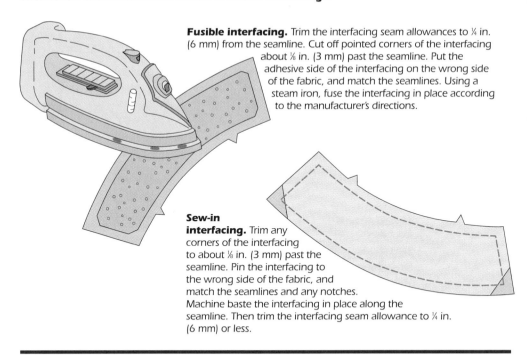

Fusible interfacing. Trim the interfacing seam allowances to ¼ in. (6 mm) from the seamline. Cut off pointed corners of the interfacing about ⅛ in. (3 mm) past the seamline. Put the adhesive side of the interfacing on the wrong side of the fabric, and match the seamlines. Using a steam iron, fuse the interfacing in place according to the manufacturer's directions.

Sew-in interfacing. Trim any corners of the interfacing to about ⅛ in. (3 mm) past the seamline. Pin the interfacing to the wrong side of the fabric, and match the seamlines and any notches. Machine baste the interfacing in place along the seamline. Then trim the interfacing seam allowance to ¼ in. (6 mm) or less.

Interfacing

Interfacing is *a lightweight, woven or non-woven fabric that is put between layers of garment fabric to prevent stretching and add extra body and shape.* Interfacing fabrics are available in a variety of types, such as fusible and sew-in, and a variety of weights. **Figure 65.6** illustrates how to apply fusible and sew-in interfacings.

Facings

A facing is a piece of fabric used to finish the raw edges of a garment. Facings may be used at necklines, armholes, and waistlines. The most common type of facing is a shaped facing, which is cut in the same shape as the edge to be finished. Separate pieces for facings are included in the pattern. **Figure 65.7** on page 635 illustrates how to sew a facing.

MORE ABOUT Interfacing

Explain that manufacturers offer inter-facing in a wide range of weights and several colors. Different kinds of interfacing are available for all types of fabric, from sheers to canvas. Some interfacing adds extra body to the fabric. Other interfacings provide a crisp effect for cuffs and necklines. Urge students to ask for help in the fabric store if they are not sure which interfacing to purchase. Caution students that not following the manufacturers' directions while applying fusible interfacing can result in a wavy, bubbled fabric that cannot be smoothed out. They will have to cut the pattern piece again and start over.

Figure 65.7
STITCHING FACINGS

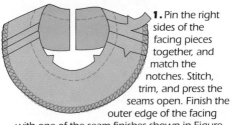

1. Pin the right sides of the facing pieces together, and match the notches. Stitch, trim, and press the seams open. Finish the outer edge of the facing with one of the seam finishes shown in Figure 65.5.

2. With right sides together, pin the facing to the garment, and match all notches. Stitch the facing to the garment. Grade, clip, or notch the seams as needed.

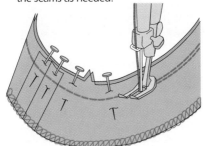

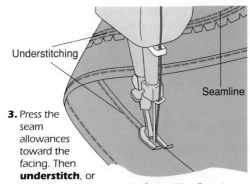

Understitching

Seamline

3. Press the seam allowances toward the facing. Then **understitch**, or <u>sew a row of stitches on the facing ⅛ in. (3 mm) or less from the seam line, through the seam allowances and facing.</u> This will keep the facing from rolling to the right side of the garment.

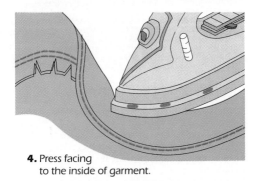

4. Press facing to the inside of garment.

Pressing

Making a professional-looking garment involves pressing—lifting the iron and lowering it back down on the garment. Pressing is not the same as ironing. When ironing, you glide the iron back and forth across the fabric. This can stretch the fabric. Pressing assures that seams lie flat, darts and gathers are shaped accurately, and facings lie smooth.

Use a steam iron or a damp press cloth—a piece of fine, plain-woven cotton, such as muslin—to create steam when pressing. Keep your fingers and face away from the steam. After pressing one section of the fabric, lift the iron, and move it to the next section. If you are using a press cloth, reposition it. Then lower the iron again. Press one whole unit before going on to the next. Here are a few more tips for pressing correctly:

ASSESS

Review

■ **Chapter Review.** Use the contents of the Chapter Review page to help students review concepts, think critically, and apply their knowledge.

■ **Study Guide.** Have students complete the Study Guide for Chapter 65 on p. 214 of the Student Workbook.

■ **Posing Problems.** Have groups write brief descriptions of two sewing challenges that could be met using techniques from this chapter. For example: What could you do if an armhole facing is raveling and won't lie flat? Collect the descriptions, select the best, and give one to each group to solve

Evaluation

■ **Chapter Test.** Use the reproducible chapter test provided in the Teacher's Classroom Resources or create your own test using the *Testmaker Software.*

■ **Alternative Assessment.** Have each student create a chart of the main steps involved in constructing a plain shirt. Under each step, they should add points to remember as they complete that step. Use their charts to determine what they learned from this chapter.

CLOSE

■ **Applying Skills.** Discuss these questions:

• Which techniques from this chapter could help you alter a pattern so it fits better?

• Which techniques could help garments last longer?

• Which techniques could help garments look their best?

• Remove pins before pressing to avoid scratching the iron or marking the fabric.
• Press on the inside of the fabric whenever possible to avoid creating a shine on the fabric. Do not use heavy pressure; let the steam do the work.
• Use a tailor's ham when pressing curved seams and darts to avoid flattening the curved shape.
• Press vertical darts toward the center of the garment. Press horizontal and diagonal darts downward toward the lower edge of the garment.

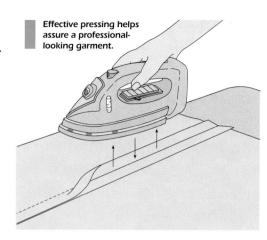

Effective pressing helps assure a professional-looking garment.

Visualizing a Whole from Its Parts

What You Learn Today . . .

All of the pattern pieces are staystitched, and all of the darts are sewn. Now you're ready to assemble the garment. It's helpful at this stage to keep in mind how the whole garment will look as you put it together. This can be difficult since, as you sew, the units are inside out and lying flat. Seeing a three-dimensional garment at this stage requires visualization, or seeing with the mind's eye.

. . . You Can Use Tomorrow

Visualizing a whole from its parts is a skill that can be useful in many different occupations. Landscape designers, for example, need to think about how plantings will fit together into a harmonious whole. Some occupations involve following a plan for assembly. Directions for putting together parts of a machine, for example, are not very different from the pattern guide sheet you use to construct a garment.

Practicing Your Skills

You can practice visualizing a whole from its parts by following the guide sheet directions for a simple shirt pattern. Use fabric cut from the pattern or the pattern pieces themselves to complete this exercise.

1. Lay out all the parts—back and front, sleeves, and collar—on a flat surface, side by side. Visualize how you would position each piece if you were going to sew them together.
2. Using straight pins, pin together the separate units of the shirt. For example, pin the seams in the sleeves, or pin the front to the back. Visualize how each unit will be joined to complete the shirt.
3. Finally, pin the sleeves and collar to the body of the shirt.

The first time you do this exercise, you will probably need to refer to the guide sheet. Try it again without looking at the guide sheet.

Assessing Your Skills

1. Were there any parts of the project you had trouble visualizing? What happened as you repeated the assembly several times?
2. Aside from the directions on the guide sheet, what other clues did you use to put together the shirt?

636   UNIT 7 Clothing and Textiles

REAL-LIFE APPLICATION

Read this to students: *After Blake slipped on her prom dress, she stood in front of the mirror. Something was wrong. The dress didn't look at all like it had when she had tried it on in the store several days ago. The velvet now looked shiny. It's softness was gone too.* Ask students what they think might have happened. *Blake or someone else probably ironed the dress to touch it up for wearing before the prom. Improper ironing may have affected the velvet, causing the shine as well as the flattened nap.*

Chapter 65

Review

Reviewing the Facts

1. What is the purpose of staystitching around edges that are curved or cut on the bias? What might happen if you don't staystitch where necessary?
2. Why are darts, tucks, and gathers used? Describe how darts and tucks differ.
3. Name five ways to finish seam allowances. How do you determine which finish to use?
4. What is the major difference between sew-in and fusible interfacing? Describe how to apply each type.
5. Why are facings used? What are the basic steps in stitching a facing?
6. What is the difference between pressing and ironing? How does each affect a garment?

Thinking Critically

1. What factors might influence your choice of interfacing?
2. What steps described in this chapter might you be tempted to eliminate if in a hurry? Choose one step, and predict how eliminating it might affect the finished garment.

Applying Your Knowledge

1. **Comparing Methods.** Cut an inward curve (similar to a facing) through two layers of fabric. Stitch a ⅝-in. (1.5-cm) seam along the curved edge. Press the seam open, and note the result. Then trim and clip the seam. Press it again and note the result. Compare results in writing.
2. **Selecting a Seam Finish.** Select one type of woven or knit fabric, and cut it into five 6 in. (15 cm) by 2 in. (5 cm) strips. Use the strips to make seam finishes: pinked, zigzagged, clean-finished, bound, and serged. Analyze the results. Which finishes worked best? Did any not work? If so, why not?

Making Connections

1. **Building Trades.** When using the unit construction technique for assembling a garment, you prepare the separate pieces first and then put them together in a specific order to create the finished garment. How do you think this technique might apply to the construction of a building? Describe at least three units of a house that might be assembled first and then added to the building. Write a short paragraph that compares unit construction of a garment with unit construction of a house.
2. **Technology.** In what ways have sewing machines and sergers simplified basic garment construction? Describe technological advances as they apply to techniques discussed in this chapter.

Building Your Portfolio

Practicing Your Techniques
Prepare a sample of each of the techniques that can be used to shape or to assemble a garment. Mount each sample on stiff paper or cardboard, and label the techniques. Add the samples to your portfolio.

ANSWERS TO REVIEWING THE FACTS

1. It prevents the fabric from stretching as you work with it. Markings and notches might not match when you join the pattern pieces. One section of the garment might be stretched out of shape.
2. They shape a flat piece of fabric to fit the shape of the body. Darts are triangular folds of fabric stitched to a point; tucks are straight folds that do not taper at the end.
3. Pinked, zigzagged, clean-finished, bound, and serged or overlocked are ways to finish seam allowances. You choose the finish by the type of fabric and the reason for finishing the seam, which could include a fabric that ravels or a seam that will be visible.
4. The major difference is the method of application. For fusible, you trim the interfacing, place it on the wrong side of the fabric, and fuse the two with an iron. For sew-in, you baste the interfacing by machine to the wrong side of the fabric, stitch the seams, and trim the interfacing.
5. Facings finish a raw edge. Stitch the facing to the garment, trim the seam, clip or notch, turn the facing, and understitch or tack it to the garment. Press.
6. Pressing involves an up-and-down movement with the iron. Ironing is a side-to-side movement. Pressing results in flat seams, well-shaped darts and pleats, and smooth facings. Ironing a garment during its construction could stretch the fabric

---

ANSWERS TO THINKING CRITICALLY

1. You should consider the method of application, characteristics of the interfacing (woven or nonwoven, soft or crisp), and type of fabric. Interfacing should be the same weight as the fabric or slightly lighter.

2. One possible response could be: not pressing the seams or darts after they are completed. Skipping this step could affect the final appearance of the garment.

Chapter 66

FOCUS

Chapter Overview

Chapter 66 explains the basic principles for constructing collars, cuffs, sleeves, pockets, and waistbands. The chapter also includes casings, hems, ribbings, closures, and trims.

Motivator

■ **Finishing School.** Hold up a reasonably complex garment (or a pattern envelope) and ask students what else they would need to know in order to sew such a garment, for example, how to add pockets, a waistband, sleeves, a zipper, a hem.

Objectives

Discuss the chapter objectives on this page. Remind students that the objectives focus on important chapter concepts.

Vocabulary

Tell students that the term *appliqué* comes from a French verb that means to apply. An appliqué is a piece of material that is added to the outside of something made of similar material. For example, paper appliqués are used on greeting cards, wooden appliqués on cabinets, and fabric appliqués on garments.

Chapter 66

More Sewing Fundamentals

Terms to Learn

- appliqué
- ribbing
- sew-through button
- shank button

Objectives

This chapter will help you to:

- Describe **the four basic hand-sewing stitches.**
- Briefly **describe techniques for sewing each of the following: collars and cuffs, sleeves, pockets, waistbands, hems, casings, and ribbing.**
- Describe **common closures and how to attach them.**
- Identify **trimmings that can personalize sewing projects.**

638   UNIT 7   Clothing and Textiles

CHAPTER RESOURCES

Student Workbook
Study Guide, p. 216
Activity, *Fashion Details*, p. 217

Teacher's Classroom Resources
Lesson Plan, p. 70

Clothing Lab, pp. 13-35
Cooperative Learning, *Adding Details*, pp. 71-72
Extension #95, *Embroidery Stitch Sampler*, p. 101
Life Skills, *Project Planning*, p. 104

Chapter 66 Test, pp. 137-138
Performance Assessment, *Steps in Clothing Construction*, p. 103
Reteaching, *Hand Sewing and Hemming*, p. 72

Once you have used basic techniques in order to shape and assemble a garment, you are ready to apply the techniques for completing it. These techniques include methods for handling:

- Fashion details—collars, cuffs, sleeves, and pockets.
- Fitting details—waistbands, casings, ribbing, and hems.
- Closures—buttons, snaps, hooks and eyes, hook-and-loop tape, and zippers.
- Trims—braid, ruffles, lace, and appliqués.

Hand Sewing

Constructing garments usually requires some hand sewing. To make threading the needle easier, cut the thread at an angle by holding the scissors at a slant. Then, hold the needle up against a light background so that you can see the eye. Insert the thread through the eye, pull it through, cut the thread off at the desired length, and knot it.

There are two ways to secure your stitching at the end of a row. One way is to make a knot. Form a loop of thread by making a small stitch. Without pulling the loop tight, make a second small stitch in the same place. As the needle comes up, bring it through the first thread loop and pull it tight. Repeat. Then cut the thread close to the knot. The other way to secure stitching is to make two small backstitches on top of each other. **Figure 66.1** describes four basic hand stitches, including the backstitch.

Fundamental Techniques

If you are just learning to sew, you may want to practice your skills on an easy-to-sew pattern before choosing a project with more challenging features, such as collars, cuffs, sleeves, and waistbands. Once you master these techniques, however, a wider choice of patterns and styles will be available to you. Basic instructions for these and other fundamental techniques are discussed briefly in this chapter. Pattern guide sheets give precise directions for adding features to particular garments.

Finishing touches on garments, such as sewing on buttons, may require some hand sewing.

TEACH

Topic on p. 639:
- **About Hand Sewing**

Checking Comprehension

✓ Can you make a garment without hand sewing? *Not usually, since hand sewing is used for many finishing steps.*

✓ Why should you hold a needle against a light background as you thread it? *Eye of the needle will be easier to see.*

✓ What will happen if you do not secure the end of the thread before you begin to sew? *Stitches will pull out.*

RETEACHING

■ **Getting Started.** Have students practice threading a needle and methods of securing handstitching.

ENRICHMENT

■ **Sew What?** Ask students if they have heard the saying, "A stitch in time saves nine." What do they think this saying means, literally and figuratively? Do they agree or disagree?

MORE ABOUT Threading Needles

Needles with small eyes can be difficult to thread, especially for those with vision problems. Students might want to know of methods that make threading needles easier. Some needles have an eye that extends to the top of the needle, allowing the thread to be pulled down into the eye. A special needle threader can be purchased that also helps. Simply moistening the end of the thread compresses the fibers into a point that is more easily slipped through the eye.

Topics on pp. 640-641:
- **Hand-Sewing Techniques**
- **Sewing Collars, Cuffs, Sleeves, and Pockets**

Checking Comprehension

✔ Where can you find out how to construct a collar or cuffs for your sewing project? *From the pattern guide sheet.*

✔ How is a set-in sleeve different from a kimono or raglan sleeve? *A set-in sleeve is eased into the armhole seam; a kimono sleeve is cut as part of the main garment; the seam in a raglan sleeve runs from the neckline to the underarm.*

✔ What is the difference between in-seam pockets and patch pockets? *In-seam pockets are often cut as part of the garment and stitched into the side seams; patch pockets are cut separately and topstitched on the outside of the garment.*

USING VISUALS

Refer students to Figure 66.1. Discuss these questions:

1. For which stitches would the color of thread be important? *All of them. It should match for invisible stitching; it should contrast for decorative stitching.*
2. Why would you use a hemming stitch instead of machine stitching a hem? *A hemming stitch is almost invisible; machine stitching shows on the outside.*

Figure 66.1
HAND-SEWING TECHNIQUES

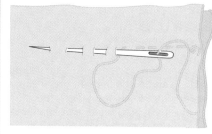

Running stitch. The simplest of stitches, this stitch is used for basting and gathering. You can form a running stitch by making tiny, even stitches $\frac{1}{16}$ in. to $\frac{1}{4}$ in. (1.5 mm to 6 mm) long. You may also create this stitch by weaving the needle in and out of the fabric several times before pulling the thread through. Do this evenly so that your stitches are all the same length.

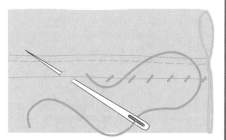

Hemming stitch. This slanted stitch is used frequently on bound, hemmed, or serged hem finishes. To form a hemming stitch, first secure the thread in the hem edge or seam allowance. Working from right to left, take a tiny, barely noticeable stitch in the garment. Place the needle between the hem edge and the garment and bring it up diagonally and out through the hem edge, about $\frac{1}{4}$ in. (6 mm) from the first stitch. Continue spacing stitches about $\frac{1}{4}$ in. (6 mm) apart.

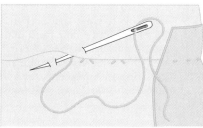

Slip stitch. This stitch is almost invisible and is used to attach a bound or turned-under edge to another piece of fabric—in linings, pockets, and trims for example. Insert the needle inside the fold of the fabric, bringing it out again about $\frac{1}{4}$ in. (6 mm) from the previous stitch. Working from right to left, pick up just one or two garment threads at the point where the needle emerges from the folded edge. Continue in this way, first sewing inside the fold and then picking up one or two threads from the inside of the garment.

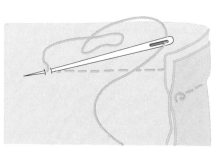

Backstitch. This durable stitch is used to repair seams. From the outside it looks like a machine stitch, but the stitches overlap on the inside. To form a backstitch, secure the thread at the beginning of the seam. Working from right to left, bring the needle through the fabric to the upper side facing you. Then, insert the needle one stitch back—about $\frac{1}{8}$ in. (3 mm)—behind the previous stitch and bring it out one stitch ahead—about $\frac{1}{8}$ in. (3 mm)—of where you brought it out last. Continue in this manner until the seam is completed. The stitches on the underside will look twice as long as those on the upper side.

640   UNIT 7   Clothing and Textiles

MORE ABOUT Hand Sewing

Hand sewing is used extensively in tailoring coats and suits. For example, the entire surface of the collar interfacing is stitched by hand to the collar facing, using small padding stitches that form a herringbone pattern. Tailors also use the padding stitch on lapels. The stitching ensures that the collar and the lapels roll correctly when the garment is worn.

Collars and Cuffs

You will find specific instructions on the pattern guide sheet for a garment's collar and cuffs. Some guidelines, however, apply to collars and cuffs generally. On a collar, the curved edges should be smooth and the collar points should be even. The underside, called the undercollar, should never show.

Most shirt collars and cuffs have a layer of interfacing to help them retaín their shape and body. To eliminate bulk, trim and grade all seam allowances. Careful stitching and pressing will help make the enclosed seams lie smooth and flat.

Sleeves

There are three basic types of sleeves. Each is joined to the garment in a different way:

- **Kimono sleeves** are cut in one piece with the top of the garment. They are usually short and loose-fitting, and they are the easiest to sew.

- **Raglan sleeves** have a diagonal seam from the neckline to the underarm on the front and the back. They are fairly easy to sew and comfortable to wear.
- **Set-in sleeves** are attached to the garment with a seam that encircles the arm near the shoulder. The sleeve itself has a larger circumference than the armhole into which it fits. This allows arm movement but makes fitting the sleeve more difficult than other types. One mark of a fine-quality garment is a set-in sleeve without puckers or gathers in the seam.

Pockets

The two most common types of pockets are in-seam and patch pockets. Often, in-seam pockets are cut as part of the garment and stitched along with side seams. Patch pockets are sewn to the outside of a garment. Many are functional, but some are merely decorative. They are often parts of garments but are also practical on tote bags, duffel bags, backpacks, and other accessories.

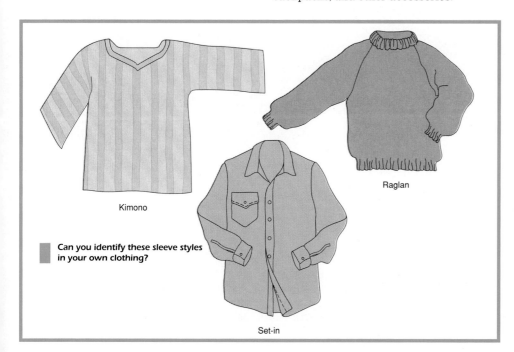

Kimono

Raglan

Can you identify these sleeve styles in your own clothing?

Set-in

Activities

■ **Is Bigger Better?** Ask students to explain the purpose of the extra fabric in a set-in sleeve (larger than armhole opening). How might the fit of the garment be affected if the sleeve pattern was the same size as the armhole? (*Critical Thinking*)

■ **Pocket Pointers.** Tell students that applying patch pockets to a plaid, striped, or printed fabric requires matching the pocket to the garment. However, cutting the pocket on the bias adds a different look to the garment and often avoids the need to match the pattern so carefully. Demonstrate how to miter square corners and notch rounded corners to eliminate bulk. (*Observation*)

ENRICHMENT

■ **Something Special.** Ask knowledgeable students to show the class how to do embroidery stitches, another form of hand stitching. They might show a simple outlining stitch, a satin stitch that fills in areas with color, lazy daisy stitches that form flowers, and cross stitches that form designs and patterns with changes in color.

MULTICULTURAL *Perspectives*

Hand stitching is a centuries-old tradition. Among the Hmong people of Laos, Thailand, and nearby countries, for example, girls as young as five begin learning how to create intricate hand-stitched patterns. As they gain skill, their stitchery earns them praise and status in the community. Some of their beautiful handiwork records the history of the culture.

DID YOU KNOW?

In sixteenth-century Europe, both men and women wore lace collars and cuffs to indicate their status and wealth: the larger and stiffer, the wealthier the wearer. Some collars, called ruffs, were so large that people could not move their heads and had to use special utensils to eat. The term *white-collar worker* is based on these collar fashions, as the large collars exempted the wearers from most physical labor. You may wish to locate photos of these collars and cuffs to show to students.

- Hemming
- Waistbands, Hems, Casings, and Ribbing

Checking Comprehension

✓ Why do waistbands need interfacing? *To prevent rolling and stretching.*

✓ How can hems be finished and secured? *By serging or applying seam binding or stretch lace. They can be secured by hand stitching, machine stitching, or fusing the hem in place.*

✓ How do you make a self-casing? *By turning under and stitching an edge of the fabric, forming a tunnel for a drawstring or length of elastic.*

✓ What does "recovery" refer to regarding knits? *The ability of a knit to regain its original shape after stretching.*

USING VISUALS

Refer students to Figure 66.2 and discuss these questions:

1. What can happen if you mark a hem for pants while wearing low shoes but wear shoes with higher heels with the finished garment? *The garment may be hemmed too short to wear with higher heels.*

2. Should you make a hem an equal distance from a person's waist or an equal distance from the floor. *An equal distance from the floor or it will probably be uneven.*

Figure 66.2

HEMMING A GARMENT

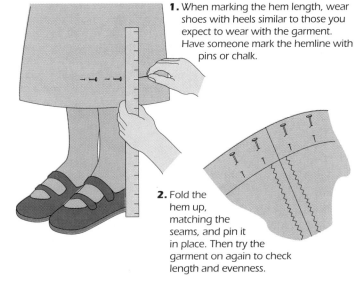

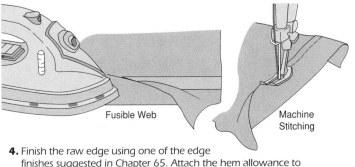

1. When marking the hem length, wear shoes with heels similar to those you expect to wear with the garment. Have someone mark the hemline with pins or chalk.

2. Fold the hem up, matching the seams, and pin it in place. Then try the garment on again to check length and evenness.

3. Use a sewing gauge, notched cardboard, or a ruler to mark the hem width plus 1/4 in. (6 mm) on the hem allowance for finishing. Trim away excess fabric.

Fusible Web

Machine Stitching

Hand Stitching

4. Finish the raw edge using one of the edge finishes suggested in Chapter 65. Attach the hem allowance to the garment by hand stitching, machine stitching, or fusing.

To topstitch a patch pocket in place, use the edge of the presser foot as a guide for straight stitching. The top corners of the pocket should be reinforced with backstitching or a stitched triangle at the corner.

Waistbands

Waistbands need to be strong and sturdy, and they should fit comfortably. Interfacing is essential to keep the waistband from rolling and stretching.

MORE ABOUT Hemming

The type of garment, type of fabric, and the amount of curve in the hem determine hem width. Hems on fairly full garments can be up to 3 inches (7.5 cm) wide, while hems on pants, sleeves, and shorts might be only 1 to 2 inches (2.5-5 cm) wide. Curved hems are made narrower than straight hems so that less fabric has to be eased in. Hemming with a single strand of thread helps keep stitches from showing on the outside. Keeping the stitches slightly loose prevents the hem from pulling or rippling. Demonstrate how to press a hem lightly so the impression of the turned-up hem is not visible on the outside of the garment.

Most waistbands call for a turned-under edge as a finish on the inside, but it is faster and easier to place one long edge of the waistband on the selvage when cutting out. Because the selvage does not ravel, this technique saves a step and eliminates the extra bulk of the turned-under edge. Another excellent way to reduce bulk in waistbands is to serge off the seam allowance on the inside edge.

Hems

A hem is usually the last step in constructing a garment. **Figure 66.2** shows the basic steps in hemming a garment.

Finish the raw edge of a woven fabric (refer to the seam finishes in **Figure 65.5** on page 633, which can be used as edge finishes) to prevent raveling. Serging the edge is an especially good choice. Hems may also be finished, however, with seam binding or stretch lace.

You may attach the hem by hand stitching (usually using a slip stitch or hemming stitch), machine stitching, or fusing. To fuse a hem, place a strip of fusible web between the garment and hem about ¼ in. (6 mm) below the finished edge.

Casings

A casing is a tunnel of fabric that holds a piece of elastic or a drawstring. Casings are often used at the waistlines of pants, shorts, skirts, dresses, and jumpsuits for an easy finish and comfortable pull-on fit. They can also be used at necklines and at the hemlines of sleeves and pants.

Most casings are self-casings, made by folding back an edge of the fabric at the edge of the garment and stitching it in place. The raw edge should be turned under ¼ in. (6 mm) or finished with a serger. Applied casings consist of separate strips of fabric or bias tape sewn to the inside of a garment—for example, at the waistline of a one-piece garment.

Leave an opening at the seam of both self-casings and applied casings to insert the elastic or drawstring. By fastening a safety pin to the end of the elastic or drawstring, you will be able to pull it through the casing.

Ribbing

Ribbing is *a stretchy knit band with recovery.* Recovery is the ability of a fabric to go back to its original shape after it is stretched. Ribbing can be used instead of a hem to finish necklines, wrists, ankles, and waistlines and to provide a snug but comfortable fit. Ribbing is used on pullover and pull-on garments, such as sweatsuits and sweaters.

To maintain stretchability, apply ribbing with a flexible stitch, such as a narrow zigzag or a serger overedge stretch stitch. Stretch the ribbing to fit the garment edge as you sew.

Closures

Closures include buttons and buttonholes, snaps, hooks and eyes, zippers, and hook-and-loop tape, as well as novelty buckles and rings. The type of closure used on a garment is often dictated by the fit. Zippers provide a close-to-the-body fit. Looser-fitting clothes use buttons and buttonholes. Snaps are used where there is little stress on the closure. Each of these types of closures is described in the following paragraphs.

Figure 66.3 on page 645 shows how to attach buttons, snaps, hooks and eyes, and hook-and-loop tapes to garments. Because the way a zipper is attached depends on what type of zipper it is and where it is found on the garment, always check the instructions that come with the zipper and your pattern guide sheet before trying to attach it.

Buttons and Buttonholes

Pattern markings show the location of buttons and the length of buttonholes. Well-made buttonholes should all be the same length and the same distance from the edge of the garment. Buy buttons when you buy a pattern and fabric. The quantity and size you'll need are listed on the pattern envelope. This also assures that the color matches.

■ **How To.** Organize the class into five groups and assign each group a construction challenge: collars, cuffs, sleeves, pockets, or waistbands. Ask each group to develop a series of illustrations with captions that describe how to construct the assigned garment detail.

■ **Special Cases.** Have students note whether the patterns for their current projects include collars, cuffs, sleeves, pockets, waistbands, or hems. If so, have them study the printed pattern instructions. Ask students to share with the whole class any special directions that are not included in, or are different from, the text.

■ **To Stretch or Not to Stretch.** Discuss what might happen if ribbing is attached to a garment with ordinary machine stitching. *(Critical Thinking)*

SPECIAL NEEDS Strategies

Attention Deficit. Inexperienced sewers often find construction details frustrating because of the concentration and the motor skills required. To help such students gain competence, have them create samples of the construction details before adding them to their sewing projects. Another option is to provide them with step-by-step samples.

REAL-LIFE APPLICATION

Read the following to students: *Chelsey had just finished sewing a new skirt, which she wore to school the next day. "Did you make it?" a classmate asked. When several friends also noticed right away that the skirt was home sewn, Chelsey finally asked her good friend Eva how she knew. Reluctantly Eva responded.* Ask students what Eva might have said. *Answers will vary. Possibly hem was puckered or stitches showed through to front side. Another possibility is lack of ironing to press bottom crease in hem.*

Topics on pp. 644-645:
- Closures—Buttons and Snaps
- Adaptations for Disabilities

Checking Comprehension

✓ Why is it important for a button to have a shank? *Without it, the button will be sewn tightly against the garment, making it difficult to push the button through a buttonhole.*

✓ Why doesn't a shank button have holes through it? *It is attached to the garment by the built-in shank on the back of the button.*

✓ Would a snap be used to hold together the edges of a neckline that just meet? *No, the sides must overlap.*

Managing Your Life

Have students read "Clothing Adaptations for People with Disabilities."

Answers to Applying . . .

1. Temporary disabilities: limited mobility caused by broken bones; limitations following surgery. Permanent disabilities: missing or paralyzed limbs; limited mobility, or other neurological conditions.
2. Increased independence; greater ease in dressing; less frustration.

644

Managing Your Life

Clothing Adaptations For People with Disabilities

Getting dressed is often a challenge for people with temporary and permanent disabilities. A task as simple as opening a zipper can be frustrating. Creating products for people with disabilities is a growing business. Notions available in every fabric store may also be used to make dressing easier. Here are a few examples:

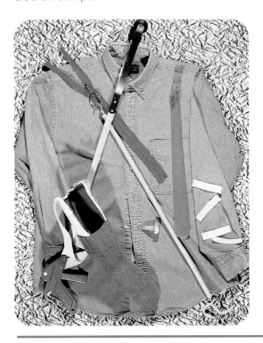

- **Buttons.** Large buttons and toggles are generally easier to handle than smaller ones. A button hook, a rod attached to a spring steel loop, is another option. By sliding the loop over the button and through the hole, the button can be pulled into place. Button extenders make it unnecessary to deal with buttons at all. They hold shirt cuffs together, allowing arms to slip through easily.
- **Zippers.** Attaching a large metal ring, a tassel, or a chain to a zipper makes zipping easier. Zipper pulls, similar to button hooks, are also available. Sewn into leg or arm seams, zippers can allow garments to fit over braces and casts.
- **Hook-and-loop tape.** Zippers, buttons, and snaps can also be replaced by hook-and-loop tape, which is possible to open and close with just one hand. To retain the look of the garment, buttons can be restitched on top of the buttonholes.
- **Dressing sticks.** Hooks, shoehorns, and leather thongs attached to poles allow users to push or pull items into place. Rigid or flexible molds called sock starters hold socks in position as they slide onto the foot.

Applying the Principles

1. What are some examples of temporary and permanent disabilities that might require adaptations to clothing?
2. Name several benefits that dressing adaptations might provide.

There are two kinds of buttons: sew-through and shank. A **sew-through button** is *a button that has two or four holes in it*. To allow for the thickness of the buttonhole when the button is closed, you'll need to make a thread shank when you sew this type of button on. A **shank button** is *a button that has a built-in shank, or loop, on the back*. The button does not have any holes in it.

644 UNIT 7 Clothing and Textiles

Snaps

Sew-on snaps are suitable for overlapping areas where there is little strain, such as at the neckline to hold a facing edge flat. Snaps consist of two parts: a ball and a socket. Heavy-duty snaps can be used instead of buttons and buttonholes on jackets and shirts of sturdy, heavyweight fabrics.

REAL-LIFE APPLICATION

Read the problems below and ask students to suggest several possible causes and solutions for each one:

- Kevin sewed ribbing at the ankles of his sweatpants, but the stitching around both ankles has broken.

- Sheila made a skirt that buttons at the waistline, but the button keeps popping open.
- Shirene used a snap to close the neckline of her blouse, but her stitches show on the outside.

Figure 66.3
CLOSURES

How to Sew on a Button

Sew-through button. You will need to make a thread shank to sew on this type of button. Secure the thread to the underside of the garment at the button location. Then, bring the needle up through the fabric and one hole of the button. Lay a toothpick or a large pin on top of the button between the holes. Bring the needle over the toothpick and down through a second hole. Sew several more stitches over the toothpick or pin and down through the fabric.

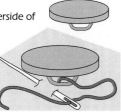

End stitches with the needle and thread under the button between the button and the garment. Remove the toothpick or pin, and wind the thread several times around the thread under the button to create the thread shank. Push the needle through to the underside of the fabric and secure it.

Shank button. Secure the thread to the underside of the fabric at the button location. Sew a shank button in place with several small stitches through the shank and into the fabric. Secure the thread to the underside of the fabric.

How to Sew on a Snap

The ball section of the snap should be sewn on the underside of the overlap at least ⅛ in. (3 mm) from the edge. Then sew the socket on the upper side of the underlap so that they are perfectly aligned. You can mark the socket position by closing the ball side over the fabric piece and pushing a pin through the ball to the underlap. Make several small stitches through each hole, carrying the thread under the snap from one hole to the next. Be sure that no stitches show on the outside of the garment. Secure your stitches when you begin and finish your work.

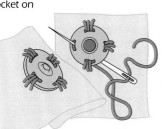

REAL-LIFE APPLICATION

To prevent buttons from pulling off coats, two sew-through buttons are sometimes used instead of one. A continuous thread is used to sew one button on the outside of the coat and a smaller button on the inside. The outside button has a thread shank to make it easier to button the coat.

When snaps are used on coats or other heavy garments, special large (sometimes covered) snaps are used.

Activities

More than Decoration. Ask students to explain why the spacing of buttonholes is important, visually and functionally. (*Problem Solving*)

ENRICHMENT

■ **Toys That Teach.** Have students design toys that include as many types of closures as possible, such as stuffed animals with shirts and skirts. The goal is to teach young children how to use closures and give them an opportunity to practice using them. Some students might enjoy creating their designs in fabric. Perhaps they could donate their finished products to a child care center.

FAMILY AND COMMUNITY OUTREACH

Ask students if they know of people who have button collections. Perhaps one or more collectors could share their collections with the class. Have students learn about the history of buttons and the characteristics that make some buttons valuable to collectors.

CROSS-CURRICULAR ACTIVITY
Art

Ask students to sketch garments that use closures as key elements in their design. Some of the closures, especially buttons, might have no function. Other closures close the garment. Have students point out the ways they have incorporated both working and decorative closures.

Topics on pp. 646-648:

- Closures—Hooks and Eyes, Hook-and-Loop Tape, Zippers
- Trims

Checking Comprehension

✓ How do you decide which kind of hook to use with a hook-and-eye closure? *Use a loop eye if the garment edges just meet, a straight eye if the edges overlap.*

✓ How does a zipper foot help? *Helps stitch close to the zipper teeth.*

✓ Where can you find out how to insert a zipper into a garment? *The pattern guide and/or the zipper package.*

✓ How can you make an appliqué? *By cutting a simple design from firmly woven fabric and sewing it to the garment with a close zigzag.*

USING VISUALS

Refer students to Figure 66.3. Discuss these questions:

1. How can you sew snaps or hooks and eyes on invisibly? *By making the stitches only through the facing and not catching the outside fabric.*

2. What can you use to help make a thread shank for a sew-through button? *A pin or a toothpick.*

3. Why should you sew the hook side down to the fabric under the curved hook? *To make sure it lies flat against the garment.*

Figure 66.3 (Continued)

CLOSURES

How to Sew on Hooks and Eyes

On edges that meet, sew the hook ⅛ in. (3 mm) from the edge with several small stitches through each hole. Finish with three or four stitches across the end of the hook, under the curve, to make sure it lies flat against the garment. Position the eye so that it is opposite the hook and extends slightly beyond the garment edge. Attach the eye with several small stitches around each hole.

How to Sew on Hook-and-Loop Tape

Position the loop section on the overlap and the hooks on the underlap at least ¼ in. (6 mm) from the edge. Attach rectangular strips or squares to fabric by machine stitching around all four sides. Attach the circles with a machine-stitched triangle.

Hooks and Eyes

There are several kinds of hook-and-eye fasteners. General-purpose hooks and eyes are used where there is little strain on the fastener, as at a neckline. If the finished edges of a garment just meet, a hook with a round (or loop) eye is used. (**Figure 66.3** shows how to sew on this type of hook and eye.) If the edges overlap, a hook with a straight eye is the appropriate one to use.

Special hooks and eyes are used at waistbands. These hooks are strong and flat so that they will not slide out of the eye.

Hook-and-Loop Tape

Hook-and-loop tape is a type of fastener consisting of two square, rectangular, or circular pieces of nylon tape that stick to each other when pressed together. One side has tiny hooks and the other has tiny soft loops. These closures are common on parkas, jackets, camping equipment, pillows, and tote bags. They are particularly useful on clothing for children and for people with disabilities, who may have difficulty opening and closing other closures.

DID YOU KNOW?

The concept of hook-and-loop fasteners was first proposed in the 1940s by Swiss engineer George deMaestral. He had noticed that woodland cockleburrs stuck to his pant legs after he brushed against them. As he examined the burrs under a microscope, he discovered the hook-and-loop structures that made them cling. Thus, the inspiration for Velcro®.

STRATEGIES That Work

Timesaving Tips

Having too little time is often cited as a reason for not sewing. If you have had the same thought, consider sewing basic garments using these timesaving items:

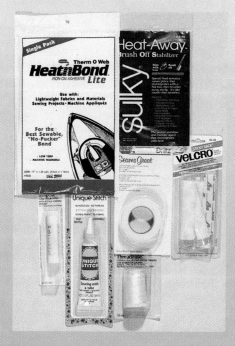

- **Fabric glue sticks.** Instead of basting hems, zippers, and trims by hand, glue them with fabric glue. The glue can also be used for repairing or adjusting pattern pieces.
- **Dissolving basting tape.** Another way to eliminate tedious basting is to apply basting tape. It dissolves the first time you wash the garment.
- **Fusible web and fusible thread.** These make quick work of hemming. They can also be used to stabilize seams and to attach lace, trims, and appliqués. When applied properly, fusing lasts through normal washing and dry-cleaning.
- **Fusible hook-and-loop tape.** Instead of taking the time to sew on buttons, snaps, and zippers, use fusible hook-and-loop tape.
- **Iron-on hemming tape.** A strip of this tape can be ironed over the raw edge of a seam. This is helpful when the hem is shallow or the fabric is very bulky.

Making the Strategy Work

Think . . .

1. Suppose that you notice the hem of your jacket is coming down as you're leaving for school. What could you do?
2. What should you consider when deciding whether or not to use a fusible product?
3. Why would iron-on hemming tape be helpful for bulky fabrics?

Try...

Try one or two of the tips described in this feature. Present the results to your classmates. Compare the effectiveness of various methods.

Activities

■ **The Professional Touch.** Discuss factors that make some garments with trim look homemade. Ask students to suggest ways they might add trim to purchased garments. (*Observation*)

■ **Zip It Up.** Demonstrate the use of the zipper foot in inserting zippers. Point out the importance of stitching in a straight, even line and using thread that closely matches the fabric. (*Observation*)

RETEACHING

■ **Closure Chart.** Have students create a chart that lists the types of closures and situations in which each type should and should not be used. For example, a snap could be used to fasten a cuff but not a skirt. Discuss the advantages and disadvantages of each closure type.

STRATEGIES THAT WORK

Have students read "Timesaving Tips."

Answers to Think . . .

1. Use a fabric glue stick.
2. Whether the fabric can withstand the heat needed to fuse the product.
3. If you use iron-on tape, you would not need to turn under the edge of the bulky fabric.

CROSS-CURRICULAR ACTIVITY
Art

Have students personalize a T-shirt with embroidery, trims, or appliqués.

MORE ABOUT Zippers

Although Whitcomb L. Judson first exhibited the zipper in 1893, a number of other inventors devised variations on this device. Probably the first extensive use of zippers occurred in 1917, when the United States Navy produced windproof flying suits with slide fasteners. During the 1920s and 1930s, slide fasteners began to be used on men's and women's clothing. They were not referred to as zippers until 1923, when a man named B. G. Work of the B.F. Goodrich Company called the slide fasteners on the company's overshoes zippers. Zippers are available in both metal and nylon and in many lengths, colors, and styles.

Review

■ **Chapter Review.** Use the contents of the Chapter Review page to help students review concepts, think critically, and apply their knowledge.

■ **Study Guide.** Have students complete the Study Guide for Chapter 66 on p. 216 of the Student Workbook.

■ **Sewing Tips.** Organize the class into pairs and assign each pair a construction challenge from this chapter, including types of closures. Ask each pair to prepare a chart with the title of the construction detail, a short list of do's and don'ts for beginning sewers, and a diagram or two for clarity. Invite the whole class to comment on the strengths and any omissions in each pair's chart.

Evaluation

■ **Chapter Test.** Use the reproducible chapter test provided in the Teacher's Classroom Resources or create your own test using the *Testmaker Software*.

■ **Alternative Assessment.** Evaluate students' samples or the techniques they used in adding collars, cuffs, buttons, and so on to their current sewing projects.

■ **Details Count.** Ask students to name construction skills they have learned in Chapters 65 and 66 that can make their hand-sewn garments look professional a smooth cap on a set-in sleeve, evenly spaced darts without puckers, an even and invisible hem).

Zippers

Detailed instructions for inserting zippers are given on each zipper package. Zippers can be inserted in a seam in two ways: centered, with a row of stitching on each side of the zipper, or lapped, with just one row of stitching showing on the outside. A special zipper foot on the sewing machine makes it easy to stitch close to the zipper teeth.

In fly-front zipper applications, the overlap side of the zipper is stitched to a facing, not to the garment. Topstitching holds the facing and the zipper in place. Separating zippers are used in jackets and sweatshirts. The zipper splits open into two pieces instead of being stopped at the bottom. The type of zipper and the method of application you use will depend on the location of the zipper in the garment.

Trims

Trims, such as braid, ruffles, and lace, add a personal touch to a garment, accessory, or household item. Trims may be hand sewn, machine stitched, fused, or serged.

An **appliqué** (a-pluh-KAY) is *a cutout fabric decoration sewn or fused onto a different fabric background*. Appliqués are popular on children's clothing. You can buy them or make them yourself. If you make them, use a firmly woven fabric that does not ravel easily and a shape without intricate edges.

■ **What kinds of trims do you see in this photo?**

Embroidery can also be used to personalize a pocket, a pillow, or a tote bag or to create a unique design on a T-shirt or a place mat. Many electronic sewing machines have embroidery patterns and designs built into them.

DID YOU KNOW?

In ancient Rome, the color, design, and width of the trim on hems indicated the wearer's social class and occupation. Today's trims include sew-on beads, sequins, pearls, gemstones, and even small mirrors. These trims indicate the wearer's taste and creativity in clothing styles.

MORE ABOUT *Sewing Fundamentals*

Sewing skills come with practice. Help students see that they need to set high standards but also allow themselves to make the occasional mistakes that are part of learning a new skill.

Reviewing the Facts

1. What are the four basic hand-sewing stitches, and how are they used?
2. What are the three basic styles of sleeves? Describe how each is joined to the garment.
3. What are the two basic types of pockets? List any other pockets with which you are familiar.
4. What are the steps in hemming a garment?
5. Briefly describe two closures and how to attach them.
6. List three types of trim that can personalize a sewing project.

Thinking Critically

1. If you had to decide between finishing something by hand or by machine, what would you consider in making your decision? What are the advantages and disadvantages of each method?
2. What factors might affect the depth of a skirt hem and how you choose to finish it?

Applying Your Knowledge

1. **Evaluating Alternatives.** Choose three garments or other items from pattern catalogs or your own wardrobe. Study the closures on the items, and tell why you think each type of closure was chosen for each opening. Then suggest alternative closures for each item, including ones that could be used by people with disabilities.
2. **Rating Work.** Compare an expensive and inexpensive garment in terms of quality. Evaluate such details as collars, sleeves, cuffs, pockets, waistbands, casings, hems, fasteners, and trims. How does the work differ? Does the most expensive garment always include the best work? Summarize your findings in a written report or display board.

Making Connections

1. **History.** If available, visit a museum or historical costume collection and analyze construction methods. Summarize your findings in a written report.
2. **Social Studies.** The United States is home to people from many different cultures. Make a list of clothing that you might see, such as kimonos or dashikis, that are distinctive to other cultures. Compare details to garments you typically see.
3. **Art and Design.** Using catalogs and fashion magazines, find a basic garment, such as a shirt, a pair of pants, or a dress. Suggest five variations of the basic garment using details described in this chapter. Describe in writing how each variation would change the look or fit of the garment.

Building Your Portfolio

Providing Sewing Samples
Create five samples of construction fundamentals discussed in this chapter—a collar, a hem, a zipper, a snap, and an appliqué, for example. Create a short caption for each sample telling how you did it, and put each sample and caption in a plastic sheet protector. Add the sheets to your portfolio.

CHAPTER 66   More Sewing Fundamentals   649

ANSWERS TO REVIEWING THE FACTS

1. The running stitch is used for seams, basting and gathering; the hemming stitch for hem finishes; the slipstitch for attaching linings, pockets, and trims; the backstitch for repairing seams.
2. A *kimono sleeve* is cut as part of the garment; a *raglan sleeve* is joined with a seam from the neckline to the underarm on the front and back of the garment; a *set-in sleeve* is eased into the armhole with a seam that encircles the arm near the shoulder.
3. In-seam and patch; other pocket types may include slash, piped, and flap.
4. Mark the hem, pin it up, mark the hem width, trim extra fabric, finish the edge, and sew to the garment.
5. Any two closures in the chapter (or others familiar to students). For example, a shank button has a loop on the back that is stitched by hand to the garment; the two sides of hook-and-loop tape stick to each other and are stitched by machine to the garment.
6. Any three: braid, lace, beads, ribbon, fabric flowers, appliqués (or others).

ANSWERS TO THINKING CRITICALLY

1. Machine stitching is faster and more durable, but it is also more visible and requires some experience to achieve neat results. Hand stitching is less visible and easier to remove, but it takes more time.
2. Hem depth is determined by style of the garment (as with straight or curved edge) and the weight of the fabric. Extra fullness in a curved edge requires a narrower hem. Fullness must be eased in so the hem will lie flat. A heavy fabric usually has a narrower hem than a light fabric and requires seam binding or serging to avoid turning under the hem edge.

Chapter Overview

Chapter 67 suggests ways that students can make old or ill-fitting clothes wearable again by adjusting the hems, altering the seams, or changing the styles. Students also learn how to use fabric dye and paint. The chapter encourages new uses for the garments and fabrics and the fibers in old clothing.

Motivator

■ **Cut-Offs.** Ask students if they have ever shortened the legs of a pair of jeans and worn them as shorts. What are some advantages of doing this?

Objectives

Discuss the chapter objectives. Remind students that the objectives focus on important chapter concepts.

Vocabulary

This chapter focuses on the word *recycle*. Remind students that the prefix *re-* often means again. A *cycle* is "a series of events that occurs regularly and leads back to the starting point." Ask students to explain some natural cycles, such as the water cycle. Then discuss ways that recycling applies to clothing.

Chapter 67
Redesigning and Recycling

Terms to Learn

• recycle
• redesign

Objectives

This chapter will help you to:

• Describe **ways to get more use out of your favorite garments.**
• Demonstrate **how to make old or ill-fitting clothes wearable again.**
• Suggest **uses for clothes that you can no longer wear.**

650   UNIT 7   Clothing and Textiles

CHAPTER RESOURCES

Student Workbook
Study Guide, p. 218
Activity, *To Tell the Truth*, p. 219

Teacher's Classroom Resources
Lesson Plan, p. 71

Cooperative Learning, *Fabric Creativity*, pp. 73-74
Decision Making, *Redesigning and Recycling*, p. 25
Extension #96, *New Uses for Old Fabric*, p. 102

Life Skills, *Creative Makeovers*, p. 105
Chapter 67 Test, pp. 139-140
Performance Assessment, *Recycling or Redesigning a Garment*, p. 104
Reteaching, *Decisions About Old Clothing*, p. 73

In Chapter 58 you learned a good technique for taking charge of your wardrobe. You divided your clothing into three categories. One of these included clothes that you don't wear because you don't like them, they no longer fit, or they are beyond repair.

In that group were there any pants that were too short or an outfit that was no longer in style? You don't have to throw these clothes away. You might be able to **redesign** a garment—*change something so that it's more in fashion or has a fresh new look*. Perhaps you can **recycle** another—*find a new use* for it.

Redesigning and recycling offer many personal rewards. You can use your creativity to alter a pair of pants that fit poorly, redesign a shirt bought at a garage sale, or change a garment in your closet to better suit your tastes. Extending the life of your clothes is a good way to save money.

Redesigning a Garment

One of the easiest ways to make a garment wearable again is to change the way it fits. You may be able to do this by simply adjusting the hems or seams. If you are ready for a completely new look, consider changing the style of the garment entirely.

Adjusting Hems

Knowing how to adjust hems is a useful skill. Sudden growth can make a pair of pants too short. Fashion changes are often reflected in skirt hemlines, and adjusting several hems is less expensive than buying new garments. **Figure 67.1** shows the steps in adjusting a hem.

Figure 67.1
ADJUSTING HEMS

1. To lengthen or shorten a hem, remove the stitching and press out the old crease. Try on the garment, and have someone mark the new hem length with pins or chalk.

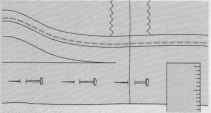

2. Turn the hem to the inside along the marked line, and pin it in place. If the hem is too wide, cut off any extra fabric, and finish the raw edge with seam tape or one of the edge finishes mentioned in Chapter 65.

3. Sew the hem in place, keeping the stitches slightly loose to avoid puckering. Make sure that the stitches do not show on the outside of the garment.

Note: If there is too little fabric for lengthening the garment, stitch a strip of wide hem facing to the bottom edge. Turn the facing to the inside along the new hemline, and sew it in place. You could also use iron-on hemming tape or add a fabric band or ruffle.

CHAPTER 67   Redesigning and Recycling   651

Topics on p. 651:
- **Redesigning and Recycling Defined**
- **Adjusting Hems**

Checking Comprehension

✔ How do redesigning a garment and recycling it differ? *Redesigning means giving a garment a new look; recycling means finding a new use for it.*

✔ How can redesigning clothes save money? *You can get more wear from old outfits instead of buying new.*

Activities

■ **Ups and Downs.** Ask if hems are adjusted more often because the wearer has grown or because fashions have changed. (*Observation*)

■ **Examining Hems.** Have students examine the hems in the clothing they are wearing. Which have enough fabric to be lengthened? Which have noticeable wear at the hem creases that might show if lengthened? What are ways to deal with these problems?

USING VISUALS

Refer students to Figure 67.1. Ask:
1. Why is it important to press out the old hem, even if you are shortening a garment? *If not pressed out, the new hem might be uneven.*
2. Why should you have someone mark the new hem for you? *Likely to be uneven.*

MORE ABOUT Alterations

Seams and hems sometimes show wear marks and creases when let out. Some fabrics also show the needle holes after stitching is removed. Fading can also be a problem if the newly revealed fabric is darker than the part that has always been exposed to light. In altering, students might cover some areas with braid or other trim. If the problem cannot be solved, however, alteration is not be a good idea if the garment doesn't look good enough to wear. On the other hand, if hems are being shortened or seams and darts are being taken in, these situations are not a problem.

Topics on pp. 652-653:

- **Altering Seams**
- **Changing Styles**
- **Dyeing and Painting Fabric**

Checking Comprehension

✓ What is a disadvantage of serge seams in making alterations? *They are usually only ¼ inch (6 mm) wide, so they can't be let out.*

✓ What are some ways to change the style of a garment? *Answers will vary.*

✓ What fabric colors are easiest to dye? *Light colors.*

✓ Why should you clean equipment carefully after using it to dye fabric? *If any dye remains, it may stain other clothing.*

✓ How do you tie-dye fabric? *Tie sections of it tightly before placing it in the dye solution. The dye will penetrate unevenly, creating patterns of color.*

652

Figure 67.2
ALTERING SEAMS

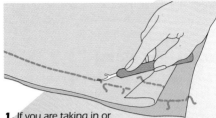

1. If you are taking in or letting out a seam, first remove the old stitching as needed.

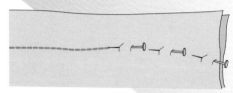

2. Try the garment on inside out, and have someone pin the new seamline. Baste the new seam.

3. Try on the garment again to check the fit. Stitch the new seam, tapering the new seam to the old one. Overlap the old stitching lines by 1 in. (2.5 cm), and backstitch to secure the seam.

4. Press the new seam open.

Altering Seams

You may need to alter seams if you have purchased a garment that is a little too big or too small. You may also want to alter seams if you lose or gain weight.

It is easier to take in seams than to let them out. Before letting out a seam, always check the seam allowance to make sure that there is enough fabric to make the change. Many ready-made garments have serged seams that are less than ¼ in. (6 mm) wide. **Figure 67.2** shows the steps in altering seams.

Changing the Style

You can also change the style of clothes to get more use out of them. Consider making changes in one of the following ways:

- **The way the garment is used.** You can transform a garment from one type into another. Pant legs can be shortened to make cropped pants or shorts; a coat can be made into a jacket.
- **The shape of the garment.** Reshape a garment. By taking in the side seams, you can turn full legs into narrow legs on pants or bring a loose-fitting garment closer to the body. Shortening a garment also changes its shape.
- **The garment's details.** Give a shirt or blouse a new look by shortening the sleeves, removing a collar, or adding patch pockets. Knitted ribbing can replace collars or cuffs.

MORE ABOUT Redesigning

Tips for redesigning:

- To taper pants, take in both the outer and inner seams the same amount. If pants are too short, cut them off at a desirable length (from mid-calf to desired length of shorts) and hem them.

- If shirt cuffs become worn or too short, cut them off, hem the bottom of the sleeves, and form roll-up cuffs.
- If a sweater or sweatshirt has lost its shape, stitch casings at the cuffs and bottom edge and insert elastic or cording.

- **The garment's trimmings.** Add a ribbon, an appliqué, decorative buttons, or other trimmings. To update the design of a garment or accessory, replace the original buttons or trim.

Creative Measures

You can revive old or damaged clothes by adding embellishments. Patches, appliqués, trims, and embroidery can cover holes or hide stains. They can also make dull clothing bright and lively. Embellish a sweatshirt with an appliqué, costume jewelry, a painted design, or a sports-team emblem. Use these embellishments to create garments that express your individuality.

Dyeing

Sometimes the only thing wrong with a garment is its color. If you don't like the color or if it doesn't go with anything you own, consider dyeing, or changing the color of the fabric.

Clothing can be dyed at home or by a professional. For successful home dyeing, follow the directions on the dye package. Home dyeing works best when a light-colored fabric is darkened. Mix the dye with hot water. Then soak the fabric in a sink, a washing machine, or another container. You must simmer the fabric in the dye if you want it to turn very dark. Natural fibers absorb dye better than manufactured fibers.

Tie-dyeing is a special kind of dyeing in which parts of the fabric are tightly wrapped or tied so that the dye penetrates unevenly. This unevenness produces many different shades of the color or colors used.

Because dyes may stain containers and other materials, always obtain permission to use whatever equipment you will need to dye your clothes. Never dye clothes in a laundromat, because you are sharing the equipment there with other people. Also, wear old clothes and check the surrounding area when dyeing a garment. Splashing may cause you to dye more than you intended.

Fabric Painting

Fabric paint can give an old shirt a new look. Acrylic paints, tube paints, waterproof markers, and fabric-marking pens work well to cover a stain or to give a comfortable old T-shirt, sweatshirt, or skirt new life.

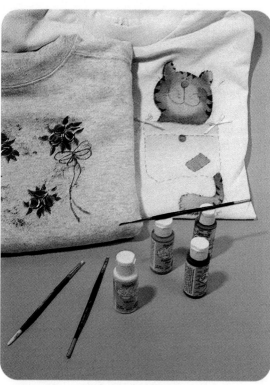

Old garments can be given a fresh look with fabric paint or dye.

CHAPTER 67   Redesigning and Recycling   653

CROSS-REFERENCE
See Chapter 57 for a review of the basic design principles.

Activities

- **Dye Quiz.** Distribute copies of the instructions from fabric dye. Have pairs of students make up five-item quizzes about the instructions. For example; What fabrics are not recommended for dyeing with this product? Ask pairs to take each other's quizzes.

RETEACHING

- **Changing Clothes.** Organize the class into groups and give each group an article of clothing to examine. Have groups discuss ways to change the garment's shape, details, or trimmings. Provide time for groups to share their ideas with the whole class. Discuss which are practical and would probably extend the life of the garment.

MULTICULTURAL *Perspectives*

Tell students that batik is a method of dyeing fabric that was first used in ancient Asia and is still popular today with fabric designers and other artists. In batik, designs are drawn on fabric with melted wax. When the cloth is dyed, the color cannot penetrate the waxed areas. After the wax is ironed out, the design remains. Have students investigate types of dyes and other dyeing techniques that have been used over the centuries by various cultures.

MORE ABOUT Dyeing

In addition to fabric, dyes can stain containers, utensils, stove tops, sinks, floors, countertops, skin, and clothing. Manufacturers recommend wearing rubber or plastic gloves when dyeing. Students should also wear old clothing and avoid getting the dye solution on anything but the material to be dyed. Explain that even cold-rinsed, colorfast dyes are not colorfast at first. They can bleed onto other fabrics and should be washed separately several times before they are washed with other clothes.

Topics on pp. 654-656:
- **Showing Compassion**
- **Recycling Garments**
- **Getting Organized**

Checking Comprehension

✓ What are some major benefits of recycling clothes? *Conserves clothing, fabrics, and fibers and helps those who receive needed clothes.*

✓ What are some ways you could recycle clothing you no longer want? *Give it to a relative or friend, sell it through a consignment shop, or give it to a charity to resell or pass on.*

Acting Responsibly

Have students read "Do You Show Compassion?" Invite them to describe any experiences they have had in helping with clothing drives.

Answers to Your Analysis

1. Not at first, but just needed increased awareness. His attitude changes as he and Kyle talk.
2. Again, not at first. Compassion seems to set in as he responds to Kyle's comments.
3. Kyle doesn't criticize Mike but effectively asks questions and offers suggestions; gets the ball rolling by taking action.
4. Give them to a friend or relative. Mike probably went along with Kyle's suggestion since he had some guilt already and realized he was not helping when he could.

Wash and dry the garment before you paint it to soften the fabric and to remove any finish that might repel the paint. Then follow instructions for the type of paint that you are using.

Some paints require heat setting to remain permanently attached to the fabric. When the paint dries, cover the painted area with a clean cloth. Use an iron at the proper setting for the fabric, and iron over the entire painted area to set the paint. Other paints cannot be heat set in this manner. Follow the instructions on the paint label.

Recycling a Garment

What if a garment can't be redesigned as part of your own wardrobe? Don't throw it away. Its fabric or fibers may still be useful for someone else if you recycle it.

Passing It On

During your teen years, you may outgrow clothing long before it wears out. Why throw garments away when there may be several more years of wear left for someone else?

One of the oldest forms of recycling clothing is the hand-me-down. Clothing that you no longer wear can be passed on to a younger

Acting Responsibly

Do You Show Compassion?

Sympathetic people are aware of the pain of others. They think of their feelings and needs as well as their own. Having compassion means that you not only understand the pain of others but also want to do something about it. Sympathy often leads to action.

Compassion In Action

Kyle ran to retrieve the basketball from where it had rolled between the Beneventi's trash cans. "What's this box of clothes, Mike? This looks like your coat."

His friend replied, "Yeah, it's a bunch of old stuff. My mom's been after me to clean out my closet ever since I moved my room to the basement. I'm just pitching all those old clothes."

Kyle was surprised. At his house, outgrown clothes were passed on to his younger brother and then sometimes even packed up for his cousins in North Dakota.

"Don't you know somebody who could use these?" he asked Mike. "Have you heard about that Coats for Kids campaign? There's a barrel you can drop old coats in at the supermarket."

Mike admitted he did feel guilty about throwing away his old clothes. "I guess I was just being lazy. You know, I did see something on television about homelessness and all the unemployment around here. I'm not helping much, am I?"

"Look, I'll show you a place where we can take that box of clothes," Kyle responded. "Let's take a quick look at what's in there first. It really won't take long, and you might be surprised at how good it makes you feel."

Your Analysis

1. Do you think Mike was sympathetic toward less fortunate people? Why?
2. Do you think Mike was being compassionate? Why?
3. Evaluate Kyle's approach in talking to Mike.
4. What other options does Mike have for his clothes? What do you think he decided to do?

REAL-LIFE APPLICATION

Read and discuss the following with students: • *Shirene often wears her grandmother's old sweater. It is soft and warm and reminds her of times she spent with her grandmother. One day Angela came to school in a bad mood. When she saw Shirene's sweater, she said, "Shirene, why don't you throw that old rag away?"* • *Lori's family often gives old clothes to charity. Just recently she said to a classmate at school. "That dress you're wearing looks just like one I used to have. We gave it to The Neighborhood Center last month."*

How can clothing that you no longer wear benefit others?

brother, sister, cousin, niece, or nephew. You can also give clothing to a friend. A shirt or sweater that is no longer right for you may be perfect for someone else.

If you don't know anyone who can use the clothes you no longer want, think about other possibilities, such as:

• Selling these garments through a consignment shop that buys and sells used clothing.

• Giving the clothing to a religious organization or a charity. The group may repair and fix used clothing and give it to people in need. Clothes that you give away may help a family that has lost everything in a fire or a flood.

Using Fabric Another Way

Even if only small pieces of the fabric are in good condition, you can save them for patchwork or craft projects. If you don't use the fabric scraps yourself, perhaps an elementary school, a retirement home, or a community group can use them for projects.

Worn-out garments of soft cotton make good dusting or polishing cloths. Remove all fasteners to prevent scratching the furniture with sharp hooks or button edges. Save all trim, decorations, and fasteners for future projects.

Reusing the Fiber

Even if the fabric cannot be redesigned or given away, the fibers may be recycled—to be used as quilt or pillow padding, for instance. Fibers may also be used as an ingredient in paper. Some cities have organizations that collect old clothes for this type of recycling.

CHAPTER 67   Redesigning and Recycling   655

DID YOU KNOW?

The Salvation Army is an international evangelical and charitable organization founded in 1865 by William Booth. It was established in the United States in 1880. The army is operated along military lines from command headquarters and has a corps of workers. Its leaders also hold military titles. In many cities, the Salvation Army operates thrift stores where it re-sells donated clothing. Proceeds from the stores and from donations to the army's holiday sidewalk bell ringers are used to support adult rehabilitation centers, emergency shelters for women and children, community centers, and summer camp programs for children.

656

ASSESS

Review

■ **Chapter Review.** Use the contents of the Chapter Review page to help students review concepts, think critically, and apply their knowledge.

■ **Study Guide.** Have students complete the Study Guide for Chapter 67 on p. 218 of the Student Workbook.

■ **Reducing Waste.** Point out that both teens and adults occasionally buy clothing they do not wear for some reason. The clothing may sit in a drawer or closet for months or years, just taking up space. Ask students to recommend ways to make the most of a poor buying decision.

Evaluation

■ **Chapter Test.** Use the reproducible chapter test provided in the Teacher's Classroom Resources or create your own test using the *Testmaker Software.*

■ **Alternative Assessment.** Have groups of students design posters that promote the recycling of clothing, fabrics, or fibers. Along with engaging visual images, they might include facts they have gathered about ways that recycled clothing, fabrics, and fibers can be put to good use. Display the posters in both the school and the community.

CLOSE

■ **Managing Resources.** Have students list the advantages of redesigning and recycling clothes. Then discuss the resources that are often used in the process. Make sure their discussion includes time, effort, and money. Ask students to describe situations in which redesigning and recycling clothing would be worthwhile.

STRATEGIES That Work
Organizing for Special Projects

When you're often busy with everyday activities and responsibilities, it can be hard to squeeze in an extra project—especially one that isn't essential to do. Redesigning a garment might easily fall into this category. Time needed for planning a project, assembling notions and tools, and just doing the work can be a strain on your schedule. What is the answer? Getting organized so that you can tackle special projects with ease can help. Try these ideas in order to be prepared for those redesigning tasks that come along:

- Maintain a good supply of notions and tools for many different types of sewing jobs, including mending as well as redesigning. Keep on hand an assortment of threads, needles, and fasteners, plus such basic tools as scissors, thimbles, pins, and a pincushion. If you have a varied supply, you won't need to run to the store every time you begin a project.
- Keep your eyes open for items to add to your notions collection. If you go to garage sales, you might buy supplies at little cost. You can collect yarn, ribbons, lace, buttons, trims, and fabrics in this way. You might even buy old garments from which you can retrieve good buttons, appliqués, and trims. Beads and jewels from old jewelry are another possibility.
- Keep the supplies you collect in a large sewing basket or container that is divided into compartments. Just putting different items in small, marked cardboard boxes can work. You'll

be less likely to put off a project when everything is easy to find.
- If you can set up a convenient work area, do so. That way, you can sit down and work in small time segments whenever your schedule allows.
- Save big jobs—for example, dyeing or painting a design—for days when you know you can set aside a block of uninterrupted time. Think of ways to combine your projects to use your time most efficiently. While soaking a shirt in a tub of dye, you could be fixing the hem on another garment.
- Plan to work on your redesigning project while listening to music or watching a program on television. Even a long hem that has to be hand-sewn won't seem to take so much time if you have something else to interest you while you work.
- Join with a friend to work on projects together. You can share ideas and conversation as you work.

Making the Strategy Work

Think . . .

1. Could collecting supplies for sewing projects ever get out of hand? Explain.
2. What obstacles can get in the way of accomplishing special sewing projects? How can you overcome them?
3. What other uses could you make of redesigned garments other than personal use?

 Try...

If you can, get together with a group of classmates who enjoy sewing projects in order to swap notions. Have everyone bring or find items that he or she doesn't need (buttons, trims, fabrics, etc.). Then arrange a system for trading so that everyone takes home something different to add to a personal collection of supplies.

REAL-LIFE APPLICATION

Read this to students: *As Brea browsed the used clothing shop, she pulled the item out for a closer look. "Hmmm," she thought, as she visualized all the possibilities for a shirt. "I can turn this $2 shirt into something special." For two years Brea had been building her wardrobe, artisti-* *cally and inexpensively. It was fun, and her efforts captured people's interest and attention. It had become a challenge.* Discuss Brea's talent. Have students theorize about Brea's personality. How might Brea use her creativity in the future?

Reviewing the Facts

1. What are three methods for redesigning garments you still want to wear?
2. How do you lengthen a hem? What could you do if the hem does not have enough fabric to lengthen?
3. List the steps for taking in a seam.
4. List two specific ways to change the style of a garment.
5. Briefly describe what dyeing and fabric painting are.
6. List three ways to recycle a garment.

Thinking Critically

1. Have you ever worn used garments, handed down by older brothers or sisters, other relatives, or neighbors? If so, how did you feel about wearing these clothes?
2. How could improving your redesigning and recycling skills lead to a small business of your own?

Applying Your Knowledge

1. **Writing Instructions.** Imagine that you have to prepare an article for a craft magazine. Make up a recycling project that uses everyday objects, such as fabric scraps or old clothing. Include specific cutting and sewing instructions and a sketch of how the finished product should look.
2. **Updating with Accessories.** Using accessories can allow you to change the look of a garment without altering the garment itself. List ways you might update your wardrobe with accessories.
3. **Drawing a Design.** Sketch a design that you could paint onto the front of a sweatshirt. The design can be of any type: geometric, pictorial, or abstract. In your sketch, indicate how you would use colors to create the finished product.

Making Connections

1. **Civics.** Use a telephone book or other local resource to find names and telephone numbers of groups or agencies in your community that collect and distribute used clothing. For two of the groups, find out any specific requirements for donations.
2. **Environmental Science.** The redesigning and recycling of clothing has many benefits. Investigate what environmental resources might be saved by redesigning and recycling clothes. Make a list of these resources, explaining briefly why you chose each one.
3. **Science.** Obtain two different fabrics—one made of natural fibers and the other made of manufactured fibers. Dye both fabrics, using fabric dye and following the package directions. What are the results? What might account for any differences?

Building Your Portfolio

Redesigning Your Garments
Choose an article of clothing from your wardrobe that could be redesigned and worn again. Make a list of possibilities for the item. Then choose one idea. Draw a "before and after" sketch and write a plan. Place the list, sketches, and plan in your portfolio.

CHAPTER 67   Redesigning and Recycling   657

Chapter 68

FOCUS

Chapter Overview

Chapter 68 helps students decide whether they have the skills and interests that could lead to a successful career in clothing or textile design, marketing, construction, or care. The chapter describes careers in three categories: entry-level, jobs that require training, and jobs that require higher education.

Motivator

Behind the Scenes. Have students identify the job titles of people who may have had something to do with the clothes they are wearing today. Write their ideas on the board. Then ask the class to put the job titles into categories, such as design, construction or manufacture, and sales. Save this list for the closure activity at the end of this chapter.

Objectives

Discuss the chapter objectives on this page. Remind students that the objectives focus on important chapter concepts.

Vocabulary

Point out that the word *coordinator* has three parts: *co-*, a prefix that means with, together; *ordinat(e)*, which means to arrange in order; and *or*, a suffix indicating a person who performs the action of the verb. Ask students to combine these three meanings to explain the duties of a coordinator.

Chapter 68 — Careers in Clothing and Textiles

Terms to Learn

- buyer
- fashion center
- fashion coordinator
- pattern maker

Objectives

This chapter will help you to:

- Identify **the interests and skills required for careers in clothing and textiles.**
- Describe **types of jobs available in clothing and textiles.**
- Describe **how to prepare for a job in the clothing and textile industry.**

CHAPTER RESOURCES

Student Workbook
Study Guide, p. 220
Activity, *Be the Boss*, p. 221

Teacher's Classroom Resources
Lesson Plan, p. 72
Extension #97, *Clothing and Textiles Careers*, p. 103

Chapter 68 Test, pp. 141-142
Performance Assessment, *A Clothing Industry Worker*, p. 105
Reteaching, *Clothing and Textiles Careers*, p. 74
Life Skills, *Assessing Skills*, p. 106

See Also:
ABCNews InterActive™ Videodiscs

A.J. is on the high school track team. While doing stretches in a new warm-up suit one day, he felt a pull on his jacket sleeve. His warm-up suit was the right size for him, but A.J. noticed that if the sleeves were cut just a bit fuller, he'd have a greater range of motion and be able to run more comfortably.

Tracy likes to watch dramas on television, but she sees things in a different way than many others do. While observing the actors' performances, she also notices the costuming. No matter what class she's in—math, science, or social studies—Tracy thinks about how it relates to her interest in clothing.

A.J. and Tracy have something in common. They're both interested in the effective use of clothing. When he gets his degree in clothing and fabric technology, A.J. will join the group of experts in fibers, fabrics, and clothing construction who work together to outfit astronauts, Olympic athletes, and other people with special clothing requirements. Tracy will apply her talents by working toward a degree in clothing design.

The clothing and textiles industry is one of the largest industries in the country. Every year new developments in fibers and fabric technology and new styles are introduced. People are needed to manufacture fabrics and sew garments. Others become entrepreneurs by starting businesses to provide products or services that consumers want or need.

Careers in clothing and textiles cover a broad range of occupations, from clothing design, to fabric manufacturing, to the sale of finished items in a retail store. Jobs are available in all aspects of the field and in all parts of the country. This chapter introduces you to some of the career opportunities.

> **Why is an interest in fabrics, color, and fashion, important for a career in clothing and textiles?**

The Qualities Needed

To be successful in a clothing career, a strong interest in clothing and a desire to work hard are essential. Competition for many of these jobs is fierce, and the jobs themselves are demanding and high-pressure. Deadlines must be met, and workers frequently put in long hours.

Positions in sales, design, and buying require the ability to predict future trends in styles, colors, and fabrics. Because success one season does not ensure success the next, job security is not as strong as it might be in other fields. However, for someone who loves fabrics and clothing design and construction, a career in the field of clothing and textiles can be immensely rewarding.

CHAPTER 68   Careers in Clothing and Textiles   659

Topics on p. 659:
- Career Opportunities
- Qualities Needed

Checking Comprehension

✓ What kinds of positions are available in clothing and textiles? *Fabric and garment design; manufacturing; sales; entrepreneurial opportunities.*

✓ What factors contribute to the industry's continued growth? *New developments in fibers and fabrics; new styles.*

✓ What pressures might someone face in the textile and garment industry? *Competition, deadlines, long hours, responsibility for predicting fashion trends, questionable job security.*

Activities

ENRICHMENT

Career Counseling. Ask the school guidance counselor to describe tests and inventories that can help students determine whether a career in clothing would be right for them. The counselor may also be able to offer specific information about the clothing industry.

Focus on Critical Thinking Skills

Ask students to identify issues related to the clothing industry that they know of, such as the popularity of second-hand clothing shops and the exporting of some manufacturing jobs to pay lower wages

Ask: Do you think these issues will remain prominent in the industry five or ten years from now? What other trends or topics do you see that may affect the field or your decision about pursuing a career in it?

Topics on pp. 660-661:

- Skills and Interests
- Design and Marketing: Entry- and Medium-Level Jobs

Checking Comprehension

✓ What skills does a stock clerk need? *Math, spelling, ability to focus on details, organization.*

✓ How do window dressers learn their skills? *Art courses; on the job; store-sponsored training programs.*

✓ What characteristics should a personal shopper have? *Good taste, ability to work within budget, good judgment in choosing clothes for others.*

FAMILY AND COMMUNITY OUTREACH

Encourage students to volunteer to work for someone as a personal shopper. Tell students to consult with their "client" on the kind of clothing desired—including the style, fabric, color, size, and price range—and then to try to find an acceptable garment, in either a store or catalog. Students should show the client their selection and discuss whether it is suitable. Have students share their experiences.

Interests and Skills

Although many types of jobs exist in clothing and textiles, the industry attracts people with similar interests and characteristics. If you can answer yes to some of the following questions, a clothing career may be for you:

- **Do you have a sense of color and design?** For almost all clothing careers, this is essential. Clothing workers need such talent to create attractive, usable products.
- **Are you well organized?** Clothing jobs often involve following many steps and combining many pieces. To get the job done, a clothing worker must plan each task carefully.
- **Do you pay attention to detail?** This trait is essential for a clothing worker, whatever the job. Close attention to detail results in a quality product—one that people will buy and recommend to friends. Consumers want to be satisfied with how they spend their clothing dollars, and they want a well-made product that will last a long time.
- **Do you want to learn about the technical side of fibers and fabrics?** Because fibers are the basic building blocks of fabrics, an understanding and knowledge of fiber characteristics is valuable. This is needed in every area of the garment industry, from the design and manufacture of clothing through clothing care.

Design and Marketing

The clothing and textile industry includes people who design and manufacture the clothing and people who market and sell the finished products. In any of these jobs, it is possible to combine an interest in fashion with a career in the world of business or art.

Entry-Level Jobs

Salespeople in retail stores help customers make decisions about their wardrobes. If salespeople know about design and color, they can help customers select clothing that looks good on them. If salespeople think about detail, they can suggest accessories and other matching items to their customers. This knowledge helps build the store's credibility and prestige. The ability to meet and work with the public, a pleasant personality, and a well-groomed appearance are qualities that employers look for in their sales personnel.

A sales position is often the first step in a retail clothing career. Some stores require a full-time salesperson to have a high school

What personal qualities are most important in a salesperson? Which qualities do you appreciate the most?

660   **UNIT 7   Clothing and Textiles**

••• REAL-LIFE APPLICATION

Read this to students: *Jeff is a salesperson in a clothing store. When he sees a customer, he busies himself nearby. He glances at the customer occasionally and waits to be asked for help. Erica is Jeff's coworker. She is quick to help customers but often remarks unkindly to Jeff that shoppers have such poor taste and choose the most unattractive styles.* Ask: Who do you think is the more helpful salesperson? Who cares more about the customer?

In Touch with TECHNOLOGY

Technology in the Garment Industry

Finding jeans that fit just right is a frustration for many. Did you know there's a store where you can order jeans directly from the manufacturer? You simply enter your waist, hip, and inseam measurements into a computer that has a direct link to the manufacturer. Your custom-made jeans can be ready in just three weeks. For reorders, you call the store with the personal ID number from the waistband label. This is just one of the ways technology is influencing the garment industry.

If you're considering a career in the industry, computer knowlege will be valuable. Clothing design and pattern making are now done frequently on the computer. In the factory, specialized pattern-making machines size and lay out designs.

Mechanical cutting machines can cut 3,500 pieces of fabric in less than three minutes. The pieces are transferred to different finishing stations by radio-controlled delivery systems. Managers or designers who want to pull a certain color or pattern from the floor do so using computer terminals.

Clothing manufacturers use software for everything from manufacturing, pricing, and order taking to inventory and shipping. One company even uses hand-held computer scanners to make sure boxes are packaged correctly. Retail clothing stores use computers to keep track of sales and inventory, as well as to maintain customer lists.

●●●●●
Thinking Critically About Technology

1. How will technology help to create new jobs in the garment industry?
2. How can future job applicants find out what new skills are needed?

---

diploma; however, many part-time employment opportunities are available for students. A part-time sales job can start you on a career path.

Another entry-level position at a department store is stock clerk. Stock clerks check incoming orders, put price tags on garments, and keep track of how the stock is moving. A stock clerk doesn't need special training, but a good background in math and spelling is helpful. It's also useful to enjoy focusing on details and to have good organizational skills.

Jobs That Require Training

Buyers are valuable people in the fashion industry. **Buyers** are *those who connect designers and garment makers with the stores where clothing is sold*. Buyers must be able to spot fashion trends many months in advance and to purchase wisely for their customers. Not all fashion trends lead to good retail sales, however. Buyers must select the styles and colors from current trends that customers in their region of the country will like.

A buyer may work for a large department store, a chain of stores, a mail-order house, or a local specialty store. In a small specialty store, the owner of the store is often the buyer. Large stores have a number of buyers who travel to fashion shows and fashion centers to select merchandise for their departments. **Fashion centers** are *buildings that house the sales offices of garment manufacturers*. New York's Seventh Avenue has many buildings that are fashion centers.

Large clothing stores have promotion and publicity departments where copywriters and artists prepare advertisements and displays.

MORE ABOUT Marketing Jobs

Jobs in marketing and advertising include market researcher; manufacturer's representative; merchandise manager; advertising manager; advertising account executive; photographer; illustrator; model; art director; and public relations manager.

DID YOU KNOW?

The Los Angeles Trade-Technical College offers an associate of arts degree and a certificate in fashion design to talented but financially struggling students. Students take four-hour classes in technical skills, which then enable them to carry out the designs they create.

Activities

RETEACHING

■ **Same Skills, Different Jobs.** Have students choose one of the positions described on pp. 660-662 and give examples of how someone with that job could use the interests and skills listed on p. 660.

In Touch With TECHNOLOGY

Have students read "Technology in the Garment Industry" and discuss the questions. Point out that new technology often eliminates jobs done by hand, perhaps by large numbers of workers. Ask: What options are available to people currently employed at such jobs?

Answers to Thinking ...
1. Answers may include: may create new positions for people who can use new machines and technology; increased worker demand if production increases; give rise to fashion software specialists.
2. Answers may include: read fashion magazines; write to companies in industry; learn what skills employer seeks in informational interview.

Topics on pp. 662-664:

• **Design and Marketing: Higher-Education Jobs**
• **Clothing Construction and Care Jobs**
• **Related Careers**
• **Preparing for a Career**

Checking Comprehension

✓ To what jobs might sewing machine operators advance? *Supervisor; sewing sample garments for designers; mending and altering; entrepreneurship.*

✓ What jobs are available to those with scientific training? *Textile engineers and chemists, dyers.*

✓ Name careers in clothing that involve other professions as well. *Fashion editor and advertising, model and modeling agency employee, photographer, video or make-up artist, stylists fashion show coordinator.*

SPECIAL NEEDS
Strategies

Inefficient Organizers. Have students organize the information in this chapter in a chart. Their charts should have two columns—one each for design and marketing jobs, the other for construction and care jobs—and a row for each level of training mentioned.

College writing and journalism courses help prepare you for a copywriter's job. Display workers and window dressers are usually people with an interest in art. In addition to what they have learned in school, these workers acquire many skills while on the job. Many larger department stores and chains offer training programs to talented candidates.

Some department stores offer their customers the services of personal shoppers. A personal shopper selects fashion merchandise that answers a particular customer's needs, saving time and energy for a busy customer. A personal shopper can also act as an image consultant for someone who wants a new look or is moving up the corporate ladder and needs a new wardrobe. A personal shopper must have good taste, be able to work within a predetermined budget, and have the ability to choose clothing that is suitable and pleasing to different customers.

Jobs That Require Higher Education

Large stores have **fashion coordinators** who *develop advertising themes and plan fashion events that will bring people into the store.* The fashion coordinators often involve community groups (such as school clubs) in their projects.

Working closely with the buyers, the fashion coordinators also make sure that different departments of the store sell clothing and accessories that go well together. They keep the buyers informed about the newest colors and styles. They want to make sure, for example, that a customer who selects a suit in a new color can find matching accessories in other departments.

Fashion coordinators are usually college graduates who majored in family and consumer sciences or art. In addition, they may attend special fashion institutes and merchandising schools to get work-study experience. They often gain experience in various positions within a clothing store.

The designer is a key person in the fashion industry. Every piece of clothing that a buyer selects, and every piece that you wear, first takes shape in the mind of a designer. Designers choose the fabric and plan every detail of new garments. They make sketches and samples from which a pattern can be made.

A college degree is not necessary to become a fashion designer, but people who become designers often enroll in college programs for fashion design. Many designers receive their training by working with experienced designers. To be successful, designers must follow fashion trends closely, understand the needs of their customers, and be creative.

■ Fashion designers plan the details of the clothing that people wear every day.

DID YOU KNOW?

In 1995, officials discovered 72 workers from Thailand were being held as virtual slaves in an El Monte, California, garment shop. They had been working up to 22 hours a day for as little as $.59 an hour and were not permitted to leave the building. The company owners were also Thais. The finished garments carried well-known labels and were sold in top-of-the-line stores. Urge students to investigate what protection exists for immigrants and other workers in the garment industry.

In addition to fashion design, job opportunities exist in fabric design, weaving, and knitting. Today many fabric designers create textures by using computers to design patterns with different kinds of yarns. The designers can quickly color the designs in a variety of combinations and print a copy of each design on paper—all by computer.

Construction and Care

The clothing industry also employs thousands of people who work behind the scenes. These workers take cloth and transform it into clothing. They may develop new fibers, dye fabrics, or sew garments. They are also involved in caring for clothing.

Entry-Level Jobs

The largest number of workers in the garment industry is sewing machine operators. These are the people who do the stitching. Most machine operators are trained on the job to sew on special machines, but they may also receive training at a technical or vocational school. Beginners start out stitching the easiest seams. Their wages begin with a legal minimum pay, but they can earn more as they gain skill and responsibility. Operators who show an ability to work with people can become supervisors.

Skilled sewers can work in other businesses. People who create the sample garments for designers must be highly skilled at machine sewing and hand sewing. Dry-cleaning companies employ menders to repair and alter customers' clothing. Large clothing stores hire alteration workers to alter garments (such as suits) to fit customers. Skilled sewers with a good business sense may even go into business for themselves to do clothing repair, alterations, and custom tailoring.

Jobs That Require Training

The pattern maker holds the highest-paid and most important production job in a garment factory. A **pattern maker** is *a skilled worker who makes a pattern from the designer's original sample.* All the patterns for a garment are copies of this first one, so accuracy is crucial. Many years of on-the-job experience are needed to become skilled in this career.

Dry cleaners must know how to choose the right chemicals to remove stubborn spots and stains without damaging a garment. They learn the techniques to use for each type of fabric and stain. Because the job involves making complex decisions, it takes 6 to 12 months to learn. This training can be obtained in a vocational school or on the job. Dry cleaners who own their own establishments also need some business training.

Jobs That Require Higher Education

Not all textiles are suitable for making clothing. To find the right types, research is necessary. Textile chemists develop new fibers and finishes. Manufactured fibers, such as nylon and polyester, as well as permanent press and water-repellent finishes, are the result of textile research. Textile engineers develop new techniques for making yarns and fabrics. They seek to improve quality and yet keep production costs down. These workers must have college degrees and be skilled in math and chemistry.

Dyers are also highly skilled workers. They work in textile mills and choose the formulas used for dyeing the fibers and fabrics. They must know chemistry and understand how the dyes and fibers will react together. They should be familiar with computers, which play a major role in controlling color and dyeing fabrics.

Related Careers

Many jobs are related to careers in clothing and textiles but are part of other industries. Fashion magazines employ fashion editors who follow the industry closely and write about trends. A career in fashion advertising requires a strong interest in clothing. Models, the individuals who manage them, and many others who work in model-

■ **In Related News . . .** Challenge students to name other products that are related to the clothing industry. What positions or opportunities exist in designing, manufacturing, and marketing those items? *(Creativity)*

Making Decisions

Have students read "Dressing for a Job Interview" and discuss the questions. Ask: How might the type of job Kelsey is interviewing for affect her choice of clothes?

Answers to What . . .

1. Wear what she chose, what Meredith suggested, or something in between.
2. Answers may include: Kelsey may be more confident wearing own choice but make poor impression; may get job but feel insincere wearing other clothes.
3. Answers may include: desire to help friend; ideas about appropriate, respectful dress
4. Answers will vary.

MORE ABOUT Related Careers

Teachers are as vital to the clothing industry as to any other. They teach courses such as family and consumer sciences, fashion merchandising, and textile design, in any number of settings—high schools, community colleges, adult education centers, vocational and trade schools, and colleges and universities. Teachers also instruct consumers as industry representatives. They may act as consultants and extension service specialists.

Review

■ **Chapter Review.** Use the contents of the Chapter Review page to help students review concepts, think critically, and apply their knowledge.

■ **Study Guide.** Have students complete the Study Guide for Chapter 68 on p. 220 of the Student Workbook.

■ **Considering Careers.** Have students write to a friend about their career plans, describing two careers they are considering. One is in design or marketing and one in construction or care. Students should explain their interest, needed skills, and training or education they need.

Evaluation

■ **Chapter Test.** Use the reproducible chapter test provided in the Teacher's Classroom Resources or create your own test using the *Testmaker Software.*

■ **Alternative Assessment.** Have students create profiles of five workers in different aspects of clothing design, marketing, construction, or care. These profiles should indicate the interests, skills, training, and education that help these people succeed in their jobs. Tell students to include jobs at each level of training mentioned in the chapter.

■ **Updating Knowledge.** Review the job titles students listed in the Motivator activity (people who may have had something to do with the clothes they are wearing). Ask what surprised students most about careers in clothing and textiles. What else would they like to know? How can they find this information?

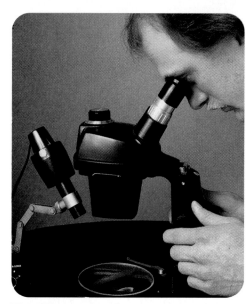

To become a chemist in the clothing and textiles industry, your preparation would include college courses in science as well as family and consumer sciences.

ing agencies are closely connected to the clothing industry. Photographers, video artists, stylists, and makeup artists, as well as those who coordinate details of the fashion shows of well-known designers, can combine their interest in art and theater with their interest in clothing.

Preparing for a Career

If you are interested in a career in the clothing and textiles industry, you can follow many avenues of experience and study. High school diplomas are required for many jobs. Technical or vocational schools, apprenticeship programs, or some other form of training after high school may be required for some positions. A college or fashion-merchandising degree will help you gain the knowledge and skills necessary for specialized positions that offer greater responsibility.

Making Decisions

Dressing for a Job Interview

"How do I look?" Kelsey asked her stepsister Meredith as she twirled around. Kelsey was headed for a job interview at Bailey's Department Store. If things worked out, she might even get to work in juniors.

Meredith frowned. "Kelsey, you're not interviewing to be a model or to show how wild your fashion sense is. I'd tone it down." Kelsey was wearing a short flowered skirt, a black silky blouse, and a flowered hat with a bright pin on the turned-up brim.

"But Meredith," Kelsey protested, "I don't want to look dowdy."

Meredith replied. "I know that, but don't forget who's interviewing you. That's the person you have to dress for."

Meredith and Kelsey began to look through Kelsey's closet. Kelsey did have a good sense of fashion. She liked bright colors and lively combinations, but she did have some conservative clothes, too.

"An outfit like this is better," Meredith said, pulling out a navy skirt and a pale pink blouse.

"But that's so plain!" Kelsey said. "They won't even notice me, let alone remember me after the interview."

Meredith shrugged her shoulders. "It's up to you," she replied.

What Would You Do?

1. What options does Kelsey have?
2. What positive and negative outcomes are possible from the various options?
3. What values might guide Meredith as she gives advice to Kelsey?
4. What would you do?

Chapter 68

Review

Reviewing the Facts

1. Identify three characteristics useful for careers in clothing and textiles.
2. What are three qualities that an employer looks for when hiring sales personnel in a retail store?
3. Describe the work that a stock clerk does.
4. What is the function of a buyer?
5. What kind of advanced training is usually necessary for a fashion coordinator?
6. Identify three jobs in clothing construction and care, one at each level.

Thinking Critically

1. What are some ways that you might use your knowledge of and skills in clothing and textiles to become an entrepreneur while in high school?
2. How can entry-level jobs help prepare individuals for other jobs within the clothing and textile field?

Applying Your Knowledge

1. **Forming Questions.** List five questions that you might want to ask on a job interview for a position in the clothing and textiles industry and five questions that an employer might want to ask you. Compare your lists with those of your classmates. Then ask and answer each others' questions to practice your interviewing skills.
2. **Comparing Professions.** Select two careers in clothing and textiles that you would like to find out more about. Ask the school librarian or career counselor to help you find career books, career encyclopedias, or magazine articles about them. Compare the details of each, and explain which you would prefer.

Making Connections

1. **Economics.** Select a type of garment to create (such as a knitted cap or a custom-decorated belt) and draw a plan for producing it. Your plan should answer such questions as: What materials and equipment will I need? How many individual items will I make at first? How will I advertise? Where will I sell it? Write up your plan and present it to the class.
2. **Language Arts.** Select a job in the clothing and textiles industry that you would like to apply for. Then write your résumé. List the qualifications that you have for the job, including interests, talents, education, and experience. Then write a letter of application that you could send with the résumé.

Building Your Portfolio

Applying Fashion Flair to Everyday Life

Assume that someone has hired you as a personal shopper. This individual has accepted a new job as a business manager and needs a new, professional-looking wardrobe. Make a plan showing what clothing you would buy for this individual. Use clothing catalogs to locate examples. Cut the examples out of the catalogs and mount them on paper. Write a summary explaining the choices you made. Include a brief description of the person you have been hired to shop for. Put the plan and the summary in your portfolio.

ANSWERS TO REVIEWING THE FACTS

1. Any three: interest in clothing; desire to work hard; competitiveness; ability to predict fashion trends; sense of color and design; organization; attention to detail, knowledge of fibers and fabric.
2. Ability to meet, work with public, pleasant personality, good grooming.
3. Checks incoming orders, puts price tags on garments, tracks sales of stock.
4. Travels to fashion shows and centers to select clothing for store.
5. College degree in fashion, family and consumer sciences, or art; work-study experience at fashion and merchandising schools.
6. *Entry-level* (any one): sewing machine operator; sample garment sewer; repair and alteration worker. *Require training* (any one): pattern maker; dry cleaner. *Higher education* (any one): textile chemist; textile engineer; dyer.

ANSWERS TO THINKING CRITICALLY

1. Answers may include: simple repairs and alterations; customize garments using paint, dye, or appliqués; making accessories.
2. Lets people learn about opportunities in company and industry, and training needed, while gaining experience. Lets person demonstrate ability that might lead to promotion.

Unit Preview

In Unit 8, students explore how living space can meet a wide range of needs and reflect the residents' personalities, interests, and values. Students compare buying with renting and learn ways to organize living space to its best advantage. The unit also covers caring for living space and avoiding home accidents. Students are urged to conserve their use of energy and water in order to protect the environment. The unit ends with a discussion of careers in the housing industry.

Content Development

Use these chapters to reinforce the following themes:

Content Strands	Chapters
Career Exploration	75
Citizenship/ Leadership	69, 74
Communication	69, 75
Decision Making	69-72, 74
Health and Safety	73
Managing Resources	70-72, 74
Personal Development	69
Technology	71, 74

Unit Motivators

■ **Pursuing Perfection.** Have students describe their dream homes. What would make a home the perfect place to live? What is the most important aspect of this home—location, size, special features, the people who live there, or something else?

■ **Home = Happiness?** Ask students this question: Does where people live make a difference in their lives? Encourage a lively discussion.

666

JOURNAL WRITING

Possible topics for student journals:

- What needs does your home meet for you?
- Would you like to own a home someday? Why?
- Are you more comfortable with neat or cluttered living space? Why?
- Which cleaning tasks appeal to you?
- Which would you rather avoid? Why?
- What could you do to improve the safety of your home?
- Why do some people have stronger feelings about protecting the environment than others do?
- What careers in housing sound appealing to you? Why?

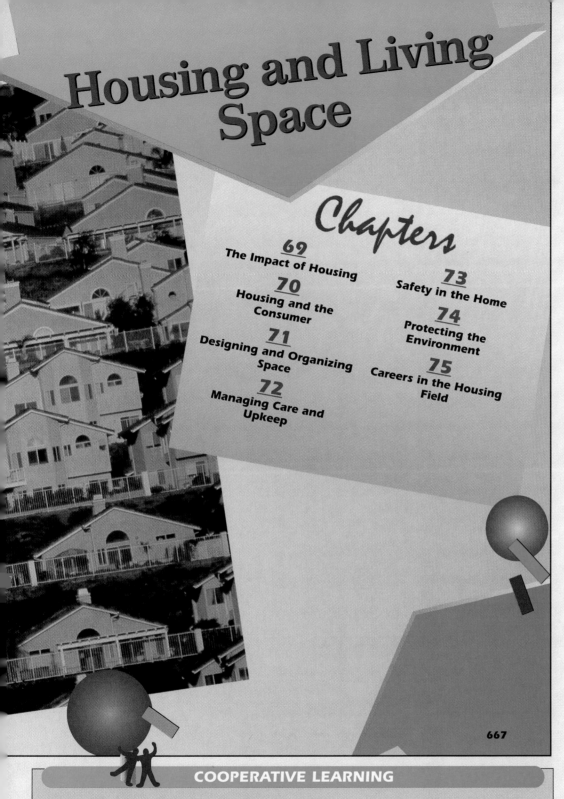

Housing and Living Space

Chapters

667

COOPERATIVE LEARNING

Cooperative Living. Form groups of three or four roommates of the same gender. Ask each group to select an unfurnished apartment in the classified section of the newspaper. Then have group members list issues to settle if living there together: furnishing the apartment; splitting costs; sharing cleaning and cooking chores; respecting space and belongings; dividing storage space; and rules for entertaining friends. Have them set up assignments and schedules and report on their agreements.

FHA Activities

These activities can be used with your FHA group or as public relations strategies:

■ **Household Hints.** Have students gather household hints from magazines, newspapers, home-improvement television shows, relatives, and neighbors. Have them use the best ideas in a booklet for young adults moving out on their own or going away to college. Suggest students group hints by topic and include illustrations when possible.

■ **On Tour.** Urge students to attend your community's next home-and-garden tour or exhibition. After the tour, discuss how homeowners or exhibitors used such concepts as the elements and principles of design.

■ **Room Makeovers.** As a fund-raiser, offer a "room makeover service." For a small fee, a team from your class will thoroughly clean and organize other students' bedrooms. The team might also rearrange furniture to improve traffic patterns, point out any safety hazards, and suggest decorating and storage ideas.

Unit Closure

REVIEW

What's New? Organize the class into seven teams; assign each team a chapter from Unit 8. Challenge teams to find a new development that relates to their chapters. Examples are a new approach to housing the homeless, a new cleaning product, and an emerging housing career.

EVALUATION

■ **Unit Test.** Have students complete the unit test in the Teacher's Classroom Resources.

■ **Testmaker Software.** You may wish to design a unit test using the *Testmaker Software*.

Chapter Overview

Chapter 69 explores the physical, emotional, and social needs that housing meets. Students learn more about factors that affect housing decisions, such as housing location and expense. The chapter also focuses on the causes of homelessness and helps students become more aware of the problems faced by homeless people.

Motivator

■ **Word Association.** Have students write down the first five images they think of when they hear the word *home*. Ask volunteers to read their responses. List them on the board and discuss any trends that appear. You may save this list for reference as students read the chapter.

Objectives

Discuss the chapter objectives on this page. Remind students that the objectives focus on important chapter concepts.

Vocabulary

Explain that *urban* means relating to or characteristic of a city. Ask students to suggest and then check the definitions of: *urbane, urbanite, urbanization, suburban, suburbia.*

Chapter 69

The Impact of Housing

Terms to Learn

- neighborhood
  crime watch
- rural
- suburban
- urban

Objectives

This chapter will help you to:

- Identify **the different needs that housing can fulfill and explain how it meets them.**
- Describe **different types of housing.**
- Identify and assess **the impact of factors that influence housing choices.**
- List **factors that contribute to homelessness.**

668   UNIT 8   Housing and Living Space

CHAPTER RESOURCES

Student Workbook
Study Guide, pp. 222-223
Activity, *What Is a Home?* pp. 224-225

Teacher's Classroom Resources
Lesson Plan, p. 73
Decision Making, *Being a Good Neighbor*, p. 26

Extension #98, *Helping the Homeless*, p. 104
Extension #99, *Being a Good Neighbor*, p. 105
Life Skills, *Identifying Your Dream Home*, p. 107
Transparency 56, *Good Neighbors*

Chapter 69 Test, pp. 143-144
Performance Assessment, *An Interview with a Neighbor*, p. 106
Reteaching, *Home, Sweet Home*, p. 75

See Also:
ABCNews InterActive™ Videodiscs

Just three days in his first apartment and Casey was already homesick. The excitement of independence was quickly fading into the reality of adjusting to a new home. His small bedroom and combined living room and kitchen gave him much less space than he was used to. The laundry room was three flights down, in the basement of his building. Finding a parking space in the renters' lot was sometimes a problem.

Even more troubling than the physical adjustments were the emotional ones. Casey wondered if he would ever get used to hearing people walking and talking just outside his door. He missed being able to look out windows in every room. He remembered growing up in his family home. I never realized everything that those four walls and roof meant to me, he thought, until I tried to start my own place from scratch.

On that first Saturday morning, Casey was setting the few personal belongings he had space for on a bookshelf in the living room. The place seemed friendlier with the picture of his family and his track trophies there. He laughed again at a cartoon poster as he hung it on the wall.

The doorbell rang. Answering it, Casey found a smiling older woman and a girl about nine years old standing outside. The girl held a plate of cookies, which she of-fered to Casey. The woman introduced herself. "Hi. I'm Rona DePaul. This is my granddaughter Faith. We live in the apartment next to the stairs. We want to welcome you to the neighborhood."

"Why, thank you; that's very thoughtful," Casey replied, accepting the cookies with a wide grin. At that moment, he was one step closer to feeling at home.

Housing in Your Life

"Be it ever so humble, there's no place like home." Those lines from an old song express something that most people have felt many times, perhaps without realizing it. Housing has an enormous effect on the quality of life. Part of the American dream, for example, is owning a home.

Why is housing so important to people? Why are decisions about housing among the most serious ones that people face? Like clothing, housing has both practical and emotional aspects that touch on very basic needs and concerns.

Housing comes in many shapes and sizes, but the people and the atmosphere inside are what make a house a home.

CHAPTER 69   The Impact of Housing   669

MORE ABOUT Homesickness

Point out that Casey is feeling homesick. People often long to return to a place where they feel they belong. Homesickness affects nearly everyone at some point—from a child spending a week at camp to an adult vacationing on another continent. People miss the sense of familiarity and belonging; they yearn to return to their homes and families. Ask students to suggest possible ways to deal with homesickness.

Topic on p. 669:
- **Why Housing Is Important**

Checking Comprehension

✓ What actions and events helped Casey feel more at home in his new apartment? *He set out some of his possessions and was welcomed by a neighbor.*

✓ Why is housing important to people? *It serves many needs.*

Activities

■ **Humble Homes.** Ask students to explain why even a "humble" home is important to the people who live there. *(Relationship)*

RETEACHING

■ **Before Your Eyes.** Ask a group of volunteers to turn the scenario on this page into a skit, expanding it as needed. Have students show verbally and visually how and why Casey's new apartment begins to feel like home.

CROSS-CURRICULAR ACTIVITY
Art

Have students create a mural of homes from around the world, using magazine and newspaper pictures, photocopies of pictures from reference books, and pictures they draw themselves.

Topics on pp. 670-671:
- **Physical Needs**
- **Emotional Needs**

Checking Comprehension

✓ How can living as a family at home help you get along with people outside your family? *Teaches you how to share space and responsibilities.*

✓ What might a home's furnishings and decorations tell you about the people who live there? *Might indicate their interests and values.*

SPECIAL NEEDS *Strategies*

Inefficient Organizers. Ask students to create a chart with the headings Physical Needs, Emotional Needs, and Social Needs. Under each heading, have them attach photos or drawings representing each of the needs mentioned in the text under that heading. For example, pictures under Physical Needs might indicate shelter and safety.

MULTICULTURAL *Perspectives*

Have students learn what the term *home* or *neighbor* signifies in another culture. For example, in some African villages, home is an entire compound occupied by extended family members. In some Russian cities, a family might crowd into a small apartment because no other housing is available. Ask students to share what they learn with the class.

Housing Meets Needs

It was a chilly, rainy afternoon. Shannon dashed from the school bus to her home. She left her boots on a mat inside the door and hung her dripping raincoat in the bathroom. In the living room, she curled up in her favorite chair to join her father and a neighbor in a cup of hot cocoa. In just five minutes, Shannon had experienced how housing meets several distinct, basic needs.

Physical Needs

Obtaining housing is often called "putting a roof over your head." This emphasizes the importance of housing in meeting physical needs. These include:

- **Shelter.** Housing offers protection from the physical elements: wind, rain, snow, and extremes in temperatures.

- **Space for possessions.** People need space to store the items that they use every day, such as food and clothing. Housing also provides a place to display things that people value.
- **Space for activities.** People need homes for personal activities—eating, sleeping, bathing, and entertaining.
- **Safety.** People and their possessions need to be secure from physical danger and theft.

Emotional Needs

Equally as important as physical needs are the emotional needs that housing can satisfy. In fact, the two are closely linked.

Belonging

Sharing a home is one of the things that unites people. Even if they are not members of the same family, people become closer by sharing space and household items. They usu-

Shared space can be arranged to provide privacy. How might that be true in a room like this one?

REAL-LIFE APPLICATION

Read the following to students: *As Rebecca Lynne sat on the edge of her older sister's bed, she watched Amanda place books and photos in a box. Amanda was leaving for college. Rebecca Lynne would have the room to herself, but she felt a pang of regret. After sharing a room for many years, the sisters had grown close. Rebecca Lynne knew she would miss Amanda in many ways.* Explore with students the positive side of sharing space in a home. What are the lifetime rewards of a relationship like this one?

ally see each other daily. Under these conditions, they naturally develop a sense of belonging, of being part of each other's lives. They come to trust and feel comfortable around each other; they know that they can be themselves. They also develop a sense of mutual rights and responsibility toward the things that they have in common. Privileges and duties associated with having a home are distributed among those who live in the home.

Privacy

Even when space is limited, everyone needs time alone—not only in obvious instances, such as when dressing or bathing, but whenever an individual feels the need to be away from others. Housing can provide privacy in the form of a bedroom, a back porch, or even a basement corner furnished with a comfortable chair and lamp. One family created privacy by hanging an old sheet in front of the bunk beds shared by the youngest brothers. Each child's bed became a secluded place in which to "get away from it all." Arranging furniture to create separate areas and putting up screens can achieve the same effect.

Personal Expression

One look around Carla's room tells you a lot about her. On one wall is painted a giant, yellow sun, its rays bursting forth. Red and purple flowers appear to spring from the floorboards and grow toward the ceiling. A poster on the opposite wall shows an African American dance troupe performing on stage. A shelf on the third wall holds a picture of Carla and her family making a huge snowman and a citation for Carla's participation in children's theater.

For many people, like Carla, housing offers an opportunity for self-expression. People can reveal their personality, interests, and past achievements in their homes. They can show their values through the items that they choose to display. For example, Carla's room included a photo of her family. People who value family history might display heirlooms handed down through several generations.

Making Decisions

Being a Good Neighbor

One warm summer evening Helena and her friends were sitting on the front stoop of Helena's apartment building. They didn't have anything in particular to do, but they were still having a good time, just talking and laughing.

Charlene was saying something in a loud voice. She was imitating the way Helena sounded when she was angry, and even Helena had to laugh. As she looked up, Helena noticed Mrs. Hawkins looking out the window.

I wonder why she's still up, Helena wondered briefly. She knew Mrs. Hawkins always went to bed early. Helena thought that the older lady looked sad, maybe even a little scared, as she peered around the corner of a drape. Helena shrugged off her concern and returned to the conversation.

A little later, Helena saw Mrs. Hawkins at her window again. Then Helena realized that she and her friends were making so much noise that Mrs. Hawkins couldn't sleep. Mrs. Hawkins wasn't sad; she was annoyed. She probably wanted to ask them to be quiet but was reluctant to do so.

Helena was about to tell her friends to keep it down. Then she stopped. What would her friends think if she told them to be quiet? She didn't want to spoil the fun. If Mrs. Hawkins was really bothered, she could come outside and ask them to be quiet. Helena liked Mrs. Hawkins, who had always been kind to her. Helena frowned as she thought about what to do.

What Would You Do?

1. Explain what Mrs. Hawkins' point of view might be.
2. What are possible outcomes of Helena saying nothing to her friends?
3. Why do you think this decision is difficult for Helena to make?
4. If Helena decides to stop the noise, could she do something other than just tell her friends to be quiet? Explain.
5. What do you think Helena should do and why?

Activities

■ **Less Is More.** Ask students if a lack of decoration in someone's room is a personal expression? In what way? (*Critical Thinking*)

RETEACHING

■ **Worth a Thousand Words.** Have students cut out magazine pictures of rooms and describe the interests, values, and goals each room reflects. Students might also discuss whether most bedrooms pictured in magazines are typical of those of average teens. If not, why are these pictures shown in the magazines?

Making Decisions

Have student read "Being a Good Neighbor." Ask them to evaluate Helena's self-confidence. What might Helena tell herself about the situation to make her decision easier?

Answers to What . . .

1. She may need or want quiet to sleep, or read, or because she's ill, but does not want to upset the teens.
2. Noise may continue; Mrs. Hawkins may become more upset, report the situation to Helena's family or landlord; neighbors' relationship may become strained.
3. She doesn't want to stop friends' fun but wants to respect neighbor's rights.
4. Could explain situation and tactfully suggest another quieter activity.
5. Answers will vary.

MORE ABOUT Privacy and Personal Space

To explore the ideas of privacy and personal space, introduce the topics with this activity. Arrange students in pairs. Have partners stand several feet apart and start a conversation. Ask them to move closer as they talk, noticing when each begins to feel uncomfortable about the other person's nearness. Discuss what this experiment demonstrates about the need for personal space.

Topics on pp. 672-673:
- **Meeting Social Needs**
- **Good Neighbors**
- **Adapting for Disabilities**

Checking Comprehension

✔ How is housing a social situation? *Families live in neighborhoods, can contribute to strong community.*

✔ How do good neighbors add to the quality of life? *Offer practical and emotional support; companionship.*

FAMILY AND COMMUNITY OUTREACH

Have students find out whether their community has a program similar to a neighborhood crime watch and what it involves. Often this kind of program is sponsored by the police department. Neighbors may be required to attend brief training sessions before signs can be posted in the neighborhood, informing potential intruders that the neighbors have banded together.

How people keep their homes can also reflect what they find important. A person who values neatness will try to keep an orderly home. Someone who favors simplicity might live with basic, practical furnishings.

A home can also reveal the goals of the people who live there. Obtaining a good education for their children, for example, is a goal of many families. To achieve this, they may fill their space with bookshelves, a desk and reading lamp, and possibly a home computer. How might a family use space to further the goal of entertaining friends?

Social Needs

Homes can be very private, individualized places. People usually live among others, however, so housing has a social aspect as well. It plays a part in strengthening ties within the community.

The Value of Good Neighbors

Eight-year-old Jeremiah watched intently as the movers unloaded the van at the house across the street. The tables, chairs, and bed frames did not interest him. At the sight of a child's bicycle and whiffle ball set, however, he grew excited. Someone to play with, he said to himself.

If he is fortunate, Jeremiah's appreciation for his neighbors will continue to grow—and be returned. Most people realize that good neighbors add quality to life. Like an extended family, they can offer practical help at times of need. They can provide emotional support during difficult times and simply "the pleasure of their company." Just knowing that there are people nearby whose faces you recognize and who share some of your concerns can be comforting.

When new neighbors move in, take time to meet them and welcome them to the neighborhood.

Focus on Relationship Skills

According to a poem by Robert Frost, "Good fences make good neighbors." Explore with students what this means. Strong relationships with neighbors are created in many ways. Some build through closeness, with people spending time together and relying on each other. Some neighborly relationships, however, require a degree of separation, characterized by people's respect for their neighbor's privacy and a willingness to not intrude.

STRATEGIES That Work

Adapting Space for Independent Living

When Michaela was on a committee to plan a neighborhood chili supper, she offered her kitchen for the cooking. The committee could gather there to prepare the chili on the day before the event. "Maybe I could do something at home," Andrea suggested, a slight note of sadness in her voice. "I don't think my wheelchair will fit through the entryway to your house."

Situations like Andrea's are a daily occurrence for the many people with disabilities. Accessing public facilities is one issue, but managing in the home is just as important. Statistics show that 70 percent of all Americans will have some kind of disability, whether temporary or permanent, sometime in their lives. Others will care for a family member with a disability. This is a strong reason for making sure that residences are planned with this need in mind. When they haven't been, modifications can be made. Here are some things that can be done:

- **Stairs.** When stairs cause difficulty, one solution is a chair lift or an elevator. Another possibility is making design changes so that the person with the disability can remain on the first floor. Outside stairs can be replaced with wooden or concrete ramps.
- **Hallways and doorways.** Wheelchairs and walkers require wide, clear paths. Bathrooms are a particular problem if they don't have enough room for a person to enter, turn around, and exit. Doorways can be widened and thresholds lowered or ramped.
- **Everyday tasks.** For people in wheelchairs, it is helpful to lower sinks, cooktops, countertops,

shelves, desks, light switches, and clothes bars. The placement of desks, sinks, and countertops should allow a wheelchair to roll under. Toilets may need to be raised. Installing grab bars near the toilet and shower or tub can help make them accessible and prevent falls. Some showers can be modified to allow a wheelchair to roll in.

- **Equipment for the visually impaired.** Household appliances can be equipped with braille controls or raised type. People with partial vision are aided by painting walls and counters in contrasting colors and putting large print on devices.
- **Equipment for the hearing impaired.** Special lights are available to signal when the doorbell or the telephone rings, when a baby cries, or when the smoke detector goes off. Nighttime emergency systems that use a flashing light or a device that causes the bed to move are effective wake-up alarms.

Making the Strategy Work

Think . . .

1. What other methods could you use to make a home more accessible and usable for someone with a disability?
2. What effect do you think the aging population will have on these kinds of needs in a home? How, in turn, will that affect you?
3. Increasing awareness promotes change. Evaluate your own sensitivity and awareness concerning the obstacles that people with disabilities face.

Try...

Do you have a friend or relative with a disability? If so, can you accommodate that person for a visit where you live? Think about any obstacles that exist in your home. List three ideas that might make it easier for someone with a disability to visit you.

Activities

■ **Comparing Roles.** Ask students to compare the actions of a good neighbor with those of a good citizen. (*Citizenship*)

RETEACHING

■ **Good Neighbors.** Have groups agree on five rules for being a good neighbor, using positive, specific terms instead of negative, vague ones. For example, "Keep down the volume on CD players and TVs" instead of "Don't make too much noise." After groups have shared their lists, ask the class to identify the behaviors that were named most often.

ENRICHMENT

■ **Contact.** Arrange for students to visit a facility designed to encourage independent living, perhaps an assisted living facility. Discuss any insights students gained.

STRATEGIES THAT WORK

Have students read "Adapting Space for Independent Living." Discuss changes that would make the school more accessible to people with physical disabilities. Students might propose some changes to school administrators.

Answers to Think . . .

1. Answers will vary.
2. More homes will need to be planned or modified to allow for disabilities. Students are likely to have aging relatives someday, will be concerned for that person's ability to function in own or student's future home.
3. Point out that often people lack empathy until faced with a situation themselves.

REAL-LIFE APPLICATION

Read this to students: *Dominic was frustrated. He had rolled his wheelchair out of the van and down the block, only to find that he couldn't get into the building where he was supposed to go. There were two steps up and the doorway was narrow. The man on the phone had said there was* *access, but where? In the back? Dominic glanced at the landscaped area that lead around the building. The bumpy brick pathway that wound through looked threatening to him.* Ask students to put themselves in Dominic's position. How would they feel?

Topics on pp. 674-675:
• Types of Housing
• Housing Locations

Checking Comprehension

✓ What are some ways to be a good neighbor? *Introduce self; show courtesy; promote safety; learn about each other.*

✓ What considerations affect housing choices? *Type of housing you want; location; how much you can afford to spend.*

✓ What are some factors that people need to consider in choosing where to live? *Their desire for familiarity or for change; climate and physical features of an area; cost of living; availability of jobs.*

✓ What are the three main kinds of communities? *Urban, suburban, and rural.*

CROSS-CURRICULAR ACTIVITY
Language Arts

Organize the class into three teams (six, if your class if large) and assign each team a housing location (urban, suburban, or rural). Have the teams put together visual and oral presentations to convince others to live in their assigned settings. Groups might describe the benefits of living in specific urban, suburban, or rural areas of your own region, if appropriate.

Being a Good Neighbor

If values inspire actions, then people who value good neighbors act in a neighborly manner. They introduce themselves when they first move in. They show courtesy—by keeping their property neat and by not playing music too loudly, for example. Apartment dwellers might carpet their floors so that their footsteps don't disturb those living in the apartment below. They would avoid letting strangers into the building.

Good neighbors learn about the families who live around them to find out how they can be better neighbors to each one. This may include forming a **neighborhood crime watch,** *a group of neighbors who band together to look out for each other's safety and property.* Members of the neighborhood watch become acquainted with their neighbors' habits, their friends, and other regular visitors. They tell one another about their plans or of changes in their routine. This helps all neighbors to be alert for any unusual occurrence that could mean trouble. They might investigate the situation themselves, if it is safe to do so, or phone the police. A neighborhood watch not only helps prevent crime; it can also promote positive, caring relationships.

Housing Decisions

Given the numerous, significant ways that housing affects a person's life, it's not surprising that most people take housing decisions very seriously. The type of housing, its location, and the resulting expenses all make a big difference in their lives and in the lives of their families.

Types of Housing

Of the many different types of housing arrangements, only a few may be practical for a particular person or family. Factors that determine which type they choose include how much space they need, how much they can afford to spend, whether they plan to stay in that geographical area, and whether they consider housing as an investment for the future. Special circumstances, such as the presence of disabilities, can further narrow their choices.

Locations for Housing

Why do you think your family chose your community as a place to live? Where would you like to live if you had the choice? People choose locations for many reasons, including:

• **Familiarity.** There are advantages to staying in a place that you are familiar with. In addition to the sense of emotional comfort and security that you may feel, your job prospects may be better in a place where you have established professional ties and a positive reputation.

• **Desire for change.** The excitement and challenge of change motivates some people to choose a setting and lifestyle that are very different from what they are used to.

• **Lifestyle needs.** A person's career goals may require a move to a place where those jobs are plentiful. People may be attracted to an area because of its climate, physical features, or low cost of living. These types of needs may lead people to change geographical locations several times during their lives.

Generally there are three types of locations for housing. Each has its advantages and disadvantages. **Urban** housing is *located in a city.* City life tends to be fast-paced and stimulating. Cities often offer great cultural, entertainment, and shopping opportunities. They provide public services ranging from public schools and libraries to regular trash pickup. Their relatively large populations, however, can also make them crowded, noisy, and dirty.

DID YOU KNOW?

In 1980, about 76 percent of Americans lived in metropolitan regions, which include urban and suburban areas. By 1992, that number had risen to 80 percent. In 1980, about 58 percent of metropolitan residents lived in the suburbs. By 1990, that number had increased to 61 percent. Thus, as the number of people living in metropolitan areas rises, the greater proportion of that group seems to be settling in suburban areas.

 The many landscapes observed where people live reflect varied ways of living. They are as different as the people within them. What type of location appeals to you?

Activities

■ **Thinking Ahead.** Discuss where students would like to eventually live. Do they plan to live in the same kind of area as their families do now? Why? *(Decision Making)*

RETEACHING

■ **Rating Reasons.** Have the class list five or six factors to consider in choosing whether to live in an urban, a suburban, or a rural area. Cost, amount of land, and public services available are examples of factors to consider. Then organize students into groups and have each group rank the list in order of importance. After each group reads the order it chose, discuss why some groups have different priorities.

FAMILY AND COMMUNITY OUTREACH

Have students use the real estate section of the newspaper to analyze the kinds of housing that are being offered locally. What benefits do each have? What price ranges are offered?

CROSS-CURRICULAR ACTIVITY
Math

Have students find out how many people in your state live in urban, suburban, and rural settings. Then have them create graphs to show the percentages.

675

Topics on pp. 676-678:
- Housing Expenses
- Homelessness

Checking Comprehension

✓ What factors affect the price of housing? *Location, size and type of housing, home and surrounding land.*

✓ What are some inexpensive ways to make a home more livable? *Paint it, make needed repairs, decorate with second-hand items.*

✓ What are the main reasons people become homeless? *Abandonment by family head, low income, mental illness, substance abuse.*

✓ Why have many lower-income people become homeless in recent years? *Drastic rise in housing expenses pushes lower-income people into homelessness.*

FAMILY AND COMMUNITY OUTREACH

Invite staff from a homeless shelter to speak with the class about the problems that bring people to the shelter and ways that young people could help the homeless, directly or indirectly. Ask if students can organize a clothing drive or fund-raiser; help serve holiday meals; volunteer at a shelter that accepts families; tutor school-age children; or teach youngsters a skill or sport.

The desire to have access to a city yet avoid the drawbacks of living in one leads many people to live in **suburban** areas. These are *mostly residential regions surrounding a city.* People who live in suburbs—suburbanites—may take advantage of jobs and leisure activities in the city or enjoy those in their community. Suburbs are smaller than cities, and their governing bodies are less complex. Many people believe that this makes life more personal and government more responsive. Suburbanites pay a price for these advantages—literally. Taxes on suburban dwellings are frequently higher than on urban homes.

Before the advances of industrialization, most housing was located in **rural** areas—*regions that are primarily countryside.* For some people, this remains the housing of choice. Though conveniences and opportunities may be limited compared to those of urban and suburban living, life in a smaller community can be rewarding. There is generally less noise and pollution. People often have more space and easier access to "the great outdoors"—woods for hiking and lakes for swimming and fishing. Many people claim that neighbors in small towns are closer and friendlier. They tend to know each other better and rely on each other more.

Housing Expenses

The cost of housing varies greatly, from a few hundred dollars to several thousand dollars a month. Whatever their payments, most people spend more money on housing than on any other single living expense.

What determines the price of housing? As you may have guessed, location is a significant factor. Housing often costs more in rapidly growing areas of the country than in less popular regions. Also, whether a home is located in an urban, suburban, or rural area affects its price. Within a single community, the cost of housing varies among different neighborhoods. The size and type of the housing unit also influence its price. Not only the structure itself, but also any grounds or land-scaping, such as a garden or fruit trees, are included in the cost.

The amount of money that people spend on housing often reflects a balance of these factors. The Gutierrez family, for example, chose a home that was smaller than they would have liked because it was located in a community with excellent public schools and services. They compromised on size in order to get the location that they wanted. Since few families can find or afford the ideal home, most make similar trade-offs based on their needs and values.

Some people want to improve their living conditions but find it difficult to do so. Lack of employment and low income may stand in the way of change. Even when people can't afford what they would like, however, they can do the best with what they have. Some fresh paint and repair work provide a new look. Creative use of inexpensive or second-hand items adds to a decor. If something better is still a dream, the reality of better housing can come with planning and preparation. Many teens, for example, who have gotten an education and a good job have been able to improve their circumstances when they were older.

Homelessness

With a heavy heart, Regina helped the Novaks load a child's toy box into her father's van. The Novaks had been good neighbors for ten years. Eighteen months ago, however, Mr. Novak had suffered a spine injury that left him unable to work. The family of four struggled to meet expenses on his disability checks and Mrs. Novak's salary from cleaning houses, but the income was too small. They had missed their last four house payments; now they were losing their home.

"Thanks for all your help," Mrs. Novak told Regina. "I don't know where we're going to put that stuff. My sister's place will be crowded enough with four more people, much less all our things. I'm so grateful she's

DID YOU KNOW?

In many communities the government provides public housing for people who have low incomes, are elderly, or are disabled. The rent is usually a set percentage of the family's income. Urban renewal projects help renovate old buildings instead of tearing them down. Under urban homesteading programs, families can buy old or abandoned houses or apartments at very low prices. They must agree to rehabilitate the home and then live in it for a certain number of years.

- **Abandonment.** Many homeless people come from families broken by divorce or abandonment. The parent who leaves the family cannot, or will not, continue to provide the financial support that the others rely on to maintain their home. This is one reason why one of every three homeless people is a child.
- **Poverty.** Expenses associated with housing have risen drastically in recent years. Lower-income people who could barely afford even inadequate housing have been pushed over the edge into homelessness. Although there are a number of government programs that help people afford a place to live, they are not nearly sufficient to meet the need.
- **Mental illness.** One-fourth of all homeless people have a mental illness that makes it difficult for them to find and hold a job. Mental health treatment can be very expensive, even for those who can afford it. As with housing programs, the government is not equipped to provide help for all who need it. These people find themselves in a frustrating cycle. With no job, they cannot afford treatment to help them cope with their illness and keep a job. They wind up unemployed, untreated—and homeless.
- **Substance abuse.** Some homeless people are drug and alcohol abusers. They may spend so much money on drugs that they cannot afford housing. They may lose their jobs because of their abuse. Substance abuse can lead to both poverty and mental illness. As substance abusers sink deeper into either of these two conditions, they become less employable and less able to function in society. Many end up on the streets.

letting us stay, though. Otherwise I don't know where we'd go."

Her words struck Regina deeply. She had always had a vague image of a homeless person as someone who came from a background far different from her own. When people said that homelessness was a person's own fault, she had been inclined to agree. Now, some very fine people—some of her best friends—were one step away from joining that population called "the homeless."

The Faces of Homelessness

Like Regina, many people have misconceptions about how and why people lose their homes. Some of the main reasons include:

CHAPTER 69   The Impact of Housing   677

Activities

■ **Cause and Effect.** Ask students how better services for people who are mentally ill or who abuse drugs might affect the problem of homelessness. *(Problem Solving)*

■ **Changing Views.** Ask students why they think many people are prejudiced against the homeless. What might be done to help the public become more aware of all the reasons for homelessness? *(Problem Solving)*

ENRICHMENT

■ **A Pound of Prevention.** Have groups discuss this question and share their answers with the rest of the class: What are some ways that people can reduce their chances of becoming homeless? After groups share their ideas, encourage the whole class to summarize them. Explore what young people can do while they are still in high school to safeguard their futures from homelessness.

FAMILY AND COMMUNITY OUTREACH

Encourage students to investigate the services in your community for people who are homeless. Different groups might research federal, state, and local governmental services and those offered by community and religious organizations. Provide time for groups to share what they learn and to discuss how easy or difficult it might be for homeless people to locate and access these services.

Focus on Relationship Skills

Encourage students to imagine that they are volunteering at a homeless shelter. Discuss the range of reactions they might receive from the adults and children who live there, and the reasons for these different responses. Then have students suggest ways they could show their respect for the challenges the homeless face.

Review

■ **Chapter Review.** Use the contents of the Chapter Review page to help students review concepts, think critically, and apply their knowledge.

■ **Study Guide.** Have students complete the Study Guide for Chapter 69 on p. 222 of the Student Workbook.

■ **Help for Homes.** Remind students that a home is just walls and doors and windows. Whether a home meets the needs of a family depends on the actions and interactions of that family. Ask students to suggest ways that teens can help make their home meet the physical, emotional, and social needs of everyone who lives there.

Evaluation

■ **Chapter Test.** Use the reproducible chapter test provided in the Teacher's Classroom Resources or create your own test using the *Testmaker Software.*

■ **Alternative Assessment.** Have students each construct a diorama that illustrates how a home could meet physical, emotional, and social needs.

■ **Home-Grown Sayings.** Have each student make up a saying that expresses feelings about "home." Provide time for student volunteers to share their sayings with the class.

Life Without a Home

Think again about the many needs that housing fulfills. Without a home, how can people meet these needs?

Homeless people sometimes find space in publicly funded or privately operated shelters. Here they can receive at least a place to eat and shower and a meal. Some shelters are able to offer personal and job counseling. They help people get an education, health care, and treatment for addictions. Such programs are expensive, however, and funds are often lacking. Every night, shelters must turn people away for lack of space.

For those who cannot or do not want to stay in shelters, life can be a struggle—and sometimes a dangerous one. Many homeless people sleep in public places, such as libraries and bus terminals, or in parks and under bridges. Some people make crude homes of tents or cardboard boxes. Others take shelter in abandoned buildings or vehicles. Physical violence is a constant threat. Meals are irregular and often consist of other people's leftovers. Sanitation is inadequate. Homeless people have few places to bathe. They often get little sleep. Not surprisingly, they are at serious risk for malnutrition and disease.

Homelessness takes an emotional toll as well. People can develop a negative self-image when they are unable to find a home. They may give up hope.

No one is certain how many people are without a home. The National Coalition for the Homeless estimates their number at between 500,000 and three million in the United States alone. Government agencies, religious organizations, and other private groups have had success in helping homeless people by providing food and shelter and a chance to learn skills, find jobs, and regain their self-esteem. Many people, however, believe that the fight against homelessness will not be won until the underlying social and economic conditions that lead to the problem are eliminated.

Habitat for Humanity is an organization of volunteers who refurbish homes in a community. People with limited financial resources have the opportunity to obtain interest-free loans to purchase these homes by helping with the work and demonstrating responsibility.

REAL-LIFE APPLICATION

Read the following to students: *Carl and his mother have moved to a homeless shelter. Carl must enter a different school for the third time in one year. He doesn't want to go, but he knows he has no choice.* Explore with students why Carl is apprehensive, what life might be like for him at school, and what could happen to make things different for him.

Chapter 69 Review

Reviewing the Facts

1. What are the four physical needs that a home can fulfill?
2. What emotional needs can a home fulfill?
3. How can an individual be a good neighbor?
4. List three basic factors to consider when choosing a place to live.
5. Identify two factors that might influence a person's choice of location for a home.
6. List two causes of homelessness.

Thinking Critically

1. Leaving the area where they grew up is difficult for some young people, even when better opportunities are elsewhere. Why is this true? What would you recommend to them?
2. If size is a major influence on cost of housing, how do you explain why a small home in a city may cost more than a larger home with more grounds in a rural area?
3. You read that the estimated number of homeless is between 500,000 and three million. Why do you think the range is so wide?

Applying Your Knowledge

1. **Writing a Description.** What type of person would you like to have as a neighbor? Write a description of the ideal neighbor. What qualities would this person have? Do you have these qualities? Why are they important to you?
2. **Setting Up a Neighborhood Crime Watch.** Imagine that you're on the planning committee for your neighborhood crime watch program. What would you want to include in the program? Make an outline of steps for setting up such a program.

3. **Making Housing Choices.** Imagine that you're looking for an apartment to rent. You have narrowed down your choices to either a tiny apartment in a very desirable neighborhood or a large apartment in a less than ideal neighborhood. Which one would you choose? Why?

Making Connections

1. **Geography.** Make a list of things that would be important to you when choosing a geographical location for your home. Consider climate, access to major cities, and other factors that you consider important. Then, using an atlas, find an area that would meet these needs.
2. **Writing.** Imagine that you're the mayor of a small town. You want to attract people to your town. Write a speech that tells them what the town has to offer and why they should consider living there.

Building Your Portfolio

Examining Location and Its Effect

Think about your home. Do you live in an urban, suburban, or rural area? Have you always lived in the same home, or have you moved to several different places? In what ways did your home and its location affect you as a child? In what ways does it affect you now? Write an essay about the location of your home and its effects on you over time. Add illustrations if you like. Place the essay and the illustrations in your portfolio.

Chapter 70
FOCUS

Chapter Overview

Chapter 70,describes some types of homes that are available. The chapter compares the advantages and disadvantages of renting and of buying and explains the basic costs involved in both approaches. Students also learn about government housing programs that help people find homes.

Motivator

■ **Moving Out.** Have students imagine that they are ready to move out of their family's home after graduating from high school or college. What options do they think they have?

Objectives

Discuss the chapter objectives on this page. Remind students that the objectives focus on important chapter concepts.

Vocabulary

The word *condominium* is formed from the prefix *con-*, meaning with, and the Latin word *dominium,* or domain. *Domain* is territory over which you have control. Ask students to suggest a definition for condominium, based on those components.

Chapter 70

Housing and the Consumer

Chapter 70

Terms to Learn

- condominium
- lease
- mortgage
- public housing
- security deposit

Objectives

This chapter will help you to:

- Describe **different kinds of housing.**
- Compare **renting and buying.**
- Explain **what a lease and a mortgage are.**
- Identify **typical housing costs.**
- Describe **types of public housing programs.**

680   UNIT 8   Housing and Living Space

CHAPTER RESOURCES

Student Workbook
Study Guide, pp. 226-227

Activity, *Decisions, Decisions*, p. 228

Teacher's Classroom Resources
Lesson Plan, p. 74

Cooperative Learning, *Living Space*, pp. 75-76

Extension #100, *Lease Terms*, p. 106

Extension #101, *Landlord and Tenant Problems*, p. 107

Life Skills, *Deciding Between Two Homes*, p. 108

Transparency 57, *Sharing Living Costs*

Chapter 70 Test, pp. 145-146

Performance Assessment, *Housing Tips*, p. 107

Reteaching, *Consumer Issues*, p. 76

See Also:
ABCNews InterActive™ Videodiscs

"I want to move out of my parents' home," Stephanie said to her friend, "but I'm worried about whether I can make it on my own." Stephanie's concern is a typical one for young people today. Some who have tried independence have returned home when finances ran short. Others struggle to make ends meet as they juggle expenses on a limited income.

How will you handle this situation when the time comes? If you're smart, you'll learn all you can about what it takes to manage before you set out for yourself.

Housing Options

When Stephanie moves away from home, where will she go? Her first residence is likely to be an apartment, although there are other possibilities. Look at the different kinds of housing described in **Figure 70.1** on pages 682-683. Which would be most likely for your first experience at living on your own?

To Rent or Buy

When people decide where to live, they have one basic question to answer. Will they rent or buy? When you buy a home, it belongs to you. If you rent a house or an apartment, you don't own it. You pay a monthly fee—the rent—to the person who owns the property.

For most young people who are just starting out, buying is not an option. They don't usually have the money it takes to purchase a home. Furthermore, they haven't had time to establish a credit record in order to qualify for a home loan.

Renting

Andre and Vicki are a young couple, both employed. They feel that now is not a good time to settle in one place, since their jobs could take them to another city in the near future. Renting makes sense to them. Also, they need a few years to save the money it takes to buy.

Carlos is a young man who just finished training as a graphic artist. He has his first job and is ready to live on his own. Renting is a logical choice for him, too.

The Lease

If you decide to rent, you are likely to face a legal necessity—signing a lease. A **lease** is *a legal contract between the renter and the property owner, usually called the landlord*. The lease states the exact amount that the renter must pay each month and the length of the rental period. It may also specify how much notice the renter must give before moving out. Most leases also list certain rules that the renter must follow. For example, many leases indicate that renters may not have pets.

If a lease is required when you rent, be sure to read it carefully before you sign. You need to understand what it says and how it may impact you in the future. Getting out of a lease can be difficult and costly.

A lease is a legal contract requiring all parties who sign it to live up to their agreements.

CHAPTER 70 Housing and the Consumer   681

TEACH

Topics on p. 681:
- **Housing Options**
- **Points of a Lease**

Checking Comprehension

✓ What basic decision do consumers make when choosing housing? *Whether to buy or rent.*

✓ What information is included in a lease? *Amount of rent, rental period, length of notice required before moving out, rules about pets, and other restrictions.*

Activities

■ **The Easy Life.** Point out that many people rent their homes when they are young and later buy homes. Ask students to describe situations in which people might choose to rent for their entire lives. *(Critical Thinking)*

■ **Making Comparisons.** Have students gather newspaper ads for rental homes and apartments. Have students choose a house and an apartment of about the same size and prepare a chart comparing the prices, locations, utilities included in the rent, lease lengths, acceptance of pets, and other features. Select some of the students' charts, and discuss situations in which a renter might prefer the home or the apartment listed in the chart. *(Decision Making)*

ENRICHMENT

■ **Sales Pitch.** Have pairs of students create television commercials or flyers for a fictional apartment or rental home. Ask students to stress features that would attract new renters. Provide time for several pairs to make their pitch to the class.

Checking Comprehension

✓ What expenses are often involved in renting a home? *Rent, the security deposit, utilities, appliances, furniture, property insurance.*

✓ Why do most landlords ask for a security deposit? *To cover any damage renters might cause.*

✓ What are some advantages and disadvantages of renting a home? *Advantages: Rent is more manageable sum than purchase price; easier to move; not responsible for maintenance. Disadvantage: Need permission to make changes.*

USING VISUALS

Refer students to Figure 70.1 to discuss the questions below.

1. What is the difference between a single-family house and a town house? *Single-family— not attached to any other building; town house— attached to other units on sides.*
2. Do people rent or own town houses? *Both— town houses can be apartments or condominiums.*
3. How many families live in a duplex? *Two.*
4. Are mobile homes always on the move? *No, usually permanently parked in mobile home park or on owners' property.*

What Can You Afford?

The cost of housing is often much more than people realize. Before you begin to look for a place to live, you need to determine the monthly payment you can afford. A good general rule is to spend no more than 28 percent of your gross income on rent.

The amount that you pay for rent is only part of what you spend on housing. Other expenses include the cost of utilities, including water, electricity, gas, and telephone service. Some of these may be covered in the rent. Ask to find out. Note, too, that some may require a deposit for hookup. You may also need to purchase furniture or buy a refrigerator and other appliances. Insurance is another household expense. You need insurance to cover personal property against loss by theft, fire, and other hazards.

Before deciding to go out on your own, you must consider all of these housing expenses. Add them to your other living expenses, such as food, clothing, entertainment, and medical care. Think about how much money you'd like to put away in savings. After you've measured all expenses against your income, you will know what you can afford.

At the time you move into rental property, you usually have to pay another cost—a **security deposit.** This is *an amount of money paid to the owner of the property by a renter to guard against financial loss caused by the renter.* The security deposit is usually equal to one or two rent payments. If the property is in good condition when you move out, you get

Figure 70.1

TYPES OF HOMES

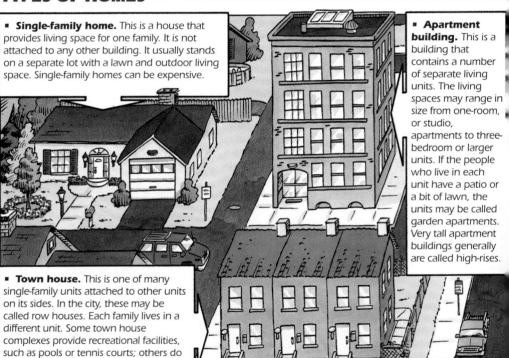

- **Single-family home.** This is a house that provides living space for one family. It is not attached to any other building. It usually stands on a separate lot with a lawn and outdoor living space. Single-family homes can be expensive.

- **Town house.** This is one of many single-family units attached to other units on its sides. In the city, these may be called row houses. Each family lives in a different unit. Some town house complexes provide recreational facilities, such as pools or tennis courts; others do not.

- **Apartment building.** This is a building that contains a number of separate living units. The living spaces may range in size from one-room, or studio, apartments to three-bedroom or larger units. If the people who live in each unit have a patio or a bit of lawn, the units may be called garden apartments. Very tall apartment buildings generally are called high-rises.

682   UNIT 8 Housing and Living Space

REAL-LIFE APPLICATION

Read the following to students: *Jana wants to live on her own, but the pay on her first job after high school is low. She knows that her income will increase in about six months, but she is eager to be independent soon. Her parents have suggested that she stay at home for a while and save some money.* Ask students to suggest possible options for Jana. Focus on the costs of living that Jana will face.

your security deposit back. If the property is damaged, the property owner may keep part or all of the security deposit to cover the cost of repairs.

As you can see, living on your own is costly. To evaluate your readiness to handle this responsibility, ask yourself these questions first:

- How much of my income will I need to spend on the monthly payments? What will be left for other expenses?
- Do I have enough money saved to pay the security deposit?
- What will the total monthly cost be for all other expenses?
- How much will it cost to move into my new residence?
- Will I still be able to afford the property if the rent and other expenses increase?

Advantages and Disadvantages

People who rent do so for many reasons. For some, renting is practical and convenient. In general, the landlord is responsible for making most repairs. Renters don't have to worry about finding or paying roofers, painters, or other home maintenance workers. If the plumbing system fails or a problem develops with the electricity, you can report the situation to the owner for repair. By carefully reading the lease, you know if there are certain repairs that you are responsible for.

Another advantage to renting is that leaving is fairly simple. Renters give notice to the landlord that they are leaving, and the owner has to find a new renter. If a lease has been signed, it may require that you give notice a specified number of days before leaving, often

Condominium. A **condominium** is <u>one of a group of apartments or town houses that people own rather than rent</u>. People who purchase a condominium agree to pay a monthly service fee. This fee covers the maintenance of common areas, such as hallways, lawns, elevators, or recreational areas. A homeowners' association governs the use and maintenance of these areas.

Manufactured home. Also called a mobile home, this is a factory-built house. It is moved by truck to a mobile home park or to the individual owner's property and is permanently placed there. In general, manufactured homes are less expensive than other single-family homes. Many of them come with furniture and built-in appliances. Some communities have special parks for manufactured homes. The location of these parks may be restricted by local zoning laws.

Duplex, triplex, or fourplex. This is a building divided into living spaces for two (duplex), three (triplex), or four (fourplex) families. The individual units can be arranged side by side or one on top of the other. Each unit has its own outside entrance.

CHAPTER 70   Housing and the Consumer   683

MORE ABOUT Mobile Homes

Many modern mobile homes are large and creatively designed. A double-width home consists of two units set side by side. Some have as many rooms as other homes. The loans people obtain to buy mobile homes often span only seven to ten years, a much shorter time than regular home mortgages. Although mobile homes tend to lose value over the years, they appeal to young couples, small families, and retired people because of the initial low cost and low monthly interest charges, compared to other types of homes.

Topics on pp. 684-686:
- Buying a Home
- Public Housing
- Responsibilities

Checking Comprehension

✓ What are some advantages and disadvantages of buying a home? *Advantages: community involvement; can make changes in home; good investment. Disadvantages: totally responsible for upkeep; more difficult to move.*

✓ How does the federal government help lower-income people find housing? *Provides low-cost public housing; helps low-income families pay rent to private landlords, and sets up urban renewal programs; loan and mortgage assistance.*

✓ What responsibilities are involved in living on your own? *Finding and furnishing home, paying bills on time, making or reporting needed repairs, keeping home clean .*

Managing Your Life

Have students read "Deciphering Real Estate Advertisements." Ask what other information people need before they can rent or buy? How do they obtain this information?

Answers to Applying . . .

1. Hardwood floors, two story, fenced yard, playroom, gas furnace, excellent closets, tennis court.
2. Answers will vary.
3. Needs repairs or remodeling.

30. It may also require that you give notice in writing. Check the lease before you sign so that you know what you will have to do when the time comes.

A disadvantage of renting is that renters cannot usually make changes to the property. A renter cannot remodel, replace carpeting, or paint the walls without first receiving permission from the owner. Sometimes simple alterations can be made, but again, check the lease or talk to the landlord. There may be rules about things like nail holes and other restrictions that you need to know.

In most cases landlords are responsive to a renter's problems. When they aren't, however, that can be a disadvantage of renting.

You may want to check with other renters in a building to see how satisfied they are.

Sharing the Rent

When the expenses are too high to pay alone, sharing a residence is an option. Such arrangements can be very helpful; however, they can also lead to disaster.

If you decide to share, think carefully about the person and the situation. Is the person reliable, trustworthy, and easy to get along with? Can the person afford the financial commitment? How will you manage? You may have to agree upfront on rules that cover sharing space, schedules, cleaning, ownership of furnishings, entertainment, finances, and guests. If you don't choose a roommate carefully, home may not be the peaceful place you want it to be.

Managing Your Life

Deciphering Real Estate Advertisements

Reading a real estate advertisement can be puzzling unless you know how to translate the abbreviations. People who place the advertisements often try to fit as much information in as few lines as possible. Someday you may want to buy a house or rent an apartment. The following advertisement shows what you might encounter:

> OPEN SUN., 2-4
> PRICE REDUCED!
> 134 Howland Ct., E. side. Brick, 1 1/2 stry, 2000 sf, 3 BR, FR, frml DR, LR, eat-in KTCH, 2 1/2 BTH, fla rm, fin bsmnt, 2 car gar, w/FP. CAC. $130s. At this price, won't last long!

Here's how to interpret this advertisement: The house, which is on the east side of town, is a 1 1/2-story brick structure with 2,000 square feet of finished living space. It has three bedrooms, a family room, a formal dining room, a living room, and an eat-in kitchen—that is, a kitchen with room for a dining table.

The house also has 2 1/2 bathrooms. (A half bath has no tub or shower.) In addition, there is a Florida, or sun, room and a finished basement. The house has a garage that will hold two cars. Finally, the house has a fireplace and central air conditioning and costs somewhere between $130,000 and $140,000.

Applying the Principles

1. Try to decipher each of the following house characteristics, which have been abbreviated as they might appear in a real estate advertisement in a newspaper: hdwd flrs, 2 stry, fncd yd, plyrm, gas furn, excel clsts, tenn ct.
2. Using the abbreviations given above or ones that you find in local housing guides, write a newspaper advertisement describing your own home or a house that would be ideal for your family. Try to give a clear description without using a lot of space.
3. If a house were described as a "handyman's special," what might you expect to find?

MORE ABOUT Mortgages

Tell students that the typical mortgage in the United States is for a 30-year period and provides about 80 percent of the purchase price of the home. The interest rate on this kind of loan was only 5 percent in 1946 but hit a high of 15 percent in 1982. A small change in the interest rate can cause a large change in a mortgage payment. Among the ways to set up a mortgage are: fixed rates that stay at the current interest rate and variable rates that change as the rate set by the federal government changes.

Buying

After renting a mobile home for several years, Sean decided that he liked the city where he was living and working. He had saved some money and thought that it was time to consider buying his own place.

Advantages and Disadvantages

Sean felt that one advantage of home ownership would be a feeling of stability. When you buy a home, you make an investment in a community. Homeowners generally want to stay in their homes for at least several years. They are more likely than renters to become involved in their neighborhoods and to participate in local government.

Unlike renters, homeowners can decorate and remodel their homes to meet their particular needs. They can add a garden, install a wheelchair ramp, or knock down a wall to enlarge a room. Homeowners need to check local building regulations before starting a remodeling project. Zoning laws in some communities regulate the kinds of changes that can be made to a structure.

For some people, the greater responsibility of home ownership is a disadvantage. Homeowners are responsible for all maintenance and upkeep of their homes. Another potential disadvantage of home ownership is that homeowners cannot move as easily as renters can since they must first find someone to buy their property.

The Costs of Ownership

Home ownership is a big expense. Most people have to take out a mortgage to pay for their home. A **mortgage** is *a long-term home loan*. With a mortgage, a bank pays for the home, and an agreement is made to pay back the money over time, usually 15, 20, or 30 years. For homeowners the ability to pay a mortgage payment can be calculated the same way that rent is—28 percent of gross income.

Buyers are usually required to make a cash payment, called a down payment, when they purchase the home. The down payment may be from 5 percent to 25 percent, or more, of the purchase price. At the time of purchase, homeowners may also have to pay closing costs that include bank fees, lawyer's fees, and other processing fees. Potential buyers usually pay an inspector to examine a home for serious flaws.

Like renting, home ownership also involves additional expenses. Besides those that you would have as a renter, you also have property taxes. These taxes generally pay for public services, such as police and fire protection, snow and garbage removal, sewer service, and street repair. They may also help pay for maintaining neighborhood schools and playgrounds. Some homeowners, including condominium owners, must pay monthly maintenance fees in addition to their mortgage payments and taxes.

Ownership as an Investment

One of the biggest advantages of buying a home is that it is an investment. Over the last 30 years, the value of homes has risen sharply in most parts of the United States. People expect to sell their homes for more money than they paid.

In order to gain from the investment, however, a house must be chosen carefully and cared for properly. Some homeowners increase the value of their homes by adding certain features, such as a new roof or additional living space.

Government Programs

Renting or buying a home can be very expensive. Some people cannot afford the monthly payments. The government helps these people by providing various forms of public housing. **Public housing** is *housing that is paid for, in part or in full, by the government.*

The governments of most large cities have developed public housing projects to accommodate low-income families, senior citizens, and people with disabilities. Residents usually pay a fixed percentage of their income for rent. The government pays the rest of the rental amount. These housing programs are

■ **Getting Started.** Ask: Why may it be more difficult for a family to afford the down payment on their first home than for down payments on later homes? *(Critical Thinking)*

■ **Building for the Future.** Have a volunteer look up the word equity in the dictionary and read the definition to the class. Explain that as homeowners pay off a mortgage, they build equity.

ENRICHMENT

■ **Fact Finding.** Invite a real estate agent to come to class and explain area housing conditions. Topics could include the types of housing available in your community; the criteria realtors use to appraise homes; current costs; zoning regulations; building codes; and tips for wise home investment. Students should prepare questions beforehand.

MULTICULTURAL *Perspectives*

Have students compare and suggest implications of the number of renters and homeowners in other nations. The annual update volume for the *Encyclopædia Britannica* is a good source for this information. Why, for example, did only 6.5 percent of the citizens of Bangladesh rent their homes in 1995, while 81.5 percent of Estonia's population were renters?

CROSS-REFERENCE

Chapter 30 discusses ways to manage money wisely. Students need to realize that living independently with success hinges on the use of these skills.

DID YOU KNOW?

If a homeowner cannot pay on a mortgage, the bank may foreclose the loan. In foreclosure, the house is sold and the money kept by the bank to pay the mortgage. The homeowner loses the home and any money paid on the mortgage. If the house sells for less than the unpaid amount of the mortgage, the bank loses money. For this reason, banks hesitate to foreclose and instead try to work out a payment plan with the homeowner.

Review

■ **Chapter Review.** Use the contents of the Chapter Review page to help students review concepts, think critically, and apply their knowledge.

■ **Study Guide.** Have students complete the Study Guide for Chapter 70 on p. 226 of the Student Workbook.

■ **Picture Pairs.** Have each student create a pair of pictures that visually contrast renting with owning a home. For example, one picture could show a renter handing the landlord dollars with wings and a homeowner stuffing money into a bank. In another pair, the landlord holds plumbing tools, while the homeowner holds similar tools. Display the pictures.

Evaluation

■ **Chapter Test.** Use the reproducible chapter test provided in the Teacher's Classroom Resources or create your own test using the *Testmaker Software.*

■ **Alternative Assessment.** Ask students to imagine that a penpal from another country has written them, asking about the housing situation in this country. Have students write a letter providing such a description.

■ **The Value of Choice.** Discuss the possible consequences if society had few or no homes for people to buy.

limited and cannot accommodate everyone who qualifies. Often, there are long waiting lists for public housing.

Public housing is just one type of government housing program. Government reimbursement programs encourage private landlords to rent their houses and apartments to low-income individuals. If the renters cannot pay their rent, the federal government pays it. Urban renewal programs are found in some cities. In these programs, the government purchases homes that are in poor condition and gives them to the local housing agency. This agency repairs the homes and then sells them to needy families at an affordable price. The federal government also has loan and mortgage assistance programs for individuals who can't afford to buy their own homes.

Accepting Responsibility

As you move closer to independence, you may be excited by the prospect of having your own living space. You will know you are ready when you are able to understand and accept the responsibilities that go along with the enjoyment.

What responsibilities will you have? For one thing, you must pay all bills on time. If you forget, you may find yourself without heat, electricity, water, or phone service as well as a damaged credit record.

You must also take good care of property. An understanding of maintenance and upkeep and knowing when and where to go for service helps. People who take care of homes contribute to the value of property in their neighborhood. They protect their own investment.

When you rent, put yourself in the place of the landlord. You would want tenants to take good care of your property. Doing so earns the respect and cooperation of a landlord. Taking care of rental property has advantages. Rental rates don't go up as fast when owners don't have to keep paying for repairs. As noted earlier, good care of property also enables renters to get back their security deposit when they move.

Being a responsible renter or homeowner takes knowledge, energy, and a caring attitude. Most people find, however, that the rewards of having a place of their own make it worthwhile. Running a household on your own can provide a feeling of great pride and accomplishment when you are ready for that step in your life.

■ When you move into a residence, what responsibilities do you have?

DID YOU KNOW?

In addition to those housing programs described, the federal government also helps supply mortgage money. It buys certain mortgages from banks, thus allowing the banks to lend money to additional homeowners for their mortgages. Many state governments, including California and New York, subsidize housing for low-income families.

Review

Reviewing the Facts

1. Describe three different styles of housing.
2. How do an apartment and a condominium differ?
3. Explain what a lease is and why it should be read carefully.
4. How can a person determine whether housing is affordable?
5. Compare the advantages and disadvantages of renting and buying?
6. Describe two government programs that help people afford housing.

Thinking Critically

1. Suppose that you work for a large company, and you are being transferred to a branch office in another town for three years. Would it be wiser to rent or buy a home? Why?
2. Recent public housing programs attempt to scatter low-income housing throughout communities instead of concentrating it in large projects. Write a paragraph explaining why you think that this is a positive or a negative idea.

Applying Your Knowledge

1. **Computing Costs.** Check the newspaper rental listings for apartments in your area. Based on those advertised, what is the average cost of rental in your area?
2. **Writing a Lease.** What do you think should be included in a lease? Write down all of the things that would be important to a landlord, and list the provisions that the landlord would want included in a lease. Then put yourself in the place of the renter. List the rules that a renter would want included. Finally, compare your lists with a standard lease agreement. What are the similarities and differences?

Making Connections

1. **Economics.** List the housing expenses that you think a typical family must pay each month. Have your list handy for a class discussion of housing costs. Which ones did you forget? If possible, find out typical costs for these expenses in your area.
2. **Language Arts.** Imagine that you are a condominium owner, and you are attending a meeting of your homeowners' association. Write a short persuasive speech that you as a homeowner might make to answer one of the following questions being discussed at the meeting: Should we put in a pool? Should we repair the roof? What should we do about the homeowner who leaves garbage in the hallway? Should we allow homeowners to have pets? Who should be responsible for shoveling snow?

Building Your Portfolio

Preparing a Housing Checklist
Imagine that you are looking for an apartment to rent or a home to buy. Develop a checklist to use as you look at various properties. What would be your requirements for a comfortable home? List the factors that you consider to be important, such as cost of rent or mortgage payments, location, square footage, utility costs, and number of bedrooms. Place the checklist in your portfolio.

CHAPTER 70   Housing and the Consumer   687

ANSWERS TO REVIEWING THE FACTS

1. Any three: single-family homes, town houses, duplexes, triplexes, fourplexes, apartments, condominiums, and manufactured, or mobile, homes. See descriptions on pp. 682-683.
2. People rent living units in an apartment but own them in a condominium. Condominium owners may also own a share of the areas that they all use and pay an additional fee to help maintain these areas.
3. A legal contract between the renter and property owner. If not read carefully, you might agree to conditions that you won't like for the duration of the contract.
4. Compare income to rent or mortgage plus all other expenses. Try to spend no more than 28 percent of gross income on rent or house payment.
5. Landlords and home owners are in charge of property upkeep, but not renters. Home owners can do what they like with property, but renters can't. Renters can leave an apartment with relative ease, but a home owner must usually sell first. Owning is an investment, but renting isn't. Owning often provides more of a tie and commitment to neighborhood and community.
6. Any two: public housing projects, rent reimbursement programs, urban renewal programs, and loan and mortgage assistance. See pp. 685-686 for descriptions.

ANSWERS TO THINKING CRITICALLY

1. Renting is sometimes the wiser choice when you know you are not going to be in an area very long. On the other hand, a wise home purchase gives you a chance to earn some equity and sell at a profit.

2. Suggest that low-income areas that are isolated from the community sometimes become unpleasant places to live. When low-income housing is scattered, its residents are more likely to become incorporated into the general community.

FOCUS

Chapter Overview

Chapter 71 describes how to use the elements and the principles of design to create attractive living areas. The chapter also gives ways to organize living space effectively, including practical ideas for storing belongings, accessorizing rooms, and sharing space with others.

Motivator

■ **Design Decisions.** Ask students what they consider when they put together an outfit to wear. List their responses on the board. Then ask what they would consider if they were decorating a room. Do the lists share factors? How do they differ?

Objectives

Discuss the chapter objectives on this page. Remind students that the objectives focus on important chapter concepts.

Vocabulary

Ask students what they think of when they hear the term *traffic pattern* (probably streets and highways). Compare what affects these kinds of traffic patterns to what affects those in a room.

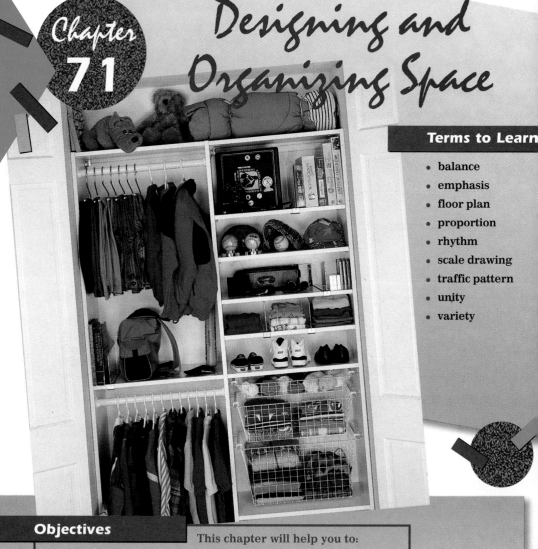

Chapter 71

Designing and Organizing Space

Terms to Learn

- balance
- emphasis
- floor plan
- proportion
- rhythm
- scale drawing
- traffic pattern
- unity
- variety

Objectives

This chapter will help you to:

- Identify **how the elements and principles of design relate to room planning.**
- Describe **how to organize your space using floor plans, analysis of traffic patterns, and creation of separate activity areas.**
- Develop **ways to increase storage, use accessories, ease cramped quarters, make rooms flexible, and share space.**

688   UNIT 8   Housing and Living Space

CHAPTER RESOURCES

Student Workbook
Study Guide, pp. 229-230
Activity, *Dream Bedroom*, pp. 231-232

Teacher's Classroom Resources
Lesson Plan, p. 75
Cooperative Learning, *Designing a Set*, pp. 77-78

Decision Making, *I Need Help*, p. 27
Extension #102, *Solving Storage Problems*, p. 108
Life Skills, *Space Planner*, pp. 109-110
Transparency 58, *Organizing Space*
Chapter 71 Test, pp. 147-148

Performance Assessment, *Creating a Floor Plan*, pp. 108-109
Reteaching, *Using Space Well*, p. 77

See Also:
ABCNews InterActive™ Videodiscs

Most people need a space of their own. Yours may be a shared bedroom, a room of your own, or a corner of the family room. Whatever it is, the space that is yours probably already contains items that express who you are. Some people like uncluttered, functional rooms that have a minimal amount of furniture. Other people prefer rooms that have lots of furniture and places to display their keepsakes. No matter what kind of space you have or what your budget is, you can give a space your personal stamp. In this chapter you will learn how to use the elements and principles of design and how to organize your space in a way that suits you.

Design for Living Space

You can make your personal space more attractive and usable by working with the basic elements and principles of design. You already know what colors and styles appeal to you. Knowing about design can help you to use your own tastes to arrange space in a way that will work best for you.

How does this room show both unity and variety?

The Elements of Design

In Chapter 57 you read about the elements of design as they relate to clothing. These elements are:

- Line
- Shape
- Space
- Texture
- Color

Figure 71.1 on page 690 shows how these elements can be applied to room design.

The Principles of Design

The principles of design are a set of guidelines or rules about how to make line, shape, space, texture, and color work together. The principles of design help you put these individual elements together in pleasing ways. The principles of design are unity, variety, balance, emphasis, proportion, and rhythm.

Unity and Variety

Designers usually advise clients to choose one color scheme and one style of furniture for a room. This helps to create a sense of **unity,** *a feeling that all objects in a room look as if they belong together.*

Unity doesn't mean that a room must have only one color or only one style in order to have a pleasant appearance. You can accent a major color, such as beige walls, with burgundy and deep green draperies and pillows. In fact, a room will be more interesting if it contains some variety. **Variety** is *the combination of different but compatible styles and materials.* For example, a simple, antique chair—such as a Shaker chair—might be combined with contemporary, open-weave drapes. You can also add variety with shapes—by hanging an oval mirror over a rectangular dresser, for example, or by using both angular and rounded tables in a room.

CHAPTER 71   Designing and Organizing Space   689

Topics on p. 689:
- **Designing Personal Space**
- **Principles of Design**

Checking Comprehension

✓ When does a room have unity? *When all objects seem to belong together.*

Activities

■ **Interpretations.** Ask: If everyone uses the same elements and principles of design, why doesn't everybody's living space look alike. *(Critical Thinking)*

ENRICHMENT

■ **Designer Packages.** Ask students to bring in examples of packaging that uses the elements of design to attract consumers' attention and persuade them to buy the product—detergent bottle that uses color or shape to make the package seem larger, for instance. Have students share their examples with the class, identifying the elements and how they make the product seem more desirable.

CROSS-CURRICULAR ACTIVITY
Language Arts

Ask students to choose two colors and write a paragraph on each, describing the feelings and energy levels they think each color evokes. After volunteers read their paragraphs aloud, encourage the class to reach some conclusions about the effects of specific colors. Have students suggest ways to use these colors effectively in a home.

Topics on pp. 690-691:
- **Elements of Design**
- **Principles of Design**
- **Making a Floor Plan**

Checking Comprehension

✓ What are two types of balance? *Formal and informal.*

✓ Is it all right for one item to stand out in a room? Why? *Yes, for emphasis.*

✓ Why should floor plans be drawn to scale? *To accurately reflect relative size of real objects.*

USING VISUALS

Refer students to Figure 71.1 to discuss the questions below:

1. How could you make the space in a room seem cozier? *Arrange furniture toward center of room.*
2. What creates vertical lines in this room? *A bookcase, wallpaper, drapes, ladder.*
3. What are some contrasting textures? *Smooth/nubby and silk/deep pile.*
4. What shapes give this room a softer feel? *Curves in bed frame, upper bunk rail, sides of desk.*
5. What are some cool colors? *Blue, green, and purple.* Warm colors? *Red, orange, and yellow.*

Figure 71.1
ELEMENTS OF DESIGN

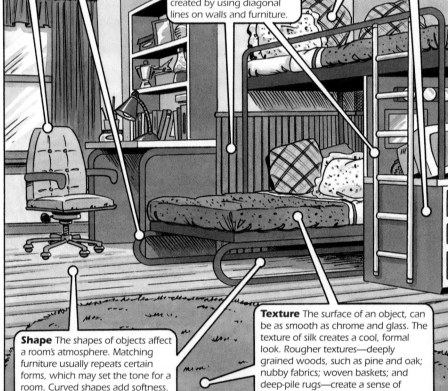

Space The way you use space can make it seem larger or smaller. Arranging furniture along a wall gives a feeling of more space. Moving the furniture toward the center makes a room seem cozier. Bright colors appear to add space, while dark colors do the opposite. You can divide large spaces into smaller areas with furniture or screens.

Line Every room is influenced by the bold lines of windows and moldings. You can create effects with the horizontal lines of a low bed, long dresser, and shelves. Vertical lines can be created with a tall bookcase and striped wallpaper. Some people like the feeling of motion and excitement that is created by using diagonal lines on walls and furniture.

Color Color has a powerful effect on a person's mood. Warm colors (red, yellow, and orange) are bold and cheerful. Cool colors (blue, green, and purple) are quiet and soothing. You can work with colors that are already there. If your walls have a light hue, for example, you can accent them with colorful accessories.

Shape The shapes of objects affect a room's atmosphere. Matching furniture usually repeats certain forms, which may set the tone for a room. Curved shapes add softness. Square and rectangular furniture provide solidity and stability. A variety of shapes bring an informal look, while many competing shapes can have an unsettling effect.

Texture The surface of an object, can be as smooth as chrome and glass. The texture of silk creates a cool, formal look. Rougher textures—deeply grained woods, such as pine and oak; nubby fabrics; woven baskets; and deep-pile rugs—create a sense of comfort and informality. Different textures can be combined for a pleasing effect.

690   **UNIT 8   Housing and Living Space**

DID YOU KNOW?

Color is affected by light. Daylight gives what is called true color, while an incandescent lightbulb gives a yellowish cast to objects. Fluorescent light, often used in stores, is more blue and gives a slightly cold look to objects.

MORE ABOUT Emphasis

The arrangement of furniture can highlight a feature in a room. For example, grouping a seating arrangement around a fireplace makes it the focal point of the room. Lighting can also be used to focus attention on a picture or other object.

Balance and Emphasis

Another effect that designers work to achieve is balance. **Balance** means *that objects are arranged in even, pleasing ways on each side of an imaginary center line.* Balance can be formal or informal. When you place identical tables at each end of a sofa and hang four pictures in a square arrangement on the wall above the center of the sofa, you are using formal balance. When you look at the center of the sofa and picture arrangement, the objects on both sides of the center are the same or have equal weight.

If you were to display several antique bottles of different sizes and shapes in an attractive arrangement on a table, you would be using informal balance. Although the bottles on both sides of the center of the table have different sizes and shapes, they leave an impression of restfulness or equality in weight.

An object that stands out in a room receives **emphasis,** or *more attention than the other objects,* and becomes the focal point, or center of interest. For example, a large, dramatic painting hung on the wall or a brightly colored rug placed on a hardwood floor can be used for emphasis in a room.

Proportion and Rhythm

Proportion is *the way that one part of a design relates in size, shape, or space to another part of the whole.* A large, oak desk from a farmhouse would be considered out of proportion when combined with a small, armless chair from an ice cream parlor. To achieve better proportion, a larger and more comfortable chair would have to be used with the desk.

Rhythm is *the regular repetition of line or shape in a room.* Rhythm in design is similar to rhythm in music. Striped fabric or pictures hung at regular intervals create a rhythm that directs the eye to move in a natural flow from object to object. Rhythm can also be created by using lines that radiate from a center point or objects that gradually increase or decrease in size.

Organizing Your Space

Keeping in mind the elements and principles of design, consider how you might organize the space that is available to you. If you decide to rearrange furniture, you will need to create a floor plan and to consider possible traffic patterns. You will also need to think about the activities that take place in this space and how the space can be organized to accommodate them.

Making a Floor Plan

A good way to assess your space is to make a **floor plan,** *an illustration of the arrangement of furniture, structural elements, and design elements in a room or home.* (See **Figure 71.2** on page 692.) A floor plan is like a map of the space as seen from a bird's-eye view. It allows you to rearrange your room on paper without actually having to move the furniture.

To make a floor plan, start by measuring your room—including walls, windows, and doors—and all of the furniture in it. Measure precisely, using a yardstick, folding ruler, or retractable metal tape measure, and record the figures on a sheet of paper. Then use graph paper to make a scale drawing of the room. A **scale drawing** is *one in which the relative sizes of objects in the drawing are the same as the relative sizes of those objects in the actual space.* Follow these steps:

1. Allow a certain number of graph paper squares to equal each foot of space that you measured. For example, if you allow two squares per foot, a room measuring 8 ft. by 12 ft. (2.4 m by 3.6 m) would be drawn as a rectangle measuring 16 squares by 24 squares.
2. Indicate the width of such features as doors and windows, and use a dotted line to show the direction in which the doors open and how much floor space they cover while opening.
3. Draw your furniture, allowing the correct number of squares per foot for each piece.

■ **Surrounded!** Ask students to look around the classroom and list objects or features that illustrate the principles of design. What other ways could the principles be applied to make the room more pleasant? *(Observation)*

RETEACHING

■ **Different Strokes.** Organize the class into three work groups (six, if your class is large). Assign each group one of these rooms: a five-year-old boy's bedroom, a doctor's waiting room, a family room in a home that includes teens. Have each group design its room with attention to space, line, texture, shape, and color.

ENRICHMENT

■ **Analyzing Curb Appeal.** Explain that in real estate, the phrase *curb appeal* describes whether the exterior of a house is likely to attract potential buyers. Have students collect exterior pictures of homes for sale from the newspaper and real estate flyers. Discuss whether the principles of design were used effectively in the exteriors of these homes to give them curb appeal?

CROSS-CURRICULAR ACTIVITY
Math

Have students follow the steps on page 691 to draw the floor plan of a room at home, including the furniture. Ask them to indicate the scale they used in their drawing. Then have them use this plan to rearrange the furniture to enhance the room's appearance, improve traffic patterns, or add usable space.

DID YOU KNOW?

Explain that the principles of design are not new ideas. Examination of the temples and monuments of ancient civilizations, such as those of the Greeks, Romans, and Incas, shows that the same principles were followed when planning these buildings. Show students a picture of an ancient building and ask them to point out applications of the principles of design.

Checking Comprehension

✓ What is the advantage of using a floor plan when rearranging furniture? *Can easily move the furniture around on the paper to find an arrangement that works well.*

✓ What is clearance space? How does it relate to traffic patterns? *Space needed to use furniture. Must be included when planning for traffic pattern.*

✓ How can you tell when you need to change a traffic pattern? *If furniture, appliances, or even a wall interferes with people moving around in the area.*

✓ Give one basic rule of organizing space. *Group furniture with other items that you use at the same time.*

USING VISUALS

After students study the floor plan in Figure 71.2, have them figure out the width and length of the room, bed, desk, and dresser, using a scale of two squares equal to one foot (30 cm).

Figure 71.2

MAKING A FLOOR PLAN

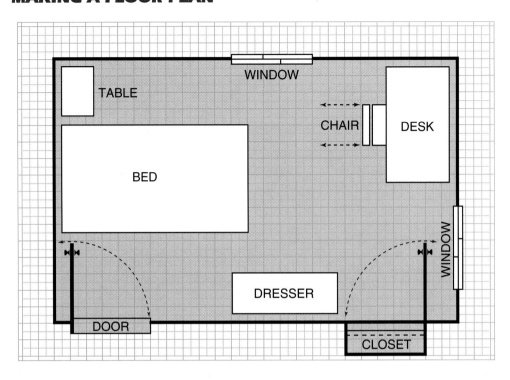

By using a floor plan, you can see how a particular arrangement of furniture will look. If you want to try another arrangement, use graph paper to draw a separate scale drawing of each piece of furniture, and cut out the drawings. Try several different layouts until you find one that you like. Doing this saves you the trouble of having to rearrange furnishings several times in order to find the best arrangement. If you are buying furniture, a floor plan can help you make sure that the pieces selected will fit well in the room.

Considering Traffic Patterns

Think about the traffic patterns in your space. **Traffic patterns** are *the most direct routes that people use to move through the space in a room.* Can you move freely from one area of your space to another without tripping over things? If you have to squeeze past a dresser every time you walk into the room, the dresser is interfering with the easy flow of traffic.

The issue of clearance space around furniture is related to traffic patterns. Certain

REAL-LIFE APPLICATION

Tell students you are going to read about problems facing three teens whose bedrooms are exactly as shown in Figure 71.2. Ask the class to offer solutions.

- *Adrienne likes to watch exercise programs on the television set that sits on her dresser. However, she would like more open space in her bedroom so she*

can do the aerobic exercises.
- *Bryant has a large collection of CDs. He would like a good way to store them in his bedroom.*
- *Chira's family is preparing to adopt Ana, a seven-year-old girl who will share Chira's room.*

types of furniture need space around them in order to be usable. For example, you need room to pull out a desk chair in order to sit comfortably at the desk. You also need enough space to be able to pull out desk drawers while working at the desk.

Creating Different Areas

In addition to sleeping, most people use a bedroom for such purposes as studying, dressing, reading, and listening to music. A bedroom might also be used as a place for private talks with a friend or as a place to get away from family noise. In addition, a bedroom is the place where clothes, schoolbooks, musical equipment, and other personal possessions are kept.

One key to organizing space is to group together furnishings and other items that you use at the same time. For example:

- A study area might include a desk, chair, bookcase, and desk lamp. Paper, pens, and pencils would be kept in the desk

drawers. A computer area—on or near the desk area—might include a computer, monitor, printer, and storage space for disks and computer games.

- A music area might contain tapes and CDs, a stereo, and—if there is space for it—a comfortable chair.
- A hobby or fitness area might include anything that is related to a pastime—a sewing machine, for example—or an exercise mat, jump rope, weights, a radio or tape player, and any other item that could be used while working out.

Design Solutions

Most people do not have the space or the budget to create a dream room that contains all of the areas they would like to have. Most design problems have to do with the need to fit clothing and possessions in a limited space and the need to have this space serve a variety of purposes. The following section describes some solutions to common design problems.

Space for Storage

Everyone needs to have space for storing possessions and protecting them from damage. Storage space should be convenient and accessible, and, with a little work, it can also be attractive. No matter what kind of space needs organization, there are a few important points to consider.

This area contains everything that is needed for efficient study.

MORE ABOUT Creating Areas

In a multipurpose room, a swing-down table can be hidden behind a door or in a cupboard and unfolded when it's needed for hobbies, such as sewing. A closet can be fitted with shelves and drawers for more storage. A pegboard on a wall can offer additional space to hang supplies and tools. Storage containers on wheels might slide under a table.

Activities

- ■ **Give Me Space!** Ask students to name room features and kinds of furniture that require extra space in a room design. (*Problem Solving*)
- ■ **Problem Placement.** Discuss the kinds of problems that can result from poorly placed furniture. Guide students to describe problems in both traffic patterns and the appearance of the room. (*Observation*)

RETEACHING

- ■ **Research.** Have groups list all the information they need about a room and its furniture to make an accurate floor plan. Have groups share items from their lists, avoiding repetition. Examples include width and height of windows and doors, and locations and measurements of closets and electrical outlets. Create a master list on the board.

ENRICHMENT

- ■ **School Traffic.** Have students analyze traffic patterns in the hallways, cafeteria, locker area, media center or library, and other busy areas of school. Have them identify bottlenecks and possible ways to improve them.

FAMILY AND COMMUNITY OUTREACH

Suggest that students evaluate the traffic patterns in their homes. They might draw a floor plan that shows high and low traffic areas and look for ways to reduce bottlenecks. Encourage students to discuss their ideas with family members.

Topics on pp. 694-696:

- **Storage Space**
- **Using Accessories**
- **Small Spaces**
- **Shared Spaces**

Checking Comprehension

✓ Why might you add accessories to a room? *To reflect your interests, improve room's appearance, serve purpose, beautify.*

✓ What can make a room look smaller? *Clutter, big furniture, too much furniture, dark colors.*

✓ Why might siblings experience conflict when they share a room? *Different needs, interests, styles.*

In Touch With
TECHNOLOGY

Have students read "Designing with Computers." Discuss the advantages of being able to see a room in three dimensions as they design it. How can this help them to better use elements and principles of design?

Answers to Thinking . . .

1. Would allow designers to work more quickly and accurately, enhancing job performance and success. However, if fewer people can do more work, some may lose their jobs.
2. Suggest it may increase creativity by helping designers see more options more completely.

In Touch with
TECHNOLOGY

Designing with Computers

Will computers eventually eliminate the need for pencils and drawing aids used by designers and architects? It seems entirely possible. More and more designers are using computer graphics programs to lay out and plan the interiors of homes and offices.

What Is the Process?

The process is computer-aided design (CAD). CAD is software that allows an architect, engineer, or designer to create the plans for an entire house, from the floor plans to the electrical system, on a computer. Using a mouse or a special stylus, a designer can create these plans in a fraction of the time that it would take to draw them by hand.

How Does CAD Work?

In laying out the floor plan of a room, for example, a designer starts with a blank grid on the computer. The designer adds the fixed elements, such as the dimensions of the room and the placement of the doors and windows. After the scale drawing of the room is completed, the designer selects furniture from a database, or catalog, and begins to lay out and plan the space in the room. Furniture styles can be selected and changed as needed.

The designer can instruct the computer to show the room in two- or three-dimensional models. With some sophisticated programs and powerful computers, it is also possible to zoom in on objects or to rotate the model in order to see the room from different angles. An architect can even walk through the space as though actually in it.

The computer can display the room in hundreds of color schemes and can change colors instantly.

The colors can be shown in a variety of textures, as well as in light and shadow. Wallpaper and carpeting can even be added.

The major benefit of computer-aided design is that it allows designers and architects to look at all possible solutions to a problem with amazing speed. In addition to being faster to execute, computer-aided design is also less expensive and more accurate than hand drawings.

Who Uses CAD?

Many high-tech engineering and architectural firms use CAD systems. As prices for the systems drop, more designers will be able to own and use them. Many colleges and universities have installed these systems for use by engineering, interior design, and architecture students.

Downscale versions of the software are available for home use too. Homeowners with personal computers can use the software to design their living space.

> **Thinking Critically About Technology**
>
> 1. What effect do you think CAD could have on people's jobs?
> 2. Do you think that computers take the creativity out of design? Why or why not?

DID YOU KNOW?

Many city planners use CAD software. It allows them to see how planned buildings will affect surrounding areas and how they will fit in with existing buildings. Automobile designers also use computers to develop new features and improve driving safety. As in other industries, CAD software saves time and money.

- **Group similar items together.** Hang or store similar items in the same area so that they will be easy to find. Rather than keeping an umbrella in the back of a bedroom closet, keep it near the front door of the home.
- **Keep often-used items within easy reach.** Avoid keeping often-used items on high shelves or in low drawers. Items that are used less frequently can be kept a bit more out of the way—in a storage box under the bed, for example.
- **Keep items clearly visible.** Storing objects in clear plastic storage containers, wire-meshed baskets, or open shelves will help you to find the objects easily. Open storage shelves and glass storage cases can also serve as display areas for your most special possessions.
- **Compartmentalize space.** Divide space in the closet or drawers into smaller categories, and designate a place for each type of item. For example, hang shirts in one section of a closet and pants in another section. Store items within drawers in boxes so that the items will stay neat and be easy to find.
- **Use walls and doors for storage.** Install hooks or pegs on walls and doors, and use them to hang jewelry, belts, and hats. Hang shoe racks, hooks, or plastic baskets on the back of the closet door. You can also hang baskets from the ceiling, but store only lightweight items in these containers.

Decorating With Accessories

When planning rooms, designers often speak of the major furnishings and the accessories. In a bedroom, the bed, dresser, and desk are the major furnishings. The small objects that add visual appeal to the room are the accessories. Accessories can improve the look of a room in a fairly inexpensive and relatively impermanent way. Posters, for example, don't cost much money and can reflect an interest in music, art, or sports. When your in-

Making Decisions

Sharing a Room

With a baby on the way, Jana's family was making plans for the new arrival. Space would be tight in their small home. Jana was given a choice: to share her bedroom with her two younger sisters or move to one end of the family room, where an area would be partitioned off for her behind a screen.

Jana's initial reaction was disappointment. It didn't seem fair that after having a room to herself, she would now lose it or have to share it. Jana began to think about the options. I'd better consider the pros and cons carefully, she thought, so that I won't regret my decision.

What Would You Do?

1. What are some pros and cons of Jana sharing her bedroom with her two sisters?
2. What are some pros and cons of choosing the partitioned space?
3. Do you think Jana should talk to anyone before making her decision? Explain.
4. If you were Janna, what would your decision be? Why?

terests change, you can buy or create new accessories to reflect that change.

Some accessories are strictly for decoration. A painting, for example, adds beauty to a room. Accessories can also be useful, however. For example, a calendar that features art prints is both useful and decorative, as are colorful baskets used to hold craft supplies. Accessories also please the senses. Plants may give a room the peaceful feeling of being in a garden. A bright quilt or cozy afghan can brighten even the darkest day.

Review

■ **Chapter Review.** Use the contents of the Chapter Review page to help students review concepts, think critically, and apply their knowledge.

■ **Study Guide.** Have students complete the Study Guide for Chapter 71 on p. 229 of the Student Workbook.

■ **Designing Do's.** Organize the class into four groups. Have two groups create a list of ten designing do's and two groups list ten designing don'ts. The do's should apply an element or principle of design or solve a problem in traffic patterns, storage, or sharing space. The don'ts should violate an element or principle or create a problem. As groups read their lists to the class, ask students to identify the element, principle, or problem related to each rule.

Evaluation

■ **Chapter Test.** Use the reproducible chapter test provided in the Teacher's Classroom Resources or create your own test using the *Testmaker Software.*

■ **Alternative Assessment.** Provide several pictures of effective and ineffective room arrangements. Ask students to explain how each room demonstrates the effective use—or violation—of the elements and principles of design. Have them suggest improvements.

CLOSE

■ **A Closer Look at Resources.** Have students discuss whether money or knowledge has the greater impact on creating a pleasing living space.

Cramped Quarters

A small room generally can't be made larger, but the way that a room is designed and the choice and arrangement of furniture can make a big difference. In cramped quarters, avoid having too many pieces of furniture or furniture that is too large. A room will also look larger and less cluttered if there are fewer items on the floor. Use hanging shelves and sturdy hooks to hold everything from a backpack to a bicycle. Don't forget to use vertical space. For example, bunk beds provide room for two people to sleep but only take up the floor space of one bed.

Bright, light colors will make a room appear to be larger. Mirrors also create the illusion of space. Placing one or two mirrors in a room—or placing a mirror on a closet door—can make the room seem larger.

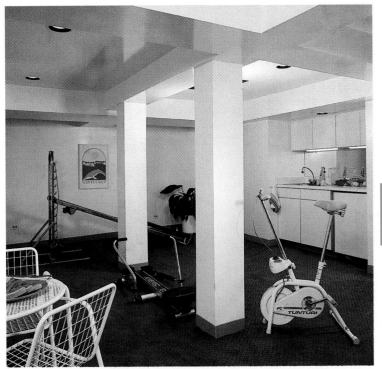

Flexibility and Sharing

In most homes, many areas are shared. Living rooms, kitchens, and bathrooms, for example, are usually used by more than one member of the family. Some families designate special purposes for rooms or parts of rooms in their homes, such as offices, workrooms, exercise rooms, or sewing rooms. Usually more than one member of the family uses the equipment that is kept in a special-purpose room. Other areas have one major use but also can be used in other ways. A den, for example, can double as a guest room if it contains a sofa bed.

If you share a room with one or more siblings, conflicts may arise over differences in interests, styles, or needs. Consideration and mutual respect will help you work out these difficulties. If possible, divide a shared room so that each of you has some area that is all your own. You may also be able to plan your schedules to allow each person exclusive use of the room for some part of the day.

When space allows, rooms can be used for special purposes, such as exercise. Often space like this is shared by family members.

696 **UNIT 8 Housing and Living Space**

DID YOU KNOW?

Tell students that attaching lighting to the walls or ceiling can save space and allow more flexible room arrangements. For example, if there is no room beside a bed for a nightstand or no nightstand is available, they can install an inexpensive wall lamp beside the bed for night-time reading. Wall lamps can also be placed above a desk so they won't take up valuable space on the desk.

Chapter 71

Reviewing the Facts

1. What are the six principles of design?
2. How do the principles of design provide guidelines for using the elements of design? Give an example for each principle.
3. Why is using a floor plan a good way to decide how to organize your space?
4. List the five storage principles.
5. How can accessories help you decorate a room?
6. Identify two ways to make a small room seem larger.

Thinking Critically

1. Consider how the five storage principles relate to the use of storage space in your room. Are your belongings stored in a space that is accessible and attractive? If so, describe how they are stored. If not, suggest ways in which you could make improvements.
2. Describe some ways in which two people can share a bedroom while maintaining a sense of privacy and personal identity.

Applying Your Knowledge

1. **Finding Ideas for Accessories.** Look through several issues of craft or decorating magazines. Report on five projects that could be made easily and inexpensively and used to accessorize a teen's room.
2. **Designing a Dream Room.** Using your own artwork or photographs from magazines, create a picture of your dream room. On an attached page, describe the elements and principles of design you used.
3. **Budgeting a Project.** Having designed a dream room, describe your reality room, based on available resources and a pleasant design that you can live with. What furniture could you repaint or refinish? What items could you buy at a yard sale or a flea market?

Making Connections

1. **Art.** Look in an art history book for a painting that you admire. Which elements and principles of design did the artist use? Write a description of the painting, explaining how the artist combined these elements and principles and why you like the painting.
2. **Business.** Use the yellow pages and newspaper advertisements to identify home-construction and home-decorating businesses in your community. Do the majority of these businesses provide full service, or are they for the do-it-yourself home repairperson? Write a brief report analyzing why one of these types of services might be more popular than the other.

Building Your Portfolio

Being Your Own Architect

Imagine that you have been hired to redesign a room in your home. With your family, discuss how the room is used and what furniture is needed. Draw a floor plan of the new arrangement. Using pictures or actual wallpaper, paint, and floor covering samples, select items that match your family's tastes. Collect furniture ideas from magazines and catalogs. Place your floor plan, samples, and a description of the new room's features in your portfolio.

ANSWERS TO REVIEWING THE FACTS

1. Unity, variety, balance, emphasis, proportion, and rhythm.
2. Principles give framework in which to use elements. Elements are "whats," principles are "hows." Examples will vary.
3. You can move furniture around on the paper without having to move it around the room.
4. Group similar items together; keep items that are used often within easy reach; keep items clearly visible; compartmentalize space; and use walls and doors for storage.
5. Accessories can reflect your interests, add beauty, be useful, and please your senses.
6. Any two: Avoid having too much furniture or furniture that is too large; keep items off the floor; use light, bright colors; hang mirrors.

ANSWERS TO THINKING CRITICALLY

1. Students' answers should apply the storage principles to their own situations and identify ways to improve their use of storage space.
2. Answers may include: put up a folding screen or other room divider; have each person decorate part of the room to reflect own interests; set up time when each person can be in the room alone.

Chapter 72

FOCUS

Chapter Overview

Chapter 72 gives tips for keeping living space clean and orderly. Students learn about regular cleaning tasks and different ways that families handle them.

Motivators

■ **Date with a Broom.** Discuss: How do you decide when your room or home needs to be cleaned? By a schedule? When someone tells you to clean it? Point out that knowing how and when to perform home care tasks is part of maturity and independence.

■ **Who Cares?** Have students estimate the percentage of home-care tasks handled by each person in their home. Do they feel tasks are evenly distributed? Why or why not?

Objectives

Discuss the chapter objectives. Remind students that the objectives focus on important chapter concepts.

Vocabulary

The verb form of *maintenance* is *maintain,* to keep in an existing state or to preserve from decline. Ask students how the term *maintenance* might apply to caring for a home. What things do people maintain in their homes, and why?

Chapter 72 — Managing Care and Upkeep

Terms to Learn

- preventive maintenance
- routine
- task rotation

Objectives

This chapter will help you to:

- Describe the benefits of caring for living space.
- Identify different ways to divide household tasks.
- Explain how to clean and maintain areas inside and outside of a home.
- Analyze how preventive maintenance can reduce costs.
- List preventive maintenance tasks.

698   **UNIT 8   Housing and Living Space**

CHAPTER RESOURCES

Student Workbook
Study Guide, p. 233
Activity, *Cleanup Commander*, p. 234

Teacher's Classroom Resources
Lesson Plan, p. 76
Decision Making, *Planning Ahead* p. 28

Extension #103, *Household Cleaning Hints,* p. 109
Life Skills, Time for Cleaning, p. 111
Chapter 72 Test, pp. 149-150
Performance Assessment, *Advertising a Cleaning Product,* p. 110

Reteaching, *Caring for Your Living Space*, p. 78

See Also:
ABCNews InterActive™ Videodiscs

When Devon first moved out of his parents' home and into an apartment, he and his roommate, Sean, didn't clean very often. After a few months, it began to show. The piles of magazines and papers, the grime in the corners of the kitchen, and the ring in the bathtub started to bother Devon. When visiting friends kidded him about the dirt, he decided it was time to act.

Devon spent an entire day—and a lot of energy—scrubbing the apartment and organizing his belongings. While he worked, he decided that he and Sean needed to put some effort into keeping the place clean. That evening, when Sean got home from work, they talked about it.

"I know cleaning isn't your favorite thing in the world—it sure isn't mine—but we need to do it more regularly," Devon said. "Maybe if we split up the jobs and do them once a week, the apartment won't get so dirty."

Sean agreed. "I guess I haven't been doing my share. Maybe if we write down what needs to be done, I won't be so tempted to ignore it."

Why Care for Space?

Imagine that you lived in a home like Devon and Sean. After a long day at school, you would come home to a mess. Seeing magazines scattered around and dishes piled in the sink might make it difficult for you to relax. With your possessions thrown all over the place, you would have trouble finding anything when you needed it.

You can avoid these problems by properly caring for your space. Caring for your space offers many benefits. You can probably think of many. Here are a few.

• **Saving money.** Caring for possessions makes them last longer and stay in better condition. Replacing items that have been carelessly treated can be expensive.

• **Saving time.** Living in a tidy space is easier than living in a cluttered one. Whether you are looking for a notebook or a pair of shoes, you can find items more easily if you always put them in the proper place. Wouldn't you prefer to spend time doing activities you enjoy instead of hunting for something that's misplaced? In addition, cleaning a little bit on a regular basis takes less time than doing it all at once.

• **Improving well-being.** Your living space can affect your state of mind. A messy space may make you feel anxious, pressured, or depressed. A clean and organized home can make you feel proud and comfortable.

Establishing a Routine

Establishing a **routine,** or *set sequence* for doing household tasks, makes the job easier. Developing a routine and sticking to it simplifies home care and upkeep for everyone. Creating a routine also helps ensure that no part of the home is neglected.

How does caring for your possessions help you save money and time?

Topics on p. 699:
• **Reasons to Care**
• **Setting Up a Routine**

Checking Comprehension

✓ How can caring for your living space save money? *Possessions last longer when you care for them.*

✓ How can you help make sure no cleaning tasks are forgotten? *Set up a routine.*

Activities

■ **Kids at Work.** Ask students to suggest home-care tasks that younger family members could assume. What tasks might be done by preschoolers? School-age children? Teens? (*Critical Thinking*)

RETEACHING

■ **Bed and Bath Benefits.** Ask students how the three benefits of caring for living space might apply to a bedroom and a bathroom.

ENRICHMENT

■ **Roles and Relationships.** The text suggests that family roles in managing a home are changing. Do students agree? Do family members share household responsibilities? What evidence do students see of changing roles?

DID YOU KNOW?

A national survey of 1,246 couples indicated that women spend an average of 32.3 hours a week on housework (not including child care) whether or not they work outside the home. Men spend an average of 8.7 hours a week on home-care tasks (not including lawn care and home repairs). On the average, women who work 35 or more hours outside the home devote about 26 additional hours a week to home care, while women who are full-time homemakers spend about 38.5 hours on housework. The survey included family-related tasks outside the home, such as grocery shopping and running errands.

Checking Comprehension

✓ What are the advantages of rotating household assignments? *No one becomes bored; everyone learns a variety of skills.*

✓ What are some examples of daily tasks? *Making the bed, putting away schoolbooks and clothes, emptying wastebaskets, cleaning up the kitchen, and taking out the garbage and the recycling container.*

✓ What are some common weekly tasks? *Straightening drawers, closets, and shelves; changing bed sheets; dusting, vacuuming and sweeping; and cleaning the bathroom.*

✓ What are two ways of scheduling weekly tasks? *Do one task a day or all on one day.*

BALANCING
WORK AND FAMILY

Have students read "Developing a System for Cleaning." Invite volunteers to share family systems for assigning household tasks. Do they know effective methods for completing home-care tasks?

Whether you live with other family members, with roommates, or on your own, you have a responsibility to help manage the household. The need for everyone to help manage a home is more important now than ever. Today, most families cannot afford to have one member stay at home and care for the house full-time. Each person in the family needs to help, simply to get all the jobs done.

Assigning Tasks

How does your family schedule household duties? In some families, the parent or parents decide who does what. In others, family members meet together to divide responsi-bilities. In some families, one person is responsible for a particular job, perhaps because he or she prefers it or is better at it. Other families divide tasks on a room-by-room basis.

Another approach is called **task rotation,** in which *a job is passed from one family member to another.* You might be responsible for handling the trash one week, with someone else doing it the next week. Task rotation cuts down on the boredom that comes from doing the same thing all the time. It also helps every family member learn a variety of skills.

Making Adjustments

Of course, all people do not have the same view of cleanliness and order. One person may see a room as cluttered if objects are left lying out, while another may not mind the dis-

BALANCING Work AND Family

Developing a System for Cleaning

Standards of cleanliness in the home have changed over the years. With fewer stay-at-home parents, people have less time to devote to household care and maintenance. This doesn't mean that they don't want clean homes. Many have simply lowered their standards somewhat and continue to look for more efficient ways to get things done.

For many households, the best solution is teamwork. In one family, the children may take responsibility only for their own rooms. In another, they may also be responsible for such specific tasks as cleaning bathrooms and vacuuming. When finances allow, some families hire housekeeping services to clean their homes. For others, spot cleaning—quickly wiping dirty areas that may be noticed—has taken the place of more thorough cleaning. In fact, sales of spot-cleaning products have increased, while all-purpose cleaners have become less popular.

The most successful systems are based on responsibility, rewards, and consequences. In addition, systems should be monitored and evaluated. A "job jar" can be used for daily tasks or special projects. Family members draw pieces of paper from the jar to determine their tasks. A chart that lists daily tasks to be checked off as they're completed is another idea. A certain number of checks at the end of a week could be rewarded with a special treat or activity. Consequences for not performing a task help insure that jobs get done. Occasional family meetings provide opportunities for everyone to discuss the system.

Using teamwork and a system approach may not guarantee that family members enjoy every household task. This approach, however, does ensure that the responsibilities are shared in a fair manner and that the work gets done.

Suppose That . . .

Assume that you have three siblings, ages 11, 9, and 5. You all live with one parent, who has a full-time job. Develop a system your family could use to get housecleaning tasks done regularly. In your system, explain the use of standards, rewards, monitoring, and consequences.

DID YOU KNOW?

Around the world, women much of their time on housework, but their efforts are not counted in their nations' gross domestic product (GDP). However, when a family hires someone to clean and cook, that work is counted in the GDP. GDP is the production of goods and services that are bought and sold in a nation. The higher the GDP, the more productive the nation. Some experts believe that including housework in the GDP would increase respect for these tasks, which are mainly handled by women.

order as long as the carpet is clean and the furniture is dusted. Communicating helps household members set standards for housekeeping that all can agree on.

People living in the same household also need to make allowances for special circumstances. When Alejandro was working on a major project for school, he had to leave papers and materials spread out on the dining room table for a few days. He couldn't finish the work in one day, and that was the best space available. Alejandro was considerate enough to talk to his family before he started the project. Fortunately, everyone understood the need to live with a little short-term disorder. Similarly, when one family member is unusually busy or not feeling well, others may have to take on that person's tasks.

Neatness and Cleanliness

Keeping your space neat and clean can become an everyday habit. By taking some simple steps each day, you keep each task manageable. If you don't enjoy cleaning, find ways to make it more acceptable. Listen to the radio or a book on tape while you work.

Daily and Weekly Tasks

Here are some daily activities that contribute toward a neat and clean home:

- Making your bed after getting up in the morning.
- Putting schoolbooks away after studying.
- Putting clothes and shoes in their proper places and putting dirty clothes in the laundry basket.
- Checking the wastebaskets to see if they need to be emptied.
- Cleaning the kitchen counters and table and washing the dishes after each meal.
- Checking the garbage and recycling container to see if they need to be taken out.

Other tasks need to be done only about once a week. You may choose to perform one job each day, or you may decide to do them all at one time during the week. Here are some weekly tasks that need to be done:

- Straightening your dresser drawers, closets, and shelves.
- Changing the sheets on the bed.
- Dusting the furniture and other objects.
- Vacuuming or sweeping the floor.
- Cleaning the bathroom.

Some jobs, such as washing windows and waxing floors, only need to be done occasionally. In addition, many families do a thorough spring or fall housecleaning once a year.

Cleaning Indoors

When you clean, use the right tools and products for specific tasks. Follow the directions on the containers. Using a product incorrectly can ruin what you are cleaning or be dangerous. For instance, combining ammonia and liquid bleach can cause life-threatening toxic fumes to form.

When someone in the house suffers from an allergy to dust mites, regular vacuuming can prevent allergic reactions.

Activities

■ **Fairness in Families.** Have students suggest factors to be considered in dividing household tasks among family members. *(Problem Solving)*

■ **Chill Out!** Pair students and have them assumeopposing points of view siblings might have about caring fora shared room. Have themtry to reach agreement. *(Relationship)*

■ **Attitude Adjustment.** Have students describe common attitudes among teens toward home-care tasks. Discuss how these attitudes might be improved by changing routines or rotating tasks. *(Management)*

ENRICHMENT

■ **Cleaning Goals.** Have students each set a specific goal to improve the way they care for their living space, such as making the bed every morning or washing the dinner dishes three nights a week. After students work toward their goals for a week, have them report on progress.

FAMILY AND COMMUNITY OUTREACH

Have students interview older relatives or neighbors about home-care tasks when they were teens. Students might ask: What kinds of home-care tasks did you do as a teen? Were any of those different from household tasks today? How were tasks divided among family members? How has technology affected household tasks over the years?

REAL-LIFE APPLICATION

Read this to students: *Jordan's room was such a mess that he could barely walk through it. His mother always closed the door to his room, especially when people visited. Then one day Jordan noticed that the dishes hadn't been done for a couple days, and "things" were piling up in the living room. Fixing a snack became as difficult as finding a place to sit to watch television.* Ask students to respond to this scenario. What do they think is happening and why?

Checking Comprehension

✓ How can you tell whether wallpaper can be washed? *Test the cleaner in a hidden spot.*

✓ What supplies do you need to clean a toilet? *A toilet brush, disinfecting cleaner, and perhaps rubber gloves.*

✓ What are some outdoor cleaning tasks? *Picking up trash, mowing lawn, raking leaves, sweeping paved areas, caring for garden.*

SPECIAL NEEDS *Strategies*

Inefficient Organizers. Have pairs set up charts of daily, weekly, and occasional home-care tasks, also identifying jobs as indoor, outdoor, preventive maintenance tasks.

CROSS-CURRICULAR ACTIVITY

Math

Have groups list the supplies and equipment needed to clean a small apartment, and then research or estimate the cost of each item. Tell them to assume the supplies last an average of two months. What is their monthly maintenance cost?

702

Follow these procedures for cleaning different areas inside your home.

- **Walls.** Check the walls for dirt and fingerprints. Use a sponge dampened with a cleaning solution to wipe spots off of walls, doors, moldings, switch plates, drawers, and cabinets. Some paint and wallpaper cannot be washed with a strong cleaner, so if you're not sure, test the cleaner in a hidden spot. When washing walls in an entire room, always start at the bottom of the walls and work toward the top to avoid streaks on the walls.

- **Washing windows.** When washing windows on the inside, apply a window-cleaning product. Then dry the window with a lint-free cloth or paper towel to avoid streaking.

- **Furniture and other objects.** Wooden furniture needs an occasional dusting. You can use a dust cloth or duster, with or without a dusting spray. You may wish to occasionally use furniture polish or wax to protect the wood. Check picture frames, books, knickknacks, lamps, and even plant leaves. They can collect dust, too. Upholstered furniture should be vacuumed to remove dust and lint. Turn the cushions over from time to time so the fabric will wear evenly.

- **Floors.** Carpeted floors should be vacuumed weekly. Clean spills immediately with a sponge and gentle liquid detergent or with a brush and cold water. Clean smooth floors with a broom or dust mop. Vinyl and tile floors can be washed with a mop and water or with floor-cleaning products. To shine and protect floors, occasionally use wax on hardwood floors or an acrylic floor finish on vinyl floors. Doing so prevents spills from ruining the finish.

▌ *Sanitizing the bathroom on a regular basis helps maintain family health.*

- **Bathrooms.** Use a sponge or cloth and scouring powder or liquid to clean the sink basin and bathtub or shower. Then rinse the surfaces thoroughly. Use a toilet brush and disinfecting cleaner to sanitize the inside and outside of the toilet. You may want to wear rubber gloves when cleaning the bathroom.

Cleaning Outdoors

Because they are exposed to weather, outdoor areas require special care. Outdoor areas also show others how you feel about your home. Keeping the outside of your home neat and clean shows that you take pride in where you live.

Check all outdoor areas every day before dark. Put toys, sports equipment, and tools in their proper places. Cover outdoor furniture and equipment. These steps create a neat appearance and prevent weather damage.

Caring for the outdoors might include any of the following weekly tasks:

- Picking up trash on the lawn and under bushes.
- Mowing the lawn or raking leaves.
- Sweeping the walkway, driveway, patio, porch, or balcony.

Focus on Time Management Skills

Home-care can be overwhelming unless you organize your time. Discuss these strategies:

- Define clear goals (wash dinner dishes every evening).
- Assign responsibilities.
- Analyze the steps (identify essential ones and how to complete them).

- Try new products that might make tasks easier or eliminate steps.
- Be prepared with supplies that work. Collect them ahead.
- Adjust your attitude. Think about how good you will feel when the area is clean, or play music to help make tasks more pleasant.

Managing Your Life

Pets and Sanitation

Pets are a valued part of many families. Without proper care, however, a pet can create unsanitary situations in a home.

Pets, of course, need food, water, shelter, and exercise. Someone has to take responsibility for providing these necessities. Just as housecleaning tasks are assigned, pet care must be too.

Dogs and cats need to be fed once or twice a day. Their water should always be fresh. The area around food and water bowls tends to get dirty quickly and must be wiped often. Any food or water spills should be cleaned up immediately.

Most pet owners find that their pets are happy when they have their own space. Dogs and cats seem to like a particular spot of their own. This area should be kept clean to avoid an accumulation of dirt and hair. Some pets such as birds or hamsters, need special cages.

Proper removal of a pet's body wastes is essential for good sanitation. Dogs are taken outside to relieve themselves. Indoor cats often have litter boxes that must be changed regularly and the area around them cleaned. To keep the home and its grounds clean,

dog and cat owners need to scoop up and dispose of solid wastes.

Pets that are allowed outdoors sometimes create additional concerns. People need to make sure that fleas on a dog or cat do not transfer to carpets and furniture. Once a home is infested, getting rid of fleas is a difficult and sometimes costly process.

Proper home management includes taking good care of pets and their environments. The health of family members depends on it.

Applying the Principles

1. What daily and weekly tasks are added to the household routine when pets are present?
2. What special approaches to cleaning might be necessary?
3. Why is teamwork helpful when completing chores related to pet care and household maintenance?

- Weeding and caring for vegetable or flower gardens.

Because the outside of windows are exposed to the weather, they get much dirtier than the inside. When washing outside windows, first remove heavy dirt using warm, soapy water, then dry the windows with old towels. Next, apply a window cleaner and wipe it away with a dry, lint-free cloth or paper towel. Cleaning these windows about once a month takes away the dirt and allows the sun to shine in.

Preventive Maintenance

Many home-care tasks provide short-term benefits. Washing dishes today makes plates available for meals tomorrow. Preventive maintenance, however, produces benefits for

the long run. **Preventive maintenance** means *making sure that structures and equipment in the home are running properly.*

For example, keeping a range clean reduces the chance of grease building up and catching fire. Cleaning up crumbs and putting away leftovers prevents insects from entering the kitchen.

Preventive maintenance can save time and money. For instance, the Kanjis' roof was in poor condition for some time. Then a heavy storm struck, and the roof began to leak. The Kanjis not only had to pay for a new roof, they also had to fix the walls inside.

Whether your family owns or rents its home, certain basic maintenance tasks need to be performed. Even if you rent, you need to look for problems and report them to your landlord.

Activities
■ **An Ounce of Prevention.** Ask students to suggest decorating tips or storage methods that would help reduce home-care responsibilities. (Example: Avoid displaying knickknacks to reduce dusting time.) *(Problem Solving)*

RETEACHING
■ **A Clean Classroom.** Have students create a plan for cleaning the classroom. They should define the goals, assign tasks, list needed supplies, and estimate the time involved. If you wish, have the class carry out its plan and evaluate the results.

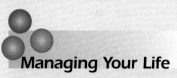

Managing Your Life

Have students read "Pets and Sanitation." Invite volunteers to describe how pets are cared for in their homes. What problems do they have to address?

Answers to Applying . . .
1. Answers may include: providing food and water; keeping the pet and its sleeping, eating, and eliminating areas clean; and providing attention.
2. Answers may include: disinfecting more areas; vacuuming more to keep pet hair down.
3. One family member might not always be available to provide care or have enough time to handle all the tasks involved.

Review

■ **Chapter Review.** Use the contents of the Chapter Review page to help students review concepts, think critically, and apply their knowledge.

■ **Study Guide.** Have students complete the Study Guide for Chapter 72 on page 233 of the Student Workbook.

■ **Excuses, Excuses.** Point out that many teens and some adults tend to put off or avoid home-care tasks. Ask students to suggest the main excuses or reasons people might offer. List the reasons on the board and discuss ways to counter them.

Evaluation

■ **Chapter Test.** Use the reproducible chapter test provided in the Teacher's Classroom Resources or create your own test using the *Testmaker Software.*

■ **Alternative Assessment.** Have pairs set up a plan to keep a shared apartment clean and neat. Ask them to include a daily and weekly cleaning schedule with assigned responsibilities and a preventive maintenance schedule.

■ **Personal Challenges.** Ask students to explain how one of their own personality traits or habits could cause—or has caused—a problem in assuming responsibility for home-care tasks. How might—or do—they overcome this problem?

The following maintenance jobs should be done once every year:

- **Building exterior.** In the spring, inspect the paint, roof, foundation, gutters, and downspouts. Take care of any needed repairs promptly, either by arranging for the repair yourself or contacting the landlord to do so.
- **Furnace and central air conditioner.** Have a professional inspect the furnace in the fall and the air conditioner in the spring to make sure that the units will operate safely and efficiently when they are needed.
- **Fireplaces and wood-burning stoves.** Have the chimney flues cleaned by an expert to reduce the risk of fire. If they are used often, the flues should be cleaned again in mid-winter.

The following maintenance tasks should be performed twice a year:

- **Smoke detectors.** Replace the batteries and clean the units to prevent dust from accumulating and setting off the alarm. Test the detectors to make sure that they work properly. Choose a regular time to do this, perhaps when the fall and spring time changes.
- **Refrigerator.** Vacuum the condenser coils at the bottom to prevent the refrigerator from overheating and shutting down. Check the manufacturer's directions for maintenance.
- **Clothes dryer.** Clean accumulated lint out of the vent pipe's lint tray to keep the dryer working efficiently.
- **Garage door.** Lubricate the tracks to keep the door running smoothly.

The following maintenance jobs should be done once a month:

- **Furnace and air conditioner.** Clean or replace the filters during heavy use.
- **Water heater.** Follow the manufacturer's recommendations for flushing out mineral deposits that collect in the bottom before they build up.

Changing air conditioner and furnace filters regularly helps these systems function properly.

- **Drains.** Run an enzyme-based drain cleaner through sink and tub drains to prevent them from clogging.

Home, Sweet Home

You can help make your home a comfortable, enjoyable place. A home gives you space to store the things you need and care about. It provides space for eating, doing schoolwork, and simply enjoying yourself. Your home is also a place that you share with others.

Each person in a household generally uses his or her own space in personally satisfactory ways. On the other hand, how that space is cared for can affect the entire household. For example, Rose chooses to do her painting in her room. Once, however, she was careless and spilled paint on the carpet. If the paint cannot be cleaned, her family may have to pay to replace the carpeting. Help your family—and yourself—by using your space responsibly.

Focus on Management Skills

Many books and articles have been written offering tips on household cleaning. One of these is *Another Use For . . .* by Vicki Lansky (Book Peddlers of Deephaven, Minnesota: 1991). Students may have books of this type at home that they could bring to class. Conversations with family members may also yield interesting tips to share. You might wish to have students collect helpful hints to share with the class or format on the computer as a handout.

Review

Reviewing the Facts

1. How can you benefit from caring for your living space?
2. What are the advantages of establishing a routine for household tasks?
3. Give two examples each of a daily, a weekly, and an occasional household task.
4. List four tasks a person might do to maintain outdoor areas.
5. What preventive maintenance tasks should be done twice a year?

Thinking Critically

1. When looking at the methods of assigning household tasks—assigning specific tasks to individuals, assigning specific areas to individuals, and rotating tasks—which do you think is preferable? Why?
2. Describe the effect you think each of the following has on preventive maintenance: laziness, procrastination, financial problems.

Applying Your Knowledge

1. **Assigning Household Responsibilities.** Assume that you have been asked by a family of four (an employed mother, a 17-year-old daughter, and two sons, age 15 and age 10) to evenly divide the following tasks: picking up items throughout the house, vacuuming, dusting furniture, carrying out the garbage, cleaning the garage, cleaning the kitchen, cleaning two bathrooms, and mowing the lawn. How would you assign the tasks fairly? Explain.
2. **Handling Conflicts.** In a group of two to four students, act out one of the following situations, assuming that members of a household have different attitudes toward cleanliness and household tasks: sharing a room; two roommates living in college dorm; at-home parent enters work force.

3. **Maintaining Your Own Space.** List all the tasks that you are responsible for in maintaining your own space. Use the list to prepare a weekly schedule showing when you will perform each task. Are there any tasks that should be done monthly or yearly?

Making Connections

1. **Environmental Science.** Many common household cleaners contain ingredients that are poisonous and harmful to the environment. Investigate what alternative cleaning methods and products you might use to make household care safer and less damaging to the environment.
2. **Technology.** If you could invent any device to make household maintenance easier, what would it be? Draw a sketch, and write a brief description of your invention, explaining how it works and what household tasks it would simplify or eliminate.

Building Your Portfolio

Making a Schedule
Design a time chart that schedules all the routine tasks and some of the special ones that must be completed at your home on a daily, weekly, and occasional basis. You may set up the chart for yourself only or for everyone involved. You may want to consult other family members for their ideas, too. Determine how much time you might spend at each task. Add this chart to your portfolio.

1. You will save money because possessions will last longer. You will save time looking for lost articles and will reduce time spent on major cleaning. Finally, you will feel less stressed and more comfortable in a clean, organized home.
2. Simplifies home care and helps ensure that all necessary tasks are completed on a regular basis; is also a way to divide tasks fairly among those living in the home.
3. Any two: daily—making the bed, putting schoolbooks and clothes away, washing the dishes, cleaning the kitchen, and emptying garbage containers; weekly—straightening closets and drawers, changing sheets, dusting furniture, vacuuming or sweeping, and cleaning the bathroom; occasionally—washing windows and walls, waxing floors, and spring or fall cleaning.
4. Any four: putting away items, covering outdoor equipment, washing outside windows, picking up trash, mowing the lawn, raking leaves, sweeping paved areas, and weeding and caring for a garden.
5. Check smoke detectors and replace the batteries, vacuum the refrigerator coils, remove lint from the vent pipe on the clothes dryer, and grease the tracks for the garage door.

ANSWERS TO THINKING CRITICALLY

1. Answers may refer to factors such as different interests, time constraints, schedules, and skills of those living in the home.
2. Laziness may mean that preventive maintenance doesn't get done or that someone else has to take on the responsibility. Procrastination may cause problems to occur before tasks get done. Financial problems may keep people from doing tasks that involve costs, causing problems to become worse and their remedies more expensive.

Chapter 73 — Safety in the Home

Chapter 73

FOCUS

Chapter Overview

Chapter 73 discusses the most common types of home accidents and gives strategies to prevent them. It also mentions specific ways students can help children, the elderly, and people with special needs stay safe.

Motivator

■ **Home Stories.** Invite volunteers to describe minor accidents they have experienced or witnessed. What caused the accident? Was it avoidable? Save the list for review at the end of the chapter.

Objectives

Discuss the chapter objectives on this page. Remind students that the objectives focus on important chapter concepts.

Vocabulary

In addition to installing a carbon monoxide detector, knowing the symptoms of carbon monoxide poisoning can help prevent it. If family members experience otherwise unexplained headaches, drowsiness, or nausea while at home, carbon monoxide may be to blame.

Terms to Learn

- carbon monoxide detector
- pilot light
- smoke detector

Objectives

This chapter will help you to:

- List the most common dangers in the home.
- Infer the causes of home accidents.
- Develop strategies for preventing home accidents.
- Describe ways that you could take responsibility for the safety of others.

706   UNIT 8   Housing and Living Space

CHAPTER RESOURCES

Student Workbook
Study Guide, p. 235
Activity, *An Ounce of Prevention,* p. 236

Teacher's Classroom Resources
Lesson Plan, p. 77

Extension #104, *Household Safety,* p. 110
Life Skills, *Safety Check,* p. 112
Transparency 59, *Be Prepared!*
Chapter 73 Test, pp. 151-152

Performance Assessment, *Home Safety Tips,* p. 111
Reteaching, *Safety Prescription,* p. 79

See Also:
ABCNews InterActive™ Videodiscs

If you are like most people, you probably think of your home as a comfortable, safe place. Actually, most homes contain a number of hazards. Every year, millions of people in the United States are injured and thousands of deaths occur where most people think that they are safest—in their homes. Most accidents that happen in the home can be prevented, however. You can help take responsibility for home safety by understanding potential dangers in the home and taking steps to prevent accidents.

Assessing the Dangers

A home is a constantly changing environment. People and pets come and go, objects are moved from place to place, and the structure itself ages. Potential household dangers

Since it may be difficult to spot problems, ask people with special needs what you might do to help them feel safer in your home.

appear and change as well. Before you can take steps to avoid accidents, you need to know what the dangers are. Here are some of the most common types of home accidents:

- **Falls and bumps.** Falls are the greatest cause of all injuries and deaths in the home. Although children and older people fall most often, anyone can fall down a flight of stairs or slip on a wet floor.
- **Cuts.** Knife and scissors cuts are easily avoidable if sharp objects are stored and used properly. Power tools and such equipment as saws and lawn mowers can also cause serious injuries.
- **Poisonings.** According to the American Red Cross, more than 90 percent of all poisonings take place in the home, and most of the victims are under 5 years old. Young children are unable to read warning labels and commonly put things in their mouths. Therefore they need to be protected from poisonous substances.
- **Fire and electrical problems.** Fire and electrical problems are the second greatest cause of accidental home deaths. While most fires are caused by carelessness with cooking or cigarette smoking, many fires are the result of problems in the home's electrical system. These include faulty wiring, overloaded outlets, broken appliances, and frayed cords. Electrical shock is also a significant cause of accidental home deaths.

Preventing Home Accidents

Human factors as well as physical conditions cause home accidents. If you are alert to these factors and know how to avoid them, you can prevent accidents and possibly even save a life. Two of the most common reasons for accidents are:

CHAPTER 73   Safety in the Home   707

DID YOU KNOW?

Facts about accidental deaths:
- The total number of accidental deaths in homes decreased from 29,000 in 1950 to 26,700 in 1994.
- In 1994, the cost of home injuries

reached $94.3 billion. This is equivalent to a $78,700 rebate on each new single-family home built that year. It's also equivalent to nearly half of the property taxes paid in 1994.

TEACH

Topic on p. 707:
- Home Dangers

Checking Comprehension
✓ What is the first step in preventing accidents in your home? *Becoming aware of possible dangers there.*
✓ What are the two greatest causes of home accidental deaths? *Falls; fire and electrical problems.*
✓ Why are children likely victims of poisoning? *Can't read labels; often put things in mouth.*

Activities
■ **It Has Been Said.** Some people say: "What you don't know can't hurt you." Have students write a short evaluation of this statement in relation to home safety. Read responses aloud; discuss.

RETEACHING
■ **Accident Ahead.** Ask the class to describe some specific situations in which home accidents are likely to occur.

ENRICHMENT
■ **A Closer Look at Accidents.** Discuss these questions with students: If an injury is predictable under certain conditions, can the injury be called an accident? What kinds of home injuries are truly unavoidable and unforeseeable?

CROSS-REFERENCE
See Chapter 23 for safety precautions when small children are in a home.

Topics on pp. 708-709:

- Reasons for Accidents
- Making a Home Safer
- Preventing Falls

Checking Comprehension

✓ What are the two main human factors that cause accidents? *Carelessness and physical limitations.*

✓ How can small children be kept safe around stairways? *Install gates at the top and bottom of stairs; lock basement doors.*

FAMILY AND COMMUNITY
O U T R E A C H

Have students gather information about first aid training programs offered in your community. Then ask them to help publicize these programs by preparing a flyer that includes program type, dates and times, locations, costs, phone numbers, and sponsoring groups. Discuss attention-getting designs for the flyers. Students might distribute the flyers or post them on school bulletin boards. The class could also prepare messages about the programs for the school's announcements.

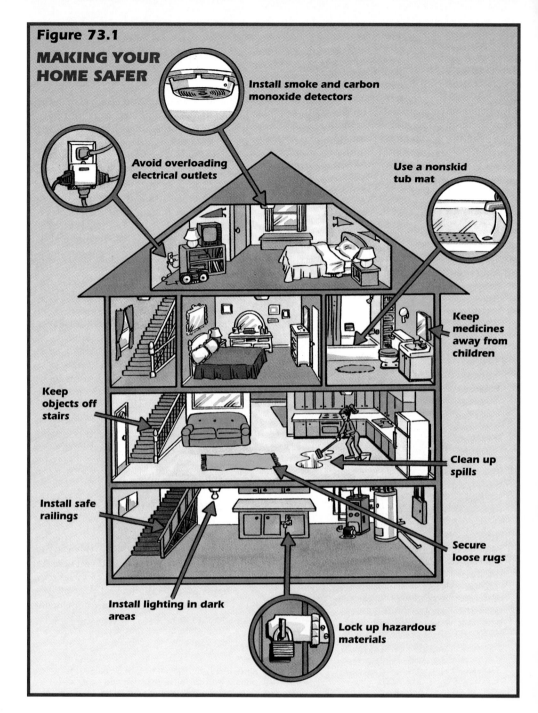

Figure 73.1

MAKING YOUR HOME SAFER

Install smoke and carbon monoxide detectors

Avoid overloading electrical outlets

Use a nonskid tub mat

Keep medicines away from children

Keep objects off stairs

Clean up spills

Install safe railings

Secure loose rugs

Install lighting in dark areas

Lock up hazardous materials

708   UNIT 8   Housing and Living Space

MORE ABOUT Falls

To protect infants and children from falls:

- Raise crib sides as high as possible and lock them in place when baby is in crib.
- Watch a baby in a carrier on a table, counter, or couch. Baby may jiggle the carrier, causing it to fall.

- If possible, open windows from the top instead of bottom. Don't allow children to sit on sills or lean against screens.
- Avoid long clothing children might trip over. Keep shoes tied. Avoid dress-up clothes with trains or capes.
- Don't let a toddler try to climb into a high chair.

- **Carelessness.** Many accidents happen when people are under stress or when they are upset. People who are in a hurry or tired are also more likely to have an accident.
- **Physical limitations.** Young children have not developed the physical coordination and awareness required to avoid many accidents. Elderly people and people with disabilities are also at a greater risk, because they may not be able to react quickly enough in an emergency.

Keeping human factors in mind, you can begin to look for and correct safety hazards in your home. **Figure 73.1** shows some sound strategies for preventing home accidents.

Preventing Falls

Falls can happen anywhere, but they are most likely to occur on cluttered surfaces, slippery floors, and stairs. Keep toys, books, and newspapers off the floor, especially in heavy traffic areas. People can also slip on freshly cleaned or waxed floors. Placing a handwritten sign that says "CAUTION: WET FLOORS" can warn others to walk carefully.

Here are some additional ways to keep floors safe:

- Wipe up spills immediately.
- Anchor throw rugs with carpet tape or nonskid mats.
- Arrange furniture to be out of the path of traffic.

BALANCING Work AND Family

When You're in Charge

Teens today are often left in charge of the homefront for a while. They may take responsbility just for themselves, but they may also be expected to watch over younger siblings. Teens and younger children need to follow certain guidelines that promote their safety.

The rules and routines set by parents should be followed. Typical guidelines cover such issues as when homework should be done, use of the television, snacks, use of appliances, telephone limits, friends in the house, going other places, and emergency procedures.

Such "house rules" help provide order. You become a role model for younger siblings when you support the rules. Children are more likely to be receptive to rules set by the family than just by you. Establishing a set routine makes the time go faster. By offering a treat to a young sibling—such as watching television after doing homework—you provide something to look forward to and gain the child's cooperation.

Dealing with strangers is a safety issue. Make sure younger children never open the door to strangers

or let them in the house, and you do the same. Telephone callers should not be told that adults are not present. Simply saying that a parent is unavailable and take a message. You can teach a young child what to say.

Learn how to handle emergencies. Every member of the family should know what to do if there's a fire in the house and how to reach emergency services. Knowing basic first aid is especially important when you are in charge alone.

What kind of support system is available to you? If possible, keep the names and telephone numbers of trustworthy neighbors handy. Some communities provide hot line numbers that can offer assistance or advice. These and other emergency numbers should be readily available in case you need them.

Suppose That . . .

You are home alone with your five-year-old sister. Your mother will be home after work in two hours. A friend, who lives a few blocks away, calls and asks you to come over and listen to a new CD. What would you do?

■ **The Immortal Years.** Discuss why teens tend to worry much less about accidents or injury then do adults. (*Critical Thinking*)

RETEACHING

■ **Caution Collage.** Have students copy warnings from appliances, tools, other equipment, and hazardous substances and combine them creatively with drawings and magazine pictures into a collage on safety.

ENRICHMENT

■ **Designing Labels.** Have students choose a potentially dangerous tool or appliance and design a label that warns users at a glance of accidents that might occur from using it. Provide space to display labels.

BALANCING
WORK AND FAMILY

Have students read "When You're in Charge." Try these related activities:

- Have students suggest ways to answer the phone or the door without indicating they are home alone.
- Discuss the value of a community safe home program—a network of homes where adults are usually present and children get help in an emergency. Students could help publicize an existing program or talk with school or community leaders about starting one.

DID YOU KNOW?

To prevent suffocation in children:
- Keep plastic bags away from children; do not use bags to protect crib mattresses.
- Keep ropes, cords, and long scarves out of the reach of children.

- Don't let children run or play when they have food in their mouths.
- Don't leave an infant alone with a bottle propped in his or her mouth.

Topics on pp. 710-712:
- **Preventing Cuts, Poisoning, Electrical Accidents, and Fires**
- **Taking Responsibility**

Checking Comprehension

✔ How should knives and other sharp tools be stored in kitchen drawers? *With handles toward the person opening the drawer.*

✔ Why should adults avoid calling medicine "candy"? *May tempt children to search for it and eat it.*

✔ How can using extension cords help prevent problems? *Distributes appliances among several outlets instead of overloading one.*

✔ What is a pilot light and why should it always be burning? *A thin stream of gas used to light stove burners, furnaces, and water heaters. If not burning, gas may be entering the home.*

Making Decisions

Have students read "Childproof Medicine."

Answers to What . . .

1. He wants bottle grandfather can open, but is concerned sister might be able to open it too.
2. Answers will vary. Either way, Ben and grandfather should agree on a safe place to store the bottle, especially since some children can open "childproof" caps.

- Shorten long electrical cords and speaker wires, or secure them to base boards with adhesive-backed electrical wire anchors.
- Use stepladders to reach high places.
- Keep rooms and hallways well-lighted, so that people can see where they're going.

Stairways are a high-danger area. Make sure that they are well-lighted. Keep them clear of clutter, and remove throw rugs from stairway tops. If you have small children in the home, install gates at the tops and bottoms of open stairways. Be sure to keep basement doors locked to prevent elderly family members and children from falling down these stairways.

Many falls happen in the bathtub and shower because surfaces are slippery. Nonskid mats or strips that stick to the tub floor can help prevent falls. A tub seat and handrails on the wall near the tub or toilet can assist elderly family members or those with disabilities.

Preventing Cuts

Cuts from tools and equipment most often occur in the kitchen, in workrooms, and in outdoor areas. Always pay close attention to what you are doing when you use knives and other tools. Sharp objects should be stored properly and used only as intended. Here are additional ways to prevent cuts.

- Store knives (with protective sheaths) and kitchen tools with their handles toward the person opening the drawer.
- Keep knives and scissors away from young children.
- Store power tools, clippers, and saws securely and out of traffic paths. Cover the blades when not in use. Don't leave cords dangling from countertops.
- When operating power tools and machinery, wear earplugs, gloves, and goggles. Don't wear jewelry or loose clothing that might get caught in blades or motors.
- Always wear shoes with closed toes—not sandals—when operating a lawn mower or a trimmer. Leather shoes offer better protection than canvas ones. To reduce

710   UNIT 8 Housing and Living Space

Making Decisions

Childproof Medicine

Ben often ran errands and did odd jobs for his grandfather. Since Mr. Arturo had arthritis in his hands, many things were difficult for him to do.

One day Ben was getting a presciption filled for his grandfather. As Ben stood waiting, the pharmacist turned to him and said, "What kind of cap do you want on this bottle, a childproof one?"

Ben stood for a moment without speaking. He thought about his grandfather's hands, remembering that he had trouble gripping objects. Opening containers was especially difficult. Then he thought about his three-year-old sister, who often spent time at their grandfather's apartment.

"Do you have a preference?" the pharmacist asked. Ben wasn't sure what to say.

What Would You Do?

1. Why is Ben hesitating with his answer?
2. What do you think Ben should do and why?

your chances of slipping, do not mow wet grass. Make sure children and others are not in the vacinity.
- Turn off the power, and unplug any tool before you adjust or fix it.

Preventing Poisoning

Most poisonings occur in the kitchen, bathroom, or bedroom. Young children are most at risk because their curiosity leads them to explore things that they don't know are dangerous. To help avoid accidental poisoning, follow these guidelines:

- Know what poisons are in your home. These include many types of medicines, cosmetics and perfume, cleaning prod-

DID YOU KNOW?

To increase home safety, replace spring-bolt locks with dead-bolts. Sliding bolts at door tops add more protection. Restraining rods in the lower track of sliding glass doors make them difficult to open. You can see who's outside with a viewer in a solid door. Timers can turn lights on and off, making the home seem occupied. Steel grills over the inside of first-floor windows and fire escapes can keep intruders out. However, family members should be able to open these grills quickly in case of fire.

ucts, gasoline, kerosene, fertilizer, paint and paint thinner, and insect and weed killers.

- Lock or attach childproof latches to all cabinets, medicine chests, and drawers that contain poisonous items. Be sure children don't gain access to handbags that contain medicines.
- Choose medicines, cleaners, and other poisonous products that come in child-proof containers.
- Never refer to medicine as "candy" when speaking to children. Keep medicines out of reach, preferably in locked cabinets and closets.
- Never put medicines or other dangerous substances in containers that don't have warning labels.

Besides emergency telephone numbers for the police, fire department, ambulance service, and hospital, keep the telephone number of the nearest poison control center next to each phone in your home. If someone swallows a poisonous substance, call the center, and follow the staff's instructions. Have the container in your hand when you call and take it with you to the hospital. You can call 911 or another central emergency number if available.

Poisonings can also occur when certain gases are inhaled. Carbon monoxide is a tasteless, colorless, and odorless gas that is extremely poisonous. In the home, it can be produced by a defective heater or fireplace, a clogged chimney, automobile exhaust, and other sources, including gas appliances. A **carbon monoxide detector** is *a device that sounds an alarm when a dangerous level of carbon monoxide is reached.* Yearly inspection of heating systems and the installation of a carbon monoxide detector will help prevent accidental poisonings from this gas.

Preventing Electrical Injuries

Most electrical injuries occur because of problems with plugs, wiring, outlets, and extension cords, and through improper use of appliances. Follow these precautions can help you prevent electrical accidents:

- **Plugs and outlets.** Pull furniture away from the walls, and inspect electrical cords for loose plugs or exposed wiring. When there are children in the house, cap all unused outlets with childproof covers.
- **Extension cords.** Avoid plugging too many electrical appliances into the same outlet to prevent circuit overload and fires. If you need to plug in many items,

What safety hazards do you see in this drawing?

■ **This Way Out.** Have students locate school smoke detectors. Are they stategically placed? Review fire drill procedures. Do students see ways to improve them? Have someone knowledgeable show students how to use the school's fire extinguishers.

■ **Just in Case.** Have students learn and report about homeowner's insurance by talking with their families or contacting insurance companies.

ENRICHMENT

■ **Informed Consumers.** Have students consult consumer buying guides on home fire extinguishers and smoke detectors. Ask them to find out what criteria were used for evaluation? Which brands are recommended?

CROSS-CURRICULAR ACTIVITY
Health

Have students find out how electrical shock affects the body, especially the heart. Ask them to describe immediate measures that can save a person's life and ways to treat burns or other injuries caused by the shock.

FAMILY AND COMMUNITY OUTREACH

Have volunteers learn about fire protection in your community, focusing on the following questions: Where are the fire stations? What is the average response time? Are the firefighters full-time employees or volunteers? What equipment do they use?

REAL-LIFE APPLICATION

Read the following to students: *Theodore and Justin just discovered that the smoke detector in their apartment has no batteries. It's the landlord's responsibility to replace the batteries, so they plan to mention it to her the next time they pay their rent.* Ask students if they think this is the best way to deal with this problem. Why not? What would they do in the same situation?

Review

■ **Chapter Review.** Use the contents of the Chapter Review page to help students review concepts, think critically, and apply their knowledge.

■ **Study Guide.** Have students complete the Study Guide for Chapter 73 on p. 235 of the Student Workbook.

■ **Class Check.** Have students complete a safety check of the classroom and other school areas. What suggestions do they have?

Evaluation

■ **Chapter Test.** Use the reproducible chapter test provided in the Teacher's Classroom Resources or create your own test using the *Testmaker Software.*

■ **Alternative Assessment.** Have students draw a home diagram similar to Figure 73.1. Have them add details that are likely to cause accidents, for example, poisonous substances stored in low cabinets and frayed electrical cords. Ask students to add captions explaining why their additions may lead to accidents and the preventive measures that should be taken.

■ **20-20 Hindsight.** Have students review the list of accidents they described in the "Home Stories" activity at the beginning of the chapter. Ask again if students think any of these accidents could have been prevented. If so, how?

---

use extension cords to distribute the plugs among several outlets. Keep extension cords out of foot traffic areas, but do not run them under carpeting or rugs.

- **Appliances.** Check the wiring of all appliances for safety. Cords should be well covered with insulation and not frayed. Unplug small appliances, and put them away when they are not in use. Regularly wipe or vacuum dust away from appliance motors. Never use electrical appliances with wet hands, or while standing on a wet surface, since this may cause a serious electrical shock. Also, never use appliances in the bathtub or near a full sink—they might fall into the water and cause electrocution.

Preventing Fires

While no home can be made entirely fireproof, several steps can be taken to reduce the risk of fire. Checking electrical outlets and appliances is the first step. Many of the tips for preventing electrical injuries will also prevent fires. In addition, never store items near a heater or furnace, and don't let papers, wood, or oily rags pile up—especially near a range, fireplace, or an electrical source. Be particularly careful when you use any portable space heaters. Some tip over easily and might then come into contact with flammable materials. Always follow the manufacturer's instructions, and do not leave space heater unattended.

In the kitchen, avoid clutter near the range. Keep the kitchen clean to prevent grease fires. If you have a gas range, check the pilot light to be sure that it is working properly. A **pilot light** is *a thin stream of gas that burns constantly and is used to light the burners.* Finally, because many fires start in the kitchen, keep a fire extinguisher there.

Always use matches, lighters, and candles safely. Be sure that burned matches are cold and wet before throwing them away. Keep matches and lighters out of the reach of small children. Make sure that no one in your home smokes in bed.

Sometimes despite all precautions, a fire occurs. The most dangerous home fires are those that begin at night, while people are asleep. Installing a **smoke detector,** *a device that sounds an alarm when it senses smoke,* can reduce the risk of injury or death from a fire. Smoke detectors should be installed on every level of a home, and the alarm should be easily heard in all bedrooms. Change the batteries every six months.

A major part of fire safety is knowing how to leave a home if a fire starts. Plan and practice using at least two escape routes, and use the buddy system for small children, elderly people, and people with disabilities. Smoke inhalation during fires causes more deaths than burns do. Family members can protect themselves from smoke by covering their mouths and noses with a wet cloth. and crawling below the level of smoke as they leave the home.

Taking Responsibility

To prevent home accidents, you need to be aware of the dangers that exist, stay on guard, and plan for prevention. Keep the following tips in mind:

- **"Childproof" your home.** To protect young children, you may ineed to closie off bathrooms, moving poisonous plants, locking cabinets, or closing pool gates.
- **Offer assistance to those with special needs.** Provide help in reaching items, climbing stairs, and getting in and out of a shower or a bathtub. If someone with reduced mobility lives in your home, consider installing ramps and railings.
- **Prepare in advance for such emergencies, as fire and severe weather.** This includes moving a person with special needs to a first-floor bedroom, providing a bell to ring for help, and regularly checking on the person.

712   **UNIT 8 Housing and Living Space**

DID YOU KNOW?

Explain that a fire goes through four stages. In the first stage, it smolders, but people nearby see no smoke or flame and feel no heat. Smoke appears in the second stage, and in the third stage flames spring up. The fourth stage is characterized by intense heat. A smoke detector can detect fire in its first stage. The detector is set off by the invisible gases generated by the smoldering fire.

Chapter 73 Review

Reviewing the Facts

1. What are the five most common types of household accidents?
2. Identify four ways to prevent falls.
3. What telephone numbers should be kept next to each telephone in the home?
4. Name four ways to prevent electrical problems.
5. Where should smoke detectors be placed?
6. Identify individuals for whom you should take special responsibility in the home.

Thinking Critically

1. Why do human factors increase the likelihood of accidents? What steps might be taken to reduce the likelihood of human failure?
2. Do you think that taking responsibility for the safety of people with disabilities increases or decreases their independence? Why?

Applying Your Knowledge

1. **Planning an Escape.** Draw a floor plan that shows of doors, windows, stairways, and outside fire escapes. Then diagram a plan for escaping a fire. When possible, indicate two ways to reach the ground from each room—especially from bedrooms. Mark each route in different colors.
2. **Suggesting Safety Measures.** How could you make your home safer for someone disabled? List as many modifications as you can think of, explaining their benefits to someone with physical limitations.
3. **Selecting a Rental Home.** Imagine that you, your spouse, and your toddler want to rent a residence. Compile a safety checklist that could be used when evaluating a safe place to live. What safety features would you look for? Rank these requirements in order of importance. What might indicate that the residence is not safe?

Making Connections

1. **Drama.** With a group of classmates, write a short, humorous skit that illustrates one or more principles of home safety and accident prevention. Perform your skit for the rest of the class.
2. **Technology.** Today's "smart homes" have computer-operated cameras and alarm systems that warn occupants of emergencies while simultaneously alerting the police, fire department, and hospital. As the costs for these and other technologies decrease, "smart homes" will become more accessible to the average family. Describe an emergency situation in which having a "smart home" would make a difference. What safety measures would people living in "smart homes" still need to take?

Building Your Portfolio

Performing a Safety Check
Using a preprinted safety checklist or one you develop yourself, evaluate the safety of your home. Make notes on problems. For example, you might write, "Extension cord in living room is in good condition but has been placed under the rug in a heavy traffic area." Also note whether your family takes such safety precautions as practicing fire drills, establishing escape routes, and using smoke detectors. Discuss your report with your family and place it in your portfolio.

Chapter 74

FOCUS

Chapter Overview

Chapter 74 describes the main sources of energy and helps students become more aware of their own use of electricity. They learn how to reduce their use of energy at home, conserve water, and reduce waste in other ways.

Motivator

■ **Trust Fund.** Discuss this quote by Alden Whitman: "Our ideals. . . should be based on the proposition that each generation in turn becomes the custodian rather than the absolute owner of our resources—and each generation has the obligation to pass this inheritance on to the future."

Objectives

Discuss the chapter objectives on this page. Remind students that the objectives focus on important chapter concepts.

Vocabulary

The prefix *hydro-* in hydroelectric means water, as in hydrophobia (fear of water) and hydroplane (a racing boat that skims the surface of water, or the skidding caused when a film of water prevents tires from contacting wet pavement) and hydrotherapy (water therapy).

Chapter 74

Protecting the Environment

Terms to Learn

- energy
- hydroelectric power
- insulation
- nonrenewable resource
- peak usage period
- R-value
- weather stripping

Objectives

This chapter will help you to:

- **Explain** what energy is and how it is used in the home.
- **Assess** ways to use energy-conservation strategies to increase the comfort level of your home and lower energy bills.
- **Identify** ways to conserve water in the home.
- **Describe** how you can incorporate the concepts of reducing, reusing, and recycling into your daily routine.

714   UNIT 8   Housing and Living Space

Shi-chung closed his checkbook with a smile of satisfaction. He had just finished paying his utility bills, and he figured out that they were 14 percent lower than they had been at this time last year—even with the cold weather coming early. As he left the study, Shi-chung turned off the desk lamp and the radio. Then he went into the living room, where he closed the drapes to keep the warmth inside. Shi-chung has earned lower utility bills—he has been working hard to conserve energy in his home.

What Is Energy?

Most people are concerned about saving money on their utility bills, and many are also concerned about conserving the planet's energy resources. **Energy** is *usable power or the resources for producing usable power*. In the home people use energy for many types of work—to run appliances, for example, and for heating and cooling.

Sources for home heating vary. The three most common energy sources for home heating are electricity, fuel oil, and natural gas. Some homes have an alternative heating source, such as a wood-burning stove or a coal-burning furnace. Still others use solar panels, which absorb heat from the sun and circulate it throughout the home.

Projects that improve a home's energy efficiency—such as adding insulation—pay off in lower utility bills. What are some other benefits.

Sources of Electricity

One of the most important energy sources in most homes—along with natural gas and fuel oil—is electricity. Electricity is provided to homes and businesses by utility companies. It can be generated in three main ways. Most utilities produce electricity by burning fossil fuels, such as oil, coal, or natural gas. These fuels are all **nonrenewable resources,** that is, *substances that cannot be replaced once they are used*. Other utilities use **hydroelectric power,** which is *electricity generated by the force of falling water*. Finally, electricity can come from nuclear reactors.

Uses of Electricity

In many homes the early evening hours are the busiest time of the day. Family members use electricity for everything from cooking dinner to watching television. This time of the day is a **peak usage period** in many homes, *the time when the most energy is consumed*.

If you have ever experienced a power blackout during a peak usage period or a storm, you know how helpless you feel without electricity. In fact, almost everything we do requires electrical energy of some kind. **Figure 74.1** on the next page lists just a few uses of electricity in the home.

Other Sources of Energy

In addition to electricity, natural gas and fuel oil are sources of energy in the home. Four important pieces of home equipment can run on natural or propane gas—the heating system, the water heater, the clothes dryer, and the range. Oil can be used to fuel the heating system and the water heater.

MORE ABOUT Nuclear Power

In 1994, France had 56 operating nuclear reactors; Japan, 49; and the U.S., 109. In 1994, those 109 generated 22 percent of the electricity used in the U.S. The number of American reactors jumped from 70 in 1980 to 111 in 1990, but no new reactors have started up since then, and 2 have shut down.

Topics on pp. 716-717:

- Electricity in the Home
- Saving Energy
- Heating and Cooling

Checking Comprehension

✓ During winter, at what temperature should a furnace thermostat be set? *At 68° when people are home during the day; at 58° when they are away and at night.*

✓ During summer, at what temperature should an air conditioner be set? *At 15° below the outside temperature, but no lower than 78°.*

✓ What is R-value ? *How well insulation prevents loss of heat or cold.*

✓ How can you prevent heated or cooled air from escaping a home? *Cover electrical outlets, install windows with double or triple panes, apply caulk cracks, add weather stripping around doors and windows.*

USING VISUALS

Refer students to Figure 74.1. Have them ask older family members or neighbors how many of the appliances on the list were used in their homes when they were teens. Allow students to compare what they learn and draw conclusions about changes in energy use over the years.

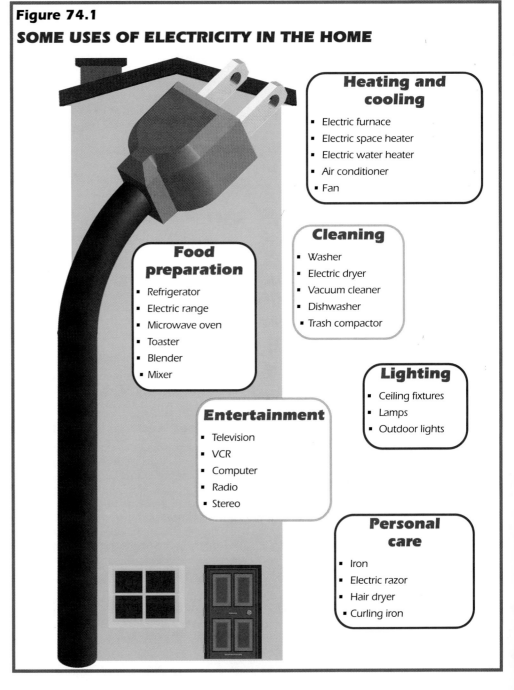

Figure 74.1

SOME USES OF ELECTRICITY IN THE HOME

Heating and cooling
- Electric furnace
- Electric space heater
- Electric water heater
- Air conditioner
- Fan

Cleaning
- Washer
- Electric dryer
- Vacuum cleaner
- Dishwasher
- Trash compactor

Food preparation
- Refrigerator
- Electric range
- Microwave oven
- Toaster
- Blender
- Mixer

Lighting
- Ceiling fixtures
- Lamps
- Outdoor lights

Entertainment
- Television
- VCR
- Computer
- Radio
- Stereo

Personal care
- Iron
- Electric razor
- Hair dryer
- Curling iron

MORE ABOUT Heating and Cooling

Explain that many homes now use heat pumps for heating and cooling. The device collects heat from outside the home, stores it, and pumps the heat through the home when it is needed. To cool, the pump transfers heat from indoors to a coil outside, where the heat disperses into the air.

Conserving Energy

To manage your energy costs at home, you first need to know how you use energy. Approximately 40 percent of the average home's energy bill is for heating the home, and 15 percent is for heating water. Cooling the home totals 7 percent. The other 38 percent goes toward all the appliances, machines, and lights that run on electricity. Your own family's energy use may be somewhat different because climate, the size of your family, and the size and age of your home all affect how much energy you use.

Heating and Cooling

No matter what source of heating and cooling your home uses, winter winds and summer sun affect the comfort level of your home. Although the weather can't be controlled, the amount of heated or cooled air used in a home can be. Because heating and cooling make up almost half of an average family's energy bill, these are two areas in which managing the use of energy has a noticeable effect. The following tips can help you conserve heating and cooling energy and cut fuel bills:

- In the heating season, set your thermostat to 68°F (20°C) when family members are home during the day. Lower the thermostat to 58°F (14°C) while you're asleep or away from home for more than four hours. Reducing the temperature of your home by 5 degrees for four or more hours each day can help you save 5 to 10 percent on your fuel bill.
- Install thermostats in more than one room if possible. This helps control the temperature better, heating only the rooms that are in use.
- Close heating vents or turn off radiators in rooms not in use.
- Instead of turning up the thermostat, wear an extra layer of clothing or a heavy sweater to stay warm.
- Use fans instead of air conditioners whenever possible. Fans are less costly to run.

- If you need to use central air conditioning, set the thermostat to 15 degrees below the outside temperature or no lower than 78°F (26°C).
- Use draperies and blinds to help control the temperature. On cold days, open drapes on the sunny side of your home; close drapes on cloudy days or as soon as the sun sets to keep the heat in. During the summer, keep your home cooler by closing drapes and shades on the sunny side.
- If you have a fireplace, close the damper when it is not in use to prevent warm air from escaping up the chimney.
- Turn the thermostat on your water heater to "medium," "normal," or 120°F (50°C).

Another way to keep your home more comfortable and conserve energy is to install insulating materials. **Insulation** is *material that is sandwiched between inside and outside walls or placed above ceilings to prevent heat loss in winter and heat gain in summer.* In some homes good insulation can lower heating bills by 30 to 35 percent.

Insulation is measured by its **R-value**—its *ability to resist heat loss or gain.* The higher the R-value, which is represented by a number, the better the insulation. Such building materials as wood and glass have low R-values, while insulating materials, such as fiberglass, have high R-values. Because heat rises, ceiling and attic insulation should have a higher R-value than wall insulation. Usually homes in colder climates need insulation with a higher R-value, such as 19 or 22, than homes in warmer areas.

Another strategy is to reduce the amount of heated or cooled air that escapes from tiny leaks and cracks in the home. You can put covers over outlets, install windows with double or triple panes of glass, apply caulking to cracks and moldings, and add weather stripping around doors and windows. **Weather stripping** is *material used to prevent air leaks around doors and windows.* It is usually made of rubber, fiber, vinyl, or metal.

Activities

- **Telltale Sign.** Have students pretend that it snowed heavily last night. All the homes in their neighborhood have snow-covered roofs—except one. What does this tell students about that home's insulation? *(Critical Thinking)*
- **Other Options.** Provide students with literature on wood- and coal-burning stoves. Have them compare prices and find out the advantages and disadvantages regarding safety, savings, and efficiency. Discuss whether these options would be good choices for homes in your community.

RETEACHING

- **Keeping Weather in Its Place.** Ask students to use classroom objects to show how insulation and weather stripping work.

ENRICHMENT

- **A Year of Bills.** Have students chart their families' energy bills for a year to see how energy use changes with the seasons. Discuss how this cycle would vary if students lived in northern Montana; Charleston, South Carolina; Dallas, Texas. (Do not require students to share their families expenses with classmates.)

CROSS-CURRICULAR ACTIVITY
Science

Have student pairs demonstrate how opening or closing window coverings can help heat or cool a living space.

REAL-LIFE APPLICATION

Read this to students: *The landlord pays the cost of heating Jennifer's apartment, so she often turns the thermostat up to 74° or higher on cold days. She figures she's not paying the fuel bills, so she might as well be comfortable.* Ask students what problems may result from Jennifer's approach. Guide students to recognize that her actions will lead to eventual increases in her rent and also waste natural resources.

Topics on pp. 718-720:
- **Using Appliances and Lighting**
- **Water Conservation**
- **Reduce, Reuse, Recycle**

Checking Comprehension

✓ Name two ways to save energy when using a dishwasher. *Wash only full loads; use energy-saving cycle.*

✓ How can you save water while brushing your teeth? *Don't run water continuously.*

✓ What is the difference between precycling and recycling? *Precycling is not making waste in the first place. Recycling is finding other uses for used materials.*

In Touch With TECHNOLOGY

Have students read "The Smart House." Ask them to identify the kinds of automation already found in many homes, such as remote controls and automatic timers on lights. (Answers to questions will vary.)

CROSS-CURRICULAR ACTIVITY
Language Arts

Have students write to the utility company, the state cooperative extension (located at land-grant colleges), or conservation groups in your region for more tips on conserving energy.

Appliances and Lighting

Appliances and lighting use a significant amount of energy in the home. If you buy energy-efficient appliances and are thoughtful about both lighting and appliance use, you can conserve energy and save on utility bills. Here are some specific strategies for conserving energy:

- Buy a frost-free refrigerator or keep the refrigerator defrosted so that it works more efficiently. Don't leave the refrigerator door open longer than you have to.

- Wash only full loads of dishes and use the energy-saving cycle if you have a dishwasher.
- Wash clothes on warm- or cold-water settings, especially for the rinse cycle. Most laundry detergents are as effective in cold water as in hot water.
- Clean the lint filter in the clothes dryer after each load to keep the dryer more energy-efficient. Do not overdry clothes.
- Dry clothes by hanging them on a clothes rack or clothesline when possible.

In Touch with TECHNOLOGY

The Smart Home

How smart is your home? Can it turn off the lights? Can it lock the doors and windows? Can it turn on the water in the bathtub so that your bath is ready when you get home?

Some homes are able to do these things and more, through the technology of home automation. In a "smart home," appliances equipped with microchips can "talk" to each other. This type of home has many conveniences and is energy efficient.

The level of automation in a "smart home" can range from a central on-off system for lights to a fully automated home in which the climate, security, entertainment, and other systems are controlled through an electronic "command post."

The simplest approach to home automation is a module into which electric appliances can be plugged. The module is then controlled by a hand-held cordless device similar to a TV remote control. The system can be programmed to turn heat up or down automatically or to turn televisions, VCRs, stereos, and lights on or off.

The fully automated home requires complete rewiring or installation at the time the home is built. Any appliance can be plugged into the home's automated system and activated from any of the control panels located throughout the home. In

some cases, appliances can also be controlled from a telephone or television.

Engineers estimate that energy costs can be reduced by 20 to 50 percent through the use of the most fully automated home. This "supersmart" home can turn out lights when no one is in the room, automatically control the water temperature usage in a dishwasher, and control the home's temperature and humidity.

The engineers and architects who are designing such homes are trying to make them as owner-friendly as possible. Today's teens, who have grown up with computers, will probably find it easy to adapt to a fully automated home.

Thinking Critically About Technology

1. Which features of the automated home appeal to you the most? Why?
2. Do you think that this type of home automation would simplify or complicate your life? Explain your answer.

DID YOU KNOW?

Tell students that appliances vary considerably in the amount of electricity they use. A clock that is constantly plugged in might use only 2 watts an hour, while a clothes dryer that is turned on once or twice a week may use over 200 watts an hour. Thus, the yearly cost to run the clock continuously may be only $1.50, but the occasional use of the dryer may be nearly $90.00.

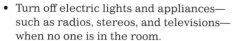

When buying large appliances, read the EnergyGuide labels for information about operating costs. You can then compare the energy efficiency of different brands and models.

- Turn off electric lights and appliances—such as radios, stereos, and televisions—when no one is in the room.
- Replace high-wattage bulbs with low-wattage ones if light isn't needed for reading or close work. Use fluorescent bulbs in the kitchen, bathroom, and workroom—they use less energy than incandescent bulbs.

Large appliances use a great deal of energy. When you plan an appliance purchase, compare the EnergyGuide labels on various brands and models. These labels estimate the cost of running the appliance for one year. You can use EnergyGuide labels to find the model that uses energy most efficiently.

Check appliances for other energy-saving features as well. For example, dishwashers should have the option of skipping the drying cycle, and washing machines should have several choices of temperature and water depth.

Conserving Water

Such energy sources as oil, natural gas, and coal are not the only resources individuals should conserve. Safe water is essential to all life, yet it is becoming increasingly scarce. By following these suggestions, you and your family can avoid wasting this precious resource:

- Use a dishpan or put a stopper in the sink drain when washing dishes by hand. Washing and rinsing dishes under continuously running water wastes about 30 gal. (115 L) of water per meal.
- Take showers instead of baths and keep them short. A typical bath uses 10 to 20 gal. (38 to 76 L) of water, whereas a 5-minute shower uses 8 to 12 gal. (30 to 45 L).
- Don't let water run continuously while you shave, brush your teeth, or work at the sink. Turn faucets off completely after you use them.
- Fix dripping faucets and other water leaks promptly. A faucet leaking one drop of water per second wastes 192 gal. (725 L) of clean water per month.
- Avoid overwatering your lawn or garden. Sprinklers should be set to water during the night or early morning hours. Watering in the heat of the day requires more water to achieve the same result and can burn the roots of the grass.

Taking Responsibility

You may have seen or heard the slogan "Reduce, Reuse, and Recycle." These are three responsible ways that people can conserve resources and reduce pollution. Remember that what you buy today will become tomorrow's trash. Here are some ways you can help protect the environment:

DID YOU KNOW?

The home appliance that has gained the most in popularity over the past 25 years is the microwave oven. Only 14 percent of homes had a microwave in 1980, but 84 percent had one by 1993. In comparison, 82 percent of homes had a color television set in 1980, and 98 percent had one in 1993. Clothes washers and refrigerators were in nearly the same percentage of homes (about 75 and 86 percent, respectively) in both 1980 and 1993.

Activities

■ **Water, Water, Everywhere.** Remind students that water evaporates, forms clouds, and falls again as rain. Why, then, are people worried about running out of water? *(Problem Solving)*

■ **Needs and Wants.** Have students each choose one appliance they use often and do without it for a week. Then discuss whether they still think they need that appliance. *(Management)*

USING VISUALS

Refer students to Figure 74.2. How does the information apply to them? What kinds of refills do students buy? When might it be wasteful to buy one large bottle instead of two smaller ones?

MULTICULTURAL *Perspectives*

Have students choose a culture and find out how water sources have affected its movement and settlement patterns. Have students write brief reports and include maps tracing the culture's movements.

FAMILY AND COMMUNITY OUTREACH

Have students plan a campaign to persuade people to conserve electricity or water. Students could design posters, buttons, and messages to read during morning announcements.

720

Review

■ **Chapter Review.** Use the contents of the Chapter Review page to help students review concepts, think critically, and apply their knowledge.

■ **Study Guide.** Have students complete the Study Guide for Chapter 74 on p. 237 of the Student Workbook.

■ **Saving Energy.** Have students observe other people for a day and take notes on how energy is wasted. What suggestions do they have?

Evaluation

■ **Chapter Test.** Use the reproducible chapter test provided in the Teacher's Classroom Resources or create your own test using the *Testmaker Software*.

■ **Alternative Assessment.** Ask groups to each list five or six actions that would promote energy and water conservation at school. After group members discuss the list, ask them to choose one idea, plan how to accomplish it, and put their plan into action. For example, they might decide to put up posters encouraging students and staff to turn off lights in empty rooms.

CLOSE

■ **Contributing to Conservation.** Have groups each list four or five ways that teens can encourage energy conservation in the community. As groups share their ideas, list them on the board. Ask students how they could carry out some of these ideas and urge them to do so.

• **Reduce.** Decrease the amount of trash you generate. **Figure 74.2** shows methods of precycling, which means avoiding making waste in the first place. When you precycle, you consider what it will take to get rid of an item before you buy it.

• **Reuse.** You can reuse things in many ways. Whenever you buy a product, think of how its container or packaging might be used for another purpose. Try to repair broken items rather than throwing them away and buying new ones. Some items, such as outgrown clothing, can be given to someone you know or to charitable groups that will distribute them to be used by others.

• **Recycle.** If your community a has recycling program, contribute such items as cans, glass, newspapers, plastic containers, and corrugated cardboard. Take used motor oil, which is a hazardous waste, to a recycling center or a designated auto service center. Recycle old appliances through your community's waste management facility.

Taking responsibility also means learning more about environmental issues. If you don't know how your community's recycling programs work, find out by calling the appropriate branch of local government. If your school doesn't have a recycling program, offer to start one. Your actions and commitment to protecting the environment can reap benefits for your community and your world.

Figure 74.2
PRECYCLING

■ Look for items you can buy in bulk (not packaged), such as flour, rice, and cereal. Some stores provide refillable containers for bulk items.

■ Buy refills when possible for products like laundry detergent.

■ Buy products you use often in large sizes. One large bottle creates less packaging waste than two smaller ones.

■ Look for products that use a minimum amount of packaging material.

■ For small purchases, don't use a grocery bag.

■ Buy frozen juice concentrate and mix it with water in a pitcher instead of buying juice in bottles. Reuse single-serving juice and iced tea bottles to carry drinks in your lunch.

■ If your supermarket recycles grocery bags, be sure to return yours. Better yet, take your own cloth bags to carry groceries.

DID YOU KNOW?

Students might be interested in the 1993 energy consumption for selected states, reported in trillions of BTUs. Ask them to explain the low figure for Vermont, where winters are long and cold.

State	BTUs
Texas	10,081.1
Tennessee	1,832.4
Maryland	1,245.8
Iowa	965.8
Nevada	446.1
Vermont	141.8

Review

Reviewing the Facts

1. What is energy?
2. List three ways that utility companies produce electricity.
3. Describe three ways to conserve heating and cooling energy.
4. What is an EnergyGuide label?
5. List five ways that you can save water.
6. How can individuals "reduce, reuse, and recycle"?

Thinking Critically

1. How could a person who is building his or her own home plan for energy conservation?
2. Do Americans take enough action to conserve energy and protect the environment? Why or why not?

Applying Your Knowledge

1. **Energy Conservation Checklist.** Using the tips in the chapter as a basis, create a checklist that can be used in your home to help save energy. For example, you might figure out which side of your home gets the most sun during the day and suggest, "In the winter, open drapes on the south side of the apartment in the morning. Close those drapes each evening." How many different conservation techniques can you put to use in your home? What new ones can you think of?
2. **Making Smart Purchases.** Imagine that you are shopping for a new refrigerator. You have narrowed down your decision to two models. The first costs $650, and the EnergyGuide label says it costs $75 a year to run. The second costs $585, and the EnergyGuide label says it costs $100 a year to run. Which would you choose to buy? Explain your decision.

Making Connections

1. **Environmental Science.** Consider your personal role in protecting the environment. Make a list of about five nonfood products you use, such as notebook paper, shampoo, and batteries. Describe how you use each product, how often you use it, the product's packaging, and how you dispose of the product and the packaging. Evaluate whether you use such products wisely, then note any ways that you might be able to reduce, reuse, or recycle them.
2. **Science.** Do you ever stop to think about what happens to the items that you put out each week for recycling collection? Research one type of material—paper, plastic, aluminum, or glass—to find out how it is recycled. What products are made from the recycled material? Prepare a brief report on your findings.

Building Your Portfolio

Designing a Conservation Message

Design a postage stamp or a T-shirt that encourages people to conserve energy. Think of an illustration and a slogan that convey your message. For example, you could show a beautiful waterfall and the slogan, "Waterpower—Don't Waste It!" Include a description or a sketch of the stamp or T-shirt in your portfolio.

ANSWERS TO REVIEWING THE FACTS

1. Usable power or the resources for producing usable power.
2. Burning fossil fuels, using hydroelectric power, and generating nuclear power.
3. Any three from page 717.
4. A guide that estimates the cost of running the appliance for one year.
5. Any five: Don't run water continuously while washing dishes, brushing teeth, or shaving; take showers instead of baths; fix dripping faucets; and avoid overwatering a lawn or garden.
6. To reduce, decrease the amount of trash you produce. To reuse, find more uses for products, repair broken items, and donate outgrown clothing to groups that can use it. To recycle, save cans, glass, newspapers, yard trimmings, and other items for a recycling service.

ANSWERS TO THINKING CRITICALLY

1. Answers may include: install multiple thermostats, add ceiling fans, use insulation with a high R-value, choose windows with double or triple panes of glass, add caulking around cracks and moldings, install weather stripping around doors and windows, and consult EnergyGuides in choosing large appliances.
2. Answers will vary. Ask students what specific steps they would like to see taken.

Chapter Overview

Chapter 75 introduces students to housing careers. They learn about related interests and skills and about specific jobs in housing design, construction, sales, and maintenance.

Motivator

■ **Career List.** Ask students to list careers in the housing industry. Do they tend, like many people, to think primarily of construction jobs? There are many other types, and they will learn more about them in this chapter.

Objectives

Discuss the chapter objectives. Remind students that the objectives focus on important chapter concepts.

Vocabulary

Ask students if they have ever heard the term *carbon copy*. Explain that it refers to carbon paper, which was used to make copies before photocopying was available. Similarly, the term *blueprint* used to refer to a mechanical drawing with white lines on a blue background. Today's blueprints are usually blue or black lines on a white background, but they still have the same name.

Chapter 75

Careers in the Housing Field

Terms to Learn

- architect
- blueprint
- construction
- crew
- trade association

Objectives

This chapter will help you to:

- Identify **interests and skills needed for careers in housing.**
- Describe **types of jobs available in design, construction, and sales.**
- Describe **types of jobs available in home maintenance.**

CHAPTER RESOURCES

Student Workbook
Study Guide, p. 239
Activity, *On the Job*, p. 240
Teacher's Classroom Resources
Lesson Plan, p. 79

Cooperative Learning, *Looking into Careers*, pp. 79-80
Extension #106, *Careers in Housing*, p. 112
Life Skills, *Write a Job Description*, pp. 115-116

Chapter 75 Test, pp. 155-156
Performance Assessment, *Housing Careers*, p. 114
Reteaching, *Housing Careers*, p. 81
See Also:
ABCNews InterActive™ Videodiscs

Along with food and clothing, shelter is one of the basic human needs. To meet the demand for comfortable, affordable housing, the housing industry provides jobs and careers for hundreds of thousands of people. The business of housing has many facets—planning, designing, building, selling, furnishing, decorating, and maintaining—and therefore many opportunities for employment. The largest segment of careers in housing is in **construction**, *the building of homes and other buildings*. More than one-and-a-half million homes are built every year. These homes may be single-family dwellings or multiple-family units.

Workers in the building industry include carpenters, masons, plumbers, plasterers, electricians, painters, and paperhangers. Carpenters are by far the largest group in the building industry.

While construction creates many specialized jobs, other aspects of the housing industry present additional opportunities. These include jobs for designers, decorators, drafters, architects, realtors, land developers, and people who repair and maintain homes.

The Qualities Needed

People who work in the housing industry do not work only with structures. First and foremost, they work with people. Whether they are designing, constructing, selling, or maintaining a home, individuals who work in this business must be interested in people and their differing needs and lifestyles. If you have some of the following interests and skills, a career in housing may be a good choice for you.

> Why would working as a drafter or architect be a good career choice for someone with an interest in art?

Interests

The interests you have today can tell you a lot about what you might choose for a career in the future. Can you answer yes to any of the following questions?

- **Do you like changing your room—selecting new colors for the walls or rearranging your furniture?** Perhaps you are the person that friends and family come to for help with decorating. Your interest in color and design may mean that you will enjoy a career in a field such as interior design.

- **Are you interested in learning how buildings are created and how to use the materials that go into construction?** Many construction jobs involve working with wood, concrete, plastics, bricks, and electrical wiring. Other jobs require knowledge of how plumbing, heating, or air conditioning works.

- **Are you interested in graphic arts or computer graphics?** An interest in these activities could lead to you a career as a drafter or architect.

CHAPTER 75   Careers in the Housing Field   723

TEACH

Topic on p. 723:
- **Interests for Housing Careers**

Checking Comprehension

✓ What is the most important skill needed in the housing industry? *The ability to work with people.*

✓ What kinds of interests might lead to a career in the housing industry? *Interior decorating, building, graphic arts or computer graphics.*

Activities

■ **Misconceptions.** Discuss why some people might think a career in housing does not require good people skills. *(Relationship)*

RETEACHING

■ **From Hobby to Housing.** Have students list their hobbies and the interests and skills these hobbies help them develop. Which hobbies might lead to a career in the housing industry?

CROSS-CURRICULAR ACTIVITY
Math

Have students locate statistics on housing starts for the past ten years—*Statistical Abstracts of the United States* and *Business Statistics* are suggested sources—and design graphs that illustrate the annual totals. Have students identify trends and explain what they indicate for people in housing careers.

MORE ABOUT Finding a Job

Like jobs in other fields, those in the housing industry are advertised in many ways. Some companies list entry-level jobs with high school career counselors. Many jobs are offered through newspaper want ads, while government job openings are often posted on bulletin boards in post offices and government buildings. Labor unions may hire carpenters, plumbers, electricians, and other skilled workers for some companies, so qualified people would apply at the appropriate union location.

Topics on pp. 724-725:
- **Career Skills**
- **Design, Construction, and Sales Jobs**

Checking Comprehension

✓ How do landscape gardeners often learn their trade? *On-the-job training at nursery.*

✓ What do interior designers do? *Update home's appearance; make it more comfortable and functional.*

✓ What information do real estate agents need from home buyers? *Size, neighborhood, and price of home they want.*

724

What types of skills do you think a roofer needs to be successful on the job?

Skills

You may have many skills that will help you succeed in a career in the housing field. Do you have any of the following skills?

- **Can you picture a finished product by looking at a plan?** Many jobs in housing require you to visualize, or see in your mind, how a completed project will look. Carpenters, for example, must be able to read a **blueprint**, *the architect's plan or mechanical drawing.* When interior designers study a floor plan, they can imagine how the furnishings will look and even how the arrangement might be improved.
- **Do you work well with your hands?** Many jobs in housing—for example, installing electrical systems—involve working with your hands.
- **Do you communicate and work well with people?** Designers, builders, and salespeople work closely with their clients, learning what they want and helping

them to feel comfortable with their final decisions. Clients who are satisfied with housing professionals are likely to recommend them to friends and associates.
- **Do you pay attention to detail?** Many jobs in housing require thoroughness and following plans very carefully. A cabinetmaker must make the tops of cabinet doors line up perfectly. A building inspector must check every inch of a house for safety hazards.
- **Are you in good physical condition?** Some jobs in the housing industry are physically demanding, requiring many hours of physical labor each day. Construction workers and landscapers, for example, must be in good physical condition.

Design, Construction, and Sales

A major segment of the housing industry involves planning, building, and selling homes. These jobs are open to people who have the interests and have learned the skills that are in demand.

Entry-Level Jobs

The housing industry includes many jobs at this level. Landscape gardeners plant and care for bushes, trees, flowers, and other plants around buildings. They generally work outdoors, and many jobs in this field are seasonal. There is a growing demand, however, for gardeners to work year-round in offices and shopping malls taking care of indoor plants. Some landscape gardeners have their own businesses, traveling between different locations.

Caring for plants properly requires a great deal of knowledge. Many landscape gardeners receive on-the-job training at a nursery. Although no specific education is necessary to become a landscape gardener, certification is needed to apply pesticides.

Construction workers do many different jobs, nearly all of which require individuals to work with their hands. Many construction workers begin their work as apprentices, helpers who are trained on the job and who may also receive classroom instruction. Construction workers usually work as part of a **crew,** *a group of workers cooperating in producing housing.*

Retail wallpaper, fabric, and furniture stores often have home furnishings coordinators. They help customers select colors, fabrics, and furniture for new homes or redecorating projects. These workers must have a high school diploma and knowledge of furniture and fabrics.

Jobs That Require Training

Someone who has some experience as a home-furnishings coordinator may consider additional training and education to become an interior designer. Interior designers plan space and furnish or update the appearance of their clients' homes. They also suggest ways to make homes more comfortable and functional. For example, a designer might use light colors and fabrics and carefully selected furniture to make a small living room appear larger. Interior designers are trained to work with color, line, form, texture, and composition, or the actual placement of furniture in a room or space.

Most designers are members of the American Society of Interior Designers (ASID). They may work for furniture stores or architects or have their own businesses.

Acting Responsibly

Can You Be Flexible?

People who are flexible know how to adapt to changing circumstances. When you're flexible, you're ready to meet new challenges, new situations, new conditions, and new limitations. You have backup plans and alternatives ready to put into action if necessary.

Flexibility in Action

The people in Shontelle's office know what it means to be flexible. No two days are alike, so they can't plan a rigid schedule. Sometimes Shontelle has to fight with her sense of order when demands cause change, but she has learned to do so.

Shontelle works part-time in a real estate office. She answers the phone and types contracts for the agents. On some days Shontelle spends most of her time just fielding calls.

Shontelle was having one of those days last week when three agents approached her at different times with typing jobs. Shontelle knew that she would be pressed to get things done for them because of the constant phone calls. It was time to explore the options—time for flexibility.

Through experience Shontelle had discovered different ways to manage the trying moments. She could ask Christie for help if she was available. She could check times and dates with the agents to see which jobs were the highest priority. She could talk to her boss about transferring calls to the answering service for a while. She could also arrange to work a few extra hours.

Shontelle quickly shifted into flexibility mode. She ran through all the options, deciding what would work best on that day. Within seconds she had a plan in mind, and she was ready to take action.

Your Analysis

1. What might happen if Shontelle were not flexible?
2. Why do you think Shontelle's employer appreciates having her as an employee?
3. Describe a situation in which you showed flexibility.

Focus on Decision-Making Skills

Explain that many people in the housing industry set up their own businesses. Have students identify some jobs in housing that might lend themselves to self-employment. Then discuss the advantages and disadvantages of being on one's own. What kinds of decisions must be made before a person is ready to become self-employed? What kinds of skills would she or he need?

Activities

■ **Learned or Innate?** Discuss which of the skills listed on page 724 can be learned. How would you learn those skills? *(Critical Thinking)*

RETEACHING

■ **Comparing Skills.** Have students list 15 things they do well and compare their lists with the skills on page 724. How many of the skills needed in the housing industry do they have? How are these skills important in the careers described on these two pages?

ENRICHMENT

■ **Resolving Conflicts.** Ask pairs of students to select a career in the housing industry. Have them act out a situation in which someone has to resolve a problem with a client. For example, an interior decorator and a homeowner might disagree on paint color. Have pairs demonstrate how good conflict resolution techniques help resolve the problem.

Acting Responsibly

Have students read "Can You Be Flexible?" Discuss what might have happened if Shontelle had simply left after four hours and told the office manager she had made other plans for the afternoon.

Answers to Your Analysis

1. Might interrupt flow of office work; certain tasks would not get done, which would upset others.
2. She is positive, can make decisions and solve problems.
3. Answers will vary.

Checking Comprehension

✓ How do city planners help communities? *Guide and predict growth; suggest ways to meet future needs.*

✓ What places use maintenance services? *Homes, office buildings, hospitals, day-care centers, nursing homes, retirement communities, hotels.*

✓ What is a resident caretaker? *Person who lives in an apartment building and is responsible for cleaning and maintaining common areas and grounds.*

✓ Name some home service jobs that might require training at a technical college? *Repairing major appliances or home systems; exterminating pests; cleaning carpet and upholstery.*

FAMILY AND COMMUNITY OUTREACH

Invite a city planner to tell the class about the community's master plan and to answer students' questions.

Building contractors, sometimes called general contractors, organize every aspect of the construction of a new home, a home renovation, or the construction of an addition. Their responsibilities include estimating costs of labor and materials, hiring and scheduling construction workers, purchasing materials, and arranging for building equipment. They usually work with subcontractors, who specialize in one aspect of construction (such as plumbing or roofing). These jobs require a high school diploma and technical or vocational training.

A real estate agent helps people buy and sell homes. Buyers consult with a real estate agent and explain what size home they want, what neighborhood in a town or city they would like to live in, and how much they can afford to pay for a home. The real estate agent tries to find a house or condominium that matches the client's needs and budget. A career in real estate requires special training in housing, financing, and sales. Real estate agents must have a high school diploma and must pass a written exam to receive a license to practice.

Real estate agents work with both buyers and sellers of homes.

Jobs That Require Higher Education

Architects are the *people who design buildings and homes*. They may design houses or huge apartment buildings. They may create a new home, design a renovation for an older home, or plan an addition to an existing dwelling.

Architects must know about building materials and people's living patterns. They must also be able to visualize a completed project while it is still on the drawing board. Computer skills and the ability to work with computer-aided design (CAD) are especially important to architects. Architects must have a five-year college degree in architecture, including course work in design, engineering, and liberal arts. Those starting out generally work for another architect for three years and then take an exam to obtain a license.

City planners, sometimes called urban developers, work for local governments to guide the growth of a new area or the rejuvenation of a neighborhood. They predict the potential population of an area and plan for facilities and services such as housing, schools, shopping, recreation, and transportation. City planners suggest ways to meet future needs so that city structures and services can grow in coordination with the population. City planners must have a college degree and computer skills.

Land developers purchase large tracts of land and create new neighborhoods. The plans sometimes include shopping areas and offices as well as housing. Land developers must have knowledge and experience in a number of related areas—real estate, construction, and financing—as well as an advanced degree in business administration, engineering, or architecture. Land development is a business that involves a high degree of risk, since a property may or may not be sold once it is built.

MORE ABOUT City Planners

Point out that city planning is an increasingly important field. Towns and cities have to use their resources wisely, and city planners can make sure that the community gets the most for its money and takes advantage of its natural resources. Discuss with students the kinds of issues that face city planners in your community, such as whether to permit a new mall to be built.

From School to Work

Customer Service

What You Learn Today . . .

Do you get along well with people? Do you like to help others solve problems? These are interpersonal skills. Finding ways to resolve conflicts in family situations can help you develop interpersonal skills. Working out differences with classmates can help you develop still others. Interpersonal skills are worth developing for more than just your personal life. These skills will be marketable as you look for a job.

. . . You Can Use Tomorrow

You can probably name stores where you like to shop and others that you avoid. Customer service is probably one of the reasons why. More and more companies are training employees in customer service to attract, then keep, customers.

What exactly is customer service? It is the extra effort employees put forth to make customers feel valued and satisfied. When several companies produce similar products, customer service can tip the balance for or against a product. When companies sell services, service quality becomes even more crucial.

What characteristics do good customer-service employees have? Managers say that such employees are inventive and flexible. They support customers and offer sympathy. They are informed and well spoken.

Practicing Your Skills

You can practice customer-service skills whenever you help others find solutions to problems. For example:

- **Identify the problem.** Help the person describe what needs to be fixed or solved.
- **Suggest and evaluate solutions.** What would work for the person? Is it practical?
- **Take action.** Find out what you can do to help.
- **Evaluate the results.** Did you help solve the problem? Why or why not?

Assessing Your Skills

1. Which of the skills mentioned in this feature do you possess? Explain.
2. Describe a situation in which you or someone else used customer-service skills.
3. Explain how you could use customer-service skills to attract and keep customers in a housing-related business.

Home Maintenance

The home-maintenance industry is among the largest in the country. This field employs people for every aspect of home upkeep—from installing alarm systems to repairing leaky roofs.

Entry-Level Jobs

As the demands of work and family increase, more people than ever are hiring others to clean and maintain their homes. Home maintenance is a service business that requires efficiency and a courteous manner.

These positions offer good opportunities for part-time work and evening hours. Houses and apartments aren't the only structures that require cleaning and maintenance services. Office buildings, hospitals, day-care centers, nursing homes, and retirement communities need these services too. Hotels and motels also have a growing demand for cleaning and maintenance workers.

One type of cleaning and maintenance position is a resident caretaker. Someone with this job is responsible for cleaning and maintaining common areas of apartment complexes such as lobbies, elevators, stairwells,

---

Activities

- **Service with a Smile.** Ask students if they think it's more important for home maintenance workers to have better cleaning skills or better people skills. (*Relationship*)
- **Stereotyping.** Discuss how ideas based on traditional gender roles might make it difficult for both women and men to pursue certain careers in the housing industry. (*Critical Thinking*)

RETEACHING

- **Getting Started.** Ask students to identify high school classes, classes offered in the community, hobbies, volunteer activities, and part-time jobs they could pursue to prepare themselves for any of the jobs discussed in this chapter.

ENRICHMENT

- **Setting Standards.** Organize the class into three groups. Have each group develop a set of criteria for hiring someone to handle one of these tasks in a home: cleaning, appliance repair, or a home improvement project. As groups share their criteria, encourage the rest of the class to look for similarities.

From School to Work

Have students read "Customer Service." Have they ever encountered store employees who were too helpful? How do you know when helpfulness becomes interference?

Answers to Assessing . . .

All answers will vary.

REAL-LIFE APPLICATION

Read this to students: *Jerome is interested in interior design, but some people he knows poke fun at his interest. Connie would like to try carpentry, but her uncles say that's a "man's job."* Ask students if they think Jerome and Connie should pursue their interests. Are they likely to receive more negative input? How should they respond? What can be done to help people enter any career that interests them?

Review

■ **Chapter Review.** Use the contents of the Chapter Review page to help students review concepts, think critically, and apply their knowledge.

■ **Study Guide.** Have students complete the Study Guide for Chapter 75 on p. 239 of the Student Workbook.

■ **Job Chart.** Give each student a blank chart with these two columns: Design, Construction, and Sales and Home Maintenance. Along the left side, label the vertical rows with these three categories: Entry-Level Jobs, Jobs That Require Training, and Jobs That Require Higher Education. Have students fill in as many jobs as they can, placing them in the correct categories.

Evaluation

■ **Chapter Test.** Use the reproducible chapter test provided in the Teacher's Classroom Resources or create your own test using the *Testmaker Software*.

■ **Alternative Assessment.** Have each student select a job title from this chapter. Ask them to draw a picture of the ideal person for that job title, indicating in some creative way the ideal person's interests, skills, and perhaps physical qualifications.

■ **Looking Ahead.** Ask students to predict how changes in the way people live might affect future careers in the housing industry. What appliance will become more popular? Will people want to build different kinds of living spaces? Which careers in housing might disappear?

laundry rooms, and courtyards, as well as the grounds. Resident caretakers live in the complex they maintain.

Salesclerks who work in hardware or home improvement stores offer help to people who are doing maintenance or renovation work in their homes. These salesclerks advise people about what materials to buy and how to use tools and materials correctly and safely. Most salesclerks get their experience from on-the-job training.

Jobs That Require Training

Many jobs in home service and repair require special training. Some individuals learn how to repair major appliances (such as refrigerators) or how to fix heating, electrical, or plumbing systems. Other workers are responsible for exterminating pests or cleaning carpets and upholstery.

In most jobs of this type, the company or employer provides training. Some firms pay for employees to take special courses. Training for these careers is also available from some vocational high schools, technical colleges, and correspondence courses.

Jobs That Require Higher Education

A college degree in family and consumer sciences may lead to work in the field of housing. Some consumer specialists work as part of the extension service, an educational program available in almost every county in the United States. The U.S. Department of Agriculture provides consumer education through these extension services.

Some public utility companies and appliance and housewares companies hire consumer specialists as home service advisors. These professionals serve as a link to the public, helping individuals learn about product use and care. Consumer specialists may be involved in writing brochures, demonstrating products, answering consumer questions, or providing educational workshops.

■ Apprenticeships help you learn a trade by working with experienced professionals in the field.

Preparing for a Career

Did this chapter interest you in a career in housing? Here are some steps you can take to prepare for a career in design, construction, sales, or home maintenance.

On-the-job experience is a great start. Try getting a part-time job in a related field—for example, as a salesclerk in a home-remodeling or hardware store—while you are going to school. Find out if there are apprenticeships with construction companies or general contractors that are available to high school graduates. A technical school will also help you get the necessary skills.

If you are interested in a particular area of the housing field, write to a **trade association,** *a professional group that provides information to, and supports the interests of, people who work in a particular field.* If you are interested in a real estate career, for example, you might write to The American Society of Real Estate Counselors in Chicago. To find an association related to your career interests, consult *The Encyclopedia of Associations* in the reference section of the library.

ℱocus on Entrepreneurial Skills

Many enterprising teens form small home-related businesses to help put themselves through college. Have students develop plans for a business such as a cleaning, lawn-care, or handy-person service. They should list the tools and supplies needed, set rates, and create advertisements or flyers to publicize the business. Further development might include plans for assistants they might employ and the skills these people would need.

Chapter 75

Review

Reviewing the Facts

1. Identify three interests or skills that might be useful for someone considering a career in housing.
2. What is a blueprint?
3. Give examples of two entry-level jobs in home design, construction, or sales.
4. How do workers in home-maintenance jobs gain training?
5. Give three examples of job activities of consumer specialists who work in the housing field.
6. Identify three steps that a person could take to prepare for a career in housing.

Thinking Critically

1. Compare and contrast what it might be like to work on a construction crew with what it might be like to work in a job alone. What kinds of skills would be useful for a member of a construction crew? How might the skills for a person working alone be similar and different?
2. Of the housing careers described in this chapter, which one do you find most appealing? Why? What interests and skills do you have that might apply to this career?

Applying Your Knowledge

1. **Researching a Career.** Choose one career in the field of housing that interests you. Do library research on the career or conduct an interview with someone in that career. Summarize your findings in a written report. Include a description of any interests, skills, and aptitudes you have that relate to the career.
2. **Analyzing the Tools.** Choose three careers named in this chapter or others related to the housing field. List or describe the tools a person would use in each of the

careers. Check resources for ideas if you are unfamiliar with the tools that would be used.

Making Connections

1. **History.** Compare a housing career of today with its counterpart from the past. For example, you might research how an architect's job has changed over the years or investigate the way apprenticeships in the building industry have changed.
2. **Technology.** Technology will affect the design, construction, sales, and maintenance of homes in the future. Can you predict some changes? How will this impact careers in the housing field? Share your thoughts with a partner.

Building Your Portfolio

Designing a Dream House
Imagine that you are an architect, an interior designer, or a landscape designer. You want to design a dream home that you would build if you had all the necessary resources and could live anywhere. Describe it in detail. It could be a two-room log cabin deep in the woods or an ultramodern town house in a large city. Design the aspect of the home that interests you most—the exterior, the interior, or the landscaping.

TABLE OF FOOD VALUES

	Amount	Cal-ories	Car-bohy-drates (g)	Fat (g)	Pro-tein (g)	Cal-cium (mg)	Iron (mg)	Vita-min A (RE)	Vita-min C (mg)	Cho-les-terol (mg)	Sodium (mg)
Milk, Yogurt, and Cheese Group											
Cheese, American process	1 oz/28 g	105	Tr	9	6	174	0.1	82	0	27	406
Cheese, Cheddar	1 oz/28 g	115	Tr	9	7	204	0.2	86	0	30	176
Cheese, cottage, creamed	½ c/125 ml	112	0.1	5	14	67.5	0.15	54	Tr	17	455
Cheese, cottage, dry	½ c/125 ml	62.5	0.5	Tr	12.5	23	0.15	6	0	5	10
Chocolate milk	1 c/250 ml	210	26	8	8	280	0.6	73	2	31	149
Ice cream, 16% fat	½ c/125 ml	175	16	12	2	75.5	0.05	110	5	30	58
Milk, whole	1 c/250 ml	150	11	8	8	291	0.1	76	2	33	120
Milk, low-fat 2%	1 c/250 ml	121	12	5	8	297	0.1	139	2	18	122
Milk, skim	1 c/250 ml	85	12	Tr	8	302	0.1	149	2	4	126
Yogurt, fruit	1 c/250 ml	230	42	3	10	343	0.2	25	21	10	133
Yogurt, plain, skim milk	1 c/250 ml	125	17	Tr	13	452	0.2	5	2	4	174
Yogurt, plain, whole milk	1 c/250 ml	140	11	7	8	274	0.1	68	1	29	105
Yogurt, frozen, low-fat	½ c/125 ml	110	24	0	3	100	0	0	0	0	50
Meat, Poultry, Fish, Dry Beans, Eggs, and Nuts Group											
Bacon, fried crisp	3 slices	110	Tr	9	4	2	0.3	0	10	16	303
Beef, lean (roasted)	3 oz/85 g	220	0	13	25	5	2.8	Tr	0	81	43
Beef, hamburger, lean	3 oz/85 g	230	0	16	21	9	2.1	Tr	0	76	70
Chicken (roasted) (½ breast)	3 oz/85 g	140	0	3	27	13	0.9	5	0	73	64
Chicken (fried) (½ breast)	3.5 oz/98 g	220	1	9	31	16	1.2	15	0	87	74
Eggs (hard-cooked)	1 egg	80	1	6	6	25	0.6	84	0	213	62
Egg substitutes	¼ cup/50 ml	30	1	0	6	20	1	0	0	0	100

Food	Amount									
Fish, flounder (baked)	3 oz/85 g	80	0	1	17	13	0.3	10	1	59	101
Ham, boiled (1 slice)	1 oz/28 g	65	0	6	5	3	0.8	0	0	16	375
Kidney beans (red beans)	1 c/250 ml	230	42	1	15	74	4.6	1	0	0	968
Lamb leg (roasted)	3 oz/85 g	205	0	13	22	8	1.7	0	0	78	57
Lentils	1 c/250 ml	210	39	Tr	16	50	4.2	4	0	0	26
Nuts, peanuts, salted	1 c/250 ml	840	27	72	37	107	3	0	0	0	626
Nuts, walnuts	1 c/250 ml	785	19	74	17	113	2.9	15	0	0	12
Peanut butter	2 T/30 ml	190	6	16	8	10	0.6	0	0	0	150
Peas, dried, split	1 c/250 ml	230	42	1	16	22	3.4	8	0	0	26
Pork (roasted)	3 oz/85 g	275	0	19	24	3	0.7	3	0	84	61
Sardines	3 oz/85 g	175	0	9	20	372	2.5	56	0	85	425
Seeds, sunflower (dry, hulled)	½ c/120 g	405	14.5	34.5	17.5	87	5.15	35	0	0	Tr
Tofu	1 piece, 2½" 3½" x 1"	85	1	5	9	108	2.3	0	0	0	8
Tuna, canned in oil	3 oz/85 g	170	0	7	24	7	1.6	20	0	55	303
Turkey, dark meat (roasted)	3 oz/85 g	175	0	7	26	0	2.0	0	0	72	67
Veal cutlet	3 oz/85 g	185	0	9	23	9	2.7	0	0	109	56

Fruit Group

Food	Amount									
Apple	1 (2¾/63 mm)	80	20	1	Tr	10	0.4	7	6	0	Tr
Apricots	3 med.	55	14	Tr	1	18	0.5	277	11	0	1
Banana	1 med.	100	26	Tr	2	10	0.8	9	12	0	1
Blueberries	1 c/250 ml	90	22	1	1	22	1.5	15	20	0	9
Cantaloupe	½ melon	80	20	Tr	2	38	1.1	861	90	0	24
Dates	10 dates	220	58	Tr	2	47	2.4	4	0	0	Tr
Grapefruit juice	¼ c/60 ml	25	6	Tr	0.25	6	0.05	Tr	24	0	1
Grapes, seedless	10 grapes	35	9	Tr	Tr	6	0.2	4	2	0	1
Orange	1 (3"/76 mm)	65	16	Tr	1	54	0.5	27	66	0	Tr
Orange juicea	¼ c/60 ml	30	7.25	Tr	0.5	6	0.1	19	30	0	2
Peach, peeled	1 (2½"/63 mm)	40	10	Tr	1	9	0.5	47	7	0	Tr
Pear, Bartlett	1 (2½"/63 mm)	100	25	1	1	13	0.5	3	7	0	Tr
Pineapple, cubed, raw	1 c/250 ml	80	21	Tr	1	26	0.5	4	26	0	2
Prunes, dried	4 med.	110	29	Tr	1	22	1.7	97	1	0	2
Raisins (snack package)	½ oz/14 g	40	11	Tr	Tr	9	0.5	Tr	Tr	0	2

(Continued on next page)

TABLE OF FOOD VALUES (Continued)

	Amount	Calories	Carbohydrates (g)	Fat (g)	Protein (g)	Calcium (mg)	Iron (mg)	Vitamin A (RE)	Vitamin C (mg)	Cholesterol (mg)	Sodium (mg)
Vegetable Group											
Beans, green, raw	1 c/250 ml	45	7	Tr	2	63	0.8	83	15	0	4
Bean sprouts	1 c/250 ml	35	7	Tr	4	20	1.4	2	20	0	6
Broccoli	1 c/250 ml	40	7	Tr	5	71	1.2	218	140	0	17
Cabbage, shredded	1 c/250 ml	15	4	Tr	1	34	0.03	9	33	0	13
Carrot, raw	1 stick	30	7	Tr	1	27	0.5	2,025	6	0	25
Celery, raw	3 stalks	15	6	Tr	Tr	48	0.3	15	12	0	105
Corn, sweet kernels	1 c/250 ml	130	31	1	5	5	0.3	41	8	0	8
Lettuce, iceberg	¼ head	20	2.6	Tr	0.8	18	0.45	44	5	0	12
Peas, green, frozen	1 c/250 ml	125	19	Tr	0.8	30	2.3	107	21	0	139
Pepper, green sweet, raw	1 med.	15	4	Tr	1	7	0.5	39	94	0	2
Potato, baked	1 med.	145	33	Tr	4	8	1.1	0	20	0	8
Potatoes, french fried	10 pieces	155	18	7	2	9	0.7	0	5	0	108
Spinach	1 c/250 ml	40	6	Tr	5	245	4	1,474	18	0	126
Tomatoes, canned	1 c/250 ml	50	10	Tr	2	62	1.2	145	41	0	391
Tomato, raw	1 med.	25	6	Tr	1	9	0.6	139	28	0	10
Tomato juice	1 c/250 ml	40	10	Tr	2	22	1.6	136	29	0	881
Bread, Cereal, Rice, and Pasta Group											
Bagel	1 med.	200	43	2	7	29	1.8	0	0	0	245
Bread, white enriched	1 slice	70	13	1	2	21	0.6	Tr	Tr	0	129
Bread, whole-wheat	1 slice	65	14	1	3	24	0.8	0	Tr	0	180
Bread, pumpernickel	1 slice	80	17	Tr	3	27	0.8	0	0	0	177
Corn flakes, fortified (25% RDA)	1 c/250 ml	95	21	Tr	2	V	V	V	13	0	V
Crackers, saltines	4 crackers	50	8	1	1	2	0.5	0	0	0	165
English muffin, plain, enriched	1 muffin	140	25	1	5	96	1.7	0	0	0	378
Egg noodles, enriched	1 c/250 ml	200	37	2	7	16	1.4	110	0	50	3
Granola cereal w/ raisins and nuts	⅓ c	125	38	5	3	18	0.9	2	0	0	58
Oatmeal, instant (flavored)	1 packet	160	26	2	5	168	6.7	460	0	0	254
Pasta, enriched (macaroni, cooked, etc.)	1 c/250 ml	190	39	1	7	14	1.4	0	0	0	1

Grains (continued)

Food	Amount										
Pita bread	1 pita	165	32	1	6	49	1.4	0	0	0	339
Rice, instant, enriched, cooked	1 c/250 ml	180	40	Tr	4	5	1.3	0	0	0	0
Rice, enriched, cooked	1 c/250 ml	185	41	Tr	4	33	1.4	0	0	0	0
Rice, puffed, whole-grain	1 c/250 ml	60	13	Tr	1	3	0.3	0	0	0	0
Wheat flakes, fortified, 25% U.S. RDA	1 c/250 ml	105	24	Tr	3	43	4.5	375	16	0	354
Wheat, puffed, whole-grain	1 c/250 ml	55	12	Tr	2	4	0.6	0	0	0	0
Wheat, shredded, whole-grain	1 lg. biscuit	90	20	1	3	11	1.2	0	0	0	3

Fats, Oils, and Sweets

Food	Amount										
Butter	1 T/15 ml	100	Tr	12	Tr	3	Tr	106	0	0	116
Cheese, cream	1 oz/28 g	100	0.2	10	2	23	0.3	124	0	31	84
Cream, heavy	1 T/15 ml	80	0.1	6	Tr	10	Tr	63	Tr	21	6
Cream, light	1 T/15 ml	30	1	3	Tr	14	Tr	44	Tr	10	6
Cream, sour	1 T/15 ml	25	1	3	Tr	14	Tr	23	Tr	5	6
Honey	1 T/15 ml	65	17	0	Tr	1	0.1	0	Tr	0	1
Margarine, regular	1 T/15 ml	100	Tr	12	Tr	3	Tr	139	0	0	132
Mayonnaise	1 T/15 ml	100	Tr	11	Tr	3	0.1	12	10	8	80
Oil, corn	1 T/15 ml	125	0	14	0	0	0	10	0	0	0
Salad dressing, Italian	1 T/15 ml	80	1	9	Tr	1	Tr	3	10	0	162
Salad dressing, Italian, low-calorie	1 T/15 ml	5	Tr	1	Tr	Tr	Tr	Tr	10	Tr	136
Sugar	1 T/12 ml	45	12	0	0	0	Tr	0	0	0	Tr

Combinations/Miscellaneous

Food	Amount										
Chili with beans	1 c, canned	340	30	16	19	82	4.3	15	8	28	1,354
Doughnuts, glazed	1 doughnut	235	22	13	4	17	1.4	Tr	0	21	222
Pierogies	3 pierogies	180	34	2	6	0	0	0	0	15	340
Pizza, cheese	1 slice	290	22	9	15	220	1.6	106	2	56	699
Popcorn, plain	1 c/250 ml	25	5	Tr	1	1	0.2	0	0	0	0
Taco	1 taco	195	18	11	9	109	1.2	57	1	21	456
Veggie burger (made w/ brown rice, oats, mushrooms, mozzarella cheese)	1 burger	140	Tr	2.5	8	Tr	2	Tr	10	0	180

Note: All fruits and vegetables fresh unless noted. Vegetables fresh cooked unless noted. Metric equivalents are approximate.

Key: [a]Made from concentrate. c = cup. T = Tablespoon (Tbsp.). Tr—Nutrient present in trace amounts. V—Varies by brand; consult label. Information about nutrients in other foods can be found on the "Nutrition Facts" labels on food packages.

Nutrient Guidelines—RDIs and DRVs

The Food and Drug Administration has established RDIs—Reference Daily Intakes—for 19 vitamins and minerals. RDIs give a recommended amount for each nutrient. They serve as a general guideline for adults and children four or more years of age.

In the past, RDIs were known as U.S. Recommended Daily Allowances (U.S. RDA). The name was changed as part of new food label rules announced in 1993.

Table 1—Reference Daily Intakes (RDIs)

Nutrient	Adults and children 4 or more yrs.		Nutrient	Adults and children 4 or more yrs.	
Vitamin A	1,000	RE	Calcium	1	g
Vitamin D	400	IU	Phosphorus	1	g
Vitamin E	30	IU	Magnesium	400	mg
Vitamin C	60	mg	Iron	18	mg
Thiamine (B1)	1.5	mg	Zinc	15	mg
Riboflavin (B2)	1.7	mg	Iodine	150	mcg
Niacin	20	mg	Copper	2	mg
Vitamin B6	2	mg			
Folate	0.4	mg	RE	= Retinol Equivalent	
Vitamin B12	6	mcg	IU	= International Unit	
Biotin	0.3	mg	g	= gram	
Pantothenic acid	10	mg	mg	= milligram ($\frac{1}{1000}$ g)	
			mcg	= microgram ($\frac{1}{1,000,000}$ g)	

DRVs, or Daily Reference Values, were also established by the Food and Drug Administration in 1993. They give guidelines for nutrients not included in the RDIs.

For some nutrients, the amount recommended for good health depends on the number of calories a person consumes each day. The DRVs for these nutrients are based on a daily intake of 2,000 calories.

The DRVs for some nutrients—total fat, saturated fat, cholesterol, and sodium—are stated as an upper limit. For good health, the goal is to stay under the DRV for these nutrients.

You will not see the terms RDI or DRV on food labels. Instead, both are referred to simply as "Daily Value."

Table 2—Daily Reference Values (DRV)

Nutrient	Adults and children 4 or more yrs.			Nutrient	Adults and children 4 or more yrs.	
Total Fat	Less than	65	g*	Total carbohydrate	300	g*
Saturated Fat	Less than	20	g*	Fiber	25	g*
Cholesterol	Less than	300	mg	Protein	50	g*
Sodium	Less than	2,400	mg	Potassium	3,500	mg

*(Assumes an intake of 2,000 calories per day)

Glossary

Note: Numbers in parentheses indicate the chapter in which the term appears.

A

abstinence The decision not to engage in sexual activity. (19)

abuse Behavior that threatens the physical or mental health of another person; often directed by a family member against a child, spouse, or elderly family member. (17)

accessories Scarves, belts, ties, jewelry, hats, and other items that enhance an outfit. (58)

accountable Willing to accept the consequences of one's actions and words. (3)

acquaintance rape Sexual relations forced on an individual during a date. Also called *date rape*. (17)

action plan A program of behavior for achieving a particular goal. (6)

active listening Concentrating on what is said in order to understand and remember a message. (9)

active play Activities that are primarily physical and that employ large-motor skills. (24)

addiction A physical or mental dependence on continued doses of a substance. (2)

additive A substance added to food before it is sold. (42)

administration Management in institutions and public agencies. (35)

adolescence The period of life when a person grows from being a child to being an adult. (1)

adoptive family A family where one or more children not born into the family are made permanent members of that family by law. (14)

aerobics Sustained, rhythmic exercises that improve the efficiency of the heart and lungs. (39)

AIDS Acquired immunodeficiency syndrome. A disease that attacks the body's immune system. (19)

alcoholism A physical and mental dependence on alcohol. (17)

alternative A choice or option. (5)

amino acids The chemicals that make up all proteins. (37)

analogous color scheme Two or more colors that are next to each other on the color wheel. (57)

annual percentage rate (APR) How much a finance charge is in relation to the amount of money borrowed. (31)

anorexia nervosa An eating disorder that involves an extreme urge to lose weight by starving oneself. (39)

appliance A piece of kitchen equipment run by electricity or gas. (43)

appliqué A cutout fabric decoration sewn or fused onto a different background. (66)

apprenticeship program A program in which beginning workers learn skilled trades from experienced workers, such as carpenters, electricians, and plumbers. (7)

aptitude A natural talent or ability. (7)

architect A person who designs buildings and homes. (75)

arcing Sparks that can damage a microwave oven and start a fire. (49)

assertiveness The ability to make decisions and carry them out with confidence. (10)

attitudes Thoughts and judgments people have about the world around them. (1)

automated teller machine (ATM) A computer that allows bank customers to perform banking transactions on their own. (29)

B

backstitch To sew in reverse by using the reverse lever on a sewing machine. (65)

backup plan An alternative course of action for doing something if the original plan does not work out. (27)

bait and switch Advertising that is used to draw a buyer into a store under false pretenses. (32)

balance When objects are arranged in an even, pleasing way on either side of an imaginary line. (71)

barter To trade resources with someone else. (27)

basal metabolism The minimal amount of energy required to maintain the automatic functions of the body. (39)

beat To mix ingredients vigorously so that air is introduced into them. (47)

Better Business Bureau (BBB) An organization of businesses that promise to follow fair business standards, which helps resolve consumer complaints. (34)

bias The line diagonal to the lengthwise and crosswise grains of a fabric. (64)

blend A yarn made from two or more different fibers. (61)

blended family A husband and a wife, at least one of whom has at least one child from a previous relationship. (14)

blueprint An architect's plan or mechanical drawing. (75)

bobbin A small spool that holds the bottom thread in a sewing machine. (63)

body language A person's posture, facial expressions, gestures, and way of moving. (9)

boil To heat a liquid at a high temperature so that bubbles rise continuously to the surface and break. (48)

boycott A strategy in which consumers organize to refuse to buy a company's product. (34)

braise To brown a food in a small amount of fat, then cook it slowly in a small amount of simmering liquid until tender. (48)

broil To cook food directly over or under a glowing heat source. (48)

budget A plan for spending and saving money. (30)

buffet A style of meal service in which plates, flatware, and food are arranged on a serving table, from which diners serve themselves. (54)

bulimia An eating disorder that involves bouts of extreme overeating followed by attempts to get rid of the food eaten. (39)

buyer A person who connects designers and garment makers with the stores where clothing is sold. (68)

C

calorie A unit of heat energy; the amount of energy a food provides. (37)

capital The money needed to start and run a business. (35)

carbohydrates The nutrients that provide the body with ready energy. (37)

carbon monoxide detector A device that sounds an alarm when a dangerous level of carbon monoxide is reached. (73)

caregiver A person who takes responsibility for raising children on a long-term or short-term basis. (21)

casserole A dish which can be used for both cooking and serving. (48)

chamber of commerce An organization that represents small businesses in a town or city. (34)

character Moral strength and integrity. (3)

checking account An account that holds your money and allows you to pay for things by writing a check rather than using cash. (30)

childproofing Making safe for children. (23)

child support In the case of a divorce, the amount of money that the court orders a parent to pay to help support his or her children. (16)

cholesterol A white, waxlike substance that plays a part in transporting and digesting fat. (37)

chop To cut into small, irregular pieces. (47)

citizen A member of a community, such as a school, city, or nation. (12)

classic A style that stays popular for a long time. (59)

client A person who uses the services of a helping professional. (20)

clique A small, exclusive group of people within a peer group. (18)

coagulate To change from a liquid state to a thickened mass. (52)

codependency A tendency to allow someone else's problem to control your behavior. (17)

commitment A state of obligation two people have to each other, and a dedication to making a relationship work. (19)

communication The sending and receiving of messages between people. (9)

community resources People, facilities, and organizations that help you enjoy life, improve your skills, solve your problems, and achieve your goals. (27)

competence The qualities and skills needed to perform a task or participate fully in an activity. (6)

complementary color scheme A scheme that uses colors that are direct opposites on the color wheel, such as blue and orange. (57)

compound interest Money a person earns on a bank deposit plus previous interest. (30)

compromise A way of solving a problem in which each person gives up something in order to reach an agreement that satisfies both of them. (8)

concentrate A juice product from which most of the water has been removed. (51)

condominium One of a group of apartments or town houses that people own rather than rent. (70)

confidence Belief in yourself and your abilities. (6)

confidentiality Privacy. (17)

conflict A struggle between people who disagree. (11)

conform To go along with current custom. (56)

conscience The inner voice that tells a person what is morally right. (3)

conserve To save or use carefully. (27)

construction The building of homes and other buildings. (75)

consumer A person who buys and uses products and services. (32)

consumer action panels (CAPs) Groups formed by industries to handle consumer complaints. (34)

contracting Making an agreement with another person about how a goal will be achieved. (6)

cooperation The willingness and the ability to work with others. (8)

cooperative play The social development skill in which preschool children seek out play groups of three or four children. (22)

co-sign To agree to be responsible for loan payments if the other party fails to make them. (31)

cost per wearing The total of the purchase price of a garment and the cost of cleaning it, divided by the number of wearings. (59)

cream To beat shortening or another fat with sugar until the mixture is light and fluffy. (47)

credit An arrangement in which someone receives money, merchandise, or a service now and promises to pay for it later. (31)

credit application A form asking for details about an applicant's job, bank accounts, and past credit history. (31)

credit limit A maximum total that can be charged. (31)

creditor A bank, business, or individual to whom money is owed. (31)

crew A group of people working together to produce something. (75)

crush An intense, usually short-lived feeling of fascination for someone who does not return the feeling. (19)

custody The legal responsibility for housing and caring for children. (16)

customary system The standard system of measurement in the United States, which measures in teaspoons, tablespoons, cups, pints, quarts, ounces, and pounds. (46)

cut A section or part of a meat carcass. (53)

cut in To mix a solid fat, such as shortening, with dry ingredients using a cutting motion. (47)

D

daily value A reference amount for a particular nutrient based on the recommendations of health experts. (42)

danger zone The range of temperatures in which bacteria grow most rapidly—between 60° and 125°F (16° and 52°C). (44)

dart A triangular fold of fabric stitched to a point to shape the fabric to body curves. (65)

date rape Sexual relations forced on an individual during a date. Also called *acquaintance rape*. (17)

deadline The time or date by which a task must be completed. (28)

decision-making process A procedure that can be followed when a person has to choose among different options. (5)

defensive driving Paying attention at all times to pedestrians, cyclists, and other drivers. (2)

dehydrated Having had all the liquid removed. (52)

depression An emotional disorder characterized by prolonged periods of sadness, hopelessness, lack of energy, and inability to enjoy life. (17)

designer A person who creates new styles. (56)

detergent A cleaning agent made from chemicals that removes soil and holds it in suspension in water. (60)

developmental tasks The skills and abilities that children master during each stage of their development. (22)

Dietary Guidelines for Americans Guidelines developed by the U.S. government that offer a number of recommendations for improving eating habits. (38)

dietitian A professional who is educated in food and nutrition and their relationship to health and fitness. (26)

directional cutting Cutting with the grain of the fabric. (65)

directional stitching Stitching with the grain of the fabric. (65)

direct mail ad An advertisement that is delivered directly to consumers' homes. (32)

discrimination Differences in treatment that are based on prejudice rather than individual merit. (8)

distract To lead children away from something they should not do by creating interest in another activity. (24)

dovetail To overlap activities in order to save time. (28)

dress code A set of rules describing required or appropriate clothes. (56)

dry-clean To clean fabrics with special chemicals rather than detergents or soap and water. (60)

dyeing The process of using a substance to change the natural color of a fiber, yarn, or fabric. (61)

ease The extra room a pattern allows for clothing to fit comfortably. (64)

eating disorder Extreme eating behavior that can lead to serious health problems and even death. (39)

electronic funds transfer The method of moving money from one bank account to another with the use of computers. (29)

emotional maturity Fully developed emotions, or feelings, and the ability to handle them well. (25)

emotional support Words and actions that reassure others and share positive feelings. (15)

empathy Understanding someone else's feelings and point of view. (3)

emphasis When one object receives more attention than other objects in the room. (71)

end-of-season sale A sale that is held to clear out merchandise to make room for the next season's styles. (59)

energy Usable power or the resources for producing usable power. (74)

enriched Processed foods, especially grain products, in which nutrients lost in processing have been replaced. (38)

entrée Main dish. (41)

entrepreneur A person who starts and manages his or her own business. (7)

entry-level job A job for which little or no experience is needed. (20)

environment The circumstances, objects, people, and conditions that surround a person. (1)

equivalent The same amount expressed in a different way using a different unit of measurement. (46)

etiquette Accepted rules of behavior in a culture. (54)

evaluate To analyze the consequences of an action or a decision by studying it carefully. (5)

expectations The wants and needs that each person believes a relationship will fulfill. (8)

expenses The items that you spend your money on. (30)

expiration date The last day a product is considered fresh. (42)

extended family A family group consisting of parents, children, and other close relatives. (14)

eye contact Direct visual contact with another person's eyes. (9)

eye-hand coordination The ability of the eyes and the hand and arm muscles to work together to make complex movements. (22)

fabric Material, or cloth, made from yarn. (61)

facilitate To help bring about play without controlling what a child does. (24)

facing An extra piece of fabric sewn on the outside and turned to the inside to finish an edge. (59)

fad A fashion that is popular for a short time. (59)

fad diet A diet that promises quick and easy weight loss. (39)

family style A style of meal service in which the food is brought to the table in bowls and on serving platters, which are passed from person to person until everyone is served. (54)

fashion center A building that houses the sales offices of garment manufacturers. (68)

fashion coordinator A person who develops advertising themes and plans fashion events to bring people into a store. (68)

fats Nutrients that are the most concentrated sources of energy, which are needed by the body to transport and store other nutrients and to help regulate temperature and growth. (37)

fat-soluble vitamins Vitamins that travel through the bloodstream in droplets of fat, such as vitamins A, D, E, and K. (37)

fax An exact copy, or facsimile, of text or pictures that is sent over phone lines. (29)

feedback Two-way communication in which a listener lets a speaker know that he or she is trying to understand the message being delivered. (9)

feed dogs Two small rows of metal teeth on a sewing machine that advance the fabric evenly for each stitch. (63)

fetus An unborn child. (25)

fiber An indigestible threadlike cell that helps to move food through the digestive system; *also,* the tiny strands of a fabric that, when twisted together, make up yarns. (37, 61)

figure type Size category determined by height and body proportion. (62)

finance charge An addition to the purchase price of an item bought on credit that is the cost of using the creditor's money. (31)

financial stability The ability to meet everyday living costs. (25)

finish A substance added to a fabric to change the appearance, feel, or performance of the fabric. (61)

first aid Emergency care or treatment given right away to an ill or injured person. (23)

fitness The ability to meet the demands of day-to-day life. (39)

fixed goal A goal that can be met only at a certain time. (4)

flatware A knife, a fork, and a teaspoon. (54)

flexible goal A goal that has no definite time limit in which it needs to be accomplished. (4)

floor plan An illustration of the arrangement of furniture, structural elements, and design elements in a room or home. (71)

fold To gently add an air-filled ingredient to a mixture by using a spoon or a rubber scraper. (47)

food-borne illness An illness caused by eating food that is contaminated with harmful bacteria. (44)

Food Guide Pyramid A guide developed by nutritionists that places food groups in a pyramid shape according to the amount of food needed each day from each group. (38)

formal clothing Clothes worn for dressy occasions, such as suits and ties, tuxedos, dresses, or gowns. (56)

fortified A food product to which additional nutrients have been added. (38)

foster family A family that assumes temporary legal responsibility for one or more children. (14)

G

garment industry The many companies involved in designing and manufacturing clothing. (56)

gathers Small, soft folds of fabric created by sliding the fabric along two parallel rows of matching basting. (65)

generic product A product that has a plain package and is less expensive than a national or store brand. (42)

gluten An elastic, protein substance found in wheat flour. (50)

grace period A period of time in which borrowed money can be repaid without incurring a finance charge. (31)

grain The direction in which the threads run in a fabric. (64)

grate To reduce a food into very small particles by rubbing the food against the small holes of a grater. (47)

H

Heimlich maneuver Action taken to aid a person who is choking, in which abdominal pressure is used to force the object that is interfering with breathing from the throat. (23)

hem The bottom edge of fabric that is turned up and sewn to the wrong side of the garment. (59)

heredity The set of characteristics that a person inherits from parents and ancestors. (1)

hidden costs The expenses of time, energy, and money not included in the purchase price of an item. (33)

homogenized Milk that has had its creamy fats blended into the liquid. (52)

hormones Chemicals released in the body that trigger physical changes. (1)

hue A specific color name. (57)

human resources Personal resources, such as knowledge, skills, imagination, energy, time, family, and friends. (27)

hunger The body's physical signal that it is short of energy and needs food. (36)

hydroelectric power Electricity generated by the force of falling water. (74)

hygiene A person's level of cleanliness. (2)

I

illusion An image that fools the eye. (57)

image ad An advertisement that attempts to associate a product with a popular image or a positive emotion so that people will want to try it. (32)

"I" messages A means of communicating in which a person says how he or she feels about something, rather than criticizing someone else. (9)

immunizations Vaccines developed to prevent specific diseases, such as polio, diphtheria, and measles. (23)

improvise To come up with new ideas when a plan or part of a plan doesn't work out. (27)

impulse buying Purchasing something that you did not intend to buy. (33)

inclusion The practice of placing children who have disabilities with those who do not together in classrooms for all or part of the school day. (22)

income The money you take in and have available to spend. (30)

individuality The unique way of being and expressing yourself that makes you different from others. (56)

infomercial A program that is usually devoted to selling one product and includes product demonstrations and ordering information. (32)

information ad An advertisement that provides information about a specific product or service, highlighting specific information such as the product's size, color, price, and special features. (32)

informational interview A meeting in which a person can ask questions and receive advice about a career. (7)

ingredient Any one of the individual food items needed to make a recipe. (41)

inseam measurement The length of the pants leg from the bottom to the seam where the two legs meet. (59)

insulation Material that is sandwiched between the inside and outside walls or placed above the ceiling to prevent heat loss in winter and heat gain in summer. (74)

intensity The brightness or dullness of a color. (57)

interest A payment in exchange for the right to use a person's or an institution's money. (30)

interfacing A lightweight, woven or nonwoven fabric that is placed between layers of garment fabric to prevent stretching and to add extra body and shape. (65)

Internet An international network of computers. (29)

inventory The amount of each product that is in stock at any one time. (55)

ironing Sliding a hot iron over fabric to smooth out wrinkles. (60)

J

jealousy The feeling that the person you care about is more interested in someone or something else than in you. (19)

joint custody Responsibility for children that is shared between the mother and the father after divorce. (16)

K

knead To use the heels of your hand to press dough down and away from your body. (50)

L

lactose intolerant Unable to digest lactose, the form of sugar that is found in milk. (40)

large-motor skills Control over the large muscles of the body, such as those in the arms and the legs. (22)

launching stage When children leave home to support themselves and develop own lifestyle. (16)

layout A diagram included in sewing instructions that shows how to place the pattern pieces on fabric. (64)

lease (verb) To rent; (noun) A legal contract between a renter and a property owner, who is usually called the landlord. (31, 70)

legumes Dry beans and peas. (38)

lifelong learning Education and training that continue throughout life. (7)

lockstitch A sewing machine stitch that uses a thread above the fabric to join the bobbin thread coming from below the fabric. (63)

long-term goal Something a person plans to accomplish sometime in the future, perhaps in six months, a year, or longer. (4)

looper Part of a serger that performs the same way a bobbin does in a conventional sewing machine. (63)

loyalty Faithfulness to others. (18)

M

malnourished Impaired in health, growth, or functioning because of inadequate nutrient intake. (40)

manufactured fiber Fiber formed completely or in part by chemicals. (61)

marbling Fine streaks and flecks of fat within the lean area of meat. (53)

markdown A reduced-price item. (59)

material resources Physical objects, such as possessions and money, that a person can use to accomplish goals. (27)

maturity Responsible, adultlike behavior and attitudes. (3)

meal patterns Daily routines for eating. (40)

media The means of communication by which ads are broadcast or displayed, such as television, magazines, and direct mail. (32)

mediation Means of settling a conflict in which an unbiased third party helps to settle differences. (11)

mentor Someone who acts as a teacher and a guide. (13)

menu The list of foods that a restaurant offers. (41)

metric system The measurement system used in most of the world, which measures in grams and liters. (46)

microwave A type of energy wave, similar to a radio wave, that operates at a very high frequency. (49)

mildew A fungus that may grow on damp fabric, causing stains that appear as small, black spots. (60)

mince To chop food until the pieces are as small as they can be made. (47)

minerals Simple substances that form part of many tissues and are needed to keep body processes operating smoothly. (37)

modeling Shaping one's behavior after that of another person. (6)

moderate Avoiding extreme amounts. (38)

money order A piece of paper that is sold in banks, post offices, and some stores and that can be used like a check. (30)

monochromatic color scheme A scheme that uses tints and shades of only one color. (57)

morality An understanding about what is right and what is wrong. (22)

mortgage A long-term loan that people take out when they buy a home. (70)

multisized pattern A pattern that has three or more separate cutting lines for different pattern sizes on each pattern piece. (62)

N

national brand A product sold across the country. (42)

natural fiber Fiber that comes from plants or the hair of animals. (61)

natural resources Things found in nature that people can use, such as air, water, soil, plants, animals, minerals, and sources of mechanical energy. (27)

neglect When a parent fails to meet a child's basic needs. (17)

negotiation The use of compromise to reach an agreement. (11)

neighborhood crime watch A group of neighbors who band together to look out for each other's safety and property. (69)

networking Making contacts with others to exchange job information. (13)

nonrenewable resources Substances that cannot be replaced once they have been used. (74)

nonverbal Without words. (9)

notions Sewing supplies—including thread, zippers, buttons, and trimmings—needed to complete a project. (62)

nuclear family A husband and a wife and their children. (14)

nurture To promote development in all areas by meeting needs throughout a lifetime. (14)

nutrient density The relationship between the number of calories a food has and the amount and types of nutrients it provides. (38)

nutrients The chemicals found in food that help the body work properly. (37)

nutrition The way that your body uses food. (36)

O

obese Weighing at least 20 percent or more above the healthy weight recommended. (39)

objective Able to see the facts of a situation without becoming emotionally involved. (20)

object permanence The concept in which an infant learns that people or things exist even when they are gone from sight. (22)

organically grown Produced without the use of manufactured chemicals. (42)

P

parallel play Behavior in which toddlers play alongside one other, rather than together. (22)

paraprofessional A worker who is trained to assist a professional. (20)

pare To cut away the skin of a fruit or vegetable. (47)

parenting The responsibility of caring for a child in order to promote the child's development. (21)

parliamentary procedure A democratic method for allowing people to voice their opinions in order to reach a majority decision. (12)

pasteurized Liquid milk that has been heated and cooled to kill harmful germs. (52)

pattern A set of written directions and printed, paper pieces showing how to put a sewing project together. (62)

pattern catalog A book that shows all the patterns available from one company. (62)

pattern maker A skilled worker who makes a pattern from the designer's original sample. (68)

peak usage period The time when the most energy is consumed. (74)

pediatrician A physician who cares for children. (26)

peel To remove the skin of fruits and vegetables. (46)

peer A person your own age. (1)

peer mediation A process in which specially trained students help other students resolve conflicts peacefully. (11)

peer pressure Influence from friends and people your age to act in a certain way. (10)

perishable Tending to spoil easily. (43)

personal development Working toward one's potential. (1)

personal inventory A review of your skills and interests. (20)

personality The combination of characteristics and actions that makes you different from every other person. (1)

pilot light A thin stream of gas that burns constantly and is used to light a gas burner on a range. (73)

place setting The arrangement of the tableware that each diner will need for a meal. (54)

poach To cook whole foods in a small amount of simmering liquid so that they keep their original shape. (48)

point-of-sale terminal A machine that allows a person to use an ATM card instead of cash to pay for groceries or other merchandise. (29)

pollution The introduction of dirt and poison into the environment. (27)

positive reinforcement A reward for achievement. (6)

potential The capability of becoming something more than you are right now. (1)

prejudice Bias against an individual or group. (8)

premature Born before development is complete. (25)

prenatal care Care for the mother and baby before birth. (25)

preservative A substance added to food to keep it fresh and tasty longer. (42)

pressing Lifting an iron and setting it down on fabric, not sliding it back and forth. (60)

pretreatment The application of stain-removal techniques before laundering a garment. (60)

preventive maintenance Making sure that structures and equipment in the home are running properly. (72)

principal The amount of money in a bank account. (30)

prioritize To decide which needs and wants are more important than others. (4)

processed Food that has been changed from its raw form before being sold. (37)

processed meat Meat—such as hot dogs, bacon, and luncheon meat—that has been seasoned, smoked, or prepared in some way before it is brought to the store. (53)

procrastinate To put things off. (28)

produce A term used to describe fresh fruits and vegetables. (51)

proportion The way that one part of a design relates in size, shape, or space to another part of the whole. (71)

proteins Nutrients that are necessary for building and repairing body tissues; the basis of all the body's cells. (37)

public housing Housing that is paid for, in part or in full, by the government. (70)

pull date The last day a product may be sold. (42)

puree To mash food until it is smooth. (47)

Q

quick bread A bread that uses baking soda or baking powder to rise. (50)

quiet play Activities that engage the mind and small-motor skills and do not call for much movement. (24)

R

rape Sexual relations forced on someone. (17)

recall A call for an unsafe product to be returned to the maker to be fixed or destroyed. (34)

recipe Detailed instructions for preparing particular foods. (41)

reciprocity Giving and getting in return. (18)

recycle To find a new use for a garment. (67)

redesign To change a garment so that it is more in fashion or has an exciting, new look. (67)

redress The right to have a wrong corrected. (34)

reference A written report about someone's work from his or her previous employer. (26)

reflex An automatic, involuntary response. (22)

refusal skills Techniques to resist negative pressures effectively. (10)

rehearsing Practicing, or learning by doing an activity over and over. (6)

relationships The connections a person has with other people. (8)

resource Something that a person needs in order to accomplish a goal. (4)

responsible Reliable and accountable for one's actions or behavior. (3)

résumé A written summary of your work experience, education, and interests, which you give to prospective employers. (20)

retrain To learn new skills. (13)

return policy A store's rules for returning or exchanging merchandise. (34)

rhythm The regular repetition of line or shape. (71)

ribbing A stretchy, knit band able to go back to its original shape after it's been stretched. (66)

role model A person who sets an example for others. (12)

roles The parts you play when you interact with others. (8)

rotate To turn a dish a quarter- or a half-turn in a microwave oven to allow microwaves to penetrate food on all sides. (49)

rotation A system in which older supplies are used before newer ones. (43)

routine A set sequence of events. (72)

rural Regions that are primarily countryside. (69)

R-value Measurement of an insulation's ability to resist heat loss or gain. (74)

S

sanitation Storing, washing, and cooking food properly—as well as keeping the kitchen, appliances, tools, and yourself clean—in order to prevent the growth of harmful bacteria. (44)

sauté To cook small pieces of food in a small amount of fat over low to medium heat. (48)

savings account An account that holds the money you deposit and pays you interest on it. (30)

scale drawing A drawing in which the relative sizes of objects are the same as the relative sizes of those objects in the actual space. (71)

seam The line of stitching that joins the pieces of a garment together. (59)

seam allowance The fabric between the line for cutting and the line for stitching. (64)

seasonal More plentiful at certain times of the year. (51)

seconds Items that are slightly imperfect or out of production. (33)

security deposit An amount of money paid to a landlord by a renter to guard against financial loss. (70)

self-concept How you define who you are. (1)

self-control A person's ability to use sense to overrule emotions. (19)

self-esteem The value, or importance, you place on yourself. (1)

selvage The finished edge of a fabric. (64)

sensory toys Objects that stimulate the senses with different textures, shapes, sounds, and colors. (24)

sequence The order in which tasks are to be done. (45)

serger A high-speed, overlock sewing machine that trims, sews, and overcasts in one step. (63)

sew-through button A button that has two or four holes through it and no shank. (66)

sexual harassment Unwanted or unwelcome sexual advances. (19)

sexually transmitted disease (STD) An illness transmitted from one person to another as a result of sexual contact. (19)

shade A darker value of a color, created by adding black to the color. (57)

shank button Button that has a built-in shank, or loop, on the back but no holes through it. (66)

shield To cover parts of food with aluminum foil to protect them from overcooking in a microwave oven. (49)

shoplifting Stealing items that are displayed for sale in a store. (34)

short-term goal Something that a person wants to accomplish soon. (4)

sibling A brother or sister. (14)

simmer To heat liquid to a temperature just below the boiling point. (48)

simple interest Interest that is paid only on the principal. (30)

size range The size category a person fits into. (59)

small-claims court Proceedings in which consumers present their claims and a judge decides the case. (34)

small-motor skills Control over the small muscles of the body, such as those in the hands and the fingers. (22)

smoke detector Battery-operated device that sounds an alarm when it senses smoke. (73)

snag A loop of yarn that gets pulled out of a knit. (60)

sociability The quality of being friendly and enjoying other people's company. (13)

special purchase An item a store has bought for a lower-than-usual price. (59)

spoilage Damage caused by bacteria, yeasts, or molds that make food look or smell bad. (51)

standing time The time allowed for food to continue to cook after the microwave oven is turned off. (49)

staples Basic food items used regularly. (42)

status Position within a group. (56)

staystitching Sewing a row of regular machine stitches through one layer of fabric in order to prevent stretching. (65)

steamer A metal basket that allows steam to pass through it as it holds food above boiling water. (48)

stereotype A set of traits that every person in a particular group is assumed to have. (8)

stir-fry To stir and cook small pieces of food very quickly at high heat in very little fat. (48)

store brand A product made especially for the store or the chain that sells it. (42)

stress A body's response to the demands being put on it. (2)

substance abuse The use of illegal drugs or the misuse of legal drugs. (17)

suburban Mostly residential regions surrounding a city. (69)

support system The network of individuals and groups that people can turn to for help. (15)

T

table service Restaurant service in which servers take the order at the table, bring the food, and clean up after the meal. (54)

task rotation Passing a job from one family member to another. (72)

teamwork Working together to reach a common goal. (8)

technology The application of scientific methods to help people meet their needs and wants. (29)

texture The way the surface of a fabric looks and feels. (57)

time-out A way of handling misbehavior that requires a child to sit quietly for a period of time, usually about a minute for each year of age. (23)

tint A lighter value of a color, created by adding white to the color. (57)

tipping Giving extra money to servers in appreciation of good service. (54)

tolerance Accepting and respecting other people's customs and beliefs. (8)

trade association A professional group that provides information to, and supports the interests of, the people who work in a particular field. (75)

traffic pattern The most direct routes that people use to move through the space in a room. (71)

traumatic Causing severe emotional shock that needs time to heal. (16)

tuck A fold of fabric, stitched from top to bottom, that is used to shape a garment. (65)

U

understitching A row of stitches used to stitch a facing and a seam allowance together. (65)

Underwriter's Laboratory An agency that tests electrical products for safety. (33)

unit construction Preparation of separate garment pieces first, before assembling them in a specific order. (65)

unit price The price of an item per ounce, pound, or other accepted unit of measure. (42)

unity A feeling that all objects in a room look as if they belong together. (71)

urban Located in a city. (69)

utensils Kitchen tools and containers, such as knives, measuring cups, pots, and pans. (43)

V

value The lightness or darkness of a color. (57)

values A person's beliefs, feelings, and ideas about what is important. (3)

vandalism Deliberately destroying or damaging the property of others. (34)

variable Any condition that determines how long a food needs to be cooked in a microwave oven and at what power level. (49)

variety A combination of different but compatible styles and materials. (71)

variety meat Organ meats, such as liver, heart, or kidney. (53)

verbal Using words. (9)

versatile Having many different uses. (58)

view A variation on a sewing pattern design. (62)

visualize To imagine yourself doing a task or activity that you want to learn. (6)

vitamins Nutrients that help the body stay healthy, function properly, and process other nutrients. (37)

volume The amount of space taken up by an ingredient. (46)

volunteer Someone who puts caring into action by offering his or her services free of charge. (12)

W

wardrobe The clothes that you own. (58)

warranty A written statement from a manufacturer or retailer promising to repair or replace a defective product or to refund the customer's money. (33)

water-soluble vitamins Vitamins that are easily absorbed and can move through the body dissolved in water. (37)

weather stripping Material used to fill gaps between the door and the door frame and around windows to prevent air leaks. (74)

wellness An overall state of well-being or total health. (2)

work center An organized area where specific kitchen tasks can be performed. (43)

work plan An action plan that includes a list of all the tasks a person has to do and how long each task will take. (45)

work triangle The paths connecting the refrigerator, sink, and range. (43)

Y

yarn Strands that are formed when fibers are twisted together. (61)

yeast bread Bread that rises through the action of a tiny plant called yeast. (50)

yield The number of servings or the amount a recipe makes. (41)

Glossary/Glosario

Note: Numbers in parentheses indicate the chapter in which the term appears.

A

abstinence/abstinencia La decisión de no tomar parte en actividades sexuales. (19)

abuse/abuso Conducta que amenaza la salud física o mental de una persona: usualmente dirigido en contra de un niño, un esposo, o un anciano por otro miembro de la familia. (17)

accessories/accesorios Pañuelos, cinturones, corbatas, alhajas, sombreros y otros artículos que realzan un traje.

accountable/responsable Dispuesto a aceptar las consecuencias de sus propias acciones y palabras. (3)

acquaintance rape/violación por un conocido Ser forzado a tener relaciones sexuales durante una cita. También se llama *violación durante una cita*. (17)

action plan/plan de acción Un programa de conducta para alcanzar una meta en particular. (6)

active listening/escuchar atentamente Concentrarse en lo que dice otra persona para poder comprender y recordar un mensaje. (9)

active play/juego activo Actividades que son principalmente físicas y emplean las habilidades motoras de los músculos grandes (24)

addiction/adicción Una dependencia física o mental del uso continuo de dosis de una sustancia. (2)

additive/aditivo Una sustancia que se le añade a los alimentos antes de venderlos. (42)

adolescence/adolescencia El período de la vida en que una persona cambia de niño en adulto. (1)

adoptive family/familia adoptiva Una familia en la que uno o más niños se convierten en miembros permanentes de ella por medios legales. (14)

aerobics/ejercicio aeróbico Ejercicio rítmico prolongado para aumentar la eficiencia del corazón y los pulmones. (39)

AIDS/SIDA Síndrome de inmunodeficiencia adquirida. Una enfermedad que ataca el sistema inmunológico del cuerpo. (19)

alcoholism/alcoholismo La dependencia del alcohol. (17)

alternative/alternativa Una selección u opción. (5)

amino acids/aminoácidos Las sustancias químicas que componen todas las proteínas. (37)

analogous color scheme/patrón de colores análogos Dos o más colores adyacentes en la rueda de colores. (57)

annual percentage rate (APR)/tasa de interés anual La cantidad cobrada como cargos de financiamiento en relación a la cantidad del préstamo. (31)

anorexia nervosa/anorexia nerviosa Un trastorno alimenticio que produce un deseo extremado de privarse de comida para perder peso. (39)

appliance/aparato de cocina Cualquier aparato de cocina que funciona por medio de electricidad o gas. También se puede llamar electrodoméstico. (43)

appliqué/aplicación Un pedazo de tela cortada que se cose o se pega a la tela de fondo para decorarla. (66)

apprenticeship program/programa de aprendizaje Un programa en el que los trabajadores principiantes aprenden oficios de trabajadores con experiencia, tales como carpinteros, electricistas, y plomeros. (7)

aptitude/aptitud Un talento o habilidad nata. (7)

architect/arquitecto Una persona que diseña edificios y casas. (75)

arcing/corto circuito Chispas eléctricas que pueden dañar un horno de microondas y empezar un fuego. (49)

assertiveness/firmeza La habilidad de tomar decisiones y llevarlas a cabo con confianza. (10)

attitudes/actitudes Las ideas y opiniones que tiene la gente del mundo a su alrededor. (1)

automated teller machine (ATM)/cajero automático Una computadora que le permite a los clientes de un banco realizar sus propias operaciones bancarias. (29)

B

backstitch/pespuntear Coser hacia atrás, utilizando la palanca de revés en una máquina de coser. (65)

back-up plan/plan de respaldo Una manera distinta de hacer algo si el plan original no da resultado. (27)

bait and switch/engatusar Una técnica publicitaria usada para atraer al comprador a una tienda con pretextos engañosos. (29)

balance/equilibrio El arreglo de objetos de manera atractiva y pareja a los dos lados de una línea imaginaria. (71)

barter/trocar Intercambiar recursos con otra persona. (27)

basal metabolism/metabolismo basal La cantidad mínima de energía necesaria para mantener las funciones automáticas del cuerpo. (39)

beat/batir Mezclar los ingredientes rápidamente para introducir aire en ellos. (47)

Better Business Bureau (BBB)/Agencia para el Mejoramiento del Negocio Una organización de comerciantes que prometen llevar sus negocios de manera justa, que ayuda a resolver los problemas de los consumidores. (34)

bias/biés La línea que está en diagonal a los hilos de urdimbre y de trama de una tela. (64)

blend/combinación Estambre hecho de dos o más tipos de fibras distintas. (61)

blended family/familia combinada Una familia en que por lo menos uno de los esposos tiene uno o más hijos de una relación anterior. (14)

blueprint/plano arquitectónico El dibujo o plan de un arquitecto. (75)

bobbin/bobina Un carretel pequeño que sujeta el hilo de abajo en una máquina de coser. (63)

body language/lenguaje corporal La postura, expresiones faciales, gestos, y manera de moverse de una persona. (9)

boil/hervir Calentar un líquido a una temperatura alta hasta que las burbujas suban continuamente y se rompan en la superficie. (48)

boycott/boicot Una estrategia en que los consumidores se organizan para no comprar los productos de una compañía. (34)

braise/guisar Sofreír un alimento en una cantidad pequeña de grasa y después cocinarlo en un poco de líquido hasta que esté tierno. (48)

broil/asar a la parrilla Cocinar un alimento directamente arriba o debajo de una fuente de calor encendida.

budget/presupuesto Un plan para gastar y ahorrar dinero. (30)

buffet/bufet Un estilo de servir comidas en el que los platos, cubiertos y alimentos están arreglados en una mesa de servir de la cual los comensales se sirven por sí mismos. (54)

bulimia/bulimia Un trastorno alimenticio en el cual se come exageradamente y después se trata de eliminar lo que se comió. (39)

buyer/comprador Una persona que pone a los diseñadores y fabricantes de ropa en contacto con las tiendas donde se vende la ropa. (68)

C

calorie/caloría Una unidad de energía del calor que se utiliza para medir la cantidad de energía que proporciona un alimento. (37)

capital/capital El dinero necesario para comenzar y llevar una empresa. (35)

carbohydrates/carbohidratos Los nutrientes que le dan al cuerpo energía rápida. (37)

carbon monoxide detector/detector de monóxido de carbono Un aparato que toca una alarma cuando se ha llegado a un nivel peligroso de monóxido de carbono. (73)

caregiver/cuidador Una persona que se responsabiliza por la crianza de niños a largo o a corto plazo. (21)

casserole/fuente de hornear Cazuela que se puede usar para cocinar y para servir. (48)

chamber of commerce/cámara de comercio Una organización que representa a los pequeños negocios de un pueblo o ciudad. (34)

character/carácter Fuerza moral e integridad. (3)

checking account/cuenta corriente Una cuenta que contiene el dinero de una persona y le permite escribir cheques para pagar por cosas en lugar de dinero.

childproofing/arreglar a prueba de niños Hacer un sitio seguro para los niños. (23)

child support/sustento de los hijos En caso de divorcio, la cantidad de dinero que la corte ordena a uno de los padres a pagar por el mantenimiento de sus hijos. (16)

cholesterol/colesterol Una sustancia blanca y parecida a la cera que ayuda a transportar y digerir la grasa. (37)

chop/picar Cortar en pedazos pequeños, de distintos tamaños. (47)

citizen/ciudadano Un miembro de una comunidad, tal como una escuela, ciudad o nación. (12)

classic/clásico Un estilo que se mantiene popular por mucho tiempo. (59)

client/cliente Una persona que utiliza los servicios de un profesional. (20)

clique/camarilla Un grupo pequeño de personas que se mantienen separados del resto de sus contemporáneos. (18)

coagulate/coagular Cambiar de un estado líquido a una masa espesa. (52)

codependency/codependencia La tendencia a permitir que los problemas de otra persona dominen la conducta de uno. (17)

commitment/compromiso Una obligación que existe entre dos personas, y su dedicación a que su relación tenga éxito. (19)

communication/comunicación El mandar y recibir mensajes entre personas. (9)

community resources/recursos de la comunidad Gente, instalaciones y organizaciones que te ayudan a disfrutar de la vida, mejorar tus habilidades, resolver tus problemas y lograr tus metas. (27)

competence/competencia Las cualidades y habilidades necesarias para hacer una labor o participar plenamente en una actividad. (6)

complementary color scheme/patrón de colores complementarios Un diseño que utiliza colores que están directamente opuestos en la rueda de colores, tales como el azul y el anaranjado. (57)

compound interest/interés compuesto El dinero que el banco paga por lo que uno tiene depositado, más el dinero que había pagado antes. (30)

compromise/acuerdo mutuo Un modo de resolver un problema en el cual cada persona cede algo para llegar a una solución que satisface a los dos. (8)

concentrate/concentrado Un producto hecho de jugo al que se le ha sacado la mayor parte del agua. (51)

condominium/condominio Uno de un grupo de apartamentos o casas de hilera que la gente compra en vez de alquilar. (70)

confidence/confianza Creer en sí mismo y en sus habilidades. (6)

confidentiality/confidencialidad Privacidad. (17)

conflict/conflicto Una lucha entre dos personas que no están de acuerdo. (11)

conform/ajustarse Adaptarse a las costumbres actuales. (56)

conscience/conciencia La voz interna que le dice a una persona lo que está moralmente correcto. (3)

conserve/conservar Ahorrar o usar con cuidado. (27)

construction/construcción La fabricación de casas u otros edificios. (75)

consumer/consumidor Una persona que compra y usa productos y servicios. (32)

consumer action panels (CAPs)/paneles de ayuda para el consumidor Grupos organizados por industrias para resolver los problemas de consumidores. (34)

contracting/contratar Hacer un acuerdo con otra persona sobre como lograr una meta. (6)

cooperation/cooperación La voluntad y habilidad de trabajar con otros. (8)

cooperative play/juego cooperativo La habilidad en niños preescolares de jugar en grupos de tres o cuatro, que forma parte de su desarrollo social. (22)

co-sign/co-firmar Aceptar la responsabilidad de pagar por un préstamo si la otra persona no hace los pagos. (31)

cost per wearing/costo por uso El total del costo de una prenda más el costo de limpiarla, dividido por el número de veces que se usa. (59)

cream/batir hasta que esté cremoso Mezclar manteca vegetal u otra grasa con azúcar rápidamente hasta que la mezcla esté ligera y esponjosa. (47)

credit/crédito Un arreglo bajo el cual uno recibe dinero, mercancía o un servicio ahora y promete pagar por él más adelante. (31)

credit application/solicitud de crédito Un formulario que pide detalles acerca del trabajo, cuentas de banco y antecedentes de crédito de una persona que desea que le extiendan crédito. (31)

credit limit/límite de crédito La cantidad máxima que uno puede cargar a una cuenta de crédito. (31)

creditor/acreedor Un banco, negocio o persona a quien se le debe dinero. (31)

crew/equipo Un grupo de personas trabajando juntos para producir algo. (75)

crush/enamoramiento Un sentimiento intenso de fascinación por una persona que no siente lo mismo y que dura poco tiempo. (19)

custody/custodia La responsabilidad legal de albergar y cuidar a niños. (16)

customary system/sistema de medidas estadounidense El sistema de medir tradicional en Estados Unidos, que utiliza cucharaditas, cucharadas, tazas, pintas, galones, onzas y libras. (46)

cut/corte Una sección de una res. (53)

cut in/mezclar en forma de cortes Mezclar una grasa sólida, tal como la manteca vegetal, con ingredientes secos como si se estuviese cortando con un cuchillo. (47)

D

daily value/valor diario La cantidad de un nutriente específico que los expertos en la salud recomiendan. (42)

danger zone/zona peligrosa Las temperaturas entre las cuales las bacterias crecen con mayor rapidez—entre 60° y 125°F (16° y 52°C). (44)

dart/pinza Un doblez triangular en un pedazo de tela que se cose hasta formar una punta y se usa para ajustar la tela a las curvas del cuerpo. (65)

date rape/violación durante una cita Ser forzado a tener relaciones sexuales durante una cita. También se llama *violación por un conocido.* (17)

deadline/plazo de entrega La hora o fecha en que se tiene que completar un trabajo. (28)

decision-making process/proceso para tomar decisiones Un procedimiento que se puede seguir cuando una persona tiene que escoger entre distintas opciones. (5)

defensive driving/manejar de manera defensiva Prestar atención continuamente a los peatones, ciclistas y otros choferes. (2)

dehydrated/deshidratado Que se le ha quitado todo el líquido. (52)

depression/depresión Un trastorno emocional caracterizado por largos períodos de tristeza y falta de esperanza, de energía y de habilidad para disfrutar de la vida. (17)

designer\diseñador Una persona que crea nuevos estilos. (56)

detergent/detergente Un agente limpiador hecho de sustancias químicas que quita la suciedad y la mantiene en suspensión en el agua. (60)

developmental tasks/tareas de desarrollo Las destrezas y habilidades que los niños tienen que llegar a dominar durante cada etapa de su desarrollo. (22)

Dietary Guidelines for Americans/Recomendaciones dietéticas para los estadounidenses Pautas desarrolladas por el gobierno de EE.UU. que ofrecen un número de recomendaciones para mejorar los hábitos alimenticios.

dietician/dietista Un profesional que tiene conocimientos sobre los alimentos y la nutrición y su relación a la salud y el buen estado físico. (26)

directional cutting/cortar con el hilo Cortar en la dirección del hilo de la tela. (65)

directional stitching/coser con el hilo Coser en la dirección del hilo de la tela. (65)

direct mail ad/anuncio por correo Un anuncio que se envía directamente a las casas de los consumidores. (32)

discrimination/discriminación Diferencias en el trato de personas que están basadas en prejuicio en vez de mérito personal. (8)

distract/distraer Interesar a los niños en una actividad nueva para alejarlos de algo que no deben hacer. (24)

dovetail/organizarse Hacer varias tareas a la vez para ahorrar tiempo. (28)

dress code/pautas de vestir Una serie de reglas describiendo la ropa obligatoria o adecuada. (56)

dry-clean/limpiar en seco Limpiar telas con sustancias químicas especiales en vez de agua y jabón. (60)

dyeing/teñir Usar una sustancia para cambiar el color natural de una fibra, estambre o tela. (61)

E

ease/holgura La anchura extra que tiene un patrón para permitir que una prenda de vestir quede cómoda. (64)

eating disorder/trastorno alimenticio Hábitos de alimentación exagerados que pueden llevar a graves problemas de salud y hasta la muerte. (39)

electronic funds transfer/transferencia de fondos electrónica El método de pasar dinero de una cuenta de banco a otra a través de computadoras. (29)

emotional maturity/madurez emocional Emociones o sentimientos bien desarrollados y la habilidad de controlarlos. (25)

emotional support/apoyo emocional Palabras y acciones que tranquilizan a los demás y comparten sentimientos positivos. (15)

empathy/empatía El comprender los sentimientos y el punto de vista de otra persona. (3)

emphasis/énfasis Cuando un objeto recibe más atención que los demás objetos en la habitación. (71)

end-of-season sale/venta de fin de temporada Una venta especial que se celebra para liquidar mercancía y hacer espacio para los estilos nuevos. (59)

energy/energía Poder utilizable o los recursos para producirlo. (74)

enriched/enriquecido Alimentos procesados, especialmente de fécula, a los que se le añaden los nutrientes que se perdieron al procesarlos. (38)

entrée/plato fuerte El plato principal. (41)

entrepreneur/empresario Una persona que empieza y dirige su propio negocio. (71)

entry-level job/trabajo de principiante Una posición para la cual se necesita poca o ninguna experiencia. (20)

environment/medio ambiente Las circunstancias, objetos, gente y condiciones que rodean a una persona. (1)

equivalent/equivalente La misma cantidad expresada de distinto modo por medio de distintas medidas. (46)

etiquette/educación Las reglas de conducta de una cultura. (54)

evaluate/evaluar Estudiar cuidadosamente y analizar las consecuencias de una acción o decisión. (5)

expectations/expectativas Las esperanzas que tiene una persona de que una relación le proporcionará lo que necesita y realizará sus deseos. (8)

expenses/gastos Los artículos en que gastas tu dinero. (30)

expiration date/fecha de vencimiento El último día en que un producto se considera fresco. (42)

extended family/familia extensa Un grupo familiar que consiste de padres, hijos, y otros parientes. (14)

eye contact/mirar a los ojos Contacto visual directo con otra persona. (9)

eye-hand coordination/coordinación entre la vista y los músculos motores La habilidad de los ojos y los músculos de las manos y brazos de trabajar juntos para hacer movimientos complejos. (22)

F

fabric/tela Material o tejido hecho de hilos. (61)

facilitate/facilitar Ayudar a los niños a que jueguen, sin controlar lo que hacen. (24)

facing/vuelta Un pedazo de tela que se cose por la parte de afuera de una prenda y se vira hacia adentro para terminar el borde. (59)

fad/moda pasajera Una moda que es popular por poco tiempo. (59)

fad diet/régimen de adelgazamiento rápido Una dieta que promete poder perder de peso rápida y fácilmente. (39)

family style/estilo de familia Una manera de servir las comidas en que se traen los alimentos a la mesa en fuentes que se pasan de persona a persona hasta que todos se han servido.

fashion center/centro de modas Un edificio donde están ubicadas las oficinas de ventas de fabricantes de ropa. (68)

fashion coordinator/coordinador de publicidad Una persona cuyo trabajo es idear temas publicitarios y eventos de modas para atraer al público a una tienda. (68)

fats/grasas Los nutrientes que contienen la mayor concentración de energía y que el cuerpo necesita para transportar y almacenar otros nutrientes y para regular su temperatura y crecimiento. (37)

fat-soluble vitamins/vitaminas liposolubles Vitaminas que se transportan por el torrente sanguíneo en gotitas de grasa, tales como las vitaminas A, D, E y K. (37)

fax/fax Una copia exacta o facsímil de un texto o ilustraciones que se manda a través de las líneas telefónicas. (29)

feedback/reacción Una comunicación entre dos personas en la cual el que escucha le hace saber al que habla que está tratando de entender su mensaje. (9)

feed dogs/dientes Dos filas de dientes metálicos en una máquina de coser que mueven la tela una distancia fija para que las puntadas queden parejas. (63)

fetus/feto Un niño que todavía no ha nacido. (25)

fiber/fibra Células en forma de hilo que no se pueden digerir y que ayudan a mover los alimentos a través del sistema digestivo; *también* pequeñas hebras que se tuercen juntas para formar el hilo. (37, 61)

figure type/tipo de figura Una de las categorías de tallas de ropa que son determinadas por la estatura y las proporciones del cuerpo. (62)

finance charge/cargos de financiamiento Cantidad de dinero añadida al costo de un producto comprado a crédito, por el uso del dinero del acreedor. (31)

financial stability/estabilidad económico La habilidad de cubrir los gastos de vida diarios. (25)

finish/acabado Una sustancia que se le añade a una tela para cambiar su apariencia, textura o utilidad. (61)

first aid/primeros auxilios Cuidados de emergencia que se le dan inmediatamente a una persona que está enferma o herida. (23)

fitness/salud total La habilidad de enfrentarse a las exigencias de la vida diaria. (39)

fixed goal/meta fija Una meta que se puede lograr en un momento dado. (4)

flatware/cubiertos Un cuchillo, un tenedor y una cucharita. (54)

flexible goal/meta flexible Una meta que no tiene un límite de tiempo determinado para lograrse. (4)

floor plan/plano del piso Una ilustración de la disposición de los muebles, los elementos estructurales y los elementos de diseño de una habitación o casa. (71)

fold/incorporar Añadir un ingrediente lleno de aire a una mezcla con movimientos suaves, utilizando una cuchara o espátula de goma. (47)

food-borne illness/enfermedad portada por los alimentos Una enfermedad causada por comer alimentos que están contaminados por bacterias dañinas. (44)

Food Guide Pyramid/Pirámide de los Alimentos Una guía creada por nutricionistas que coloca los distintos grupos de alimentos dentro de una pirámide para indicar la cantidad que se debe comer de cada grupo cada día. (38)

formal clothing/ropa de etiqueta Ropa que se usa en ocasiones de vestir, como un traje con corbata, esmoquin, vestido o traje de noche. (56)

fortified/enriquecido Un alimento al que se le han añadido nutrientes adicionales. (38)

foster family/familia de acogida Una familia que asume la responsabilidad legal por uno o más niños temporariamente. (14)

G

garment industry/industria del vestido Las compañías que toman parte en el diseño y la manufactura de ropa. (56)

gathers/frunces Pliegues pequeños y suaves que se hacen al deslizar la tela a lo largo de dos costuras hilvanadas paralelas. (65)

generic product/producto genérico Un producto que está empaquetado sencillamente y es más barato que una marca nacional o de una tienda. (42)

gluten/gluten Una sustancia elástica formada de proteínas que se encuentra en la harina de trigo. (50)

grace period/período de gracia Un período de tiempo en el que se puede pagar un préstamo sin tener que pagar cargos de financiamiento. (31)

grain/hilo La dirección en que van los hilos de la tela. (64)

grate/rallar Reducir un alimento a partículas muy pequeñas al restregarlo contra un rallador. (47)

H

heimlich maneuver/maniobra de Heimlich Acción que se toma para ayudar a una persona que se está asfixiando, en la cual se utiliza presión abdominal para expulsar de la garganta un objeto que no le permite respirar. (23)

hem/dobladillo El borde de la tela que se dobla y se cose al revés de la prenda. (59)

heredity/herencia El grupo de características que uno hereda de sus padres o antepasados. (1)

hidden costs/costos no aparentes Los gastos de tiempo, energía y dinero que no están incluidos en el precio de compra de un artículo. (33)

homogenized/homogeneizada Leche que tiene la grasa cremosa mezclada con el líquido. (52)

hormones/hormonas Sustancias químicas en el cuerpo que producen cambios físicos. (1)

hue/tono El nombre específico de un color. (57)

human resources/recursos humanos Recursos personales, como conocimientos, habilidades, imaginación, energía, tiempo, familia y amigos. (27)

hunger/hambre La señal física que da el cuerpo cuando le falta energía y necesita alimento. (36)

hydroelectric power/energía hidroeléctrica La electricidad que se obtiene a partir de la corriente del agua. (74)

hygiene/higiene Lo limpia que está una persona. (2)

I

illusion/ilusión Una imagen engañosa. (57)

image ad/anuncio de imagen Un anuncio que trata de asociar un producto con una imagen popular o una emoción positiva para que la gente quiera probarlo. (32)

"I" messages/mensajes sobre sí mismo Una manera de comunicarse en la cual el que habla explica sus sentimientos sobre un asunto en vez de criticar a otra persona. (9)

immunizations/inmunizaciones Vacunas hechas para prevenir enfermedades específicas, como la polio, la difteria y el sarampión. (23)

improvise/improvisar Idear algo nuevo cuando un plan o parte de un plan no da resultado. (27)

impulse buying/hacer compras impulsivas Comprar algo que uno no tenía intención de comprar. (33)

inclusion/inclusión La práctica de poner a los niños discapacitados en la misma aula que a los que no tienen problemas, durante todo o parte del día escolar. (22)

income/ingresos El dinero que tienes de entrada y que está disponible para gastar. (30)

individuality/individualidad La manera única que tienes de ser y expresarte que te hace distinto a los demás. (56)

infomercial/comercial informativo Un programa dedicado a vender un producto que incluye demostraciones e información para hacer un pedido. (32)

information ad/anuncio informativo Un anuncio que proporciona información sobre un producto o servicio específico, destacando cierta información, tal como el tamaño, color, precio o características especiales. (32)

informational interview/entrevista informativa Una cita en la cual una persona puede hacer preguntas y recibir consejos acerca de una carrera. (7)

ingredient/ingrediente Cualquiera de los alimentos individuales que son necesarios para hacer una receta. (41)

inseam measurement/entrepierna El largo de los pantalones desde los bajos hasta la costura que une las dos piernas. (59)

insulation/material aislante Material que se instala entre las paredes de adentro y afuera o sobre el techo para alejar el frío y conservar la calefacción en invierno. (74)

intensity/intensidad Lo brillante o fuerte que es un color. (57)

interest/interés Un pago que se hace a cambio del derecho de usar el dinero de una persona o institución. (30)

interfacing/entretela Una tela ligera, de telar o no, que se pone entre dos de las piezas de una prenda para evitar que se estire o para darle cuerpo o mejor forma. (65)

Internet/Internet Una red internacional de computadoras. (29)

invetory/inventario La cantidad de un producto que está almacenado en un momento dado. (55)

ironing/planchar Deslizar una plancha caliente sobre una tela para quitarle las arrugas. (60)

J

jealousy/celos El sentimiento que la persona a quien uno quiere está más interesada en otra persona. (19)

joint custody/custodia en conjunto El compartir la responsabilidad de los hijos entre los dos padres después de un divorcio. (16)

K

knead/amasar Apretar la masa con la base de las manos hacia abajo y adelante. (50)

L

lactose intolerant/intolerancia a la lactosa No poder digerir la lactosa, el tipo de azúcar que contiene la leche. (40)

large-motor skills/habilidades motoras de los músculos grandes El control de los músculos grandes del cuerpo, como los de los brazos y las piernas. (22)

layout/distribución Un diagrama que es parte de las instrucciones y que muestra cómo colocar las piezas de un patrón sobre la tela. (64)

lease/arrendar/contrato de arrendamiento (verbo) Alquilar; (sustantivo) documento legal que detalla el acuerdo entre el dueño de una propiedad y la persona que la alquila. (31, 70)

legumes/legumbres Frijoles secos. (38)

lifelong learning/aprendizaje por vida Educación y entrenamiento que continúan durante toda la vida. (7)

lockstitch/puntada de máquina Una puntada a máquina en la cual el hilo que está arriba de la tela engancha el hilo de la bobina que está debajo de la tela. (63)

long-term goal/meta a largo plazo Algo que una persona planea lograr en el futuro, en seis meses o un año o más. (4)

looper/gancho Parte de una remalladora que tiene la misma función que una bobina en una máquina de coser regular. (63)

loyalty/lealtad Serle fiel a los demás. (18)

M

malnourished/malnutrido Tener la salud, el crecimiento o el funcionamiento afectado por la falta de nutrientes adecuados. (40)

manufactured fiber/fibras artificiales Fibras que están formadas totalmente o en parte de materiales químicos. (61)

marbling/vetas de grasa Pequeñas rayas o partículas de grasa que se encuentran en la carne. (53)

markdown/saldos Mercancía a descuento. (59)

material resources/recursos materiales Los artículos, tales como las posesiones o el dinero, que una persona puede usar para lograr metas. (27)

maturity/madurez Conducta y actitudes responsables y adultas. (3)

meal patterns/pautas de comidas Las rutinas diarias de comer. (40)

media/medios de comunicación Los modos de transmitir información que se usan para emitir anuncios, tales como la televisión, las revistas y el correo. (32)

mediation/mediación Un método de resolver conflictos en el que un tercero sin interés en el asunto ayuda a solucionar el problema. (11)

mentor/mentor Alguien que actúa de maestro o guía. (13)

menu/menú La lista de platos que sirve un restaurante. (41)

metric system/sistema métrico El sistema de medidas que se usa en la mayor parte del mundo, que usa gramos y litros. (46)

microwave/microonda Un tipo de onda enérgica, similar a la onda radioeléctrica, que opera a una frecuencia muy alta. (49)

mildew/moho Un hongo que puede crecer en una tela húmeda y dejar pequeñas manchas negras. (60)

mince/picar en trozos menudos Picar un alimento en los pedazos más pequeños posibles. (47)

minerals/minerales Sustancias simples que forman parte de los tejidos del cuerpo y que son necesarias para que funcione debidamente. (37)

modeling/modelar Ajustar la conducta propia a la de otra persona. (6)

moderate/moderado Que evita las cantidades extremas. (38)

money order/giro Un documento que se vende en bancos, oficinas de correos y algunas tiendas que se puede usar como un cheque. (30)

monochromatic color scheme/patrón de color monocromo Un diseño que utiliza tintes y matices de un solo color. (57)

morality/moralidad El entendimiento que tiene alguien acerca del bien y el mal. (22)

mortgage/hipoteca Un préstamo que se saca para comprar una casa. (70)

multisized pattern/patrón para múltiples tallas Un patrón de costura en que cada pieza tiene líneas de cortar para tres o más tallas. (62)

N

national brand/marca nacional Un producto que se vende en todo el país. (42)

natural fiber/fibra natural Una fibra que proviene de plantas o el pelo de animales. (61)

natural resources/recursos naturales Cosas que provienen de la naturaleza y que la gente puede utilizar, tales como el agua, la tierra, las plantas, los animales, los minerales, y las distintas fuentes de energía. (27)

neglect/abandono El descuido por los padres de las necesidades básicas de un niño. (17)

negotiation/negociación El uso de concesiones para llegar a un acuerdo mutuo. (11)

neighborhood crime watch/vigilancia del vecindario Una agrupación de vecinos que velan mutuamente por el bienestar y la propiedad de todos. (69)

networking/interconectar Ponerse en contacto con otros para intercambiar información acerca del trabajo. (13)

nonrenewable resources/recursos no renovables Sustancias que no se pueden reemplazar una vez que se han usado. (74)

nonverbal/no verbal Sin palabras. (9)

notions/artículos de mercería Artículos pequeños—tales como hilo, cremalleras, botones y adornos—que se usan para completar una prenda. (62)

nuclear family/familia nuclear El esposo, la esposa y sus hijos. (14)

nurture/cuidar Satisfacer las necesidades de una persona para estimular su desarrollo total. (14)

nutrient density/densidad nutritiva La relación entre el número de calorías que tiene un alimento y la cantidad y tipos de nutrientes que proporciona. (38)

nutrient/nutriente Las sustancias químicas que se encuentran en los alimentos que ayudan al cuerpo a funcionar debidamente. (37)

nutrition/nutrición La manera en que el cuerpo utiliza los alimentos. (36)

O

obese/obeso Que pesa por lo menos un 20 por ciento más del peso recomendado. (39)

objective/imparcial Que puede ver la realidad de una situación sin emoción. (20)

object permanence/permanencia de objetos La comprensión por los niños pequeños que las personas y objetos continúan a existir aun cuando están fuera de vista. (22)

organically grown/cultivados orgánicamente Producido sin el uso de sustancias químicas artificiales. (42)

P

parallel play/juego paralelo Conducta en la cual los niños juegan uno al lado del otro en vez de juntos. (22)

paraprofessional/ayudante de un profesional Un trabajador que está entrenado para asistir a un profesional. (20)

pare/pelar Cortarle la cáscara a una fruta o vegetal. (47)

parenting/crianza de los hijos La responsabilidad de cuidar a los hijos para estimular su desarrollo. (21)

parliamentary procedure/procedimiento parlamentario Un método democrático de permitir que la gente exprese sus opiniones para llegar a una decisión mayoritaria. (12)

pasteurized/pasteurizada Leche que se ha calentado y enfriado para matar los gérmenes. (52)

pattern/patrón El conjunto de instrucciones y piezas de papel impreso que enseñan cómo se confecciona una prenda. (62)

pattern catalog/catálogo de patrones Un libro que enumera todos los patrones que vende una compañía. (62)

pattern maker/patronista El trabajador que hace el patrón de una prenda de la muestra original del diseñador. (68)

peak usage period/período de uso máximo Las horas en que más energía se usa. (74)

pediatrician/pediatra Un médico que atiende a los niños. (26)

peel/pelar Quitarle la cáscara a las frutas y vegetales. (46)

peer/contemporáneo Una persona de la misma edad. (1)

peer mediation/mediación de contemporáneos Un proceso en el que estudiantes con entrenamiento especial ayudan a otros estudiantes a resolver problemas pacíficamente. (11)

peer pressure/presión de contemporáneos La influencia de amigos y personas de la misma edad a actuar en cierta forma. (10)

perishable/perecedero Que tiende a echarse a perder con facilidad. (43)

personal development/desarrollo personal Trabajar para alcanzar el potencial personal de sí mismo. (1)

personal inventory/inventario personal Una revisión de las habilidades e intereses de uno mismo. (20)

personality/personalidad La combinación de características y acciones que diferencian a uno de todas las demás personas. (1)

pilot light/piloto Una llama de gas que se mantiene prendida constantemente y se usa para encender la hornilla de una cocina. (73)

place setting/servicio de mesa El conjunto de vajilla, cubiertos y vasos que cada comensal necesita para una comida. (54)

poach/escalfar Cocinar alimentos enteros en una cantidad pequeña de agua hirviendo a fuego lento para que mantengan su forma original. (48)

point-of-sale terminal/terminal al punto de venta Una máquina que le permite a una persona usar una tarjeta de cobro automático para pagar por comestibles y otra mercancía. (29)

pollution/contaminación La introducción de basura y tóxicos en el medio ambiente. (27)

positive reinforcement/refuerzo positivo Una recompensa por buenos resultados. (6)

potential/potencial La capacidad de convertirse en algo más de lo que uno es ahora. (1)

prejudice/prejuicio Sesgo en contra de un individuo o grupo. (8)

premature/prematuro Que nace antes de estar completamente desarrollado. (25)

prenatal care/cuidado prenatal Cuidado para la madre y el bebé antes del nacimiento. (25)

preservative/conservante Una sustancia que se le añade a los alimentos para mantenerlos frescos y con buen gusto por más tiempo. (42)

pressing/planchar Levantar una plancha y colocarla sobre la tela sin deslizarla hacia delante y hacia atrás. (60)

pretreatment/tratamiento de antemano El uso de técnicas para quitar manchas antes de lavar una prenda. (60)

preventive maintenance/mantenimiento preventivo Asegurarse que la estructura de una casa y los aparatos dentro de ella están en buenas condiciones. (72)

principal/fondos La cantidad de dinero que hay en una cuenta de banco. (30)

prioritize/priorizar Decidir cuales necesidades y deseos son más importantes que los otros. (4)

processed/procesado Un alimento que ha sido cambiado de su forma cruda antes de venderse. (37)

processed meat/carne procesada Carnes—tales como los perros calientes, tocineta y fiambres—que han sido sazonadas, ahumadas o preparadas de algún modo antes de llevarlas a la tienda. (53)

procrastinate/dejar para luego Dejar las cosas para hacerlas más tarde. (28)

produce/productos de granja Frutas y vegetales frescos. (51)

proportion/proporción La manera en que una parte de un diseño está relacionada en tamaño, forma o espacio a otra parte del todo. (71)

proteins/proteínas Nutrientes que son necesarios para fabricar y reparar los tejidos del cuerpo; la base de todas las células del cuerpo. (37)

public housing/viviendas subvencionadas Viviendas por las cuales el gobierno paga en parte o totalmente. (70)

pull date/fecha de retirada El último día en que se puede vender un producto. (42)

puree/hacer puré Moler un alimento hasta que no tenga grumos. (47)

Q

quick bread/pan horneado rápido Un pan al que se le echa polvos de hornear o bicarbonato de soda para que se fermente. (50)

quiet play/juego tranquilo Actividades que envuelven la mente y las habilidades motoras de los músculos pequeños y no requieren mucho movimiento. (24)

R

rape/violación Relaciones sexuales forzadas. (17)

recall/retirada del mercado Devolver un producto que no es seguro al que lo fabricó para que lo arregle o destruya. (34)

recipe/receta Instrucciones detalladas para preparar un alimento en particular. (41)

reciprocity/reciprocidad Dar y recibir por turnos. (18)

recycle/reciclar Encontrar un nuevo uso para una prenda. (67)

redesign/diseñar nuevamente Cambiar una prenda para que esté más de moda o tenga una apariencia nueva. (67)

redress/compensación El derecho a que se corrija una injusticia. (34)

reference/referencia Un reporte escrito por un antiguo empleador acerca de las habilidades de trabajo de una persona. (26)

reflex/reflejo Una reacción involuntaria y automática. (22)

refusal skills/habilidades de rechazo Técnicas para resistir la presión negativa eficazmente. (10)

rehearsing/ensayar Practicar o aprender cómo se hace algo por medio de repetir la actividad muchas veces. (6)

relationships/relaciones Las conexiones que uno tiene con otras personas. (8)

resource/recurso Algo que una persona necesita para lograr una meta. (4)

responsible/formal Confiable y responsable de sus propios actos o conducta. (3)

résumé/curiculum vitae Un resumen escrito de su experiencia, educación e intereses que un candidato a un puesto le entrega a un empleador. (20)

retrain/entrenarse de nuevo Aprender nuevas técnicas o destrezas. (13)

return policy/normas de devolución Las reglas de una tienda para devolver o cambiar mercancía. (34)

rhythm/ritmo La repetición regular de línea o forma. (71)

ribbing/canalé Una banda elástica que vuelve a su forma original después de ser estirada. (66)

role model/modelo de conducta Una persona que sirve de ejemplo a otros. (12)

roles/papeles La manera en que uno actúa cuando se relaciona con otros. (8)

rotate/dar vueltas Girar un plato un cuarto o media vuelta en un horno de microondas para permitir que las microondas penetren toda la comida. (49)

rotation/rotación Un sistema en el que los suministros más viejos se utilizan antes que los nuevos. (43)

routine/rutina El orden de sucesos acostumbrado. (69)

rural/rural Regiones que son principalmente campestres. (69)

R-value/valor R Una medida de lo bien que un tipo de material aislante resiste la perdida de calor o frío. (74)

S

sanitation/salubridad La prevención del crecimiento de bacterias dañinas por medio de guardar, lavar y cocinar los alimentos debidamente y de mantener la cocina, los aparatos, los utensilios y la persona limpia. (44)

sauté/sofreír Cocinar pequeños trozos de alimentos en poca grasa sobre fuego lento o mediano. (48)

savings account/cuenta de ahorro Una cuenta en que se conserva el dinero que uno deposita y que paga interés sobre este. (30)

scale drawing/dibujo a escala Un dibujo en que los tamaños relativos de los objetos son iguales a los tamaños relativos de los objetos de verdad. (71)

seam/costura Una línea de puntadas que une dos partes de una prenda. (59)

seam allowance/orilla de la tela La cantidad de tela que hay entre la línea de cortar y la línea de coser. (64)

seasonal/de temporada Más abundante durante cierto tiempo del año. (51)

seconds/artículos con defectos de fábrica Mercancía imperfecta o que ya no se produce. (33)

security deposit/depósito Una cantidad de dinero que el que quiere alquilar le entrega al dueño de una casa como protección contra perdidas financieras. (70)

self-concept/autoconcepto La definición de una persona de sí misma. (1)

self-control/autocontrol La habilidad de una persona de usar su buen juicio para dominar sus emociones. (19)

self-esteem/autoestima El valor o importancia que uno se da a sí mismo. (1)

selvage/orillo El borde de la tela que está terminado para que no se salgan los hilos. (64)

sensory toys/juguetes sensorios Objetos que estimulan los sentidos por medio de distintas texturas, formas, sonidos y colores. (24)

sequence/sucesión El orden en que se deben hacer las cosas. (45)

serger/remalladora Una máquina de coser de alta velocidad que corta, cose y remata en un solo paso. (63)

sew-through button/botón sin vástago Botón con dos o cuatro agujeros por donde se pasa el hilo al coserlo. (66)

sexual harassment/acoso sexual La persecución de una persona con insinuaciones sexuales. (19)

sexually transmitted disease (STD)/enfermedad transmitida sexualmente Una enfermedad que se transmite de persona a persona a través del contacto sexual. (19)

shade/matiz oscuro Una gradación opaca de un color que se crea añadiéndole negro al color. (57)

shank button/botón con vástago Un tipo de botón que tiene un tallo por detrás, pero no tiene agujeros. (66)

shield/proteger Cubrir un alimento en el horno con papel de aluminio para evitar que se cocine demasiado. (49)

shoplifting/hurto en las tiendas Robarse de una tienda artículos que están en venta. (34)

short-term goal/meta a corto plazo Algo que una persona quiere realizar pronto. (4)

siblings/hermanos Hermanos o hermanas. (14)

simmer/hervir a fuego lento Calentar un líquido lo más posible sin dejarlo llegar al punto de ebullición. (48)

simple interest/interés simple Un tipo de interés que se paga sólo sobre el capital. (30)

size range/clasificación de tallas Las categorías de tallas que les sirven a distintas personas. (59)

small-claims court/tribunal de menor cuantía Una corte en la cual los consumidores presentan sus demandas ante un juez que decide el caso. (34)

small-motor skills/habilidades motoras de los músculos pequeños El control sobre los músculos pequeños del cuerpo, tales como los de las manos y los dedos. (22)

smoke detector/detector de humo Un aparato que funciona por medio de pilas y suena una alarma cuando nota que hay humo. (73)

snag/enganchón Un hilo que se prende y se sale de un tejido. (60)

sociability/sociabilidad La cualidad de ser amistoso y disfrutar de la compañía de otras personas. (13)

special purchase/compra especial Un artículo que una tienda ha comprado a un precio más bajo de lo normal. (59)

spoilage/estropicio El daño causado por bacterias, hongos, y moho que hace que las comidas luzcan y huelan mal. (51)

standing time/tiempo de reposo El tiempo que se deja que una comida termine de cocinarse sola después que el horno de microondas se ha apagado. (49)

staples/alimentos básicos Alimentos que se usan con frecuencia. (42)

status/prestigio Nivel de importancia dentro de un grupo. (56)

staystitching/poner puntadas de fijar Coser una línea de puntadas a máquina en un pedazo de tela para evitar que se estire. (65)

steamer/vaporera Un cesto de metal que sujeta los alimentos arriba del agua hirviendo pero permite que el vapor lo atraviese. (48)

stereotype/estereotipo Una combinación de rasgos que todos los miembros de un grupo se supone que tengan. (8)

stir-fry/sofreír revolviendo Cocinar pequeños trozos de alimentos rápidamente a fuego alto con muy poca grasa. (48)

store brand/marca de la tienda Un producto que se hace especialmente para la tienda o cadena de tiendas que lo vende. (42)

stress/estrés La reacción del cuerpo a las demandas que se le imponen. (2)

substance abuse/abuso de sustancias El uso de drogas ilegales o el mal uso de drogas legales. (17)

suburban/suburbano Las secciones principalmente residenciales que rodean una ciudad. (69)

support system/sistema de apoyo La red de individuos y grupos a quienes una persona puede pedir ayuda. (15)

T

table service/servicio a la mesa Un tipo de servicio de restaurante en el que los camareros toman la orden en la mesa, traen los alimentos y recogen después de la comida. (54)

task rotation/rotación de labores Pasar una tarea de un miembro de la familia a otro. (72)

teamwork/trabajo en conjunto Trabajar juntos para lograr una meta en común. (8)

technology/tecnología La aplicación de métodos científicos para ayudar a la gente a satisfacer sus necesidades y deseos. (29)

texture/textura La manera en que la superficie de una tela luce y se siente. (57)

time-out/tiempo muerto Una manera de manejar la mala conducta en los niños que los obliga a sentarse tranquilos por un período de tiempo, usualmente un minuto por cada año de edad. (23)

tint/matiz claro Una gradación de un color no subido, que se crea añadiéndole blanco al color. (57)

tipping/dar una propina Darle dinero adicional a los camareros por su buen servicio. (54)

tolerance/tolerancia Aceptar y respetar las costumbres y creencias de otras personas. (8)

trade association/asociación comercial Un grupo de negociantes que proporciona información y apoya los intereses de las personas que trabajan en ese tipo de negocio. (75)

traffic pattern/patrón de movimiento Las sendas más directas que usan las personas para moverse a través de una habitación. (71)

traumatic/traumatizante Que causa un choque emocional severo que requiere tiempo para aliviarse. (16)

tuck/alforza Un doblez en la tela que se cose de arriba abajo para darle forma a una prenda. (65)

U

understitching/costura por debajo Una línea de puntadas que se usa para coser una vuelta de tela de una prenda a la orilla de la tela. (65)

underwriter's Laboratory/Laboratorio garante Una agencia que prueba productos eléctricos para ver si son seguros. (33)

unit construction/construcción por unidad Preparación por separado de las piezas de una prenda antes de coserlas juntas en un orden específico. (65)

unit price/precio por unidad El precio de un producto por onza, libra u otra unidad aceptada. (42)

unity/unidad El sentido de que todos los objetos en una habitación van juntos. (71)

urban/urbano Ubicado en una ciudad. (69)

utensils/utensilios Instrumentos de cocina, tales como cuchillos, tazas de medir, cazuelas y trastes. (43)

V

value/opacidad Lo claro u oscuro que es un color. (57)

values/valores Las creencias, ideas y sentimientos de una persona acerca de lo que es importante. (3)

vandalism/vandalismo El destruir o dañar la propiedad de otros adrede. (34)

variable/factor variable Cualquier condición que determina por cuanto tiempo y a que nivel de potencia se tiene que cocinar un alimento en un horno de microondas. (49)

variety/variedad Una combinación de estilos y materiales que son distintos pero pegan. (71)

variety meat/vísceras Las carnes que provienen de los órganos, como el hígado, mondongo y riñones. (53)

verbal/verbal Que usa palabras. (9)

versatile/versátil Que tiene muchos usos distintos. (58)

view/modelo Una de las variaciones de una prenda que tiene un patrón de costura. (62)

visualize/visualizar Imaginarse a uno mismo haciendo una tarea o actividad que quiere aprender a hacer. (6)

vitamins/vitaminas Nutrientes que ayudan al cuerpo a mantenerse sano, funcionar debidamente y procesar otros nutrientes. (37)

volume/volumen La cantidad de espacio que ocupa un ingrediente. (46)

volunteer/voluntario Alguien que ofrece sus servicios sin cobrar por ellos. (12)

W

wardrobe/vestuario La ropa que te pertenece. (58)

warranty/garantía La promesa por escrito de un fabricante o vendedor al por menor de arreglar o reemplazar un producto defectuoso o de devolverle su dinero al consumidor. (33)

water-soluble vitamins/vitaminas hidrosolubles Vitaminas que se pueden absorber con facilidad y que se transportan por el cuerpo disueltas en agua. (37)

weather stripping/burletes Material que se usa para tapar las rendijas alrededor de las puertas y las ventanas para evitar que se escape el aire. (74)

wellness/bienestar Un buen estado de salud total. (2)

work center/centro de trabajo Un área de la cocina organizada para hacer ciertas tareas. (43)

work plan/plan de trabajo Un plan de acción que enumera todas las tareas que va a hacer una persona y cuánto tiempo van a tardar. (45)

work triangle/triángulo de trabajo Las sendas que conectan el refrigerador, el fregadero y la cocina. (43)

Y

yarn/estambre Hebras que se forman cuando se tuercen las fibras. (61)

yeast bread/pan de levadura Pan que se fermenta y crece por medio de una sustancia llamada levadura. (50)

yield/rendimiento El número de porciones o la cantidad que da una receta. (41)

Index

Q

Quality, 334, 423, 603
Quality control inspectors, 534
Quick breads, 493

R

Raglan sleeves, 641
Ramie, 589, 590
Ranges, 429
Rape, 174–175
Rayon, 591
Readiness, 257–259
Reading, 79–80, 250
Real estate advertisements, 684
Real estate agent, 726
Realism, 55–56
Rebates, 317
Recall, 346
Receiving, 93
Recipes, choosing, 415–417
Reciprocity, 184
Recycling, 654–656, 720
Redesign of garments, 651–654
Redress, 339
References, 265
Reflexes, 226
Refrigerators, 429, 430, 704
Refusal skills, 112
Regional traditions, 360–361
Rehearsing, 73
Reinforcement, positive, 72–73
Rejection, handling, 187–188
Relationships
    building, 93–95
    and clothing, 544–546
    ending, 198, 200
    influences on, 90–92
    kinds of, 89
    with older people, 147
    qualities of strong, 92
    rewards of, 89–90
Reliability, 284
Religious customs, 361, 546
Remarriage, 167–168
Renting, 681–684, 686
Repairs of clothes, 581–582
Resale shops, 568
Reservation software, 536
Resident caretaker, 727–728
Resolution, 118–119

Resourcefulness, 279
Resources, 180, 273
    community, 275
    examining, 57
    human, 273–274
    managing, 276, 277–280
    material, 274–275
    natural, 275
    using, 276
Respect, 104, 138, 153–154
Responsibilities
    accepting, 686
    personal, 49
    and sexuality, 200–202
    sharing home, 49
    showing, 50
    taking, 709, 712, 719–720
Responsible management, 280
Responsibly, acting, 47, 458
Restaurants, 406–407, 528, 536
Résumé, 141, 207, 208
Retirement, 163
Retraining, 134–135
Return policy, 346
Rhythm as design principle, 691
Ribbing, 642
Rice, 491–492, 493, 494
Roasting, 476
Role model, 126–127, 258
Roles, 90
Rotary beater, 466
Rotation, 434, 484
Routine, establishing, 699–700
Routine outings, 250
Rubber scraper, 466
Rummage sales, 333, 568
Running stitch, 640
Rural areas, 676
R-value, 717

S

Safety, 38
    for children, 238–242
    and clothes, 546–547
    in comparison shopping, 334, 335
    food, 500–501
    in housing, 706–712
    in kitchen, 437–442, 462, 465, 486

product, 346
    sewing, 618
    and technology, 295
Salmonella, 439
Salt, 384
Sanitation, 437–442, 500–501, 509, 703
Satin weave, 592
Saturated fats, 371
Sautéing, 477
Saving, learning to, 301
Savings accounts, 305–307
Savings bonds, 306, 307
Scalding, prevention of, 438
Scale drawing, 691
Schedule, 287, 446, 448–449
School, eating at, 408
School-age children, 229–231
Seams, 572, 619, 633, 652
Seasonal produce, 498
Seconds, 331
Security deposit, 682–683
Seeds, 516
Self-concept, 29, 30, 90
Self-control, 219
Self-esteem, 30–31, 71, 389
Self-knowledge, 110–111
Selvage, 619–620
Semolina, 492
Sensitivity, 544
Sequence in meal preparation, 447–448
Serger, 609–611, 633
Service fees, 307
Serving styles, 525
Set-in sleeve, 641
Sewing, 563–564
Sewing area, setting up, 621
Sewing equipment, 606–614
Sewing techniques, 601, 627–632, 639–648
Sew-through button, 644, 645
Sexual feelings, strategies for handling, 202
Sexual harassment, 201
Sexuality and responsibility, 200–202
Sexually transmitted diseases (STDs), 200
Shade as design element, 553
Shank button, 644, 645

Credits

Photos:

Ann's Portrait Designs: 29, 35, 37, 55, 125, 154, 202, 253, 255, 274, 301, 305, 307, 315, 320, 360, 362, 369, 371, 377, 381, 383, 393, 400, 405, 415, 437, 447, 450, 452, 461, 464, 467, 468, 478, 484, 486, 488, 490, 492, 494, 496, 498, 501, 504, 510, 512, 516, 517, 519, 520, 523, 531, 558, 562, 566, 639

James Ballard: 18, 102, 390

Roger B. Bean: 220, 227, 229, 246 403, 533, 715, 724, 728

Bemis Company Inc.: 245

Bernina of America, Inc.: 612

Keith M. Berry: 46, 50, 58, 78, 79, 83, 114, 127, 165, 196, 212, 237, 333 401, 431, 528, 545, 570, 582, 596, 597, 600, 602, 604, 616, 638, 644, 647, 648, 650, 653, 670, 676, 707

California Closet Company: 688

Central Illinois Sight Center: 707

Comstock: 158, 204, 219, 262, 543
   Jack Elness: 76, 356-357

Congregation Anshai Emeth: 46

Country Paintin' Palace: 653

Dacron®: 593

Leo de Wys Inc.
   Bill Bachman: 173
   David Lissy: 162
   Sipa/Gama, 36

FPG International
   Ron Chapple: 52, 82, 214-215, 216, 217
   Jim Cummins: 68
   Montes de Oca: 550
   Gerald French: 436
   Rob Gage: 44, 192
   Michael Hart: 88
   L.O.C. Inc.: 26
   Steven Jones: 225
   Michael Krasowitz: 190, 534
   James Levin: 263
   Bill Losh: 22-23
   Reggie Parker, Images Unlimited: 727
   Dick Luria: 351
   Ron Routar: 680
   Stephen Simpson: 24, 25
   Telegraph Color Library: 666-667, 675, 714
   Ron Thomas: 153

   Arthur Tilley: 60, 197, 270-271
   Tom Wilson: 132, 722

David R. Frazier Photolibrary: 133, 275, 302, 323, 675

Timothy Fuller: 406, 497

The Gamma Liaison Network: 124, 278
   Paul Avis: 145, 189
   Barbara Campbell: 224
   Roy Gumpel: 257
   Keith Lampher: 175
   Richard Shock: 226
   Sotographs: 100
   James D. Wilson/National Community Service: 124

Greater Peoria Family YMCA: 227

Jeff Greenberg: 115, 122, 128, 138, 205

Habitat for Humanity: 678

Nancy Hill, House Beautiful's Home Remodeling and Redecorating: 689

Illinois Antique Center: 333

Illinois Cycle: 58

Image Bank
   Bard Martin: 272

Index Stock Photography: 387, 693
   Matthew Borkoski: 547
   Melanie Carr: 182
   Myrleen Cate: 98
   Wallace Garrison: 244
   Powerstock: 94
   Mark Segal: 48
   Kim Weatherly: 34

Jo-Ann Fabrics: 600

Libby's: 533

Little Friends Learning Center: 403

Lippman's Furniture and Interiors: 670

Merillat: 434

National Cotton Council: 589

Nawrocki Stock Photo Inc.: 77, 137, 149, 152, 268, 348

Orlon®: 593

P.A .R.C.: 644

Peoria City Council: 50

Peoria Police Department: 127

Brent Phelps: 57, 61, 66, 70, 80, 89, 93, 130, 221, 238, 280, 313, 325, 335, 336, 455, 462, 466, 471, 472, 473, 613, 614

Infographics and Art:

Cover Photo:

J. Clarke/Picture Perfect

Other Acknowledgements:

In California: Adray's, Infiniti of Santa Monica, Lev-off Family, Love Tennis of Marina del Rey, Martin Minkardo, Myers Family, Adrienne Osmansky's Seniors, Pro-Look Sports in Santa Monica, Santa Monica High Schook, Windward School, Yimei Wong; **In Illinois:** Bradley University, House of Fabrics; **In Texas:** Cloth World, Dillard's (housewares), Ever's Hardware, Folley's (housewares), University of North Texas, USA Distributors, Inc. of Dallas.